GREECE

THE ROUGH GUIDE

ARUN + JOE
EASTER 91

ROUGH GUIDE CREDITS

Series Editor: Mark Ellingham
Editorial: Martin Dunford, John Fisher, Jack Holland
Production: Susanne Hillen
Typesetting: Greg Ward
Design: Andrew Oliver and Greg Ward

THANKS

This new edition of the Rough Guide owes a very large debt to **readers** of the previous book who took the time to write in with accounts, ideas and new information, and to those who helped us in Greece. In no special order, we'd like to thank: Florika Kyriacopoulos, Rhoda Nottridge, Michael Hathaway, Andy Wilson, Karen Silvester, Helen Carpenter, Adam Kawecki, Aziz (Theo) Dikeulius, Elizabeth Herring, Kiveli Petropoulou, John Chapple, Emil Moryannidhis, Kevin Andrews, Johnny Saunderson (again!), Andy Wilson, Jonathan Plant, Alicia Yin, Andy Warren, Heather Gourlay, Stuart Knight, Alan Grove, Pippa Jones, Ros, Ted Sumner, Dave Harris, Ruth Gates, Peter Walker, Jenny Woolf, Rona Williams, Pete Lawrence, Penelope Davies, Michael Hathaway, Diana Shaw, Morna Smith, Norma Daykin, Julia Smith, Liz Raymont, Philip Bogaert, James Salmon, Sheila Golightly, David Mackay, Mary Sharp, Sheena MacDonald, Heyns Peter, Michelle Newman, E. Frith, Dave Keech, John Flack, Doug Holton, Carola Scupham, Ken Scudder, Kellin Defiel, Carola Darwin, Linton J. Childs, Charlie Ellis, Mike Gunton, Janice Drummond, Helga Pantelides, Jan Stirling, Sandra Johnson, Yuri Bender, Gerard Stewart, Dave Harris, J. Boucher, Stephen Rees, Morten Stokkar, Andrea Wilder, Bill Higham, Kathy Price, Ken Baker, Mark Billings, Margie Curran and Pamela Blyth. Please keep in touch . . .

Thanks are also due to Rob Jones, Jules Brown and Mike Gerrard for helping out with the **editing**, to Andrew Preshous, Karen Silvester, Chris Coe and Anita Peltonen for their **research**, and to Alison Walsh for the piece on 'Disabled Travellers'.

This revised edition published by
Harrap Columbus, Chelsea House, 26 Market Square, Bromley, Kent BR1 1NA in 1989, reprinted 1990.

Original editions published by Routledge & Kegan Paul, 1982, 1984, 1985, 1987.

Typeset in Linotron Univers and Century Old Style.
Printed by Cox & Wyman, Reading.
672p.
Includes index.

British Library Cataloguing in Publication Data
Ellingham, Mark
    Greece : the rough guide – 5th ed.
    1. Greece – Description and travel – 1981 – Guide-books.
    I. Title. II. Dubin, Marc. III. Fisher, John, 1958- . IV. Jansz, Natania. V. Salmon, Tim.
    914.95'0476

ISBN 0–7471–0252–X

GREECE

THE ROUGH GUIDE

WRITTEN AND RESEARCHED BY
**MARK ELLINGHAM, NATANIA JANSZ,
JOHN FISHER, MARC DUBIN
AND TIM SALMON.**

With Additional Accounts by
Richard Hartle, Carol Phile,
Diane Fortenberry, Michael House,
Stephen Lees and Pete Raine.

Edited by
MARK ELLINGHAM
With Marc Dubin and Tim Salmon

HARRAP-COLUMBUS ■ LONDON

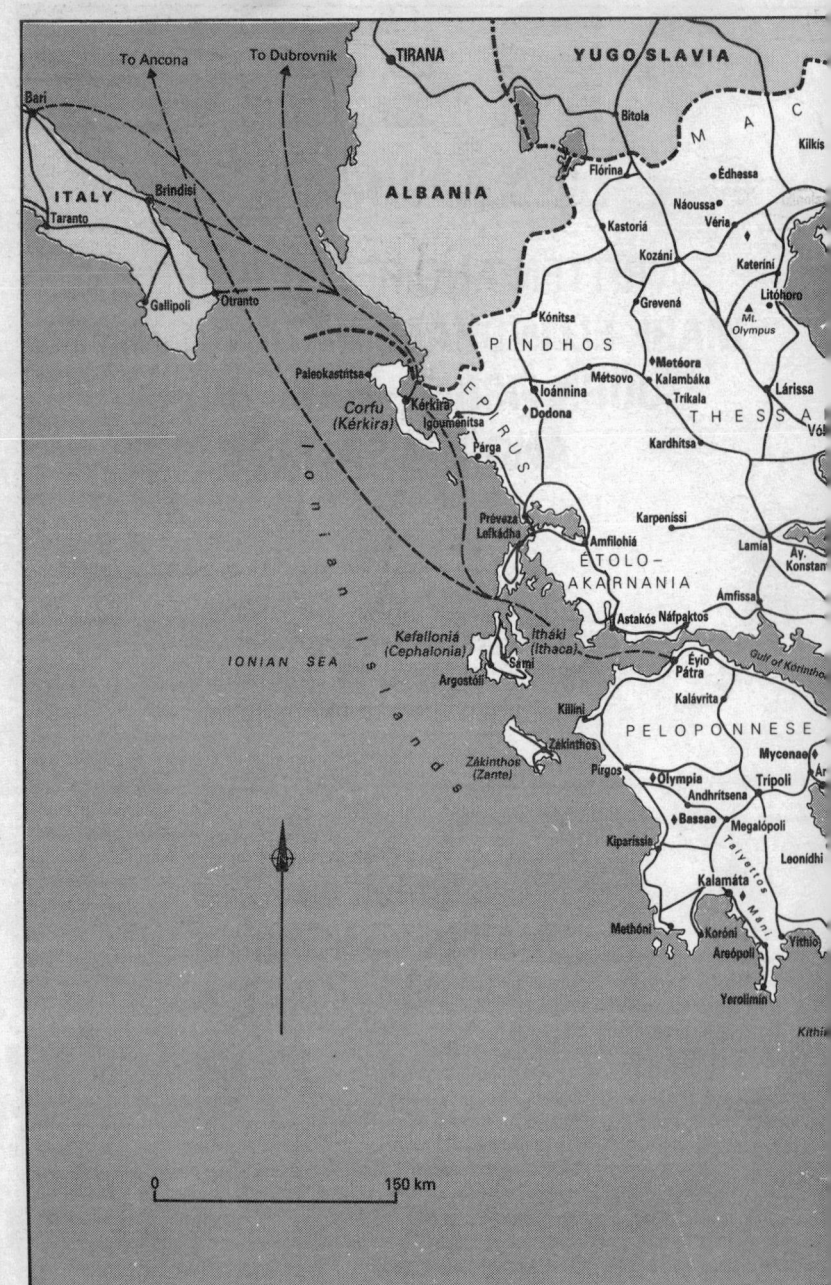

PLACE NAMES: A WARNING!

The art of rendering Greek words in Roman letters is in a state of chaos: a major source of confusion with **place names**, for which seemingly each local authority, and each map-maker, uses a different system.

The word for 'saint,' for instance, one of the most common prefixes, can be spelt Áyios, Ágios, or Ághios. And, to make matters worse, there are often two forms of a name in Greek – the popularly used *dhimotikí*, and the old 'classicising' *katharévoussa*. Thus you will see the island of Spétses written also as Spétsai, or Halkídha, capital of Évvia, as Halkís (or even Chalcís, on more traditional maps).

Throw in the complexities of Greek grammar – with different case-endings for names – and the fact that there exist long-established English versions of classical place names, which bear not the slightest relation to the Greek sounds (Mycenae for Mikínes, for example), and you have a real mare's nest.

In this book, we've used a (fairly accepted) modern system, with *Y* rather than *G* for the Greek gamma, and *DH* rather than *D* for delta, in the spelling of all modern Greek place names. We have, however, retained the accepted 'English' spellings for the **ancient sites**, and for familiar places like Athens (Athiná, in modern Greek). The accented letter of each word should always be **stressed** in pronunciation.

CONTENTS

Introduction

INTRODUCTION

With 166 inhabited islands and a landscape that ranges from Mediterranean to Balkan, Greece has enough of interest to fill months of travel. The **historic sites** span four millenia of civilisation, encompassing the renowned, such as Mycenae, Olympia, Delphi, or the Parthenon, and the obscure, where a visit can still seem like a personal discovery. The **beaches** are parcelled out along a convoluted coastline equal in length to that of (far larger) France, and they range from islands where the boat calls once a week to resorts as cosmopolitan as any in the Mediterranean. And for anyone with an interest in **walking**, the country's mountainous interior offers some of the best and least exploited hiking territory in Europe.

Modern Greece is the sum of an extraordinary diversity of **influences**. Romans, Arabs, French, Venetians, Slavs, Albanians, Turks, Italians, to say nothing of the great Byzantine empire, have all been here and gone since the time of Alexander the Great. All have left their marks: the Byzantines in countless churches and monasteries, and in ghost towns like Mystra; the Venetians in impregnable fortifications at Náfplio, Monemvassía and Methóni in the Peloponnese; the Franks in crag-top castles. Most obvious, perhaps, is the heritage of 400 years of Ottoman Turkish rule which, while universally derided, exercised an inestimable influence on music, cuisine, language and way of life. The contributions, and continued existence, of substantial minorities – Vlachs, Muslims, Jews, Gypsies – round out the list of those who have helped to make up the Hellenic identity.

All of these groups have left an indelible stamp on the character of the people, which combines with that powerful strain of **Greekness** – a quality hard to define – that has kept alive the people's sense of themselves throughout their turbulent history. With no ruling class to impose a superior model of taste or patronise the arts, the Greek people – peasants, fishermen, shepherds – created perhaps the most vigorous and truly **popular culture** in Europe. Its works can be seen in the songs and dances, costumes, embroidery, woven bags and rugs, furniture, the white cubist houses of popular image – in a thousand instinctively tasteful manifestations. Its vigour may be failing under the impact of western consumer values, but much survives, especially in remoter regions.

Of course there are formal cultural activites as well: **museums** that shouldn't be missed, in Athens, Thessaloníki and Iráklio; equally compelling buildings, like the **monasteries** of the Metéora and Mount Áthos; **castles** such as those in the Dodecanese, Lésvos, central Greece and the Peloponnese; as well, of course, as the great Mycenaean, Minoan and Classical sites. The country hosts some excellent summer **festivals**, too, bringing international theatre groups and orchestras to perform in the ancient theatres of Epidaurus, Dodona, and Herodes Atticus in Athens – magical settings in themselves.

But the call to cultural duty is muted on the whole. The sheer **hedonistic pleasures** of languor and warmth – always going lightly dressed, never suffering goosepimples in the sea, talking and tippling under the stars without a hint of a shiver – are more than enough for most northerners. Greece is a land for simple sybarites. If you're into the five-star stuff – super-soft beds, faultless plumbing, exquisite cuisine, attentive service – forget it. Hotel accommodation is mostly plain. Rooms can be box-like and stuffy. Campsites offer the minimum of facilities. Food at its best is fresh, colourful and uncomplicated – and irresistibly cheap by most European standards.

The Greek people

Greek history, politics, and contemporary culture are covered in the *Contexts* section of this book, and individual, regional factors detailed in the main text. A brief background note, however, seems appropriate, since few visitors realise just how recent and profound are the events that created the modern Greek state and national character.

Up until the early decades of this century many parts of Greece – Crete, Macedonia, the islands of the Dodecanese – were in Turkish (or in the latter case, Italian) hands. As many ethnic Greeks meanwhile lived in Asia Minor, Egypt and in the north Balkans as in the recently-forged kingdom. The Balkan Wars of 1912–13 and the exchange of 'Greek' and 'Turkish' populations in 1922–23 changed everything in a sudden, brutal manner. Worse still was to come during World War II, and its aftermath of civil war between the Communists, who formed the core of wartime resistance against the Germans, and the western-backed rightist, 'government' forces. The viciousness of this period found a more recent echo in nearly seven years of military dictatorship under the colonels' junta between 1967 and 1973.

Such memories of brutal misrule, diaspora and catastrophe remain uncomfortably close for all Greeks, despite the last decade or so of democratic stability and economic growth as a member of the European Community. The resultant identity is complex, an uneasy coexistence of opposing impulses, which cannot be accounted for merely by Greece's position as a natural bridge between Europe and the Middle East. Within a generally extroverted outlook is a strong streak of pessimism.

It is the poverty of, and enduring paucity of opportunity in, their homeland that spurs the indisputable resourcefulness of Greek entrepreneurs, many of whom choose to emigrate. Those who remain may be lulled by an (until recently) humane full-employment policy which has resulted in the lowest jobless rate in Western Europe. The downside of this is an occasionally staggering lack of initiative, but official attempts to impose a more austere economic line have been met by waves of popular strikes.

On the other hand, the meticulousness of Greek craftworkers is legendary, even if their values and skills took a back seat to the demands of crisis and profiteering when the evacuation of Asia Minor and the rapid depopulation of rural villages prompted the graceless urbanisation that most visitors remark on. Amid the contemporary sophistication and conspicuous consumption of the big towns it's easy to forget the nearness of the agricultural past and the fact that Greece is still as much a part of the Third World as of the the First.

You may find that buses operate with Germanic efficiency, but ferries sail with an unpredictability little changed since the time of Odysseus. In short, modern Greece is an exasperating, inexhaustible well of contradictions, simultaneously friendly and frustrating, and ultimately addictive.

A word on attitudes

Greece is changing rapidly under the impact of mass tourism and the twentieth century, both of which have been felt most keenly only in the last twenty to thirty years. The encounter has been painful and in many ways destructive. A largely rural, traditional and conservative society, in which until recently the Orthodox church was all but an established faith and the guardian of national identity, has been shocked to its roots. Though the Greeks are adaptable and the cash registers ring happily, at least in tourist areas, the so-called 'liberated' behaviour of many westerners is deeply distasteful to the older generations. The mind boggles to imagine the reaction of the black-clad grandparents to nudism, or even scanty clothing. But it's not just 'obvious' issues of decorum or morality. Many young foreigners travelling cheap and ragged are nettled by hostile reactions to their appearance and their assumption that they can do as they please. But doing things on the cheap and roughing it are not admirable to the Greek mind. Poverty is a fresh and uncomfortable memory, something to be ashamed of and hide. Holes in jeans are despised. Be gentle with susceptibilities.

Where and when to go

There is no such thing as a 'typical' Greek island; each has its distinctive character, appearance, history, flora, even a unique tourist clientele. And the same is true of the mainland provinces. **Landscapes** vary from the mountainous northwest and rainy, shaggy forests of the Pílion to the stony deserts of the Máni, from the soft theatricality of the Peloponnesian coastal hills to the poplar-studded plains of Macedonia, from the resin-scented ridges of Skíathos and Sámos to the wind-tormented rocks of the central Aegean. The inky plume of cypress, the silver green of olive groves, the blue outline of distant hills, an expanse of shimmering sea: these are the enduring and unfailingly pleasing motifs of the Greek landscape.

Most places and people are far more agreeable, and recognisably Greek, outside the **peak period** of late June to the end of August, when the soaring mercury (see climate chart opposite) and crowds will try the patience of saints – and your Greek hosts and the other travellers are all too human. You won't miss out on pleasantly warm weather if you come in **early June or September**, excellent times everywhere but particularly amid the Sporades and north or east Aegean islands. In **October** you might hit a stormy spell, especially in western Greece or in the mountains, but most of the time the 'summer of Áyios Dhimítrios', the Greek equivalent of Indian summer, prevails. Autumn in general is beautiful; the light is softer, the sea often balmier than the air, the colours subtler.

December to March are the coldest and least reliable months, though there are many fine days of perfect crystal visibility, and the glorious lowland flowers begin to bloom very early in spring. The more northerly latitudes and high altitudes of course endure far colder and wetter conditions with the mountains themselves snowed under from November to April. The most **dependable winter weather** is to be found in the Dodecanese, immediately around Rhodes, or in the southeastern parts of Crete. As spring slowly warms up, **March and early April** are still uncertain, though fine for visiting the Ionians or Dodecanese; by **May** the weather is dependable, and Crete, the Peloponnese, and the Cyclades are perhaps at their best, even if the sea's still a little cool for swimming.

Other factors that can affect the timing of your Greek travels are mainly concerned with the level of tourism. Standards of service invariably slip under the high-season pressure of making a fast buck, when room rates are already at their highest; more good arguments for avoiding the most popular destinations in July and August. If you can only visit in high season, then you'll do well to plan your itinerary a little away from the beaten track. Explore the less obvious parts of the Peloponnese, or the northern mainland, for example; or island-hop with an eye for the more obscure – the places where ferries don't call more than once a day, and there's not yet an airport.

Out of season, especially between November and March, you may have to wrestle with uncertain ferry schedules to the islands, and often fairly skeletal facilities when you arrive. However, you will find reasonable service on all the main routes and at least one hotel open in the port or main town. On the mainland, out-of-season travel poses no special difficulties.

CLIMATE CHART

	JAN			MAR			MAY			JULY			SEPT			NOV		
	°F Max Min		Rain days	°F Max Min		Rain days	°F Max Min		Rain days	°F Max Min		Rain days	°F Max Min		Rain days	°F Max Min		Rain days
Athens	54	44	13	60	46	10	76	60	9	90	72	2	84	66	4	65	52	12
Crete (Haniá)	60	46	17	64	48	11	76	56	5	86	68	0	82	64	3	70	54	10
Cyclades (Mikonos)	58	50	14	62	52	8	72	62	5	82	72	½	78	68	1	66	58	9
North Greece (Halkithiki)	50	36	7	59	44	9	77	58	10	90	70	4	83	64	5	60	47	9
Ionian (Corfu)	56	44	13	62	46	10	74	58	6	88	70	2	82	64	5	66	52	12
Dodecanese (Rhodes)	58	50	15	62	48	7	74	58	2	86	70	0	82	72	1	68	60	7
Sporades (Skíathos)	55	45	12	58	47	10	71	58	3	82	71	0	75	64	8	62	53	12
East Aegean (Lésvos)	54	42	11	60	46	7	76	60	6	88	70	2	82	66	2	64	50	9

$°C = (°F - 32) \times 5/9$

PART ONE

THE

BASICS

GETTING THERE

It's close on 2000 miles from London to Athens, so for most visitors flying is the only viable option. There are direct flights to a variety of Greek destinations from all the major British aiports, as well as from Dublin and Belfast. Flying time is around 3½ hours and costs are reasonable – from around £120 return out of season, £160 or so in midsummer.

Road or rail alternatives take a minimum of three days, but are obviously worth considering if you plan to visit Greece as part of an extended trip through Europe. There are two alternative routes – through Italy (and over by ferry) or via Yugoslavia – and pairing these on an outward and return leg makes for a satisfying circuit.

Australians and New Zealanders have the possibility of direct and reasonably competitive flights from Sydney or Melbourne to Athens. However, it's almost always cheaper to transit via London, picking up flights or rail tickets on from there.

FLIGHTS

Most of the cheaper flights to Greece are **charter** deals, sold either with a package holiday or, through 'consolidators', as a flight-only option. They have fixed and unchangable outward and return dates, a maximum stay of one month, and must meet the somewhat peculiar conditions of Greek law – see below. For longer stays or more

flexibility, or simply if you're travelling out of season (when few charters are available), you'll want a **scheduled** flight. As with charters, these are offered under a wide variety of fares, and are again often sold off at discount by consolidators.

Although Athens remains the prime destination for cheap fares, there are **direct flights** from Britain to Thessaloníki and Préveza on the **Greek mainland**, and to the **islands** of Crete, Rhodes, Corfu, Lésvos, Páros, Zákinthos, Skíathos, Sámos and Kós. And with any flight to Athens, you can buy an additional **domestic connecting flight** (on *Olympic*) to one of the dozen or so regional Greek airports.

CHARTERS

Travel agents throughout Britain sell **discount charter flights** to Greece. Even the high street chains frequently promote 'flight-only' deals, or heavily discount all-inclusive holidays, when their parent companies have chartered too many airline seats. The greatest variety of flights, however, tends to be from the London airports; in summer, you should have a choice between most of the dozen Greek destinations above. Flying from elsewhere in Britain, you'll find options more limited, most commonly to Athens, Corfu, Rhodes and Crete.

In Britain as a whole, the best **sources** of flights are the classified sections in *The Sunday Times*, the Saturday travel section of *The Independent*, and local evening papers. In London, scour the back pages of *Time Out*, the *Evening Standard* and the various free magazines distributed for London-resident Australasians. Obviously the more flexible you can be on dates the better your chances of a rock-bottom deal; if you're prepared to take a 'leaving tomorrow at 2am from Luton Airport' flight, you can often pick up a real bargain. Whatever, phone around at least half a dozen agents for a range of offers.

Some words of **warning** about Greek aviation law. This specifies that a charter ticket must be for no less than three days and no more than four weeks and must be accompanied by an **accommodation voucher** for at least the first few nights of your stay – check that your ticket satisfies these conditions or you could be refused entry. In practice the 'accommodation voucher' has become a formality; it has to name an existing hotel but you're not expected to use it (and probably won't be able to if you try).

The other important condition regards travel to Turkey. If you travel to Greece on a charter flight, you may **visit Turkey** (or any other neighbouring country) only as a daytrip; staying overnight, you run the risk of invalidating your ticket. Ironically, the most popular daytrip from Greece to Turkey – from Kos to Bodrum – is forbidden altogether to charter ticket holders. (Note that exact details of this regulation change frequently: for the latest situation check withe the Greek National Tourist Office – see p.12).

Student/youth charters are exempt from the voucher restriction and are allowed to be sold as one-way flights only. By combining two one-way charters you can, therefore, stay for over a month. Tickets are available to anyone under 26, and to all card-carrying full-time students under 32. The main operators of student charters are the Irish/British company USIT; see box below.

SCHEDULED FLIGHTS

The advantages of scheduled flights are that they can be pre-booked well in advance, remain valid for three months (sometimes longer) and involve none of the above restrictions on charters.

As with charters, though, deals on scheduled flights are available from most high street travel

agents, as well as from a number of specialist flight and student/youth agencies (same sources of flights as for charters). And again, you will usually do well to phone around a number of outlets to compare prices.

The Greek national **airline** Olympic generally have a range of special scheduled fares – sometimes competitive with an average charter flight. British Airways, too, often have cheap deals to Athens, as do East European airways like JAT, Balkan and Malev (these may fly via their respective capitals of Belgrade, Sofia and Budapest). It is possible to book these fares direct from the airlines, though you'll pay no more by going through an agent. (See addresses below).

FLIGHTS FROM IRELAND

Coments above on charters and scheduled flights apply equally to Ireland as a starting point. Costs, however, are generally higher and if you want to fly direct from Dublin (Aer Lingus services only) or Belfast you'll certainly be limited to the major Greek destinations.

The cheaper flights, including most of the youth/student offers, are often via London, with a tag on fare from Ireland for the connection. As ever, it's worth spending the time to shop around. The two most useful agencies are USIT and Joe Walsh Tours (see below for addresses).

AGENCIES AND AIRLINES

STUDENT/YOUTH AGENCIES

London Student Travel, 52 Grosvenor Gdns, London SW1 (☎01/730-3402). London branch of USIT.

STA Travel, 86 Old Brompton Rd, London SW7 (☎01/581-8233).

Miracle Air/Bus, 408 Strand, London WC2 (☎01/379-6055).

Both STA and USIT (useful for non-students, too) have agencies throughout Britain; see their adverts at the back of the book for addresses.

DISCOUNT FLIGHT AGENCIES

Alecos Tours, 3a Camden Rd, London NW1 (☎01/267-2092). Regular Olympic Airways consolidator.

Goldair, 321-322 Linen Hall, 162-168 Regent St, London W1 (☎01/287-1003). Specialist in connecting Athens to Turkey/Israel/Egypt.

Springways Travel, 71 Oxford St, London W1 (☎01/734-0393).

Three Greek specialists, out of hundreds.

AIRLINES

Olympic Airways, 164/165 Piccadilly, London W1 (☎01/846-9966).

British Airways, 75 Regent St, London W1 (☎01/897-4000).

JAT, 201 Regent St, London W1 (☎01/734-6252).

MALEV, 10 Vigo St, London W1(☎01/439-0577).

Balkan, 322 Regent St, London W1 (☎01/637-7637).

IRELAND

USIT, 7 Anglesea St, Dublin (☎0001/778-117). Student/youth specialists with good charter deals.

Joe Walsh Tours, 8-11 Lower Baggot St, Dublin (☎0001/789-555). General budget fares agent.

Aer Lingus, 59 Dawson St, Dublin (☎0001/795-030). For direct flights.

FLIGHTS FROM AUSTRALIA AND NEW ZEALAND

Due to the large Greek populations in Sydney and Melbourne, direct flights to Greece **from Australia** can be viable alternatives to routing through London. At various times of year you'll find special fares on *Olympic*, and although these are all to Athens you can add on a domestic flight within Greece for relatively low cost.

From New Zealand you will generally have to fly via one of the Australian airports or London.

STA Travel are usually a good bet for discount (and youth/student) flights. They have offices throughout Australia and New Zealand. Their head office addresses are:

STA , 1a Lee St, Sydney 2000 (☎212/1255)

STS, 10 O'Connel St, Auckland (☎399/191).

Try also contacting *Olympic Airways* direct:

Melbourne (84 Wiliam St, 3000 Victoria; ☎602/5400).

Sydney (44 Pitt St, NSW 2000; ☎02/251-1047).

SPECIALIST PACKAGE COMPANIES

Virtually every British **tour operator** includes Greece in their programme, though with many of the larger groups you'll find choices limited to the established resorts – notably on the islands of Rhodes, Kos, Crete, Skíathos and Corfu, and at Toló and the Halikidhikí on the mainland. If you buy one of these at a last-minute discount, you may find it costs little more than a flight – and you can use the accommodation offered as much or as little as you want.

For a more low-key and genuinely "Greek" resort, however, you'll do a lot better going through one of the smaller **specialist agencies**, who concentrate on Greece, or on holidays based around particular activities like hiking or dinghy sailing. These include:

GREEK SPECIALISTS

Greek Islands Club, 66 High St, Walton-on-Thames, KT12 1BU (☎0932/220-477). Mainly Ionian islands, also sailing – see opposite.

Laskarina Holidays, St Marys Gate, Wirksworth DE4 4DQ (☎062/982-2203).

Next Island, 113 Lower Richmond Rd, London SW15 (☎01/780-2200).

Simply Crete, 486 Chiswick High Rd, London W4 (☎01/747-1011). Crete only.

Sporades Holidays, The Coach House, Bull Lane, Winchcombe, Cheltenham, GL54 5HY (☎0242/603-747). Skíathos, Skópelos and Alónissos only.

Small World, 2 Mount Sion, Tunbridge Wells, TN1 1UE (☎0892/511-733).

Timsway Holidays, Nightingales Corner, Little Chalfont, HP7 9QS (☎02404/5541).

Twelve Islands, Angel Way, Romford, Essex, RM1 1AB (☎0708/752-653). Dodecanese only.

These companies are all fairly small-scale operations, offering competitively-priced packages with flights plus accommodation. They make an effort to find local, village accommodation and to offer islands without developed tourist resorts.

HIKING SPECIALISTS

Exodus Expeditions, All Saints Passage, 100 Wandsworth High St, London SW18 (☎01/870-0151).

Explore Worldwide, 7 High St, Aldershot, GU11 1BH (☎0252/319-448).

Sherpa Expeditions, 131a Heston Rd, Hounslow, TW3 0RD (☎01/577-2717).

The Pindhós (Pindus) mountains provide the focus for most Greek hiking holidays, though some of the companies above also feature Mt. Olympus, the Máni peninsula, Sámos and Crete. Groups are usually about a dozen people, led by experienced walkers.

SAILING SPECIALISTS

Falcon, 33 Notting Hill Gate, London W11 (☎01/221-8204).

Flotilla Sailing Holidays, 2 St John's Terrace, Harrow Rd, London W10 (☎01/969-5423).

Greek Islands Sailing Club, 66 High St, Walton-on-Thames, KT12 1BU (☎0932/220-477).

Island Sailing, The Port House, Port Solent, Portsmouth, PO6 4TH (☎0705/210-345).

Dinghy sailing and windsurfing holidays based on small flotillas of four to six berth yachts. Prices start at around £320 per week; all levels of experience. If you're a confident sailor and can muster a group of people, it's possible simply to hire a yacht from a broker; the Greek National Tourist Organisation have lists of companies.

MIND AND BODY

Skyros Centre, 1 Fawley Rd, London NW6 (☎01/431-0687). Holistic health, fitness and 'personal growth' holidays on the island of Skyros.

TRAINS

Travelling to Greece by train can be a very good deal if you're under 26 and if you plan to visit other countries en route. If not, then a return flight is likely to work out a fair bit cheaper, as well as a lot more relaxing.

YOUTH DEALS

The cheapest return train ticket to Greece from London is an **InterRail** pass (£145 from British Rail or any travel agent). This is available to anyone resident in Europe and is valid for a month's free travel on all European railways. The only extra you pay is half the price of travel in the country of issue (and, coming from Britain, on the Channel ferries). If you plan to cross over to Greece from Italy the pass will also secure reduced rate tickets on certain ferry crossings.

In Greece itself you won't get much benefit out of the pass since the railway network is slow and limited. But even so, the price equals buying a **Eurotrain** or **Transalpino** "BIJ" ticket (again available to anyone under 26), at currently just under £200 return London to Athens. Where these *BIJ* tickets have advantages is if you want to stay for longer in Greece. They have two months' validity, or can be purchased as one-ways (just over £100), and include all ferry crossings en route.

Details and tickets are available from *USIT/ Eurotrain* and *Transalpino* (see below) or any student/youth agency.

REGULAR TICKETS

The Eurotrain/Transalpino tickets represent a saving of around 30percent on the cost of a standard rail ticket. If you're over 26 and determined to travel by train, you'll pay around £300 return (£150 one way) from London to Athens. Even in peak season, it would be hard to pay more than this for a scheduled flight.

Details from British Rail.

ROUTES

There are two basic rail routes from London to Athens, either of which will take around three and a half days with the minimum of stops on the way.

With *Eurotrain/Transalpino* tickets you can make any number of stops along these routes, and can pre-specify excursions slightly off the main lines (to Florence or Rome, en route to Brindisi, for example) at little extra cost.

● London–Paris–Venice–Zagreb–Belgrade–Thessaloníki–Athens

This is the cheaper route, as it's entirely overland once you're across the channel. If you do it, you should certainly plan to break the journey, and it's worth including at least one stop in Yugoslavia (the longest and generally most crowded leg). If you want to travel straight throm Venice to Thessaloníki or Athens, try to reserve a couchette – in midsummer this needs to be done-least a month in advance. At Venice, for those intent on doing the journey non-stop, there are showers in the station, useful for the enforced two hour halt. Final advice: take advantage of the stop in Thessaloníki, and don't feel you need to rush straight to Athens.

● London–Paris–Rome–Milan–Brindisi–Corfu–Pátra–Athens

The extra expense on this route is the ferry from Brindisi to Pátra, via Corfu – but this has to be counted an attraction in itself. The possible Italian stopovers speak for themselves, though budget accordingly as Italy today is one of the most expensive nations in Europe.

Note: For a nominal fee, you can have the bulk of your luggage registered through to Athens (or any other stage of the journey), saving the hassle of carting it around at every change. Furthermore, if the railway authorities lose, damage, or delay your baggage, you are entitled to compensation – insist on obtaining the supporting documentation.

COACHES

Unless you're lucky enough to get a rock-bottom flight, coaches are the cheapest form of transport between London and Athens. Prices advertised in

RAIL TICKET OFFICES

USIT/Eurotrain, London Student Travel, 52 Grosvenor Gardens, London SW1 (☎01/730-3402).

Transalpino, 71–75 Buckingham Palace Road, London SW1 (☎01/834-9656).
British Rail European Travel Centre, Victoria Station, London SW1 (☎01/834 2345).

midseason can start very low indeed – at under £40 one way for the three- day journey.

As with flights the best source for **adverts** in London are the classified sections of *Time Out*, the *Evening Standard* and the free Australasian magazines. However, **be very wary** about going for the cheapest company unless you've heard something about them. There have been a string of accidents in recent years with operators flouting the terms of their licence, and horror stories abound of drivers getting lost or their coaches being refused entry. Some of the more disreputable operators actually start their journeys in modern, air-conditioned coaches to comply with British regulations then, once across the channel, transfer passengers to old beaten-up buses. Be equally aware of these cowboys if you are looking around Athens to buy a ticket home.

The **route** is usually via Belgium, Germany, Austria and Yugoslavia. Stops of about twenty minutes are made every five or six hours, with the odd longer break for roadside café meals. If you've booked with one of the more reliable operators you'll have three drivers working in shifts; most companies make do with two, and driving can become correspondingly hairy.

All in all, it's a journey that's really too long for comfort – even with copious supplies of food and drink – and at best you'll need a day at the end to recover. At worst it's a nightmare.

NON-COWBOY OPERATORS

Eurolines (01/730 0202). These coaches are operated by *National Express*, along with a consortium of other European state bus companies. They're comparatively expensive (£80 one way) but are safe, reliable and bookable through any National Express office.

Miracle Bus, 408 Strand, London WC2 (☎01/ 379-6055). A fairly established company who market what they feel are responsibly operated coaches. They sometimes have discounts on the *Eurolines* services. Prices from £50 one way. Summer only.

DRIVING OR HITCHING

If you have the time, driving to Greece can be a pleasant proposition. There are a multitude of possible routes, either heading down through Yugoslavia, or making for one of the Italy–Greece ferries (see over page for details).

VIA YUGOSLAVIA

The most direct approach is **through Germany and Yugoslavia**:

London–Ostend–Frankfurt–Munich–Zagreb– Belgrade–Thessaloníki–Athens.

If speed is your only consideration, and you are sharing the driving, it's feasible to cover this in three to four days. However, that would mean taking the motorway the whole way and giving yourself the briefest of overnight stops. With a week to spare, you could get a great deal more from the journey, possibly taking a wider loop through Vienna and Budapest.

An alternative to this route, only slightly longer, is **through France, Switzerland, Austria and Yugoslavia**:

London–Paris–Basel–Innsbruck–Ljubljana– Belgrade–Thessaloníki–Athens.

Again, this has the possibility of more or less continuous motorway, if you are pushed for time.

By general concensus, the most exhausting and also the most dangerous part of either journey is the long haul through **Yugoslavia**. The central highway – through Llubjana, Zagreb, Belgrade and Skopje – is one of Europe's poorest road arteries, with thundering trucks and not a lot to see en route. If you want to make something of the Yugoslav leg, far better to ease your way along the slow but beautiful coastal road, before veering inland, to skirt Albania, after Dubrovnik .

VIA ITALY

Heading for Western Greece, or the Ionian islands, it makes sense to drive via Italy – and whatever your final destination, taking a ferry on the final leg makes for a much more relaxed journey. From Italy there's a choice of six ports (though the closest, Venice and Trieste, are expensive options); in Greece you can dock at either Igoumenítsa in Epirus, Pátra in the Peloponnese, or coming from Venice at Pireás. Details follow in the box overpage.

Routes down **to Italy through France and Switzerland** are very much a question of personal preference. The fastest is probably:

Calais–Paris–Dijon–Geneva–Chamonix
which will get you to Milan with just one night en route if you follow the autoroutes (and pay their tolls). A little dawdling on minor roads, taking in something of Alsace-Lorraine, or Burgundy, makes for more of a holiday.

Whichever route you choose through France, you're likely to emerge in Italy around the Milan ring road. From here **Ancona** is under a day's drive on the autostrada; for the southern ports of **Bari, Brindisi or Otranto** you will need to count on at least one Italian overnight stay. Again, there are infinite possibilities for slower, detouring routes, inland through Umbria and the Abruzzi for example.

HITCHING

There are arguments for all the routes detailed if you're planning to hitch to Greece.

Going **via Yugoslavia** it's better to set out from Ostend, bypassing the legendary French indifference and plugging straight into a major European route. If you ask around on the ferry you might get a single lift most of the way. Yugoslavia itelf is a bad place to run out of lifts.

The **Italy route** will involve more outlay on ferries, and a harder start through France. Trains, at least, in Italy, though, are good value if you get stuck once across the border.

FERRIES TO GREECE

Regular ferries run most of the year from the Italian ports of **Ancona**, **Bari**, **Brindisi** and **Otranto** to **Igoumenítsa** (the port of Epirus in western Greece) and/or **Pátra** (at the tip of the Peloponnese). Most sail via the island of **Corfu**, and a few link other Ionian islands en route to Pátra; you can stop over at no extra charge if you get this specified on your ticket. Ferries also sail— less frequently – from **Venice** to Pireás, the port of Athens, from **Trieste** to Pátra and down the **Yugoslav coast** to Igoumenítsa.

At most times of year you can simply turn up at the main ports (Ancona, Bari, Brindisi) and buy a ticket. In July or August, however, the ferries can be packed in both directions and you'd be well advised to book ahead. A few phonecalls before leaving are, in any case, advised as the range of fares and operators (from Brindisi especially) is considerable; if you do just turn up at the port, spend an hour or so shopping around agents.

For **more information** on the companies, schedules and prices, see the listings for Igoumenítsa (p.282) and Pátra (p.207). Note that crossing to Igoumenítsa is substantially cheaper than to Pátra.

Routes

From Ancona *Marlines, Strintzis* and *Minoan* to Igoumenítsa (24 hr.) and Pátra (31 hr.); *Karageorgis* direct to Pátra (29 hr.); daily departures. *Minoan* sails via Corfu; *Strintzis* via Corfu or Dubrovnik; *Marlines* continues from Pátra to Iráklio (Crete) and Kuşadasi (Turkey).

From Bari *Ventouris* to Corfu, Igoumenítsa (12 hr.) and Pátra (16½ hr.); daily departures.

From Brindisi *Fragline* and *Adriatica* to Corfu, Igoumenítsa (10 hr.) and Pátra (19 hr.). *Hellenic Mediterranean Lines* to Igoumenítsa, Kefalloniá and Pátra. *Seven Islands* to Igoumenítsa, Corfu, Páxi, Itháki, Kefalloniá and Pátra. *Nausimar* to Corfu and Igoumenítsa. Several ferries leave every day, most between 9.30–10.30pm.

From Otranto *R-Lines* to Corfu and Igoumenítsa (9 hr.); 5 weekly, May-Oct. only.

From Venice *Adriatica* to Pireás (42 hr.) and Iráklio, Crete. Three monthly.

From Trieste *Hellenic Cypriot Mediterranean* to Brindisi and Pátra (44 hr.). Three weekly.

From Yugoslavia *Jadrolinja Lines* down the Dalmatian coast to Corfu and Igoumenítsa,

starting at Rijeka and calling at (Rab), Zadar, Split, (Hvar), Korčula, Dubrovnik, (Bar); ports in brackets are stops in high season only. One to three departures weekly.

British Agents

Karageorgis Lines, 36 King St, London W1 (☎01/499-0076). *Karageorgis.*

Sealink Travel Ltd, PO Box 29, Victoria Station, London SW1 (☎01/828-1948). *Adriatica.*

Viamare Travel Ltd, 33 Mapesbury Rd, London NW6 (☎01/452-8231). *Fragline, Hellenic Mediterranean Line, Karageorgis, Marlines, R-Lines, Strintzis, Ventouris.*

Yugotours, Chesham House, 150 Regent St, London W1 (☎01/734-7321). *Jadrolinja Lines.*

Sample Fares (Low/High Season)

Deck class passenger **to Igoumenítsa** from Bari, Brindisi or Otranto: £15-20/20-35. Car from £25/35.

Deck class passenger **to Pátra** from Bari, Brindisi or Otranto: £25-35/30-45. Car from £30/40.

50% reductions on most lines with *InterRail*.

RED TAPE AND VISAS

British, Australian and EC nationals need only a valid passport for entry to Greece, and can stay on an ordinary entry stamp for up to three months.

Temporary British passports are valid, though to travel via Yugoslavia you need either a full passport or a visa (obtained in advance at a Yugoslav consulate, or for a small fee at the border).

VISA EXTENSIONS

If you want to stay longer than three months you should officially apply for an **extension**. This can be done through the *Ipiresía Allodhapón* (Aliens Bureau), whose head office in Athens is at Halkondhíli 9, off Platía Káningos; open 8am–1pm), or, if you're somewhere more remote,

through the local police. It is advisable to complete the procedures a couple of weeks before your time runs out and also to keep all your pink, personalized bank exchange slips as confirmation that you can support yourself without working.

It's possible, although not strictly legal, to get around this law by leaving Greece for a day or so every three months, thus bypassing the bureaucracy and living in the country for as long as you like on an ordinary visitor's stay. (Just don't re-enter at the same border post!). Alternatively, you could simply ignore – or plead ignorance of – the procedures and overstay your ninety days. When you leave you'll be fined, but this amounts only to the cost of various revenue stamps to effect a retroactive extension – about fifty pence per month of actual stay.

COSTS, MONEY, AND BANKS

Greece is no longer really cheap – the days of four people renting a house for a thousand or so drachmas a week are long gone – and Common Market membership (since 1980) has brought the familiar pattern of spiralling food prices. However, the country remains a remarkably inexpensive place to stay in comparison with Northern Europe, and if you're willing to cut a few corners and avoid the more overtly developed areas, you can get by on very, very little.

SOME BASIC COSTS

Needs are simple in Greece. Once you've negotiated a room or campsite, it is only food, transport and the occasionally high admission tickets to the ancient sites that will dictate your budget. This is not a country for big consumers. On £8-12 a day you can live very well in all but the most upscale resorts, while if you're prepared to buy some of your own food in shops, it's quite possible to manage on as little as £5-7.

Ferries to the islands, the main extra expense, are reasonable. A deck class ticket from Pireás, the port of Athens, to Haniá on Crete will set you back just over £7, and for less than that there are dozens of other accessible islands. **Buses** and **trains** – the latter slightly cheaper – are similarly inexpensive. Athens to Thessaloníki, probably the longest single journey you'd think of making, is only around £7 one-way (2nd class).

A **room** for two can generally be bargained down to around £5-6 a night; **campsites** cost little more than £1.50 a person or, with discretion, you can camp on your own near the beaches for free. A solid **taverna meal**, even with considerable quantities of wine, should rarely work out above £4 a head.

All of this is of course subject to **where and when** you go. You'll pay much more for the same calibre room in Athens or the major resorts (if you can find one there at all) than in the provinces or on the lesser-known islands, while out of season rates are generally reduced by 25 to 50 percent.

Solo travellers will experience some frustration; even in city hotels, single rooms are rare, and in summer on the islands you'll invariably pay the full double rate. Food likewise is cheaper if shared, but even in the resorts with their inflated 'international' menus, you'll usually find a market or taverna where the locals eat.

For students, an **ISIC card** offers small discounts on museum and archaeological site entrance fees, plus some discounts on transport.

CURRENCY

Greek currency is the **drachma** (*dhrahmí*), currently around 270dr to the pound. The most common notes in circulation are those of 100, 500, 1000 and 5000 drachmas (*dhrahmés*), coins of 1, 2, 5, 10, 20 and 50drs; the drachma is theoretically subdivided into 100 *leptá*.

You are officially allowed to take just 3000 drachmas (about £11) into Greece with you, so the majority of your money will have to be changed after arrival. Most people take it in the form of travellers' cheques, though if you've a British bank account you might prefer to carry Eurocheques, or if you've a Girobank current account, Postcheques. A small amount of local currency is worth acquiring to tide you over the first few hours.

CHEQUES, PLASTIC AND PROBLEMS

Travellers' cheques can be cashed at all banks, and when they're closed at quite a number of hotels, agencies and tourist shops. **Eurocheques** (issued by most British banks with a Eurocheque card) are widely accepted at banks and can be written out in drachmas. Commission on travellers' cheques is paid when you buy them and also to the exchanging bank (see below). With most Eurocheques you pay a commissioning charge of around 1.6 percent to the exchanging bank plus a handling fee of around 30p per transaction against your British account.

Postcheques are almost worth getting a Girobank account to make use of. They work in a similar way to Eurocheques (again in conjunction with a cheque card) but can be exchanged at post offices rather than banks. In Greece this is a considerable advantage. You miss out on the exchange queues at banks and have access to exchange almost anywhere you go. There are small islands which have no bank but they almost all have a post office. Post cheques are issued, with a small commission, in amounts of the equivalent of £100 in local currency.

Major **credit cards** are fairly widely accepted but only by the more expensive shops, hotels and restaurants. They're useful for hiring cars, for example, but no good in the cheaper tavernas or hotels.

If you run short of money, you can get a **cash advance on a credit card**, but be warned that the minimum amount is 15,000dr (about £56). The *Emborikí Trápeza* (Commercial Bank) handles *VISA*; the *Ethnikí Trápeza*/National Bank services *Access* customers. Failing this, in an emergency, you will have to arrange to have **money sent** from home. Though this is theoretically very quick, you should in practice count on delays of three to six days for receipt of telexed funds. You can pick up the sum in foreign currency, or even travellers' cheques, but there are of course reconverting commissions (curiously, much heavier for foreign cash) and you can only do this on the day of receipt.

RECEIPTS AND CURRENCY REGULATIONS

Travellers' cheques are freely importable into Greece, but more than £350 in **cash** should be declared upon entry to minimise hassles if you want to take it out again. Similarly, if you have any reason to believe that you'll be acquiring large quantities of drachmas – i.e. you will be working, or selling something – declare everything on arrival, then request (and save) the pink, personalised **receipts** for each exchange transaction. Otherwise you can only re-exchange up to £75 worth of drachmas on departure.

BANKS

Greek **banks** are normally open Mon.–Thurs. 8am–2pm, Fri. 8am– 1.30pm. Certain branches in the major cities and tourist centres are open extra hours in the evenings and Saturday mornings to change money. Always take your passport with you as proof of identity and be prepared for at least one long queue – often you have to queue up once to have the transaction approved and again to pick up the cash.

Commissions can also vary considerably (usually 60–100dr at the bigger banks), even between branches of the same bank, so ask first.

Remember, though, that both commission and rate will be worse if you change money at a hotel or travel agent.

HEALTH AND INSURANCE

There are no required inoculations for Greece, though it's wise to have a typhoid-cholera booster, and to ensure that you are up to date on tetanus and polio.

The water is safe (and tastes wonderful) pretty much everywhere, though you will come across shortages on some of the drier and more remote islands. Bottled water is widely available if you're feeling cautious.

HEALTH HAZARDS

The main health problems experienced by visitors have to do with overexposure and the sea. Wear a hat and drink plenty of fluids in the hot months to avoid any danger of **sunstroke**, and don't underestimate the power of even a hazy sun to **burn**.

If you are sleeping on **beaches**, a wise precaution is to use insect repellent, and/or a tent with a screen to guard against sandflies – carriers of a range of diseases, including a few (rare but serious) viral infections.

Mosquitos (*kounóupia*) are less worrying – in Greece they don't carry anything worse than a vicious bite – but they can be infuriating in some parts of the country. The best solution is to burn pyrethrum incense coils (*spíres* or *fidhákia* in Greek); these are widely and cheaply available.

In the sea, you may just have the bad luck to meet an armada of **jellyfish**, especially in late summer; they come in various colours and sizes including invisible and minute. Urine or ammonia lessens the sting. Less vicious but more common are **sea urchins**, which infest rocky shorelines year-round; if you are unlucky enough to step on, or graze one, a sterilized needle, scalpel, and olive oil are effective for removing spines from your anatomy. And they should be extracted, or they will fester. A pair of goggles for swimming and footwear for walking over wet rocks should help avoid both of the above.

The worst maritime danger – fortunately very rare – seems to be the **weever fish**, which buries itself in tidal zone sand with just its poisonous dorsal and gill spines protruding. If you tread on one the sudden pain is unmistakably excruciat-

ing, and the venom is exceptionally potent. Consequences can range up to permanent paralysis of the affected area, so the imperative first aid is to immerse your foot in water as hot as you can stand. This degrades the toxin and relieves the swelling of joints and attendant pain.

The **adder** and **scorpion** are found in Greece, though both are shy; just take care when climbing over dry-stone walls where snakes like to sun themselves, and don't put hands/feet in places, i.e. shoes, where you haven't looked first!

Lastly, **hay fever** sufferers should be prepared for the early Greek pollen season, at its height from April to June. If you are taken by surprise pharmacists stock tablets and creams.

MEDICAL ATTENTION

For **minor complaints** it's enough to go to the local *farmakío* (chemist). Greek pharmacists are highly trained and dispense a number of medicines which in Britain could only be prescribed by a doctor. In the larger towns there'll usually be one who speaks good English. If you regularly use any **prescription drug** you should bring along a copy of the prescription together with the generic name of the drug – this will help should you need to replace it and also avoid possible problems with customs officials (see note about codeine, below*). **Contraceptive pills** are more readily available every year, but don't count on local availability – unfortunately abortion is still the principal form of birth control. **Condoms**, though, are inexpensive and ubiquitous – just ask for *kapótes* at any corner *períptero* (kiosk).

Homeopathic and herbal remedies are also much more widely available than in Britain, with homeopathic pharmacies in many of the larger towns. There is a large **homeopathic** centre in Athens at Nikosthénous 8, Platía Plastíra, Pangráti (☎709-8199) and a nearby homeopathic pharmacy at Ivíkou 8, corner Eratosthénous (☎722-2774), plus anywhere else you see the characteristic green cross.

For serious **medical attention** you'll find English-speaking doctors in any of the bigger towns or resorts; the Tourist Police (☎171 in

Athens, ☎104 elsewhere) or your consulate should be able to come up with some names if you have any difficulty. In **emergencies**, treatment is given free in state hospitals – for cuts, broken bones, etc. – though you will only get the most basic level of nursing care. Greek families routinely take in food and bedding for relatives, so as a tourist you'll find difficulties. Somewhat better are the ordinary state-run outpatient clinics (*yatría*) attached to most public hospitals and also found in rural locales; these operate on a first-come, first-served basis, so go early; usual hours are 8am–noon.

INSURANCE

British and other EC nationals are officially entitled to free medical care in Greece – but this means admittance only to the lowerst grade of state hospital (known as *yenikó nosokomío*), and, as stated above, does not include nursing care. If you need prolonged medical care, you'll need to make use of private treatment, which, as everywhere, is expensive.

Some form of **travel insurance**, therefore, is advisable. Just about any British travel agent, bank or insurance broker will sell you a comprehensive cover to include not only medical expenses but also loss or theft of baggage. If you think you might rent a car or motorbike, make sure that this is included in your policy – the vast majority of tourist accidents in Greece involve falling off two-wheelers.

For medical claims, keep all receipts, including those from chemists. You will have to pay for most medical care on the spot (insurance claims can be processed if you have hospital treatment) but it can all be claimed back.

Claims on stolen items need to be registered with the local police station. This can occasionally be tricky as many officials simply won't accept that anything could be stolen on their patch, or at least don't want to take responsibility for it. But be persistent and if necessary enlist the support of the local Tourist Police or tourist office.

A warning needs to be sounded about **codeine, which has recently been banned in Greece. If you import any – and it is fairly common in headache drugs lincluding Codeine, Panadeine, Veganin, Solpadeine and Codis – you just might find yourself in serious trouble. So check labels carefully.*

THE EOT, INFORMATION AND MAPS

glossy, regional pamphlets, good for getting an idea of where you want to go, even if the actual text should be taken with an occasional grain of salt. Also available from the EOT are a reasonable fold-out map of Greece, a large number of sheets on special interests, from annual festivals to lead-free petrol stations, and a (highly approximate) ferry timetable.

The National Tourist Organization maintains **offices** in most European capitals (though not Dublin), Australia and North America. Addresses include:

London 195-7 Regent St, W1 (☎01/734-5997).
Amsterdam Leidsestraat 13 (☎254-212).
Copenhagen Vester Farimagsgade 3.
Stockholm Grev Turegatan 2 (☎211-113).
Sydney 51-57 Pitt St (☎241-1663).

In Greece, you will find **EOT offices** in most of the larger towns and resorts. The principal office is in Athens, inside the National Bank of Greece on Síntagma Square. Here, in addition to

The first place to head for information is the National Tourist Organization of Greece (*Ellinikós Organismós Tourismoú*, or *EOT*). They publish an impressive array of free,

the usual leaflets, you can pick up weekly schedules for the inter-island ferries – not 100 percent reliable, but useful guidelines. The EOT staff are themselves very helpful for advice on ferry, bus, and train departures.

Where there is no EOT office, you can get information (and often a range of leaflets) from municipally-run **tourist offices** or from the **Tourist Police**. The latter are basically a branch of the local police; they can sometimes provide you with lists of rooms to let, and in general are helpful and efficient.

MAPS

Maps are an endless source of confusion in Greece. Each cartographic company seems to have its own peculiar system of transcribing Greek letters into English – and these, as often as not, do not match the transliterations on the road signs.

The most reliable **road maps of Greece** are Michelin #980x (1:700,000) and the Viennese Freytag-Berndt (1:650,000). These are widely available in Britain, though less easily in Athens. Freytag-Berndt also publishes a series of more detailed maps on various regions of Greece, such as the Peloponnnese and Cyclades. Individual **maps of islands** are much less consistent – many are local productions with strange hieroglyphic symbology, and they tend to be sold only on the spot. A reasonably good series, covering most islands of any size and available overseas, is published by Toubi.

Hiking/topographical maps are also uneven but getting better all the time. The Greek mountaineering magazine Korfes began in 1982

to publish 1:50,000 maps (Greek lettering only) of select alpine areas. More than thirty now exist and a new one is issued every other month as a centrefold in the magazine. To get back issues you'll probably need to visit the magazine's office at Platía Ayíou Vlassíou 16, Aharnés, Athens (☎246-1528), although the bookstore I Folia tou Vivliou (see 'Listings' in the Athens chapter) generally has a big backstock as well.

The Korfes maps are extremely accurate, based as they are on the generally unavailable maps of the **Army Geographical Service** (Yeografikí Ipiresía Stratoú). If you want to try your luck at obtaining those, visit the YIS at Evelpídhon 4, north of Aréos Park in Athens, on Monday, Wednesday, or Friday from 11.30am to 2pm only. If the officer in charge decides you have a legitimate reason to procure a map or two (not more) he will authorise your purchase. You need to bring your passport and must sign a statement decalaring that you won't sell, give away, export, photocopy, or trace said map(s), under penalty of two years' imprisonment! If you don't speak good Greek, best to ask a Greek friend to get them for you.

Easier to obtain, though less detailed at a scale of 1:200,000 and up to twenty years out of date, are the maps of the **National Statistical Service** (Ethnikí Statistikí Ipiresía), sold in Athens at Likoúrgou 14 (3rd floor, near Omonia; weekdays 8am–1.30pm). These 1:200,000 survey maps, together with a good selection of Toubi and other island maps, are also obtainable in Britain through the map shops Stanfords (12 Long Acre, London WC2; ☎01/836-1321) or McCarta (122 Kings Cross Rd, London WC1; 01/278-8278).

GETTING AROUND

The standard means of transport in Greece is the bus. Train networks are usually slow and limited. Buses, however, cover just about every route on the mainland – albeit infrequently on minor roads – and provide a basic service on the islands. The best way to supplement buses is to hire a moped or scooter, especially on the islands, where at any substantial town or resort you can find a rental outlet. Inter-island travel of course means taking ferries. These again are extensive, and given time will get you to any of the 166 inhabited isles.

GREECE: TRAINS

0   100 km

BUSES

Bus services on the **major routes** – both on the mainland and islands – are highly efficient. On **secondary roads** they're a lot less regular, but even the most remote villages will be connected by a school or market bus. As these often leave shortly after dawn, an alarm clock can be a useful travel aid. On the islands, there are usually buses to connect the port and main town for ferry arrivals or departures.

Most of these green-and-cream-coloured buses are privately run by a syndicate of companies known as the **KTEL**. However, even in medium-sized towns there can be several widely scattered terminals for services in different directions, so make sure you have the right station for your departure. As a rough estimate to cost, figure on about six drachmas per kilometre travelled.

A few intercity and international routes are also served by express buses operated by **OSE**, the State Railway Organization. These always leave from the train station. Departure times are often more convenient than the KTEL or conventional rail service, with fares almost identical with those of the KTEL.

TRAINS

The Greek railway network, run by **OSE**, is limited to the mainland, and trains are invariably slower than the equivalent buses. However, they're also much cheaper – about 35 percent less on non-express services, even more on return tickets – and some of the lines are enjoyable in themselves. The best, a real treat of a ride, is the rack-and-pinion line between **Diakoftó and Kalávrita** in the Peloponnese.

If you're starting a journey at the initial station of a run you can (at no extra cost) reserve a seat; a carriage and seat number will be written on the back of your ticket. At most intermediate points, it's first-come, first-served. **Timetables** are sporadically available, printed in Greek only; the best place to obtain one is the OSE office in Athens. Trains tend to leave promptly at the outset, though on the more circuitous lines they're invariably forty minutes late by the end of the journey.

There are two **classes**: first and second. First class is rarely worth the extra money; cars are often smaller, seats may not recline as promised, and fellow passengers are less interesting.

InterRail pass holders must secure reservations like everyone else, and must pay express supplements on a few lines.

FERRIES

Ferries are of use primarily for travel to, and between, islands, though you may also want to make use of the routes between Athens and Monemvassía in the Peloponnese. There are three different varieties of boats: **ordinary ferries** (which operate the main services), **hydrofoils** (run by the 'Flying Dolphins' company on popular routes), and local **kaíkia** (small boats which in season cover short island hops and excursions). Costs are very reasonable on the longer journeys, though proportionately more expensive for shorter, inter-island connections.

Regular ferries

Usually your only consideration will be getting a boat that leaves on the day, and for the island, that you want, but when sailing from Pireás, the port of Athens, to the Cyclades or Dodecanese islands you should have quite a range of choice.

Bear in mind that **routes** taken and the speed of the boats vary enormously. A journey from Pireás to Thíra (Santoríni), for instance, can take anything from nine to fourteen hours. Before buying a ticket it's wise to establish how many stops there'll be before your island, and the estimated time of arrival. Many agents act only for one specific boat (they'll happily tell you that theirs is the only available service) so you may have to ask around to uncover alternatives; notoriously slow boats include the *Schinoussa* (formerly the *Elli*) and the *Miaoulis*.

Many **sailings from Pireás** are in the early morning, between 7.30 and 9am, but there are even more between 2 and 4pm to the Dodecanese and various islets between them and the Cyclades, and a final spate of departures between 6 and 7pm for Crete, Híos, and Lésvos.

We've indicated most of the **ferry connections**, both on the maps (see p.344-5 for a general picture) and in the 'Travel Details' at the end of each chapter. Don't take our listings as exhaustive or wholly reliable, however, as schedules are notoriously erratic, and be aware that we have given details essentially for summer departures. **Out-of-season** schedules are severely reduced, with many islands connected only once or twice a week. The most reliable, up-to-date information is available from the local port police (*limenarhío*), which maintains offices at Pireás and on most fair-sized islands.

Regular **ferry tickets** are, in general, best bought on the day of departure, unless you need to reserve space for a car. Buying tickets in advance will tie you down to a particular ferry at a particular time – and innumerable factors can make you regret that. Most obviously there's **bad weather**, which, particularly off-season, can play havoc with the schedules, causing some small boats to remain at anchor and others to alter their routes drastically. There are only three periods of the year – March 23-25, Easter weekend, and mid-August – when ferries need to be booked a couple of days in advance. Otherwise, you can usually even buy a ticket once on board (albeit with a small surcharge at times) despite what travel agents may tell you.

The cheapest class of ticket, which you'll probably automatically be sold, is **deck class**, variously called *tríti*, *gámma*, or *touristikí*. This gives you the run of most boats except for the first-class restaurant and bar. On the shorter journeys the best place to be, in any case, is on deck – space best staked out as soon as you get on board.

Motorbikes and **cars** get issued extra tickets, in the latter case up to four times as costly as simple passenger fares. This obviously limits the number of islands you'll want to drag a car to – it's really only worth it for the larger ones like Crete, Rhodes, Híos, Lésvos, Sámos or Kefalloniá. Even with these, unless you're planning a prolonged stay, you may find it cheaper to leave your car in Pireás and hire another on arrival.

Most ferries sell a limited range of **food** aboard, though it tends to be overpriced and unenticing. Honourable exceptions are the meals served by *ANEK* lines, which operates the ferries from Pireás to Haniá and Iráklio on Crete, certain of the *Ventouris* ferries serving the western Cyclades, and virtually all of the boats plying to Híos and Lésvos. On other lines it is worth stocking up with your own provisions.

Hydrofoils

'Flying Dolphin' hydrofoils are roughly twice as fast (and up to twice as expensive) as ordinary ferries. They operate mainly among the Argo-Saronic islands close to Athens, and down the east coast of the Peloponnese to Monemvassía and Kíthira, and among the northern Sporades (Skíathos, Skópelos, and Alónissos). There are also summer-only services in the Cyclades between Míkonos, Páros, Íos, Thíra and Crete, and in the Dodecanese between Rhodes, Tílos, Níssiros, Kós, Kálimnos and Pátmos.

Due to the quirks of Greek agencies, it is only possible to buy **one-way** tickets on the Dolphins. In summer, if you have a tight schedule, it is worth buying your return (or onward) ticket on arrival at an island. They are generally sold by an agent at the dock.

Schedules and tickets are available in Athens from *Wagons-Lits*, Stadhíou 5, off Síntagma square (☎01/324-2281) and in Pireás from *Ceres Hydrofoils*, Aktí Miaoúli 69 (☎01/452-7107).

Kaïkia

In season *kaïkia* (caiques) sail between adjacent islands and to a few of the more obscure. These are no cheaper than main services but can be extremely useful and often very pleasant. We have tried to detail the more regular links in the text, though many, inevitably, depend on the whims of local boat-owners or fishermen. The only firm information is to be had on the quayside.

Kaïkia, despite appearances, have a good safety record; indeed it's the larger, overloaded car-ferries that have in the past run into trouble.

MOPED AND BIKE HIRE

Motorcycles, **scooters**, **mopeds** and **bicycles** are available for hire on many of the islands and in a few of the popular mainland resorts. Motorcycles and scooters (which can, perilously, take two people) cost around £7 a day up; mopeds from £4; bikes as little as £1. All rates can be reduced with bargaining outside of peak season, or if you negotiate for a longer period of rental. To hire motorcycles (usually 125cc) you will need to show a driver's licence; otherwise all you need is a passport to leave as security.

Mopeds are perfect for all but the hilliest islands, and you can obtain them literally everywhere. Make sure you check them thoroughly before riding off since many are only cosmetically maintained and repaired. If you break down it's your responsibility to return the machine, so it's worth taking down the phone number of whoever rents them to you in case they give out in the middle of nowhere.

A warning should also be given about **mopeds and safety**. There are a constant number of accidents each year involving tourists coming to grief on rutted dirt tracks or through a mechanically dodgy machine. And in addition to your own injuries you're likely to be charged a criminally high price for any repairs needed for the bike.

Few people seem to **cycle** in Greece but it's not always such hard going as you might imagine. If you have a bicycle – especially a mountain bike, which is ideal for Greek terrain – you might consider taking it along by train or airplane (it's free if within your 20-kilo allowance). Within Greece you should be able to take it for free on most of the ferries, in the guard's van on most trains (for a small fee), and with a little persuasion on the roof of buses. Any spare parts you might need, however, are best brought along. Alternatively, you can hire a bone-breaking old model on many of the larger islands.

CAR RENTAL AND DRIVING

Cars have obvious advantages for getting to the more inaccessible parts of mainland Greece. If you're thinking of **renting** one, though, bear in mind that this is probably the most expensive country in Europe to do so — £150-190 a week (depending on season) for a compact model, once you have added on the extras like insurance.

If you want to hire a car from the outset, you may get a better price from one of the **British companies** who make deals with local firms than if you negotiate for rental in Greece itself. One of the more competitive of these outlets, who can arrange for (reliable and fully insured) cars to be picked up at most airports is **Cars Direct** (Hobbs Court, Jacob St, London SE1; ☎01/287-3402). Others include **TransHire** (71 Oxford St, London W1; ☎01/437-0951) and **Holiday Autos** (33 Dover St, London W1; ☎01/491-1087). Most travel agents can also offer car hire in Greece, though their rates are generally higher than these specialist rental agents.

From a costs standpoint, you might prefer to spend most time on public transport, with just the occasional strategic week (say in the Máni or Pilion peninsulas, where buses are sparse) in your private vehicle. **In Greece, InterRent** and **Just** are reliable medium-sized companies with branches in many towns; both are considerably cheaper than (and just as reputable) as international operators like *Hertz* and *Avis*. Specific local recommendations are given in the guide. All agencies will want either a credit card or a large cash deposit up front; minimum age requirements vary from 21 to 25. In theory an International Driver's License is also needed but in practice European, Australasian and American ones are honoured. Note that initial prices quoted may not include tax and supplemental insurance premiums; the coverage included by law in the basic rental fee is generally inadequate, so check the fine print on your contract carefully.

If you drive **your own vehicle** to and through Greece you'll need international third party insurance and a carnet in your passport. The latter normally allows you to keep a vehicle in Greece for up to three months; it is difficult, if not impossible, to leave the country without the vehicle — a frustration if you want to make a trip by ferry to Turkey, for example.

Keep in mind that Greece has the highest **accident rate** in Europe after Portugal, and many of the roads, particularly if you're unfamiliar with them, are quite perilous. Asphalt can turn into a dirt track without warning on the smaller routes, and railway crossings are rarely guarded. If you are involved in any kind of accident it's ille-

gal to drive away, and you can be held at a police station for up to 24 hours. Often the talk will be way out of proportion to the incident, but if it is serious ring your consulate immediately in order to get a lawyer (you have this right). Don't make a statement to anyone who doesn't speak, and write, very good English.

Tourists with AA/RAC or similar membership are given free **road assistance** from ELPA, the Greek equivalent, who run breakdown services based in Athens, Pátra, Lárissa and Thessaloníki. Their 'guidance service' number is 174. In an **emergency** ring the Tourist Police on 104, anywhere in the country.

TAXIS

Greek **urban taxis**, especially Athenian ones, are among the cheapest in Europe; they are well worth making use of (though see the caveats on fares in the *Athens* chapter).

In **rural areas**, taxis have no metres — you bargain. A reasonable per-vehicle (*not* per-person) charge for a sixteen-kilometre transfer on a dirt road will be about £6. Occasionally a taxi returning empty from a drop-off will offer you a ride for the equivalent of the bus fare, just to pay for their petrol.

HITCHING

Hitching is fine in Greece as long as you're not too bothered by time; lifts are fairly frequent but tend to be short. Most important, it's also one of the safer countries for women travellers, though as ever you find a great deal of confidence in numbers — the best being two, one man and one woman.

Although Greek traffic is sparse, much of it is **trucks and vans** which are good for thumbing. Rides are easiest to come by in remote areas where most people know that buses are scarce. Hitching on commercial vehicles is nominally illegal, so if you're offered a ride in a large van or lorry, especially in the load space, don't be offended if you're set down just before an upcoming town and its police checkpoints.

Thumbing may even prove the quickest form of travel if you want to take an unusual route which would otherwise involve a string of bus connections. At its best it's a wonderful method of getting to know the country — there's no finer way to take in the Peloponnese than from the back of a truck that looks converted from a lawn-mower – and a useful means of picking up some Greek. While you'll often get lifts from Greeks eager to display or practice their English there'll be as many where to communicate you're forced to try the language. As it can be all too easy to stay in Greece without picking up more than restaurant talk, this is one way of breaking out.

FLYING

Olympic Airways operates all domestic **flights** within Greece. They cover a fairly wide network of islands and larger towns, though most routes are to and from Athens, or the northern capital of Thessaloníki. Schedules can be picked up at the head office on Singroú 96, Athens (☎01/929-2111). *Olympic* also has branch offices or repre-sentatives in almost every other town or island of any size.

Fares usually work out around three times the cost of an equivalent bus or ferry journey but on long inter-island hauls (Rhodes to Kastellórizo or Kefalloniá to Zákinthos, for example) you might consider this time well bought. For obscure reasons, flights between Athens and Mílos, Skíathos, and Kalamáta are slightly better value per kilometre, so take advantage.

Olympic's island flights are often full in midseason; if they're part of your plans, **reserve** well in advance (i.e. two weeks). Be aware, too, that, like ferries, flights can be cancelled in bad weather; many of the planes are lightweight, 40-seaters and are not flown in strong winds. Also like ferries, domestic Olympic tickets are **non-refundable** and non-transferable.

SLEEPING

There are huge numbers of beds for tourists in Greece, and most of the year you can rely on turning up pretty much anywhere and finding a room – if not in a hotel, then in a private house (the standard island accommodation).

Only in July and August, the country's high season, are you likely to experience problems. At these times, it is worth striking a little off the standard tourist routes, turning up at each new place early in the day, and taking whatever is available in the hope that you will be able to exchange it for something better later on.

HOTELS AND ROOMS

Hotels are categorized by the Tourist Police from 'Luxury' down to 'E-class,' and all except the top category have to keep within set price limits. D- and E-class hotels are usually very reasonable, costing around £5-8 for a double room, £4-7 for a single. The better value places tend to be in more remote areas, as ratings depend partly on loca-tion; in Athens, inevitably, you get less for your money.

If you want a roof over your head while travel-ling about the mainland towns, you're generally going to have to depend on these small hotels – specific recommendations appear throughout the guide. In resorts, however, and throughout the islands, you can supplement them with privately-let **rooms** (*dhomátia*). These are again officially controlled and are divided into three classes ('A' down to 'C'). They are usually a fair deal cheaper than hotels, and are in general spotlessly clean. These days the bulk of them are in new, purpose-built low-rises but some are in people's homes, where you'll often be treated with disarming hospitality.

At its simplest, *dhomátia* implies a bare, concrete room, with a hook on the back of the door and toilet facilies (cold water only) outside in the courtyard; at its fanciest it could be a modern, fully-furnished place with an attached

Prices for rooms and hotels should be displayed on the back of the door of your room. If you feel you're being overcharged at a place which is officially registered, threatening to go to the Tourist Police – who will generally adopt your side in such cases – should be enough to elicit compliance. Small amounts over the posted price may be legitimately explained by tax or out-of-date forms. And just occasionally you may find that you have bargained so well, or arrived so far out of season, that you are actually paying *less* than you're supposed to.

marble bathroom. Between these two extremes you may well find that you pay extra for a hot shower (or even a cold one), that there's a choice of rooms at various prices (they'll usually show you the most expensive first) and that price and quality are not necessarily directly linked. Always ask to see the room before agreeing to take it and settle on the price.

Areas to look for rooms, and some suggestions for the best, are again included in the guide. But as often as not, they find you: owners descend on ferry or bus arrivals to fill any space they have. In smaller places you'll often see rooms advertised (sometimes in German – *zimmer*), or you can just ask at the local taverna or *kafenío* (café). Even if there are no official places around, there is very often someone prepared to earn extra money by putting you up.

Just occasionally, you encounter an incredibly officious setup where all rooms are controlled by (and only by) the Tourist Police; this can be useful but there are times and places where they'll refuse to let out any *dhomátia* until all the hotels are full, an infuriating business. In **winter**, designated to begin 1 November and end in early April, private rooms are closed pretty much across the board to keep the hotels in business. There's no point in traipsing about hoping to find exceptions – most rooms owners obey the system very strictly. If they don't, they'll find you themselves and, watching out for hotel rivals, guide you back to their place.

It has become standard practice for rooms proprietors to ask to keep your passport; ostensibly 'for the Tourist Police,' but in reality to prevent you skipping out with an unpaid bill. Some owners may be satisfied with just taking down the details, as in hotels, and they'll almost always return the documents once you get to know them, or if you need them for another purpose (to change money for example).

CHEAPER OPTIONS: HOSTELS, ROOFS, HOUSES AND VILLAS

If even rooms are beyond your budget, then an alternative can usually be found.

Youth Hostels

Greece is not exactly packed with **youth hostels** (*ksenón neotítos*) but those that there are tend to be fairly easy-going affairs: slightly run-down and a far cry from the harsh institutions you find in northern Europe. Very few of them ever ask for an IYHA card, and if they do you can usually buy one on the spot, or maybe just pay a little extra for your bed. Charges are around £2.50 a night. The only annoying factor is a curfew, most often around 11.30pm or midnight, but occasionally as early as 10pm. However, this is usually offset by the company of fellow travellers, with the hostel simply turning into a kind of members-club. Hostels can also be a good source of up-to-date information, and are sometimes handy for finding work, as when farmers march down to the rural ones at harvest time to pick up casual labour.

Hostels on the **mainland** are at Athens (3), Náfplio, Mycenae, Olympia, Pátra, Delphi, Litohóro (Mt. Olympus) and Thessaloníki. On the **islands** you'll find them only on Corfu (2), Thíra, and Crete (where there are seven – at Iráklio, Mália, Ierápetra, Réthimno, Haniá, Sitía and Mírthios).

'Student Houses' and Roofspace

In Athens there are also cheap dormitory-style '**Student Houses**', non-YHA hostels which despite their name are in no way limited to students. These – and sometimes rural/island tavernas – will also sometimes let '**roofspace**', usually providing a mattress for you to lay a sleeping bag down on, or even full bedding. If any place seems full it's worth asking about this, as it can be a cheap, cool and pleasantly uncramped alternative.

Houses and Flats

Houses or flats – and, out of season, villas – can sometimes be rented by the week or month. If you have two or three people to share costs, and want to drop roots on an island for a while, it's an option well worth considering. To arrange a rental, find a place you want to stay, get yourself known around the village, and ask around; you can occasionally pick up wonderful deals.

CAMPING

Official campsites range from ramshackle compounds on the islands to highly organized – and rather soulless – EOT-run complexes. Cheap, casual places rarely cost much above £1.50 a night per person; at the larger sites, though, it's not impossible for two of you and one tent (all separately charged) to add up to the price of a basic room.

As a general rule you don't have to worry about leaving tents or **baggage** unattended; the Greeks are one of the most honest races in Europe. The main risk, sadly, comes from other campers, and every year a few items disappear in that direction.

'Freelance' Camping

Freelance camping – outside authorised campsites – is such an established element of Greek travel that few people realize that it's officially forbidden. Since 1977, however, it has indeed been forbidden by law, and once in a while the regulations get enforced.

In effect this simply means you should exercise a reasonable degree of **sensitivity and discretion**. Obviously the police crack down on people camping rough (and littering) on popular mainstream tourist beaches, especially when a large community of campers is developing. But elsewhere, particularly in rural inland areas, nobody is really bothered. If you're near a beach, it is standard procedure to camp by a taverna; if you eat and drink there regularly, they will generally let you use their facilities.

MONASTERIES AND REMOTE VILLAGES

Greek **monasteries and convents** have a tradition of putting up travellers of the appropriate sex. On the mainland, this is still customary practice; on the islands, much less so. Wherever, you should always ask locally before heading out to one for the night. Also, dress modestly – shorts on either sex, and short skirts on women, are total anathema – and try to arrive early evening, not later than 8pm or sunset (whichever is earlier).

For **men**, the most exciting monastic experience is a visit to the 'Monks' Republic' of **Mount Áthos**, on the Halkidhikí peninsula, near Thessaloníki. This is a far from casual travel option, involving much bureaucratic procedure to obtain a permit. If you are interested, see p.325 for details.

If you are stranded, or arrive very late, in a **remote mountain** village with no tourist facilities whatsoever, you may very well find that you are invited to pass the night in someone's home. This should not, however, be counted on; the most polite thing to do is to have a meal or drink at the taverna/*kafenío* (there will always be at least one of the latter) and then, especially if it is summer, enquire as to the possibility of sleeping either in the vacant schoolhouse or in a spare room at the *kinotikó grafío* (community records office).

Camping Climates. It's warm enough to sleep out in just a sleeping bag from May until early September, so you don't really need to drag round a tent*. A waterproof bag or cover is, however, useful to keep out the late summer damp; so too is a foam pad, which lets you sleep in relative comfort almost anywhere. You will always need a sleeping bag, since even in midsummer the nights get cool, but it can be as lightweight as you can find.

*But see comments on **sandflies** under 'Health'.

EATING AND DRINKING

Greeks spend a lot of time socialising outside their homes, and sharing a meal is one of the chief ways of doing it. They're not great drinkers, but what drinking they do is mainly done at the café. The atmosphere is always relaxed and informal, and pretensions (or expense account prices) rare outside of the more chi-chi parts of Athens or major resorts.

RESTAURANTS

Greek cuisine and **restaurants** are simple and straightforward. There's no snobbery about eating out; everyone does it some of the time, and for foreigners with strong currencies it's extremely cheap – around £4 for a substantial meal with (house) wine.

In choosing a restaurant the best strategy is to go where the Greeks go. And they go late: 2 to 3pm for **lunch**, 9 to 11pm for **dinner**. You can eat earlier, but you're likely to get indifferent service if you frequent the purely touristic establishments. Chic appearance is not a good guide to quality; you'll mainly be paying for the linen napkins and stemmed wine glasses. Often the most basic are the best, so don't be put off by a restaurant that brings your order in a sheet of paper and plonks it directly on the table top, as *psistariés* (see below) often do.

It's wise to keep a wary eye on the waiters too. They are inclined to push you into ordering more than you want and then bring things you haven't ordered. They often don't actually write anything down and may work your **bill** out by examining your empty plates. Itemised tabs, when present, will be in totally illegible Greek scribble, so the opportunities for slipping in a few extra drachmas here and there are pretty good, especially in establishments which disdain menus and published prices altogether. The service charge is always included, although a small tip (20-50dr) is standard practice for the 'boy' who lays the table, brings the bread and water, and so on.

If you have children, have no fears for them. Wherever you go they'll be welcome, and no one gives a damn if they chase the cats or play tag between the tables.

Estiatória

There are two basic types of restaurant: the *estiatório* (*estiatória* is the plural form) and the taverna. The former is mainly an urban lunchtime place. What distinguishes it from the taverna is the food it serves.

Estiatória specialize in the more complicated, **oven-baked casserole dishes**: moussakás, pastítsio, stews like kokinistó and stifádho, yemistá (stuffed tomatoes or peppers), the oily vegetable casseroles called ladherá, and oven-baked meat and fish. The cooking is done in the morning and then left to stand, which is why the food is often lukewarm or even cold. Greeks don't mind this (most actually believe that hot food is bad for you), and in fact in summertime it hardly seems to matter. Besides, dishes like yemistá are actually enhanced by being allowed to cool off and stand in their own juice. Similarly, you have to specify if you want your food with little or no oil (horís ládhi), but again you will be considered a bit strange since Greeks regard olive oil as essential for digestion (and indeed it is one of the least pernicious oils to ingest in large quantities).

Wine will usually be house bulk stuff and probably resinated (see below); desserts of the pudding-and-pie variety don't exist, although fruit is always available in season and you may occasionally be able to get a yogurt served at the end of a meal.

Choosing in an *estiatório* is best done by going to the kitchen and pointing.

Tavernas

Tavernas are much more common than *estiatória*, and range from the glitzy and fashionable to rough-and-ready cabins with a bamboo awning set up by the beach. The primitive ones have a very limited menu, but the more established will offer some of the main *estiatório* dishes mentioned above as well as the standard **taverna fare**. This essentially means *mezédhes* (hors d'oeuvres) and *tis óras* (meat and fish fried or grilled to order).

Since the idea of courses is foreign to Greek cuisine, starters, main dishes, and salads often arrive together. The best thing is to order a selection of *mezédhes* and salads to share among you; that, after all, is what Greeks do. Waiters encourage you to take the *horiátiki* **salad** – the so-called Greek salad – because it is the most expensive one. If you only want tomato or tomato and cucumber, ask for *domatosaláta* or *angouro-domáta*. *Maroúli* (lettuce) and *láhano* (cabbage) are the winter and spring salads.

The most interesting **starters** are *tzatzíki* (yogurt, garlic, and cucumber dip), *melitzano-saláta* (eggplant dip), zucchini or eggplant fried in batter (*kolokithákia tiganitá*, *melitzánes tiganités*), *yígandes* (white haricot beans in vinaigrette sauce), small cheese and spinach pies (*tiropitákia*, *spanakópites*), *saganáki* (fried cheese), octopus (*okhtapódhi*), and *mavromátika* (black-eyed peas).

Of **meats**, *souvláki* (shish kebab) and *brizóles* (chops) are reliable choices. In both cases, pork (*hirinó*) is usually better than veal (*moskharísio*). The best *souvláki* is lamb (*arnísio*), but it is not often available. The small lamb cutlets called *païdhákia* are very tasty, as is roast lamb (*arní psitó*) and roast kid (*katsíki*) when obtainable. *Keftédhes* (meatballs), *biftékia* (a sort of hamburger) and the spicy sausages called *loukánika* are cheap and good, though mince is the most common source of stomach problems: beware.

Seaside tavernas of course also offer **fish**. *Kalamarákia* (fried baby squid) are a summer staple. The choicer fish, however, *barboúnia* (red mullet), *lithrínia* (pandora), *fangrí* (sea bream) and so on, are expensive. The price is quoted by the kilo, and the standard procedure is to go to the glass cooler and choose your own. The cheapest widely available fish are *gópes* (bogue) and *marídhes* (tiny whitebait, eaten head and all).

As in *estiatória*, **desserts** are more or less nonexistent. Watermelons, melons and grapes are the standard summer fruit.

Tavernas will, however, offer you a better choice of **wines**. *Cambas*, and *Boutari Rotonda* or *Lac des Roches* are good among the cheaper bottled ones. If you want something better, the *Boutari Naoussa* is hard to beat. Otherwise, go for the local wines. *Retsina* – pine-resinated wine, a slightly acquired taste – is invariably better straight from the barrel. Not as many tavernas keep it as once did, but always ask whether they have wine *apó to varélli* or *híma* – both mean, in effect, 'from the barrel'.

Some tavernas **specialise**. *Psarotavérnes*, for example, feature fish, *psistariés* serve spit-roasted lamb and goat or *kokorétsi* (grilled offal). A few concentrate on game (*kinígi*): wild boar, hare, quail or turtle dove in the autumn, when the migrating flocks fly over Greece on their way south. In the mountains of the north where there are rivers, trout, pike, and freshwater crayfish are to be found in the local eating places.

SNACKS AND BREAKFAST

The **kafenío** is the traditional Greek coffee shop or café. Although its main business is Greek coffee, it also serves spirits such as *oúzo* (aniseed-based spirit), and brandy, beer, tea (either herbal mountain tea or British-style Liptons), soft drinks, *glikó tou koutalioú* (sticky, syrupy preserves of quince, grape, fig, citrus fruit, or cherry), and the old-fashioned *ipovríhio*, which is a piece of mastic submerged in a glass of water like a submarine, which is what *ipovríhio* means in Greek. Another summer drink sold in the more modern cafés is *kafés frappé*, a sort of iced instant coffee – uniquely Greek despite its French-sounding name.

Like tavernas, *kafenía* range from the plastic and sophisticated to the old-fashioned, spit-on-the-floor variety, with marble or brightly painted metal tables and straw-bottomed chairs. An important institution anywhere in Greece, they are the central pivot of life in the country villages. In fact, you get the impression that many men spend most of their waking hours there. Greek women are rarely to be seen in the more traditional places – and foreign women may sometimes feel uneasy or unwelcome.

This is no longer true of the towns and holiday resorts. But there also, if you look carefully, you will find there is at least one café that the local men have kept intact for themselves.

Some *kafenía* close at siesta time, but many remain **open** from early in the morning until late at night. The chief socialising time is 6pm, immediately after the siesta. This is the time to take your pre-dinner *oúzo*, as the sun begins to sink and the heat cools. You will be served two glasses, one with the *oúzo*, and one full of water, to be tipped into your *oúzo* until it turns a milky white. You can drink it straight, but its strong, burning taste is hardly refreshing if you do.

Until not long ago, every *oúzo* you ordered was automatically accompanied by a small plate of **mezédhes**, on the house: bits of cheese, cucumber, tomato, a few olives, sometimes octopus or even a couple of small fish. Unfortunately these days you have to ask for, and pay for, them.

Though their number seems to be diminishing rapidly, there is a kind of drinking establishment which specializes in *oúzo* and *mezédhes*, called an **ouzerí** (same in the plural). These are well worth trying for the marvelous variety of *mezédhes* they serve.

A somewhat similar institution to the *kafenío* is the **zaharoplastió**. A cross between café and pátisserie, it serves coffee, alcohol, yogurt and honey, sticky cakes, etc., both to consume on the premises and to take away. The good establishments offer an amazing variety of pastries, cream and chocolate confections, honey-soaked Greco-Turkish sweets like *baklavás*, *kataífi* (honey-drenched 'shredded wheat'), *loukoumádhes* (puffs of batter fried in olive oil, dusted with cinnamon and dipped in syrup; if you have a sweet tooth they'll transport you), *galaktobóureka* (a melting, milky, eggy pie), and so on. If you want a stronger slant toward the dairy products and away from the pure sugar, seek out a **galaktopolío**, where you'll often find *rizógalo* (rice pudding), *kréma* (custard), and home- or at least locally-made *yiaoúrti* (yogurt), best if it's *próvio* (from sheep's milk). A sign at either establishment with the legend *pagotó politikó* means that the shop concerned makes its own Turkish-style ice cream, and the proprietors are probably from Istanbul (Konstantinoúpoli to them, thank you...) – as good as or better than the usual Italian-style fare.

Both *zaharoplastía* and *galaktopolía* are more family-oriented places than the *kafenío*, and

many also serve a basic continental-type breakfast of *méli me voútiro* (honey poured over a pat of butter) or jam (all kinds are called *marmeládha* in Greek; ask for *portokáli* – orange – if you want proper marmalade) with fresh bread or *friganiés* (melba-toast-type slivers). You are also more likely to find proper (*evropaïkó*) tea and different kinds of coffee. *Nescafé* has become the generic term for all instant coffee, regardless of brand.

Bars – *barákia* – are a recent transplant, confined to big cities and holiday resorts. They range from clones of Parisian cafés to seaside cocktail bars and mindless, imitation English 'pabs' (sic), with equally mindless videos running all day. Drinks are invariably more expensive than at a café.

CAFES, BARS AND SWEETS

Greeks generally don't eat **breakfast**. So the only egg-and-bacon kind of places are in resorts where foreigners congregate; they're expensive compared to a taverna meal. The alternatives are the sort of bread/jam/yoghurt compromises obtainable in some *zaharoplastía* or *galaktopolía*, or having a picnic breakfast with your own ingredients.

Picnic fare is good, cheap, and easily available. When buying olives, go for the fat Kalamáta or Ámfissa ones; they're more expensive, but tastier and more nourishing. *Fétta* cheese is ubiquitious – often, ironically, imported from Holland or Denmark. It can be very dry and salty, so it's wise to ask for a piece to taste before buying. The same goes for other cheeses, the most palatable of which are the expensive gruyère-type *graviera*. Yoghurts are superlative (and good stomach settlers); honey, too, is wonderful though it costs an arm and a leg. The fruit is generally good and cheap.

Snacks can be one of the distinctive pleasures of Greek eating, though they are being increasingly edged out by an obsession with *tóst* (toasted sandwiches) and pizzas. However, small kebabs (*souvlákia*) are on sale at bus stations, ferry crossings, and all over the place in towns. The same goes for *tirópites* (cheese pies), which can almost always be found at the baker's, as can *kouloúria* (crispy baked pretzel rings sprinkled with sesame seeds). Another city staple is *yíro* (doner kebab), served in *píta* bread with garnish and often *tzatzíki*.

Basics and terms

Neró	Water
Psomí	Bread
Sitarénio psomí	Wholewheat bread
Sikalénio psomí	Rye bread
Aláti	Salt
Yiaoúrti	Yoghurt
Méli	Honey
Kréas	Meat
Psári(a)	Fish
Lahaniká	Vegetables
Fitofágos/Hortofágos	Vegetarian
Avgá	Eggs
Tirí	Cheese
(Horís) ládhi	(Without) oil
Katálogo/lísta	Menu
O logariasmós	The bill
Sto foúrno	Baked
Psitó	Roasted
Sti soúvla	Spit Roasted
Tis óras	Grilled/fried to order

Soups and starters

Soúpa	Soup
Avgolémono	Egg and lemon soup
Dolmádhes	Stuffed vine leaves
Fasoládha	Bean soup
Taramósalata	Fish roe paté
Tzatzíki	Yogurt and cucumber dip
Melitzanosaláta	Eggplant dip

Vegetables

Patátes	Potatoes
Hórta	Greens (usually wild)
Radhíkia	Wild chicory
Piperiés	Peppers
Domátes	Tomatoes
Fasolákia	String beans
Angoúri	Cucumber
Angináres	Artichokes
Yígantes	White haricot beans
Koukiá	Broad (horse) beans
Melitzána	Eggplant
Kolokithákia	Zucchini
Spanáki	Spinach
Fakés	Lentils
Rízi/Piláfi	Rice (usually with sáltsa – sauce)
Saláta	Salad
Horiátiki (saláta)	Greek salad (with olives, feta etc.)
Yemistés	Stuffed vegetables
Papoutsákia	Stuffed eggplant/squash
Bouréki	Eggplant/potato/cheese pie

Meat and meat-based dishes

Kotópoulo	Chicken
Arní	Lamb
Hirinó	Pork
Vodhinó	Beef
Moskhári	Veal
Sikóti	Liver
Patsás	Tripe soup
Nefrá	Kidneys
Biftéki	Hamburger
Moussaká	Eggplant/potato/ground meat/pie
Stifádho	Meat stew with tomato and onion
Pastítsio	Noodles, bechamel, and meat pie
Hilopíttes	Small, square egg noodles with meat
Païdhákia	Lamb chops
Brizóla	Pork or beef chop
Keftédhes	Meatballs
Loukánika	Spicy sausages
Kokorétsi	Liver/offal kebab
Tsalingária	Garden snails

Fish and seafood

Garídhes	Shrimp
Okhtapódhi	Octopus
Astakós	Lobster
Kalamária	Squid
Kalamarákia	Baby squid
Glóssa	Sole
Barboúni	Red mullet
Sinagrídha	Dentex
Gópes	Bogue (cheap!)
Soupiá	Cuttlefish
Marídhes	Whitebait
Gávros	Anchovy

Sweets and fruit

Karidhópita	Walnut cake
Baklavá	Honey/nuts pastry
Rizógalo	Rice pudding
Galaktobóuriko	Custard pie
Pagotó	Ice cream
Pastéli	Sesame/honey bar
Kasséri	Hard cheese
Graviéra	Gruyère type cheese
Fráoules	Strawberries
Kerásia	Cherries
Stafília	Grapes
Portokália	Oranges
Pepóni	Melon
Karpoúzi	Watermelon
Míla	Apples
Síka	(Dried) figs
Fistíkia	Pistachio nuts

Drinks

Neró Enfialoméno	Mineral water
Bíra	Beer
Krasí	Wine
Mávro	Red
Áspro	White
Rosé/Kokkinéli	Rosé
Tsáï	Tea
Kafés	Coffee
Gálakakáo	Chocolate milk
Portokaládha	Orangeade
Limonádha	Lemonade
Gazóza	Generic fizzy drink
Boukáli	Bottle
Potíri	Glass
Stiniyássas!	Cheers!

COMMUNICATIONS: MAIL, PHONES, AND MEDIA

THE POST OFFICE

Post offices are open from about 7.30am to 2.30pm, Monday through Friday; in big towns and important tourist centres, hours may extend into the evening and even weekends. Bigger post offices will change money as well as handle mail.

Air mail **letters** take three to six days to reach the rest of Europe, five to eight days to get to North America, and a bit more for Australia and New Zealand. Aerograms are faster and surer; post cards can be inexplicably slow: up to two weeks for Europe, a month to North America or the Pacific. A modest (about 150dr) fee for express (*katsapígonda*) service cuts letter delivery time to two days for the UK and three days for North America.

For a simple letter or card, **stamps** (*grammatósima*) can also be purchased at a *períptero* (corner kiosk). However the proprietors are entitled to a ten percent commission and never seem to know the current international rates. **Post boxes** are bright yellow; if you are confronted by two slots, *esterikó* is for domestic mail, *exoterikó* for overseas.

If you are sending large purchases home, note that **parcels** should and often can only be handled in sizeable towns, preferably a provincial capital. This way your bundle will be in Athens, and on the plane, within a day or two. **Registered** (*sistiméno*) delivery is also available, but it is extremely slow unless coupled with express service.

POSTE RESTANTE

Receiving mail, the *poste restante* system is reasonably efficient, especially at the post offices of larger towns. Mail should be clearly addressed and marked *poste restante*, with your surname underlined, to the main post office of whichever town you choose. It will be held for a month and you'll need your passport to collect it.

Alternatively you can use the **American Express** mail-holding service, free of charge if you carry their cheques or hold their card, but because of new security regulations they will no longer accept delivery of even small packages. Amex offices are open Monday through Friday, plus Saturday mornings, and are conveniently spaced:

ATHENS: *American Express International*, Síntagma/Ermoú 2, P.O. Box 325.

THESSALONÍKI: *American Express International*, Venizélou 10.

IRÁKLIO (CRETE): c/o *Creta Travel Bureau*, Epimenídhou 20-22.

RHODES: c/o *Georgiadis Tourism Ltd.*, Vassiléos Sofías 41, Rhodes town.

CORFU: c/o *Corfu Tourist Center Ltd.*, 25 Avgoústou 27–29, Kérkira.

PHONES

Local calls are relatively straightforward. In many hotel lobbies or cafés you'll find fat, red pay-phones which at present take a five-drachma coin and are for local calls only. In the towns you'll also find conventional phone booths. Those with a blue band on top are for local (*topikó*) calls and require five-drachma coins; those with an orange strip are intended for middle and long-distance (*iperastikó*), and are fed five-, ten-, and twenty- drachma pieces. A tone in mid-conversation warns you when you need to insert more.

It's probably easier to phone from a *períptero*, or street kiosk. Here the phone is connected to a metre, and you pay after you have made the call, thus eliminating the need to juggle small change. Local calls are very cheap, but long-distance ones are subject to a mark-up which only the owner can calculate (since only he can see the metre). For this reason, international calls from a *períptero*, though they can be dialled direct quite easily, are slightly risky because of the unpredictable cost, and are really best done only when the OTE office (see below) is closed.

For **international long distance** (*exorikó*) calls, it's cheaper to visit the nearest **OTE** (*Organismós Tiliepikinoníon tis Elládhos*) office, and you'll have to do this if you want to reverse charges or do anything else exotic. Operator-assisted calls can take well over an hour to connect, but even if you are going to dial direct on their metred phones you should be prepared for a long line. In major towns there is at least one branch open 24 hours; in smaller towns OTE can close as early as 3pm. In that case you'll have no choice but to use a kiosk, or to find a *kafenío* with a metred phone: look for a sign saying *Tiléfono me metrití*.

If you have access to a private phone you can dial the international operator (☎ 161) to get a reverse charge call put through, or dial direct: 00, followed by the country code (44 for the UK, 1 for the U.S. and Canada) and the local number without its initial zero. Calls will cost, very approximately, £2 for three minutes to the UK; rates drop very slightly in the evening.

THE MEDIA: NEWSPAPERS, MAGAZINES AND THE AIRWAVES

British **newspapers**, are fairly widely available in Greece if you are prepared to pay for them. You'll find day-old copies of the tabloids in all the resorts as well as in major towns, and most of the heavier papers can be found too – though they're in shorter supply and often a couple of days old. Local English-language alternatives include the daily *Athens News*, heavily dependent on American wires but with an interesting (and in its section 'From the Police Files', bizarre) round-up of selections in translation from the Greek press. It's on sale widely in Athens and at some of the larger cities and resorts.

Among **magazines**, far and away the best is *The Athenian*, an English-language monthly sold in Athens and all major resorts, well worth a read for its cultural/festival listings, updates on Greek life and politics, and often excellent features. *Journey to Greece*, a tabloid-format magazine sold in Athens bookshops and along the island travel circuits (particularly the Cyclades), is good for up-to-the-minute travel advice and features.

If you have a **radio** you may pick up something interesting. Greek music progammes are always accessible despite the language barrier, and with various recent successful challenges to the government's monopoly of wavelengths stations have mushroomed – listen out for the new Channel 15. The BBC World Service can be received on short wave only (15.07 and 12.09 mhz), but there are regular news bulletins and bouts of tourist information in English on local Greek stations (try 412 MW at 7.30am daily). American Armed Forces Radio can be picked up in much of Greece as well.

There are presently two centralised, government-controlled **television** stations, ERT1 and ERT2, though there are mutterings of local broadcasts beginning in the wake of the radio pirates' successes. News summaries in English are read daily at 6pm, and generally followed by a plethora of American serials and old movies, most of which are subtitled and with the original soundtrack.

BUSINESS HOURS AND PUBLIC HOLIDAYS

It is virtually impossible to generalise about Greek opening hours, except to say that they change constantly. The traditional timetable starts at a relatively civilised hour, with shops opening between 8.30 and 9.30am, and runs through until lunchtime, when there is a long break for the hottest part of the day. Things may then reopen in the mid-to late afternoon.

Tourist areas tend to adopt a more northern timetable, though, with shops and offices probably staying open right through **the day – certainly the most important archaeological sites and museums do so.**

SHOPPING HOURS

Shopping hours during the hottest months are theoretically Monday, Wednesday, and Saturday from approximately 9am until 2pm, and Tuesday, Thursday, and Friday from 9am to 1pm and 5 to 8.30pm. But there are so many exceptions to the rule by virtue of holidays and professional idiosyncracy that you can't count on getting anything done except from Monday to Friday from 9.30am to 1pm or so. **Chemists** (most of which are closed Saturday morning) are supposed to have a sign on their door referring you to the nearest one open.

In late 1988 the government, after years of stubborn resistance from shopkeepers, finally managed to push through its progamme (in Athens at least) of a unitary schedule during the colder months of the year. This may very well reduce the pollution resulting from four commutes a day but most everyone is unhappy about it. The gist of it (hours are still being contested) seems to be that things will be shut on Monday morning but open continuously on the other days of the week up to either 6 or 7pm.

ANCIENT SITES AND MONASTERIES

All the major **ancient sites** are now fenced off and, like museums, charge admission. This ranges from 50dr to 500dr, though with an **international student card** you can get reductions of up to 50 percent.

Opening hours vary from site to site. As far as possible individual times are quoted in the text, but bear in mind that these change with exasperating frequency and at smaller sites may be subject to the whim of a local keeper. The times quoted are generally summer hours, which operate from around April to the end of September. Reckon on similar days but later opening and earlier closing in winter. If you're a dedicated archaeology buff you should carry some kind of detailed **guide** with you; on the spot you'll usually find a glossy tourist picture book at best.

Smaller sites generally close for a long lunch and **siesta** (even where they're not supposed to), as do **monasteries**. Most monasteries are fairly strict on visitors' dress, too, especially for women; they don't like shorts on either sex and often expect women to cover their arms and wear skirts. They are generally open from about 9am–1pm and 5–7pm for limited visits.

PUBLIC HOLIDAYS

All of the above will be regularly thrown out of sync by any of a vast range of **public holidays and festivals**. The most important, when almost everything will be closed, are: January 1; January 6; March 25; the first Monday of Lent (February or March); Easter weekend (according to the Orthodox calendar, see below); May 1; August 15; October 28; and several days at Christmas. There are also a large number of local holidays.

FESTIVALS

Many of the big Greek popular festivals have a religious base so they're observed in accordance with the Orthodox calendar. This is similar to the Catholic liturgical year (allowing, of course, for only partial overlap in the matter of sainthood), except for Easter, which can fall several weeks to either side of the western festival.

EASTER

Easter is by far the most important festival of the Greek year – infinitely more so than Christmas – and taken much more seriously than it is anywhere in western Europe. From Wednesday of Holy Week the radio and TV networks are given over solely to religious progammes until the following Monday. It is an excellent time to be in Greece, both for the beautiful and moving religious ceremonies and for the days of feasting and celebration which follow. The mountainous island of Ídhra with its alleged 360 churches and monasteries is the prime Easter resort, but unless you plan well in advance you have no hope of finding accommodation there at that season. Probably the best idea is to make for a medium-sized village where, in most cases, you'll be accepted into the community's celebration.

The first great ceremony takes place on **Good Friday** evening as the Descent from the Cross is lamented in church. At dusk the *Epitafión*, Christ's funeral bier, leaves the sanctuary and is paraded solemnly through the streets; in many places, Crete especially, this is accompanied by the burning of effigies of Judas Iscariot.

Late **Saturday** evening sees the climax in a majestic *Anástasi* mass to celebrate Christ's triumphant return. At the stroke of midnight all lights in each crowded church are extinguished and the congregation plunged into the darkness which envelopes Christ as He passes through the underworld. Then there's a faint glimmer of light behind the altar screen before the priest appears, holding aloft a lighted taper and chanting '*Avtó to Fós...*' (This is the Light of the World). Stepping down to the level of the parishioners he touches his flame to the unlit candle of the nearest worshipper intoning '*Dévthe, lévethe Fós*' (Come, take the Light). Those at the front of the congregation and on the aisles do the same for their neighbours until the entire church is ablaze with burning candles and the miracle affirmed.

Even solidly rational atheists are likely to find this moving. The traditional greeting, as firecrackers explode all around you in the streets, is '*Hristós Anésti*' (Christ is risen), to which the response is '*Alithós Anésti*' (Truly He is risen). In the week leading up to Easter Sunday you should wish people a Happy Easter: '*Kaló Páskha*'.

The burning candles are then taken home through the streets by the worshippers, and it brings good fortune on the house if the candle arrives without having been blown out in the wind; on reaching the front door it is common practice to make the sign of the cross on the lintel with the flame, leaving a black smudge visible for the rest of the year. The Lenten fast is traditionally broken early on Sunday morning with a meal of *mayarítsa*, a soup made from lamb tripe, rice, and lemon. The rest of the lamb will be roasted for Sunday lunch, and festivities often take place through the rest of the day. The Greek equivalent of Easter eggs are hard-boiled eggs (painted red on Holy Thursday), which are given as gifts on Easter Sunday; people rap their eggs against their friend's eggs, and the owner of the last uncracked egg is considered lucky.

THE FESTIVAL CALENDAR

Most of the Greek festivals are celebrations of one or another of a multitude of **saints**. The most important are detailed below: wherever you are, it is worth looking out for a village, or church, bearing the saint's name, a sure sign of celebrations – sometimes across the town or island, sometimes quiet and local. Detailed below, too, are a scattering of **secular** holidays, most enjoyable of which are the pre-Lenten carnivals.

January 1st
New Year's Day in Greece is the feast day of **Áyios Vassílios**, their version of Santa Claus, and is celebrated with church services and the baking of a special loaf, *vassilópitta*, in which a coin is baked which brings its finder good luck throughout the year.

January 6th
The **Epiphany**, when the *kalikántzari* (hobgoblins) who run riot on earth during the twelve days of Christmas are rebanished to the nether world by various rites of the Church. The most important of these is the blessing of baptismal fonts and all outdoor bodies of water. At lakeside and seaside locations, the priest casts a crucifix into the deep, with local youths competing for the privilege of recovering it. As these competitions have tended to get a little out of hand in recent years, the custom is now honoured more in the breach than in the observance.

Pre-Lenten Carnivals
These span three weeks, climaxing during the seventh weekend before Easter. **Pátra Carnival**, with a chariot parade and costume parties, is one of the largest in the Mediterranean, with events from January 17th until 'Clean Monday', the last day of Lent; on the last Sunday before Lent there's a grand parade. Interesting, too, are the *boúles* or masked revels which take place around **Macedonia** (particularly at **Náoussa**), and the outrageous 'Goat Dance' on **Skíros** in the Sporades. The **Ionians**, especially Kefalloniá, are also good islands for Carnival, while **Athenians** celebrate by going around hitting each other on the head with plastic hammers – a source of real street-gang brawls a few years back!

March 25
Independence Day and the **Feast of the Annunciation** is both a religious and national holiday, with, on the one hand, parades and danc-

ing to celebrate the beginning of the revolt against Turkish rule in 1821, and, on the other, church services to honour the news being given to Mary that she was to become the Mother of Christ. There are major festivities on **Tínos**, **Ídhra (Hydra)**, and many other places, particularly any monastery or church named Evangelístria or Evangelismós.

April 23

The **Feast of St. George (Áyios Yióryios)**, the patron of shepherds, so there are frequently big rural celebrations, such as the dancing and feasting that occurs at **Aráhova**, near Delphi. St. George is also the patron saint of **Skíros**, so this day is celebrated in some style there too. If the date falls before Easter, i.e. during Lent, the festivities are postponed until the Monday after Easter.

May 1

May Day, the great urban holiday when townspeople traditionally make for the countryside to return with bunches of wild flowers. Wreaths are hung on their doorways or balconies until they are burnt on Midsummer's eve.

May 21

The Feast of **Áyios Konstantínos** and his mother, **Ayía Eléni**, the first Orthodox Byzantine rulers. There are firewalking ceremonies in certain **Macedonian villages**, and elsewhere the day is celebrated rather more conventionally as being the nameday for two of the more popular Christian names in Greece.

June 29

The **Feast of Saints Peter and Paul (Áyios Pétros and Áyios Pávlos)**. More nameday celebrations to watch out for.

June 30

The **Feast of the Holy Apostles (Ayíi Apostolí)**. Widely celebrated.

July 17

The **Feast of Ayía Marína.**

July 20

The **Feast of Profítis Ilías (the Prophet Elijah)** is widely celebrated at the countless hill- or mountain-top shrines of Profítis Ilías. The most famous is on **Mt. Taíyettos**, near Spárti.

July 26

Feast of Ayía Paraskeví, with big village festivals, especially in **Epirus**.

August 6

The **Feast of the Metamórfosi (Transfiguration)**, another excuse for celebrations. In fact in between mid-July and mid-August there are religious festivals every few days, especially in the rural areas, and between these and the summer heat ordinary business comes to a virtual standstill.

August 15

The **Apokímisis tis Panayías (Assumption of the Blessed Virgin Mary)**. This is the day when people traditionally return to their home village, and in many places there will be no accommodation available on any terms. Even some Greeks will resort to sleeping in the streets. There is a great pilgrimage to **Tínos**, and major festivities at **Páros** and at Olímbos on **Kárpathos**.

September 8

The **Yénesis tis Panayías (Birth of the Virgin Mary)**, with special services in most churches, and a double cause for rejoicing on **Spétses** where they also celebrate the anniversary of the **Battle of the Straits** of Spétses, which took place on 8 September 1822. A re-enactment of the battle takes place in the harbour, followed by fireworks and feasting well into the night.

September 14

A last major summer festival, the **Exaltation of the Cross**.

October 26

The **Feast of Áyios Dhimítrios**, another popular nameday, particularly celebrated in **Thessaloníki**, of which he is the patron saint. New wine is traditionally tapped on this day, a good excuse for general inebriation.

October 28

Óhi Day, the year's major patriotic shindig – a national holiday with parades, folk-dancing, and feasting to commemorate Metaxas' apocryphal one-word reply to Mussolini's 1940 ultimatum: 'Ohi!' (No!).

November 8

Another popular nameday, the **Feast of the Archangels Michael and Gabriel (Mihális and Gavriél)**.

December 6

The **Feast of Áyios Nikólaos**, the patron of seafarers, with many chapels dedicated to him, and obviously a good time is to be had in any place with maritime connections.

December 25

A much less festive occasion than Greek Easter, **Christmas** is still an important religious feast celebrating the birth of Christ, and in recent years it has started to take on more of the trappings of the western Christmas, with decorations, Christmas trees and gifts.

December 31

New Year's Eve, when, as on the other twelve days of Christmas, children sing the traditional *kalénda* (carols). Adults tend to sit around playing cards, often for money. The *vassilópitta* may be cut at midnight, to mark the start of another year of what sometimes seems like a non-stop round of celebrations.

In addition to the specific dates mentioned, there are literally scores of **local festivals**, or *paniyiriá*, celebrating the patron saint of the village church. With some 330-odd possible named saints' days you're unlikely to travel around Greece for long without stumbling on something. A good source of information if you want to deliberately coincide – and avoid being told 'If only you'd been here last week!' – is the monthly *Athenian* magazine, which has listings and some background on forthcoming events.

ENTERTAINMENTS AND EVENTS

CULTURAL FESTIVALS

The major summer cultural events in Greece take place under the aegis of the **Athens Festival** (mid-June to mid-September). This encompasses a wide range of performances, including modern and ancient theatre, ballet, opera, jazz and classical music. For most people the highlights are the open-air **performances of Classical drama** in the ancient theatres of Epidaurus (in the Peloponnese) and the Herodes Atticus in Athens. Those at Epidaurus take place at weekends (when there are special buses from Athens); at Herodes Atticus (which also hosts ballet and symphony concerts) they are usually spread through the week. There's also a kind of **fringe festival** with some rock, jazz and experimental dance groups at another (modern) open-air theatre on Likavitós hill.

Details and tickets for both festivals can be obtained from the Athens Festival offices at Stadhíou 4 (on Omónia square) or Voukourestíou 1. It's worth calling in very soon after you arrive in Greece since the more prestigious events often sell out.

You might also pick up an annual leaflet published by the EOT called 'Greek Festivals' which includes details of other **local festivals** of music, drama and dance. Among these are sporadic performances of Classical plays in the ancient theatres of Thássos, Dodona, and Philippi.

Other important **regional events** include the Thíra music festival, in September; a festival of song on Itháki, in July; the Rhodes festival, September through November; the Iráklio festival in September; a general arts festival on Lefkádha, mid- to late August, including poetry, theatre, and great dancing by foreign and Greek troupes; the *'Ipirotiká'* events during August in Ioánnina, featuring everything from Theodorakis to the Tashkent ballet; and two biggies in Thessaloníki, a film festival in September and the *'Dhimitria'* general festival in October.

THEATRE AND CINEMA

Ordinary **indoor theatre** gets suspended during the summer months but from around September to May there's a lot of activity – Athens alone has some 45 theatres ns ranging from classics to reviews.

Cinemas are cheap and screen a large proportion of American and British movies, often undubbed with Greek subtitles, and in summer a number set up outside. An outdoor movie is worth catching at least once – indoor shows never quite seem the same once you've seen an open-air screening of Kirk Douglas in *The Odyssey* on Ithaca . . . .

For more details on events in Athens, particularly the film, nightclub, and music scene, see the main guide.

PARTICIPATORY SPORTS

The Greek seashore offers endless scope for water sports, with windsurfers for rent in most resorts, and, less regularly, waterskiing facilities. On land, the greatest attraction lies in hiking, through what is one of Europe's most attractive and unspoilt mountain terrains. Winter also sees possibilities for skiing at one of a dozen or so low-key centres.

Spectating, the twin Greek obsessions are soccer and basketball. Both are constantly to be seen on TV, as well as by attending matches.

WATER SPORTS

The last few years have seen a massive growth in the popularity of **windsurfing** in Greece. The country's bays and coves are ideal for beginners, and boards can be hired in literally hundreds of resorts. Particularly good areas include the islands of Lefkádha, Zákinthos, Náxos, Lésvos, Corfu and Crete, and Methóni in the Peloponnese. You can almost always pay for an initial period of instruction, if you've not tried the sport previously. Rates are very reasonable – about £5 an hour.

Waterskiing is available at a number of the larger resorts, and a fair few of the smaller ones, too. By the crippling rental standards of the ritzier parts of the Mediterranean it is a bargain, with twenty minutes' instruction often available for around £8-10. At Párga in Epirus **parasailing** is also possible.

Sailboats and dinghies are rented out by the day or week at many of the country's naval clubs. For details, contact the Greek Sailing Federation (Xeonofóndos 15a, Athens; ☎01/323-5560).

Because of the potential for pilfering submerged antiquities, **scuba diving** is restricted to a very few recognized centres, on the islands of Míkonos, Corfu, Paxí, and Lefkádha, and on the mainland's Halkidhikí peninsula. A leaflet, 'Sea Areas for Underwater Activities', is published by the EOT.

Greece also has *lots* of white water, especially in Epirus, so if you're into **river rafting** there is much potential. There are periodic articles and advice (in Greek) in the outdoors magazine *Korfes*.

SKIING

Skiing is a comparative newcomer to Greece, in part because snow conditions are unpredictable, and runs generally short. However, there are now a dozen **ski centres** scattered about the mountains, and what they lack in professionalism is often made up for in the absence of a pretentious *après-ski* scene. Costs are an attraction, too – much lower than in northern Europe, at around £6 a day for rental of skis and boots, plus £4 a day for a lift pass.

The season generally lasts from the beginning of January to the end of April, with a few extra weeks possible at either end depending on snow conditions.

The most developed of the resorts is on **Parnassós**, the legendary mountain near Delphi. It's easily accessible from Athens; throughout the season two Athenian companies run buses up to the resort, returning the same day. Avoid weekends (which can be chaos) and you may have the resort more or less to yourself. The easiest company to find is *Klaoudatos*, a big department store on Dimarhíou street, near Omónia square. In winter they devote a floor to skiing, including ski rental (though this is simpler at Parnassós itself). The resort has slopes for beginners and enough to keep most experienced skiers happy, at least for a couple of days. Its main problem is that the lifts are often closed due to high winds.

Other ski centres include **Veloúhi**, above Karpeníssi in central Greece, and **Métsovo** in Epirus, which has ample other attractions besides the skiing. The latter is, however, at a lower altitude than Parnassós, so the season is shorter. **The Pílion** is another enjoyable region to ski in as part of a general holiday. Buses run to its ski centre (at Haniá) from Vólos. All of these centres rent out ski equipment for casual visitors.

In the **north** there are more centres at Náoussa, Flórina, Sérres, and elsewhere. The snow here is a little more reliable, though access is generally more difficult.

Further details are available from the EOT, who publish a leaflet entitled 'Ski Centres and Mountaineering Shelters', or from the Greek Skiing and Alpine Federation (Karayióryi 7, Athens; ☎01/323-4555).

HIKING

Greeks are just becoming used to the notion that anyone should want to walk for pleasure, yet if you have the time and stamina it is probably the single best way to see the country. This guide includes descriptions of a number of the more accessible mountain hikes, as well as suggestions for more casual walking. In addition, you may want to acquire one or both of the specific Greek hiking guides (both written by *Rough Guide Greece* editors, see 'Books' in *Contexts*).

See also 'Information and Maps' for details of hiking maps available.

SPECTATOR SPORTS

Football is far and away the most popular sport in Greece – both in terms of participating and

watching. The most important (and most heavily sponsored) teams are *Panathanaïkós* and *AEK* of Athens, *Olympiakós* of Pireás, and *PAOK* of Thessaloníki. Other major teams in the provinces include *Lárissa* and the Cretan *Ofí*. If you're interested, matches are easy enough to catch during the winter/spring season. In mid-autumn you might even see one of the Greek teams playing European competition, though the clubs, and the national squad, have fallen on somewhat hard times of late.

Not so the nation's **basketball** team, which recently won the European Championship – cheered all the way with enormous enthusiasm. Many of the football clubs also own basketball teams, though *Arís* of Thessaloníki are the current domestic leaders.

FEMINISMÓS

Women's right to vote wasn't universally achieved in Greece until 1956, and less than a decade ago adultery was still a punishable offence, with cases regularly brought to court.

The **Greek Women's Movement** has a long tradition, but in recent years it has conspicuously emerged. By far the largest organisation is the *Women's Union of Greece*, founded in 1976. This espouses an independent feminist line and is responsible for numerous consciousness-raising activities across the country, though it remains

too closely linked to the governing party, PASOK, for most women's comfort. PASOK were elected to power with a strong theoretical progamme for women's rights, and their women's council review committees, set up in the early, heady days, effected a landmark reform with the 1983 **Family Law**. This prohibited dowry and stipulated equal legal status and shared property rights between husband and wife.

Subsequently, however, many women's groups, including those set up by PASOK, have become disillusioned by the government's lack of commitment to follow through on **practical demands** for improved child care, health, and family planning. Contraception is not available as part of the skeletal Greek public health service meaning that many women rely on abortions – only recently made legal under specified conditions, and running (as for many years past) to an estimated 70-80,000 a year.

Other, more autonomous groups, have been responsible for setting up advice and support networks, highlighting women's issues within trade unions, and campaigning for changes in media representation.

None of this is easy in a country as polarised as Greece. In many rural areas women rely heavily on traditional extended families for security, and are unlikely to be much affected by legislative reforms or city politics.

CONTACTS

If you're interested in making contact with a feminist group or centre, there are comprehensive listings in the women's *Imerolóyio* (Diary) published in Athens by *Eyroptyp* (Kolónou 12– 24). Groups listed below are the more accessible contacts, particularly if you don't have a good command of Greek. Most suspend activities for the month of August.

Multinational Women's Liberation Group of Athens, Mavromihális 69, Athens. The group, formed mainly of expatriate women, produce an English language newsletter, *OUT*. They meet every week at *The Women's House* (Románou Melódhou 4, Likavitós, Athens; ☎01/281-4823), a centre which operates a bar on Tuesday and Thursday nights, and where the **Autonomous Group of Gay Women** also meets. The building isn't labelled; it's on the side road off Dhafnomíli street, the second building on the right, up two flights of stairs.

Greek Women's Liberation Movement Tsimíski 39, Athens.

Women's Bookshops: *Selana*, Sína 38, Athens; *Ton Yinekon*, Massalías 20, Athens.

Federation of Greek Women (*Omospondhía Yinekón Elládhas*). Focusses on women at work, unequal pay and job discrimination; active in organising Women's Peace Movement. Many branches throughout Greece – in Athens at Akadhimías 52 (☎01/361-5565).

Movement of Democratic Women (*Kínisi Dhimokratikón Yinekón*). Interested in family law and sexual liberation. Athens branch at Yenadhíou 5 (☎01/365-0661).

Union of Greek Women (*Énosis Yinekón Elládhas*). Emphasis on problems of peasant women and Medierannean women in general, and responsible for forming the Council of Equality. Branches in all the major towns: in Athens at Enianón 8 (☎01/823-4937).

Greek Women's Anti-Nuclear Movement, Emmanuél Benáki/Nikitára 6 (☎01/362-1855).

DISABLED TRAVELLERS

It is all too easy to wax lyrical over the attractions of Greece: the steep narrow alleys, the ease of travel by bus and ferry, the thrill of clambering round the great archaeological sites. It is almost impossible, on the other hand, for the able-bodied travel writer to see these attractions as potential hazards for anyone who has some difficulty in walking or is wheelchair-bound or suffers from some other disability. The cheering line 'facilities for the disabled are not well developed in Greece' is often the only reference to disabled people in the available travel literature.

In all honesty this guide is barely more practical in this respect than any other. However, don't be discouraged. It is possible to enjoy an inexpensive and trauma-free holiday in Greece if some time is devoted to gathering information before arrival. The following guidelines come from a rheumatoid arthritis sufferer, but the general principles should be applicable to all physically challenged travellers.

Attitudes

There are **organised tours and holidays** specifically for disabled people, but if you want to be more independent that is perfectly possible, provided that you do not leave home with the vague hope that things will turn out all right, and that 'people will help out' when you need assistance. The best form of assistance, unexpected and unasked for, is likely to be cheerfully given in Greece, but it cannot be relied on. Local attitudes – and comments – may be astonishingly outdated. You must either be completely confident that you can manage alone, or travel with an able-bodied friend (or two). When you have special personal needs, the confidence to travel alone or with one other person, to plan and organise your trip, comes only with preparation.

Become an authority on where you must be self-reliant and where you may expect help, especially regarding transport and accommodation. For example, to get between the terminals at Athens airport, you will have to fight for a taxi; it is not the duty of the airline staff to find you one, and there is no trace of an organised queue.

Be wary, too, since much existing or readily available information is **out of date** – you should always try to double-check. A number of addresses of contact organisations are published below. The EOT is a good first step as long as you have specific questions to put to them; they publish a useful questionnaire which you could send to hotels or owners of apartment/villa accommodation.

It is also vital that you **be honest** – with travel agencies, insurance companies, the organisations you write to for information, companions, the people you meet along the way and, above all, with yourself. Know your limitations and make sure others know them. If you do not use a wheelchair all the time but your walking capabilities are limited, then remember that you are likely to need to cover greater distances while travelling (often over tougher terrain and in hotter weather than you are used to). So if you use one, take a wheelchair with you, have it serviced before you go, and carry a repair kit; rough roads play havoc with nuts, bolts and tires.

Insurance and Preparations

If you're getting travel **insurance**, read the small print carefully to make sure that people with a pre-existing medical condition are not excluded. And use your travel agent to make your journey simpler: **airlines** or coach companies can cope better if they are expecting you, with a wheelchair provided at airports and staff primed to help. A medical certficate of your fitness to travel, provided by your doctor, is also extremely useful; some airlines or insurance companies may insist on it.

The best place to start is with a **list** of all the facilities that will make your life easier while you are away. You may want a ground floor room, or access to a large elevator; you may have special dietary requirements, or need level ground to enable you to reach shops, beaches, bars, and places of interest. Again, be realistic, and accept that you may not be able to expect the level of comfort and convenience you have at home. You should also keep track of all your other special needs, making sure, for example, that you have extra supplies of drugs – carried with you if you fly – and a prescription including the generic name in case of emergency. Any kind of drug, clothing, or equipment which might be hard to find in Greece you should carry spares of; if there's an association representing people with your disability, contact them for information on what to take and what to leave behind.

And if all of this sounds like hard work, the rewards should be worth it.

Useful Contacts

National Tourist Organization of Greece (EOT): Addresses on p.12. Their specific information is skimpy and out-of-date, but they try, and can advise at least on terrain and climate.

National Institution of Rehabilitation for the Handicapped: Odhós Hassías, Néa Lióssia, KA 1322, Athens. Will advise disabled visitors.

National Foundation of Disabled (KAPAS): Leofóros Dhiamantídhou, Paléa Psihikó, Athens. Contact in case of emergency.

Evyenía Stravropoúlou, Lavinia Tours: Egnatía 101, 541 10 Thessaloníki. Will advise disabled visitors and has tested many parts of Greece in her wheelchair. She also organises tours within Greece.

RADAR: 25 Mortimer St, London W1 (☎01/637-5400). Publishes fact sheets and an annual guide to accommodation and facilities abroad, and issues a list of insurance companies who arrange policies for disabled travellers.

POLICE, TROUBLE, AND HARASSMENT

It's now well over a decade since the colonels' junta was dislodged and Greece ceased to be a police state. As everywhere, there are a few mean characters around, but in general your average Greek policeman is not likely to have too much of a power complex, and you need to do something pretty insensitive to risk arrest. The most common causes of a brush with authority – all of them technically illegal – are nude bathing or sunbathing, camping outside an authorized site, and (a major crime in the Greek book) taking or possessing cannabis products or any other drug.

Nude bathing is, currently, legal on only a very few beaches (on Míkonos, for example), and is deeply offensive to many more traditional Greeks – exercise considerable sensitivity to local feeling and the kind of place you're in. Generally, stay away from families, the main entrance of a beach, and any tavernas. If a beach has become fairly established for nudity, or is well secluded, it's highly unlikely that the police are going to come charging in. Where they do get bothered is if they feel a place is turning into a 'hippie beach' or nudity is getting too overt on mainstream tourist stretches. But there are no hard and fast rules; it all depends on the local cops. Most of the time the only action will be a warning but you can officially be arrested straight off – facing as much as three days in jail and a stiff fine.

Very similar guidelines apply to **freelance camping** – though for this you're still less likely to incur anything more than a warning to move on. The only real risk of arrest is if you are told to move on and fail to do so. In either of the above cases, even if the police do take any action against you, it's more likely to be a brief spell in their cells than any official prosecution.

Drug offences are a far more serious matter. The maximum penalty for 'causing the use of drugs by someone under 18', for example, is life imprisonment and a 10-million-drachma fine. Theory is by no means practice but foreigners caught in possession of quite small amounts of grass do get jail sentences of up to a year – much more if there's evidence that they've been supplying others.

If you get arrested for any offence you have a right to contact your **consulate** who will arrange a lawyer for your defence. Beyond this, there is little they can, or in most cases will, do.

SEXUAL HARASSMENT

Very many women travel independently around Greece without being harassed or feeling intimidated. Greek machismo is strong, but less upfront than the equivalent in, for example, Spain or Italy. Most of the hassle you are likely to get is from a small minority of Greeks who migrate to the **main resorts and towns** in summer in pursuit of 'liberated, fun-loving' tourists. Indigenous Greeks, who are increasingly hospitable as you become more of a fixture in any one place, treat these outsiders, known as *kamákia* ('harpoons'), with contempt. The obvious stake outs are beach bars and discos. Words worth remembering for an unambiguous response include 'Stamáta' (stop it), 'afísteme' (leave me alone) and 'fíyete' (go away).

Camping is generally easy and unthreatening, although away from recognized sites it is often wise to attach yourself to a local family by making arrangements to use nearby private land. In the more **remote mountains and inland areas** you may feel more uncomfortable travelling alone. The intensely traditional Greeks that you meet may have trouble understanding why you are unaccompanied, and might not welcome your presence in their exclusively male *kafenía* – often the only place where you can get a drink. Travelling with a man, you're more likely to be treated as a *kséni*, a word meaning both (female) stranger and guest.

Very few Greek women **hitch**, although a fair number of tourists do. Much the same rules of caution apply as elsewhere in Europe: accept rides from couples and you'll feel secure enough.

FINDING WORK

The EC notwithstanding, short-term work in Greece is always on an unofficial basis and for this reason it will generally be where you can't be seen by the police or you're badly paid – or, more often, both. There's a little more dignity to permanent employment, though as elsewhere in Europe this is largely limited to teaching English.

TEMPORARY WORK

Tourism-Related Work

Most tourists working casually in Greece find jobs in **bars or restaurants** around the main tourist resorts. Women will generally find these jobs easier to obtain than men – who should count themselves lucky to get work washing up, though 'trained' chefs could fare better.

If you're waiting or serving, most of your wages will probably have to come from tips but you may well be able to get a deal which includes free food and lodging; evening-only hours can be a good shift, leaving you a lot of free time. The main drawback may be the machismo and/or chauvinist attitudes of your employer. (Ads in the *Athens News* for 'girl bar staff' are probably best ignored; the work tends to be drinking rather than serving, with a commission on whatever you sell).

Corfu, with its big British slant, is usually the most rewarding place to look for bar work, though its resorts are perhaps less of an attraction for living. Start looking, if you can, around April or May; you'll get better rates if you're taken on for a season.

On a similar level you might be able to get a job pitching or selling for **tourist shops** on Corfu, Rhodes, or Crete, or (if you've the expertise) helping out at one of the **windsurfing** 'schools' that have sprung up all around the coast.

Outside the tourist season there can be **building/painting/signpainting** work preparing for the influx; ask around at Easter-time. **Yacht marinas** can also prove good hunting-grounds though less for the romantic business of crewing (still a possibility if you've got the charm and arrogance) than scrubbing down and repainting. Again your best possibilities are likely to be on Rhodes, Corfu, or Crete; the Zéa port at Pireás is actually the biggest marina, but non-Greek owners don't tend to rest up there for long.

Selling and Busking

You will almost certainly do better by working for yourself. Travellers report rich pickings during the tourist season from **making and selling jewellery** (or importing it from Turkey to sell) on island beaches, or on boats. Once you've managed to get the stuff past the customs officials (who will be skeptical, for instance, that all those trinkets are presents for friends), there rarely seem to be problems with the local police, though it probably pays to be discreet.

Busking can also be quite lucrative. Playing on the Athens metro, it's possible to make around 1500dr in a two-hour session. In resorts, you might just strike luckier if you've talent, and even back in Athens the western-style pubs occasionally hire foreign musicians for gigs.

Agriculture

Harvesting and other agricultural jobs are invariably low-paid but provide a winter fallback for some long-term travellers. It's predominantly male work, however, with the fields often quite a rough scene, while some Greeks, in addition, see fit to pay women a lower daily rate.

If you're still intent on doing it, the most promising course is to ask around among fellow travellers at youth hostels – at some of which you'll find employers recruiting casual labor.

The best **areas, month by month** are:

November-February: Oranges, in the region bounded by Mycenae, Árgos, Náfplio and Tólo – though be aware that the police here are the most unpleasant in Greece. Lemons at Mistrás, near Spárti, and Kiáto on the coast by Kórinthos, after the oranges are gone. On Crete the season may continue into **April or May**, especially at Paleóhora and Falassárna in the west.

March: Artichokes at Iría, near Tólo.

June: Peaches around Véria in Macedonia.

October-November: Olive harvest, most notably near Ámfissa (near Kalamáta), on Crete, and possibly Lésvos.

EMPLOYMENT

Teaching English

Language schools (*frontistíria*) have expanded rapidly through Greece, and English is the most popularly required tongue. To get a job in a school it helps to have a TEFL (Teaching of English as a Foreign Language) certificate, or a university degree, though neither are essential, nor do you need to speak Greek. You will, however, find work much easier to come by if you've got a degree or certificate – take it with you, along with any other impressive documents you can muster.

The simplest way to get a teaching job is to apply before leaving. There are ads published weekly – particularly from August to October – in *The Guardian* newspaper (Tuesday Education) and in the weekly *Times Educational Supplement*. Once accepted, you should get one-way air fare from London paid, accommodation, and a salary of £50-80 a week – enough to live on in Greece, since you pay no tax for the first year you work. The other big advantage of arranging work from abroad is that the red tape of work permits and teaching licenses will be cleared up for you before you set off.

If you're already in Greece and want teaching work there are in theory a number of bureaucratic obstacles, such as obtaining a license. In practice, however, schools are rarely bothered, and if you're around at the right time (try at the end of August) you're likely to find a place. The best technique is to approach *frontistíria* directly – dozens are listed in the phonebook for all larger towns, and many are jointly owned and will send you to an affiliate if they don't have a vacancy. Teaching is essentially a winter exercise; the schools close down from the end of May until mid-September, operating only a few special courses in June and July.

It's general practice to supplement your income by giving **private lessons**, and for this the going rate is around £4-8 an hour. Many teachers finance themselves exclusively on private lessons and, although you still officially need a teaching permit for this, few people experience any problems with it. The *British Council* in Athens can sometimes put you in touch with people who want lessons and you can also advertise in the *Athens News*.

Au-Pair Work

The popularity and scale of private English teaching also means that English-speaking women are heavily in demand as **au-pairs**. As ever, such positions tend to be exploitative and low-paid but if you can use them to your own ends – living reasonably well and learning Greek – there can be mutual benefits. It's unwise to arrange anything until you're in Greece, so you can at least meet and talk terms with your prospective family, and in Athens you should find little difficulty fixing something up. Posts are advertised in the daily *Athens News* and there are quite a number of specialist agencies. These include:

International Staff (Th. N. Camenos), Botási 12, Athens.

Miterna, Ermoú 28, Athens.

Working Holidays, Níkis 11, Athens.

XEN (Greek YWCA), Amerikís 11, Athens.

A final word on (semi-) permanent employment: try if at all possible to get your employer to contribute on your behalf to IKA, the Greek **social security** scheme, thus affording you some minimal medical insurance coverage. They may well decline to mention its existence when hiring you.

DIRECTORY

AIRPORT TAX There is no tax on exit or arrival.

ANIMAL WELFARE is not a Greek strongpoint: cats, dogs, donkeys, horses, etc. are rarely considered worthy of veterinary treatment. The Greek Animal Welfare Fund has a network of (English-speaking) contacts around the country, willing to help animals in distress. For the local representative phone their Athens office (☎01/643-5391 or ☎01/644-4473).

BACKPACKS Unless you're camping, hiking, or travelling long-term, you may be best off without a backpack. Light canvas duffle bags are a lot easier to cart around on buses (packs often have to be tied on to the roof) and create a useful aura of respectability . . .

BARGAINING isn't a regular feature of life though you'll find it possible with private rooms and some off-season hotels. A useful idea with rooms is to offer to use your sleeping-bag, saving the washing of the sheets.

BRING an alarm clock (for early buses and ferries), and a flashlight (if you camp out).

CONSULATES See listings for Athens and Thessaloníki.

CONTRACEPTIVES Condoms (*kapótes*) are available from city kiosks or *farmakía*; the pill, too, can be obtained from a *farmakío*.

ELECTRICITY is 220 volt AC, 110 DC in a few remote spots. Wall outlets take double round-pin plugs as in the rest of continental Europe.

FERRY DEPARTURE TAX A departure tax is levied on all international ferries – currently 1000dr per person and per car.

FILMS *Fuji* films are reasonably priced; *Kodak* and *Ektachrome* expensive.

GAY LIFE is centred on Míkonos, still the most popular European gay resort after Ibiza in Spain. Lesser action on Rhodes and Íos; for women, to a modest extent, on Lésvos (appropriately). Homosexuality is legal over the age of 17 and (male) *bi*sexuality quite widely accepted. See also the 'Listings' in the *Athens* chapter.

GREEK LANGUAGE COURSES abound in Athens – see the city's 'Listings' for addresses.

KIDS/BABIES are worshipped and indulged, perhaps to excess, and present few problems travelling. Baby foods and nappies are ubiquitous and concessions are offered on most forms of transport. Private rooms establishments are more likely to offer some kind of babysitting service than the more impersonal hotels.

LAUNDRIES (*plintíria*) are rare except for the expensive drop-off kind. Ask rooms owners for a *skáfi* (laundry trough) or bucket (*koúvas*); they often freak out if you use basins, Greek plumbing being what it is.

MEDICAL EMERGENCIES ☎166 for hospital cases.

PERÍPTERA are street-corner kiosks. They sell everything from pens to razors, stationery to soap, candy to condoms, cigarettes to plastic crucifixes . . . and are often open when nothing else is.

TAMPONS are sold at *farmakía* and some kiosks.

TIME Greek summertime begins at 12.01 am on the last Sunday in March, when the clocks go ahead one hour, and ends at 12.01 am the last Sunday in September when they fall back. Be alert to this, as scores of visitors miss planes, ferries, etc. every year; the change is not well publicised. Greek time is two hours ahead of the UK, three hours when the countries' respective changes to summertime fail to coincide.

TOILETS Public ones are usually in parks or squares, often subterranean; otherwise try a bus station. Throughout Greece you toss paper in adjacent wastebaskets, *not* in the bowl.

Metric Weights and Measures

1 metre = 1.09 yards	1 yard = 0.91 metres
1 kilometre = 0.62 miles	1 mile = 1.61 kilometres (km)
100 grams = 3½ ounces	1 ounce = 28.3 grams
1 kilogram = 2.2 pounds	1 pound = 454 grams
1 litre = 2.12 pints	1 pint = 0.47 liters
10 litres = 21 pints	1 gallon = 3.78 liters

PART TWO

THE
MAINLAND

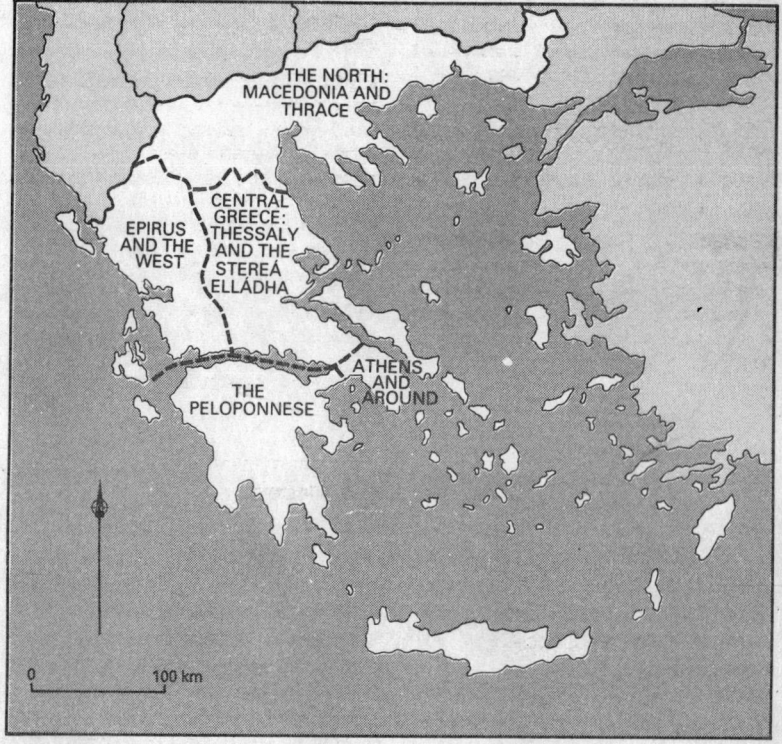

THE NORTH:
MACEDONIA AND
THRACE

CENTRAL
GREECE:
THESSALY
AND THE
STEREÁ
ELLÁDHA

EPIRUS
AND THE
WEST

ATHENS
AND
AROUND

THE
PELOPONNESE

0   100 km

CHAPTER ONE

ATHENS AND AROUND

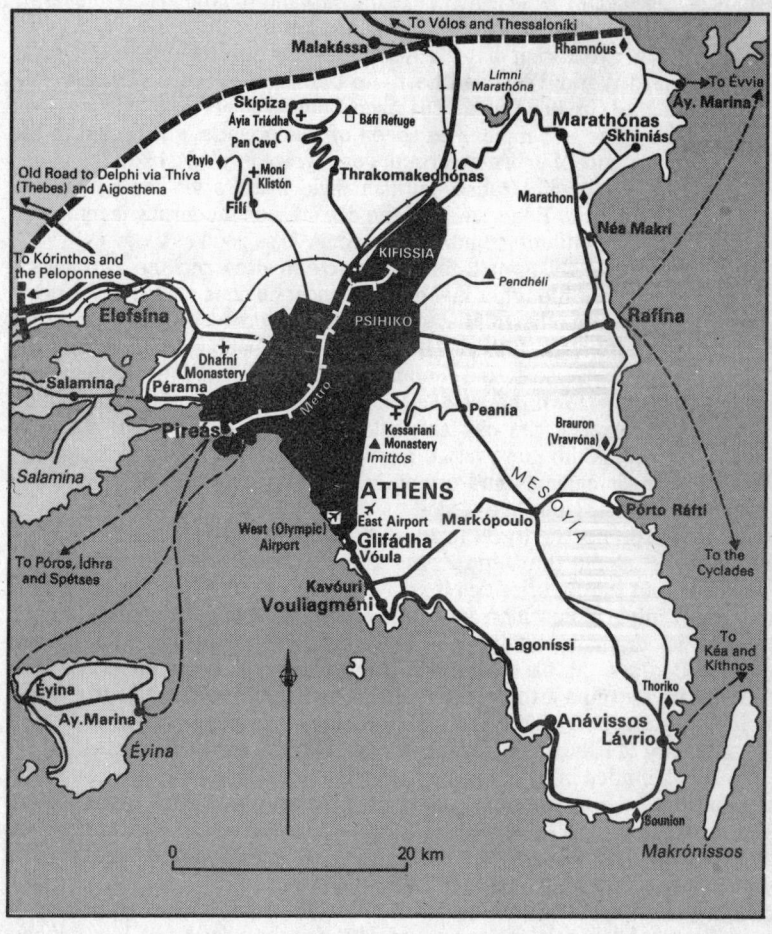

Athens (*Athína* in its Greek form) is not a graceful city. It looks terrible from just about every approach; its air pollution is dire; and its traffic and post-war architecture are a disaster. For many of the 3-million-plus visitors who pass through each year, it can seem a dutiful stop. Time is spent at the Acropolis; more at the vast National Archaeological Museum; and an evening or two amid the increasingly rip-off joints of Pláka, the one surviving old quarter. Most then get out fast, disillusioned at such sparse evidence of the past and so little apparent charm.

It is not a vision that holds great promise. Yet somehow the city has the character – an exhausting but always stimulating mix of urban and rural, First and Third World, West and East – to transcend it. Since World War II, the population of Greater Athens has risen from 700,000 to 3.8 million – over a third of the nations' people. The speed of this process is reflected in the city's shambolic mix of urban and rural: goats graze in yards, carts are pulled along streets thick with traffic, Turkish style bazaars vie for space with outlets for Armani and Benetton. And the city's hectic modernity is tempered with an easy-going attitude: tomorrow, it seems, is as good as today.

Once you accept this, you'll find the **ancient sites** and the Acropolis – supreme monument though it is – only the most obvious of **Athens' attractions**. There are some beautiful cafés, terraced tavernas and street markets; startling views from the hills of Likavitós and Filopáppou; and, around the foot of the Acropolis, scattered monuments of the Byzantine, medieval and nineteenth-century town that seemed so exotic to Byron and the Romantics. As you might expect, the city also offers the best eating to be found in Greece, as well as the most varied nightlife: traditional music in the winter months, open-air cinemas and drama in summer, plus the whole range of style in bars, music clubs and discos.

Outside Athens, the travel focus shifts more exclusively to ancient sites; the beaches along the Attic coast are functional enough escapes for Athenians, but hardly priorities if you are moving on to the islands. Of the sites, the Temple of Poseidon at **Sounion** is the most popular trip, and rightly so, with its dramatic cliff-top position above the cape. Lesser-known and lesser-visited are the sanctuaries at **Rhamnous** and **Brauron** (Vravróna), both rewarding ruins with beaches nearby; and, for the committed, the burial mound at **Marathon**, though this is more literary pilgrimage than sight, and the sanctuary of **Eleusis** (Elefsína), stranded amidst industrial sprawl.

Equally hemmed in by Greater Athens, but worth a visit, is the **monastery of Dhafní**, whose mosaics are among the greatest works of all Byzantine art. And for relief from all this culture there are of course the **mountains** that ring the city – Párnitha, most compellingly – where springtime walks reveal some of the astonishing range of Greek wild flowers.

Finally, a note on the three **ports** of Attica. **Pireás** (Piraeus), effectively an extension of Athens, is the main terminus for the island and international ferries, as well as for most Greek industry. It's reached from central Athens on the single-line metro or direct from the airport. The other two ports, **Rafína** and **Lávrio**, are on the east coast, connected by bus with the city; the former is a useful (and underused) departure point for many of the Cycladic islands, the latter serves the islands of Kéa and Kíthnos (see 'Travel Details' at the end of this chapter).

ATHENS (ATHÍNA)

ATHENS has been inhabited continuously for over 7000 years. Its *acropolis*, supplied with springwater, protected by a ring of mountains, and commanding views of all approaches from the sea, was a natural choice for prehistoric settlement and for the Mycenaeans, who established a palace-fortress on the rock. Its development into a city-state and artistic centre continued apace under the Dorians, Phoenicians and various dynastic rulers, reaching its apotheosis in the fifth century B.C. This was the Classical period, when the Athenians, having launched themselves into an experiment in radical democracy, celebrated their success with a flourish of art, architecture, literature and philosophy that has pervaded Western culture ever since.

Yet, for all the claims of its ancient past, and for all its natural advantages, the city was not the first-choice **capital of modern Greece**. That honour went to Náfplio in the Peloponnese, where the War of Independence was masterminded by Capodistria, and where the first Greek National Assembly met in 1828. Athens at the time was still a provincial backwater, whose population, 250,000 in Classical times, had declined to around 1500 Greek and 400 Turkish families under Ottoman rule. Had Capodistria not been assassinated – the victim of a vendetta carried out by a Maniot clan – the capital would most likely have remained in the Peloponnese, if not at Náfplio, then at Trípoli, Kórinthos (Corinth), or Pátra, all much more established and sizeable towns.

But following Capodistria's death, in 1831, the 'Great Powers' of Western Europe intervened, inflicting on the Greeks a king of their own choosing – **Otho**, son of Ludwig I of Bavaria – and in 1834 transferring the capital and court to Athens. The reasoning was almost purely symbolic and literary. Athens was not only insignificant in terms of population and physical extent but was at the edge of the territories of the new Greek state, which was yet to include Northern Thessaly, Epirus and Macedonia or any of the islands beyond the Cyclades.

Medieval and Turkish Athens

The **ancient history** of Athens, to the end of the Roman period, is covered with the archaeological sites (see pps. 68 and 82). The period from the **decline of Rome** to the nineteenth century is swiftly summarised. Having survived for over a millenium as a cultural and intellectual centre, the city lost influence in the wake of two radical religious and political developments. The first was the emergence of **Christianity**; the second, the division of the Roman empire into eastern and western halves. At Byzantium (Constantinople) – capital of the eastern **Byzantine** empire – a new Christian focus soon outshone Athens, whose schools of philosophy continued to teach a pagan Neoplatonism. In 529 the schools were finally closed by Justinian I and the temples, including the Parthenon, reconsecrated as churches. Athens was designated an archbishopric but it features little in the chronicles of the age.

Ironically, at least from a Greek nationalist perspective, the city underwent something of a revival under the foreign powers of the Middle Ages. In the aftermath of the piratical Fourth Crusade, Athens, together with the Peloponnese and much of the region north to Thessaly, passed into the hands of the **Franks**. At the Acropolis they established a ducal court (of some magnificence, according to contemporary accounts) and for a century Athens was back in the mainstream of Europe. Frankish control, however, was based on little more than a provincial aristocracy. In 1311 their forces met with **Catalan** mercenaries, who had a stronghold in Thebes, and were driven to oblivion in a swamp. The Catalans, having set up their own duchy, in turn gave way to **Florentines** and, briefly, **Venetians**, before the arrival in 1456 of **Sultan Mehmet II**, the Turkish conqueror of Constantinople.

Turkish Athens was never much more than a garrison town. The links with the West, which had maintained some sense of continuity with the Classical and Roman city, were severed. The Acropolis became the home of the Turkish governor, and the Parthenon a mosque; visitors were reduced to a handful of French or Italian ambassadors to the Sublime Porte and the occasional traveller or painter. The town does not seem to have been oppressed by Ottoman rule; the Greeks enjoyed some autonomy, and both Jesuit and Capuchin monasteries were permitted. However, life in the village-like quarters around the Acropolis drifted back to a largely rural and market existence, while at Pireás, the great port, still partially walled, was left to serve just a few dozen fishing boats.

Records of the Ottomans' four centuries of occupation largely concern the **monuments**. In 1687 the Venetians, under the Doge Francisco Morosini, laid siege to the Acropolis. A 'fortunate shot', fired by a Swedish mercenary general from the Hill of Filopáppou, ignited the Turkish powderstore in the Parthenon and rent the temple in two. At the end of the eighteenth century came the Western looters: Elgin levering away sculptures from the Parthenon, the French ambassador Fauvel gathering his share for the Louvre. Byron, a sympathetic luminary amidst all this unenlightened activity, visited in 1810–11, in time to see the last of Elgin's ships loaded with the marbles.

Independence was just two decades away. In 1821, in common with a score of other towns across the country, the Greeks in Athens rose in rebellion. They occupied the Turkish quarters of the lower town – the current Pláka – and laid siege to the Acropolis. The Turks withdrew but five years later were back to reoccupy the Acropolis fortifications, while the Greeks evacuated to the countryside. When the Ottoman garrison finally left in 1834, and the Bavarian architects moved in, Athens was at its lowest ebb.

Modern Athens

The **nineteenth-century development** of Athens was a gradual and fairly controlled process. While the archaeologists stripped away all the Turkish and Frankish embellishments from the Acropolis, a modest city took shape along the lines of the Bavarians' neoclassical grid. Pireás, meanwhile, grew into a port again, though until this century its activities continued to be dwarfed by the main Greek shipping centres on the islands of Síros and Ídhra (Hydra).

The first mass expansion of both municipalities came suddenly, in 1923, as the result of the tragic Greek-Turkish war in **Asia Minor**. The settlement of this involved the exchange of Greek and Turkish ethnic populations, the determination of identity being made solely on the basis of religion. A million and a half Greeks, mostly from the age-old settlements along the Asia Minor coast, but also many Turkish-speaking communities from inland Anatolia, arrived in Greece as refugees. Over half of them settled in Athens, Pireás, and the neighbouring villages, changing at a stroke the whole makeup of the capital. Their integration, and survival, is one of the great events of Athens' history – ancient and modern. It is still evident today. The web of suburbs that straddle the metro line from Athens to Pireás, and sprawl out into the hills, bear the names of their refugees' origins: *Néa Smírni* (New Smyrna), *Néa Iónia*, and the rest. At the beginning they were exactly that: refugee villages with populations from one or another town, built in ramshackle fashion, often with a single water source for two dozen families.

The merging of these shanty-suburbs and their populations with the established communities of Athens and Pireás dominated the years before **World War II**. With the war, however, new concerns emerged. Athens was hit hard by German occupation; during the winter of 1942 there were an estimated 2000 deaths from starvation each day. In late 1944, when the Germans had finally left (Allied policy was to tie them down in the Balkans), the capital saw the first skirmishes of **civil war**, with British forces being ordered to fight against their previous Greek partners in the Communist resistance army, ELAS. Physical evidence of the ensuing month-long Battle of Athens, the *Dhekemvrianá*, can still be seen in the bullet-pocked walls.

From 1946–49 Athens was a virtual island in the civil war, with road approaches to the Peloponnese and the north only tenuously kept open. During the 1950s, though, the city started to expand rapidly. A massive **industrial investment** programme – backed largely by the Americans, who had won Greece for their sphere of influence – took place, and, concurrently, the capital saw huge **immigration** from the war-torn, impoverished countryside. The open spaces between the old refugee suburbs began to fill and, by the late 1960s, Greater Athens covered a continuous area from the slopes of mounts Pendéli and Párnitha down to Pireás and Elefsína.

This enormous population increase and attendant industrial development have had disastrous effects. On a visual level, much of the city is unremittingly ugly; old buildings were demolished wholesale in the name of quick-buck development, particularly during the colonels' junta of 1967–73. Only now – too late – are planning measures being enforced. More seriously, with around half the country's industry and over two-thirds of its cars crammed into Greater Athens, the capital has found itself with one of the world's worst **pollution** problems. A sulphurous cloud, the *néfos*, makes regular appearances, trapped by the circle of mountains and hovering above the city. It causes the acute respiratory diseases most frighteningly demonstrated by the number of deaths during the freak heat waves of the last two summers.

Symbolically, some might say, the ensuing acid rain is eating away at the Parthenon marbles.

For the last ten years the only antipollution measures have been restrictions on the use of private cars. The last conservative government limited weekend driving to alternate weekends, according to whether you had odd or even number plates. The current one, PASOK, despite vociferous protests in opposition, merely replaced this system with limitations on weekday use: alternate days for odd- and even-numbered plates. Meanwhile most shops, offices and businesses persist in closing for a three-hour summer siesta, making for four rush hours a day and doubling the pollution and other traffic problems that most cities have to face.

But not all is gloom. Dimitris Beïs, the former PASOK mayor, endowed the city with thousands of trees, shrubs, and patches of garden, and an ever-growing number of pedestrian-only streets. There is also increasing awareness of the nineteenth-century architectural heritage – what's left of it – with many old houses being restored and repainted. It's the **long-term solutions** that are more problematic: decanting industry and services into the provinces, where there is no infrastructure and where no self-respecting Athenian wishes to live, and creating a mass transport network capable of meeting the needs of a modern capital city. The current mayor, Miltiades Evert – a fairly independent spirit from the conservative Néa Dhimokratía party – seems to be making a start, having initiated a trial section of tunnel for the long-discussed metro extension. However, with Athens bidding to host the centennial modern Olympics in 1996, there is still a long way to go.

Arriving and getting around the city

As a visitor, you're likely to spend most time in the central grid of Athens, a compact, walkable area. Only on arrival or departure at the various far-flung stations and terminals do you have to confront the confused urban sprawl. Details on coming into the city are given opposite and overleaf.

Once into the centre it's a simple matter to **orient** yourself. There are four strategic reference points: the squares (*platíes*) of **Síntagma** and **Omónia**, the hills of the **Acropolis** (unmistakable with its temple crown) and (to the northeast) **Likavitós**. Once you've established these as a mental compass you shouldn't get lost for long – anyone will point you back in the direction of Síntagma or Omónia at the (approximate) pronunciation of their names.

Síntagma (Platía Sintágmatos, 'Constitution Square', in its full title) lies midway between the Acropolis and Likavitós. With the Greek Parliament building on its uphill side, and banks and airline offices grouped around, it is to all intents and purposes the centre of the capital.

Almost everything of daytime interest is within twenty to thirty minutes' walk of Síntagma. To the northeast, the ritzy **Kolonáki** quarter curls around the slopes of **Likavitós**, with a funicular up the hillside to save you the final climb. To the east, behind the Parliament, the jungly **National Gardens** function as the city's chief lung and meeting place; beyond them are the 1896 Olympic stadium and the attractive neighbourhoods of **Pangráti** and **Méts**, both good for drinking and eating options. To the southwest, lapping up to the base of the **Acropolis**, spread the ramshackle but much-commercialised lanes of **Pláka**, the lone surviving area of the nineteenth-century, pre-independence village.

Northwest of Síntagma, two broad thoroughfares, **Stadhíou** and **Panepistimíou** (officially but ineffectually renamed Venizélou), run in just under a kilometre to **Omónia** (fully, Platía Omonías, 'Harmony Square'). This is the nearest Athenian equivalent to Picadilly Circus or Times Square: a bit seedy, with fast-food cafés and a scattering of porno shows in the back streets around. To the north, beyond Panepistimíou, is the neighbourhood of **Exárhia**, slightly 'alternative', with a concentration of lively bars. South of Omónia, stretching down to **Ermoú** street and the borders of Pláka, lies the main commercial centre, crammed with offices and shops for everything from insurance to machine tools.

The city's main **EOT tourist office** is located inside the National Bank of Greece on the Stadhíou corner of Síntagma. It's an invaluable source of information, dispensing ferry timetable sheets (use these as guidelines only!),

---

Points of arrival

Arriving in Athens has been greatly simplified by the introduction of five new **express bus lines**. These blue-and-yellow double-decker coaches connect the two airport terminals, the centre of the city, the train and bus (KTEL) stations, and the port of Pireás.

The **Athens routes** are:
Line A Airport (East terminal)–Stíles–Síntagma–Omónia–Váthis–Karaïskáki–KTEL Kifissoú.
KTEL Kifissoú–Karaïskáki–Omónia–Síntagma–Stíles–Airport (East terminal).
Line A As above, but running to and from the West (Olympic) air terminal.
Line B Airport (East terminal)–Stíles–Síntagma–Omónia–Váthis–Karaïskáki–Stathmí (train stations)–KTEL Liossión.
KTEL Liossión–Karaïskáki–Omónia–Síntagma–Stíles–Airport (East terminal).
Line B As above, but running to and from the West (Olympic) air terminal.

The most obvious stops for the centre of town are Omónia and Síntagma; Stíles is useful if you plan to stay in the Veikoú/Koukáki area.

The **Pireás route** is:
Express #19 Airport (East terminal)–Airport (West terminal)–Fáliro–Mégaro–Telonío–Aktí Tzelépi.
Aktí Tzelépi–Telonío–Fáliro–Airport (West terminal)–Airport (East terminal).

For hydrofoils at the Zéa port the best stop is Telonío; Mégaro is by the international ferry dock; Aktí Tzelépi fronts the main harbor, where most island ferries leave and ticket agents are concentrated.

Lines A, A, B, and B run **every twenty minutes** (every hour midnight–6am). The Pireás #19 bus runs **every thirty minutes** (every ninety minutes midnight–6am). Each service has a 100dr flat fare (150dr from midnight to 6am). Useful free **plans** indicating the lines and the metro are widely available in hotels, travel agents, tourist offices, etc., in Athens.

EXPRESS BUS STOPS

LOCAL BUSES

A Dhafni, Eléfsina
B Rafina, Soúnion, Lávrio
C Glifádha, Voúla and the Beaches

★ Metro stations

0   500 metres

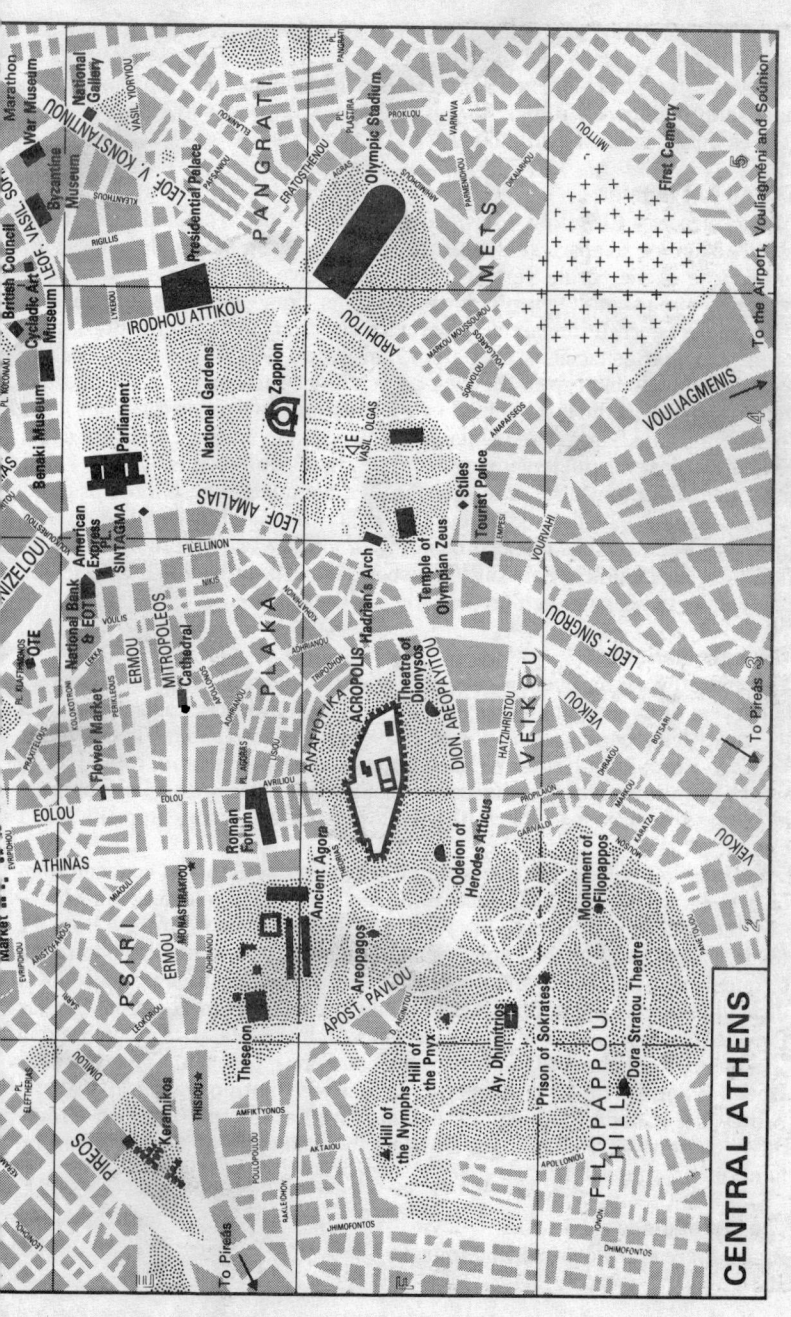

CENTRAL ATHENS

along with maps and pamphlets for Athens and other parts of the country. To complement our plans and the free EOT map, a good, **large-scale map** of the city is the street-indexed *Falk-Plan* (hard to obtain in Athens: see the bookshop listings on p.104). If you're planning a long stay, an **A-Ω** atlas (Greek only) is available from kiosks and bookshops.

The airport terminals

Athens airport – **Ellinikón** – has two distinct sections, **West** and **East**. They stand 1500m or so apart with separate entrances five minutes' drive away on either side of the perimetre fence; when you leave, it's important to specify which one you want. **Olympic Airways** flights, domestic *or* foreign, operate from the western terminal; all **other airlines** from the eastern. Both have **money exchange** facilities, open from 7am–11pm.

The airport is 9km from the city, so you'll need transport to get into the centre. As well as the bus detailed (see *Arrival* box), Olympic run a bus from their terminal to Singroú and Síntagma, leaving from outside the airport door.

The simplest way to get into town and to a hotel, however, is by **taxi**, which at around 700dr to central Athens or Pireás is a modest cost split two or more ways. Make sure before setting out that either the meter is switched on or a price has been established; overcharging of tourists can be brutal. You may find (see our comments on 'City Transport', opposite) that you'll have fellow passengers in the cab; each drop-off will pay the full fare.

The train stations

There are two train stations, almost adjacent, a couple of hundred metres northwest of Omónia, off Dheliyáni street. The **Stathmós Laríssis** handles the main lines coming from the north – from Thessaloníki, Yugoslavia or Western Europe, and Turkey. The **Stathmós Peloponníssou**, three blocks south, is the terminal for the narrow-gauge line circling the Peloponnese, including the stretch to Pátra (the main port for the ferries from Italy and Corfu).

From either station, you are within five minutes' walk of the concentration of hostels around Ioulianoú (above the National Archaeological Museum – see the following section). For hotels elsewhere, yellow trolley **bus #1** (30dr) passes right by the Laríssis station (to get to it from the Peloponníssou terminal, use the giant metal overpass) and makes a strategic loop down through Omónia, along Stadhíou to Síntagma, then down Leofóros Amalías (beside the National Gardens) to Hadrian's Arch (for Mets), and finally along Veikoú to Koukáki (on the south side of Filopáppou hill). The **Express Buses B** and **B** (100dr) also link the stations with downtown (see above).

Be wary of **taxis** (both official and unofficial) at the train stations – some thrive on newly-arrived tourists, shuttling them a couple of blocks for several hundred drachmas.

The bus stations

Again, there are two principal terminals.

Coming into Athens **from Northern Greece or the Peloponnese**, you'll find yourself at **Kifissoú 100**, a 25-minute bus ride from the centre. The simplest way into town is to take Express Bus **A** or **Á** (see box). Alternatively, bus #051 (30dr) takes a more circuitous route; its most convenient stop is at the corner of Vilará/Menándhrou, just off Omónia.

Routes from central Greece (see p.121 for specific destinations) arrive rather closer in at **Liossíon 260**, north of the train stations. Express buses **B** and **Ḃ** (100dr) will take you into town (see box), or you could take the blue city bus #024 or less frequent #723 (both 30dr flat fare) to Síntagma.

In addition, there are **OSE buses**, run by the railway company, which arrive at the two train stations. **International bus companies** arrive at, and leave from, a variety of locations. Most will take you to the train station or to Kifissoú 100; a few drop passengers right in the city centre.

Pireás: the ferries

If you arrive by boat at **Pireás**, the simplest access to Athens is by **metro** to the stations at Monastiráki, Omónia, or Viktorías. Trains run from 6am to midnight, with a flat fare of 30dr (free from 5–8am). For the airport, take express #19 (see box).

Taxis from Pireás to central Athens should cost around 700dr – but see the comments above under 'The Airport Terminals'.

There's a map of Pireás, showing the metro station and harbours, on p.111.

City transport: buses, the metro and taxis

All public transport networks operate from around **5am to midnight**, with a skeleton service on some of the buses in the small hours. Between **5am and 8am** all services are **free**, in an effort to discourage car drivers.

City Buses

Athens' **bus network** is extensive and very cheap, with a 30dr flat fare (drop your money in the slot – no tickets and definitely no change given). However, it's very crowded at peak times, unbearably hot in summer traffic jams, and when you can walk in preference, you probably will.

Individual routes, where relevant, are detailed in the text. The most straightforward are those of the **yellow trolley buses**, numbered 1 to 12. #1 (see opposite) connects the Laríssis train station with Omónia, Síntagma, and Veikoú/Koukáki. #2, #3, #5 and #12 all link Síntagma with Omónia and the National Archaeological Museum on Patissíon.

In addition, there are scores of **blue city buses**, all with three-digit numbers and serving an infinity of lines out into the straggling suburbs and beyond.

The Metro

The single-line **metro** (30dr flat fare) is next to useless except for journeys to the termini of Pireás in the south, Kifissiá in the north. Monastiráki, Omónia and Platía Viktorías are the only central stops.

Taxis

Greek taxis are the cheapest anywhere in Europe, and an option always worth bearing in mind. Fares around the city will rarely run above 250 or 300dr, though the minimum fare now is 200dr for any journey.

The officially licensed taxis are painted yellow with a special red number plate. Make sure the meter is switched on (and properly zeroed) and if it's 'not working' keep your confidence when you come to pay. To try and make ends meet on government-regulated fare limits, taxi drivers will often pick up a whole string of passengers along the way. This is technically illegal but universally practised. There is no fare-sharing: each passenger (or group of passengers) pays the full fare for their journey. So if you're picked up by an already-occupied taxi, memorise the meter reading at once; you'll pay from that point on. When hailing an occupied taxi, yell out your destination. The driver then decides whether you suit him or not. Luggage is extra, about 50dr a piece.

When you need them most – between 11pm and 6am – taxis can be dauntingly elusive. If you're leaving the city (especially if you've got to make a flight), try and get your hotel to phone one for you. The only approximation of a **taxi rank** is on the Óthonos (National Gardens) corner of Síntagma. This is also the only place in the city where you've a chance of a cab during the rush hours between 1.30–2.30pm and 7.30–8.30pm.

A Note on Addresses.
The Greek for street is **odhós** but, in both addressing letters and talking, people usually refer only to the name of the street: Ermoú, Márkou Moussoúrou, etc. The practice is similar with **platía** (square) and **leofóros** (avenue). In written addresses, the house number is also written after the street name, thus: Ermoú 13. We have adopted the same practice.
Grid keys throughout this chapter refer to the main map of Athens printed on p.48–49; for more detail on the Pláka area, see the map on p.58.

Phone Numbers
If you are dialling from outside the municipality, the **area code** for both Athens and Pireás is ☎01-.

Finding a place to stay

Hotels and **hostels** can be packed to the gills in midsummer – August especially – but for most of the year there are enough beds to go around, and to suit most wallets and tastes.

On the **budget level**, expect to pay around 1700 to 2400dr for a double room in an E-class; as little as 500 to 700dr a person if you're prepared to share a three- to six-person room. **Moving upmarket**, doubles in D-class hotels rarely run much above 3000dr a night; 4000dr or so in a relatively luxurious C-class or one of the fancier pensions.

The **recommendations** below are geared towards the lower end of the range – D- and E-class hotels, C- and B-class pensions and hostel-style places – and are listed in roughly ascending order of price. At the end of each area, however, we've included a couple of slightly more upmarket C-class hotels which seem worth the extra money for comfort.

Looking for a room, it makes sense to phone before turning up. If you just set out and do the rounds, you'll find somewhere, but in summer, unless you're early in the day, it's likely to be at the third or fourth attempt. If you have the money for a C-class hotel (or above) you can book through the **hotel reservations** desk beside the tourist office in the National Bank of Greece on Síntagma. For cheaper places, you're on your own. Find a street kiosk (there are hundreds in Athens) and ask to use their phone; you pay after you've finished making all the calls – there's no need to find coins. Virtually every hotel and hostel in the city will have an English-speaking receptionist.

Once you locate a vacancy, **ask to see the room** before booking in. Standards vary greatly even within the same building, and you can avoid occasional overcharging by checking the government-regulated room prices displayed by law in each room on the back of the door.

Listings following are organized according to **area** – an important consideration for more than just ease of access. Many of the hotels around Pláka and Omónia, for instance, are victim to round-the-clock noise; if you want uninterrupted sleep, better to head for the neighbourhoods south of the Acropolis (Méts, Veikoú, Koukáki) or to the north between the National Archaeological Museum and the railway stations.

Prices quoted are intended only as a guideline, with Greek inflation running at a current 20 percent a year. They are basically summer rates; **out of season** most prices drop by a quarter to a half – more if you negotiate rates for a three or more nights' stay.

● In and around Pláka/Síntagma

There aren't a lot of cheap options in **Pláka** these days: the last few years saw police raids on the unofficial 'student inns', strict licensing of those that remained, and a definite overall swing towards gentrification. For the best of the cheap hostels, check instead the National Archaeological Museum area (below).

Pláka, however, is still an area to consider, especially if you're after a D- or C-class hotel. The whole quarter, despite its tourist tat, is highly atmospheric, and above all very central, within easy walking distance of all the sites, Síntagma, and the Monastiráki metro station (for Pireás).

Thisseus Inn, Thisséos 10, *E3* (☎324-5960). You don't get much more central than this – three blocks west of Síntagma – nor much cheaper. No frills, but clean enough, with top floor bar and lounge. 1000dr per person in dbls, 900dr per person in trpls/quads.

George's Guest House, Níkis 46, *E3* (☎322-6474). One of the cheapest and most enduring of the hostel-type places, located just a block west of Síntagma. Various-sized dorms (mattresses on floor) and some doubles. Fills early but worth a try at 700–850dr per person (according to room size).

Student Inn, Kidhathinéon 18, *E3* (☎324-4808). Another central hostel – but one that's gone downhill over the years, and is prone to night-time revellers outside; 2am curfew. Sgls 1500–1600dr; dbls 2000–3300dr.

XEN (YWCA), Amerikís 11, *D3* (☎362-6970). **Women-only** hostel just north of Síntagma – not in Pláka – that provides clean, relatively quiet rooms, a self-service restaurant, a small library, and Greek classes. Well worth considering. The YMCA (**men-only**) equivalent nearby, the *XAN* (Omírou 28, *D3*; ☎362-4291), is less inspiring.

Solonion **(E)**, Spírou Tsángari 11, *F3* (☎322-0008). Eccentric and (usually) friendly staff in grand, if slightly run-down, building. Sgls 1700dr; dbls 2100dr.

Phaedra **(D)**, Herefóndos 16 at the Adhrianoú junction, *F3* (☎322-7795). Plain, clean, and dead quiet at night, at the junction of two pedestrian malls. Prices fluctuate wildly with season; summer rates 2500dr sgl, 3000dr dbl. In summer, **roofspace** mattresses (an attractive option for the cool and the stars) are available for about 1000dr per person.

Cleo's Guest House, Patroú 3, *E3* (☎322-9053). A bit cell-like but reasonably comfortable dbls for 2000–4000dr (cheaper off-season).

Pension Kouros **(C)**, Kódhrou 11, *E3* (☎322-7431). Okay facilities and on a pedestrianised street (the continuation of Voulís – two blocks south and west of Síntagma). Sgls (only three) 1600dr; dbls 2600dr.

Pension Dioskouri **(C)**, Pittákou 6, *F3* (☎324-8165). Gloomy rooms, though well-furnished, with a garden and a good locale (one block in from Leofóros Amalías). Dbls 2600dr.

Phoebus **(C)**, Pétta 12, *F3* (☎322-0142). Probably the best C-class in Pláka. Three minutes walk from Síntagma down Filellínon (Pétta is off Níkis). Sgls, 2900dr; dbls 3800dr.

Pension Myrto **(B)**, Níkis 40, *E3* (☎322-7237). Again good value for its class, with baths in all rooms and a small bar. Just off Síntagma. Dbls 3900dr.

Acropolis House **(B)**, Kódhrou 6, *E3* (☎322-2344). A very clean, well-sited pension (see *Kouros* above for directions) and surprisingly good value. Sgls 2900dr; dbls 3500dr up.

● Ermoú/Athinás: the Bazaar Area

If the Pláka is bohemian/chic Athens, this district is the city at its (occasionally gritty) most authentic. Noise there is in abundance, plus the odd bordello or cockroach, but also every other material thing you could possibly want – and it's a very short walk to the major sites.

Hermion **(D)**, Ermoú 66c, *E2* (☎321-2753); *Anatoli* **(E)**, Ermoú 69, *E2* (☎321-3057). Not the city's most salubrious hotels, with mixed reviews as to cleanliness and management. But low prices (dbls 2000dr), and an excellent coffee shop, *Hermes*, down the road at no.56.

Ideal **(D)**, Eólou 39, corner Voréou, *E2* (☎321-3195). 19th c. building with the odd balcony facing the Acropolis; reasonable if somewhat decayed rooms, friendly management. Sgls 1400dr; dbls 2100dr.

Tembi **(D)**, Eólou 29, *E2* (☎321-3175). Just around the corner from the *Ideal* and similar in price and most respects.

Sofokléous street. Note that many of the hotels on this street, and on adjacent **Athinás**, up towards Omónia, are worked by prostitutes. This needn't rule them all out – the *Serreon* (Sofokléous 32; D; ☎523-2606; dbls 1400dr), for example, is cheap and clean – but be aware of your environment. Three to avoid are the *Pindharos, Parnassos,* and *Kosmikon*, at any of which you'd get little sleep...

● South of the Acropolis: Koukáki/Méts

Koukáki is just south of the Acropolis, edging up to the hill of Filopáppou; **Méts** spreads behind the Olympic Stadium, over to the east. Both are attractive parts of the city, with the occasional street that owes more to the last century than the present one. Though slightly out of the way – twenty minutes' walk from Síntagma or the heart of Pláka – they compensate with some excellent neighbourhood tavernas, cafés, and grocery shops.

Joseph's House, Márkou Moussoúrou 13, *F4* (☎923-1204). Under new management, this elegant old building looks set to become one of the city's better (as well as most attractively sited) budget hostels – casting off a somewhat seedy past. Prices a little on the high side: dbls 2000dr; triples 2600dr. Roofspace also available; kitchen.

Villa Olympia (D), Karatzá 16, Veikoú, *G2* (☎923-7650). A helpful, British-managed pension which sets you up for the day with full English breakfast. Call ahead as they only have sixteen beds. Sgls 1300dr; dbls 2000dr.

Lito (D), Missaraliótou 15, corner of Kariatídhon/Zítrou, *C3* (☎323-8461). Co-managed with *Phaedra* in Pláka, but rather cheaper. Sgls 2200dr; dbls 2700dr.

Marble House (C), in a quiet alley off A. Zínni 35, *G3* (☎923-4058). Probably the best value in Koukáki, with a very helpful French/ Greek management. It's often full, however, so call ahead. Sgls 1500dr up; dbls 2200dr up.

Clare's House (C), Sorvoloú 24, Méts, *F4* (☎922-2288). Immaculate pension which moved out here from the Pláka. Prices are high but include a bath in most rooms, and breakfast. Dbls 4000dr and up.

● Around the National Archaeological Museum: Exárhia and Platía Viktorías

These areas north of Omónia – **Exárhia** to the east of the National Archaeological Museum, **Platía Viktorías** to the west – are again out of the tourist mainstream. The local restaurants are good value, the train stations (and metro Viktorías) a short walk away, and at night there are the clubs and bars around Exárhia. Due to all of these factors, the area now has the main concentration of 'student hostels,' offering cheap triples and larger dormitories as well as standard double rooms. Most of these are very well run, offering friendly advice and useful services – and they're greatly recommended over the city's official youth hostel, way out in Kipséli and listed here only for the sake of completeness.

Athens Connection, Ioulianoú 20, just east of Patission, *B2* (☎822-4592). Perhaps the best of the student hostels, with single and double rooms as well as four-bed dorms, generally knowledgeable reception, money change and ticket-booking facilities, and a basement bar. 800–1200dr per person, depending on the room.

Iokastis' House, Aristotélous 65, corner of Ioulianoú, *B2* (822-6647). A similar set-up to the above, and very close by. Bar, travel agency, luggage storage, etc. 800–1500dr per person.

Joy's Hotel, Aharnón 74/Férron 38, *B2* (☎823-1012). Another reliable hostel-type place, slightly closer to the stations. Clean, helpful and good value, with per-person rates from 600dr (dorm bed) to 1550dr (in a dbl with bath); also triples, quads.

Paradise Inn, Mézonos 4, Platía Váthi, *C1* (☎524-1109). The most convenient of a chain of three 'Paradise' hostels, all of which feature singles, doubles, triples, and dorm beds. This one also has a cheap bar and an interested management. Rates from 600–1600dr per person. If the inn is full they may have space in the nearby *Dido* annex (Viktór Oúgo 13, *C1*; ☎524-6906) or send you on to the rather dingily-located *California* on the edge of Pláka (Leokoríou 7, off Ermoú, *E2* ; ☎323-8789).

Hotel Orpheus (C), Halkondíli 56, Platía Váthi, C2 (☎522-4996). Well run hostel-cum-hotel with student discounts on 1–4 bed rooms.

Athens Youth Hostel, Kipséli 57, just north of A3 (reservations: ☎822-5860). If all the above are full, you *might* just want to try a night at the city's official IYHF hostel. Phone first, though, as it's a 15-minute bus ride away (yellow trolleys #2, #4 or #9 from Patission, by the National Archaeological Museum). 650dr per person.

Hotel Museum (C), Bouboulínas 16, corner Tossítsa. Nicely placed hotel, right behind the National Archaeological Museum and parkland. Sgls 2100dr, dbls 3000dr.

Hotel Dryades (C), Dhriadón 4, off Anexartisías, near corner of Themistokléous, *C3*. A small, quiet hotel at the top end of the Exárhia quarter, behind the National Archaeological Museum. Sgls 1800dr; dbls 2600dr. Co-managed with adjacent, slightly cheaper *Hotel Orion* (D), which has a kitchen.

Hotel Exarhion **(C)**, Themistokléous 55, Platía Exárhia (360-1256). Similar to – and close by – the above. Dbls 3200dr.

● Campsites

The city's **campsites** are all some way out – and not especially cheap. Unless you have a camper-van to park it's hard to think of a good reason for using them. However, for the committed, the two most convenient are detailed below; at either, phone ahead to book space.

Athens Camping (☎581-4113). A reasonable site with the usual facilities, 7km out on the road to Kórinthos (right-hand side). Costs 300dr per person plus 250dr for a tent. Bus #822/823 from Athens (corner of Leonidhíou/Dheliyóryi: west of Omónia, *D1*), or bus #802/#845 from Pireás; driving, leave the city centre along Leof. Athinón.

Dhafni Camping (☎598-1150). Poorer facilities and crowded due to its location, right next door to the Wine Festival grounds (see p.94), and the famous monastery. Charges much the same as *Athens Camping*. Clearly signposted on the left of the road next to the monastery; 20 min. by bus (almost any whose number begins with '8') from Platía Eleftherías, halfway between Omónia and Keramikós; driving, head down towards Keramikós and take Ierá Odhós, which later becomes the main highway to Dhafní and Elefsína.

Camping out rough in Athens would not be a good idea. Police patrol many of the parks, especially those by the train stations, and tales of tourists being mugged while sleeping out are not uncommon. Even the train stations themselves are no real refuge, closing up when services stop and unceremoniously cleared of any stragglers. If you can't afford a night in a room, or on a roof, dump your luggage somewhere and spend it in a bar.

● Long-Term Residence

Finding a flat in Central Athens, if you decide to stay and work, is quite tricky at present. Ironically, this is due to the government's removal of rent control: landlords seem to be holding back, waiting for prices to rise. Your best bet is probably a scan of the ads in the English-language *Athens News*. Traditionally, everyone just paced the streets, looking for signs, usually red on white, announcing *ENOIKAZETAI* (To Let). They used to be all over the city, stuck on doors, walls, windows, or lamp posts – and hopefully will gradually reappear.

Average **prices** have also shot up to match demand. You would be doing well to find a two-roomed apartment for under 20,000dr a month. On top of the rent, you will nearly always have to pay *kinóhrista*, an all-encompassing term for services, lighting, heating, and sometimes cleaning, too. Kolonáki, Ambelókipi, and Méts are the fashionable quarters; one notch down are Pangráti (beyond Méts) or Koukáki (around the base of the Filopáppou hill), with Exárhia and Pláka/Anafiótika still a little down the scale.

If you are planning to live in Athens, *Athens: A Survival Handbook* (Efstathiadis) is exhaustive and invaluable.

The Neighbourhoods

Athens as a city – rather than a location of ancient sites and museums – is peculiarly neglected: few visitors get to grips with more than the Pláka, and even that as little more than an approach to the Acropolis. Yet though the

neighbourhoods may lack the style and monuments of most of their European capital counterparts, they are worth at least a casual exploration. The **bazaar** area, around Athinás and Eólou, retains an almost Middle Eastern atmosphere in its life and trade; the **National Gardens**, elegant **Kolonáki** and the hill of **Likavitós** offer escape from the maelstrom, as do the more low-key quarters of **Méts**, **Koukáki** and **Pangráti**, and **Kessarianí**; while **Dhafní**, out in the suburbs to the west, has a Byzantine monastery the equal of any in Greece.

Pláka itself, though, with its alleys and staired streets built on the Turkish plan, is the most rewarding area for daytime wanderings. In addition to its Roman sites (detailed on p.82) and various museums (p.85-92), it offers glimpses of an exotic and rural past, refreshingly at odds with the concrete blocks of the metropolis. An attraction, too, is its recent pedestrianisation, with cars banished from all but a few main streets. And if you can coincide, there is plenty to look at, if perhaps few bargains to be found, in the Sunday morning **flea market** (smaller on other days) around Monastiráki square.

Pláka and Monastiráki

Visiting Athens in 1832, its last winter of Turkish rule, the Rev. Christopher Wordsworth wrote: 'The town of Athens is now lying in ruins. The streets are almost deserted: nearly all the houses are without roofs. The churches are reduced to bare walls and heaps of stone and mortar . . . A few new wooden houses, one or two more solid structures, and the two lines of planked sheds which form the bazaar are all the inhabited dwellings that Athens can now boast'. He was staying near the Thiseion temple, 'on the extreme edge of the modern town . . . There are few other buildings near . . . At a little distance to the south a peasant is now engaged in ploughing the earth . . .' – his field the ancient Agora.

Wordsworth's 'modern town' was essentially today's **Pláka**, roughly the area between Síntagma, Odhós Ermoú and the Acropolis. It's the one part of Athens with real charm and architectural merit. Once away from Síntagma, the narrow winding streets and stairs are lined with nineteenth-century neoclassical houses, some grand, some humble and home made. The tiled roofs are edged with terra-cotta sphinxes, goddesses and foliage designs. The grander facades are decorated with pilasters and capitals and wrought iron balconies. Gateways open on courtyards filled with greenery and overlooked by wooden verandas. Poor and working-class for most of this century, the quarter is gradually being renovated and gentrified.

From Síntagma: central Pláka

An attractive approach to Pláka is to follow **Odhós Kidhathinéon**, a pedestrian walkway starting near the English and Russian churches on Odhós Filellínon, south of Síntagma. It leads gently downhill, past the Popular Arts Museum (see p.90) on a leafy square with one of the few remaining old-time cafés on the corner, on through café-crowded Platía Pláka to Hadrian's street, **Odhós Adhrianoú**, which runs nearly the whole length of Pláka from the Thiseion to Hadrian's Arch.

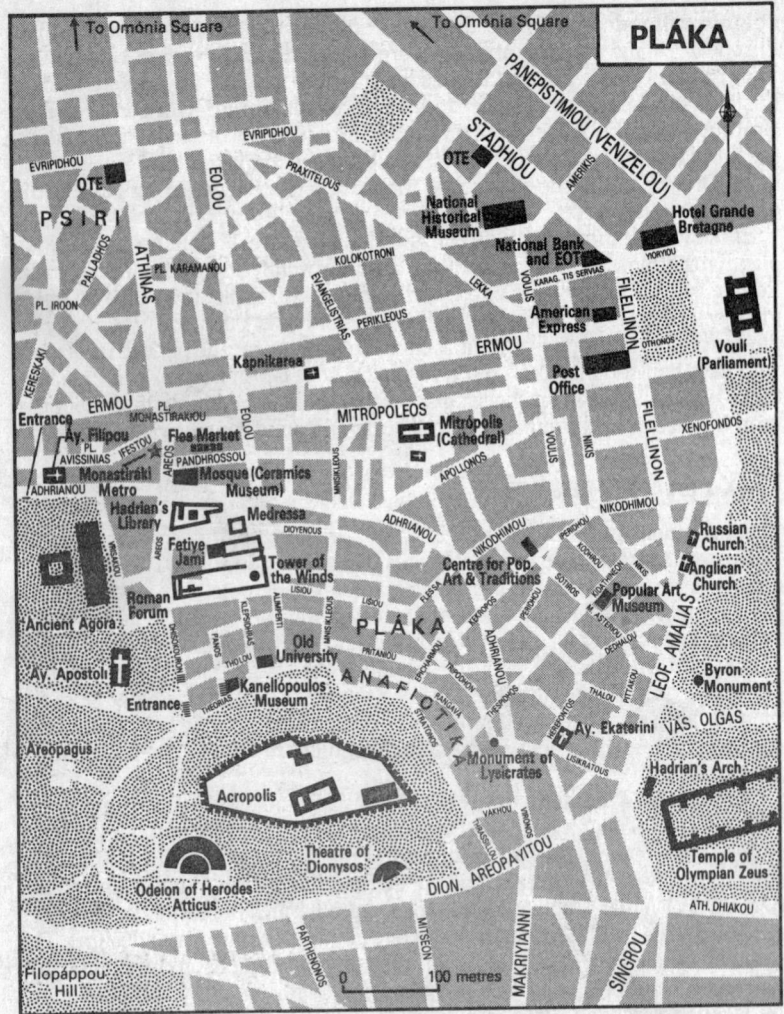

The rightward section of Adhrianoú, past the newly restored neoclassical Demotic School, is largely commercial – souvenir shops and sandals – as far as the **Roman Forum** (see p.83). Left, just a few metres on, there's a quiet and attractive sitting space (and partial excavation) around the fourth century **Monument of Lysicrates**, erected to celebrate the success of a prize-winning dramatic chorus (see p.83). Built into a Capuchin convent for several centuries, the story goes that Byron, who wrote part of *Childe Harold* here, used it as a study; at the time Athens had no inn and the convent was a regular lodging for European travellers. The street beyond, **Vironos**, is named after Byron ('O Lórdhos Víronos' to Greeks). At its far end, facing you across the road, is the old Makriyánni police barracks, revered by Greek rightists for its stout resistance to Communist attack during the 1944 *Dhekemvrianá*. Part of it is currently being transformed into a museum to contain replicas of Acropolis statuary, but there are further plans to excavate on the site and also to build a new Acropolis Museum – scheduled for 1996, the centenary of the modern Olympic Games – with space for the Elgin Marbles, hopefully by then recovered from the British Museum.

Continuing straight ahead from the Kidhathinéon-Adhrianoú intersection up **Odhós Thespídhos** you reach the edge of the Acropolis precinct. Up to the right the whitewashed cubist houses of **Anafiótika** cheerfully proclaim an architect free zone amidst the highest crags of the Acropolis rock. The buildings here were erected by workers from the island of Anáfi (near Thíra/Santoríni) employed in the mid-nineteenth century construction of Athens. Unable to afford land, they took advantage of a law stating that if a roof and four walls could be thrown up overnight, the premises were yours at sunrise. In appearance, the houses, and the two churches that serve them, are the image of those the Cycladic islanders had left behind. Today, sadly, many stand empty on their mule-width lanes and steps – their fate doubtless gentrification and tweeness.

The west side: Monastiráki

The other side of Pláka, along Ermoú and Mitropóleos, is noisier, busier, and more geared to the Greek life of the city. Neither street lays any claim to beauty, though the bottom (west) half of **Ermoú**, with its metalworkers and other craftsmen, has an attractive workaday character; the top half has unhappily transformed the pretty Byzantine church of the **Kapnikaréa** (11th–13th c.) into a traffic island. Churches, too, are the chief feature of **Odhós Mitropóleos** (Cathedral Street). A dusty, tiny chapel crouches below the concrete piers of the Ministry of Education and Religion; the **Mitrópolis** itself, an undistinguished nineteenth-century cannibal of dozens of older buildings, carves out a square midway along; and the old cathedral stands alongside it, a beautiful little church (12th c.) cobbled together from plain and carved blocks as ancient as Christendom itself.

From the bottom corner of the cathedral square, just recently reclaimed for pedestrians, **Odhós Pandhróssou** introduces the **Monastiráki Flea Market** – not that its name is really justified by the rich and conventional jewellery and fur shops that pack the first section. In fact, not many genuine market shops remain at all this side of Platía Monastirakioú. With the exception of a couple of specialist icon dealers, everything is geared to the tourist. Among them, but still a curiosity, is the shop of *Stavros Melissinos*, the 'poet-sandalmaker of Athens', at no.89. Melissinos enjoyed a quirky sort of fame in the 1960s, hammering out sandals for The Beatles, Jackie Onassis and the like; it is said that Lennon sought him out specifically for his poetic musings on wine and sea, which he continues to sell alongside the footwear.

Platía Monastirakíou, full of nut sellers, lottery tickets, fruit stalls, kiosks and cars, gets it name from the little monastery church (*monastiráki*) at its centre, tenth-century in origin and currently undergoing restoration. The area around has been a marketplace since Turkish times, and maintains a number of features from its Ottoman past. On the south side of the square, rising from the walls of Hadrian's Library (see p.83) and the shacks of Pandhróssou, the eighteenth-century **mosque of Tzistarákis**, minus minaret, is now home to the Museum of Traditional Greek Ceramics (see p.91). The building is not very distinguished, but retains calligraphic inscriptions (stating the founder and date) above the entrance, and a series of niches used as outside *mihrabs* (indicating the direction of prayer) for occasions when worshippers could not all fit into the main hall. Another mosque, the **Fetiye Jami** ('Mosque of the Conquest'), serves as an archaeological warehouse in the corner of the Roman forum, while to the south, across the street from the picturesque **Aéridhes** (the Roman 'Tower of the Winds', see p.83) are the remains – a gateway and single dome – of a **medressa**, an Islamic college, or 'seminary'.

Odhós Aréos, alongside Hadrian's Library, was once wholly dedicated to the recycled tyre business – they were made into shoe soles and indestructible baskets. It's now mainly bamboo furniture and wickerwork shops. At its end, round behind the Roman forum, are some of the quietest, prettiest and least spoiled streets in the whole of Pláka – many of them ending in steps for the ascent to **Theorías**, the last lane below the Acropolis. **Panós** is a good approach. Left at the top of its steps is a nineteenth-century mansion housing the little-visited Kanellópoulos Museum (see p.91). A block beyond, straddling Klespídhras and Alimpérti, is a building thought to be the oldest in Athens – the **Panepistímio**, site of the university (the first in modern Greece) in the 1830s.

West of Monastiráki square, the market caters more and more for local needs, with clothes and tools, records and second-hand books in **Odhós Iféstou**; old furniture, bric-a-brac, and camping gear in **Platía Avissinías** (on Sundays here, especially); chairs, office equipment, wood-burning stoves, mirrors, canaries and sundry other goods in **Astíngos**, **Ermoú**, and around; plus used motorbikes (Sunday mornings only) at the bottom of Ermoú. Beside the church of **Ayíou Filípou**, there's a market in hopeless jumble-sale rejects, touted by a cast of eccentrics – again, especially on Sundays. There's a tiny *kafenío*, too, and the *Estiatorio Ipiros*, not much to look at, but serving good Greek fare, and cheap.

The main **entrance to the Agora** (see p.80) is just south of Platía Avissinías on Adhrianoú, across the cutting where the **metro** (for Pireás) re-emerges into open air after tunnelling under the city centre. Odhós Adhrianoú here is at its most appealing, with a couple of good antique shops, a shady *kafenío* beloved of cats, and the best views of the Acropolis. Following the Agora fence round to the southwest you'll come to another good café vantage-point on **Apostólou Pávlou**, which shares the same view. On the hill above is the old **Observatory**, surrounded by a last enclave of streets untroubled by tourism or redevelopment: no special features, just a pleasant wander.

The Bazaar: Athinás to Omónia

A broad triangle of streets, based on **Odhós Ermoú** and flanked by Pireós (officially Tsaldhári) in the west and Stadhíou in the east, reaches north to its apex at Omónia. Through the middle run **Athinás** and **Eólou**. This is the modern bazaar whose shops, though stocked mainly with imported manufactured goods, still reflect their origins in their unaffected decor, unsophisticated packaging, and – most striking – by their specialisation. As was once the case throughout Europe, each street has a concentration of particular shops and wares, almost untouched by any modern notions of marketing.

Hence the Monastiráki end of Athinás is dedicated to tools; food shops are gathered around the central market in the middle; glass to the west; paint and brasswork to the east; clothes in Eólou and Ayíou Márkou. Praxitélous is full of lettering merchants; Platía Klafthmónos of electrical goods. Department stores are close to Omónia. The crumbling houses of Psirí, between Athinás and Keramikós, are riddled with dingy workshops. Always raucous and teeming with shoppers, *kouloúri* (pretzel) sellers, gypsies and other vendors, the whole area is great free entertainment.

The best single bit is the **central market**, on the corner of Athinás and Evripídhou. The building itself is a grand nineteenth-century relic, with fretted iron awnings sheltering forests of carcasses and mounds of hearts, livers, and ears – no place for the squeamish. In the middle section of the hall is a fish market, all manner of luscious fruits of the sea squirming and glistening on the marble slabs, while across the street brilliant displays of fruit and vegetables are flanked by miserably caged pullets, rabbits and canaries (the latter not for eating). On the surrounding streets, perhaps more enticing, are rows of entirely traditional grocers, their stalls piled high with sacks of pulses, salt cod, barrels of olives and wheels of cheese. *Oúzo* addicts should definitely head this way for what could be the drinking experience of their career: *Finopoulos*'s old-fashioned, stand-up *ouzerí* on the Athinás-Evripídhou corner. Just watch the traffic as you stagger out.

Slightly to the north is the **flower market**, gathered around the church of Ayía Iríni on Eólou. This has stalls through the week but really comes alive with the crowds on a Sunday morning. An additional feature of **Eólou** is its views. Walk it north to south, coming from Omónia, and your approach takes you towards the rock of the Acropolis, with the Erechtheion's slender columns and pediment peeking over the crag edge.

Bargain hunters aren't well served in the bazaar unless they stick to traditional Greek goods: pistachios, olives, herbs and the like. But **shoes** are an exception. Well made from sound leather, Greek shoes are surprisingly cheap by European standards. There's a bevy of shops between Panepistimíou and Akadhimías, just to the north of the neoclassical **National Library** and **University** buildings – themselves worth a look, since their garish decoration gives an alarming idea of what the Classical monuments must have looked like when their paintwork was intact.

Omónia itself has little to offer. A continuous turmoil of people and cars, it is Athens at its most western and big-city. There are escalators (the only public ones in Greece) down to the **metro**, and, at the top, every kind of junk food imaginable – the pride of returned Greek-Americans. The central fountain works only occasionally and the baby palms are remorseful replacements for their predecessors, cut down in the 1950s lest foreigners thought Greece 'too Asiatic'.

To the north, just below the National Archaeological Museum on Patissíon, a more interesting landmark is the **Politehnío**, a neoclassical building with gardens and an iron fence housing the university's school of engineering and science. It was here in 1973 that the students launched their protests against the fierce repressions of the colonels' junta, occupying the building and courtyards, and broadcasting calls for widespread resistance from a pirate radio transmitter. Large numbers of Greeks defied the military cordons to demonstrate support and to smuggle in food and medicines. The colonels' answer came on the night of November 16. Snipers were positioned in neighbouring houses and ordered to fire indiscriminately into the courtyards while tanks broke down the gates – with students still clinging on. Nobody knows how many of the unarmed students were killed – official and unofficial figures range from twenty to 300 – since their bodies were secretly buried in mass graves. Although the junta's leader, Papodopoulos, was able publicly to congratulate the officers involved, a new, more urgent sense of outrage was spreading; within a year of the massacre the dictatorship was toppled. Evidence of the incident can still be seen today, in the bullet-marked pillars and staircases.

The anniversary of the massacre is invariably commemorated by a march on the U.S. Embassy, outpost of the the colonels' greatest ally. These demonstrations are occasionally broken up by violence; in 1985 a student was shot dead by the police. The date is also, less aptly, commemorated in the title of Greece's most notorious active terrorist group, *Dhekaeftá Noémvri,* with several assassinations to their name and not a single arrest.

Exárhia, fifty or so square blocks squeezed between the National Archaeological Museum and Stréfi hill, is perhaps the city's liveliest and most enjoyable nighttime location, becoming home, over the last few years, to a concentration of *ouzerí*, nightclubs and genuine music tavernas. It has also, in the press at least, become synonymous with Athens' lost youth, the so-called anarchists who frighten the sedate and respectable by staving in car windscreens, splattering walls with black grafitti and setting off the occasional incendiary device. The junkies and sporadic police raid notwithstanding, the reality is not so extreme as Greeks – who like their city pretty savoury – would lead you to believe.

Síntagma, the National Gardens and the Stadium

All roads lead to Platía Sintágmatos – **Síntagma** square – so you'll find yourself there sooner or later. Geared to tourism, with the main EOT branch (in the National Bank), post office (extended hours), American Express, airline and travel offices grouped around, it has convenience but not much else to recommend it. The cafés, well patrolled by Greek males on the lookout for foreign affairs, are overpriced and dangerously exposed to lead-poisoning, but make an easy rendezvous spot.

Most of the square's buildings are modern and characterless, though earlier times prevail on the uphill (east) side where the **Voulí**, the Greek National Parliament, looks over proceedings. It was built as the royal palace for Greece's first monarch, the Bavarian King Otho, in the 1830s. In front goose-stepping *Evzónes* in tasselled caps, kilt, and woolly leggings – a prettified version of traditional mountain costume – change their guard at intervals, to the rhythm of the camera shutters.

The square's only other building to have survived post-war development is the vast **Hotel Grande Bretagne** – Athens' grandest – whose name recalls the (generally disastrous) role Britain has often taken upon itself to play in the affairs of Greece. In the course of one of the more nefarious episodes of British meddling it nearly became the tomb of Winston Churchill. He had arrived on Christmas Day 1944 to sort out the *Dhekemvrianá*, the 'events of December': a month of serious street-fighting between British forces and the Communist-led ELAS resistance movement, whom the British were trying to disarm. ELAS saboteurs had placed an enormous explosive charge in the drains, intending to blow up various Greek and Allied VIPs, but removed it when they realised they might get Churchill as well.

'Síntagma' means 'constitution' and derives from the fact that Greece's first was proclaimed by a (needless to say) reluctant King Otho from a palace balcony in 1843. The square is still the principal venue for mass **demonstrations**, most recently a rash of trade-union protests against the governing socialists. At election times the major political parties always stage their final campaign rallies here – a pretty impressive sight, with around 100,000 singing, flag-waving Greeks packed into the square.

At the back of the Voulí, the former palace gardens now known as the **National Gardens** form the most refreshing acres in the whole city: not so much a flower garden, more a luxuriant tangle of trees, shrubs and creepers, whose shade, duck ponds, and sparkling irrigation channels provide palpable relief from the heat and smog of summer. The grounds include a scraggy mini-zoo, a botanical museum, a summer open-air cinema and two of the oldest and nicest cafés in the city. The *Kafenío–Ouzerí Aigli*, the most famous of these, stands (with the summer open-air cinema) just to the right of the **Zappíon**. This grand neoclassical exhibition hall was for a period the Greek Radio headquarters but is now used mainly for press and business conferences. The other café, the *Oasis*, is a cool counterpart to the *Aigli*'s spot in the sun, sited by the east (uphill) exit of the park on to Iródhou Attikoú. There are few better places in the city than the gardens to read or wait for an evening ferry or plane. They are locked at sunset.

Iródhou Attikoú also fronts the **Presidential Palace**, the royal residence until Constantine's exit from the scene in 1967, where more *evzónes* stand sentry duty. The current, embarrassingly pompous incumbent, Mr. Sartzetakis ('Don't call me Mr. Sartzetakis. I'm the President,' he once rebuffed onlookers), is the first president to take up residence here since Greece became a republic in 1974. The surrounding streets, with a full complement of foreign embassies and hardly a store or taverna, are considered very posh. The main conservative party, *Néa Dhimokratía*, has its headquarters in Odhós Rigílis nearby, as does the army's Officers' Club, scene of much anti-democratic intriguing in the past.

At the bottom of Iródhou Attikoú is the preternaturally white **Olympic Stadium**, rebuilt (on ancient foundations) for the first Olympiad of modern times in 1896, and still used by local athletes. It slots tightly between the pine-covered spurs of Ardhittós hill, to the south of which are the only two central neighbourhoods outside Pláka to have retained something of their traditional flavour – **Méts** and **Pangráti**.

Méts and Pangráti

Particularly in **Méts**, a steep hillside quarter on the southwest side of the stadium, there are almost complete streets of pre-World War II houses with tiled roofs, shuttered windows, and courtyards with spiral metal stairs and potted plants. They're a sad reminder of how beautiful this out-of-control city must have been, even recently. More specific attractions are the concentration of tavernas and bars (see p.97) in Márkou Moussoúrou and Arhimídhous, and the **Próto Nekrotafío**, the 'First Cemetery,' at the top end of Anapáfseos (Eternal Rest) street. The cemetery shelters just about anybody who was anybody in twentieth-century Greek public life; the humbler tombs of singers, artists and writers are interspersed with ornate mausolea of soldiers, statesmen and 'good' families, whose descendants come to picnic, stroll and tend the graves. One of 'the unregarded wonders of Athenian life,' Peter Levi called it; 'the neoclassical marbles run riot, they reflower as rococo, they burst into sunblasts of baroque'.

Pangráti is the unremarkable but pleasant quarter to the north and east of the Stadium. Platía Plastíra, Platía Varnáva and Platía Pangratíou are the focal points, the first with a vast old-fashioned *kafenío* where you can sit for hours on a leafy terrace for the price of a coffee. Pangratioú is the rallying place for the neighbourhood's youthful posers; Varnáva has several tavernas, as does nearby Odhós Arhimídhous, which is taken over every Friday by an impressive produce market. Another Pangráti eating area is down towards Leofóros Konstantínou, in the rather claustrophobic streets opposite the memorial to Harry Truman, recently restored to his pedestal after being belatedly blown up by leftists in reprisal for the notorious Doctrine promulgated in 1947 to justify U.S. intervention in the Greek civil war. The poet Seféris lived not far away in Odhós Ágras, an attractive stair-street flanking the northeast wall of the Olympic stadium. For several years this street also boasted one of the city's more original graffiti: 'The *KNITES* (members of the Communist Party youth movement) are free as birds. Give them a little hash so they can fly even higher'.

Kolonáki, Likavitós, and the North

Kolonáki is the city's most chic central address and shopping area. Although no great shakes architecturally, it enjoys a superb site on the south-facing slopes of Likavitós (Lycabettus), looking out over the Acropolis and National Gardens. From its summit, on a clear day (preferably after rain) you can make out the mountains of the Peloponnese.

The lower limits of Kolonáki are defined by Akadhimías and Vassilíssis Sofías, where in grand neoclassical palaces France, Italy and Britain have their embassies. The middle levels are for shopping, and the highest purely residential. The heart of the district is **Kolonáki square**, officially called Platía Filikís Eterías. Its location should be committed to memory, for beneath the central garden, where kids, pensioners, nannies, and pigeons compete for limited bench space, glistens the city's almost unique and certainly cleanest public toilet. Other possible lures include the excellent, quick-serving *Estiatorio Kioupi* in a basement near the Skoufá corner; the kiosks with their stocks of foreign papers and magazines; and the British Council library on the downhill side, where you can read the paper for free. The numerous cafés here are posy and expensive – they're the principal display ground for Kolonáki's extremely well-heeled natives.

Kolonáki's streets also contain an amazing density of small, classy **shops**, with the accent firmly on **fashion and design**. In a half-hour walk around the neighbourhood you can view the whole gamut of consumer style. Patriárhou Ioakim, to the east of the square, and Skoufá with its cross-streets to the northwest, comprise the most promising area, along with the peripheral Voukourestíou-Valaorítou-Amerikís block just below Akadhimías.

For more random strolling, the highest tiers of Kolonáki are pleasant, with the vertical streets ending in long flights of steps, planted with oleander, jasmine, and other flowering shrubs. The one **café** spot up here is at Platía Dhexamenís, a small and attractive square close to the Likavitós loop road, where in summertime tables are set under the trees around the **Dhexamení**, a covered reservoir begun by the Emperor Hadrian.

Not far away, at the corner of Dhorás Dhistría and Ploutárhou, a **funicular** begins its ascent to the summit of **Likavitós** (8am–10pm, about every 20 min. in summer). For the more energetic, the principal path up the hill begins here, too, rambling up through the woods. Once on top, the chapel of Áyios Yióryios provides the main focus – a spectacular place to celebrate the *Anástasi* or Resurrection if you're around at Easter. There's a **café** on the adjacent terrace, with eats, and another, less plastic, halfway down. Both have morning and sunset views spectacular enough to excuse the inflated prices and unenthusiastic service.

Various other paths lead up and around the hill, and a **road** runs round the southwest corner, overlooking another quarter of narrow lanes and steep stairs in the vicinity of Odhós Dhoxapatrí and Sína, where the French Institute puts forth the gallic message. The road ends at the open-air **Likavitós Theatre**, used primarily as a music venue during the Athens Summer Festival (see p.101). If you come down by the southeast slopes, you emerge in the very lovely but privileged little enclave that the British and American Archaeological Schools have managed to retain for themselves on Odhós Souidhías. Here too is the **Yennádhion Library**, with large collections of books on Greece and an unpublicised drawer full of Edward Lear's watercolour sketches; good-quality and reasonably-priced reproductions are on sale.

Beyond Likavitós, points of interest become more and more diffuse. Just a short distance north, the **Panathenaïkós** football ground stands on Leofóros Alexándhras, which marks the outer limits of downtown Athens.

Across the street, the new Hall of Justice occupies the site of the notorious Averoff prison, from where many political prisoners were marched off to execution at Goudhí in the civil war years. The decrepit housing estate alongside, about the only one of its kind in the city, still bears the scars of a 1944 battle when the partisans tried to get their hands on some British-held Nazi collaborators. Behind it the land rises again to the quarry-hacked ridge of Tourkovoúni and Damária, another section of the city's broken spine which pops up on and off all the way from Filopáppou to Kifissiá.

North into the Suburbs: Kifissiá

Kifissiá, Athens' most desirable suburb, edges up the leafy slopes of Mount Pendéli, about 8km north of the city centre. A surprising 300m above sea level and a good five degrees cooler than central Athens, it drew the pre-war bourgeoisie as a suitable site for summer residence. Their villas, neoclassical, Swiss, Alsatian, and blatant fantasy, still hold their own amid the newer concrete models. Indeed, despite the encroachments of speculative apartment blocks and trendy boutiques, the suburb's village character is still noticeable. If you need a more purposeful focus than merely wandering among trees and gardens, you could find it in the collections of the **Goulandhrís Natural History Museum** (see p92) on Ódhos Levídhou.

Centre of the old 'village' is the crossroads still called Plátanos, though the mighty plane tree that gave it its name was long since swept away by the traffic flow. It's just at the uphill end of the gardens opposite the **Kifissiá metro** station – last stop on the line from Pireás and Athens and much the easiest approach. The hub is the two or three streets around Plátanos, with *Varsos*, the old-fashioned patisserie specialising in home-made yoghurts, jams, and sticky cakes, a pole of attraction for the whole quarter. The young (and rich) hangout is the *Edelweiss* café, ten minutes' walk away in Kefalaríou.

Completely untouristed, Kifissiá offers numerous good eating possibilities. The big problem is transport: it's almost impossible to find your way about its dark streets at night without a car. A good lunchtime stop which will serve most people's purposes is the *Estiatorio O Platanos* by the above-mentioned crossroads. If however you do have your own vehicle, Káto Kifissiá, downhill from the metro station, is the best area to head for.

Dhafní (Daphne) and Kessarianí

Athens pushes its suburbs higher and wider with each year and the **monasteries of Dhafní and Kessarianí**, once well outside the city limits, are now approached through more or less continuous building. However, each retains a definite countryside setting and makes for a good escape from the central areas.

They are easily reached by taxi or by local **city transport**. For Dhafní (9km west of the centre) take more or less any bus prefixed #8 (#818, #853, #862 are most frequent) from Platía Elefthérias (*D1*); the monastery is signposted on the right of the road, about twenty minutes' ride. For Kessarianí, take blue bus #224 from Akadhimías (*D3/4*) to the last stop, from where the church is a thirty- to forty-minute climb up the lower slopes of Mt. Imittós.

Classical enthusiasts may want to continue from Dhafní to the site of **Eleusis** (see p.119), a further twenty-minute ride on the same bus routes. Committed (and preferably not too discriminating) drinkers could stay on at Dhafní for the **wine festival** (see p.94), held every evening in the summer.

Dhafní

Dhafní Monastery is one of the great buildings of Byzantine architecture. Its design – the classic Greek-cross-octagon – is a refinement of a plan first used at Óssios Loukás, on the road to Delphi. Its mosaics are considered among the great masterpieces of the Middle Ages.

The Byzantine monastery replaced a fortified fifth-century church, which in turn had been built from the ruins of a sanctuary of Apollo; the name is derived from the *daphnai* (laurels) sacred to the god. Both the church and the fortifications which enclose it incorporate blocks from the ancient sanctuary; a porch, present until two centuries ago, featured complete Classical columns, but was among the targets of Lord Elgin's looting. The fortifications (and remains of a Gothic cloister) also show evidence of later building under the Cistercians, who replaced Dhafní's Orthodox monks after the Frankish conquest of Athens in 1204. The Byzantines, ironically, had occupied their building for little over a century. When the monastery was established in 1070 the Greek church was undergoing an intellectual revival but the state was in terminal collapse. The following year the Normans took Bari, the last Byzantine possession in Southern Italy, and the Seljuk Turks defeated the Byzantine army in Armenia – a prelude to the loss of Asia Minor and, before long, Greece itself.

Inside the church, the **mosaic cycle** is remarkable for its completeness, giving a full display of Byzantine iconography as well as artistic power. There are scenes from the life of Christ and the Virgin, saints (a predominance of Eastern figures from Syria and elsewhere in the Levant), archangels and prophets. But the great triumph is the *Christ Pantokrator* (Christ in Majesty) on the dome. Lit by the sixteen windows of the drum, and set against a background of gold, this stern image directs a tremendous and piercing gaze, his finger poised on the Book of Judgment. It is a perfect encapsulation of the strict orthodoxy of Byzantine belief, rendered poignant by the troubled circumstances in which it was created.

The monastery today is unoccupied; the Cistercians were banished by the Turks, and Orthodox monks, allowed to return in the sixteenth century, were expelled in turn for harbouring rebels during the War of Independence. After a long period of closure, following severe damage during the 1981 earthquake, the complex, much-repaired, is again open to regular **visits**: Mon.– Sat. 8.45am–3pm, Sun. 9.30am–2.30pm.

Kessariani

What it loses in an architectural comparison with Dhafní, **Kessariani monastery** makes up for in its location. Just 5km from the middle of the city, it is high enough up the slopes of Imittós to escape the *néfos* and the noise, but not, sadly, the attentions of the city's arsonists, who burnt a sizeable patch of the surrounding pine woods in summer 1988. The sources of the river Ilissos provide for extensive gardens hereabouts, as they have since ancient times (Ovid mentions them), and today's Athenians still come to collect water from the local fountains.

The monastery buildings date, like Dhafní, from the eleventh century, though the frescoes in the chapel are much later – executed during the sixteenth and seventeenth centuries. In contrast to Dhafní's clerics, Kessarianí's abbot agreed to submit to Roman authority when the Franks took Athens, so the monastery remained in continuous Greek (if not quite Orthodox) occupation through the Middle Ages. It today maintains a small group of monks, who allow **visits** to the monastery proper Monday to Saturday 9am to 3pm, Sunday 10am to 3pm. Outside these hours you can while the time away in the well-maintained grounds, full of picnickers until sunset in summertime.

On the **way up to the monastery**, which is fairly obvious from the bus terminal, don't overlook the neighbourhood of Kessarianí. Lively and working-class, it has a casual, ramshackle aspect about its streets, which were used as a 1920s location for the recent Greek movie *Rembetiko*. There are a handful of good tavernas around the square off to the left, four stops before the end of the bus stop.

Ancient Athens

Perhaps the most startling aspect of ancient, Classical Athens is how suddenly it emerged to the power and glory for which we remember it – and how short its heyday proved to be.

In the middle of the **fifth century B.C.**, Athens was little more than a country town in its street layout and buildings. These comprised a scattered jumble of single-storey houses or wattled huts, intersected by narrow lanes. Sanitary conditions were notoriously lax: human waste and rubbish were dumped outside the town with an almost suicidal disregard for plague and disease. And on the rock of the Acropolis, a site reserved for the city's most sacred monuments, stood blackened ruins – temples and sanctuaries burnt to the ground during the Persian invasion of 480 B.C.

There was little to suggest to a traveller that the city had entered a unique phase of its history in terms of power, prestige, and creativity. Following the victories over the Persians at Marathon (470 B.C.) and Salamis (460 B.C.), Athens stood unchallenged for a generation. It grew rich on the export of olive oil and of silver from the mines of Attica, but above all from the control of the Delian League – an alliance of Greek city-states formed as insurance against Persian resurgence. The Athenians removed the League's treasury from the island of Delos to their own acropolis, ostensibly on the grounds of safety, and with its revenues their leader Pericles was able to create the so-called **Golden Age** of the city. Great endowments were made for monumental construction; arts in all spheres were promoted; and, most important, a form of **democracy** emerged.

This had its beginnings in the sixth century B.C. reforms of Solon, under which the political rights of the old landowning class had been claimed by farmer- and craftsmen-soldiers. With the emergence of **Pericles** the process of democratisation was radically overhauled, aided in large part by the Delian League's wealth – which enabled office-holders to be paid, so making it possible for the poor to play a part in government. Pericles's constitution ensured that all policies of the state were to be decided by a general assembly of Athenian male citizens (6000 was a quorum). The assembly, which met outside at either the **Agora** or the **Pnyx**, elected a council of 500 members to carry out the everyday administration of the city and a board of ten *strategoi* or generals to guide it. Pericles, one of the best known and most influential of the *strategoi*, was as vulnerable as any other to the electoral process – if sufficient numbers cast their lot (*ostra*) against him his citizenship would be forfeited (he would be literally ostracised).

In line with this system of democratic participation, a new and exalted notion of the Athenian citizen emerged. This was a man who could shoulder political responsibilty, take public office, and play a part in the **cultural and religious events** of the time. The latter assumed ever-increasing importance. The city's Panathenaic festival, honouring its protectress deity Athena, was upgraded along the lines of the Olympic Games to include drama, music, and athletic contests.

Athenians rose easily to the challenge. The next five decades were to witness the great dramatic works of Aeschylus, Sophocles, and Euripides, and the comedies of Aristophanes. Foreigners such as Herodotus, the inventor of history, and Anaxagoras, the philosopher, were attracted to live in the

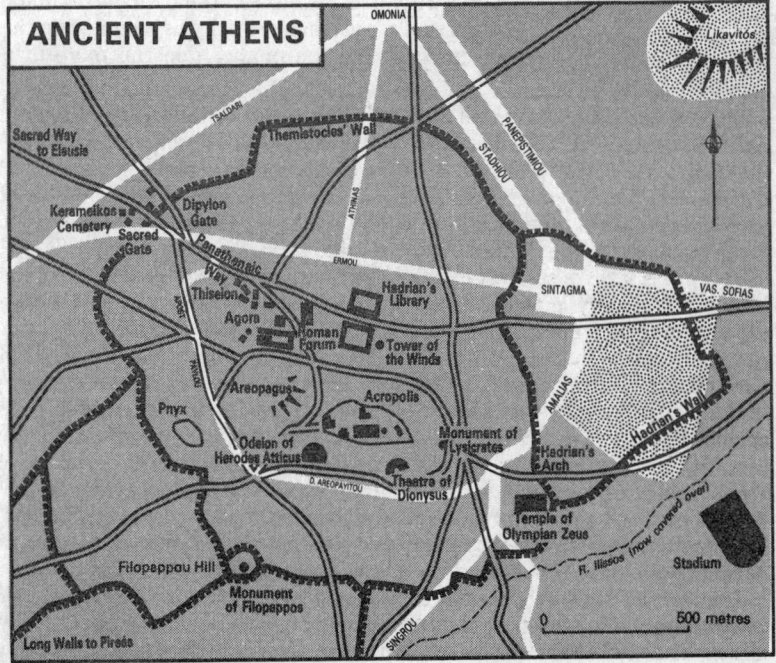

city. And they, in turn, were surpassed by native Athenians. Thucydides wrote *The Peloponnesian War*, a pioneering work of history with its documentation and analysis; Socrates posed the problems of philosophy that were to exercise his follower Plato and to shape the discipline to the present day.

But it was the great civic **building programme** that became the most visible and powerful symbol of the age. Under the patronage of Pericles and with vast public funds made available from the Delian treasury, the architects Ictinus, Mnesicles and Callicrates, and the sculptor Pheidias, transformed the city. Their buildings, justified in part as a comprehensive job-creation scheme, included the Parthenon and Erechtheion on the Acropolis; the Thiseion (or Hephaisteion) and several stoas (arcades) in the Agora; a new Odeion (theatre) on the south slope of the Acropolis hill; and, outside the city, the temples at Sounion and Rhamnous.

Athenian culture flourished under democracy, but the system was not without its contradictions and failures. Only one in seven inhabitants of the city were actual citizens; the political status and civil rights that they enjoyed were denied to the many thousands of women, *metics* (foreigners) and slaves. While the lives of men became increasingly public and sociable with meetings at the Agora or Pynx and trips to the gymnasiums and theatres, **women** remained secluded in small and insanitary homes. Their subordination was reinforced by a decree (451 B.C.) which restricted their property rights, placing them under the control of fathers, husbands, or guardians. Only forty women were appointed priestesses – one of the few positions of female power – at any one time. The vast majority, like the slaves, would labour in home workshops or manage their husband's household; Aeschylus summed up the prevailing attitude when he declared that the mother does no more than foster the father's seed.

Athenian democracy and **Athenian imperialism** were inextricably linked and the latter could be as brutal and exploitative as any imperial force before or since. Its atrocities included the wholescale massacre of the male population of Melos – although acts of mercy against rebellious allies were also documented – and the building programme of Pericles itself relied on easy pickings from weaker neighbours and allies. In the *polis* of Athens the achievements of democracy could be overshadowed, too, with attacks on the very talents it had nurtured and celebrated. Aristophanes was impeached; Pheidias and Thucydides were exiled; Socrates was tried and executed.

But, historically, the fatal mistake of the Athenian democracy was allowing itself to be drawn into the **Peloponnesian war** against Sparta, its most persistent rival, in 431 B.C. Pericles, having roused the assembly to a pitch of patriotic fervor, died of the plague two years after war began, leaving Athens to a series of far less capable leaders. In 415 B.C. a disastrous campaign in Sicily destroyed a third of the navy; in 405 B.C. defeat was finally accepted after the rest of the fleet was destroyed by Sparta in the Dardanelles; in a demoralised state Athens succumbed to a brief period of oligarchy.

Through succeeding decades Athens was overshadowed by Thebes, though it recovered sufficiently to enter a new phase of democracy, the **age of Plato**. However, in 338 B.C., nearly one and a half centuries after the original defeat of the Persians, Athens was again called to defend the Greek city-states, this time against the incursions of **Philip of Macedon**. Demosthenes, said to be as powerful an orator as Pericles, spurred the Athenians to fight, in alliance with the Thebans, at Chaironeia. There they were routed, in large part by the cavalry commanded by Philip's son, Alexander, and Athens fell under the control of the Macedonian empire. As such it was favoured, particularly under **Alexander the Great**, a former pupil of the Athenian Aristotle, who respected both the city and its democratic institutions.

Following Alexander's death came a more uncertain era, with periods of independence and Macedonian rule, until 146 B.C. when the **Romans** swept through southern Greece, making it into an imperial province (see p.82).

The Acropolis

Open Mon.–Sat. 7.30am–6pm, Sun. 8am–5pm (Acropolis Museum same hours but closed Tues. am); entrance 500dr, students 250dr.

For all its archetypal familiarity, the **rock of the Acropolis**, with the ruins of the Parthenon rising above it, is a powerfully imposing sight. Pericles had intended the temple to be a spectacular landmark, a 'School for Hellas' and symbol of the city's imperial confidence. As such it was famous throughout the ancient world. Even Pericles, however, could not have anticipated that in 2000 years the ruin of his temple would achieve even greater fame, symbolising no less than the emergence of Western civilisation itself; less likely still that he would have envisaged 3 million annual tourists. As Donald Horne points out in *The Great Museum*, it would be hard to imagine the ruins having such a wide appeal if they had retained more of their former glory; if the Parthenon 'still had a roof, and no longer appealed to the modern stereotype for outline emerging from rough stone,' or if 'we repainted it in its original red, blue and gold and if we reinstalled the huge, gaudy cult-figure of Athena festooned in bracelets, rings and necklaces'.

Yet it's hard not to feel a sense of wonderment as you catch glimpses of the ancient ruins from the modern streets below. The best of these street level **views** are along Eólou, where the Parthenon forms the focal point of the horizon. Up above, calmer and quieter vantage points include the nearby hills of Likavitós, Ardhittós, and Filopáppou, where you can look on undisturbed from among the pineglades; a walk to one of these is highly recommended. For unless you visit well out of season, only at opening or closing hours (and to a certain extent around lunchtime) are you able to escape the crowds to get a real sense of the complex.

The main **approach** to the ruins is the path that extends above Odhós Dhioskoúron, where it joins Theorías at the northwest corner of Pláka. Two alternatives – though both perhaps better as ways down from the rock – are to make your way through the ancient Agora (entrance on Adhrianoú, *E2*; see p.80) or, from the south side of the slope, around the footpath beside the Odeion of Herodes Atticus, (*F2*).

Some History

The Acropolis's natural setting, a craggy mass of limestone plateau, watered by springs and rising an abrupt 100 metres out of the plain of Attica, has made it a focus and nucleus during every historical (and prehistorical) phase of the city's development.

The site was one of the earliest settlements in Greece, drawing a **Neolithic** community to its slopes around 5000 B.C. In **Mycenaean** times it was fortified with Cyclopean walls (parts of which can still be seen), enclosing a royal palace and temples where the cult of Athena was introduced. City and goddess were integrated by the **Dorians** and, with the union of Attic towns and villages in the ninth century B.C., the Acropolis became the heart of the first Greek city state, sheltering its principal public buildings. So it was to remain, save for an interval under the **Peisistratid tyrants** of the seventh and sixth centuries B.C., who reestablished a fortified residence on the rock. But when the last tyrant was overthrown in 510 B.C. the Delphic Oracle ordered that the Acropolis should remain forever the **province of the gods**, unoccupied by humans.

It was in this context that the monuments visible today were built. More or less all of the substantial remains date from the **fifth century B.C.** or later. There are outlines of earlier temples and sanctuaries but these are hardly impressive, for when the Persians sacked Athens in 480 B.C. they were burnt to the ground. For some decades, until Pericles promoted his grand plan, the temples were left in their ruined state as a reminder of the Persian action. But with that threat removed, in the wake of Athenian military supremacy and a peace treaty with the Persians in 449 B.C., the walls were rebuilt and architects set to draw up plans for a reconstruction worthy of the city's cultural and political position.

Pericles' rebuilding plan was both magnificent and enormously expensive but it won the backing of the democracy, for many of whose citizens it must have created both wealth and work paid for from the unfortunate Delian League's coffers. The work was under the general direction of the architect and sculptor **Pheidias** and it was completed in an incredibly short time. The Parthenon took only ten years to finish: 'every architect', wrote Plutarch, 'striving to surpass the magnificence of the design with the elegance of the execution'.

Their monuments survived unaltered – save for some modest Roman embellishments – for close to a thousand years until, in the reign of the Emperor Justinian, the temples were converted to **Christian** worship. In subsequent years the uses became secular, too, and embellishments increased, gradually obscuring the Classical designs. Fifteenth-century Italian princes held court in the *Propylaia*, the entrance hall to the complex, and the same quarters were later used by the **Turks** as their commander's headquarters and as a powder magazine. The Parthenon underwent similar changes from Greek to Roman temple, from Byzantine church to Frankish cathedral, before several centuries of use as a Turkish mosque. The Erechtheion, with its graceful female figures, saw service as a harem. A Venetian diplomat, Hugo Favoli, described the Acropolis in 1563 as 'looming beneath a swarm of glittering golden crescents', with a minaret rising from the Parthenon. For all their changes in use, however, the buildings would have resembled – very much more than today's bare ruins – the bustling and ornate ancient Acropolis, covered in sculpture and painted in bright colours.

Sadly, such images remain only in the prints and sketches of that period. Having survived more or less intact for well over two thousand years, the Acropolis buildings finally fell victim to the demands of war, blown up during the successive attempts by the Venetians to oust the Turks. In 1684 the Turks demolished the temple of Athena Nike to gain a brief tactical advantage. Three years later the Venetians, laying siege to the garrison, ignited a Turkish gunpowder magazine in the Parthenon, and in the process blasted off its roof and set a **fire** that raged within its precincts for two days and nights. The apricot-coloured glow of the Parthenon marbles so admired by the neoclassicists of the eighteenth century was one of the more aesthetic results.

Arguably surpassing this destruction, at least in the minds of today's Athenians, was **Lord Elgin**'s 'removal' of the Parthenon's frieze in 1801. As British Ambassador to the Porte he obtained permission from the Turks to erect scaffolding, excavate, and remove stones with inscriptions. He interpreted this concession as a licence to make off with almost all of the bas-reliefs of the Parthenon's frieze, most of its pedimental structures and a caryatid from the Erechtheion – which he later sold to the British Museum. There were perhaps justifications for Elgin's action at the time – the Turks' tendency to use Parthenon stones in their lime kilns, and possible further ravages of war – though it was controversial even then and opposed notably by Byron. Today, however, the British Museum's continued retention of the 'Elgin Marbles' (a phrase that Greek guides on the Acropolis, who portray Elgin unequivocally as a vandal, do not use) rests on legal rather than moral claims. Hopefully the museum will soon find a graceful pretext to back down; the 100th anniversary of the modern Olympics, likely to be held in Athens in 1996, could provide the perfect opportunity.

As for the **buildings** themselves, their fate since the Greeks regained the Acropolis after the War of Independence has not been entirely happy. Almost immediately after the war Greek archaeologists began clearing the Turkish village that had developed around the Parthenon-mosque; a Greek regent lamented in vain that they 'would destroy all the picturesque additions of the middle ages in their zeal to lay bare the ancient monuments'.

Much of this early work was indeed destructive. The nineteenth-century iron clamps and supports that were used to reinforce the marble structures have since rusted and warped, causing the stones to crack. Meanwhile, earthquakes have dislodged the foundations; generations of visitors have slowly worn down the Parthenon's surfaces; and, more recently, acid rain, caused by car and industrial pollution in the city, has been turning the marble to dust. Over the last decade, since a 1975 report predicted the collapse of the Parthenon, visitors have been barred from its actual precinct, and a major, long-term restoration scheme has been in progress. Inevitably this has its frustrations for visitors, with many of the buildings scaffolded and the whole Acropolis at times taking on the appearance of a building site. However, attempts have been made to keep this as discreet as possible – a giant crane was designed that could be folded and concealed behind the temple columns – and it is certainly less depressing than the previous decay.

● THE SITE

Today, as throughout its history, the Acropolis offers but one entrance – from a terrace above the Agora. Here in Classical times the Panathenaic Way extended along a steep ramp to the massive Periclean *propylaia*; the modern path makes a more gradual, zigzagging ascent through an arched Roman entrance, the Beule Gate, added in the third century A.D.

The Propylaia and Athena Nike temple

The Acropolis's monumental entrance, or **Propylaia**, was constructed by Mnesicles upon completion of the Parthenon, in 437 B.C., and its axis and proportions aligned to balance the temple. It was built from the same Pentelic marble (from Mt. Pendéli, northeast of the city), and in grandeur and architectural achievement was no mean rival to the Parthenon temple. In order to offset the difficulties of a sloping site, Mnesicles combined for the first time standard Doric columns with the taller and more delicate Ionic order. The ancient Athenians, awed by the fact that such wealth and craftsmanship should be used for a purely secular building, ranked this as their most prestigious monument.

The halls had a variety of uses, even in Classical times. To the left of the central hall (which before Venetian bombardment supported a great coffered roof, painted blue and gilded with stars), the *Pinakotheke* exhibited paintings of Homeric subjects by Polygnotus. Executed in the mid-fifth century B.C., these were described 600 years later by Pausanias in his Roman-era *Guide to Greece*. There was to have been a similar wing-room to the right, but Mnesicles's design trespassed on ground sacred to the Goddess of Victory and the premises had to be adapted as a waiting room for her shrine.

This, the simple and elegant **Temple of Athena Nike**, was begun late in the rebuilding scheme (probably due to conflict over the extent of the Propylaia's south wing) and stands on a precipitous platform overlooking Pireás and the Saronic Gulf. Pausanias recounts that it was from this bastion that King Aegeus, watching for the return from Crete of his son Theseus, threw himself to his death; Theseus, having slain the Minotaur, had forgotten his promise to change his black sails for white. The temple's frieze, with more attention to realism than triumph, depicts the Athenians' victory over the Persians at Plateia. Amazingly the whole building was reconstructed, from its original blocks, in the nineteenth century; the Turks had demolished the building two hundred years previously, using it as material for a gun emplacement. Recovered in this same feat of jigsaw-puzzle archaeology were the reliefs from its parapet – among them *Victory Adjusting Her Sandal*, the most beautiful exhibit in the Acropolis Museum.

In front of this small temple stood a **Sanctuary of Brauronian Artemis**. Its precinct was home to a colossal bronze representation of the Wooden Horse of Troy, but the sanctuary's function remains obscure, and only scant remains of its foundations can be seen. More noticeable is a nearby stretch of **Mycenaean wall** (running parallel to the Propylaia) which was incorporated into the Classical design.

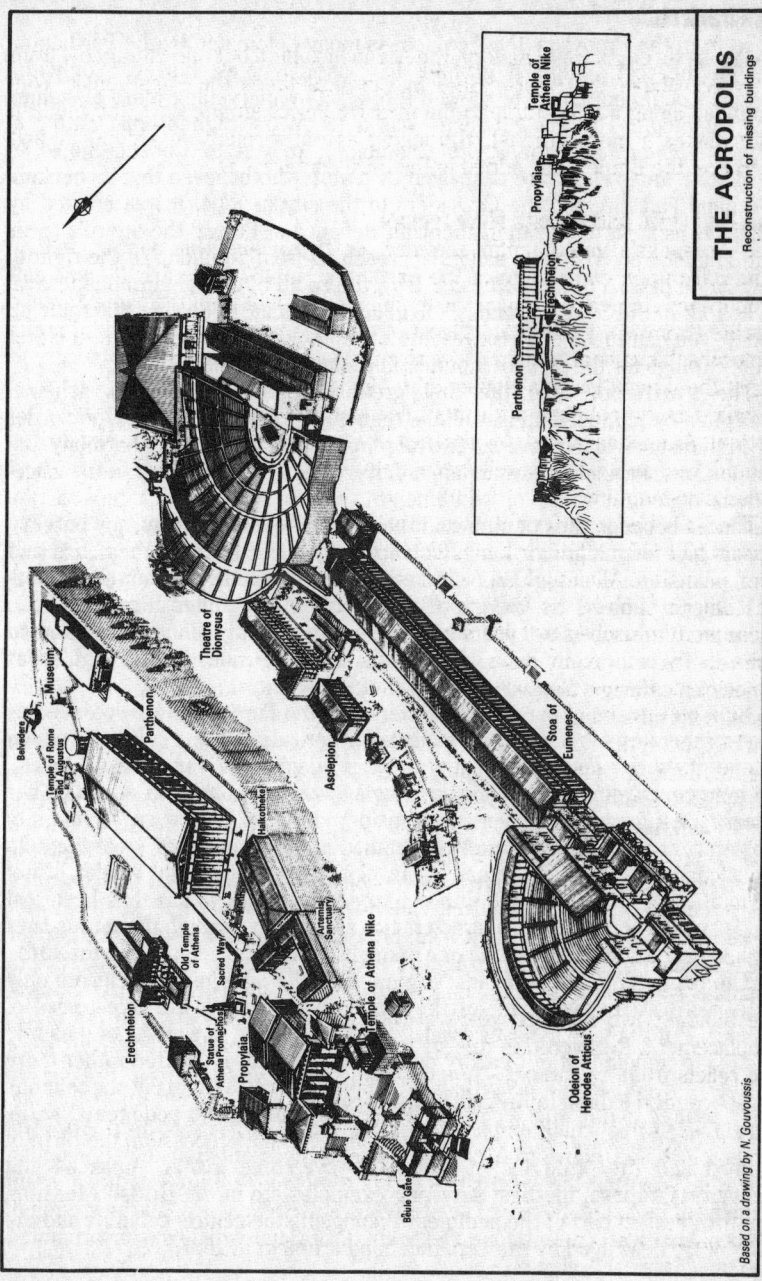

THE ACROPOLIS
Reconstruction of missing buildings

Temple of Athena Nike

Propylaia

Parthenon

Erechtheion

Museum

Belvedere

Temple of Rome and Augustus

Parthenon

Theatre of Dionysus

Asclepion

Stoa of Eumenes

Pinakotheke

Artemis Sanctuary

Old Temple of Athena

Statue of Athena Promachos

Sacred Way

Propylaia

Temple of Athena Nike

Odeion of Herodes Atticus

Blue cave

Based on a drawing by N. Gouvoussis

The Parthenon

Seen from the Propylaia, the Acropolis is today dominated by the Parthenon, set on the rock's highest ground. In Classical times, however, only the temple's pediment could be viewed through the intervening mass of statues and buildings. The ancient focus was a ten-metre high bronze *Statue of Athena Promachos* (Athena the Champion), moved to Constantinople in Byzantine times and there destroyed by a mob who believed that its beckoning hand had directed the Crusaders to the city in 1204. It was created by Pheidias as a symbol of the Athenians' defiance of Persia; the figure's spear and helmet were visible to sailors approaching from Sounion. To the right of the statue passed the *Panathenaic Way*, the route of the quadrennial festival in honour of the city's patroness, the goddess Athena. Following this route up today, you can make out grooves cut for footholds in the rock and, to either side, cuttings for the rows of innumerable statues and offerings.

The **Parthenon** was the first great building in Pericles's scheme. Designed by Ictinus, it utilises all the refinements available to the Doric order of architecture to achieve an extraordinary and unequalled harmony. Its proportions, for instance, maintain a universal 9:4 ratio, not only in the calculations of length:width, or width:height, but in such relationships as the distances between the columns and their diametre. Additionally, any possible appearance of malproportion is corrected by meticulous mathematics and craftsmanship. All straight-appearing lines are in fact slightly curved, an optical illusion known as *entasis* (literally 'strain' or 'intensification'). The columns (themselves swelled slightly to avoid seeming concave) are slanted inwards by 6cm, while each of the steps along the sides of the temple was made to incline just 12cm over a length of 70 metres.

Built on the site of earlier archaic temples, the Parthenon was intended as a new sanctuary for Athena and a house for her cult image, a colossal wooden statue of *Athena Polias* (Athena of the City) decked in ivory and gold plate, with precious gems as eyes and sporting an ivory gorgon death's-head on her breast. Designed by Pheidias and considered one of the Seven Wonders of the Ancient World, the statue was installed in the semi-darkness of the *cella* (cult chamber) where it remained an object of prestige and wealth, if not veneration, until at least the fifth century A.D. The sculpture has been lost since ancient times but its characteristics are known through numerous later copies (including a fine Roman one in the National Archaeological Museum).

The name 'Parthenon' means 'virgins' chamber' and initially referred only to a room at the west end of the temple occupied by the priestesses of Athena. But the temple never rivalled the Erechtheion in sanctity and its role tended to remain that of treasury and artistic showcase, devoted rather more to the new god of the *polis* than to Athena herself. Originally its columns were painted and it was decorated by the finest frieze and pedimental sculpture of the Classsical age, depicting the Panathenaic procession, the birth of Athena and the struggles of Greeks to overcome giants, Amazons and centaurs. Of these, the best surviving examples are in the British Museum, but the greatest part of the pediments, alongside the central columns and the *cella*, were destroyed by the Venetian bombardment in 1687.

The Erechtheion

To the north of the Parthenon, beyond the foundations of the Old Temple of Athena, stands the **Erechtheion**, the last of the great works of Pericles to be completed. It was built over ancient sanctuaries which in turn were predated by a Mycenaean palace. Here, in symbolic reconciliation, were worshipped both Athena and the city's old patron of Poseidon-Erechtheus; the site, according to myth, was that on which they had contested possession of the Acropolis. The myth (which probably recalls the integration of the Mycenaeans with earlier pre-Hellenic settlers) tells how an olive tree sprung from the ground at the touch of Athena's spear, while Poseidon summoned forth a seawater spring. The Olympian gods voted Athena the victor.

Pausanias wrote of seeing both olive tree and seawater in the temple, adding that 'the extraordinary thing about this well is that when the wind blows south a sound of waves comes from it'. Today, as with all the buildings on the Acropolis, entrance is no longer permitted, and large expanses of it are marred by scaffolding. Its elegant Ionic porticoes, though, are all worth close attention, particularly the north one with its fine decorated doorway and frieze of blue Eleusinian marble. On the south side, in the **Porch of the Caryatids**, the Ionic line is transformed into the tunics of six tall maidens holding the entabulature on their heads. The statues were modelled on the widows of Carya, a city which was punished for its alliance with the Persians by the slaughter of its menfolk and the enslavement of the women. There is little suggestion however of grieving or humbled captives in the serene poses of the Caryatid women. The ones in situ are now, sadly, replacements; two of the originals are in the Acropolis Museum, a third was looted by Elgin. The stunted olive tree growing in the precinct was planted by an American archeologist in 1917.

The Acropolis Museum

Placed discreetly on a level below that of the main monuments, the museum contains all of the portable objects removed from the Acropolis since 1834 (with the exception of a few bronzes in the National Archaeological Museum). Over the last decade, as increasing amounts of stone and sculptures have been removed from the ravages of environmental pollution, the collection has grown considerably.

In the first rooms to the left of the vestibule are fragments of pedimental sculptures from the **old Temple of Athena** (7th-6th c. B.C.) which give a good impression of the vivid colours that were used in temple decoration. Farther on there is the **Moschophoros**, a painted marble statue of a young man carrying a sacrificial calf, dated 570 B.C. and one of the earliest examples of Greek art in marble. Room 4 displays one of the chief treasures of the building, a unique collection of **Korai**, or maidens, dedicated as votive offerings to Athena at some point in the sixth century B.C. Between them they represent a shift in art and fashion, from the simply contoured Doric clothing to the more elegant and voluminous Ionic designs. The figures' smiles also change subtly, becoming increasingly loose and natural.

The only pieces of the **Parthenon frieze** left in Greece are in Room 7. Having been sundered from the temple by the Venetian explosion, and subsequently buried, they escaped the clutches of Lord Elgin. They portray scenes of Athenian citizens in the Panathenaic procession; the fact that mortals featured so prominently in the decoration of the temple indicates the immense collective self-pride of the Athenians at the height of their Golden Age. The room adjoining it contains the graceful and fluid sculpture of **Athena Nike** adjusting her sandals. Finally, in the last room are two authentic and semi-eroded **caryatids** from the Erectheion, displayed behind a glass screen in a carefully rarified atmosphere.

The west and south slopes of the Acropolis

Most visitors to the Acropolis leave by the same route they arrived – north through Pláka. For a calmer, and increasingly panoramic, view of the rock it is worth taking the time to explore something of the **west slope of the Acropolis**, punctuated by the hills of the Areopagus, Pnyx, and Filopáppou, each of which had a distinct function in the life of the ancient city.

The **south slope** is rewarding, too, with its Greek and Roman theatres and the remains of stoas and sanctuaries. It can be approached from the Acropolis, with an entrance just above the Herodes Atticus theatre, though its main entrance is some way to the south along Leofóros Dhionissíou Areopayítou.

No less important, these sites all give access to the neighbourhoods of **Veikoú** and **Koukáki**, two of the least spoiled quarters in Athens, with some of the city's best tavernas (see p.97).

The Areopagus, Pnyx and Filopáppou Hill

Rock-hewn stairs ascend the low hill of the **Areopagus** immediately below the entrance to the Acropolis. The 'Hill of Mars' was the site of the Council of Nobles and the Judicial Court under the aristocratic rule of ancient Athens. During the Classical period the court lost its powers of government to the Assembly (held on the Pnyx) but it remained the court of criminal justice, dealing primarily with cases of homicide. Aeschylus used this setting in *The Eumenides* for the trial of Orestes, who, pursued by the Furies' demand of 'a life for a life', stood accused of murdering his mother Clytemnestra. The hill was used as a campsite by the Persians during their siege of the Acropolis in 480 B.C., and in the Roman era by Saint Paul, who preached the Sermon on an Unknown God, winning amongst his converts Dionysius 'the Areopagite', who became the city's patron saint.

There are various foundation cuttings on the site, and the ruins of a church of Áyios Dhioníssios (possibly built over the court), though nothing is actually left standing. The Areopagus's historic associations apart, it is notable mainly for the views, not only of the Acropolis, but down over the Agora and towards Kerameikos.

Following the road or path over the flank of the Acropolis, you come out on to Leofóros Dhionissíou Areopayítou, by the Herodes Atticus theatre. Turning right, 100m or so down (and across) the avenue, a network of paths leads up **Filopáppou Hill**, also known as the 'Hill of the Muses' (*Lófos*

Moussón). This strategic height has played an important, if generally sorry, role in the city's history. It was from here that the shell that destroyed the roof of the Parthenon was lobbed; more recently, the colonels placed tanks on the slopes during their coup of 1967. (Avoid the area at night, when it has a reputation for rapes and muggings.)

The hill's summit is capped by a somewhat grandiose monument to a Roman senator and consul, Filopappos, who is depicted on its frieze driving his chariot. Again, it is a place above all for views. To the south is the Dora Stratou Theatre (or Filopáppou Theatre) where Greek music and dance performances (see p.102) are held. North, along the main path, and following a line of truncated ancient walls, is the church of **Áyios Dhimítrios**, an unsung gingerbread gem, preserving its original Byzantine frescoes. In the cliff face across from this to the south you can make out a kind of cave dwelling, known (more from imagination than evidence) as the **prison of Socrates**.

Farther to the north, above the church, rises the **Hill of the Pnyx**, an area used in Classical Athens as the meeting place for the democratic assembly. All except the most serious political issues, such as ostracism, were aired here, the hill on the north side providing a convenient semicircular terrace from which to address the crowds of at least 6000 citizens (a quorum) that met more than forty times a year. All could vote and, at least theoretically, all could voice their opinions, though the assembly was harsh on inarticulate or foolish speakers. There are remains of the original walls, used to form the theatre-like court, and of stoas for the assembly's refreshment. The arena is today used for the *son-et-lumière* (not greatly recommended) of the Acropolis, which takes place on most summer evenings.

Beyond the Pnyx, still another hill, **Lófos Nimfón** (hill of the Nymphs') is dominated by a nineteenth-century observatory and gardens, occasionally open to visitors.

The south slope of the Acropolis
Entrances above the Herodes Atticus theatre and on Leof. Dhionissíou Areopayítou. Open weekdays 8am–4pm, Sun. 10am– 4pm.

The second-century Roman **Odeion of Herodes Atticus**, restored for performances of music and Classical drama during the summer festival (see p.107), dominates the south slope of the Acropolis hill. It is open, however, only for shows, and the main interest on the slope lies in the earlier Greek sites to the east.

Pre-eminent among these is the **Theatre of Dionysus**, beside the main site entrance. One of the most evocative locations in the city, it was here that the masterpieces of Aeschylus, Sophloncles, Euripides, and Aristophanes were first performed. It was also the venue for the annual festival of tragic drama, where each Greek citizen would take his turn as member of the chorus. The ruins are impressive; rebuilt in the fourth century B.C., the theatre could hold some 17,000 spectators – considerably more than the Herodes Atticus's 5000 to 6000 seats. Twenty-five of the theatre's sixty-four tiers of seats survive. Most notable are the great marble thrones in the front row, each of which is inscribed with the name of an official of the festival or of an important priest;

in the middle sat the Priest of Dionysus and on his right the representative of the Delphic Oracle. At the rear of the stage along the Roman *bema* (rostrum) are reliefs of Dionysus flanked by squatting Sileni.

To the west of the theatre extend the ruins of the **Asclepion**, a sanctuary devoted to the healing god Asclepius (see p.142) and built around a sacred spring. The curative centre was probably incorporated into the Byzantine church of the doctor-saints, Kosmas and Damian, of which there are prominent remains. Nearer to the road are the foundations of the Roman **Stoa of Eumenes**, a colonnade of stalls which stretched to the Herodes Atticus Odeion.

The Ancient Agora

North entrance by the Areopagus; south entrance on Adhrianoú, E2; open Mon.-Sat. 7.30am–7.30pm, Sun. 8am–5pm; museum closed Tues.

The **Agora** (market) was the nexus of ancient Athenian city life. Competing for space were the various claims of administration, commerce, market and public assembly. The result was ordered chaos. Eubolus, a fourth-century poet, observed that 'you will find everything sold together in the same place at Athens: figs, witnesses to summonses, bunches of grapes, turnips, pears, apples, givers of evidence, roses, medlars, . . . water clocks, laws, indictments'. Before shifting location to the Pnyx, the assembly also met here, and continued to do so for cases of ostracism for most of the fifth and fourth centuries B.C.

Originally the Agora was a rectangle, divided diagonally by the Panathenaic Way and enclosed by temples, administrative buildings, and long porticoed *stoas* (arcades of shops) where idlers and philosophers gathered to exchange views and listen to the orators. Women were not in evidence; secluded by custom, they would delegate any business in the Agora to slaves. In the centre of the rectangle was an open space, defined by boundary stones at the beginning of the fifth century B.C., which was considered sacred and essential to the life of the community. Those accused of homicide or other serious crimes were excluded from it by law.

Perhaps appropriately the site is today a confused, if extensive, jumble of ruins, dating from various stages of building between the sixth century B.C. and the fifth century A.D. The best overview, as stated, is from the Areopagus, by the north entrance. For some idea of what you are surveying, however, the place to head for is the **Museum**, housed in the totally reconstructed **Stoa of Attalos**. Here you can get some measure of the original buildings and also find your bearings from plans of the site displayed within. The *stoa* itself was a $1.5 million project of the American School of Archaeology in Athens. It is, in every respect bar one, an entirely faithful reconstruction of the original. What is missing is colour. In Classical times the exterior would have been painted in bright red and blue (like the Minoan palaces of Crete). However, as Donald Horne observed in *The Great Museum*, 'they couldn't bring themselves to paint it. To have been authentic would have made it seem untrue to the modern stereoptype of the Classical'. The building in Athens which most accurately resembles the ancient models is the University on Panepistimíou street. Built by a Dane in the 1830s, this features polychrome decoration and frescoes. Judge for yourself.

Back on the Agora site, the most prominent ruins are those of the various *stoas*, including the recently excavated 'Painted Stoa', where Zeno expounded his Stoic philosophy, and of the city's gymnasiums and council hall (*bouleuterion*). Somewhat above the general elevation, to the west, is the **Thiseion**, or Temple of Hephaistos. The best preserved, though perhaps least admired, of all Doric temples, it lacks the curvature and 'lightness' of the Parthenon's design. It was the first building begun in Pericles's programme, though not the first completed. Significantly its dedication is to the patron of blacksmiths and metalworkers, yet another sign of the Athenians' willingness to take pride in their human virtues and bring their religion closer to earth. Its remaining *metopes* depict the labours of Hercules and the exploits of Theseus, hence the popular name. The barrel-vaulted roof dates from the Byzantine conversion of the temple into a church of St George.

Kerameikos (Kerameikós)

Entrance at Ermoú 148, E1; open daily 9am–3pm; museum closed Tues.
The Kerameikós site, encompassing the principal cemetery of ancient Athens, provides a fascinating and quiet retreat from the Acropolis. It is little visited by tourists and in addition has something of an oasis feel about it, with the brook Iridhanós, brimful of water lilies, flowing across it from east to west providing an atmosphere of lush coolness.

From the entrance the double line of the **Long Walls**, which ran to the port at Pireás, can be seen; the inner wall was hastily cobbled together by the men, women and children of Athens while Themistocles was pretending to negotiate a mutual disarmament treaty with Sparta in 479 B.C. The barriers are interrupted by the great **Dipylon Gate** where travellers from Pireás, Eleusis, and Boeotia entered the ancient city, and the **Sacred Gate**, used for the Eleusinian and Panathenaic processions. These followed the Sacred Way, once lined by colonnades and bronze statues, into the Agora. Between the two gates are the foundations of the **Pompeion**, where preparations for the processions were made and where the main vehicles were stored.

Branching off from the Sacred Way is the **Street of the Tombs**, begun in 394 B.C. and now excavated along a hundred or so metres. Both sides were reserved for the plots of wealthy Athenians. Some twenty, each containing numerous commemorative monuments, have been excavated, and their original stones, or replicas, replaced on the site. The flat vertical *stelai* were the main funerary monuments of the Classical world; the sarcophagus belonged to Hellenistic and Roman times. The sculpted crescent with the massive conglomerate base to the left of the path is the *Memorial of Dexileos*, the twenty-year-old son of Lysanias of Thorikos, who was killed in action at Corinth in 394 B.C. The adjacent plot contains the *Monument of Dionysios of Kollytos*, in the shape of a pillar *stele* supporting a bull carved from Pentelic marble. As with any cemetery, however, it is the more humble monuments, such as the statue of a girl with a dog on the north side of the street, that connects past and present in the shared experience of loss. From the terrace overlooking the tombs, Pericles delivered his famous funeral oration dedicated to those who died in the first years of the Peloponnesian War. His propaganda coup inspired thousands more to enlist in a campaign where one-third of the Athenian force was to be wiped out.

The **Oberlaender Museum**, named after the German-American manufacturer who financed it, contains an extensive collection of *stelai*, terra-cotta figures, vases and sculptures from the site. Among them, that of *Ampharete Holding Her Infant Grandchild* and *The Boxer*, with a cauliflower ear and thongs of a glove tied around his wrist, in Room 1, are remarkable in their detailed execution. The terracotta figures and vases of Room 2 include some of the earliest art objects yet found in Greece.

Roman Athens

When the **Romans** ousted the Macedonian rulers of Athens, incorporating the city into the vast new province of Achaia in 146 B.C., Athens continued to enjoy rare political privileges. The city's status as a respected seat of learning and great artistic centre had already been firmly established throughout the ancient world. Cicero and Horace were educated here and Athenian sculptors and architects were supported by Roman commissions. Unlike Corinth, though, which became the administrative capital of the province, the city was endowed with relatively few imperial Roman **monuments**, Hadrian's Arch being perhaps the most obvious exception. Athenian magistrates, exercising a fair amount of local autonomy, tended to employ architects who would reflect the public taste for the simpler *propylaion*, gymnasium, and old-fashioned theatre, albeit with a few Roman amendments.

The city's Roman **history** was shaped pre-eminently by its alliances, which often proved unfortunate. The first major onslaught on what had become a prestigious backwater of the empire occurred in 86 B.C., when Sulla punished Athens for its allegiance to his rival Mithridates by burning its fortifications and looting its treasures. His successors were more lenient. Julius Caesar preferred a free pardon after Athens had sided with Pompey; and Octavian, who extended the old *agora* by building a forum, showed similar clemency when Athens harboured Brutus following the Ides of March. The most frequent visitor was the **Emperor Hadrian**, who used the occasions to bestow grandiose monuments, including his eponymous arch, a magnificent and immense library and (though it had been begun centuries before) the Temple of Olympian Zeus. A generation later **Herodes Atticus**, a Roman senator born in Marathon, became the city's last major benefactor of ancient times. His great wealth came purely and simply from a lucky find; his father had stumbled upon a vast treasure buried in an old house and, with permission from the Emperor, kept it all.

The Roman Forum, Tower of the Winds, and Other Sites in Pláka
Forum site entrance on Eólou, E2; open daily 9am–3pm.
Heading south from Monastiráki square along Eólou you come to a large irregular-shaped excavation site bounded by railings. This was the **Roman Forum**, built as an extension of the older *agora* by Julius Caesar and

Augustus. It has been under substantial excavation in recent years, and while much of it is closed to visitors, what is open to view can be somewhat obscure. Among the more prominent ruins are a large **public latrine**, a number of shops and a stepped *propylaion* (at the south-east corner). The main entrance to the forum was through the relatively intact **Gate of Athena Archegetis**, consisting of a Doric portico and four columns supporting an entablature and pediment. It was erected with funds from Julius Caesar and Octavian. On the pilaster facing the Acropolis is engraved an edict of Hadrian announcing the rules and taxes on the sale of oil.

The best preserved and easily the most intriguing of the ruins, though, is the graceful, octagonal structure known as the **Tower of the Winds** (*Aéridhes* in Greek). It was designed in the first century B.C. by Andronicos of Cyrrhos, a Syrian astronomer, and served as a compass, sundial, weather vane and water clock – the latter powered by a stream from one of the Acropolis springs. Each face of the tower is adorned with a relief of a figure floating through the air, personifying the eight winds. On the *north* side (facing Eólou) is Boreas blowing into a conch shell; *northwest*, Skiron holding a vessel of charcoal; *west*, Zephyros tossing flowers from his lap; *southwest*, Lips speeding the voyage of a ship; *south*, Notos upturning an urn to make a shower; *southeast*, Euros with his arm hidden in his mantle summoning a hurricane; *east*, Apiliotis carrying fruits and wheat; and *northeast*, Kaikias emptying a shield full of hailstones. Beneath each of these it is still possible to make out the markings of eight sundials. The semicircular tower attached to the south face was the reservoir from which water was channelled in a steady flow into a cylinder in the main tower; the time was read by the water level viewed through the open northwest door. On the top of the building a bronze Triton used to revolve with the winds.

Bordering the east end of the site, stretching between Áreos and Eólou, stand the surviving walls of **Hadrian's Library**, an enormous building which once enclosed a cloistered court of a hundred columns.

At the eastern end of Pláka, Odhós Lissikrátous gives on to a small, fenced-off archaeological park known as the **Street of the Tripods**, where winners of the ancient dramatic contests dedicated their tripod-trophies to Dionysus. The **Monument of Lysicrates**, a tall and graceful stone and marble structure from 335 B.C., stands as a surprisingly complete example of these ancient exhibits. A four-metre-high stone base supports six Corinthian columns rising up to a marble dome on which, in a flourish of acanthus leaf carvings, a winning tripod was placed. The inscription on its architrave tells us that 'Lysicrates of Kikyna, son of Lysitheides was *choregos*; the tribe of Akamantis won the victory with a chorus of boys; Theon played the flute; Lysiades of Athens trained the chorus; Evainetos was archon'. The monument was incorporated into a French Capuchin convent in 1667 (see p.58).

Hadrian's Arch, the Temple of Olympian Zeus, and the Stadium
Entrance on Leof. Amalías, F4; Olympian Zeus site open Mon.–Sat. 9am–3pm, Sun.10am–2pm.
Beside what is now one of the most hazardous road junctions in Athens stands **Hadrian's Arch**, erected by the Emperor to mark the edge of the

Classical city and the beginning of his own. On the near side its frieze is inscribed 'This is Athens, the ancient city of Theseus,' and on the other 'This is the City of Hadrian and not of Theseus'.

Directly behind, the colossal pillars of the **Temple of Olympian Zeus** make some justification for this show of arrogance. The largest temple in Greece, and according to Livy, 'the only temple on earth to do justice to the god', it was dedicated by Hadrian in 131 A.D., some 700 years after the tyrant Peisistratos had laid its foundations. Hadrian marked the occasion by contributing a statue of Zeus and a suitably monumental one of himself (both now lost). Of the temple, just sixteen of the original 104 Pentelic marble pillars remain erect, though the column drums of another (which fell in 1852) litter the ground, giving a startling idea of the project's size. Almost equally impressive is the fact that in the Middle Ages a stylite made his hermitage on the temple architrave.

A walk across the National Gardens from the Olympian Zeus temple will bring you out on Leofóros Ardhittoú, across which is the **Stadium**, a nineteenth-century reconstruction on Roman foundations. This site was originally marked out in the fourth century B.C. for the Panathenaic athletic contests, but in Roman times, as a grand gesture to mark the presidency of the Emperor Hadrian, it was adapted for an orgy of blood sports, with thousands of wild beasts baited and slaughtered in the arena. Herodes Atticus (see above) later undertook to refurbish the 60,000 seats of the entire stadium; his white marble gift was to provide the city with a convenient quarry throughout the ensuing seventeen centuries. The stadium's reconstruction dates from the modern revival of the Olympic Games in 1896 and to the efforts of another wealthy benefactor, the Alexandrian Greek, Yiorgos Averoff. Its appearance – pristine whiteness and meticulous symmetry – must be very much as it was when first restored and reopened under the Roman senator.

Above the stadium to the south, on the secluded **Hill of Ardhittós**, are a few scant remnants of a Temple of Fortune, again constructed by Herodes Atticus. The short climb is amply repaid with one of the best views of the city.

The Museums

Just about every visitor to Athens goes to the **National Archaeological Museum**, and rightly, for the concentration of ancient Greek art here is probably the best in the world. But the city's other museums are consistently undersubscribed. Collections such as the **Benáki**, **Kanellópoulos** and **Cycladic Art** have exhibits that occasionally equal the National's, displayed amid far more intimate and sympathetic surroundings. Greek traditional culture is also well represented by there's a rewarding batch of **folk and popular art** museums in Pláka.

A **warning on opening hours**, which are included here with some trepidation. They are notorious for changing: without notice, from one season to another, from year to year, or from one week to the next due to staff short-ages (the National Archaeological Museum closed for a while at 2.30pm on this account). Monday or Tuesday are the most common closing days. To be absolutely certain of admission, as at any museum or site in Greece, it's best to visit between 9am and 12 noon; you may find a place closing for the day at 1pm.

Admission prices, in a similar state of flux, aren't detailed. As a general guideline, reckon on 300dr for the main attractions (400dr for the National Archaeological) and 75-150dr for the others; student cards secure a 50-75 percent discount at state-owned museums (including the National Archaeological).

Where a museum has regular summer and winter hours they are detailed as: 9/10am–7pm/2pm (summer: 9am–7pm; winter 10am–2pm).

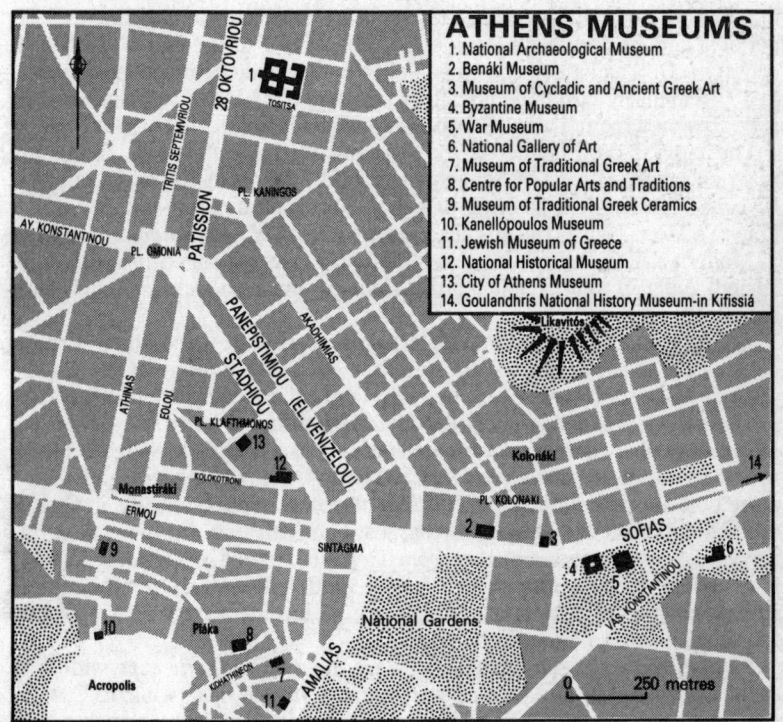

ATHENS MUSEUMS
1. National Archaeological Museum
2. Benáki Museum
3. Museum of Cycladic and Ancient Greek Art
4. Byzantine Museum
5. War Museum
6. National Gallery of Art
7. Museum of Traditional Greek Art
8. Centre for Popular Arts and Traditions
9. Museum of Traditional Greek Ceramics
10. Kanellópoulos Museum
11. Jewish Museum of Greece
12. National Historical Museum
13. City of Athens Museum
14. Goulandhrís National History Museum-in Kifissiá

The National Archaeological Museum

Patissíon 28, C2/3; Tues.–Sat. 8am–7/5pm, Sun. 8am– 6/5pm, closed Mon.; Thira and Numismatic sections close at 3pm and 1.30pm respectively.

The National Archaeological Museum is a treasure house of Cycladic, Minoan, Mycenean, and Classical Greek art. And its riches would be even greater if, for example, the 'Elgin marbles' were not still, inexcusably, in London, the sculptures from Aeyina's Temple of Aphaia in Munich and the *Venus de Milo* in Paris – to name but a few of the major missing works from Greece's widely looted heritage.

But this is a tribute to the creators' genius. The museum itself would not score so highly. The exhibits are crowded and unimaginatively displayed; the labelling is perfunctory; and there isn't a single explanatory panel. Without a guide of some kind (the account below provides pointers – or there are books on sale in the foyer), you wouldn't be much wiser after a visit.

The museum's main divisions are **Prehistoric**, with Mycenae predominating, **Sculpture** from the Archaic (8th c. B.C.) to Hellenistic (3rd–2nd c. B.C.) periods, and **Pottery** from Geometric (9th c. B.C.) to the end of the fourth century A.D. Smaller self-contained collections include **bronzes** in Rooms 36 to 40, immensely covetable **jewellery** in Room 32, and the brilliant Minoan-style **frescoes from Thira (Santorini)** upstairs in Room 48.

The biggest crowd-puller is the **Mycenaean hall** (Room 4), facing the main entrance, with all of Schliemann's gold finds from the grave circle at Mycenae. To the left, as hard to get a look at on a summer's day as the Louvre's Mona Lisa, is the so-called funerary *Mask of Agamemnon* [a] in Case 3. Modern dating techniques prove this must have belonged to some more ancient Achaian king, yet it fits the Homeric myth so well that such facts scarcely seem to matter.

The Mycenaeans' consummate art was small-scale decoration – rings, cups, seals, inlaid daggers – and requires eye-tiring scrutiny of the packed showcases to appreciate. Don't be entirely mesmerised by the death masks, or the superb golden-horned *Bull's Head* [b] in Case 27. In Case 5 there's a lovely duck-shaped vase of rock crystal; in Case 3, with the 'Agamemnon' mask, a magnificent inlaid dagger. Case 8 has jewellery, daggers, and a miniature golden owl-and-frog from Nestor's palace at Pylos; alongside, in Case 9, are baked tablets of Linear B, the earliest Greek writing. On the wall in this section are Cretan-style frescoes from Tiryns of chariot-borne women watching spotted hounds in pursuit of boar, and bull-vaulting reminiscent of Knossos. More finds from Tiryns in Case 15 include a huge ring depicting four demons presenting gifts to a goddess.

Another highlight – in Case 32 [c] – are the glorious *Vafío cups*, with their scenes of wild bulls and long-tressed, narrow-waisted men, while in Case 33 an equally eye-catching cup is decorated with twining octopuses and dolphins. Further references to Homer abound. In Case 18 there's a magnificent *Boar's Tusk Helmet* and an ivory lyre with sphinxes adorning the soundboard; on the frescoes in the corner of the room you can pick out Achilles-style figure-of-eight shields.

NATIONAL ARCHAEOLOGICAL MUSEUM

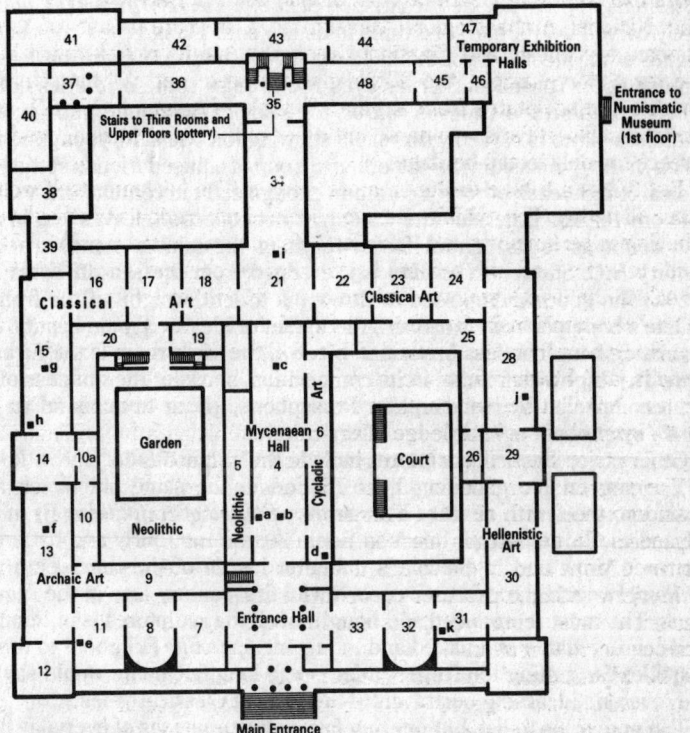

To the right of the Mycenaean hall, Room 6 houses a large collection of **Cycladic art** – pre-Mycenaean pieces from the islands. Many of these suggest the abstract forms of modern Cubist art – a link at its most striking in the much-reproduced *Man playing a Lyre* **[d]**. Another unusual piece, at the opposite end of the room, is a sixteenth-century B.C. cylindrical vase depicting a ring of fishermen carrying fish by their tails. The most common and characteristic of the sculptures are folded-arm figurines, among them a near full-size nude.

To the left of the Mycenaean hall, Room 5 contains **Neolithic** finds, primarily from excavations in Thessaly.

Most of the rest of the ground floor is occupied by **Sculpture**. Beginning in Room 7, on the left of the museum's main entrance, the exhibition evolves chronologically (and this is the best way to see it, at least for the first time) from the Archaic through the Classical and Hellenistic periods (Rooms 7-31) to the Roman- and Egyptian-influenced (Rooms 41-43). The gradual development from the stiff, stylised representations of the seventh century B.C. towards ever freer and looser naturalism is excitingly evident as you go through these cold and rather shabby rooms.

Early highlights include the Aristion *Stele of a Young Warrior* [e], with delicately carved beard, hair, and tunic folds in Room 11, and the Croesus *kouros* (statue of an idealised youth) in Room 13 [f]; both are from the late sixth century B.C.. You need sharper eyes not to miss some of the less obvious delights. Behind the Croesus *kouros*, for instance, and quite untrumpeted, a statueless plinth is carved with reliefs showing, on one side, young men exercising in the gymnasium, on the other a group of amused friends setting a dog and cat to fight each other – a common enough sight in contemporary Greece.

Room 15, which heralds the **Classical art** collection, leaves you in rather less doubt as to its central focus. Right in the middle stands a mid-fifth century B.C. *Statue of Poseidon* [g], dredged from the sea off Évvia in the 1920s. The god stands poised to throw his trident, weight on the front foot, athlete's body perfectly balanced, the model of idealised male beauty. A less dramatic, though no less important, piece in the same room is the *Eleusinian Relief* [h], highly deliberate in its composition, showing the goddess of fertility, accompanied by her daughter Persephone, giving to mankind an ear of corn – symbol of the knowledge of agriculture.

Other major classical sculptures include the virtuoso *Little Jockey* (Room 21 [i]) urging on his galloping horse, found in the same shipwreck as the Poseidon; the fourth century B.C. bronze *Ephebe of Antikithira* [j] in Room 28; and the three portrait heads in Room 30: a *Boxer*, burly and battered the furrowed brow and intellectual's unkempt hairdo of the third-century B.C. *'Philosopher'* and the expressive, sorrowful first-century face of the *Man from Delos*. The most reproduced and bought of all the sculptures is in Room 31: a first-century statue of a naked and indulgent *Aphrodite* [k] about to rap Pan's knuckles for getting too fresh – a far cry (a long fall, some would say) from the reverent, idealising portrayals of the gods in Classical times.

Too numerous to list, but offering fascinating glimpses of everyday life and changing styles of craftsmanship and perception of the human form, are the many *stelai* or carved gravestones. They are to be found in several of the Classical rooms. Also worth mention is Room 20, where various Roman copies of the lost Pheidias *Athena*, the original centrepiece sculpture of the Parthenon, are displayed. And in Room 32 is the *Heléne Stathatos Collection* of gold jewellery – amazing pieces all – from the ancient and Byzantine worlds.

Upstairs, keep a reserve of energy for the **Thíra rooms**. A visual knockout, these have been reconstructed in situ, their walls frescoed with monkeys, antelopes, and flowers, and furnished with painted wooden chairs and beds. Discovered at Akrotiri on the island of Thíra (Santoríni), they date from around 1450 B.C., contemporary with the flourishing Minoan civilisation on Crete.

The other upper rooms are occupied by a dizzying succession of **pottery**. Rooms 49 and 50 are devoted to the Geometric Period (1000-700B.C.); 52 and 53 to sixth century black-figured pottery; 54 to black- and red-figured pots; and 55 and 56 to the mainly funerary white urns and fourth-century pottery. But beautiful though many of the items are, there is absolutely nothing in the way of explanation, and this is probably the section to omit if you are running short of time or stamina.

In the south wing of the museum, entered separately from ToSsítsa street, is the extensive **Numismatic Collection**. This takes in over 400,000 coins, from Mycenaean times (with the Homeric double-ax motif) to Macedonian, though only a fraction are on display – and again with little imagination.

The Benáki Museum

Koumbári 1/corner Vassilíssis Sofías, D4; daily 8.30am–2pm; closed Tues.

Not to be missed – as it is by 90 percent of tourists – is this private collection, given to the state by an Egyptian-Greek collector. Constantly surprising and fascinating, the exhibits range through Chinese ceramics, Mycenaean jewellery, Greek costumes and folk artifacts, Byronia, and other memorabilia of the Greek War of Independence, even a reconstructed Muslim palace reception hall. These and the Benáki's new displays of acquisitions of jewellery and other items from the Helène Stathatos collection are worth an hour or two of anyone's time.

Among the more unusual exhibits, not easily accessible elsewhere, are collections of early Greek gospels, liturgical vestments, and church ornaments rescued by Greek refugees from Asia Minor in 1922 (*Rooms 4 and 10*); some dazzling embroideries from various parts of the islands and mainland in *Room 21* upstairs; and some unique historical material – on the Cretan statesman Eleftherios Venizelos, Asia Minor, and the Cretan Revolution in *Room 9*, and material on the 1821 rising against the Turks upstairs.

An additional attraction, if you've been dodging traffic in the streets all day, is the **rooftop café**, with good snacks and views over the nearby National Gardens. A **shop**, by the entrance, stocks a fine selection of books on Greek folk art, records of regional music and some of the best posters and postcards in the city.

Museum of Cycladic and Ancient Greek Art

Neofítou Dhouká 4 – second left off Vassilíssis Sofías after the Benáki museum, D4; Mon., Wed., Thurs., Fri. 10am–4pm, Sat. 10am–3pm (free); closed Sun. and Tues.

For display, labelling, explanation, and comfort, this small, new, private museum is streets ahead of anything else in Athens. Though the collections are restricted – to the Cycladic civilisation (3rd millenium B.C.), pre-Minoan Bronze Age (2nd millenium B.C.), and the period from the fall of Mycenae to the beginning of historic times around 700 B.C., plus a selection of pottery – you learn far more about these periods than from the corresponding sections of the National Archaeological Museum.

If Cycladic art seems an esoteric field, don't be put off. This display establishes the characteristic marble bowls and folded-arm figurines with their sloping wedge heads as objects of supreme purity and simplicity. Their interest for twentieth century artists like Moore, Picasso, and Brancusi becomes immediately obvious. And you can see in the figurines the remote ancestry of the Archaic style that evolved into the great sculptures of the Classical period.

To round off the experience, there's a **shop**, **bar** and shaded courtyard with a mosaic and a fountain.

Smaller Museums

Byzantine Museum

Vassilíssis Sofías 22 – 400m from the Benakí, D5; Tues.– Sat. 9am–3pm, Sun. 9am–2pm; closed Mon.

The setting is perhaps the best feature: a peaceful, courtyard-ed villa with as rural a feel as is possible in central Athens. To enjoy the exhibits — almost exclusively icons – requires some prior interest, best developed by a trip to the churches at Mystra, Dhafní or Óssios Loukás. Labelling is generally Greek-only and sadly you are told little of the development of styles, which towards the sixteenth century show an increasing post-Renaissance Italian influence from the presence of the Venetians in Greece.

War Museum

Vassilíssis Sofías 24, just beyond the Byzantine museum, D5; Tues.–Sun. 9am– 2pm; closed Mon.; Free.

The only 'cultural' endowment of the 1967-74 junta, this becomes predictably militaristic and right-wing as it approaches modern events – the Asia Minor campaign, the civil war, Greek forces in Korea, etc. Earlier times, however, are covered with a more scholarly concern and this gives an interesting insight into changes in warfare from Mycenae through to the Byzantines and Turks. Among models are a fascinating series on the acropolises and castles of Greece, both classical and medieval.

National Gallery of Art

Vassiléos Konstantínou 50, past the War Museum by the Hilton, E5; Tues.–Sat. 9am–3pm, Sun. 10am–2pm; closed Mon.

The National Gallery has a rather disappointing core collection of Greek art from the sixteenth century to the present. Its temporary exhibitions, though, can be worth catching; keep an eye out for posters or check listings in *The Athenian* magazine.

Popular Arts Museum

Kidhathinéon 17, Pláka, E3; Tues.–Sun. 10am–2pm; closed Mon. Free.

A beautiful, small museum in the heart of Pláka. On the first floor is a display of (mainly 18th and 19th c.) weaving, pottery, and embroidery, which reveals both the sophistication and the strong Middle Eastern influence of traditional Greek arts. On the third and fourth levels are traditional and ceremonial costumes from almost every region of the country.

Most compelling of all is the display on the **second floor** of a reconstructed village house with a series of wall paintings by **Theophilos** (1873-1934). A 'primitive' artist from the island of Lésvos, Theophilos was one of the characters of nineteenth-century Athens, dressing in War of Independence outfits and painting murals on tavernas and cafés for a meal or a small fee. Originals – usually scenes from peasant life or of battles from the War of Independence – survive in situ in Lésvos and in the Pílion, though they have only in the last decade or two been recognised as worth preserving.

Centre for Popular Arts and Traditions

Angelikís Hatzimiháli 6, off Kidhathinéon, Pláka, E3; Tues./Thurs. 9am–8pm, Wed./Fri./Sat. 9am–1pm & 5– 8pm, Sun. 9am–1pm; closed Mon.; Free.

An interesting supplement to the above: costumes, cloth, musical instruments, and so forth, well displayed in another grand Pláka mansion.

Museum of Traditional Greek Ceramics

Platía Monastiráki, E2; closed since the 1981 earthquake but scheduled for re-opening some time in 1989-90.

Housed in the Tzistarákis mosque, whose interior and *mihrab* (niche indicating the direction of Mecca, and hence prayer) were at last sight perhaps more interesting than the exhibits themselves.

Kanellópoulos Museum

Panós, Pláka, E3; Daily 8.45am–3pm, Sun. 9.30am–2.30pm; closed Tues.

Though there is nothing here that you won't have seen examples of in the bigger museums, this eclectic collection of treasures, exhibited in the topmost house under the Acropolis, has a calm appeal of its own. The bulk of the exhibits are icons but there is also Byzantine jewellery, Coptic textiles, and odds and ends of Cycladic, Minoan, and Classical art (among the pots, on the top floor, a mini 'Kama Sutra' vase, as the guard points out to male visitors).

Jewish Museum of Greece

Amalías 36 – above the French consulate, F3; Mon.–Fri. 9am– 1pm; closed weekends; Free.

Art and religious artifacts from the very ancient Jewish communities scattered throughout Greece. Highlight is a complete reconstruction, in miniature, of a medieval synagogue.

National Historical Museum

Platía Kolokotróni, off Stadhíou, D3; Tues.–Fri. 9am–2pm, Weekends 9am–1pm; closed Mon.

Exhibits are predominantly Byzantine and medieval, but with a strong section on the War of Independence that includes Byron's sword and helmet. Housed in the former Parliament building.

City of Athens Museum

Paparigopoúlou 7, Platía Klafthmónos – off Stadhíou, D3; Mon., Wednesday, Fri. 9am–1pm

A recently inaugurated, high-quality museum, housed in the original Royal Palace, residence of the German-born King Otho in the 1830s. Exhibits (prints mainly, and still somewhat sparse), feature an interesting – if also, in the modern light, depressing – model of the city as it was in 1842, with just 300 houses.

Goulandhrís Natural History Museum

Levídhou 13, Kifissiá – 10 min. walk from the metro; Mon.–Sat. 9am–1pm and 5–8pm (winter 9am–2pm only), Sun. 10am–4pm; closed Fri.

These modest but well-displayed collections have especially good coverage on Greek birds and butterflies and endangered species like the monk seal or sea turtle (*Caretta caretta*). Housed in a grand marble mansion, with a 250,000-specimen herbarium attached, the museum is a good reason to visit Kifissiá (see p.66). There is a café and a shop which sells superb illustrated books, postcards, posters, flower prints, seashells, etc.

See also the Acropolis (p.77), Agora (p.80) and Kerameikos Museums (p.81); also the Archaeological Museum in Pireás (p.110).

The Facts

The listings and recommendations below are up-to-date at the time of press, but obviously restaurants, bars, and nightlife venues change fast and often. Useful additional **sources of information** include the English-language *Athenian* magazine (monthly, 250dr) and *Athens News* papers (daily, 60dr). *The Athenian* has particularly good coverage of forthcoming art, dance and music events, including the summer Athens Festival, some interesting features, and a useful 'Organizer' with listings of all airline offices, embassies, and foreign banks.

If you can read Greek, the weekly *Athinórama* and daily newspapers provide fairly comprehensive listings; *Défi* magazine is good for music events.

Eating and drinking

As you'd expect in a city that houses almost half the Greek population, Athens has the best and the most varied **restaurants and tavernas** in the country. It's hard to imagine this in parts of the Pláka, but walk out to other, less touristed neighbourhoods and you have ample choice. Most places, too, are not just sources of good food but of a good night out.

The sections below are devoted mainly to **restaurant meals**, grouped according to quarter and with a division into cheap (under 850dr per person) and less so (up to 1250dr). Preceding these are run-downs on **breakfast** (most Athenians don't take it), **snacks** (on which you could, contentedly, live), *ouzerí* (ditto – but better), **bars** and **tea houses** (which are among the few fallbacks for vegetarians).

● BREAKFAST AND SNACKS

As elsewhere in Greece, a thimbleful of coffee is sufficient for most Athenian **breakfasts**. However, it's little problem finding a bakery, yoghurt shop and fruit stall to set yourself up for the day. In Pláka, the *Rekor* bakery, just below Kidhathinéon on Adhrianoú (*F3*), has whole-grain bread (a rarity), as does the (even better) bakery at Veikoú 45 (in Veikoú, *G3*).

Alternatively, the city caters well enough for western tastes in and around the Pláka. For a bacon/egg/juice breakfast, the cheapest and friendliest place is at **Níkis 26** (*E3*); nearby, a second choice is at Kidhathinéon 30, two doors up from Adhrianoú (*F3*), and a third at Kidathinéon 10, near the corner of Moní Asteríou (*E3*).

Around Omónia, the *Bretannia* (at the corner of Athinás, *D2*) is a wonderful old cafétaria, open twenty hours a day and serving up the best *rizógalo* (rice pudding with cinnamon) and yoghurt you'll find. Some of the best *loukoumádhes* – hot puffballs of dough served in syrup – are to be found at the stall near the corner of Panepistímiou and Ippokrátous. Or try one of the places listed under 'Teahouses and Coffeeshops' below.

Later in the day a host of **snack** stalls and outlets get going. If your budget is low you can fill up on them exclusively, forgetting sit-down restaurants altogether. If it's not, you'll still probably indulge. The standard snacks are *souvláki me píta* (kebab in Arabic bread), *tirópites* (cheese pies) and *spanakópites* (spinach pies), along with *bougátzes* (cream pies) and a host of other speciality pastries.

The best downtown **souvláki stands** cluster at the beginning of Mitropóloeos street (*E2*), just behind Monastiráki; other good ones include *Kostas'*, at Adhrianoú 116 (*E3*), and another on the corner of Dhrákou and Veikoú (*F3*). For the various **pastry snacks**, try two adjacent shops on Kolokotróni, near the corner of Lékka, or – well worth the little bit extra – *Noufara* on Kolonáki square.

Tea houses and coffee shops

With a couple of honourable exceptions (*Floca*, most famously), **tea houses** and Western-style **coffee shops** are a recent phenomenon in Athens. Quiet, rather consciously sophisticated places, they're essentially a reaction against the traditional and basic *kafenía*. Most are concentrated around the Pláka and in Kolonáki and the more upmarket suburbs.

Koperti, Sína 46, *D3*. Popular, youthful *salon de thé* in a handsome old shop close to the French Institute.

De Profundis, Angelikís Hatzimihális 1, Pláka, *E3*. A trendy-looking tea house but surprisingly reasonably-priced; herb teas, quiches, small entrées, pastries. Open 5pm to 3am; weekends noon to 3am.

To Tristrato, corner Dedhálou/Angélou Yéronda, Pláka, *F3*. Coffee, fruit juices, and salads, eggs, puddings, cakes; comfortable but expensive. Open 10am to midnight.

Orea Elladha, mezzanine of *Centre for Hellenic Tradition*, Pandhróssou 36, Monastiráki, *.F3*, Coffee and snacks; open all day.

Tchai-Tchai, Skoufá 3, Kolonáki, *D4*. Relaxed, if somewhat arty, tearoom. A nice place to go for a quiet beer – but not for tea which is absurdly priced at 350dr a cup! Open 10am–3pm & 5pm– 2am.

Floca, Panepistímiou (in the arcade), *D3*. The oldest-established Athenian café-pâtisserie – and still the best. Their *chocalatina* (cream chocolate cake) is without rival.

● OUZERÍ AND BARS

Ouzerí are very Greek and, sadly, increasingly rare. They are essentially bars selling *oúzo* (occasionally just *oúzo*), beer and wine, along with *mezédhes* (hors d'oeuvres) to reduce the impact. A special treat is a *pikilía* (usually about 500-650dr), a selection of all the *mezédhes* available. This will probably include fried shrimp, pieces of squid, cheese, olives, tongue, cheese pies, sausage, etc.; see 'Food' in *Basics* for *mezé* translations.

Added to the end of this section are a handful of **bars** and **pubs** where you can go to drink and snack. The more exciting of the city's bars, however, are music-orientated and are covered with the music clubs on p.106.

To Yerani, Tripódhon 14, corner Epihármou, Pláka, *F3*. Lively, wood-panelled *mezé* bar with terrace. Open lunchtimes and evenings.

Apotsos, Panepistimíou 10 (at the end of the arcade), *D3* . A lunchtime-only bar with a wide range of *mezédhes*. A landmark, frequented by journalists, politicians, writers and the rest.

To Athinaikon, Themistokléous, near corner with Panepistimíou, *D3*. An old *ouzerí* in a new location but retaining style – marble tables, old posters, etc. Variety of good-sized *mezédhes*. Closed Sundays.

Café-Bar Dhodhoni, Sólonos 64 (parallel to Panepistimíou, 3 blocks northeast), *D3*. A packed student hangout opposite the law school. Delicious snacks.

Salamandra, Mantzanárou (off Sólonos), Kolonáki, *D4*. *Mezédhes* bar in a restored neoclassical house. Open evenings as well as lunchtimes.

Dhexameni, Platía Dhexamenís, Kolonáki, *D4*. Unnamed café-*ouzerí* that serves drinks and snacks in summer under the trees. Shaded and cheap.

Ouzeri Finopoulos, corner Athinás/Evripídhou, in the bazaar, *D2*. The drinker's bar. Stand at the dented, water-swilled counter and take your *oúzo* by the tumbler . . . no food.

Ouzeri I Gonia, corner Emmanuél Benáki and Arahóvis, Exárhia, *C3*. Fine for snacks (on display in trays), beer, *oúzo*. Establish prices before ordering.

Cafe Neon, Platía Omonías, *D2*. An old, cavernous café-bar with no pretensions. Always crowded (this is a real meeting-place) and open until the small hours.

Rozaki, Evranónos 4, off Platía Plastíra, Pangráti, *F5*. Pink decor (as implied by the name), *oúzo*, wine, and *mezédhes*.

Mets, Márkou Moussoúrou 14, Méts, *F4*. Trendy but unsnobbish French-style brasserie. A limited menu meal runs around 2000dr with wine; the food is good but the wine's grossly overpriced.

Balthazar, Vournázou 14/Tsóha 27, near the Panathenaïkos football ground in Ambelókipi. Another 'in' brasserie (the bar part's more fun) installed amid the palm-tree gardens and ground floor of a palatial old mansion. A long list of cocktails; food and snacks around 1200-1500dr.

Larry's Bar, Likavitoú 20, Kolonáki, *D4*. American bar that serves perhaps the city's best cocktails. Clientele is mainly expatriate/upmarket, but the drinks give genuine value for money at 700dr or so a shot.

Serious Drinking

For a night of really excessive drinking, the **Dhafní Wine Festival**, open every evening from the second week of July through to the first week of September, is hard to beat. For around 400dr admission, you receive a goblet, refillable with as many different wines as you can handle. Most are pretty rough numbers (aficionados suggest mixing sweet with dry) but you tend to have a good time. The food, incidentally, is neither free nor cheap, let alone appetising, so eat before you go.

The site is next to the Dhafní campsite – a twenty-minute bus ride from Platía Eleftherías (just off Pireós street, between Omónia and Keramikós); numerous buses (all have numbers beginning with 8) leave every quarter of an hour and return throughout the evening. Alternatively, taxis are usually available (about 350dr one way).

● RESTAURANT MEALS

If it is character you are after, **Pláka**'s hills and lanes can still provide a pleasant evening's setting for a meal, despite the aggressive touts and general tourist hype. But for good-value and good-quality fare, only one in ten of the quarter's restaurants and tavernas is these days worth a second glance. If you're staying any length of time in the city, it's best to strike out into the ring of neighbourhoods around: to **Méts**, **Pangráti**, **Exárhia**, **Veikoú/Koukáki**, or the more upmarket **Kolonáki**. None of these are more than a half hour's walk, or a cheap taxi hop, from the centre – effort that is well repaid in increased menu choice and a more authentic and often livelier atmosphere.

All **listings** below are divided into area and cost, starting with options for a full meal at under 850dr a person, and moving on to more upmarket choices, where you'll pay 850–1500dr (very rarely more).

Pláka

Selections here represent just about all of note that **Pláka** has to offer. Most, sadly, are on the periphery of the quarter, rather than on the more picturesque squares and stairways. At those, don't be bamboozled by the touts, positioned at crucial locations to draw you across to their tavernas' tables; and don't be lulled into confidence by the menus' declarations that 'prices are controlled by the market police' – this is duly negated by the shrinking-portion trick.

Under 850dr

To Kosmikon, corner Adhrianoú/Kidhathinéon, *F3*. A cheap *psistariá* run by a friendly couple; speciality is roast chicken. Closed Wednesdays, mobbed at all other times.

Damingos, across Kidhathinéon from the above at no.41, *F3*. Dour service, but good value if you pick plates carefully; barrelled wine, excellent *bakaliáro skordhaliá* (cod with garlic sauce). Evenings only; closed midsummer.

More upmarket

To Fagadhiko, Adhrianoú 81, *E3*. Reasonable casserole-food taverna; popular with locals and tourists alike.

To Ipoyio, Kidathinéon 30 (in the basement), *E3*. Wide range of grills, vegetable *mezédhes*, bulk wine. Evenings only; closed June 1–Sept. 30.

Psarra, corner of Erehthéou/Erotokrítou, *E3*. Virtually the only decent establishment in the heart of Pláka's honky-tonk district and thankfully in one of its most attractive squares. Famous for seafood grills; exclusively outdoor seating.

O Zafíris, Thespídhos 4a, *F3*. Renowned game taverna, though at its best in autumn and winter.

Eden, Fléssa 3, *E3*. A rare vegetarian/macrobiotic restaurant whose quality fluctuates violently – you may strike lucky. Open evenings and/or lunchtime, depending on season.

● Monastiráki and the Bazaar

The shift from Pláka to Monastiráki is refreshing. In the streets of the commercial quarter people eat for a serious fill. There is a definite character about the quarter, too, at its best around the Flea Market.

Under 850dr

Ipiros, Platía Ayíou Filíppou, *E2*. An old restaurant in a great location, right at the heart of Flea Market. If the food – casserole dishes – is occasionally listless, the prices and quantity are fair enough.

Kea, Panós 6, *E2*. Average food but a fine outdoor setting, beside the old mosque and trailed with vines.

Bairaktaris, Platía Monastirakioú 2, *E2*. Huge, old restaurant with walls lined in retsina barrels. Straightforward menu. Closes 11pm.

Psistaria I Platia, Platía Iróön (a couple of minutes' walk from Monastiráki along Miaoúli), *E2*. Vegetable *mezédhes*, grilled northern Greek dishes; packed with locals at lunch. ·

In the meat market (entrances at Edhoú 80 and off Athinás), *D2*. The meat-market building is not everyone's prime eating site but the restaurants within know how to cook the goods – and feature *patsás* (tripe soup) for the more hardened. Open from around 6am until 3pm.

Around Omónia

Another no-nonsense, commercial location, whose only drawback is the dubious cleanliness of some of the places in the Omónia square arcades.

Under 850dr

Galaxias, *Greek Taverna*, *D2*. Best of the underground eateries on the pedestrian walkway.

Ioannis' & Dora's, Mavromiháli, just off Sólonos, *C3*. Caters to the business crowd, who demand – and get – delicious food.

Platía Viktorías/Exárhia

A small but good cluster of places, handy for the National Archaeological Museum, the better value student hostels, and for going on to the clubs ...

Under 850dr

Vangelis, Sahíni, off Liossíon (100m up from Platía Váthis), *C2*. Simply one of the friendliest – and most traditional – tavernas in the city.

O Lefteris, Ioulianoú 84. Walled-in garden taverna with casserole food.

Ouzeri, Elpídhos 14, Platía Viktorías. Seafood and *pikilíes* with your drinks.

Hlorofili, Soultáni 12, corner Solomoú, *C3*. Rare vegetarian restaurant; dinner only.

More upmarket

Kostoyiannis, Zaími 37 (behind the Nat. Arch. Museum, off Ioulianoú), *C3*. One of the city's best – much frequented by crowds from the theatres and cinemas around. Quality *mezédhes* and delicacies like rabbit stew. Highly recommended. Evenings only; closed Sunday.

Kolonáki and Likavitós

Kolonaki has a chic, upmarket reputation which puts off a lot of travellers. Nonetheless, between the piano bars there are some surprising finds.

Under 850dr (!)

I Rouga, Kapsáli 7 (in a cul-de-sac), just off Kolonáki square, *D4*. Small taverna open for supper only; menu changes daily. Closed summer.

O Vrahos, Likavitoú 8, *D4*. A tiny, sympathetic lunchtime *estiatório*. No frills but some character. Open weekdays only.

To Grafio, Dhexamení, *D4*. Cool, modern restaurant with a wide selection of *mezédhes* and a very pleasant location.

More upmarket

Taverna Dhimokrítos, Dhimokrítou 23/corner Tsakálof, *D4*. An excellent, unstuffy taverna at odds with the Kolonaki image; open for lunch and dinner. Closed late summer.

Likavitos Hill Restaurant, Xanthíppou (under the *Saint George Lycabettus Hotel*), *D4*. If you want a change from taverna fare, try this terrace restaurant, halfway up Likavitós, which serves up excellent pasta and salad amid leafy surroundings. Closed in winter.

Pangráti and Méts

These two neighbourhoods have perhaps the city's best concentration of eating places. All selections below are a short (if generally uphill) walk across Ardhittoú and past the Olympic stadium.

Under 850dr

O Megaritis, just above *Virinis* at Ferekídhou 2, corner Arátou. Casserole food, barrel wine, indoor/outdoor seating. Open all year.

Vellis, Platía Varnáva/corner Stilpónos (between Pangráti and Méts), *F5*. Limited choice, but very characterful little place on the square. One of the last of a dying breed of working-men's wine-with-food shops. Evenings only; indoor and outdoor seating.

Taverna Dhiana, Platía Varnáva/corner Melísson, *F5*. Good oven-food and bulk retsina. Open lunchtimes only.

O Ilias, corner Stasínou/Telesílis (near Leofóros Konstantínou), *E5*. A very good and very popular taverna – not a lot of room, so always crowded. Tables outside in summer.

More upmarket

O Virinis, Arhimídhous 11 (off Platía Plastíra), *F5*. Good quality, regular-priced taverna, with its own house wine and a wide variety of *mezédhes*. Garden in summer.

Karavitis, Arktínou 35, off Leofóros Konstantínou, *F5*. Old-style taverna with bulk wine, *mezédhes*, clay-cooked entrées. Indoor/outdoor seating.

Neroútsos, Arhimídhous 2-6/corner Platía Plastíra, *F5*. Basement restaurant serving first-rate, traditional oil-soaked fare – clean, efficient, and courteous. Lunchtime only.

O Anthropos, Arheláou 13 (between Vassiléos Yioryíou and Spírou Merkoúri), *E5*. Fish restaurants are always expensive in Athens – and at around 2000dr a head this is no exception. But the cooking here is excellent, with an effort to offer something different, more interesting salads, and so on. Popular and crowded.

O Mandis, Evyeníou Voulgaréos 68, near *Joseph's House* hostel, *F4*. Great for traditional dishes like *spetzofaï* (pepper/sausage stew from Mount Pílion), rabbit stew, snails and also vegetable plates; impeccable service and, by Greek standards, a very wacky decor.

Manesis, Márkou Moussoúrou 3, *F4*. Good value, especially if you piece together a meal from their *mezédhes*, which include such novelties as *loukaniko flambé*. Walled garden in summer. Evenings only.

Ta Pergoulia, Márkou Moussoúrou 16. Delicious, unusual *mezédhes* – order seven or eight and you'll have a fair-sized bill but a big meal. Closed in summer.

Veikoú/Koukáki

This is one of the most pleasant parts of the city to spend the middle of a day or round off an evening, having wandered down from the south slope of the Acropolis or Filopáppou hill. It's very much residential Athens – uneventful and a bit early-to-bed. However, Veikoú street, especially, has an incredible concentration of bakeries, ice-cream parlours, *psistariés*, and tavernas, all with local, family-oriented prices.

Under 850dr

O Periklis, Veikoú 38, *G3*. By day a barber shop; by night a walled-in passage to the side becomes arguably the cheapest restaurant in town. Huge portions of simple but well-prepared food. Closed May-October.

O Yeros tou Morea, Arváli 4, Koukáki, *G2*. Best for lunch when the oven food and *mezédhes* are fresh. Full of Koukáki bachelors, of all ages, who can eat here more cheaply than at home.

I Gardhenia, Anast. Zínni 29, Koukáki, *G3*. Casserole food in a cool, cavernous setting. Lunchtime only in summer.

I Gonia, corner Zán. Moreás Andhroútsou 34, *G2*. One of the cheapest *psistariés* around, serving excellent grilled chicken and *kondosoúvli*. Small and popular, so come early for a table. Open lunchtime and evenings.

To Sokáki, Aryiríou 6 (an alley off Veikoú, near the Mitsi cinema), *G2*. Slightly more upmarket but pleasant *psistariá*; speciality grilled chicken and *mezédhes*.

More upmarket

Terpsilarigios, Stratéon 3 (off Mitséon), Veíkou, *G3*. Istanbul-Greek management prepares sumptuous *table d'hôte* (choice of four entrées) for 900dr or so, including wonderful house red wine. Evenings only – and only forty seats so call for reservations (922-7692). Closed Sun., all through mid-May to mid-September (and whenever else they feel like it). Hard to find, but a find.

Irodhio, Angelikári 1 (up Rátzieri steps, just off Propiléon at the Acropolis end), Veikoú, *G3*. Beautiful premises, reasonable *mezédhes*, slightly pricier casseroles; a very short walk from the Herodes Atticus theatre.

Ouzadhiko to Meltemi, A. Zinní 26. A new, modest-priced *ouzerí* that shields its customers from street traffic with banks of greenery.

Music and other nightlife

Traditional **Greek music** – *rembétika* and *dhimotiká* – can, at its best, provide the city's most compelling night entertainment. To partake, however, you really need to visit during the winter months; from around Easter through to October most clubs and *boîtes* close their doors, while the musicians head off to tour the countryside and islands. A very few authentic places do continue into the summer (they're listed below) but for the most part what remains is a tourist travesty of overamplified and overpriced *bouzouki* noise – at its nadir, not surprisingly, in the Pláka.

As for other forms of live music, there are small indigenous **jazz** and **rock** scenes, perennially strapped for funds and venues but worth checking out. The major **classical** music performances tend to be part of the summer Athens Festival – for which see overpage.

Discos and **music bars**, a relatively new arrival to Athens nightlife, are very much in the European mold. The clubs in the city, like the Greek music *boîtes*, tend to close during the summer, unless they can draw with roof terraces. The hip Athenian youth, meanwhile, move out to a series of huge hanger-like disco-palaces in the coastal suburbs.

For **information** and knowledgeable advice on all kinds of Athens music – traditional, rock and jazz – look in at the record shop *Pop 11* (Pindhárou 38/ corner Tsakálof, Kolonáki). They have posters up for almost all interesting events and usually have tickets on sale for rock, jazz, or festival concerts.

● TRADITIONAL MUSIC

An introduction to Greek traditional and folk music is included in *Contexts*. In Athens, the various styles can co-exist or be heard alternate evenings at a number of music halls or *boîtes*. Most gigs start pretty late – there's little point in arriving much before 10.30pm – and stay open until 3 or 4am, though officially places are supposed to close at 2am. After midnight (and a few drinks) people tend to loosen up and start dancing; at around 1am there's generally an interval, when patrons may move to other clubs down the street or across town. Whether you club-hop or not, music halls can turn out expensive outings: be prepared to spend 2000dr-plus per person, and at weekends try to reserve ahead – ideally for a group of four or more.

Listings below are a slightly hit-and-miss affair as places open, close, move or change opening times with all too frequent regularity. *Athinórama* is a useful (though by no means exhaustive) check.

Rembétika

For anyone with an interest in folk sounds, *rembétika*, the old drugs-and-outcast music brought over by Asia Minor Greeks, is worth the effort to catch live. The form was revived in the early '80s and, though clubs are on the decline, there are good sounds still to be heard.   Unless otherwise indicated, all of the clubs below are in or near the quarter of Exárhia (most in the two to three blocks immediately around its square).

Taksimi, Isávron 29, off Hariláou Trikoúpi, *C3* (☎363-9919). Crowded salon on third floor of neoclassical building; no food, no cover, but reckon on 1200dr per person for drinks. Large, young house band with baglama, bouzouki, guitar, accordeon and two female singers. Material tends to be 1950s songs, interspersed with *laíka* – blander, modern songs. Closed Wednesdays.

Frangosyriani, Arahóvis 57, Exárhia, *C3* (☎360-0693). The band's emphasis (very good female vocalist, similar instrumentation to *Taksimi*) is again on '50s material, mainly by Bellou and Tsitsanis, with a few earlier standards thrown in. Drinks, no food, and 800-1000dr minimum charge, depending on the day of the week. Closed Thursday.

Minore, Notará 34 (☎823-8630), closed Monday. *Rembetiki Istoria*, Ippokrátous 181 (☎642-4937). Closed Monday and Tuesday. Two other Exárhia possibilities.

Marabout, Panórmou 113, near Leofóros Alexándhras in Ambelókipi (look for a sign with a toucan!), *off map*. The first revival club for rembetíka and still one of the most popular – mobbed at weekends. For four nights of the week the music is taped, other times they feature *laterna* (hurdy-gurdy) by an old man who was jailed recently (at age 74) for a knife fight over a woman! Expensive food and drink; no reservations. Open year-round.

To Palio Mas Spiti, Odhemissíou 9, Kessarianí (☎721-4934). The best and most authentic of the surviving clubs – a real neighbourhood place with decent food, reasonable drinks, no minimum charge and no amplification. The part-owner, Girogos Tzortizis, plays baglama, alongside a bouzoukiist, guitarist and singer; excellent house album on sale. Closed Sunday.

Dhimotiká (Folk) Music

A real mix of styles at these clubs – everything from Zorba-like Cretan *santoúri* music to wailing clarinet from the mountains of Epirus, from ballroom dancing to salsa. The principal areas for venues are Kipséli (particularly around Patissíon) and, to a lesser extent, Ambelókipi. If you walk the streets of these quarters you're likely to see posters for events – probably the best way to find out what's on.

Listings below cover some of the more distinctive or enduring clubs. Most are rather pricier than their *rembétika* equivalents.

Ravanastron, Dhimitsánas 60, Ambelókipi (☎644-9534). A newish club, featuring Greek and Turkish traditional music played on lyra, fiddle, oud, saz and tzourás.

Latin, Kalidhromíou 69, Exárhia, *G3* (☎364-5978). Another new (and ground-breaking) venue which mixes salsa, Peruvian folk, traditional Greek sounds, according to the night of the week.

To Panayiri ton Trellon, Evelpídhon 97, beyond Aréos Park, *A4* (☎884-3595). Mainland and island music. Closed Tuesday and from mid-May to mid-October.

Elatos, Trítis Septemvríou 16 at Platía Lavríou (☎523-4262). Assorted *dhimotiká*. Closed Wednesday.

Nostalgia, Kalímnou 11, Kipséli, *A2* (☎865-7902). Features *kantádhes* (ballads from the Ionian islands), Greek and ballroom dancing. Closed Monday and in summer.

● JAZZ

With the closure of *Tzaz Club* in Pláka, Athens seems to be left with just one regular jazz venue:

The Half-Note, Nikifórou Ouranoú 2, corner Patriárhou Fotíou, below the Likavitós Theatre in Pefkáki, *C4* (☎364-1842). Live jazz most nights but closed Tuesdays and for much of the summer.

All is not lost, however, for there are some enterprising events through the spring and summer under the aegis of the **Praxis Festival of Jazz and Contemporary Music**. Greek and foreign musicians collaborate on many of these concerts, sponsored by the Praxis record label (who issue subsequent recordings). ☎362-3397 for information.

● ROCK: LIVE VENUES AND MUSIC BARS

The tiny indigenous rock scene is beset by difficulties. Instruments are the most expensive in Europe, audiences the smallest, and the whole activity is still looked upon with some official disfavour – clubs frequently being raided and closed by the police. However, there are an ever-increasing number of music bars, especially in Exárhia (*C3*), which host the occasional gig and generally have a dance floor of sorts.

Among the more durable, if not necessarily artistically worthy, local groups are *Mousikes Taxiarhies*, *Socrates* and *Villa 21*.

Kittaro, Ipírou 48, between the train stations and Archaeological Museum, *C2*; *Tracks*, Singroú 49, south of the National Gardens, *G3*; *Club 22*, Vouliagménis 22, *G4*. Live bands most weekends – and some weekdays – at each of these establishments; fairly contemporary recorded sounds most other nights.

Surabaja Johnny, Kleovoúlis 32, near Papadhiamandopoúlou, Ayíou Thomá district, *off map*; ☎777-0547. Similar to those above but with bands (generally soft-rock) most nights. A modern venue for hip Greeks and ex-pats (who do much of the playing).

Enalax, Mavromiháli 137 (on the east edge of Exárhia), *C4*. Hub of Athens' new wave scene – a big, cool place with minimalist interior. Don't turn up much before midnight, and count on 500dr a shot for cocktails.

Green Door, Kallidhromíou, Exárhia, *C3*. Another lively Exárhia venue – and as semi-permanent as they come. A good place to ask about new places in the neighbourhood.

Stadhio, corner Márkou Moussoúrou/Ardhittoú, Méts, *F4*. A high-tech, fashionable bar, pricey (cocktails 800dr) but with good music and a terrace open to the stars and to views of the Acropolis.

The Doors, Marína Antípa 145, Áno Illiopóli, *off map*. Friendliest, cheapest (150dr for a mix) and definitely the loudest of a cluster of bars in and around Áno Illiopóli's main square. Music here – and at its neighbours – covers most tastes from soul to heavy metal. Áno Illiopóli slopes up towards Mt. Imittós: a 15-min. taxi drive from the centre.

Blues Pub, Vatopedhíou 13 (off Panórmou, northeast of Likavitós), Ambelókipi, *off map*. Old fashioned R'n'B discs in a comfortable, unpretentious bar; a friendly crowd, too, despite the highish prices.

The Big Apple, Néa Filadhélfia (in the main square), *off map*. '70s music for '70s people: a place to get smashed to Led Zeppelin on the cheap (if this idea appeals . . .). Néa Filadhélfia is a northwest suburb, 15–20 min. by taxi from the centre.

Retro, Mithímnis 41 (off Amerikís square), Kipséli, *just off map*. '60s music in a small, easy-going disco-bar.

Aigli, at the Zappíon in the National Gardens, *E4*. The city centre's trendiest evening café, full of rich young things in their designer best; music is pretty standard, no admission charge but drinks are *very* pricey; closes around 3.30am.

● DISCOS

The 'music bars' detailed above are probably the most enjoyable of downtown Athens' disco options. The 'real' discos, however, take place way out of town – past the airport and on to the seaside suburbs of Glifádha (16km from Athens) and Voúla (20km). Athens youth moves out here in force at weekends. If you join them, keep in mind that the taxi ride will be only the first (and least consequential) expense; admission prices, however, usually include a first drink.

Bitchoulas, Vassíleos Yioryioú 66, *off map*. One of the smaller discos, playing mainly new wave/rock. Just past the airport on the road to Glifádha.

Dorian Grey, Vouliagméni 568, *off map*. Huge disco-palace with a dazzling light show and regular dance sounds; drinks 1000dr. Closed Monday and Tuesday.

Aftokinisi, Ay. Ellenikoú 5, Glifádha, *off map*. Another vast disco, in a similar vein to Dorian Grey, in the next suburb on.

Aerodhromio, opposite the airport, *off map*. Hippest of a crop of discos around Voúla – the suburb after Glifádha – which is where the weekend action is currently deemed to be. The dance floor is open-air, so you can watch the planes passing overhead. Open till 4am.

Gay discos and clubs

The scene is fairly discreet but Athens does have a handful of clubs with an established gay (male) reputation. For lesbians, *Snob* (An. Polémiou 10, Kolonáki; closed Tues.) is about the only promising venue.

Alexandheri, Anagnostopoúlou 44; *Alekos Island*, Tsakálof 42, *D4*. Relaxed, slightly middle-of-the-road, gay bars in the Kolonáki district.

Grafitti, Xánthou 9, near Omónia. Predominantly gay disco-bar; somewhat abrasively New Wave.

Xomino, Granazi, both on Singroú street (south of the National Gardens), which is also the transvestite cruising area, *G3*.

> **LATE NIGHT EATING:** The restaurants in the **Central Market** on Athinás (*D2*) are open through the small hours: regular haunts for truck drivers and a smattering of clubbers unable to face nighttime sleep.

Festivals, Theatre, Dance and Cinema

Festival events

The summer **Athens Festival** has, over the years, come to encompass cultural events in just about every sphere: Classical Greek theatre most famously (in performance at the Herodes Atticus theatre on the south slope of the Acropolis), but also established and contemporary dance, classical music, big-name jazz, traditional Greek music, and even a smattering of rock shows. As well as the Herodes Atticus theatre, which is memorable in itself on a warm summer's evening, the festival spreads to the open-air theatre on

Likavitós hill, the Veákio amphitheatre in Pireás and (with special bus excursions) to the great ancient theatre at Epidaurus (see p.142).

The festival runs from early June until mid-September. Programs of performances are best picked up as soon as you arrive in the city, and for theatre, especially, you'll want to move fast to get tickets.* The main **festival box office** is in the arcade at Stadhíou 4 (*D4*; ☎322-1459/3111; weekdays 8.30am–1.30pm and 6–8.30pm); the various theatre box offices are open on the day of performance. Schedules of the main drama/music events are available in advance from EOT offices abroad (though they don't handle tickets or reservations).

As a prelude to the summer festival season, from March through the summer, there is also the **Praxis Festival of Jazz and Contemporary Music** (see 'Jazz', above).

Theatre and Dance

Unless your Greek is fluent, the contemporary **Greek theatre** scene is likely to be inaccessible. As with Greek music, it is essentially a winter pursuit; in summer, the only theatre on stage tends to be satirical and (to outsiders) totally incomprehensible revues.

However, one event that needs no translation is the *Karagiózis,* or **shadow-puppet play**, presented at the Haridhímos Theatre, just behind the Lysicrates monument in Pláka (*F3*). Karagiozis is the archetypal Greek underdog – wily, greedy, and wheedling in his attempts to deceive his Turkish overlords, and a perfect terror to his intimates. Other characters include Alexander the Great, the Jew, various heroes of the revolution . . . whatever the puppeteer decides on. Of late the shows have become more overtly political – anti-nuclear, anti-NATO; all suitable material, for to be topical is part of the tradition. Performances begin at 9pm nightly, from mid-May through September.

On the **dance** front, the most worthwhile 'permanent' performance is that performed by the **Dora Stratou Ethnic Dance Company** in their own theatre on Filopáppou hill (*G1*). Gathered on a single stage are traditional music, choreography and costumes you'd be hard-put to encounter in a year's travel around Greece. Performances are held nightly at 10.15 (8.15 and 10.15 on Wed. and Sun.) from May to October. To reach the theatre, walk up the busy Areopayítou Street, along the south flank of the Acropolis, until you see the signs. Tickets (650–850dr) can almost always be picked up at the door; take your own refreshments.

For details of the growing **contemporary dance** scene, consult the back sections of *The Athenian* magazine – the best source, too, for events at the various **foreign cultural institutes**. Among these, the *Hellenic American Union* (Massalías 22, *D3*), *British Council* (Platía Kolonáki 17, *D4*), *French*

There are cheap tickets and student reductions for most festival shows – the main problem, as stressed, being that they sell out quickly, particularly for ancient drama at Herodes Atticus. If this happens, however, don't necessarily give up: at Herodes Atticus the young and ticketless are often admitted a few minutes before the start to sit on the wall at the back. It's worth hanging around; the entrance is on Dhionissíou Areopayítou.

Institute (Sína 29/Massalías 18, *D3*) and *Goethe Institute* (Omírou 14-16, *D3*) host many free or low-cost concerts, films, lectures and exhibitions, not necessarily emanating from their home culture.

Cinema

Athens is – surprisingly perhaps – a great place to catch up on movies. There are literally hundreds of indoor cinemas in the city, many of them moody relics of the '20s and '30s, whilst in summer **outdoor** screens spring up all over the place – in parks, abandoned lots, anywhere there's space.

Admission, whether at indoor or outdoor venues, is extremely cheap, owing to heavy government subsidy of the theatres, and films are always shown in the original langauge with Greek subtitles (a good way to increase your vocabulary, by the way). For **listings**, the *Athens News* does an imperfect job of distilling the quality Greek and foreign offerings from the grade-B bedroom romps and kung fu flicks; their daily selection, moreover, is notoriously unreliable and there's no real substitute for checking current posters at the entrance.

Among **indoor cinemas**, a cluster regularly showing English-language films can be found in three main areas: Patissíon/Kipséli; downtown, on the three main thoroughfares connecting Omónia and Síntagma; and Ambelókipi. **Oldies** and **art films** tend to be shown at the *Asti* on Koraï downtown (*D3*), the *Attikon* (Stadhíou 19; *D3*) and the *Alkionis* (Ioulianoú 42, Platía Viktorías, *B2*) and the *Studio* (Stavropoúlou 33, Platía Amerikís, Kipséli, *off map*). Catch **horror/cult films** at the *Plaza* (Kifissiás 118, Ambelókipi, *off map*) , the *Philip* (Platía Amerikís/Thássou 11, *off map*), the *Amalia* (Dhrossopoúlou 197, *off map*) and *Alfaville* (Mavromiháli 168, *C4*).

The summer **outdoor screens** are less imaginative in their selections – second-run offerings abound – though to attend simply for the film is to miss much of the entertainment's purpose. You may in any case never hear the soundtrack above the din of Greeks cracking *passatémpo* (pumpkin seeds), drinking, and conversing. The most central and stable outdoor venue is to be found by the Zappíon in the National Gardens.

Consuming Interests: Markets and Shops

You can buy just about anything in Athens – for a price – and, even on a purely visual level, the city's **markets** and **bazaar** areas are worth an hour or two's wandering (see p.59). Among the markets, don't miss the Athinás foodhalls (a previously mentioned source of exceptional and cheap meals), nor, if you're into bargain-sifting through junk, the Sunday morning **flea markets** in Monastiráki and Pireás.

● THE MARKETS

The Athens **flea market** spreads over a half dozen or so blocks around Monastiráki square each Sunday from around 6am until noon. In parts it is an extension of the tourist trade – the shops in this area are promoted as a 'flea market' every day of the week – but there is authentic Greek junk, too, notably along (and off) Iféstou and Pandhróssou streets (*E2/3*). The real McCoy is just a bag of odds and ends strewn on the ground – dive in.

For the more seriously inclined, **Pireás** – at similar times on Sunday mornings – has less tourists and more goods. There is business antique trading among the stalls, as well as the more simple commerce of ordinary people offloading ordinary (sometimes extraordinarily ordinary) everyday items. The market is concentrated in a couple of streets just behind the Aktí Possidhónios seafront (see the plan on p.111).

In addition, many **neighbourhoods** have a *laikí agorá* – **street market** – on a set day of the week. Usually running from 7am to 2pm, these are inexpensive, enjoyable and offer household items and dry goods for sale as well as meat, cheese and produce. The most centrally located ones are: **Monday**, Hánsen in Patissíon (*A20*); **Tuesday**, Levoú in Kipséli (*off map*) and Láskou in Pangráti (*off map*); **Friday**, Xenokrátous in Kolonáki (*D5*) and Arhimídhous in Méts (*F5*); and **Saturday**, Plakendías in Ambelókipi (one of the largest; *off map*) and Kallidhromíou in Exárhia (*C3*).

Finally, if you're after live Greek **plants or herbs**, there's a Sunday-morning gathering of stalls on Vikéla street in Patissíon (*off map*) and daily plants/flowers on sale at the Platía Ayía Iríni near Ermoú (*E2*).

● SPECIALIST SHOPS

A selection of the most functional and the most fun:

Books

Compendium, Níkis 28 (upstairs), off Síntagma (*E3*). Friendliest and best value of the English-language bookstores, featuring Penguins, Picadors, *Rough Guides* and other English-language paperbacks, plus a small secondhand section.

Eleftheroudhakis, Níkis 4 (*E3*). Probably the best source of books about Greece – in English and Greek – and a good general English-language stock, too.

Pantelidhes, Amerikís 11 (*D4*). Combines (some of) the virtues of the above two but in a cramped space.

I Folia tou Vivliou, Panepistimíou 25 (*D4*), in the arcade. Best selection of fiction and social science paperbacks in the city.

Estia, Sólonos 62 (*D30*). Big Greek bookshop, specialising in modern history, politics, folk traditions, etc.

Vassiotis, Iféstou 24, Monastiráki (*E2*). Huge basement secondhand bookshop with an arrangement that looks like a bomb hit it.

Camping, hiking and biking supplies

Army/Navy, Kinettoú 4, on Ayíou Filíppou square (*E2*). Large central store good for ponchos, stoves, mess kits, etc.

Pindhos, Leofóros Alexándhras 4, across from the Attica KTEL bus stop on Mavromatéon (*B3*). State-of-the-art hiking/climbing gear (Lowe packs, ice axes, skis, foam pads, etc).

Iféstou street, off Monastiráki square (*E2*). Numerous stalls along Iféstou sell used, military surplus and off-brand canteens, boots, jungle gear, sleeping bags, duffels, etc.

Tsipidhis, Stournára 51/Leof. Kifissiás 131 (*C2*); *Alberto's*, Patissíon 37 (in the arcade, *B2*); *Theodhorakou*, Ahárnon 40 (*C2*). Bike repairs, parts and sales.

National Statistical Service (*Ethnikí Statistikí Ipiresía*), Likoúrgou 14 (*D2*). Topographic maps for hikers (1:200,000 scale). Open weekdays 8am–1.30pm; bring your passport. The office has a sale of old surplus maps on the last day of each month.

Crafts

National Welfare Organisation, Voukourestíou 24a (*D4*). Rugs, embroideries, copperware – traditional craft products made in remote country districts under the sponsorship of this welfare outfit. The place to go if you're looking for something genuinely 'typical Greek'.

YWCA, Amerikís 11 (*D3*). The XEN (YWCA) runs a small shop on the left of the entrance, selling a small stock of goods similar to the above.

ADC, Valaorítou 4 (*D4*). A highly original modern potter has her base here. Prices aren't cheap, but nor are they exorbitant considering this is one of the world's best.

Stavros Melissinos, Pandhróssou 89, off Monastiráki (*E3*). The 'poet-sandalmaker' of Athens – see p.59. The sandals perhaps translate better than the poems but nevertheless an inspiring (and not especially inflated) place to be cobbled.

Records

If you hear music you like, or want to explore Greek sounds of bygone days (or the present), refer to the discography in *Contexts* and then try the selections below. Worth knowing, too, is that new rock LPs (pressed in Greece) are very cheap – though beware they haven't warped in the sun.

Pop 11, Pindhárou 38/corner Tsakálof, Kolonáki (*D4*). The best general record shop – huge stocks of traditional and contemporary music (*all* Greek rock is here!), house label pressings of *rembétika* discs and a fount of knowledge.

Musiki Gonia, corner Panepistimíou/Ippokrátous (*D3*). An even larger range of traditional Greek music – though less helpful and unwilling to play anything for listening.

Iféstou street (*E2*). A trio of shops on Iféstou, west of Monastiráki square, are worth a browse for Greek music: the basement *7 + 7*; an unnamed arcade stall next door to *Vassiotis*; and another, also unnamed, at the corner of Astíngos and Ayíou Filíppou. All will let you listen to short sections of potential purchases.

Sweets and speciality food

Ionás, Sólonos 52, Kolonáki (*D4*). Dark, old-fashioned shop run by three brothers from Constantinople, who brought with them the secrets of oriental sweet-making. Nothing to look at from the outside, but the promised land for sticky-cake addicts.

Aristokratiko, Kolonáki square (*D4*). Mountains of chocolates and *loukoúmia* (Turkish delight), sold by the weight.

La Chocolatière, Skoufá/corner Dhimokrítou, Kolonáki (*D4*). The most exquisite chocolates and cakes in town. Come for a present if you're invited to a Greek's nameday, or simply to indulge.

Fruit and nuts shop, corner Likavitoú/Alex. Soútsou, Kolonáki (*D4*). A nameless shop – but renowned for its roast pistachios, almonds, walnuts and *oúzo*.

The Tibetan Centre, Korinthías 25, Ambelókipi (*off map*); *Health House*, Pireós 14-16, Omónia (*D2*); *Health Shop #1*, Iraklítou 9a, Kolonáki (*D4*); *Katerina Pasali*, Evripídhou 20, Central Bazaar (*D2*); *Propolis*, Fedhíou 3 (parallel to Panepistimíou, *D3*); and *To Stari*, Dhimitrakopoúlou 53, Koukáki (*G3*). All central and convenient outlets for **vegetarian/ health** foods. Herbs and herb teas are sold dry and fresh at most street markets and at the Athinás bazaar.

Listings

Airlines *Olympic* (Ticket office at Óthonos 6, on Síntagma, *E3*; ☎929-2555; main office at Leof. Singroú 96, *G3*; ☎929-2111); *Alitalia* (Níkis 10, *E3*; ☎324-4315); *Balkan* (Níkis 23, *E3*; 322-4315); *British Airways* (Óthonos 10, *E3*; ☎322-2521); *Egyptair* (Óthonos 10, *E3*; ☎323-3575); *El Al* (Óthonos 8, *E3*;

☎323-0116); *KLM* (Voulís 22, *E3*; ☎324-2991); *SAS* (Sína 6, *D3*; 363-4444); *PanAm* (Óthonos 4, *E3*; 323-5242); *Turkish Airlines* (Filellínon 19, *E4*; 322 2569); *TWA* Xenofóndos 8, *E4*; ☎323-6831). **Note** that almost all these addresses – Singroú apart (which is south of the Temple of Olympian Zeus) – are within 100m or so of Síntagma.

Airport enquiries ☎981-1201 for Olympic flight enquiries; ☎906-9466 for all other carriers.

American Express Poste Restante and money changing at the main branch at Ermoú 2 (1st floor), on the corner of Síntagma (*E3*). Mail desk open Mon.–Fri. 8.30am-5.30pm, Sat. 8.30am–1.30pm; banking facilities open Mon.–Thur. 8.30am– 2pm, Fri. 8.30am–1.30pm, Sat. 8.30am–12.30am.

Banks The *National Bank of Greece* in Síntagma (*E3*) stays open for **exchange** Mon.–Fri. 8 am–8 pm, Sat.–Sun. 8 am–2 pm. Other banks, keeping normal hours of Mon.–Thurs. 8am–2pm, Fri. 8am–1.30pm only, include the *Commercial Bank* (Sofokléos 11, *D2*), *Ionian & Popular Bank* (Panepistimíou 45/corner Pezmazóglou, *D3*), *Barclays* (Voukourestíou 15, off Panepistimíou, *D4*, ☎361-9222), *Midland Bank* (Sekéri 1a, Kolonáki, *D5;* ☎364-7410), and *National Westminster* (Stadhíou 24, *D3*; ☎325-0924). *Royal Bank of Scotland* have a branch in Pireás (Aktí Miaoúli 61; ☎452-7483).

Bicycles Good bike shops include: *Tsipidhis* (Stournára 51/Leof. Kifissías 131, *off map*); *Alberto's* (Patissíon 37, inside the arcade, *C2*); and *Theodhorakou* (Aharnón 40, *B2*). The *Greek Cycling Federation* is at Bouboulínas 28 (☎833-1414).

Buses For information on buses out of Athens (and the respective terminals) see 'Travel Details' at the end of this chapter.

Camera repair Most central at *Pikopoulos*, Lékka 26 (off Ermoú, *E3*), 3rd floor. All makes; remove easily lost accessories and get an estimate.

Car hire A number of companies are to be found along Leofóros Singroú (*F3*), including *Just* (43), *InterRent* (4), *Thrifty* (24) and *Autorent* (118); the latter two give student discounts.

Car repairs, tyres, and assistance Good for VW van repair is *Stamatis Papageorgiou*, Leof. Singroú 216 (*off map*). Other (reputably) reliable garages include; *Mavtis*, Leof. Singroú 8, *F3* (Citroens); *Leonidas Fragos*, Mínos 21, Kinosárgous, off Leof. Vougliaménis 104 on the way to the airport, *off map* (Fiats and Simcas); Thisséos 7, *E1* (Renaults) and Thisséos 226 (*off map*, Austin Minis). Tyre shops are grouped between 60-80 Tritis Septemvríou (north of Omónia, *B2*). **ELPA** – the Greek AAA equivalent – gives free **help and information** to foreign motorists at Leof. Mesoyíon 2 (northeast of Likavitós, *off map*) and at the Athens Tower in Ambelókipi. For **Emergency Assistance** ☎104 (free).

Dentists Free treatment at the Evangelismos Hospital (Ipsilándou 45, Kolonáki, *D5*) and at the Pireás Dentistry School (*Odhondoiatrikó Skolío*, corner Thivón/Livadhiás). If you're insured for private fees check the ads in the *Athens News* or ask your embassy for addresses.

Embassies/Consulates BRITAIN, Ploutárhou 1, Kolonáki, *D5* (☎723-6211); IRELAND, Vass. Konstantínou 7, *E5* (☎723-2771); AUSTRALIA, Mesoyíon 15, *off map* (☎360-4611); NEW ZEALAND, An. Tsóha 15, Ambelókipi, *off map* (☎641-0311); NETHERLANDS, Vass. Konstantínou 5-7 (☎723-9701); DENMARK, Filikís Eterías 15 (☎724-9315); NORWAY, Vass. Konstantínou 7, *E5* (☎724-6173); SWEDEN, Vass. Konstantínou 7, *E5* (☎729-0421); USA, Vas. Sofías 91, *off map* (☎721-2951); CANADA, Ioánnou Yennadhíou 4, *D5* (☎723-9511).

Visa sections: EGYPT, Zalakósta 1, *D4* (Mon.–Fri. 8am–noon); ISRAEL, Marathonodhrómon 1, Paleó Psihikó, *off map* (Tues.–Fri. 10am–noon); TURKEY, Vass. Yioryíou 8, *E5* (Mon.– Fri. 8.30am–noon); HUNGARY, Kalvoú 10, Paleó Psihikó, *off map* (Mon., Wed., Fri. 10am–noon); BULGARIA, Akadhimías 12, *D4* (Mon., Wed., Fri., Sat. 10am–noon); YUGOSLAVIA, Évrou 25, *off map* (Mon.–Fri. 9–11.30am); INDIA, Mérlin 10, *D4* (Mon.–Fri. 10am–noon). **Note**: Unless you are resident in Greece, it takes four weeks or more to obtain an Indian visa; if you need one, it's easier to fly to Nepal and obtain it there.

Emergencies Dial the tourist police (☎171, 24hr.) for medical or other assistance. In case of a **medical emergency**, if you can travel safely don't wait for an ambulance. Get a taxi straight to the hospital address that the Tourist Police give you.

Football The Athens team *Panathinaikós*, owned by the shipping magnate Yiorgos Vardinoyannis, is Greece's wealthiest and as a rule most successful club. Catch them at the 25,000-capacity stadium on Leof. Alexándhras (*B5*). Their traditional rival, *Olympiakós* of Pireás (owned until recently by Koskotas, the man at the centre of the 1988 Bank of Crete scandal) plays at the Karaïskáki stadium (by the Néo Fáliron metro stop, see the Pireás map on p.111). Also worth looking out for are *AEK*, which has had some recent European success. Football being an obsession in Greece (there are *daily* sports papers), fixtures are not hard to discover: just ask at a kiosk or bar.

Gay groups The *Autonomous Group of Gay Women* meet weekly at *The Women's House* (see 'Women's movement', below). *AMFI*, the (predominantly male) Greek Gay Liberation Movement, has an office at Zalóngou 6 (Mon.–Fri. 6–11pm) and produces a regular magazine (in Greek).

Greek language courses Try the *Hellenic American Union*, Massalías 22, *D4*; the *Ionic Centre*, Strat. Sindésmou 12, *D4*; the *Athens Centre*, Arhimídhous 48, Pangráti, *F5*; the *Hellenic Language School*, (Zalóngou 4, *D4*; or the *XEN* (YWCA), Amerikís 11, *D3*.

Hiking The *EOS* (Hellenic Alpine Club) headquarters is at Eólou 68–70 (☎321-2429).

Hospital clinics For minor injuries the *Hellenic Red Cross* (Trítis Septemvríou/Kapodhistríou, *C2*) is fairly good; the *Woman's House* (see below) has addresses of English-speaking gynaecologists.

Inoculations for travellers *Vaccination Centre*, Leofóros Alexándhras 196/corner Vas. Sofías, Ambelókipi, *off map*. Open Mon.–Fri. 8am–noon only for quick, clean shots: cholera, typhoid, tetanus, typhus, yellow fever (this last only given Tues. and Fri.). Most jabs are free. ☎642-7846 for details.

Kiosks Remember that an Athenian kiosk (*períptero*) will stock virtually everything not on this list, from soap to plastic crucifixes.

Laundry Numerous cleaners shops will do your laundry for you – at a price; there are real live coin-ops at Angélou Yerónda 10, off Platía Fillimoussís Eterías ('Platía Pláka', *F3*), at Xenofóndos 10 (*F3*) nearby and at Veïkoú 107 (below Platía Koukakíou).

Lost property The transport police have a lost property office (*Grafío Haménon Andikiménon*) at Áy. Konstantínou 33 (*D2*) (☎523-0111).

Luggage storage Best arranged with your hotel; many places will keep the bulk of your luggage for free while you head off to the islands. *Pacific Ltd.* (Níkis 24, *E3*) stores luggage for 1000dr a piece per month; 350dr per week.

Mount Athos permits See *Chapter Five* for details, if you're planning a trip to Athos. In Athens, the Ministry of Foreign Affairs (Zalakósta 2, off Leof. Vas. Sofías, *E4*) is the first stop in securing a permit; office hours are Mon.–Fri. 8am–1pm.

Opticians Quick repairs at *Paraskevopoulos* (Stadhíou 4, *D3*); also at Karyióryi Servías 8-10 (*E3*).

OTE See *Phones* below for details of the OTE offices.

Parcel post To send home personal effects, use the post office in the arcade behind Stadhíou 4 (7.30am–3pm, weekdays only). Paper and string are supplied – *you* bring box and tape. 'Surface/air lift' will get parcels home to North America or Europe in two weeks. For souvenirs, a branch at Níkis 37 (*E3*) expedites shipments and minimizes duty/declaration problems.

Peace movement Contact the *International Group for Nuclear Disarmament* (☎895-8349 or 252-9846).

Pharmacies (*farmakía*) Most pharmacists speak English. The *Marinopoulos* branches (in Patissíon and Panepistimíou streets, *C2/D3*) are particularly good and also sell homeopathic remedies, as does (supposedly) any establishment with a green cross outside.

Phones You can phone locally from a *períptero* (kiosk); pay on completion of your call(s). Blue-topped booths may be quieter but require exact change. International calls can be made from orange-topped phone-kiosks or at the OTE offices at Stadhíou 15 (*D3*) and Patissíon/28 Oktovríou (*B2*), open 17 and 24 hours a day respectively.

Post Offices (*Tahidhromío*) For ordinary letters and parcels up to two kilograms, the branch on Síntagma (corner Mitropóleos, *E3*) is open Mon.–Fri. 7.30am–8pm, Sat. 8am–3pm, Sun. 9am– 1.30pm.

Poste restante Main post office for Athens is at Eólou 100, just off Omónia, *D2* (Mon.–Sat. 7.30am–8.30pm).

Swimming pools There's a public pool in the university at Patissíon 281 (*C2/3*). The *Park Hotel*, Leof. Alexándhras, Ghízi (north of Likavitós, *B3*), has a rooftop pool free for the price of a drink or two.

Tourist Police Head office at Leof. Singroú 7 (behind the Temple of Olympian Zeus). ☎171.

Train tickets The *OSE* (Greek State Railways) offices at Sína 6 (behind the National Library/University, *C1*) and Karólou 1 (near Omónia, *D3*) give out information and sell tickets and InterRail passes; international tickets and information at Filellínon 21 (*D4*).

Travel agencies Most budget and youth/student agencies are to be found just off Síntagma, in and around Filellínon and Níkis streets. The cheapest ferry tickets to Italy are usually sold through the Irish student travel company *USIT* (Filellínon 1; ☎324-1884) or *Transalpino* (Níkis 28). Among other agencies, *Highway Express* (Níkis 40), *Periscope* (Filellínon 22), *Himalaya* (Filellínon 7) and *Arcturus* (Apóllonos 20) are worth scanning for air travel deals. For the hardy, the widest range of north-bound coaches is still available at *Magic Bus* (Filellínon 20). All these addresses are *E3/F3*.

Women's movement Most accessible of the women's groups is the *Multinational Liberation Group of Athens* (Mavromiháli 69, ☎867-0523). Like most other organisations, they meet (currently at 8.30pm, Wed.) at *The Women's House*, Románou Melódhou 4, Likavitós, *C3* (☎281-4823).

Work/residence permits, visa extensions Aliens' Bureau (*Ipiresía Allodhapón*), Halkokondhíli 9, Pl. Káningos, *C3*; open Mon.–Fri. 8am–1pm but go early or you won't get seen.

ATTICA

Attica (*Attiki*), the region encompassing the capital, is not much explored by tourists. Only the great romantic ruin of the **Temple of Apollo at Sounion** is on the excursion-circuit. The rest, if seen at all, tends to be for the functional reason of escaping to the islands – from the ports of **Pireás**, **Rafina** (whose ferry journeys can be quicker and cheaper to many of the Cyclades), or **Lávrio** (which serves Kéa and Kíthnos).

The neglect is not surprising. The mountains of Imittós, Pendéli, and Párnitha, which surround Athens on three sides, are progressively less successful in confining the urban sprawl, and the routes out of the city to south and west are unenticing to say the least. But if you're planning on a reasonable stay in the capital, a day trip or two, or a brief circuit by car, can make a rewarding break. And there is much of Greece in microcosm to be seen within an hour or two's ride: mountainside at **Párnitha**, beautiful minor sites in **Brauron** and **Rhamnous**, and the odd unspoiled beach, too, between the resorts.

Pireás (Piraeus)

PIREÁS has been the port of Athens since Classical times. Today it is a substantial metropolis in its own right, containing much of Greater Athens' industries, as well as the various commercial activities associated with a port: banking, import-export, freight, and so on. For most visitors, however, it is Pireás's inter-island ferries that provide a focus, and the reason for coming.

There is little to distinguish the city as you approach; its scruffy web of suburbs merging with those of Athens.

The ancient port was founded at the beginning of the fifth century B.C. by Themistocles, who realised the potential of its three natural harbours. His work was consolidated by Pericles with the building of the 'Long Walls' to protect the corridor to Athens. During Byzantine and medieval times the place was deserted – there was just one building, a monastery, at the end of the War of Independence – but from the 1830s on the city grew by leaps and bounds. The original influx into the port was a group of immigrants from Híos, whose island had been devastated by the Turks; later came populations from Ídhra, Crete and the Peloponnese. By the time of World War I Pireás had outstripped the island of Síros as the nation's first port, its strategic position in the Mediterranean highlighted by the opening of the Suez and Corinth canals (in 1862 and 1893 respectively).

It was natural that in 1923, with the exchange of populations with Turkey, over 100,000 Asia Minor Greeks decided to settle in the city. This doubled the population and gave Pireás a semi-underworld culture – expressed most enduringly in the 'outcast' music, *rembetika*, played in hashish dens along the waterside. Sadly, the culture was suppressed in the early 1950s. What you find today is little different from anything in Athens, save for the numbers (and diversity) of the sailors waiting between boats. Economically, the port is at present on a mild upswing, boosted by a couple of pushy, go-ahead mayors and perhaps also by the public prominence of one of its deputies, the former actress and current Minister of Culture, Melina Mercouri.

The Port

Pireás is unashamedly a functional place, with its port despatching up to sixty ships a day in season, both to the islands and to a range of international destinations.

There are few sights. The ancient walls are long gone, and the junta years saw misguided demolition of most later buildings of character. But there's a nice enough **park** (three blocks back from the main harbour, intersected by Vassiléos Konstantínou); a scattering of genuine antique/junk shops, full of peasant copper and wood, plus a big **Sunday morning flea market**, near Platía Ipodhamías, at the top end of Goúnari (behind the railway station). Nearby are a couple of respectable museums. The **Archaeological Museum** (Hariláou Trikoúpi 31; daily 9am–3pm, Sun. 10am–2pm; closed Tues.) holds most of interest, including superb bronzes of Artemis and Athena dragged up from the harbour. The **Naval Museum** (Tues.–Sat. 9.30–12.30) is more specialist, tracing developments with models and the odd ancient piece.

Culturally, there's not a great deal going on, though a summer festival, run alongside that of Athens, features events in the open-air theatre back from the yacht harbour of Mikrolímano (or Tourkolímano, as it has been called for centuries). In winter there's always **football**: Olympiakós are the big Pireás team, rivals to the capital's AEK and Panathenaïkós. Swimming is best kept for your arrival on the islands, even though the more hardened locals wade out into the polluted waters from the **beach** west of the Zéa Marína.

PIREÁS

1. Argo-Saronic Ferries and Eyina Hydrofoil
2. Crete and Aegean Ferries
3. Aegean Ferries
4. International Ferries
5. Flying Dolphins for Póros, Idhra, Spétses, Monemvassía, etc

To Athens

AKTI KONDHILI

Train Station (Peloponnese)

TH. RETSINA

Train Station (Northern Greece)

AK. KALIMASIOU

DH. MOUTSÓPOULOU

KERASKAKI

DH. GOUNARI

AF. POSEIDONOS

SKILITSI

New Market

ETH. ANDISTASEOS

Post Office

FILONOS

Main Harbour

To Athens

ATHINON

AKTI MIAOULIS

Theatre

KOLOKOTRONI

VASSILEOS KONSTANTINOU

Custom House

FILONOS

KOLOKOTRONI

VASSILEOS KONSTANTINOU

Bus 041 for Athens

TROKHIDHROMON

LEOFOROS YIORYIOU ANDHROÚTSOU

VASSILISSIS SOFIAS (EL VENIZELOU)

Archaeological Museum

Naval Museum

AKTI MOUTSOUPOLOU

Zéa Marina

YOUGLÁ

THEATROU

Olympiákos Stadium

TSAVELLA

Néo Fáliron Metro

Open-air Theatre

FALIROU

K. SERFA

Mikrolímano

Express ⌗19 Bus stops
A. Mégaro
B. Telónio
C. Aktí Tzelépi

Perhaps the most fulfilling pursuit is to check out some of the port's excellent **eating options**. If you're simply looking for food to take on board, or breakfast, you'll find numerous places (as well as several budget restaurants) around the market area, back from the waterside Aktí Miaoúli/Eth. Andistáseos, open from 6.30am onward. For more substantial meals, there are a string of *ouzerí* and seafood tavernas along Aktí Themistokléous, west of the Zéa Marina, most of them pretty good and normally priced. Or, for a real blowout, there is *Vassilena's* (Etolikoú 72), an old grocery store whose set menu provides *mezédhes* enough to defy all appetites; at 1500dr a head it's not cheap, but enough Athenians consider it worth the drive out that most evenings you need to book ahead for a table (☎461-2457). Very much more upmarket, though serving some excellent seafood, are the line of tavernas around Mikrolímano – a nice stroll over the hill, in any case.

Few visitors **stay** in Pireás, and most of the hotels are geared to a steady clientele of seamen, resting between ships. For this reason, picking a place at random is not always a good idea. Two more or less recommendable possibilities are the *Enos* (Andistáseos 14, off Goúnari) and the slightly more savoury *Galaxia* (Sahtoúri 18, off Aktí Miaoúli). Both cost around 900dr single, 1100dr double.

Sleeping rough in Platía Karaïskáki, as some exhausted travellers end up doing, is unwise. If thieves or the police don't rouse you, streetcleaners armed with hoses certainly will – at 5am.

Getting to Pireás

The easiest way to get to Pireás from Athens is on the **metro**. There are central stops in Athens at Omónia and Monastiráki squares; the journey takes about 25 minutes to the Pireás train station stop (the end of the line). Metro trains run from 5.30am to midnight: they're free until 8am, thereafter the flat fare is 30dr.

The alternatives are to go by bus or taxi. **Green bus #041** (about every 20 min. during the day; hourly from 1am-5am) will deposit you on Vassiléos Konstantínou, half a dozen blocks from the docks, but they're very slow. The new **express buses** (see *Athens: Points of Arrival*) are quicker and a particularly useful link with the airport. **Taxis** run at about 700dr from the centre of Athens or the airport – worth considering, especially if you're taking one of the hydrofoils from the Zéa Marína (see below).

The Ferries

If you're staying in Athens prior to heading out to the islands, it is worth calling in at the EOT office in Síntagma to pick up a **schedule of departures**. These are never to be relied upon implicitly, but they do give a reasonable indication of what boats are leaving, when and for where. Most of the boats

---

Aegean departures (Cyclades, Dodecanese, North/East Aegean). Leave from either Aktí Possidhónios, the quay right in front of the metro station (*2*), or from Aktí Kondhíli (perpendicular to Possidhónios), or from the end of the promontory (Aktí Tzelépi) by Platía Karaïskáki (*3*).
Crete. Most ferries dock at Aktí Possidhónios (*2*) but a few may also use the promontory by Platía Karaïskáki (*3*).
Argo-Saronic. Ordinary ferries (and the **hydrofoils for Éyina**) leave further down Aktí Possidhónios (*1*), 10 min. walk from the metro.
International destinations (Limassol, Haifa, Alexandria, etc). Leave farther around the main harbor (*4*), towards the Customs House (where you should check passports before boarding).
Hydrofoils. Except for departures direct to Éyina, these leave from the Zéa Marina, a twenty-minute uphill walk from the metro. Tickets are on sale from the *Flying Dolphins* office at the quay about an hour before departure: to be sure of a particular departure in season, it is wise to book ahead in Athens. Equally, if your schedule is tight, book your ticket back to Pireás as soon as you arrive at the destination; return tickets, confusingly, are not issued.

leave between 7am and 8.30am or 2 and 3pm, though for Crete, Híos, and Lésvos there are additional evening departures from 6 to 7pm.

Buying tickets is not necessary until you arrive at Pireás, unless you're taking a car on board (in which case consult agents in Athens). The best plan is to get to Pireás early, say at 6.30am, and check with the various **shipping agents** around the metro station and in the quayside Platía Karaïskáki. Keep in mind that many of these act only for particular lines; for a full picture of the various boats sailing ask at three or four outlets. Prices for all domestic boat journeys are standardised but the quality of the craft and circuitousness of routes vary greatly. If you are heading for Thíra (Santorini) or Rhodes, for example, try to get a boat that stops at only three or four islands en route; for Crete settle for direct ferries only.

Boats for different destinations leave from a variety of points along the main harbour, *usually* following the pattern in the box opposite, but leave time for wayward ships and look for the signs (indicating name of boat and a clockface with departure time) hung in front of the relevant boats on the waterside railings or on the stern of the boats themselves.

Sounion, the 'Apollo Coast' and Lávrio

The seventy kilometres of coast south of Athens – the tourist-board-dubbed **'Apollo Coast'** – has some good but highly developed beaches. At week-ends, when Athenians flee the city, the sands fill fast, as, by night, do the innumerable bars, restaurants, and discos. If this is what you're after, then resorts like Glifádha and Vouliagméni are functional enough. But for most foreign visitors, the coast's lure is at the end of the road, in the form of the Temple of Poseidon at **Cape Sounion**.

Access to Sounion (Soúnio in the modern spelling) is straightforward. There are **buses** on the hour and half-hour from the KTEL terminal (D on the Athens map; *B2*) on Mavromatéon at the southwest corner of Áreos Park; they have an additional and more central (but in summer, very full) stop ten minutes later on Filellínon street, south of Síntagma (corner of Xenofóndos, in front of the *Middle East Airways* office). There are both coastal (*paraliakó*) and inland (*mesoyiakó*) services, the latter slightly longer and more expensive. The coast route normally takes around two hours; last departures back to Athens are posted at the Sounion stop.

For Glifádha–Voúla and Vouliagméni–Várki – the main resorts – there are additional, more regular, city buses from the Zappíon gardens (stop E on the Athens map; *F4*). Most frequent are #115, #116 and #117.

The Temple of Poseidon at Sounion

Site open daily 9am until sunset; Sun. from 10am.
Cape Sounion – Akrí Soúnio – is one of the most imposing spots in Greece, a clear landmark for boats sailing between Pireás and the islands, and an equally dramatic vantage point in itself to look out over the Aegean. On its tip stands the fifth-century B.C. **Temple of Poseidon**, built in the time of Pericles as part of a major sanctuary to the sea god.

The temple's fame is due above all to Byron, who visited in 1810, carved his name on the nearest pillar (an unfortunate precedent), and commemorated the event as the finale of his hymn to Greek independence, the *Isles of Greece* segment of *Don Juan*:

Place me on Sunium's marbled steep,
  Where nothing, save the waves and I,
May hear our mutual murmurs sweep;
  There, swan like, let me sing and die:
A land of slaves shall ne'er be mine –
  Dash down yon cup of Samian wine!

In summer, at least, there is faint hope of solitude, unless you slip into the site before the tours arrive. But the temple is as evocative a ruin as Greece can offer. Doric in style, it was probably built by the architect of the Thiseion in the Athens agora. That it is so admired and visited, in contrast to the Athens temple, is due mainly to its site, but also perhaps to its state of ruin – preserving, as if by design, sixteen of its thirty-four columns. The view from the temple takes in the islands of Kéa, Kíthnos, and Sérifos, to the southeast, Éyina and the Peloponnese to the west.

The rest of the site is of more academic interest. There are remains of a fortification wall around the sanctuary; a *propylaion* (entrance hall) and *stoa*; and, to the north, the foundations of a small temple to Athena.

Below the promontory are several **coves** – the most sheltered a five-minute walk east from the car park and site entrance. The main Soúnio beach is more crowded, but has a group of tavernas at the far end – fairly reasonably priced, considering the location. If you want to stay, there are a couple of **campsites** just around the coast: *Camping Bacchus* (the nearest; ☎0292/39-262) and *Sounion Beach Camping* (5km; ☎0292/39-358).

The Resorts and Lávrio

Although some Greeks swim at Pireás itself, few would recommend the sea much before **GLIFÁDHA**, half an hour's drive from the capital. The major resort along the 'Apollo Coast', merged more or less indistinguishably with its neighbour VOÚLA, it is lined with seafood restaurants, ice-cream bars, and discos, as well as a couple of marinas and a golfcourse. Its popularity, though, is hard to fathom, built as it is in the shadow of the East Airport. The only possible appeal is in the beaches, the best of which is the *Astir*, privately owned and with a 200dr admission charge; others are gritty. Hotels are all on the expensive side, and in any case permanently occupied in season by package firms; there is a **campsite** at Voúla (☎01-895-2712).

VOULIAGMÉNI, which in turn has swallowed up KAVOÚRI, is a little quieter than Glifádha, and a little ritzier. Set back from a small natural lake, it boasts a waterski school, some extremely chi-chi restaurants, and an EOT pay-beach. Again, budget accommodation is hard to come by, though there is a **campsite** (and another EOT pay-beach) just to the south at **VÁRKIZA**.

South of Várkiza, there are further beaches en route to Soúnio, though unless you've a car to pick your spot they're not really worth the effort. The resorts of **LAGONÍSSI** and **ANÁVISSOS** are in the Glifádha mould, and only slightly less crowded despite the extra distance from Athens.

Ten kilometres north of Soúnio, around the cape, **LÁVRIO** has daily ferry connections with Kéa and a couple weekly with Kíthnos. Its ancient predecessor, Laurion, was famous for its silver mines – a mainstay of the Classical Athenian economy and worked almost exclusively by slaves. The port today remains an industrial and mining town, now for less precious minerals, and houses the country's main transport camp for political refugees – mostly Turks and Kurds, with a scattering of East Europeans, awaiting resettlement in North America, Australia, or Europe. The island offshore, **Makrónissos**, now uninhabited, has a more sinister refugee past: it was here that communists were imprisoned in 're-education' labor camps during and after the civil war.

If you are in Lávrio with time to kill, the site of **ancient Thoriko** lies down a zigzag track from the village of PLÁKA, 5km north. A defensive outpost of the mining area in Classical times, the town has prominent ruins of a theatre, engineered into an irregular slope in the hill.

Lávrio can be reached by **bus** from the Mavromatéon terminal in Athens, or from Soúnio.

East: Imittós, The Mesóyia, and Brauron

The area east of Athens is one of the least visited parts of Attica. The mountain of **Imittós** (Mt. Hymettus) forms an initial barrier, with Kessarianí on its cityside flank. Beyond extends the plateau of the **Mesóyia** (literally 'midland'), a gentle landscape whose villages have a quiet fame for their *retsina* and for their churches, many of which date to Byzantine times. On towards the coast, there is the remote and beautiful site of **ancient Brauron**, and the developing resort of **Pórto Ráfti**.

The Mesóyia
The best-known attraction of the Mesóyia is at the village of **PEANÍA**, on the east slope of Imittós. This is the **Koutoúki cave** (daily 10am–5.30pm), with its spectacularly illuminated stalactites and stalagmites and multicoloured curtains of rock. It is fairly easily reached by taking the Athens–Markópoulo bus, stopping at Peanía, and then walking up. Close by the village (just east on the Spáta road) is the chapel of **Áyios Athanásios**, built like so many churches in the region with old Roman blocks and fragments.

MARKÓPOULO, the main Mesóyia village, shelters a further clutch of chapels. Within the village, in a walled garden, stand the twin chapels of **Áyia Paraskeví** and **Ayía Thékla**; ring for admission and a nun will open them up to show seventeenth-century frescoes. Over to the west, on the road to **KOROPÍ**, is one of the oldest churches in Attica, tenth century **Metamórfosi**. The keys to this can be obtained from the church of the Análipsi in Koropí.

Heading east from Markópoulo, the road runs past the unusual double-naved **Ayía Triádha** (2½km out) and on to the coast at **PÓRTO RÁFTI**, whose bay, protected by islets, forms an almost perfect natural harbour. It is in the throes of development, with an EOT pay-beach and a fair number of tavernas, but remains a good place to stay if you can find a room. On the islet of Rafti, facing the harbour, is a huge, curious Roman statue of a woman tailor, probably intended as a beacon.

From here, if you've your own vehicle, you can make your way along the coast road to VRAVRÓNA and the site of Brauron.

Brauron

Site and museum open daily 9am–3pm; Sun. 9.30am–2.30pm; closed Tues.
BRAURON is one of the most enjoyable (though also inaccessible) minor Greek sites. It lies just outside the modern village of VRAVRÓNA (40km from Athens), in a marshy valley at the base of a low, chapel-topped hill.

The remains are of a **Sanctuary of Artemis**, centred on a vast *stoa*. This was the chief building of the Artemis cult, founded, legendarily, by Iphigeneia (whose 'tomb' has also been identified). It was she who, with Orestes, stole the image of Artemis from Tauris (as commemorated in Euripides's *Iphigeneia at Tauris*) and introduced worship of the goddess to Greece. The main event of the cult was a quadrennial festival, now something of a mystery, in which young children dressed as bears to enact a ritual connected with the goddess and childbirth. The 'Stoa of the Bears', where these initiates would have stayed, has been substantially reconstructed, along with a stone bridge; both are fifth-century B.C. and provide a graceful focus to the semi-waterlogged site. Somewhat scantier are the ruins of the temple itself, whose stepped foundations can be made out. At the site **museum**, a short walk from the ruins, various finds from the sanctuary are displayed, along with some explanation of the cult.

Getting to Vravróna from Athens will involve a walk if you're dependent on public transport. There are two alternative approaches. Either get a bus from the Mavromatéon terminal (D on the Athens map, *B3*) to Markópoulo, 8km southwest; or take bus #304 from the Thissío metro (*E1*) to the village of LOÚTSA, 5km north.

Rafína, Marathon and Rhamnous

The port of **RAFÍNA** has ferries to half a dozen of the Cyclades, as well as nearby Évvia. It is connected regularly with Athens: a forty-minute bus trip (from Mavromatéon) through the 'gap' in Mt. Pendéli. Boats aside, the appeal of the place is mainly gastronomic. Though much of the town has been spoilt by tacky seaside development, the little fishing harbour with its line of roof-terrace seafood restaurants remains one of the most attractive spots on the Attic coast. A lunchtime outing is an easy operation, given the frequency of the bus service. Evenings, when it's more fun, you need to arrange your own transport back, or make for the beachside **campsite** at nearby KÓKKINO LIMANÁKI. The town's half dozen hotels are often full; the three cheapest – *Corali* ☎0294/22-477, *Kymata* ☎0294/23-406, and *Rafína* ☎0294/23-460 – are in the Platía N. Plastíra.

The village of **MARATHÓNAS**, 42km from Athens, is on the same bus route. Four kilometres before you arrive, the **Tímvos Marathóna** stands to the side of the road: the ancient burial mound raised over 192 Athenians who died in the city's famous victory over the Persians in 490 B.C.; though ten metres high, it feels a strangely uninspiring monument. A kilometre to the west is a small **archaeological museum** (open, as is the mound precinct, Mon.–Sat. 9am–3pm, Sun. 8.30am-2.30pm; closed Tues.), with a sparse collection of artifacts mainly from the local Cave of Pan, a shrine felt to have aided the victory. Closer to the town is another burial mound, the Tímvos Platéon, built for the Athenians' only allies in the battle. The village itself is a dull place, with just a couple of cafés and restaurants for the passing trade. A more impressive site is **Límni Marathóna** – Marathon Lake – to the west, with its huge marble dam, which provided Athens' entire water supply until the 1950s.

The coast around ancient Marathon takes in some good stretches of sand, walkable from the tomb if you want to cool off. The best and most popular beach is to the north at **SKHINIÁS**, a long, pine-backed strand full of windsurfers at the weekends. There is a **campsite**, *Camping Marathon*, midway on the road from Marathónas.

Farther north are the ruins of **RHAMNOUS**, in a beautiful and totally isolated setting above the sea. Amongst the scattered and overgrown remains is a Doric **Temple of Nemesis**, goddess of retribution. Pausanias records that the Persians who landed nearby before their defeat incurred her wrath by carrying off a marble block – upon which they intended to commemorate their conquest of Athens. There are also the remains of a smaller temple dedicted to Themis, goddess of justice. (Site open Mon.–Sat. 8.45am–3pm, Sun. 9.30am–2.30pm). To get there you really need your own transport.

Párnitha and Phyle

Scarcely an hour's bus ride north from the city centre, **Mount Párnitha** is an unexpectedly vast and virgin tract of forest, rock and ravine. If you've no time for expeditions further afield, Párnitha will give you a taste of what Greek mountains are all about, including a good selection of mountain flowers. If you're here in March or April, it is certainly worth a visit in its own right. Snow lies surprisingly late on the north side, and in its wake carpets of crocus, alpine squills, and mountain windflower spring from the mossy ground, while lower down you find aubretia, tulips, dwarf iris, and a whole range of orchids.

There are numerous waymarked paths on the mountain (look for red discs and paint splodges on the trees). The principal and most representative ones are the approach to the Báfi refuge up the Hoúni ravine, and the walk to the Skípiza spring. These, along with a couple of lesser excursions, to the ancient fort at Phyle and the Cave of Pan, are detailed below.

To the Báfi Refuge

To get to the start of this walk, take bus #726 from the corner of Aharnón and Stournári (top side of Platía Váthi; *C2* on the main Athens map) to Menídhi and change (free) to the #724 on to the suburb of Thrakomedhónes, whose topmost houses are beginning to steal up the flanks of the mountain beside the mouth of the Hoúni ravine. Get off at the highest stop and keep on, bearing left, up Odhós Thrákis to where the road ends at the foot of a cliff beside two new blocks of flats. Keep straight ahead along the foot of the cliff and in a few metres you come on the start of the path. It turns down left into a dry streambed, before crossing and continuing on the opposite bank.

It's about two hours to the refuge, curving slowly leftward up the craggy, well-defined ravine, at first through thick scrub, then through more open forest of Greek fir. You cross the stream two or three times. At a junction reached after about 45 minutes, signposted 'Katára–Mesanó Neró–Móla', keep straight ahead. At the next fork some ten minutes later, keep right. After a further five minutes, at the top of a sparsely vegetated slope, you get your first glimpse of the pink-roofed refuge high on a rocky spur in front of you. Another twenty minutes brings you to the confluence of two small streams, where a sign on a tree points left to Ayía Triádha (see below), and a second path branches right to Móla and Koromiliá. Take the third, middle, path, up a scrubby spur. At the top a broad path goes off left to meet the ring road leading to Ayía Triádha. Turn right, down into the head of a gully, where the path doubles back and climbs up to the **refuge**. Normally the refuge warden provides board and lodging but it would be wise to check opening times with the Athens EOS (see p.107) in advance as the schedule changes periodically. Water is always available at the back of the building.

To the Skípiza spring

For the walk to the Skípiza spring you need bus #714, again from Menídhi (#726 from Aharnón/Stournári). Get off at the chapel of Ayía Triádha in the heart of the mountain. There are two connections a day: at 6.30am, returning at 8am; and at 2pm, returning at 4pm. If you get stuck, you can continue to the *Hotel Mt. Parnes* and take the *téléférique* down.

Skípiza is an hour and a half to two hours' walk away. From the bus stop by the chapel, walk west past the *Hotel-Chalet Kiklamina*, continuing straight onto the ring road. After the first ascent and downhill, you come after fifteen minutes to the Paliohóri spring on the right of the road in the middle of a left-hand bend, opposite a piece of flat ground marked with pointed-hat pipes. The path begins by the spring, following the course of a small stream up through the fir woods. It's well-defined, beautiful, and clearly marked by discs on the trees.

From Skípiza you can continue right around the summit to **Móla** (1½ hr.) and from there, in another hour, back to the Báfi refuge. Alternatively, by setting your back to the Skípiza spring and taking the path that charges up the ridge almost directly behind, you can get to **Báfi** in around forty minutes. Turn left when you hit the tarmac road after about half an hour; follow it ten minutes more down to the ring road and turn left again. In a few paces you are in the refuge parking lot. To get back to Ayía Triádha by the road it's about 6km (an hour's walk).

Phyle

Over to the west of the main Párnitha trails, another route up the mountain will take you to the nearly complete fourth-century B.C. Athenian fort of **Phyle**, about an hour and three quarters' on foot beyond the village of FILÍ (known locally as HASIÁ). Buses to Filí leave near the Aharnón/Stournári stop on Odhós Soúrmeli (*C2*). On the way up to the fort you pass the unattractively restored fourteenth-century monastery of Klistón in the mouth of the Goúra ravine which splits through the middle of the Párnitha range. The walking unfortunately is all on asphalt, but the fort, built to defend the road from Athens to Thebes, is impressive.

The Cave of Pan

Another highly evocative spot for lovers of Classical ghosts is the **Cave of Pan**, which Menander used as the setting for one of his plays. It's not easy to find, but whatever anyone tells you, the easiest access is from the ford where the forest track from Áyia Triádha to Roumáni crosses the Goúra stream. Follow down the true right bank of the stream for five minutes, then, where the gully opens out a bit, cross over and steeply up the left bank. The way is marked by cairns of stones, but they are well-lichened and don't show very clearly. About ten minutes later, just downstream from the confluence of two streams and about twenty metres above the water, you come to the cave, a large overhang shaded by a plane tree.

Eleusis and west to the Peloponnese

The main **highway to Kórinthos** (Corinth) is about as unattractive a road as any in Greece. For the first thirty or so kilometres you have little sense of leaving Athens, whose western suburbs merge into the industrial wastelands of first Elefsína and then Mégara. Offshore, closing off the bay, is the grim and much-polluted island of Salamína. A train or bus direct to Kórinthos or beyond is in many ways the wisest option. Only the site of **ancient Eleusis** is in any way a temptation to stop, and even this is really for the academic.

Eleusis
Daily 8.45am–3pm, Sun. 9.30am–2.30pm.

The Sanctuary of Demeter at **ELEUSIS** was one one of the most important in the Greek world. Here, for two millenia, at the beginning of the Sacred Way to Athens, were performed ritual ceremonies – the mysteries – that had an effect on their ancient initiates the equal of any modern cult. According to Pindar, who undertook the rites in Classical times, and like all others was bound by pain of death not to reveal their content, anyone who had 'seen the holy things (at Eleusis) and goes in death beneath the earth is happy, for he knows life's end and he knows the new divine beginning'.

The basis of the cult was established in Mycenaean times, perhaps as early as 1500 B.C., around the figure of Demeter (Ceres to the Romans), the goddess of corn, and the myth of her daughter Persephone's annual descent into, and resurrection from, the underworld. It was, in some ways, an ancient prefigurement of the Easter ritual: the earth's crops', and its god's, simultaneous rebirth in the miracle of fertility. By the fifth century B.C. the cult had developed into a sophisticated annual festival, attracting up to 30,000 from throughout the Greek world. They gathered in Athens, outside the *propylaia* on the acropolis, and, after various rituals, including mass bathing and purification in Phaleron Bay, followed the Sacred Way to the sanctuary here at Eleusis.

The **ruins** are obscure in the extreme, dating from several different ages of rebuilding and largely reduced to foundations; any mystic imaginings are further hampered by the spectacularly unromantic setting. The best plan is to head straight for the museum, which features models of the site at various stages of its history. This will at least point you in the direction of the **Telesterion**, the windowless Hall of Initiation, where the priests of Demeter would exhibit the 'Holy Things' and speak 'the Unutterable Words'.

To reach the site from Athens, take **bus** #818, #853 or #862 (signposted Elefsína, Skaramangás or Asprópirgos) from Platía Eleftherías (C on the main Athens map; *D2*). Ask to be dropped at the *Heroon* (Sanctuary), to the left of the main road, a short way into Elefsína. The trip can easily be combined with a visit to the monastery at Dhafní (see p.67), on the same road and bus routes.

On from Elefsína

Northwest from Elefsína the **old road to Thebes and Delphi** heads into the hills. This route is covered in the *Central Greece* chapter; it's highly worthwhile, with its detours to ancient Aegosthena and the tiny resort of Pórto Yermenó. At MÉGARA another, more minor road heads north to reach the sea at the village of ALEPOHÓRI, where it deteriorates to a track to loop around to Pórto Yermenó.

Heading directly **west** there are shingle beaches – more or less clear of the pollution – along the old, parallel coastal road at KINÉTA and ÁYII THEÓDHORI. The scenery is good, too, with the Yeránia mountains to the north, those of the Peloponnese across the water. You leave Attica at ISTHMÍA, a village beside the **Corinth Canal**, where most of the buses set you down for a drink by the bridge.

LOUTRÁKI and PERAHÓRA, north of ISTHMÍA, are technically part of Attica but, since they are more easily reached from Kórinthos, are covered in *The Peloponnese* chapter following.

travel details

BUSES

● **Attica** Buses for most destinations in **Attica** (i.e. within this chapter) leave from the **Mavromatéon terminal** (250m north of the National Archaeological Museum, at the junction with Leof. Aiexándhras, 'D' on the Athens map, *B2*). Exceptions are specified in the text.

Destinations include: Sounion (every half hour; 1½ hr.); Rafína (every half hour; 1½ hr.); Marathon Tomb (hourly; 1 hr.).

● **Peloponnese and western/northern Greece** Most buses leave from the terminal at **Kifisoú 100**, easiest reached on the **express bus B or B̄** (see 'Points of Arrival'). Alternatively, take the #051 bus from the corner of Vilará and Menándhrou (near Omónia; 'F' on the map, D2) to the end of its route (about 20 min.).

Destinations include: Agrínio (15 daily; 5 hr.); Árgos (hourly; 2 hr. 45 min.); Árta (8 daily; 6 hr.); Corfu (4 daily; 11 hr.); Édhessa (3 daily; 8½ hr.); Igoumenítsa (3 daily; 8½ hr.); Ioánnina (8 daily; 7½ hr.); Kórinthos (hourly; 1½ hr.); Lefkádha (4 daily; 7 hr.); Mycenae/Náfplio (hourly; 2 hr./3 hr.); Pátra (hourly; 3½ hr.); Olympia (4 daily; 6 hr.); Pílos (2 daily; 6½ hr.); Thessaloníki (7 daily; 7½ hr.); Trípoli (12 daily; 4 hr.); Zákinthos (2 daily; 7 hr.).

● **Central Greece** Buses for most other destinations in central Greece leave from the **Liossíon 260** terminal, easiest reached on the **express bus A or Á**. Alternatively, take either: bus #024 at the Amalías entrance of the National Gardens (by Síntagma, E4), almost to the end of its route (about 25 min.; the stop is 200m south of the terminal); or the metro from Omónia/Monastiráki to the Áyios Nikólaos stop (800m east of the terminal; coming out, go under the rail line, turn left and look out for the coaches).

Destinations include: Delphi (5 daily; 3½ hr.); Halkídha (hourly; 1½ hr.); Karpeníssi (3 daily; 6 hr.); Lamía (hourly; 3¼ hr.); Lárissa (6 daily; 5 hr.); Óssios Loukás (2 daily; 4 hr.); Thíva/Thebes (hourly; 1½ hr.); Tríkala (10 daily; 5½ hr.); Vólos (9 daily; 5 hr.).

OSE buses Express buses from the train station to Pátra, Lárissa, Pírgos, Thessaloníki, Véria, etc.

TRAINS

Trains for **Kórinthos and the Peloponnese** leave from the **Stathmós Peloponíssou**, those for **northern Greece** from **Stathmós Laríssis**; both are just west of Deliyiánni (B/C1). The #1 trolley takes you there, as do Express Buses B and Á. The stop for both stations is the same, but to get to the Peloponnese terminal use the metal overpass starting right next to the main-line station.

Tickets and information for both can be obtained at the more central OSE office at Sína 6 (D3).

HITCHING

● **To Kórinthos/Peloponnese/Patras** Bus to Dhafní; National Road 8 starts at the junction of Leof. Athinón and Ierá Odhós.

● **To Lámia and the north** Bus to the Lióssion 260 terminal (as above), then walk north to the start of National Road 1.

● **Old road to Delphi** Bus to Elefsína.

ISLAND FERRIES

● **Pireás** Ferries and hydrofoils to the Argo-Saronic, Monemvassía, Crete, the Cyclades, Dodecanese and North and East Aegean islands. See p.112 for details on how to get to Pireás.

● **Lávrio** Ferries daily to Kéa; a few weekly to Kíthnos. Bus from Mavromatéon ('D', B2).

● **Rafína** Ferries daily to Mármari, Káristos and Stíra on Évia; most days to Ándhros, Tínos, Síros, Míkonos, Páros and Náxos; less regularly to Amorgós. The Cycladic ferries generally leaves in the **late afternoon or evening**, a boon if you've missed the morning Pireás boats to the islands. Buses from Mavromatéon ('B', D2).

Guideline **schedules** *for all ferries from the EOT in Síntagma (E3), or more reliable information from individual agencies or the port police in Rafína (☎0294/23-300) and Lávrio (☎0202/25-249).*

For Lávrio or Rafína sailings, buy actual tickets at the agencies at the ports, both of which are well-connected by bus to the Mavromatéon terminal in Athens.

See the 'Travel Details' at the end of each island-group section for details on frequency of sailings.

INTERNATIONAL FERRIES

From Pireás Destinations include: Alexandria, Egypt (via Iráklio, Crete; 2 weekly); Algiers, Tripoli, Tunis, Malta, Naples, Varna [Bulgaria] (monthly); Limassol [Cyprus] and Haifa (3–4 monthly, via Rhodes or Crete); Larnaca [Cyprus] (2 monthly); Odessa [USSR] (2 monthly); Lattakia [Syria] (2 monthly); Venice (3 monthly).

DOMESTIC FLIGHTS

Olympic Airways operate flights from the **West Airport** (see *Points of Arrival*) to the following destinations:

Áktion (Préveza), Alexandhroúpoli, Haniá (Crete), Híos, Iráklion (Crete), Ioánnina, Kalamáta, Kárpathos, Kássos, Kastoriá, Kavála, Kefalloniá, Kérkira (Corfu), Kíthira, Kós, Kozáni, Lárissa, Léros, Límnos, Mílos, Míkonos, Mitilíni (Lésvos), Páros, Ródhos (Rhodes), Sámos, Sitía (Crete), Skíathos, Skíros, Thessaloníki, Thíra (Santoríni) and Zákinthos.

Note: Some of the island routes are seasonal.

CHAPTER TWO

THE PELOPONNESE

The appeal of the **Peloponnese** (*Pelopónissos* in Greek) is hard to overstate. This southern peninsula, technically an island since the cutting of the Corinth Canal, seems to have the best of almost everything Greek. Its ancient sites include the Homeric palaces of Agamemnon at **Mycenae** and of Nestor at **Pílos**; the best preserved of all Greek theatres at **Epidaurus**; and the sanctuary of **Olympia**, host for a millenium of the Olympic Games. The medieval remains are scarcely less rich, with the fabulous Venetian, Frankish and Turkish castles of **Náfplio**, **Methóni** and **Kórinthos**; the strange towerhouses and churches of the **Máni**; and the extraordinary Byzantine towns of **Mystra**, **Monemvassía** and **Yeráki**. The Peloponnesian **beaches**, especially along the west coast, are among the finest and least developed in the country. And, last but by no means least, the **landscape** itself is inspiring, dominated by range after range of forested mountains, and cut by some of the lushest valleys and gorges to be imagined.

Perhaps the most satsifying feature from a traveller's point of view is that the Peloponnese will fill (and fulfill) any amount of **time** that you devote to it. The Argolid, the area richest in ancient history, is just a couple of hours from Athens, and if pushed you could complete a circuit of the main sights here, plus Mystra and Olympia, in four or five days. If you had a month to explore the peninsula, you'd still be omitting numerous possible rewards.

A surprise for many first-time visitors is how the big-name sights – though they live up to expectations – cease to be the highlights. The Peloponnese is at its most enjoyable and intriguing when you venture a little **off the beaten track**: in the old **hill towns of Arcadia** like **Karítena** and **Dhimitsána,** the bizarre semi-desert of the **Máni** in the south; or the trip along the startling **rack-and-pinion railroad** leading inland from Dhiakoftó on the north coast.

If travelling about the peninsula by public **transport**, you'll be dependent mainly on the buses, which are fast and regular on the larger routes, and get to most other places at least once a day. The Peloponnesian train line, now a century old, is in a poor state, especially on its highly scenic southern loop, with trains having to plod their way around for fear of defective sleepers. Hiring a **car** would be worthwhile if you can afford it, even for just a few days – exploring the south from Kalamáta or Spárti, or Arcadia from Náfplio or Trípoli. **Hitching** can fill in the gaps, though rides from locals tend to be short.

THE MOREA: SOME HISTORY

The ancient history of the Peloponnese is comparatively well-known (see 'Historical Framework' in the *Contexts* section). Less so, however, the region's **medieval history**, which is unique, and probably more complex than that of any other part of Greece. As the medieval ruins provide an unexpected focus and fascination for many travellers, a few background notes might be useful.

The Peloponnese retained a nominally Roman civilisation well into the sixth century. But subsequently, following attacks from barbarian tribes of Avars and Slavs, the peninsula hosted a rapid and at times bizarre jumble of occupants and rulers.

First to hold sway were the **Byzantines**, the eastern rulers of the old Roman empire, who established their courts, castles, and towns from the ninth century on. They were rivalled in the Morea – as the Peloponnese was then known – principally by the Franks and Venetians. The **Venetians** settled along the coast, founding trading ports at Monemvassía, Pílos, and Koróni which endured, for the most part, into the fifteenth century. The **Franks**, led by the Champlitte and Villehardouin clans, arrived in 1204, fresh from the sacking of Constantinople in the piratical Fourth Crusade. They swiftly conquered large tracts of the peninsula, and divided it into feudal baronies under a Prince of the Morea.

Towards the middle of the thirteenth century, however, there was a remarkable **Byzantine revival**, which spread from the court at Mystra to exert power over the peninsula once again. A last flicker of 'Greek' rule, it was eventually extinguished by the **Turkish conquest**, between 1458–60, and was to lie dormant, save for sporadic rebellions in the Máni, until the nineteenth-century **War of Greek Independence**. In this, the Peloponnese played a major part. The banner of rebellion was raised near Kalávrita, in Arcadia, by Yermanos, Archbishop of Pátra. The Greek forces' two most successful leaders – Mavromihalis and Kolokotronis – were natives of, and carried out most of their actions in, the Peloponnese. The battle which decided the war, Navarino Bay, was fought off the west coast at Pílos. And the first Greek parliament was held here, too, at Náfplio.

More Recent History

After independence, the exercise of power passed swiftly away from the Peloponnese to Athens, where it was to stay. The peninsula's contribution to the early Greek state was on the whole a disaffected one. Capodistrias, the first Greek president, was assassinated by Maniots, in revenge for his treatment of the Mavromihalis clan. Meanwhile the other great Peloponnesian war leader, Kolokotronis, was imprisoned for 'antidemocratic' activity.

Throughout the nineteenth and early twentieth centuries, the region developed important ports at Pátra, Kórinthos and Kalamáta, but like so much of the country its interior reverted to backwater status. It was little disturbed until **World War II**, during which the area saw some of the worst German atrocities, much brave resistance in the mountains, but also some of the most shameful collaboration. The **civil war** left many of the towns polarised and physically in ruins. In its wake there was substantial **emigration** from both towns and countryside, to the U.S. in particular, as well as to Athens and other Greek cities.

Today, the Peloponnese has a reputation for being one of the most traditional – and politically conservative – regions of Greece. The people are held in rather poor regard by other Greeks, though to outsiders they are unfailingly hospitable. The most significant recent events, sadly, have been **earthquakes**, at Kórinthos in 1981, and at Kalamáta in 1986; the effects of both remain visible.

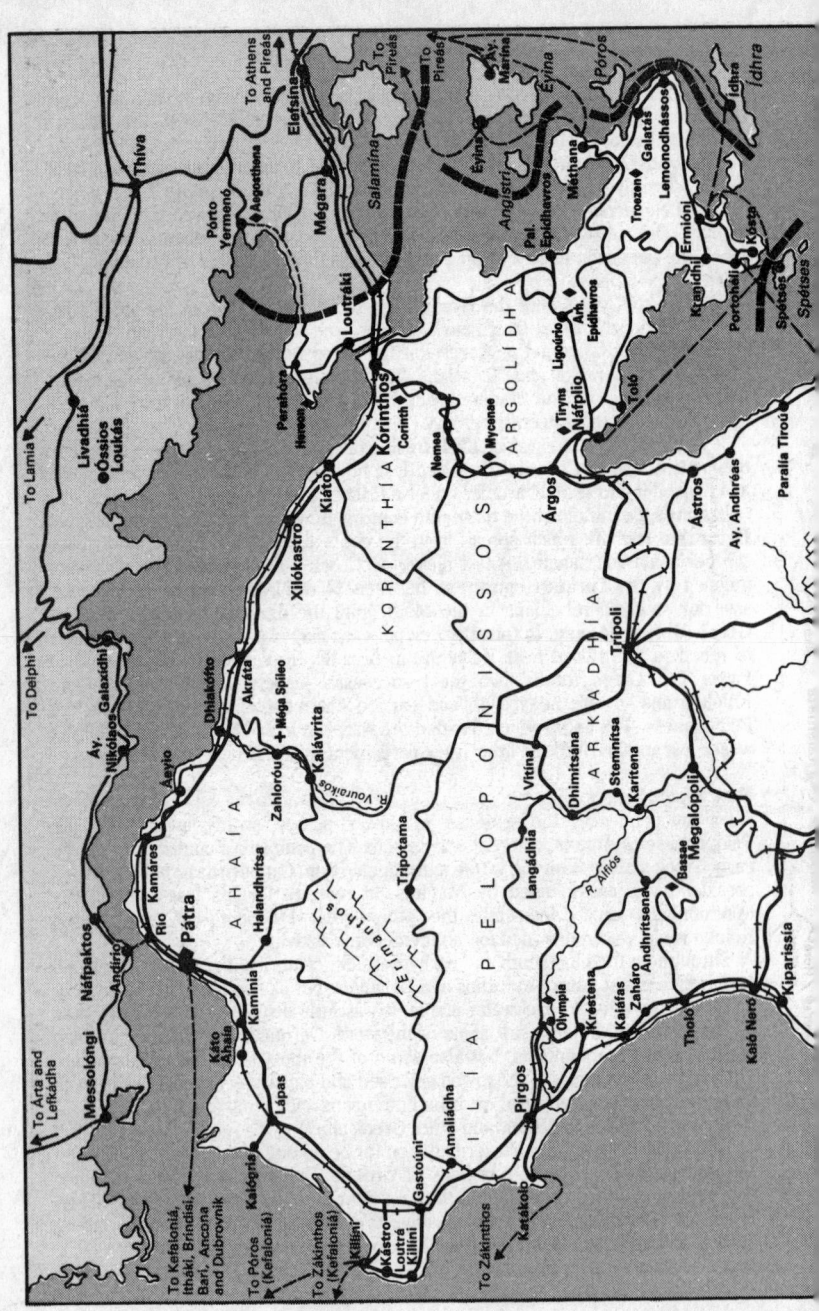

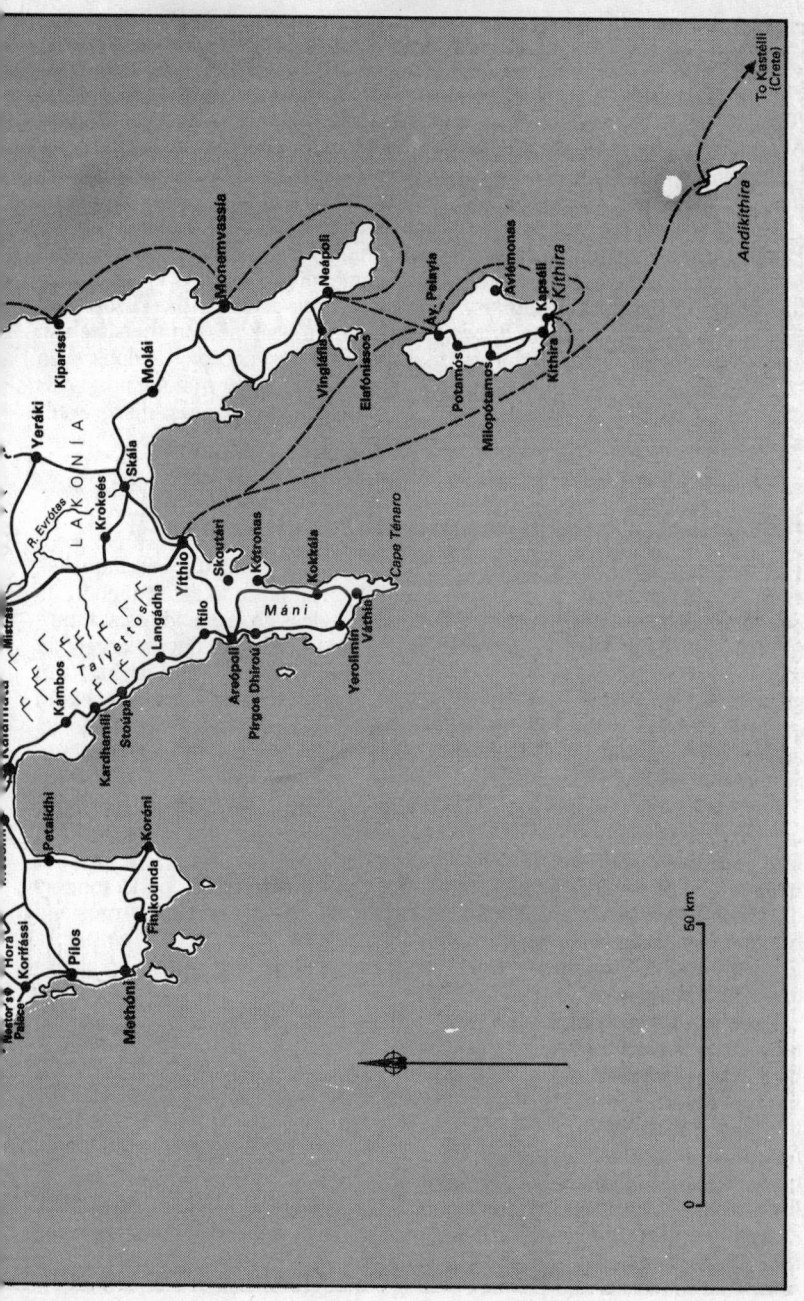

THE ARGOLID

The usual approach from Athens to the Peloponnese is via **Kórinthos** (Corinth) into the Argolid; buses and trains run this way at least every hour. Alternatively – and attractively – you could enter the Argolid by ferry or hydrofoil, via the islands of the **Argo-Saronic** (see *Chapter Six*); routes run from Pireás, through the islands, to Náfplio and then south to Monemvassía.

The Argolid has the greatest concentration of ancient sites in the Peloponnese – indeed, in Greece. Within a highly compact area, all within an hour or so's journey of each other, are Agamemnon's fortress at **Mycenae**, the great theatre of **Epidaurus**, and lesser sites at **Corinth**, **Tiryns** and **Árgos**. Inevitably the region draws crowds and in peak season the sites can lose a little magic under the pressure. But this is best accepted – don't even consider omitting the region from your travels – and when ruin-hopping palls there are a handful of **coastal resorts**, at their best (and least discovered) along the bus routes south from Árgos.

Kórinthos: ancient and modern Corinth

The modern city of **KÓRINTHOS** (CORINTH) was levelled by earthquakes in 1858, 1928 and again in 1981. It's a slightly grim place in consequence, its buildings reconstructed in prudent but characterless concrete to resist future tremors. For itself, there's no particular reason to visit: the city is largely an industrial-agriculture centre, its economy bolstered by the drying and shipping of currant-grapes, for centuries one of Greece's few successful exports. But for visitors Corinth does have the lure of easy access to its ancient predecessor, Arhéa Kórinthos, 7km southwest, as well as to Perahóra on the western tip of Attica.

Orientation is straightforward. The centre of Kórinthos is its **park**, bordered on the longer sides by Ermoú and Ethnikís Andístassis streets. The **bus station for Athens**, as well as most local destinations (Ancient Corinth; Isthmía and Loutráki; Neméa), is on the Ermoú side of the park; **longer-distance buses** (to Spárti, Kalamáta, Trípoli, as well as Mycenae, Árgos and Náfplio) use a terminal on the other side of the park, on the corner of Ethnikís Andístassis and Aratoú. The **train station** is a couple of blocks toward the waterside.

Hotels are reasonably easy to find, with three or four on the main road into town from the train station and a couple, less expensive, on the waterside. Best of the cheaper options, both around 1200dr a double, are *Hotel Belle-Vue* (on the waterside; ☎0741/22-088) and *Hotel Byron* (Dhimokratías 8, opposite the train station; ☎0741/22-631). A little more upmarket is the C-class *Hotel Ephira* (Konstantínou 52, a block back from the Ethnikís Amerikís side of the park; ☎0741/22-434). If you get stuck, there's a **Tourist Police** post on Ermoú, just down from the bus station. Or there are a couple of **campsites** along the gulf to the west: *Corinth Beach* at Dhiavakíta (☎0741/27-967) and *Blue Dolphin* at Léheo (☎0741/25-7667). Neither is especially enticing, in somewhat industrial and polluted settings, though *Corinth Beach*, at least, is well-equipped, and both have **beaches** and tavernas nearby. **Eating** in Kórinthos isn't spectacularly good. There are a few tavernas, and rather more fast-food/souvlaki places along the waterside, all modestly priced.

Ancient Corinth

Buses to ancient Corinth (marked *Arhéa Kórinthos*) leave modern Kórinthos every hour, on the hour, from 8am to 9pm; they return on the half hour.

The ruins of the **ancient city**, which displaced Athens as capital of the Greek province in Roman times, occupy a rambling site below the imposing acropolis hill of **Acrocorinth**, littered with medieval remains. To explore both you need a full day, or better still, to stay at the site. A modern **village** spreads back around the main ancient site and there are a scattering of **rooms** to rent in the back streets – follow the signs or ask at the cafés – and, if you can face the climb, at Acrocorinth (see below). The two campsites detailed above are also within a three-kilometre walk.

The Ancient Site

Open daily 8am–7pm, Sunday 9am–7pm; 400dr.

The ruins of ancient Corinth spread over a vast area, and include sections of ancient walls (the Roman city had a fifteen-kilometre circuit), outlying stadiums, gymnasiums and necropolises. However, only the central area – around the Roman forum and the Classical Temple of Apollo – is preserved in an excavated state; the rest, odd patches of semi-enclosed and often overgrown ruin, you come across unexpectedly while walking about the village and up to Acrocorinth. The whole is impressive, if also somewhat obscure, but it only begins to suggest the majesty of this once supremely wealthy city, which was a key centre of the ancient world throughout the Greek and Roman eras.

Possession of Corinth not only meant the control of trade between northern Greece and the Peloponnese, but, with the city's twin ports on either side of the isthmus, a link between the Ionian and Aegean seas – the west and east of the Mediterranean. Not surprisingly, its ancient (and medieval) history was chequered with invasions and power struggles, and in Classical times by Corinth's intense rivalry with Athens (against whom it sided with Sparta in the Peloponnesian War). But the city suffered only one break in its historical continuity: in 146 B.C., when the Romans, having defeated the Greek city states of the Achaean League, razed it to the ground. For a century the site lay in ruins before being refounded, on a majestic scale, by Julius Caesar in 44 B.C.: initially as a colony for veterans, later as the provincial capital. Once again it grew rich on trade – with Rome to the west, Syria and Egypt to the east – and its population revived to 300,000 (compared to 750,000 at its peak in Classical times).

The new wealth of Roman Corinth was increasingly matched by pleasures, as the city became a byword for luxury with its access to exotic goods. Sex, too, was part of the image. Corinthian women were renowned for their beauty and much sought after as *hetairai* (courtesans); in Corinth itself a temple to Aphrodite/Venus, on the acropolis, was served by over a thousand sacred prostitutes. Saint Paul stayed in Corinth for eighteen months in 54 A.D., though his attempts to reform the citizens' ways were met only by rioting in response, tribulations recorded in his two Epistles to the Corinthians. The city endured until rocked by two major earthquakes, in 522 and 551, which brought down the Roman buildings, and again depopulated the site until a Byzantine revival in the eleventh century.

Inevitably, it is remains of the Roman city that dominate the **main excavated site**, just behind the road where the buses pull in. The area is entered from the south side, which leads you straight into the **Roman agora**, an enormous marketplace flanked by the foundations of a huge *stoa*, once multi-levelled, with 33 shops on the ground floor. Adjoining it in the middle is a *bema*, a marble platform used for public announcements. To the east (right) are remains of a Christian basilica and the starting lines of a Greek race track, covered in the Roman period by administrative buildings. Across the agora to the north is another trace of the Greek city, a **Sacred spring**, covered over by a grill but with its bronze lions' head spouts (5th c. B.C.) still in situ.

More substantial is the elaborate Roman **Fountain of Peirene**, just above the starting line of the racetrack. This is one of two natural springs in Corinth – the other is on the acropolis – and its cool water was channelled into a magnificent fountain and pool in the courtyard. The fountain house was (like many of Athens' Roman public buildings) the gift of the wealthy Athenian and friend of the Emperor Hadrian, Herodes Atticus. The waters still flow through the underground cisterns and supply the modern village. Above the fountain, approached down a flight of steps, is an excavated stretch of what was the main approach to the city, the **Lechaion Way**. Fifteen metres wide, drained, and paved in marble, this remained in use for centuries; it leads today to the site's exit.

The real focus, however, is a survival from the Classical Greek era: the fifth century B.C. **Temple of Apollo**, whose seven austere Doric columns stand slightly above the level of the forum, flanked by foundations of another marketplace and baths. Over to their west is the site **museum**, housing a large collection of domestic pieces, some good Roman mosaics and (outside) a frieze depicting the labours of Heracles (Hercules), several of which (Nemea, Stymphalia, Lernea) were set in the Corinth region. The city's other mythic fame, incidentally, is as the home of the infant Oedipus and his step-parents, prior to his travels of discovery to Thebes.

A number of miscellaneous smaller excavations surround the main site. To the northwest, just across the road from the enclosing wire, there are outlines of two **theatres**: a Roman *odeion* (once again endowed by Herodes Atticus) and a larger Greek amphitheatre, adapted by the Romans for gladiatorial sea battles. To the north, by the (signposted) *Xenia Hotel*, are inaccessible but visible remains of an **Asclepion** (dedicated to the healing god), including a fountain.

Acrocorinth

Towering 600m above the lower town, **Acrocorinth** is an amazing mass of rock still largely encircled by two kilometres of wall. The ancient acropolis of Corinth, it became during the Middle Ages one of Greece's most powerful fortresses, besieged by successive waves of invaders, who considered it the key to the Morea. It's a long climb up – at least an hour and a half – but unreservedly recommended. Amid the sixty-acre site you wander through a jumble of semi-ruined chapels, mosques, houses and battlements, erected in turn by Greeks, Romans, Byzantines, Frankish Crusaders, Venetians and Turks. And looking down over the Saronic and Corinthian gulfs, you really sense the strategic importance of the fortress's position.

The Turkish remains are unusually substantial. Elsewhere in Greece evidence of the Ottoman occupation has been physically removed or at least defaced. Here, halfway up the hill, you can see a midway point in the process: the still functioning **Fountain of Hatzi Mustafa**, Christianized by the addition of great carved crosses. The outer of the citadel's **triple gates**, too, is largely Turkish; the middle is a combination of Venetian and Frankish; the inner, Byzantine, incorporating fourth-century B.C. towers.

Within the citadel (open 24 hr., no charge), the first summit, to the right, is enclosed by a **Frankish keep** – as striking as they come and which last saw action in 1828 during the War of Independence. Keeping along the track to the left, you pass some interesting (if perilous) cisterns, remains of a Turkish bath house and crumbling Byzantine chapels. In the southeast corner of the citadel, hidden away in the lower ground, is the **upper Peirene spring**. This is not easy to find as it's underground; look out for a narrow, overgrown entrance, from which a flight of iron stairs leads down some three metres to a metal screen. Here broad stone steps descend to a pool of water (which has never been known to disappear), out of which stands a fourth century B.C. arch, seemingly guarding the pool and darkness beyond. To the north of the fountain, on the second and higher summit, is the site of the **Temple of Aphrodite** mentioned above; after its days as a brothel, it saw use as a church, mosque and belvedere.

There are no modern buildings up at Acrocorinth, save for a **café-restaurant**, which offers three or four **rooms** to let.

Around Kórinthos: the Canal, Loutráki, Perahóra and Neméa

Besides the **Corinth Canal**, which you can't help but pass en route between Kórinthos and Athens, a number of minor sites are accessible by bus (at least most of the way) from Kórinthos. **Perahóra**, on the Attic peninsula, is the most distant and rewarding; a possible approach for car-drivers from Athens is by way of Mégara and Alepohóri. **Neméa** – as in the lion of Hercules' labour – is a brief detour beyond Kórinthos, off the road to Árgos or Mycenae.

The Corinth Canal and Isthmía

The **Corinth Canal** seems like a tiny strip of water until a huge freighter assumes toy-like dimensions as it passes hundreds of metres below. As a project the canal dates back at least to Nero – who performed initial excavations with a silver shovel – but it was only in the 1890s that the technology became available to cut across the six-kilometre isthmus. Along with the more or less contemporary Suez, it made an important contribution to the development of Pireás as a Mediterranean port and shipping centre, though the canal's projected revenue in tolls was itself never realised. Today, in this age of supertankers, it is something of an anachronism, though no less exciting to pass through, if you take one of the boats from Pireás to the Ionian.

Approaching on the main Athens road, you cross the canal near its eastern end. At the bridge there's a café, where buses from Athens tend to stop if they're going beyond Kórinthos. At the western end of the canal, by the old Kórinthos–Loutráki ferry, there are remains of Roman platforms, on to which boats would be hauled and then dragged across the isthmus on logs.

The site of **ANCIENT ISTHMÍA**, Greek/Roman Corinth's eastern harbour on the Saronic Gulf, lies just to the south of the canal: a little before the modern village of ISTHMÍA if you are coming along the road from Kórinthos (buses from Koliatsoú/Ermoú). There is nothing very notable to see, though the ancient settlement was an important one, with its **Sanctuary of Poseidon** (foundations only remain) and panhellenic Isthmian games. The latter, which ranked with those of Delphi, Nemea and Olympia, have left scant evidence in the form of a stadium and theatre along with a host of curiosities, including starting blocks used for foot races, in the small adjacent **museum** (open 8.45am–3pm, Sun. 9.30am– 2.30pm; closed Tues.; site same hours).

Loutráki and Perahóra

Six kilometres north of the canal, the spa resort of **LOUTRÁKI** was the epicentre of the 1981 Corinth earthquake. It may once have had its charms but today the concrete line of hotels – far more than the place justifies – casts a leaden air over the town. Greeks come here in force for the 'cure' (Loutráki produces the country's leading bottled mineral water), the hot springs and the long pebbly beach. There are reasonably-priced pensions if you decide to stay, but with more than a weekend to escape from the capital, or from Kórinthos, it all seems a bit functional.

Still, Loutráki is connected half-hourly by bus with Kórinthos (20 min.) and with Isthmía, and in the town you can hire a moped (from one of the outlets off the main street) to explore the site of ancient Perahora on Cape Melangávi, 20km around the gulf. There are also buses from Loutráki to Perahóra.

The **route to the cape** is enjoyable in itself, looping above the sea in the shadow of the Yeránia mountains, which are now recovering from fires that devastated the pines in 1986. En route the road offers a loop through the modern village of PERAHÓRA (11km) before heading out to the cape along the shore of **Lake Vouliagméni**, a beautiful lagoon with quiet swimming, a couple of tavernas with rooms and a campsite.

ANCIENT PERAHORA (or the Heraion Melangavi, as it's also known) stands right on the tip of the peninsula, commanding a marvellous, sweeping view of the coastline and mountains along both sides of the gulf. The site's position is its chief attraction, though there are identifiable ruins of two sanctuaries – the **Hera Akraia** and **Hera Limenia** – as well as the submerged **stoa** of the ancient port. The latter provides great snorkelling opportunities, but beware the potentially dangerous currents beyond the cove.

If you have a car, there's a grand and rather wild route east from the cape, around the Alkionid Gulf to PÓRTO YERMENÓ (see *Chapter Three*). There are beaches along the way, though little settlement or development, and the final stretch of road from KÁTO ALEPOHÓRI is scarcely more than a track. The area, Perahóra especially, is described by Dilys Powell in *An Affair of the Heart*.

Ancient Nemea

The location for Hercules' slaying of the lion, **ANCIENT NEMEA** lies 4km off the road to Árgos and Mycenae. The ruins are just outside the village of IRÁKLIO and 6km before modern NEMÉA (which is on a bus route from Kórinthos).

Like Olympia, Nemea held athletic games (supposedly inaugurated by Hercules) for the Greek world and it was a sanctuary rather than a town. Its principal remains are of the **Temple of Nemean Zeus**, currently four slender Doric columns surrounded by other fallen and broken drums, but all slowly being reassembled by a team of Berkeley archaeologists. Nearby are a **palaestra** with **baths** and a Christian basilica, built with blocks of the temple; outside the site, half a kilometre east, is a **stadium** whose starting line has been unearthed. The chief attraction for enthusiasts, however – and this is not really a site for the casually interested – is the **museum**, a newly endowed and imaginative building with excellent contextual models and displays relating to the biennial games.

Moving on from Nemea, you can walk back down to the Árgos road, then try your luck at hitching (or possibly waving down a bus) on to Mycenae. Alternatively, it's possible to cut across the hills into Arcadia, via another Herculean locale – the Stymphalian Lake.

This, known in modern Greek as the **Límni Stimfalías**, is really more marsh than lake: an enormous depression with seasonal waters, ringed by the dark peaks of Mt. Killíni. With no habitation for miles around, save for the ruins of a thirteenth-century Frankish Cistercian **abbey** (east of the road), it easily lends itself to the Herculean legend. The lake was reputed to be the home of great birds who preyed upon travellers, suffocating them with their wings before eating their flesh. Hercules killed them as his fifth labour.

If you don't have your own transport the most promising approach to the lake is from KIÁTO on the Gulf of Kórinthos; the road, much better than that from Neméa, has the occasional bus. The nearest place to stay is at **KASTANIÁ**, an attractive mountain village 20km to the west. Unless you can find a private room, however, it's an expensive night at the one, B-class, *Xenia* hotel (☎0747/31-283).

Mycenae (Mikínes)

Tucked into a fold of the hills just east of the road from Kórinthos to Árgos is Agamemnon's citadel, 'well-built Mycenae, rich in gold' (Homer). Nowhere in Greece does the place better fit the legend. It was uncovered in 1874 by the German archaeologist Heinrich Schliemann (who also excavated the site of Troy), impelled by his single-minded belief that there was a factual basis to Homer's epics. Schliemann's finds of brilliantly-crafted gold and sophisticated tomb-architecture bore out the accuracy of Homer's epithets.

The modern village of **MIKÍNES** is 2km from the Kórinthos–Argos road and the railroad station; the walk in (many buses will drop you at the turning rather than the village) is along a beautiful straight road lined with eucalyptus trees, through which glimpses of the citadel appear, flanked by the twin mountains of Zára and Ilías. The site is a further two kilometres uphill from the village.

Unless you have your own transport, you'll probably want to stay at Mikínes – which is heavily touristed by day but quiet once the site has closed and the tour buses departed. The cheapest options are the *Restaurant Iphigeneia*, halfway up the single street, which doubles up as a **youth hostel** (with plenty of roofspace), and the two **campsites**, *Camping Mycenae* and *Camping Atticus*, both fairly central. Alternatives include **rooms** to let in village houses or the C-class *Hotel Belle Hélène* (☎0751/66-255; doubles around 2000dr), up the hill towards the site. The latter was the house used by Schliemann during his excavations, and used to be managed by two brothers, Agamemnon and Menelaus; as a hotel it has seen visits from Virginia Woolf and Debussy, whose signatures are displayed along with other notables in the foyer. The village has plenty of **restaurants**, all geared to the lunchtime bus-tour trade; don't expect too much.

The Site

Open daily 8am–7pm, Sun. 8am–6pm; winter 9.30am–3.30pm; 500dr, students 250dr.

The Mycenae–Árgos region is one of the longest-occupied in Greece, with evidence of Neolithic settlements from around 3000 B.C. But it is from a period of three centuries at the end of the second millenium B.C. – the **Mycenaean civilisation** that flourished in southern Greece from around 1550-1200 B.C. – that the principal remains of the excavated site and its associated drama belong.

According to legend, as related in Homer's *Iliad* and *Odyssey* and Aeschylus's *Oresteia*, the city of Mycenae was founded by Perseus, the slayer of the gorgon, Medusa, before it fell into the fated hands of the **House of Atreus**. Atreus had brought down the gods' wrath on his descendants with the murder of his nephews and nieces, whom he fed to his brother and their father Thyestes. His son Agamemnon, after commanding the Greek forces in the Trojan War, returned to Mycenae to suffer the consequences: death in his bath at the hands of his wife Clytemnestra and her lover Aegisthus. The tragic cycle was completed by Agamemnon's son, Orestes, who took revenge

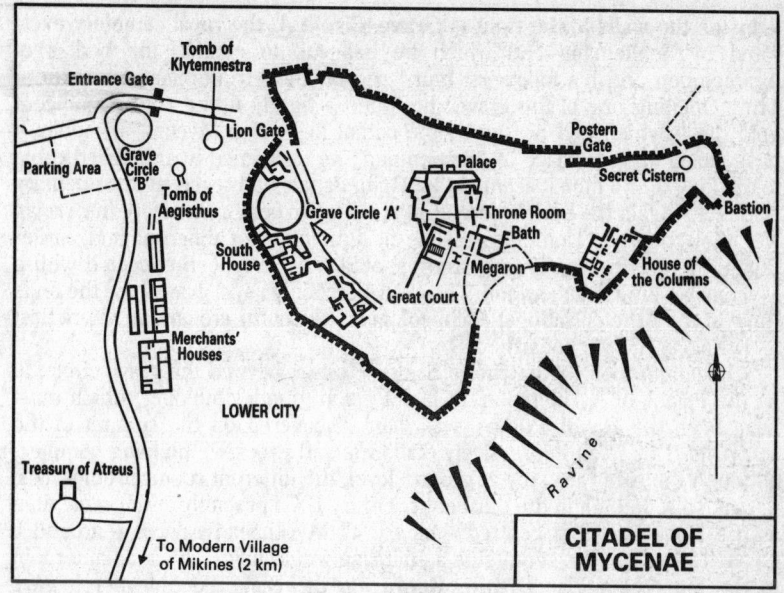

CITADEL OF MYCENAE

by murdering his mother, and was haunted by the Furies before Athena finally lifted the curse on the house.

The archaeological remains of Mycenae fit remarkably easily with the tale, at least if it is taken as a poetic rendering of dynastic struggles, or, as most scholars now believe, a merging of stories from various Myceneaean periods. The buildings unearthed by Schliemann show signs of occupation from around 1950 B.C., as well as two periods of intense disruption, around 1200 B.C. and again in 1100 B.C. – at which stage the town, though still prosperous, was abandoned. No coherent explanation has been found for these events, since the traditional 'Dorian invasions' theory has fallen from favour, but it seems that war among the rival kingdoms was a major factor in the Mycenaean decline. These struggles seem to have escalated as the civilisation developed in the thirteenth century B.C., and excavations at Troy have revealed the sacking of that city – quite possibly by forces led by a king from Mycenae – in 1240 B.C.

The **Citadel of Mycenae** seems to have been replanned, and heavily fortified, during this period. It is entered through the famous **Lion Gate**, whose huge sloping gateposts bolster walls termed 'Cyclopean' by later Greeks in bewildered explanation of their construction. Above them a graceful carved relief stands out in confident assertion of its powerful and advanced domain: Mycenae at its height led a confederation of Argolid towns (Tiryns, Argos, Asine, Hermione), dominated the Peloponnese and exerted influence throughout the Aegean. The motif of a pillar supported by two muscular lions was probably the royal symbol of the Mycenaean royal house, for a seal found on the site bears a similar device.

Inside the walls to the right is **Grave Circle A**, the royal cemetery excavated by Schliemann and which he believed to contain the bodies of Agamemnon and his followers, murdered on their triumphant return from Troy. Opening one of the graves he found a tightly fitting and magnificent gold mask which had preserved the actual flesh of a Mycenaean noble; 'I have gazed upon the face of Agamemnon', he exclaimed in an excited cable to the king. For a time it seemed that Homer's tale had received documentary evidence. In fact the burials date from at least two centuries before the Trojan war though given Homer's possible accumulation of different and earlier sagas, there is no reason why they should not have been conected with a Mycenaean king Agamemnon. They were certainly royal graves, for the finds (now in the Athens National Archaeological Museum) are among the richest archaeology has yet unearthed.

Schliemann took the extensive **South House**, beyond the grave circle, to be the Palace of Agamemnon. In fact a much grander building, which must have been the **Royal Palace**, was later discovered on the summit of the acropolis. This is an impressively elaborate and evocative building complex; although the ruins are only at ground level, the different rooms are not hard to make out. Rebuilt in the thirteenth century B.C., probably at the same time as the Lion Gate, it is centred – as are all Mycenaean palaces – around a **Great Court**. On the south side a staircase would have led via an anteroom to the big rectangular **Throne Room**; on the east, a double porch gave access to the **Megaron**, the grand reception hall with its traditional circular hearth. The small rooms to the north are believed to have been **royal apartments** and in one of them the remains of a red stuccoed bath have led to its fanciful identification as the very spot of Agamemnon's murder.

Equally evocative are the **ramparts** – with the sounds of bells drifting down from goats scratching about the mountainside – and, above all, the **secret cistern** at their east end. This was created, presumably in troubled times, in the twelfth century B.C.; whether it was to stand siege from outsiders, rival Mycenaeans, or perhaps an increasingly alienated peasantry, is not known. Steps lead down to a deep underground spring and it's still possible to descend the whole way; you will need a torch – and take care, as there's a drop into the 70-metre-deep water at the final turn of the twisting passageways. Nearby is the **House of Columns**, a large and stately building with the base of a stairway leading to an upper storey.

Outside the walls of the citadel lay the main part of the town; only the ruling elite of Mycenaean society could live within the citadel itself. Extensive remains of **merchants' houses** have been uncovered near to the road, beside a second grave circle. In them, Linear B tablets recording the spices used to scent oils were found along with large amounts of pottery, the quantity suggesting that the early Mycenaeans may have engaged in a considerable trade in perfume. The discovery of the tablets has also caused a reassessment of the sophistication of Mycenaean civilisation for they show that, here at least, writing was not limited to government scribes working in the royal palaces as had previously been thought, and that around the citadel may have been a commercial city of some size and wealth.

Alongside the merchants' houses are the remains of another grave circle ('B'), dating to around 1650 B.C. and possibly representing an earlier, rival dynasty to the kings buried in 'A', and two **tholos** (circular chamber-type) tombs, speculatively identified by Schliemann as the **Tombs of Clytemnestra and Aegisthus**. The former, closer to the Lion Gate, dates from around 1300 B.C. and so may key with the Trojan timescale; the latter is some two centuries earlier.

Across the road from the main site is another – and infinitely more startling – *tholos*, known as the **Treasury of Atreus** or 'Tomb of Agamemnon'. This was certainly a royal burial vault at a late stage in Mycenae's history, contemporary with the 'Clytemnestra Tomb', so the attribution to Agamemnon or his father is as good as any – if the king was indeed the historic leader of the Trojan expedition. At all events, it is an impressive monument to Mycenaean building skills, a beehive-like structure built without any use of mortar. It is entered (on the same ticket as for the main site) through a majestic fifteen-metre corridor. Above the chamber doorway is a great lintel formed by two immense slabs of stone – one of which, a staggering nine metres long, is estimated to weigh 118 tons.

The Argive Heraion

Four kilometres from Mycenae, on the minor road east of Árgos to Náfplio, is the little-visited **Argive Heraion**, an important sanctuary in Mycenaean and Classical times and the site where Agamemnon is said to have been chosen as leader of the Greek expedition to Troy.

There are various Mycenaean tombs in the neighbourhood, but the principal remains of the Heraion are from the fifth century B.C., a complex of temples, baths, and a *palaestra* built on three interconnecting terraces. The site is unrestricted and makes an enjoyable afternoon's walk from Mikínes – a little over an hour away if you follow the track southeast from the village, paralleling the road to Monastiráki/Ayía Triádha/Náfplio. The shrine is located just above the village of HÓNIKAS, which has the occasional bus to Árgos; AYÍA TRIÁDHA, 4km on, has more frequent connections to Náfplio.

Árgos

ARGOS, 10km south of the Mikínes junction on the main Kórinthos road, is said to be the oldest inhabited town in Europe. Passing through the town – a gloomy farming centre redeemed by a few open squares and neoclassical buildings – you wouldn't guess it. However, a brief stop is called for, if only for the excellent museum (a stone's throw from the bus station), the generally ignored Greek/Roman ruins and (if you can coincide) the marvellous **Wednesday market**, which attracts peasants from all the hill villages around.

The **Archaeological Museum** (8.45am–3pm, Sun. 9.30am–2.30pm; closed Tues.) is just off the main market square. It's an interesting visit after

Mycenae, containing a good collection of Mycenaean tomb objects and armour along with extensive pottery from the region. The region's Roman occupation is well represented, too, with some fine sculpture and mosaics.

The principal **Roman ruins** (9am–3pm, Sunday 10am–2pm: but not entirely fenced in) are in fact a few minutes' walk down the Trípoli road, struggling to hold their own next to a tyre yard. Though very much a minor site they are surprisingly extensive. The **theatre**, built by Classical Greeks and adapted by the Romans, looks oddly narrow from the road, but climb up there and it feels immense. It's estimated to have held 20,000 spectators, 6000 more than Epidaurus and rivalled on the Greek mainland only by those at Megalopolis and Dodona. Alongside are the remains of an *odeion* and **Roman baths**. If parts of the modern town could be cleared back, other substantial remains would presumably be revealed.

Above the site and the town looms the ancient acropolis, capped by a largely Frankish **medieval castle**. Massively cisterned and guttered, the sprawling ruins offer the views you'd expect – but it's a long haul up.

Practicalities

You may well need to change buses in Árgos: its connections are considerably better than those of Náfplio. There are two **KTEL stands**, a block apart from each other and the central square; the one to the south, on Vassiléos Yioryíou, is for buses back toward Athens and various points in the Argolid; the other, on the corner of Nikitáras and Dhanáou, on the east side of the square, is for Trípoli, Spárti and downcoast toward Leonídhi.

If you need lunch between buses, try the good, very cheap, anonymous **restaurant** 20m east of the main square on Nikitáras. Staying shouldn't prove necessary, unless you find Náfplio completely full – a possibility in high season. A good modest standby, north of the main square, is the *Apollo Inn* (Kórai 15; ☎0751/28-012).

Tiryns (Tírinthos)

In Mycenaean times **TIRYNS** stood by the sea, commanding the coastal approaches to Árgos and Mycenae. Today the Aegean sea has receded, leaving the fortress stranded on a low hillock in the plains – alongside the Argolid's principal modern prison. It's not the most enchanting of settings, which in part explains why this accessible, substantial site is so little visited. After the crowds at Mycenae, however, the opportunity to wander about Homer's 'wall-girt Tiryns' in near-solitude is worth taking.

The site lies just to the left of the road coming from Árgos (7km), with Náfplio 5km south. Buses will drop and pick up passengers, on request, at the café opposite.

The Citadel

Mon.–Sat. 9am–3pm, Sun. 9.30am–2.30pm; 200dr, students 100dr.

As at Mycenae, Homer's epithets are a remarkable match. Tiryns' dominant aspect is its walls, formed of huge Cyclopean stones. The Roman guidebook writer Pausanias, happening on the site in the second century A.D., found them 'more amazing than the Pyramids' – a claim that seems a little exaggerated, even considering that the walls then stood twice their present height. But as an example of military architecture, over 3000 years old, the fortress is undeniably impressive.

The sophistication of the site and its unequivocally military purpose (or at least, later adaptation) is clear as soon as you climb up the **entrance ramp** to the citadel. This was wide enough to allow access to chariots, but designed to make any invading force immediately vulnerable. Their right hand, unshielded side would be exposed along the whole way, and at the top, the ramp forced a sharp turn – again surveyed by defenders from within. The **gateways**, too, were (and remain) considerable barriers to final access to the courtyard; the outer one is similar in design to Mycenae's Lion Gate, though sadly its lintel has gone so there is no heraldic motif to confirm any dynastic link between the two sites.

In the thickness of the courtyard's outer wall is one of the long **stone-vaulted corridors** which are the citadel's most dramatic feature. A passage from the courtyard leads to a large forecourt and from there a staircase continues to a 21-metre-long gallery, off which are numerous storage chambers. Sheep have for years taken refuge from storms in these galleries and the stone walls have been left brightly polished from their movements.

Of the **palace** itself only the limestone foundations survive, but it is somehow more substantial than Mycenae and you can gain a clearer idea of its structure. The walls above would have been of sun-dried brick, covered in stucco and decorated with frescoes. Fragments of these were found on the site: one depicting a boar hunt, the other a life-sized frieze of courtly women (they are now in Náfplio's museum). Entering from the forecourt you emerge on to a spacious **colonnaded court**, with a round sacrificial altar in the middle. A typically Mycenaean double porch leads directly ahead to the **Megaron** (great hall), where the throne, its base surviving, is set before a massive round clay hearth. **Royal apartments**, as at Mycenae, lead off on either side; the women's quarters are thought to have been to the right, while to the left is the bathroom, its floor – a huge, single flat stone – intact. A tower further off to the left gives access to a **secret staircase**, as at Mycenae. It's not easy to find, even now without the hindrance of walls, and winds down to an inconspicuous **postern gate**.

The site beyond the *megaron* is separated by an enormous inner wall and has been fenced off for archaeological exploration after two underground cisterns were discovered at the far end.

Náfplio (Nauplia, Navplion)

NÁFPLIO is a rarity amongst large Greek towns. It is lively, beautifully sited and has a rather grand, fading elegance, inherited from the days when it was the fledgling capital of modern Greece. The seat of government was here from 1829–34 and it was in Náfplio that the first prime minister, Capodistrias, was assassinated by vengeful Maniot clansmen; here too that the Bavarian Prince Otho, put forward by the European powers to be the first King of

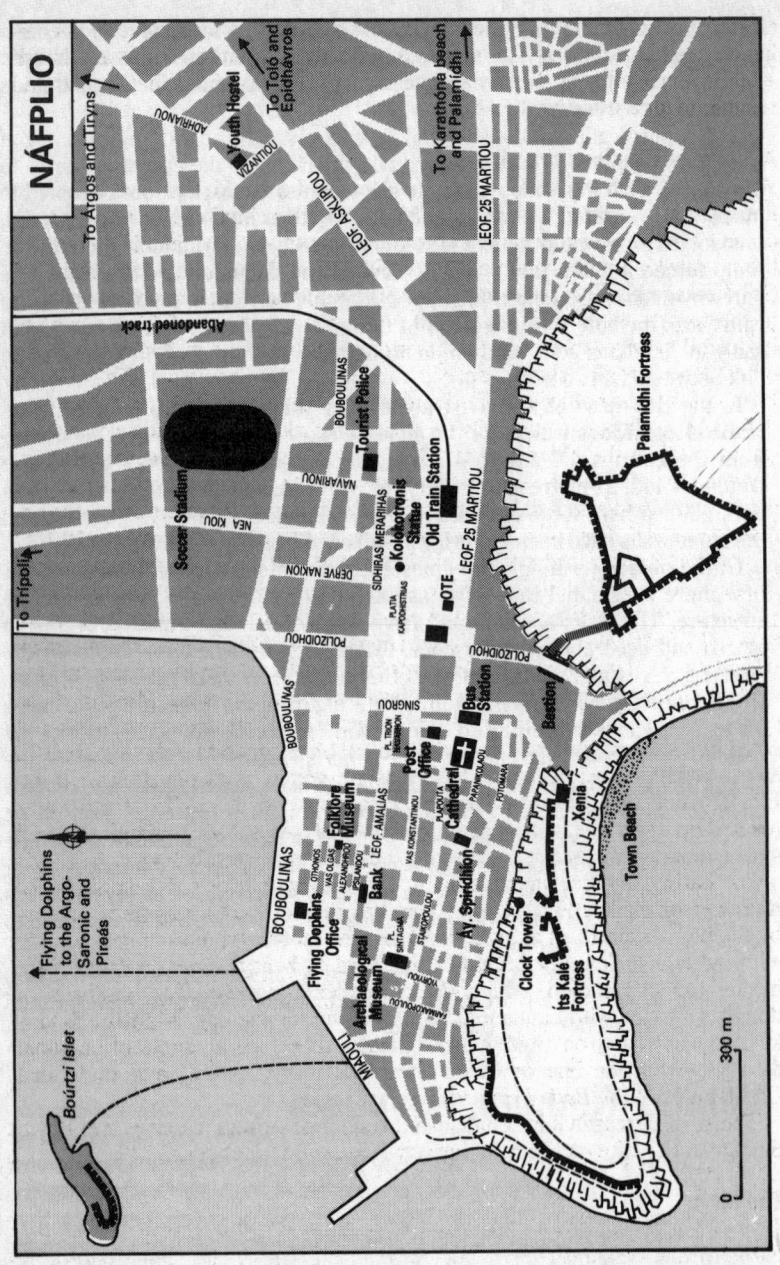

NÁFPLIO

To Argos and Tíryns

Youth Hostel

ADHRIANOU

VIZANTIOU

To Tolò and Epidhávros

LEOF. ASKLIPIOU

To Karathóna beach and Palamídhi

To Trípoli

To Trípolis

Abandoned track

Soccer Stadium

NEA KIOU

DERVE NAXIOU

NAVARINOU

BOUBOULINAS

Tourist Police

SIDHIRAS MERARHIAS

Kolokotrónis Statue

PLATIA KAPODISTRIOU

Old Train Station

OTE

LEOF. 25 MARTIOU

POLIZOIDHOU

POLIZOIDHOU

Palamídhi Fortress

Flying Dolphins to the Argo-Saronic and Pireás

Boúrtzi islet

BOUBOULINAS

BOUBOULINAS

Archaeological Museum

Flying Dolphins Office

OTHONOS

VAS OLGAS

ALEXANDROU

STAIKOPOULOU

PL. SINTAGMATOS

VAS KONSTANTINOU

PAPANIKOLAOU

PAPADHOPOULOU

FARMAKOPOULOU

Bank

LEOF. AMALIAS

Folklore Museum

SINGROU

PL. TRION NAVARHON

Post Office

KAPODISTRIOU

SOFRONI TZANNI

Cathedral

Av. Spiridhon

FOTOMARA

Bus Station

Bastion

Clock Tower

Its Kalé Fortress

Xenía

Town Beach

MIAOULI

0   300 m

Greece, had his initial royal residence. Today it's in some danger of becoming too popular for its own good – with hotel rooms at Athens rates and above – but it remains by far the most attractive base for exploring the Argolid and resting up for a while by the sea.

Accommodation and practicalities

Wedged between the sea and a fortress-topped headland, the town is easy to find your way around. Arriving by **bus** – the train station has been purely ornamental for over a decade – you are set down at a terminal just south of the interlocking main squares, **Platía Navárhon/Platía Kapodhístrias**, on Ódhos Singroú. All services use this same terminal. An alternative approach to the town – or more likely a route onwards – is by the 'Flying Dolphin' **hydrofoil** service; there are (summer-only) connections to Spétses and the other Argo-Saronic islands, and to Pireás and Monemvassía. The 'Flying Dolphins' booking office is at Bouboulínas 2, by the harbour.

Accommodation is generally overpriced for what you get, especially if you want to stay in the older part of town, west of the squares and bus station. Rooms here are thin on the ground and of fairly poor quality – rarely with more than a cold-water sink in the corner. The most reasonable are at the co-managed *Hotel King Otto* (Farmakopoúlou 3; ☎0752/27-585) and *Hotel Lito* (Zigomála 28, at the base of Its Kale fortress; ☎0752/28-093)); prices at either run around 1700dr double, 1350dr single. Alternatively, of a slightly lower standard but with similar prices, you could try the *Epidavros* (Ipsilándou; ☎0752/27-541), *Akropol*, (Vassilíssis Ólgas 7; ☎0752/27-796) or *Emborikon* (Plapoúta 31, by the bus station; ☎0752/27-339). If you're going to stay several nights, prices may work out lower at private **rooms**. Most of these cluster on the slope south of the main square, or there are a few below the *Hotel Lito*; others, generally cheaper, are out on the road to Toló. A fallback if all else is full (as can happen in high season), or you're travelling alone, is the (not too pleasant) **youth hostel** on Vizantíou (☎0752/24-720) in the new town. The town campsite closed a couple of years back, though it's still shown on many maps; the nearest are at Toló/Assíne (see below).

For **eating**, try the tavernas along the waterside street Bouboulínas; *To Koutouki*, on Staikopoúlou; *O Veryis*, on Vassilíssis Ólgas; a very basic taverna by the bus station (best at lunchtime); or several others, more upmarket and with outdoor tables. For breakfast, it's hard to beat the *zaharoplastío* right beside the bus station, which does excellent *loukoumádhes* (puffballs of dough sprinkled with cinnamon) to set you up for the day. **Nightlife** is low-key, concentrating on Bouboulínas, though there are a couple of seasonal discos (an outside one on Kilkís, near the tourist police) and traditional Greek music at the *Boite Lychnari*.

There is a reasonable English-language **bookshop**, *Odyssey*, on Platía Síntagma. For bike and **moped** hire try *Nikopoulos*, Bouboulínas 49.

The town

There's ample pleasure in just wandering about Náfplio: looking around the harbourfront, walking over to the rocky town beach, and, when energy is sufficient, exploring the great twin fortresses on the headland.

Rich in historical associations since medieval times, the **Palamídhi**, the principal fort, was one of the key military points of the War of Independence. The Greek commander Kolokotronis – of whom there's a majestically bewhiskered statue in the Platía Kapodhistrías – laid siege to the castle for over a year before finally gaining control. After independence, ironically, he was imprisoned in the fortress by the new Greek government; wary of their attempts to curtail his powers, he had kidnapped four of the parliament's members.

The fortress (open 8am–5.30pm, Sunday/off season 10am–3pm; 200dr, students 100dr) is most directly approached by a stairway from the end of Polizídhou street, by the side of a Venetian bastion, though there is also a circuitous road up from the town. On foot, it is a long climb – 899 stone-hewn steps – and, when you reach the summit, a bewilderingly vast complex. Within the outer walls are three self-contained castles. All were built by the Venetians between 1711–14, and the city's symbol, the Lion of Saint Mark, appears above the various gateways. The middle fort, San Niccolo, was the one used to imprison Kolokotronis; it was later a notorious prison during the civil war.

The **Íts Kalé** ('Inner Castle' in Turkish), to the west, occupies the ancient acropolis, whose walls were adapted by successive medieval restorers. The fortifications are today far less complete than those of the Palamídhi, and the most intact section, the lower Torrione castle, has been adapted to house a *Xenia Hotel*. There's little of interest, but the hotel has meant a road is carved out over the headland and this brings you down to a small **EOT pay beach**, overcrowded in season but a nevertheless enjoyable spot to cool off in the shadow of the forts. In the early evening it usually has just a few swimmers. Another beach – a slightly longer, rocky but free stretch – can be reached by following the road clockwise **around the headland** for a few hundred metres. Keep walking along the path and in half an hour you'll emerge back at Náfplio's port.

The third fort, **Boúrtzi**, occupies the islet offshore from the harbour – accessible by *kaíkia* (200dr return) in summer. Built in the fifteenth century, the castle has seen various modern uses. In the last century it was the home of the town's public executioner; during this one it was, for a while, a luxury hotel. Melina Mercouri claims to have consummated her first marriage there.

In the town itself, there are a few minor sights – mainly from the Turkish past – and two excellent museums. **Platía Sintágmatos**, the main square, is the focus of most interest. On and around it survive three converted **Ottoman mosques**: one is now a cinema; another, in the southwest corner, was the original *Voulí* (Parliament building); a third has been reconsecrated as the cathedral of Áyios Yióryios. In the same area are a pair of handsome **Turkish fountains** – one recessed into the south wall of the theatre-mosque, the other on Kapodhistrías, opposite the church of Áyios Spirídhon.

The **Archaeological Museum** (9am–1pm and 5–7pm in season, 9am–3pm out; closed Tues.; 200dr, students 100dr) occupies a dignified Venetian mansion on the west side of Síntagma. It has some good collections, as you'd expect in a town at the heart of the Argolid sites, including a unique and more or less complete suit of Mycenaean armour and reconstructed frescoes from Tíryns. Equally worthwhile is the new **Folk Art Museum** (same hours as archaeological museum; free) on Ipsilándou. This features superb and imaginatively displayed embroideries, costumes and traditional household tools and goods, all presented in the context of their use and production. An adjoining shop sells unusually high-quality handicrafts.

More handicrafts are on sale at the convent of **Áyia Móni**, 2km east of Náfplio on the Epídhavros road, just north of the village of Ária. The monastic church, one of the most accomplished Byzantine buildings in the Peloponnese, dates back to the twelfth century. From the outer wall bubbles an eighteenth century fountain, identified with the ancient spring of Kanthanos, in whose waters the goddess Hera bathed each year to restore her virginity. Modern Greeks similarly esteem the water, though its powers are not as miraculous as hitherto.

Beaches near Náfplio

The closest 'proper' beach to Náfplio is at **KARATHÓNA**, a fishing hamlet just over the headland beyond the Palamídhi fortress. You can't reach this by going along the shore – the way is blocked by cliffs – but there's a good modern road inland, heading out of town on Leofóros 25 Martíou. It's an hour's walk or a ten-minute bus ride (mornings, in season, only). The sandy beach stretches for a couple of kilometres, with a single taverna at its far end. It was to have been developed during the junta years, when the road here was built along with the concrete foundations of a hotel, but the project was suspended in the 1970s and has yet to be revived. At present Karathóna attracts quite a few Greek day-trippers in season, along with a handful of foreigners in camper-vans. If you want to set up a tent, there's nobody to tell you otherwise.

Toló and Kastráki

TOLÓ, by contrast with Karathóna, is one of the Argolid's fastest-growing resorts, all but swamping its narrow sands with a line of thirty or more hotels and campsites. Out of season it could be quite a pleasant resort; in midsummer it's way too crowded for comfort, redeemed only by the views of the islets of Platía and Romví on the horizon and a good range of watersports equipment for hire. However, if you've been unable to find a room in Náfplio, then you may want or need to stay. The three **campsites** – *Camping Stars*, *Lido I* and *Lido II* – all charge much the same rates and should have space; hotels are liable to block-reservations by charter companies, but it's usually possible to find **rooms** by asking around or following the signs. Toló is connected by bus with Náfplio every hour (last back at 8.30pm), or, considerably more expensive, by 'Flying Dolphin'.

A pleasanter alternative to Toló, especially for campers, is the longer beach at **KASTRÁKI**, 3km east; coming from Náfplio by bus, ask to be set down where the road reaches the sea – it forks right to Toló, left (500m) to Kastráki. Here too development is underway, but it's some years behind that of Toló, limited to a scattering of small-scale hotels and *Camping Assini* (☎0752/59-387), right by the beach with windsurfing equipment for hire. If you get tired of the water, wander along the beach to the scrub-covered rock by the Náfplio road junction. This is, or was, **Ancient Assine**, an important Mycenaean and Classical city destroyed by the jealous and more powerful Argos in retribution for their having sided with the Spartans against them. There's little to see, other than a 200-metre length of ancient wall, but it's an oddly atmospheric spot.

Dhrépano

Further around the coast **east from Kastráki**, the road runs on to **DHRÉPANO**, a sizeable village with a campsite (*Plaka Beach*), beyond which is the **Vivári lagoon** with a couple of good fish tavernas on its shore. You can continue this way for another 10km until the road dwindles to a poor track by the beach and campsite at **PARALÍA IRÍON**.

Epidaurus (Epídhavros)

EPIDAURUS is most famous and most visited for its remarkably preserved ancient theatre, built by Polycleitus in the fourth century B.C. With its extraordinary acoustics, this has become a major venue for the Athens Festival productions of Classical drama – principally Sophocles, Euripides, and Aeschylus – which are performed Friday and Saturday nights from June through September. Great spectacles in this setting, they are worth arranging your plans around whether or not you understand the modern Greek in which they're spoken. **Tickets** are available at the site on the day of performance, or in advance in Athens (at the festival box office) or Náfplio (from *Olympic Airways* at Bouboulínas 2). In Athens you can buy all-inclusive tickets for performances and return bus travel. There are also special evening buses to return to Náfplio after the show. English translations of the plays are available at Epidaurus and at the bookshop in Náfplio.

Normally there are four buses **daily** from Náfplio to the site; they are marked *Asklipion* and shouldn't be confused with those to the modern villages of NEA or PALEÁ EPÍDHAVROS, each 15km distant. The nearest village to the site is LIGOÚRIO, 5km north.

Most people take in Epidaurus as a daytrip, but if you want to stay it's possible to **camp** near the car park (rich green lawn); on days of performances, you must wait until an hour after the play's end before setting up a tent. Alternatively, there's an expensive *Xenia* **hotel** at the site, or two more modestly-priced places (*Hotel Koronis*, ☎0753/22-267; *Hotel Asklepios*, ☎0753/22-251) in Ligoúrio. For evening meals, the nearest restaurant to the site is the *Oasis* on the Ligoúrio road; if your money is tight, bring a picnic.

The Theatre and Asclepion

Site open Mon.–Sat. 8am–7pm, Sun. 8am–6pm; 500dr, students 300dr.
From the sixth century B.C. to Roman times, Epidaurus was a major spa and religious centre, and its Sanctuary of Asclepius the site of pilgrimage from throughout the ancient world. The sanctuary's dedication to Asclepius, the

legendary son of Apollo, perhaps owes its origin to an early healer from northern Greece who settled in the area. There were Asclepian sanctuaries throughout Greece – Athens has ruins of one on the south slope of its Acropolis – and they were sited, rationally enough, alongside natural springs. Epidaurus, along with the island of Kos, was the most famous of them all, and probably the richest. The sanctuary was much endowed by wealthy visitors and hosted a quadrennial festival – including drama in the ancient theatre – which immediately followed the Isthmian games. Its renown was at a height in the fourth and third centuries B.C.; Rome, ravaged by an epidemic in 293 B.C., sent for the serpent that was kept in the sanctuary.

This aspect of the site, however, along with most of the associated Asclepian ruins, is an incidental for most visitors. For Epidaurus' **ancient theatre** is a sight – not a ruin or anecdote – par excellence. With its backdrop of rolling hills, this 14,000-seat arena merges perfectly into the landscape; so well in fact that it was rediscovered and unearthed only last century. Constructed with mathematical precision, it has an extraordinary appearance of balance and, as guides on the stage are forever demonstrating, near-perfect natural acoustics. These are such that you can hear coins – even matches – dropped in the circular *orchestra* from the highest of the 54 tiers of seats. Aside from repairing these tiers – constructed in white limestone (red for the dignitaries at the front) — restoration has been comparatively minor, retaining the beaten earth stage, for instance, as in ancient times.

Close by the theatre is a small **museum** (no additional charge), which it's best to visit before exploring the somewhat obscure site of the sanctuary. The site finds displayed here show a progression of medical skills and cures used at the Asclepion; there are tablets recording miraculous and outrageous cures (like the man cured from paralysis after being ordered to heave the biggest boulder he could find into the sea) and also quite advanced surgical instruments. Additionally, the museum has some excellent reconstructed models of the site, helpful for visualising since most of the ruins are just foundations. In 86 B.C., by which time Epidaurus's reputation was probably in decline, the Roman consul Sulla, leader of the forces invading the Peloponnese, looted the sanctuary and destroyed its buildings.

Nethertheless the **Sanctuary**, which is as large a site as Olympia or Delphi, holds considerable fascination. For the ruins here are all of buildings with identifiable functions: hospitals for the sick, dwellings for the priest-physicians, and hotels and amusements for the fashionable visitors to the spa. Their setting, a wooded valley thick with the scent of thyme and pine, is self-evidently that of a health farm.

The site begins just past the museum, where there are remains of Greek **baths** and a huge **gymnasium** with scores of rooms leading off a great colon-naded court; in its centre the Romans built an **odeion**. To the left is the outline of the **stadium**, used for the ancient games. To the right, a small **Sanctuary of Egyptian Gods** reveals a strong presumed influence on the medicine used at the site.

Just beyond the stadium are the foundations of the **Temple of Asclepius** and beside it a rectangular building known as the **Abaton**. Patients would sleep here to await visitation from the healing god, who probably appeared in a more physical manifestation than expected; harmless snakes are believed to have been kept in the building and released at night to give a curative lick.

The strong significance of the serpent at Epidaurus – Asclepius was thought to assume its form – is elaborated in the next building you come to: the circular **Tholos**, one of the best-preserved buildings on the site and designed, like the theatre, by Polycleitus. Its inner foundation walls form a labyrinth which it is believed was used as a snakepit – and according to one theory a primitive form of shock therapy for mental patients. The afflicted would crawl in darkness through the outer circuit of the maze, guided by a crack of light towards the middle where they would find themselves surrounded by writhing snakes. Presumably, on occasions, it worked.

The Coast West to Náfplio

The coastline around the southern tip of the Argolid can be a good scenic ride, especially the cliff-hugging corniche road between Fanári and Galatás, but its resorts are generally overdeveloped. If you've a car then you can pick your beaches and take a leisurely route back to Náfplio. If you haven't, you'll probably travel this way only if heading for one of the **Argo-Saronic islands** (see *Chapter Six*). MÉTHANA has direct connections to Éyina; GALATÁS to Póros; ERMIÓNI to Ídhra (Hydra) and Spétses; KÓSTA and PORTOHÉLI to Spétses.

Paleá Epídhavros

The closest beach to Epidaurus is **PALEÁ EPÍDHAVROS**, with black sands, a couple of hotels and a **campsite**. It's a functional enough place to stop en route to or from Athens but has a slightly down-at-heel air. Farther south the main road takes on more promise as it loops around the coast. **MÉTHANA**, on its own peninsula, is a minor spa, whose devotees are attracted by warm sulphur springs. **GALATÁS**, only 200m across the water from Póros, has the best scenery (pine hills, backed by mountains) and the most interesting excursions.

Close by the village of TRIZÍNA are ruins of **Ancient Troezene**, the birthplace of Theseus and location of his domestic dramas with Phaedra and Hippolytus as recounted by Euripides and Racine. Such remains as there are are spread over a wide site, most conspicuous are the three ruined Byzantine chapels constructed of ancient blocks and a tower whose bottom half is third century B.C., its top medieval. This stands at the lower end of a gorge, the course of an ancient aqueduct, which you can follow in half an hour's walk to the **'Devil's Bridge'** (*Yéfira tou Dhiavólou*), a natural rock formation spanning the chasm.

Following the coast road south for a couple of kilometres beyond Galatás, you reach **Limonódhassos**, an enormous grove of lemon trees above the small beach of **Alikí** (see Póros in *Chapter Six*). A path, signposted 'Restaurant Cardassi', leads through the grove, past irrigation channels to a taverna.

Beyond this point, the road is comparatively new, created to open up additional resorts close to Athens. **PLÉPI** (or 'HYDRA BEACH') is a 'villaurbanisation', visited by boats from beachless Ídhra opposite. **ERMIÓNI** is better: an old established village enclosed by a rocky bay, saved from development perhaps by lack of a sandy beach. **KÓSTA** and **PORTOHÉLI**, on either side of a bay, are gradually merging into each other, forming a somewhat soulless resort: a mix of charter hotels and facilities for yachters exploring the Argo-Saronic.

The **route back to Náfplio** from Portohéli runs inland, via attractive KRANÍDHI, scrambling its way slowly up through the mountains. It is covered by a twice-daily bus, which meets the ferry from Spétses.

South from Náfplio: the coast to Leonídhi

The coast **south from Náfplio** is one of the least known and least exploited in the Peloponnese – a state that, alas, is unlikely to continue for very much longer. It is mountainous terrain, increasingly so as you move south towards Monemvassía where the few coastal villages seem carved out from their dramatic backdrop. None offers more than basic facilities, and the beaches are pebble rather than sand, but for anyone seeking sea and calm they're as good as they come.

Access is easiest from Árgos, either by **bus** (2 departures daily to Leonídhi, which has connections on as far as Kosmás) or by **hydrofoil** (the 'Flying Doplphins' to Monemvassía usually stop en route at Pláka, Paralía Kiparíssi and Limáni Yérakas).

Beware – few of the villages covered in this route have banks or facilities for **changing money**, so carry enough with you for your stay.

Ástros and Tirós

The initial section of coast from Náfplio to Ástros and Áyios Andhréas is low-lying: less spectacular than the sections further south, but pleasant enough. The first village of any size is **PARALÍA ÁSTROS**, whose houses are tiered against a headland shared by an ancient acropolis (minor ruins) and medieval fort. Back from the beach, which extends for 6km of sand and gravel south of the fishing harbour, there are half a dozen tavernas and a similar number of hotels and **private rooms**, most modestly priced. The village is an attractive place though in season the one spot on this coast that could be described as touristed; if it's isolation you're after, best to keep going.

Just south, a trio of surprisingly neat and compact villages – the inland settlements of ÁSTROS, KORAKAVÓUNI and ÁYIOS ANDHRÉAS – perch on the foothills of **Mt. Párnon** as it drops to meet the lush, olive-green plain. A little beyond Áyios Andhréas (10km from Ástros) the road curls down to the coast and the first in a series of fine-pebbled swimming coves, crammed between the massive spurs of Párnon. There are **rooms** at several of the coves and one official **campsite** (*Arcadia Camping*), but if you plan to stay bring plenty of food from Ástros. The first conventional lodging is at **PARALÍA TIROÚ**, no great shakes with its cement quay and houses, but with an excellent pebble beach just beyond the windmill-crowned headland. **TIRÓS** proper, 3km inland, is an attractive hill village with numerous **rooms** to let, and a visitable monastery, Panayía Kariás.

Leonídhi, Pláka and Inland

Gigantic red cliffs which wouldn't look out of place in the American Southwest confine **LEONÍDHI**, 4km inland and the terminus of the Árgos bus route. It is a prosperous agricultural town, and therefore has little need to encourage tourists – most of whom in any case end up down by the sea at Leonídhi's diminutive port, Pláka.

PLÁKA is a tiny place, consisting mainly of **rooms** to let, the inexpensive *Hotel Dionysos*, and a couple of seafront tavernas/cafés, both of which have good food. Even better, and cheaper, is the taverna across the river (dry in season) to the north; it features homemade wine so good that you need considerable willpower to leave. If you want to camp, this side of the river is also a better bet; the beach on the south has 'No Camping' signs everywhere.

The road **inland from Leonídhi** is worth taking for its own sake. Climbing up into Párnon, it follows a ravine for the first 13km, at which point there's a signpost off to the **Moní Elónis**. Set in a niche in the cliffs, this is approached by a downward sloping path, ending at an impregnable gateway. If all looks closed pull the wire, which passes along the cliff to a large bell. Visitors seem to be welcome and the nuns show you around a small chapel crammed with icons and lanterns. Beautiful cold water with supposedly curative powers is available from a well set high in the cliff above the monastery. **Continuing south**, past the Elónis turning, you reach the high mountain village of **KOSMÁS**, with a grand *platía*, an inn and a couple of tavernas. Straddling the most important pass of Párnon, it can be a chilly place in spring or winter, but beautiful too, with its streams, cherry and walnut trees, and forests of fir all around. Beyond the village the road deteriorates into a brief unpaved section, through an uninhabited valley, then lurches slowly down to the village and Byzantine ruins of YERÁKI (see p.158).

This inland route is easily negotiable by car. On public transport, there is a mid-afternoon minibus from LEONÍDHI to KOSMÁS, but nothing for the 18km on to Yeráki. Yeráki itself has bus connections with SKÁLA (whence you can reach MONEMVASSÍA or YÍTHIO) and with SPÁRTI.

Kiparíssi and Liméni Yérakas

South of Leonídhi the coastline grows wilder and more sparsely inhabited, with just a couple of coastal settlements cut into the cliffs. **KIPARÍSSI**, the first of these, is a smaller version of Leonídhi: a main village 2km inland with a tiny port, PARALÍA KIPARÍSSI. Despite appearances on most maps, there's a passable road from here to MOLÁI, on the Spárti-Monemvassía road.

Final stop on the 'Flying Dolphins' route down to Monemvassía is the hamlet of **LIMÉNI YÉRAKAS**, which, with its larger inland village, YÉRAKAS, is in similar mold to Kiparíssi.

Trípoli: the Crossroads

TRÍPOLI is a major crossroads of the Peloponnese, from which most travellers either head north towards Olympia (the routes are covered in 'Arcadia and the North'), or south to Spárti and Mystra, or Kalamáta. Alternatives include more direct routes to the coast – west to Kiparissía, or east to Náfplio or Ástros/Leonídhi – and the Peloponnese railway, which continues its meandering course from Kórinthos and Árgos to Kiparissía and Kalamáta.

Few people decide to stay. A large, modern town, the administrative centre of Arcadia province and home of one of the country's largest army barracks, Trípoli doesn't exactly bombard you with its charm. It has no sights to speak of, either: medieval *Tripolitsa* was destroyed by retreating Turkish forces during the War of Independence, after Greek forces, led by Kolokotronis, had earlier massacred the town's entire population. The city's ancient predecessors, the rival towns of Tegéa to the south and Mantinea to the north, are the only local points of interest (see below).

Getting in and out of Trípoli can be fairly complicated. The major **bus terminal**, serving all destinations in Arcadia and the northern Peloponnese, is on Platía Kolokotróni, one of the main squares. For service to Messinía, Kalamáta and Pílos, walk west down Yioryíou to the Platía Ayíou Vassilíou, where these buses leave from outside the *Restaurant Ethnikon*. If you're going to Pátra or Kalávrita, turn right of the *platía* and walk 1km north on Ethnikís Andístassis, then turn left at the park for the tiny terminal. For buses south to Spárti, tickets are sold inside, and buses depart from outside, a small *zaharoplastío* on Vassilíssis Ólgas, some 300m south of Platía Kolokotrónis.

If you need to spend a night, the E-class **hotel** *Kynouria* (Vassilíssis Ólgas 79; ☎071/222-463) has spotless doubles with hot water; or, for a little more, there's a good C-class, *Hotel Alex* (Vassiléos Yioryíou 26; ☎071/223-465).

Ancient Tegea

Eight kilometres south of Trípoli, **ANCIENT TEGEA** was the main city of the central Peloponnese in Classical and Roman times, and, refounded in the tenth century, an important town again under the Byzantines. The diffuse and partially excavated site lies just outside the village of ALÉA (3 buses daily from the Platía Ayíou Vassilíou terminal in Trípoli).

The buses stop in the village beside a small **museum** (8.30am–2.45pm, Sun. 9am-2pm; closed Tues.; 200dr, students 100dr), well stocked with sculptures from the site. Turning left as you leave, a road leads in 100m to the main remains, the **Temple of Athena Alea**, in whose sanctuary two kings of Sparta (with which Tegea was allied) took refuge.

Keeping on the road past the site, it's a twenty-minute walk to the village of PALEA EPISKOPÍ, whose church – a huge modern pilgrim shrine – incorporates part of ancient Tegea's theatre and a number of Byzantine mosaics. Remains of the agora lie to the west. The village also has a couple of tavernas.

Nestáni and Mantinea

The direct Kórinthos-Trípoli highway, now nearing completion, will emerge on to the plains close to the village of **NESTÁNI**, and if you find yourself coming this way it is worth a brief detour: a lovely place, set below a gigantic stump of rock.

ANCIENT MANTINEA lies 5km to the west of the highway. The traditional rival of Tegea, it invariably allied with Athens when Tegea stood with Sparta, with Sparta when Tegea joined Thebes. Its site is unenclosed, the principal remains being the circuit of fourth century B.C. **walls** – still more or less intact, though much reduced in height. Alongside is a wonderfully eccentric modern **church**, a bit of a pastiche but still in the Byzantine tradition and superbly sited with the peaks of Mt. Ménalo as backdrop.

Mantinea is served by a daily bus from Trípoli but really only worth the detour for drivers. The route beyond loops around Ménalo and then forks: north towards Kalávrita, west through VITÍNA (with a reasonable hotel) and on to DHIMITSÁNA.

THE SOUTH: LAKONÍA AND MESSINÍA

Draw a line on a map from Kalamáta over the Taíyettos mountains, through Spárti and across to Leonídhi. This, broadly, is **Lakonía**, the ancient territories of the Spartans. It's a dramatic country of harsh mountains and, but for the lush strip of the Evrótas valley, of poor, rocky soil – terrain that has kept it isolated throughout history. **Taíyettos** itself is a formidable barrier, looming ahead of you for miles if you approach from Trípoli, and providing an exciting exit or entrance in the form of the Langádha Pass, between Spárti and Kalamáta.

Landscapes apart, the highlights here are **Byzantine and medieval sites**: the extraordinarily preserved towns of **Mystra** and **Monemvassía** above all, but also lesser sites such as **Yeráki** or the churches and bizarre towers of the remote and semidesertic **Máni** peninsula.

Moving west across the region, you enter **Messinía**, with its mellower countryside, and marvellously little-developed coast. There are good beaches at Messinía's own medieval sites – the twin fortresses of **Koróni** and **Methóni** – but if you are looking for sands to yourself in the Peloponnese, and you're unbothered by a near-total lack of facilities, you could do no better than explore the **shore north of Pílos**. En route are the remains of **Nestor's Palace**, foundations only, but the most important ancient site in the south and like Mycenae keying remarkably with the Homeric legend.

Spárti (Sparta)

Thucydides predicted that if the city of Sparta were deserted, 'distant ages would be very unwilling to believe its power at all equal to its fame'. The city had no great temples or public buildings and throughout its period of greatness remained unfortified – Lycurgus, architect of the Spartan constitution, declaring that 'it is men not walls that make a city'.

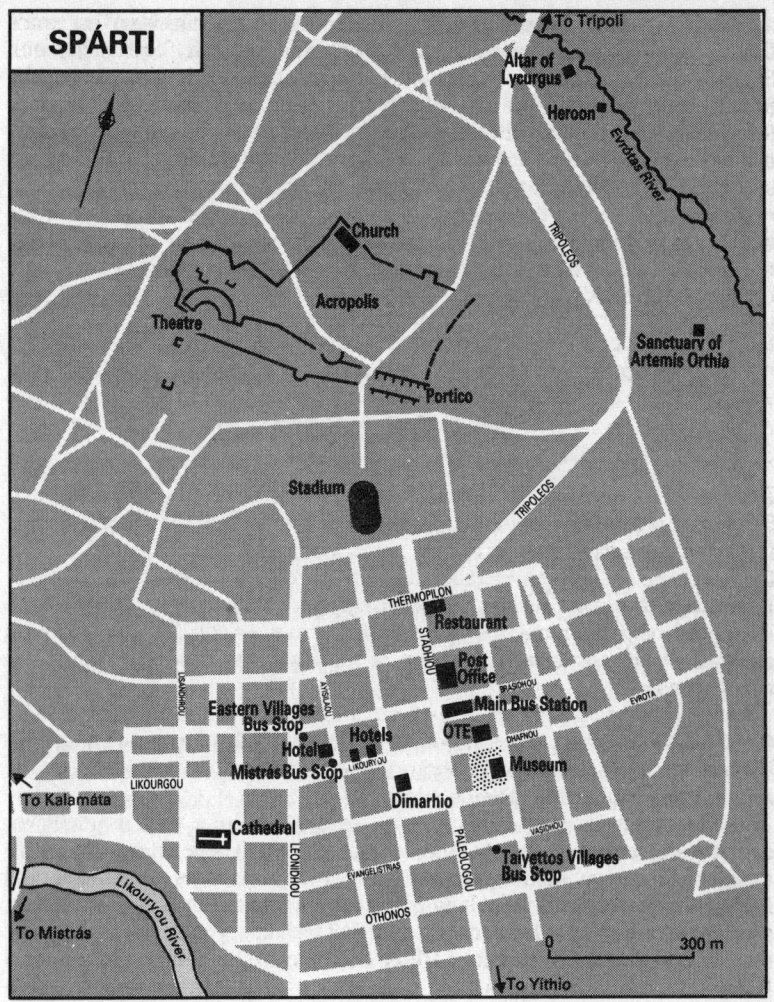

SPÁRTI

To Trípoli

Altar of Lycúrgus

Heroon

Evrótas River

Church

Acropolis

Theatre

Sanctuary of Artemis Orthia

Portico

TRIPOLEOS

Stadium

TRIPOLEOS

THERMOPILON

Restaurant

STADHIOU

Post Office

VRASIDOU

Main Bus Station

EVROTA

Eastern Villages Bus Stop

LISANDHOU

AYISILAOU

OTE

DHAFNOU

Hotels

Hotel

Mistrás Bus Stop

LIKOURYOU

Museum

LIKOURGOU

Dimarhio

VASIOHOU

To Kalamáta

Cathedral

LEONIDHOU

EVANGELISTRIAS

PALEOLOGOU

Taíyettos Villages Bus Stop

Likouryou River

OTHONOS

0   300 m

To Mistrás

To Yíthio

Modern **SPÁRTI**, consequently, has few ruins to speak of, though descending through the hills into the Shangri-La fertility of the Evrótas valley you can sense how strategically located was the ancient city-state. The ancient 'capital' occupied more or less the site of today's town, though it was less a city than a grouping of villages, commanding the Laconian plain from a series of low hills to the east of the river. It was at the height of its powers from the eighth to the fourth century B.C., the period when Spartan society followed Lycurgus's laws, defeated Athens in the Peloponnesian War, established colonies around the Greek world, and eventually lost hegemony through defeat to Thebes. A second period of prosperity came under the Romans – for whom this was an outpost in the south of Greece, with the Máni never properly subdued – but from the third century A.D. Sparta declined as nearby Mystra became the focus of Byzantine interest.

Practicalities

It is likely to be a visit to Mystra that brings you to Spárti and if you arrive reasonably early in the day you may well decide to move straight on. With its rough retsina, crude taverna food and rows of tractor dealers, Spárti isn't the most rewarding of Greek towns. But on the plus side, it does usually have enough beds to go around, with most of the cheaper **hotels** grouped about the central square. Among the best of these are the *Panhellinion* (Paliológou; ☎0731/28-031) and the *Kypros* (Leonidhíou 72; ☎0731/26-590), D- and E-class respectively. Cheapest of all, charging a per-person rate, is the E-class *Hotel Sparti* (Ayissiláou 46; ☎0731/21-343).

There are two **campsites** out on the Mystra road. Nearest, 2½km from Spárti, is *Camping Mystra* (☎0731/22-724) which charges a stiff 350dr per person plus 200dr per tent but compensates with a swimming pool; it is open year-round. Two kilometres further on – and thus closer to Mystra – is the new *Camping Castle View*, a very clean, well-managed site with a shop, snack-bar, restaurant and lower rates. Take the Mystra bus for either.

Eating in Spárti is unlikely to be a highlight, at least in the places about the square. There are a couple of fair restaurants, though: *Kali Kardia* at Ayissiláou 39, and a *psistariá* up at the north end of Stadhíou, just as it begins to bend into Tripoléos.

Getting out of Spárti is straightforward. The **main bus terminal** (for Trípoli, Athens, Monemvassía, Kalamáta and the Máni) is on Vassídhou, just off Stadhíou. **Buses for Mystra** leave (hourly on weekdays; less frequently at weekends) from the corner of the main street Likoúrgou and Ayissiláou; schedules are posted on the window of the café there. Additional stations for local villages include one on Meneláou, east of Stadhíou, for **Taíyettos**; and another at Ayissiláou 47, across from the open market.

Ancient Sparta

Traces of ancient Spartan glory are in short supply but there are some ruins to be seen to the north of the city if you follow the track behind the football stadium to the **acropolis**, tallest of the Spartan hills. An immense **theatre** here, built into the side of the hill, can be quite clearly traced, even though today most of its masonry has gone – hurriedly adapted for fortification when the Spartans' power declined and, later still, used in the building of the Byzantine city of Mystra. Above the theatre, to the left, are the foundations of a Temple to Athena. At the top of the acropolis sits the more substantial Byzantine church and monastery of Óssios Nikónas.

About 500 metres along the Trípoli road, a path descends to the remains of the **Sanctuary of Artemis Orthia** where Spartan boys underwent endurance tests by flogging. Pausanias records that young men often expired under the lash and adds that the altar had to be splashed with blood before the goddess was satisfied. Perhaps it was this aspect which attracted the Romans to revive the custom; the main ruins here are of the grandstand they built for onlookers to watch the spectacle.

Neither of these sites is enclosed, all movable artifacts and mosaics having been transferred to the town's small **Archaeological Museum** (9am–3pm, Sun. 9.30am–2.30pm; closed Tues.). Among its more interesting exhibits are a number of votive offerings found on the sanctuary site – knives set in stone that were presented as prizes to the Spartan youths and solemnly rededicated to the goddess.

Mystra (Mistrás)

A glorious, airy place, hugging a steep flank of Taíyettos, Mystra is arguably the most exciting and dramatic site that the Peloponnese can offer. Winding up the hillside is an astonishingly complete Byzantine city which once sheltered a population of some 42,000; you wander along winding alleys, through monumental gates, past medieval houses and palaces and above all into a sequence of churches, several of which yield superb and radiant frescoes. It is, in effect, like wandering into a massive museum of architecture, painting, and sculpture – and being placed within a different age.

Some history

That Mystra is here at all is an extraordinary quirk of history. The castle on its summit was built in 1249 by Guillaume II de Villehardouin, fourth Frankish Prince of the Morea, and together with the fortresses of Monemvassía and the Máni it guarded his territory. The Franks, however, were driven out of Mystra in 1271 and an isolated triangle of land in the southeastern Peloponnese became the **Despotate of Mystra**, a last province of the Greek Byzantine empire and for many years its virtual capital. While the walls of Constantinople enclosed little more than a pillaged and half-ruined city, Mystra hosted a defiant and splendid rebirth of Byzantine power. Its rulers – usually the son or brother of the eastern emperor, often the heir apparent – recaptured and controlled much of the Peloponnese, which became the largest of the ever-shrinking Byzantine provinces. It was to endure for two centuries before falling, amid internal struggling, to the Turks in 1460 – seven years after Constantinople.

Mystra's political significance was, however, overshadowed by its **artistic achievements**. Through the fourteenth and the first decades of the fifteenth, centuries it was the principal cultural and intellectual centre of the Byzantine world, sponsoring, amidst these highly uncertain conditions, a renaissance in the arts and attracting the finest of Byzantine scholars and theologians – among them a number of members of the imperial families, the Cantacuzenes and Paleologues. At the court here the humanist philosopher Gemisthus Plethon rediscovered and reinterpreted Plato; his followers, who moved to teach in Italy after Mystra's fall, exercised wide influence in

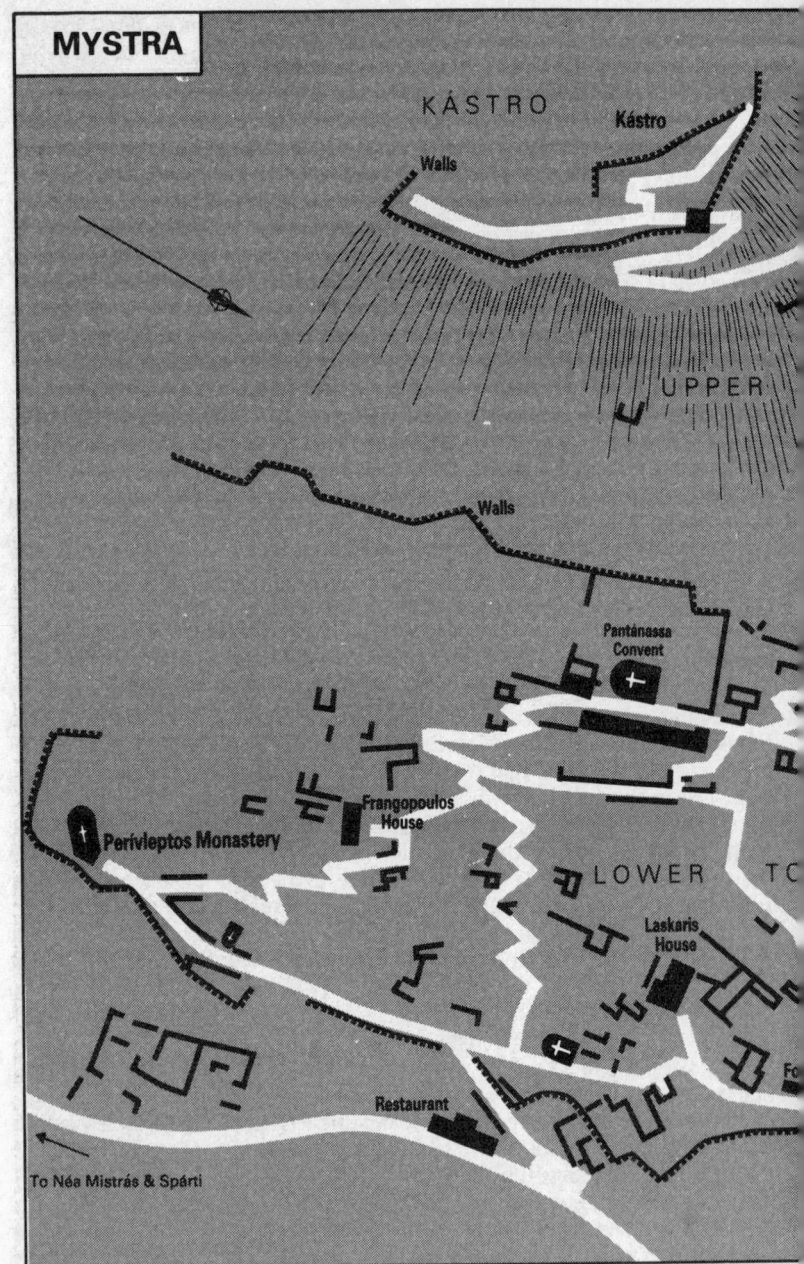

MYSTRA

KÁSTRO

Kástro

Walls

UPPER

Walls

Pantánassa
Convent

Frangopoulos
House

Perívleptos Monastery

LOWER   TO

Laskaris
House

Restaurant

Fo

To Néa Mistrás & Spárti

Parking

Walls

Upper Entrance

Ay. Sofia

Náfplio Gate

Palatáki

aos

vassia
e

Mosque

Despots' Palace

Refectory

Afendikó

Vrontohión
Monastery

Ay. Theódhori

Mitrópolis

Walls

Lower
Entrance

Xenia

0   100 m

Renaissance Florence and Rome. Here too, more tangibly, a last flourish of Byzantine architecture took form, with the building of a magnificent Despots' palace and a perfect sequence of churches, multidomed and brilliantly frescoed. It is these, remarkably preserved and sensitively restored, that provide the focus of this extraordinary site.

The town's post-Byzantine history follows a familiar Peloponnesian pattern. It was occupied by the Turks from the mid-fifteenth to late-seventeenth centuries, then taken briefly by the Venetians – under whom the town again rose to prosperity with a population of over 40,000. Decline set in with a second stage of Turkish control, from 1715 on, and destruction with the War of Independence, the site being evacuated after fires in 1770 and 1825. Restoration began in the first decades of this century, was interrupted by the civil war (it was for a while a battle site) and renewed in earnest in the 1950s.

The Byzantine city

Mon.–Sat. 8.45am–3pm, Sun. 9.30am–2.30pm; off season the site may close as early as 3pm.

The site of the Byzantine city comprises three main parts: the *Katohóra* (lower town), with the city's earliest and most important churches; the *Anohóra* (upper town), grouped around the vast shell of a royal palace; and the *Kástro* (castle). There are two entrances on the road up from the modern village of Néa Mistrás (see below); buses from Spárti make stops at both. Before setting out it is a good idea to stock up on refreshments; there is a (pricey) restaurant near the lower gate and a drink stall by the upper, but nothing within the site. Unless you're determinedly energetic, it makes sense to take the bus to the top entrance, then explore a leisurely downhill route.

The Upper Town and Kástro

Following a course from the upper entrance, the first identifiable building that you come to is the church of **Ayía Sofía** which served as the chapel for the Despots' Palace – the enormous structure beyond. The chapel's finest feature is its floor, made from polychrome marbles. Its frescoes, notably a *Pantokrator* (Christ in Majesty) and *Nativity of the Virgin*, have survived reasonably well, protected until recent years by coatings of whitewash applied by the Turks, who adapted the building as a mosque. Recognisable parts of the refectory and cells of its attached monastery survive also.

The **Kástro**, reached by a path that climbs directly from the upper gate, maintains the Frankish design of its original thirteenth-century construction, though it was repaired and modified by all successive occupants. There is a walkway around most of the keep, whose views allow an intricate panorama of the town below. The castle itself was the court of Guillaume II de Villehardouin but was used primarily as a citadel in later years.

Heading down from Ayía Sofía, there is a choice of routes. The right fork winds past ruins of a Byzantine mansion, the **Palatáki** or 'Small Palace', and **Áyios Nikólaos**, originally a Turkish building. The left fork is more interesting, passing the massively fortified **Náfplio Gate**, which was the principal entrance to the upper town, and the vast, multi-storeyed complex of the

Despots' Palace, parts of whose Gothic structures probably date to the Franks. Most prominent among its numerous buildings is a great vaulted audience hall, built at right angles to the line of the building, with ostentatious windows regally dominating the skyline; this was once heated by eight great chimneys and sported a painted facade. Behind it are mainly the ruins of official public buildings. To the right of the lower wing, flanking one side of a square used by the Turks as a marketplace, are the remains of a **mosque**.

The Lower Town

At the **Monemvassía Gate**, which links the upper and lower towns, there is a further choice of routes: right to the Pantánassa and Perívleptos monasteries; left to the Vrontohión monastery and cathedral. If time is running out it is easier to head right first, then double back down to the Vrontohión.

When excavations were resumed in 1952, the last thirty or so families, then still living in houses in the lower town, were moved out to Néa Mistrás. Only the nuns of the **Pantánassa convent** remained. Today they make a fair living from showing their church to visitors and from selling embroidery – beautiful work if you can imagine a use for it. The church, whose name means 'Queen of All', is perhaps the finest that survives in the town, perfectly proportioned in its blend of Byzantine and Gothic. Its **frescoes** date from various centuries, with some superb fifteenth-century work including *Scenes from the Life of Christ* in the gallery (entered by an external staircase). David Talbot Rice, in his classic study *Byzantine Art*, wrote of these frescoes that 'Only El Greco in the west, and later Gauguin, would have used their colours in just this way'. Many of the frescoes in the church were painted between 1687 and 1715, when Mystra was held by the Venetians.

Farther down on this side of the lower town is a balconied Byzantine mansion, the **House of Frangopoulos**, once the home of the Despotate's chief minister – who was incidentally the founder of the Pantánassa. Beyond it is the diminutive **Perívleptos monastery**, whose single-domed church, partially carved out of the rock, contains Mystra's most complete cycle of frescoes, almost all of which date from the fourteenth century. They are in some ways finer than those of the Pantánassa, blending an easy humanism with the spirituality of Byzantine icon traditions. In addition, they give an excellent idea of the structured iconography of a Byzantine church. The position of each figure depended upon its sanctity and so here upon the dome, the image of heaven, is portrayed the *Pantokrator* (the all-powerful Christ in glory after the Ascension); on the apse is the Virgin, and on the higher expanses of wall are depicted scenes from the *Life of Christ in this World*. Prophets and saints could only appear on the lower walls, decreasing in importance according to their distance from the sanctuary.

Along the path leading from Perívleptos to the lower gate are a couple of minor, much-restored churches, and, just above them, the **Laskaris House**, a mansion thought once to have belonged to relatives of the emperors. Like the Frangopoulos House, it is balconied; its ground floor probably served as stables. Close by, beside the path, is an old Turkish fountain.

The **Mitrópolis**, or cathedral, immediately beyond the gateway, is the oldest of Mystra's churches, built in 1309 under the first Paleologue ruler. A marble slab set in its floor is carved with the double-headed eagle of Byzantium, commemorating the spot where Constantine XI Paleologus, the last Eastern emperor, was crowned in 1448; he was to perish, with his empire, in the Turkish sacking of Constantinople in 1453. Of the church's frescoes, the earliest, in the north aisle, depict the *Torture and Burial of Áyios Dhimítrios*, the saint to whom the church is dedicated. The comparative stiffness of their figures contrasts with the later works opposite. These, illustrating the *Miracles of Christ* and the *Life of the Virgin*, are more intimate and lighter of touch; they date from the last great years before Mystra's fall. A **museum**, adjacent to the cathedral, contains various fragments of sculpture and pottery and a few icons from the various Mystra churches.

Finally, a short way uphill, is the **Vrontohión monastery**. This was the centre of cultural and intellectual life in the fifteenth century town – the cells of the monastery can still be discerned – and it was also the burial place of the despots. There are two churches attached. **Afendikó**, the further of the two, has been beautifully restored, revealing late frescoes, similar to those of Perívleptos, with startlingly bold juxtapositions of colour.

Néa Mistrás

Buses run regularly through the day from Spárti to the two Mystra site entrances, stopping (if requested) at the campsites en route, as well as at the modern village of **NÉA MISTRÁS**.

Néa Mistrás is quite attractive in its own right: a small roadside community whose half-dozen tavernas, crowded with tour buses by day, revert to a low-key life at night. **Accommodation**, however, is limited to the oversubscribed B-class *Hotel Byzantion* (☎0731/93-309; doubles 3500dr), and a small number of rooms. These are a little overpriced but worth the extra for the setting if you can arrive early enough in the day to get a place.

On from Spárti: Mount Taíyettos, the Langádha pass and Yeráki

Moving **on from Spárti** there is a tough choice of routes: west over Mount Taíyettos along the dramatic **Langádha Pass to Kalamáta**; south, skirting the mountain's foothills, to **Yíthio and the Máni**; east to the Byzantine towns of **Yeráki and Monemvassía**.

For anyone wanting to get to grips with the Greek mountains, there is **Taíyettos** itself, one of the most dramatic and hazardous ranges, with vast grey boulders and scree along much of its length. However, there is one reasonably straightforward path to the highest peak, Profítis Ilías.

Hiking Mount Taíyettos (Taygettus)

Gazing up at the crags above the castle at Mystra, Taíyettos looks both daunting and inviting. If all you want is a different perspective on the mountain, then the simplest course is to take a bus up from Spárti to **ANAVRITÍ**, a little way to the south of Mystra and closer to the peaks. The village has a monastery, a hotel and a number of rooms to rent; vistas are superb. Any serious **hiking from Anavrití**, however, needs experience and proper equipment; and it should definitely not be undertaken alone – a sprained ankle could be fatal up here. If you are confident, there are three possibilities. The most realistic is to try to follow the partly intact *kalderími* (cobbled way) to Mystra via ÁYIOS IOÁNNIS: a long day-hike. The others involve at least one and probably two nights on the mountain and (after initial sections) have no paths to follow. These are either: setting out to the west (as did Patrick Leigh Fermor in *Mani*) to ascend the Neraidhovoúni saddle (2025m); or south, all along the top of the ridge, to Profítis Ilías (2404m). It should be stressed that these are *not* outings for the inexperienced, and you should have detailed government maps and proper equipment.

The hike to Profítis Ilías

Far more accessible for regular walkers is the reasonably well-marked **route to Profítis Ilías**. This leads off from the village of PALEOPANAYÍA, a short bus ride south of Spárti off the Yíthio road. There a dirt road, signposted by the EOS, climbs for some ten kilometres to the west up a long valley to TÓRIZA and POLIÁNNA. It's a dusty slog if you have to do it on foot, so if possible take a taxi (usually available at PALEOPANAYÍA).

Beside the track at POLIÁNNA there is a ramshackle house where in summer you can get drinks and a simple meal (possibly a bed if you need one). From here to Profítis Ilías takes about 4½ to 5 hours. The path begins on the left a few minutes beyond the house, by a rather drunken blue sign pointing into the fir forest.

Following it, you come almost immediately to a concrete junction box in a water pipeline where you turn sharp right. Five minutes later you join a forestry track, and soon after the first of the red-arrow waymarks appears. There is no difficulty in following the path thereafter, a two-hour trail through woods of Greek fir all the way to the refuge (*katafiyio*). Just before reaching it you pass the spring of Ayía Varvára, the only source of water you'll see; in summer it is often dry, so be prepared.

The **refuge** sits on a beautiful grassy knoll shaded by tremendous storm-blasted black pines. The conical peak of Profítis Ilías rises directly above; if you can get your climb to coincide with a full moon you won't regret it. There is plenty of room for camping, and the hut has a porch to provide shelter in bad weather.

The path to the summit starts at the rear left corner of the refuge and swings right on a long reach. Level and stony at first, it leaves the treeline and loops up a steep bank to a sloping meadow, where it is ineffectually marked by twisted, rusting signs with their lettering long obliterated. Keep heading right across the slope towards a distinct secondary peak until, once around a steep bend, the path begins to turn back left in the direction of the summit. It slants steadily upward following a natural ledge until, at a very clear nick in the ridge above you, it turns right and crosses to the far side, from where you look down on the Gulf of Messinía. Turn left and you climb steeply up to the summit in 25 more minutes.

There is a squat stone chapel and outbuildings on the **summit**, used during the celebrations of the feast of the prophet Elijah (Profítis Ilías) on July 19-20. The views are breathtaking: north up through the Peloponnese, south into the Máni, east and west over the sea.

Spárti to Kalamáta: the Langádha pass

The **Langádha pass**, the sixty-kilometre route across the Taíyettos from Spárti to Kalamáta, is the nearest road equivalent to a walk up the mountain. Remote and barren, with no habitation at all for the central 25-kilometre section, it unveils in a constant drama of peaks, magnificent at all times but startling at sunrise. This was, incidentally, the route that Telemachus took in *The Odyssey* on his way from Nestor's palace at Pylos to that of Menelaus at Sparta. It took him a day's journey by chariot – good going by any standards; buses today take three hours.

At TRÍPI, 14km from Spárti, there are two small D-class hotels, the *Keadas* (☎0731/98-222) and *Trypi* (☎0731/26-387). Just beyond the village the road climbs steeply into the mountains and enters the **gorge of Langádha**, a wild sequence of hairpins through the pines. To the north of the gorge, so it is said, the Spartans used to leave their sick or puny babies to die from exposure. Beyond the gorge, close to the summit of the pass, there is a summer-only, B-class **hotel**, the *Pension Taiyetos*, and a *Tourist Pavilion*. The first actual village on the route beyond Trípi is ARTEMISÍA. From here you enter another gorge before zigzagging down to Kalamáta.

Yeráki

A kilometre or two north of Spárti, a roadside sign suggests that travelers detour to 'visit the Byzantine antiquities at Yeraki'. Such signs in Greece are often over-imaginative, but in this case the advice is sound. Medieval **YERÁKI**, with its Frankish castle and fifteen chapels spread over a spur of Mount Párnon, stands a respectable third to the sites of Mystra and Monemvassía. And with adequate bus service to and from Spárti (40km) it's a mystery why the place is not more visited. There is no standard accommodation in the village, though rooms may be negotiable through the taverna.

The village

'Modern' **YERÁKI**, with its population of 1500, must be much as Néa Mistrás would have been twenty or thirty years ago, before tourism. It is visibly traditional, with graceful-arched buildings grouped over a knoll above the Laconian plain. The place suffered heavy destruction during the War of Independence, but although most of the buildings date from the nineteenth or early twentieth century, they are old enough to seem timeless.

At the top of the settlement is the very ancient **acropolis**, preserving stretches of Mycenaean walls; it's a totally unpretentious (and untended) site, used as a playground and with patches of wheat grown around the fortifications. A small **museum** in the village displays local finds.

Medieval Yeráki

All of which is pleasant enough, but might leave you wondering why you have come – until you look northeast towards the first low ridges of Párnon. Here, an hour's walk by road and then a very steep path, is **Medieval Yeráki**. One of the original twelve Frankish baronies set up in the wake of the Fourth Crusade, it remained through the fourteenth century an important Byzantine town, straddling the road between Mystra and its port at Monemvássia. The site is spectacular, with sweeping vistas over the olive-covered Evrótas plain and across to Taíyettos. It is unenclosed, though the churches with frescoes are locked; a caretaker is usually around with the keys (ask at the taverna in the village before you set out).

The most substantial remains are those of the **Kástro**, built in 1256 by the local Frankish baron, Jean de Nivelet, who had inherited Yeráki, with six other lordships, from his father. Its heavily fortified design is based on that of the Villehardouin fortress at Mystra, for this was one of the most vulnerable Frankish castles of the Morea, intended to control the wild and only partially-conquered territories of Taíyettos and the Máni. In the event, Jean retained his castle for less than a decade, surrendering to the Byzantines in 1262 and buying an estate near Kórinthos on the proceeds. Within the fortress are huge cisterns for withstanding siege, and the largest of Yeráki's churches: thirteenth-century **Áyios Yióryios**, with a Frankish heraldic shield above its door and a Gothic tomb within.

The churches on the slope below the castle also mix Frankish and Byzantine features, and many incorporate ancient blocks from Yeráki's ancient predecessor, *Geronthrai*. **Áyios Athanássios** is perhaps the most interesting, with a Gothic fresco of Joshua attacking a city of Amorites. Joshua's forces are depicted chasing the defenders to the gate of their castle: a scene, in essence, of the Frankish conquest of the Morea (upon which Amorite may have been a pun). The earliest of the churches is **Áyios Ioánnis**, built before the Franks arrived in the twelfth century and with frescoed portraits of Byzantine empresses in its roundels; with its twin cross-in-square chapel of **Áyios Sózon**, it is half-hidden among the foliage of Yeráki's kitchen gardens. **Evangelístria**, nearby, has frescoes of David and Solomon; and if the caretaker is willing, there are further frescoes to be seen in twelfth-century **Áyia Paraskeví** and thirteenth-century **Áyios Yióryios**.

Monemvassía and South to Neápoli

After Mystra you half-expect Byzantine sites to be disappointing, or at least low-key like Yeráki. **MONEMVASSÍA** is definitively neither. Set impregnably on a great island-like irruption of rock, the medieval seaport is equally as exciting as its spiritual counterpart inland: a place of grand, haunted atmosphere, whose houses and churches are all the more evocative for being populated – albeit on a largely weekend and touristic basis.

Its name – *Moni Emvasis* means 'single entrance' – is a reference to the town's approach from the mainland: across a kilometre-long causeway built this century to replace a sequence of wooden bridges. In appearance the rock resembles Gibraltar and Monemvassía in fact held a similarly strategic position through the Middle Ages, controlling the sea-lines from Italy and the West to Constantinople and the Levant. Fortified on all approaches, the town was invariably the last outpost of the Peloponnese to fall to invaders. At the outset of the thirteenth century it was the Byzantines' sole possession in the Morea, eventually being taken by the Franks in 1249, but only after three years of siege. Regained by the Byzantines as part of the ransom for the captured Guillaume de Villehardouin, it served as the chief commercial port of the Despotate of the Morea and was to all effects the capital. Mystra, despite the presence of the court, was never much more than a large village; Monemvassía at its peak had a population of almost 60,000.

Yéfira and practicalities

Monemvassía can be approached by road or more enjoyably by sea. There are twice-weekly **ferries** from Pireás, and Kastélli on Crete, and more or less daily **hydrofoils** in season, linking it to the north with Leonídhi, Spétses and Pireás, to the south with Neápoli and the island of Kíthira. Buses connect with Spárti three times daily and Yíthio (change at Mólai) once.

The boat or hydrofoil will drop you at a mooring midway down the causeway; buses arrive in the town of **YÉFIRA** on the mainland. Most accommodation is in Yéfira, a slightly amorphous waterside town, with a pebble beach and a lot of recent and impending development. By the causeway there are a couple of reasonable **hotels**: the E-class *Akroyiali* (☎0732/61-202) and D-class *Aktaion* (☎0732/61-234), both around 1700dr for a double. There are half a dozen other pensions and **rooms** places, too, most at similar or slightly cheaper prices; just follow the signs. The nearest **campsite**, *Camping Paradise* is 3½km north of Yéfira – a bit of a walk but near a good beach.

Rooms on the rock are a lot more expensive – in season, at least – and are in short supply. However, if you've the money, or a group of people to split costs, the *Hotel Malvasia* (☎0732/61-435) is one of the most attractive in the country. Its rooms are in two adjoining mansions (signposted from Monemvassía's main street), beautifully restored and furnished; prices can run around 3500dr a double in high season. A few other rooms on the rock are sporadically available for rent if you ask around at the shops and taverna on the main street; prices are comparable to the *Malvasia*.

The Rock: medieval Monemvassía

From Yéfira nothing can be seen of Monemvassía's town, and little more is revealed as you walk across the causeway, past a spectral-looking garage with a rattling Mobil sign. But, with the rock rising sheer above, the powerful spirit of the place is asserted, and turned to reality when the road is suddenly barred by huge castellated walls. Once through the fortified entrance gate, wide enough only for person or donkey, everything finally appears: piled upon one another amid narrow stone streets and alleyways are houses with tiled roofs and walled gardens, distinctively Byzantine churches, and high above, the improbably long castle walls protecting the town on the summit.

History

The impregnability of this site, which was only ever taken by siege, dictated an unusually individual history. It was founded by the Byzantines in the sixth century, becoming immediately an important port. Following a brief period of Frankish occupation, it returned to **Byzantine** rule, and experienced something of a golden age, in the thirteenth century. Populated by a number of noble Byzantine families, the town reaped considerable wealth from estates inland, from the export of wine (the famed *Malmsey*, mentioned by Shakespeare) and from roving corsairs who preyed on Latin shipping heading for the East. When the rest of the Morea fell to the Turks in 1460, Monemvassía was able to seal itself off, placing itself first under the control of the Papacy, later under the **Venetians**. Only in 1540 did the Turks gain control, the Venetians having abandoned their garrison after Suleiman the Magnificent's victory at Préveza.

Turkish occupation precipitated a steady decline, both in prestige and population. However, Monemvassía was again in the forefront of events during the War of Independence – the first of the major Turkish fortresses to fall, after a terrible siege, in April 1821. Subsequently, with the Turkish inhabitants massacred, the need for such strongholds at an end and (at the end of the nineteenth century) shipping routes changing with the opening of the Corinth Canal, the town drifted into a village existence, its buildings for the most part allowed to fall into ruin. By the last war (during which 4000 New Zealand troops were evacuated from the rock) only eighty families remained; today there are just ten. Many of the houses, though, have been restored over the past two decades and at weekends there is a fair summer population of Athenians, along with a scattering of fortunate expatriates. Their presence, increasingly, is added to by tourists – Monemvassía having recently, and rightly, found its way back onto the map.

The Town

Standing at the **gateway** to the rock there is the same sense of luxury and excitement as at Mystra: the prospect of being able to walk each street, explore every possible turn of this extraordinary place.

The **LOWER TOWN**, once sheltered forty churches and over 800 homes, an incredible mass of building which explains the intricate network of alleys. A single main street – up and slightly to the left from the gateway – shelters most of the restored houses, as well as a café, two tavernas, and a scattering of shops. The **tavernas** add much-needed life to the rock, and are beautiful locations in the evening, when the day-trippers have gone. One is owned by the Ritsos family, relatives of Yannis Ritsos, one of Greece's leading living poets (and an important member of the Communist party), who was born on the rock.

At the end of the street is the lower town's tiny main square, with a well in its centre and a *kafenío* along one side. Foremost, however, is the great, vaulted **Mitrópolis**, the cathedral built by the Byzantine Emperor Andronicus II Comnenus when he made Monemvassía a see in 1293. The largest medieval church in southern Greece, it is dedicated to Christ in Chains (*Hristós Elkómenos*). Across the square the domed church of **Áyios**

Pávlos was transformed by the Turks into a mosque and now shelters a small museum of local finds; it is rarely open. Unusually for Ottoman Greece, the Christian cathedral was allowed to function during the occupation – and must have done so beside this mosque.

Down towards the sea is a third church, the **Hrissafítissa**, with its bell hanging from a bent-over old cypress tree in the courtyard. It was restored and adapted by the Venetians in a second, eighteenth-century, occupation when for twenty-odd years they took the Peloponnese from the Turks. Continuing on here by the sea, past the *Hotel Malvasia*, you can get to a small strip of concrete and rocks for swimming.

The climb to the **UPPER TOWN** is highly worthwhile, not least for the solitude, since most of the day-trippers stay down below. Its fortifications, like those of the lower town, are substantially intact; indeed the **entrance gate** retains its iron slats. Within, the site is a ruin, though infinitely larger than you could imagine from below. In medieval times its population was much greater than that of the lower town, though it is today deserted – the last resident having moved down in 1911. Close by the gateway is the beautiful thirteenth-century **Ayía Sofía**, the only fully intact building, its candles flickering anarchically in the wind. It was founded as a monastery by Andronikos II, along a plan similar to that of Dhafní, though the outbuildings have long since crumbled to foundations.

Beyond the church extend acres of ruins: the stumpy bases of Byzantine houses and public buildings, and, perhaps most striking, a vast **cistern** to ensure a water supply in time of siege. Monemvassía must have been more or less self-sufficient in this respect, though its weakness was its food supply, all of which had to be imported from the mainland. In the last siege, by Mavromihalis's Maniot army in the War of Independence, the Turks were reduced to eating rats – and, so the propagandists claimed, Greek children.

There is a drop of 270m below the Ayía Sofía, and the cliffs and cistern are uncovered. It's therefore wise to descend before dusk. At sunset, though, it really is a glorious place, charged with derelict grandeur.

Neápoli

Isolated at the southeastern tip of the Peloponnese, **NEÁPOLI** is easiest reached by hydrofoil: there are 'Flying Dolphins' from Monemvassía and Yíthio, and connections on to Kíthira. Alternatives include a daily bus from Spárti (3hrs) or the twice-weekly Pireás-Monemvassía-Kíthira-Crete ferry.

The town is an unremarkable but pleasant enough resort, more developed than you expect for the location and patronised almost exclusively by Greeks. There are several **hotels** and a very few rooms to let; the E-class *Hotel Neapolis* (☎0732/41-339), by the port, is good value.

Sandy **beaches** line both sides of the town. That to the north leads around to the village of VINGLÁFIA, where you can negotiate for a fishing boat across to the islet of **Elafónissos**. This has a single fishing hamlet and a couple of excellent beaches – one, Káto Nísso, reputedly on the verge of development. There are two B-class **pensions**, both June-September only: the *Aster tis Elafonissou* (0732/49-271) and *Elafonissos* (0732/49-268).

To the south of Neápoli a road leads through ÁYIOS NIKÓLAOS and then deteriorates to a dirt track (very tricky for cars) across the last sliver of peninsula to the hamlet of VELANÍDHIA. Neither place has accommodation.

The Island of Kíthira (Kythera)

Kíthira is one of the least well-known Greek islands. Set apart from the main archipelagos, including the Ionian to which it technically belongs, it is connected most easily with the ports of Neápoli and Yíthio, and Kastélli on Crete – all somewhat remote. In one respect, however, it does have a reputation: Kíthira is *the* emigrant island to beat all others. Since the war, it has lost over 75 percent of its population to Australia, and the remainder – who know Australia as 'Big Kíthira' – are kept going largely by remittances sent home.

As such, the island has a very different feel than most. There is an insularity about the place and a reticence towards outsiders which can leave you feeling a bit of an intruder. Local hotels and tavernas do a good business with vacationing Kíthiran-Australian families and can seem unconcerned about other customers. They can be full, too; this is not an easy island to find a room, either in season, or out (when few places stay open).

The landscape, underfarmed and slightly ghostlike, has seen a more than usually troubled past, with no less than eighty invasions. Along with Monemvassía, Kíthira was once an important military and trading outpost, again only really losing its function (and population) with Greek independence and the opening of the Corinth Canal. Its early settlers included Phoenicians, Minoans, and Romans; in Byzantine times it was a fief of a Monemvassía family and a refuge for nobles after the fall of the mainland to the Turks; later it was Venetian, then Turkish, and briefly Russian, until being ceded with the other Ionian islands back to Greece by the British in 1864. Most of these occupiers, the Venetians especially, have left traces on a land – 30km by 15km – that is substantial by Greek island standards.

Orientation

Most ferries call at both the island **ports**: Ayía Pelayía in the north and Kapsáli, below Kíthira's capital, Hóra, in the south; hydrofoils run only to Ayía Pelayía. Kíthira's main road links these three points and you can hitch easily enough from one to the other or take a taxi; don't rely on the bus, which runs just once daily. From the **airport**, 5km off the road at Potamós, again either hitch or take a taxi.

There are **rooms** – in short supply in season – at Ayía Pelayía, Hóra, and Kapsáli (which also has an official **campsite**). Unofficial camping is possible, though not widespread; the beach at Vroúlea usually has a small summer community. To get around, a hired **moped** (available at either Hóra or Kapsáli) is invaluable.

Leaving Kíthira, check on the confusing schedules for boats and hydrofoils (the pattern is indicated in the 'Travel Details' at the end of this chapter) at the port offices in Ayía Pelayía or Kapsáli, or at the travel agent in Hóra. *Olympic Airways* has an office at the village of Potamós.

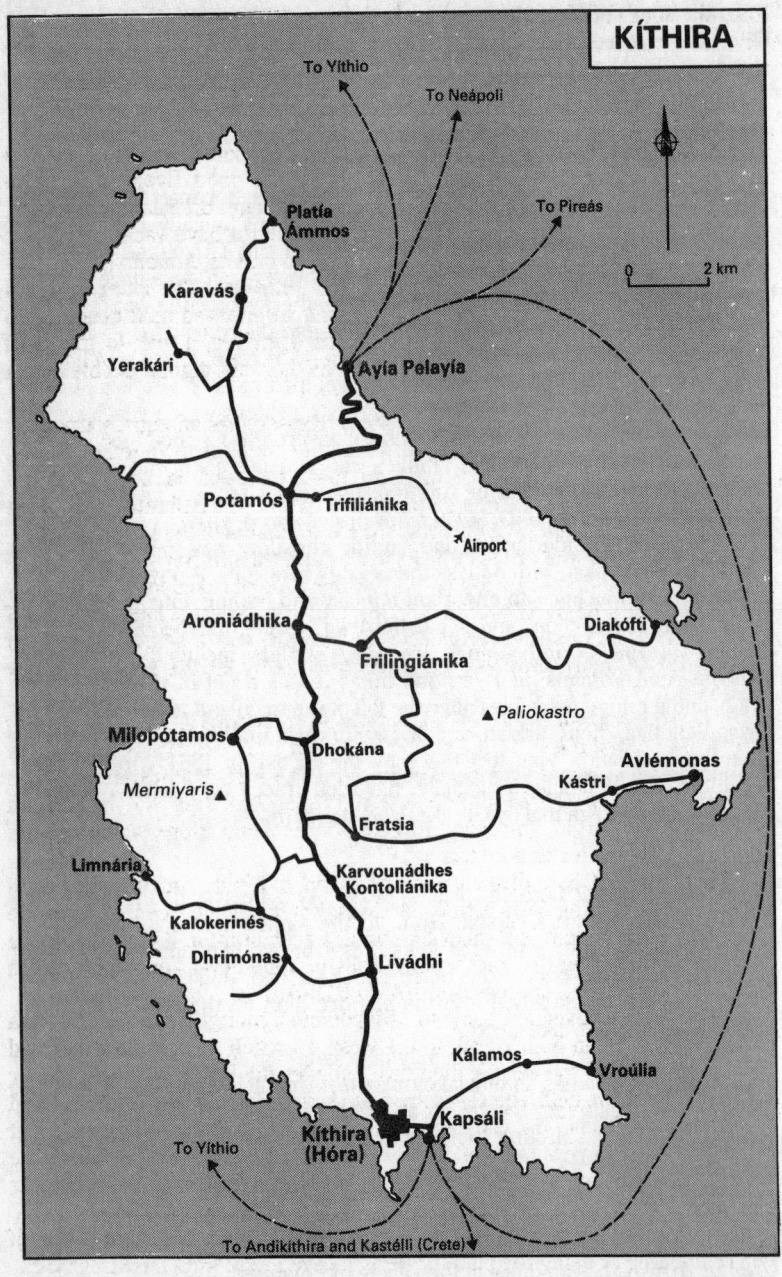

KÍTHIRA

To Yíthio

To Neápoli

To Pireás

0   2 km

Platía Ámmos

Karavás

Yerakári

Ayía Pelayía

Potamós   Trifiliánika

Airport

Aroniádhika   Diakófti

Frilingiánika

Paliokastro

Milopótamos   Dhokána   Avlémonas

Kástri

Mermiyaris

Fratsia

Limnária   Karvounádhes
Kontoliánika

Kalokerinés

Dhrimónas   Livádhi

Kálamos   Vroúlia

Kíthira   Kapsáli
(Hóra)

To Yíthio

To Andíkithira and Kastélli (Crete)

Kapsáli, Hóra and the interior

Given the choice, most visitors stay on the ferry to **KAPSÁLI** which, in addition to its harbour function, is Kíthira's only real resort. Set on an isthmus between double pebble-sand bays, it is certainly picturesque – a stage-setting enhanced out to sea by Avgó (Egg) islet, legendary birthplace of Aphrodite. Accommodation, however, is not plentiful. There are some reasonable **rooms** in a mansion owned by Emmanuel Komnenos (a good Byzantine Kíthira name) and a few others signposted around the village; the island **campsite**, though, 250m up the road to Hóra, is more likely to have vacancies (open mid-June–September only). At the waterside, two outlets, *Mihalis* (☎0733/31-008) and *Panayiotis* (☎0733/31-004) hire out **mopeds**. The latter also has windsurfers and canoes. To the east of Kapsáli an unpaved road heads off to the village of KÁLAMOS (5km). Just before it arrives, a fork to the right veers down to the coast at **VROÚLIA** (5km further on), a good pebble beach with a single taverna.

HÓRA (or KÍTHIRA), a steep 2km above Kapsáli, has an equally dramatic site, its Cycladic-style houses tiered about the walls of a Venetian **castle**. Along with several of the mansions in the town, the castle is carved with the Venetian coats of arms, the winged Lion of St. Mark. A small **museum** (open 8am–3pm, closed Tues.; free) nearby houses remnants of the island's numerous occupiers. **Rooms** are slightly easier to find than in Kapsáli. The supermarket is a good first stage to enquire, or there's a reasonable-value pension (owned by Eleni Kalliyeri, ☎0733/31-026). Other facilities include a couple of **banks**, an **OTE**, **post office** and **petrol station**, and a second branch of *Panayiotis* with more **mopeds for hire**. *Zorba* is by far the best of the few tavernas.

North from Kapsáli and Hóra, the main road runs through LIVÁDHI (4km; with a few rooms to let), where a fork heads left to DHRIMÓNAS, and, 3km further west, the island's principal monastery, **Panayía Mirtidhíon**. With its blackened icon of the Virgin, this attracts pilgrims from the island and beyond on the Virgin's birthday, August 25. Set amid cypresses above the cliffs, it has rooms for visitors to stay.

MILOPÓTAMOS, at the centre of the island, is Kíthira's main attraction: a village luxuriant as an oasis with its streams, watermill and trees. Right at the heart of the settlement is a valley-like park, a restaurant in its midst. On the hillside below, within the fragmenting walls of a medieval Venetian fort, lies Milopótamos's ruined predecessor, KÁTO HÓRA.

The reason most visitors come to Milopótamos, though, is to see the **Ayía Sofía caves**, half an hour's walk to the west. To reach them, follow the road forking right out of the village, then turn left after the bridge and look out for stairs carved in the cliff. The caves are open regularly only in July and August (3–7pm; closed Tues.) but you can usually locate the guide in Milopótamos at other times of the year (ask for Andreas at the taverna). They are worth the effort to see, spreading across a sequence of chambers; one of these, used as a church in days of Turkish rule, is whitewashed and frescoed.

Milopótamos can be reached off the main island road at MÍTATA (easier if you're hitching or using the bus), or along a paved road from DHRIMÓNAS.

Ayía Pelayía, the north and the east

Few travellers stay in the north of Kíthira, though it has the better beaches and, arguably, the friendlier villages. **AYÍA PELAYÍA**, the island's main port, is one such, with a likely collection of rooms and, slightly more luxurious, the *Hotel Kytheria* (☎0733/33-321; doubles around 2400dr). The town itself is no beauty, with a line of modern buildings along the waterside, but functional enough. It has a small beach of its own; another – better though more remote – is at **PLATÍA ÁMMOS**, 8km north via the village of KARAVÁS.

South of the port, and reached by following a track off to the left of the road to Potamós, are the ruins of Kíthira's medieval capital, **PALEÓ HÓRA**. It is not easy to spot from the road – and was not intended to be. Throughout the Middle Ages Kíthira was threatened by pirates, initially Saracen Arabs from Crete, later Turks. Paleó Hóra, concealed by great spurs of rock, survived through to 1537, when it was discovered and sacked by Barbarossa; the island was for a time deserted before being resettled by the Venetians. The remains of the town (in parts merged with the rocks) and the views are worth the haul. For some refreshment **POTAMÓS**, the north's largest village, is about the same distance from Paleó Hóra as Áyia Pelayiá. Its main distinction is a **Sunday market**, Kíthira's liveliest regular event.

The **east of the island** is very lightly populated, though there is a loop of road if you hire a moped and want to explore. The loop leaves the main road at ARONIÁDHIKA, 4km south of Pótamos. SKANDHÍA, to the south, was ancient Kíthira's port, and there are remains of an acropolis at the old *hóra*, a spot known as KASTRÍ. At AVLÉMONAS, 2km east, there is a beach and a seasonal taverna with a few rooms to let, beside the decaying remains of a Venetian fort.

Andikíthira

The tiny island of **ANDIKÍTHIRA** has twice-weekly connections on the Kíthira-Kastélli run. Rocky and poor – it has only just received electricity – its few dozen inhabitants are divided between two settlements, POTAMÓS and SOHÓRIA. One for the isolates, and one our research is yet to include. Reports welcome!

Yíthio (Gythion)

YÍTHIO, Sparta's ancient port, is the gateway to the dramatic Máni peninsula (see the section following) and in its own right one of the south's most attractive seaside towns. Its somewhat low-key harbour, with intermittent ferries to Pireás, Kíthira and Crete, gives on to a graceful nineteenth-century waterside of tiled-roof houses. There's a beach within walking distance and rooms are easy to find. In addition to this the town has as exotic a site as any in Greece. Out to sea, tethered by a long narrow mole, is the **islet of Marathónissi**, ancient Kranae, where Paris of Troy, having abducted Helen from Menelaus's palace at Sparta, dropped anchor, and where the lovers spent their first night.

Buses drop you close to the centre of town and finding a **room** should be a matter of a stroll along the waterside. Just off the main square on Vassiléos Pávlou there's a D-class hotel, the *Kranae* (no.15; ☎0733/22-249), slightly seedy but characterful, and the C-class *Pantheon* (no.33; ☎0733/22-284). Another C-class hotel, the *Laryssion* (☎0733/22-021), is nearby at Grigoráki 7. Four or five room establishments huddle by the port police; others up the steps from the waterside, or, cheapest of all, west along the seafront. Standards for these vary considerably, as do prices, so look around; doubles start around 1200dr. If you want to **camp**, there are a couple of official sites at MAVROVOÚNI beach, which begins 3km south of the town off the Areópoli road: *Gythion Beach* (April–Oct.; ☎0733/23-441) and, beyond it, *Mani Beach* (April–Sept.; ☎0733/23-450). There is also a C-class hotel at Mavrovoúni, the *Milton* (☎0733/22-091).

For eating, the waterside is again the obvious location – though pick carefully from among the five tavernas, several have inflated prices. A much more genuine local taverna, *Petakos'*, is to be found tucked against the sports stadium at the north end of town; portions, mostly spit-roasts, are vast and very cheap. Two other outlets you may want to make use of are the *Ladopoulou* **bookshop** (worth scouring for books on the Máni), and *Motor Mani* (by the causeway, on the Areópoli road; ☎0733/22-853), which hires out **mopeds** by the day and, by negotiation, for longer periods. The latter is well worth considering for an exploration of the Máni and, if you're heading that way, **banks** too should be visited.

Kranae is the town's main sight, an alluring place to while away the afternoon, with fair swimming off the rocks. Amid its trees and scrub are a slightly battered fortress built in the 1780s by the Turkish-appointed Bey of the Mani to guard the harbour against his lawless countrymen. For an aerial view, climb through the town on to the hill behind – Yíthio's ancient acropolis. The settlement around it, Laryssion, was quite substantial in Roman times, enjoying a wealth from the export of murex, the purple-pigmented mollusc used to dye imperial togas.

Much of the ancient site now lies submerged but there are some impressive remains of a **Roman theatre** to be seen at the northeast end of the town. Follow the road marked 'Tahidhromio' (post office) for about 300m. This ends at an army barracks, a great sign in the road says 'STOP' and there the theatre is before you – 80m in diameter and with most of its stone seats intact. It shows perfectly how ages blend into one another in Greece: built into the side is a Byzantine church (now ruined) and that, in turn, has been adapted into the outer wall of the barracks. Back in town there's a small **museum**, thoroughly in keeping with this mood, displaying a mildly chaotic collection of local finds; it's by the *Hotel Laryssion* and, in theory at least, open from Monday to Saturday, 8am to 1.30pm.

For swimming, there are a number of coves within reach of Yíthio, on both sides of which rise an intermittent sequence of cliffs. The **beach** at MAVROVOÚNI, by the campsites detailed above, is one of the best; a smaller strand by the town has a nominal admission charge. Alternatively, if you've transport, there are the superb beaches in Váthi Bay, further along off the Areópoli road (see p.171).

The Máni

The southernmost peninsula of Greece, **the Máni** stretches from Yíthio in the east and Kalamáta in the west down to Cape Ténaro, mythical entrance to the underworld; its borders, passable by road at just three points, are the vast grey peaks of Mt. Taíyettos and its southern extension, Sangiás. It is a wild landscape, an arid Mediterranean counterpart to Cornwall, say, or the Scottish highlands, and with an idiosyncratic culture and history to match. Nowhere in Greece does a region seem so close to its medieval past – a past which went largely unchanged until the end of the last century.

The mountains offer a key. Formidable natural barriers, they provided a refuge from, and bastion of resistance to, each and every occupying force of the last two millenia. The Dorians never reached this far south in the wake of the Mycenaeans, Roman occupation was perfunctory and Christianity only took root in the interior in the ninth century (some 500 years after the establishment of Byzantium). Throughout the years of Venetian and Turkish control of the Peloponnese there were constant rebellions, climaxing in the Maniots' uprising on 17 March 1821, a week before Archbishop Yermanos raised the Greek flag at Kalávrita to launch the War of Independence.

Alongside this national assertiveness, however, went an equally intense and violent internal society – at its most extreme in the Maniots' bizarrely elaborate tradition of **blood feuds**. These were the result of an intricate feudal society that seems to have developed across the peninsula in the fourteenth century. After the arrival of refugee Byzantine families, an aristocracy (known as Nyklians) arose and the clans gradually developed strongholds in the tightly-clustered villages. The poor, rocky soil was totally inadequate for the population – even given the Maniot's traditional trade in piracy – and for the next five centuries the clans clashed frequently and bloodily for land, power and prestige.

The feuds became ever more complex and gave rise to the building of clan strongholds: marble-roofed **tower houses** which could be raised only by those of Nyklian descent. From these local forts the clans – often based in the same village – conducted their vendettas according to a strict system of rules. The object was to annihilate the enemy's tower house completely, as well as the male population of their clan. The favourite method of attack was to smash the prestigious tower roofs; the forts consequently rose to four and five storeys.

Feuds would be signalled by the ringing of church bells and from this moment the adversaries would confine themselves to their towers, firing with all available weaponry at each other. The battles could last for years, even decades, with women (who were safe from attack) shuttling in food, ammunition and supplies. With the really prolonged feuds, temporary truces were declared at harvest times, then with business completed the battle would recommence. Ordinary villagers – the non-Nyklian peasantry – would, meanwhile, evacuate for the duration of the conflict. The feuds could end in two ways: destruction of a family in battle, or by total surrender of a whole clan in a gesture of *psihikó* ('a thing of the soul'). In the latter instance the clan would file out to kiss the hands of enemy parents who had lost 'guns' (the Maniot term for male children) in the feud; the victors would then dictate strict terms by which they could remain in the village.

The feuds were probably prolonged, and certainly exploited, by **the Turks**. The first Maniot uprising against them had taken place in 1571 – a year after the Ottoman occupation – and there were to be renewed attempts, involving plots with Venetians, French and Russians, through the succeeding centuries. But the Turks, wisely, opted to control the Máni by granting a level of local autonomy, investing power in one or other clan whose leader they designated 'Bey' of the region. The position provided a focus for the obsession with arms and war that worked well until the nineteenth-century appointment of Petrobey Mavromihalis. With a power base at Liméni he managed to unite the clans in revolution, and his Maniot army, which at one stage had to fight a rearguard action for a foothold in the Peloponnese, was to prove vital in the success of the War of Independence.

Perhaps unsurprisingly the end of the war and the formation of an **independent Greece** was not quite the end of Maniot rebellion. Mavromihalis swiftly fell out with the first president of the nation, Capodistrias, and, with other members of the clan, was imprisoned by him at Náfplio – an act which led to the president's assassination at the hands of Petrobey's brothers. The monarchy, which was then foisted on the emerging nation by the European powers, initally fared little better. In 1833 King Otho decided to break the anarchic outpost of his kingdom by destroying the Maniot tower houses. His first force of troops was ambushed, stripped naked and ransomed back to the state; a second detachment of 6000 soldiers was also repulsed. In the end a more pragmatic solution was found, with one of the king's German officers visiting the Máni to enlist soldiers in a special Maniot militia. The idea was adopted with enthusiasm, and was the start of an enduring tradition of Maniot service in the military. The last full-scale feud, however, took place as late as 1870, in the village of Kítta, and required a full detachment of the Greek army to put down.

In this century, sadly, all has been decline, with persistent **depopulation** of the villages. In places like Váthia and Kítta, which once held populations in the hundreds, the numbers are now down to single figures, predominantly the old. Socially and politically the region is notorious as the most conservative in Greece. The Maniots reputedly enjoyed an influence during the colonels' junta; they voted almost 100% for the monarchy in the 1974 plebiscite; and this is one of the very few parts of Greece where you still see visible support for the far-right EPEN party.

Visiting the Máni

The Máni divides into two: Éxo (Outer) and Mésa (Inner, or Deep).

Deep Máni is the classic territory: its jagged coast relieved only by the occasional cove, its land a mass of rocks. It has one major sight, the remarkable caves at Pírgos Dhiroú which are now very much on the tourist circuit. Beyond this point, though, tourists, mainly Germans, are more committed. The attractions are in small part the coastal villages, like Yerolimin on the west coast, or Kótronas on the east; more in the walking, and in exploring the

THE MÁNI

tower houses and churches. Of the former, a fair number survive – their groupings most dramatic at Kítta, Váthia and Flomohóri. The churches are harder to find, often hidden away from actual villages, but worth the effort. Many were built during the tenth and twelfth centuries, when the Maniots enthusiastically embraced Christianity; almost all retain frescoes.

In **Éxo Máni** – the coast up from Areópoli to Kalamáta – the emphasis shifts much more to beaches. Stoúpa and Kardhamíli are both beautiful resorts, developing now but far from spoiled. And the road itself is an experience, threading precipitously up into the foothills of Taíyettos before looping down to the sea.

For travelling in either part of the region, two **books** are unreservedly recommended. These are Patrick Leigh-Fermor's *Mani* (Penguin), a marvellous study of its history, interwoven with travels in the 1950s, and Peter Greenhalgh and Edward Eliopoulos's *Deep Into Mani* (Faber), an anecdotal and practical guide compiled from a journey in 1980. This latter is invaluable if you want to locate Maniot churches – only a small selection of which are detailed below.

Getting around can be time-consuming in Deep Máni with just two buses a day from Areópoli to Yerolimín and one around the eastern side of the peninsula from Areópoli to Kotrónas/Láyia. You may therefore want to consider hiring mopeds from Yíthio (see above), or a car from Spárti or Kalamáta. An alternative is to make use of the handful of taxis, generally negotiable at Areópoli, Yerolimín and Kótronas, as well as at Yíthio (if you want to explore Passavá en route to Areópoli).

And finally, keep in mind that the Deep Máni has no regular **bank**. Though you can change travellers cheques at the post offices in Yerolimín or Areópoli, it's wise to collect as much as you think you'll need for a visit either at Yíthio or Kalamáta.

Into the Máni: Yíthio to Areópoli

The road from Yíthio into the Máni begins amid a fertile and gentle landscape, running slightly inland of the coast (and the Yíthio/Mavrovoúni beach), through tracts of orange and olive groves.

About 12km beyond Yíthio, however, the Máni seems suddenly to assert itself as the road enters a gorge below the Turkish **Castle of Passavá**. The castle is one of a pair – with Kelefá to the west – guarding the Máni, or perhaps more accurately guarding against the Máni. It's quite a scramble up, with no regular path, but the site is ample reward, with views out across two bays and for some miles along the defile from Areópoli. It has hosted a fortress since Mycenaean times; the present version is an eighteenth-century Turkish rebuilding of a Frankish fort (contemporary with Mystra) which the Venetians had destoyed on their flight from the Peloponnese in 1684. It was abandoned by the Turks in 1780 following the massacre of its garrison by the Maniot Grigorakis clan – their vengeance for the Turks' arrest and execution of the clan chief.

Shortly after Passavá a turning to the left, signposted 'Belle Hélène', leads down to a long sandy beach at **Váthi Bay**. At the southern end are two small hotels: the E-class *Megas Alexandros* (☎0733/22-039) and B-class *Belle Hélène* (☎0733/22-867; April-Oct.). The road beyond the beach deteriorates rapidly though it is possible to continue through woods to the village of AYERANÓS, with a couple of tower houses, and thence, if you can find your way among the numerous rough tracks, to SKOUTÁRI, below which is another good beach, with some Roman remains. A better road to Skoutári leaves the main Yíthio–Areópoli road at KARIOÚPOLI, itself dominated by an imposing tower house-fort.

Continuing towards Areópoli from Passavá, the landscape remains fertile until the wild, scrubby mass of Mt. Kouskoúni signals the final approach to Deep Máni. You enter another pass, with **Kelefá Castle** (see 'Outer Mani') above to the north, and beyond it the five southern peaks – the *Pendadháktilos* – of Taíyettos. Areópoli, as you curl down from the hills, radiates a real sense of arrival.

Areópoli, Pírgos Dhiroú and Around

An austere-looking town, **AREÓPOLI** sets an immediate mood for the region. It was until the last century secondary to Ítilo, 6km north, as the gateway to Deep Máni, but the modern road has made it to all intents the region's centre. Its name – the Town of Ares, god of war – was bestowed for its efforts in the struggle for independence: it was here that Mavromihalis (commemorated in a statue in the main square) declared the uprising. The town's other sights are archetypically Maniot in their apparent confusion of ages. The **Taxiárhis** cathedral, for example, has primitive reliefs above its doors which look twelfth-century until you notice their date – 1798. Similarly, although its tower houses, as throughout the region, could readily be described as medieval, most of them were built in the early 1800s. One of the towers, the *Pirgos Kapetanakou*, has been restored by the EOT as a 'Traditional Guesthouse'; the rooms are beautiful if you can afford the rates (4000dr for a double in season; ☎0733/51-233). Cheaper **rooms** are advertised at a number of ordinary houses, mostly grouped around the cathedral; or there's a pension in the main square (☎0733/51-307), and the C-class *Hotel Mani* (☎0733/51-269). There is also a **bank** (open Tues. and Thurs. evening only), a **post office** and **OTE**.

Areópoli stands back a kilometre or so from the sea – an enjoyable walk. The best local beach is at **LIMÉNI**, Areópoli's port, 3km to the north, whose scattering of houses are dominated by the restored tower house of Petrobey Mavromihalis. There's a taverna, with **rooms** to let, on the waterside.

Moving south from Areópoli it is 8km to the village of **PÍRGOS DHIROÚ**, where the road forks off to the famed caves. The village has an isolated 25-metre-high tower house, but is otherwise geared to the cave trade, with numerous tavernas and cafés, and several rooms to let (the best along the route to the caves). The **Pírgos Dhiroú caves** are 4km further on, set beside the sea and a small beach. They are very much a packaged attraction, with long queues for admission in season and a fairly hefty entrance charge (500dr; children 250dr). However, unless caves leave you cold, all is worthwhile. Visits consist of a half-hour punt around the underground waterways of the **Glifádha caves**, well-lit and crammed with stalactites. Their reflections a remarkable sight in the two-to-twenty-metre-deep water. You are then allowed a brief tour on foot of the **Alepótripa caves**, huge caverns (one 100m by 60m) in which recent excavation has unearthed much evidence of prehistoric occupation. The caves are open from 8.30am to 7.30pm in summer, 8am to 3pm off season. Buy a ticket as soon as you arrive: this gives you a priority number for the tours. In midseason the wait can be up to four hours, so it's best to arrive as early as possible in the day with gear to make the most of the beach. If time is short, taxis from Areópoli will take you to the caves then wait and take you back; prices, especially split four ways, are reasonable.

The narrow plain between Pírgos Dhiroú and Yerolimín – 17km along the main road – is one of the more fertile stretches of Deep Máni, and supported, until this century, an extraordinary number of villages. It retains a major concentration of **churches**, many of them Byzantine, dating from the eleventh to the fourteenth centuries. These are especially hard to find, though well-detailed in Peter Greenhalgh's *Deep Into Mani*. Among Greenhalgh's favourites **on the seaward side** are the church at HAROÚDHA (3km south of Pírgos), Trissákia church by a reservoir near TSÓPOKAS (5km south of Pírgos) and Ayía Varvára at ÉRIMOS (8km south of Pírgos). Equally rewarding is a walk along the **old road** east of, and parallel to, the main road. This begins near the village of DHRÍALOS and rejoins the main road beyond the tower houses at MÍNA. Midway is VÁMVAKA and its eleventh-century church of Áyii Theódhori, with superb carved marbles and decorative brickwork.

An easier excursion from the main road is to the village of **MÉZAPOS**, whose deepwater harbour made it one of the chief settlements of Máni until the road was built in this century. There are a few **rooms** to let (ask at the café), and some good walks. The best is to the **Castle of the Maina** at TIGÁNI ('Frying Pan') rock, 4km around the cliffs, past the Byzantine church of Episkopí (with a well-preserved cycle of frescoes). Tigáni is as arid a site as any in Greece – a dry Monemvassía – whose fortress, probably constructed by the Franks, seems scarcely man-made, blending as it does into the terrain. It's a jagged walk out to the castle across rocks fashioned into pans for salt gathering; within the walls are ruins of a Byzantine church and numerous cisterns. If you ask at the café in Mézapos it's sometimes possible to negotiate a boat trip out to Tigáni, or even around the cape to Yerolimín.

Continuing by road, **KÍTTA**, once the largest and most powerful village in the region, boasts the crumbling remains of over twenty tower houses. It was here in 1870 that the last feudal war took place, eventually being suppressed by a full battalion of 400 regular soldiers. Over to the west, visible from the village, are another eruption of tower houses at Kítta's traditional rival, **NÓMIA**.

Yerolimín and south to Cape Ténaro

After the journey from Areópoli, **YEROLIMÍN** (Yeroliménas, Gerolimena) has an end-of-the-world air. It is the end of the bus line, anyway, and a good base for exploring the southern extremities of the Máni. Despite appearances, the village was only developed in the 1870s – around a jetty and warehouses built by a local (a non-Nyklian migrant) who had made good on the island of Síros. There are a few shops, a post office (closes at 2.30pm), a couple of cafés and two very simple E-class hotels, run by cousins. Of these the *Akroyali* (☎0733/54-204) has the better restaurant, the *Akrotenaritis* (☎0733/54-205) has slightly cheaper rooms at around 1200dr a double. At the dock occasional boat trips are offered, when the local owners feel like it, around Cape Ténaron (see below). For swimming, the best beach near the town is 2km south at an inlet known as Yiáli, overlooked by the ruins of a tower house and windmill.

Two kilometres to the north of Yerolimín, **BOULARÍÍ** is well worth the walk: a village divided into 'upper' and 'lower' quarters which retain well-preserved tower houses and, in varying states of decay, some 21 churches. The two most impressive are tenth-century Áyios Pantelímon (roofless and unlocked, with several frescoes) and eleventh-century Áyios Stratigós (locked – keys are with the priest at Eliá village), with a reputedly spectacular series of frescoes from the twelfth to the eighteenth centuries.

South from Yerolimín a good road continues to **ÁLIKA**, where it divides, one fork leading east through the mountains to Láyia (see the following section), the other on to Váthia and across the Marmári isthmus to Páliros. Between Álika and Váthia there are good coves for swimming. One of the best, reached by following a riverbed (dry in summer) about midway to Váthia, is a place known as KIPÁRISSOS. On the headland above are scattered Roman remains, including (amid the walled fields) the excavated remains of a sixth-century basilica.

VÁTHIA, a group of tower houses set uncompromisingly on a scorching mass of rocks, is one of the most dramatic villages in Deep Máni. It features in the travels of Colonel Leake – one of the best sources on Greece in the early nineteenth century – who was warned to avoid going through it as a feud had been running between two families for the previous forty years. Today it has a ghost-town feel with under a dozen people left, despite the efforts of the EOT who have restored a couple of the tower houses as guest lodges (☎0733/54229; doubles 6000dr in season). Other than these, there's just a makeshift (and sporadically open) café selling drinks from a refrigerator.

From Váthia the road south to the cape starts out uphill – edging around the mountain in what appears to be quite the wrong direction. It slowly descends, however, bringing you out at the beach and hamlet of **PÓRTO KÁYIO** (7km from Váthia). There's a taverna here, which may be able to find you a room if you decide to stay. Above the village a track winds west around the headland, capped by ruins of a Turkish castle contemporary with Kelefá, to sandy beaches at the double bay of MARMÁRI.

Moving on to the Máni's last, barren peninsula the road continues for a couple of kilometres up to a hilltop church and a parking area. A track from here extends a few hundred metres more to the nearly-deserted hamlet of PÁLIROS. But heading for the cape follow instead a clearly-defined **path** (which comes up from Pórto Káyio) leading off to the south from the parking area. This passes Páliros well to the west and reaches (in 45 min.) MIANÉS, another hamlet with a single-figure population. Beyond here the trail dwindles as it descends towards the sea, skirting a knoll crowned with the squat **chapel of Asomatíí**, constructed largely of materials from an ancient Temple of Poseidon.

To the left (east) as you face the chapel is the little pebbly bay of ASOMATÍÍ, often with a fishing boat at anchor, on whose shores is the small **cave** said to be the mythical entrance to the underworld*. To the right (west) of the Asomatíí hill the main path, marked now by red dots, continues along the shore of another cove and through the metre-high foundations of the Roman town which grew up around the Poseidon shrine; there is even a good mosaic in one structure. Following the trail to its end, along a walled path with 180° views of the sea, you'll reach the lighthouse on **Cape Ténaro** (about 25 min. from Asomatíí). The keepers here used to welcome visits but, sadly, the lights were automated in 1986.

Láyia, Kótronas and the east coast

The east coast of Deep Máni is most easily approached from Areópoli, whence there's a daily bus to Kótronas, the largest settlement. However, if you have transport, or you're prepared to walk and hitch, there's a satisfaction in doing a full loop of the peninsula, crossing over to Láyia from Yerolimín or Pórto Káyio. For much of its length the road has to cling to the mountains, with sheer cliffs dropping to the sea; the landscape is almost remorselessly barren, little more than scrub and prickly pears, for this is the Deep Máni's **'Sunward coast'**, far harsher than the 'Shadow coast' of the west side.

From the fork at Álika (3km south of Yerolimín) it is about an hour and a half's walk by road to Láyia. Coming from Pórto Káyio it takes around three hours, though the route, at times on narrow tracks, is more dramatic, passing the virtually deserted hilltop village of KOROGONIÁNIKA.

LÁYIA, when you arrive, is worth all the effort: a multitowered village which perfectly exemplifies the feudal setup of the old Máni. Four Nyklian families lived in the town and their four independently sited settlements, each with its own church, survive. One of the taller towers, so the locals claim, was built overnight by the four hundred men of one clan, hoping to gain an advantage at sunrise. During the eighteenth century the village was the residence

---

*Patrick Leigh Fermor, in *Mani*, writes of another 'Gate of Hades' cave, which he swam into on the western shore of Mátapan, just below Marmári. Other claimants to the title, elsewhere in Greece, include the Necromanteion of Ephira near Párga in Epirus.

of Deep Máni's doctor – a strategic base from which to attend the war-wounded across the peninsula. There is a friendly taverna with a few **rooms** to rent.

Láyia is 2km from the coast but the first village beyond, **ÁYIOS KIPRIANÓS**, is by the sea, and inexplicably towerless. It too has a few rooms. **KOKKÁLA**, 5km on, is larger, enclosed by a rare patch of greenery, and boasts a harbour, a couple of cafés (**rooms** again available) and a shop. It also has walking possibilities. Three kilometres to the northwest, up on the mountainside, is a spot known as Kiónia (columns) with the foundations of two Roman temples; from there a path reputedly leads over the mountain to Mína. Reports welcome if anyone tries this.

KÓTRONAS – back on the bus route – is more popular, frequented by a fair number of Germans each summer, and with other nationalities slowly catching on. All for good reason since this fishing village, with its pebble beach (sandy strips further around the bay) and causeway-islet, makes a good last stop in the region. **Rooms** are offered in several of the village houses, though they can be in short supply in August. If they're full, camping should create few problems, and there are even shops. The land hereabouts is reasonably fertile, and **FLOMOHÓRI**, half an hour's walk in the hills behind, has maintained a reasonable population as well as a last imposing group of tower houses.

Outer Máni: Areópoli to Kalamáta

The forty kilometres of road between Areópoli and Kalamáta is as dramatic and beautiful as any in Greece, a virtual corniche between Mount Taïyettos and the Gulf of Messinía. En route the first few settlements are classic Maniot villages, their towers packed against the hillside; as you move north, with the road dropping to near sea level, there are three or four small resorts – increasingly popular but as yet far from spoiled. For walkers, there is a reasonably well-preserved *kalderími* (cobbled track) paralleling (or shortcutting) much of the asphalt route, and a superb gorge hike just north of Kardhamíli.

ÍTILO, 11km from Areópoli, is the transport hub for the region. If you are heading towards Kalamáta, either from Yíthio or Areópoli, you'll need to change here. The town, with its tiny harbour of KARAVOSTÁSSI (or NÉO ÍTILO), was formerly capital of the Máni, and from the sixteenth to the eighteenth century was the region's most notorious base for piracy and slave trading. The Maniots traded amorally and efficiently in slaves, selling Turks to Venetians, Venetians to Turks, and, at times of feud, the women of each others' clans.

Irritated by their piracy and hoping to control the important pass to the north, the Turks built the **Castle of Kelefá**. This is just a kilometre's walk from Ítilo across a gorge and its walls and bastions, built for a garrison of five hundred, are still substantially intact. Also worth exploring from Ítilo is the monastery of **Dhekoúlou**, down towards the coast; its setting is beautiful and there are some fine medieval frescoes in the church. Ítilo itself looks tremendous from a distance, though close up it is a little depressing – its population aging and in decline, and many of the tower houses collapsing into decay.

Karavostássi, with a couple of **hotels**, is a better base; both hotels, however, are pricey, with the cheaper of the two, the C-class *Hotel Itilo* (☎0733/51-300) charging 4500dr a double in season.

Continuing, if you want to walk for a stretch of the route, you can pick up the *kalderími* out of Ítilo – follow the main road initially and look out for the path below. As it continues north the track occasionally crosses the modern road but it is distinct at least as far as RÍNGLIA, and probably (we've not tried) beyond to Kardhamíli. The most interesting of the villages along this mountainous leg of the way are **LANGÁDHA**, for its setting, bristling with towers, and **NOMITSÍS**, with a number of Byzantine churches.

The beaches begin at **ÁYIOS NIKÓLAOS**, which has a few roadside rooms and the modest E-class *Hotel Mani* (☎0721/54-238), and extend more or less continuously through to Kardhamíli. **STOÚPA** (or Stoúfa) has possibly the best sands: two glorious beaches separated by a headland, each sloping into the sea and superb for anyone with children. The village is now geared very much to tourism, with numerous **rooms** to let, several small hotels (cheapest is the C-class *Stoupa*, ☎0721/54-308), a **campsite** (*Camping Kalogria*, ☎0721 94-319; five-minutes' walk from the first beach – with a children's playground), a supermarket (which will change money and cheques) and a fair number of tavernas. But the setting, with banana trees lending an exotic air, justifies at least the present state of development. Out of season (August brings crowds of Germans) it is certainly recommended.

KARDHAMÍLI, 10km north, is in a similar vein, with a great long pebble beach fronted by acres of olive trees, and a group of tower houses edging into the hills. For a while the village seemed to be developing as the main Outer Máni resort but Stoúpa seems to have overtaken it and there is still only one proper hotel (the D-class *Dioskouri*, ☎0721/73-231). If you want a **room**, however, you shouldn't have to look very far. As well as a number of cheapish (1500dr double) village places (a particularly nice house in an orchard, owned by the Mandagari family, is worth asking for at their grocery store), there are a couple of brand new apartments which let rooms with kitchen and bathroom for around 2500dr a night. There is the usual network of women passing you from one to the other until you find space. Of an evening the old abandoned tower houses, slender-spired church and ruins of other fortified buildings, or the acropolis behind the modern village, make an enjoyable wander. There are a couple of tavernas (best is *Lilla*'s on the shore), and two bars on the main road. As at Stoúpa, there is no bank or post office.

Beyond Kardhamíli the road leaves the coast, which rises to cliffs around a cape, before dropping back to the sea in the bay around Kalamáta. But as the Taíyettos rears up again, a magnificent **gorge** cuts its way inland from KÉNDHRO (easiest approached along the jeep track from KÁMBOS). To reach the gorge follow the track out of the village and you'll see a paved path (which runs along its course to PIGÁDHIA) down below to the left. Pigádhia is a beautiful-looking village, though deserted save for one family; it has a water supply. From here it's simplest to retrace your steps but if you're feeling energetic and happy to camp en route there is a jeep track through the mountains to the Kalamáta–Spárti road.

Kalamáta and beyond

KALAMÁTA is by far the largest city of the southern Peloponnese with a long-established export trade in olives and figs from the Messinian plain, and, until recently, a prospering industrial base. In 1986, however, the city was near the epicentre of a severe earthquake which killed twenty people, left 12,000 families homeless and did 40 billion drachmas worth of damage. But for the fact that the quake struck in the early evening, when many people were outside, the death toll would have been much higher. As it was, large numbers of buildings were – and, three years later, remain – levelled throughout the town. The intensity of the damage was in part due to the city's position over several subterranean streams; but most, it seems, was the legacy of poor 1960s construction, with incorrectly mixed concrete, insufficient reinforcing and misaligned supporting piers. The effects have been disastrous, causing economic depression across the whole Kalamáta area and an estimated 50 percent drop in the city's population of 60,000.

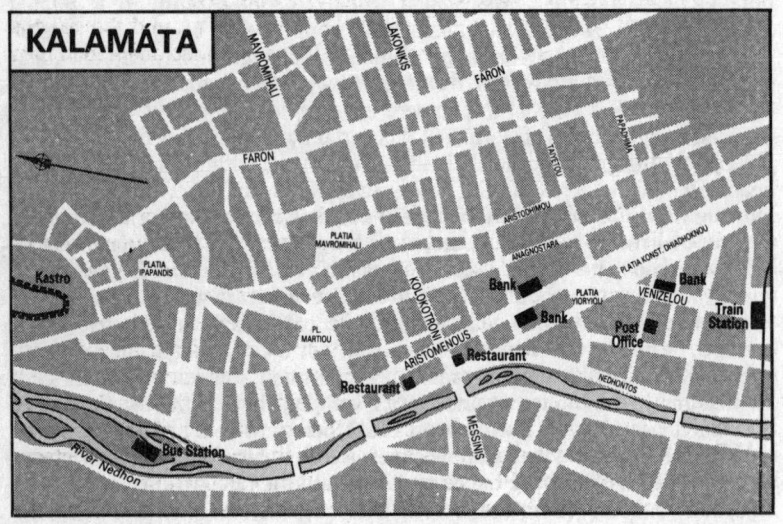

Practicalities

For visitors Kalamáta always had a slightly grim aspect and today it is certainly not a place to linger. If you can, try and get transport straight through; if not, then arrive early to make **connections**. The most regular buses run north to Megalópoli/Trípoli and south to Koróni; the magnificent route over the Taíyettos to Spárti, like that to Areópoli, is covered twice a day. Trains pass through Kalamáta along the slow but enjoyable route to Kiparissía (and ultimately to Olympia) or inland to Trípoli and Árgos.

Arriving, orient yourself by the main square, **Platía Yioryíou**, with most of the banks and the post office in the streets around. The **train station** is 300m to the south, with a **tourist police** post; the **bus station** is about 600m north along by the river – follow Aristoménous street and look out for a large plastic roof. For the hurried, there is a daily **flight** to Athens (40 min.); tickets are sold at the *Olympic* office on Aristoménous, from outside of which there's a shuttle bus to the airport. For **car hire**, phone or visit the two rival agencies: *Maniatis* (Iatropoúlou 1, opposite the post office; ☎0721/27-694) and *Stavrianos* (Nethóndos 89; ☎0721/23-041).

If you want or need to stay, there are very few **hotels** left centrally; best value is the C-class *Galaxias* (Kolokotróni 14; ☎0721/28-891; doubles around 4000dr). In general you'll do better down by the waterside, 3km from the centre (take bus #1), where there are two cheaper places with doubles around 2500dr on Santaróza street: *Hotel Nevada* (no.9; ☎0721/82-429) and *Pension Avra* (no.10; ☎0721/82-759). The town **beach** here is functional if unenticing, though the harbour itself has a welcome touch of life and activity. There are some **campsites** along the stretch to the east (the nearest, about 2km, is *Camping Patista*, ☎0721/29-525; Apr.–Oct. only) but unless stuck you'd do better heading east towards Petalídhi (see below).

With time to fill, the most pleasing area of the city is around the **Kástro** (Mon.–Sat. 8am–7pm), built by the Franks and destroyed and adapted in turn by the Turks and Venetians; ironically it survived the quake with little damage.

Ancient Messene

The ruins of **ANCIENT MESSENE**, a fortified capital thrown together by the Messenians as protection against the Spartans, lie 22km northwest of Kalamáta. The city achieved some fame in the ancient world as a showcase of military architecture and the highlights of the widely dispersed site are the outcrops of its giant walls, towers and gates. It's a tricky place to get to, however, unless you're driving. Buses run only twice a day from Kalamáta and you'll either have to return to the city or try your luck hitching on. With a car it's a fairly easy detour en route to either Kiparissía, Pílos or Petalídhi/ Koróni. The site shares the slopes of Mt. Ithómi with the pretty village of MAVROMÁTI, and, as you climb higher towards the summit, offers spectacular views of the region of Messinía and the southern Peloponnese.

The fortifications were designed as the southernmost link in a defensive chain of walled cities (including Megalopolis and Argos) masterminded by the Theban leader Epaminondas to keep the Spartans at bay. Having managed to halt the Spartans at the battle of Leuctra in 371 B.C. he set about building a nine-kilometre circuit of walls and restoring the Messenians to their native acropolis. The Messenians, who had almost continually resisted Spartan oppression from the eighth century B.C. onwards, wasted no time in re-establishing their capital; according to Diodorus the city was built in eighty-five days.

The most interesting of the remains is the **Arcadia gate** at the north side of the site, through which the modern road still runs. This consisted of an outer and inner gate separated by a circular courtyard made up of massive chunks of stone precisely cut to fit together without mortar. The outer gate, the foundations of which are fairly evident, was flanked by two square towers from where volleys of javelins and arrows would rain down on attackers. The inner gate, a similarly impregnable barrier, comprised a huge monolithic doorpost, half of which still stands.

Farther to the south, and signposted 'Ithomi: Archeological site' on the road running northwest from Mavromáti, is a newly excavated **Sanctuary of Asclepius** (open Mon.–Sat. 8.45am–3pm, Sun. 9.30am–2.30pm). This site, which was first mistakenly marked out as the *agora*, consisted of a temple surrounded by a porticoed courtyard. The bases of some of the colonnades have been unearthed along with traces of some of the benches. Next to it you can make out the site of a theatre or meeting place.

Other remains are to be seen by climbing up Mt. Ithómi, an hour on foot along a steep path forking from the road at the Laconia gate. Along the way you pass remains of an Ionic **Temple of Artemis**. At the top is the small **Monastery of Vourkanó**, founded in the eighth century on the site of a temple of Zeus; spread below you are the lush and fertile valleys of Messinía.

Towards Koróni: Petalídhi

Beaches stretch for virtually the entire distance southwest from Kalamáta to Koróni, along what is steadily developing as a major resort coast. At present, however, it is more popular with Greeks than foreigners, and the resorts, tucked away in the pines, are primarily **campsites**.

The best of the beaches are around the village of **PETALÍDHI**, 40km from Kalamáta. The campsites here – particularly the B-class *Eros Beach* (☎0722/31-209) and *Zervas Beach* (☎0722/31-009) – are geared primarily to car-campers with mini-enclosures as well as a few straw cabins for rent. But although expensive, costing little less than the price of a room, they're well-organised and well-planned. Slightly cheaper are the C-class campsites, *Petalidhi Beach* (☎0722/31-154) and *Sun Beach* (☎0722/31-200). All are open from April through October.

Koróni and Methóni

The twin fortresses at **Koróni** and **Methóni** were the Venetians' oldest, and longest-held, possessions in the Peloponnese: strategic outposts on the route to Crete and known through the Middle Ages as 'the eyes of the Serene Republic'. Today they shelter two of the most attractive small resorts in the south.

If you have a car, the two towns form an obvious route either from Kalamáta to Pílos or vice versa. Relying on public **transport** the 47km road across the peninsula can be a problem, for Koróni has its bus connections with Kalamáta (7 daily in summer; 30km) while Methóni's are with Pílos (8 daily; 12km). From Methóni there are buses east along the coast to Finikoúnda (16km) but no further; the remaining 31km has to be hitched, cycled (mopeds are hired out at Koróni) or walked.

Koróni

Set against a fortified bluff and commanding grand views across the Messenian gulf to the Taíyettos peaks, **KORÓNI** is picturesque and strikingly-sited. The town is beautiful in itself, too, with tiled and pastel-washed houses arrayed in a maze of stair-and-ramp streets which can have changed little since the medieval Venetian occupation.

It is not, alas, undiscovered. The Germans arrived in the early 1980s and in recent years have been buying up houses in the town and surrounding countryside. However, the process is decidedly low-key and outside high season Koróni still feels scarcely touristed. There seems to be a local policy of spreading visitors into the immediate region. Signs in cafés point you towards rooms on farms away from the town and even at the beach, Zánga, there's little real development.

To be sure of a room in season, it's worth trying to phone ahead. In the town there are two D-class **hotels**, and one rather cheaper E-class: respectively, the *Flisvos* (☎0725/22-238), *Panorama* (☎0725/22-224) and *Diana* (☎0725/22-312). Looking for **rooms** on arrival, try the places to the right of the fishing port as you face the water, and don't leave it too late in the day or you'll be down to (illegal) camping by the beach. The better and more authentic tavernas are the two *inomayiría* – barrel-wine and oven-food places – on the main shopping street, and the *Bellevue* (follow its signs) up by the castle. Many people make wine in their basement and the heady local brew figures prominently in the nightlife.

The **citadel**, Koróni's 'sight', is one of the least militaristic-looking in Greece, crowning rather than dwarfing the town. Much of it is given over to private houses and garden plots but the greater part is occupied by the sprawling **nunnery** of Timíou Prodhrómou, whose chapels and outbuildings occupy nearly every bastion. From the southwest gate of the fortress stairs descend to the park-like grounds of **Panayía Elestría**, a church erected at the end of the last century to house a miraculous icon – unearthed with the assistance of the vision of one Maria Stathaki (buried close by). The whole arrangement, with fountains, shrubbery and benches for watching the sunset, is more like the Adriatic than the Aegean.

Continuing downhill you reach the amazing **Zánga beach**, a two-kilometre stretch of sand which sets the seal on Koroni's overall superiority as a place to relax, drink wine, and amble about a countryside lush with vineyards, olives and banana trees. There is a line of tavernas on the beach and by night a solitary disco.

Methóni

In contrast to the almost domesticated castle at Koróni, **METHÓNI**'s **fortress** is as imposing as they come – massively bastioned, washed on three sides by the sea, and cut off altogether from the land by a great moat on its fourth. It was maintained by the Venetians in part for its military function, in part as a staging post for pilgrims en route, via Crete and Cyprus, to the Holy

Land, and from the eleventh to the nineteenth centuries it sheltered a substantial town. Within the gates (open Mon.–Sat. 8am–7pm, Sun. 9am–7pm) are the remains of a Venetian cathedral – the Venetians' Lion of St. Mark emblem is ubiquitous – along with a Turkish bath, dozens of houses and some awesome underground passages; a torch is helpful for exploring. Walking around the walls, a sea gate midway along leads out across a causeway to a fortified islet, Boúrtzi, where the Venetian forces made their last stand against the Turks in 1500.

The modern **village**, on the 'mainland' opposite, is geared more conspicuously to tourism than Koróni and can get very crowded in season, when hundreds of travellers descend to swim and windsurf in the shallow bay by the fort. Lodgings, however, are reasonably priced, and rarely too difficult to find if you arrive in good time. Cheapest and possibly most pleasant of the **hotels** is the D-class *Iliodyssio* (☎0723/31-225), near the moat. The E-class *Rex* (☎0273/31-239), on the beach, and *Dionysos* (☎0273/31-317) are similarly priced. Otherwise there are three more expensive D-class and two C-class hotels, a B-class pension and the usual collection of **rooms**. At the east end of the beach there's also a **campsite**, *Camping Methoni* (April–Oct. only), with showers and reasonable prices. The village has a **bank**, **OTE** and **post office**, all easily located in the three-street-wide grid.

Finikoúnda

East from Methóni most of the Pílos-based buses continue as far as **FINIKOÚNDA** (14km), a small fishing village with a superb cove-beach. Over recent years this has gained a reputation as a travellers' resort, with half the summer intake camping freelance, the others housed in a variety of **rooms** arranged through one or other of the tavernas. It can be a fun, laid-back place and draws considerably fewer visitors than either of the fort towns to either side.

Pílos and Nestor's Palace

PÍLOS in many ways resembles Náfplio. It is an unusually stylish town (the more so after Kalamáta), has a pair of medieval castles and occupies a superb and dominant position on one of the finest natural harbours in Greece. A better base for exploring this part of the Peloponnese would be hard to imagine – particularly given its romantic associations with the Battle of Navarino, and, more anciently, with Homer's 'sandy Pylos', the domain of 'wise King Nestor' whose palace (see below) has been identified 16km to the north.

Practicalities

Getting your bearings is easy. Pílos is not a large town and buses drop you close by the central square and the port. Finding a place to stay in season can be a struggle, however, and you may find it worthwhile to phone ahead for a room. There are three good-value D-class **hotels**: the *Navarinon* (above the south side of the harbour; ☎0723/22-291), *Trion Navarhon* (Platía Tríon Navarhón 24; ☎0723/22-206) and *Astir* (Yioryíou Krassanoú 1; ☎0723/22-204); prices at any run about 1750dr a double. A few private rooms are also advertised, at similar prices. If you're stuck Methóni is an alternative – 12km to the south and connected four times a day by bus.

Mopeds or **cars**, ideal for taking in both Methóni and Nestor's palace, are available at *Venus Rent* (☎0723/22-312) on the road north out of town. Cars are also hired out at the *Hotel Miramare* (☎0723/22-226).

Navarino Bay and the Town

Arriving at Pílos your gaze is inevitably drawn to the bay, virtually landlocked by the offshore island of Sfaktiría. Its name, Ormós Navarínou – **Navarino Bay** – commemorates the battle that effectively sealed Greek independence from the Turks on the night of October 20 1827. The battle itself seems to have been accidental. The 'Great Powers' of Britain, France and Russia, having established diplomatic relations with the Greek insurgent leaders, were attempting to force an armistice on the Turks. To this end they sent a force of 27 warships to Navarino, where Ibrahim Pasha had gathered his forces – 16,000 men in 89 ships. The declared intention was to coerce Ibrahim into leaving Messinía, which he had been raiding.

In the confusion of the night an Egyptian frigate, part of the Turks' supporting force, fired its cannons and full-scale battle broke out. Without having intended to take up arms for the Greeks, the 'allies' found themselves responding to attack and, extraordinarily, sank and destroyed 53 of the Turkish fleet without a single loss. There was considerable international embarrassment when news filtered through to the 'victors' but the action had nevertheless ended effective Turkish control of Greek waters and within a year independence was secured and recognised.

For a dramatic view of the battle site it is worth enquiring at the port about **boat trips** to the island, on which stands a monument to the Russian sailors. A small **museum** in the town, just off the main waterside square on Filellínon street, also boasts various remains from the battle, along with archaeological finds (9.30am–3.30pm, Sun. 10am–3pm; closed Tues.; 100dr, students 50dr). However the main pleasures of Pílos are the hillside alleys and waterside streets, or, more purposefully, visiting the two fortresses.

The best-preserved of these is the **Néo Kástro**, close by the port on the south side of the bay. Built by the Turks, it offers walks right around the arcaded battlements. Until recent years the castle served as a prison and its inner courtyard is divided into a warren of narrow yards separated by high walls. Most Greek prisons – internally, at least – are fairly open and this peculiar feature is explained by the fact that it was the nearest garrison to the Máni. So frequently was it filled with Maniots imprisoned for vendettas, and so great was the crop of internal murders, that these pens had to be built to keep the imprisoned clansmen apart. The **Paleó Kástro**, whose hill almost touches the island at the north end of the bay, was the city's ancient acropolis. It too has substantial walls, though just rubble within.

Nestor's Palace

Site open 8am–3pm, Sun. 9am–3pm; 200dr, students 100dr. Museum at Hóra open 9am–4pm, Sun. 10am–4pm, closed Tues.; 200dr, students 100dr. Excellent site guide by Carl Blegen on sale at entrance (200dr).

Nestor's Palace was discovered just before World War II, in 1939, and so its excavation – unlike Mycenae, or most of the other major Greek sites – has been a product of modern archaeological techniques. In consequence its remains are the best preserved of all the Mycenaean royal palaces, though they shelter rather prosaically beneath a giant plastic roof. The palace is located 17km from modern Pílos. Using public transport take any of the buses from Pílos to Kiparissía; these follow the main road inland past Korifássi to the site and then to its museum at the village of HÓRA (4km beyond).

Flanked by deep, fertile valleys, the palace looks out towards Navarino Bay – a location perfectly in keeping with the wise, measured and peaceful king described in Homer's *Odyssey*. The scene placed here in the epic is the visit of Telemachus, the son of Odysseus, who journeys from Ithaca to seek news of his father from the king. Arriving at the beach, accompanied by the disguised goddess Pallas Athena, he comes upon Nestor with his sons and court making a sacrifice to Poseidon. The visitors are welcomed and feasted, 'sitting on downy fleeces on the sand', and although the king has no news of Odysseus he promises Telemachus a chariot so he can enquire from Menelaus at Sparta. First, however, the guests are taken back to the palace, where Telemachus is given a bath by Nestor's 'youngest grown daughter, beautiful Polycaste', emerging, anointed with oil, 'with the body of an immortal'.

The Site

By some harmonious quirk of fate a bathtub was in fact unearthed, and the **palace ruins** as a whole are potent ground for Homeric imaginings. The walls stand to a metre in height enabling you to make out a very full plan. They were originally half-timbered (like Tudor houses), with upper sections of sun-baked brick held together by vertical and horizontal beams, and brilliant frescoes within. Even in their diminished state they suggest a building of considerable prestige – as indeed might be expected, for Nestor sent the second largest contingent, 'ninety black ships', to Troy.

Remains are of a massive complex in three principal groups: the **main palace** in the middle, on the left an earlier and **smaller palace**, and on the right either **guardhouses** or **workshops**. The basic design will be familiar if you've been to Mycenae or Tiryns: an internal court, guarded by a sentry box, gives access to the main sections of the building.

The main palace contained some 45 rooms and halls. The great **throne room** with its traditional open hearth lies directly ahead of the entrance through a double porch. It was here that the finest of the frescoes, depicting a griffin (perhaps the royal emblem) standing guard over the throne, was discovered; it is now in the museum at Hóra. Around are arranged domestic quarters and **storerooms**, which yielded literally thousands of pots and cups during excavations; the rooms may have served as a distribution centre for the produce of the palace workshops. Farther back, the famous **bathroom**, its terracotta tub in situ, adjoins a smaller complex of rooms, centred on another throneroom, identified as the **queen's quarters**.

Archaeologically the most important find was a group of several hundred tablets inscribed in **Linear B**. These were discovered on the very first day of digging in the two small rooms to the left of the entrance courtyard. They were the first such inscriptions to be discovered on the Greek mainland and proved conclusively a link between the Mycenaean and Minoan civilisations – for, like those found by Sir Arthur Evans at Knossos on Crete, the language was unmistakably Greek. The tablets were baked hard in the fire which destroyed the palace around 1200 B.C., perhaps as little as one generation after the fall of Troy.

The Museum

The museum at **HÓRA** adds significantly to a visit to the site. If you've no transport, it shouldn't be too hard to hitch a ride up to it.

Pride of place in the display goes to the **palace frescoes**, one of which, bearing out Homer's descriptions, shows a warrior in a boar's-tusk helmet. Lesser finds include much pottery, some beautiful gold cups and other objects gathered both from the site and from various Mycenaean tombs in the region.

Upcoast to Pírgos: Kiparissía and the beaches

The **beaches** north from Pílos to Pírgos are on a different scale to those elsewhere in the Peloponnese – fine sands, long enough (and undeveloped enough) to satisfy the most cynical Australian or Californian. That they aren't better known is something of a mystery – one accounted for in part by the poor communications, which for those without their own vehicle demand a slow and patient progress.

Pílos to Kiparissía

If you return to the KORIFÁSSI turning from Nestor's Palace you can take a very rough and beautiful track, flanked by orange and olive orchards up towards Kiparissía. This road keeps within a couple of kilometres of the sea for most of its course and there are isolated villages along the way: unbothered by tourism and perfect for anyone with a tent and the will to stop, walk and swim. By one of those chance patterns of emigration, just as Kíthira is home to Greek-Australians, the villages here seem to have a concentration of returned Greek-Americans, virtually all of them having done a stint of work in New York or New Jersey. Ex-Vice-President Spiro Agnew was perhaps the most infamous local boy.

It's perhaps just as enjoyable to stop at random along this stretch as to head for any particular targets. However, if you are looking for the rudiments of accommodation and a little more than a village café then MARATHÓPOLI or FILIATRÁ hold most promise. **MARATHÓPOLI** has a couple of standard **pensions** beside a long beach – rockier than most along this coast. At **FILIATRÁ**, where the track rejoins the asphalt road, there's a single D-class **hotel**, the *Trifylia* (☎0761/32-289).

From FILIATRÁ you can pick up regular OSE (rail company) buses to KIPARISSÍA.

Kiparissía

As the junction of the rail lines from Kalamáta and Pírgos, **KIPARISSÍA** is a surprisingly small and congenial town. Within walking distance are long, near-deserted sands and rocky cliff paths, and the town itself is unpretentious and atmospheric. It is positioned hard against the Eyaléo mountains, with a Byzantine-Frankish **castle** crowning the range's first outcrop, the hill above the town. Around the castle spreads the abandoned old quarter of Kiparissía, whose overgrown streets and graceful, apricot-wash houses were deserted after heavy damage in the civil war and are now left to goats and chickens.

Down below, the modern town goes about its business, with a small harbour and real shops – nothing yet of the tourist boutiques. It's a pleasant place to rest up, and certainly preferable to a night in Kalamáta if you're en route by train or bus to Olympia. There are two excellent and cheap **restaurants** in the central Platía Kalantzakoú; a good, down-to-earth **pension**, the *Trifolia*; three C-class hotels (the *Vassilikon*, ☎0761/22-655, Alexopoúlou 7, is the least costly); some rooms; and a **campsite**, *Camping Hani* (☎0761/23-330; open all year), on the beach. The town also has a **bank**, **OTE** and **post office**, all gathered around the main square.

North to Pírgos: Kaiáfas

North from Kiparissía the road and rail lines continue a kilometre or so back from the coast, with the occasional **campsite** advertising its particular stretch of beach. At **ZAHÁRO**, the one largish village, there is a little more, with shops, a couple of inexpensive C-class hotels by the train station (*Rex*, ☎0625/31-221; *Nestor*, ☎☎0625/31-206) and an even cheaper E-class (*Diethnes*, Ayíou Spiridhónos; ☎0625/31-208).

Arguably the best of the beaches is the last, before the routes head inland, at **KAIÁFAS**. This is an enormous strand, backed by great sand dunes and pine groves, which, despite the village's status as a spa-resort, are decidedly underdeveloped. If you want to camp, the sands are a fairly established, though unofficial site. Alternatively, wander 1km inland to the very different atmosphere of the town, strung out alongside its lagoon. Frequented mainly by Greeks seeking hydrotherapy cures, this has nine **hotels** and pensions, almost all of them budget-priced.

If you're **headed to Olympia by train** from here, you can save the detour to PÍRGOS (not an exhilarating stop) by getting a connection at ALFIÓS, a tiny station at the junction of the Olympia line and as bucolic a halt as any on the network.

ARCADIA AND THE NORTH

Arcadia (*Arkadhía* in modern Greek) lives up to its name. This rambling central province of the Peloponnese contains some of the most beautiful landscapes in Greece: rich rolling hills crowned by a string of medieval towns, and the occasional Classical antiquity. The best area of all is around **Andhrítsena** and **Karítena**, where walkers are rewarded with the luxuriant (and rarely-visited) **Lousíos gorge**, and archaeology-buffs by the remote, though currently scaffolded, **Temple of Bassae**. En route, if approaching from Trípoli, you may also be tempted by the ancient theatre at **Megalópoli**. The one site everyone heads for is, of course, **Olympia**, whose remains, if at times obscure, are again enhanced by the scenery.

Beaches are not a highlight in this northwest corner, nor along the **north coast** between Pátra and Kórinthos. However, if you are travelling this way, or are arriving in or leaving Greece at the (modern) port of Pátra, a detour along the **rack-and-pinion Kalávrita railway** should on no account be missed.

If heading for Delphi, or central or western Greece, car-drivers and pedestrians alike can save backtracking to Athens by using the **ferry link** across the Gulf of Kórinthos at Río-Andírio.

Megalópoli (Megalopolis)

Modern **MEGALÓPOLI** is an important road and bus junction, and your first thoughts on arrival are likely to be directed towards getting out. Like Trípoli, it's a dusty, characterless place, with a garrison army presence, and little in the way of hotels or food – altogether an empty joke on its adoption of its ancient name, 'Great City'. However, the impulse should be resisted, at least for an hour or two, for outside the city is one of the Peloponnese's most extensive and least touristed ancient sites.

Practicalities

Megalópoli has good **bus connections** with Trípoli (and on to Árgos and Athens), and Kalamáta. Arrive at a reasonable hour and you should be able to make either of these transfers. Moving north or west **into Arcadia** is slightly more problematic, with just one bus daily to Karítena/Andhrítsena (currently at noon). However, hitching is a viable proposition along this route, as local drivers are aware of the paucity of transport; if you're feeling wealthy, or can share costs, it's also possible to negotiate a taxi to Karítena. The **rail line** from Megalópoli has been closed down but OSE operates buses to Lefktró for train connections west to Kiparissía or east to Trípoli/Árgos.

Should you need to stay in Megalópoli, and it's not something to plan on, there are four D-class **hotels**; cheapest is the *Hotel Pan* (Papanastassíou; ☎0791/22-270). Other facilities – banks, post office, OTE etc – are to be found around the central square, Platía Gortinías.

Ancient Megalopolis

Site open daily 9am–6pm; theatre unrestricted access.

Ancient Megalopolis was one of the most ambitious building projects of the Classical age, a city intended by the Theban leader Epaminondas, who oversaw construction from 371–368 B.C., to be the finest of a chain of Arcadian settlements containing the Spartans. However, although no expense was spared on its construction, nor on its extent – nine kilometres of walls alone – the city never took root. It suffered from sporadic Spartan aggression and the citizens, transplanted from forty local villages, preferred, and returned to, their old homes. Within two centuries it had been broken up, abandoned and ruined.

As you walk out towards the site, 2km along the Andhrítsena road then left along a track signposted 'Ancient Theatre', it seems a past very much in keeping. The countryside is beautiful enough, a fertile valley broken only by a power station, with beyond the riverbed just a low hill: no sign of any ruins. Suddenly, though, you round the corner of the hill and it reveals its function: carved into its side is the largest **theatre** built in ancient Greece. Only the first few rows are excavated but the rest is clearly visible: mounds and ridges of earth shelving right to the summit where, from the back rows, trees look on like immense spectators.

The theatre was built to seat 20,000 citizens and the **Thersileion** (Assembly Hall) at its base could hold 16,000, but today you're likely to be alone at the site, save for the custodian (who has plans of the ruins). Out beyond the enclosed part of the site you can wander over a vast area, and with a little imagination make out the foundations of walls and towers, temples, gymnasiums and markets. 'The Great City', wrote Kazantzakis, 'has become a great wasteland' – but it's the richest of wastelands, gently and resolutely reclaimed by nature.

Karítena and beyond: Gortys, Stemnítsa and Dhimitsána

North of Megalópoli the best of Arcadia lies before you: minor roads which curl through a series of lush valleys and below the province's most exquisite medieval hill towns. The obvious first stop and most enjoyable base for exploring the region is **Karítena**. From here you can visit the dramatic and remote site of **ancient Gortys** and explore the **Loúsios Gorge**, above which, outrageously sited on 300-metre-high cliffs, is the eleventh-century **Monastery of Áyios Ioánnis Pródhromos**.

Moving on there is a choice of roads. The **'main' route** loops west through Andhrítsena to Créstena, from where you can pick up irregular buses to Olympia. To the northwest an **alternative route** (covered below) winds around the edge of the Ménalo mountains to the delightful towns of **Stemnítsa** (Ipsoúnda) and **Dhimitsána**, beyond which you could hitch to Karkaloú and – somewhat tortuously – through Langádhia towards Olympia.

If you have time on your hands perhaps the most attractive option is to explore the region north as far as Dhimitsána, then backtrack to Karíténa to proceed on to Olympia via Andhrítsena. Coming **from Trípoli** this is an almost rational route: there are regular buses to Vitína/Karkoloú, just a few kilometres north of Dhimitsána.

Karítena

Set high above the Megalópoli–Andhrítsena road, **KARÍTENA** may look familiar; with its medieval bridge over the river Lousíos, it graces the 5000-drachma note. The village has a population today of just 300, but there were at least ten times that figure until the last century – and much more during the Middle Ages, when it was a place of some standing.

Like many of the Arcadian hill towns hereabouts, its history is a mix of Frankish, Byzantine and Turkish contributions, the Venetians having passed over much of the northern interior. It was founded by the Byzantines in the seventh century and had attained a population of some 20,000 when the Franks took it in 1209. They made it the hundred-year capital of a large barony under Geoffroy de Bruyères, the paragon of chivalry in the medieval ballad 'The Chronicle of the Morea' and virtually the only well-liked Frankish overlord.

It was Geoffroy who built the **castle** crowning the village; the Turks added the towers. Down below there are two eleventh-century Byzantine churches worthy of interest: the **Panayía**, in town, with a Romanesque belfry, and **Áyios Nikólaos**, to the west above the river, with magnificent frescoes (enquire at the *kafenío* in the square for the keys). Continuing downhill from Áyios Nikólaos you eventually come to the **medieval bridge**, now missing its central section (replaced by planking) but an intriguing structure nonetheless, with a small Byzantine chapel built into one of the central pillars.

Karítena has just one, unclassified, **hotel**, the *Karitena* set on the edge of the town in the valley behind the Áyios Nikólaos church. The hotel (doubles around 1750dr) has hot water in the afternoon, great beds (lots of blankets – nights here are cold), and can offer evening meals on request. Even if you don't stay, the town's local rosé wine – supposedly hangover-free – is worth sampling.

Gortys, Pródhromos and the Lousíos Gorge

The site of ancient Gortys can be approached either from Karítena (9km to the southwest) or from Stemnítsa (7½km to the northeast). Walkers may want to make a circuit starting or ending in Stemnítsa, possibly camping overnight at Gortys, or staying at the nearby monastery of Pródhromos. By car or taxi there is also a dirt road from Karítena to the village of ASTÍLOHOS, 2km southwest of Gortys.

Approaching from Karítena under your own steam it's easiest to follow the road toward Dhimitsána north for 7km to the hamlet of ELLINIKÓ; you may be able to hitch this section of the journey. From the edge of the village a dirt track signposted 'Gortys' descends west; after a rough six kilometres it ends at the bank of the Loúsios and you cross to the ruins on the other side via an old bridge.

Ancient Gortys

Ancient Gortys is one of the most stirring of all Greek sites, set beside the rushing river which in ancient times was the Gortynios. The relics are widely sown amongst the vegetation on the west (true right) bank of the stream, but the main attraction, below contemporary ground level and not obvious until well west of the little chapel of Áyios Andhréas, is the huge excavation containing the remains of a **temple** to Asclepius, god of healing, and an adjoining **bath**, both dating from the fourth century B.C.

The most curious feature of the site is a circular portico enclosing round-backed seats which most certainly would have been part of the therapeutic centre. It's an extraordinary place, especially if you camp with the roar of the Loúsios to lull you to sleep. The only drawback is the climate: temperatures up here plummet at night, no matter what the season, and heavy mists, wet as a soaking rain, envelope the mountains from midnight to mid-morning.

The Loúsios Gorge and Monastery of Pródhromos

The farmland surrounding Gortys belongs to the monks of Pródhromos, who have carved a donkey path along the **gorge of the Lousíos** between Áyios Andhréas (10th. c) and the monastery. It's about two hours' walk upstream, with at first a gradual and later a steady ascent over a well-graded, switchbacked trail. A set of park benches by a formal gate heralds arrival at the cloister, and the whole area is well stamped about by the monks' mules. If you look up through the trees above the path, the monastery, stuck on to the cliff like a swallow's nest, is plainly visible a couple of hundred metres above.

The interior of **Pródhromos** (or Prodhrómou, as it's known locally) does not disappoint this promise; the villagers who gave me directions there accurately described it as *politisméno* (cultured) as opposed to *ágrio* (wild). Once inside it is surprisingly small; there were never more than about fifteen tenants, and currently there are twelve monks, four of them very young and committed.

Visitors are received in the *arhondaríki* (guest lounge and adjoining quarters), and then shown the tiny frescoed *katholikón* (chapel), and possibly invited to evening services there. Strictest rules of dress apply but the monks welcome visitors who wish to stay the night. The only problem, especially on weekends, is that there are only a dozen or so beds, and people from Trípoli and even Athens make pilgrimages and retreats here, arriving by the carload along a circuitous dirt track from Stemnítsa. Be prepared for this possibility, and arrive in time to get back to level ground to camp.

Beyond Pródhromos the path continues clearly to the nearby monasteries of **Paleá and Néa Filosófou**: the older dating from the tenth century but virtually ruined and easy to miss since it blends into the cliff on which it's built, the newer (seventeenth-century) one locked and abandoned, but with fine frescoes inside; ask the monks at Pródhromos for the keys or content yourself with a peek in through the door grille. From here north the trail becomes almost impassable, though there is a jeep track from near Néa Filosófou upstream to Dhimitsána.

As noted, there is also a jeep road between Pródhromos and Stemnítsa, off which forks a branch to Ellinikó (and, with another turning, Gortys), but if you are walking it is pleasant, and quicker, to follow the old *kalderími* (cobbled trail) from the monastery to the town – a climb, but not a killing one, of about ninety minutes through scrub oak with fine views over the valley. Usually one of the monks or lay workers will be free to point to the start of the path; once clear of the roadhead confusion by the modern little chapel at the edge of the canyon, there's little possiblity of getting lost. Descending from Stemnítsa, head out of town on the asphalt road to Dhimitsána and (just after the town-limits sign) bear down and left on to the obvious beginning of the upper end of the path.

Another track (as opposed to the paved road) runs between Stemnítsa and Ellinikó, so in eight or nine walking hours (best spread over two days) it's quite easy to do a loop through all the points mentioned.

Stemnítsa

Fifteen kilometres north of Karítena, **STEMNÍTSA** (or IPSOÚNDA, in its official, but little-used, Hellenised form) was for centuries one of the premier metalsmithing centres of the Balkans. Although much depopulated, it remains a fascinating town, with a small folklore museum, a revived artisan school (and workshop near the bus stop), and a handful of quietly magnificent medieval churches.

The town is divided by ravines into three distinct quarters: the Kástro (the ancient acropolis hill), Áyia Paraskeví (east of the stream) and Áyios Ioánnis (west of it). The **Folklore Museum** (daily 4–6pm, plus 11am–1pm at weekends; closed Tues.) is in the latter, just off the main road, and repays the trip out in itself. The ground floor is devoted to mock-ups of the workshops of indigenous crafts such as candle-making, bell-casting, shoe-making, and jewellry. The next floor up features recreations of the salon of a well-to-do family and a humbler cottage. The top storey is taken up by the rather random collections of the Savopoulos family: plates by the Asia Minor refugee ceramics master Avramides, textiles and costumes from all over Greece, weapons, copperware, and eighteenth- and nineteenth-century icons. Across the way you can visit an **artisan school**, staffed by the remaining local silver-, gold-, and coppersmiths to slow migration to the city; it has a current enrolment of twenty-five.

Next door to the school is the seventeenth-century basilica of **Tríon Ierarhón**, most accessible of the town's churches; its caretaker lives in the low white house west of the main door. To visit the other churches, all of which are frescoed and locked, requires more determined enquiries to unearth a key. The *katholikón* of the monastery of **Zoodhóhos Piyí**, again seventeenth-century, has perhaps the finest setting, on the hillside above Áyia Paraskeví, but the tiny windows do not permit much of an interior view.

The little adjoining monastery hosted the first *yerousía*, or convention, of guerilla captains in the War of Independence, giving rise to the local claim that Stemnítsa was Greece's first capital. Near the summit of the Kástro hill are the two adjacent chapels, tenth- and twelfth-century in turn, of **Profítis Ilías** and **Panayía Vaferón**, the former with a convenient window for fresco-viewing, the latter with an unusual colonnade. The last of the town's five churches, **Áyios Pantelímonas**, is located at the west edge of the town, to the left of the asphalt road leading to Dhimitsána.

Options for **staying** and eating are limited. If you can afford it, the C-class *Hotel Trikolonion* (☎0795/81-297) has doubles for around 2400dr, and some highly luxurious suites in a fine traditional building. The alternative is a single, cheaper room rented by the Lagos family just off the *platía*. You can get fed at a wonderful no-name **taverna**, with murals of Classical and revolutionary heroes, at the end of a garden lane behind the clock tower, or, in the warm months only, at the *Inomayirion I Klinitsa* near the goldsmith's studio and the bus stop. Speaking of **buses**, there's only one daily bus to/from Trípoli, with the morning Trípoli-bound bus coming from Dhimitsána; you may have to hitch nine asphalted kilometres to Dhimitsána.

Dhimitsána

Like Stemnítsa, **DHIMITSÁNA** has an immediately seductive appearance, its cobbled streets and tottering houses straddling a twin hillside overlooking the Lousíos river. Views from the village are stunning. It stands at the head of the gorge, and looking downriver you can just see the stack of the Megalópoli power plant and the bluff that supports Karítena. To the east are the lower folds of Ménalon, most visible if you climb up to the **Kástro**, whose stretch of 'Cyclopean' walls attests to its ancient use.

In the town itself a half-dozen churches with tall, squarish belfries recall the extended Frankish, and especially Norman, tenure in this part of the Morea during the thirteenth century. Yet none should dispute the deep-dyed Greekness of Dhimitsána. It was the birthplace of Bishop Yermanos, who first raised the flag of rebellion at Kalávrita in 1821, and of the hapless Patriarch Grigoris V, hanged in Constantinople upon the Sultan's receiving news of the insurrection mounted by his co-religionist. During the hostilities the ubiquitous Kolokotronis maintained a lair and a powder mill in the then well-nigh inaccessible town. Even before the War of Independence the Kolokotronis clan used the nunnery of **Emyalón** (open daily 9am–2pm; 3km towards Stemnítsa) as a hideout.

The choice of **lodging** is almost identical to that in Stemnítsa. There is a small five-bed inn on a *platía* in the east part of town, whose proprietress is reluctant to let to lone or short-term travellers, and, 1½km out on the road to Stemnítsa, the C-class *Hotel Dimitsana* (☎0795/31-518), with doubles about 3000dr in season (otherwise open to negotiation). *Taverna Kallithea*, just across the road from the hotel, is Dhimitsána's best; other than that there's a lone *souvláki* stall in town, and the eminently avoidable *Vlahos*, a stygian basement dive.

Dhimitsána to Olympia

If you choose to proceed directly north and west **from Dhimitsána to Olympia**, keep in mind that through buses are few, and that you may have almost as many changes and stops as backtracking south to join the Karítena–Andhrítsena route. Even the first stage, from Dhimitsána to Karakoloú, can be tricky, with the infrequent buses running into town (from Trípoli, via VITÍNA, which has a handful of pricey C- and B-class hotels) mostly leaving via Stemnítsa. You are likely to have to walk, hitch or use a taxi at some point.

By far the most enjoyable, planned halt on this route is **LANGÁDHIA** (18km toward Olympia), whose tiers of houses and bubbling sluices both tumble downhill to the river far below the road. Often you can stop on a late morning bus, eat lunch, and pick up the next through service with little lost time. If you decide to stay the night, there's an E-class **hotel**, the *Kentrikon* (☎0795/43-221).

Andhrítsena and the Temple of Bassae

Moving on from Karítena towards Andhrítsena the hills become mountains – Líkeo and Mínthi – with the Alfiós river falling away to the north. Only slightly less remote than the twists of road around Dhimitsána, it remains a superb route to take, for its own sake and more.

ANDHRÍTSENA, 28km from Karítena, is a beautiful stop and the traditional base from which to visit the Temple of Bassae up in the mountains to the south. Though very much a roadside settlement today, it too was a major hill town through the years of Turkish occupation and the first century of independent Greece. It is remarkably untouched, with wooden houses spilling down to a stream, whose clear, ice-cold headwaters are channelled into a fountain – set within a tree – in the central square.

Cheap **accommodation** is in short supply, the *Hotel Vassae* having finally shut down after years of crumbling elegance on the main square. This leaves just the D-class *Pan* (☎0626/22-213), at the far end of town by the Shell station, with clean, comfortable rooms, but in-season prices of 2000dr double, and the C-class *Theoxenia* (☎0626/22-219), pricier still, on the Karítena side of town. **Restaurants** are a better bet, with a number of good options on the main square, including one serving very substantial fare up the steps beside the old *Hotel Vassae*.

The Temple of Apollo at Bassae

Fourteen kilometres into the mountains from Andhrítsena, the **Temple of Apollo** at Bassae (Vassés, in the modern idiom) has the most remote and arguably the most spectacular site in Greece. For many years it was thought to have been designed by Ictinus, architect of the Parthenon, though this theory has recently fallen from favour. However, after the Thiseion in Athens, it remains the best-preserved Classical monument in the country.

There, for the moment at least, the superlatives must cease. For romantic though it was in the past, the temple is currently swathed in a gigantic grey marquee supported on metal girders and set in concrete with wire stays; its entablature and frieze lie dissected in neat rows on the ground to one side. No doubt the restoration is badly needed for its preservation but, while it is in progress, the effect is pretty deadening.

If you are not put off – and the mountain setting remains awesome – the road up to the temple begins to climb from behind the church in Andhrítsena. The simplest aproach is to share a taxi, which should charge around 1000dr for the round-trip, waiting an hour at the site. On foot it's a pretty agonising ascent of 14 kilometres, with little likelihood of a lift. The site has a daytime guardian but is unenclosed. It's a lonely place, and must have felt even more so in ancient times.

The **temple** was erected in dedication to Apollo Epikourios ('the Succourer') by the Phigalians. It is known that they built it in gratitude for being spared from plague but beyond this it is something of a puzzle. It is oddly aligned (facing north) and, being way up in the mountains, is only visible when you are comparatively near. There are oddities too in the architecture: the columns on its north side are strangely thicker than in the rest of the building, and incorporated into its *cella* was a single Corinthian column, the first known in Greece (though now vanished save for its base). Unusually again, the cult statue, probably a four-metre-high bronze, would have stood in front of this pillar.

On from Bassae or Andhrítsena

Leaving the Bassae/Andhrítsena area, you've a myriad of choices.

From Andhrítsena there's one daily bus back up toward Karítena/ Megalópoli and two down to Pírgos. If you are headed for Olympia, take the Pírgos bus and get down in KRESTENA, from where you can hitch/taxi the 12km side road up to the site. You'll certainly save time and maybe some money.

For the adventurous, an unsurfaced track winds down through the mountains **from Bassae to the coast** at THOLÓ. It's a dusty, very bumpy ride of middling interest, but for the unhurried there's the opportunity to stop at PERIVOLIA (10km). This mountain hamlet has a two-kilometre dirt road connecting it with the similarly diminutive FIGÁLIA (no accommodation), close by the ruinous but enormous, Classical walls of **ancient Phigalia**. A trail at Figália leads down (in 2½–3 hr.) to the river Nédhas and on to PLATÁNIA village, from where you can hitch and bus your way to Kiparissía.

Olympia (Olimbía)

The historic associations and resonance of **OLYMPIA**, which for over a millenium hosted the ancient Panhellenic games, are rivalled only by Delphi or Mycenae. Its site, too, ranks with this company. For although the actual ruins of the sanctuary are confusing and jumbled, the setting is as perfect as could be imagined: a luxuriant valley of wild olive and plane trees, spread beside the the twin rivers of Alfiós (Alpheus) and Kládhios, and overlooked by the pine-covered hill of Krónos. Despite the crowds, it deserves and demands a lengthy visit.

The Games: Some History

The **origins of the games** at Olympia are rooted in legends – the most dominant relating to the god Pelops, revered in the region before his eclipse by Zeus, and to Hercules, one of the earliest victors. Historically, the contests probably began around the eleventh century B.C., growing over the next two centuries from a local festival to the quadrennial celebration attended by states from throughout the Greek world.

The impetus for this change seems to have come from the Oracle of Delphi, which, with the local ruler of Elis, Iphitos, and the Spartan ruler Lycurgus, helped to codify the Olympic rules in the ninth century B.C. Among their most important introductions was a sacred truce, the *Ekeheiria*, announced by heralds prior to the celebrations and enforced for their duration. It was virtually unbroken throughout the games' history – Sparta, ironically, was fined at one point – and as host of the games, Elis, a comparatively weak state, was able to keep itself away from political disputes, growing rich meanwhile on the associated trade and kudos.

From the beginning, the main **Olympic events** were athletic. The earliest was a race over the course of the stadium – roughly 200 metres. Later came the introduction of two-lap (400m) and 24-lap (5000m) races, along with the most revered of the Olympiad events, the pentathlon. This encompassed running, jumping, discus and javelin events, whose competitors were gradually reduced to a final pair for a wrestling-and-boxing combat. It was, like much of these early Olympiads, a fairly brutal contest. Even more so was the Pancratium, introduced, alongside chariot racing, in 680 B.C. In this – one of the most prestigious events – contestants fought each other, naked and unarmed, using any means except biting or gouging each others' eyes; the olive wreath had on one occasion to be awarded posthumously, the victor having died at the moment of his opponent's submission. The chariot races, similarly, were extreme tests of strength and control, only one team in twenty completing the seven-kilometre course without mishap.

The great **gathering of people and nations** at the festival extended the games' importance and purpose well beyond the winning of olive wreaths; assembled under the temporary truce, nobles and ambassadors negotiated treaties, and merchants chased contacts and foreign markets. Sculptors and poets, too, would seek commissions for their work. Herodotus read aloud the first books of his history at an Olympian festival to an audience that included Thucydides – who was to date events in his own work after the winners of the Pancratium.

In the early Olympiads, **rules of competition** were strict. Only free-born – and male – Greeks could take part, and the rewards of victory were entirely honourary: a palm, given to the victor immediately after the contest, and an olive branch, presented in a ceremony closing the games. As the games developed, however, the rules were loosened to allow athletes from all parts

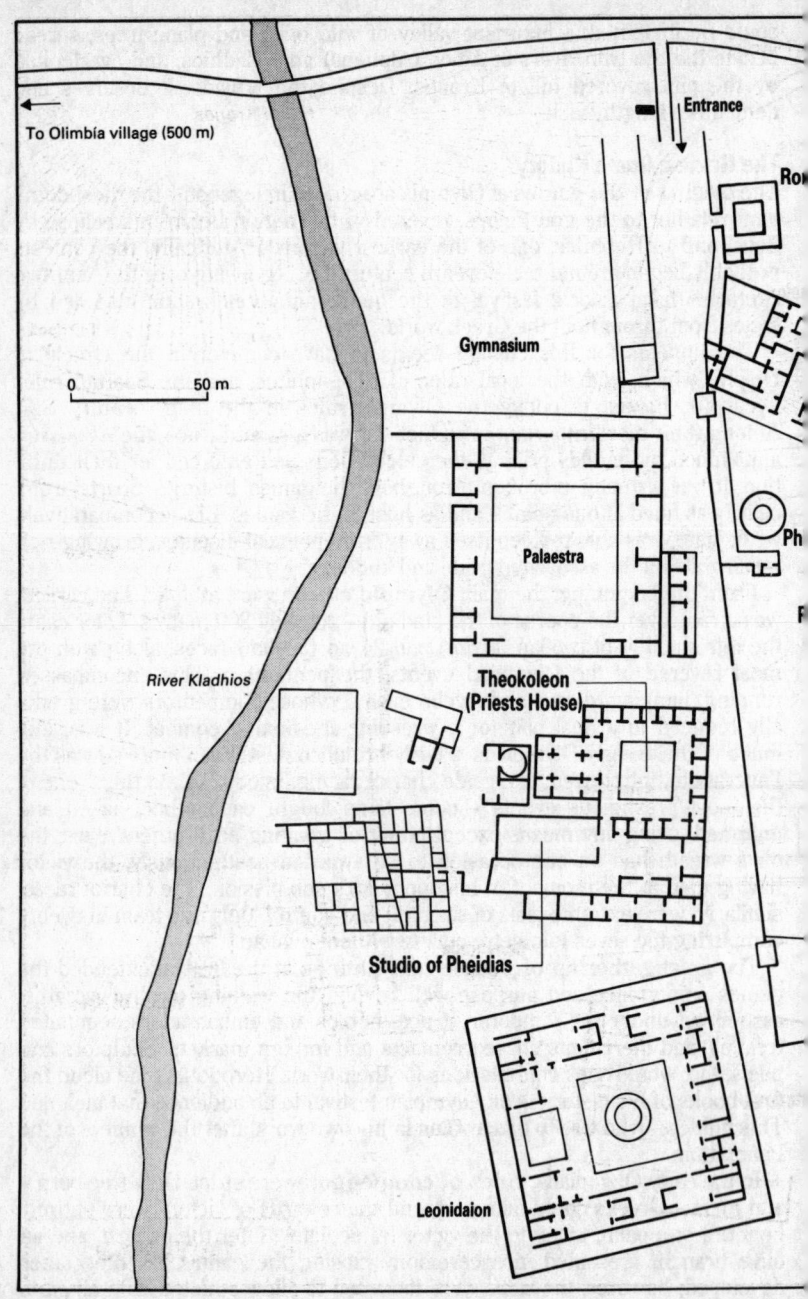

Entrance

Row

To Olimbía village (500 m)

Gymnasium

0   50 m

Palaestra

Ph

River Kladhios

Theokoleon
(Priests House)

Studio of Pheidias

Leonidaion

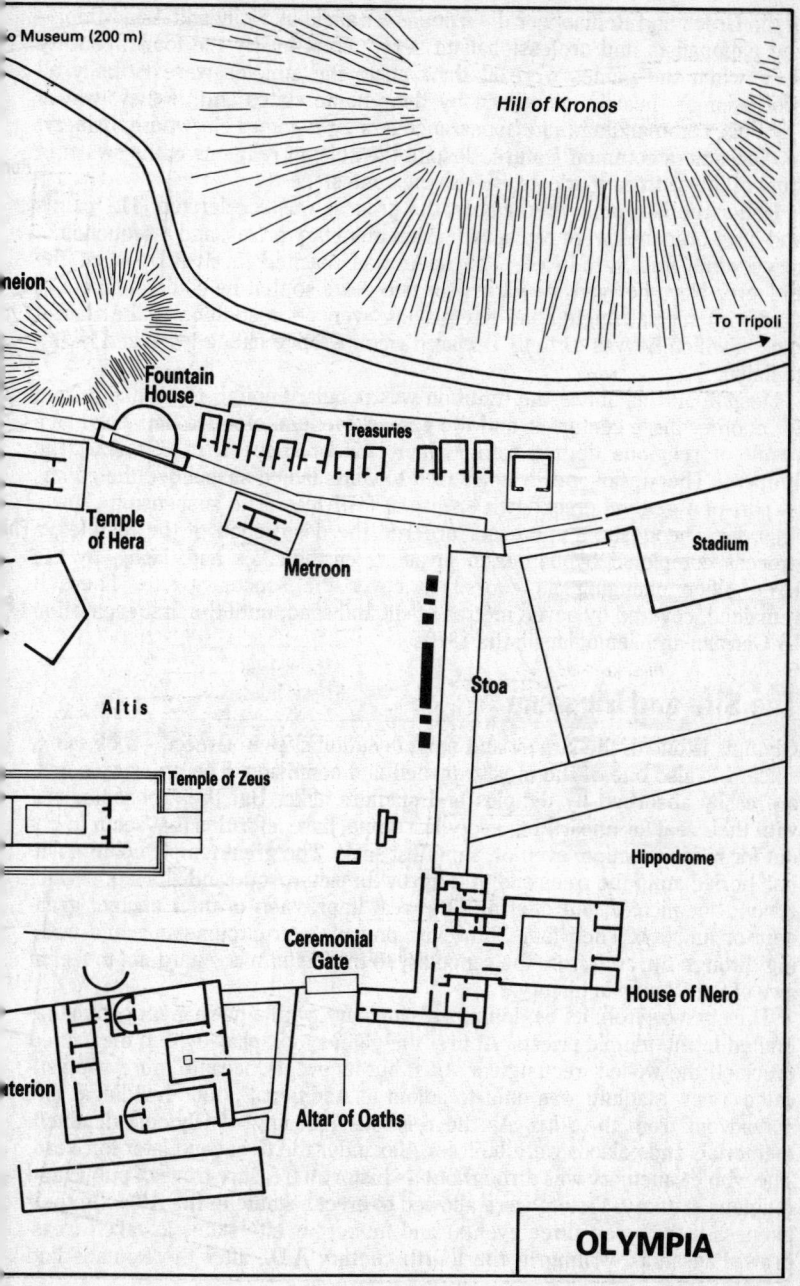

o Museum (200 m)

Hill of Kronos

neion

To Trípoli

Fountain
House

Treasuries

Temple
of Hera

Metroon

Stadium

Altis

Stoa

Temple of Zeus

Hippodrome

Ceremonial
Gate

House of Nero

uterion

Altar of Oaths

OLYMPIA

of the Greek and Roman world – from as far afield as Sicily and Asia Minor – and nationalism and professionalism slowly crept in. By the fourth century B.C., when the games were at their peak, the athletes were virtually all professionals, heavily sponsored by their home states and, if they won at Olympia, commanding huge appearance money at games elsewhere. Bribery, too, became a common feature, despite the solemn religious oaths sworn in front of the sanctuary priests prior to the contests.

Under the **Romans**, predictably, the process was accelerated. The palms and olive branches were replaced by rich monetary prizes, and a sequence of new events was introduced. The nadir was reached in 69 A.D. when the Emperor Nero delayed the games for two years so that he could compete in (and win) special singing and lyre-playing events – in addition to the chariot race in which he was tactfully declared victor despite falling twice and failing to finish.

Despite all this abuse the tradition was popular enough to be maintained for another three centuries, and the games' eventual **closure** happened as a result of religious dogma rather than lack of support. In 393 A.D. the Emperor Theodosius, newly converted to Christianity, suspended the games as part of a general crackdown on pagan festivities. The suspension proved final, for Theodosius's successor ordered the destruction of the temples, a process completed by barbarian invasion, earthquakes and, lastly, by the river Alfiós changing its course to cover the sanctuary site. There it remained, covered by seven metres of silt and sand, until the first excavation by German archaeologists in the 1870s.

The Site and Museum

Olympia is one of the largest and most beautiful sites in Greece – a blessing, since it is also one of the most crowded and confusing. The crowds, in fact, are easily absorbed by temples and stadium alike. But the archaeologists, with their zeal for unearthing every last stone, have left ruins that seem to cry out for reconstruction, even on a modest scale. The great temple columns lie half-buried amid the trees and undergrowth: picturesque and shaded, perfect ground for picnics, but offering little real impression of their ancient grandeur or function. Their fame, however, prevails over circumstance and walking through the arch from the sanctuary to the stadium it is hard not to feel in awe of the Olympian history.

The site was from its beginnings a sanctuary, with a permanent population limited to the temple priests. At first the games took place within the sacred precinct, the walled, rectangular *Altis*, but as events became more sophisticated a new stadium was built to adjoin it. Additional public buildings, too, spread out from the *Altis*. As the religious meaning of Olympia declined, memorials and palaces were built for Alexander the Great and later for Nero. The whole sanctuary was throughout its history a treasure-trove of public and religious statuary. Victors were allowed to erect a statue in the *Altis* (in their likeness if they won three events) and numerous city states installed treasuries. Pausanias, writing in the fourth century A.D., after the Romans had already several times looted the sanctuary, fills almost a whole book of his *Guide to Greece* with descriptions. An idea of this wealth is suggested today not only by the site but by a spectacular collection of sculpture in the museum.

The Sanctuary

Open Mon.–Sat. 8am–7pm; Sun. 9am–6pm; off-season 9am–3pm daily. Admission 400dr, students 200dr.

The entrance to the site leads along the west side of the *Altis* wall, past a group of public and official buildings. On the left, beyond some Roman baths, is the **Prytaneion**, the administrators' residence where athletes were lodged and feasted at official expense. On the right are the ruins of a **Gymnasium** and **Palaestra** (wrestling school), used by the competitors during their obligatory ten months of training at Olympia prior to the games.

Beyond these stood the Priests' House, the **Theokoleon**, a substantial colonnaded building in the southeast corner of which is a structure adapted as a Byzantine church. This was originally the **studio of Pheidias**, the fifth-century B.C. sculptor responsible for the great cult statue in Olympia's Temple of Zeus (and for that of Athena in the Parthenon). It was identified by following a description in Pausanias, and by the discovery of tools, moulds for the statue, and a cup engraved with the sculptor's name. The dimensions of the studio are exactly those of the inner sanctuary, or *cella*, in which the statue was to be placed. To the south of the studio lie further administrative buildings, including the **Leonidaion**, a large and doubtless luxurious hostel endowed for the most important of the festival guests. It was the first building visitors would reach along the original approach road to the site.

Admission to the *Altis*, the Sacred Precinct, was in the earlier centuries of the games limited to free-born Greeks – whether spectators or competitors. Throughout its history it was male-only, save for the sanctuary's priestess. An Olympian anecdote records how a woman from Rhodes disguised herself as her son's trainer to gain admission, but revealed her identity in the joy of his victory. She was spared the legislated death penalty, though subsequently all trainers had to appear naked.

The main focus of the precinct, today as in ancient times, is provided by the great Doric **Temple of Zeus**. Built between 470 and 456 B.C., it was as large as the (contemporary) Parthenon: a fact quietly substantiated by the vast column drums littered on the ground. The temple's decoration, too, rivalled the finest in Athens; partially recovered, its sculptures of Pelops in a chariot race, of Lapiths and Centaurs, and the Labors of Hercules, are now exhibited in the museum. In the *cella* was exhibited the great gold-and-ivory cult statue by Pheidias, one of the seven wonders of the ancient world. Here too the Olympian flame was kept alight, from the time of the games until the following spring – a tradition continued at an altar for the modern games.

The smaller **Temple of Hera**, behind, was the first built in the *Altis*; prior to its completion in the seventh century B.C., the sanctuary had only open-air altars, dedicated to Zeus and a variety of other cult gods. The temple, rebuilt in the Doric style in the sixth century B.C., is the most complete building on the site, with some thirty of its columns surviving in part, along with a section of the inner wall. The levels above this wall were just sun-baked brick, the lightness of which must have helped to preserve the sculptures – most notably the *Hermes of Praxiteles* – found amid the earthquake ruins.

Between these two temples of Hera and Zeus is a grove described by Pausanias, and identified as the **Pelopeion**. In addition to a cult altar to the Olympian hero, this enclosed a small mound formed by sacrificial ashes, among which excavations unearthed many of the terracotta finds in the museum. The sanctuary's principal altar, dedicated to Zeus, probably stood just to the east.

West of the Temple of Hera, and bordering the wall of the *Altis* are remains of the circular **Philippeion**, the first monument in the sanctuary to be built to secular glory. It was begun by Philip II after the Battle of Chaeronea gave him control over the Greek mainland, and may have been completed by Alexander the Great. To the east of the Hera temple is a small, second-century A.D. **fountainhouse**, the gift of the ubiquitous Herodes Atticus. Beyond, lining a terrace below at the base of the Hill of Kronos, are the **state treasuries**. All except two of these were constructed by cities outside of Greece proper, as they functioned principally as storage chambers for sacrificial items and sporting equipment used in the games. They are built in the form of temples, as at Delphi; the oldest and grandest, at the east end, belonged to Gela in Sicily. In front of the treasuries are the foundations of a fourth-century B.C. Doric temple, the **Metroon**, dedicated to the mother of the gods.

The ancient ceremonial entrance to the *Altis* was on the south side, below a long **stoa** taking up almost the entire east side of the precinct. At the corner was a house built by Nero for his stay during the games. The emperor also had the entrance remodelled as a triumphal arch, fit for his anticipated victories.

Through the arch, just outside the precinct, stood the **Bouleuterion** or Council House, where before a great statue of Zeus the competitors took their oaths to observe the Olympian rules. As they approached the stadium the gravity of this would be impressed upon them; lining the way were bronze statues paid for with the fines exacted for foul play, bearing the name of the disgraced athlete, his father and his city.

Finally, though, it's neither foundations nor columns that make sense of Olympia but the 200-metre track of the **Stadium** itself, entered through a football-tunnel-like arch. The starting and finishing lines are still there, with the judges' thrones in the middle and seating ridges banked to either side. Originally unstructured, the stadium developed with the games' popularity, forming a model for others throughout the Greek and Roman world. The tiers here eventually accommodated up to 20,000 spectators, with a smaller number on the southern slope overlooking the **Hippodrome** where the chariot races were held. Even so, the seats were reserved for the wealthier strata of society. The ordinary populace – along with slaves and all women spectators – watched the events from the Hill of Krónos, then treeless and a natural grandstand to the north.

The Archaeological Museum

Open 8am–7pm daily, except Sun. 9am–5pm and Tues. 11am–5pm; off season 9am–3pm. Admission 400dr, students 200dr.

Olympia's museum lies a couple of hundred metres north of the site. With some of the finest Classical and Roman sculptures in the country, it clearly makes good use of the high admission fee.

Among the finds displayed are a variety of objects relating to the games – including *halleres*, or jumping weights – and a large number of statues and fragments. The most famous of the individual sculptures are the **Head of Hera** and the **Hermes of Praxiteles**, both dating from the fourth century B.C. and discovered in the Temple of Hera. The Hermes is one of the best-preserved of all Classical sculptures, and remarkable in the easy informality of its pose; it retains traces of its original paint. On a grander scale is the **Nike of Paionios**, originally ten metres high. Though no longer complete, it hints at how the sanctuary must once have appeared, crowded with statuary.

The best of the smaller objects are housed in Room 4. These include several fine bronzes, among them the **Helmet of Mitiades**, captured by the Athenians at the Battle of Marathon and found with votive objects dedicated in the stadium, and a superb terracotta group of **Zeus abducting Ganymede**.

The centrepiece of the museum, however, is the statuary from the **Temple of Zeus**, displayed in the vast main hall. This includes three groups, all of which were once painted. From the *cella* is a frieze of the **Twelve Labours of Hercules**, delicately moulded and for the most part identifiably preserved. The other groups are from the east and west pediments. The east, reflecting Olympian pursuits, depicts Zeus presiding over a **Chariot race between Pelops and Oinamaos**. The story has several versions. King Oinamaos, warned that he would be killed by his son-in-law, challenged each of his daughter Hippomadeia's suitors to a chariot race. After allowing them a start he would catch up and kill them from behind. The king (depicted on the left of the frieze) was eventually defeated by Pelops (on the right with Hippomadeia), after – depending on the version – assistance from Zeus (depicted at the centre), magic steeds from Poseidon, or, most un-Olympian, bribing Oinamaos'scharioteer to tamper with the wheels.

The west pediment, more safely mythological, illustrates the **Battle of Lapiths and Centaurs** at the wedding of the Lapith king Peirithous. This time Apollo presides over the scene while Theseus helps the Lapiths defeat the drunken centaurs, seen – with fairly brutal realism – attacking the women and boy guests.

Olimbía village: practicalities

Modern **OLIMBÍA** is little more than a couple of streets, a village that has grown up simply to serve the excavations and tourist trade. Nevertheless, it's a pleasant place to stay – certainly preferable to PÍRGOS (see overpage) – with the prospect of good countryside walks along the Alfiós river and around the hill of Krónos.

Accommodation is fairly easy to come by, with a swift turnaround of clientele and a range of hotels and private rooms. If you're travelling alone, the **youth hostel** (on the main street, Kondhíli 18; ☎0624/22-580) is the cheapest option, and the 11.30pm curfew is unlikely to prove frustrating; the hostel is open all day except between 10am and 1pm. Between two people, **rooms** in private houses can end up being better value. You're likely to be offered one on arrival; otherwise most are signposted on the road parallel to and above Kondhíli. The main **campsite**, *Camping Diana* (☎0624/22-314), has a pool and good facilities, just off the main road. *Camping Olympia* (☎0624/22-745), on the Pírgos road, is marginally less expensive and less well-endowed.

Among **hotels**, the cheapest is generally the D-class *Heraeum* (Kondhíli 39; ☎0624/22-539), which may drop rates if asked. Other D-class options include the *Pelops* (Varía 2; ☎0624/22-543), *Praxiteles* (Spiliopoúlou 7; ☎0624/22-592) and *Hermes* (Kondhíli 63; ☎0624/22-577). If you want more comfort, there are a couple of dozen C- and B-class hotels, though many of these are block-reserved by tour groups.

For **eating**, most of the tavernas offer standard tourist meals at mildly inflated prices. The *Stadhion*, Greek-American run, at the west end of town, is a reasonable *psistariá*; and if you're preparing a picnic, bread from the bakery on the road to Kréstena is excellent. Among other facilities, Olimbía has a **bank** and **OTE** on the main street, a **post office** (just uphill), and an unusually good selection of **English-language books** at the back of the *Galerie d'Orphée* crafts shop.

The village itself has little in the way of diversion, save a somewhat dutiful **Museum of the Olympic Games** (8am–3.30pm, Sun. 9am–4.30pm; 120dr), with commemorative postage stamps and the odd memento. A display on the history of the excavations would be more enlightening; German archaeologists continued work during the last war, unearthing the stadium allegedly on the orders of Hitler.

Getting to Olympia

Most people arrive at Olympia **via Pírgos** which is on the main Peloponnese rail line and has frequent bus connections with Pátra and a couple daily with Kalamáta/Kiparissía. **Buses** leave 16 times daily between Pírgos and Olympia, though with a break between 12.30 and 3.30pm and a last service at 9pm. The last **train** from Pírgos to Olympia leaves at 6pm.

The only other direct buses to Olympia are **from Trípoli**, via LANGÁDHIA. These run three times daily in either direction. If you are approaching **from Andhrítsena**, either take the bus to Pírgos and change, or stop at KRÉSTENA and hitch or taxi the final 12km on from there.

The Coast From Pírgos to Pátra

Despite the proximity of Olympia and Pátra, this **northwest corner** of the Peloponnese is not much explored by foreign visitors. Admittedly, it's not the most glamorous of coasts, but for a day or two's beach stop, **Kalógria** or the old port of **Katákolo** are functional and pleasant.

Ferry connections may add further purpose to your travels. From Killíni there are regular crossings to Zákinthos, and in summer to Kefalloniá. Katákolo also has (summer-only) *kaíkia* to Zákinthos.

Pírgos and Katákolo

PÍRGOS has a grim recent history. When the Germans withdrew at the end of World War II it remained under the control of Greek Nazi collaborators, who, after negotiating surrender with the resistance, opened fire on their entry to the town. Full-scale battle erupted and for five days the town burned. Today, it's a drab, 1950s-looking place, which few casual visitors have a good word to say about. If you can avoid an enforced overnight stay, do so. The hotels are overpriced, the food uninspiring, diversions nonexistent. The main escape routes are to Pátra, Kiparissía or Olympia (by train or bus); or, closer at hand, to Katákolo by local bus #4. The bus and train stations are around 100m apart, and not hard to find your way between. Among the **hotels**, there are five C-class places, the D-class *Acropole* (Ermoú 7; ☎0621/22-925), and E-class *Emporikon* (Ahiléos 2; 0621/22-925).

Katákolo

Thirteen kilometres west of Pírgos, **KATÁKOLO** is somewhat more enticing: a decayed, ramshackle old port with good beaches close by. Until the last few decades, and improved road connections with Pátra, it controlled the trade for Ilía province. Today only a few tramp steamers rust at anchor, though the navy calls occasionally and, oddly, the port remains a stop for Italian cruise ships, including the *Orient Express*. What the cruise passengers make of the caved-in warehouses and the little two-street town is hard to say. But arriving from Pírgos it feels an easy place to settle into. There are three **hotels**: a C- and two D-class, cheapest of which is the *Delfini* (☎0621/41-214); alternatively try the **rooms** establishments at the top of steps leading from the road, with cabins fronted by peach and apricot trees. For **meals**, there are a handful of excellent tavernas on the quay.

Katákolo's beach, the **Spiátza**, stretches away for miles to the north, a popular spot with Greeks, many of whom own shuttered little cottages set just back from the sea. It is sandy, though hard-packed: more of a spot for football or jogging, with the sea too shallow for swimming. However, a thirty-minute walk north, past the overgrown castle, will take you to much better swimming at **Áyios Andhréas** beach, 200 metres of sloping, outcrop-studded sand, with views over a few attendant islets and out to Zákinthos. There are summer tavernas here and a few rooms to let. An even better beach is to be found at **SKAFÍDHIA**, 3km north of Katákolo and accessible by road via KORAKOHÓRI. It is a quiet, attractive strand despite the presence of a *Club Med* holiday complex to its north.

To the south of Katákolo there's a pleasant twenty-minute walk out to the **lighthouse**, set on a plateau among arbutus and pine.

Loutrá, Killíni, and Hlemoútsi

North from Pírgos, road and rail meander through a series of uneventful market towns. For the coast there are two forks: at GASTOÚNI for the spa of LOUTRÁ KILLÍNIS (occasional bus); and at KAVÁSSILAS where a rail line (7 trains daily) and road (buses from Pátra) head down to KILLÍNI proper.

At the north end of **LOUTRÁ KILLÍNIS'** long beach you'll find a crop of upmarket (A- and C-class) hotels catering for the resort's spa-trade. But walk south and the development soon gives way to sand dunes, seasonal home to a crowd of unofficial campers, mostly German, French and Italian. Joining them should pose no problems, though there is also a legitimate EOT **camp-site**, *Camping Killini* (☎0623/96-270) back on the road towards VARTHOLOMIÓ and GASTOÚNI.

Using Loutrá or Killíni as a base, it's worth taking time to hitch or walk to the village of **KÁSTRO**, 6km from either town at the centre of the sandy cape. Looming above the village is the Frankish **Castle of Hlemoútsi** (or Chlemoutzi), a vast hexagonal structure built by Guillaume de Villehardouin, the founder of Mystra, in 1220. Its function was principally to control the province of Achaia, though it served also as a strategic fortress on the Adriatic. Haze permitting, there are sweeping views across the straits to Zákinthos, and even to Kefalloniá and Itháki, from the well-preserved and restored ramparts.

Killíni

Cheerless little **KILLÍNI** (reachable by taxi from Loutrá, as well as buses from Pátra) has little more to offer than its **ferry connections**. It is the princi-pal port for Zákinthos (3-7 daily departures) and in season has boats (1-3 departures daily) to Póros on Kefalloniá. Be warned, however, that ferry and train arrivals/departures are perversely designed to just miss each other, so count on an enforced two-to-three-hour stopover and an expensive meal at the harbour, unless you get a combined bus/ferry ticket from Pátra. In any case try to avoid an overnight stay, since the choice is between sleeping on the beach or two expensive hotels (cheapest is the C-class *Glaretzas*; ☎0623/92-937).

Kalógria

Midway between Killíni and Pátra, **KALÓGRIA** is an eight-kilometre strand of beach, bordered by a swathe of pine forests. A fair proportion of Pátra descends at the weekend as it's the nearest good beach to the city, but it's also a respected place (both the sands and, for its birdlife, the forest) and permanent development remains low-key. It is not actually a village – the nearest bona fide town is METÓHI – but instead a line of tavernas and stores, well used to unofficial summer campers. At the far north end of the beach there's a hotel and *Barracuda Club* complex. A novelty for wildlife aficionados are the estuaries nearby in which you may find yourself swimming alongside harmless metre-long watersnakes.

Pátra (Patras)

PÁTRA is the largest town in the Peloponnese and, after Pireás, the major port of Greece. You can go from here to Italy, Yugoslavia, and Turkey, as well as to the Ionian islands and Crete; and the city is the key for the transport network for the mainland too, with connections throughout the Peloponnese and, via the ferry at Rió, across the straits to Delphi or western Greece.

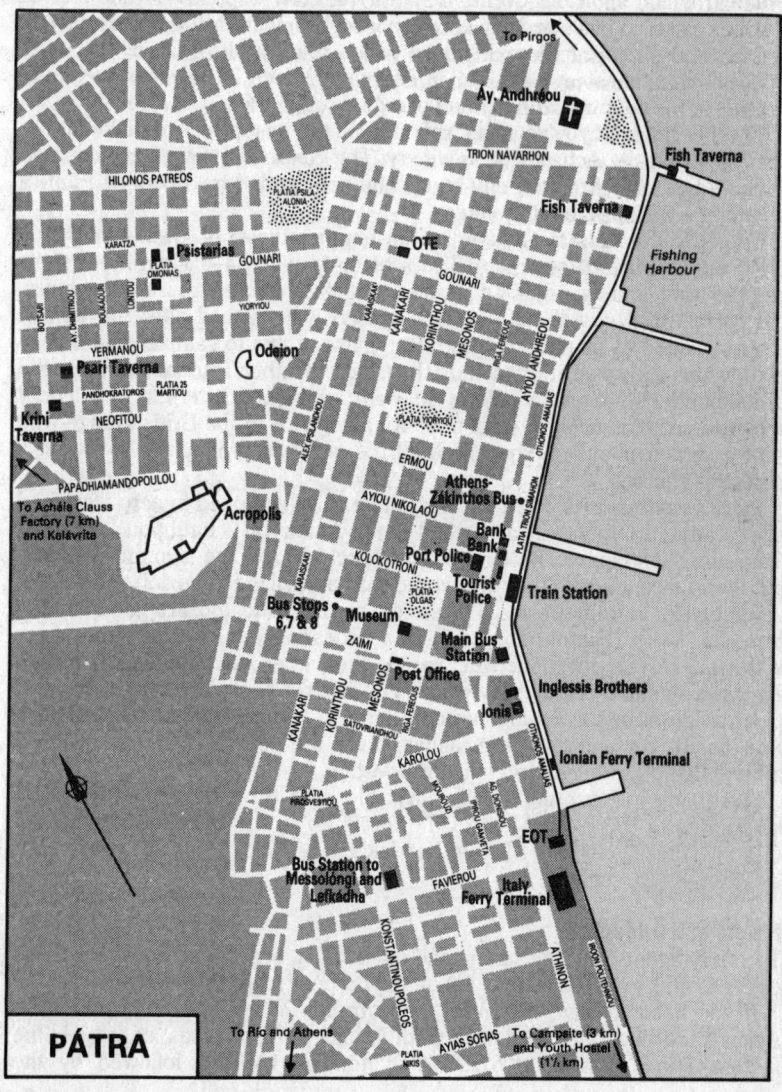

PÁTRA

The City and nearby

Unless you arrive late in the day from Italy, you shouldn't need to spend more than a few hours in the city. A conurbation of close to 200,000 souls, it's not the ideal holiday retreat: there are no beaches, no particular sights, and the hotels are positioned on noisy streets, with traffic noise well into the night and earlier than you'd want to get up. Nor is there much effort to make the place attractive to visitors, save for the recently-instigated **International Festival** which sponsors events from July to early September. The festival features classical plays and the occasional rock concert in the Roman *odeion*, and art and photographic exhibitions which bring a bit of life to the warehouses by the harbour. **Carnival**, in February/March, is however one of the biggest in the country, with a grand parade through the city centre.

At other times, if you've an afternoon to fill the best places to make for are the castle and the Achaïa Clauss winery. The **castle** is mainly Venetian: not exciting but away from the city bustle and surrounded by a park. It's only a ten-minute walk up from the water.

To get to the **Achaïa Clauss** factory, 9km southeast of town, take the #7 bus from Kandakári (see map). Tours (9am–1pm and 4–6.30pm; free) show you the wine- and *ouzo*-making process, and feature some treasured, century-old barrels of *Mavrodhafni* – a dark dessert wine named after the woman Clauss wanted to marry. You're given a glass of this to sample (and a postcard, which they post) on reaching the factory's rather Teutonic bar, an echo of its founder's nationality. Along the walls are signed letters from celebrity recipients of *Mavrodhafni* (first prize for arrogance to the British judge who sent a signed photo); a shop sells all the factory's products if you want a bottle for yourself.

Pátra's **restaurants** seem to constitute a fairly wretched bunch – fast-food places around Óthonos Amalías and Ayíou Andhréou – until you look away from the city centre. Better options here include the two no-nonsense *estiatória* facing each other across the road at Ipsilándou no.140 and no.159, seven blocks in from the sea. The streets by the castle, too, are good hunting grounds. *Krini* (Pantokrátoros 57) is a endearingly basic lunchtime place, with wine barrels down one side; around the corner *Psari* (Ayíou Dhimitríou 75) has a similar feel – open evenings. For fish, the best places are a couple of tavernas down by the fishing harbour, home to a somewhat half-hearted fleet. And finally, for spit-roast specialities, there are several *psistariés* grouped around Platía Omonías and Platía Pirosvestíou.

Swimming in Pátra isn't really advisable, with the sea polluted for some kilometres to the west. Most of the locals go to the **beaches** around Río (7km northeast; city bus #6 from Kandakári), or Kalógria (32km south-west; bus from KTEL station).

Hotels and transport

The ferry agents, railway station and main KTEL bus station could hardly be easier to find, grouped as they are on the harbour road, Óthonos Amalías.

If you need to stay, the main concentration of low-budget **hotels** is on Ayíou Andhréou, one block back from Amalías. The cheapest of these is the D-class *Delphi* (no.63; ☎061/273-050; doubles 1350dr), followed by the

THE FERRIES

Innumerable ticket agents along the waterfront each sell different permutations of **ferry crossings to Italy** on one or more of the lines detailed below. It is worth spending an hour or so researching these, especially if you're taking a car, since costs, journey times and routes all differ from one company to another.

En route to Italy it is possible to make stopovers on Kefalloniá, Itháki (Ithaca), Páxi and, most commonly, Igoumenítsa and Corfu (Kérkira); or in Dubrovnik, Yugoslavia. Individual tickets to any of these **Greek island stops** (or Dubrovnik) are also available from Pátra.

A few **general points**:

Fares All companies offer a variety of fares for cabin, *aircraft* seats, and deck passage (the basic price quoted below), plus reductions according to age, student, or rail-card status.

Embarkation tax of (currently) 1000dr per person and per car is levied on all international departures.

Stopovers are free if you specify them when booking, though you may have to pay re-embarkation taxes.

Checking in at the company's respective port agent is essential if you have booked tickets in advance, or bought them through a travel company other than the official agent. This should be done at least three hours before departure. For companies who have no exclusive agent in Pátra, you should go directly to the departures hall, where all companies have a booth staffed before sailings.

ROUTES AND AGENTS

Fragline Brindisi (18½ hr.), via Igoumenítsa and Corfu; daily. Passage £15 (low), £35 (high). *Inglessis Bros.*, Óthonos Amalías 5; ☎061/277-676.

Hellenic Mediterranean Lines Brindisi (19 hr.), via Kefalloniá; daily. Passage £28 (low), £46 (high). *Hellenic Mediterranean Lines Co. Ltd,,* Sarandopórou 1/Athinón; ☎061/429-520.

Seven Islands Brindisi (23 hr.), via Kefalloniá, Itháki, Páxi, Igoumenítsa and Corfu; daily. Passage £24 (low), £32 (high). *Inglessis Bros.* (see *Fragline*, above). *Tsimaras*, Óthonos Amalías 14; ☎061/277-783. These agents each handle a different *Seven Islands* line boat.

Adriatica Brindisi (19 hr.), via Igoumenítsa and Corfu; daily. Passage £21 (low), £32 (high). No exclusive agent in Pátra.

Ventouris Bari (16½ hr.), via Igoumenítsa and Corfu; daily. Passage £18 (low), £24 (high). *Express Shipping Agencies Co.*, Óthonos Amalías 85; ☎061/222-958.

Karageorgis Ancona (29 hr.), direct; Mon. and Thurs. Passage £22 (low) £27 (high). *Proslentis-Petropoulou*, Óthonos Amalías 32; ☎061/270-994.

Marlines Ancona (34 hr.), via Igoumenítsa; weekdays only. Passage £25 (low), £33 (high). Coming back from Italy a *Marlines* boat leaves Pátra every Sunday morning for Iráklio (Crete) and Kusadasi (Turkey). *Marlines*, Óthonos Amalías 56; ☎061/226-666.

Strintzis Ancona (31 hr.) via Igoumenítsa and Corfu; Mon., Weds., Thurs., Sat. Passage £21 (low), £28 (high). Ancona (34 hr.), via Dubrovnik (19 hr., free stopover; Tues. only). Passage to Dubrovnik $35 (low), $45 (high); double to Ancona. *Tsimaras* (see *Seven Islands*, above).

Minoan Lines Ancona (34 hr.), via Igoumenítsa and Corfu; 5 weekly. Passage £26 (low), £33 (high). No exclusive agent in Pátra.

Hellenic Cypriot Mediterranean Line Trieste (44 hr.); Tues., Thurs., Sat. Passage £25 (low), £30 (high). No exclusive agent in Pátra.

Most companies designate a **high season** of mid-June to mid-September.
Frequency of departures detailed are for the high season period.

Kentrikon (no.10; ☎061/277-276). Slightly quieter at much the same prices is the E-class *Parthenon* (Ermoú 25; ☎061/277-288), a block in from Platía Tríon Simáhon, the principal waterside square. The main low-budget alternative to these options is the city's **youth hostel** (Iróon Politehníou 68; ☎061/427-278)), a kilometre-plus walk south from the ferry terminal. Housed in a nineteenth-century mansion, it's clean and cheap, with roof space as well as dormitory rooms, and no curfew. Lastly, in the same direction as the hostel there's a beach **campsite** (☎061/424-130), 3km beyond the city.

The **EOT** office, by the customs house at the harbour, can be helpful for information. For **money exchange**, if you arrive late or need to buy last-minute drachmas for embarkation tax, the *National Bank of Greece*, just back from the waterside, keeps special evening hours (5.30–8.30pm).

Buses go almost everywhere from Pátra: back to Athens, to most points of the Peloponnese, and into central and western Greece (Lefkádha, Ioánnina, etc) via the ferry at Río-Andírio. The main **KTEL** station, midway along the waterside, has buses to Athens, Killíni, Pírgos and other towns in the Peloponnese, as well as to Ioánnina. For Lefkádha (change at Agrínio) and Messolóngi you need the **KTEL Étolo-Akarnanía** on Favieroú, near the domed church above the Ionian island ferry terminal. You can pick up the Athens-**Zákinthos** bus on Othónos-Amalías, just north of the railway station – an alternative to the regular Killíni port departure. Heading to **Delphi**, take local bus #6 (from Kandakári, five blocks back from the waterside) to the **Río-Andírio ferry**, cross over and take a local bus to Náfpaktos and then a regular bus on from there. Moving on by **train** from Pátra, keep in mind the detour along the narrow-gauge line to Kalávrita (see the following section).

Hitching out of town, for Athens take the Río bus (#6) and walk up to the toll point by the National Road; for central and western Greece take the ferry across to Andírio and try your luck there; for Pírgos walk out for 100m or so past the massive modern church of Ayíou Andhréou.

A good value **car hire** outlets is *Just* (Óthonos Amalías 37; ☎061/27 5-495). **Olympic Airways** is represented at the *Hotel Astir* (Ayíou Andhréou 16; ☎061/222-901).

The north coast and the Kalávrita railway

From Pátra you can reach Kórinthos in two hours by bus along the **National Highway**, or half an hour longer on the **train** line; Athens itself is only another hour and a half beyond. To go this way without taking the time to detour along the **Kalávrita railway**, however, would be to miss one of the best treats the Peloponnese has to offer – and certainly the finest train journey in Greece. Even if you have a car, this railway should still be part of your plans. Beyond, if you're unhurried, it is worth taking the old **coast road** along the Gulf of Kórinthos; this runs below the new highway, often right by the sea.

Along the coast road: the Río ferry and beaches

The resorts and villages lining the Gulf of Kórinthos are nothing very special, though none too developed either. At most of them you find little more than a campsite and a couple of seasonal tavernas.

RÍO, connected by local bus #6 from Pátra, signals the beginning of swimmable water – though most travellers stop here only to make use of the **ferry across the gulf** to Andírio. This runs every twenty minutes through the day (every 30 min. at night) shuttling cars (400dr) and passengers (60dr) across to the central mainland. It is a long-established crossing, testimony to which are a pair of diminutive Turkish forts on either side of the gulf. As detailed in the Pátra section, there are onward connections at Andírio for Delphi (via Náfpaktos) and to Messolóngi and Lefkádha to the west. If you are crossing over into the Peloponnese from Andírio you might be tempted to stop by the sea here, rather than at Pátra. There are a couple of C-class hotels and three **campsites**: *Rio Mare* (on the beach; ☎061/99-2263), *Rion Camping* (☎061/99-1585), and *George* (☎061/99-1323).

Moving east, there are good beaches, and further campsites, around **ÉYIO**. The best sands are at the village of RHODHODHÁFNI, 2km northwest of Éyio; the *Corali Beach* (☎0691/71-558) campsite here is right on the beach. At Éyio itself a **ferry** (cars and passengers) traverses the gulf three times daily (7.30am, 1.30pm and 5pm; passengers 200dr, cars 1000dr; June-Sept. only) to ERATINÍ, well-poised for Delphi.

It is at **DHIAKOFTÓ** that the rack-and-pinion railway heads south into the Vouraíkos gorge for Kalávrita (see below). If you arrive late in the day it's worth spending the night, so as to do the journey in daylight. The town is, too, an attractive alternative to staying overnight in Pátra. Accommodation is plentiful, with five D-class **hotels** and another, very cheap, unclassified and unnamed, near the beginning of the Kalávrita rail line. Best value of the D-class places are the *Acropole* (☎0691/41-226) and *Helmos* (☎0691/41-236). For meals, avoid the bars in the village and cross the railway tracks instead: a ten-minute walk will bring you down to a small harbour with a couple of reasonable tavernas overlooking the water.

Beyond Dhiakoftó there are minor resorts at Akráta and Xilókastro. **AKRÁTA**, a small town with a beach hamlet a kilometre distant, is a little crowded with four **campsites** set along a rather drab, exposed stretch of beach. DHERVÉNI, another 8km east, is more attractive, though you'll need to camp as there's no official accommodation. **XILÓKASTRO**, a popular weekend escape from Kórinthos, has both good beaches and accommodation, and a pleasant setting below Mt. Zíria. Cheapest of its **hotels** are the D-class *Hermes* (Ioanoú 81; ☎0743/22-250) and *Kyani Akti* (Tsaldhári 68; ☎0743/22-225), or E-class *Kentrikon* (Tsaldhári/Petrídhi; ☎0743/22-223).

The Kalávrita rack-and-pinion railway

Even if you have no interest in trains, the **rack-and-pinion railway from Dhiakoftó to Kalávrita** is a must. It's a crazy feat of engineering, rising at gradients of up to one in seven as it cuts through the course of the

Vouraíkos gorge. En route is a toy-train fantasy of tunnels, bridges and precipitous overhangs; midway is the riverside hamlet of Zahloroú, a wonderful place to stay the night, with the historic monastery of Méga Spílio set in the cliffside above.

The line was built by an Italian company between 1885 and 1895 to bring minerals down from the mountains to the sea. Its steam locomotives were replaced some years ago – one remains by the line at Dhiakoftó – but the railway itself retains all the charm of its period. The tunnels, for example, have delicately carved windows, and the narrow bridges zigzagging across the Vouraikós seem engineered for sheer virtuosity. It takes about an hour to get from Dhiakoftó to Zahloroú, and about another half hour from there to Kalavríta. However, the pace is satisfyingly unhurried, including, when I last travelled down, a stop to let a chicken cross the line.

The best part of the trip is **the stretch to Zahloroú**, along which the gorge narrows to a few feet at points, only to open out into brilliant, open shafts of light beside the Vouraikós, clear and fast-running even in midsummer. To make the most of it you could walk back in around three hours – timing your hike to avoid trains in the tunnels! – but even in the train you get a sense of adventure, with everyone rushing from one side of the carriage to the other like five-year-old kids. Considering that the gorge is a fair rival to Samaria in Crete, it's suprisingly little touristed.

Zahloroú and Méga Spílio

As perfect a railway stop as could be imagined, **ZAHLOROÚ** is a tiny hamlet echoing with the sound of the Vouraikós river, which splits it into two neighbourhoods. It's a lovely, peaceful place with a couple of restaurants, both of which offer **rooms**. The nearest, the *Romantzo*, is in fact a bona-fide D-class hotel, very reasonably priced. The *Messinia*, 100m beyond, is even cheaper – Greek-American run and very friendly, allowing travellers to sleep on their roof if they can't afford a room.

The **Monastery of Méga Spílio** (Great Cave) is a 45-minute walk from the village up a rough donkey track along the cliff. It is reputedly the oldest monastery in Greece, though it has burnt down and been rebuilt so many times that you'd hardly guess it. The last major fire took place in the 1930s after a keg of gunpowder left behind from the War of Independence exploded. Visits are allowed to both women and men, though dress conduct is strict: skirts for women (though the monks do lend these, from their positively indecent collection of denim wraps) and long sleeves and trousers for men.

The view of the gorge from the monastery is for many the principal attraction. However, the cloister was once among the richest in the Greek world, owning properties throughout the Peloponnese, in Macedonia, Constantinople and Smyrna. In consequence, its treasury, arranged as a small museum, is outstanding, including among its icons a charred black image of the Virgin, one of three paintings in Greece said to be by the hand of St. Luke. It was the reason for the monastery's foundation, having been discovered, after a vision by saints Theodhoros and Simeon, in the large cave behind the church.

Men are allowed to **stay overnight** at the monastery, though the monks like visitors to arrive before 8pm, serving up a rough repast before closing the gates.

Kalávrita

From Méga Spílio a huge new road has been hacked down to **KALÁVRITA**. The train line is more in harmony with the surroundings, though coming from Zahloroú the drama of the route is diminished as the gorge opens out. The town itself is beautifully positioned, with Helmós and the Aroánia mountains as backdrop, though it wears a sad edge. During the last war the Germans carried out one of their most brutal reprisal massacres, killing the entire male population – 1436 men and boys – and leaving the town in flames.

Rebuilt, it is both depressing and poignant. The first and last sight is a mural, opposite the station which reads: 'Kalavrita, founder member of the Union of Martyred Towns, appeals to all to fight for world peace'. The clock-tower on the church stands for ever at 2.34 – the hour of the massacre. And out in the countryside behind the town is a moving and beautiful shrine to those massacred, its way grafittied with the single word 'Peace' at regular intervals.

The Nazis also burnt the **Monastery of Ayía Lávra**, 6km out of Kalávrita and – as the site where Yermanos, Archbishop of Pátra, raised the flag to signal the War of Independence – one of the great Greek national shrines. It too has been rebuilt, along with a small historical museum.

Staying at Kalávrita has a sense of pilgrimage for Greeks, though it's probably not for the casual visitor. If you miss the last train back to Zahloroú (currently at 5.55pm) there are a few **hotels**; cheapest is the *Paradissos* (☎0692/22-303). Buses also run from Kalávrita to Pátra four times daily.

Mount Helmós

At 2341m, **Mount Helmós** is the most imposing peak of the northern Peloponnese, and only sixty metres short of the summit of Taíyettos to the south. It thrusts clear of the other ridges of the Aroánia range, a dozen or so kilometres to the southeast of Kalávrita. However, the walk from Kalávrita is not an interesting approach. To get the most from hiking on the mountain you need to climb up from the village of SÓLOS, on the west side – a five-hour-plus walk which takes you to the Mavronéri waterfall, source of the legendary river Styx which souls of the dead had to cross in order to enter Hades.

The hike from Sólos

To reach the path opening at Sólos, start at AKRÁTA on the Pátra-Kórinthos road. From here it's a slow but beautiful haul up a winding dirt road. Buses run only three times a week, but hitching isn't too difficult in high summer.

SÓLOS is a tiny place, a nearly-deserted cluster of stone cottages on a steep hillside just below the fir trees. Facing it across the valley is the larger but more scattered village of PERISTÉRA, past which runs the easiest of the routes to Mavronéri.

Follow the **track through Sólos**, past the *magazí* (café-shop), where you can get a simple meal. Past the last houses the track curves around the head of a gully. On the right, going down its wooded flank, is a good path which leads to a bridge over the river in the bottom. Just beyond (15 min.; this and all subsequent times are from Sólos), you reach another track. There is a chapel on the left, and on the wall of a house on the right a sign saying 'Pros Gounariánika' pointing up a path to the left. Follow it past a church on a prominent knoll and on to the track again, where, at 75 minutes out, you turn left to the half-ruined hamlet of GOUNARIÁNIKA. From there continue steadily upward along the west (right) flank of the valley through abandoned fields until you come to a stream-gully running down off the ridge above you on your right. On the far side of the stream the fir forest begins. It's an ideal **camping place** (2½ hr.; 1½ hr. going back down).

Once into **the woods** the path is very clear. After about an hour (3½ hr.) you descend to a boulder-strewn **stream bed** with a rocky ravine to the right leading up to the foot of a huge bare crag, the east side of the Neraidhórahi peak visible from Kalávrita. Cross the stream and continue leftward up the opposite bank. In June there are the most incredible wild flowers, including at least half a dozen different orchids, all the way up from here.

After fifteen-minutes' climb above the bank you come out on top of a grassy knoll (3¾ hr.), then dip back into the trees again. At the four-hour mark, you turn a corner into the mouth of the **Styx ravine**. Another five minutes' walk brings you to a deep gully where enormous banks of snow lie late into the spring. A few paces across a dividing rib of rock there is a second gully, where the path has been eroded and you have to cross some slippery scree.

Here you come to a wooded spur running down from the crag on the right. The trail winds up to a shoulder (4hr. 20 min.), descends into another gully, and then winds up to a second shoulder of level rocky ground by some large black pines (4½ hr.) known as *To Dhiásselo tou Kinigoú* (the Hunter's Saddle). From there you can look into the Styx ravine. Continue down the path towards the right until it dwindles at the foot of a vast crag (4¾hr.). You can now see the **Mavronéri waterfall**, a 200-metre-long, wavering plume of water pouring off the red cliffs up ahead.

To get to it, angle across the scree bank without losing altitude – for the track is obliterated soon after the saddle – until you reach the base of the falls (5½ hr.). There's a small cave under the fall, where a rare columbine grows.

travel details

BUSES

Buses detailed have similar frequency in each direction, so entries are given just once; for reference check under both starting-point and destination.

Connections with Athens Kórinthos (hourly; 1½hr.); Mikínes (Mycenae)/Árgos/Tíryns/Náfplio (hourly to 9.30pm; 2 hr./2½ hr./2¾ hr./3 hr.); Spárti (7 daily; 6 hr.); Olympia (3 daily; 6 hr.);

From Kórinthos Mycenae/Árgos/Tíryns/Náfplio (hourly; ½ hr./1 hr./1¼ hr./1½ hr.); Loutráki (half-hourly; 20 min.); Neméa (5 daily; 45 min.); Trípoli (9 daily; 1½ hr.); Spárti (8 daily; 4 hr.); Kalamáta (7 daily; 4 hr.).

From Árgos Náfplio (half hourly; ½ hr.); Mikínes (Mycenae; 6 daily; ½ hr.); Neméa (3 daily; 1 hr.); Ástros/Leonídhi (3 daily; 1 hr./3 hr.); Trípoli (9 daily; 1 hr. 20 min.); Spárti (8 daily; 3 hr.);

Andhrítsena (daily at 10am; 3½ hr.); Olympia (3 daily on weekdays; 4½ hr.).

From Náfplio Epidaurus (3 daily; 45 min.); Toló (half-hourly; 25 min.); Trípoli (6 daily; 50 min.).

From Trípoli Megalópoli (8 daily; 40 min.); Spárti (6 daily; 1½ hr.); Olympia (3 daily, in stages; 5 hr.); Pátra (via Lámbia; 2 daily; 4 hr.); Pírgos (3 daily; 3 hr.); Andhrítsena (1 daily; 1 hr.); Dhimitsána (2 daily; 1½ hr.); Kalamáta (6 daily; 2 hr.); Pílos (2 daily; 3 hr.); Kiparissía (2 daily; 2 hr.); Megalópoli (8 daily; 35 min.).

From Spárti Místras (10 daily; 15 min.); Monemvassía (3 daily; 3 hr.); Kalamáta (2 daily; 2½ hr.); Yíthio (6 daily: 1 hr.); Neápoli (3 daily; 4 hr.).

From Yíthio Areópoli (4 daily; 50 min.); Monemvassía (2 daily; 2½ hr.).

From Areópoli Yerolimín (2 daily; 1 hr.); Kalamáta (4 daily via Ítilo; 2½ hr.).

From Kalamáta Koróni (7 daily; 1½ hr.); Ítilo/Areópoli (3 daily; 1½ hr.); Pátra (2 daily; 4 hr.); Pílos (8 daily; 1 hr.); Megalópoli/Trípoli (10 daily; 1 hr./1 3/4 hr.).

From Pílos Methóni (4 daily; 15 min.); Kalamáta (9 daily; 1 hr. 20 min.); Kiparissía (4 daily; 2 hr.).

From Megalópoli Andhrítsena/Pírgos (1 daily; 3 hr./4 hr.); Trípoli (8 daily; 40 min.).

From Pírgos Olympia (hourly, but none between 12.30-3.30pm; 45 min.); Andhrítsena (2 daily; 2 hr.); Pátra (10 daily; 2 hr.); Kiparissía/Kalamáta (2 daily; 1 hr./2 hr.).

From Pátra Kalávrita (4 daily; 2½ hr.); Zákinthos (3 daily; 2½ hr. including ferry from Killíni); Ioánnina (2 daily; 5 hr.); Kalamáta (2 daily; 4 hr.); Vólos (daily; 6 hr.).

TRAINS

There are two main Peloponnesian lines:

Athens-Kórinthos-Dhiakoftó-Pátra-Pírgos-Kiparissía-Kalamáta 3 trains daily make the full run in each direction. Another 3 daily run between Athens and Pátra, two continuing to Pírgos, the other as far as Pátra. Another 2 trains daily cover the route between Pátra and Kiparissía.

Approximate journey times between points are:
Athens-Kórinthos (1½-2½ hr.)
Kórinthos-Dhiakoftó (1-1½ hr.)
Dhiakoftó-Pátra (1 hr.)
Pátra-Pírgos (2 hr. 10 min.)
Pírgos-Kiparissía (1 hr.-1 hr. 20 min.)
Kiparissía-Kalamáta (1 hr. 40 min.).

Athens-Kórinthos-Mikínes(Mycenae)-Árgos-Trípoli-Kalamáta 4 trains daily cover the full route, in each direction.

Approximate journey times are:
Athens-Kórinthos (1½-2½ hr.)
Kórinthos-Mikínes (50 min.)
Mikínes-Árgos (10 min.)
Árgos-Trípoli (1½ hr.)
Trípoli-Kalamáta (2 hr. 40 min.).

In addition, there are the following branch lines:
Pírgos-Olympia 5 daily (50 min.).
Pírgos-Katákolo Daily at 2:18pm (25 min.).
Kavássila-Killíni 7 daily (35 min.).
Dhiakoftó-Zahlaroú-Kalávrita 6 daily; Diakoftó-Zakhlaroú (50 min.); Zahlaroú-Kalávrita (20 min.).
Lefktrá-Megalópoli Service replaced by OSE coaches, connecting with services to Lefktrá (between Árgos and Kalamáta).

FERRIES

Pireás-Monemvassía-Neápoli-Kíthira-Yíthio-Kíthira-Andíkithira-Kastelli (Crete)
Every Monday and Thursday at 9am the *Ionion* leaves Pireás, stopping at Monemvassía (8 hr.), Neápoli (10 hr.) and Ayía Pelayía (Kíthira; 12 hr.), then looping back to the mainland at Yíthio (14 hr.) before finally heading south for Kapsáli (Kíthira), Andíkithira and Kastélli (Crete; 6 hr. from Yíthio). The Monday boat normally stops at Kiparíssi and Yerakás en route to Monemvassía. The boat **returns from Kastélli** on Tuesdays and Fridays, calling at Neápoli and/or Monemvassía on its way back to Pireás. Departure times (and ports of call) can, however, fluctuate. For current, reliable information, it's worth contacting the very helpful *Rozakis* agency in Yíthio (☎0733/22-229).

From Killíni Zákinthos (3-7 daily; 2 hr.); Kefaloniá (1-3 daily; 1½ hr.).

From Pátra Corfu and Igoumenítsa (several times daily; 7-9 hr./8½-10 hr.); Kefalloniá, Itháki and Páxi (most days; 8½ hr./9½ hr./13½ hr.); Iráklio, Crete (weekly; 18 hr.); also to Brindisi, Ancona, Bari, Trieste (Italy); Split, Dubrovnik (Yugoslavia); and Kuşadasi (Turkey). See under 'Pátra' for details.

Across the Gulf of Kórinthos Andírio-Río (every 20 min., 30 min. at night; 20 min.); Éyio-Áy. Nikólaos (3 times daily; 35 min.; June-Sept. only).

HYDROFOILS

'Flying Dolphin' hydrofoils run between the following ports:

Leonídhi/Kiparíssi/Monemvassía to Spétses, Póros, and Pireás.

Neápoli/Kíthira to Pireás.

Méthana to Éyina and Póros.

Ermióni to Ídhra (Hydra) and Spétses.

Náfplio (summer only) to Monemvassía, Toló, Spétses, Póros and Pireás.

For details and frequencies of services, which vary drastically with season, contact local agents or the 'Flying Dolphins' main office in Pireás (Themistokléous 8; ☎01/452-7107).

SUMMER-ONLY EXCURSION BOATS

From Katákolo Zákinthos (3 times a week; 2½ hr.).

Galatás to Póros and Ídhra (Hydra).

Portohéli Water-taxis to Spétses according to demand (20 min.).

FLIGHTS

To/from Athens Kalamáta (daily; 50 min.); Kíthira (daily in season, less frequently out; 50 min.).

CHAPTER THREE

CENTRAL GREECE: THESSALY AND THE STEREA ELLADHA

C entral Greece has a slightly indeterminate character. For most visitors it's a region of highlights – **Delphi** above all, and farther to the north the unworldly rock-monasteries of the **Metéora** and the luxuriant woods and beaches of the **Pílion**. Few of its general characteristics are exciting: vast agricultural plains occupy much of the land, dotted with rather drab market and industrial towns.

This is not to suggest that you hurry through the area. The **Stereá Elládha** – literally 'Greek Continent' – takes its name from having been, with Attica and the 'island' of the Peloponnese, the sole mainland territory of post-Independence Greece. It corresponds to the ancient divisions of Boetia and Phocis, the domains respectively of Thebes and Delphi. For modern travellers it is dominated by the **routes to Delphi**, but if you have time there are rewarding detours. At the monastery of **Óssios Loukás** are preserved the finest Byzantine frescoes in the country; at **Glá**, just off the National Road, is the largest and most obscure of the Mycenaean sites; while from **Aráhova** you can climb the fabled **Mount Parnassós**.

The central plains of **Thessaly** (*Thessalía*) formed the bed of an ancient inland sea – rich agricultural land which was ceded reluctantly to the modern nation by the Turks in 1878. The province's attractions lie on the periphery, chained in by the mountain ranges of Ólimbos (Olympus), Píndhos (Pindus), Óssa and Pílion (Pelion). Picking a route is a hard choice. To the east, the island-like peninsula of the **Pílion**, an outstanding scenic attraction easily combined with island-hopping to the Sporades, extends from the major city and port of Vólos. To the west, **Kalambáka** gives access to the Metéora (not to be missed) and across a dramatic pass over the Píndhos to Epirus.

To the east, looming across a narrow gulf, and joined by an actual bridge at Halkídha, is the long island of **Évvia**. Though this feels in many ways an extension of the mainland (from which there are also three short ferry crossings), it is nonetheless a bona fide island. For this reason it is covered with the Sporades (see *Chapter Eleven*).

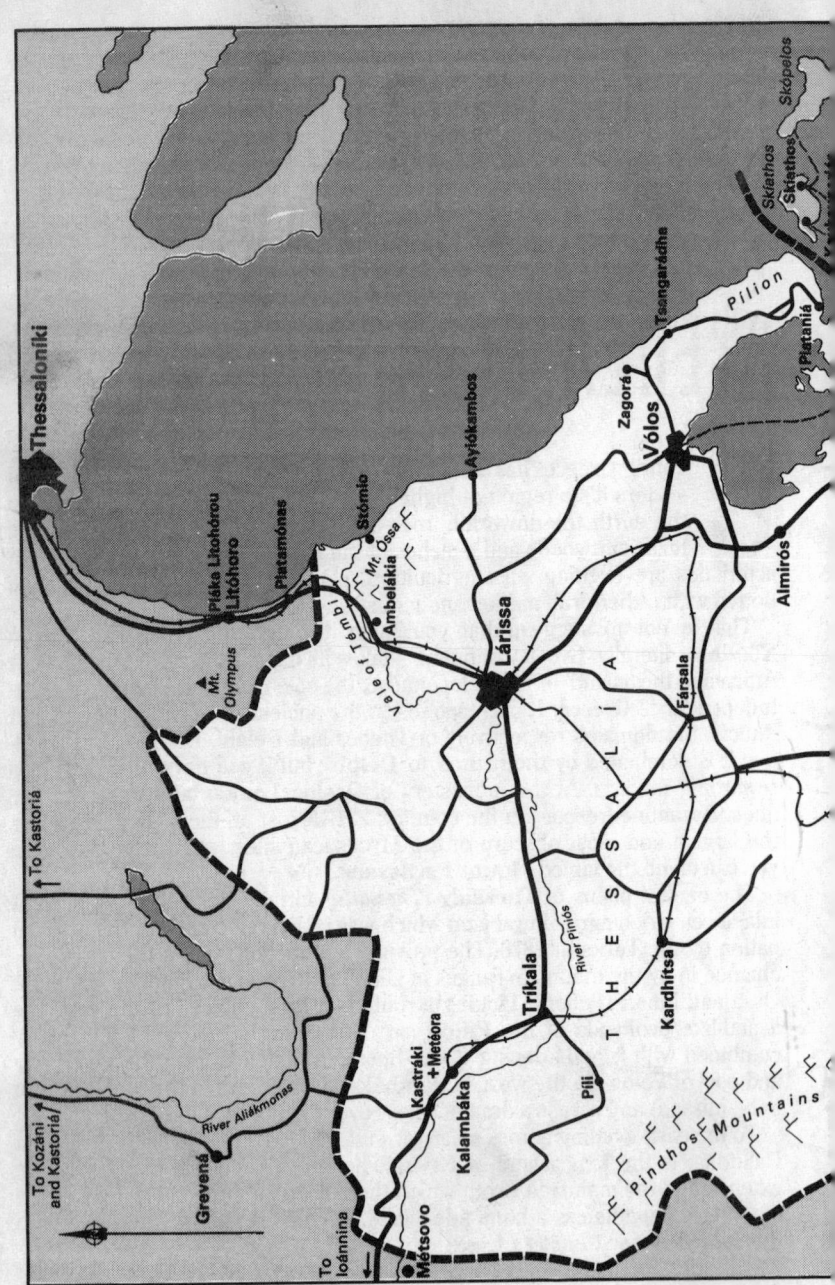

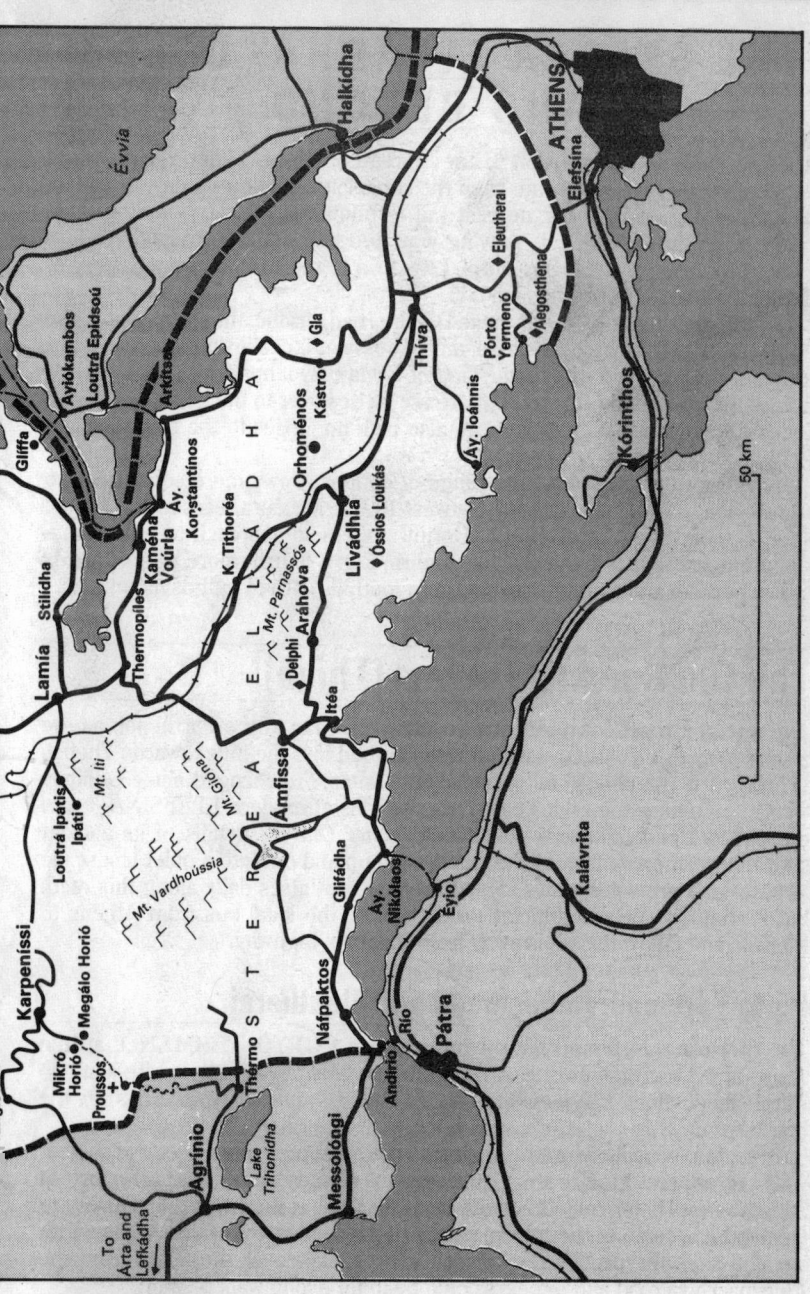

THE STEREÁ ELLÁDHA: DELPHI AND BEYOND

The inevitable focus of a visit to the Stereá is **Delphi**, 150km northwest of Athens. Buses cover the route from the capital several times a day, or can be picked up at Livádhia, the nearest rail terminus. However, if you're in no hurry, there are rewards in slowing your progress: taking the 'old road' to Thíva (Thebes), or detouring **from Livádhia** to the Byzantine monastery of Óssios Loukás, or to Mycenaean **Glá**.

To the northeast of the Athens-Delphi road, traffic thunders along the **National Road** towards Lárissa and Thessaloníki, skirting the coast for much of the way, with the long island of Évvia only a hundred or two metres across the gulf. Along this route there are ferries over to the island at Arkítsa, Áyios Konstantínos (where you can also pick up ferries to the Sporades and to Límnos) and Glíffa.

Moving **on from Delphi** the range of options grows more complex. Two routes head north into Thessaly – west to the Metéora, east to the Pílion; another, southwest to the Gulf of Corinth, offers an approach to – or from – **the Peloponnese**, via the ferry at Andírio-Río; a fourth, more remote, leads to **Karpeníssi** and through the southern foothills of the Píndhos mountains.

The Old Road to Thebes (Thíva)

The **ancient road from Athens to Delphi** began at the Parthenon as the Sacred Way to Eleusis, and from there climbed into the hills towards Thebes (Thíva). It is possible to follow this route, almost unchanged since Oedipus trod it, by taking the minor road into the hills at modern ELEFSÍNA. From the polluted and industrial port (see *Chapter One* for details of its ancient site) things improve fast, as the road winds up and out into a quiet landscape of pines and grey stony hills. There are just two buses daily along this road, but it shouldn't be too difficult to hitch: take the local bus from Athens to Elefsína and follow the signs away from the main highway.

Pórto Yermenó, Aegosthena and Eleutherai

The first place to tempt you off the route is **PÓRTO YERMENÓ**, a little resort at the extreme northeast corner of the Gulf of Kórinthos, with just one **hotel**, the C-class *Egosthenion* (☎0263/41-226), and a few tavernas on the beach.

Here, too, beneath Mount Kithairon, is the best preserved circuit of ancient walls anywhere in Greece – the fourth century B.C. Classical fort of **Aigosthena**. Historically it is quite insignificant but the ruins themselves are tremendous, some of the towers rising 10–12m above the walls. As ever with isolated sites the problem is transport: no buses cover the 23km from the Elefsína-Thíva road and hitchers could be in for a long walk or wait.

Eleutherai

Back on the Thíva road, a kilometre on from the Pórto Yermenó turning, you pass by another Classical fortress, fourth-century B.C. **ELEUTHERAI**. This is visible from the road, to the right, and it is again well preserved. The north side of the fort is almost intact and eight of its circuit of towers survive to varying degrees.

Thíva (Thebes)

The modern town of **THÍVA** (Thebes) lies 20km on from Eleutherai, built over the site of its mighty, ancient predecessor. For this very reason, however, it boasts scant remains of the past: archaeologists have had little leeway in excavating the crucial central areas, and the most interesting visit is to the excellent town **museum** (8.45am–3pm, Sun. 9.30am–2.30pm; closed Tues.; 200dr, students 100dr). This is to be found at the far (downhill) end of Pindharoú, the main street; look out for the Frankish tower in its forecourt. Among many fine exhibits are a unique collection of painted Mycenaean sarcophagi depicting, in bold expressionistic strokes, women lamenting their dead.

There are no direct **buses** from Thíva to Delphi but services run frequently to Livádhia (whence there are regular connections) and a couple of times a day to Halkídha, gateway to Évvia. You're unlikely to have reason to stay, unless waiting for one of these. Cheapest of the three **hotels** is the *Niobe* (Epaminónda 63; ☎0262/27-949), officially C-class but with lower than usual rates.

Livádhia, Orhómenos, Glá and Chaironea

LIVÁDHIA is a pleasant and prosperous town on the banks of the Herkína, a river of ancient fame which emerges from a dark gorge at the base of a fortress. It is an attractive place to stop, and a curious one, too, with a unique duo of sights from ancient and medieval times.

The ancient curiosity is the site of the **Oracle of Troiphonos**, a ten-minute walk from the main square, beside an old Turkish bridge. Here the waters of the Herkína rise from a series of springs, now channelled beside a (signposted) *Xenia* restaurant. Above the springs, cut into the rock, are niches for votive offerings – in one of which, a large chamber with a bench, the Turkish governor would sit for a quiet smoke. In antiquity they marked the Springs of Memory and Forgetfulness where all who sought to consult the Oracle of Troiphonos had first to bathe. The actual oracle, a circular structure which gave entrance to caves deep in the gorge, has been tentatively identified at the top of the hill, near the remains of an unfinished Temple of Zeus. It was visited by Pausanias, who wrote that it left him 'possessed with terror and hardly knowing himself or anything around him'.

The **castle**, again a short walk from the centre (along Odhós Froúrio), provides the medieval interest. In itself it is impressive: a well-bastioned square structure, built in the fourteenth century and a key early conquest in the War of Independence. But it is the history that's most interesting. The castle was the stronghold of a small group of Catalan mercenaries, the Grand Company, who took control of central Greece in 1311 and, appointing a Sicilian prince as their ruler, held it for sixty years. They were a tiny, brutal band who had arrived in Greece from Spain in the wake of the Fourth Crusade. They wrested control from the Franks, then established in Athens and Thebes, in a cunning deviation from traditional rules of engagement. As the Frankish nobility approached Livádhia, the vastly outnumbered Catalans diverted the river to flood the surrounding fields. The Frankish cavalry advanced into the unexpected marsh and were cut down to a man.

The town is today a minor, provincial capital with a trade in milling cotton from the area. It is completely off the tourist route and so an enjoyable pause before, or after Delphi. Arriving by **bus** you'll be dropped near the central square, Platía Dhiákou. The **train station** is 3km out but arrivals are met by a shuttle bus into town. Staying, you should have no problem finding a **hotel** room. There are a couple of C-class and two (somewhat ramshackle) D-class places – the latter, *Viotia* (☎0261/28-350) and *Erkyna* (☎0261/28-227), almost next door to each other at Ódhos Láppa no.3 and no.6, overlooking the river. Round the corner from them is the excellent *Taverna Tambahna*.

Orhómenos and Glá

Just 10km east of Livádhia (10 min. by local bus; every hour) is the site of **ANCIENT ORHOMENOS**, inhabited from Neolithic to Classical times and as the capital of the Minyans one of the wealthiest Mycenaean cities.

Near the middle of the drab modern village is the **Treasury of Minyas** (9am–3pm, Sun. 10am–2pm), a stone *tholos* similar to the tomb of Atreus at Mycenae. Its roof has collapsed but it is otherwise complete and its inner chamber, hewn from the rock, has an intricately carved marble ceiling. Beside it are the remains of a fourth-century B.C. theatre, and behind, on the rocky hilltop, a tiny fortified acropolis from the same period. Across the road is the ninth-century Byzantine **Church of the Dormition**, built entirely of blocks from the theatre and column-drums from a Classical temple – as is the minute Byzantine church in the main square.

Gla

Continuing east, in a highly worthwhile diversion, it's a further twenty minutes by bus (5 daily, but they stop early) to the village of **KÁSTRO**, right next to the National Road to Lárissa. If you walk through the village, cross the highway and then walk 100 metres south along it (towards Athens) you come to an unsignposted road behind a *Shell* garage and tyre store. This leads in 200m to the Mycenaean Citadel of Gla.

An enormous and extraordinary site, **GLA** (unrestricted entrance) stands within a three-kilometre circuit of 'Cyclopean' walls: a far larger citadel than either Tiryns or Mycenae. Almost nothing, however, is known about the site, save that it was once an island in Lake Copais (which was drained in the last century) and that it may have been an outpost of the Minyans.

The **walls** and city gates still stand to five metres in places. Inside, on the higher ground, a huge Mycenaean **palace** has been revealed. Further down, and currently being excavated, is a vast walled area believed to have been the **marketplace**, but almost anywhere you walk in this rarely visited site you come across evocative traces of its former buildings. One word of warning; there are said to be snakes among the ruins, so tread with care.

Chaironeia

Directly north of Livádhia, on the main road to Lamía, is the site of one of the most famous battles of ancient Greece. This is **Chaironeia**, where in 338 B.C. Philip of Macedon won a resounding victory over an alliance of Athenians, Thebans and Peloponnesians put together by Demosthenes. The defeat was in essence the death of the old city-states, from whom control passed forever into foreign hands: first Macedonian, later Roman.

Set beside the road, at modern HERÓNIA, is a remarkable six-metre-high **stone lion**, originally the funerary monument to the Thebans (or, some say, to the Macedonians) killed in the battle. The site of the battle lies 3km to the east, towards the village of AKONDHÍO, where a Macedonian burial mound is still to be seen near the river. Herónia itself was a minor ancient town, home of the writer Plutarch, and there are remains of the **acropolis** fortifications, with a theatre at its base, above the village.

The Oedipus crossroads and Óssios Loukás

West from Livádhia the scenery becomes ever more dramatic as Mount Parnassós and its attendant peaks loom high above the road. At 24km, about halfway to Delphi, you reach the so-called 'Schist Crossroads', junction of the ancient roads from Thebes, Delphi, Daulis and Ambrossos. (The crossroads is today signposted to Dávlia, modern Daulis; the old road in fact lay below the new one, in the gorge).

It is this spot that Pausanias identified as the site of **Oedipus's murder of his father**, King Laertes of Thebes, and his two attendants. According to the myth, Oedipus was returning on foot from Delphi while Laertes was speeding in the opposite direction on a chariot. Neither would give way, and in the altercation that followed Oedipus killed the trio, oblivious of who they were. It was, as Pausanias put it, 'the beginning of his troubles'. Continuing to Thebes, Oedipus solved the riddle of the Sphinx, which had been ravaging the area, and was given the hand of widowed Queen Jocasta, his mother.

If you are driving, you can turn left at the crossroads and follow a minor road to DHÍSTOMO, and thence **to the Monastery of Óssios Loukás**. Relying on public transport to the monastery, it's easiest to get a bus direct to Dhístomo from Livádhia. Óssios Loukás is 8km southeast of Dhístomo. Only a couple of buses a day run direct to the monastery, but there are more regular connections from Dhístomo to Kiriakí; you can take one of these and ask to be dropped at the fork to Óssios Loukás (leaving just a 2½km walk).

Alternatively, it's possible to get a taxi in **DHÍSTOMO**, which also has a couple of D-class hotels if you get stuck overnight. It is a drab place, though, with a tragic wartime history – the Germans having shot the entire adult population in 1944, as reprisal for a guerilla attack.

Óssios Loukás Monastery

The **Monastery of Óssios Loukás** was a precursor of that last defiant flourish of Byzantine art that produced the great churches at Mystra in the Peloponnese. It is modest in scale, but from an architectural or decorative point of view, ranks as one of the great buildings of medieval Greece. The setting, too, is exquisite – as beautiful as it is remote; hidden by trees along the approach from Dhístomo, the monastery's shady terrace suddenly opens out on to a spectacular sweep of the Elikónas peaks and countryside.

Ten monks still live in the monastic buildings around the courtyard, but the monastery is essentially maintained as a museum. A small seasonal hotel and restaurant have been built within the grounds. The monastery itself is **open to visits** daily in summer from 8am to 2pm and 4 to 6pm; 8am to 5pm for the rest of the year. Skirts or long trousers (no shorts) must be worn.

The main structure comprises two domed churches, the larger *katholikón* of Óssios Loukás and the attendant chapel of the Theotókos. They are joined by a common foundation wall but otherwise share few architectural features.

The Churches

The **Katholikón**, built in the early eleventh century, is dedicated to a local beatified hermit, St. Luke of Stiri (not the Evangelist). The building formed a model for the octagonal style of church, and was later copied at Dhafní and at Mystra. Externally it is modest, with rough brick and stone walls surmounted by a well-proportioned dome. The inside, however, is startling. A conventional cross-in-square plan, its atmosphere switches from austere to exultant as the eye moves along walls lined in red and green marble to the gold-backed mosaics on the high ceiling. Light filtering through marble-encrusted windows reflects across the curved surfaces of the mosaics in the narthex and the nave and bounces on to the marble walls, bringing out the subtlety of their shades.

The original **mosaics** were damaged by an earthquake in 1659, and in the dome and elsewhere have been replaced by unmemorable frescoes. But other surviving examples testify to their effect. The mosaic of *The Washing of the Apostles' Feet* in the narthex is one of the finest; its theme is an especially human one and the expressions of the Apostles, seen varying between diffidence and surprise, do it justice. This dynamic and richly humanised approach is again illustrated by the *Baptism*, high up on one of the curved squinches that support the dome. Here the naked Jesus reaches for the cross amid a swirling mass of water, an illusion of depth created by the angle and curvature of the wall. The church's original **frescoes** are confined to the vaulted chambers at the corners of the cross plan and though less imposing than the mosaics are far more sympathetic in colour and shade to their subjects, particularly that of *Christ Walking toward the Baptism*.

The church of the **Theotókos** (literally 'God-Bearing', i.e. the Virgin Mary) is a century older than the *katholikón*. From the outside it overshadows the main church with its elaborate brick decoration culminating in a highly Eastern-influenced, marble-panelled drum. The interior, though, seems gloomy and crouched by comparison, highlighted only by a couple of fine Corinthian capitals and an original floor mosaic.

Finally, do not miss the vivid frescoes in the **crypt** of the *katholikón*, entered on the lower right side of the building. If you have a torch, bring it, since the same darkness which has preserved the colours also hides them.

Aráhova

Arriving at **ARÁHOVA**, the last town east of Delphi, you are properly in the Parnassós country. The peaks stand tiered above, tamed only slightly by the road cut to a ski-resort – the winter weekend haunt of BMW-driving Athenians. If you want to ski, see 'Sport' in *Basics* for details.

The town, despite the winter skiing (and *après-ski*) intrusions, and despite being split in two by the Livádhia-Delphi road, is a delight. Its houses are predominantly traditional in style, twisting up narrow lanes into the hills and poised to the south on the edge of the olive-choked Pleistos gorge. If you're not making for any other mountain areas it is well worth an afternoon's pause before continuing to Delphi (just 11km further on), and if you've got your own transport you might consider staying here as a base for visiting the site. At the cheaper end of the scale, there are two D-class **hotels**, the *Apollon* (☎0267/31-427) and *Parnassos* (☎0267/31-307), plus a very few rooms in private houses.

The village is renowned for its strong wines, honey, *flokáti* (sheep-hide) rugs, and woollen weavings; all are much in evidence in the roadside shops, though some of the goods are nowadays imported from Albania and northern Greece. Also of note is Aráhova's **Festival of Áyios Yióryios** (23 April, or the Tuesday after Easter if this date falls within Lent), which is centred on the church at the top of the hill. If you can coincide it's one of the best events to catch genuine folk-dancing and almost 48 hours of unrelieved feasting! At other times you'll have to make do with one of the excellent local **tavernas** – try *Karathanasi* for carnivorous fare, *To Elato* for more vegetables.

Delphi (Dhelfí)

With its site raised on the slopes of a high mountain terrace and dwarfed to either side by the great and ominous crags of Parnassós, it's easy to see why the ancients believed **DELPHI** to be the centre of the earth. But more than the natural setting or even the occasional earthquake and avalanche were needed to confirm a divine presence. This, according to Plutarch, was achieved through the discovery of a rock chasm which exuded strange vapours and reduced all comers to frenzied, incoherent and undoubtedly prophetic mutterings.

The Oracle: some history

The first **oracle** established on this spot was dedicated to Gea (or 'Mother Earth') and to Poseidon ('the Earth Shaker'). The serpent Python, son of Gea, was installed in a nearby cave and communication made through the Pythian Priestess. Python was subsequently slain by Apollo, whose cult had been imported from Crete (legend has it that he arrived in the form of a dolphin – hence the name *Delphoi*). The Pythian Games were instigated on an eight-year cycle to commemorate the feat, and perhaps also to placate the ancient deities.

The place was known to the Mycenaeans, whose characteristic votive offerings (tiny striped statues of goddesses and worshipping women) have been discovered near the site of Apollo's temple. Following the arrival of the Dorians in Greece at the beginning of the twelfth century B.C., the sanctuary became the centre of the loose-knit association of Greek city-states known as the Amphyctionic League. The territory still belonged, however, to the city of Krissa, which as the oracle gained in popularity began to extort heavy dues from the pilgrims arriving at the port of Kirrha. In the sixth century B.C. the league was called to intervene, and the first of a series of **Sacred Wars** broke out. The league wrested Delphi from the Krissaeans and made it an autonomous state. From then on Delphi experienced a rapid ascent to fame and respect, becoming within a few decades one of the major sanctuaries of Greece, with its oracle tried and tested and generally thought to be the arbiter of truth.

For over a thousand years a steady stream of **pilgrims** worked their way up the dangerous mountain paths to seek divine direction in matters of war, worship, love or business. On arriving they would sacrifice a sheep or a goat and, depending on the omens, wait to submit votive questions inscribed on leaden tablets. The Pythian Priestess (a simple and devout village woman, of 50 or more years) would chant her prophecies from a tripod positioned over the oracular chasm. More importantly, an attendant priest would then 'interpret' her utterings and relay them to the enquirer in hexameter verse.

Many of the answers were equivocal: Croesus, for example, was told that if he embarked on war against neighbouring Cyrus he would destroy a mighty empire – he did and destroyed his own. But it's hard to imagine that the oracle would have retained its popularity and influence for so long without offering predominantly sound advice. Indeed, Strabo wrote that 'of all oracles in the world it had the reputation of being the most truthful'. One explanation is that the Delphic priests were simply better informed than any other corporate body around at the time. As the centre of the **Amphyctionic League**, which became a kind of 'United Nations' of the Greek city states and, as Peter Levi describes it, 'a keystone of their disjointed unity', it amassed a wealth of political, economic, and social information. And from the seventh century B.C. on, Delphi had its own network of informants throughout the Greek world.

The **influence** of the oracle spread abroad with the age of Classical colonisation and as its patronage grew so did its spectrum of informants. It reached a peak in the sixth century B.C., attracting powerful benefactors such as Amasis, King of Egypt, and the unfortunate King Croesus of Lydia; many of the Greek city-states also dedicated treasuries at this time. The Temple of Apollo was elaborately rebuilt in 548 B.C., and the Pythian Games were reorganised (along the lines of Olympia) to become one of the four great Panhellenic festivals.

Privileged position and enormous wealth, however, made Delphi an obvious prey to Greek rivalries. The first Sacred Wars left it autonomous but in the fifth century B.C. the oracle began to be too closely identified with individual states. Worse, it maintained a defeatist, almost treacherous attitude towards the Persian invasions – only partially mitigated when a Persian force, sent by Xerxes to raid Delphi, was crushed at the entrance to the Sanctuary by a well-timed earthquake.

It never quite regained the same level of trust (and consequently of power) after these instances of bias and corruption. However real **decline** did not set in until the fourth century B.C. with the resumption of the Sacred Wars and the emergence of Macedonian control. Following prolonged squabbling amongst the Greek city states the Sanctuary was seized by the Phocians in 356 B.C., leading to Philip of Macedon's intervention to restore control to the Amphyctionic League. Seven years later, when the league again invited Philip to settle a dispute, this time provoked by the Amphissans, he responded with the invasion of southern Greece. The independence of the city states was brought to an end at the Battle of Chaironeia; Delphi's political intriguing was effectively over.

Under Macedonian and later Roman control the oracle's role became increasingly domestic and insignificant, dispensing advice on marriages, loans, voyages and the like. The Romans thought little of its utterances and of its treasure; Sulla plundered the sanctuary in 86 B.C. and Nero, outraged by the oracle pronouncing judgment on the murder of his mother, carted away some 500 bronze statues. Finally, with the demise of paganism under Constantine and Theodosius in the fourth century A.D., the oracle became defunct.

Excavations

In modern times, the sanctuary site was rediscovered towards the end of the seventeenth century and explored, haphazardly, from the 1840s onwards. Real **excavation** of the site came only in 1892 when the French School of Archaeology leased the land – then occupied by a hamlet – in exchange for a French government agreement to buy the Greek currant crop. There was little to be seen other than the outline of a stadium and theatre but the villagers were persuaded (with the help of an army detachment) to move to the site of the modern village 1km west and digging commenced. Over the next decade most of the excavations and reconstruction visible today were completed.

The most interesting development in Delphi's recent history came through the efforts of the poet Angelos Sikelianos and his wife Eva Palmer to set up a 'University of the World' in the 1920s. The project eventually failed, though it inspired an annual **Delphic Festival**, held now in June of each year with performances of Classical drama in the ancient theatre.

The Sites

Split by the road from Aráhova, the ancient site divides essentially into three parts: the **Sacred Precinct**, the **Marmaria** and the **Castalian spring**. In addition there is a worthwhile (though poorly presented) **museum**. All in all it's a large and complex ruin, best taken in two stages, with the sanctuary ideally at the beginning or end of the day, or at lunchtime, to escape the crowds. Admission is a steep 400dr to the sanctuary, and a further 400dr for the museum (students 120dr); the Marmaria and Castalian Spring, however, are free.

Visting the sites, make sure you have sturdy footwear as there's a lot of clambering up rough stone steps and paths. And if you're planning to make a full day's visit, take food and drink – consumed, most enjoyably, in the stadium with its seats and panorama of the sanctuary.

The Sacred Precinct

Open 8am–6.45pm; Sun. 8am–5.45.

The **Sacred Precinct**, or Temenos (Sanctuary) of Apollo, is entered, as in ancient times, by way of a small **Agora**, enclosed by ruins of Roman porticoes and shops for the sale of votive offerings. The paved **Sacred Way** begins after a few stairs and zigzags uphill between the foundations of memorials and treasuries to the Temple of Apollo. Along each edge is a litter of statue bases where gold, bronze and painted marble figures once stood; Pliny counted more than 3000 on his visit, and that was after Nero's infamous raid.

The choice and position of these **memorials** was dictated by more than religious zeal; many were used as a deliberate show of strength or often as a direct insult against a rival Greek state. For instance the **Offering of the Arcadians** on the right of the entrance (a line of bases which supported nine bronzes) was erected to commemorate their invasion of Laconia in 369 B.C. and pointedly placed in front of the Lacedaemonians' own monument. Beside this, and following the same logic, the Spartans celebrated their victory over Athens by erecting their **Monument of the Admirals** – a large recessed structure, which once held 37 bronze statues of gods and generals – directly opposite the Athenian's **Offering of Marathon**.

Farther up the path, past the Doric remains of the **Sikyonian Treasury** on the left, stretch the expansive foundations of the **Siphnian Treasury**, a grandiose Ionic temple erected in 525 B.C. Siphnos had rich gold mines and intended the building to be an unrivaled show of opulence. Fragments of the caryatids which supported its west entrance, and the fine Parian marble frieze which covered all four sides, are now in the museum. Above it is the **Treasury of the Athenians**, built, like the city's 'Offering', after Marathon (490 B.C.). It was reconstructed in 1904-06 by matching the inscriptions that completely cover its blocks. These include honourific decrees in favour of Athens, lists of Athenian ambassadors to the Pythian Festival, and a hymn to Apollo with its musical notation in Greek letters above the text.

Next to it are the foundations of the **Bouleuterion**, or council house, a reminder that Delphi needed administrators, and a little higher up is a circular area known as the **Threshing Floor** where a morality play enacting the

DELPHI: THE SACRED PRECINCT

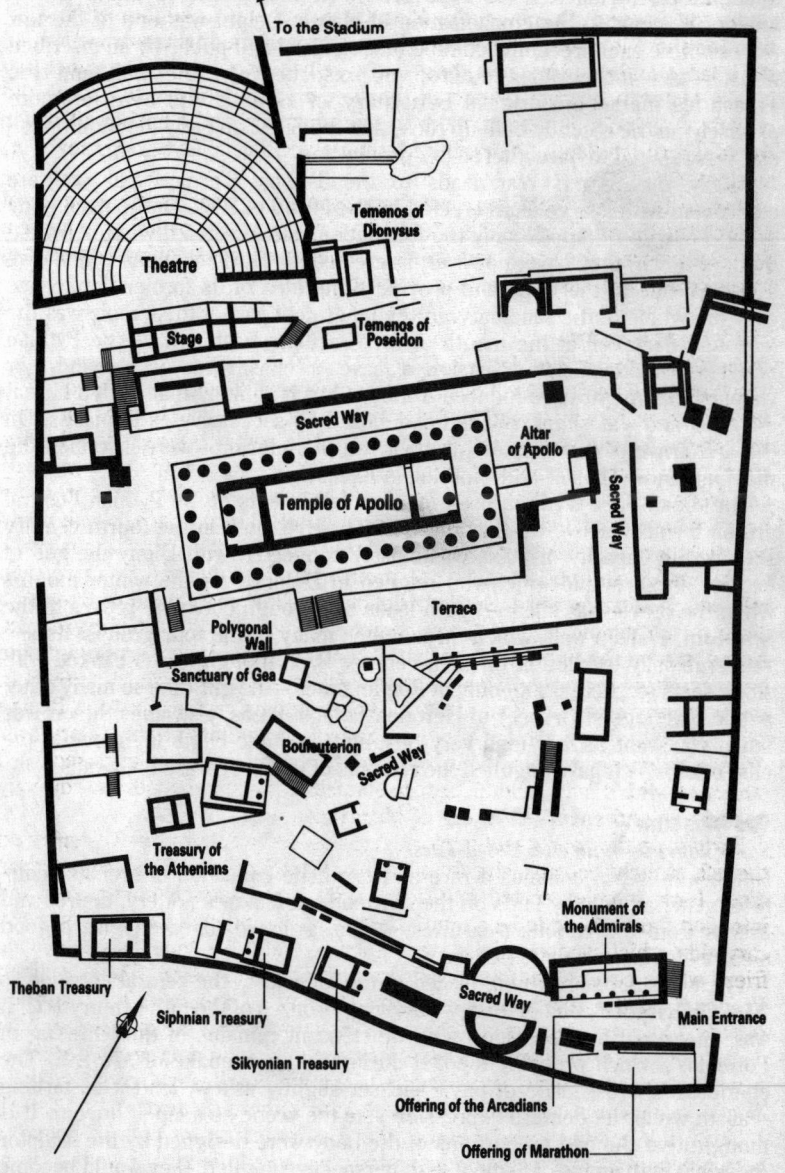

To the Stadium

Temenos of Dionysus

Theatre

Stage

Temenos of Poseidon

Sacred Way

Altar of Apollo

Temple of Apollo

Sacred Way

Terrace

Polygonal Wall

Sanctuary of Gea

Bouleuterion

Sacred Way

Treasury of the Athenians

Monument of the Admirals

Theban Treasury

Sacred Way

Siphnian Treasury

Main Entrance

Sikyonian Treasury

Offering of the Arcadians

Offering of Marathon

killing of the serpent was presented every seventh year. Above is the remarkable **Polygonal Wall** whose irregular interlocking blocks have withstood, intact, all earthquakes. It too is covered with inscriptions but these almost universally refer to the emancipation of slaves; Delphi was one of the few places where such freedom could be made official and public by an inscribed register. An incongruous outcrop of rock between the wall and the Treasuries marks the original **Sanctuary of Gea**. It was here, or more precisely on the recently built-up rock, that the Sibyl, an early itinerant priestess, was reputed to have uttered her prophecies.

Finally the Sacred Way leads to the Temple Terrace and you are confronted with a large altar, erected by the island of Híos. Of the main body of the **Temple of Apollo** only the foundations stood when it was uncovered by the French; they have, however, re-erected six Doric columns which give a vertical line to the ruins and provide some idea of its former dominance over the whole of the sanctuary. In the innermost part of the temple was the *adyton*, a dark cell at the mouth of the oracular chasm where the Pythian priestess would officiate. No sign of cave or chasm has been found, nor vapours that might have induced a trance, but it is likely that such a chasm did exist and was simply opened and closed by successive earthquakes. On the architrave of the temple – probably on the interior – were inscribed the maxims 'Know Thyself' and 'Nothing in Excess'.

The theatre and stadium used for the main events of the Pythian Festival are on terraces above the Temple. The **Theatre**, built in the fourth century B.C. with a capacity of 5000, was closely connected with Dionysus, god of ecstasy, the arts and wine, who reigned in Delphi over the winter months when the oracle was silent. A path leads up through cool pine groves to the **Stadium**, a steep walk which discourages many of the tour groups. Its site was artificially levelled in the fifth century B.C., though it was banked with stone seats (capacity 7000) only in Roman times – the gift (like so many other public buildings in Greece) of Herodes Atticus. It easily swamps the crowds but if you want further (and very beautiful) solitude climb up above to the pine trees which have engulfed the remains of fourth-century B.C. walls.

The Museum
Same hours as main site; closed Tues.

Delphi's museum contains a rare and exquisite collection of archaic sculpture, matched only by finds on the Acropolis. It features pottery, figures and friezes from the various treasuries, which, grouped together, give a good picture of the sanctuary's riches.

The most famous exhibit, placed at the far end of the central corridor, is **'The Charioteer'**, one of the few surviving bronzes of the fifth century B.C. It was unearthed in 1896 along with other scant remains of the 'Offering of Polyzalos', which probably toppled during the earthquake of 373 B.C. The charioteer's eyes, made of onyx and set slightly askew, lend it a startling realism while the demure expression sets the scene as a lap of honour. It is thought that the odd proportions of the body were designed by the sculptor (possibly Pythagoras of Samos) with perspective in mind; they would become 'corrected' when the figure was viewed, as intended, from below.

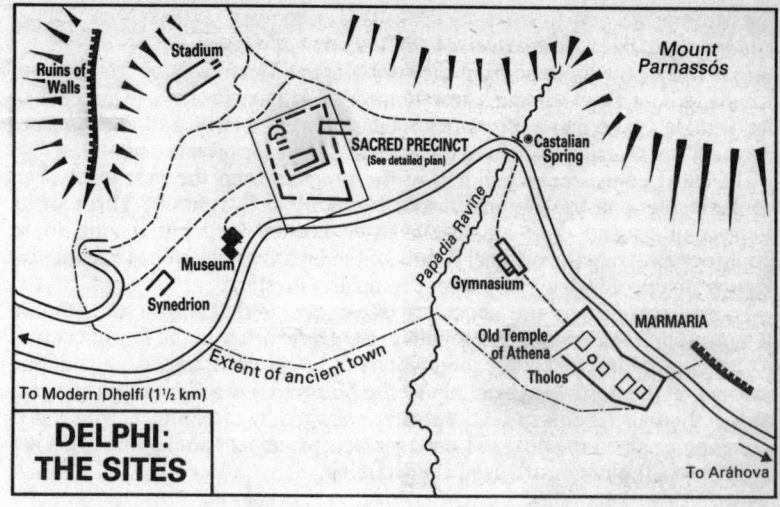

DELPHI:
THE SITES

Other major pieces include two huge **Kouroi** (archaic male figures) from the sixth century B.C. in the second room at the top of the stairs. To the right of this room, in the 'Hall of the Siphnian Treasury', are large chunks of the beautiful and meticulously-carved **Syphnian frieze**; they depict Zeus and other gods looking on as the Homeric heroes fight over the body of Patroclus and the gods battling with the giants. In the same room is an elegant Ionic sculpture of the winged **Sphynx of the Naxians** (ca. 560 B.C.). Back along the main corridor is the **Athenian Treasury**, represented by fragments of the metopes which depict the labours of Hercules, the adventures of Theseus and a battle with Amazons. Further on and to the right, the **Hall of the Monument of Daochos** is dominated by a group of three colossal dancing women, carved from pentelic marble around an acanthus column. It is likely that the figures, celebrating Dionysus, formed the stand for a tripod.

Interspersed with these more obvious exhibits are cases containing small pieces of minutely-detailed carving in marble and ivory, and similarly detailed bronze and silver castings.

The Castalian spring
Site partially fenced in; free admission.

Following the road east of the sanctuary, towards Aráhova, you reach a sharp bend. To the left, marked by niches for votive offerings and by the remains of an archaic fountain house, the celebrated **Castalian spring** still flows from a cleft in the Phaedriades cliffs. Visitors to Delphi (who originally had to be male) were obliged to purify themselves in its waters, usually by washing their hair, though murderers had to take the full plunge. Byron, impressed by the legend that it succoured poetic inspiration, jumped in. (This is no longer possible except illicitly, since the spring is fenced off).

The Marmaria

8.45am–3pm, Sun. 10am–3pm; closed Tues.; free admission.

Across and below the road from the spring is the **Marmaria**, or Sanctuary of Athena, whom the Delphians worshipped as Athena Pronoia ('Guardian of the Temple'). The name *Marmaria* means 'marble quarry' and derives from the medieval practice of filching the ancient blocks for private use.

The most conspicuous building in the precinct (and the first to be seen from the road) is the **Tholos**, a fourth-century B.C. rotunda. Three of its dome-columns and their entablature have been set up but though these amply demonstrate the original beauty of the building (which has become *the* popular image of Delphi) its purpose remains a mystery.

At the entrance to the sanctuary stood the **Old Temple of Athena**, destroyed by the Persians and rebuilt in the Doric order in the fourth century B.C. a hundred metres away; foundations of both can be traced. Outside the precinct on the northwest side (above the Marmaria) is a **Gymnasium**, again built in the fourth century B.C., but later enlarged by the Romans who added a running track on the now collapsed terrace; prominent among the ruins is a circular (cold) plunge bath used after training.

Dhelfí: the village

The modern village of Dhelfí is entirely geared to tourism: An insubstantial place, its attraction lies in its mountain site, proximity to the ruins, and access to Mount Parnassós (see the following section).

Like most of the Greek site villages it has a quick turnaround of visitors so finding a place to stay should present few problems. There are upwards of thirty hotels and pensions, various rooms to let, and an excellent **youth hostel** (Appollónou 29, on the upper road; ☎0265/82-268). Best value of the **pensions** are *Maniatis* (Issáia 2; ☎0265/82-134) and *Odysseus* (Fillelínon 1; ☎0265/82-235), both the equal of the cheaper hotels. The village's two official **campsites** are none too close: *Apollon* (1½km west – follow the road out towards Ámfissa) and *Delphi* (☎0265/28-944; nearly 4km down the road towards Itéa).

Eating is best at *Taverna Vakhos*, right next to the youth hostel – incredibly cheap, tasty and with views down to Itéa, but only open from May to September. Otherwise try the no-name *psistariá* opposite *Hotel Pan* at the west end of town, or *Stammatis* 200m further out.

Buses out of Dhelfí can pose problems. There are two stops, owing to the one-way street scheme. For buses to Ámfissa (whence you can pick up connections north), Itéa and Náfpaktos, wait just downhill from the youth hostel on Apollónou. For eastbound services, to Livádhia or Athens, wait at the indicated *kafeneío* on the lower Pavloú street. More of a difficulty, since all coaches originate elsewhere, is that seats allocated for the Dhelfí ticket booth are limited and they sell out some hours in advance. If you're going to be stuck standing all the way to Athens it's better to get down at Livádhia and continue by train.

There are **banks**, a **post office**, **tourist office** and **OTE** along the main street.

Mount Parnassós

For a quick sniff of the Greek mountain scene, **Parnassós** is probably the most convenient peak in the land. It is no longer a wilderness, with the ski-station above Aráhova and its accompanying paraphernalia of lifts, cafés and access roads. But equally, it's no Piccadilly Circus. Routes are normally practicable from May through September.

Parnassós's highest and finest peak is **Liákoura** (2457m), which can be aproached either from the Delphi side or from around the mountain to the north. The latter is the best ascent, starting **from Áno Tithoréa**, but it involves taking a bus or train and then local taxi to the trailhead – plus camping out on the mountain. If you want a more casual look at Parnassós, it's probably best to walk up **from the Delphi side**. This is very enjoyable as far as the EOS (Hellenic Alpine Club) refuge – about six hour's walk – and you could either turn back here or a couple of hours' lower down on the Livádhi plateau (hitching here is possible) if you don't fancy a night on the mountain and the final, rather dull, four hours' slog up to Liákoura. For the energetic, it's possible to **traverse the whole massif** in around fifteen hours' walking, starting from Delphi and descending at Áno Tithoréa, or vice versa.

If you're driving, there are metalled **roads** up the mountain from Aráhova and Graviá and a rally-style track from Amfíklia. These could easily be combined with a walk.

The snow season, for **skiing**, usually lasts from December to March. If you don't have your own car, it's easiest to buy a package from an Athens travel agent.

The Delphi to Liákoura hike

To reach the path up the mountain, take the right hand, uphill road (approaching from Athens) through Dhelfí village. At the top of the slope turn right on a lane that doubles back to a house where the poet Sikelianos once lived – there's a bust of him outside – close to the perimeter fence of the archaeological site. Climb up the bank through some almond trees and follow the fence to its highest point where a cobbled mule path, or *kalderími*, begins zigzagging up the slope above you in broad reaches. The view from here is fantastic, stretching back over the Gulf of Kórinthos to the mountains of the Peloponnese.

The cobbles come to an end by a large concrete inspection cover in the Delphi water supply (1 hr.; this and all subsequent times are from the start of the walk at Delphi). Here you turn left up the gully in front of you towards the heart of the mountains, with the water conduit running beside the path. At 1 hr. 40 min., you reach a spring and watering troughs, with some shepherds' huts scattered under the trees. Climb the low rise behind the spring and follow the track to the right into the firs. You re-emerge from the woods (2 hr. 30 min.) with a view ahead of the rounded mass of the Yerondóvrahos peak (2367m), which guards the southwestern approaches to the summit.

Another fifteen minutes (2hr. 45 min.) brings you to a spring, followed by a chapel and lean-to on the left, with a patch of grass that would do for camping. Just beyond is a muddy tarn backed by a low ridge. To the left rises a much steeper ridge, on whose flank lies the ancient **Corycian cave**. Though famous and sacred to Pan, it's not very interesting, and getting there involves an unpleasant scramble and a long detour from the track.

Better to keep going, and come out on to the wide **Livádhi plateau** crossed by the ski-road from Aráhova, with some low stone cottages straight ahead. Some way left of these is a scattering of modern buildings near a bridge. Strike out across the fields to the bridge (3 hr. 40 min.), cross the road (you can **hitch back from here**, with luck, to Aráhova, if you've had enough!) and continue up the true* left bank of the usually dry gully. A hundred metres upstream the track crosses over and one branch leads to a modern taverna where you can get snacks and drinks. Behind it two fir-clad bluffs stand to either side of the defile mentioned above. Go down to the bank of the stream and across a patch of **meadow**. At its further edge an eroded gully begins. The path, marked by rusting red discs on the trees, starts in the corner of the meadow. Clear at first, it then disappears. But you'll pick it up again in a few minutes if you keep fairly close to the true right bank of the stream.

After passing a spring on your left (4 hr.) you soon enter the fir woods again. Ten minutes later a steep scree-filled clearing again obliterates the path. Keep up the left edge into the trees in the top left corner. Straight on up, you come out on a low saddle by a rusty sign pointing to the HAC refuge (4 hr. 20 min.). Here you turn diagonally right up a stony slope with trees on your right, over the brow of the rise and into the woods again, where the path at last is perfectly clear. Along the contour and slightly downhill, with the peak of Yerondóvrahos looming ahead, you eventually rejoin the stream in the bottom of the defile to your right. Cross to the true left bank for a few hundred metres before returning to the right and emerging into a large open meadow encircled by firs (5 hr.) where the path finally gives out.

Turn immediately left up the left-hand edge of the meadow, through some trees into the open and you come to a very rough track by an old well. Follow the track up to the **Athens Ski Club road** (5 hr. 25 min.), where you can either turn right and continue up the road or cut diagonally right uphill across country to the **EOS refuge at Sarandári** – about twenty minutes' walk (5 hr. 45 min.).

Hitching back from here is more difficult than from the Livádhi plateau. Your only hope is a farmer or shepherd with a pick-up truck. If you want to turn back, it's best to retrace your steps as far as the Livádhi plateau road, where chances of a ride are better. Whatever you do, don't follow the road down on foot, or you'll use up the rest of the day.

Continuing to Liákoura
For the intrepid, intent on continuing to Liákoura or beyond, the worst stint is going to be the next three hours or so – and there's no supply of water for the next six, so be prepared. Times given below are from the **Athens Ski Club**, where the road ends in a hollow.

---

* 'True' means facing upstream (i.e. the flow of the river).

The ski club is a short distance beyond the refuge. To reach the **Yerondóvrahos peak**, just plod up the ridgeline to your right.

To continue on **up to the Liákoura summit**, the start of the path is marked with red paint by the fourth pylon of the ski-lift creeping up the bare slope in front of you. It first bears left past a stunted tree and then on towards a second small tree on a ridge 400 metres away; here it veers right and sharply up towards a large cairn liberally splashed with red paint. Beyond this landmark the way continues through a gully between two ridgelets.

As you climb out of this trough note a cairn on the left and another red dot to the right; Yerondóvrahos looms above. The greater part of the ski resort, forlorn and unsightly in summer, sprawls to your left. After a brief level stretch the path descends to the first of four sheepfolds, shortly after to vanish under the ski-run. When this happens, head straight up a bulldozer track to the top of the graded ridge in front of you until you come to a distinctive right-angle junction. Do not continue toward Yerondóvrahos, but bear off left on to the wide track aiming towards the last pylon of one of the ski-lifts. Soon the path acquires a neat stone edge and occasional red dots on the way to a second stone hut (2 hr. 30 min.).

Thereafter the path climbs abruptly up a rock stairway splattered with red arrows on to a low spur of Yerondóvrahos. Through two consecutive patches of meadow, past a vertical rock pinnacle with crude shelters at its foot, the path bends leftward, drops into a third pasture, and climbs out to a low saddle from which you look across directly to Liákoura. At your feet a valley descends leftwards towards the EOT ski station at FTERÓLAKA, reached via the track on the far side – a good escape route in bad weather. Go down past the shepherds' huts in the hollow, and turn right on to the track towards a low point in the ridge, keeping an eye open for the paint blazes which mark the way to Liákoura, now above you on the left.

The **final ascent** is an easy twenty-minute scramble more or less up to the ridge line (for a total of about 4 hr.). On a clear morning, especially after rain, you're supposed to be able to see Mount Olympus in the north, the Aegean to the east, the Ionian to the west and way down into the Peloponnese to the south. The best viewing is said to be in mid-summer; all too often you can see only cloud.

For the descent to Áno Tithoréa/Velítsa, reverse the directions which follow.

Áno Tithoréa/Velítsa to Liákoura

This alternative route up Parnassós to Liákoura involves first a train or bus to KÁTO TITHORÉA, which is on the Livádhia-Amfíklia road and the Athens-Thessaloníki railway. You then need to get to the higher, twin-village of ÁNO TITHORÉA, a four-kilometre haul easiest accomplished by taxi (usually available: bargain for the price beforehand). It's best to arrive early in the day and plan on camping out on the mountain as lodging can be difficult to find.

From the *platía* in Áno Tithoréa head southwest out of town until you reach some park benches overlooking the giant Velítsa ravine. Adjacent is a 'waterfall', in reality a leak in an aqueduct, which crosses the path beginning here a few minutes above the benches. A hundred metres further, bear left away from what seems to be the main track and descend toward the bed of the canyon. Once you're on the far side you can see the aqueduct again, now uncovered. Follow it until you reach the isolated chapel of Áyios Ioánnis (1 hr. from Áno Tithoréa).

Once past the chapel, bulldozer scrapings cease and a fine alpine path heads off through the firs before you. The way is obvious for the next ninety minutes, with tremendous views of the crags filing up to the Liákoura summit, on your right across the valley. You emerge on a narrow neck of land, with a brief glimpse over the Ayía Marína valley and monastery to the east (left). The path, faint for an interval, heads slightly downhill and to the right to meet the floor of the Velítsa at the Tsáres spring (3hr. 30 min.). This is the last reliable water, so best fill up.

On the far bank of the river, head up a steep, scree-laden slope through the last of the trees to some sheep pens (4 hr.), then climb up to another pastoral hut (4 hr. 30 min.) at the base of the defile leading down from the main summit ridge. Beyond this point the going is gentler for much of the final ascent to the northwest (top right-hand) corner of this valley. A brief scramble up a rock fall to a gap in the ridge and you are at the base of Liákoura (5 hr. 30 min.). Orange paint-splashes – primarily orientated for those descending – stake out the way to the summit.

Down to the Gulf of Kórinthos: Delphi to Náfpaktos

All buses heading southwest of Delphi toward the Gulf of Kórinthos stop first at **ITÉA**, a gritty little town (literally, owing to the bauxite-ore dust everywhere) where you may have to change buses for the next leg of the journey.

GALAXÍDHI, 17km southwest of Itéa, is the first place you may want to break the journey voluntarily: a quiet, mirage-like port whose nineteenth-century shipowners' houses spring out of a virtual desert. The village has no real beach, which perhaps explains the near absence of tourists. Walking around the landscaped headland, however, you'll find some pebbly **coves**, with chapel-crowned islets offshore. Another worthwhile walk is to the **Moní Metamórfosi**, an archetypal rural monastery which looks out over the bay towards Parnassós. It's an hour's walk to the west, through terraced fields and olive groves; take the track under the main road at the western edge of the village and look out for a footpath to the right after about twenty minutes.

Accommodation in Galaxídhi is limited to the relatively expensive but delightful *Pension Ganimede* (☎0265/41-328), Italian-run with a beautiful garden and home-made jams and drinks; or to the cheap, old-fashioned *Hotel Possidon* (☎0265/41-271). The best of the **tavernas** is more or less across the street from the *Ganimede*.

Beyond Galaxídhi is some of the sparsest scenery of the Greek shoreline; there are few villages and none which seems to warrant a stop. At **ÁYIOS NIKÓLAOS**, however, there's a summer (June–Sept.) ferry across the gulf to **ÉYIO**: an alternative approach to the Peloponnese to the crossing at

Andírio–Río, 60km further west. The ferries leave Áyios Nikólaos three times daily, at 8.30am, 3.30pm and 6.30pm; the journey takes 45 minutes, and costs 200dr for passengers, 1000dr per car.

The one place that stands out to the west of Galaxídhi is **NÁFPAKTOS**, a lively little resort sprawling along the seafront below a rambling Venetian castle. Two hours by bus from Delphi, and an hour by bus and ferry from Pátra, it's a convenient journey break, though surprisingly most of its visitors are Greek. The **Kástro** provides a picturesque backdrop to town, and enjoyable rambling to the top of its fortifications. At their base they run down to the sea, enclosing the old harbour and the **beach** – entered through one of the original gates. On the outskirts of town to the west there's a longer stretch of beach with a few tavernas. **Lodgings** can be in short supply in summer, though you should end up with something from the dozen hotels and scattering of rooms. Best value of the D-class places are the *Aegli* (Ilárhou Tzavéla 75; ☎0634/27-271) and *Diethnes* (Messolongíou 3; ☎0634/27-342). A good **campsite**, *Camping Platanitis*, is 4½km west of the town towards Andírio; to get there catch a blue city-bus from the main square (the last one leaves at 10pm).

Moving **on from Náfpaktos** there are services northwest to Agrínio (where you can pick up services to Ioánnina or Lefkádha), and east to Itéa and Ámfissa (for connections north into Thessaly). The same local city buses detailed for the campsite (above) run to the ferry at Andírio.

The Andírio–Río Ferry

The ferry at **ANDÍRIO** runs every fifteen minutes from 6.45am to 10.45pm and every half hour at night; journey time to Río is 15 minutes, and fares are 60dr per passenger, 400dr per car. Once across to Río you can generally pick up a city bus immediately for Pátra. If you're driving, count on a half hour or so wait. There's a cheapish restaurant across from the little fortress gate on the strait.

For the continuation of this route **west to Messolóngi and Agrínio** see *Chapter Four*.

North to Lamía

Lamía is a half-day's journey north from Delphi, with a connection at Ámfissa: a pleasant, mountainous route skirting Parnassós and, to the northwest, Mount Íti. At the historic pass of **Thermopylae** the road joins the **coastal highway** from Athens.

Inland via Ámfissa

The inland road north from Delphi climbs slowly through a sea of olive groves to **ÁMFISSA**, a small town set in the foothills of Mt. Yióna. Like Livádhia it was a base for the Catalan Grand Company, who have left their mark on the **castle**, originally Frankish, of the ancient acropolis. If you have time to fill between buses, its ruins are a short and obvious walk – if only to enjoy the shade of the pine trees and examine a few stretches of Classical polygonal masonry. In town the **market** quarter is good for a stroll. Ámfissa was once one of the major bell-making centres in the Balkans, and copper-alloy sheep bells are still produced and sold here. The local olives – green and salty – are also acclaimed.

Serious **walkers** may want to use Ámfissa as a jumping-off point for the mountains west and north towards Karpeníssi: **Gióna, Vardhoússia, and Oxía**. There are routes through from Ámfissa (and from Lidhoríki, west of Ámfissa) **to Karpeníssi**. Most travellers, however, roll north on the dramatic **Lamía road**, dividing Mounts Parnassós and Gióna, or the **rail line** from Livadhiá to Lamía. The railway is one of the most dramatic stretches of line in Europe and has a history to match. It runs through the foothills of Mt. Íti and over the precipitous **defile of the Gorgopótamos** river, where in 1942 the Greek resistance – all factions united for the first and last time, under the command of the British intelligence officer C. M. Woodhouse – blew up a railway viaduct, cutting one of the Germans' vital supply lines to their army in North Africa. Since PASOK came to power, the anniversary on November 25 is commemorated as a great national event.

The coastal highway

The **Athens–Lamía** coastal highway is fast, efficient and generally dull. For the first 90km or so it runs a little inland, though skirting various pockets of inland lake, like Límni Ilíki, north of Thíva. The most interesting stop, along with Thíva, is the Mycenaean citadel of **Glá**, by the village of KÁSTRO (see p.220).

There are various links with the island of Évvia (see *Chapter Eleven*): first at HALKÍDHA, where there's a causeway; then by ferry at **ARKÍTSA** to LOUTRÁ EDHIPSOÚ (about every hour, last at 11pm; 50 min.; passengers 200dr, cars 1000-2000dr). Arkítsa itself is a rather upmarket resort, popular mainly with Greeks.

ÁYIOS KONSTANTÍNOS is a useful port – the closest to Athens if you're heading for the Sporades (again see *Chapter Eleven*). There are daily car **ferries**, usually around midday, to Skíathos and Skópelos (occasionally continuing to Alónissos); and a weekly departure (usually on Mondays) to Áyios Efstrátios, Límnos and Kavála; ☎01/417-8084 for information. In summer there are also 'Flying Dolphin' **hydrofoils** (no cars carried) to Skíathos, Skópelos, and Alónissos; these are considerably quicker, though about 30 percent more expensive; information ☎01/452-7107. There should be no reason to stay in Áyios Konstantínos but if you're stranded there are eight or so **hotels** in the town (try the *Pension O Tassos*, ☎0235/31-610; or *Hotel Poulia*, ☎0235/31-663) and a **campsite** on the beach (*Camping Blue Bay*, ☎0235/52-1098). A better beach, if you find yourself waiting some time in Konstantínos for a ferry, is at **KÁMENA VOÚRLA**, 9km north; this is, however, very much a resort, used mainly by Greeks attracted by the spas here and at neighbouring Thermopílio.

Just before joining the inland road the highway enters the famous **Pass of Thermopylae**, where Leonidas and 300 Spartans made a last stand against Xerxes' 30,000-strong Persian army in 480 B.C. The pass was in ancient times much more defined, a narrow defile with Mt. Gióna on its west and the sea – which has silted and retreated nearly 4km – to the east. The tale of Spartan bravery is described at length by Herodotus. Leonidas, King of Sparta, stood guard over the pass with a mixed force of 7000 Greeks, confident that it was the only approach an army could take to enter Greece from Thessaly. At night, however, Xerxes sent an advance part of his forces along a mountain trail and broke through the pass to attack the Greeks from the rear. Leonidas ordered a retreat of the main army, but remained in the pass himself, with his Spartan guard, to delay the Persians' progress. He and all but two of the guard fought to their deaths.

LOUTRÁ THERMOPILÍON, midway through the pass, is named for the hot springs present since antiquity. It retains the grave mound of the fallen Spartans, opposite a modern memorial to Leonidas.

Lamía and northward

LAMÍA is a busy provincial capital and an important transport junction for travellers. It sees few overnight visitors, however, since there are no particular sights. If you are in no hurry, there are few better places to get an idea of small-town Greek life.

The town straddles a valley between two hills, on the northern of which is the shell of a Catalan **fortress**, a military reserve today, though with possible access at weekends. Down below, Lamía is arranged around four main squares. **Platía Parhoú** is at the end of the feeder roads to National Road No. 1. It stakes out the heart of the shopping area, with most of the banks grouped around. The **buses**, too, including the local service from the train station (6km out), all arrive in this southeast quarter, though their terminals are scattered. Arrivals/departures of the Ámfissa and Karpeníssi services use a terminal on Márkou Bótsari; those for Lárissa, Tríkala and the north one on Thermominó; those for Vólos, the corner of Levadhítou and Rozáki-Ángeli.

Most of the **hotels** are nearby, with a concentration of the cheapest places on Rozáki-Ángeli: *Rex* (☎0231/21-366) at no.22; *Thermopylae* (☎0231/28-840) at no.36; and *Athina* (☎0231/20-700) at no.41; all are D-class. A couple of others, nicely sited, are on Platía Laoú (see below): the *Emborikon* (☎0231/22-654) and *Neon Astron* (☎0231/26-245).

The town's social hub is **Platía Eleftherías**, full of outdoor cafés and restaurants, where people parade in an evening *volta*. The cathedral and town hall occupy two sides of the square, the latter pockmarked by bullets dating from riots during the colonels' junta. Every Sunday the flag above is lowered in solemn ceremony, to the wayward accompaniment of the local band. Steps below the cathedral lead down to an *ouzerí*, good for a *mezé* and a drink.

Below Eleftherías is **Platía Laoú**, shaded by plane trees which in autumn are crowded with migratory birds. Here is the town's main taxi rank and an all-night kiosk. In the paved streets off to the right are a number of very cheap pasta-and-chicken **restaurants**. Even cheaper, and open until 6am, is the restaurant at the base of the steps on the south side of the square, by the fish and meat market; this is used chiefly by prostitutes and their pimps. If you prefer a bit more attention to cuisine, good tavernas elsewhere in town include *Yioryos* in Markopoúlou, *Foudha* near the Tríkala bus station, and *Psilidhas* on the road out of town towards Stilídha and Vólos.

For a look at **bread-making** by the oldest of old-fashioned methods, leave Laoú by the road behind the *zaharoplastío* and follow it for 200 metres into the old part of town. The bakery is on the left, recognisable by the quarter-glazed windows and stable door. Another noteworthy bakery, supplying the best *tirópites* in Greece, is to be found between Laoú and Eleftherías; look for its blue shutters.

Other diversions in Lamía include genuine live **bouzouki music**, not tainted by the sophisticated tastes of Athenians, nor pandering to tourists, on the Stilídha road, opposite the high school; a **theatre** on Ipsilandoú, used for art exhibitions and in winter as an art-film cinema; and a scattering of winter-only **'pubs'**, among them *59* on Markopoúlou and *Decadence* on Víronos, both with loud music and not a lot of atmosphere. On **Saturdays** the streets below Párhou turn into a **market**, very lively and with everything from goats to plastic combs on sale. And finally, every **Sunday** there is a **puppet show** in the small theatre 200m up the road past the OTE; it's designed for children, telling classic Greek stories that are understandable even with a very hazy knowledge of the language.

North from Lamía

Heading north from Lamía there's a choice of three routes: to Tríkala and Kalambáka, to Lárissa, or around the coast to Vólos. None are especially memorable. FÁRSALA and KARDHÍTSA, on the routes to Lárissa and Tríkala respectively, are small, very ordinary country towns.

The **Vólos road**, however, has a little more to delay your progress. At **AYÍA MARÍNA**, 12km from Lamía, there are some fine seafood tavernas along the beach – a popular weekend trip for Lamian families. A couple of kilometres further, **STILÍDHA** was once one of the major ports of the Aegean – it was here that Maria Callas's grandfather outsung a visiting Italian opera star and started a legend. It is today chiefly concerned with olive-oil bottling and cement: not an inspiring prospect, though there is a good beach with a **hotel** (*Stilis Beach*) and **campsite** (*Camping Paras*; April-October only; ☎0238/52-8022). Look out for nesting herons on the road back to Lamía.

The best beach along this route is at **GLÍFFA**, 30km further north, though it is 9km off the highway and hard to get to without your own transport. It has the mainland's northernmost **ferry crossing to Évvia**: 7 times daily to ÁYIOKAMBOS (last at 6pm; 30 min. journey; passengers 150dr, cars 900dr). Rooms are fairly plentiful – offered both in private houses and by half a dozen **hotels** (cheapest is the E-class *Oassis*, ☎0238/61-201). **AKHÍLIO**, 7km north, is less attractive, though it has a **campsite**.

Finally, rounding the Pagasitic Gulf towards Vólos, car-drivers might want to stop at **NÉA ANHÍALOS**, where five early Christian basilicas have been uncovered. Their mosaics and the small site museum are interesting, perhaps enough to make it worth risking a three-hour wait between buses.

West to Karpeníssi – and some hiking

The road **west from Lamía** climbs sinuously out of the Sperhíos river valley, allowing glimpses along the way of Mounts Íti, Gióna and Vardhoússia, just 10km to the south. If you're looking to do some **hiking**, there are spectacular routes on Mt. Íti (or Oita), easiest approached from the village of Ipáti. The **Karpenissí valley**, too, lends itself to walking trips: a countryside of dark fir forest and snow-fringed mountains, which the EOT promote (with some reason) as 'the Greek Switzerland'. Neither area sees more than a few dozen summer tourists.

Ipáti and foot-paths on Mt. Íti

Mt. Íti is an unusually accessible mountain. There are buses almost hourly from Lamía to **IPÁTI**, its main trailhead; if you arrive by train, these can be picked up en route at the Lamía station, LIANOKLÁDHI. Be sure not to be dropped off the bus at the sulphurous spa of LOUTRÁ IPÁTIS, 5km south.

Ipáti is a small village, gathered below a medieval castle. It has two **hotels**, catering mainly for Greek families. Both are good value: the C-class *Panorama* (☎0231/59-222) and D-class *Panhellinion* (☎0231/59-640). There are also a couple of reasonable tavernas.

Trails into Mt. Íti can be ambitious undertakings, and require detailed maps and/or one of the hiking guides. A limited trek, however, should be feasible if you've reasonable orientation skills. From the village a path loosely marked by red splashes of paint leads in around four hours to an EOS refuge at **Trapezítsa** (usually locked, but with a spring and camping space nearby). This is a steep but rewarding walk, giving a good idea of Íti's sheer rock ramparts and high lush meadows.

On to Karpeníssi

After scaling a spur of Mount Timvristós, and passing the turnoff to a tiny **ski centre** (uncrowded and with equipment to hire), the main road west drops down to **KARPENÍSSI**. The site is spectacular, huddled at the base of the peak and head of the Karpenissiótis valley, which extends south all the way to the wall-like Mount Panetolikó. The town itself is entirely nondescript having been destroyed in the World War II by the Germans and again during the civil war. On the latter occasion, in January 1949, it was captured and held for a week by Communist guerillas. During the fighting here an American pilot was shot down, having, as C. M. Woodhouse observes in *Modern Greece*, 'probably the unenviable distinction of being the first American serviceman to be killed in action by Communist arms'.

Except in mid-summer or skiing season, **accommodation** is easily found in Karpeníssi. Within a block of the central square a dozen or so hotels compete for your attention. The cheapest are the D-class *Panhellinion* (Tsitsára 9; ☎0237/22-330) and E-class *Velouchi* (Zinopoúlou 64; ☎0237/22-264), but there's a broad selection in all categories. As the provincial capital of Evritanía, the town has most facilities you might need, along with a good selection of places to eat and drink. A couple of passable **tavernas** and a *souvláki* bar are to be found on Etoloú, immediately around the corner from the *Panhellinion*.

Walks around Karpeníssi

Within easy walking distance (4km) of town is the traditional mountain village of **KORISKHÁDHES**, whose stone houses display the ornate wooden balconies typical of the region. There's one *kafenío* where you can order *mezédhes* and gaze over the trees at Mount Helidhóna. To get there follow the road south out of town (towards Proussós) and look for the turning to the right after about 1km.

If your appetite is whetted for more, a twice-daily bus trundles 13km downriver, again along the Proussós road, to **MEGÁLO** and **MIKRÓ HORIÓ** ('Big' and 'Little Village'). Both have **inns** and the possiblity of day hikes up the respective peaks presiding over them.

Beyond these villages, the valley narrows to a gorge, the road loses its asphalt, and only one daily bus braves the hair-raising drive to the monastery and village of **PROUSSÓS** (33km out of Karpeníssi). The **monastery** is large and much rebuilt after a succession of fires (always a hazard with candles), and presently tenanted by just five monks. Visitors are welcomed and shown such curiosities in the ninth-century *katholikón* as paper made from the skin of goat-kid embryo or an icon of the Panayía – with its eyes gouged out. (According to the monks, the Communist *andártes* of the 1940s were responsible for this, though the Turks were wont to perform the same sacrilege, as well as credulous villagers attributing magical powers to the dust thus obtained.) In summer the monastery will host men for a one-night stay; otherwise there are a couple of tavernas in the **village** (1km further on) and probably a bed or two – necessary since the bus won't reappear until the following day.

West from Karpeníssi

The roads west from Karpeníssi climb high into the mountains of Panetolikó, the southernmost extension of the Píndhos. In winter they're generally impassable, but through the summer they're serviceable, if boneshaking.

The most remote and dramatic – with 'no bus service – is the route on **south from Proussós**, 33km of dirt track which eventually brings you out at **THÉRMO**, on the shores of Lake Trihonídha. There you are within striking distance (and daily bus ride) of AGRÍNIO, with its connections to Patrá and Ioánnina.

The direct **Karpeníssi-Agrínio** road is in a better state, though it still takes the one morning bus a good five hours to cover. It breaks for a lunch stop at the tidy village of **FRANGÍSTA**, sandwiched between various river crossings. If you wish to explore the Ágrafa wilderness to the north, leave the bus at the nearby turnoff for KERASOHÓRI. Beyond the turning, the bus lumbers past the giant **Kremastón dam** on the Tavropós, Trikeriótis, and Aheloós rivers, skirts Panetolikó, then winds down through tobacco-planted hills to Agrínio. The beauty of the first half of the journey cannot be overemphasised.

THESSALY

The highlights of travelling through **Thessaly** are easily summarised. To the east, curling down from the industrial port-city of Vólos, is the **Pílion** (Pelion). The villages on this lush, orchard-covered peninsula are among the most beautiful in Greece: an established resort area for Greeks, though still surprisingly undiscovered by tourists. To the west – a sight not to be missed in any mainland exploration – are the extraordinary 'monasteries in the air' of the **Metéora**.

The **central plains** are to be passed through, rather than visited. **Lárissa**, the region's capital, provides efficient connections by bus, and rather slower ones by train, to Vólos and to Kalambáka (via Tríkala).

Heading north or west from Thessaly, you will find yourself in one or other mountain range. The dramatic route over the Píndhos, from Kalambáka to Ioánnina, is covered in *Chapter Four*. North from Kalambáka there are reasonable roads, though few buses, into western Macedonia, with the lake-side town of Kastoriá an obvious focus. Most travellers, however, head north from Lárissa towards Thessaloníki, a very beautiful route in the shadow of Mount Olympus.

For details on climbing Mt. Olympus, see *Chapter Five*.

Vólos

Arriving at **VOLOS** you have little hint of the Pílion's promise. This is Greece's fastest-growing industrial city, and a major port depot for lorry-drivers, who cross with the ferry here to Tartous in Syria. It is not a pretty sight: a remorselessly modern, concrete sprawl, rebuilt after an earthquake in 1955 and now edging to its natural limits against the Pílion foothills behind.

That said, you may well find yourself spending a night, or at least a few hours, in the town. In addition to serving as a gateway to the Pílion, Vólos is the main **port for the Northern Sporades** – Skíathos, Skópelos and Alónissos. As with Áyios Konstantínos, there are both regular ferries and (around 30 percent more expensive) the quicker 'Flying Dolphins' hydrofoils. Ferries leave two to four times daily for Skíathos and Skópelos, with at least one continuing to Alónissos; the last departure is generally at 7pm (Sun. 1pm); ☎01/417-8084 for information. Hydrofoils run two to three times daily to all three islands, occasionally continuing from Alónissos to Kími on Évvia, and on Sunday to Skíros. If you are interested in the sailing to **Tartous**, the boat generally leaves on a Saturday evening; ☎01/413-3835 for information.

The ferries all depart from the central harbour, and most other services are to be found within a couple of blocks. The **bus station** is on Metamór-fosséos; the **post office** on P. Melá; the **EOT** on the main square, Platía Rigá Feréou. If you want to **hire a car** to explore the Pílion, try *Theofanidis Hellas* (Iassónos 137, parallel to the waterside but a block in; ☎0421/32-360).

Hotels are fairly plentiful with a concentration of D- and E-class places in the grid of streets behind the port. *Acropolis* (Koraí 49; ☎0421/25-984) and *Europa* (Koraï 18; ☎0421/23-624) are reasonably appointed and as cheap as

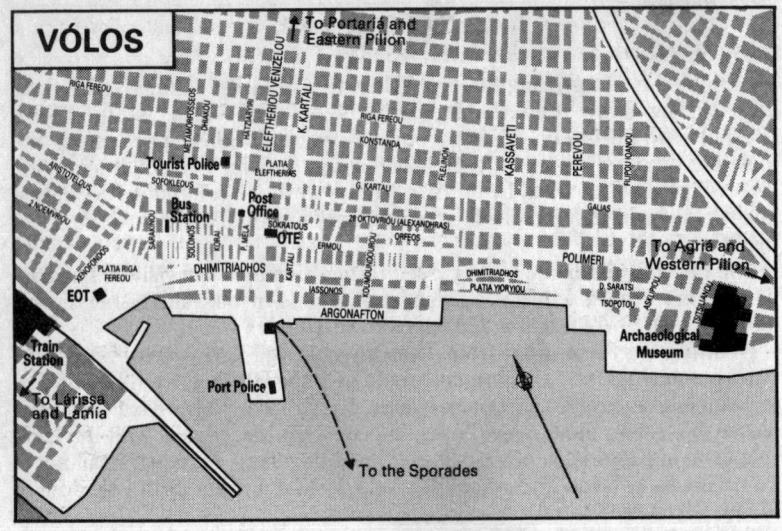

they come; *Iasson* (P. Melá 1; ☎0421/26-075), on the waterside, is marginally pricier. **Eating out** can be an expensive proposition in the centre and some of the cheaper *souvláki* joints are not very clean. There's a superlative taverna, however, on Orféos (five blocks back from the front), and two others, both good value, facing each other on Kartáli, in the first block up from the quay.

To fill in time, the **Archaeological Museum** (8.45am–3pm, Sun. 9.30am–2.30pm; closed Tues.) is highly recommended. Imaginatively laid out and clearly labelled in English, it features a unique collection of painted grave *stelai* which depict, in now faded colours, the everyday scenarios of fifth century B.C. life. It also has one of the best collections in Europe of Neolithic pottery, tools, and figurines; these are from the local sites of Sesklo and Dimini and, exhibited with models and diagrams, give a real insight into the sophistication of fourth- and fifth-millennium B.C. civilisation. (The Sesklo and Dimini sites can themselves be visited – they're respectively 15km and 3km from Volos – but are of essentially specialist interest.)

The villages of Mount Pílion

There is something decidedly un-Greek about the **Pílion peninsula**, with its lush orchards of apple, walnut and chestnut trees, and dense forests of beech and oak. Scarcely a rock is visible along the slopes and the sound of water bubbles up everywhere from crevices. Its **villages** are equally idiosyncratic, spread out over a wide area due to the availability of water, and with the quarters linked by winding cobbled paths. They formed a semi-autonomous district during the Turkish occupation, and during the eighteenth century became something of a nursery for Greek culture, which encompassed not only an Orthodox education (including semi-underground schooling) but a revival of folk art and traditional architecture.

The villages have changed little in appearance over the centuries, and offer rich rewards with their mansions (many restored in recent years), churches and rambling *platíes*. A common feature of these squares is the vast plane tree, perennially sheltering the village café. The churches are equally distinctive, built in a low, wide style, often with wooden cloisters and a detached belltower. A couple of villages – **Makrinítsa** and **Vizítsa** – have been restored by the EOT as showpieces of the region, but almost every hamlet has a mansion, church or at least a view. **Naturalists** are in for good things, too. The Pílion's temperate climate is 20°F cooler in summer than the rest of Thessaly, and its high and low slopes take in two quite different types of flora. Unusually for Greece, there is also a strong regional **cuisine**. Don't leave without sampling specialities such as *spédzofai* (sausage and pepper stew), *kounéli stifádho* (rabbit casserole), or *gidá brastí* (a delicious goat *pot-au-feu*).

The peninsula breaks into three regions, with the best concentration of villages on, or just inland from, the **northeast coast**. The **west coast** is less scenically interesting, with generally lower-altitude villages and much more beach development. The **south**, sparsely populated, has just one resort, Platanía, and a few tiny inland hamlets.

Travelling between the Pílion villages can be tricky. **Buses** cover two main routes: Vólos-Hánia-Zagorá (4-8 daily, depending on season) and Vólos-Kalá Nerá-Miliés-Tsangarádha (4-7 daily). Both, however, retrace their routes on arrival. If you want to complete a loop of the peninsula you're dependent on just a couple of daily buses which connect Tsangarádha with Zagorá; likewise, heading south, Plataniá is connected only with Vólos-Kalá Nerá-Argalastí (2 daily). Alternatives are to hire a car in Vólos (worth considering if you are pushed for time); some very uncertain hitching; or **walking**. The latter can be slow progress, with roads backtracking around the slopes, seeming never to get any closer to villages just across the way. For walkers there are a few surviving *kalderimiá*, the old cobbled mule **paths**, to provide shortcuts.

Moving **on from the Pílion**, there are summer *kaíkia* from Plataniá to Koukounariés on **Skíathos**.

The north and east

As detailed above, the main axis of this route is Vólos-Zagorá. However, before crossing over to the coast, consider pausing en route on the mountain itself. Both Makrinítsa and Portariá have intrinsic attractions and make good first or last stops out of Vólos; they each have frequent bus connections with Vólos.

Anakassía, Portariá, Makrinítsa and Hánia

The first of the Pílion villages, **ANAKASSÍA** is just 4km out of Vólos, and few casual visitors give it more than a passing glance. What they miss is a small but very beautiful museum, dedicated to the 'naive' painter **Theophilos** (1873-1934). A grand eccentric, originally from Lésvos, Theophilos lived for periods in both Athens and Vólos, where he wandered around, often dressed in War of Independence garb, painting frescoes for anyone prepared either to pay or feed him. In the Pílion you find his work in the most unlikely places, mostly untrumpeted, including a number of village tavernas and *kafeneía*. Here, the museum (open around 9am–6pm daily) occupies the **Spíti Kondós**, an eighteenth century mansion whose first floor is entirely frescoed with scenes from the War of Independence.

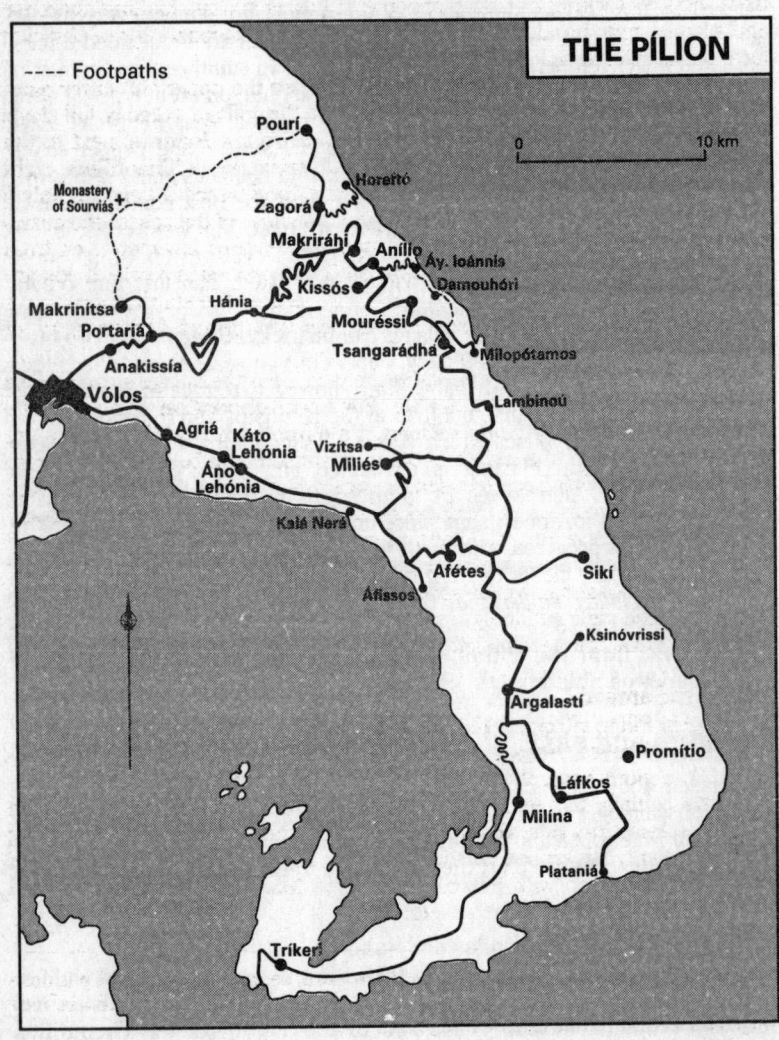

THE PÍLION

PORTARIÁ, 10km on, has a more mountainous feel: a quiet roadside village with a startling soundtrack of running streams. Its chief glory, as so often in the Pílion, is its main square, shaded by a tremendous plane tree. There are several **rooms** advertised, and several small hotels – cheapest of which is the C-class *Alkistis* (☎0421/99-178).

From Portariá many buses detour north and west to **MAKRINÍTSA**, 17km from Volos and 600m up the mountain. If your time in the Pílion is severely limited, this is probably the best single target. Founded in 1204 by refugees from the first sacking of Constantinople, it boasts six outstanding churches and a monastery, in addition to the much-touted mansions – three of which have been restored as lodges by the EOT.

There's a 200-metre altitude difference between the upper and lower quarters of Makrinítsa, so to get a full sense of the village takes a full day's rambling. Most impressive of the churches are **Áyios Ioánnis**, next to the fountain on the shady main *platía*, and the **Monastery of Theotókos**, right under the clock tower. Many of the sanctuaries and frescoes here are only a few centuries old but the marble relief work on some of the apses (the curvature behind the altar) is the best of its type in Greece. A few metres on from the Áyios Ioánnis square there are **Theophilos frescoes** in a café. If you are looking for a major walk in Pílion, the village is also the starting point for a long **trail** over to POURÍ (see below), via the deserted monastery of Sourviás.

Makrinitsa's EOT lodges are expensive, and even the village's two E-class pensions charge 3000dr for a double. For **accommodation** at only a little above normal prices try *Yanni's Rooms*, a red-fronted house 150m above the main square, or one of a couple of other establishments between the square and road's end. *Kafe-Bar Pakoulorizos*, again just above the square, is the place to eat, specialising in the local *spédzofai*. Travelling on over the mountain, beyond Portariá, the road hairpins up to the **Hánia pass**, and the village of the same name, a stark cluster of modern houses. To the south a road leads in 4km to a small, winter **ski resort** (open Jan.–March). Once over the Hánia pass the view suddenly opens to take in the whole east coast, as you spiral down to a fork: leading left to Zagorá, right towards Tsangarádha.

Zagorá and around

The largest Pílion village, **ZAGORÁ** has a life more independent of tourism* than its neighbours, and a fair amount of recent building alongside the traditional. It supports several shops, an OTE and post office, and a bank agent – the latter actually the electrical and general store, *Raftopoulos*, in the main square of Áyios Yióryios. **Rooms** come a little cheaper than elsewhere, too; there are plenty advertised, in addition to the regular E-class *Hotel Charavgi* (☎0426/22-550). And with bus connections to Makriráhi, Tsangarádha, and Horeftó, the village can make a useful base.

---

*Zagorá is the centre for apple-picking on Pílion: hard, demanding work, which is done mainly by pickers from Egypt. The Egyptians are a tightly-knit bunch, and in 1987 waged a successful strike against a wage cut.

Zagora's beach is 8km down the mountain at **HOREFTÓ** (2 buses a day, but good hitching). It's a deservedly popular strand: a small fishing village with fine sand, several seasonal tavernas, a few signposted rooms for rent and half a dozen **hotels**, of which the cheapest, oddly enough, is the C-class *Votsala* (☎0426/22-001), its rates below those of the D-class *Aegeus* (☎0426/22-778) and E-class *Cleopatra*, (☎0426/22-606). The village also has a couple of **campsites**, one official, *Camping Seahorse* (☎0426/22-180), the other (left at the end of the road, and over some rocks) not.

The road to **POURI**, the last in the Pílion, is a spectacular approach to the tiny village, overhung by almost tropical-looking, dripping slopes. This is also the northeastern trailhead for the four-hour walk up to the Monastery of Sourviás (see Makrinítsa).

Around to Tsangarádha

Bearing right at the junction below Hania brings you shortly to **MAKRIRÁHI**, which serves as the terminus for buses going on south and around to Tsangarádha, and occasionally beyond to Mílies.

The first stop of real interest is **KISSÓS**, virtually buried in foliage and ascending in terraces up the mountainside above the road. The village church, eighteenth-century **Ayía Marína**, is among the best on the peninsula; while the combination **taverna-inn** of Sofoklis Garoufalias, with good, simple food and rooms, makes it an excellent base to explore the area.

Half-overgrown tracks wander tentatively from Kissós up toward the ski-lift ridge. You're less likely to get lost on the way to **ÁYIOS IOÁNNIS**, 6km downhill. This is connected by a solid, modern road, and has become the eastern Pílion's major resort, complete with windsurfing boards and water-skis for hire. In July or August, despite the sixteen or so hotels, it can be hard to find a room, so popular is it with Greek holidaymakers. If you're prepared to camp, you should be okay; there are again official and (and on the less developed southern beach) unofficial sites. Cheapest of the **hotels** are the *Anessis* (☎0426/31-223) and *Avra* (☎0426/31-224).

Even if you don't intend to stay in Áyios Iaoánnis, you might want to consider getting a bus down for a bit of Pílion walking. Many of the mountain's old trails have been bulldozed or allowed to revert to forest. But heading south, past the beaches, from Áyios Ioánnis, there's an erratically signposted **path** along the coast to **DAMOUHÓRI**, a tiny hamlet set amid olive trees on the shore of a secluded fishermen's cove. At the base of a giant ravine just beyond is a further, spectacular, stairway trail up to Tsangarádha. From certain points along the way you've glimpses of up to six villages simultaneously plus a good stretch of coast. You emerge at Tsangarádha (about 2hr. walk from Áyios Ioánnis) in its Áyios Stéfanos quarter.

TSANGARÁDHA is one of the larger Pílion villages, though it divides into four quite distinct quarters, scattered along several kilometres of road. Each is grouped around a *platía* and church, and they are still connected by cobbled paths. **Áyios Stéfanos** has the best-value **hotel**, the *Pension San Stefano* (☎0423/49-213). The finest square is that of of **Áyia Paraskeví**, completely shaded by what is reputedly the largest plane tree in Greece – a thousand years old and with a trunk that would take eighteen men to encircle. **Taxiárhis**, the next *platía* south, is just off the road, near the bus stop; there are a number of **rooms** for rent nearby.

Between these last two squares a side road descends 8km to the secluded cove of **MILOPÓTAMOS**, popular in season with a couple of tavernas.

The west and south

South of Tsangarádhas, vegetation becomes more scarce and villages more spread out. With patience, it's possible to bus or hitch around to the west coast via Miliés. For conections south, you need to loop down to the west coast at Kalá Nerá.

Miliés and Vizítsa

MILIÉS, like Tsangarádha, was an important cultural centre in the eighteenth century and retains a number of imposing mansions and the brilliantly frescoed church of **Taxiárhis**. In the central square there are a few signposts to **rooms** and a wonderful bakery selling *tirópsomi* (cheesebread), the local speciality.

Above the village, 3km up into the mountain, is the equally inviting **VIZÍTSA**, preserved as another 'traditional settlement' by the EOT, which has converted (as at Makrinítsa) a number of mansions into guesthouses. If you have the money, they'd be superb places to stay; rates run between 2500-7500dr, depending on season and the number of beds (reservations ☎0423/86-373). For the less affluent, there are a few **rooms** available through the village *kafenío*.

An extremely overgrown **path** leads from Miliés to Tsangarádha in around 4½ hr., a longer walk in the opposite direction.

The west coast

If it were anywhere else in Greece, the Pílion's west coast would have to be recommended as at least a stopping-off point. However, with a limited amount of time to spend on the mountain, it seems a shame not to use as much as possible of it over in the eastern or central villages.

Virtually the whole **west coast** between Vólos and Kalá Nerá has been developed. At **AGRIÁ**, in particular, there are rashes of hotels and neon-garish tavernas, popular mainly with Greeks, but also Germans and French. The appeal is mainly the ease of access from Vólos; the narrow strip of beach and waterside seems all too close to the road.

As you head south, things gradually improve. Around **KÁTO GADZÉA** the traffic thins, olive groves edge the route and there are some lower-key **campsites**. **KALÁ NERÁ**, however, the main south terminal of the route, is again a major commercialised resort.

South to Plataniá

To get a better idea of the low-lying, olive-grove countryside of the western Pílion, press on south from Kalá Nerá to the junction of **ARGALASTÍ**, a regional centre for the south with a few **rooms**.

From here you can get sporadic transport to **MILÍNA**, a tiny beach village with a seasonal **campsite**. For the enthusiastic, there's a rough dirt track on from here to the end of the peninsula at **TRÍKERI**, a yet smaller hamlet set 2km above its beach.

Alternatively, pick up one of the Vólos buses (2 daily in summer) to **PLATANIÁ**, a small but surprisingly crowded Greek resort with a half dozen **hotels**. Cheapest are the D-class *des Roses* (☎0423/65-568) and E-class *Kyma* (☎0423/65-569) and *Platania* (☎0423/65-565); if you find these full 'free-lance' camping shouldn't present a problem. The beach is excellent.

In season, there are **kaíkia from Plataniá** to Koukouariés beach on Skíathos, and excursions to the beach at Tríkeri.

Lárissa, the Vale of Témbi and Tríkala

LÁRISSA stands at the heart of the Thessalian plain: a large, market centre aproached across a prosperous but dull landscape of wheat and corn fields. It is for the most part modern and unremarkable, but retains a few old streets (Venizélou, most notably) which hint at its recent past as a Turkish provincial capital. From above the town looms a medieval castle, with the military still in residence.

As a major **road and rail junction**, the town has efficient connections with most places you'd want to reach: Vólos to the east; Tríkala and Kalambáka to the west; and Lamía to the south. Travelling north, the national highway cuts along the coast towards Thessaloníki: a highly scenic route which passes through the **Vale of Témbi** beneath Mounts Olympus and Óssa.

Should you need to stay in Lárissa, there are numerous **hotels**. Cheapest are a group of three D-class places in the square by the train station (1km from the central square, Platía Stratoú): *Diethnes* (☎041/234-210), *Neon* (☎041/236-268) and *Pantheon* (☎041/236-726). The most pleasant place to while away a few hours is the **Alcazar** park, beside the Piniós, Thessaly's major river.

The Vale of Témbi

If you have time, or a vehicle, a worthwhile first stop in the Témbi region is **AMBELÁKIA**, a small town on the foothills of Mount Óssa. In the eight-eenth century this small community supported the world's first industrial co-operative, producing, dying and exporting textiles, and maintaining its own branch offices as far afield as London. With the co-operative came a rare and enlightened prosperity. At a time when most of Greece lay stagnant under Turkish rule, Ambelakia was largely autonomous; it held democratic assem-blies, offered free education and medical care, and even subsidised weekly performances of ancient drama. The brave experiment lasted over a century, eventually succumbing to the triple ravages of war, economics and the indus-trial revolution. In 1811 Ali Pasha raided the town and a decade later any chance of recovery was lost due to the collapse of the Viennese bank in which the town's collective wealth was deposited, as well as by the advent of aniline dyes.

Until World War II over 600 palatial mansions survived. Today there are just 36, most in poor condition. You can still get some idea of the former local prosperity, though, by visiting the restored **Mansion of George Schwartz**. The home of the co-operative's last president, this *arhondíko* (open 9.30am-3.30pm; closed Tues.) is built in grand, old-Constantinople style. Schwartz, incidentally, was a Greek, despite the German-sounding name – which was the Austrian bank's translation of his real surname, Mavros (Black).

The town is connected by bus with Lárissa (3 daily); or you can walk up in about an hour from the TÉMBI train station.

Two kilometres beyond the Ambelákia turn-off you enter the **Vale of Témbi**. The valley, nearly 10km long, has been cut by the Piniós over the eons, between the steep cliffs of the Olympus (Ólimbos) and Óssa ranges. In antiquity it was sacred to Apollo and one of the few possible approaches into Greece; this was the path taken by both Xerxes and Alexander the Great. It remained an important passage during the Middle Ages. Halfway down (on the right) are the ruins of the **Kástro tis Orías** (Castle of the Beautiful Maiden), one of four Frankish guardposts. Marking the northern end of the pass is a second medieval **fortress** at PLATAMÓNAS, this time built by the Crusaders. Walkers might consider a hike along the valley – which can also be traversed by canoe on the Pínios. However, both National Road 1 and the railway forge through Témbi, impinging somewhat on its beauties.

A side road, close by the first castle, takes you the 13km to **STÓMIO**, an attractive seaside town at the mouth of the Piniós. The dense beech trees of Ossa march right down to the shore, making Stómio at least part mountain village – the *platía* is some 30m above sea level and most of the buildings are old. Outside of summer (when northern Europeans mob the place) you shouldn't have much trouble finding a **room**. There are five small hotels, including the E-class *Argithea* (☎0495/91-323) and *Drossia* (☎0495/91-365), and a free municipal **campsite** behind the beach. The **beach** itself is tremendous, reached across a wooden bridge over the Piniós estuary (which will also reward birdwatchers). Take care, however, with stingrays – a perennial hazard on the sandy sea floor hereabouts.

PLATAMÓNAS marks the beginning of **Macedonia** and heralds a rather grim succession of overdeveloped resorts fronting the narrow, pebbly beaches of the Thermaíkos gulf. Inland, though, the mountain spectacle continues, with **Mount Olympus** (Óros Ólimbos) casting ever-longer shadows. The trailhead for **climbing Olympus** is LITÓHORO, 7km inland. For details see *Chapter Five*.

West to Tríkala

West from Lárissa, the road (and 5 daily buses) trails the Piniós to Tríkala, where you may need to change buses for Kalambáka and the Metéora. The railway makes a similar number of connections between Vólos, Lárissa, Tríkala and Kalambáka, though it loops around to the south, through the market town of KARDHÍTSA.

Tríkala

TRÍKALA, a lively metropolis after the agricultural plains towns of central Thessaly, spreads along the banks of the Lethéos, a tributary of the Piniós. It was a major centre for the nineteenth-century Turkish province and retains many of the era's houses, stacked about the clock tower at the south end of town. Close by the bus station a Turkish mosque survives too, a graceful accompaniment to the town's numerous stone churches. Around the **Fortress**, adapted by the Turks from a Byzantine structure, are attractive gardens and the meagre remains of a **Sanctuary of Asclepius**. The cult of the healing god (see Epidauros, *Chapter Two*) is, by some accounts, said to have originated here.

The liveliest part of the town, with numerous cafés and restaurants, is around the central Platía Vassiléos Yioryíou on the riverside. The bus station is on this side of the river, a couple of blocks away; the train station across on the other (west) bank. Accommodation should pose few problems, with two good cheap **hotels** near the square, upriver from and west of the bus stop: the E-class *Panhellinion* (Vassilísis Ólgas 2; ☎0431/27-644) and comparably-priced C-class *Palladion* (Víronos 4; ☎0431/28-091).

Píli

It takes some effort of will to delay immediate progress to Kalambáka and the Metéora. For Byzantine aficionados, however, **PÍLI**, 20km west of Tríkala (frequent buses) is a rewarding excursion. A twenty minute walk upstream from the village leads to the thirteenth-century church of **Pórta Panayía**, one of the unsung beauties of Thessaly, with original frescoes and mosaics. The site, too, is memorable, at the entrance to a mountain gorge. The church is generally locked and unattended, but the key can be obtained from a care-taker who lives nearby (the low house on the hillside). Following the gorge for a kilometre further upstream, you come to a well-preserved Roman bridge. The village has a single D-class **hotel**, the *Babanara* (☎0431/22-325).

Kalambáka and the Metéora monasteries

There are few more exciting places to arrive at than Kalambáka. The town itself you hardly notice, for the eye is immediately drawn up in an unremitting vertical ascent to the weird grey cylinders of rock overhead. These are the outlying monoliths of the extraordinary **valley of the Metéora**. To the right you can make out the monastery of Áyios Stéfanos, firmly entrenched on a massive pedestal; beyond stretch a chaotic confusion of spikes, cones and cliffs – beaten into bizarre and otherworldly shapes by the action of the prehis-toric sea that covered the Plain of Thessaly around fifty million years ago.

The Monasteries: Some History

The monasteries of the Meteora are as enigmatic as they are spectacular. Teetering high up on detached and seemingly inaccessible pinnacles of rock, their origins remain unknown. Legend has it that Saint Athanassios, who founded Méga Metéoron (the Great Meteoron), the earliest of the buildings, flew up to the rocks on the back of an eagle. More rational historians suggest that the villagers of Stáyi, the medieval precursor of Kalambáka, may have become adept at climbing, and helped the original monks up. Whatever, the difficulties of access, and building, are hard to overstate; a German guide has recently been published for rock climbers in the Metéora, and its routes are almost all graded 'advanced'. The name *metéora* means literally 'rocks in the air'.

The earliest religious communities in the valley emerged in the late tenth century, when **hermits**, seeking refuge from the turbulence of the age, made their homes in the caves which score many of the rocks. In 1336 they were joined by two monks from Mount Athos, Gregorios, Abbot of Magoula, and his companion, **Athanassios**. Gregorios returned shortly to Athos but he left Athanassios behind, ordering him to establish a monastery. This Athanassios did, whether supernaturally aided or not, and despite imposing a particularly austere and ascetic rule he was quickly joined by many brothers, including, in 1371, **John Palaeologos**, who refused the throne of Serbia to become the monk Ioasaph.

The royal presence was an important aid to the **endowment** of Meteorite monasteries, which followed swiftly on all the accessible, and many of the inaccessible rocks. They probably reached their zenith during the Ottoman reign of Suleiman the Magnificent (1520-66), by which time 24 of the rocks had been surmounted by monasteries and hermitages. The major establishments accumulated considerable wealth, flourishing on the revenues of estates granted to them in distant Wallachia and Moldavia, and in Thessaly itself. These they retained, more or less intact, through to the eighteenth century, at which time monasticism here, as elsewhere in Greece, was beginning to **decline**.

Along the way there were numerous disputes over power and precedence between the monasteries. However, the principal factors in the Metéora's fall from glory were physical and economic. Many of the buildings, especially the smaller hermitages, were just not built to withstand centuries of use and, perhaps neglected or unoccupied, gradually disintegrated in the air. The grander of the monasteries suffered depopulation, conspicuously so in the nineteenth century as a modern Greek state was established to the south – with Thessaly itself excluded. And in the present century the crisis accellerated, as the monastic lands and revenues, already much reduced from their heyday, were nationalised for the use of Greek refugees from Asia Minor after the Greco-Turkish war of 1920-23.

In the 1950s five of the monasteries were struggling along with little more than a dozen monks between them – an epoch superbly chronicled in Patrick Leigh Fermor's *Roumeli*. Ironically, before their expropriation for **tourism** over the last two decades, they had begun to revive, attracting a number of young and intellectual brothers. Today, put firmly on the map by appearances in such films as James Bond's *For Your Eyes Only*, the four most accessible monasteries, although still maintained as religious houses, are essentially museums. Only two, **Ayía Triádha** and **Áyios Stéfanos**, continue to function with any real monastic purpose.

Kalambáka and Kastráki

Visiting the Metéora demands a full day, which means staying at least one night at Kalambáka or at the village of Kastráki, 2km north and right in the shadow of the rocks.

KALAMBÁKA has no particular allure, save for its position near the rocks. The town was burnt by the Germans in the last war and, save for its old cathedral, little of character remains. It's nonetheless a pleasant enough base with a fairly plentiful supply of rooms – both in private houses and hotels. Arriving by bus or train, in season, you are likely to be offered a **room** by waiting householders. If not, there are numerous signs on the road into town from the bus station. **Hotels** are pricier, with above-usual rates. Try the C-class *Odyssion* (Kastrakioú; ☎0432/22-320) or E-class *Epirotikon* (Ioaninón 33; ☎0432/23-372).

The old **Cathedral**, or Mitrópolis, stands a couple of streets above its modern predecessor, at the top end of the town. It was founded in the seventh century on the site of a temple to Apollo and incorporates various classical drums and fragments in its erratically designed walls. Inside are fourteenth-century Byzantine frescoes and, most unusually in a Greek church, a great marble pulpit placed in the central aisle.

KASTRÁKI is twenty minutes' walk out of Kalambáka; there's a slight shortcut if you follow a footpath out of the northwest corner of the town. Along the way to the village you pass *Camping Kastraki*, the first of three **campsites** here (there are others, less well sited, on the Tríkala and Ioánnina roads). This site seems always to be full; perhaps because it's the nearest to walk to, though a small swimming pool also gives it an edge. Kastráki's two other, more central, grounds seldom have more than a dozen or so tents between them. If you don't want to camp, the village also has a fair number of **rooms** advertised, as well as a wonderful, very cheap E-class **hotel**, the *Kastraki* (☎0342/22-286), right below the rocks.

The Monasteries

There are six Metéora monasteries, each open to visits at different **hours**. If you want to see them all in a day, start early to take in Áyios Nikólaos, Varlaám and Méga Metéoron before 1pm, leaving the rest of the day for Roussánou, Ayía Triádha and Áyios Stéfanos. The road route from Kastráki to Áyios Stéfanos is just under 10km (6 miles). **Walking**, you can cut a little off this by veering off the tarmac and on to the old tracks. Certainly to experience the valley it really should be walked.

Returning, you may feel otherwise. The 'circuit' stops at Áyios Stéfanos and the route signposted Kalambáka just before Ayía Triádha is a highly indirect 5km. However, in season there are a couple of daily buses from Kalambáka up the road to Méga Metéoron/Varlaám; reasonable possibilities of hitching; or, if you've left yourself daylight and have sturdy footwear, a very rough trail down the gorge to Kalambáka from below Ayía Triádha.

Before setting out it is worth buying **food and drink** to last the day; there are only a couple of drinks/fruit stalls on the circuit, by the Mega Metéoron road. And finally, don't forget to carry money with you: each monastery levies an admission charge – currently 100dr.

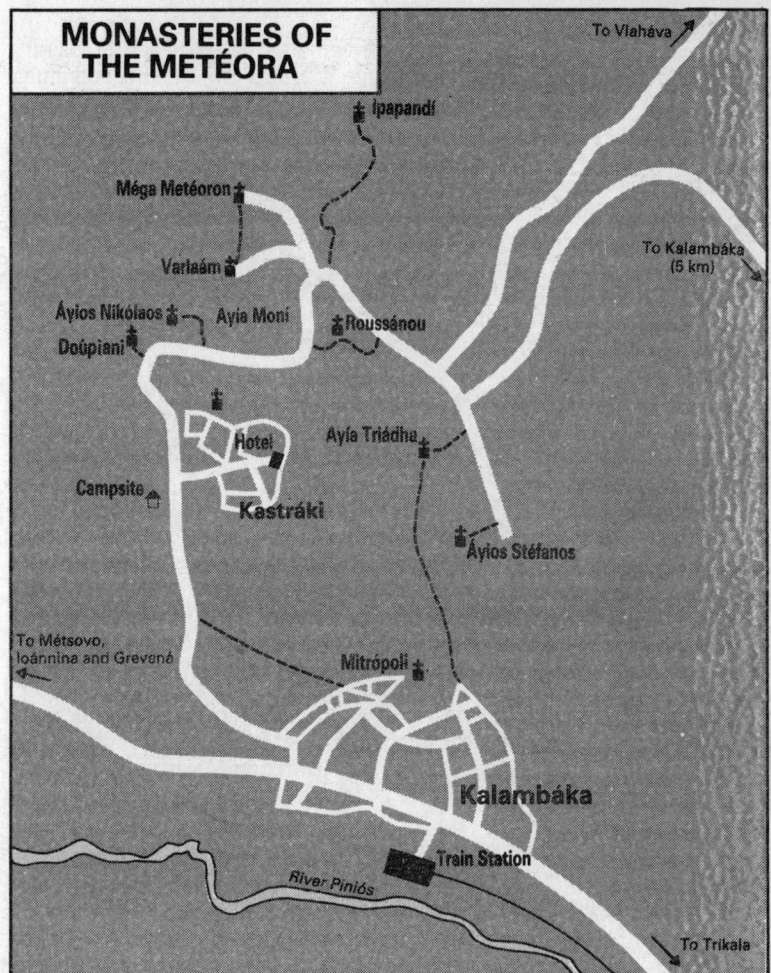

MONASTERIES OF THE METÉORA

To Vlaháva

Ipapandí

Méga Metéoron

Varlaám

To Kalambáka (5 km)

Áyios Nikólaos   Ayia Moní

Doúpiani   Roussánou

Hotel

Ayía Triádha

Campsite

Kastráki

Áyios Stéfanos

To Métsovo, Ioánnina and Grevená

Mitrópoli

Kalambáka

Train Station

River Piniós

To Trikala

Opening hours for the monasteries are as follows:
Áyios Nikólaos 9am–6pm (summer); 9am–1pm and 3–6pm (winter).
Varlaám 9am–1pm & 3:20–6pm; closed Friday.
Méga Metéoron 9am–1pm and 3:20–6pm; closed Tuesday.
Roussánou 9am–6pm.
Ayía Triádha 8am–1pm and 3–6:30pm.
Áyios Stéfanos 8am–1pm and 3–6:30pm; closed Monday.

Dress code is operated strictly at all the monasteries. For women this means wearing a skirt – not trousers; for men, long trousers. Both sexes must cover their arms (no T-shirts). Garments are not lent to visitors by the monasteries.

The circuit

From Kastráki the road loops around between huge outcrops of rock, passing below (20 min. walk) the chapel-hermitage of **Doúpiani**, the first communal church of the early monastic settlements.

A further ten minutes' walk and you reach a track to the left, which winds around and up a low rock to **Áyios Nikólaos**. A small, recently-restored monastery, this has some superb sixteenth-century frescoes in its *katholikón* (main chapel) by the Cretan painter Theophanes. Next to it on a needle-thin shaft is **Ayía Moní**, inaccessible now, and ruined and empty since an earthquake in 1858.

Bearing off to the right, fifteen minutes or so further on, a barely visible path ascends to the tiny and compact convent of **Roussánou** (or Ayía Varvára), approached across dizzying bridges from an adjacent rock and again recently restored and opened. This has perhaps the most extraordinary site of all the monasteries, with walls built right on the edge of a sharp and imposing blade. Its frescoes, particularly bloody scenes of martydom and judgment, were painted in 1660. (Roussánou can also be reached by a track from the 'upper' fork of the road.)

A short way beyond Roussánou the road divides, the left fork heading toward Varlaám and the Mega Metéoron.

Varlaám is one of the earliest-established monasteries, standing on the site of a hermitage established by Saint Varlaam – a key figure in Meteorite history – shortly after Athanasios's arrival. The present building was founded by two brothers from Ioánnina in 1517 and is one of the most beautiful in the valley. The *katholikón* is small but glorious, supported by painted beams and with walls and pillars totally covered in frescoes. A dominant theme, well suited to the Metéora, are the desert ascetics; more conventionally, there is a highly vivid Last Judgment, with a gaping Hell's Mouth, and, dominating the hierarchy of paintings, a great Pantokrator (Christ in Majesty) in the dome; they were painted in 1548 and 1566. In the refectory is a small museum of icons.

Varlaám also retains intact its old **Ascent Tower**, with a precipitous reception platform and dubious windlass mechanism. Until the 1920s the only way of reaching the monasteries was by being hauled up in a net drawn by rope and windlass, or by the equally perilous retractable ladders. Leigh Fermor, who stayed at Varlaám in the 1950s, reported the anecdote of a former abbot; asked how often the rope was changed, he gave the macabre, if logical, reply: 'When it breaks'. Steps were eventually cut to all of the monasteries on the orders of the Bishop of Trikala, unnerved no doubt by the vulnerability of his authority on visits. Today the ropes are used only for carrying up supplies and building materials.

From Varlaám a path shortcuts the road approach to **Méga Metéoron**. This, always the grandest of the monasteries, is also the highest – built on the 'Broad Rock' 550m above the surrounding ground. It had extensive privileges and held jurisdiction over the area for several centuries; in a fine eighteenth-century engraving (displayed in the museum) it is depicted literally towering above the others. Its *katholikón* is certainly the most magnificent, a beautiful cross-in-square church surmounted by a lofty dome. It, too, was rebuilt in the sixteenth century; the original chapel, constructed by Athanasios and Ioasaph, forms just the *hieron*, the sanctuary behind the *iconostasis*, or altar screen. The other monastery rooms comprise a vast, arched cluster of buildings. The refectory houses a **museum**, featuring a number of exquisite carved-wood crosses, and the ancient domed and smoke-blackened kitchen can also be visited. But the Mega Metéoron's real power lies in its position, and in the mystery of how Athanassios ever got up on to the rock.

If you are visiting the valley in midsummer, you may, by this point, be impressed by the buildings but depressed by the crowds – which blur much of the wild, spiritual romance of the valley. The remaining monasteries, on the 'south loop' are less visited. However, for a real escape, it's worth taking the path leading north from just past the Varlaám/Great Meteora fork. This will bring you out, in around half an hour's walk, at the abandoned four-teenth-century monastery of **Ipapandí**, a cave containing a small church.

Returning to the main branch it's about two hours' walk to **Ayía Triádha** (Holy Trinity), approached up 130 steps carved into a tunnel in the rock. You emerge into a light and airy cloister where the monks are hard at work building and renovating. There is less to be seen than elsewhere (the tour buses, mercifully, do not stop) and most of the frescoes in the *Katholikón* are black with age (donations are appreciated towards their resto-ration). All told, though, a visit here is a refreshing change, for the life of the place, under the head resident monk (not yet an abbot), remains essen-tially monastic; in the near future it may even be possible for men to stay the night.

Although Ayía Triádha teeters above a deep ravine and the little garden ends in a precipitous drop, nevertheless there is a **track** at the bottom of the monastery's steps back to Kalambáka. This is about 3km in length, saving a long trudge back around the circuit, though it is not the easiest going, includ-ing a crawl under a huge stone. After a rainstorm, it is probably not worth attempting.

Áyios Stéfanos, the last and easternmost of the monasteries, is a further forty minutes' walk from Ayía Triádha, appearing suddenly at a bend in the road. Again it is active, occupied this time by nuns, though the buildings are a little disappointing. The *katholikón* is whitewashed and simple, while the rock on which it stands is spanned by a bridge from the road. Its view, of course, is amazing – like every turn and twist of this valley – but if you're pushed for time it's the obvious one to leave out.

On from Kalambáka

West from Kalambáka runs one of the most dramatic roads in Greece, the **Katára Pass** across the Píndhos mountains to MÉTSOVO and IOÁNNINA. This route, taking you into northern Epirus, is covered at the beginning of the next chapter.

North from Kalambáka a road leads into Macedonia, through GREVENÁ and then forks – north to KASTORIÁ, or east to KOZÁNI, VÉRIA and THESSALONÍKI (see *Chapter Five*). The **Grevená road**, despite its uncertain appearance on most maps is quite reasonable; its only drawback is that there's just one daily bus (mid-morning) and not a lot of other transport. Quite a scenic route, it edges through the Hásia and Voúrinos mountains, though without a great deal of intrinsic interest. **GREVENÁ**, once a Klephtic stronghold against the Turks, is now just another dull concrete town; and **KOZÁNI** is no less forgettable – you'll pause just long enough to catch onward buses. If you've time or your own transport, consider pausing at **SIÁTISTA**, just above the Thessalian frontier and the point where the road splits for Kozáni or Kastoriá. This small town, a fur centre like Kastoriá, has good, if also mostly semi-ruinous, eighteenth-century Macedonian mansions, and a small museum. One of the mansions has recently been converted to a C-class **hotel**, the *Arhondikon* (☎0465/21-298).

travel details

BUSES

Buses detailed have similar frequency in each direction, so entries are given just once; for reference check under both starting-point and destination.

Connections with Athens Thíva/Livádhia (hourly; 1½ hr./2 hr. 10 min.); Delphi (4-6 daily; 3½ hr.); Lamía (hourly; 3 hr. 15min.); Karpeníssi (3 daily; 6hr.); Vólos (9 daily; 5 hr.); Lárissa (6 daily; 5 hr.); Tríkala (8 daily; 5 hr. 15).

From Elefsína Thíva [Thebes] (2 daily; 1½ hr.).

From Thíva Livádhia (hourly; 1 hr.); Halkídha (2 daily; 1 hr. 20 min.).

From Livádhia Aráhova/Delphi (7 daily; 40 min./1 hr.); Dhístomo, for Óssios Loukás (10 daily; 45 min.); Óssios Loukás, direct (daily at 1.30pm; 1 hr.).

From Delphi Itéa (6 daily; 30 min.); Ámfissa (4 daily; 40 min.); Náfpaktos (5 daily – not direct; 2 hr. 30 min.);

From Itéa Galaxídhi/Náfpaktos (5 daily; 1 hr. 10 min./2 hr.).

From Náfpaktos City bus to Andírio for most connections.

From Andírio Messolóngi/Agrínio (12 daily; 1½ hr.).

From Ámfissa Lamía (3-4 daily; 2 hr. 30 min.).

From Lamía Karpeníssi (1 daily; 5 hr.); Vólos (2 daily; 3 hr.); Lárissa (4 daily; 3 hr. 30 min.); Tríkala, via Kardhítsa (4 daily; 3 hr.).

From Karpeníssi Agrínio (1 daily; 5 hr.).

From Vólos Lárissa (hourly; 1½ hr.); Tríkala (4 daily; 2½ hr.); Thessaloníki (4 daily; 3 hr. 20 min.); Portariá/Makrinítsa (9 daily; 40 min./50 min.);

Zagorá (4 daily; 1 hr. 40 min.); Platanía (2 daily; 2 hr.).

From Lárissa Stómio (3 daily; 1 hr. 25); Litóhoro junction (almost hourly; 1 hr. 45); Tríkala (every half hour; 1 hr. 25); Kalambáka (hourly; 30 min.).

From Tríkala Kalambáka (hourly; 30 min.); Kalambáka-Métsovo-Ioánnina (4 daily; 30 min./2 hr./4 hr.); Kalmbáka-Grevená (1 daily; 30 min./2 hr.).

From Kalambáka Métsovo/Ioánnina (3 daily; 1½ hr./3½ hr.); Grevená (daily; 1½ hr.).

TRAINS

Athens-Thíva-Livádhia-Lianokládhi (Lamía)-Lárissa

9 trains daily, in each direction.
Approximate journey times:
Athens-Thíva (1 hr. 20 min.–1½ hr.)
Thíva-Livádhia (30–35 min.)
Livádhia-Lianokládhi (1 hr. 10 min.–1 hr. 25 min.)
Lianokládhi-Lárissa (3 hr.–3 hr. 20 min.).

Lárissa–Kateríni–Thessaloníki 6 daily in each direction.
Approximate journey times:
Lárissa-Kateríni (1 hr. 10 min.)
Kateríni-Thessaloníki (1 hr. 10 min.).

Vólos-Lárissa-Platamónas-Litóhoro-Kateríni-Thessaloníki 3 daily in each direction.
Approximate journey times:
Vólos-Lárissa (1 hr. 20 min.)
Lárissa-Platamónas (1 hr.)
Platamónas-Litóhoro (25 min.)
Litóhoro-Kateríni (20 min.)
Kateríni-Thessaloníki (1 hr. 50 min.).

Lárissa-Vólos 13 daily in each direction (1 hr.).

Vólos-Fársala-Kardhítsa-Tríkala-Kalambáka
3 daily in each direction.
Approximate journey times:
Vólos-Farsála (1 hr. 40 min.)
Farsála-Kardhítsa (1½ hr.)
Kardhítsa-Tríkala (35 min.)
Tríkala-Kalambáka (35 min.).

Athens-Halkídha Almost hourly (1 hr. 35 min.).

FERRIES

From Áyios Konstantínos Daily to Skíathos and Skópelos (occasionally continuing to Alónissos); weekly (usually Mon.) to Áyios Efstrátios, Límnos and Kavála – ☎01/417-8084 for information.

From Vólos 2-4 daily for Skíathos and Skópelos, at least one continuing to Alónissos – information ☎01/417-8084; weekly (usually Sat. evening) to Tartous, Syria.

From Platániá (Pílion) Daily kaíki to Koukounariés, Skíathos (summer only).

To Évvia Arkítsa-Loutrá Edhipsoú (hourly, last at 11pm; 50 min.); Glífa-Ayiókambos (7 daily, last at 6pm; 30 min.).

Across the Gulf of Kórinthos Andírio-Río (every 20 min., 30 min. at night; 20 min.); Áyios Nikólaos-Éyio (3 times daily, summer only; 35 min.).

HYDROFOILS

'Flying Dolphins' run between the following ports:

From Áyios Konstantínos 2 daily in eason to Skíathos, Skópelos and Alónissos.

From Vólos 2-4 daily to Skíathos and Skópelos, with at least one continuing to Alónissos; last departure generally 7pm (1pm on Sunday).

For details of services, which vary drastically with season, contact local agents or the 'Flying Dolphins' main office in Pireás (Themistokléous 8; ☎01/452-7107).

FLIGHTS

From Lárissa Athens (4 weekly); Thessaloníki (2 weekly).

CHAPTER FOUR

EPIRUS AND THE WEST

Epirus (more correctly, *Ípiros*) has the strongest regional identity in mainland Greece. It owes this character to its mountains: the rugged peaks and passes, forested ravines, and turbulent rivers of the **Píndhos** (Pindus) **range.** They have protected and isolated it from outside influence and interference, securing it a large measure of autonomy even under Turkish rule.

Because of this isolation the region's role in Greek affairs was peripheral in ancient times. There are just two archaeological sites of importance; both of them oracles both chosen for their end-of-the-world isolation. At **Dodona**, the sanctuary includes a spectacular Classical theatre, at **Ephyra**, the weird remains of a Necromanteion, or 'Oracle of the Dead', touted by the ancients as the gateway of Hades.

In more recent times, **Lord Byron** has been the region's greatest publicist. Visiting in 1809 when the tyrannical ruler Ali Pasha was at the height of his power, Byron's tales of passionate intrigue, fierce-eyed brigandage, and colourful braggadocio came just at the right moment to send a frisson of horror down romantic western spines. The poet later, of course, distinguished himself in the southern extension of the region – the tongue-twistingly-named province of **Étolo-Akarnanía** – by taking command of the Greek War of Independence forces, and dying, at Messolóngi.

Despite eventual Greek victory in the War of Independence, however, the Turks remained in Epirus, to be ousted finally only in 1913. A disputed frontier territory through the nineteenth century, the region never recovered its former prosperity. When the Italians invaded in 1940, followed by the Germans in 1941, its mountain fastnesses became first the stronghold of the Resistance, then a battleground for rival political factions, and finally, after 1946, the chief bastion of the Communist Democratic Army in the **Civil War**. The events of this period – see 'The Civil War in Epirus', overpage – are among the saddest of modern Greek history, and continue to reverberate today.

However, the **mountains** are still the place to head for in Epirus. The people are the friendliest and most hospitable you could find. Many aspects of the traditional way of life are still in force. Latinate-speaking Vlach* and Doric-speaking Sarakatsan shepherds still bring their flocks to the high mountain pastures in summer. Bears raid the cherry trees in springtime and wolves keep a hungry eye out for stray ewes.

---

*For some background on **the Vlachs**, see 'The Greek Minorities' in *Contexts*.

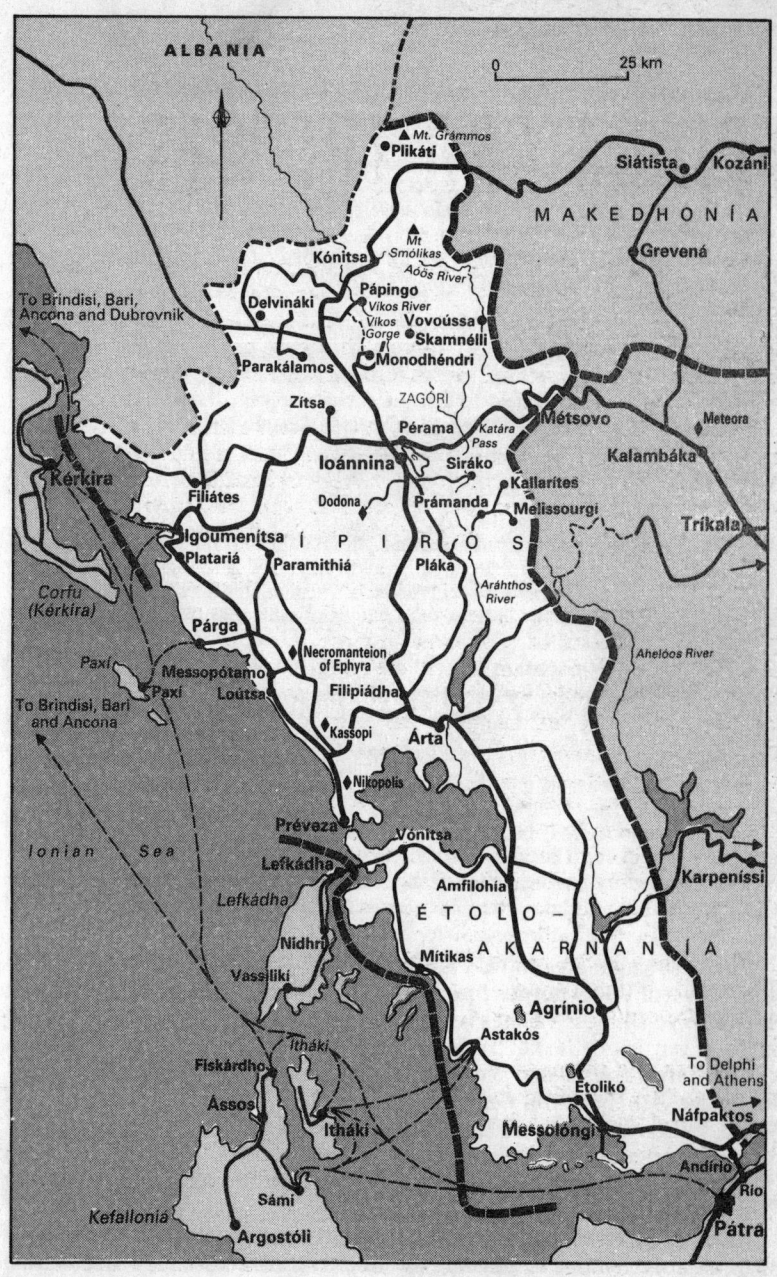

The Civil War in Epirus

The vicissitudes of the **Civil War** dashed any hopes of a reasonable existence in the mountains. Victims of reprisals by one side or the other, villagers fled to safety in cities, and many never returned. Wherever you go in the back country you'll hear people talk of these times. Some blame the Communists, others the Nationalists; some think the People's Courts and other aspects of the Communist wartime administration were the greatest thing they ever witnessed; others say they were merely an excuse for settling private scores (witness Nicholas Gage's *Eleni* – see 'Books' in *Contexts*). People of all persuasions blame the British: 'They set us at each other's throats', they say, and with much justice.

Over the last decade, many men who fought as communists in ELAS, either as volunteers or conscripts, have returned to their villages – some of them after twenty or thirty years of exile in the USSR and eastern bloc countries. You see them sitting at café tables drinking and chatting with their former sworn enemies. Others were carried off as children to Albania, and worked in labour camps before being distributed to various east European states, where, as they readily admit, they received an excellent education as engineers, doctors, or other skilled workers. Interestingly, even the bitterest often say they led better, more fulfilling lives in exile than since their homecoming.

The right claim that this *pedhomázema* – the roundup of children – was a cynical and merciless ploy to train up an army of dedicated revolutionaries for the future. The left retort that it was a prudent evacuation of noncombatants from a war zone. Which merely illustrates the futility of arguments over who committed more atrocities.

One thing, however, is certain. The Right won, with the backing of the British and, more especially, the Americans. They used that victory to maintain a thoroughly undemocratic and vengeful regime for the best part of the following quarter century. Many Epirot villagers, regardless of political conviction, believe that the poverty and backwardness in which their communities have remained was a deliberate punishment for being part of Communist-held territory during the civil war. They were constantly harassed by the police, who controlled the issue of all sorts of licences and permits needed to find work, travel, put your kids in school, run a business and so forth. Only, really, in the 1980s have things changed, and the past begun to be treated as another, and separate, age.

The best single area to visit is around **Mts. Gamíla** and **Smólikas**, with the **Aóös** and **Víkos gorges** to walk and the splendid **villages of the Zagóri**. Buses serve all these villages regularly, if not daily, though walking is surely the best way to get the full flavour of the place. **Hiking routes** are detailed in the text; others, expanded and with fuller maps, are to be found in the specialist guides (see 'Books' in *Contexts*). Most of the routes are arduous and lonesome, rather than difficult. But all the same this is high mountain country, with its own rather unpredictable microclimate, so you shouldn't set off on the longer, more ambitious itineraries unless you are already familiar with basic trekking skills.

Among less strenuous travelling highlights are some of the roads themselves – above all that negotiating the **Katára pass** across the Píndhos from Kalambáka to Ioánnina. En route is **Métsovo**, perhaps the easiest location for a taste of mountain life, though sadly increasingly commercialised of late. **Ioánnina**, Ali Pasha's capital, is a town of some character, with its island and lake, and the main transport hub for trips into the Zagóri. Other than **Árta**, prettily set and with some fine Byzantine churches, there are few other urban attractions.

The coast, both in Epirus and Étolo-Akarnanía, is in general disappointing. **Igoumenítsa** is a useful ferry terminal for Corfu and for routes to Italy and Yugoslavia, but will win few admirers. **Párga**, the major Epirot resort, has been developed beyond its capacity. To the south, you enter a low, marshy landscape of lakes and land-locked gulfs – of interest only to the birdwatcher. For beach escapes in this part of the world you need islands, fortunately close at hand in the Ionian group – Lefkádha is actually connected to the mainland by a movable bridge.

THE PÍNDHOS

Even if you have no plans to go hiking, the **Píndhos range** deserves a few days' detour. The remoteness and traditional nature of life, the air, the peaks – all constitute a Greece unseen by most tourists.

The best of the main **routes** is Kalambáka–Métsovo–Ioánnina. If you are coming from central Greece, this is a perfect introduction to Epirus; arriving by ferry at Igoumenítsa, it's quite the most attractive route into the mainland.

Walkers will want to make directly for **Ioánnina**, to the north of which the excitements begin. They range from relatively easy day-walks, such as the increasingly trodden **Víkos gorge**, to the most peak-oriented ramblings you can devise.

The Katára pass: Kalambáka to Métsovo and Ioánnina

West of Kalambáka, the **Katára pass** cuts across the central range of the Píndhos to link Thessaly and Epirus. The route, the only motor road that is kept open year-round, is one of the most spectacular in the country – worth taking for the sake of the journey alone. It is also, in fact, the shortest east–west crossing in Greece, though distances here are deceptive: the road switchbacks and zigzags through folds in the enormous peaks, rising to 1705m around Métsovo, and from November to March the snowline must be crossed.

Three buses daily cover the route, starting/ending in Tríkala and Ioánnina. If you're driving, allow half a day for the journey from KALAMBÁKA to IOANNINA (114km), and in winter check on conditions before setting out. Hitching from Kalambáka, take a lift only if it's going through to Ioánnina or Métsovo, for there's little but mountain forest in between.

Métsovo

MÉTSOVO stands almost astride the Katára pass, a high mountain village built on two sides of a ravine and encircled by a mighty range of peaks. It is a startling site, matched, albeit in a slightly showcase way, by the village's traditional architecture and life. Immediately below the Ioánnina road begin the first of its eighteenth- and nineteenth-century stone houses with their wooden balconies and quarried roof slates. They wind down the ravine along an intricate network of rock-paved paths to the main *platía*, where the old men loiter, magnificent in full traditional dress, from flat black caps to pompommed feet; the women, enveloped in rich blue weave, have a rougher attire.

If you arrive outside of the main summer season, and if you stay overnight and take the time to walk in the valley, the village can seem magical. Through the summer, however, your experience may not be so positive. Métsovo has become a favorite of the coach trips, and its beauty veers uneasily towards the artificial and 'quaint'. Souvenir shops selling 'traditional' handicrafts (some of them nowadays imported from Albania) proliferate, while the stone of the mansions is increasingly marred by the ceramic-pink of new construction.

Nonetheless, it seems a shame to pass through Métsovo too speedily, for its mansions are among the finest in Epirus, and its history (and current status) unique. Positioned on the only commercially and militarily viable route across the Píndhos, it won a measure of independence, both political and economic, from the earliest days of the Turkish conquest. These privileges were greatly extended in 1659 by a grateful Turkish vizier, who, restored to the Sultan's favour, wanted to say a proper 'thank you' to the Métsovite shepherd who had hidden and protected him during his disgrace.

As the town grew in prosperity, the Vlachs – who occupy Métsovo and a dozen villages in the Píndhos roundabout – traded their sheep products further and further afield. Metsovite merchants established themselves in Constantinople, Vienna, Venice and elsewhere, and expanded into other businesses. Vlachs played a major role in Balkan haulage, for instance, (mules, of course) and the hotel business – the *caravanserais*, where the mule convoys halted.

Métsovo's present prosperity, and the preservation of its traditions, are largely due to the munificence of Baron Tossitsas, banker scion of a Metsovite family living in Switzerland. He left his colossal fortune to a fund that has financed sawmills, dairy farming and a cottage weaving industry, along with the village museum and its small ski resort north of the Ioánnina road.

The museum comprises the family mansion, the **Arhondíko Tossítsas** (open 8am–1pm and 3–5.30pm; ring for admission). This has been restored to the full glory of its eighteenth-century past, and with its panelled rooms, rugs and fine collection of Epirot crafts and costumes, gives a real sense of the wealth and grandeur of the town of the era. Today the mansion serves also as a handicrafts centre, stocking what must be the most tasteful and finely woven cloth, rugs, and blankets to be found in Greece – in a different class to the standard goods in the village shops. They are expensive, but not outrageously so, considering the quality of the work, all handwoven on household looms.

The Métsovo streets are worth an hour or so's exploration. However, for a glimpse of a more authentic mountain community, walk across to the village's other half, **Anílio** (meaning 'sunless', i.e. north-facing), the hamlet that faces it across the ravine of the Metsovítikos river. A fine old *kalderími*, or cobbled path, joins them, but it's a bit of a gruelling trek down and up and back again. Like Métsovo, its population is Vlach-speaking; and its life is genuinely traditional.

Practicalities

Métsovo has quite a range of **accommodation**, and outside of the ski season you should find little problem in getting a room. The cheapest are the E-class *Athinae* (☎0656/41-217), on the main square, and the (excellent) *Acropolis* (☎0656/41-672), at the top end of town, to the right of the road down from the Kalambáka-Ioánnina road.

For **eating** try *Kryfofolia*, on the main square, near the *Athinae*, or *Barba Takis* (signposted). When catching a **bus** on from the town to Ioánnina or Kalambáka, it's wise to walk up to the main road; not all of them loop down to the village's bus station by the main square.

On towards Ioánnina: the eastern Zagóri

For a taste of wilder, remoter scenery, and a truer, grittier picture of contemporary mountain life, you might consider breaking the journey to Ioánnina. At the HÁNI BALDHOÚMA junction, 32km west of Métsovo, a road heads north along the valley of the Várdhas river and through the predominantly Vlach villages of the **eastern Zagóri**. It's a winding, precipitous dirt road most of the way, but plied by a daily bus from Ioánina. You can pick it up at HÁNI BALDHOÚMA on the Métsovo-Ioánina road around 2pm (check before setting out). It snakes uphill through surprisingly lush country to Greveníti, where forest – black pines, extending virtually all the way to Albania – takes over.

GREVENIÍTI, FLAMBOURÁRI, ELATOHÓRI and the beautiful **MAKRINÓ** (an hour's glorious walk across the ravine) are all Vlach villages. The first three have basic **inns** (*ksenónes*) or rooms and places to eat. All are badly depopulated, never having recovered from wartime destruction by the Germans pursuing Resistance fighters. But what is left of them is very attractive: stone-roofed churches (especially the monastery in Makrinó), vine-shaded terraces, courtyards full of flowers and logs stacked for the winter.

VOVOÚSSA lies right on the Aóös river, its milky green waters spanned by a high-arched fourteenth-century bridge. Either side, wooded ridges rise steeply to the skyline. Just downstream a stretch of riverbank meadow makes an idyllic camping site (turn left off the road on to the old path just past the Vovóussa roadsign) if the thought of bears in the vicinity doesn't alarm you. I found three fresh prints in the riverside mud here, but the locals swear they are timid creatures and avoid contact with humans. Otherwise, there is a large riverside **hotel** in the village, and a couple of *psistariés*; both are open more or less year round.

Though the road continues from VOVOÚSSA to PERIVÓLI and on to GREVENÁ, the Ioánnina bus goes no further. You'd have to get yourself to Perivóli (uninhabited from November to May) to pick up the Grevená buses, or – if you're prepared for some real wilderness hiking through beautiful but totally uninhabited land – strike north to Dhístrato for buses to Kónitsa.

Ioánnina

Coming from Métsovo, you approach **IOÁNNINA** through more spectacular folds of the Píndhos, emerging high above the great lake of Pamvótis. The town, once the capital of Ali Pasha, stands upon its edge, a rocky promontory jutting out into the water, its fortifications punctuated by towers and minarets as if to declare its history. For from this base Ali, 'the Lion of Ioannina', carved from the Turks a kingdom encompassing much of western Greece, an act of contemptuous rebellion that portended wider defiance in the Greeks' own War of Independence.

Ali Pasha's capital

The great figure in Ioánninan and Epirot history, Ali Pasha was a distinctly ambivalent 'heroic rebel'. His only consistent policy was that of ambition and self-interest, and as frequent as his attacks on the Turkish Porte were his acts of appalling and vindictive savagery against his Greek subjects.

He was born in 1741 in Albania and rose to power under Turkish patronage, being made Pasha of Tríkala in reward for his efforts in the Sultan's war against Austria. His ambitions, however, were of a grander order and that same year, 1788, he seized Ioánnina, an important town since the thirteenth century and with a population of 30,000 – probably the largest in Greece at the time. Paying sporadic and usually token tribute to the Sultan, he operated from this power-base for the next 33 years, allying in turn and as the moment suited him with the British, French and Turks.

In 1809, when his dependence upon the Porte was nominal, Ali was visited by the young **Lord Byron**, whom he overwhelmed with hospitality and attention. Byron, impressed for his part with the rebel's daring and stature, and the lively revival of Greek culture in Ioannina (which, he wrote, was 'superior in wealth, refinement and learning' to any town in Greece), commemorated the meeting in *Childe Harold*. The portrait that he draws, however, is an ambiguous one, well aware that there are 'deeds that lurk beneath' the Pasha's splendid court and deceptively mild countenance which 'stain him with disgrace'.

In a letter to his mother Byron was still more explicit, concluding that 'His highness is a remorseless tyrant, guilty of the most horrible cruelties, very brave, so good a general that they call him the Mahometan Buonaparte . . . but as barbarous as he is successful, roasting rebels, etc, etc'. Of the rebels, the most illustrious was Katsandonis the Klepht, whom Ali captured wracked by smallpox in a cave in the Ágrafa mountains. He imprisoned the unfortunate wretch in a soaking lakeside dungeon, and finally executed him by breaking his bones in public with a sledgehammer.

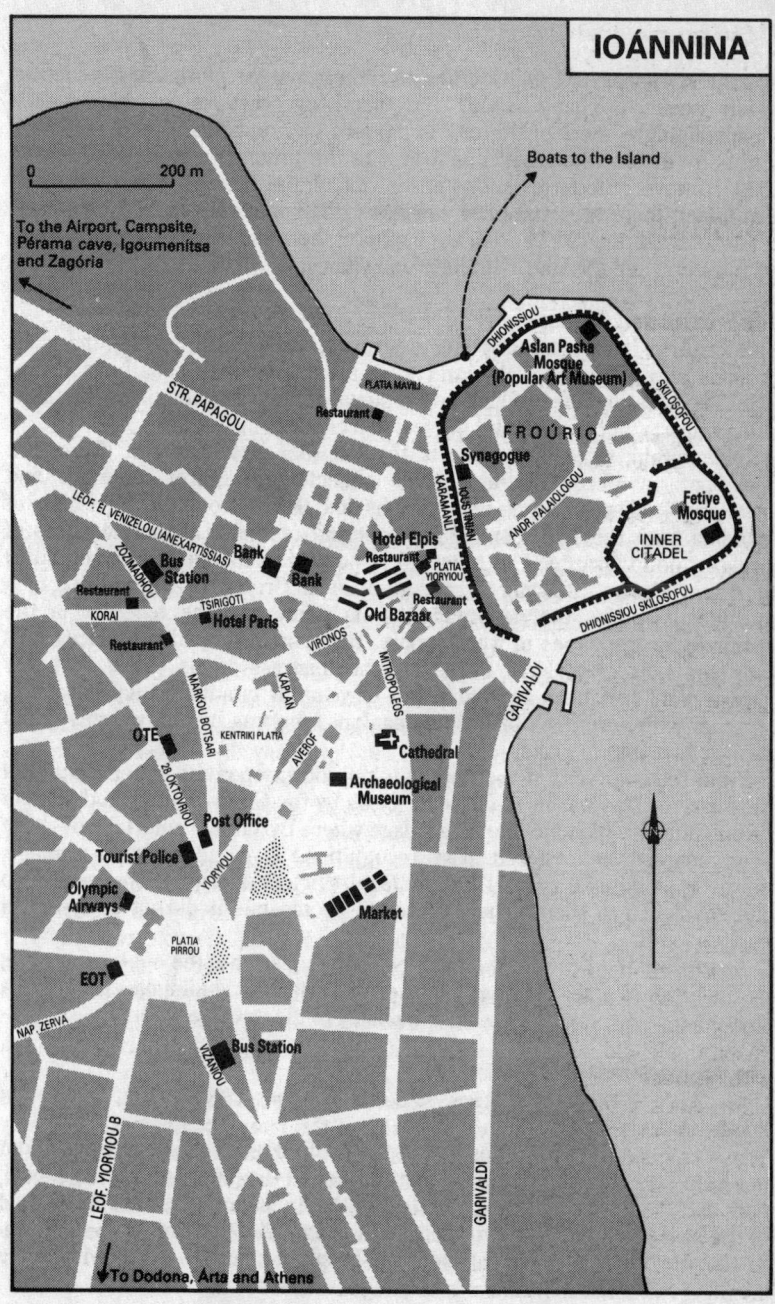

IOÁNNINA

0   200 m

To the Airport, Campsite,
Pérama cave, Igoumenítsa
and Zagória

Boats to the Island

STR PAPAGOU

PLATIA MAVILI

Restaurant

DHIONISSIOU

Aslan Pasha
Mosque
(Popular Art Museum)

FROÚRIO

SKILOSOFOU

LEOF. EL VENIZELOU (ANEXARTISSIAS)

Synagogue

KARAMANLI

TSIRISI NIKOLI

ANDR. PALAIOLOGOU

Fetiye
Mosque

ZOSIMADOU

Bank

Bus
Station

Hotel Elpis

Restaurant

PLATIA
YIORYIOU

INNER
CITADEL

Restaurant

KORAI

TSIRIGOTI

Bank

Restaurant

Hotel Paris

Old Bazaar

Restaurant

VIRONOS

DHIONISSIOU SKILOSOFOU

MARKOU BOTSARI

KAPLAN

MITROPOLEOS

GARIVALDI

OTE

KENTRIKI PLATÍA

AVEROF

Cathedral

28 OKTOVRIOU

Post Office

Archaeological
Museum

YIORYIOU

Tourist Police

Olympic
Airways

PLATIA
PIRROU

Market

EOT

NAP ZERVA

VIZANDOU

Bus Station

LEOF. YIORYIOU B

GARIVALDI

To Dodone, Árta and Athens

The Town

It is the stories of Ali Pasha's cruelties rather than the glories of his success which seem to hang about the surviving vestiges of his capital. Disappointingly, most of the city is modern and undistinguished – in itself testimony to Ali, who burnt much of it to the ground when under siege in 1820. However, the fortifications of his citadel, the Froúrio, survive more or less intact; there are crumbling mosques, their minarets capped by storks' nests, to evoke the old Turkish atmosphere; there's an excellent archaeological museum; and the lake, with its island village, is a delight.

The Froúrio and Bazaar

The **Froúrio** is an obvious point to stroll towards. In its heyday the walls dropped abruptly to the lake, and were moated on their (south) landward side. The moat has been filled, and a quayside now extends below the lakeside ramparts, but there is still the feel of a citadel.

Once within, signs direct you to the **Popular Art Museum** (Mon.–Fri. 8am–3pm), a splendidly ramshackle collection of Epirot costumes and jewellery. It displays, too, photographs and relics from the liberation of Ioánnina from the Turks in 1913, a sobering reminder of the closeness of foreign rule in Greece. The museum is housed in the well-preserved **Jami of Aslan Pasha**, allowing a rare glimpse in Greece of the interior of a mosque; it retains the decoration on its dome and the recesses in the vestibule for the shoes of worshippers. Here, in 1801, tradition places Ali's rape and murder of Kyra Phrosyne, the mistress of his eldest son. Her 'provocation' had been to refuse the 62-year-old tyrant's sexual advances; together with seventeen of her companions, she was bound, weighted, and thrown alive into the lake.

From the courtyard of the Jami you look down upon the **inner citadel** of the fortress. This was used for some years by the Greek military and most of its buildings – which include Ali's palace where Byron was entertained – have been adapted or restored past recognition. A circular tower remains, however, along with the old **Fetiye Jami** (Victory Mosque), now sealed up and consigned to silent decay. Close by the mosque is purported to be Ali Pasha's tomb.

Apart from the Froúrio, the most enjoyable quarter is the old **bazaar** area, by the citadel's gate. This has a cluster of Turkish-era buildings, as well as a scattering of silversmiths – once a mainstay of the town's economy.

The Archaeological Museum

Open daily 8.45am–3pm, Sun. 9.30am–2.30pm; closed Tues.; admission 200dr, students 100dr.

The actual centre of town lies just to the south of the bazaar, grouped about the Kentrikí Platía and the Platía Pírrou. Just off the latter, set beside a small park and the town's modern cathedral, is the **Archaeological Museum**, one of the best you'll find in the provinces. It is a must if you are planning a visit to the theatre and oracle of Dodona. Displayed here – along with some exceptional crafted bronze seals – are a fascinating collection of lead tablets inscribed with questions to the Oracle. Memorable too, though unlabelled in the corner by the door, is an object that looks like an anchor chain: this is the windlass mechanism from the extraordinary Necromanteion of Ephyra (see p.284).

Nissí and Lake Pamvótis

The island of **Nissí**, on the sadly polluted Lake Pamvótis, is connected by half-hourly motor-launches (5am-11pm) from the quay northwest of the Froúrio. Its village, founded in the sixteenth century by refugees from the Máni in the Peloponnese, is flanked by a beautiful group of four monasteries, providing perfect focus for an afternoon's visit. Stay on through the evening and you can eat at a string of restaurants on the waterfront, watching superb sunsets over the encircling reed-beds.

The **Monastery of Pantelímon**, just to the east of the village, is perhaps the most dramatic of Ioánnina's Ali Pasha sites. In January 1822, he was assassinated here, his hiding place having been revealed to the Turks, who had finally lost patience with the wayward ruler. Trapped in his rooms on the upper storey, he was shot from the floor below. The fateful bullet holes in the floorboards form the centrepiece of a small museum to the tyrant, along with a few prints and knick-knacks like Ali's splendid hubble-bubble. Pantelímon stands a little to the east of the village.

South and west of the village are three other **monasteries**: Áyios Nikólaos Filanthropinoú, Stratigopoúlou and Panayías. They are signposted and stand within a few hundred yards of one another along a lovely treeswept lane; each is maintained by a handful of nuns, who allow brief visits (ring for admission). The monasteries are attractively situated, with pleasant courtyards, though visits essentially consist of being shown the main chapel, or *katholikón*. All of these feature frescoes, in various stages of decay or preservation. The finest are those of **Áyios Nikólaos**, portraying some extraordinarily bloody and graphic seventeenth-century scenes of early Christian martyrdoms. Beyond the monasteries the path loops around the island to bring you out near Pantelímon.

The Pérama Caves

Five kilometres north of Ioánnina, the village of PÉRAMA boasts what are reputed to be Greece's largest **caves**. They were discovered during the last war by a guerrilla in hiding from the Germans and are indeed immense, extending and echoing for kilometres beneath a low hill.

Tours (45 min.) are given virtually all day in summer, and until around 4pm the rest of the year. They're refreshingly low-key, the guide even encouraging you to tap the stalagmites to produce bell tones, something frowned upon in most other visitable caves.

To reach the village, take a #8 blue city bus from Platía Eleftheríou; the caves are a short walk inland from the bus stop.

The road splits shortly after Pérama: one fork leading north to the mountain village of DHRÍSKOS, with superb views down over Ioánnina and the lake; the other circling the lake, with a beachside café midway around. With a car it's a very pleasant route.

Ioánnina practicalities

If you arrive early enough in the day, it is worth heading straight out to the **island**, whose two inns offer the most attractive (and the best-value) **accommodation** available. The best is run by the Della family; enquire at the store a short way inland from the quay (☎0651/25-481). This generally has rooms, although at weekends or in summer you may find them taken by trekking groups en route to the Píndhos. *Pension Varvara* (☎0651/24-396), next door, is a good alternative.

In the town most cheap lodging is in the area between the bazaar and the Zozimádhou bus station. Best of the lot is the D-class *Elpis* (Neoptolémou 10; ☎0651/25-323), within sight of the old town walls; a second choice is the co-managed *Paris/Pandohio Agapi* (Tsirigóti 6; ☎0651/20-541); two others, a little pricier, and a lot noisier, are sited on the Kéntriki Platía. For the really budget-minded, there are also a few rather grim-looking *pandohía* (workers' hostels) along Tsirigóti.

Camping, unusually for a city, provides an attractive alternative. *Camping Limnopoulo* is just 2km out of town, on the road to Pérama; connections by bus #8, as for Pérama above.

For **meals**, the island is again the best location with its village tavernas; whether you risk lake specialities like eel (*héli*), crayfish (*karavídhes*), trout (*péstrofa*), *glínia* (a local fish) and frogs' legs, though, is a hard choice – the waters are none too sanitary. Whatever, the lakeside tavernas have the finest sites. Back in town, more standard fare can be found in the bazaar near the Froúrio gate; try the *Pantheon* restaurant, or for grills an unnamed *psistariá* opposite the old walls, halfway around the bend to the *Hotel Elpis*. At lunchtimes there's another excellent *psistariá* on Zozimádhou, 300m above the bus station and just below the *Hotel Egnatia*. Ioánnina is also home to the *bougatza* (custard-tarts), fresh at breakfast time from *Sakellaríou* at Avéróf 3.

In July and August, the town provides a focus for the **Epirotika festival**, which includes music and theatre performances, plus the odd cultural exhibition. Some years there are one or two performances of Classical drama at the ancient theatre of Dodona (see below). Most of the events, however, take place in a hillside theatre, known as Frontzos, just outside the town. There is also a pleasant summer restaurant at Frontzos, with fine views down to the town and lake.

Arriving at, or leaving, Ioánnina, you'll find yourself at one of two **bus terminals**. The main station is at Zozimádhou 4, serving most points north and west: Métsovo/Kalambáka, Igoumenítsa, Kónitsa and the villages of the Zagoría. A smaller terminal at Vizantíou 28 connects Árta, Préveza, Dodona and all villages in the south or east parts of Epirus. It is advisable, especially before weekends, to buy tickets the day before. If you're confused by the chaos – there are two to three schedule placards and twice that many ticket windows at each station – check out times and departure points at the friendly **EOT** office or at the **Tourist Police**.

For locations of other useful services – the **OTE**, **post office**, and **banks** – see the map. Ioánnina **airport** is on the Pérama road, again served by bus #8.

Dodona

There is a certain romantic egocentricity in being a tourist which demands that a site should not only be beautiful beyond one's expectations but should also be a personal and private discovery. If you ever feel like this go to **DODONA**, 22km southwest of Ioánnina. Here in a wildly mountainous and once-isolated region lie the ruins of the Oracle of Zeus – the oldest in Greece – dominated by a vast and elegant theatre which was meticulously restored at the end of the last century.

'Wintry Dodona' was already known to Homer but **the oracle** is probably far older; the worship of Zeus and of the sacred oak tree at Dodona seems to have been connected with the first Hellenic tribes who arrived in Epirus around 1900 B.C. Its origins are shadowy. Herodotus gives an enigmatic story about the arrival of a dove from Egyptian Thebes which settled in an oak tree and ordered a place of divination to be made. Significantly the word *peleiae* meant both dove and old woman so it's possible that the legend Herodotus heard refers to an original priestess – possibly captured from the East and having some knowledge or practice of divination. The oak tree, stamped on the ancient coins of the area, was central to the cult. Herodotus recorded that the oracle spoke through the rustling of its leaves in sounds amplified by copper vessels suspended from its branches. These would then be interpreted by frenzied priestesses and strange priests who slept on the ground and never washed their feet.

Many oracular inscriptions were found scattered around the site when it was excavated in 1952. Now displayed in Ioánnina's archaeological museum, they give you a good idea of the personal realm of the oracle's influence in the years after it had been eclipsed by Delphi. More interestingly, they also offer a glimpse of the fears and inadequacies that motivated the pilgrims of the age to journey here, asking such everyday domestic questions as: 'Am I her children's father?' and, memorably, 'Has Pleistos stolen the wool from my mattress?'

The Theatre and Site
Open 7.30am–7.30pm, Sun. 10am–6pm in summer; winter 9am–5pm.
Entering the site through the outline of a third-century B.C. **Stadium**, you are immediately confronted by the massive western retaining wall of the **Theatre**. One of the largest on the Greek mainland and rivalled only by Argos and Megalopolis, it was built during the time of Pyrrhus (297–272 B.C.). Later, the Romans made adaptations necessary for their blood sports, building a protective wall over the lower seating and also a drainage channel, cut in a horseshoe shape around the *orchestra*.

The theatre is used annually for ancient drama performances in the *Epirotika* festival (see Ioánnina 'Practicalities'), which must be terrific. For this is one of the most glorious settings in Greece; the seats face out across a green, silent valley to the slopes of Mount Tomaros like one peak challenging another.

At the top of the *cavea*, or auditorium, a grand entrance gate leads into the **Acropolis**, an overgrown and largely unexcavated area. The foundations of its walls, mostly Hellenistic, are a remarkable four to five metres wide.

Beside the theatre, and tiered uncharacteristically against the same slope, are the foundations of a **Bouleuterion** (council house), beyond which lie the complex ruins of the **Sanctuary of Zeus**, site of the ancient oracle.

There was no temple at all in the sanctuary until the end of the fifth century B.C. Worship centred upon the Sacred Oak, within which the god was thought to dwell, standing alone within a circle of votive tripods and cauldrons. Building began modestly with a small, stone temple precinct, though by the time of Pyrrus this enclosure was made of Ionic colonnades. In 219 B.C. the Sacred House was sacked by the Aetolians and a larger temple was rebuilt with a monumental *propylaion*. This survived until the fourth century, when the oak tree was hacked down by Christian reformists.

It is the remains of the later precinct that can be seen today. They are easily distinguishable by an oak planted at the centre by a reverent archaeologist. Remains of an early Christian **Basilica**, constructed over a Sanctuary of Herakles, are also prominent nearby.

Access

Few people make the detour to Dodona so the site, and DODHÓNI the little village to the west of it, are completely unspoilt.

Transport, however, is accordingly sparse, with only two buses a day from Ioannina: at 6am (8am on Sunday) and 2pm. Hitching back from the site should be feasible in summer, or a round trip by taxi from Ioánnina with an hour at the site can be negotiated for about 2000dr. Alternatively, you could always stay the night here. There are some lovely spots to camp, a friendly if basic taverna in the village, and a tiny B-class **pension** at the site, the *Xenia Andromachi* (☎0651/91-196; doubles 2400-3000dr).

Villages of the south Píndhos

Most hikers arriving at Ioánnina have their sights firmly set to the north – on the Víkos gorge and the Zagória villages. If you're feeling adventurous, however, and are not too particular about where you sleep or what you eat, the villages of the **south Píndhos** provide an interesting alternative. A daily 2pm bus from Ioánnina (Zozimádhou station) will take you southeast to Ágnanda, Prámanda and other remote villages on the beetling flanks of the Athamánia range: a bare ridge of three mountains, plainly visible from Ioánnina. There are no special sights, but you'll get a solid, undiluted experience of Epirot life.

Many of the villages can also be approached from the south. Buses run a couple of times daily in either direction along the secondary road between Árta and Ioánnina stopping at PLÁKA (with a fine bridge over the

Arakhthós), and a schoolbus continues along the sideroad east into the mountains as far as MELISSOURGÍ.

Prámanda and Melissourgí

Twelve kilometres into the mountains from Pláka, ÁGNANDA is the first village of any size but heavily damaged in the last war, it's not particularly attractive, nor does it have reliable accommodation. Better to continue on to **PRÁMANDA**, last village on the Ioánnina provincial bus routes, where there's a rather primitive *ksenónas* and a couple of *psistariés*. The village itself, while no more distinguished architecturally than Ágnanda, at least enjoys a wonderful setting, strewn across several ridges, dominated by Mt. Kakardhítsa behind, and commanding fine views of the Kallaritikós valley. Nearby there is a huge cave, inhabited in Neolithic times; ask any villager for directions.

MELISSOURGÍ, 6km to the southeast, is more rewarding, having escaped damage during the war. Its buildings and large church are a grand if sombre unity in traditional grey schist. There is one tiny inn – not to be counted on in midsummer, when it is likely to be booked by holidaying village relatives – and a taverna. But more importantly Melissourgí is the jump-off point for rambles on the **Kostelláta plateau** to the south. This upland separates 2429-metre Kakardhítsa, which looms sheer and above the village from the more pyramidal Tzoumérka (2399m); you can cross these high pastures, heading south, in a day and a half. There are intermittent *stánes*, or summer sheepfolds, if you need water or directions. You would descend to either Theodhorianá or Dhrossopiyí, both at the edge of the Ahelóös river basin and both with daily buses to Árta.

Kípina, Kallarítes and Siráko

If you instead bear north from Pláka, you're reliant on the school bus, or your own footpower, to continue up the Kallaritikos valley. The bus runs as far as the hamlet of **KÍPINA**, with its nearby **Monastery**, founded in 1381 and hanging like a martin's nest from the cliff face.

Beyond this point a wonderful *kalderími* climbs the 500m up to **KALLARÍTES**, perched superbly above the upper reaches of its eponymous river. One of the southernmost Vlach settlements in the Pindhos, this depleted village was a veritable El Dorado until the close of the last century. Fame and fortune were based on its specialisation in gold- and silver-smithing, and even today the smiths of Ioánnina are mostly of Kallaritiote descent – as is Bulgari, one of the world's most celebrated contemporary jewellers. Though all but deserted except during summer holidays, the grand houses of the departed rich are kept in excellent repair by their descendants. The cobbled *platía*, with its old-fashioned shops and statue commemorating local emigré Kallaritiotes, who helped finance the Greek Revolution, has probably remained unchanged for a century. There is a very basic **ksenónas** (☎0659/61-251) with ten beds, no running water, and rough food; for eating, the two grills by the square are preferable.

Just beyond the village the awesome **Hroússias river chasm** separates Kallarítes from its neighbour SIRÁKO, visible high up the west bank but a

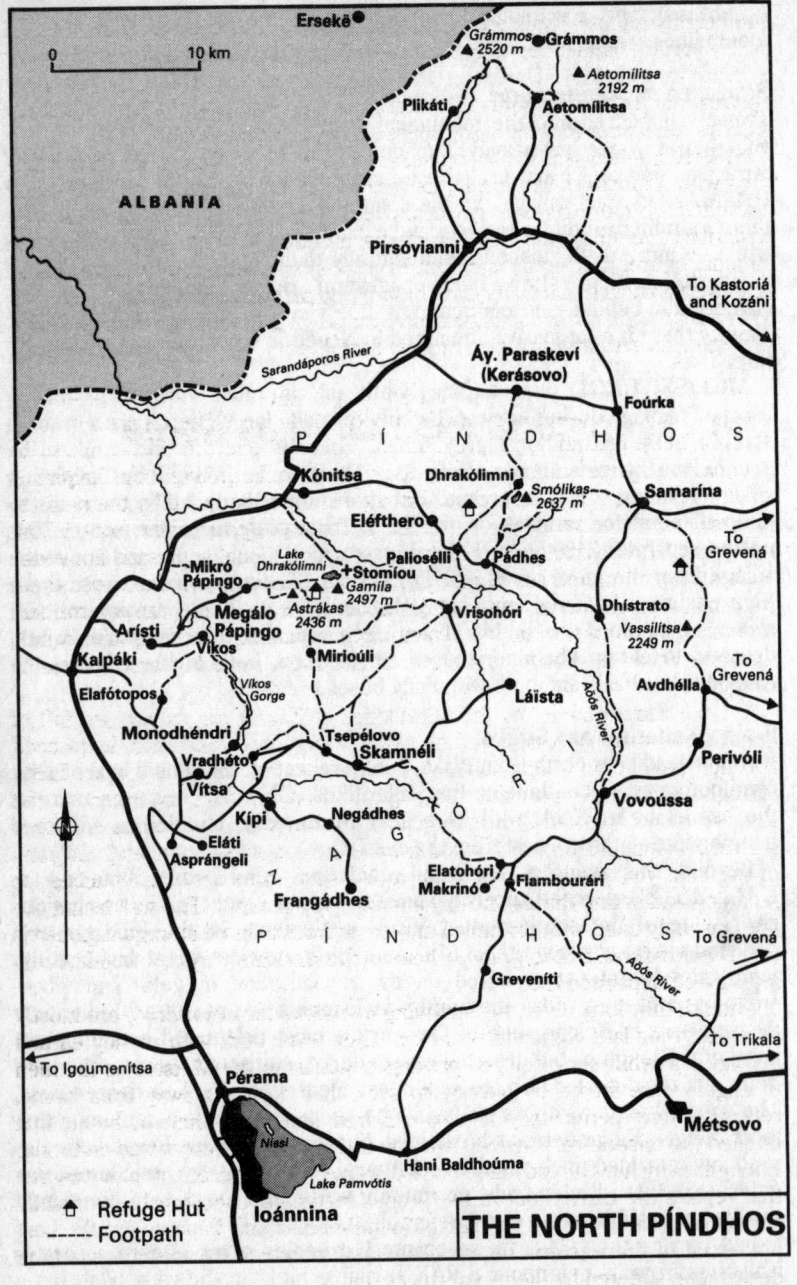

ALBANIA

Ersekë

Grámmos 2520 m
Grámmos
Aetomílitsa 2192 m

Plikáti

Aetomílitsa

Pirsóyianni

To Kastoriá and Kozáni

Sarandáporos River

P Í N D H O S

Áy. Paraskeví (Kerásovo)

Foúrka

Kónitsa

Dhrakólimni

Smólikas 2637 m

Samarína

Eléfthero

To Grevená

Mikró Pápingo

Lake Dhrakólimni

Paliosélli

Pádhes

Megálo Pápingo

Astrákas 2436 m

+Stomíou

Gamíla 2497 m

Vrisohóri

Dhístrato

Vassilítsa 2249 m

To Grevená

Arísti

Víkos

Kalpáki

Mirioúli

Elafótopos

Víkos Gorge

Láista

Avdhélla

Monodhéndri

Tsepélovo

Skamnéli

Perivóli

Vradhéto

Vovoússa

Vítsa

Kípi

Negádhes

Eláti Asprángeli

Elatohóri Makrinó

Flambourári

Frangádhes

P Í N D H O S

To Grevená

Greveníti

Aóös River

To Tríkala

To Igoumenítsa

Pérama

Métsovo

Níssi

Hani Baldhoúma

Lake Pamvótis

Ioánnina

THE NORTH PÍNDHOS

⌂ Refuge Hut
---- Footpath

0   10 km

good eighty minutes' walk away. The trail is steep and spectacular including a nearly vertical 'ladder' hewn out of the rock face (quite manageable if you've a head for heights). Down on the bridge over the river you can peer upstream at a pair of abandoned watermills; the canyon walls here are steep and the sun shines for only a few hours a day even in summer.

SIRÁKO, when you finally arrive, is even more strikingly set than Kallarítes with its fortress-like locale; its well-preserved mansions, archways and churches are more reminiscent of those in Zagória. Not to be upstaged by Kallarítes, the village has also erected a number of monuments to various national figures (including the poet Krystallis) who hailed from here. There is a taverna and a couple of *kafenía* but no regular accommodation.

The road back out to Ioánnina from Siráko is a different one than that serving Ágnanda and Prámanda, exiting via Mihalítsi.

The Zagorohória and the Víkos Gorge

Few parts of Greece are more surprising, or more beguiling, than **Zagóri**. A wild, infertile region, it lies to the north of Ioánnina, bounded by the roads to Kónitsa and Métsovo in the west and south and by the river Aóös in the northeast. The beauty of its landscapes is unquestionable: barren limestone wastes, rugged mountains deeply furrowed by foaming rivers and resurgent streams, miles of forest. But there is not a cultivatable inch anywhere, and scarcely a job for any of its few remaining inhabitants. The last place, in fact, that one would expect to find some of the most imposing architecture in Greece.

Yet the **Zagorohória**, as the 46 villages of Zagóri are called, are full of grand stone mansions, enclosed by semi-fortified walls and with deep-eaved porches opening on to immaculately cobbled streets. Inside, if you are lucky enough to get a glimpse, the living quarters are upstairs, arranged on the Turkish model. Instead of furniture, low platforms line the rooms on either side of an often elaborately hooded fireplace. Strewn with rugs and cushions of the kind you see in the museum in Métsovo, they serve as couches for reclining and sitting during the day and sleeping at night. The wall facing the fire is usually lined with pannelled and sometimes painted storage cupboards called *misándhres*. In the grander houses the intricately fretted wooden ceilings are often painted too.

Though they look older, the surviving mansions (or *arhondiká*) are mostly nineteenth- or late eighteenth-century. They were built with money earned abroad. For while they enjoyed privileges similar to the Metsovites the men of Zagóri were forced by poverty to seek their fortunes away from home, returning only periodically to sire children and build them a home that implied the miseries of *ksenitiá* (living in foreign parts) were worth enduring. Though many have already fallen into disrepair, the government now ensures that repairs are carried out in the proper materials, checking the unsightly spread of cheap and easy tin roofs. Monodhéndhri and Pápingo are the best preserved of the western Zagóri villages, all of which escaped the wartime devastation suffered by their eastern cousins.

As for the countryside, much the best way of savouring its joys is on foot, **trekking** the dozens of still extant paths which, gliding through forest and sheepfold or slipping over passes and hogbacks, connect the outlying villages.

'Packhorse' bridges

An additional pleasure as you stumble down boulder-strewn ravine beds that are bone-dry an hour after a thunderstorm is coming upon one of the many fine high-arched 'packhorse' bridges that abound in the Zagóri. One-, two- or three-arched, these bridges, and the old cobbled tracks, were the only link with the outside world for these remote communities until motor roads were opened up in the 1950s. They were erected mainly in the nineteenth century by gangs of itinerant craftsmen and were financed by local worthies.

Like the semi-nomadic Vlach and Sarakatsan shepherds of Epirus, these wandering construction gangs or *bouloúkia* were away from home between the feasts of Áyios Yióryios (St. George's Day) in April and of Áyios Dhimítrios in October. As in other mountainous regions of Europe – the Alps, for example – they came from remote and poor communities, Pirsóyianni and Vóurbiani in particular in the Kónitsa area and Ágnanda, Prámanda and Houliarádhes southeast of Ioánnina. Closely guarding the secrets of their trade with their own invented private language, they travelled the length and breadth of Greece and the Balkans, right up to World War II.

While you're in the Zagóri region a good side trip would be to go out to **Kípi** to take a look at the half-dozen fantastic bridges in the vicinity of the village.

The Víkos Gorge

In the northwest corner of the region, the awesome trench of the **Víkos gorge** – its walls nearly 1000 metres deep in places – cuts through the limestone tablelands of Mount Gamíla, separating the villages of western and central Zagóri. Quite the equal of the Samariá gorge in Crete, a hike through or around Víkos, depending on your abilities and time, is the highlight of any visit to the area. Since 1975 a national park has encompassed both Víkos and the equally attractive Aóös River canyon to the north. Development is just beginning but for the past decade British and French trekking companies have been coming here so almost every hamlet within spitting distance of the canyon, and in fact any sizeable village elsewhere in the Zagóri, is able to provide a **bed and a meal** at short notice.

The **walk along the gorge** is not difficult to follow, and takes about five hours at a reasonable speed. Another hour will get you as far as the hamlet of Víkos, above the north end of the gorge. If you want a roof over your head for the night, allow two hours more from the gorge end to reach one of the Pápingo villages.

Walking the gorge

The usual starting point for the walk is the handsome village of **MONODHÉNDRI**, perched right on the rim of the gorge near its south end. There is a daily bus connection with Ioánnina (except Sun.) and accommodation at nearby VÍTSA (only 15 min. walk below by a footpath) in a renovated *arhondikó*. Monodhéndri has plans for a *ksenónas* (hostel) of its own, too; meanwhile nobody seems to mind if you pass the night in the porch outside the church. There's a taverna on the plane-shaded *platía*, where it is always pleasantly cool even on the hottest days, and another (good for breakfast) by the bus stop.

The lane leading off from the far end of the *platía*, signposted 'Pros Vikon', leads to the eagle's nest monastery of **Áyia Paraskeví**, teetering on the very brink of the sheer drop into the gorge. Renovation has rather spoilt its air of mystery, but if you continue on around the adjacent cliff face – a good head for heights permitting – the path eventually comes to a dead-end near a well-hidden cave where the villagers used to barricade themselves in times of danger.

Much the clearest **path into the gorge** starts beside the church in Monodhéndri's main square. It is paved for most of the way down to the river bed, whose stony course you can quite easily parallel for the first hour or so of the walk. There are occasional splashes of red paint directing the way, but in reality all you need to do is to keep straight, occasionally crossing from one to the other side of the riverbed or climbing for a while through the wooded banks.

About three hours out of Monodhéndri you draw even with the mouth of the Mégas Lákkos ravine, the only breach in this wall of the gorge; its water is drinkable. Another hour's level tramping brings you past a small white shrine with a recessed well next to it; a further hour yet (5 hr. from Monodhéndri) sees the gorge begin to open out and the sheer walls recede.

On to Víkos and the Pápingos

As the gorge widens you are faced with a choice. Continuing straight, on the best-defined path, takes you close to a beautiful eighteenth-century chapel, past which the route becomes a newly-paved *kalderími* (mule path), climbing up and left to the hamlet of **VÍKOS** (also known as VITSIKÓ). This route has been kept in good repair by the locals who use it to get down to the church for the August 15th festival of the Panayía, to whom it's dedicated.

Most walkers, however, prefer to search out the **route on to the two Pápingo villages**. This has recently been repaved, and signposted from the gorge end; finding and following it is straightforward. It's just under two hours' walk to MEGÁLO PÁPINGO, half an hour more if you head for MIKRÓ, so if darkness is approaching plan accordingly. Midway, after a steep, predominantly scree-laden climb from the riverbed, and before some weathered, toothlike pinnacles, another clear sign indicates the respective forks left and right for Megálo and Mikró. The paths to either village are again simple to follow.

MEGÁLO PÁPINGO is, as its name suggests, the larger of the two villages: a sprawl of fifty or so houses along a tributary of the Voïdhomátis river. It has a 17-bed **inn** with a café-grill, run by Koulis Hristodhoulos (☎0653/41-238) who can also advise on walks towards Gamíla (see below). A second, smaller inn is run by Kalliopi Ranga (☎0653/41-081). There is also a summer **tourist office**, a sign of the times in what was until recently a little-visited region.

Around half the size of its neighbour, **MIKRÓ PÁPINGO** crouches below an outcrop of grey limestone rocks known as the *pírgi* (towers). It has just one **inn**, run by Klearhos Staras (☎0653/41-230), which offers both beds and meals.

Returning to Ioánnina, there are buses five times a week from either of the Pápingo villages. If you strike unlucky, the best course is to walk to the village of **KÁTO KLIDHONIÁ**, with regular buses, on the Kónitsa-Ioánnina highway; it's around two and a half hours, via the abandoned hamlet of Áno Klidhoniá, on a better-than-average path.

Further hikes: Mount Gamíla

For walkers keen on further, fairly arduous hiking, there are a number of routes on from the Pápingo villages, up and across the Gamíla range.

Astrákas: the refuge and around

All onward hikes, east into Gamíla, begin with the steep but straightforward ascent to the **refuge on Astrákas col**, clearly visible from Megálo Pápingo. To reach this you need to make first for Mikró Pápingo: an hour's walk, coming from Megálo Pápingo, along a jeep track that has more or less subsumed the old track.

From the top of Mikró Pápingo a well-signed, bona fide path begins. You pass a chapel (Áyios Pantelímon), then head through forest to a spring (Antálki; about 40 min. from Mikró Pápingo). From here the forest thins as you climb towards a second spring (Tráfos; 1 hr. 40 min. from Mikró). Twenty minutes beyond Tráfos a signposted trail branches right towards the Astrákas peak – a three-hour round-trip. If you ignore this path, and keep straight, you will reach the **EOS refuge**, perched on the saddle joining Astrákas with Mt. Lápatos, in around 35 minutes (3 hr. from Megálo Pápingo). A trickle of summer hikers base themselves here for the trek up Astrákas or walks further afield on Gamíla. The keys can be obtained at the tourist office in Pápingo.

Northeast of the refuge, on the far side of the boggy Tsoumáni valley below, the gleaming **lake of Dhrakólimni** looms on the very edge of the Gamíla range. This is about an hour from the refuge. **Gamíla summit** proper, 2497m, is a good two hours' climb to the east of the refuge.

South to Tsepélovo

A more obvious **onward trek from Astrákas** is the five-hour route across Gamíla, via the head of the Mégas Lákkos gorge, to the village of **TSEPÉLOVO**. There is only one tiny spring en route and it's a grassy and stony mountainside. The destination is one of the finest of the Zagorohória. English-speaking Alekos Gouris, who runs the store on the village *platia*, also keeps a taverna and **rooms** and is generally very helpful to walkers. There's also a good value B-class pension, the *Fanis* (☎0653/81-271).

This side of Gamíla is treeless and rather dull, apart from the villages themselves. So it is worth going on to SKAMNÉLI, the next village, and beyond, for there the forest begins again and continues around into the beautiful **ravine of the Aóös**. The road ends at VRISSOHÓRI in the west, and at Láista in the east. There is an infrequent bus service to Ioánnina from both. **LÁISTA** has an incongruously large **hotel**, the E-class *Avra* (☎0653/81-286), and a fine, though damaged, church; **SKAMNÉLI** has a new B-class **pension**, the *Platanos*. If you're interested in mountain wildflowers, there's no better place to look than in the Goura valley directly above Skamnéli.

VRISSOHÓRI, though, is the most worthwhile destination for it's the start of an easy and very lovely three-hour path (signposted *Pros Yefíran* – 'To the Bridge' – by the monastery at the entrance to the village) to Palioséli and Pádhes on the far side of the valley, on the southern flank of Mount Smólikas (see below). Like the two Smólikas villages, Vrissohóri is Vlach. Tiny and part derelict (no rentable accommodation), it appears about to be swallowed up by the encroaching woodland.

The northern Píndhos: Kónitsa, the Aóös, Smólikas and Grámmos

KÓNITSA is a sleepy little town, its most memorable features a bridge and a view. The **bridge**, built over the Aóös, is a real giant, built around 1870 but looking far older. The view comes from the town's amphitheatrical setting on the slopes of Mount Trapezítsa; below spreads the broad flood plain where the Aóös and Voïdhomátis rivers mingle with the Sarandáporos before flowing through Albania to the sea.

The town was besieged by the Communist Democratic Army over the New Year, 1948, in a last and unsuccessful bid to establish a provisional capital. Much was destroyed in the fighting, though parts of the old bazaar and a tiny Turkish neighbourhood near the river survive. If you want a **room**, there are two *ksenónes* in the bazaar: the *Melissa* and another, unnamed, on the opposite side of the street about 200m away; both are cheap and basic. There are also four hotels – one in each class from B to E; the D-class *Tymfi* (☎0655/22-035) and E-class *Egntia* (☎0655/22-881) are both on the central *platía*. Also on this square are a **bank**, a good taverna (at the south end), several *psistariés*, and the **bus terminal** (seven buses daily to Ioánnina; connections to most villages in the sections below).

From Kónitsa itself, there are rewards in an afternoon's walking. To the south of the town, the **Aóös valley** is protected as a national park. A clear path, parallel to the river, leads in 6km to the newly-restored **Monastery of Stomíou**, perched on a bluff overlooking the narrowest part of the Aóös.

Unhappily a dam is scheduled to be built in or above the narrows, drying up the idyllic lower reaches of the river, which in summer is swimmable. But for now it's still around to be enjoyed.

If you want to continue on foot be warned that the vegetation is dense on the shaggy slopes hereabouts – which are one of the last pristine habitats for lynx, roe deer and birds of prey. The paths south to the Astrákas area all have blockages, requiring a good four hours' of scrambling and ideally a local guide.

Mt. Smólikas, Samarína, and South

At 2637m, **Mount Smólikas**, to the east of Kónitsa, is the second highest peak in Greece. It dominates a beautiful and very extensive range, covering 100 square kilometres of mountain territory, all of it above 1700m, and one of the last heartlands of traditional shepherd life – best witnessed in summer at the Vlach village of Samarína.

Lake Dhrakólimni

From Kónitsa one afternoon bus a day rolls through the mountains to DHÍSTRATO, stopping en route at **PALIOSÉLI** and **PÁDHES**. Both villages have rooms: at the *kafenío* in Palioséli (☎0655/22-040), and rentedout at the café-restaurant run by Vassilis Kourtinos in Pádhes.

From either of these two villages you can follow paths through thick forests of black pines (and perhaps past the occasional brown bear) to **Dhrakólimni** (around 4 hr. walk; not to be confused with the lake of the same name in the Gamíla range). The path **up from Pádhes** is easier to find with only two critical turnings. Forty-five minutes above the village you need to bear right at a wayside shrine. Some three hours later, just before the path reaches a major stream, angle diagonally up to the left across a grassy slope towards the top of the ridge, where the path becomes clear again. **Coming up from Palioséli** the trail is distinct as far as a new wooden refuge (Náni), above a spring and sheepfold, about halfway along; from here you have to follow your nose, compass (or, preferably the *Korfes* map) through forest before emerging at the lake.

From the ridge above **the lake** (a good camping place) you can reach the **summit of Smólikas** within an hour or so. It is not unusual to see chamoix near the top.

The easiest way off of the mountain is the scenic three-hour **path down to Áyia Paraskeví** (also known as Kerásovo). This starts at the sheepfold (*stani*) in the vale between the lake and the peak. Alternatively, you can make your way **east to Samarína** (see below).

Dhrakólimni to Samarína

If you've a good head for heights, and you're not carrying a full pack, it's possible to walk along the ridge of Smólikas from Dhrakólimni much of the way to Samarína. However, it is a lot safer and more straightforward to head back down from the lake to the bona fide **Pádhes-Samarína path**. To do so, follow the course of the stream below the lake to the southwest; after about an hour's descent you meet the marked route. Bear left (northeast), following sporadic yellow blazes on the rocks.

After about half an hour, if you have joined the path at the stream (some three hours in all, coming from Pádhes) you pass a couple of sheepfolds on the left. Here bear to the right (northeast), towards a gap in the ridgeline, looking for markers on the last dwindling trees or rocks. Once through the 'gap' you cross the Smólikas watershed proper, descending into the rather lunar, northwest-facing cirque which eventually drains down to Áyia Paraskeví. Next you traverse the base of one of Smólikas' secondary peaks as prelude to creeping up a scree-laden rock 'stair'. From the top of this climb – the last en route – the markers change from yellow to red, and a line of small cairns descends diagonally across a broad flat-topped ridge.

Follow these cairns until the path wriggles down through a rocky gully, levelling out on another neck of land. To the left of this is a dry gully (avoid) and way off to the right (south) can be glimpsed the other of Smólikas's lakes, as large or bigger than Dhrakólimni but difficult of access. Try not to stray in either direction in poor visibility – there are steep drops down the mountain to either side.

There is only one stunted landmark pine before you encounter the leading edge of the black pine forest, at the foot of Bogdháno peak, which is capped by an altimeter. The trail threads between this knoll and Gorgoloú, at the foot of which lies Samarína. Twenty minutes or so beyond this pass the Bogdháno spring oozes from serpentine strata. Then you begin to descend once more in earnest through thick forest, with the Soupotíra spring gurgling into a log-trough set in a beautiful mountain clearing. Lower down the woods end abruptly and you'll emerge on a bare slope directly above Samarína.

Samarína

Although **SAMARÍNA** looks a bit of a mess – it was burnt several times during the war and Civil War – it's a thriving and friendly place and very proud of its Vlach traditions. It's only inhabited in the summer (at 1600m it's the highest village in Greece), when it fills up with Vlachs from the plains of Thessal – and their sheep, some 50,000 of them. The high point of the year is the Feast of the Assumption on August 15, when there is much music and merry-making and the place is swamped by nostalgic Vlachs from all over the country.

The interior of the main church, the **Panayía**, is superb, with frescoes and painted ceilings and an intricately carved iconostasis, where the angels, soldiers and biblical figures are dressed in mustachios and *fustanélles* (the Greek kilt). Though it looks a lot older, like many other churches in the region, it dates from around 1800. Its special hallmark is an adult black pine growing out of the roof of the apse, and no one can remember a time without it. Also very fine are the frescoes in the church of **Áyios Sotíras**, fifty minutes' walk along the rough forest track that leads to Dhístrato and back into the Aóös valley.

The improbably large stone building which confronts you at the top of the village is a **hotel** and there is another basic inn by the *platía*, but both of these may well be full during the summer in which case the only other lodging, with more chance of a vacancy, is the *Hotel Kiparíssi*, out on the east edge of town. No one will mind, though, if you camp a bit out of town, and there are numerous *psistariés* (and even an OTE office) on the square.

Leaving Samarína can be tricky. There is a bus for Grevená from June to September, but not every day, though a lift is not too hard to get if you ask around. Your other options are on foot: walking the 17-kilometre jeep track south to Dhístrato, or a similar distance (and surface) northwest to Foúrka.

Mount Grámmos

It was on **Mount Grámmos** that the Democratic Communist Army made its last stand in the Civil War. Their eventual retreat into Albania followed a bitter campaign which saw tens of thousands of deaths and the world's first use of napalm (supplied by the United States). The upper slopes of the mountain remain totally bare, and walking in the range you still see rusting cartridges scattered about, as well as trenches from the fighting.

If you want to visit the range, and peer down into the forbidden wilds of Albania, the simplest approach is from Kónitsa. At 2pm each day there's a bus to Plikáti, the most useful base for a day's hike. Coming from the Gámila/Smólikas area you're best off walking out to Áyia Paraskeví, which has a daily bus to Kónitsa; if you time it right you could get off at the junction with the main road and flag down the Plikáti bus without backtracking to the town.

Plikáti and a hike up Grámmos

There's a singularly end-of-the-world feel to **PLIKÁTI** – as indeed there should be, for this is the closest Greek village to the Albanian frontier. It's a traditional-looking place, with stone houses, a tiny permanent population, a couple of **inns** and a combination taverna/general store.

At 2520m, **Mount Grámmos** is one of the four loftiest Greek peaks. In making the ascent – a practicable day trip from Plikáti – the easiest strategy is to angle north-northeast up the gentler slopes leading to Perífano (2442), second highest point in the range, rather than tackling head-on the badly eroded and steep incline immediately below the main peak. The trail in the indicated direction is clear for the first two hours out of the village, crossing the river and switchbacking up through bushes and then beech trees before petering out at a sheepfold. Just above this are the last water sources on this side of the ridge – various trickles feeding a pond. Bearing west along a plain trail you can thread along the crest for roughly an hour to the **summit**, its cairn covered in a babel of multilingual initials and graffiti. Below, to the west, stretches the cultivated Albanian valley to the barns and tractors of Erseka, 5km distant. Don't entertain thoughts of entering on a lark, as armed guards hidden in pillboxes might well have no compunction about shooting.

THE COAST AND SOUTH

After the functional aspects of **Igoumenítsa**, and the out-of-season attractions of **Párga**, there's precious little to recommend on the **Epirus coast**. Head inland a short way, however, and things look up. Close by Párga, the **Necromanteion of Ephyra** is an intriguing ancient detour, and the ruins of **Nikópolis** break the journey to Préveza. Best of all, perhaps, is **Árta**, a pleasant and interesting provincial town, approached either around the Amvrakikós gulf, or, most impressively, along the plane-shaded Loúros river gorge from Ioánnina.

Moving south into **Étolo-Akarnanía** the landscape becomes increasingly desolate, and most travellers bound for Lefkádha or **Andírio**, with its ferry across to the Peloponnese, will be interested mainly in how to transit as efficiently as possible. For committed beach-seekers there is **Mítikas**, south of Vónitsa; and for hard-nosed romantics, **Messolóngi**, though unglamorous, retains its name, situations and Byron's buried heart.

Igoumenítsa and Around

IGOUMENÍTSA is Greece's third passenger port, after Pireás and Pátra, with hourly ferries to Corfu, several daily to Italy, and more sporadic connections to Yugoslavia and to the lesser Ionian islands of Kefalloniá, Itháki, and Páxi. In itself, however, the town is unappealing. It was levelled during the last war, and, rebuilt in a sprawling, functional style, is a place most travellers aim to pass through in the day. If you're Italy or Yugoslavia bound, this means arriving early, or at least making an advance reservation, as the majority of ferries leave early- or mid-morning. See the details overpage.

If you need to **stay** the night budget hotels are plentiful if uninspiring. The town is not large and most are to be found either along, or just back from, the waterside. The two cheapest are generally the E-class *Hotel Rhodos* (Kíprou 19; ☎0665/22-248), near the main square, and *Pension Ktematias*, 75m inland and north of the square on Venizélou. Campers might prefer to take a local bus to the beaches at KALÁMI or PLATARIÁ, respectively 10km and 12km south. Both have **campsites** and tavernas.

Arriving in Igoumenítsa from Italy or Yugoslavia, a word of warning. If you miss the banks (which close at 2pm) you're dependent on travel agents for **changing money** and rates are not good. Best to buy a few drachmas on board. The same, of course, applies if you forget that you need to pay departure tax before leaving the port.

Out from Igoumenítsa

If you find yourself stuck for the day in Igoumenítsa, the best escapes are probably to the **beach**. Closest strands are those at KALÁMI and PLATARIÁ, mentioned with the campsites above. Both these, and PÁRGA (see the following section) have regular bus connections with Igoumenítsa.

THE FERRIES

If you arrive late and stay overnight in Igoumenitsa you can at least shop around carefully for tickets. Most ferries leave for Italy early evening or mid-evening, and travel offices tend to stay open until around 9pm. Fares available vary widely. From June 1 to October 1 (or thereabouts) the cheapest crossing to Italy tends to be *R-Line*'s service to Otranto, via Corfu. A more unusual getaway is the *Jadrolinija* sailing up the **Damatian coast** of Yugoslavia – far and away the most pleasant way of entering Yugoslavia from Greece, allowing grand views of Albania en route. If you specify stopovers in Yugoslavia the trip can become something of a budget mini-cruise.

A few general points:

Fares All companies offer a variety of fares for cabin, 'aircraft' seats and deck passage (the price quoted below, for low/high season), as well as reductions according to age, student or rail card status.

Cars are carried on all ferries. *R-Line* charges £20–40 for a car up to 4.25m, depending on season.

Season All frequencies of ferry crossings detailed are for the summer; out of season, all services are reduced.

Embarkation tax of (currently) 1000dr per person and per car is levied on all international departures.

Stopovers Unlike sailings from Pátra, ferries from Igoumenitsa to Italy or Yugoslavia are not allowed to sell tickets with a stopover on Corfu. You can, however, take the regular Corfu ferry over and then pick up most ferry routes on from there. Stopovers are allowed on Yugoslavia departures, but should be specified in advance.

Checking in If you have bought tickets in advance, or from a travel agent other than the official agent listed below, you must check in (to the respective official agent, or to their booth at the port) at least two hours before departure.

● **International routes and agents include:**

R-Line Otranto (9 hr.), via Corfu; Tues.-Sat. only, 10am. Passage £16 (low), £30 (high). *G. Pitoulis*, Leof. Vassileós Pavloú; ☎0665/22-001.

Fragline Brindisi (10½hr.), via Corfu; daily at 6.30am. Passage £15 (low), £34 (high). *Revis Brothers*, Ethnikís Andístassis 34; ☎0665/22-104.

Hellenic Mediterranean Lines Brindisi (10 hr.), usually via Corfu; daily at 7am (and at 11.50pm in high season). Passage £23 (low), £40 (high). *Hellenic Mediterranean Lines*, Ethnikís Andístassis 30; ☎0665/22-180.

Seven Islands Brindisi (7½ hr.), via Corfu; daily at 8:30am. Passage £20 (low), £28 (high). No exclusive port agent.

Adriatica Brindisi (10 hr.), via Corfu; daily at 7am. Passage £20 (low), £28 (high). No exclusive agent.

Nausimar Brindisi (10½ hr.), via Corfu; daily (9.30pm or 9pm). Passage £18 (low), £24 (high). *Nausimar*, Ethnikís Andístassis 60; ☎0665/25-351.

Ventouris Bari (10–12½ hr.), via Corfu; daily at 8.30pm/9:30pm. Passage £15 (low), £20 (high). *Milano Travel*, Áyii Apóstoli 11B; ☎0665/24-237.

Marlines Ancona (24 hr.), direct; Thurs. (2pm), Sun. (11pm). Passage £25 (low), £33 (high). *Marlines*, Ethnikís Andístassis 42; ☎0665/23-301.

Strintzis Ancona (23 hr.), via Corfu; Mon./Wed. (9pm), Fri./Sat. (7.15am). Passage £38 (low), £50 (high). *G. Pitoulis*, Ethnikís Andístassis 20; ☎0665/23-970.

Minoan Ancona (23½ hr.), via Corfu; daily except Wed./Sun. (9am). Passage £26 (low), £33 (high). No exclusive agent.

Jadrolinja Corfu-(Bar)-Dubrovnik-Korčula-(Hvar)-Split-Zadar-(Rab)-Rijeka; Tues., Wed., and Fri. in high season, Tues. only the rest of the year; ports in brackets are served only once a week and in high season only. Passage to Dubrovnik, £22 (low), £28 (high). *Jadrolinja* office at the quay; ☎0655/22-409.

Inland, the easiest and most rewarding target is **FILIÁTES**, 19km northwest and linked with frequent buses. A traditional Epirot town, with well-preserved mansions, and the thirteenth-century Monastery of Yiromeríou, nearby, this makes a pleasant half-day excursion.

More difficult to reach, other than by car, is the old hill town of **PARAMITHIÁ**, 38kms east and south (1 or 2 buses daily). This was once an important centre for copper working, with reputedly superb architecture. However, much was destroyed in the last war and during the 1950s, and today just one artisan remains amid sparse traces of latter-day prosperity. The narrow lanes, Byzantine church of the Assumption and old castle provide a certain focus. But it's really worth a stop only if you're heading south to the remarkable **Necromanteion of Ephyra** (below) – a detour you would certainly need your own vehicle for if you're planning to return to Igoumenítsa the same day.

Párga

PÁRGA used to be a wonderful place: a small resort town, somewhat in the Náfplio mould, with a superb beach and a crescent of tiered houses set below a Norman-Venetian castle. The beaches are still as good as ever, with their views out to sea of a trail of rocky islets and in the distance Páxi. But the town, with its ancient, arched lanes, has recently become swamped by an ever-growing tide of cement apartment blocks – and the accompanying crowds. In season, at least, it's hard to recommend as anything more than a stopover point before taking the local ferry across to Paxí, and even this needs to be reserved a good day ahead in season.

The town's fate is sadder still given its highly evocative and idiosyncratic history. From the fourteenth to eighteenth century Párga was a lone Venetian toehold in Epirus, complementing the Serene Republic's offshore possessions in the Ionian islands. The Lion of St. Mark – symbol of Venice – is still present on the blufftop **Kastro** (open all day). Later, the Napoleonic French took the town for a brief period, leaving additional fortifications on the largest **islet**, a 200-metre swim from the harbour beach. The place enjoyed a stint of independence at the start of the nineteenth century when the little city-state was self-sufficient through the export of olives, still a mainstay of the region's agriculture. After that, the British acquired Párga and sugsequently sold it to Ali Pasha. The townspeople, knowing his reputation, decamped to the Ionian Islands; the area was then resettled by Muslims who remained until exchanged in 1924 for Greeks from the area around Constantinople.

Beaches and practicalities

Párga's **beaches** line three consecutive bays, split by the headland of the fortress hill. Immediately beyond the castle (and on foot easiest reached by the long stairway from the castle gate) is **Váltos beach**, over a kilometre in length as it sprawls around to the hamlet of the same name. **Lihnós**, 3km in the opposite (southeast) direction, is a similarly huge beach. Both have **campsites**; another, *Parga Camping* (☎0684/31-130), is sited 600m inland to the north among olive groves.

Rooms are plentiful if a little pricey: someone will probably approach you on arrival at the bus station or ferry quay. If you want to stay in a traditional building try the *Vassilas House* or *Petros House* pensions, both in the market area. Hotels are generally reserved en masse in season.

For **food**, the *To Kantouni* taverna at the rear of the market, on Platía Ayíou Dhimitríou, serves good cheap meals, as does its nearest neighbour across the square. Up by the castle are a couple more decent places to eat; on the waterside *To Souli* and *Ta Thalassinopoulia* are probably the best of the bunch.

Buses link Párga with Igoumenítsa and Préveza four times daily, more in season; if you've missed a direct departure try hitching the 12km up to Mórfi junction on the Igoumenítsa-Préveza road. *Parga Tours* and *West Travel*, both on the waterside, hire **mopeds** – worth considering for the trip to the Necromanteion of Ephyra detailed below. The latter also runs **boat tours up the Aherónda river** to the Necromanteion, allowing good views of the delta birdlife en route. Both tour agents sell tickets for the daily (in season) **kaíki to Paxí**.

The Necromanteion of Ephyra

The **Necromanteion of Ephyra**, or Sanctuary of Persephone and Hades, is perhaps the strangest of all Greek sites. It is sited on a low, rocky hill, above what in ancient times was the mouth of the Aherónda – the mythical Styx, river of the underworld – and from Mycenaean to Roman times it maintained an elaborate Oracle of the Dead.

The oracle never achieved the stature of Delphi or Dodona but its fame was sufficient for Homer, writing (it is assumed) in the ninth century B.C., to use it as the setting for Odysseus's visit to Hades. This he does explicitly, with Circe giving Odysseus the directions:

> *You will come to a wild coast and to Persephone's grove, where the hill poplars grow and the willows that so quickly lose their seeds. Beach your boat there by Ocean's swirling stream and march on into Hades' Kingdom of Decay. There the River of Flaming Fire and the River of Lamentation, which is a branch of the Waters of the Styx, unite around a pinnacle of rock to pour their thundering streams into Acheron. This is the spot, my lord, that I bid you seek out . . . then the souls of the dead and departed will come up in their multitudes.*

The Sanctuary

Open 9am-3.30pm, Sun. 10am-4.30pm.

The trees of Homer's account still mark the sanctuary's site today, though the lake, which once enclosed the island-oracle, has receded to the vague line of the Aherónda skirting through the plain: from the sanctuary you can pick out its course from the vegetation. As for the sanctuary itself, its **ruins**, flanked by a second-century Christian basilica, offer a disappointingly convincing exposé of the confidence tricks pulled by its priestly initiates.

According to contemporary accounts, pilgrims arriving on the oracle-island were accommodated for a night in windowless rooms. Impressed by the atmosphere, and by their mission to consult with the souls of the dead, they would then be graciously relieved of their votive offerings. Finally, as their turn came, they were sent groping along a labyrinth-corridor into the heart of the sanctuary where, further disorientated by hallucinogenic vapors, they were lowered into the antechamber of Hades itself to witness whatever spiritual visitation the priests might have devised.

The remains of the sanctuary allow each room to be identified; there is a useful plan at the entrance. At the centre is a long room with high walls, flanked by chambers used for votive offerings. And from here metal steps lead to the underground chamber where the necromantic audiences took place. Originally this descent was by means of a precarious windlass mechanism – which is now (rather sadly) deposited in Ioánnina's archaeological museum.

Access

The Necromanteion stands on a rocky hill just above the village of MESOPÓTAMO, 22km south and east of Párga; it is signposted also from the village of KASTRÍ, 5km east, on the Igoumenítsa-Préveza bus route. The easiest access, of course, is by tour from Párga (see opposite).

Although it seems hard today to think of the Aherónda here as the pathway to hell, only a few kilometres to the east the river saws a course into the mountains, its waters cutting deep into the rock strata and disappearing into mysterious chasms. If you are intrigued, make your way to GLIKÍ, on another sideroad between Paramithiá and Préveza. There you can follow the course of the river through a **gorge** that is reputedly one of the country's finest – and least known. To this book's shame, none of us has made the trip: reports welcome.

Only 4km from the Necromanteion, there is a good beach at the village of AMMOUDHIÁ, still a surprisingly undeveloped alternative to Párga.

South to Préveza: Nikópolis

The approach from Igoumenítsa/Párga to Préveza has a few further, minor sites before edging out on to the land-locked Amvrakikós (Ambracian) Gulf, where in 31 B.C. Octavian defeated Antony and Cleopatra at the Battle of Actium. The most substantial of them, suitably enough, is Octavian's 'Victory City' Nikópolis, 7km north of Préveza.

First, however, if you are travelling by bus, you will pass a turning to the village of **KAMARÍNA**, just to the east of National Road 19, overlooked by the monastery and monument of Zalóngo (4km from the village) and the ruins of ancient Kassopi.

The **Monastery of Zalóngo** is a staple of Greek schoolbook history, lent immortal fame by the defiant mass-suicide of the 'Souliot women'. The Souliots, who acted as Byron's bodyguard during the War of Independence, were a independent-spirited tribe of Orthodox Christians dwelling in the coastal barrier ranges between the Ionian and the Loúros River. For the last decades of the eighteenth century, and the first of the nineteenth, they conducted a perennial rebellion against Ali Pasha and the Turks, which in 1806 led to Turkish troops cornering a large band of Souliots in the Zalóngo monastery. As this refuge was overrun, about sixty Souliot women and children fled to the summit of the cliff above, and to the amazement of the Muslim troops approaching to enslave them, the mothers danced one by one, with their children in their arms, over the edge of the precipice. A modernistic bronze sculpture commemorates their supreme gesture.

Slightly to the northwest, on a similar bluff, are the remains of ancient **Kassopi**, a minor Thesprotian city state. The ruins, dating mainly from the fourth century B.C., are at present under excavation. However, you can view the walls and column bases of the central agora, stoas, a tiny theatre and a *katagoyeion* or guest hostelry. Principally, though, the site – 600m above the level of the sea, clearly spread out below you – demonstrates the unerring ancient Greek sense of geomancy.

Nikopolis

NIKOPOLIS – 'Victory City' – was founded by Octavian on the site where his army had camped prior to the Battle Of Actium. An arrogant and ill-considered gesture, it made little geographical sense: the settlement was on unfirm ground, water had to be transported by aqueduct from the springs of the Louros and a population had to be forcibly imported from towns as far afield as Náfpaktos. However, such delusionary posturing was perhaps understandable. At Actium, Octavian had first blockaded and then largely annihilated the combined fleets of Antony and Cleopatra, gathered there for the invasion of Italy. The rewards were sweet, subsequently transforming Octavian from a military commander into the Emperor Augustus.

Nikopolis's history was largely undistinguished, with much of its original population drifting back to their homes. As the Roman Empire declined, the city suffered sacking by Vandals and Goths. Later, in the sixth century A.D., it was restored by Justininan and flourished for a while as a Byzantine city. But within four centuries it had sunk again into the earth, devastated by the combined effect of earthquakes and Bulgar raids.

The Site and Museum
Open 9am–3pm, Sun. 10am–3pm.
Nikopolis's far-flung and overgrown ruins lie 7km north of Préveza. From the road they look impressive. A great theatre stands to the east and as you

approach the museum, past remnants of the baths, there is a formidable stretch of fortified walls. But, walking around, the promise of this enormous site is unfulfilled; there are few remains that reward closer inspection, and the most interesting of these are the mosaics of an early Christian basilica beside the museum.

The **Museum** itself houses a rather miscellaneous array of Roman sculpture. Its caretaker's main function, however, is to unlock the Roman and Byzantine mosaics unearthed amidst the foundations of the sixth-century **Basilica of Doumetios** nearby. The finest and best preserved of these depicts the Creation, crowded with trees, flowers, fruits and birds, and framed by a well-stocked sea. The caretaker will then point you in the direction of a Roman **Odeion** dating from the original construction of the city; it has been well restored for use in a small annual drama festival.

Backtracking past the scant foundations of another sixth century church, the double-aisled **Basilica of Bishop Alkyon**, it's a three-kilometre walk to the main **Theatre**, its arches still standing amidst dangerously crumbling masonry. To the left the sunken outline of the **Stadium** can just be made out, below the modern village of Smirtoúna. Octavian's own tent was pitched upon the hill above the village, and a massive podium remains from the commemorative monument that he erected. On a terrace alongside, recent excavations have revealed the foundations where he dedicated to the gods the 'beaks' (ramming protruberances) of some of the captured warships.

Préveza

Modern **PREVEZA**, at the tip of the gulf, is a drab, insignificant successor to Nikopolis. For most visitors it's of interest solely as a transport hub. South, car-ferries ply across the gulf every half hour (10pm–6am), with a nominal charge for the brief trip; across the gulf you can pick up buses to Vónitsa and less frequently to the 'island' of Lefkádha. North, there are regular buses (500m from the ferry dock, on the harbour quay) towards Árta and Ioánnina; from a separate station, on the Nikópolis road, for Párga and Igoumenítsa.

If you need to stay, there are a half dozen or so **hotels**. None is especially inviting; the C-class *Aktaeon* (Kolovoú 1; ☎0682/22-258) is the best value. Nearest **campsite** is *Camping Monolith* (June-Sept. only), on the beach 10km north; take any bus running through Kanáli. Foodwise, you'll be hard put to avoid the ubiquitous *tost* establishments in the bazaar; aside from these there's one place specialising in grilled, fresh sardines near the main *platía*.

Árta

ÁRTA is one of the most pleasant towns in western Greece: a quiet place, very much the provincial centre, with a good scattering of medieval buildings and a fine situation. Set back from the marshes of the Amvrakikós gulf, it lies in a loop of the broad Árakhthos river, flanked, as you enter the town, by an old **packhorse bridge**. This – the Bridge of Arta – is the subject of folksongs throughout Greece. Legend maintains that the builder, continually thwarted by the current, took the advice of a bird and sealed up his wife in the arch: the bridge held but the woman's voice haunted the place everafter.

Arriving by bus, you'll be dropped at a terminus on the riverbank, on the northern outskirts of town. It's a ten – minute walk into the centre, marked by Platía Skoufá. From the square, Skoufá and Pírrhou streets wind through the oldest quarter of town, which still has much of the Turkish bazaar about it. The cheapest of the **hotels** are both on Skoufá: E-class *Rex* (no.9; ☎0655/27-563) and the unclassified *Pantheon* (no. 126). Slightly pricier is the C-class *Anessis* (Mitropolitoú Xenopoúlou 7; ☎0655/25-991). With very few tourists, Árta's restaurants, concentrated mainly in the bazaar area, are good workaday affairs.

The Churches and Káto Panayía

Árta was known anciently as Ambracia, the capital of Pyrrhus, King of Epirus, and the base for his hard-won ('Another such victory and I am lost') campaigns in Italy. Sparse remains from the period – the foundations of a temple and *odeion* – have been excavated on Odhós Pírrhou, the street leading from the main square to the Froúrio (castle).

Much more impressive, however, is the legacy of Árta's second period of greatness, when, following the fall of Constantinople, it became, like Mystra, an autonomous Byzantine state – the **Despotate of Epirus**.

Most striking and certainly most bizarre of the churches from this epoch is the **Panayía Paragorítissa** (9am–3pm, Sun. 10am–1pm; small charge), a grandiose multi-domed cube that rears above Platía Skoufá. The church's interior is perhaps best described as 'Byzantine Gothic', the main dome being held by an extraordinary cantilever system that looks unwieldy and unsafe, its insecurity exaggerated by a looming *Pantocrator* (Christ in Majesty) mosaic. The church was built in 1282-89 as part of a monastic complex; today a small archaeological museum occupies part of the old refectory.

Two smaller Byzantine churches also survive in the town. Both have a more conventional structure but are enlivened by highly elaborate brick and tile decorations on the outside walls. **Ayía Theódhora**, containing the fine marble tomb of the Byzantine Emperor Michael II's consort, stands in a courtyard halfway down Pírrhou. A little further, opposite the market, is the small but very beautiful fourteenth-century **Áyios Vassílios**.

Amid the orange groves surrounding Árta a number of monasteries were built during the Despotate, many of them by members of the imperial Angelos dynasty. Within easy walking distance (2km out on the Komninon road) is **Káto Panayía**, perhaps the only monastery in Greece with an automated electric door. Its thirteenth century *katholikón*, in a shaded couryard guarded by peacocks, again has extravagant exterior decoration.

Around the Amvrakikós gulf and south to Messolóngi

Árta is a bright spot on the road around the Amvrakikós gulf. Further around, and in fact all the way south to the coast, there is little to prompt a stop. The best quick escape is to **Lefkádha** (see *Chapter Twelve*), which can be reached either via Amfilohía-Vónitsa, or on one the few direct buses daily from Ioánnina which run through Filipiádha and Préveza. If you're approaching from Árta you might try flagging down a Ioánnina-Lefkádha bus at the Filipiádha junction.

AMFILOHÍA is promisingly situated at the head of the gulf, but in reality is a very dull small town. The chance for a swim would seem a redeeming feature on the map, but the water is too murky. If you can get a through bus, do so.

If you needed to stay the night, **VÓNITSA**, 38km west, would be the best choice. Again it's not an exciting place, and still frustratingly distant from real sea. But there's a quiet waterside, squares lined with plane trees, a substantial castle above, and a number of modest hotels. The two cheapest are both D-class: *Avra* (☎0643/22-205) and *Leto* (☎0643/22-246). Local, infrequent buses cover the 14km to **ÁKTIO**, the south ferry terminal across the gulf from Préveza.

The **coast** proper, south from Vónitsa, offers just one attractive resort in **MÍTIKAS**. With its rows of rickety houses strung along a pebbly shore, this looks out on to the hulking island of Kálamos; development is minimal. South from here the coast road runs through **ASTAKÓS**, a village whose name means 'lobster'. Patrick Leigh Fermor, in *Roumeli*, fantasises about arriving at this gastronomic-sounding place; it turns out to be a crashing non-event, and it hasn't changed much since. Come only if you want to take the ferry across to Itháki.

Slightly more enticing is **ETOLIKÓ**, perched on a causeway across the Messolóngi gulf. Although a predominantly modern town, it has a few reminders of a medieval past, plus two D-class **hotels** (cheaper than any options in Messolóngi): the *Alexandra* (☎0632/22-243) and *Liberty Inn* (☎0632/22-206). From here Messolóngi itself is just 10km south, past the salt factories which today are the area's mainstay.

AGRÍNIO, to the east, serves as a transport link for this whole area, with buses to Árta/Ioánnina, Karpeníssi, and south to **ANDÍRIO**, where there are local 'city' buses to Náfpaktos, as well as the ferry across the Gulf of Corinth to the Peloponnese.

Messolóngi: O Lórdhos Víronos

Messolóngi, for Greeks and visitors alike, is irrevocably bound with the name of **Lord Byron**, who died in the town, to dramatic world effect, while commander of the Greek forces during the **War of Indepenence**.

Byron had arrived at Messolóngi, a squalid and inhospitable town surrounded by marshland, in January 1824. The town, with its small port allowing access to the Ionian islands, was the western centre of resistance against the Turks. The poet, who had contributed much of his personal fortune to the war effort, as well as his own fame, was enthusiastically greeted with a 21-gun salute.

On landing, he was made commander-in-chief of the 5000 soldiers gathered at the garrison: a role which was as much political as military. The

Greek forces, led by Klephtic brigand-generals, were split among themselves and each faction separately and persistently petitioned him for money. He had already wasted months in Kefalloniá trying to assess their claims and quarrels before finalizing his own military plan – to march full force on Náfpaktos and from there take control of the Gulf of Corinth – but in Messolóngi he was again forced to delay.

Occasionally Byron despaired; 'Here we sit in this realm of mud and discord', he wrote in his journal. But while other Philhellenes were returning home, disillusioned by the squabbles and larceny of the Greeks, or appalled by the conditions in this damp, stagnant town, he stayed, campaigning eloquently and profitably for the cause. Outside his house, he drilled soldiers; in the lagoon he rowed, and shot, and caught a fever. It was, bathetic though the story may seem, the most important contribution he could have made for the struggle. On April 19 Byron died, pronouncing a few days earlier, in a moment of lucid resignation, 'My wealth, my abilities, I devoted to the cause of Greece – well, here is my life to her!'

The news of the poet's death reverberated across Northern Europe, swelled to heroic proportions by his admirers. Arguably it changed the course of the war. When Messolóngi fell again to the Turks, two years later, there was outcry in the European press, and the French and English forces were finally galvanised into action at Navarino Bay (see Pílos). Byron, ever since, has been a Greek national hero. Almost every town in the country has a street – *Víronos* – named for him; there's a brand of cigarettes (perhaps the ultimate Greek tribute); and, perhaps more important, the respect he inspired was for many years generalised to his fellow countrymen – only to be dissipated in this century by British interference in the Civil War and bungling in Cyprus.

The modern town

The one part of the legend that doesn't measure up is **MESSOLÓNGI** itself. As in Byron's time, it's a miserable, desperately unromantic place – wet through autumn and spring, and conspicuously drab. If you come here on a pilgrimage, plan on moving ahead within the day. Lodgings are cheerless and overpriced (Etolikó, see above, is preferable), with the cheapest, if you're stuck, being the E-class *Diethnes* (Iróön Politehníou 17; ☎0631/2-365).

You enter the town by the **'Gate of the Sortie'** where during the Turks' year-long siege in 1826, 9000 men, women and children attempted to break out. In one wild dash they managed to get free of the town, leaving a group of defenders to destroy it in their wake. But they were betrayed and in the supposed safety of nearby Mount Zígos were ambushed and massacred by a large Albanian force.

Just inside the gate on the right is the **Garden of Heroes**, where a tumulus covers the bodies of the town's unnamed defenders; beside it is a **Statue of Byron** erected in 1881, under which is buried the poet's heart.

In the town, traces of Byron are sparse. **The house** which he lived and died in was destroyed during World War II and its site is marked by a clumsy memorial garden. It is on Odhós Levídhou, which is reached from the central square by walking down to the end of Trikoúpi and turning left.

Back in the central square, Platía Vótsari, the **Dhimarhío** (town hall) houses a small 'Museum of the Revolution', with some emotive paintings of the independence struggle (including a reproduction of Delacroix's *Gate of the Sortie*) and a rather desperate collection of Byronia – padded out with postcards from Newstead Abbey and the branch of an elm from his old school, Harrow.

travel details

BUSES

Buses detailed have similar frequency in each direction, so entries are given just once; for reference check under both starting-point and destination.

Kalambáka-Métsovo-Ioánnina (3 daily; 1½ hr./3 hr.).

From Ioánnina Athens (8 daily; 7½ hr.); Metsovo (4 daily, 1½ hr.); Dodona (2 daily, 6am/2pm Mon.-Sat.; 40min); Igoumenítsa (9 daily; 2½ hr.); Árta (10 daily; 2½ hr.); Préveza (10 daily; 2½ hr.); Kónitsa (7 daily; 1½ hr.); Paramithiá/Párga (1 daily; 2 hr./3 hr.); Kastoriá, via Kónitsa (2 daily, change at Neápoli; 6 hr.); Monodhéndri/Elafótopos (1 daily, except Sun.); Tsepélovo (2 daily; 1 on Sun.); Vrissohóri, via Tsepélovo (3-4 per week); Pápingo (5 weekly).

From Kónitsa Paliosélli/Pádhes (1 daily, except Sun.); Ayía Paraskeví (1-2 daily); Plikáti (1 daily, except Sun.).

From Igoumenítsa Párga (4 daily; 1½ hr.); Préveza (2 daily; 3 hr.).

From Árta Párga (4 daily; 1½ hr.); Préveza (4-5 daily; 1 hr.).

From Préveza Lefkádha (4 daily; 45 min.); Parga (7 daily; 1½).

From Vónitsa Áktio (3 daily; 30 min.); Lefkádha (4 daily; 2½ hr.).

From Agrínio Messolóngi-Andírio (12 daily; 1 hr./1½ hr.); Karpeníssi (1 daily; 5 hr.); Corfu (bus/ferry, 2 daily in season; 4 hr.).

FERRIES

From Igoumenítsa Corfu (hourly, last at 10pm; 2 hr.); Paxí/Kefalloniá/Itháki (daily in season, every other day out; 1½ hr./5½ hr./10½ hr.). Also to Ancona, Bari and Brindisi (Yugoslavia); Bar, Dubrovnik, Hvar, Korçula, Rab, Rijeka, Split and Zadar (Yugoslavia). See 'Igoumenítsa' for details.

From Párga Paxí (daily in season, book day before; 2 hr.).

Préveza-Áktio Every half hour (6am-10pm), every hour (10pm-6am); 5 min.

From Astakós Daily (mid-morning) to Itháki, almost year-round.

CHAPTER FIVE

THE NORTH: MACEDONIA AND THRACE

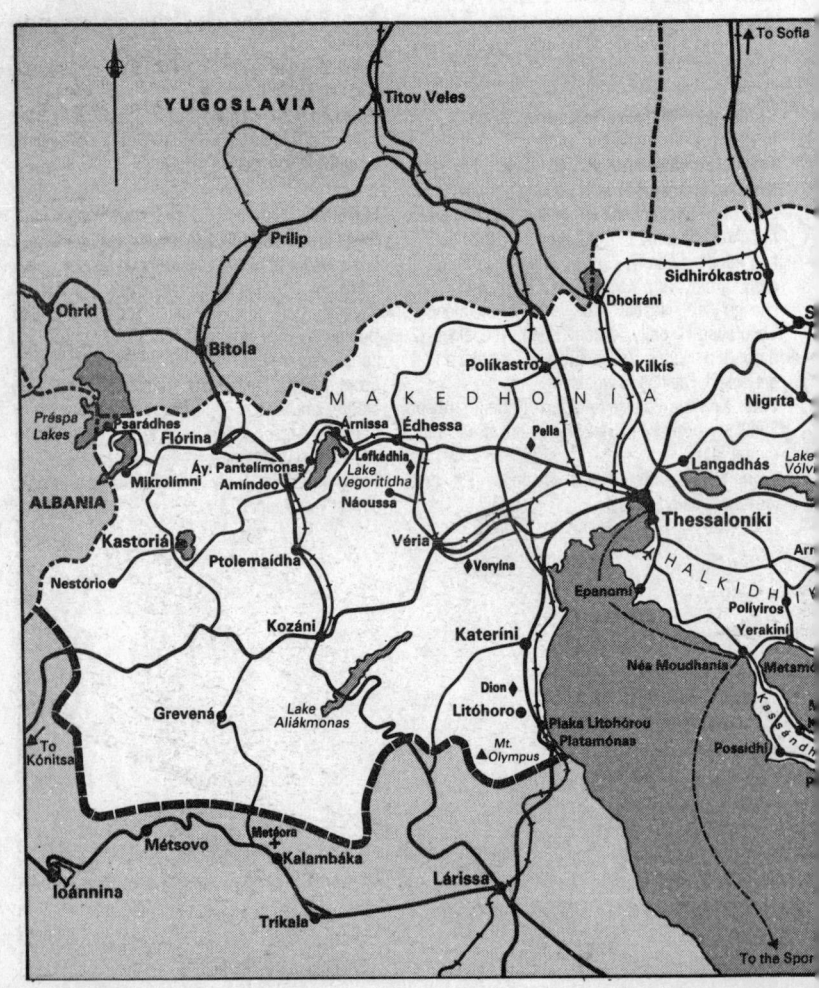

T he two northern provinces – **Macedonia** and **Thrace** – have been part of the Greek state for little more than two generations. Macedonia (*Makedhonía*) was surrendered by the Turks after the Balkan wars in 1913; Thrace (*Thráki*) only in 1923. As such, the region stands slightly apart from the rest of the nation – an impression reinforced for visitors by scenery and climate that are essentially Balkan. Macedonia is characterised by lake-speckled vistas to the west, and, to the east, moving towards Thrace, by heavily cultivated flood plains and the deltas of rivers finishing courses begun in Yugoslavia or Bulgaria. The climate can be harsh, with steamy summers and bitterly cold winters, especially up in the Rhodópi mountains that form a natural frontier with Bulgaria.

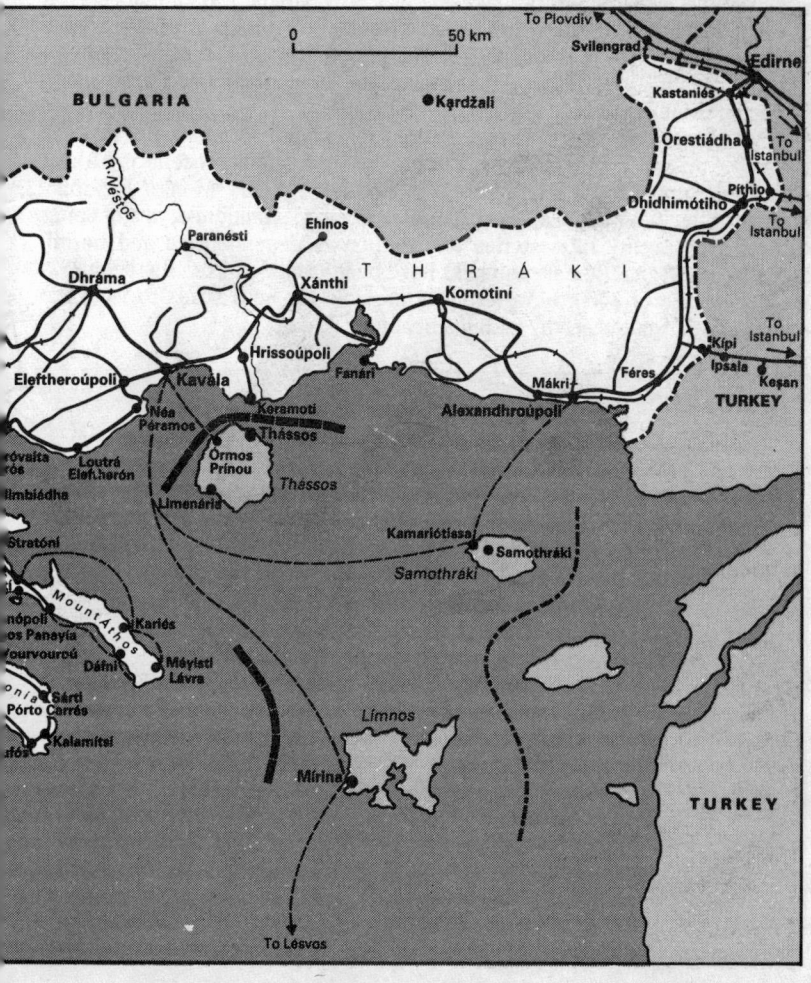

These factors, along with a relative dearth of beaches, may explain why the north is so little known to outsiders – even to those who have travelled throughout the rest of the mainland and islands. The only areas to draw more than a scattering of summer visitors are **Halkidhikí**, the three-pronged peninsula trailing below Thessaloníki that provides the city's beach-playground, and **Mount Olympus**, a mecca for walkers in the south of the province. For the rest, few travellers look beyond the dusty, poplar-lined trunk routes to Yugoslavia and Turkey.

With a more prolonged acquaintance, the north may well grow on you. Part of its appeal lies in its vigorous day-to-day life, independent of tourism – most evident in the relaxed Macedonian capital of **Thessaloníki** (Salonica) and its chief port **Kavála**. Another part lies, as in Epirus, in the mountain areas of the west, around **Flórina** and the lakeside city of **Kastoriá**. Monuments are on the whole modest, though the recent discovery of Philip II of Macedon's tomb at **Veryína**, if it is opened to visitors, will change that assessment. Meanwhile, there are lesser Macedonian and Roman sites at **Pella** and at **Philippi**, Saint Paul's first stop in Greece.

If you are male, over 21, and interested enough in monasticism – or Byzantine art and architecture – to pursue the applications procedure, **Mount Áthos** may prove to be a highlight of a Greek stay. This 'Monks' Republic' occupies the mountainous, eastern-most prong of Halkidhikí, maintaining control over twenty monasteries and numerous dependencies and hermitages. **Women** (and female animals) have been excluded from the peninsula since a decree of 1060; however, it is possible for both sexes to view the monasteries from the sea by taking a boat tour.

A Note on Macedonia

The name 'Macedonia' is a geographical term of long standing, applied to an area which has always been populated by a variety of races and cultures.

The original **Kingdom of Macedonia**, which gained pre-eminence under Alexander the Great and Philip II, was a Greek affair – governed by Greek kings and inhabited by a predominantly Greek population. Its early borders spread south to Mt. Olympus, west to present-day Kastoriá, east to Kavála, and north into parts of modern Yugoslavia. It lasted, however, for little more than two centuries. In subsequent years the region fell under the successive control of **Romans, Slavs, Byzantines, Saracens and Bulgars**, before eventual subjugation, with southern Greece under Ottoman **Turkish** rule.

In the late nineteenth century, when the disintegration of the Ottoman Empire began to throw into question future national territories, the name Macedonia denoted simply the region. Its population included Greeks, Slavs, and Bulgarians – who referred to themselves and their language as, respectively, *Makedhones, Makedonski*, and *Macedoneni* – as well as large numbers of Jews, Serbs, Vlachs, Albanians and Turks. The first **nationalist struggles** for the territory began in the 1870s, when small armies of Greek *andartes*, Serbian *chetniks* and Bulgarian *comitadjis* took root in the mountain areas, coming together against the Ottomans in the first Balkan War.

THESSALONÍKI AND WESTERN MACEDONIA

Thessaloníki is fulcrum, and focus, to Macedonian travel. If you are heading for the west of the province – **Kastoriá**, **Édhessa** or **Flórina**, all covered in the sections following – you will usually do best to go by bus or train from the capital. The train ride between Édhessa and Flórina, edging around Lake Vegorítidha, is one of the most scenic in the country; Kastoriá, for those who like their towns remote, is also highly worthwhile.

The biggest attraction in these parts of Macedonia, however, has to be **Mount Olympus** (Óros Ólimbos). The fabled home of the gods soars into the air above the town of Litóhoro, easily approached from the highway or rail line between Lárissa and Thessaloníki.

Thessaloníki (Salonica)

Second city of Greece and administrative centre for the north, **THESSALONÍKI** (or Salonica, as the city was known until this century) has a very different feel to Athens: more modern, cosmopolitan and for the most part wealthier. Situated at the head of the Thermaikós gulf it also seems more open – you're never far from the sea, and the air actually circulates.

Following Turkish defeat, things swiftly became more complex. The Bulgarians laid sole claim to Macedonia, but were defeated, and a 1912 Greco-Serbian agreement divided the bulk of Macedonian territory between the two states along language/population lines. During World War I, however, the Bulgarians occupied much of Macedonia, along with Thrace, until their capitulation in 1917. There followed exchanges of Greek and Bulgarian populations – a small part of Slav-speaking Macedonia remaining in Bulgaria; followed, seven years later, by the arrival and settlement of tens of thousands of Greek refugees from Asia Minor.

During World War II the Bulgarians occupied Macedonia again, as allies of Nazi Germany. Their defeat by the Allies led to withdrawal and seems to have vanquished ambitions. The Bulgarian leader, Todor Zhivkov, has renounced all territorial claims and 'minority rights' for 'Greek-Bulgarians'. The position of Yugoslavia, though, which under Tito established the Socialist Republic of Macedonia in its share of the historical territory, has been more ambiguous. During recent decades there have been Yugoslav propaganda attempts to suggest Slav affinities with the ancient Macedonian kingdom, and, by extension, with the present Greek population. Given the current state of the Yugoslav union, the issue has become quiescent, but visas for Yugoslav Macedonians are still treated with wariness by the Greeks. And archaeology in this province is very much a political as well as an academic issue.

This 'modern' quality of the city is due largely to a disastrous fire, which in 1917 levelled most of the old labyrinth of Turkish lanes; the city was rebuilt eight years later on a grid plan with long central avenues running parallel to the sea. The result is a more liveable city, though less interesting than Athens. It is also one with a distinctively northern European aspect, stimulated by its major university and international trade centre.

Until just a few decades ago the city's population was as mixed as any in the Balkans. Besides the Turks, who had been in occupation for close on five centuries, were Slavs, Albanians and the largest European **Jewish** community of the age – 100,000 before the first waves of emigration to Palestine began in the 1920s. Numbers remained at around 60,000 up until World War II when all but a fraction were deported to the concentration camps, in the worst atrocity committed in the Balkans. It was this operation in which the Austrian president Kurt Waldheim was involved – or, rather, which he claims not to have noticed.

You can get glimpses of 'Old Salonica' today in the walled **Kastrá** quarter of the city, on the hillside beyond the modern grid of streets. Even amidst the post-1917 streets below, there are pockets of Turkish buildings – mostly uncared for, and doubtless earmarked for redevelopment. For most visitors, however, it is Thessaloníki's excellent **archaeological museum**, with its spectacular exhibits from the tombs of Philip of Macedon and Alexander the Great, that stands out. Add to this, if you have developed a taste for Byzantine monuments, a unique array of **churches** dating from Roman times to the fifteenth century that constitute a showcase of the shifting styles of Orthodox religious architecture.

The downside, for visitors as well as residents, is a series of problems all too reminiscent of Athens. Industries and city alike discharge their waste, untreated, into the Thermaikós gulf, and the traffic on the front is often at a standstill. The present *Nea Dhimokratía* mayor, Sotiris Kouvelas, elected on promises of a cleanup, has plans for a metro line and seaward extension of the waterfront. Whether they come to anything remains to be seen; so far, his only claim to fame has been to defy the government in Athens by introducing satellite television – officially forbidden in Greece.

Orientation and accommodation

Arriving in Thessaloníki is in general straightforward. The **train station** is just a short walk from the central grid of streets and the waterfront. The various **bus terminals** are scattered around (see the 'Listings' at the end of the city section for getting out) but will mostly drop you within a half dozen blocks of the train station. Coming from the **airport**, 16km out, there are *Olympic Airways* buses (to their office on Níkis, near the seafront) and fairly modest-priced taxis.

Once within the grid, get your **bearings** by the three main avenues, **Ayíou Dhimitríou**, **Egnatía** and **Tsimíski**. All run parallel to the seafront, on the east side of which stands the city's symbol – the **White Tower**, or Lefkós Pírgos. **Kastrá**, the most pleasant part of town, is about fifteen minutes' walk from the sea.

The **local buses** #10 and #11 are useful – both ply the length of Egnatía. From Platía Eleftherías (just back from the port: see map), bus #5 runs down to the archaeological and folklore museums, and #22 heads north to the uppermost walls of Kastrá and the quarter known as Eptapirgíou. Buses are free before 8am. During summer you can also catch launches next to the White Tower for the beaches at Peréa and Ayía Triádha.

Accommodation

Outside of the festival season (see below), inexpensive hotels are reasonably easy to find – if not as a rul, very attractive.

The main concentration of D- and E-class places, along with a scattering more upmarket, and the occasional bordello, are found along the busy Egnatía avenue. In roughly ascending price order, these include:

Thessalonikon (Egnatía 9). Dirt cheap – in all senses of the words. Unclassified.

Argo (Egnatía 11; ☎031/519-770). A much more congenial E-class.

Atlantis (Egnatía 14; ☎031/540-131). Another, similar E-class. Best rooms face on to a side street.

Avgoustos (Elénis Svoronoú 4; ☎031/522-550). Quieter location, a block north of Egnatía. D-class.

Ilios (Egnatía 27; ☎031/512-620). D-class.

Atlas (Egnatía 40; ☎031/537-046). D-class.

Alexandhria (Egnatía 18; ☎031/536-185). D-class.

Lido (Egnatía 60; 223-805). D-class.

If you're staying for more than a night or two, it is worth hunting out a more pleasant, downtown location. For example:

Tourist (Mitropóleos 21; ☎031/270-501). Good value D-class by the cathedral, two blocks from the water.

Continental (Komnínon 5; ☎031/277-553); *Rea* (Komnínon 6; ☎031/278-449). A pair of good C-class hotels, little more expensive than the *Tourist* and nearby – Komnínon leads back from the sea between *platías* Eleftheriás and Aristotélous.

The city's **youth hostel** (Príngipos Nikoláou 44; ☎031/225-946) is noisy, ill-equipped, adds tax to the standard charge and seems to be run for minimum inconvenience to the wardens. It closes from 10am to 4pm and operates an 11pm curfew; IYHA card required for the privilege. For **women**, a much better hostel alternative is the **XAN** (YWCA) at Ayías Sofías 11 (☎031/276-144), well-run and well-maintained, opposite the cathedral. (The *XEN* (YMCA) is basically a sports hall and has no accommodation facilities).

The closest **campsites** are at the rather uninspiring beaches of Peréa and Ayía Triádha (20km and 22km respectively; bus #69 from Platía Eleftherías or, in summer, a boat from the White Tower).

Finally, for anyone with train tickets or a rail pass, the **train station** is a last-resort place to sleep. There are a fair number of early morning trains and most summer nights see a number of groups of travellers there. The staff don't seem to mind, moving people out of the booking hall at around 11pm to an out-of-the-way waiting room.

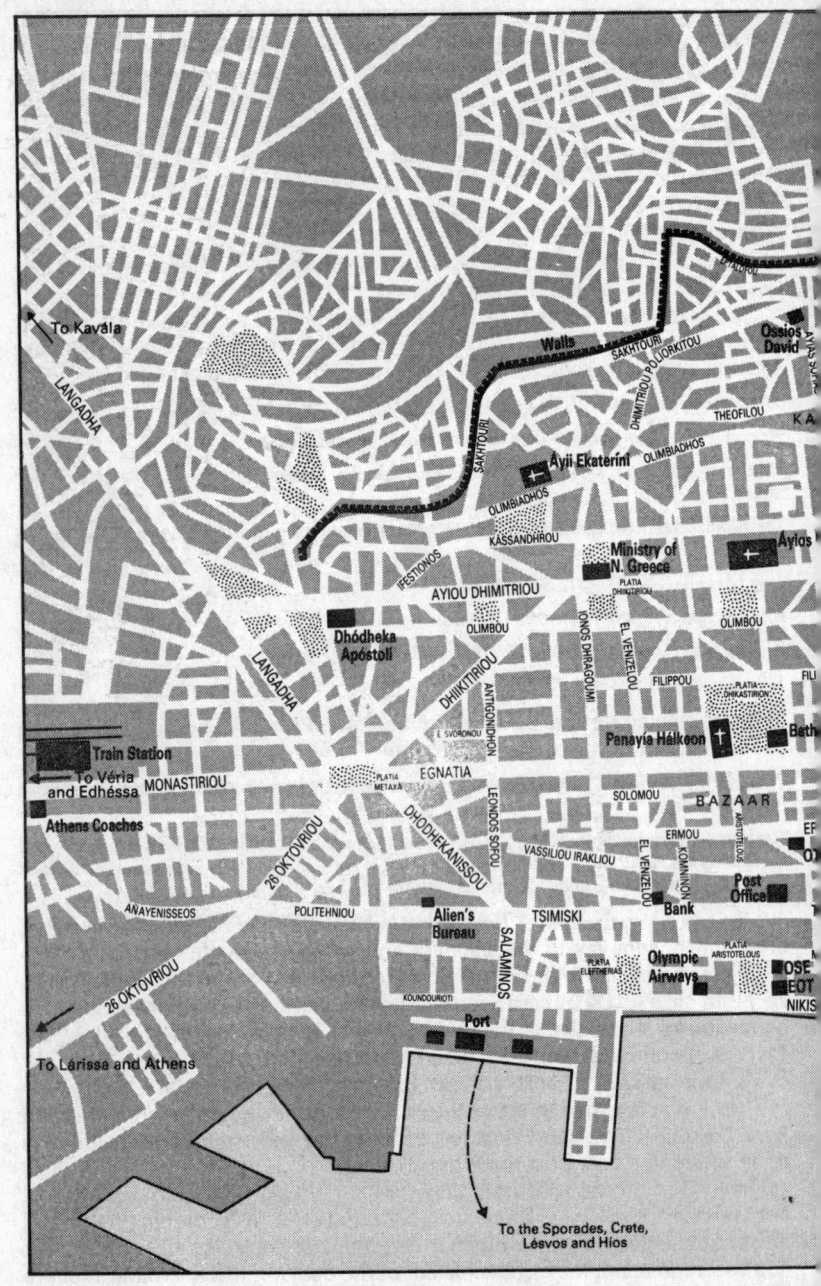

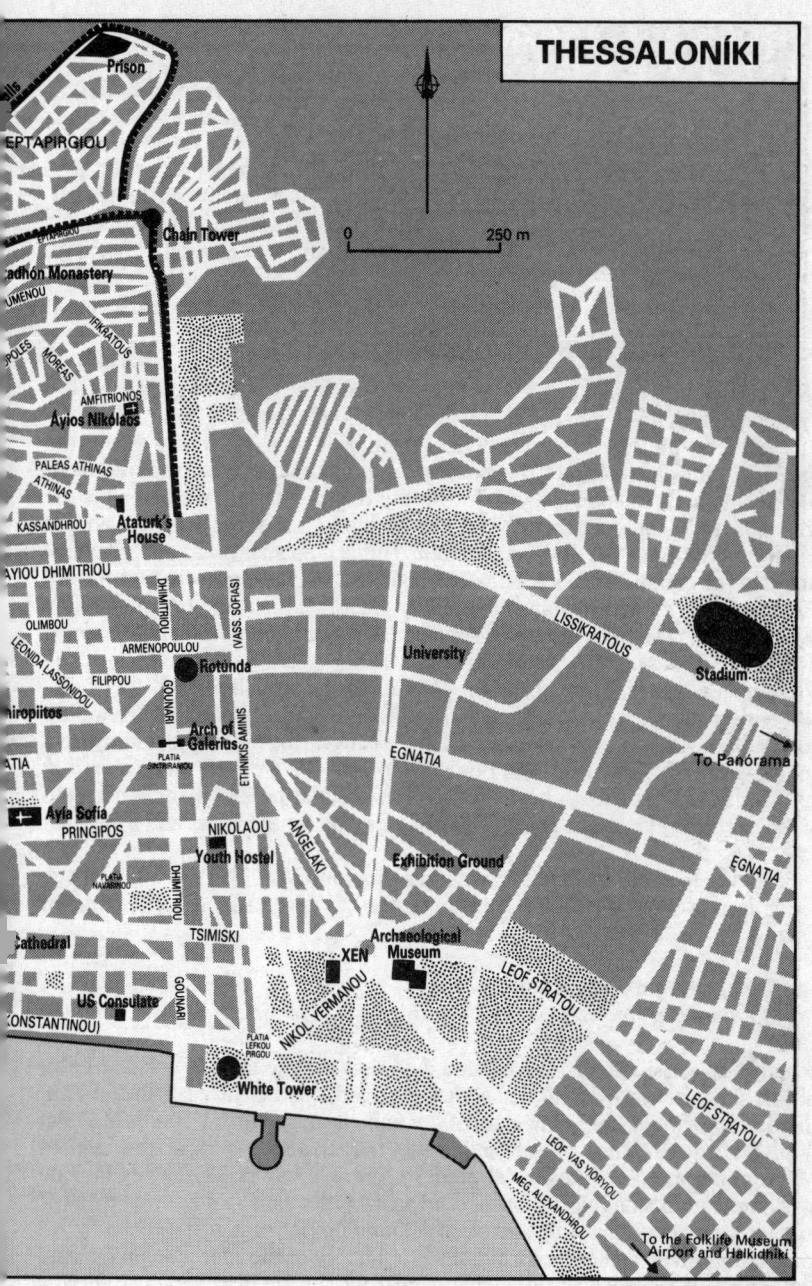

THESSALONÍKI

Prison

EPTAPIRGIOU

Chain Tower

0   250 m

adhón Monastery

UMENOU

IPAGATOUS

POLES

MOREAS

AMFITRIONOS

Áyios Nikólaos

PALEAS ATHINAS

ATHINAS

KASSANDHROU

Ataturk's House

AYIOU DHIMITRIOU

OLIMBOU

DHIMITRIOU

ARMENOPOULOU

(VASS. SOFIAS)

LEONIDA LASSONIOU

FILIPPOU

GOUNARI

Rotunda

University

LISSIKRATOUS

Stadium

hiropiitos

ATIA

Arch of Galerius

ETHNIKIS AMINIS

PLATIA DIKITIRANIOU

EGNATIA

To Panórama

Ayía Sofía

PRINGIPOS

NIKOLAOU

DHIMITRIOU

ANGELAKI

Youth Hostel

Exhibition Ground

EGNATIA

PLATIA NAVARINOU

Cathedral

TSIMISKI

GOUNARI

Archaeological Museum

XEN

LEOF STRATOU

US Consulate

CONSTANTINOU)

NIKOL VERMANOU

PLATIA LEFKOU PIRGOU

White Tower

LEOF STRATOU

LEOF. VAS YIORYIOU

MEG. ALEXANDROU

To the Folklife Museum Airport and Halkidhiki

Downtown: the museums and Kastrá

Wanderings in Thessaloníki's town centre are best given direction by the Byzantine churches – detailed in full in the section following. If your interest is a casual one, the two finest are Áyios Dhimítrios and Ayía Sofía. Along the way, take time to look into the **bazaar** area, just south of Egnatía between Dhragoúmi and Aristotélous, which with the Kastrá quarter (see below) is the area most redolent of nineteenth-century Turkish – and Jewish – Thessaloníki. It is said that until the last war, *Ladino* (Judaeo-Spanish) was the principal language of commerce here. Almost opposite, on Egnatía itself, is a former Turkish **bath**, its doorway surmounted by elaborate stalactite ornamentation. Down towards the waterfront on Tsimíski a sole **synagogue** remains; it can be visited by ringing for the caretaker at no. 24.

The focus however, has to be the **White Tower**, which formed the south-east corner of the city's Byzantine and Turkish defences, fronting a sea wall. It now looks a little stagey, isolated on the seafront, but is a graceful symbol nonetheless, which appears Big Ben style, on the TV news. It was restored in 1985 for Salonica's 2300th birthday celebrations and houses a small museum of the city's development. You can climb to the top for the views and a pleasant café.

From the tower you are within a couple of minutes' walk of the archaeological museum. For the folklife museum, the #5 bus can be picked up on Tsimíski.

The Archaeological Museum

Open 8am–7pm; Sun. 8am–6pm; closed Tues.; admission 400dr (students 200dr).

Whatever else you do in Thessaloníki, find time for the superb **Veryína exhibition** at the archaeological museum. Displayed – and clearly labelled in both English and Greek – are almost all of the finds from the Royal Tombs of Philip II of Macedon (father of Alexander the Great) and others at the ancient Macedonian capital of Aegae (at modern Veryína, see p. 315). They include startling amounts of gold – masks, crowns, wreaths, pins and figurines – all of extraordinary craftsmanship and often astounding richness.

Through these and other local finds, the history of the Macedonian dynasty and empire is traced: a surprisingly political act, for the discoveries at Veryína have been used by Greece to emphasise the fundamental 'Greekness' of the modern provinces of Makhedonía and Thráki. Although to an outsider these territories might seem an accepted and inviolable part of Greece, their recent occupation by Turks and Bulgarians is still very much part of Greek political memory. The sites, too, are a significant part of the debate; during the Bulgarian occupation of Macedonia during World War II, for example, there was a deliberate policy of vandalism towards 'Greek–Macedonian' remains.

Folklife–Ethnological Museum of Macedonia
Vassilíssis Ólgas 68; 9.30 am–2pm; closed Thurs.; free.

This is the best museum of its kind in Greece, with well-written commentaries (in English and Greek) accompanying displays on housing, costumes, day-to-day work and crafts. The exhibits, on weaving and spinning especially, are beautiful. And there is a sharp, highly un-folkloric emphasis on context: on the role of women in the community, the clash between tradition and progress, and the yearly cycle of agricultural and religious festivals. Even the traditional costumes are presented in a manner that goes beyond the mere picturesque.

The collection is housed in an elegant turn-of-the-century mansion, just a fifteen-minute walk (or short bus ride) from the archaeological museum.

Kastrá: the 'Turkish' quarter
Sections of the fourteenth-century **Byzantine ramparts**, constructed with brick and rubble on top of old Roman foundations, crop up all around the northern part of town. The best-preserved portion begins at a large circular keep, known as the 'Chain Tower' (for its encircling stringcourse), in the northeast angle. It then rambles north around the district of **Eptapirgíou**, enclosing the old acropolis (now the city prison) at the top end. On its south side the wall is trailed by Eptapirgíou street and edged by a small strip of park – a good place to sit and scan the town. Nearby, small *psistariés* and *kafenía* come alive in the late afternoon and evening.

Below Eptapirgíou is **Kastrá**, the main surviving quarter of 'Turkish' Thessaloníki. Although they are gradually becoming swamped by new apartment blocks, the streets here remain ramshackle and atmospheric – a labyrinth of timber-framed houses and winding steps. The churches of Óssios Davíd and the Vlatadhón Monastery (see overpage) are both quiet and interesting sanctuaries.

If you approach or leave Kastrá on its east side, it is worth casting an eye at the Turkish Consulate at the bottom of Apostólou Pávlou. In the pink building beside it **Kemal Ataturk**, first president and creator of the modern state of Turkey, was born. The consulate maintains the house as a small museum, with its original fixtures. To visit you must apply for admission at the main building, with your passport (Mon.–Fri. 9am–1pm and 4–6pm). Security is tight, and for good reason – Ataturk has been held largely responsible for the traumatic exchange of Greek and Turkish populations in 1923. In 1981 a Turkish celebration of the centenary of his birth had to be called off after a Greek stunt pilot threatened a kamikaze-dive at the house.

Roman and Byzantine Salonica: the churches

Macedonia became a **Roman** province in 146 B.C. and Salonica, with its strategic position for both land and sea access, was the natural and immediate choice of capital. Its fortunes and significance were boosted by the building of the *Via Egnatia*, the great road linking Rome (via Brindisi) with Byzantium and the East, along whose course Philippi and Kavála were also to develop.

Christianity had slow beginnings in the city. **Saint Paul** visited twice, being driven out on the first occasion after provoking the Jewish community. On the second, in 56, he stayed long enough to found a church, later writing the two Epistles to the Thessalonians, his congregation. It was another three centuries, however, before the new religion took full root. **Galerius**, who acceded as eastern emperor on Byzantium's break with Rome, provided the city with virtually all its surviving monuments – and its patron saint, Dhimitrios, whom he martyred. The first resident Christian emperor was **Theodosius** (375-395), who after his conversion issued from the city the Edict of Salonica, officially ending paganism.

Under Justinian's rule (527-65) Salonica became the second city of **Byzantium** after Constantinople, and it remained so, under constant pressure from Goths and Slavs, until its sacking by Saracens in 904. The storming and sacking continued under the Normans of Sicily (1185) and with the Fourth Crusade (1204), when the city became for a time capital of the Latin Kingdom of Salonica. It was, however, restored to the Byzantine Empire of Nicea in 1246, reaching a cultural 'Golden Age', amid the theological conflict and political rebellion of the next two centuries, until Turkish conquest and occupation in 1430.

Roman Salonica

Remains of Salonica's formative years in the early eastern empire are thin on the ground. The **Rotunda**, later converted to a church (see opposite), is the most striking. It originally formed part of a larger complex linking the **Arch of Galerius** with a palace and hippodrome. The arch, the surviving span of a dome-surmounted arcade over a group of Roman palaces, was built to commemorate the emperor's victories over the Persians in 297 A.D.; its piers contain reliefs of the battle scenes interspersed with symbolic poses of Galerius himself. Scant remains of the palaces can be seen, below the level of the modern street, on pedestrianised Goúnari.

Elsewhere in the city ruins of the **Roman Agora** were unearthed in the 1970s in the vast Platía Dhikastírion; they have yielded little in the way of structures, though they're still being excavated. Rather more prominent is an **Odeion** in the north corner of the square.

The churches

Almost all the main Byzantine churches can be found in the central area, so a 'Grand Tour' of them is not difficult – but then it isn't very grand either. Under the Turks most of the buildings were converted for use as mosques, a process which obscured many of their original features and destroyed the majority of their frescoes and mosaics. Further damage came with the 1917 fire and more recently with the earthquake of 1978. Restoration seems a glacially slow process, guaranteeing that most of the sanctuaries are shrouded in scaffolding at any given moment. But these disappointments acknowledged, the churches of Thessaloniki remain an impressive and illuminating group, considered below in rough chronological order, rather than by their placement in the urban grid.

The church of **Áyios Yióryios**, popularly known as the *Rotunda*, is the oldest and strangest of the collecton. It was designed, but never used, as an imperial mausoleum (possibly for Galerius) and converted to Christian use in the late fourth century by adding a sanctuary, a narthex and rich mosaics. Later it became one of the city's major mosques; the minaret (the tower from which prayer was called) remains. Sadly the church's interior has been closed since the 1978 earthquake. If it has reopened, the superb mosaics of peacocks, elaborate temples and martyred saints are definitely worth time.

The most prevalent of Roman public buildings was the **basilica**: a large wooden-roofed hall, with aisles split by rows of columns. It was ideally suited for conversion to Christian congregational worship, a process achieved simply by placing a canopied altar at what became the apse, and dividing it from the main body of the church (the nave) by a screen (a forerunner to the iconostasis). The baptistry, a small distinct building, was then added to one side. The upper reaches of wall were adorned with mosaics illustrating Christ's transfiguration and man's redemption, while at eye level stood a blank lining of marble. (Frescoes, a far more economical medium, did not become fashionable until much later – around the thirteenth and fourteenth centuries – when their scope for expression and movement was realised.)

Two fine examples of massive yet simple churches are Áyios Dhimítrios and the Ahiropíitos. Both originated in the fifth century, though they have been heavily restored and indeed rebuilt since.

Áyios Dhimítrios is dedicated to the city's patron saint and stands on the site of his martyrdom. Even if you know that it is the largest church in Greece, its immense interior comes as a surprise. Tall facades supported on red, green and white columns run alongside the nave. However, amid so much space and white plaster the few small surviving mosaics make an easy focal point; five are grouped to either side of the iconostasis and of these three date back to the church's second building in the late seventh century. The mosaic of *Áyios Dhimítrios with the Church's Founders* was described by Osbert Lancaster as 'the greatest remaining masterpiece of pictorial art of the pre-Iconoclastic era in Greece'; it contrasts well with its contemporary neighbour, a warm and humane mosaic of the saint with two young children. The **crypt**, unearthed after the great fire, contains the *martyrion* of the saint – probably an adaption of the Roman baths in which he was imprisoned – with its famous peacock mosaic. The church is open 8am to noon and 4 to 7pm (winter: 8am–3.30 pm); the crypt is closed on Tuesday.

Panayía Ahiropíitos has similar arcades, with monolithic columns and often highly elaborate capitals – a popular development under Theodosius. Only the mosaics beneath the arches survive, depicting birds, fruits and flowers in a rich Alexandrian style.

By the sixth century architects had succumbed to eastern influence and set about improving their basilicas with the addition of a **dome**. For inspiration they turned to the highly effective Ayía Sofía in Constantinople – the most striking of all Justinian's churches. Aesthetic effect, however, was not the only accomplishment, for the structure lent itself perfectly to the prevailing representational art. The **mosaics and frescoes** adorning its surfaces became physically interrelated or counterposed, creating a powerful spiritual aid. The eye would be uplifted at once to meet the gaze of the *Pantocrator* (Christ in Majesty) illuminated by the windows of the drum. Between these windows the prophets and apostles would be depicted, and as the lower levels were scanned the liturgy would unfold amid a hierarchy of saints.

Thessaloniki's **Ayía Sofía**, built early in the eighth century, follows closely its more illustrious namesake. Its dome, ten metres in diameter, bears a splendid *mosaic of the Ascension*: Christ, borne up to the heavens by two angels, sits resplendent on a rainbow throne; below them a wry inscription reads 'Ye Men of Galilee, Why stand ye Gazing up into Heaven?' Once again, the dome is in the process of restoration; the rest of the interior decoration was repatched after the 1917 fire.

The most successful shape to emerge during all these later experiments with the dome was the '**Greek Cross-in-Square**' – four equal arms that efficiently absorb the weight of the dome, passing it from high barrel vaults to lower vaulted chambers fitted inside its angles. Architecturally it was a perfect solution; a square ground plan was produced inside the church with an aesthetically pleasing cruciform shape evident in the superstructure. Best of all, it was entirely self-supporting.

By the mid-tenth century it had become the conventional form. Architects, no longer interested in new designs, began to exploit the old, which proved remarkably flexible; subsidiary drums were introduced above corners of the square, proportions were stretched ever taller, and the outer walls became refashioned with elaborate brick and stone patterning.

The eleventh-century **Panayía Hálkeon** is a classic though rather unimaginative example of the form. Far more beautiful is the church of **Dhódeka Apóstoli**, built with three more centuries of experience and the bold Renaissance influence of Mystra (see *Chapter Two*). Its five domes rise in perfect symmetry above walls of fine brickwork, though its interior no longer does it justice. **Ayía Ekateríni**, its contemporary, has still finer brickwork exploiting all the natural colours of the stones.

Finally, tucked into the heart of the old Turkish quarter are three highly worthwhile churches. Fourteenth-century **Áyios Nikólaos Orfanós** is a barn-like basilica, preserving its original frescoes. **Óssios Davíd**, a tiny fifth-century church, does not really fit into any architectural progression, since the Turks, overzealous in their conversion, hacked most of it apart. However, it has arguably the finest mosaic in the city, depicting a clean-shaven (fifth century style) *Christ appearing in a Vision*, to the amazement of the prophets Ezekiel and Habakkuk. Nearby, the **Monastery of Vlatadhón** is noteworthy for its peaceful, tree-shaded courtyard, a perfect place to complete a tour.

Out from the centre: woods and beaches

The big weekend escape from Thessaloníki is to the three-pronged Halkidhikí peninsula – detailed on p. 321. To get to its better beaches, however, requires more than a day trip. If you just want a respite from the city, or a walk in the hills, better to think in terms of Thessaloníki's own local villages and suburbs.

Panórama and Hortiátis

These two villages are perched on the hillside overlooking the city – 9km and 15km to the east, respectively.

PANÓRAMA, the closer, is exactly what its name suggests: a high, hillside viewpoint looking down over Thessaloníki and the gulf. To accompany the views, there are a number of cafés, tavernas, and **zakoroplastía**. The best known of these is *Elenidhi-To Ariston*, which serves up the premier local speciality, *trígona* (custard-filled triangular confections), wonderful *dondurma* (Turkish style ice cream) and *salépi* (a beverage made from the ground-up root of *Orchis mascula*). The village can be reached by #59 bus from Platía Dhikastiríon, or (not too expensive) by taxi.

Still more of a retreat is **HORTIÁTIS**, set in an area known as *Hília Dhéndhra* (Thousand Trees). This is accessible on the #17 city bus from Egnatía. Again, it offers sweeping views over the city, some popular places to eat, and good walking among the pines.

Beaches

To swim near Thessaloníki you need to get well clear of the gulf, where the pollution is all too visible. This means heading southwest towards Kateríni and the beaches below Mount Olympus (along the fast National Road), or north towards Halkidhikí.

If all you want is a meal by the sea then you can take local buses #72 or #69 clockwise **around the gulf**. Bus #69 runs to PERÉA (with a campsite, and a good inexpensive grill, *O Fotis*), AYÍA TRIÁDHA (another campsite, and rooms) and NÉA MIHANIÓNA: small resorts, with good seafront tavernas but rather unpleasant beach. Bus #72 takes you a little further around the bay to ÓRMOS EPANOMÍ, with a better strand and a third campsite. The first point where the sea is anything like clear, however, is **NÉA KALLIKRÁTIA**, an hour by bus from the Halkidhikí terminal (see *Listings*).

Eating, drinking, and nightlife

Thessaloníki has a less obvious restaurant and nightlife scene than Athens. Looking around the city centre you might imagine that there's little available aside from fast-food *tóst* and *souvláki*. Once you have found where the locals eat, however, there's both choice and quality; and finding a bar should present few problems at any hour of the day or night.

Restaurants

First, the **town-centre** options, all contained within the central grid:

Ta Koumbarakia, Egnatía 140. Modest-priced restaurant with outdoor tables always packed for Macedonian-style grills, salads (including pickled *tursí*) and seafood. Tucked behind the little chapel of the Transfiguration.

O Vangos, off Egnatía in the same area, close to the university. Another good outdoor option – cheap, well-cooked meat dishes.

O Loutros, corner Komnínon/Vassilíou Iraklíou (between Egnatía and the port). A delicious fish taverna housed in an old Turkish bath near the flower market; excellent retsina.

Inside the bazaar. In the area enclosed by Aristotélous, Iraklioú, Egnatía and Dragoúmi, there are some good kebab stalls (one or two open in the evening) and numerous lunchtime booths serving *patsás* (tripe soup).

Tsarouhas, Olímbou. The most famous of the city's *patsatzádhika*, if you're curious about the above delicacy.

Olymbos Naoussa, Níkis 5. Old-fashioned restaurant on the waterside. Lunch only, and go early before it fills with businessmen.

Ódhos Politéhniou Another good area for kebab houses. Try the group nearby the Aliens Bureau (at no. 53).

Bistrot Mandragore, Mitropóleos 98. A large and elegant wine-and-*mezédhes* bar, run by a man who twice won the state lottery. Closed in summer.

The **Kastrá** area is also good ground for food-hunting, with some nicely situated tavernas. Just wandering around, or up (in the area between Ayíou Dhimitríou and Kassandhroú), you should find somewhere that takes your fancy – and at much lower prices than in the main grid. Perhaps the best is:

Palio Skholio, Iktinoú. Situated on the first floor in this pedestrian arcade.

Farther afield, east of the main grid, there are some excellent restaurants and snacks to be found. The best (though also the most expensive) are in the seafront suburb of **Kalamariá**, 3km from the centre. The most useful buses to get there are #1 and #3, which run down from Mitropóleos along Vassilíssis Ólgas.

Krikelas, Vassilíssis Ólgas 284 (just beyond the Folklife Museum). A fairly pricey option, but the chef here is reputedly the best in Greece, drawing on almost a half century of experience; large menu, good service.

O Yiorgos, Márkou Bótsari 133. Superb *yíros* (lamb kebabs).

Ta Pringiponissia, Krítis 60 (near 25 Martíou; 600m beyond the Folklife Museum). Delicious Turko-Greek food in a pleasant two-level building; you make your selection from proferred plates of hot and cold *mezédhes*. Closed Sunday.

Archipelagos, *Il Fignatta*, *Chez André*. Kalamariá's three most popular restaurants. The first is good-quality Greek food; the second, Italian; the third, French-Swiss. If you try one of them, move on for ice creams to *Afrodite*, if only for its decor – a Greek idea of where the Carrington family might hang out.

Roma Pizza, Néa Plastiriá 24, Hariláo. For those in need of a fill of pizza, this is an outlet of the best chain in the country. Hariláo is a suburb 3km northeast of the White Tower; go by taxi.

Finally, the city has some good **desserts**. You can get excellent ice-cream at *I Ovaia* (Páliou Patrón Yermanoú 7), and freshly-baked American-style cookies by the kilo at Egnatía 144.

Bars

A good place to start an evening is pedestrianised Dhimitrío Goúnari. The main *vólta,* or promenade, takes place along here, working its way between the seafront and the Arch of Galerius. Platía Navarínou, just west of Goúnari, is also a lively centre.

Bars and **clubs** are to be found mainly on the seafront and parallel Korómila. Some of the more trendy places tend to be out along the road towards Kalamariá. Among them are:

Blue Window, near the Estía (student hostel) up behind the university. Live music.

Dheka Vima, Flemíng, off Vassilíssis Ólgas. A good *bouzoúki* joint; closed June to September.

Roots, near the White Tower. Popular student haunt, with dancing to a live band and regular *bouzoúki* music.

Lotos, by the White Tower. Regular music bar.

An Plo, Amnesia, Swing, Tottis. Currently the trendiest bars on the front proper.

Penny Lane, Korómila. 'English-style' pub.

Shic, Layamargeríta 5 (between Mitropóleos and Níkis). Piano bar and feminist meeting place. Closed in summer.

Entasis, Korómila 29. Bar-coffee shop with a (partly) gay clientele.

If you are looking for a place just to drink and have snacks, rather than the most modern that Thessaloníki can offer, then there's always the **OTE tower** in the International Fair Ground. This makes a complete revolution every twenty minutes, stays open until 2am, and is surprisingly reasonably priced. For hardened drinkers, the bar at the **train station** stays open through the small hours.

Listings

Air tickets *Olympic Airways* is on the waterside at Níkis 7; they run buses to the airport at Mikrá (16km out). See 'Travel Details' at the end of this chapter for destinations. Airport information: ☎031/411-977.

American Express Venizélou 10, for mail pick-up.

Bank The *National Bank of Greece* in the train station keeps late evening and weekend hours.

Bicycle hire Outlet at Filíppou 66.

Books *Molho* (Tsimíski 10) has an excellent stock of English-language books and magazines. Well worth a browse, whether you're hankering after *The New Statesman* or *The Face,* or looking for a volume on Mount Áthos. Try also *Promitheus,* Ermoú 75.

British Council Leof. Vass. Konstantínou 3. Free library and reading room. Also various cultural events, mainly in the winter months.

Bus terminals These are confusingly spread out, though mostly in the train station area. They include: Alexandhroúpoli (Koloniári 31, behind the train station); Athens (Monastiríou 67; opposite the train station; run by OSE, the rail company, which sells tickets); Halkidhikí (Karakássi 68, way out near the 'Bótsari' stop of the #10 bus line); Ioánnina/Kalambáka (Hristoupipsoú; west side of the city); Kavála (Langadhá 69; northwest of Egnatía); Vólos, Kastoriá, Flórina, Pélla and western Macedonia (Anayenisséos 22; south of the train station).

Camping gear Try *Petridhis,* Vassilíou Iraklíou 43.

Car hire *InterRent* (Anthéon 5; ☎031/826-333) is one of the best value agencies.

Coin-op laundries Three, fairly closely spaced in the centre: *Bianca* (Antoniádhou 3, near the Arch of Galerius); *Zerowatt* (Episkópou 2; around the corner); and *Canadian* (Platía Navarínou, north of Tsimíski).

Consulates Important for getting letters of introduction for Áthos permits. The British consulate was cut in 1985, and UK and Commonwealth citizens are represented by Honorary Consul Yiorgos Doukas, Venizélou 8. Netherlands (Komnínon 26, ☎031/227-477).

Ferries In season there are 'Flying Dolphin' hydrofoils (Monday, Wednesday and Friday) to Néa Moudhanía (Halkidhikí), Skíathos, Skópelos and Alónissos; details and tickets from *Egnatía Tours,* Kamboínion 9 (☎031/ 223-811). Regular ferries run on Monday to Haniá on Crete, on Saturday to Lésvos and Híos; tickets from *V. Karakharissis,* Koundouríotou 19 (westward continuation of Níkis; 2nd floor; ☎031/532-289).

Football Thessaloníki's main team is PAOK, whose stadium is in the east of the city – off our map, though visible on square A5 of the map in the EOT Thessaloníki pamphlet.

Ministry for Northern Greece This is on Platía Dhikitiríou; for processing permits for Mount Áthos make your way to Room 218.

Phones OTE office on Ermoú, corner Karólou Díehl. Open 24 hours.

Post Office Main office (for Poste Restante) at Tsimíski 45; open 7.30am–8pm, Mon.–Fri. only.

Records The best store is *Studio 52* (Goúnari 46; basement), stocking a wide selection of traditional Greek music as well as rock, jazz and classical.

Shoes The city has dozens of shoe shops. Two old-established stores offering excellent quality are *Sevastakis* and *Petridhis* (Tsimíski 23 and 38, respectively). Trendiest styles are at *Moccassino* (Tsimíski 22). Cheap buys in the bazaar area and along Svoloú or Egnatía.

Tourist Office The main EOT office is at Platía Aristotélou 8; open Mon.–Fri. 8.30am–8pm, Sat. 8am–1pm.

Trains All depart from the giant terminal down on Monastiríou, the southwestern continuation of Egnatía. If you want to buy tickets or make reservations, in advance the OSE office at Aristotélou 18 is more central and more helpful.

ANASTENARIÁ: The Fire Walkers of Langadhás

On 21 May, the feast day of Saints Constantine and Helen, villagers at **LANGADHÁS** (20km north from Thessaloniki) perform a ritual barefoot dance across a bed of burning coals.

The festival rites are of unknown and strongly disputed origin. It has been suggested that they are remnants of a Dionysiac cult, though devotees assert a purely Christian tradition. This seems to relate to a fire, around 1250, in the Thracian village of Kósti: holy icons were heard groaning from the flames and were rescued by villagers, who emerged miraculously unburnt from the blazing church. The icons, passed down by their families, are believed to ensure protection. Equally important is piety and purity of heart: it is said that no one with any harboured grudges or unconfessed sins can pass through the coals unscathed. The Greek church authorities, meanwhile, refuse to sanction any service on the day of the ritual; it has even been accused of planting glass among the coals to try and discredit this 'devil's gift'.

Whatever the origin, the rite is still performed each year – now something of a tourist attraction, with an admission charge and repeat performances over the next two days. It is nevertheless strange and impressive, beginning around 7pm with the lighting of a cone of hardwood logs. A couple of hours later their embers are raked into a circle and, just before complete darkness, a traditional Macedonian *daoúli* drummer and two lyra players precede about sixteen women and men into the arena. These *anastenarídhes* (literally 'groaners'), in partial trance, then shuffle across the coals for about a quarter of an hour.

In recent years they have been the subject of various scientific tests. So far the only established clues are that the dancers' brain waves indicate some altered state – when brain activity returns to 'normal' they instinctively leave the embers – and that their rhythmical steps maintain minimum skin contact with the fires. There's no suggestion of fraud, however. In 1981 an Englishman jumped into the arena, was very badly burned, and had to be rescued by the police from irate devotees and dancers.

If you go to the *anastenariá*, arrive early at Langadhás – by 5.30pm at the latest – in order to get a good seat. Be aware, too, that the event has a fairly circus-like commercialism, though this in itself can be quite fun.

Other *anastenarídhes* 'perform' at **MELÍKI**, near Véria, and at the villages of **AYÍA ELÉNI** and **ÁYIOS PÉTROS** near Sérres. Crowds, though, are reputed to be just as large and fire-walkers fewer; there doesn't seem much advantage in their remoteness.

If you're in Greece, anywhere, and moderately interested, you can catch the show on the **ERT TV news** at 9pm. Their cameramen are at Langadhás, too.

Travel agents *Magic Bus* (Tsimíski 32; ☎031/283-280) runs buses to Istanbul (quicker and more comfortable than the train), and – rather less recommended – to London. Agents for flights are to be found along Tsimíski.

Pella

PELLA was the capital of Macedonia throughout its greatest period and the first real capital of Greece, after Philip II forcibly unified the country around 338 B.C. It was founded some sixty years earlier by King Archelaus, who transferred the royal Macedonian court here from Aigai (see Veryína), and from its beginnings was a major centre of culture. The royal palace was decorated by Zeuxis and said to be the greatest artistic showplace since the time of Classical Athens. Euripides wrote and produced his last plays at the court, and here too Aristotle was to tutor the young Alexander the Great – born, like his father Phillip II, in this city.

The site today, split by the road to Édhessa, is an easy and rewarding day trip from Thessaloníki. Its main treasures are a series of pebble mosaics, some in the museum, a couple in situ. For an understanding of the context, it is best to visit after looking around the archaeological museum at Thessaloníki.

The Site
Open 8.45 am–3pm, Sun. 9.30am–2.30pm; closed Tues.
When Archelaus founded Pella it lay at the head of a broad lake, connected to the Thermaíkos gulf by a navigable river. By the second century B.C. the river had begun to silt up and the city fell into decline. It was destroyed by the Romans in 146 B.C. and never rebuilt. Today its **ruins** stand in the middle of a broad expanse of plain, 40km from Thessaloníki and the sea.

The city was located by chance finds in 1957; preliminary excavations have revealed a vast site covering over one and a half square miles. As yet, only a few blocks of the city have been fully excavated but they have proved exciting. To the right of the road is a grand official building, probably a government office; it is divided into three large open courts, each enclosed by a *peristyle*, or portico (the columns of the central one have been re-erected), and bordered by wide streets with a sophisticated drainage system.

The three main rooms of the first court have patterned geometric floors, in the centre of which were found superb, intricate **pebble-mosaics** depicting scenes of a lion hunt, a griffin attacking a deer, and Dionysus riding a panther. These are now in the **musuem** (across the road, same hours as the site). But in the third court three mosaics have been left in situ; one, a stag hunt, is complete, and astounding in its dynamism and use of perspective. Others represent the rape of Helen and a fight between a Greek and an Amazon.

It is the inherently graceful and fluid quality of these compositions which sets them apart from later Roman and Byzantine mosaics and which more than justifies a visit. The uncut pebbles, carefully chosen for their soft shades, blend so naturally that the shapes and movements of the subjects seem gradated rather than fixed, especially in the action of the hunting scenes and the sloping movement of the leopard with Dionysos. Strips of lead or clay are used to outline special features; the eyes, all now missing, were probably made of semi-precious stones.

The **acropolis** at Pella is a low hill to the left of the modern village. Excavation is in progress on a sizeable building but at present it's illuminating mainly for the idea it gives you of the size and scope of the site.

Access
Pella is easiest reached from Thessaloníki. Just take any of the Édhessa **buses** from the Anayennisséos terminal; they run more or less half-hourly through the day and stop by the Pella museum. If you arrive late and want to stay, the nearest hotels are in the town of Yiannitsá, 12km west on the road to Édhessa.

Continuing to **Aegae/Veryína** by public transport, you'll need to get a bus, or walk, back down the Thessaloníki road to the junction at Halkidhóna. From here you can pick up the Thessaloníki-Véria buses.

Dion

ANCIENT DION, in the foothills of Mount Olympus, was the Macedonians' sacred city. At this site – a harbour before the sea receded – the kingdom maintained its principal sanctuaries: to Zeus (from which the name *Dion*, or *Dios*, is derived) above all, but also to Demeter, Artemis, Asclepius, and, later, to foreign gods such as the Egyptian Isis and Serapis. Philip II and Alexander both came to sacrifice to Zeus here before their expeditions. Inscriptions found at the sanctuaries referring to boundary disputes, treaties, and other affairs of state suggest the political and social importance of the city's festivals exceeded a purely Macedonian domain.

Most exciting for visitors, however, are the finds of mosaics, temples and baths that have been excavated over the last five years – work that remains in progress. These are not quite on a par with the Veryína tombs, but still rank among the major discoveries of Macedonian history and culture. If you are heading for Mount Olympus, they are certainly worth a half-day detour. At the village of DHIÓN, just north of Litóhoro beach, take a side road inland, to the east, past remains of a theatre. The main site lies ahead.

The site is open daily in summer from 9am–7.30pm (Weds. 9am–3pm; closed Tues.; 400dr). The main visible excavations are of the vast **public baths** complex and, outside the city **walls**, the **sanctuaries** of Demeter and Aphrodite-Isis. In the latter a small temple has been unearthed, along with its cult statue – which remains in situ. The finest mosaics so far discovered (and which may be open to view) are in a former banquet room; they depict the god Dionysos on a chariot. Christian **basilicas** attest to the town's later years as a Roman bishopric in the fourth and fifth centuries A.D.

The integrity of the site and its finds is due to the nature of the city's demise. At some point in the fifth century a series of earthquakes prompted an evacuation of the city, which was then swallowed up by mud from the mountain.

Back in the village a small **museum** (same hours; admission included with site ticket) houses most of the finds. The sculpture, perfectly preserved by the mud, is impressive, and accompanied by various tombstones and altars.

Upstairs, along with extensive displays of pottery and coinage, is a collection of everyday items, including surgical and dentists' tools perhaps connected with the sanctuary of Asclepius, the healing god.

Note that the village cannot be approached directly from Mount Olympus. An army firing range bars the way.

Mount Olympus (Óros Ólimbos)

Highest, most magical and most dramatic of all Greek mountains, **Mount Olympus** (*Ólimbos* in Greek) rears nigh on 3000 metres straight from the shores of the Thermaíkos gulf. Dense forests cover its slopes and its wild flowers are without parallel even by Greek standards. To make the most of it you need to allow two to three days' hiking.

Equipped with decent boots and warm clothing, no special expertise is necessary to get to the top in summertime (mid-June to October), though it's a long hard pull requiring a good deal of stamina. Winter climbs, of course, are another matter. At any time of year Olympus is a mountain to be treated with respect: its weather is notoriously fickle and it does claim lives.

Litóhoro and Olympus basics

The best base for a walk up the mountain is the village of **LITÓHORO** on the eastern side. Unexciting in itself, in good weather it affords intoxicating eve-of-climb views into the heart of the range.

To reach Litóhoro is easy. From the train station (9km distant) there's a connecting bus; or you can get a bus direct from Thessaloníki or Kateríni. Cheapest lodgings are at the **youth hostel** (☎0352/81-202) or D-class *Hotel Park* (☎0352/81-252), respectively above and below the square. For a more comfortable **hotel**, well-heated in winter and only marginally more expensive, try the *Myrto* (☎0352/81-398) in the main street. In the square there are a few rather uninspired tavernas.

Accommodation on Olympus itself is better organised than on any other mountain in Greece. There are two staffed **refuges**: the relatively luxurious and expensive *Spílios Agapitós* at 2100 metres (open May 15–October 15; ☎0352/81-800), and the more Spartan *Yiósos Apostolídhis* hut at 2700 metres (open only in July and August, though its glassed-in porch is always available for climbers in need; ☎0352/82-300). Both serve food, the latter pretty basic. *Spílios Agapitós* gets very full in summer, so it might be wise to phone ahead; the wardens speak English.

Any other provisions you need have to be bought in Litóhoro. You'll need to stock up with water, and, before you leave, be sure to get a free EOS leaflet with **map** from the kiosk in the square.

The mountain

To reach the Olympus footpaths you need first to cover 18km of **forest track to Priónia**. If you can afford it, the simplest solution is to hire a taxi. Lifts are possible in season, too. Trying to walk is real drudgery, though you could break the journey at the **Stavrós refuge** (after 10km) or at the ruined **Monastery of Áyios Dhioníssios** in the ravine bottom, about 2km short of Priónia.

As for the actual **ascent routes**, there are two main trails: one beginning at PRIÓNIA, where a primitive taverna operates by the spring in summer; the other at a spot called DHIAKLÁDHOSI (14km up), marked by a signboard displaying a map of the mountain. Both are beautiful. The first is more frequented and more convenient, and is described below.

The ascent from Priónia

The path begins just uphill from the taverna by an EOS signpost giving the time to the refuge as 2½ hours (allow 3 hr.). You cross a stream (last water before the *Spílios Agapitós* refuge) and start to climb steeply up through woods of beech and black pine. The path is well-trodden and there is no danger of getting lost. As you gain height there are superb views across the Mavrólongos ravine to your left and to the peaks towering above you.

The *Spílios Agapitós* **refuge** perches on the edge of an abrupt spur, surrounded by huge storm-beaten trees. Zolotas, the warden, can be short-tempered, so let him know in good time if you want a meal and a bed. It's best to stay overnight here, as you need to make an early start for the three-hour ascent to Mítikas, the highest peak at 2917 metres. The peaks frequently cloud up towards midday and you lose the view, to say nothing of the danger of catching one of Zeus's thunderbolts, for this was the mythical seat of the gods. Besides, nights at the refuge are fantastic: a log fire blazes; you watch the sun set on the peaks, and dawn come up over the Aegean; there are billions of stars.

The path continues behind the refuge (last water source on the mountain), climbing to the left up a steep spur among the last of the trees. In an hour you reach a signposted **fork** above the treeline. Straight on takes you to Mítikas, via the ridge known as Kakí Skála (1½hr.). Right leads to the *Yiósos Apostolídhis* hut in one hour, with the option after forty minutes of taking the very steep Loúki couloir left up to Mítikas; if you do this be wary of rockfalls.

For the safer **Kakí Skála route** continue up the right flank of the stony featureless valley in front of you, with the Áyios Andónios peak up to your left. An hour's dull climb brings you to the summit ridge between the peaks of Skolió on the left and Skála on the right. You know you're there when one more step would tip you over a 500-metre sheer drop into the Kazánia chasm: take great care. The Kakí Skála ('Evil Stair') begins in a narrow cleft on the right just short of the ridge; paint splashes mark the way. The route keeps just below the ridge, so you are protected from the drop into Kázania. Even so, those who don't like heights will feel pretty uncomfortable.

You start with a slightly descending rightward traverse to a narrow nick in the ridge revealing the drop to Kazánia – easily negotiated. Continue traversing right, skirting the base of the Skála peak, then climb leftwards up a steepish gully made a little awkward by loose rock on sloping footholds. Bear right at the top over steep but reassuringly solid rock, and across a narrow neck. Step left around an awkward corner and there in front of you, scarcely 100 metres away, is **Mítikas summit**, an airy, boulder-strewn platform with a trigonometric point, tin Greek flag, and visitors' book.

In reasonable conditions it is about forty minutes to the summit from the start of Káki Skála; three hours from the refuge; five and a half hours from Priónia.

A stone's throw to the north of Mítikas is the **Stefáni peak**, also known as the Throne of Zeus, a bristling hog's back of rock with a couple of nastily exposed moves to scale the last few feet.

Back - or on - from Mítikas

You can either go back the way you came, with the option of turning left at the signpost (see above) for the *Apostolídhis hut* (2½hr. from Mítikas by this route), or you can step out, apparently into space, in the direction of Stefáni and turn immediately down to the right into the mouth of the Loúki couloir. It takes about forty minutes of downward scrambling to reach the main path where you turn left for the hut, skirting the impressive northeast face of **Stefáni** (1 hr.), or go right, back to the familiar signpost and down to *Spílios Agapitós* (2 hr. altogether).

The advantage of going on to the **Apostolídhis hut** is that you can then descend by the magnificent but long **Petróstrounga path**. With your back to the refuge (there's often a small herd of chamois around here towards dusk), turn left and cross the flattish grassy ground known as the 'Plateau of the Muses' to its edge, where the path bends round the head of a precipitous drop. Thence it follows the ridge dividing the Enipéas ravine on your right from the Pápa Réma ravine to the north as far as a rounded bump with a survey point on top. Here the path winds down to a flat-topped ridge just clear of the highest trees. In two to two and a half hours from the hut, you come out on a rock-strewn shoulder among scattered Balkan pines, with a sheepfold among the boulders to your left. This is **Petróstrounga**.

From here you drop down into a grassy bowl and enter the trees again, where there is a signposted **fork** (a spring 15 min. to the right). Keep straight on, and straight again at another fork a little way beyond. Thereafter the path descends strong and clear through mixed woods of beech and pine to a little patch of meadow known as **Bárba**, and thence to the Priónia track at Dhiakládhosi (4½ hr. going down; at least 6 hr. up; see above), where you are faced once more with the problem of getting back to Litóhoro.

Véria and Veryína

VÉRIA has no particular site or monument but it is one of the more interesting northern Greek towns. The central streets preserve much of their old Turkish atmosphere, including a largely untouched nineteenth-century bazaar quarter, as well as a unique collection of 'disguised' churches, which see few tourists from one year to the next.

Perhaps the best point to start exploring is the **Laographic Museum** (open 9am–2pm and 5–8pm; if closed knock at the office next door) on Odhos Xánthi, off the Belvedere. This contains an appealing collection of traditional fabrics, costumes, embroidery, and carpets, as well as agricultural and cooking implements. It is worth enquiring here about possibilities of admission to the town's numerous seventeenth- and eighteenth-century **churches**. Some fifty or so survive from an era when Ottoman law forbade their building and use. They are to be found hidden behind (or disguised as) townhouses. Most, inevitably, are tricky to find and many are now decaying and kept locked. One that's not – and which gives a good idea of their long, low structures – is near the new cathedral on Mitropóleos, the main road out of town to Kozáni. If you're determined, a good area to hunt out others is around Makariótissa and Ilías streets.

For the most part, however, Véria seems more a place to wander about, particularly in the streets off Vassiléos Konstantínou, the main thoroughfare into town from the bus station. Midway along this street is the old **Mitrópolis** (cathedral). Opposite is a gnarled plane tree from which, in 1436, the Turks hanged the town's archbishop. Farther down – past some fine *kafenía* in the old bazaar section – narrow, dark streets of balconied wattle-and-timber houses sprawl towards the river.

The town's **Archaeological Museum** (daily 9am–3pm, Sun. 10am–4pm; closed Tues.) has a few of the lesser finds from Veryína but contains mostly Roman oddments from the area; it's about 500m out of town on Leofóros Ánixos, the beginning of the road to Veryína.

Staying, you'll find the town's two D-class **hotels** on the Kendrikí Platía: *Aristidhis* (no.71; ☎0331/26-355) and *Veroi* (no.4; ☎0331/22-866). Private rooms are not in evidence. If you want to camp, Veryína (see below) is a better choice.

Veryína: ancient Aigai

Excavations at **VERYÍNA**, twenty minutes by bus from Véria, have revolutionised Macedonian archaeology over the past decade. A series of chamber tombs, unearthed here by Professor Manolis Andronikos, are now unequivocally accepted as those of Philip II and members of the Macedonian royal family. This means that the site itself must be that of Aigai, the original Macedonian royal capital before the shift to Pella, and later its necropolis. Finds from the site and tomb, the richest in Greece since the discovery of Mycenae, are exhibited at Thessaloniki's archaeological musem. The tombs, however, are still in the process of excavation and documentation. The few sites to be seen here are somewhat minor and disappointing: not, on balance, worth much of a detour.

As yet the village hasn't been exploited for the growing number of hopeful tourists. But there are a few tentative tavernas and rooms to let; camping is easy too, in the pleasant surroundings.

Ancient Aigai and the sites

Ancient Aigai is documented as the sanctuary and royal burial place of the Macedonian kings. It was here that Philip II was assassinated and buried – and tradition maintained that the dynasty would be destroyed if any king were buried elsewhere, as indeed happened after the death of Alexander the Great in Asia. Until Andronikos' finds in 1977, Aigai had long been assumed lost beneath modern Édhessa, a theory which is now completely discarded.

What Andronikos unearthed, under a tumulus just outside the village of Veryína, were two large and undoubtedly Macedonian **chamber tombs**. The first had been looted in antiquity but retained a wall painting of the rape of Persephone by Hades, the only complete example of an ancient Greek painting that has yet been found. The second, a grander vaulted tomb with a Doric facade adorned by a superb painted frieze of a lion hunt, was – incredibly – ntact. Among its treasures emerged a marble sarcophagus, within it a gold casket of bones bearing the exploding star symbol of the royal line on its lid, and, still more significantly, five small ivory heads, among them representations of both Philip II and Alexander. It was this definitive clue that led to the identification of the tomb as that of Philip II.

Buses to Veryína stop at the crossroads, from where the 'Royal Tombs' and other sites are frustratingly signposted.

The so-called **Tomb of Veryína**, not to be confused with Philip's, can be visited. It lies some way from the recent discoveries, about half a kilometre up the hill from the village. Excavated by the French in 1861, its form is that of a temple with an Ionic facade of half-columns closed by two pairs of marble doors. Inside stands an imposing marble throne with sphinxes carved on the sides, armrests and footstool. Its royal neighbours are said to be similar in design.

A few hundred metres further on, occupying a low hill, are the ruins of the **Palace of Palatitsa** (8.45am–3pm, Sun. 9.30am–2.30pm; closed Tues.; 300dr). This was probably built in the third century B.C. as a summer residence for the last great Macedonian king, Antigonus Gonatus. It is now little more than foundations but amid the confusing litter of poros drums and capitals you can make out a triple *propylaion* (entrance gate) opening on to a central courtyard. This is framed by broad porticoes and colonnades which, on the south side, preserve a well-executed if rather unexciting mosaic. For all its lack of substance it is an attractive site, dominated by a grand old oak tree looking out across the plains of Veryína – scattered with Iron Age tumuli (10th–7th c. B.C.) and who knows what more.

Édhessa, Lefkádhia and Náoussa

ÉDHESSA, like Véria, is a pleasant Macedonian stopover, its modest fame attributed to the waters which flow through the town. Coming down from the mountains to the north, they flow swiftly through the middle of town and then, just to the east, cascade down a dramatic ravine, luxuriant with vegetation, to the plain below. From the train station, walk straight for 400m until you see the walled-in river, paralleled by Tsimíski street. Turn left and you will come to the **waterfalls**, the focus of a park with a *Xenia* hotel (☎0381/22-995; good out-of-season rates) and a couple of cafés. For the **Byzantine bridge** turn right from here and follow the river for about 600 metres. Paths also lead down the ravine, providing access to caves below.

The town itself is a little ordinary, but the various riverside parks and wide pedestrian sidewalks are a rare Greek pleasure, and the train and bus stations are both well placed for breaking a journey. If you're looking for cheaper **accommodation**, the E-class *Hotel Olympia* (18 Oktovríou 69; ☎0381/23-544), near the train station, is clean, friendly and quiet. The D-class *Olympion* and *Pella*, by the bus station, are both pricier and noisier. Simple but good and inexpensive **food** is served at the taverna *I Varhoula*, again near the train station, at 25 Martíou 10; at *Tsarouhakis* (18 Oktovríou 32); and at *To Roloi*, near the clock tower and OTE.

Lefkádhia and Náoussa

If you have your own transport, both Lefkádhia and Náoussa justify a stop along the road between Édhessa and Véria.

The village of **LEFKÁDHIA** lies just off the main road, heralded by a signpost bearing the legend 'Two Royal Tombs'. There are in fact four Macedonian tombs here, though only one is open to the public. This, the so-called **Great Tomb** (west of the road), is the largest Macedonian temple tomb yet discovered. It dates from the third century B.C. and was probably built for a general – who is depicted in one of the surviving frescoes with Hermes (the Conductor of Souls). Other frescoes represent the judges of Hades. The tomb has an elaborate and grand double-storied facade, one half Doric, the other Ionic; the frieze on its entablature shows a battle between Persians and Macedonians. The other three tombs are nearby – one (presumably that of the road sign) with a huge Ionic front. Lefkádhia itself has not been positively identified with any Macedonian city, but it is thought possibly to have been Mieza, where Aristotle taught.

Four kilometres south is a turning (west) to **NÁOUSSA**, a small country town which produces what is arguably Greece's finest wine – the *Boutari* red. It's reputed to have the country's best apples and peaches too, and hosts one of Macedonia's most elaborate pre-Lenten carnivals. All in all, a good watering-hole, and with two E-class **hotels**: *Kentrikon* (Konstantinídhi 9; ☎0332/22-409) and *Megas Alexandhros* (Platía Emboríou; ☎0332/27-511).

West from Édhessa: Flórina and the lakes

West of Édhessa lies **Límni Vegoritídha**, the first of a series of lakes that punctuate the landscape towards Kastoriá and up to, and across, the Yugoslav border. The rail line between Édhessa and Flórina traces the lake's west shore: a fine journey which could be broken at either of the two village train stops, Árnissa and Áyios Pantelímonas.

ÁRNISSA has perhaps the better setting, opposite an islet and amidst apple orchards. The village itself is a little drab, though it does have the convenience of an E-class **hotel**, *Megali Hellas* (☎0381/31-232). To its north rises **Mount Kaimaktsalán**, scene of one of the bloodiest and more important battles of World War I, which raged intermittently from 1916 to 1918 until a Yugoslav force managed to break through the German-Bulgarian lines. The 2524-metre summit marks the Greek-Yugoslav frontier and bears a small memorial chapel to the fallen. If you can get a lift to the end of the road at Kalívia, it's a beautiful walk beyond.

The more attractive of the villages, however, is **ÁYIOS PANTE-LÍMONAS**, with its red-roofed houses crowned by a windmill, and with a small beach if you're prepared to swim in the slightly algae-ridden waters. There is a taverna, which may be able to arrange accommodation. Otherwise camping should present no problem. The place sees few tourists.

Flórina

FLÓRINA is the last town before the Yugoslav border 13km to the north. As such, it is quite a lively market centre, both for Greeks from this region and for Yugoslavs in search of goods unobtainable over the frontier. You can get just about anything here, including Yugoslav *dinars* – though they are (currently) sold at better rates in Yugoslavia itself.

There is little of intrinsic interest. Other than crossing into Yugoslavia, the main reason for a visit is to see the Préspa lakes (40km west), or get onward transport to Kastoriá. If you stay, best of the cheap **hotels** is the unclassified *Hotel Patera*, behind the fruit market; otherwise try the D-class *Diethnes* (☎0385/22-778). For Macedonian food at its best, follow the locals to *Taverna Orea Ellada* on the main square.

The Préspa lakes

The entire area of the **Préspa lakes** is a protected ornithological refuge, as well as a highly sensitive political region – on the borders of Greece, Yugoslavia and Albania. In past years it has been necessary to obtain a permit from the police in Flórina or Kastoriá before setting out; this shouldn't at present be the case, though it might be wise to check.

The smaller of the two lakes, **Mikrí Préspa**, lies almost entirely in Greece. Deep and cliff-girt, it has just one shoreside village, MIKROLÍMNI, at the road's end on the south side. If you've come for the birdlife – which is unique – it's said to be possible to hire a boat for some lake exploration. Just don't drift across into Albania: the guards are prone to the occasional potshot at intruders.

Megáli Préspa is the highest and second largest lake in the Balkans, with extensive reed beds. Most of its waters, however, are inside Yugoslavia. On the Greek side the end of the infrequent bus line is PSARÁDHES, a handsome but very derelict, old-fashioned village – still Macedonian-speaking. Lodging is available at a pretty basic family taverna.

Transport to Yugoslavia

The one, *slow* daily train (3.30p.m.) from **Flórina to Bitola**, Yugoslavia, sounds like a bad deal compared to the four daily buses (morning and mid-day) to the frontier post at NÍKI. But from the latter it's 18km to Bitola and you'll have to hitch the first 6km to MEDZITLIJA, where Yugoslav bus services begin.

One consolation at NÍKI is that there's a bank at which you can exchange drachmas for dinars. Rates, however, as at Flórina, are worse than in Yugoslavia, so don't change more than you need for the day.

Kastoriá

Set on a peninsula extending deep into a chill-blue lake, **KASTORIÁ** is one of the most interesting and attractive towns of mainland Greece, despite its proliferation of tower blocks. It is a wealthy place and has been so for centuries as the centre of the Greek (and Balkan) fur trade; its very name means 'beavers'. It is not a trapping centre, and never really was, but instead boasts a considerable industry of furriers who make up coats, gloves and other items from fur scraps imported from Canada and Scandinavia. For visitors, the main appeal lies in the town's traces of former prosperity. From the seventeenth to nineteenth centuries, when the town was perhaps at its peak, survive half a dozen splendid *arhondiká* – mansions of the old fur families. Dotted about as well are some fifty Byzantine and medieval churches.

Arriving by bus, you'll find yourself at the edge of the peninsula. Finding a **hotel** can be a struggle, as the town's business means places are full pretty much year-round. They are also expensive, so if you plan on staying try to phone ahead. There is just one D-class, the *Palladion* (Mitropóleos 40; ☎0467/22-493), centrally positioned, though don't count on getting a room. Two of the cheaper C-class options are by the bus station on Grámmou: *Anessis* (no.10; ☎0467/29-410) and *Acropolis* (no.16; ☎0467/22-537). Another, *Keletron*, is on the street's extension, 11 Noemvríou, at no.52 (☎☎0467/22-676). The last place to fill is generally the *Xenia du Lac* (Platía Dhexamenís; ☎0467/22-565), which, although graded A-class, has out-of-season rates around 3500dr double. The best area for **restaurants** is around Platía Omonías. The *Stakhi* bakery, below the square, is good for *bougátzes* (custard tarts), *tirópites* and pizzas. If you need to return to Athens in a hurry, Kastoriá has an **airport**; details of flights from *Olympic Airways* at Megálou Alexandhroú 15 (☎0467/24-455).

The best part of town, for a sense of what Kastoriá must once have been, is the lakeside quarter and former Christian ghetto of **Kariádhi**, around Platía Immanouíl. In nearby Ódhos Kapitán Lázou (at no.10) the seventeenth-century Aïvazís family mansion has been turned into a **Folklore Museum** (9am–12.30pm and 2–5pm). The house was inhabited until 1972 and its furnishings and ceilings are in excellent repair. It's well worth the visit. The caretaker here, on request, will show you some of the other surviving *arhondiká*. The most notable – the nearby **Basára** and **Natzí**, and the **Sapountzí** to the north – are marked on the map.

Kastoriá's **churches** are harder to visit. Although hours of admission are posted on some of the doors, they are irregularly kept. To be sure of entry it's best to enquire of the two *fílakes* (caretakers) at one of the *kafenía* in Platía Omonías. One has keys for Taxiárhes, Áyios Nikólaos and Koumbelidhikí;

KASTORIÁ

the other for Áyii Anáryiri and Áyios Stéfanos. **Áyii Anáryiri** dates from the eleventh century, with three layers of frescoes spanning the following two hundred years. Only one of the frescoes, *Áyios Yióryios and Áyios Dhimítrios*, has been cleared of grime. **Áyios Stéfanos** is of the twelfth century and has been little changed over the years. Its frescoes are negligible but it does have an unusual women's gallery, or *yinaikonítis*. **Áyios Nikólaos Kasnítsi** is currently under restoration, inside and out; when this is complete, its frescoes should have been returned to their former glory. **Taxiárhes**, the oldest (9c.) church, hides various treasures beneath layers of soot and damp; some of its more visible frescoes, such as that of the *Virgin and Archangels*, are fourteenth-century. Lastly, the **Panayía Koumbelidhikí**, so named because of its unusual dome (*koumbet* in Turkish) has the best-preserved and illuminated frescoes, including a highly unusual portrayal of God the Father in a ceiling mural of the Holy Trinity. The building was done in stages, with the apse completed in the tenth century and the narthex in the fifteenth. The dome was meticulously restored after being destroyed by Italian bombing in World War II.

Kastoriá also suffered heavily during the Civil War. Platía Ván Flít, by the lakeside at the neck of the promontory, commemorates the US general – Van

Fleet – who supervised the Greek Nationalist Army's operations against the Communist Democratic Army in the final campaigns of 1948-49. The town was nearly captured by the communists in 1948, and Vítsi, the conical peak dominating the north shore of the lake, was, together with Mount Grámmos, the scene of their last stand in August 1949. The little square is appropriately shabby. However, most of the destruction of Kastoriá's architectural heritage is not due so much to munitions as to 1950s neglect and 1960s developers.

If tracking down buildings seems too frustrating a pursuit, perhaps the nicest thing to do in Kastoriá is to follow the footpath which runs all around the **lake shore**. Although the lake itself is heavily polluted, the path has been deliberately created by one of Greece's few environmentalists. It has almost a country-park atmosphere and wildlife abounds – frogs, tortoises and water-snakes especially. At the far end of the peninsula, about an hour's walk, is the **Mavrótissa monastery**, with more frescoes, and a **campsite** (for those oblivious to mosquitoes).

Finally, if you have transport, you might make a trip 14km west to OMORFOKLISSIÁ, an eerie village of mud houses inherited from Turkish peasants. It has a Byzantine church with a huge, primitive wooden statue of Saint George.

HALKIDHIKÍ AND EASTERN MACEDONIA

Halkidhikí, easily reached by bus from Thessaloníki, is the clear highlight of Macedonia's eastern half. Its first two peninsulas, **Kassándhra** and **Sithonía**, shelter the north's main concentration of beaches; the third, **Áthos**, the country's finest, though most secretive, monasteries.

Moving east, there are a few more good beaches en route to **Kavála**, but little of interest inland, with a scattering of small market towns serving a population that – as in neighbouring Thrace – produces the main Greek tobacco crop.

Halkidhikí: Kassándhra, Sithonía and secular Áthos

The squid-shaped peninsula of Halkidhikí begins at a perforated edge of lakes east of Thessaloníki and extends into three prongs of land – Kassándhra, Sithonía, and Áthos – trailing like tentacles into the Aegean sea.

Mount Áthos, the easternmost peninsula, is in all ways separate: a 'Holy Mountain', whose monastic population, semi-autonomous from the Greek state, excludes all women – even as visitors. For men who wish to experience Athonite life, a visit involves suitably Byzantine procedures which are detailed, with the monastic sights, in the main Áthos section. The most that **women** can do is to glimpse the buildings from offshore. It is possible to take *kaíki* rides from the two small resorts on the periphery of the peninsula – Ierissós and Ouranoúpoli; this 'secular' part of Áthos is covered overpage.

Kassándhra and **Sithonía**, by contrast, host some of the fastest-growing holiday resorts in Greece. Up until the last five years these were popular mainly with Greeks – they are still Thessaloníki's beach-playground – but they're now in the process of a staggering development, with most European package-tour companies maintaining a presence. On Kassándhra, especially, almost any reasonable beach is accompanied by a crop of villas or a hotel development, while huge billboards advertise campsite complexes miles in advance. A still larger billboard at the entrance to the Kassándhra peninsula reminds you that camping outside the authorised grounds is strictly prohibited, although you may have no other choice if you're so bold as to show up in high season without a reservation. One consolation is that most beaches here are equipped with free freshwater showers.

Both Kassándhra and Sithonía are connected to Thessaloníki by a network of fast new roads which extend around their coastlines; buses run frequently to all the larger resorts. In spite of this, neither peninsula is that easy to travel around if you are dependent on public **transport**. You really have to pick a place and stay there, perhaps hiring a moped for local excursions.

Kassándhra

Kassándhra, the nearest prong to Thessaloníki, is also by far the most developed. Unless you're very pushed for time and want a couple of days' escape from Thessaloníki, it's best to keep on to Sithonía or, better still, the top end of Áthos. Apart from resorts, there is very little to Kassándhra. Its population took part in the independence uprising of 1821, but was defeated and massacred; as a result, up until the last decades there were only a few small fishing hamlets.

On the peninsula's west coast, the first resort you come to, **NÉA MOUDHANÍA** has hydrofoils in summer to Skiáthos, Skópelos and Alónissos. The second, **NÉA POTÍDHEA**, at the neck of the peninsula, is a tiny place, overlooked by a medieval watchtower. It is generally jammed to the gills in season, however, as are both **SANÍ** and **POSSÍDHI** with their international campsites. **KALLITHÉA**, just beyond Possídhi, is a slightly better option if you want a straightforward resort. There are a large number of **rooms** to let – not just package hotels – and you can rent bikes and mopeds on the main street, or windsurfers on the beach. Don't expect much character, though.

On the east coast, **HANIÓTIS** has a good long beach and a few ordinary-sized hotels and tavernas; *Camping Kera Maria*, just outside the resort, is low-key. But at both **PALIOÚRI** and **KRIOPIYÍ** it's back to the huge 'holiday-campings'.

Sithonía

Things improve considerably as you move east across the Halkidhikí and away from the frontline of tourism; the landscape too becomes increasingly green and hilly, culminating in the isolated and spectacular scenery of the Holy Mountain, looming across the gulf lapping Sithonía's east coast. As for the peninsula itself, **Sithonía** is more rugged but better cultivated than Kassándhra, and it has more pre–touristic village communities. Pine forests cover much of its slopes, giving way to olive groves at the coast. The small pebbly inlets with relatively discreet pockets of hotels make a welcome change from sprawling beach resorts.

Suitably enough, **METAMÓRFOSSI**, on the road between Kassándhra and Sithonía, signals this transportation. Its beach is only adequate but there's good swimming to be had, and the village has a quiet, easygoing air. In addition to three or four **hotels** (cheapest is D-class *Golden Beach*, ☎0375/22-063), there are various **rooms** to let (the *Bibis* and *Vassilis* apartments are good value) and a **campsite**, *Camping Sithon*, a couple of kilometres from the village. There are a fair number of tavernas in and around the village square, as well as a solitary summer disco.

Moving on to Sithonía proper, it's best to follow the road around the east coast – facing Áthos. The only problem is the lack of bus services. There are regular runs from Thessaloníki down the west coast and around as far as Sárti, and from Poliyíros you can get connections along the east coast as far as Vourvouroú. No buses, however, run between Vourvouroú and Sárti.

ÓRMOS PANAYÍA, first of the east coast resorts, is on a human scale, slowly developing around its tiny harbour village; **rooms** are fairly easily come by and there are beaches within walking distance. Excursion **boats** leave from the village to sail around Áthos, though they're often pre-reserved for tourists bussed in from the big Halikidhiki resorts. Neighbouring **VOURVOUROÚ** is probably Sithonía's best beach, set in a tremendous bay with (as yet) only two small hotels, one B-, the other D-class (*Vourvourou*, ☎0375/91-261).

Farther down the east coast, **SÁRTI** has a long, coarse sandy beach. The village, discovered it seems only by Germans, has a less 'package' feel than most, with numerous signposted **rooms** on offer. In the small, busy square there are some good tavernas; also mopeds for hire. To the south are a series of small coves. At the first of these, **ÁYIOS IOÁNNIS**, a short way from the road, a small official **campsite** flanks the sandy bay; others, further south, have no development and attract the odd pocket of freelance summer campers.

As you round the peninsula, beyond the small resort of KALAMÍTSI, hills spill out into the sea, creating a new series of bays, and vultures circle the rocky hills above the road. At **KOUFÓS**, just above the cape, a tremendous bay shelters amid sheer white cliffs. It's a tempting base, with two **campsites**: the tiny *Camping Nikolaos* and, 200m beyond, *Camping Porto Kuphos* with more facilities.

Beyond here, however, you are back into resort territory, beginning with Greece's largest planned holiday complex, **PÓRTO CÁRRAS**. Set up by the Carras wine dynasty, this takes Spanish Marbella as its model, featuring its own conference hall, shopping centre and vineyards. On the beach outside the complex you can parasail, in addition to the more usual water sports. If you're struck by the notion, then you might want to stay a few days at nearby **NÉA MARMARÁS**, though come expecting the crowds. This has six camp-sites (capacity over 3000) and numerous hotels in the space of a few kilo-metres. Its most attractive quarter is on the south side, opposite the beach, where there are pleasant **rooms** above the *Restaurant Xenia*.

East to secular Áthos and beyond

From Órmos Panayía a dirt road winds around the coast through the villages of PIRGADHÍKIA and GOMÁTI to Ierissós, at the top of the Áthos peninsula. No buses run this route, however, and if you're dependent on public trans-port you'll need to backtrack along the coast to YERAKÍNI and then **inland** to Halkidhikí's capital, **POLÍYIROS**, a small market town with an unexciting archaeological museum. From here, buses for Ierissós head through the hills, past ARNÉA, which has some fine old parts and a reputation for weav-ing; it could be worth a few hours' stopover, or if you decide to stay longer it has a single **hotel**, the E-class*Arni* (☎0372/22-259).

IERISSÓS, with a good long beach facing the rising sun and a coastline which extends towards the enormous Cape Arápis, is probably the best 'sec-ular Áthos' resort. **Boat tours** leave daily in summer on a loop around the Holy Mountain. Unless they are all-male (in which case they're allowed to dock at the monastery of Ivíron) they have to stay 500 metres from the coast, but the views of the monasteries are something, at least. The village has a few rooms to let and a couple of **hotels** – the basic and cheap E-class *Akanthos* (☎0377/22-359) and D-class *Marcos* (☎0377/22-518); there is also a bank, though it is open just two days a week.

The road beyond Ierissós passes through NÉA RÓDHA, then veers left to follow the remaining stretch of **Xerxes' canal**, cut by the Persian invader in 48 B.C. to spare his fleet the shipwreck at the tip of Áthos that had befallen the previous expedition eleven years before. You emerge on the southwest, facing the coast at **TRIPITÍ** (5km), whence boats ply to the tiny **island of Amolianí** (regular crossings in summer; nominal charge). On the island's further side is a beautiful beach, with a **campsite** and small taverna – perfect for a few days' relaxation. For scuba diving enthusiasts, it's worth noting that this is one of the few areas of Greece where the sport is permissible. If you're interested, ask in Tripití about hire of equipment.

Last settlement before you reach the restricted monastic domains is the fishing village of **OURANÓPOLI**. This is the port for visitors to the Holy Mountain (see following) and again operates summer **boat trips** to Áthos, as well as the short hop (boats about every half hour) to Amolianí. The village is popular with Greeks and so retains a more native feel than most of the

Halkidhikí resorts – despite an initially disarming array of **room** and **hotel** signs. At least accommodation is generally available, with excellent value rooms, three D-class and two E-class hotels (the latter are *Galini*, ☎0377/71-217; and *Ouranopolis*, ☎0377/71-205).

Ouranópoli's village beach is a little crowded, though it compensates with hire of windsurfers and even small motor boats. Other intermittent strands stretch for 5km north – beyond the Byzantine **Phosphori tower** where Sydney Loch, author of *Áthos: the Holy Mountain* (written in the 1950s but still as good a guide as any to the monasteries), lived for almost thirty years. Ouranópoli, like many villages on the 'tentacles' of Halkidhikí, was settled by refugees from Asia Minor in 1923; the Lochs, a Scots-Australian missionary couple, ran a school for carpet-making – a cottage industry still much in evidence.

On towards Kavála

Heading towards Kavála from Áthos or Sithonía is surprisingly tricky, since buses from Políyiros or Ierissós/Ouranópoli run only back to Thessaloníki.

You can, however, take the bus to **STRATÓNI** on the eastern coast – paying passing homage to Aristotle's birthplace at **STÁYIRA** – from where a rough road twists 19km through the hills above the coast to **OLIMBIÁDHA**. This is a feasible but slow hitch, or you could negotiate in Stratóni, itself an ugly seashore mining town, for a taxi. Don't try hitching the mountainous road that heads inland just before Stáyira; though well drawn on some maps it is really no more than a forest track.

STAVRÓS, another 17km beyond Olimbiádha, is a gentle resort with a beautiful seafront terrace of plane trees. It's popular but not at all spoiled, with five inexpensive **hotels** (cheapest is the E-class *Avra Strymonikou*, ☎0397/61-278) and good possibilities for camping.

From either Olimbiádha or Stavrós you can take the daily (morning) bus to the main Thessaloníki-Kavála highway.

Mount Áthos: the Monks' Republic

The population of **Mount Áthos** has been exclusively male – domestic animals included – since an edict, the *avaton*, issued by the Byzantine Emperor Constantine Monomachos in 1060. Known in Greek as the *Áyion Óros* (Holy Mount), it is an administratively autonomous part of the country – a 'monks' republic' – on whose slopes are gathered some twenty monasteries, together with a number of smaller dependencies and hermitages.

Most of the monasteries were founded in the tenth and eleventh centuries. Today, all survive in a state of considerable decline but they remain unsurpassed in their general and architectural interest and for the art treasures they contain. If you are male, over 21 years old, and have a genuine interest in monasticism or Greek Orthodoxy, or simply in the remarkable Byzantine and medieval architecture, a visit is strongly recommended. It takes a few days to arrange, either in Thessaloníki or Athens (see 'Permits and Practicalities', below) but the rewards more than justify your efforts.

In addition to the historic and architectural aspects of Áthos, it should be added that the peninsula is one of the most beautiful parts of Greece. With only the occasional farm vehicle, and a sporadic boat service along the coast, a visit by necessity involves walking between settlements – amid dense woods, along the slopes of the mountain, or on paths above what is perhaps the Mediterranean's last untouched coastline. For many visitors, this as much as the experience of monasticism is the highlight – maybe even the spiritual highlight – of time spent on the Holy Mountain.

The Theocratic Republic: some history

By a legislative decree of 1926 Áthos has the status of **Theocratic Republic**. It is governed from the small town and capital of Kariés by the *Ayía Epistasía* (Holy Community), a council of twenty elected representatives from each of the monasteries. At the same time Áthos remains a part of Greece. All foreign monks must adopt Greek citizenship and the Greek government is represented by a governor and a small police force.

Each monastery has a distinct place in the **Athonite hierarchy**: Méyisti Lávra holds the prestigious first place, Kastamonítou ranks twentieth. All other settlements are attached to one or other of the twenty monasteries; these range from *skíti* (a group of houses, often scarcely distinguishable from a monastery) through *kellí* (a kind of farmhouse) to *isikhastírio* (a solitary hermitage, often a cave). As many laymen as monks live on Áthos, mostly employed in agriculture by the monasteries.

The **development of monasticism on Áthos** is a matter of some controversy, and foundation legends abound. The most popular is that the Virgin Mary was blown ashore here on her way to Cyprus and while overcome by the great beauty of the mountain a mysterious voice consecrated the place in her name. Another tradition asserts that Constantine the Great founded the first monastery in the fourth century – but this is certainly far too early. The earliest historical reference to Athonite monks is to their attendance at a council of the Empress Theodora in 843; probably there were some monks here by the end of the seventh century. Áthos was particularly appropriate for early Christian monasticism, its deserted and isolated slopes providing a natural refuge from the outside world – especially from the Arab conquests in the east, and the iconoclastic phase of the Byzantine Empire (eighth to ninth centuries). Moreover its awesome beauty, which had so impressed the Virgin, facilitated communion with God.

The most famous of the **early monks** were Peter the Athonite and Saint Euthimios of Salonica, both of whom lived in cave-hermitages on the slopes in the mid-ninth century. In 885 an edict of Emperor Basil I recognised Áthos as the preserve solely of monks, and gradually hermits came together to form communities known as *cenobia* (literally 'common living'). The year 963 is the traditional date for the foundation of the first monastery, **Méyisti Lávra**, by Athanasios the Athonite; the Byzantine Emperor Nicephoros Phocas provided considerable financial assistance. Over the next two centuries, with the protection of other Byzantine emperors, foundations were frequent, the monasteries reaching forty in number (reputedly with a thousand monks in each) alongside many smaller *kelliá*.

Troubles for Áthos, after this early growth, began at the end of the eleventh century. The monasteries suffered sporadically from pirate raids and from the settlement of three hundred Vlach families who joined the monks on the mountain. After a reputedly scandalous time, however, these shepherds were ejected and a new imperial *chryssobul* was issued, confirming that no female, human or animal, be allowed to set foot on Áthos. It is this edict that remains in force today.

During the twelfth century, the monasteries gained an international – or at least, **pan-Orthodox** – aspect, as Romanian, Russian and Serbian monks flocked to the mountain in retreat from the turbulence of the age. Áthos itself was subjected to Frankish raids during the Latin Occupation of Constantinople (1204-61) and even after this faced great pressure from the Unionists of Latin Salonica to unite with western Catholics; in the courtyard of Zographou there is a monument to the monks who died to preserve the independence of Orthodox Christianity. In the early fourteenth century the monasteries suffered two disastrous years of pillage by Catalan mercenaries but they recovered, primarily through Serbian benefactors, to enjoy a period of great prosperity in the fifteenth and sixteenth centuries.

After the fall of the Byzantine Empire to the **Ottomans**, the fathers wisely declined to resist maintained good relations with the early Sultans, one of whom paid a state visit. The later Middle Ages brought economic problems, with taxes and confiscations, and many of the monasteries reverted to an *idiorhythmatic* system, a self-regulating form of monasticism where monks live and worship in a community but work and eat individually. However, Áthos remained the spiritual centre of Orthodoxy and in the seventeenth and eighteenth centuries it built and maintained its own schools.

The mountain's real decline came after the **War of Independence**, in which many of the monks fought alongside the Greek *klephts*. In Macedonia they were easily subdued and as the region remained under Turkish control they paid the price. A permanent Ottoman garrison was established on the mountain and monastery populations fell sharply as, in the wake of independence for southern Greece, monasticism became less of a focus for Greek Orthodox Christianity.

In **this century** foreign Orthodox monks, especially Russians, following the 1917 revolution, tried to step in to fill the vacuum. But the Athonite Fathers have always resisted any move that might dilute the Greek quality of the Holy Mount. Up until recently, numbers continued to drop at an alarming rate – the current population is estimated at 1700, compared to 20,000 in its heyday. Today, however, it seems that some monasteries, notably Filothéou, Simópetra and Ayíou Pávlou, are experiencing a modest revival. Whether this is a positive trend for Áthos, or simply the effect of the Greek church relocating young novices from monasteries closed elsewhere, is hard to establish.

Permits and practicalities

Until a few years ago foreigners could visit Áthos quite easily, but in the early 1970s the number of tourists grew so great that the monasteries could no longer cope. Nowadays a considerable amount of bureaucracy precedes a visit by all non-Greeks. The only stipulation that has been dropped is the old rule that all visitors should have beards – a further check on women. In its place is a general ban on long hair; the monks do not welcome those they imagine to be 'hippies', despite their own tied-back locks.

The first step in **acquiring a permit** to visit and stay on Áthos is to get a **letter of recommendation** from your government (Department of Religious Affairs) or from any of its consulates. This is easiest done in Athens or Thessaloníki; see respective listings for addresses. The letter should be purely a formality, though most consulates make a charge. If you apply in Greece they will probably give you a list of regulations and information, not all of which are correct or relevant; don't be alarmed. It is best to present yourself as a university-level scholar of art, religion, or architecture – or at a stretch, philosophy – or as a 'man of letters', which designation covers just about any published (or hopeful) writer.

Take the consular letter either to the **Ministry of Foreign Affairs in Athens** (Zalakósta 2; Mon.–Fri. 11am–1pm: be persistent, this is the right place) or to the **Ministry for Northern Greece in Thessaloníki** (room 218; in Platía Dhikitírou; Mon.–Fri. 8am–2pm). You will there be issued with a permit valid for four days' residence on Áthos, which must be used within a month and which may have a day specified for beginning the visit. In summer this might not be on the date of your choice since only ten non-Greeks are allowed to enter each day.

To get to Áthos take the **bus** from Thessaloníki (Halkidhikí terminal, Karakássi 68) to OURANÓPOLI or IERISSÓS (see 'Secular Áthos'.) From Ouranópoli a **boat** leaves daily for **Dháfni**, the main port of Áthos, in mid-morning; if you're setting out on the day your permit starts, best take the 6am departure from Thessaloníki. From Ierissós there is also a daily boat to **Ivíron** and other monasteries on the east coast. As you board either boat you'll be asked for the permit and for your passport, which you later collect in Kariés, the capital of Áthos. The boat rides take around two hours.

On arrival, you should proceed immediately to **KARIÉS**. There is generally a connecting bus from both Dháfni and Ivíron; if not, you can walk (in about an hour) or hitch a monastic vehicle with little difficulty. At Kariés, make your way to the **police** (*astinomía*) to retrieve your passport and permit, then finally walk across the central square to the **ecclesiastical authorities** (the *Epistasía*) in the yellow building; here you get your final permit, the *dhiamonitírion* (1000dr), which admits you to stay at any of the Athonite monasteries. The permit lasts for four days but if you want to stay longer ask at this stage and you will probably be granted a few days more at no extra cost. You will also be given a card to return to the police at Ouranópoli or Ierissós after you leave Áthos; failure to do so may disqualify you from a return visit.

The way of life

With the *dhiamonitírion* you will be staying in the monasteries free of charge. If you offer money it will be refused, though at some of the monasteries you're encouraged to buy candles and icon-reproductions by way of donation.

Accommodation is in dormitories, and fairly spartan, but you're always given sheets and blankets – you don't need to haul a sleeping bag around. The monasteries are largely self-sufficent in food and the diet is based on tomatoes, beans and other vegetables; wine is served with every meal, including breakfast. You might want to carry some provisions (like fruit and chocolate) for the long walks between monasteries; there are a few shops in Kariés.

Some knowledge of Greek language is obviously useful, though you can get by at most monasteries on a combination of English and French. The standard wayside greeting, on your part, is '*evlóyite*' (your blessing), to which monks reply '*O Kyrios*' (the Lord's blessing on you).

You will find that your whole day is shifted around to fit in with sunset and sunrise. Quite apart form being thirteen days behind the outside world (the Julian Calendar is still observed), the Athonite day *begins* at sunset, when most clock towers read twelve o'clock. Very few monasteries have electricity and you will be expected to go to bed early. When you arrive at a monastery you should inquire for the *arhondaris* (guest-master), who is responsible for you during your visit; he is usually on hand to welcome you with an *oúzo* and *loukoúmi*.

While on the mountain there are a few customs that should be observed. You should be fully clad at all times, even when going from dormitory to bathroom; smoking, singing, or whistling are forbidden, wherever you are on the mountain; and if you want to photograph the monks you should always ask prior permission. When in any of the chapels, do not stand with your hands behind your back (which is considered an overbearing stance), nor cross your legs while seated.

Walking between monasteries it's a great help if you have the *Korfes* map of the peninsula (try the bookshops listed for Athens or Thessaloníki). If not, there are vaguely helpful pamphlets, with maps, on sale in Kariés. Either way you'll still need to ask specific instructions from the monks for each stage of your walk; the old paths are often overgrown and difficult to find. You can supplement walking between monasteries with the daily kaíki services which ply more or less daily between the main establishments on each coast. The boat up along the west coast (towards the 'border') sails each morning from Ayía Anna at around 11am.

Athonite terms

Cenobitic/Idiorhythmatic. This is the major distinction between monasteries. At cenobitic establishments the monks eat together, hold all property in common and have rigidly defined days with frequent common worship. Those that are idiorhythmatic are more individual – the monks eat in their own quarters and study or worship when and as they wish. Over the last two to three years many of the formerly idiorhythmatic monasteries have reverted to cenobitic status. At the time of writing it seems that only Vateopédhi, Ivíron, Stavronikíta and Pantokrátoros remain idiorhythmatic.

Arhondáris Guest-master of a monastery, responsible for all visitors.

Arsanás Harbour annexe of each monastery, where the *kaíkia* call; they can be some distance from the monastery proper.

Katholikón Main chapel of a monastery.

Trapezaría Refectory, or dining room.

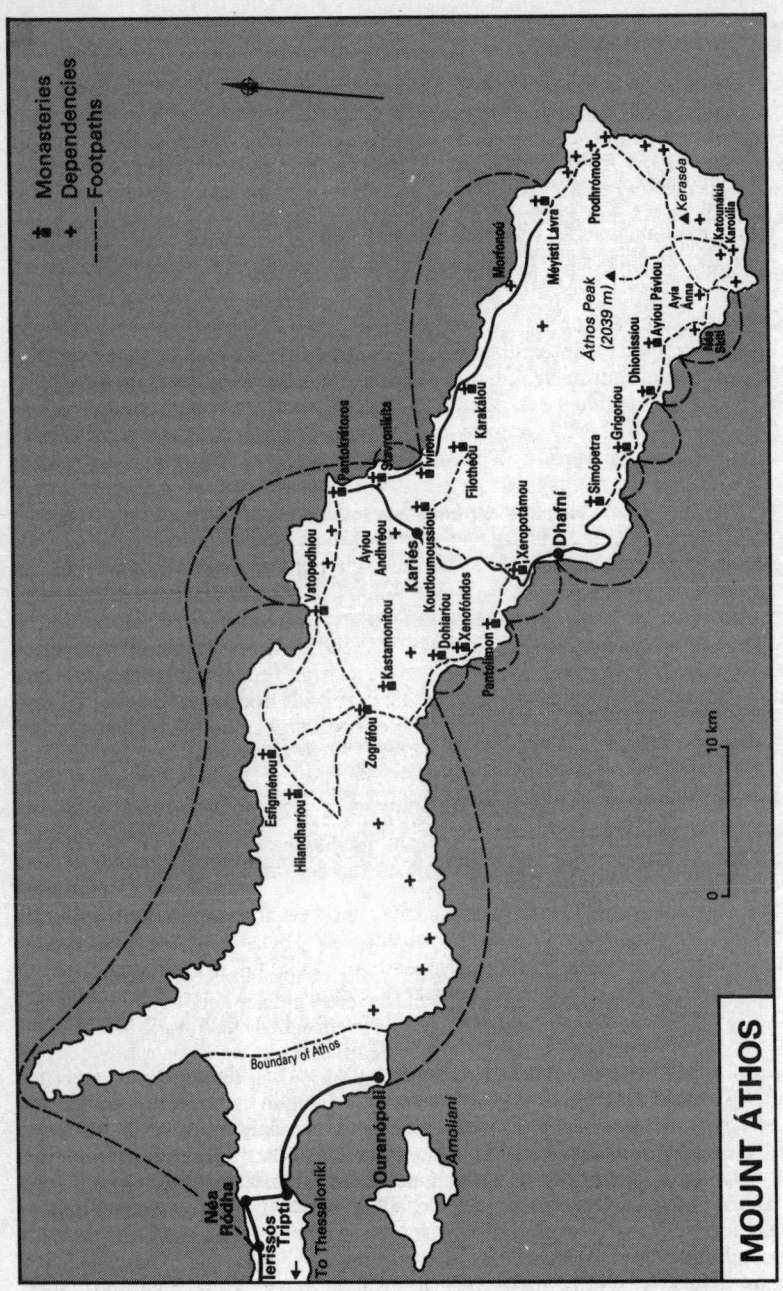

MOUNT ÁTHOS

† Monasteries
+ Dependencies
--- Footpaths

Morfonoú
Megísti Lávra
Prodhrómou +
Athos Peak
(2039 m) ▲
Keraséa ▲
Katounákia
Karoúlia
Ayiou Pávlou
Ayía
Ánna ▲
Néa
Skíti
Dhionissíou
Grigoríou
Simópetra
Ayíou Pandelímon
Dháfni
Karakálou
Filothéou
Ivíron
Stavronikíta
Pandokrátoros
Kariés
Koutloumoussíou
Ayíou Andhréou
Dohiaríou
Xenofóndos
Xeropotámou
Pandelímon
Vatopedhíou
Kastamonítou
Zográfou
Esfigménou
Hilandharíou

Boundary of Áthos

Néa
Ródha
Ierissós
Triptí
To Thessaloníki
Ouranópoli
Amolianí

0   10 km

The monasteries

Obviously you can't hope to visit all twenty monasteries on a short visit, so the accounts below concentrate on the more interesting and accessible. Perhaps the simplest route, if you are limited to four days, is to take in a **southern loop** from Kariés, spending the first night in Filothéou, then making your way to Méyisti Lávra either on foot or by boat from Ivíron, with a last stop at Ayíou Pávlou or one of its neighbouring monasteries on the west coast. If you travel by boat from Ayíou Pávlou back to Ouranópoli, you will sight most of the major establishments along the way.

Kariés and the east coast

Having obtained your *dhiamonitírion* in **KARIÉS**, take a look inside the **Protatón**, the church in the main square. The second oldest on Áthos, it dates from 965 and has exceptional fourteenth-century frescoes. Also worth a look, and only a short walk away on the town's outskirts, is the magnificent *skíti* of **Ayíou Andhréou**, a Russian dependency of the great Vatopédhi monastery, today virtually deserted. If you've a lengthy permit, or plan to cross the peninsula in a first day's walk over to Grigoríou or Simópetra, you might want to make use of one of the **inns** in Kariés.

But for most visitors there seems no reason not to walk straight on out to a monastery: the closest are Koutloumousíou, Ivíron, Stavronikíta and Filothéou, any of which you could easily reach before sunset, the hour when Athonite monasteries close their doors. Check the noticeboard in the government building before setting out, however, as from time to time some monasteries are closed to visitors. This was the case with Koutloumousíou not long ago, due to fire damage – an all too frequent occurrence on the peninsula.

Around half an hour's walk from Karyes, **IVÍRON** was founded late in the tenth century by Iberian (Russian Georgian) monks. It ranks third on the Athonite hierarchy, possessing an immensely rich library and treasury – though the monks, perhaps jaded by being an easy first stop, seem reluctant to show vistors around. As an idiorrhythmatic monastery, hospitality relies very heavily on the individual *arhondáris*.

STAVRONIKÍTA, in contrast, is a small and very friendly cloister, an hour and a half's walk out of Kariés. If you fix your sights here make sure you come early: it's been known for the guesthouse to be full in midsummer. Like most Athonite structures, the monastery is built like a fortress perched on rocks above the sea, offering a pleasant introduction, if little in the way of artistic treasures.

From Stavronikíta it is a short walk north along the coast to **PANTOKRÁTOROS**, similar in design and again with many buildings restored and replaced after a series of fires. Only eighteen monks live here but they are exceptionally kind. Since this is another idiorrhythmic monastery, the guest-master will be cooking solely for himself and any guests.

While not conspicuously hospitable, **VATOPEDHÍOU**, a couple of hours' walk further north, is one of the most worthwhile monasteries to visit. Second in the Athonite hierarchy and fabulously situated above the sea, this grand complex seems more like a fortified town. It is also the most modernised establishment; electricity has been installed and there are rumours of colour television. It was founded in the tenth century, has superb Byzantine mosaics in its *kathólikon*, an impressive display of relics and ikons in its treasury and a library of over 10,000 volumes and illuminated manuscripts. Incidentally, here (as everywhere on Áthos) you'll find difficulty in seeing the treasury and library. The usual system is that one monk only has the keys, and he is invariably busy; the best times to make a request are immediately after a main service or (if you're in a *cenobium*) during meals.

Southeast of Kariés, only a couple of hours' walk, **FILOTHÉOU** is a good first or last night's stop. It is not impressive from any artistic or architectural point of view, but it is a good monastery to discover a little about Athonite life. At least one monk will usually be able to set aside time to talk with visitors. The food here, too, is remarkably good, which may sound trivial on reading but assumes some importance after several days of hard bread, cold beans, off-smelling cheese and vinegary wine. From Filothéou it is four to five hours' walk to Méyisti Lávra.

Over to the west coast

If you are crossing over from the east to the west coast, a good walk is that between Vatopedhíou and Pantelímon, via Zográfou and Dohiaríou.

ZOGRÁFOU is about two and a half hours' walk west of Vatopédhi; the path is quite difficult to find so get clear instructions. The monastery is populated by Bulgarian monks – just twelve of them nowadays, though the rambling seventeenth-century buildings must once have accommodated hundreds of brothers. A walk down the empty corridors past old, uncared-for cells is a stirring experience and helps you appreciate the enormous workload (not least the upkeep of the buildings) which now falls on so few monks. The monastery is dedicated to Áyios Yióryios. 'Zográfou' means 'of the painter', in reference to a tenth-century legend: the Slavs who founded the monastery couldn't decide on a patron saint, so they put a wooden panel by the altar, and after lengthy prayer a painting of St. George appeared.

ÁYIOS PANTELÍMON is another foreign monastery – often referred to just as *To Roússiko* (The Russian). It's inhabited by twenty Russians, four Romanians and one Greek, an ethnic predominance strongly reflected in the onion-shaped domes of the architecture and in the softer and more angelic faces of the frescoes. Do not miss the early morning service held here, in the church on the top storey of the building next to the bell tower; the church is exceptionally rich in gold, which looks even more impressive when illuminated by candles. The service is in Russian. In many monasteries non-Orthodox visitors are not allowed to enter the main body of the church during services but here you are permitted. Pantelímon's library contains several illuminated manuscripts and some interesting photographic albums documenting its more recent history.

The next coastal monastery south, the other side of Dháfni, is **SIMÓPETRA** (also known as Símonos Pétras – Simon Peter) which, though entirely rebuilt in the wake of a fire a century ago, is perhaps the most architecturally striking on Áthos. With its multiple storeys, ringed by wood balconies overhanging sheer 300-metre drops, it resembles nothing so much as a Tibetan lamasery. The community is cenobitic and apparently growing – there are some forty monks. As at Pantelímon, you may be allowed to attend a service.

To reach Simópetra from Pantelímon, it's best to go by truck, or boat, as the trails here (and to Kariés) are a mess. But from Simópetra, clear paths lead all the way south around the tip of Áthos to Méyisti Lávra.

GRIGORÍOU, surrounded on three sides by the sea, lies ninety minutes' walk downcoast. Another ninety minutes from here and you will reach **ÁYIOU DHIONISSÍOU**, whose architecture (similar to Simópetra) has escaped fires in recent centuries, preserving some of the best frescoes on the mountain. This is an austerely cenobitic community.

A hard forty-five minute trek further separates you from **AYÍOU PÁVLOU**, less spectacular and set back from the coast but, with its growing number of monks (currently 125), perhaps the most active monastery on Áthos.

From Ayíou Pávlou it's possible to walk a very full day through the various *skítis* – including the enormous Romanian **Prodhrómou** – to Méyisti Lávra. But you might consider breaking the journey at **Keraséa** to climb **Áthos peak** (2033m) proper; this will use up a full day of your permit but it is well worth it. You can ask for monastic hospitality at Keraséa or, if you're well-equipped, sleep at the combination hospice chapel of the Panayía, five hours' walk up the side trail to the summit. Get up an hour or so before sunrise for the final push to the top, crowned by the squat church of Metamórfosi (festival August 6).

Méyisti Lávra

The oldest and foremost of the monasteries, **MÉYISTI LÁVRA** (Great Lávra) lies towards the end of the east coast. It is by far the most impressive establishment on Áthos, with no less than fifteen chapels inside its walls; unique among the twenty, too, it has never suffered from fire.

The **katholikón** was completed in 1004 and its plan copied in all others on Áthos. Its frescoes, painted by Theophanes the Cretan in 1535, are particularly fine. Theophanes also executed the frescoes in the *trapezaría*, the most notable of which is of *The Last Supper*, not surprisingly a very popular theme in refectories. The Great Lavra's treasury and **library** are both extraordinarily rich, the latter containing over 2000 manuscripts.

Kavála

KAVÁLA, backing on to the lower slopes of Mount Simbólon, is the second largest city of Macedonia and the principal port for northern Greece. Coming in through the suburbs there seems little to commend a stay. But the centre, at least, is pleasant and characterful, grouped about the old nineteenth-century harbour area and its old tobacco warehouses. A citadel towers above from a rocky promontory to the east, and an elegant Turkish aqueduct leaps over modern neighbourhoods into the old quarter on the bluff.

The town was known anciently as Neapolis and, as such, served as the terminus of the Via Egnatia and the first European port of call for merchants and travellers from the Middle East. It was here that Saint Paul landed on his way to Philippi (see overpage), on his initial mission to Europe. In later years, the port and citadel took on considerable military significance, being occupied in turn by Byzantines, Normans, Franks, Venetians, Turks and (during each of the world wars) Bulgarians.

Practicalities

For once most points of utility or interest are central. The main **bus station** is on the corner of Mitropolitoú, near the main anchorage; buses for Alexandhroúpoli stop by a café called *Poda* on adjoining Filikís Eterías.

In the main square, Platía Eleftherías, you'll find an **EOT** office, which can provide details (and sell tickets) for the summer drama festivals at Philippi and on Thássos. They can also be of help with schedules for ferries from Kavála (see below), and those from Alexandhroúpoli to Samothráki.

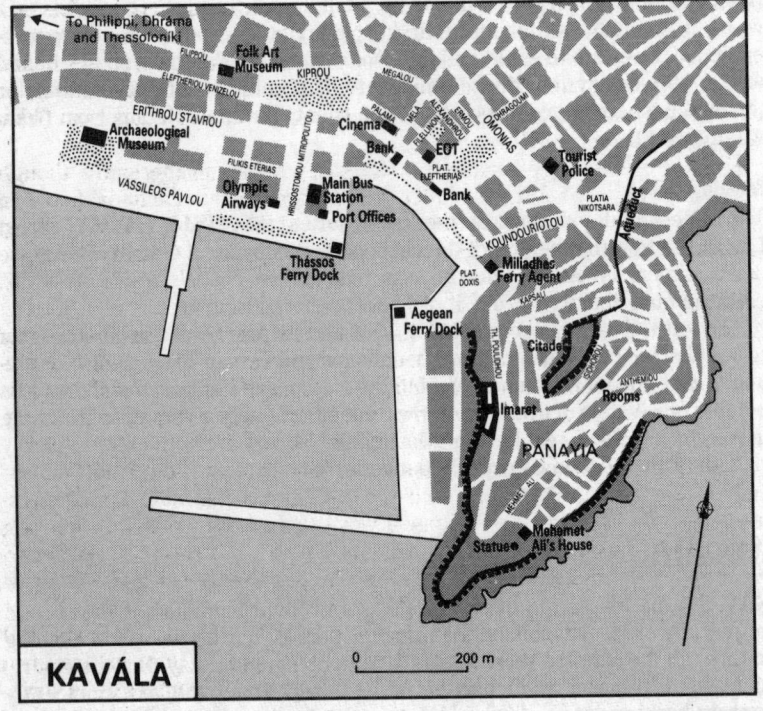

KAVÁLA

0   200 m

Hotels are in short supply and in season it's wise to phone ahead and book a room. All three of the D-class places are in the grid of streets around Eleftherías: *Attikon* (Megaloú Alexándrou 8; ☎051/222-257), *Parthenon* (Spetsón 14; ☎051/223-205) and *Rex* (Kriézi 4; ☎051/223-393). Moving up to C-class try either the *Acropolis* (☎051/223-543) or *Panorama* (☎051/224-205), repectively at 53c and 32c Eleftheríou Venizélou, west of the square. The only private rooms advertised in the centre are those of *Yiorgos Alvanos* at Anthemíou 35 (☎051/228-412), in the heart of the old Panayía quarter – worth trying for if you arrive early in the day. Eating, take your pick from a row of seafood **restaurants** along the harbour front. If funds are limited, the *Zythestiatorion*, opposite the bus station on Venizélou, is reasonable.

An alternative place to stay, frequented by many Greeek tourists, is the beach-suburb of Kalamítsa, to the west of town. Farther out still are a string of **campsites**; the nearest is *Camping Batis* (5km west), reached by bus #8 or local taxi.

Ferries sail from Kavála to **Thássos** almost hourly in season; most run to the port of Órmos Prínou, though a few continue to the capital, called Thássos or Liménas (an hour-long journey). Out of season, when services drop to just two boats daily, you may be better off taking the bus to Keramotí (46km southwest; hourly service) and the ferry on from there to Thássos/Liménas. Other ferry services are less predictable. In season, there are generally three weekly departures to **Samothráki** (Mon., Thurs., Sat.; 3¾hrs), and two to **Límnos** (Tues., Weds.; the latter continuing to Lésvos). These, or other, boats may continue to Híos, or to Áyios Efstrátios. Details from *Nikos Miliadhes*, Karaóli Dhimitríou 36.

KERAMOTÍ, if you're heading for Thássos, provides an alternative, though unexciting, base. It's a small, rather drab village, with a functional beach, a campsite and three hotels: D-class *Evropi* (☎0591/51-277) and the very cheap E-class *Eleftheria* (☎0591/51-230) and its annexe *Exasteron* (☎0591/51-230).

Old Kavála

Although the remnants of Kavála's Turkish past are understandably neglected, the **Panayía** quarter above the port preserves a scattering of eighteenth- and nineteenth-century buildings, and considerable atmosphere. It is by far the most attractive part of town to explore, wandering amid the twisting wedge of lanes and up toward the citadel.

The most conspicuous and interesting of its buildings is the **Imaret**, overlooking the harbour on Ódhos Poulidhoú. An elongated, multi-domed structure covered in Islamic inscriptions, it was originally an almshouse housing three hundred *softas*, or theological students. Today, in a sorry state of decay, it serves as a warehouse; admission may be possible if you find anyone at work.

The building was endowed by **Mehmet Ali**, the Pasha of Egypt and founder of the dynasty which ended with King Farouk. Born in Kavála in 1769, his birthplace, at the corner of Pavlídhou and Méhmet Alí, is maintained as a monument. It provides an opportunity, rare in Greece, to look over a prestigious Turkish house. To visit its wood-panelled reception rooms, ground-floor stables and first-floor harem, ring for the caretaker.

Another caretaker will unlock the **Citadel** so you can explore the Byzantine ramparts and dungeon; in season it hosts a few festival performances, mainly dance, in its main court.

Down toward the middle of town the **aqueduct**, built on a Roman model in the reign of Suleiman the Magnificent (1520-66), spans the traffic in Platía Nikotsára, north of Panayía's narrow maze of streets.

Finally, by the harbour, the two museums are of moderate interest. The **Archaeological Museum** (8.30am–2.30pm; closed Tues.) is at the west end of the waterfront, just off Erithroú Stavroú. It contains a fine dolphin mosaic, a reconstructed Macedonian funeral chamber and many terra cotta figurines decorated still in their original paint. Close by, next to an old tobacco warehouse on Odhós Filíppou, is the **Folk Art and Modern Art Museum** (daily 9–11am and 6–9pm). Along with various collections of traditional costumes and household utensils, this has some interesting rooms devoted to the locally-born sculptor Polignotos Vigis.

Philippi

As you might expect, **PHILIPPI** was named after Philip II of Macedon, who wrested the town from the Thracians in 356 B.C. However, it owed its importance and prosperity to the Roman building of the Via Egnatía. With Kavála-Neápolis as its port, it was essentially the easternmost town of Roman-occupied Europe.

Here also, as at Actium, the fate of the Roman Empire was decided on Greek soil – at the **Battle of Philippi** in 42 B.C. Following their assassination of Julius Caesar, Brutus and Cassius had fled east of the Adriatic, and, against their better judgement, were forced into confrontation on the Philippi plains with the pursuing armies of Antony and Octavian. The 'honourable conspirators', who could have successfully exhausted the enemy by avoiding action, were decimated by Octavian in two successive battles, and as defeat became imminent first Cassius, then Brutus killed himself – the latter running on his comrade's sword with the Shakespearian sentiment 'Caesar now be still, I killed thee not with half so good a will'.

Saint Paul visited Philippi in A.D. 49 and so began his mission in Europe. Despite being cast into prison he retained a special affection for the Philippians, his first converts, and the congregation that he established was one of the earliest to flourish in Greece. It provides the principal remains of the site – several impressive, although ruined, basilican churches.

The Site
Open sunrise to sunset; 150dr, students 80dr.
Philippi is easily reached from Kavála, just 14km distant; buses (which continue to Dhráma) leave at least half-hourly, dropping you by the road which now splits the site.

Most conspicuous of the churches is the **Direkler**, on the left of the modern road. This was an unsuccessful attempt by its sixth-century architect to improve the basilica design by adding a dome. In this instance the entire east wall collapsed under the weight, leaving only the narthex convertible for worship. The central arch of its west wall and a few pillars of reused antique drums stand amid remains of the Roman **forum**.

A line of second-century porticoes spreads outwards in front of the the church, and on their east side are the foundations of a colonnaded octagonal church which was approached from the Via Egnatia by a great gate. Behind the Direkler, and perversely the most interesting and best preserved building of the site, is a huge monumental **public latrine** with fifty of its original marble seats still intact.

Across the road near the further of the two entrances, stone steps climb up to a terrace passing on the right a Roman crypt, reputed to have been the **prison of Saint Paul** and appropriately frescoed. The terrace flattens out on to a huge paved atrium that extends to the foundations of another awesomely large basilica church. Continuing in the same direction around the base of a hill you emerge above a **theatre** cut into its side. Though dating from the original town it was heavily remodeled as an amphitheatre by the Romans – the bas-reliefs of Nemesis, Mars and Victory (on the left of the stage) all belong to this period. It is used for the annual ancient drama festival, held every weekend from mid-July to early August. The **museum**, above the road at the far end of the site, is rather dreary.

The best general impression of the site – which is very extensive despite a lack of obviously notable buildings and of the battlefield behind it, can be gained from the **Acropolis**, a steep climp along a path from the museum. Its own remains are predominantly medieval.

THRACE (THRÁKI)

Greek sovereignty over **western Thrace** was confirmed only in 1923 and its status as a transportation zone into eastern (Turkish) Thrace is highlighted by the presence of 120,000 Turks (or, more properly, Greek Muslims). One-third of the province's population, these Turkish-Muslim communities are highly visible in the main towns of Xánthi, Komotiní and Alexandhroúpoli, as well as in their distinctive – and separate – villages, bristling with minarets and surrounded by tobacco fields.

The **Thracian 'Turks'** were the only Muslims in Greece exempt from the 1923 population exchange; in return Greeks were allowed to remain in Istanbul and on the islands of Imbros and Tenedos. Over the years the Turkish government has repeatedly abrogated the terms of the pact and the Turkish Greeks now number only a few thousand, primarily in Istanbul. Greece has rather more scrupulously honoured the agreement, though many Thracians allege a systematic discrimination by the state bureaucracy, impeding such factors as land sales or improvements, access to bank loans and tractor licences, and educational development. Greek spokesmen counter that the visible backwardness of the Muslims in Greece reflects a deeply traditional outlook which resists modernisation on either the political or technological level. There is probably truth in both assertions. Certainly the 'Turks' of western Thrace are devoutly religious and in many other respects live unmindful of the secular reforms in Ataturk's Turkey.

Ethnic composition aside, there is little in the modern province to delay your progress. Most travellers take a bus straight through to **Alexandhroúpoli**, for the ferry to Samothráki, or a privately operated bus (from Thessaloníki or Kavála) direct to **Istanbul**. If you are in no hurry the **train line** forges a circuitous but scenic route below the foothills of the Rodhópi mountains. The best section of this journey is the **Néstos valley** between Paranésti and Xánthi.

Xánthi and Komotiní

Shortly after the turning to KERAMOTÍ you cross the Néstos river which with the Rhodópi mountains forms the border of Thrace. The Greek/ Turkish, Christian/Muslim make-up is almost immediately apparent in the villages: the Turkish ones, long established, with their tiled, whitewashed houses; the Greek settlements, often adjacent, built in drab modern style for the refugees of the 1920s.

XÁNTHI (KSÁNTHI), the first town of any size, is perhaps the most interesting point to break a journey. Here the two ethnic groups live side by side, with apparent ease. There is a busy market area, good Turko-Greek food and a very attractive old quarter, up the hill to the north of the main square. The town also has a new university, which lends an optimistic air to the place, while a highly pungent air is produced by the unique brand of local cigarettes, *Kiretsiler*, sold in fine blue-and-gold packs. There are a couple of D-class **hotels**, *Lux* (Stavroú 18; ☎0541/23-004) and *Raris* (☎0541/20-531), or, for not a lot more, the C-class *Dimokritus* (28 Oktovríou 41, parallel to the market; ☎0541/25-111).

Leaving Xánthi to the east you pass through a gorge, capped by the ruins of a Byzantine fort and with a number of monasteries nearby. If you have transport, a thirty-kilometre detour to the northeast would take you to **EHÍNOS**, a fine-looking town that is the main market for surrounding communities of Pomaks – Bogomil-Christian Slavs forcibly converted to Islam in the sixteenth century. They still speak a degenerate dialect of Bulgarian with generous admixtures of Greek and Turkish.

KOMOTINÍ, 48km east of Xánthi, is more markedly Turkish with its fourteen functioning mosques. Social mixing is less common, though Orthodox and Muslim continue to live in the same neighbourhoods. On the left of the road leading into town (prominently signposted) is an interesting **Archaeological Museum** (daily 9am–5pm), giving a lucid overview of Thracian history by means of plans and finds from local sites.

Alexandhroúpoli and on to Turkey

ALEXANDHROÚPOLI has little to recommend it: a border town and military garrison, its nearby beaches and summer wine festival seem something of an afterthought. Surprisingly, though, it can get very crowded in season, with overland travellers and Greek holiday-makers competing for limited space in the few hotels and the gritty beach campsites. The best places to stay are the inexpensive **hotels** right near the train station: the C-class *Olympion* (Malyarón 12; ☎0551/28-091), D-class *Majestic* (Platía Troúman 7; ☎0551/26-444) and E-class *Aktaeon* (Karaóli 74; ☎0551/28-078). **Food** is a bright spot. Excellent meals are to be had at *I Neraidha*, a couple of blocks from the train station and across from the town hall. The **Wine Festival** takes place through July and August at the EOT-run *Camping Alexandhroupoli* (bus #5 from the train station or a half-hour walk).

Looking about the town, there are no obvious sights, and the heavy military presence can be oppressive – especially for single women. The Turkish ghetto, literally on the wrong side of the tracks, may or may not whet the appetite for the 'genuine' article across the border.

Heading for the island of **Samothráki** (see *Chapter Ten*) there are twice daily (7am and 4pm) ferries in season; more or less daily (usually around 10am) out of season. Tickets are sold at a cluster of waterfront agencies opposite the ferry dock, which is within sight of the train station.

Routes on to Turkey and Bulgaria

Crossing into Turkey from Alexandhroúpoli, you are presented with a bewildering choice of routes.

By bus

Simplest, if you can get a ticket, is to go by bus **direct to Istanbul**. There are several departures daily, one run by OSE (tickets from the train station), the others by private companies (ask at travel agents). The problem is that most of the buses start in Thessaloníki and most by this stage are full.

An alternative is to take a local bus to the border at **KÍPI** (6 departures daily). You are not allowed to cross the frontier here on foot, but it is generally no problem to get a driver to shuttle you the 500m across to the Turkish post – and possibly to give you a lift beyond. The nearest town is IPSALA (5km), but if possible get as far as KEŞAN (30km), from where buses to Istanbul are much more frequent.

By train

Going by **train to Istanbul** should be simpler but the only through connection leaves Alexandhroúpoli at 5:40pm and there are no reservations; you have to show up at the station at 5pm and buy a ticket. This route crosses the border at PÍTHIO and takes about fifteen hours more (including a long halt at the frontier) to reach Istanbul.

You might, therefore, prefer to go by day, taking a train (at around 11am, 3pm or 5.40pm) through Píthio and on to **KASTANIÉS**, opposite Turkish

EDIRNE. As at Kípi, you are forbidden to walk across this frontier but the border guards are usually cooperative and will help you get a vehicle over. Once at Edirne, hotels are easy to find, you can eat well, and buses run in little over three hours to Istanbul.

En route, **DHIDHIMÓTIHO** makes a good last stop in Greek Thrace: an old Byzantine town completely enclosed in double fortifications (hence the name, which means 'double wall'). Among the buildings is a very large and impressive synagogue which the townspeople ransacked during World War II at the instigation of the Nazis – who had spread about the (false) rumour that treasure was secreted in its walls.

Into Bulgaria

There is one train daily into Bulgarian Thrace, leaving Alexandhroúpoli at 5:28am and reaching SVILENGRAD four hours later. By road the crossing from ORMÉNIO is now open 24 hours a day.

From Svilengrad (which has just one, 5-star, hotel), it is best to plan on moving on the same day towards PLOVDIV.

travel details

BUSES

All buses detailed have similar frequency in each direction, so entries are given just once; for reference check under both starting point and destination.

Connections with Thessaloníki Athens (*KTEL/ OSE*; numerous; 8 hr.); Pélla/Édhessa (hourly; 1 hr./1¾ hr.); Kateríni, for Mt. Olympus (hourly; 1½ hr.); Véria (hourly; 1¾hr.); Vólos (4 daily; 4 hr.); Flórina (5 daily; 3½ hr.); Kastoriá (5 daily; 4½ hr.); Kalambáka/Ioánnina (4–5 daily; 4½ hr./7½ hr.); Sárti, via Políyiros (4 daily; 4½ hr.); Vourvouroú, via Políyiros (3 daily; 3 hr.); Arnéa–Ierissós/ Ouranópoli, via Arnéa (5–7 daily; 3½ hr., 2 hr.); Kavála (hourly; 3 hr.); Alexandhroúpoli (5 daily; 6 hr.); Istanbul (daily *OSE* service, others privately operated; 14 hr.); Sofia (Thursday/Friday; 7½ hr.).

Kateríni–Litóhoro (hourly; 1½ hr.; for Mt. Olympus)

From Véria Kozáni (8 daily; 1½ hr.); Édhessa, via Náoussa (6 daily; 1½ hr.)

From Édhessa Kastoriá (4 daily; 2½ hr.); Flórina (5–6 daily; 2 hr.)

From Kastoriá Flórina (1 direct, daily; 3 hr.; other indirect services via Amíndeo)

From Flórina Níki, Yugoslav frontier (4 daily; 45min.)

From Kozáni Grevená (8 daily; 1 hr.)

From Kavála Philippi (every 20min.; 20min.); Keramotí (frequently; 1 hr.); Xánthi/Komotiní (every half hour; 1 hr./2 hr.); Alexandhroúpoli (5 daily; 3 hr.)

From Alexandhroúpoli Dhidhimótiho (8–9 daily; 2 hr.); Kípi (6 daily; 20min.); Istanbul (daily *OSE* and other private coaches; 8 hr.)

TRAINS

Thessaloníki–Kateríni–Lárissa–Athens 6 daily in each direction.

Approximate journey times:
Thessaloníki–Kateríni (1½hr.)
Thessaloníki–Lárissa (2 hr. 20 min.)
Thessaloníki–Athens (8¾ hr.)

Thessaloníki–Kateríni–Litóhoro– Platamónas–Lárissa–Vólos 3 daily in each direction.

Approximate journey times:
Thessaloníki–Litóhoro/Platamónas (2 hr. 10min./2 hr 35min.)
Thessaloníki–Vólos (5 hr.).

Thessaloníki–Véria–Édhessa–Flórina 6 daily in each direction; connections from Édhessa to Kozáni 4 times daily; 1 train daily leaves Flórina (3.30 p.m.) for Bitola, Yugoslavia.

Approximate journey times:
Thessaloníki–Véria (1 hr.)
Véria–Édhessa (¾hr.)
Édhessa–Flórina (1½ hr.).

Thessaloníki–Sérres–Dhráma–Xánthi–Komotíni–Alexandhroúpoli 5 trains daily.
Approximate journey times:
Thessaloníki–Dhráma (3 hr.)
Dhráma–Xánthi/Komotíni (1¾ hr./2½ hr.)
Xánthi–Komotíni (2 hr.).

Thessaloníki–Yugoslavia/Bulgaria
Thessaloníki–Sofia, via Promahon (2 daily; 13 hr.).
Thessaloníki–Belgrade–Venice, via Gevyéli (3 daily; 12 hr./32 hr.).

Alexandhroúpoli–Turkey/Bulgaria
Alexandhroúpoli–Istanbul Direct night train (5:40p.m.), arriving Istanbul around 8.30 a.m., after a 2-hr. wait at the border. N.B. This train is often delayed by up to 3 hr.
Alexandhroúpoli–Dhidhimótiho–Orestiádha–Kastaniés 5 daily; 2 hr./2½ hr./3 hr.
Alexandhroúpoli–Svilengrad (Bulgaria) 1 daily (5:28a.m.); 4 hr.

N.B. *OSE* also operates **long–distance buses** from Thessaloníki to Istanbul, Sofia, Belgrade, Milan, Paris, London, Vienna, and Germany; they're not cheap.

FERRIES
From Thessaloníki: Weekly to Lésvos and Híos (usually on Sat. or Sun.); weekly to Haniá, Crete (usually Mon.).

From Kavála 5–10 daily, depending on season, to Thássos (Órmos Prinoú); weekly to Samothráki; 2 weekly to Límnos and Áyios Efstrátios, one of which continues to Lésvos; also, in season, occasional service to Híos, Sámos and select Dodecanese.
From Keramotí 6–8 daily, year–round, to Thássos (Thássos town/Liménas).
From Alexandhroúpoli 1–2 daily to Samothráki in season, 6 weekly out; 1 weekly to Límnos/Lésvos.

HYDROFOILS
From Thessaloníki Mon., Wed., and Fri. in season to Skíathos, Skópelos and Alónissos, via Néa Moudhaniá (Halkidhikí).
For details of service, contact local agents or the 'Flying Dolphins' main office in Pireás (Themistokléous 8; ☎01 452–7107).

FLIGHTS
Thessaloníki connections Flights **within Greece** to Athens (8–10 daily), Ioánnina (2 weekly), Iráklio, Crete (2 weekly), Lárissa (2 weekly), Lésvos (daily), Límnos (daily), Pátra (2 weekly), Sámos (weekly), Skíathos (3 weekly). Also **international flights** to Amsterdam, Budapest, Dusseldorf, Istanbul, Larnaca (Cyprus), London, Munich, Paris, Stuttgart, Vienna, and Zurich.
From Alexandhroúpoli Athens (4 weekly).
From Kastoriá Athens (6 daily).
From Kozáni Athens (daily).

PART THREE

THE
ISLANDS

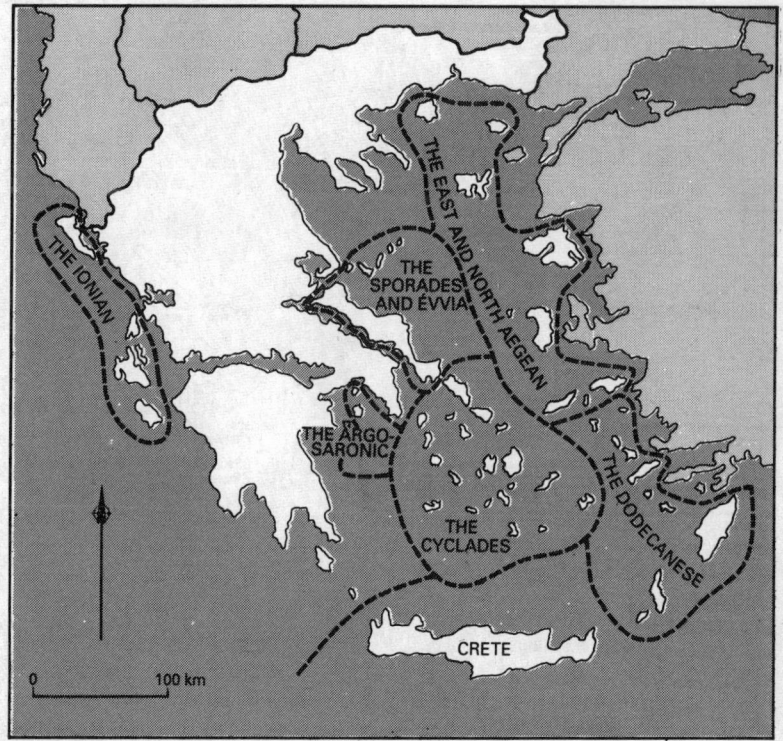

THE IONIAN

THE EAST AND NORTH AEGEAN

THE SPORADES AND ÉVVIA

THE ARGO-SARONIC

THE CYCLADES

THE DODECANESE

CRETE

0   100 km

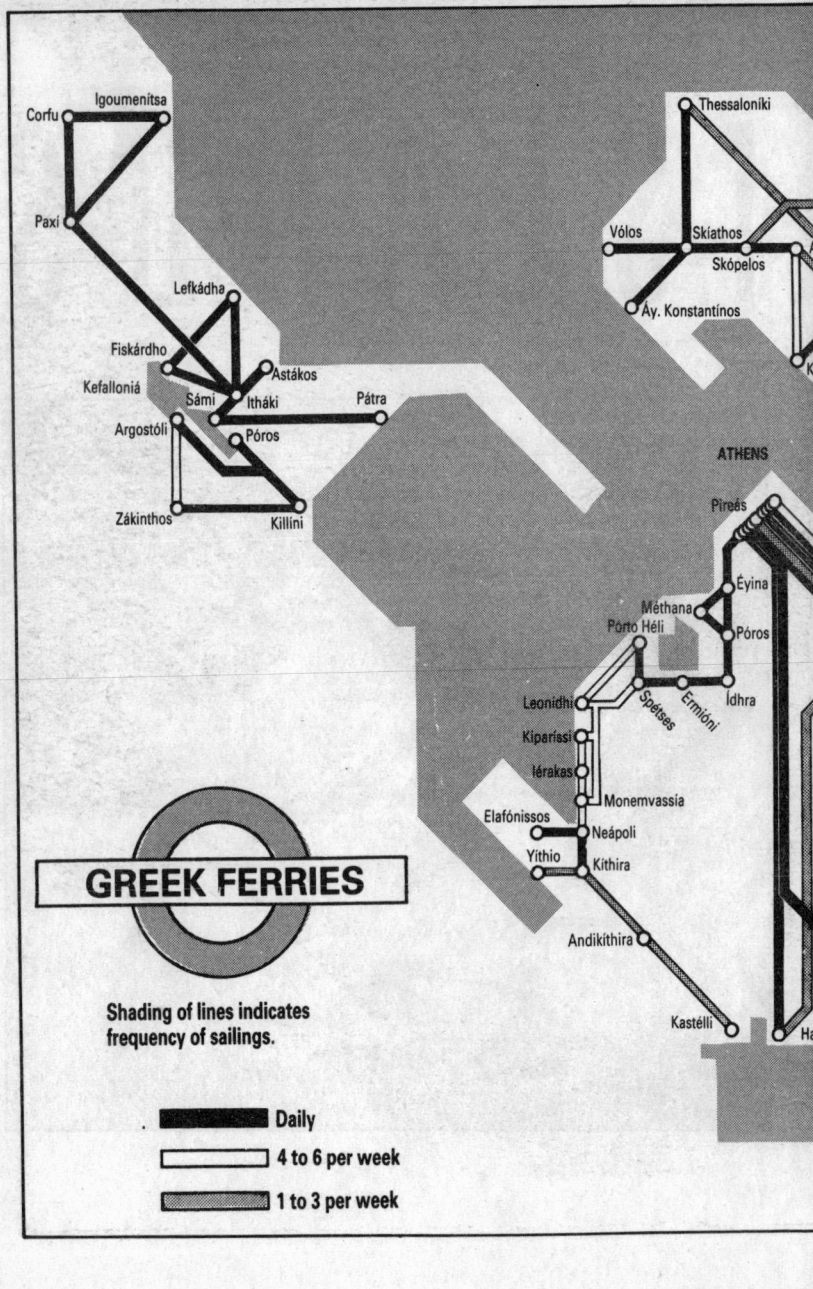

GREEK FERRIES

Shading of lines indicates
frequency of sailings.

Daily
4 to 6 per week
1 to 3 per week

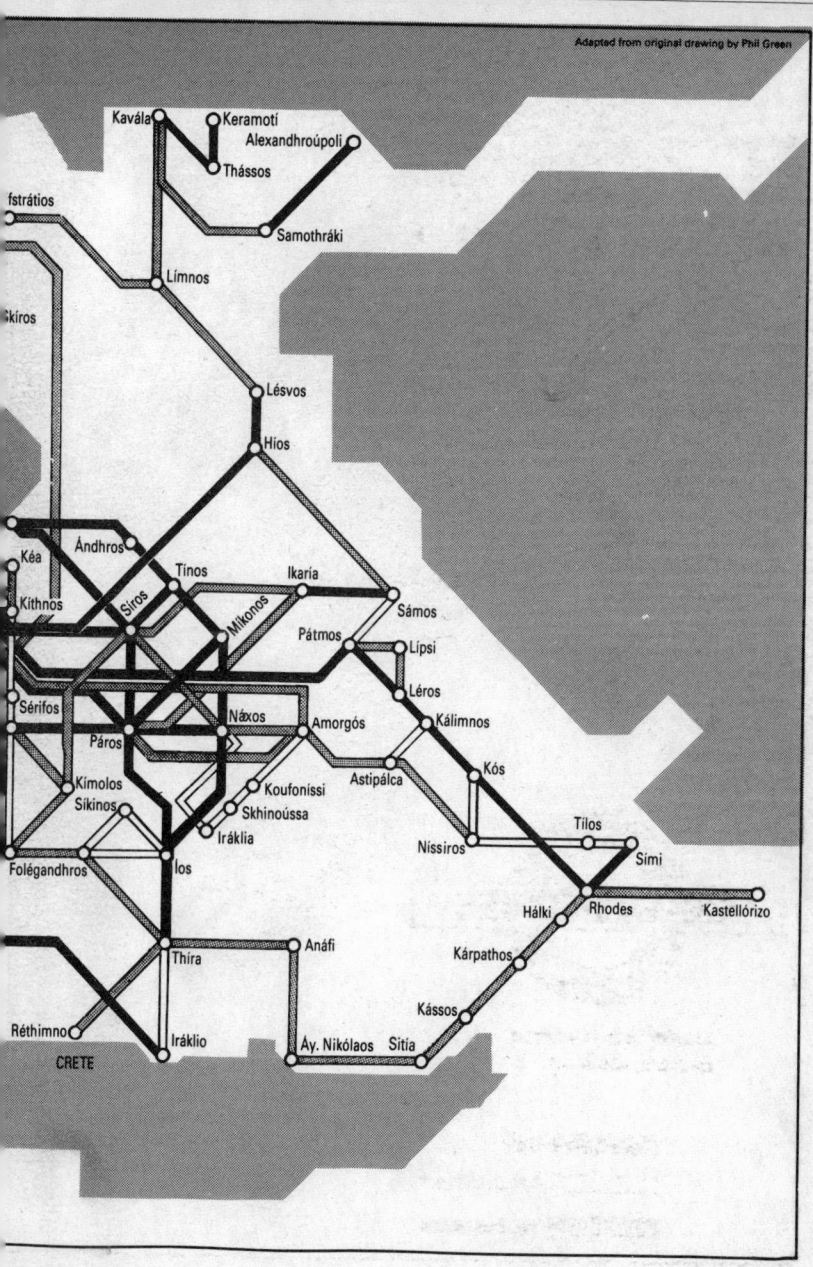

Adapted from original drawing by Phil Green

Kavála
Keramotí
Alexandhroúpoli
Thássos
fstrátios
Samothráki
Límnos
Skiros
Lésvos
Híos
Kéa
Ándhros
Kíthnos
Tínos
Ikaria
Síros
Sámos
Mikonos
Pátmos
Lípsi
Léros
Sérifos
Náxos
Amorgós
Kálimnos
Páros
Kós
Kímolos
Koufoníssi
Astipálca
Síkinos
Skhinoússa
Tílos
Iráklia
Níssiros
Símí
Folégandhros
Íos
Hálki
Rhodes
Kastellórizo
Thíra
Anáfi
Kárpathos
Réthimno
Iráklio
Áy. Nikólaos
Sitía
Kássos
CRETE

CHAPTER SIX

THE ARGO-SARONIC

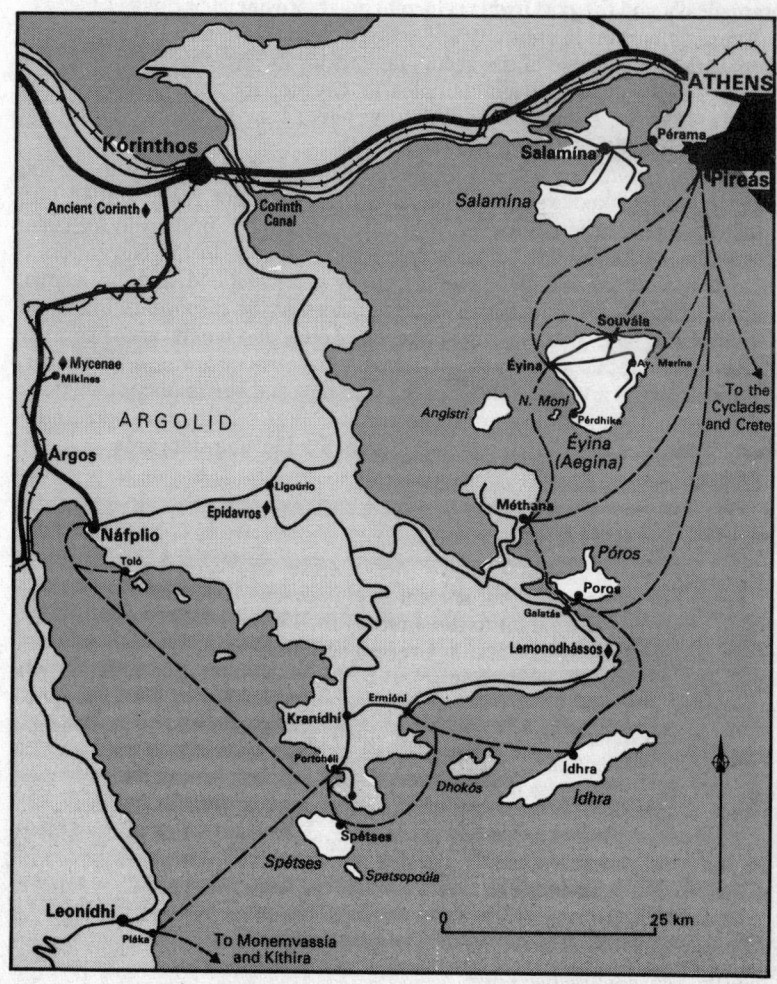

The rocky, volcanic chain of **Argo-Saronic** islands, most of them barely an olive's throw from the Argolid, differ to a surprsing extent not just from the mainland but from one another too. Less surprising is their massive popularity, with Éyina (Aegina) especially becoming something of an Athenian suburb at weekends. Ídhra (Hydra), Póros, and Spétses are not far behind in summer, though their emphasis tends to be more on cruise and package tourists. More than any other group, these are islands very much at their best out of season, when populations fall dramatically and the port towns return to quiet, provincial-backwater life.

Éyina, important in antiquity and more or less continually inhabited since then, is the most fertile of the group, famous for its pistachio nuts, as well as for one of the finest ancient temples in Greece. Its main problem – the crowds – can be escaped by avoiding weekends, or by taking the time to explore its satellite isles, **Angístri** and **Moní**.

The three southerly islands, **Spétses**, **Ídhra** and **Póros**, are to varying extents pine-cloaked; relatively infertile, they were not really settled until medieval times, when refugees from the mainland – principally Albanian Christians – established themselves here. In response to the barrenness of their new home the islanders adopted piracy as a livelihood, and the seamanship and huge fleets thus acquired were placed at the disposal of the Greek nation during the War of Independence. Today foreigners and Athenians have replaced locals in the rapidly depopulating harbour towns, and windsurfers and sailboats are faint echoes of the warships and *kaíkia* once at anchor.

Of the fifth island of the group, **Salamína**, there's little to be noted other than its position, awash in the pollution from the Elefsína shipyards.

Éyina (Aegina)

It seems incredible today, but ancient Aegina was a major power in Classical times, with trade carried on to the limits of the known world, a sophisticated silver coinage system (the first in Greece) and prominent athletes and craftsmen. But during the fifth century B.C. the islanders made the political mistake of siding with their fellow Dorians, the Spartans, and Athens seized on this as an excuse to act on a long-standing jealousy; her fleets defeated Aegina's in two separate sea battles and, after the second, the population was expelled and replaced by more tractable colonists.

Today, though the island is essentially regarded as a beach annexe of Athens, it is visited also for the sake of the remarkable Temple of Aphaia. This is located on the east coast of the island, close to the port of Ayía Marína. If it is your primary goal, best take one of the ferries that in season run directly to that port. If you plan to stay, then make sure your boat will dock at Éyina town, the island capital. Ferries also occasionally stop at Souvála, between the two ports.

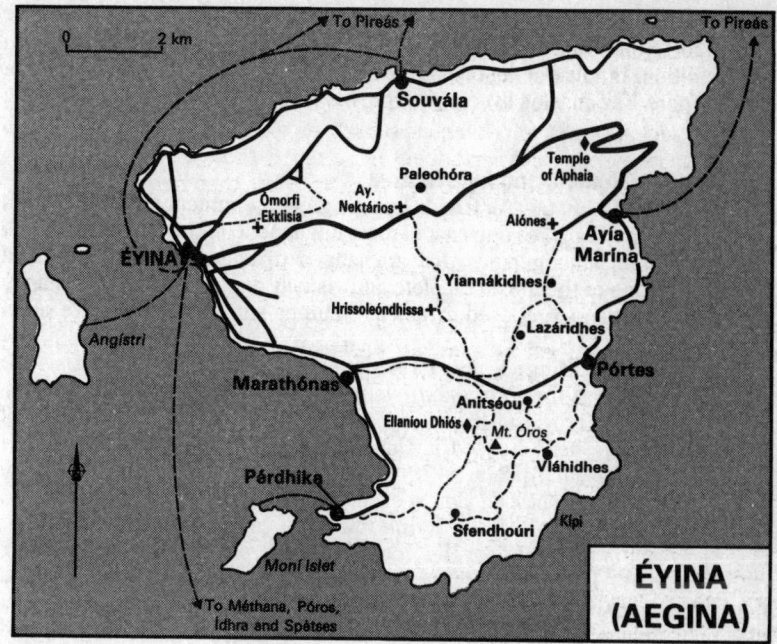

Éyina town

A solitary column of a Temple of Aphrodite beckons as your ferry steams around the point into the harbour at **ÉYINA TOWN**. The bus stop and moped rental are conveniently located a couple of hundred metres to the left of the jetty as you disembark, handy for a daytrip exploration of the island. But the capital is a pleasant enough place to stay, with some grand old buildings from the time (1826-28) when it served as the first capital of Greece after the War of Independence. There are a few D- and E-class **hotels** scattered throughout town, particularly near the bus stop in front of the post office; otherwise look for **rooms** inland.

The **harbour** is workaday rather than picturesque, and all the more appealing for that. Fishermen talk and tend their nets, and *kaíkia* loaded with produce from the mainland bob at anchor. There are some decent tavernas right on the water, and an *ouzerí* where you can have octopus and pistachios (the island's main product) with your drink while you watch the produce and seafood being carried inland to the fish market and the small bazaar district surrounding it.

The Archaeological Museum (now in the Kolóna district north of town) is definitely not worth a detour, the paucity of its exhibits reflecting the various calamities that have befallen the island more than anything else. The town churches too are mostly undistinguished, though fifteen minutes' walk east of the port you'll find thirteenth-century **Ómorfi Ekklisía** with frescoes in fair condition. In Livádhi, just to the north of Éyina town, a plaque marks the house where Kazantzakis lived and wrote his most celebrated book, *Zorba the Greek*.

The Temple of Aphaia and Ayía Marína

The Doric **TEMPLE OF APHAIA**, Éyina's great monument and dating from the fifth century B.C., lies due east of town but almost on the other side of the island, standing among pines that are tapped to make the excellent local retsina. It is one of the most complete and visually complex ancient buildings in Greece, with superimposed arrays of columns and lintels evocative of an Escher drawing.

Less than two centuries ago its pediments (as important a part of the national heritage as the Parthenon) were intact and virtually perfect, depicting two battles at Troy; but they were 'bought' from the Turks by Ludwig of Bavaria and have been housed in the Munich Glyptothek since 1813. The dedication is unusual: Aphaia, a Cretan nymph who had fled from the lust of King Minos, was worshipped almost exclusively on Aegina.

To **get to the temple from Éyina** town you can go by bus, though the best approach is by hired bicycle. There's a coast road via the uninteresting resort of SOUVÁLA, but if under your own power it's better to take the inland road which passes the monastery of **Áyios Nektários** (a local worthy who died only sixty years ago and was canonised in highly irregular fashion) and ruined, deserted **PALEOHÓRA**, the island's old capital. The town was built here in the ninth century A.D. as protection against piracy and only abandoned in 1826, after independence from the Turks. A dozen or so of the reputed 365 churches and monasteries remain in recognizable state, but nothing of the town itself; when the islanders left, they simply dismantled their houses and moved them to modern Éyina.

AYÍA MARÍNA, 13km from Éyina town, lies on the south side of the Aphaia temple ridge. A major resort, its beach is often so crowded with Athenians that it is only really worth coming here for the ferries. Rooms and restaurants are both expensive, though scores of backpackers brave the insect life to camp in the olive groves behind the beach – not a great prospect. Beyond the town the road continues south to another beach at **PÓRTES**, where the rough road turns inland to cross the island, passing just under Mt. Óros and hitting the west coast near Marathónas.

The south and centre

The south and centre of the island constitute good walking country. Coming from Marathónas, you can walk up past Pahía Ráhi hamlet on a mixture of jeep tracks and paths to the turning for the final ascent of **Mt. Óros**.

Just off the trail and within sight of the Pórtes–Marathónas road are the massive foundations of the shrine of **Ellaníou Dhiós**, Éyina's third temple, with the monastery of Taxiárhes squatting amidst the massive masonry. At the top, an hour from the road, the chapel of Análipsi is unremarkable – but not so the fantastic view, stretching over the entire island and much of the Argo-Saronic Gulf. Óros (532m, 1700ft) is the archipelago's highest point. From the summit you can pick out the hamlets of Vláhides, Anitséou and Sfendóuri, as well as the islolated beach of Kípi. More **paths** in this largely roadless portion of the island link these points with Pórtes and Pérdhika; there is also a direct path from nearby the ancient temple to Pérdhika.

From Alónes, a hamlet west of Ayía Marína, you can walk through the settlements of Yiannákidhes and Lazáridhes to the nunnery of **Hrissoleóndissa**, whose dozen or so inmates may still offer hospitality to suitably-clad visitors. A more popular route, used on religious feast days, begins from Áyios Nektários monastery.

For such a well-visited island, Éyina is rather short of attractive swimming spots. Ayía Marína, the only really sandy beach, is bearable out of season, but other than Kípi and Pórtes your best bet is in the vicinity of **PÉRDHIKA**. This itself is a fishing village, twenty minutes by bus from Éyina town, with a small beach. It is certainly the best place to stay on the island besides the main town. Everyone camps on the abandoned naval reserve on the side of the bay opposite the village, a series of partly shaded terraces.

Alternatively, there are *kaíkia* from here across to **Moní Islet**, where there's an official EOT campsite, a seasonal taverna and tremendous skin diving. The **campsite**, incidentally, is quite lively and has plenty of water – a pressing problem back on Éyina where the thirsty pistachios lower the water table several feet annually.

Angístri

ANGÍSTRI, the other of Éyina's satellite isles, is served by *kaíki* several times daily from the Éyina town harbour; the trip takes half an hour. There's a lone village, frequented seasonally by Germans, for whom twenty or so (mostly D- and E-class) hotels have sprung up. There are a couple of small beaches, uncrowded by Éyina standards. The 600-plus islanders still preserve some of their old customs, with the women wearing long embroidered skirts and yellow scarves.

Póros

Separated from the mainland by a 400-metre strait, Póros (literally 'the ford') only just qualifies as an island. But qualify it does, making it fair game for the package tours in summer. Its proximity to Pireás also means a weekend invasion by Athenians, so if you want to see just how many people can fit onto a Greek island try Póros on a summer Saturday.

Attractions on the island are, in any case, limited. The beaches are few and poor, especially compared to neighbouring Éyina and Spétses, and the most enjoyable excursions are across on the mainland around Galatás. If you do decide to stay, there are village **rooms to let** and a range of **hotels**, from cheapish family-run ones to pricier A- and B-class. Camping is not encouraged: there are prominent 'No Camping' signs and no official campsite.

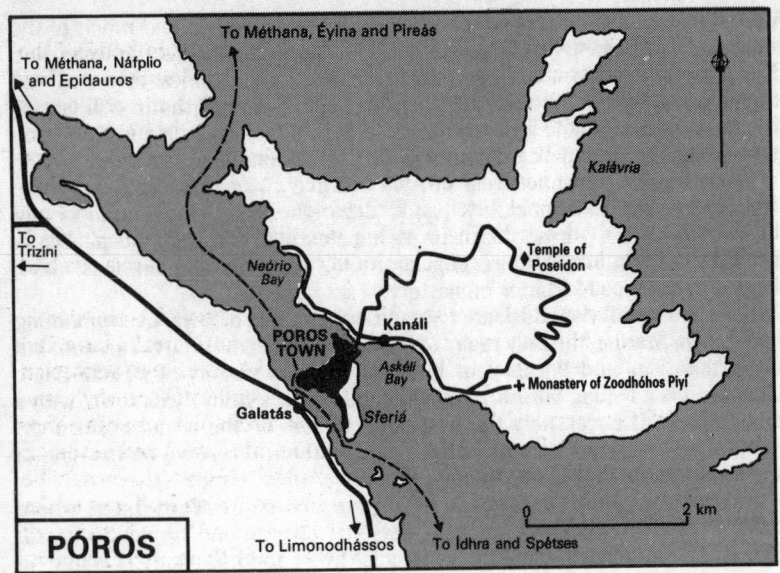

Perhaps the most interesting feature of the island is its topography. Póros is in fact two islands, Sferiá and Kalávria, separated from each other by a shallow engineered canal. 'The canal reminds you of Venice' according to one local guide book – a phrase which must have gained something in the translation.

Póros town and Sferiá

Ferries drop you at **PÓROS**, the only town, which rises steeply on all sides of the tiny volcanic peninsula of Sferiá. The harbour and town look very attractive as the boats come in, though less so as you notice the numbers of tourist shops on the front. The cafés and the waterfront have a certain animation about them or are just plain noisy, according to your taste and mood. Either way, you probably won't want a room right in the midst of it so walk uphill through the quieter back streets in the general direction of the clock tower, which also offers a good view of the town and mainland.

As with many island towns, you only need to move a few streets back from the seafront to see the quieter places where the islanders themselves live and shop. Down on the quay good-value **eateries** include *Grill Oasis* and *Ta Dhilina*, at the far end away from the ferry dock, while in the town the *Three Brothers* restaurant is pricier but recommended. There's also a small fish market and plenty of produce stalls.

Kalávria

Most of Póros's **hotels** are to be found on Kalávria, the main body of the island, just across the canal beyond the Naval Cadets' Training School. They stretch for 2km or so on either side of the causeway, with some of those to the west ideally situated to catch the dawn chorus: the Navy's marching band. If you're not into early-morning martial music, head beyond the first bay where the fishing boats tie up. Alternatively, turn right around Askéli Bay, where there are some hotels and villas with good clear water, but not much in the way of beaches. The best is Kanáli, near the beginning, which usually charges admission – a reflection both of Póros's commercialism and the premium on sand.

At the end of the four-kilometre stretch of road around Askéli is the simple eighteenth-century **Monastery of Zoödhóhos Piyí**, whose monks have fled the tourists and been replaced by a caretaker to collect the admission charges. It's a pretty spot, with a couple of tavernas under the nearby plane trees – though they may well be shut out of season. From here you can either walk up across to the far side of the island through the pines and olives, or bike along the road. Either route will keep you fit and allow you to escape the new developments in and around the town. Either will also lead you to the few columns and ruins that make up the sixth-century B.C. **Temple of Poseidon**, but keep your eyes open or you may miss them. Here, supposedly, Demosthenes, fleeing from the Macedonians after taking part in the last-ditch resistance of the Athenians, took poison rather than surrender to the posse sent after him. A road leads on and back down in a circular route to the 'grand canal'.

On the mainland: Limonodhássos

The adjacent mainland offers more rewarding escapes and diversions, with or without your own transport. Frequent skiffs will take you (and a bike) over to the village of GALATÁS for a few drachmas, and from there you can head east to the immense lemon groves known as **Limonodhássos**. On foot from Galatás the groves are about a thirty-minute walk.

Though one travel brochure says there are 300,000 lemon trees here, the more general consensus tallies about 30,000, not that it matters much as you pick your way along the various paths that meander through them, all heading upwards to an inspiringly positioned taverna where a charming old Greek serves fresh lemonade as you sit on the terrace and look out at the magnificent view, the more so when the trees are in blossom or in fruit. According to Henry Miller's *Colossus of Maroussi*: 'In the spring young and old go mad from the fragrance of sap and blossom'.

Infrequent buses also cover the six road-kilometres northwest from Galatás to the village of modern Trizíni (Dhamalá), a base for excursions on foot to the remains of **ancient Troezene** and the Yéfira tou Dhiavoloú, a natural rock bridge crossing a deep gorge (see p.144). Unfortunately the beauty of the area has been marred by road building but the half-day outing from Póros is still a good trip, not least for the chance of glimpsing a rare black butterfly endemic to the ravine.

From Galatás there's also a morning bus to Náfplio, which will drop you at **Epidaurus** (see *Chapter Two*), about halfway; the next bus will pick you up again in mid-afternoon, allowing a few hours at the theatre and site. During the summer Epidaurus Festival there are coach excursions from Póros for the weekend performances of ancient drama.

Ídhra (Hydra)

The port and town of **ÍDHRA**, with its tiers of substantial stone mansions and white, tiled houses climbing up from a perfect horseshoe harbour, is a very beautiful spectacle. Unfortunately, thousands of others think so too, and from Easter until September it's packed to the gills. The front becomes one long outdoor café, the hotels are full and the discos flourish. Once a fashionable artists' colony, established in the 1960s as people restored the grand old houses, it has experienced a predictable metamorphosis into one of the more exclusive and expensive resorts in Greece. But this acknowledged, a visit is still to be recommended, especially if you can get here some time other than peak season.

The town and nearby beaches
The town's dozens of **mansions** were built mostly during the eighteenth century, on the accumulated wealth of a remarkable merchant fleet of 160 ships which traded as far afield as America and, during the Napoleonic Wars, broke the British blockade to sell corn to France. Fortunes were made and the island also enjoyed a special relationship with the Turkish Porte: govern-

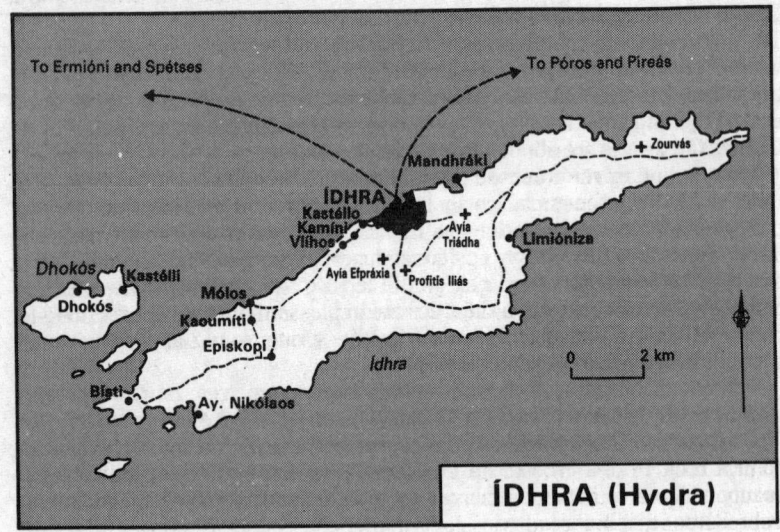

ing itself, paying no tax, but providing sailors for the Sultan's navy. A particularly large wave of immigrants arrived here in the 1770s – persecuted minorities from all over the Greek mainland joining those who had arrived as early as the fifteenth century – and by the 1820s the town's population stood at nearly 20,000, an incredible figure when you reflect that today it is under 3000. During the War of Independence, Hydriot merchants provided many of the ships for the Greek forces and inevitably many of the commanders.

Their houses, designed by architects from Venice and Genoa, are still the great monuments of the town; ask the tourist police for help in locating, among others, the **Votsís** and **Ikonomoú** *arhondiká*. The interior of the **Koundouriótis** and **Voulgarís** houses can also be occasionally visited. The **Tsombadhoú** villa on the harbour is now a maritime academy, and the **Tombázis** a school of fine arts.

Ídhra is also reputedly hallowed by no less than 365 churches (the same number as on several other islands!), the most important being the cathedral of **Panayía Mitropóleos**, built around a courtyard down by the port, with a distinctive clocktower.

Staying on Ídhra means finding a room in the port, or if you're lucky at Vlíhos (see below). There are a number of **pensions** along the waterside. Most have similar prices – 30 percent or so above usual island rates – and your main concern is likely to be finding space rather than quality. Reasonable-value places to start a hunt (or if you're organised, phone ahead) include the C-class *Leto* (☎0298/53-385) and D-class *Argo* (☎0298/52-452), *Dina* (☎0298/52-248) or *Sofia* (☎0298/52-313), or the pleasant, unclassified *Douglas* (☎0298/52-599). If you still have no luck, try asking around the fishermen's quarter of Kamíni, a kilometre to the west. *Ta Tria Adhelfia* is a good, inexpensive, friendly taverna next to the cathedral.

The island's only sandy beach is at **MANDHRÁKI**, 2km east of town along a concrete track; it's the private domain of the *Miramare Hotel*, although the windsurfing centre is open to all. On the opposite side of the harbour a coastal path leads around to a pebbly but popular stretch, just before **KAMÍNI**, where there's a good year-round taverna, *George and Anna's*. Continuing along the water on the now unsurfaced mule track you'll come to **KASTÉLLO**, another small, rocky beach with the ruins of a tiny fort.

Just thirty minutes' walk beyond Kamíni (or a boat ride from the port) will bring you to **VLÍHOS,** a small hamlet with three tavernas, **rooms** and a historic nineteenth-century bridge. **Camping** is tolerated here (though nowhere else closer to town) and the swimming in the lee of an offshore islet is good. Farther out, the island of **Dhokós** is only seasonally inhabited by goatherds and people tending their olives.

The interior

There are no motor vehicles of any kind on the island (except for two lorries to pick up the rubbish), and no metalled roads away from the port, for Ídhra is mountainous and its interior accessible only by foot or donkey. The practical result of this is that most visiting tourists don't venture outside the town, so with a little walking you can find yourself in a quite different kind of island.

Following the streets of town upwards and inland you reach a path which winds up the mountain (in about an hour's walk) to the **Monastery of Profítis Ilías** (Prophet Elijah) and the **Convent of Ayía Efpraxía**. Both are beautifully situated; the nuns at the convent (the lower of the two) offer hand-woven fabrics for sale. Further on, to the left if you face away from the town, is the **Monastery of Ayía Triádha**, occupied by a few monks (no women admitted). From here a path continues east for two more hours to the cloister of **Zourvás** in the extreme east of the island.

The donkey path continues west of Vlíhos to **Episkopí**, a high plateau planted with olives and vineyards and dotted by perhaps a dozen summer homes (no facilities). An inconspicuous turning roughly half an hour below leads to Mólos Bay, dirty and sea-urchin infested, and to the more pleasant farming hamlet of **KAOUMÍTI**. From Episkopí itself faint tracks lead to the western extreme of the island, on either side of which the bays of **BÍSTI** and **ÁYIOS NIKÓLAOS** offer solitude and good swimming.

The south coast, too, if you're energetic and armed with a map, is scattered with coves, best at **LIMIÓNIZA** (beyond Ayía Triádha). Most of these more distant spots are served by **boat excursions** in season from Ídhra town, though, and the charms of walking on Ídhra in any case took a severe blow in 1985 when a disastrous fire devastated much of the forest between Profítis Ilías and Episkopí; the land is only beginning to recover.

Spétses (Spetsai)

Spétses, the island where John Fowles once lived (and used, thinly disguised as Phraxos, as the setting for *The Magus*), is very green and very small. If you're feeling lively you could walk the whole way around it in a day. Whatever, you can easily wander off 'away from its inhabited corner (where Spetses is) truly haunted . . . its pine forests uncanny'. Sheltered pebble bays teeming with fish are scattered along much of the coastline and a number of paths link them with the dirt perimeter track of the island.

The island, like the rest of the group, is popular – alarmingly so in season. However, it absorbs its tourists with more than usual grace. The discos haven't yet blighted the charms of the old waterfront town and the best beach on the island, Ayii Anáryiri, has had its development limited, remarkably, to a scattering of holiday villas. On the minus side, up until the recent emergence of Takis – Spetses' 'King of Tourism' – as mayor, the island's streets and roads have been neglected, its beaches left littered and hotels allowed to pump untreated sewage out into the bay. Hopefully, change is in sight.

Spétses town

SPÉTSES, or Kastélli, is the port and town, and, while less immediately strik-ing than Ídhra or even Póros, has more character than either. It shares with Ídhra the same history of nineteenth-century mercantile adventure and pros-perity, and the same leading role in the War of Independence which made its foremost citizens the aristocrats of the newly independent Greek state. Pebble-mosaic courtyards and streets sprawl between 200-year-old mansions, whose architecture is quite distinct from the Peloponnesian styles across the straits. Horse-drawn cabs connect the various quarters of town, spread out along the waterfront.

The sights of Spétses town are principally its majestic old houses and gardens. The town **museum**, occupying the magnificent Mexis family mansion, has a display of relics from the War of Independence, including the bones of the Spetsiote admiral-heroine Lascarina Bouboulina. Just outside the town, Fowles aficionados will notice **Anáryiros College**, a curious Greek recreation of an English public school where Fowles taught; it is now vacant, save for the occasional conference or kids' holiday programme. Like the massive Edwardian **Hotel Possidonion**, another *Magus* setting, on the waterside, it was endowed by Sotirios Anaryiros, the island's great nine-teenth-century benefactor. An enormously rich self-made man he was also responsible for planting the pine forest that now covers the island. His former house, behind the *Hotel Roumani*, is a monument to bad taste, decked out like a pharaoh's tomb.

Perhaps more interesting is a walk east from **Dápia**, the cannon-studded main harbour. At the end of the road is **Baltíza** inlet, where half a dozen yards continue to build *kaíkia* in the traditional manner; the shipyard recreated the *Argo* for Tim Severin's 'Jason Voyage' a couple of years back. En route, you pass the old smaller harbour, and the church of **Áyios Nikólaos** with its graceful belfry and giant pebble mosaics.

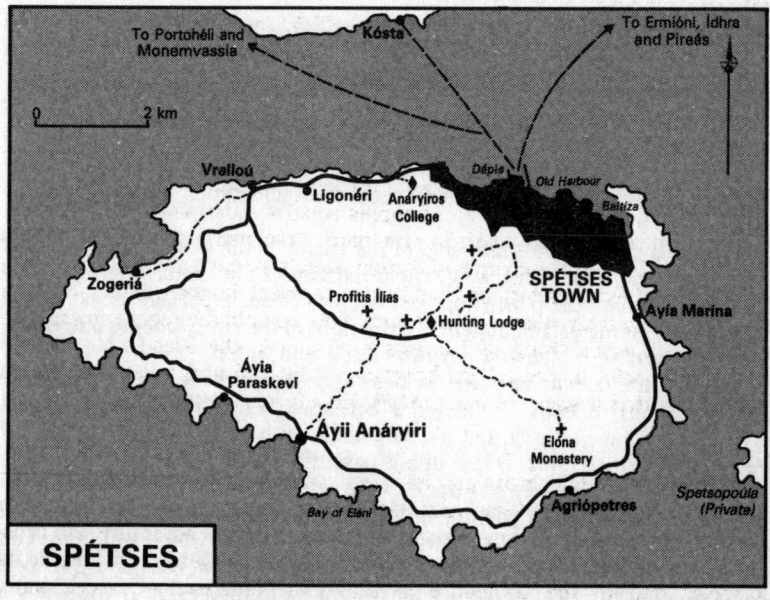

Nearly all visitors stay in Spétses town and all kinds of **accommodation** are available, from the above-mentioned *Hotel Possidonion* (☎0298/72-208; surprisingly low rates out of season) to simple **rooms** in people's houses. If you can get one, the best rooms are in a grand old house behind the Sotirios Anaryiros mansion – illustrious quarters and not too expensive. Well worth trying also is the blue-balconied *Hotel Saronikos* (☎0298/72-646), a lovely old D-class place just by the Flying Dolphin quay at Dápia. If you don't fancy pounding the streets yourself, then go to *Takis's Tourist Office*, fifty paces from the end of the jetty, and see what they can come up with. For **camping** head out to the shade of tamarisks behind Lámpara Beach, 700m west-northwest of the dock – this seems to be tolerated if somewhat exposed.

Food and drink can be expensive and if your money's short you'll prob-ably need to hunt around. Among cheaper places are *Taverna Haralambos,* on Baltíza inlet, by the smaller harbour. The only traditional taverna is *Lazaros*'s (400m inland and uphill from Dápia: ask directions), though it can't cope with large parties. *Mimosa*, near the Anáryiros College, has an attractive garden, but the best (if also the priciest) food is served up at *Trehandiri*, next to the church of Áyios Nikólaos on the way to the old harbour. By day, Stambolis's *kafenío*, below the *Hotel Saronikos*, remains steadfastly traditional.

Finally a word for the two Dápia **crafts shops**, *Pityousa* (behind the *Soleil Hotel*) and *Kaiki* (on the first street in from the front). Both are superior establishments with genuine pieces from the Pireás markets and (at *Pityousa*) some imaginative 'naïve' art by the owner.

Around the island

For **swimming** you need to get clear of the town. Walkable beaches are at **Ayía Marína** (twenty minutes east, with a taverna), at various spots beyond the **old harbour**, and several other spots half an hour away in either direc-tion. The tempting islet of Spetsopoúla, just offshore from Ayía Marína, is unfortunately off-limits. It's the private property of shipping magnate Stavros Niarchos, of dubious repute, who maintains it as a pleasure park for his asso-ciates; his yacht (the largest in Greece) can sometimes be seen moored offshore.

Áyii Anáryiri, on the south side of the island, is the best, if also the most popular, beach: a beautiful, long, sheltered bay of fine sand. There's a self-service taverna on the beach and, just behind, *Tassos*'s, Spétses' finest (and a well-priced) eating establishment. To the right of the cove, looking out to sea, there's a sea cave, which you can swim out to and within.

To avoid the crowds and the reckless speedboat-driving waterski instruc-tors, try to arrive early – ideally for breakfast before any boats or buses arrive. You'll have to walk, but it's only about an hour through the woods, if you take the road from Dápia uphill past the police station and *Lazaros*'s taverna, then continue up the track to the top of the wooded ridge dominat-ing the town. Turn right past the little cabin, which is a hunter's lodge, and a few minutes beyond turn left down a signposted track, which will bring you out by the first houses in Áyii Anáryiri. Turn right on the road and you soon come to a left turn which takes you straight on to the beach. If you fancy a slightly longer walk, you can detour near the hunters' lodge to the chapel of Profítis Ilías, right at the centre of the island, with 360-degree views and a well with bucket for the thirsty.

For the more sedentary, Áyii Anáryiri can also be reached from Dápia by *kaíki* (regular departures) or expensive boat-taxi; or by moped or the island bus (4 departures daily), a bumpy half-hour ride via Ayía Marína.

The road actually encircles Spétses, though it's in poor condition between Vréllou and Áyii Anáryiri and if you hire a moped or bike you may well find yourself carrying your machine over obstacles. Heading **west from Dápia** around the coast, the road is concreted until the houses run out after a kilometre or so; thereafter it is a dirt track which winds through pine trees and around inlets. The forest stretches from the central hills right down to the shore and it makes for a beautiful coastline with little coves and rocky promontories, all shaded by trees. **VRELLOÚ** is one of the first places you come to, at the mouth of a wooded valley known locally as 'Paradise'. It is a fairly apt description except that like so many of the beaches it becomes polluted every year by tourists' rubbish. However, the entire shore is dotted with coves (claimed to be particularly safe swimming for children) and in a few places there are small tavernas – at **ZOGERIÁ**, for instance, where the scenery more than makes up for the inadequate little beach.

Working your way anti-clockwise around the coast towards Áyii Anáryiri you reach **ÁYIA PARASKEVÍ** with its small church and beach – one of the most beautiful coves on Spétses and an alternate stop on the *kaíki*. The road and coves continue after Áyii Anáryiri, though often at some distance from each other until you loop back to Ayía Marína.

travel details

Ordinary Ferryboats

From the central harbour at **Pireás** at least 10 boats daily run to Ayía Marína (1 hr.) and Éyina (1½ hr.); 5 daily to Póros (3½ hr.); 1 or 2 a day to Ídhra (4½ hr.) and Spétses (5½ hr.). About 4 connections daily between Éyina and Póros.

Most of the ferries stop on the mainland at Méthana (between Éyina and Póros) and Ermióni (between Ídhra and Spétses); it is possible to board them here from the Peloponnese. Some continue from Spétses to Portohéli. There are also constant boats between Póros and Galatás (10 min.) from dawn until late at night, and boat-taxis between Spétses and Portohéli.

N.B. There are more ferries at weekends and fewer out of season (although the service remains good); they leave Pireás most frequently between 7am and 9am, and 1pm and 6pm. Do not buy a return ticket as it saves no money and limits you to one specific boat. The general information number for the Argo-Saronic ferries is ☎01/451-1311 or 411-5801.

'Flying Dolphin' Hydrofoils

Approximately hourly services from the central harbour at Pireás to **Éyina** only 6am–8pm in season, 7am–7pm out; 40 min.

All hydrofoils going beyond Éyina leave from the **Zea Marina**: 4 to 15 times daily to Póros (1 hr.), Ídhra (1 hr. 40 min.), and Spétses (2–2½ hr.). All these times depend upon the stops en route, and frequencies vary with the season.

Éyina is connected with the other three islands twice a day; Póros, Ídhra, and Spétses with each other 3 to 5 times daily. Some hydrofoils also stop at Méthana and Ermióni and all of those to Spétses continue to Portohéli (15 min. more). This is a junction of the hydrofoil route – there is usually one a day onwards to Toló and Náfplio (and vice versa; 30 and 45 min.) in season and another (almost year-round) to Monemvassía (2 hr.). The Monemvassía hydrofoil continues 2 to 4 times a week to the island of Kíthira.

N.B. Once again services are heavily reduced out of season, though all the routes between

Portohéli and Pireás still run. Hydrofoils are usually twice as fast and twice as expensive as ordinary boats, though to Éyina the price is little different. You can only buy one-way tickets, so if you need to return on a certain day buy your ticket back, *on arrival*, from the local agent. In season, it's not unusual for departures to be fully booked.

Details and tickets available from local agents and in Athens from *Wagons-Lits*, Stadhíou 5, Síntagma (☎01/322-8650). The Pireás ticket office is at Themistokléous 8 (☎01/452-7107). Tickets can also be bought at the departure quays.

CHAPTER SEVEN

THE CYCLADES

Named for the circle they form around the sacred island of Délos, the **Cyclades** (*Kikládhes*) are the most satisfying Greek archipelago for island-hopping. On no other group do you get quite such a strong feeling of each island as a microcosm, each with its own distinct traditions, customs and (very definitely) path of modern development. Most of these small worlds are small enough to walk around in a few days, giving you a sense of completeness and identity impossible on, say, Crete or most of the Ionian islands.

There is some unity. The majority of the islands – Ándhros, Náxos, Sérifos and Kéa notably excepted – are arid and rocky, and most share the 'Cycladic' style of brilliant-white, cubist architecture. The extent and impact of tourism, however, is dramatically haphazard, so that although some English is spoken on most islands, a slight detour from the beaten track – say from Íos to Síkinos – could have you groping for your Greek phrasebook.

But whatever the level of tourist development, there are only two islands where it has come completely to dominate their character. These are **Íos**, the original hippie-island and still a paradise for hard-living backpackers, and **Míkonos**, by far the most popular of the group, with its teeming old town, nude beaches and highly sophisticated clubs and often gay bars. After these two, **Páros**, **Sífnos**, **Náxos**, and **Thíra** (Santoríni) are currently the most popular, their beaches and main towns drastically overcrowded in August. But away from the resort areas these islands have, for the most part, escaped the ravages of mass development and seem able to absorb visitors with remarkable ease. To avoid the hordes altogether, the most promising islands are **Síkinos**, **Kithnos**, **Kímolos** or **Anáfi**, or even (going to extremes) the minor islets around Náxos. For a different view of the Cyclades, visit **Tínos** and its imposing church, a major spiritual centre of the Greek Orthodox world – crowded out at the peak seasons of pilgrimage in late March and mid-August. The one major ancient site is **Delos** (Dhílos), certainly worth making time for: the commercial and religious centre of the Classical Greek world, it's visited most easily on a day trip, by *kaíki* from Míkonos.

When it comes to **moving on**, many of the islands are handily connected with Crete (in season), while from Náxos or Amorgós you can loop on to the Dodecanese ferry-circuits. Similarly, you can get from Síros and Páros to Ikaría and Sámos (in the eastern Aegean). A useful source of information (including up-to-date ferry schedules) is *Journey to Greece*, a newspaper sold in Athens bookshops, on the ferries out of Pireás and on most of the islands themselves. It's also worth noting that the Cyclades often get frustratingly **windy**, particularly in early spring, while they're the group worst affected by the *meltémi*, which blows sand and tables about with equal ease throughout much of July and August. Delayed and cancelled ferries are not uncommon, so if you're heading back to Athens to catch a flight leave yourself a day or two of leeway.

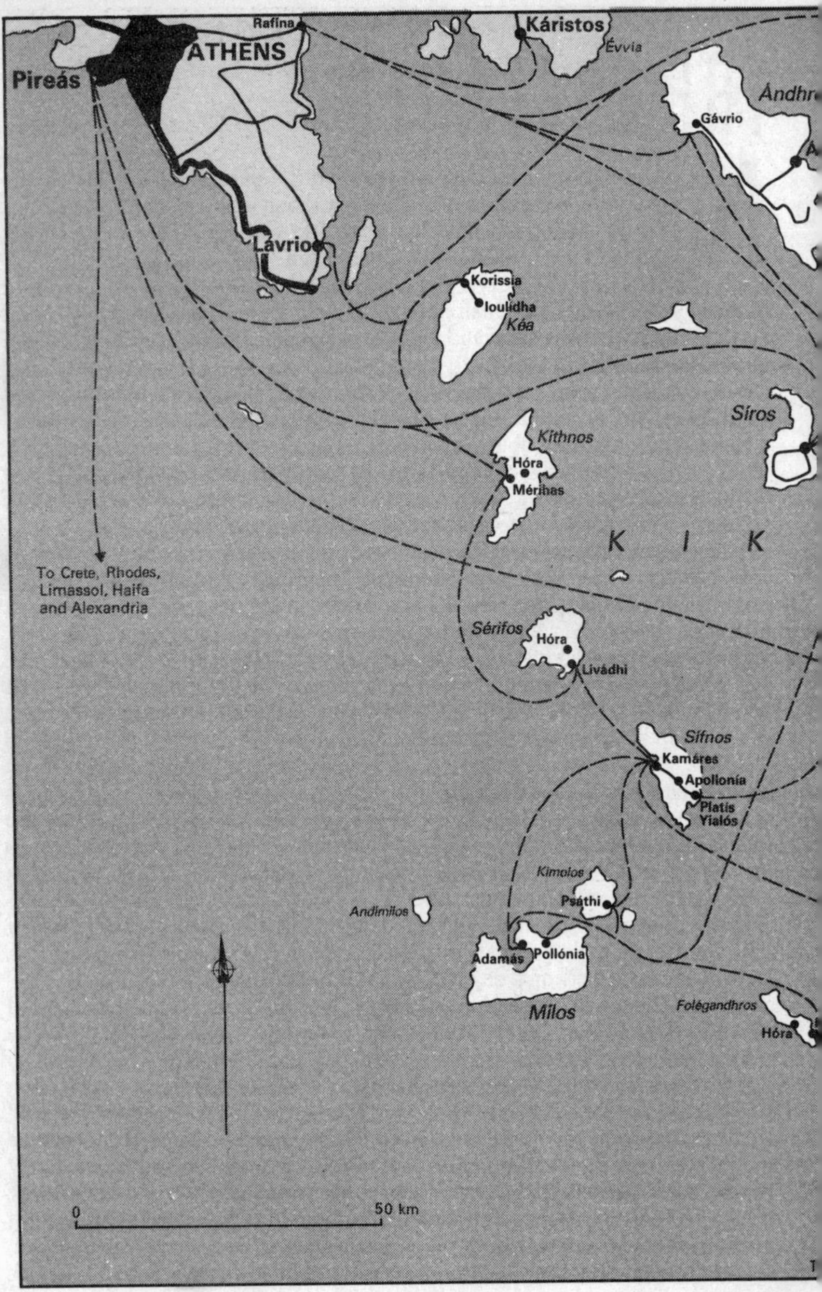

Rafína

Káristos

Évvia

ATHENS

Ándhr

Gávrio

A

Pireás

Lávrio

Korissia

Ioulídha

Kéa

Síros

Kíthnos

Hóra

Mérihas

To Crete, Rhodes,
Limassol, Haifa
and Alexandria

K I K

Sérifos

Hóra

Livádhi

Sífnos

Kamáres

Apollónia

Platís
Yialós

Kímolos

Psáthi

Andímilos

Adamás

Pollónia

Mílos

Folégandhros

Hóra

0   50 km

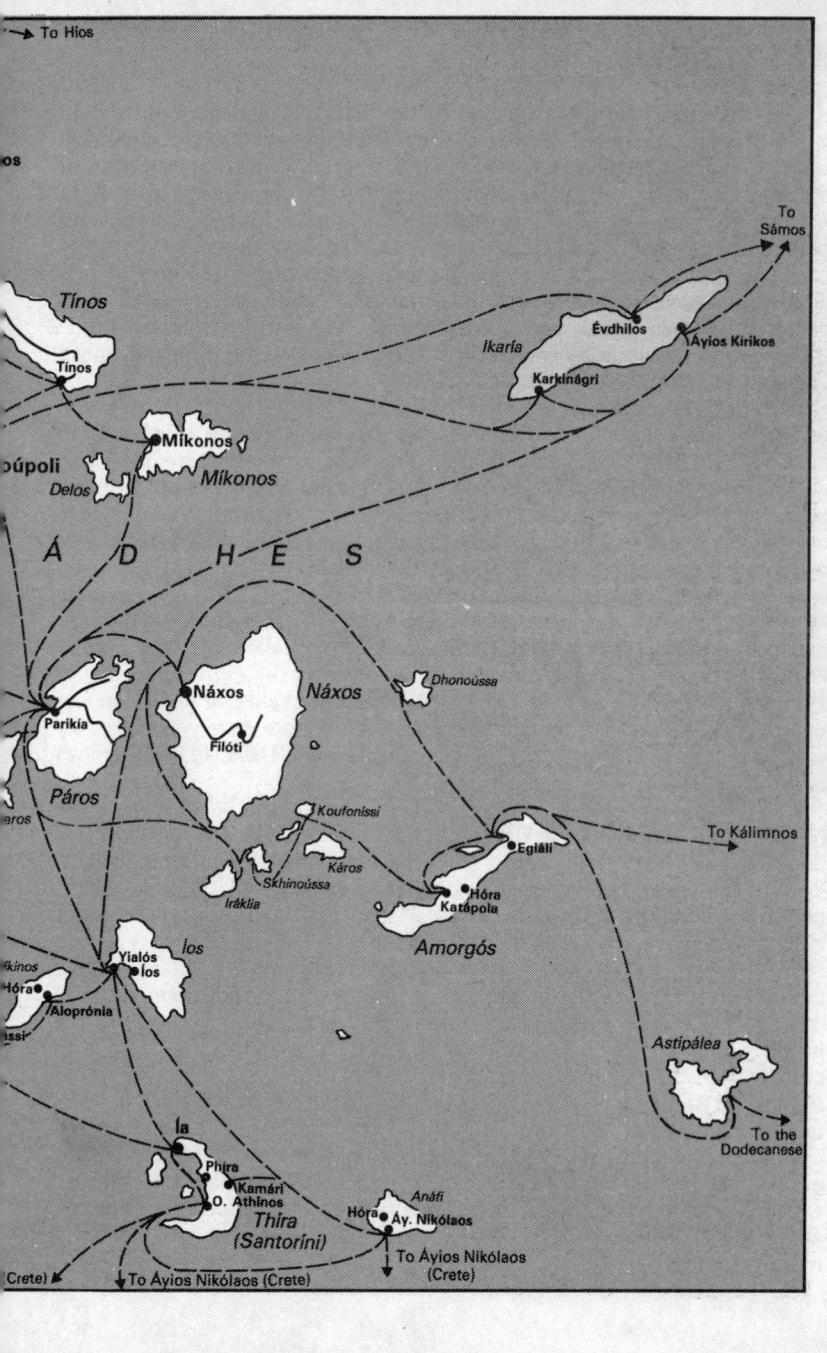

Kéa (Tziá)

Kéa is the closest of the Cyclades to the mainland and very popular in summer with Athenians. However, they (and the attendant commercialisation) confine themselves to certain small coastal resorts, leaving most of the interior quiet. During the week, when the city dwellers head back to Athens, the whole of Kéa is an enticing destination, its rocky, forbidding perimeter enlivened inland by oak and almond groves. As ancient Keos, the island was important, its strategic harbour supporting four cities, a pre-eminence which continued well into the nineteenth century until Síros became the main Greek port. Today tourists account for what sea traffic there is, with regular ferry connections with LÁVRIO on the mainland, only a two-hour bus ride from Athens.

The small northern port of **KORISSÍA** and its handful of hotels, **rooms** to let and tavernas, has fallen victim to uneven expansion and has little beauty to lose. **VOURKÁRI**, a couple of kilometres north is more attractive; the hang-out of the well-heeled yacht set. You might want to stay overnight as there are some good (but expensive) tavernas and, if you hunt around, a few rooms too. Across the bay, on the promontory, the Minoan site of **Ayía Iríni** has been under excavation since 1960, with the remains of a palace, temple and road unearthed in good condition. Another 3km along, **OTZIÁS** has an unofficial campsite with a small beach, but there's only one taverna here and you're exposed to the prevailing wind. Better, probably, to follow the path beyond Otziás as far as Kéa's only functioning monastery, the eighteenth-century **Panayía Kastrianí** – an hour's walk. It's more remarkable for its fine setting on a high bluff than for any intrinsic interest, but from here you can easily and pleasantly walk on to the island capital, IOULÍDHA, in another two hours.

Fairly regular **buses** link Otziá and Vourkári with the port, and run directly from Korissía to **IOULÍDHA**, the ancient Ioulis and birthplace of the renowned early fifth-century B.C. poets Simonides and Bacchylides. With its numerous red-tiled roofs it's by no means a typical Cycladic village, but it is beautifully situated in an arc-shaped fold in the hills. The lower reaches stretch across a spur to the **Kástro**, a half-demolished Venetian fortress incorporating stones from an ancient temple of Apollo. Fifteen minutes northeast of town, on the path to or from Panayía Kastrianí, the road passes the **Lion of Kea**, a sixth-century B.C. sculpture carved out of the living rock. Six metres long and three high, it's an imposing beast, with crudely powerful haunches and a bizarre facial expression. There are steps right down to it, but the effect is most striking from a distance. Back in town, the **Archaeological Museum** (Mon.–Sat. 9am–2pm, Sun. 10am–2pm, closed Tues.) displays finds from the four ancient city-states of Kéa, though sadly, as so often, the best items were long ago spirited away to Athens. Besides an expensive hotel in the Kástro, there's one very good **pension** (the *Filoxenia*, above the shoeshop; ☎0288/22-057), a fine place to stay if you can get a room.

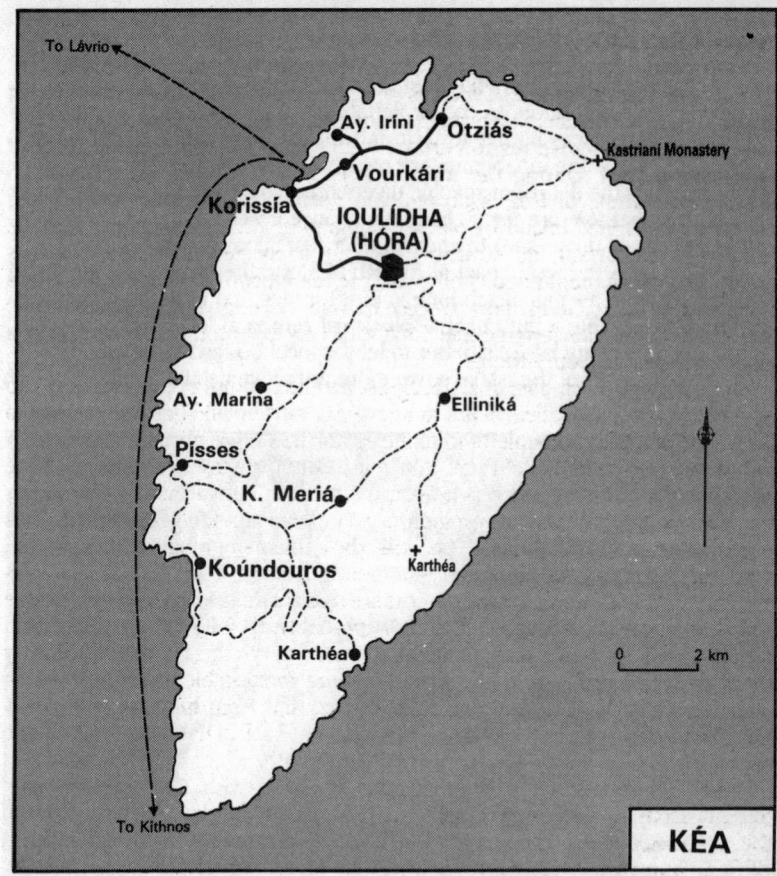

To the southwest of Ioulídha, reached on a good path from town, the crumbling Hellenistic watchtower of **Ayía Marína** sprouts dramatically from the grounds of a small nineteenth-century monastery. Beyond, towards the coast, sprawls the lovely agricultural valley of **PÍSSES**, fronted by an excellent and largely undeveloped beach – probably the best place to camp on the island (rooms and tavernas too). **KOÚNDOUROS**, the next bay south, is less appealing, a burgeoning bungalow resort catering to Athenian weekenders.

The scant ruins of ancient Poiessa are close to Písses. However, the only remains of any real significance from Kéa's past are at **KARTHÉA**, tucked away on the opposite, southeastern, edge of the island at Polis Bay. If you're interested, it's a good three hours' round-trip walk from the hamlets of KATO MERIÁ or ELLINIKÁ.

Kíthnos (Thermiá)

Though possibly the dullest and most barren of the Cyclades, a short stay on Kíthnos is a good antidote to the exploitation likely to be encountered elsewhere. Few foreigners bother to visit and the island is oddly quiet, even in midsummer, while the inhabitants are overtly friendly – all factors that easily compensate for the dearth of specific diversions. You could use it as a first or last island stop: there are ferry connections once a week with Kéa, and more frequent services (in season) to and from Sérifos, Sífnos and Mílos.

You'll dock on the west coast at **MÉRIHAS**, a rather functional ferry and fishing port (with a small beach for camping), redeemed by some good tavernas and less likeable – but cheap – blocks of rooms to let. Frankly, though, unless you're arriving late, it's better to let the local **buses** whisk you immediately away to either of the island's two more attractive destinations, HÓRA or DHRIOPÍDHA.

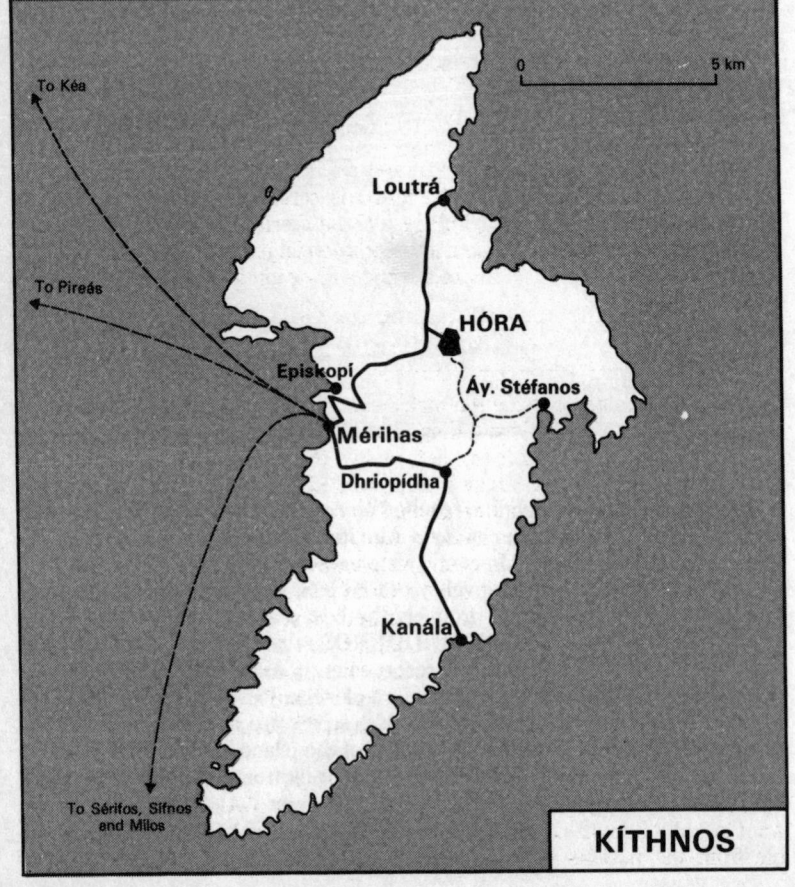

HÓRA is 6km distant, set in the middle of the island; tumbling across an east-west ridge, it's an awkward blend of Kéa-style gabled roofs, Cycladic churches with dunce-cap cupolas, and the inevitable cement monsters. If you're going to stay here, **rooms** are limited to those above the Koutoulia family shop, near the clock tower; eating is best at *To Kentron* or *Barba Stathis*, near the telephone office. Much of the year electricity is supplied by two windmills erected by a German company on the outskirts of the village.

You're handily placed in Hóra to tackle the most interesting thing to do on Kíthnos: the beautiful walk south to **DHRIOPÍDHA**. It takes about an hour, following the obvious old cobbled way that leaves Hóra (though plans are afoot to bulldoze a road over the path). Towards the end the path drops dramatically into Dhriopídha, whose pleasing tiled roofs below seem more appropriate to Spain or Tuscany than Greece. It's a surprisingly large place, once the island's capital, and built around a famous cave (the Katafíki) at the head of a valley alive with springs. There are a couple of small tavernas but nowhere to stay. For this you may want to head 6km beyond, to **KANÁLA** – twenty-odd houses and a church on a sea-washed headland, with tavernas and **rooms** in season.

From Kanála, a succession of small sandy coves extends up the east coast as far as **Áyios Stéfanos**, a chapel-crowned islet tied by causeway to the body of the island. Apart from this stretch, the only other presentable beach on the island is at **EPISKOPÍ**, one bay north of Mérihas.

By way of contrast, the much-vaunted resort of **LOUTRÁ** (3km north of Hóra and named after its thermal baths) is scruffy, its homey nineteenth-century spa closed and decaying beside the sterile modern facility – and bound to become more so since a new commercial jetty was completed. Once again, there are tavernas on the beach and a few rooms to let.

Sérifos

Sérifos has remained outside the mainstream of both history and tourism, its only fame in myth as the island kingdom to which Perseus returned with the Gorgon's head. Most visitors are deterred by the apparently barren, hilly and little-explored interio,r and stay in the port, **LIVÁDHI**, set in a wide green bay and handy for the local beaches. It's not the most attractive place on Sérifos – and to stay here exclusively would be to miss some fine walks – but it is certainly the easiest place to find **rooms** (which, elsewhere, are very sparse). It is also the one place on the island geared to tourists. You'll have to step lively off the boat to get a decent bed; best deal is the *Hotel Galanos* (☎0281/51-277) above the bakery, though there are several other places as well. To the south, the further of two beaches (Karávi) is cleaner and better for camping, as well as being totally nudist. A similar 45-minute walk to the north of the port leads to the sandy beach at **PSILÍ ÁMMOS**, where there are more rooms and a taverna, but no naturism.

An hourly **bus** connects Livádhi with the island capital HÓRA, 2km away, and, less frequently, with MEGÁLO LIVÁDHI and GALANÍ. You may well want to walk though – it's a pleasant half-hour up a cobbled way to Hóra, visible from the port as you climb. Out of season (i.e. by the beginning of

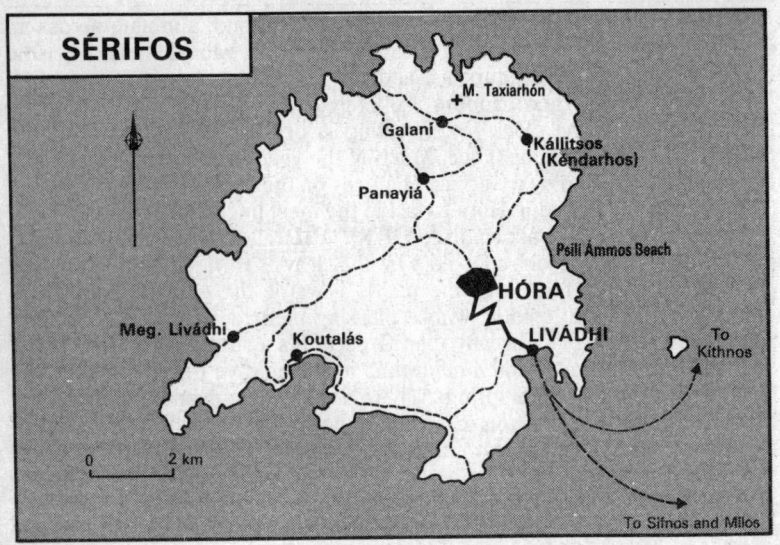

October) you'll have no choice, since the bus – and nearly everything else on Sérifos – ceases operations for the winter; expect beds and food to be severely limited.

HÓRA, pouring like milk from a rocky hog's back above the harbour, is one of the most spectacular villages of the Cyclades. At odd intervals along its alleyways you'll find part of the old castle making up the wall of a house, or a marble statue leaning incongruously in one corner. It's a quiet place, with a couple of tavernas (near the bus stop), the island's post office and one place with **rooms** to let (on the track to the cemetery). There's a path from here which leads to Psilí Ámmos, a short walk, but if you're looking for a more remote beach as a base, try **MEGÁLO LIVÁDHI**, 8km west of Hóra. Iron and copper ore were once exported from here, but cheaper African deposits sent the mines into decline and today the idle machinery rusts away. As well as the beach, there's a taverna and the possibility of rooms to let, as there is also in nearby **KOUTALÁS**, a small fishing village just to the south across the headland.

North of Hóra, the island's high water table frequently breaks the surface to run in delightful rivulets swarming with turtles and frogs; reeds, orchards, and even the occasional palm tree take advantage of the unexpected moisture. This is especially in evidence at **KÁLLITSOS** (Kéndarhos – tavernas), reached by a path from Hóra. A couple of kilometres beyond Kállitsos the sixteenth-century **monastery of Taxiarhón** has some good frescoes and Byzantine manuscripts stored in the library. Looping back towards Hóra, the fine villages of **GALANÍ** and **PANAYIÁ** (named after its tenth-century church) make convenient stops. On foot the circuit will take a full six hours, but there are tavernas and little shops in Kállitsos and Galaní – as well as isolated, remote beaches just to the north where you can sleep undisturbed.

Sífnos

Sífnos is a more immediately appealing island than its northern neighbours – more cultivated and with some fine local architecture – and it's much more popular. No bigger than Kíthnos or Sérifos, it does often get crowded; buses can be packed, and if you want a room, be quick to take any offered as you land. On the other hand its modest size means that wherever you stay, you can reach the rest of Sífnos on foot, over an excellent network of old stone pathways. Besides pottery (a traditional skill), Sifniote cooking, too, is noted: the island is nationally celebrated for its chefs, and fresh dill flavours everything. Try *stámnas*, a clay-pot speciality with meat, cheese and potatoes, and *revíthia* (garbanzo soup). However, like so many islands, Sífnos is short of both water and fresh produce – it's worth bringing a bag of fruit from Athens.

KAMÁRES, the port, is tucked at the base of high bare cliffs in the west. It can be an expensive town (in summer, expect accommodation prices to double), and it is well worth haggling – try the **rooms** above the *Katsoulakis Tourist Agency* close to the quay. There are other places along the front too, as well as the reasonable *Hotel Stavros* (☎0284/31-641) just after the church. Otherwise, there's a long beach with public showers and space to camp and more rooms to let right at the end of the sands.

An excitingly steep twenty-minute bus ride (hourly service until late at night) takes you up to **APOLLONÍA**, the *hóra*, a rambling collage of flagstones, belfries, and flowered courtyards. The island bank, post office and tourist police are all here, but **rooms**, though plentiful, are even more likely to be full than at Kamáres. If you have no luck, try asking around in the outlying districts of Katavatí or Artemónas, once distinct villages, respectively 500m north and south of the central *platía*. The town itself is becoming commercialised but there are still some good genuine tavernas, best of the lot *O Manganas* at Artemónas. The **Folk Museum** (open afternoons only) in the square by the bus stop is also well worth a look since Sífnos produces some of the finest pottery and fabrics in Greece.

As an alternative base with rooms (though there aren't many) you could try **KÁSTRO**, a three-kilometre walk (or regular bus ride) below Apollonía on the east coast. Built on a rocky outcrop with an almost sheer drop to the sea on three sides, the ancient capital of the island retains much of its medieval character. Parts of its boundary walls survive, along with a full complement of sinuous, narrow streets with two-storey houses and some fine sixteenth- and seventeenth-century churches. Venetian coats-of-arms can still be seen on some of the older dwellings, there are remains of the ancient acropolis, and fifteen minutes' walk below the town you can swim off a rocky peninsula.

At the southern end of the island, around 10km from Apollonía, is the growing resort of **PLATÍS YIALÓS**, to which there are (roughly) hourly buses from the capital. You're allowed to camp on the large sandy beach here, though it can get extremely windy. There are several tavernas, a pottery workshop, and rooms available too, but for many the ugly *Xenia* hotel at the southern end of the beach renders Platís Yialós a bit too touristy.

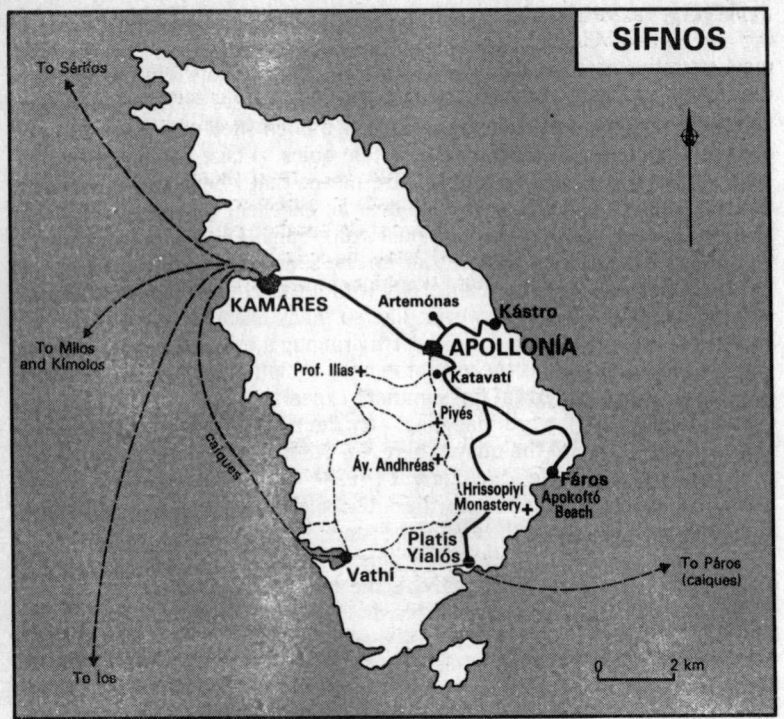

However, seasonal *kaíkia* run from here to the island of PÁROS – an immensely useful link.

Far less crowded beaches are to be found just to the northeast at adjacent **FÁROS** and **APOKOFTÓ**, both with good, cheap tavernas behind their coves (again, regular buses from Apollonía to Fáros). And close to Apokoftó, marooned on a rocky sea-washed spit and featuring on every EOT poster of the island, is the disestablished seventeenth-century **Hrissopiyí monastery**, whose cells are sometimes let out in summer. Note that Fáros has rooms to let also and makes another good fallback base when the main villages are full.

You can hire mopeds in Apollonía, but most (except those from *Svikiadhis*) are in deplorable condition and anyway the best exploration of Sífnos is done on foot. Taking the path out from Katavatí (the district south of Apollonía) you'll pass, a few minutes along, the beautiful empty **monastery of Piyés** and (half an hour later) **Áyios Andhréas** – this last offering tremendous views over the islands of Síros, Páros, Íos, Folégandhros and Síkinos. Just below the church is an enormous Bronze Age archaeological site.

Even better is the walk to **VATHÍ**, again around two to three hours from Katavatí but reached by bearing right at a white house ninety minutes past Áyios Andhréas; beyond this junction you pass another exceptional Sifniote monastery, **Taxiárhis**, where you can again stay in season. Vathí itself, a fishing and pottery village on the shore of a stunning funnel-shaped bay, is the most attractive base on the island. There are **rooms** to let and four summer tavernas. If you've just arrived on the island you could come here directly by well-publicised small boat from Kamáres (three times daily in season – mid-morning, noon, early evening).

From Vathí, an alternative hiking route back to Apollonía winds up toward the ridge of the **Profitis Ilías monastery**, a detour offering even greater views than those from Áyios Andhréas. Or another path (partly duplicating the walk in from Áyios Andhréas) leads directly back to Platís Yialós, from where there are buses until quite late (9pm in season) to Apollonía and on to Kamáres.

Mílos and Kímolos

Mílos has always derived prosperity from its strange geology. Minoan settlers were attracted by obsidian, and other products of its volcanic soil made the island important in the ancient world. Today the quarrying of barite, perlite and porcelain brings in a steady revenue, but it has left deep scars on the landscape; a large power plant adds to the industrial air as you arrive. The rocks, however, can also be beautiful – on the left of the bay as the boat enters, two outcrops known as the *Arkoúdhes* (bears) face up like sumo wrestlers. Off the north coast, and accessible only by boat, the *Glaroníssia* (Seagull Isles) are shaped like massed organ pipes, and there are more weird formations on the south coast at Kleftikó. Inland, too, you frequently come across strange, volcanic outcrops, and bubbling hot springs.

ADAMÁS, the cramped little port, was founded by Cretan refugees. Despite sitting on one of the Mediterranean's best natural harbours (created by a volcanic cataclysm similar to, but earlier than, Thira's), it's not a spectacularly inviting place, though just to the right of the quay (facing inland) you can sit in a shady square and watch the island go by. There's no shortage of places to **sleep and eat** in the port and you could do worse than to grab a **room** as soon as you can – accommodation elsewhere is sparse. Two standard hotel choices, nothing special, are the *Hotel Georgantas* (☎0287/41-636), in the square to the left of the quay, and the *Semiramis* (☎0287/41-617), further up and off (left) the road to Pláka. There are more rooms to let along the harbourfront and in the streets behind, while campers should be all right on the tamarisk-lined sandy beach east of the port. Back on the quayside the tourist office has information about boat trips, sells maps of Mílos, and hires out mopeds. Otherwise, Adamás is the hub of the island's bus service – hourly to PLÁKA, less regularly to Pollónia, and twice daily to Paleohóri via Zefiría. Incidentally, if you arrive by plane (daily from Athens), the **airport** is 5km south of the port, close to Zefiría.

ZEFIRÍA hides among olive groves below the bare hills at the far end of Mílos Bay, and used to be the capital until an eighteenth-century epidemic drove out the population. Much of the old town is still deserted, though some life has returned, especially to the taverna opposite the church. South of here the road deteriorates as it leads past LOUTRÁ PRÓVATA (some good hot springs in a more-or-less natural state), and KÍPOS, with a large Byzantine church. It peters out completely at the remote coarse-sand beach of **PALEOHÓRI**; with only two expensive tavernas and some rooms to let, it's more for day-trippers than for campers.

Most tourists stay in the north, but even here they tend to stick together, and there is little problem dodging the crowds. **PLÁKA** is the capital of the island, the most pleasant of a horseshoe of villages, with various rooms available. A stairway above the town leads up to the old Venetian **Kástro**, its roofs peculiarly sloped to channel precious rainwater into cisterns. This was where the ancient Melians made their last stand against the Athenians before being massacred in 416 B.C.

Back in town there are two small museums. An **archaeological** collection (daily 8.30am–12.30pm, Mon. and Thurs.–Sat. 4pm–6pm) contains Neolithic pottery from the Filakopí site (see opposite) and – more entertainingly – a plaster cast of the world's most famous statue, the *Venus de Milo*, found on the island in 1820 and appropriated by the French (her arms were knocked off in the melée surrounding her abduction). More significantly the **Folklore Museum** (Mon.–Tues./Thurs.–Sat. 9am–1pm and 6pm–9pm, Wed./Sun. 9am–1pm) displays a whole range of items from Mílotian life.

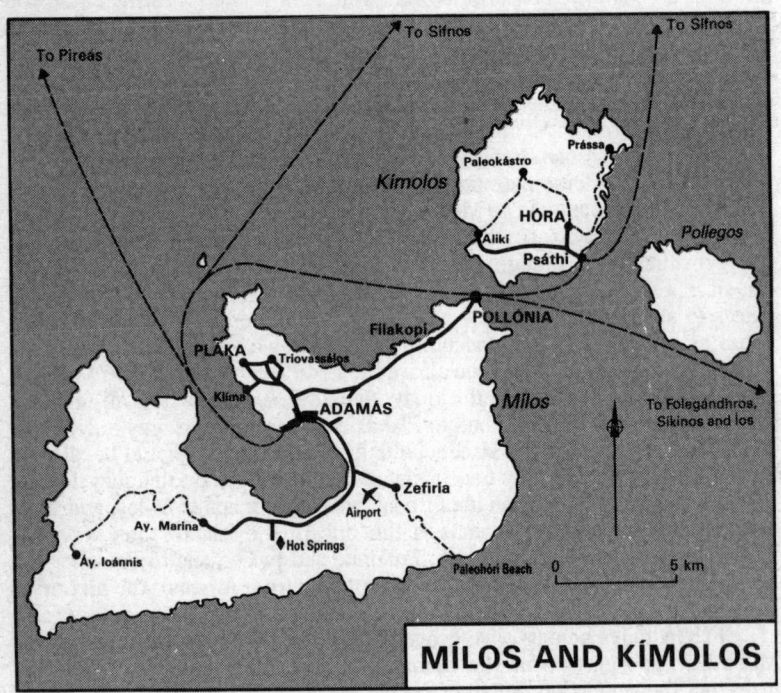

MÍLOS AND KÍMOLOS

Below Pláka the road passes the entrance to early Christian catacombs – up to 5000 bodies were buried in tomb-lined corridors. Sadly, the whole ensemble is in imminent danger of collapse and the catacombs seem permanently closed to visitors. But the ruins of **ancient Mílos**, extending down from the *kástro* almost to the sea, make the detour worthwhile. There are huge Dorian walls, the usual column fragments lying around and best of all, a well-preserved Roman **amphitheatre** facing out to sea. Two hundred metres from the theatre is a plaque marking where the *Venus de Milo* was found – and promptly delivered to the French consul for 'safekeeping' from the Turks; this was the last the Greeks ever saw of the statue until the local copy was belatedly forwarded from the Louvre in Paris. At the very bottom of the vale, **KLÍMA** is one of the best fishing hamlets on the island. There's no beach to speak of, but there is excellent seafood and a good place to both eat and stay, the aptly-named *Panorama*.

For proper beaches in the north, visit **PLATHIÉNA**, reached by leaving Pláka on a footpath towards ARETÍ and FOURKOVOÚNI; the junction for Plathiéna is signposted. Or head for **POLLÓNIA**, 10km northeast of Adamás, where three or four reasonable fish *tavernas* overlook a working fishing port and a small beach. There are a limited number of **rooms** here, usually oversubscribed since camping on the unprotected shore can be a windy proposition. You might want to head this way since the little island of KÍMOLOS (see below), easily visible, is accessible by a daily (usually early morning) *kaíki* from Pollónia – the boat can be hard to find, so ask at the pier. Just inland at **FILAKOPÍ** the remains of three prehistoric cities lie at the edge of a small cliff; the site was important archaeologically, but it hasn't been maintained and is therefore difficult to interpret.

Kímolos

Of the three islets off the coast of Mílos, Andímilos is home to a rare species of chamois and Políegos has more ordinary goats, but only Kímolos has any human habitation. Like Mílos, it has profitable rocks and used to export chalk (in Greek, *kímolos*) until its supply was exhausted. Nowadays it's a source of fuller's earth, and the fine dust of this stone is a familiar sight on the island. Rugged and barren in the interior, there is some green land on the south coast, and this is where the small population is concentrated.

Whether you arrive by ferry, or by *kaiki* from Pollónia, you'll dock at the hamlet of **PSÁTHI**, where there's a good taverna. Around the bay there are a few old windmills and the dazzlingly white **HÓRA** perches on the ridge above them, fifteen minutes' walk up. You'll find most of the island's accommodation here and indeed it seems a surprisingly large town; a maze of tortuous lanes makes it difficult at first to get your bearings. There are only a few cafés and tavernas, a handful of **rooms**, a post office – and virtually no tourists, even in August.

Another taverna and a few rooms-to-let can be found at the village of **ALIKÍ** on the southwest coast. This is flanked by a long if rather coarse stretch of sand here, and beyond the headland a smaller, more secluded beach which is better for camping.

More rewarding is the road leading northeast from Hóra to a beach at the village of **KLÍMA** and, beyond that, to the radioactive springs at **PRÁSSA**, 7km away. It's a route that takes in impressive views across the straits to Políegos and there are several shady peaceful beaches where you could camp out. Innumerable goat tracks invite exploration of the rest of the island and towards the west coast is **PALEOKÁSTRO**, where the ruins of an imposing Venetian *kástro* ring the church of **Hristós**, oldest on the island.

Ándhros

Ándhros, the second largest and northernmost of the Cyclades, is thinly populated but prosperous; its lush valleys have attracted scores of Athenian holiday villas whose red-tiled roofs and white walls stand out among the greenery. These have robbed many of the villages of life and atmosphere – turning them into scattered settlements with no nucleus, especially in the north – but on the positive side the permanent population is distinctly hospitable. Andriotes traditionally work on ships and many are only too happy to practice their English on you.

Ferries connect the island with Rafína on the mainland, only an hour from Athens on the bus. You'll arrive at the main port, **GÁVRIO**, not a pretty town but all right as a base, with a small beach, several rooms and tavernas. Consider hiring a bike as soon as you dock. It's really the only way to see the island properly given the poor state of the local bus service. Most people, with or without wheels, head 8km downcoast to **BATSÍ**, a fast-developing resort with a crop of hotels (*Avra*, ☎0282/41-216, and *Krinos*, ☎0282/41-232, the cheapest) and discos above its fine natural harbour. From either Gávrio or Batsí there's easy walking access to some beautiful inland villages – ARNÍ and KATÁKILOS especially, if you're at Batsí. Perhaps the most rewarding trip is to a well-preserved, 20-metre-high **Classical tower** at AYÍOS PÉTROS, 5km from Gávrio or 9km coming from Batsí.

A minimal bus service, whose drivers signal to each other with their revolving roof beacons, links the west coast with **HÓRA**, or **ÁNDHROS** town, an hour away. The capital and the most attractive place on the island, this is set on a rocky spur cutting across a huge bay. Much of the town is paved in marble, cut from the still-active local quarries; buildings around the bus station are grand nineteenth-century affairs, and the squares with their ornate wall fountains and gateways are equally elegant. The few **hotels** in town are a little expensive – try the *Aigli* (☎0282/22-303; opposite the big church on the main walkway), or ask around for rooms. Sometimes there's a seasonal campsite, and people also sleep on the sands of Parapórti (the southern) beach below, exposed and none too inviting. Eating out, you've a choice of four tavernas.

From the square right at the end of town you pass through an archway and down to windswept Platía Ríva, its statue of the unknown sailor scanning the sea. Beyond him lies the thirteenth-century Venetian **Kástro**, precariously joined to the mainland by a narrow-arched bridge, damaged by German munitions in the last world war. For some inexplicable reason there are three

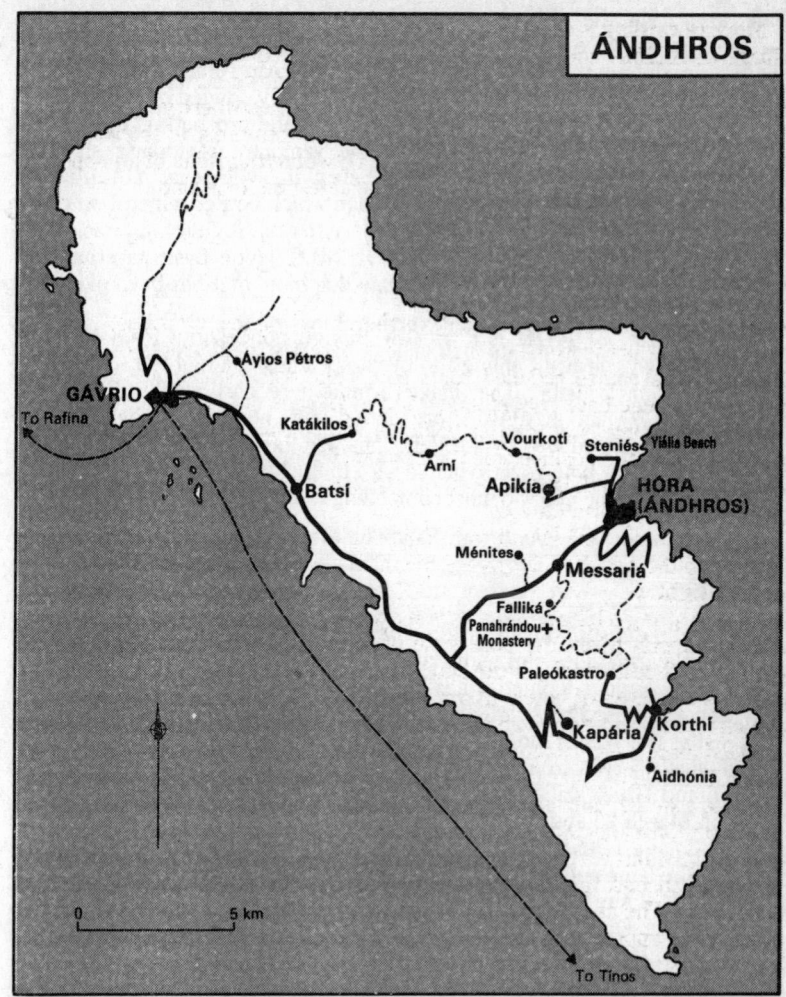

museums in town; maritime, modern art and (best) the **Archaeological Museum** (Mon.–Sat. 9am–3pm, Sun. 9.30am–2.30pm, Tues. closed), well laid out and labelled with instructive models.

Hiking inland and west from Ándhros the natural target is **MÉNITES**, a hill village just up the valley, which may have been the location of a Temple of Dionysos, said to turn water into wine; water still flows continuously from the local rocks. Nearby is the mostly abandoned medieval village of **MESSARIÁ**, with the deserted twelfth-century Byzantine church of **Taxiárhis** below. And the finest monastery on the island, **Panahrándou**, is only an hour's (steep!)

walk away, via the village of Falliká. Reputedly tenth-century, it's still defended by massive walls but occupied these days by just three monks. It clings to a cliff southwest of Hóra, to which you can return directly with a healthy two- to three-hour walk down the creek valley, guided by red dots.

Hidden by the ridge directly north of Hóra is the prosperous nineteenth-century village of **STENIÉS**, built by the vanguard of today's shipping magnates. There's a small beach just below the village at YIÁLIA. Just beyond Steniés is **APIKÍA**, a tidy little village which bottles mineral water for a living; there are a few tavernas but nowhere to stay. A delightful track once threaded up over the mountains, to VOURKOTÍ (one basic taverna) and beyond to Arní, but recent reports indicate that most of it has been ploughed under a new road.

To the south, **KORTHÍ** is a friendly though nondescript town set on a large sandy bay, pleasant enough to merit spending the night at – one hotel and a few rooms available. The villages around here, particularly AIDHÓNIA, PALEÓKASTRO and KAPÁRIA, are dotted with numerous pigeon towers (*peristereónes*), introduced by the Venetians. It's these towers, and the *fráktes* or ubiquitous dry-stone walls, which aspire to the status of an art form on the island and are in the end the most compelling monuments on Ándhros.

Tínos

There's little question about it: the character of Tínos is determined almost solely by the grandiose shrine of **Panayía Evangelístria**, erected on the spot where a miraculous icon with healing powers was found in 1822. A Tiniote nun, now canonised as Ayía Pelayía, was directed in a dream to unearth the relic just as the War of Independence was getting underway – a timely coincidence which served to underscore the age-old links between the Orthodox Church and Greek nationalism. Today, there are two major annual pilgrimages, on March 25 and August 15, when (around noon) the icon bearing the Virgin's image is carried in state down to the harbour over the prostrate forms of the lame and the ill.

The rest of the island, too, smacks of religion and tradition in varying degrees. The Ottoman tenure here was the most fleeting in the Aegean. **Exóbourgo**, the craggy mount dominating southern Tínos and surrounded by most of the island's forty-odd villages, is studded with the ruins of a Venetian citadel which defied the Turks until 1715, long after the rest of Greece had fallen. An enduring legacy of the long Latin rule is a persistent Catholic minority (almost half the population), and sectarian rivalry is responsible for the numerous graceful belfries scattered throughout the island – Orthodox and Catholic parishes vying to build the tallest. The sky is pierced, too, by distinctive pigeon towers, even more in evidence here than on Ándhros. Aside from all this, the inland village architecture is striking and there's a flourishing folk-art tradition which finds expression in the abundant local marble. If there are weak points to Tinos, they are that the religious atmosphere tends to dampen nightlife, and that beaches are few and far between, but the islanders have remained open and hospitable to the relatively few foreigners who touch down here. Any mercenary inclinations seem to be satisfied by booming sales in religious paraphernalia to the Greek faithful.

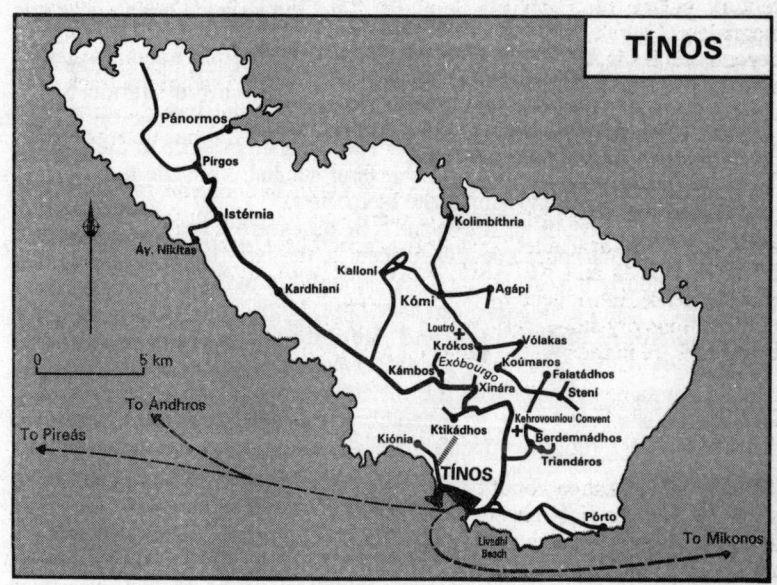

Tínos town and its beaches

Trafficking in devotional articles certainly dominates the busy port town of **TÍNOS**, with the neoclassical **church** (daily 8.30am–8.30pm) towering above at the top of Leofóros Megalohári. Approached via a massive marble staircase, the famous icon inside is all but buried under a dazzling mass of gold and silver *támmata* (votive offerings); below is the crypt (where the icon was discovered) and a mausoleum for the sailors drowned when the Greek warship *Elli*, at anchor off Tínos during a pilgrimage, was torpedoed by an Italian submarine on August 15, 1940. Museums around the courtyard display more objects donated by worshippers, who inundate the island for the two big yearly festivals.

To have any chance of securing a reasonably-priced **room** at these times you must arrive several days in advance – and even then, be prepared to do a lot of walking and asking around. At other times there's plenty of choice, though nothing is particularly cheap and you'll still be competing with out-of-season pilgrims, Athenian tourists and the sick and the disabled seeking a miracle cure. Of the hotels, the *Thalia* (☎0283/22-811) and *Eleana* (☎0283/22-561) are the two best low-budget options. Otherwise, beat the crowds by staying at *Tinos Camping* (☎0283/22-502 – follow the signs from the port, a ten-minute walk) which has tents and a few nice rooms to let. **Eating out** can be expensive; try the very reasonable *O Kipos*, a taverna a hundred metres from the *Eleana*.

The shrine aside – and all the attendant stalls, shops, and bustle – the *hóra* is none too exciting, the buildings mostly products of the late nineteenth century. But you might make time for the **Archaeological Museum** (Mon.–Sat. 9am–3pm, Sun. 10am–2pm, closed Tues.) on the way up to the church, which displays finds, including a fascinating sundial, from the local Roman Sanctuary of Poseidon and Amphitrite (see below).

Most, though not all, of the island's **beaches** are close to town; buses depart from the harbour, at a stop adjacent to the ferry quay. **KIÓNIA**, 3km northwest (hourly buses), is functional enough but marred by a luxury holiday complex, though there is a campsite here. More importantly, it's the site of the **Sanctuary of Poseidon and Amphitrite**, discovered in 1902, the excavations yielding principally columns (*kiónia* in Greek), but also a temple, baths, a fountain, and hostels for the ancient pilgrims. **PÓRTO**, 8km east, has perhaps Tínos's best beach, with another campsite nearby (and four buses daily); **LIVÁDHI**, though conveniently close (2km) to the port, is rockier and more exposed.

Inland Tínos

The best beginning to a foray **into the interior** is the stone stairway behind the Evangelístria church in Tínos town, which climbs for an hour and a half through marvellous countryside to **KTIKÁDHOS**. This is a fine village, with a sea-view *kafenío* where you can sit and wait for a late-morning onward bus (which passes by up on the main road).

Heading northwest, there's little to stop for until you pass KARDHIANÍ (rooms) and the turning for **ÁYIOS NIKÍTAS**, a somewhat overdeveloped beach with a campsite, 30km from Tínos. Better to stay on the bus to **PÍRGOS** (four daily buses), a few kilometres further north and smack in the middle of Tínos' marble-quarrying district. A beautiful village, its local artisans are renowned throughout Greece for their skill in producing marble ornamentation; ornate fanlights and bas-relief plaques adorn houses throughout the island but particularly here. With a School of Fine Arts and an attractive shady *platía*, Pírgos is popular in summer, but you should be able to find a room easily enough. The marble products were once exported from **PÁNORMOS** harbour, 4km northeast. There's a tiny beach, more rooms, a taverna and a campsite, though little to keep you there long.

The ring of villages **around Exóbourgo** mountain is the other focus of interest on Tínos. The fortified pinnacle itself, 570m (1800 ft.) above sea level, with ancient foundations as well as the ruins of three Venetian churches and a fountain, is reached by steep steps from **XINÁRA**. More rewarding, however, is **LOUTRÓ** where there's an Ursuline convent and carpet-making school to visit (leave the bus at the turning at KRÓKOS). At Kómi, 3km before Kallóní, you can take a detour for **KOLIMBÍTHRIA**, a beachlet with a campsite and tavernas, but a northerly exposure. From Loutró it's a forty-minute walk on to **VÓLAKAS**, the highest village on the island and a wind-swept oasis amidst bony rocks. Here, a dozen Catholic basketweavers fashion some of the best examples of that craft in Greece. From the village you can traipse on foot past potato fields to KOÚMAROS, where another long stair-way leads up to Exóbourgo, or turn down towards STENÍ and FALATÁDHOS, white speckles against the fertile green plain of Livadhéri.

From Stení you can catch the bus back to the harbour (seven daily). On the way down, try and stop off at one of the ring of beautiful settlements – DHÍO HORIÁ, TRIANDÁROS and BERDEMNÁDHOS, just below the impor-tant twelfth-century **convent of Kehrovouníou**. It was here that Ayía Pelayía dreamed of the icon, and the nuns still float through lavender-tinted corridors and under Lilliputian arches. The best **dovecotes** on Tínos in the region of **KÁMBOS**, west of Exóbourgo.

This is hardly an exhaustive list of Tíniote villages. Armed with a map and plenty of food, you could spend days within sight of Exóbourgo and never pass through the same village twice. Some of the old paths still exist, and the inhabitants will be absolutely bowled over at your presence. Take warm cloth-ing, though, especially if you're on a moped, as the forbidding mountains behind Vólakas and the Livadhéri plain keep things noticeably cool almost year-round.

Míkonos (Mykonos)

Originally visited only as a stop on the way to ancient Delos, Míkonos has become easily the most popular (and the most expensive) of the Cyclades. Boosted by direct air links with Britain and domestic flights from Athens, an incredible 600,000 tourists are reputed to pass through in a good year, producing some spectacular overcrowding in high summer on Míkonos's 75 square kilometres. But if you don't mind the crowds – or you come out of season, a much more attractive proposition – the prosperous capital is still one of the most beautiful of all island towns, its immaculately whitewashed houses conceal hundreds of little churches, shrines, and chapels.

The sophisticated nightlife is pretty hectic, amply stimulated by Míkonos' reputation as *the* gay resort of the Mediterranean – a title lost in recent years to places like Ibiza and Sitges in Spain. Whatever, the locals take this compar-atively exotic clientele in their stride, though considerable outrage was provoked a few years ago when Petros the Pelican, the island's official mascot, died after a depraved tourist involved him in an unnatural act. Unspoilt it isn't but the island does offer excellent, if crowded (and mainly nude) beaches, picturesque windmills, and a rolling brown interior with the sea never very far away.

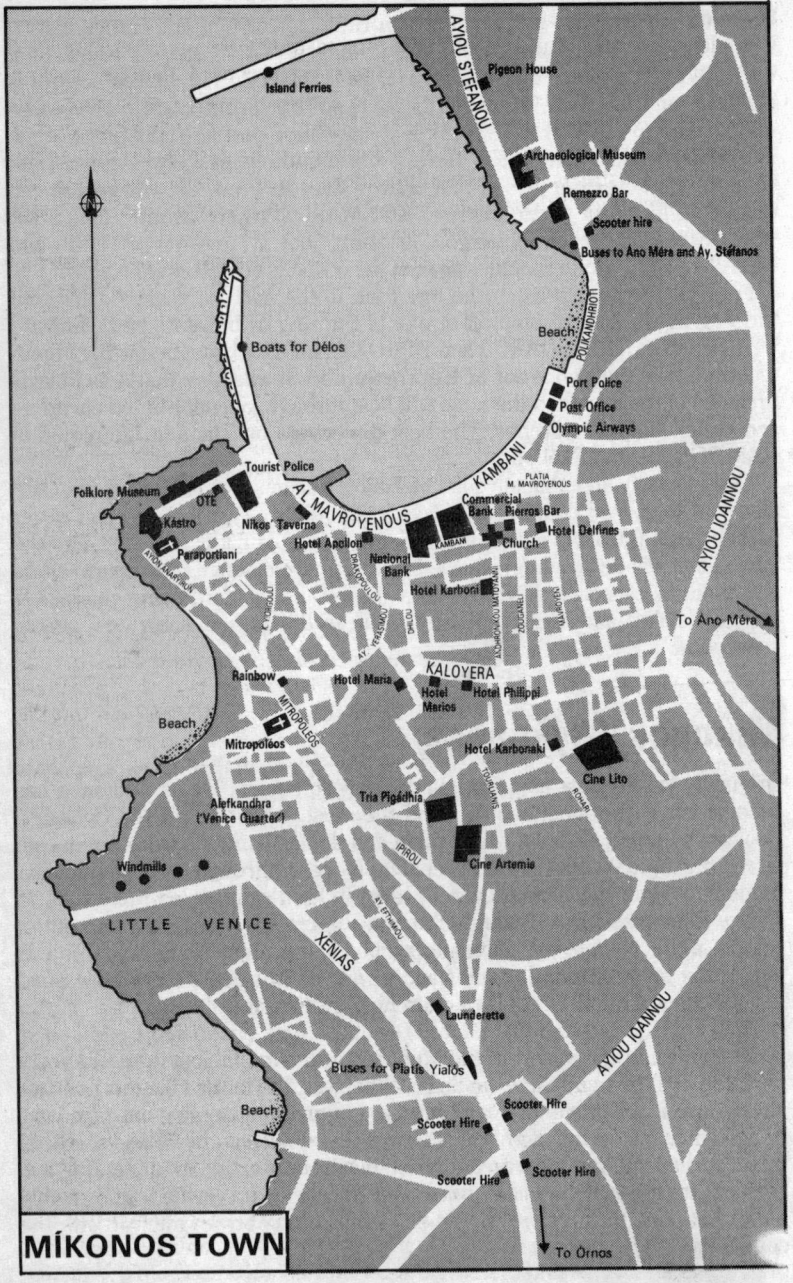

Island Ferries

AYIOU STEFANOU

Pigeon House

Archaeological Museum

Remezzo Bar

Scooter hire

Buses to Áno Méra and Ay. Stéfanos

Boats for Délos

Beach

POLIKANDHRIOTI

Port Police

Post Office

Olympic Airways

Tourist Police

KAMBANI

PLATIA M. MAVROYENOUS

Folklore Museum

AL MAVROYENOUS

Commercial Bank

Pierros Bar

OTE

Kástro

Nikos' Taverna

KAMBANI

Church

Hotel Delfines

Peraportiani

Hotel Apollon

AYIOU IOANNOU

National Bank

Hotel Karboni

To Áno Méra

Rainbow

Hotel Maria

KALOYERA

Hotel Philippi

Beach

MITROPOLEOS

Hotel Marios

Mitropoleos

Hotel Karbonaki

Cine Lito

Alefkandhra ('Venice Quarter')

Tria Pigádhia

Windmills

IPIROU

Cine Artemis

LITTLE VENICE

XENIAS

Launderette

Buses for Platis Yialós

AYIOU IOANNOU

Beach

Scooter Hire

Scooter Hire

Scooter Hire

Scooter Hire

MÍKONOS TOWN

To Órnos

Míkonos Town ...

Don't let the crowds put you off exploring **MÍKONOS** town. Marshmallow white, it's the archetypal postcard image, sugarcube buildings stacked around a cluster of seafront fishermen's dwellings with every nook and cranny scrubbed and shown off. Most people head out to the beaches during the day, so early morning or late afternoon are the best times to wander the maze of narrow streets. The labyrinthine design was intended to confuse the pirates who plagued Míkonos in the eighteenth and early nineteenth centuries and it remains effective – everyone gets lost.

Arriving, however, couldn't be simpler. If you're flying in, the **airport** is about 3km out of town, a short taxi ride away – or hop on the shuttle bus which drops you at the *Olympic Airways* office. Otherwise you'll arrive at the northern jetty, where **ferries** and cruise ships dock, to be met by a horde of owners hustling hotels and **rooms** which – if you want to stay in the town – you should attempt to procure immediately. Space is limited and rates are high (as everywhere on Míkonos); but the bus service to the main resorts is good, and most people stay out of town anyway, so you should find something. If you balk at the prices be warned that a private room here is likely to be cheaper than staying in a hotel on any of the nearby beaches. As for **hotels in town**, make for *Hotel Delfínes* (☎0289/22-292) on Mavroyéni, *Hotel Karboni* (☎0289/23-127) on Androníkou Matoyiánni, *Hotel Apollon* (☎0289/22-223) on Mavroyénous, *Hotel Maria* (☎0289/22-317) at Kaloyéra 18, *Hotel Marios* (☎0289/22-704) at Kaloyéra 5, *Hotel Philippi* (☎0289/22-294) at Kaloyéra 32, or *Hotel Karbonaki* (☎0289/23-127) at Panahrándou 21 – all are shown on our map though, again, none especially cheap. Otherwise there is an official campsite at Paradise Beach (see below), and every other beach on the island has some sort of taverna. There are occasional raids but usually the local police allow you to sleep out anywhere except on the beach in Míkonos town itself; the only problem will be persuading a bar to keep your baggage, as there's no official left-luggage office.

The harbour curves around past the dull, central Polikandhrióti beach; behind it is the **bus station** for Toúrlos, Áyios Stéfanos and Áno Méra (for all of which, see below). Just beyond, next to the post office, is the *Olympic Airways* office. Continue around the seafront to the southern jetty for the **tourist police** (☎0289/22-482; at the base) and *kaíkia* to Delos. A second bus terminus, for beaches to the south of town, is right at the other end of Hóra, beyond the windmills – and shown on the map. Buses to all the most popular beaches and resorts run very frequently, and until very late in the evening.

You don't need any maps or hints to scratch around the convoluted streets and alleys of town; getting lost is half the fun. There are, however, a few places worth seeking out if you require more direction to your strolling. Coming from the ferry quay, you'll pass the **Archeological Museum** (daily 9am–3pm except Sun. and Tues.) on your way into town; some good Delos pottery – and a superb *souvláki* bar next door. Alternatively, behind the Delos jetty, the **Folklore Museum** is housed in an eighteenth-century mansion and crams in a larger-than-usual collection of bric-a-brac, including a vast four-poster bed. The museum shares the same promontory as the old Venetian *kástro*, the entrance to this part of Hóra marked by Míkonos' oldest and best-known church, **Paraportianí**. It's a fascinating hodge-podge, four chapels amalgamated into one with little symmetry. The shore leads around to the area known as 'Little Venice' because of its high, arcaded Venetian houses built right up to the water's edge. Its real name is **Alefkándhra**, a trendy district packed with art galleries, chic bars and discos. Back off the seafront, behind Platía Alefkándhra, are Míkonos' two **cathedrals**: Roman Catholic and Greek Orthodox. Beyond, the famous **windmills** look over the area, disappointingly shabby but location for all kinds of photos. Instead of retracing your steps along the water's edge, follow Enóplon Dhinámeon (left off Mitropóleos) to **Tría Pigádhia** fountain. The name means 'three wells' and the legend has it that should a maiden drink from all three she was bound to find a husband, though these days she'd be more likely to end up with a waterborne disease.

The **nightlife** in town is every bit as good as it's cracked up to be – and every bit as expensive. There is little for those on a tight budget, so treat yourself for an evening if you can. It's impossible to list every current hot-spot and, given the confusing street plan, chances are you wouldn't find half of them anyway. However, amid the possibilities, you might check one or two of the following. *Remezzo* (near the archeological museum) is one of the oldest and classiest bars, a nice place to watch the sunset. Off the main Platía Mavroyénous is *Pierro's* (actually on Matoyánni), once an exclusively gay bar, now mixed, and in the square itself is *The Seagull*, a good pub. The area around Kaloyéra is a promising place for food: the *Edem Garden* (top of Kaloyéra) is a popular gay restaurant with an adventurous menu, and *El Greco* and *The Sesame Kitchen* are two other semi-reasonable eateries.

More drinking haunts are over in the Alefkándhra area; try *Kástro's* for an early evening cocktail, moving on later to *Montparnasse*, which is fairly swanky – to the extent of boasting a visitor's book. Save time too for K. Yiorgoúli street, off Mitropóleos; the *City Bar* here is the campest spot in town, with marble and columns everywhere, a sweeping staircase, and a nightly drag show (there is another one at the *Windmill Disco* at 1am). Just around the corner is *Nikos' Taverna*, reasonable and recommended; close by, *Down Under* and *Scandinavia Bar* are both cheap, jovial, and non-stop party bars. Other good stops for food are at the *Cathedral* restaurant (by the two cathedrals at Platía Alefkándhras), serving great fish; the expensive but well-sited *Pelican*, behind the cathedral on the seafront; and *El Greco*, at Tría Pigádhia, for romantic surroundings. Finally, two more discos: *La Mer*, a yuppie spot, and the *Rainbow*, young, mixed and sweaty, both at the northern end of Mitropóleos. If you're still standing after 3am, gravitate toward *The Yacht Club*, which bops until sunrise.

...and its beaches

Closest **beaches** to Hóra are those to the north, at TOÚRLOS (2km away) and – better – ÁYIOS STÉFANOS (4km), both developed resorts and connected by very regular bus service to Míkonos. There are rooms to let (as well as the package hotels) at Áyios Stéfanos, away from the beach. Other nearby, mainstream destinations are the resorts on the southwest peninsula, fairly undistinguished beaches tucked into pretty bays at ÁYIOS YIANNIS and ÓRNOS. Better to make for **PLATÍS YIALÓS**, 4km south, though you won't be alone. One of the longest established resorts on the island, it's not remotely Greek any more but it makes a good base for reaching other more fashionable beaches – there's a **kaíki service** from Míkonos town which connects almost all the beaches east of Platís Yialós. **PSAROÚ**, next door, is very pretty, 150m of white sand backed by foliage and calamus reeds, but covered in sunbathers unless it's dawn, dusk, or out of season. All these places are among the straightest on the island, to some extent still regarded by the Greeks as family beaches.

The beach here is divided up among the various hotels, plus there's waterskiing and windsurfer hire – but absolutely no possibility of finding a room between mid-June and mid-September unless you've reserved well in advance. A dusty footpath beyond Platís Yialós' beach crosses the deserted fields and caves of the headland, leading to the gorgeous, pale-sand **PIRÁNGA** beach, popular with campers. There's some good snorkelling to be done around the east flank of the bay, cluttered with volcanic rocks, starfish, and sea urchins. More footpaths lead further across the clifftops and drop down to **PARADISE BEACH**, well sheltered by its headland, predominantly nudist, and packed full of beautiful people. The crescent of fine white sand makes it a handsome place to stay; there's an official campsite (☎0289/ 22-129, April to October) and two tavernas (*Freddie's* sells English newspapers). The next bay east contains **SUPER PARADISE** beach (officially Plindhrí), again accessible by footpath or by *kaíki*. This has a good, friendly atmosphere, and a couple of tavernas. Its reputation used to be as a gay and nudist beach, though nowadays it's pretty mixed.

Probably the best beach on Míkonos, though, is the last port of call for the *kaíkia*, **ELÍA**. The longest on the island, it's a broad sandy stretch with a verdant backdrop, split in two by a rocky area. Almost exclusively nudist, it boasts an excellent restaurant, *Mathaios*. If the crowds have followed you this far, one last escape route is to follow the bare rock footpath over the spur at the end of Elía beach (the one with the white house). This cuts upwards for grand views east and west and then winds down to **KALÓ LIVÁDHI**, a stunning beach adjoining an agricultural valley scattered with little farmhouses. It hardly seems part of the same island, though even here there's a restaurant (a good one to boot) at the far end of the beach.

The rest of the island

If your time is limited, you'll find any of the beaches already listed good enough for your purposes. There are others, though, further away from the *hóra*, as well as a few non-sandy destinations worth making the effort for.

East of Elía, and 12km by road from the town, **AYÍA ÁNNA** boasts a beach and taverna, with the cliffs above granting some fine vistas. Almost-adjacent **KALAFÁTI** is more of a tourist community, its white-sand beach supporting a few hotels, restaurants and a disco. There's a local bus service from here to ÁNO MÉRA (see below) or you can jump on an excursion boat to **Tragoníssi**, the islet just offshore: spectacular coastal scenery, seals and wild birds. The rest of the east coast is difficult – often impossible – to reach.

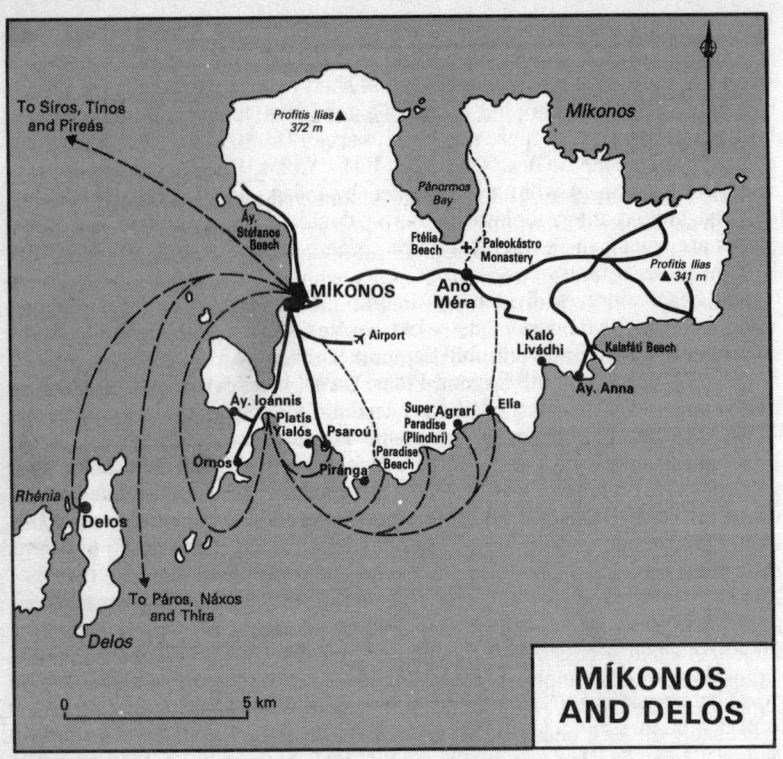

**MÍKONOS
AND DELOS**

There are some small beaches, none better than elsewhere and only worth the effort for loners, while the region is dominated by the peak of Profítis Ilías, sadly spoiled by a huge radar dome and military establishment.

The **north coast** suffers persistent battering from the *meltémi*, and for the most part is bare, brown and exposed. The one notable exception is relatively sheltered **PÁNORMOS BAY**, site of an ancient city of Míkonos. There are two beaches, though both are prone to savage, windy sandblasting. From Pánormos, it's an easy walk to the only other settlement of any size on the island – **ÁNO MÉRA** (rooms available), slightly inland and 8km from Míkonos. It works hard at remaining a traditional agricultural village and normal Greek life still thrives here. In the *platía* there's a proper *kafenío* and fresh vegetables are sold; ouzo and a local cheese are produced; and there's just one hotel. The red-roofed church near the square is the sixteenth-century **monastery of Panayía Tourlianí**, in which it's worth viewing the collection of Cretan icons and unusual eighteenth-century marble baptismal fount. It's not far either to the late twelfth-century **Paleokástro monastery** (also known as Dárga), just north of the village, in a magnificent green setting on an otherwise barren slope. To the northwest are more of the same dry and wind-buffeted landscapes, though they do provide some enjoyable, rocky walking with good views across to neighbouring islands. Using such tracks as exist, it's a short stroll down to Áyios Stéfanos and buses back to the *hóra*.

Delos (Dhílos)

The remains of **ancient Delos**, Pindar's 'unmoved marvel of the wide world', though skeletal and swarming now with lizards (and tourists), give some idea of the past grandeur of this sacred isle a few sea-miles west of Míkonos. The ancient town lies on the west coast on flat, sometimes marshy ground which rises in the south to **Mount Kínthos**. From the summit – an easy walk up – there's a magnificent view of almost the entire Cyclades; the very name of the archipelago means 'those (islands) around (Delos)'.

The *kaíki* to Delos leaves Míkonos at 9am (2 to 7 weekly, depending on the season; 600dr round-trip) and returns at 12.30pm, without loud warning. This gives you three hours on the island – barely enough time to take in the main attractions – but sadly, the campsite and the tiny *Xenía* lodge have closed, so it's no longer possible to stay the night. If you want to make a thorough job of the site, you'll have to come on several morning excursions or take a private afternoon charter tour, both expensive options. In any case, take your own food and drink as the tourist pavilion's snack bar is a rip-off.

Some history

Delos' ancient fame was due to the fact that Leto gave birth to the divine twins Artemis and Apollo on the island, although its fine harbour and central position did nothing to hamper development. When the Ionians colonised the island around 1000 B.C. it was already a cult centre, and by the seventh century B.C. it had become the commercial and religious centre of the Amphictionic League.

Unfortunately Delos also attracted the attention of Athens, which sought to increase its prestige by controlling the island; the wealth of the Delian Confederacy, founded after the Persian Wars to protect the Aegean cities, was harnessed to Athenian ends, and their officials took over the Sanctuary of Apollo itself for a while. Athenian attempts to 'purify' the island started with a decree that no one could die or give birth on Delos – the sick and the pregnant were taken to the islet of Rheneia – and culminated in the simple expedient of banishing what remained of the native population.

Delos reached its peak in the third and second centuries B.C. after being declared a free port by its Roman overlords. In the end, though, its undefended wealth brought ruin. First Mithridates (88 B.C.), then Athenodorus (69 B.C.) plundered the treasures, and the island never recovered. By the third century A.D. Athens could not even sell it, and for centuries after every passing seafarer stopped to collect a few prizes.

The site

You land with the Sacred Harbour on your left, the Commercial Harbour on your right; straight ahead is the **Agora of the Competialists** (Roman merchants or freed slaves who worshipped the *Lares Competales*, the

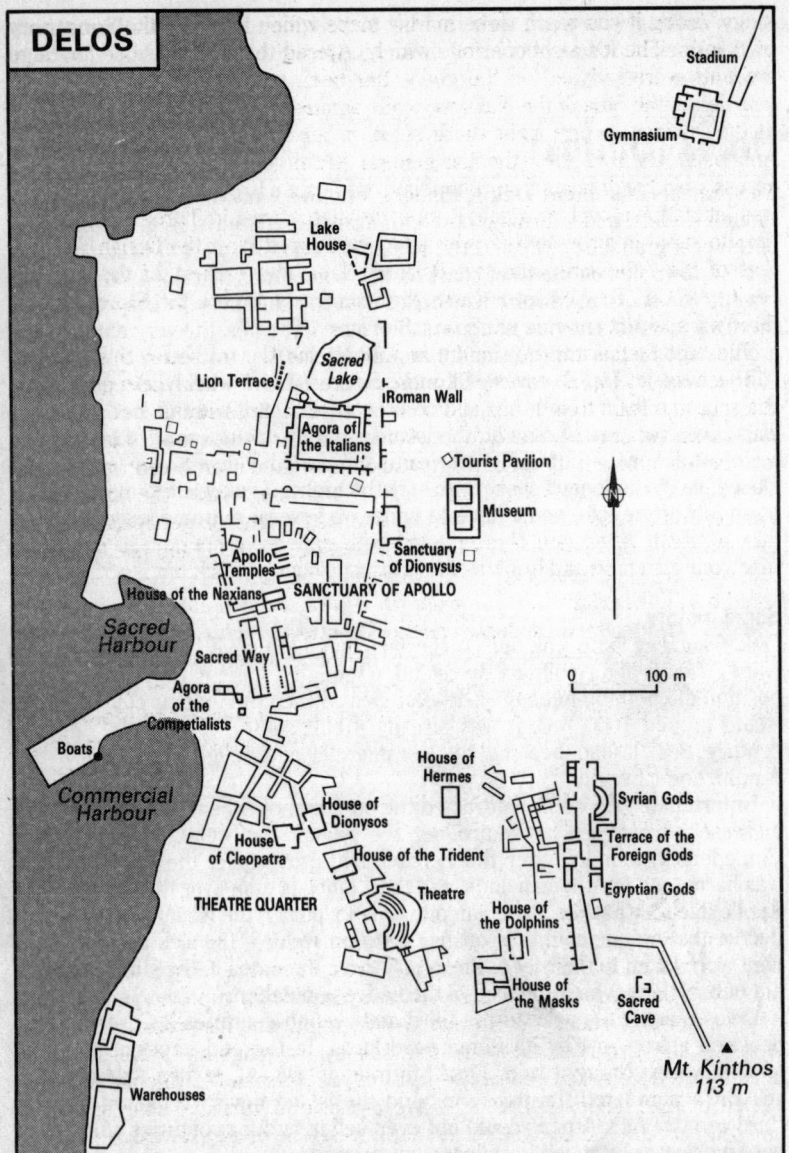

DELOS

Stadium

Gymnasium

Lake House

Lion Terrace

Sacred Lake

Roman Wall

Agora of the Italians

Tourist Pavilion

Museum

Apollo Temples

House of the Naxians

SANCTUARY OF APOLLO

Sanctuary of Dionysus

Sacred Harbour

Sacred Way

Agora of the Competialists

0   100 m

Boats

Commercial Harbour

House of Hermes

House of Dionysos

House of Cleopatra

House of the Trident

Syrian Gods

Terrace of the Foreign Gods

Egyptian Gods

THEATRE QUARTER

Theatre

House of the Dolphins

House of the Masks

Sacred Cave

Warehouses

Mt. Kínthos
113 m

guardian spirits of crossroads) who have offerings to Hermes in the middle
(a round and a square base). The **Sacred Way** leads north from the far left
corner; it used to be lined with statues and the grandiose monuments of rival

kings. Along it you reach three marble steps which lead into the **Sanctuary of Apollo**. The forest of offerings which covered this entire area – for huge amounts were lavished on the god – has been stripped by plunderers. On your left is the Stoa of the Naxians, while against the north wall of the House of the Naxians to the right there stood in ancient times a huge statue of Apollo. In 417 B.C. the Athenian general Nicias led a procession of priests across a bridge of boats from Rheneia to dedicate a bronze palm tree; when it was later blown over in a gale it took the statue with it. Three **Temples of Apollo** stand in a row to the right along the Sacred Way: the Delian Temple, that of the Athenians, and the Porinos Naos, the earliest of them (sixth century B.C.). To the east towards the museum you pass the **Sanctuary of Dionysus** with its marble phalli on tall pillars.

The best finds from the site are in Athens, but the **museum** (if it's open) still justifies a visit. To the north is the **Sacred Lake** where Leto gave birth clinging to a palm tree. It has lost both its water and its swans, but a modern wall marks where they used to be. Guarding it are the superb **Lions**, their lean bodies masterfully executed by Naxians in the seventh century B.C. Of the original nine, three have disappeared and one adorns the Arsenale at Venice; don't try to ride the remaining five, as the guards get apoplectic. On the other side of the lake is the City Wall, built (in 69 B.C.) too late to protect the treasures. The houses to the north have some mosaics.

Set out in the other direction from the Agora of the Competialists and you enter the residential area, known as the **Theatre Quarter**. Many of the walls and roads remain but there is none of the domestic detail that makes Pompeii, for example, so fascinating. Some colour is added by the mosaics; one in the House of the Trident, better ones in the **House of the Masks**. The finest on Delos is there, a vigorous portrayal of Dionysus riding on a panther's back. The **Theatre** itself seated 5500 onlookers and, though much ravaged, offers some fine views. Behind the theatre, a path leads past the Sanctuaries of the Foreign Gods and up Mount Kínthos for more panoramic sightseeing.

Síros (Syros)

Don't be put off by first impressions of Síros. From the ferry it looks grimly industrial, but away from the Neórion shipyard things improve quickly. Very much a working island with no real history of tourism, it's probably the most Greek of the Cyclades; there are few holiday trappings and what there are exist for the locals. You probably won't find, as Herman Melville did when he visited in 1856, shops full of '. . . fez-caps, swords, tobacco, shawls, pistols, and orient finery . . .' But you're still likely to see Síros as a refreshing change from having to compete with the beautiful people. Of course outsiders do come to the island and the nice beaches are hardly undeveloped, but everywhere there's the underlying assumption that you're on borrowed territory belonging to an inherently private people.

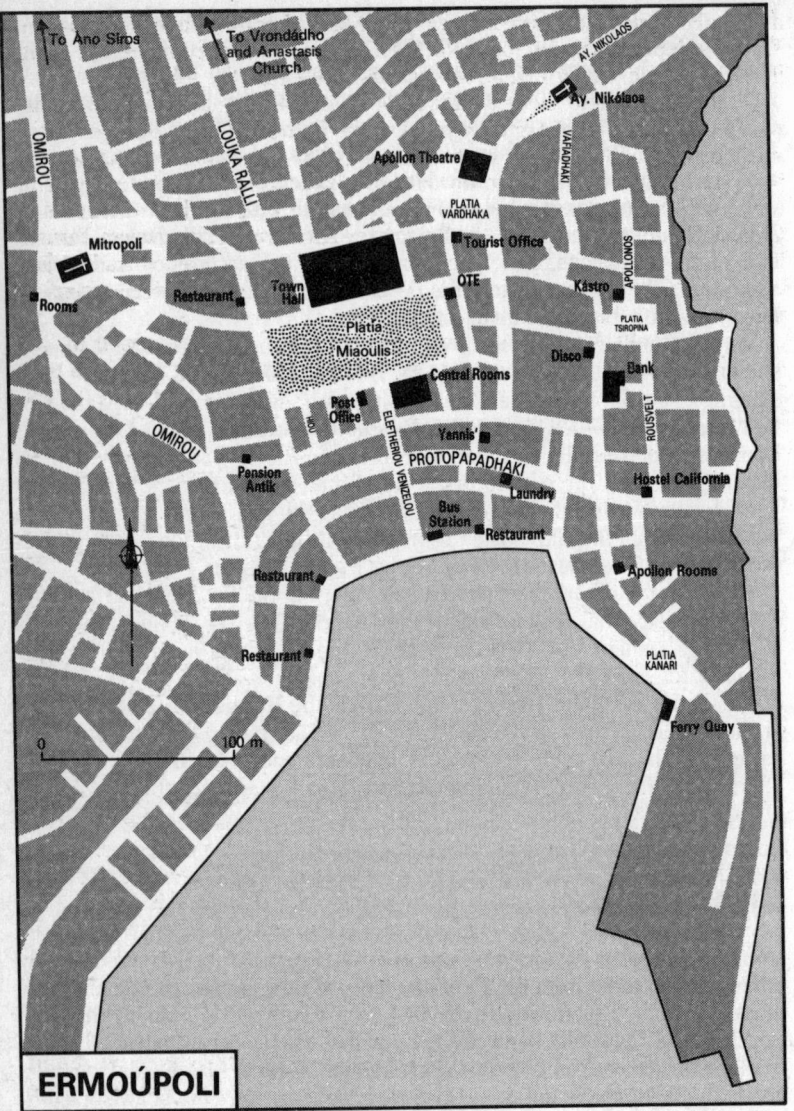

ERMOÚPOLI

Arriving: Ermoúpoli

The main town and port of **ERMOÚPOLI** was founded during the War of
Independence by refugees from Psará and Híos and became Greece's chief
port in the nineteenth century. Pireás has left it an age behind, but it's still
the largest town in the Cyclades, and their capital. Medieval Síros was largely

a Catholic island, but there was an influx of Orthodox refugees during the War of Independence and today the town has two distinct communities living in their respective quarters, on two hills rising up from the sea.

On the taller hill to the left is the intricate medieval quarter of **Áno Síros**, with a clutch of Catholic churches below the Cathedral of St. George. There are fine views of the town below and, close by, the **Cappuchin monastery of St. Jean**, founded in 1535 to do duty as a poorhouse. It takes an hour of tough walking (up Omírou) to reach this quarter, passing the Orthodox and Catholic cemeteries on the way – the former full of grand shipowners' mausoleums, the latter with more modest monuments and French and Italian inscriptions. (You can halve the time needed by turning on to the stair-street named Andhréa Kárga, part way along.)

The other hill, **Vrondádho**, hosts the Orthodox quarter, topped by the wonderful church of the **Anástasi** with its domed roof and great views over Tínos and Míkonos, weather permitting. If it's locked, ask for the key at the priest's house to the left of the church.

Ermoúpoli itself, the **lower town**, is worth at least a night's stay, with grandiose buildings a relic of its days as the first port of Greece. Between the harbour and **Áyios Nikólaos**, the fine Orthodox church to the north, you can stroll through its faded splendour. The **Apollon Theatre**, slowly being restored over the last two decades, is a copy of La Scala in Milan and once presented a regular Italian opera season; today local theatre and music groups put it to good use. The long, central **Platía Miaoúlis** is named after an admiral of the revolution whose statue stands there; in the evenings the population parades in front of its arcaded *kafenía*, while the children ride the mechanical animals. Up the stairs to the left of the Town Hall is the small **Archaeological Museum** (Mon.–Sat. 9am–3pm, Sun. 10am–2pm, Tues. closed) with three rooms of finds from Síros, Páros and Amorgós. To the left of the clock tower more stairs climb up to Vrondádho.

The **quayside** is still busy, though nowadays it deals with more touristic than industrial shipping; Síros is a major crossover point on the ferryboat routes. Also down here is the **bus station**, along with the tourist police and several **bike hire** places. Between them shops sell the *loukoúmia* (Turkish delight) and *halvadhópita* (sweetmeat pie) for which the island is famed.

Keeping step with a growing level of tourism, **rooms** have improved in quality and number in recent years; many are in garishly decorated (if crumbling) neoclassical mansions. Good choices include *Apollon Rooms* (☎0281/22-158) at Odhisséou 8 and the *Hostel California* around the corner; *Kástro Rooms*, on Platía Tsiropína; the *Pension Antik* (☎0281/26-849 – follow the little white signposts); and *Yianni's Guest House* (☎0281/28-665) on Emm. Riódhou. A notch up, both in price and quality, are the well-sited *Hotel Hermes* (☎0281/28-011) on Platía Kanári, overlooking the port, or for a real slice of luxury, the *Xenon Ipatias*, beyond Áyios Nikólaos. Siros is finally beginning to fill up in peak season; at such times the agency *Travel Team* (on the waterfront) may be able to find you unadvertised accomodation.

For **eating**, the most authentic of the harbour tavernas are *Mavrikakis* and the nearby *Ouzeri To Dhelfíni*. *Mama Ana's*, by the bus stop, looks like a tourist trap but is in fact quite good. Just off Platía Miaoúlis, at Híou 53, the new, as yet unnamed taverna run by the Syllivari family is also excellent, and reasonable. Finally, way up in Vrondádho, try either *Tembelis* (Anastáseos 17, corner Kalavrítou, just below the church), where the cooking makes up for the limited seating and grouchy service, or *Folia* (Athanasíou Dhiakoú 2), more expensive but serving such exotica as rabbit and pigeon.

Incidentally, Síros still honours its contribution to the development of *rembétika* (see 'Music' in *Contexts*); *bouzoúki* great Markos Vamvakaris hailed from here and a *platía* has been named after him in Áno Síros. Taverna-clubs such as *Lilli's* (up in Áno Síros) and *Rahanos*, with music on weekends, also take their place beside a batch of more conventional disco-clubs down near the Apollon Theatre. There are several more *bouzouki* bars scattered around the island, mostly on routes heading to beach resorts.

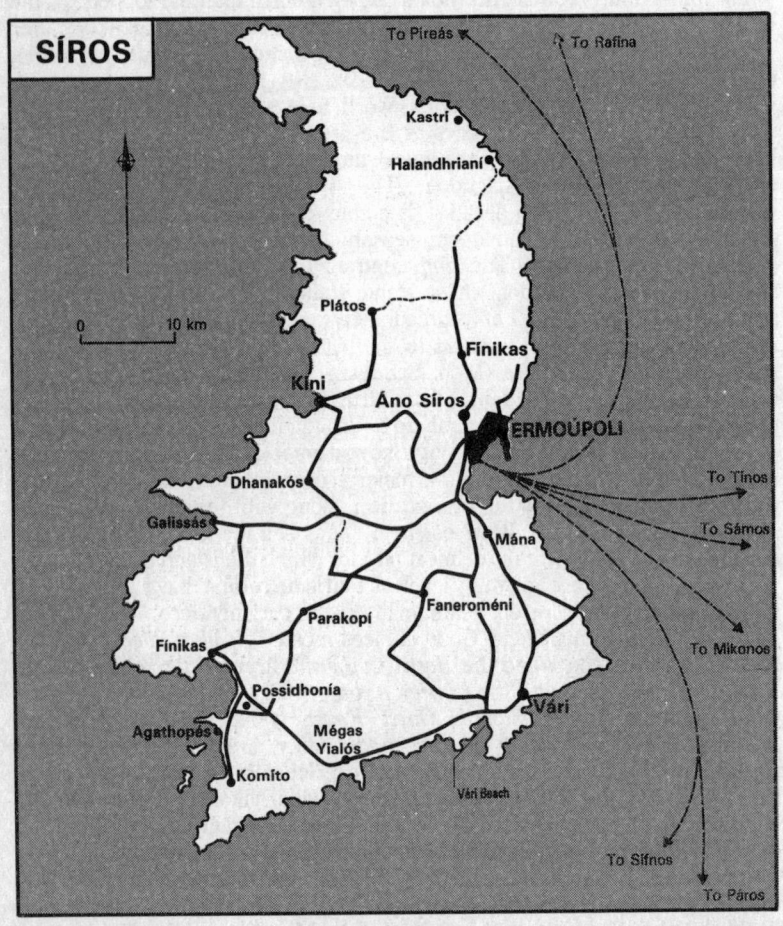

Around the island

The main loop road (the capital to Gallissás, Fínikas, Mégas Yialós, Vári and back) and the road west to Kíni is good: it's cheapest and easiest to get to these places on the buses which ply the routes half a dozen times daily. Elsewhere expect potholes especially to the **north** where the land is barren and high, with few villages. Here, any exploration has to be done on foot, setting off beyond Áno Síros. But the nature of the meandering, stony tracks and the absence of inviting coves and beaches discourages any real effort in this direction.

Stick, instead, with the well-trodden **south**. Closest to the capital, fifteen minutes away by bus, is the coastal settlement of **KÍNI**. Though the community is more villas than village, there are two separate beaches and an excellent taverna (*Iliovasilima*), rarely overrun even in summer. **GALISSÁS**, a few kilometres south (but reached by different buses), is developing along different lines. Fundamentally an agricultural village, it's being slowly but surely taken over by backpackers attracted by the island's only **campsites** (*Camping Yianna* plus one other) and a very pretty beach, much more protected than Kini's. There are, too, numerous adequate **rooms** and three bona fide hotels (cheapest is *Petros*, ☎0281/42-067), as well as mini-markets for the campers. Galissas's identity crisis is exemplified by the proximity of bemused, grazing dairy cattle, a heavy-metal music pub, and upmarket handicrafts shops. Still, the people are welcoming, and if you need to get away, you can hire a moped, or walk ten minutes past the headland to the nudist beach of San Vákou (fresh springwater, 'freelance' camping).

A pleasant one-hour walk (or ten-minute bus ride) south from Kíni brings you to **FÍNIKAS**, purported to have been settled originally by the Phoenicians (though *finikas* also means 'palm tree' in Greek). It's a more mainstream resort with a narrow and gritty beach, tamarisk-lined but right next to the road. The *Cyclades* (☎0281/42-255) is the cheapest and cosiest of the hotels here, with a reasonable restaurant.

Fínikas is separated by a tiny headland from its neighbour **POSSIDHONÍA** (or Delagrazzia), a nicer spot with some idiosyncratically ornate mansions and a bright blue church right on the edge of the village. It's worth walking ten minutes further south, past the naval yacht club and its patrol boat, to **AGATHOPÉS**, with a sandy beach, a little islet just offshore, and one hotel, the *Delagrazia* (☎0281/42-225). **KOMITÓ**, at the end of the unpaved track leading south from Agathopés, is nothing more than a stony beach fronting an olive grove.

The bus and road swing east to **MÉGAS YIALÓS**, a small resort below a hillside festooned with brightly painted houses. The long, narrow beach is lined with shady trees and there are pedal-boats for hire. **VÁRI**, with the adjacent Ahládhi cove, is more – though not much more – of a town, with its own small fishing fleet. Beach-goers are in a fishbowl, as it were, with tavernas and **rooms** looming right overhead, but it is the most sheltered of the island's bays – something to remember when the *meltémi* is up. And if you've not tracked one down yet, on the road between here and the capital there's an excellent *bouzoúki* club, the *Nereida*.

Páros and Andíparos

Páros has some of the finest beaches in the Cyclades, but to visit it for these alone, as increasing crowds seem to do every summer, is to miss much. Gently furled around a single peak, the island manages quietly and undramatically to be one of the most beautiful of the group. With a little of everything – old villages, monasteries, fishing harbour and a labyrinthine capital – Páros is a good point to begin your island wanderings. Unfortunately, plenty of others agree. It isn't yet dominated by tourism to the same degree as Míkonos or Íos, although prices are inching steadily upward, and in peak season it's touch-and-go when it comes to finding rooms and beach space. At such times, the attractive inland settlements or the satellite island of Andíparos handle the overflow.

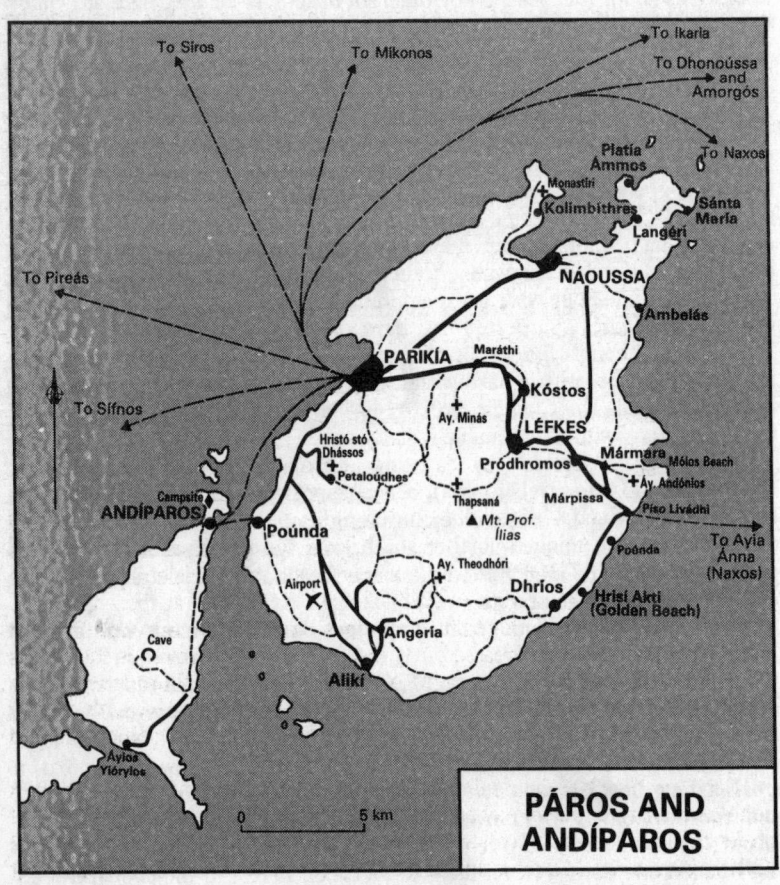

Parikía and around

PARIKÍA, the *hóra*, sets the tone for the rest of Paros, with its ranks of typically Cycladic white houses punctuated by the occasional Venetian-style building and church domes. All ferries dock here, and the busy waterfront is jam-packed with bars, restaurants, hotels and ticket agencies. The front, and the outskirts of town close to the beach, have sadly yielded to the tourists. But the jumble of houses beyond, designed to keep out wind and pirates alike, is little altered.

Just outside the central clutter, the town also has one of the most architecturally interesting churches in the Aegean – the **Ekatondapilianí**, or 'Church of One Hundred Gates' (daily 7am–noon and 4–8pm). The original construction was overseen in the sixth century by Isidore of Miletus but the work was carried out by his pupil Ignatius. It was so beautiful on completion that the master, consumed with jealousy, is said to have grappled with his apprentice on the rooftop, flinging them both to their deaths. They can be found today kneeling at the column bases across the courtyard: master tugging at his beard in repentance, pupil clutching a broken head. Restored at intervals ever since, the church was substantially altered after a severe earthquake in the eighth century, but its essentially Byzantine aspect remains, its shape an imperfect Greek cross. Enclosed by a great wall to protect its icons from pirates, it is in fact three churches interlocking with one another; the oldest, the chapel of Áyios Nikólaos to the left of the apse, is an adaptation of a pagan building dating from the early fourth century B.C. Behind Ekatondapilianí, the **Archaeological Museum** (Mon.–Sat. 8am–2pm, Sun. 8am–1pm, closed Tues.) has a fair collection of antique bits and pieces, its prize exhibit a piece of the *Parian Chronicle*, a social and cultural 'history' of Greece up to 264 B.C., recorded on marble.

These two sights apart, the real attraction of Parikía is simply to wander the town itself. Arcaded lanes lead past Venetian-influenced villas, traditional island dwellings and the three ornate wall fountains donated by the Mavroyénnis family in the eighteenth century. Of the minor churches, the most interesting is the seventeenth-century Presentation, with fine frescoes. The town culminates in a seaward Venetian **Kástro**, whose surviving east wall is constructed of masonry pillaged from ancient temples to Demeter and Apollo. The beautiful, arcaded church of Áyios Konstantínos and Ayía Eléni crowns the highest point, from where the fortified hill drops sharply to the quay in a series of hanging gardens.

If you're staying in town, you'll want to get **out into the surroundings** at some stage, if only to the beach. The most rewarding excursion is the hour's walk up to **Áyii Anáryiri** monastery, perched on the bluff above town; this is reached on an unsurfaced road which starts just past the museum. It's a great picnic spot, with cypress groves, a gushing fountain and some splendid views.

There are **beaches** immediately north and south of the harbour, though none particularly attractive when compared to Paros's best. In fact, you might prefer to avoid the northern stretch altogether, though there's a campsite at KRÍOS, 3km away. Heading **south** along the asphalt road is better: the first unsurfaced side track you reach leads to a small, sheltered beach; fifteen minutes further on is **PARASPÓROS**, with another campsite (☎0284/21-944) and a better beach; while the same distance again brings you to the best of the bunch, **AYÍA IRÍNI**. Here, there's more camping, good sand and a taverna.

Continuing in the same direction, but a much longer two-hour haul each way, is **PETALOÚDHES**, the so-called 'Valley of the Butterflies', a walled-in oasis where millions of Jersey tiger moths perch on the foliage during the early summer. There's a small admission fee and a snack bar (operating after June 15 only; grounds shut 1–4pm). The trip pays more dividends in conjunction with a visit to the eighteenth-century nunnery of **Hristós sto Dhássos**, at the crest of a ridge twenty minutes to the north. Only women are allowed in the sanctuary, although men can get as far as the courtyard. The succession of narrow drives and donkey paths linking both places begins just south of Parikía, by the *Ksenon Ery*. Petaloúdhes can be reached from Parikía by bus (in summer), by moped, or on an overpriced excursion by mule.

Practicalities

Páros is fast becoming a major hub of inter-island ferry services, approaching even Síros in this respect. Boats **dock** in Parikía by the windmill, which houses a summer tourist information centre. Although there's a bus timetable posted here, the **bus stop** itself is 100m or so to the left – routes extend to Náoussa in the north, Alikí in the south, and Dhríos on the island's east coast (with another very useful service between Dhríos and Náoussa). Most of the island is flat enough for bicycle rides, but mopeds are more common and you can hire them at several places in town. The **airport** is around 12km from town, close to Alikí – from where six daily buses run to Parikía.

As for **places to stay**, Parikía is a pleasant and central base, but absolutely mobbed in summer. You'll be met off the ferry by locals offering rooms, and it's a good idea to capitulate straight away. Most of the hotels tend to be reserved wholesale by tour operators, and you'll have to be quick to grab space in the remaining cheaper places. Try the *Hotel Kondes* (☎0284/21-246), very close to the windmill by the *ITS Travel Agency*; or the *Constantine Passos*, which is further up the course of the dry riverbed, on the left-hand side. *Oasis Rooms* (☎0284/21-227) near the post office is fairly cheap too, and there are more rooms to let along the sea front, turning right from the quayside.

Currently, the best value **food** is to be had at *I Aligaria*, on the square behind the ferry dock; *Katataktes*, a meat grill inland on Gravári; *Corfo Leone*, just back from the waterfront on a small square; and the *Koutouki Manasis*, serving oven food for locals a couple of alleys inland from this square. The *Palm* self-service café near the *Aligaria* is fine for breakfast. A word of warning, however: most Paros tavernas are run by outsiders operating under municipal concession, so year-to-year variation in proprietors and quality is marked.

Parikía has a wealth of **pubs**, **bars** and low-key **discos**, not as pretentious as on Míkonos or as raucous as on Íos, but certainly everything in between. The most popular cocktail bars extend along the seafront, all tucked into a series of open squares and offering competing 'Happy Hours'. A thriving cultural centre, *Arhilohos* (near Ekatondapilianí) caters mostly to the needs of locals, with occasional film screenings.

The rest of the island

The second port of Páros, **NÁOUSSA** was recently an unspoiled town, a sparkling labyrinth of winding, narrow alleys and simple Cycladic houses. Alas, a rash of new concrete hotels has all but swamped its character, though down at the small fishing harbour, oblivious of the tourists, fishermen still tenderise octopi by thrashing them against the walls. Despite the development, the town is a good place to head for as soon as you reach Páros; it's noted for its nearby beaches, while **rooms** are marginally cheaper than in Parikía – track them down with the help of Katerini Simitzi's tourist office on the main square. Hotels are more expensive, though out of season haggle for reduced prices at the *Madaki* (☎0284/51-475) the *Drossia* (☎0284/51-213), and the *Stella* (☎0284/51-317). There's a campsite too, out of town towards Kolimbíthres (see below), and various tavernas – all of which, for a change, are pretty good, specialising in fresh fish and seafood. (Avoid the self-service cafés, which unlike those in Parikía are rip-offs.) The local festival, a shindig celebrating an old naval victory over the Turks, takes place annually on August 23.

Some good-to-excellent beaches are within walking distance of Náoussa, and a summer *kaíki* service also connects them. To the west, an hour's tramping brings you to **KOLIMBÍTHRES** (Basins), where there are three tavernas and the wind- and sea-sculpted rock formations which give the place its Greek name. A few minutes beyond, **MONASTÍRI** beach – below the abandoned Pródhromos monastery – is similarly attractive, and partly nudist. Go northeast and the sands are better still, the barren headland spangled with good surfing beaches: **LANGÉRI** is backed by dunes; the best surfing is at **SANTA MARÍA**, a trendy beach connected with Náoussa by road; and finally there's **PLATIÁ ÁMMOS** on the northeasternmost tip of the island.

More energetically, you might take the 45-minute walk southeast to **AMBELÁS** hamlet as the start of a longer trek down the **east coast**. Ambelás itself has a small taverna and a good beach, and from here a rough track leads south, passing several undeveloped stretches on the way. After about an hour you reach **MÓLOS** beach, impressive and not particularly crowded, and – twenty minutes later – **MÁRMARA**. There are rooms to let here and it's an attractive place to stay, though the marble that the village is built from and named after has largely been whitewashed over.

If Mármara doesn't appeal to you, then serene **MÁRPISSA** just to the south may do so – a maze of winding alleys and aging archways overhung by floral balconies and clinging to the hillside. There are rooms here too and you can employ a spare hour making the climb up the conical Kéfalos hill, on whose fortified summit the last Venetian lords of Páros were overpowered by the Ottomans in 1537. Today the monastery of **Áyios Antónios** occupies the site and the grounds are locked, so to enjoy the views over eastern Páros and the straits of Naxos fully get the key from the priest in Márpissa before setting out. Don't, incidentally, be tempted to seek rooms down on the coast at **PÍSO LIVÁDHI**, the port for all the villages hereabouts. Once a quiet fishing village, it's been ruined by package tourism: concrete mushrooms, no soul and – in July and August – no chance of a bed. The only good reason to visit would be to catch a (seasonal) *kaíki* to Ayía Ánna on Naxos.

The road runs **west** from Píso Livádhi **back to the capital**, and while there are regular buses you'd do better, if you have time, to return on foot. A medieval flagstoned path once linked both sides of the island; parts of it survive in the east between Mármara and the villages around Léfkes. First-encountered **PRÓDHROMOS** is an old and fortified farming settlement with more defensive walls girding its nearby monastery. **LÉFKES** itself, an hour up the track, is perhaps the most beautiful and unspoilt village on Páros. The town flourished from the seventeenth century on, its population swollen by refugees fleeing from coastal piracy; indeed it was the island's *hóra* during most of the Ottoman period. Léfkes's marbled alleyways and amphitheatrical setting are unparalleled and, despite the presence of an oversize hotel, a disco and a taverna on the outskirts, the area around the *platía* remains unspoilt. There are no rooms to let and the central *kafenío* and bakery observe their siestas religiously.

Half an hour further, through olive groves, **KÓSTOS** is a simple village and a good place for lunch in the one taverna. Any traces of path disappear at **MARÁTHI**, on the site of the ancient marble quarries which once supplied much of Europe – with a torch you can poke around the abandoned workings. The last slabs (considered second only to Carrara marble) were mined here by the French in the nineteenth century for Napoleon's tomb. From Maráthi, it's easy enough to pick up the bus on to Parikía, but if you want to continue hiking, strike south for the monastery of **Áyios Minás**, twenty minutes away. Various Classical and Byzantine masonry fragments are worked into the walls of this sixteenth-century foundation, and the friendly couple who act as custodians can put you on the right path up to the convent of **Thapsaná**. From here, other paths lead either back to Parikía (two hours altogether from Áyios Minás), or on up to the island's summit for the last word in views over the Cyclades.

There's little to stop for **south of Parikía** until **POÚNDA**, 6km away, and then only to catch the ferry to Andíparos (see below). What used to be a sleepy hamlet is now a concrete jungle, a far cry from the days when you left the Poúnda church door open to summon the boat over from the smaller island. Neighbouring **ALIKÍ** appears to be permanently under construction – though there's an excellent beachside restaurant here (by the large tamarisk tree) – and the new airport is close by, making for lots of unwelcome noise. The end of the southern bus route is at ANGERÍA (rooms). About 3km inland is the **convent of Áyii Theodhóri**, whose nuns specialise in weaving locally commissioned articles and are further distinguished as *paleomeroloyítes*, or old-calendarites – meaning that they follow the medieval Orthodox (Julian) calendar, a few weeks behind everyone else.

Working your way around the **south coast**, there are two routes east to Dhríos. Either retrace your steps to Angería and follow the (slightly inland) coastal jeep track, which skirts a succession of isolated coves and little beaches; or keep on, across the foothills, from Áyii Theodhóri (a shorter walk). Aside from an abundant water supply and surrounding orchards,

DHRÍOS village is modern and characterless, lacking even a well-defined *platía*. Between here and Píso Livádhi to the north are several sandy coves – HRISSÍ AKTÍ (Golden Beach), TZIRDHÁKIA, MEZÁDHA, POÚNDA and LOGARÁS – all prone to pummelling by the *meltémi*, yet all favoured to varying degrees by campers. The piles of rubbish left at Hrisí Aktí in particular seem to augur either police action, a controlled campsite, or both, in the near future. Note that the only real facilities – shops, rooms, and food – are in Dhríos, though there are tavernas at Golden Beach and Logarás (and sometimes a semi-official campsite at the latter).

Andíparos

In recent years the islet of Andíparos has become something of an open secret among those who consider Páros to be irredeemably sullied. In 1981 the island only had one bar, and as late as 1984 cars were unheard of; now there are at least fifteen places to drink, and in July and August there's a steady stream of vehicles through the one village. This is not to say that Andíparos is horrendously commercialised – it isn't, yet. But in high season it can be full of the very people you were trying to escape from.

Most of the population of 500 live in the single northern **village**, built around a broad *platía* which is actually the inner courtyard of the fifteenth-century *kástro* – a similar arrangement to that on Síkinos. A few of the buildings on its periphery survive to their original heights, and there's the usual complement of domed Cycladic churches a pleasant surprise for those expecting the usual unremarkable architecture of minor islets. Both **kaíkia** from Poúnda (ten minutes) and **boats** from Parikía (summer only, one hour) dock at the island's village. There are several tavernas, some small hotels (the two cheapest *Mandalena*, ☎0284/61-206 and *Anargyros*, ☎0284/61-204) and a part-time bank, as well as a very popular campsite (☎0284/61-221) (ten minutes' walk north) with an adjacent nudist beach. You might be offered a room in someone's house – worth taking if it happens.

It's the great **cave** in the south of the island that is the chief attraction for daytrippers. In these eerie chambers the eccentric Marquis de Nointel celebrated Christmas Mass in 1673 while 500 bemused but well-paid Parians looked on; at the exact moment of midnight explosives were detonated at the entrance to emphasise the enormity of the event. Although electric light and cement steps have diminished much of its mystery and grandeur, it remains impressive. Two buses a day run from the port to the cave; should you fail to coincide with them it's a stoney ninety-minute hike from the village, or you can jump on one of the morning boats which will transfer you down the coast to within a short, if tiring, walk of it. In the off-season you'll have to fetch the key for the cave from the village.

For real seclusion, walk over to **ÁYIOS YIÓRYIOS** on the southwest coast. There are already signs of developers' interest, but for the moment its lovely little sandy coves remain uncluttered. A bus and a mobile cantine make the journey out here twice a day from the village.

Náxos

Náxos is the largest and most fertile of the Cyclades, and with its green and mountainous interior seems immediately distinct from many of its neighbours. The difference is accentuated by the unique architecture of many of

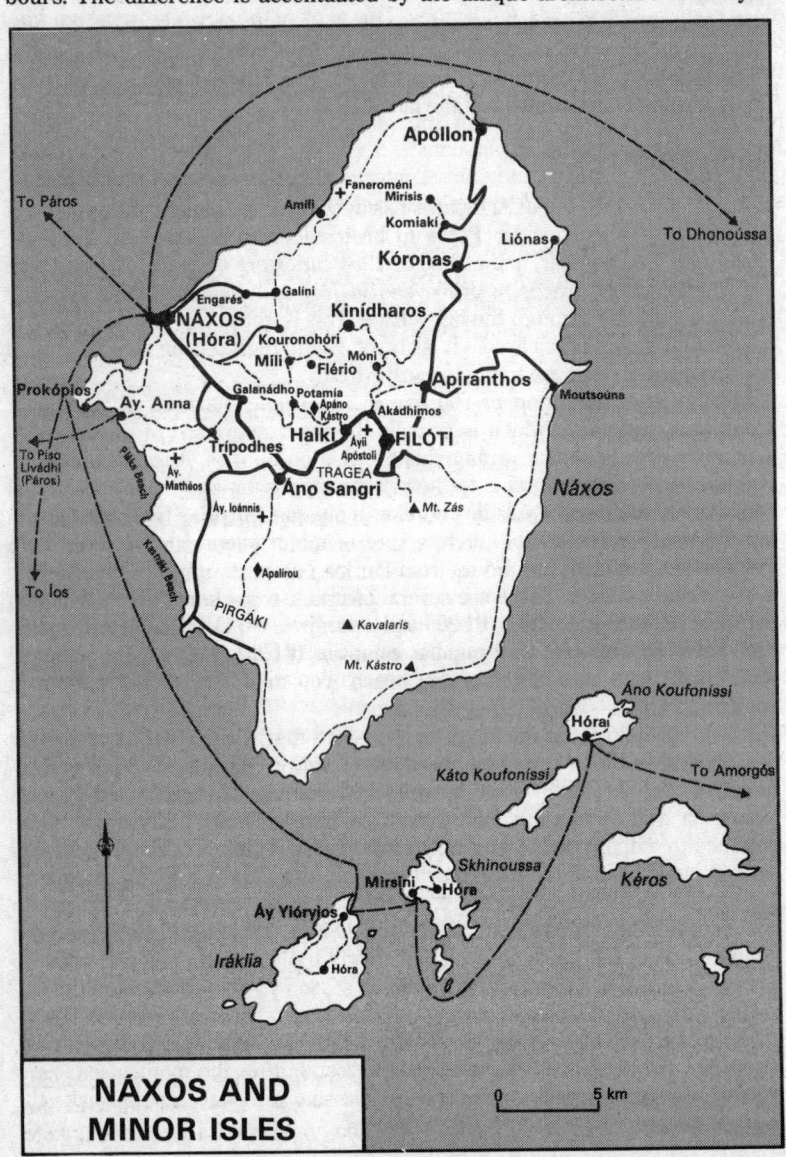

NÁXOS AND MINOR ISLES

0   5 km

the interior villages: the Venetian occupation (13th–16th c.) left towers and fortified mansions scattered throughout the island, while late medieval Cretan refugees bestowed a singular character upon Náxos's eastern settlements.

Today Náxos could easily support itself without tourism by its production of potatoes, olives, grapes and lemons. This adds to the down-to-earth, worka-day atmosphere. There's no tourist police post, no airport (though one is planned), and few locals know more than a smattering of English or French. That's not to say that you'll be alone; more people are arriving each year, refusing to be scared off by half-true tales of the gruffness of the villagers. And the island, certainly, has plenty to see if you know where to look: intri-guing central valleys, a windy but spectacular north coast, and marvellously sandy beaches in the southwest – these last some of the best in Greece.

Náxos town and the southwest coast

A long causeway protecting the harbour on the north connects **NÁXOS** town (or Hóra) with the islet of Palátia, where legend has Theseus abandoning Ariadne on his way home from Crete. The huge stone portal of a **Temple of Apollo** still stands there, built on the orders of the tyrant Lygdamis in the sixth century B.C. but never completed. Most of the *hóra*'s life goes on down by the port or in the streets just behind it, and this crowded esplanade has a hearteningly traditional life. In one shop you can sample *kitron*, the island's lemon liqueur, a firewater that comes in three strengths, while on the quay an *ouzéri* serves grilled octopus as *mezédhes* with their drinks.

Move into the back alleys and there's an almost medieval atmosphere to Hóra; indeed, at times the silent, claustrophobic alleys can be positively creepy. Narrow streets behind the harbour lead up past crumbling balconies and through low arches to the fortified **Kástro**, from where Marco Sanudo and his successors ruled over the Cyclades for the Venetians. Only two of the original seven towers – those of the Sanudo and Glezos families – remain, though the north gate (approached up Apóllonos) survives as a splendid example of a medieval fort entrance. The Venetians' Catholic descendants, numbers dwindling, still live in the old mansions which encircle the site, many with ancient coats-of-arms above crumbling doorways. Other brooding relics survive in the same area: a seventeenth-century Ursuline convent, the Roman Catholic Cathedral (restored in questionable taste in the 1950s, though still displaying a thirteenth-century coat-of-arms inside), and one of Ottoman Greece's first schools, the *French School*, opened in 1627 for Catholic and Orthodox students alike (including, briefly, Nikos Kazantzakis). This now houses an excellent **Archeological Museum** (daily except Tues. 9am–2.30pm), whose wide historical range of finds – mostly pottery – indi-cates that Náxos was continually occupied throughout antiquity, from Mycenean to Roman times.

For the most part it's a quiet town, and an attractive place to stay. **Ferries** dock along the harbour causeway and the **bus station** is at its landward end – services (up to five daily) for Apóllon in the far north, via Áno Sangrí, Halkí, Filóti and Apíranthos (for all of which see below), and less often to the beaches at Ayía Ánna and Pirgáki. Here, too, you'll find a free left-luggage place (beside the *Penguins* restaurant) and a good bike hire office. There's rarely any problem about finding **rooms** as there are loads of places in the old quarter. One, the *Hotel Dionyssos* (☎0285/22-331, near the *kástro* just off Amfitrítis), has fairly cheap rooms, a youth hostel in the basement, and roof space on top. Three more options close to the quay are the *Hotel Proto* (☎0285/22-394, Protopapáki 13, behind where the buses park); the *Hotel Oceanis* (☎0285/22-436), Damiráli 11, to the left and one street back from the water); and some rooms on the same street, behind the *Proto*. Much of the evening **action** goes on along the quayside, where cafés and restaurants are abundant enough, if a bit on the expensive side. For local fresh fruit and vegetables, something of a rarity in the Cyclades, there's often a morning **market** outside the *Agricultural Bank*.

There's nothing merely functional about the **beaches** within easy reach of Náxos town; they're considered to be the island's best. For some unusual swimming just to the north of the port, beyond the causeway, **GROTTA** is easiest reached. Besides the eponymous caves, the remains of submerged Cycladic buildings are visible, including some stones said to be the entrance to a tunnel leading to the unfinished Temple of Apollo.

The finest targets, though, are all **south** of town, the entire southwestern coastline boasting a series of excellent beaches acessible by bus. **ÁYIOS YIÓRYIOS**, a lengthy sandy bay on the brink of hotel development, is within walking distance. There are several tavernas here, a windsurfing school, and you can **camp** officially just off the beach or unofficially in the dunes behind. A pleasant hour's walk south through the salt marshes brings you to **PROKÓPIOS** beach (cheapish hotels and basic tavernas), whose peaceful days are again surely numbered. Or follow the tracks a little further to **AYÍA ÁNNA** (habitually referred to as 'Ayi'Ánna'), a small fishing and potato-shipping port where there are plenty of **rooms** to let and a few modest tavernas (plus summer *kaíkia* to Píso Livádhi on Páros). Away from the built-up area the beach here is nudist and, again, though there's an official campsite, people set up tints along behind the sand.

Beyond the headland stretch the five lovely kilometres of **PLÁKA** beach, a vegetation-fringed expanse of white sand which comfortably holds the summer crowds of nudists and campers. There are only a couple of buildings right in the middle of Pláka beach, so bring your own provisions. For real isolation, stalk off to the other side of Mikrí Vígla headland (there's a narrow footpath across the cliff edge) to **KASTRÁKI** beach; almost as good, and with a single taverna. Be warned, however, that the sea at the southern end of this beach (at Alikó promontory) catches the sewage swept down from Náxos town. From Kastráki, it's an hour's walk up to the castle of **Apalírou** which held out for two months against the besieging Marco Sanudo. The fortifications are relatively intact and the views are magnificent. Even more remote is **PIRGÁKI** beach, last stop on the coastal bus route and 21km from Náxos town. There's a hotel complex under construction but for the moment it remains a pretty place.

A word of warning for campers: although this entire coast is relatively sheltered from the *meltémi*, the plains behind are boggy and you should bring some sort of mosquito repellent along, as well as plenty of fresh water.

The rest of the **southern coast** – indeed, virtually the whole of the southeast of the island – is almost completely deserted, and studded by mountains. You'd have to be a very dedicated and well-equipped camper/trekker to get much out of the region.

Central Náxos . . . and the Tragéa

Although buses for Apóllon (in the north) link up the central Naxian villages, the core of the island – between Náxos town and Apíranthos – is best explored by moped or on foot. Much of the region is well off the beaten track, a rewarding excursion if you've had your fill of the beaches.

Out of Hóra, you quickly arrive at the neighbouring villages of **GLINÁDHO** and **GALANÁDHO**, forking respectively right and left. Both are scruffy market centres, Glinádho built on a rocky outcrop above the Livádhi plain, Galánadho displaying the first of Náxos's fortified mansions and an unusual 'double church'. This is a combined Orthodox chapel and Catholic sanctuary separated by a double arch, reflecting both the tolerance of the Venetians during their rule and of the locals to established Catholics afterwards. Continue beyond Glinádho to **TRÍPODHES** (the ancient Biblos), 9km from Náxos town. Noted by Homer for its wines, it's an old-fashioned agricultural village with nothing much to do except enjoy a coffee at the shaded *kafenío*. If you're looking for a longer walk, there's a rough road (past the parish church) which leads down the colourful Pláka valley – past an old watchtower and the Byzantine church of Áyios Mathéos (mosaic pavement) – and ends at the glorious Pláka beach (see above).

Going east, the twin villages of SANGRÍ are next, on a vast plateau at the head of a long valley. You can also reach them by continuing to follow the left-hand fork, past Galanádho, a route which allows a look at the domed eighth-century church of **Áyios Mámas** (on the left), once the Byzantine cathedral of the island but neglected during the Venetian occupation and now a sorry sight. Either way, **KÁTO SANGRÍ** boasts the remains of a Venetian castle, while **ÁNO SANGRÍ** is a comely little place, all cobbled streets and fragrant courtyards. A half hour's stroll away, on a path leading south out of the village, is a small Byzantine chapel, **Áyios Ioánnis Yíroulas**; the site originally held a Classical temple of Demeter, then a Christian basilica, and there are marble chunks and column fragments all around – and a breathtaking view down to the sea.

From Sangrí the road twists northeast into the **Tragéa** region, a densely fertile area occupying a vast highland valley. It's a good jumping-off point for all sorts of exploratory rambling, and **HALKÍ** is a fine introduction to what is to come. Set high up, 16km from Hóra, it's a noble and silent town with some lovely churches. Tourists wanting to stay here are a rarity and, though nothing is organised, you might get a room in someone's house. The olive and citrus plantations surrounding Halkí are criss-crossed by paths and tracks, the groves dotted with numerous Byzantine chapels (invariably locked) and the ruins of fortified *pírgi* or Venetian mansions. If you're interested, the **Panayía Protóthronis** church with its eleventh-to-thirteenth-century frescoes, and the romantic **Grazia (Frangopoulos)** *pírgos*, both in Halkí itself, are open for inspection – but only in the morning. Between Halkí and

Akadhímos, but closer to the latter, sits the peculiar twelfth-century 'piggy-back' church of **Áyii Apóstoli**, with a tiny chapel (where the ennobled donors worshipped in private) perched above the narthex.

A delightful circular path starts from Halkí. There's a footpath north to KALÓXILOS and, beyond, both a track and a road to **MONÍ**. Just before the village, you pass the sixth-century monastery of **Panayía Dhrossianí**, a group of stark grey stone buildings with some excellent frescoes; the monks allow visitors at any time, though there are coach tours too from Náxos town. Moní itself enjoys an outstanding view of the Tragéa and the surrounding mountains – and has a taverna from which you can enjoy both. A dirt road leads on to KINÍDHAROS with its old marble quarry, above the village, and a few kilometres beyond a signpost points you down a rough track to the left, to **FLÉRIO** (also commonly called Melanés).

This is the most interesting of Naxos' ancient marble quarries, for in and above a private, irrigated orchard are the two famous **kouri**. Idealised statues of classical (sixth century B.C.) youth, they were left recumbent and unfinished because of flaws in the material. Even so, they're finely detailed figures, over 5m (15 ft.) in length. The second Flério *koúros* lies up a hillside some distance above the oasis; local children will help you to find it.

From Flério you could retrace your steps to the road and head back to the *hóra* via MÍLI and KOURONOHÓRI (with its ruined Venetian castle), both pretty hamlets and connected by footpaths. More adventurously, ask to be directed south to the footpath which leads over the hill to the Potamía villages. At **ÁNO POTAMÍA**, first met with, there's a fine taverna and a rocky track back towards the Tragéa. Once past the valley the landscape becomes craggy and barren, the forbidding Venetian fortress of **Apáno Kástro** perched upon a peak just south of the path. This is believed to have been Sanudo's summer home, but the fortified site goes way back if the Mycenean tombs found nearby are any indication. From the fort, paths lead back to Halkí in around an hour. Alternatively you can continue further southwest down the Potamía valley toward Hóra, passing first the ruined **Cocco** *pírgos* – said to be haunted by one Constantine Cocco, victim of a seventeenth-century clan feud – on the way to **MÉSO POTAMÍA**, joined by some isolated dwellings with its twin village **KÁTO POTAMÍA**, nestling almost invisibly among the greenery flanking the creek.

At the far end of the gorgeous Tragéa valley, **FILÓTI**, the largest village in the region, lies on the slopes of Mount Zas (or Zeus) – which, at 1000m (3300 ft.), is the highest point in the Cyclades. Essentially agricultural, the village's only concession to tourism is a garish fast-food restaurant. Water shortages caused a mass exodus in the 1960s and Filóti never really recovered. However, there are – perhaps as a consequence – plenty of **rooms** and old houses to let and you could do worse than use Filóti as a base. From the village, it's a walk of only an hour or so to the summit of Zás, a climb which provides an astounding panoramic view of virtually the whole of Náxos and its Cycladic neighbours. **APÍRANTHOS**, a hilly, winding 10km beyond, shows the most Cretan influence of all the interior villages. The houses, of mostly unwhitewashed local stone, present a mottled grey and tan aspect, and the inhabitants are reserved and dignified, though helpful when approached (and reputed to be the best musicians on the island). Among the subdued houses there's a small **museum** and two Venetian fortified mansions, while the *platía* contains a miniature church with a three-tiered belltower. Ask to be pointed to the start of the spectacular path up over the ridge behind; this ends either in Moní or Kalóxilos, depending on whether you fork right or left respectively at the top.

Apíranthos has a beach annexe of sorts at **MOUTSOÚNA**, 12km to the east. Emery mined near Apíranthos used to be transported here, by means of an aerial funicular, and then shipped out of the port. The industry collapsed recently and the sandy cove beyond the dock now features a growing colony of vacation villas. The coast south of here is completely isolated, the road petering out into a rutted track – ideal for self-sufficient campers, but again take sufficient water.

Northern Náxos

Even if you've got your own vehicle, it really isn't worth trying to push it any further than Apíranthos; leave the concentration to the bus driver while you enjoy the really startling landscape en route to APÓLLON.

Jagged ranges and hairpin bends confront you before reaching KÓRONOS, the halfway point. From this village, a road off to the right threads through a wooded valley to **LIÓNAS**, a tiny and very Greek port with a pebbly beach. It's not the greatest of diversions and you'd do best to continue, past SKÁDHO, to the high, remote village of **KOMIAKÍ** – original home of the *kitron* liqueur. This is a pleasing, vine-covered settlement, the starting point for perhaps the most extraordinary walk on Náxos. Head up the mountainside and cross the ridge (there is a path) as far as an improbably long marble staircase which winds 300m down into the valley. It's overwhelmingly tempting to climb down this 'Jack and the Beanstalk' fixture (though bear in mind that you'll need to come back up at some point): the views are marvellous, the experience exhilarating, and the hamlet at the bottom, **MIRÍSIS**, enchanting. People from Komiakí migrate downwards in spring and summer to tend and harvest their crops; there are no amenities and all the food is locally produced in this veritable oasis.

Back on the main road, a series of slightly less hairy bends lead down a long valley to **APÓLLON** (Apóllonas). An embryonic resort, it's rather tatty so far, with the beach marred by washed-up tar. There are, however, **rooms** to let above the shops and tavernas, and one major attraction – the **kouros**. On the approach to the village, an unsurfaced road leads to this largest of Náxos' abandoned stone figures. Lying in situ at a former marble quarry, it's 10½m (35 ft.) long but, compared to those at Flério, disappointingly lacking in detail. Here since 600 B.C., it's a singular reminder of the Naxians' traditional skill; the famous Delian lions (see 'Delos' preceding) are also made of Apollonian marble. Not surprisingly, busloads of tours descend upon the village during the day, but by nightfall Apóllon is a peaceful place, with a minimal but traditional nightlife. The local festival, yearly on August 29, is one of Náxos' best.

Apollón is as far as the bus goes, but with sturdy wheels it's possible to loop back to Náxos town on the northern coastal route: windswept, bleak, and far removed from the verdant centre of the island. Make sure that you're equipped for this trip, since there are few settlements along the way if you get into trouble. As of 1989, reputedly, the road is to be paved and a twice-daily bus service between Hóra and Apóllon will be introduced.

Ten kilometres past Naxos's northern cape sprouts the beautiful **Ayía pírgos**, another foundation (in 1717) of the Cocco family. There's a tiny hamlet nearby and, 7km further along, a track leads off to **ÁVRAM** beach, an idyllic spot with a family-run taverna and **rooms** to let. Just beyond HÍLLIES VRÍSSES, the only real village in this region, is the abandoned **monastery of Faneroméni**, built in 1606. Nearby, there's another deserted beach, **AMITÍ**, and then the track leads inland, up the Engarés valley, to ENGARÉS and **GALÍNI**, only 6km from Hóra. The road at last becomes paved here, and on the final stretch back to the port passes a unique eighteenth-century Turkish fountain-house and the fortified monastery of **Áyios Ioánnis Hrissóstomos**, where a couple of aged nuns are still in residence. A footpath from the monastery, or the road below, will lead you straight back to town.

Minor Isles: Koufoníssi, Skhinoússa, Iráklia and Dhonoússa

In the patch of the Aegean beween Náxos and Amorgós there is a chain of six small islands neglected by tourists, by guidebooks and by the majority of Greeks, few of whom have ever heard of them. **Kéros** (ancient Karos) is an important archaeological site but has no permanent population and **Káto Koufoníssi** is inhabited only by goatherds. The other four islands, however – **Áno Koufoníssi**, **Skhinoússa**, **Iráklia** and **Dhonoússa** – are all inhabited, served by ferry, and can be visited. They have few facilities – no electricity (except on Koufoníssi), scarce water, few provisions in the shop(s), limited choice of food at the restaurant(s), no post office and no organised method of changing money – though this, of course, is most of the reason why you're going. Some knowledge of Greek, at least phrasebook-level, is going to be necessary and you should be prepared to be regarded as a distinct curiosity. However, this said, if you're looking for peace and solitude – what the Greeks call *isikhía*– you should be able to find it.

Several times weekly in summer a Pireás-based **ferry** (the *Skhinoússa* or *Nireus*) calls at each of the islands, linking them with Náxos and Amorgós and (usually) Páros, Síros, Sérifos and Sífnos. Dhonoússa has the worst connections, the ferries to or from Pireás always seeming to turn up at 4 o'clock in the morning.

Áno Koufoníssi and Kéros

Áno Koufoníssi (or just Koufoníssi) is the least primitive of the group and, unlike the rest, is beginning to attract a few Greek holiday-makers and some seasonal travellers. As it's also the smallest of these islands – you can walk around it an energetic morning – *isikhía*, at least in July and August, may be on the way out. The (single) village has recently acquired a post office and mains electricity. There is a hotel and a number of **rooms** to let, notably at the main taverna, the *Afroessa*, and in a new building, *Soroccos*. On the east coast, back from a long sandy stretch of beach, there's another (seasonal) taverna. Camping hereabouts presents no problems except that you may have to walk some way for fresh water and supplies.

From the beach, it's sometimes possible to take a *kaíki* to Kéros where you can potter around the remains of a Neolithic village. In the north of the island there's a second settlement, in this case a neglected medieval village.

Skhinoússa

Skhinoússa, a short hop to the west, is probably the quietest of all Cycladic islands, with a winter population of 85 which barely increases throughout the summer. **MIRSÍNI**, its tiny port hamlet, has a simple restaurant, but the main settlement is at **HÓRA**, concealed on arrival but less than a mile's walk up the hill. Here, there are two sparsely-stocked shops and two similarly-endowed tavernas, one of which has a few rooms to let. Otherwise it's down to camping at the coarse grey beach (others in the group are fine and yellow) ten minutes below Hóra on the southwest coast. Sitting or swimming here you can gaze out and reflect on the populated islands – Páros, Náxos, Amorgós and Íos – visible all around: a strange sensation.

Iráklia and Dhonoússa

Iráklia, at the southwestern end of the chain, and Dhonoússa, slightly isolated to the north, fall somewhere between the previous two – not as equipped for visitors as Koufoníssi nor so primitive as Skhinoússa. They are also a little larger and more mountainous, terrain for a good day's walking.

On Iráklia the old *hóra*, an hour's walk up through the hills, is now giving way to its very attractive harbour, **ÁYIOS YIÓRYIOS**, set in a fertile valley at the head of a deep inlet. The Iráklia beach, Livádhi, lies just off the road between the port and Hóra and is pretty much ideal for camping.

An increasing number of people are visiting Dhonoússa each year and the island's capacity to accomodate them has been under severe pressure. With a permanent population of less than a hundred, resources are extremely limited, so don't expect too much in the way of choice at the two tavernas and one shop. Fresh produce is scarce, though there is an excellent (summer only) bakery. The harbour village is the main settlement, and there are rooms available here (be warned that there are no other facilities of any kind elsewhere on the island). If you want to camp on the beach, you'll have to head out of town, about half an hour to the east. There's a second beach, a further hour away in the same direction, reached via the hamlets of **HARAVYÍ** and **MIRSÍNI** – or you can take an occasional *kaíki*; ask in the main village. A final excursion leads northeast to the hamlet of **KALATIRÍTISSA**, an hour from the port along a path giving impressive views of the coastline.

Amorgós

Like Kárpathos in the Dodecanese, Amorgós is virtually two islands: roads are so poor in its splendidly rugged terrain that by far the easiest way of getting between KATÁPOLA in the south and EGIÁLI in the north is by boat – all ferries call at both. Unlike Kárpathos, though, the island is often very crowded in summer, with Germans particularly. It has a post office but as yet no bank.

KATÁPOLA, the chief port, has lots of modest **rooms** and pensions – the best among them *Pension Amorgos* (☎0285/71-214), left from the quay. However, the typically very late ferry arrivals mean that you might well end up spending your first night in the fields or on the beach. Katápola is actually three combined villages: Kseró Keratídhi to the north, Katápola proper at the head of the gulf, and the hillside district of Rahídhi, below which are most of the stores and tavernas. The latter district also has Katápola's official camp-site, behind the soccer field. Steps lead up through Rahídhi from the quay to the remains of the ancient city of **Minoa**, but the view is more interesting than what little can be made out of the ruins. Beyond Minoa the path leads in a few hours to ARKESSÍNI (see below) via several hamlets and **Áyia Saránda beach** – a wonderful outing.

HÓRA is forty minutes' walk away up a steep mule track, or there's a shambling old Dodge school bus that makes the same trip several times a day. A line of decapitated windmills post themselves beyond the village's perfect Cycladic houses and bulbous churches, which halt abruptly at the edge of precipitous cliffs. There are a few simple **rooms** to let here but in

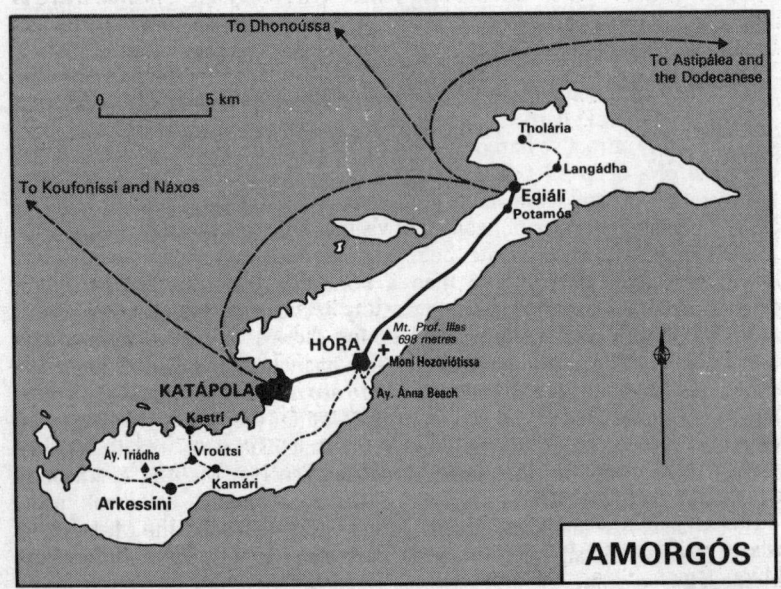

summer they're likely to be full; it's not unheard of to sleep in the streets, and the two restaurants are permanently packed; off-season it's still a tremendous place. As usual, a thirteenth-century Venetian castle surveys the island from its summit above the town. On Platía Ioannídhis there's a workshop devoted to the manufacture of *karagiózis* (shadow puppet) figures.

Near the bus stop a path leads steeply down and around the cliffs to the left. Suddenly the monastery **Hozoviótissa** is before you, its vast wall shining out white below the towering orange cliffs. Only three monks occupy the fifty rooms now, but you can still see the eleventh-century icon around which the monastery was founded, along with a stack of other treaures; visit between 8am and 2pm (or 5–7pm in summer).

In the other direction from Hóra you can walk – or take an occasional bus – to the protected white beach of **AYÍA ÁNNA**. Skip the first cove encountered in favour of the second bay, where there's spring water but no taverna. For beauty and a bit more seclusion, the countryside to the southwest is recommended. A lorry leaves Hóra for **ARKESSÍNI** daily, although you can walk it in two hours (or from Katápola as well, see above). Close to modern VROÚTSI, **ancient Arkessini** features the remains of tombs, walls, and houses. There's a well-preserved Classical tower (known locally as the *pírgos*) at nearby **AYÍA TRIÁDHA**; adjacent **modern Arkessíni** has one taverna and rooms.

EGIÁLI, the northern port, is a good five hours' walk from Hóra, through beautiful deserted country. However much of the path has been bulldozed, and going by boat is a lot easier – in summer the ferry services are augmented by regular *kaíkia*. Smaller than Katápola, Egiáli has a more attractive beach and a genial atmosphere, though again there is no shortage of people there to appreciate it. Boats are met by locals offering **rooms** and you should get something; the tavernas here are among the cheapest in the Cyclades.

POTAMÓS, just to the south, and **LANGÁDHA**, forty minutes' walk to the north, are both sleepy, untouched villages; Langádha is especially wonderful. Another half hour beyond are the **Tholária**, vaulted tombs which date from Roman times.

Íos

No other island is quite like Íos, nor attracts the same vast crowds of young people. The beach is almost as packed with sleeping bags at night as it is with naked bodies by day, and nightlife in the village is loud and long. But crowded as it is, the island hasn't been commercialised in quite the same way as, say, Míkonos – mainly because few of the visitors have much money. You're either going to decide that Íos (short for 'Ireland Over Seas', as some would have it) is the island paradise you have always been looking for and stay for weeks, as many people do, or hate it and take the next boat out, an equally common reaction.

Almost all the visitors stay along the arc delineated by the port, Yialós where you'll arrive (there's no airport), Hóra above it, and the beach at Milopótamos. It's a small area, and you soon get to know your way around.

Three **buses** constantly shuttle between the three places, with daily service running roughly from 8am to 11pm; you should never have to wait more than fifteen minutes, but at least once try the short walk up (or down) the stepped path between Yialós and the Hóra.

Despite its past popularity, **sleeping on the beach** on Íos is worth avoiding these days. Raids are becoming more frequent as the island strains under the sheer impact of youth tourism and, recently, the police have been known to turn very nasty. They prefer you to sleep in the official campsites, which, given the problem of theft is probably good advice. If you are going to sleep elsewhere, it's wise to stick in a crowd of like-minded people or keep a very low profile. A further problem is the **water shortage**, which has dire effects above all on local toilets. Things get particularly grim in Yialós; but even in the tavernas on the beach only the desperate and the foolish dare venture out the back. In the village, where there's much more choice, you may find a toilet which flushes, although officially water is too scarce to be used for so frivolous a purpose.

Practicalities

You might be tempted to grab a **room** in YIALÓS as you arrive, though it's the most expensive place on the island to stay. Owners meet arrivals off the ferries, hustling accommodation here (and in the *hóra* and at Milopótamos too); it's up to you. Just note that the official campsite in Yialós, to the right of the harbour on a scruffy beach, is the worst of the island's three – and mosquito-ridden. From the quayside, **buses** turn around just to the left, while the Yialós **beach** is another five minutes' walk in the same direction. Backed by hotels and rooms-places, it's not peaceful by any means – loud music seems to be accepted on the beach and obligatory in the tavernas, plus there are frequent uproarious gatherings: great fun if you like that sort of thing. Yialós has all the other predictable conveniences: tourist information office, a reasonable supermarket (to the right of the bus stop), and a few fairly authentic tavernas. If you stay, there's a smaller, less crowded beach at KOUMBÁRA, a twenty-minute stroll over the headland, and largely nudist. There's a taverna, and a rocky islet to explore.

Most of the cheaper **rooms** are in HÓRA, a twenty-minute walk up the mountain behind the port. There's plenty of dormitory space around as well as the usual rooms and hotels – though for the latter two options, you've got a better chance of getting something reasonable if you haggle with the intention of staying for several days. The old white village is becoming overwhelmed by the number of tourists, but with any number of arcaded streets and whitewashed chapels, it still has a certain charm. Recently a bevy of expensive fashion and jewellery boutiques have begun to appear, reflecting an increased affluence and consumerism among the once avidly anti-materialist clientele, but what the *hóra* is still really about is **nightlife**.

Every evening the streets throb to music from ranks of competing discos and clubs – mostly free, or with a nominal cover charge, to get in, but drinks tend to be expensive. In no particular order of importance, some of the best (and longest-established) places to hit are: the *Ios Club*, on a peak above the

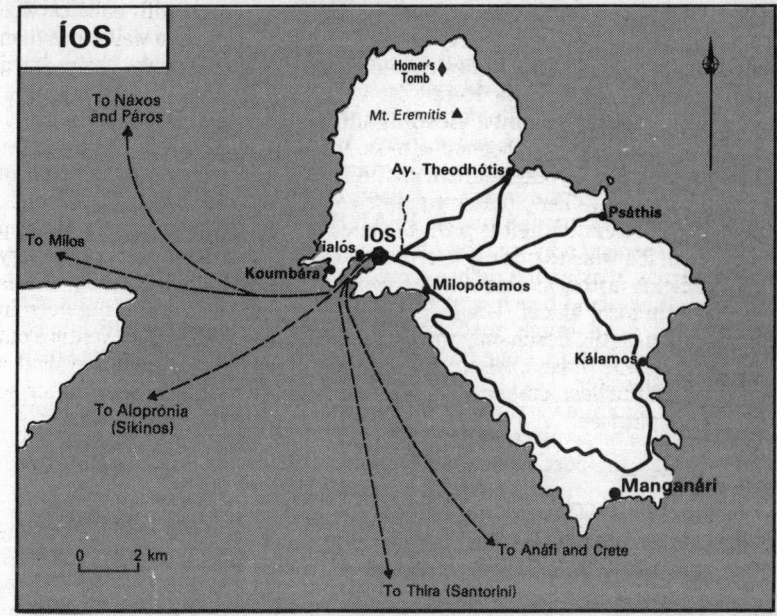

ÍOS

Homer's Tomb

Mt. Eremítis ▲

Ay. Theodhótis

To Náxos and Páros

Psáthis

ÍOS

To Mílos

Yialós

Koumbára

Milopótamos

Kálamos

To Alopronia (Síkinos)

Manganári

0   2 km

To Anáfi and Crete

To Thíra (Santoríni)

---

main road, for sunset cocktails and classical music; the *Sweet Irish Dream* below, where the Pogues and U2 are served at boiling point; the *Why Not?* pub for curries and chili; *Old Ios Jazz Club*, sometimes with live music; *Disco 69* for dancing in the street; and the *Village Pub*, with occasional visiting British bands and cheap beer. One to avoid is the *Red Lion* (near the *Sweet Irish Dream*), the province of British lager-louts and the apparent venue for international vomiting contests. There are plenty of places **to eat** too: cheapest and best are *I Folia*, near the top of the village, and *Ikoyeniaki Taverna I Stani*, at the heart of town.

Around the island

The most popular stop on the island's bus routes is **MILOPÓTAMOS**, site of a magnificent beach and a mini-resort to boot. By day, young people cover every inch of the bus-stop end of the sand, though for a bit more space head the other way, where there are dunes behind the beach. There are two official **campsites**, one at either end of the strip, *Camping Stars* (the first encountered) being better than *Camping Soulis*. There are **rooms** around (try *Draco Pension* to the right – facing the sea – of the bus stop), and one good self-service café, the *Far Out* (so named for the standard reaction to the view on the ride in). You can always walk to Milopótamos from Íos; it takes about 25 minutes, and there are also some rooms on the road down.

From Yialós, daily boats depart at around 10am (returning in the late afternoon) to **MANGANÁRI** on the south coast, where there is a beach and a posh hotel. Predominantly nudist, this is the beach to come for serious tans.

There's more to see though, and a better atmosphere, at **ÁYIOS THEODHÓTIS**, up on the east coast. A new **bus** service runs at 10am from Yialós (or ten minutes later from the stop behind the windmills in Hóra), but purists can walk there on a decaying walled track across the heart of the island. This begins just to the north of the windmills; carry water as the hike will take two to three hours. Once there, Áyios Theodhótis boasts a ruined Venetian castle which encompasses the ruins of a marble-finished town and a Byzantine church. If the beach – a good one and mainly nudist – is too crowded (unlikely), try the one at **PSÁTHIS**, another hour's stroll to the southeast. Frequented by wealthy Athenians, this small resort has a couple of pricey tavernas, making it strictly a target for a day trip rather than a place to stay. The other island beach is at **KÁLAMOS**, another three-hour walk and best reached on a rough road from the Hóra. It's very remote indeed, although at PERIVÓLIA – one hour into the walk – there are welcome shady trees and fresh water.

The only cultural diversion on the island is an expensive one. The story goes that, while on a voyage from Samos to Athens, Homer's ship was forced to put in at Íos, the poet subsequently dying on the island. Visiting **Homer's tomb** you need to hire either a donkey or a *kaíki* – and, ideally, a guide too as it's difficult to find; ask at the tourist office in Yialós. You can walk, but it's a good three hour's slog to the northeastern tip of the island, passing the Psarápirgos tower on Mt. Eremítis, until you reach the site of the ancient town of Plakatos. The town itself has long since slipped down the side of the cliff, but the rocky ruins of the entrance to a tomb remain, as well as some graves – one of which is claimed to be Homer's.

Síkinos

Síkinos has so small a population that the mule-ride or walk up from the port to the village has only recently been replaced by a bus, and until the new jetty is completed it's the last major Greek island where ferry passengers are still taken ashore in launches. With no dramatic characteristics, nor any nightlife to speak of, few foreigners seem to make the short trip over here from neighbouring Íos and Folégandhros or well-connected Páros, Náxos, or Thíra.

Yet spend the required hour walking up from the little harbour of **ALOPRÓNIA**, with its tavernas, handful of rooms, and sandy beach, and the scenery turns out to be more beautiful than the desolate first impression suggests. The double village of **KÁSTRO-HÓRA**, upon a ridge overlooking the sea, is a really charming place, quite untouched by tourism though with just enough rooms to go around. A partly ruined monastery, **Zoödhóhos Piyí** ('Spring of Life', a frequent name on the Cyclades), crowns the rock above, and there are two or three *very* basic tavernas.

To the west an hour's walk leads through a landscape lush with olive and arbutus to **EPISKOPÍ**, where elements of an ancient temple-tomb have been ingeniously incorporated into a church dating from the seventh century. An hour and a half in the opposite direction lies **PALEOKÁSTRO**, the patchy remains of an ancient fortress. If you turn down and right (south) from this

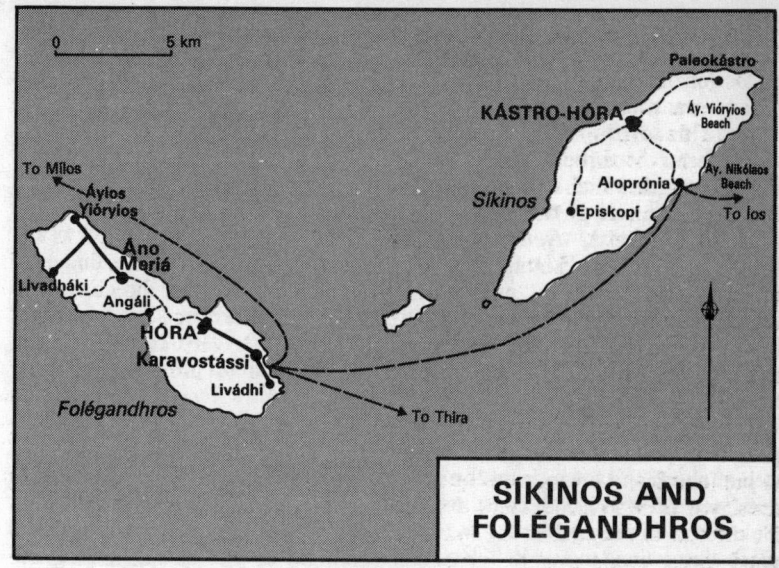

SÍKINOS AND
FOLÉGANDHROS

path you'll come to a pair of beaches, **ÁYIOS YIÓRYIOS** and **ÁYIOS NIKÓLAOS**, which face Íos; the former cove has a well.

In addition to the regular ferries there are infrequent local *kaíkia* to and from Íos and Folégandhros. There is no bank, but you can sometimes change cash at the store in Aloprónia.

Folégandhros

The cliffs of Folégandhros rise sheer in places over 300m (1000 ft.) from the sea, until the early 1980s a deterrent to tourists as they always were to pirates. It is traditionally an island of political exile, and was used as such in recent decades, but life in the high barren interior has been eased since the junta years by the arrival of electricity and the construction of a road from the harbour to Hóra. A growing number of visitors – mostly German – have begun to tax the island's limited tourist facilities, but rampant commercialisation is still a few years away. **Rooms** are in short supply, however, and since many **ferries** arrive at around 9.30pm you should be prepared to camp, at least for the first night or two.

KARAVOSTÁSSI, the port, is a popular base, its tavernas and much-sought-after hotel and rooms a short walk from the pebbly beach. A little further around, in the next bay, is the hamlet of **LIVÁDHI** and the island's official campsite (sporadically supplied with water); the beach here is fine and shaded, the two seasonal tavernas mediocre.

But the island's real character and appeal is to be found in the spectacular **HÓRA**, perched on a cliff-top plateau some 45 minutes' walk (or a quick bus ride) from the dock; hourly bus service from morning until late at night. Villagers and foreigners – scores of them in high season – mingle at the tavernas under the lentisk trees, passing the time. Toward the cliff's edge, and entered through an arcade, the defensive core of the medieval **Kástro** is marked by ranks of of two-storey houses, their repetitive, nearly identical stairways and slightly recessed doors pleasing to the eye.

In the kástro, the *Danassis* (☎0286/41-230) is one of the longest established and cheaper **hotels**; if you can wangle a room it's also the most dramatic place to stay on the island, with some rooms looking directly out on to the alarming drop to the sea. Otherwise, there are at least two other government-classified lodgings, including the *Fani-Vevis* (☎0286/41-237) and the *Odysseas* (☎0286/41-239), and a handful of rooms on the outskirts of the village. If you're really stuck for accomodation, *Pavlos's Rooms*, between Hóra and Karavostássi, is often the last outfit to run out of vacancies. A combination **OTE/post office** (no bank) completes the list of amenities.

Just above the town, from the square where the bus stops, a zig-zag path with views down to both coastlines leads to the beautiful church of **Análipsi**. Below it is **Hrissospiliá**, a cave with stalactites, but you'll need a boat and close instructions to find it.

Northwest of Hóra a road threads its way through **ÁNO MERIÁ**, the other village of the island, deteriorating after several kilometres into what is merely a wide dirt track. There's a taverna about halfway along, an excellent **folk museum** (daily 4–7pm), and, just possibly, rooms. Several times a day the bus trundles out here to drop people off at the footpaths down to the various sheltered beaches on the south and west of the island. Most notable of these is **ANGÁLI** (aka Vathí), an hour's walk west of Hóra. Here you'll find two or three tavernas and some rooms; camping is tolerated but nudism isn't. For that, paths lead twenty minutes east or west to **FIRÁ** or **ÁYIOS NIKÓLAOS** beaches respectively. Alternatively there is seasonal *kaíki* service once or twice daily between Karavostássi and the Angáli area. **LIVADHÁKI** and **ÁYIOS YIÓRYIOS** beaches, accessible on foot from the last two Áno Meriá bus stops, are more remote and unspoiled. Away from the beaches the countryside is pristine, still largely devoted to the cultivation of barley which supported many of the Cyclades before the advent of tourism.

Thíra (Santoríni)

As the ferryboat manoeuvers into the great caldera of Thíra, the land seems to rise up and clamp around it. Gaunt, sheer cliffs loom hundreds of feet above, nothing grows or grazes to soften the view, and the only colours are the reddish-brown, black and gray pumice striations layering the cliff face. The landscape tells of a history so dramatic and turbulent that legend hangs as fact upon it.

From as early as 3000 B.C. the island developed as a sophisticated outpost of Minoan civilisation until, around 1450 B.C., catastrophe came: the volcano-

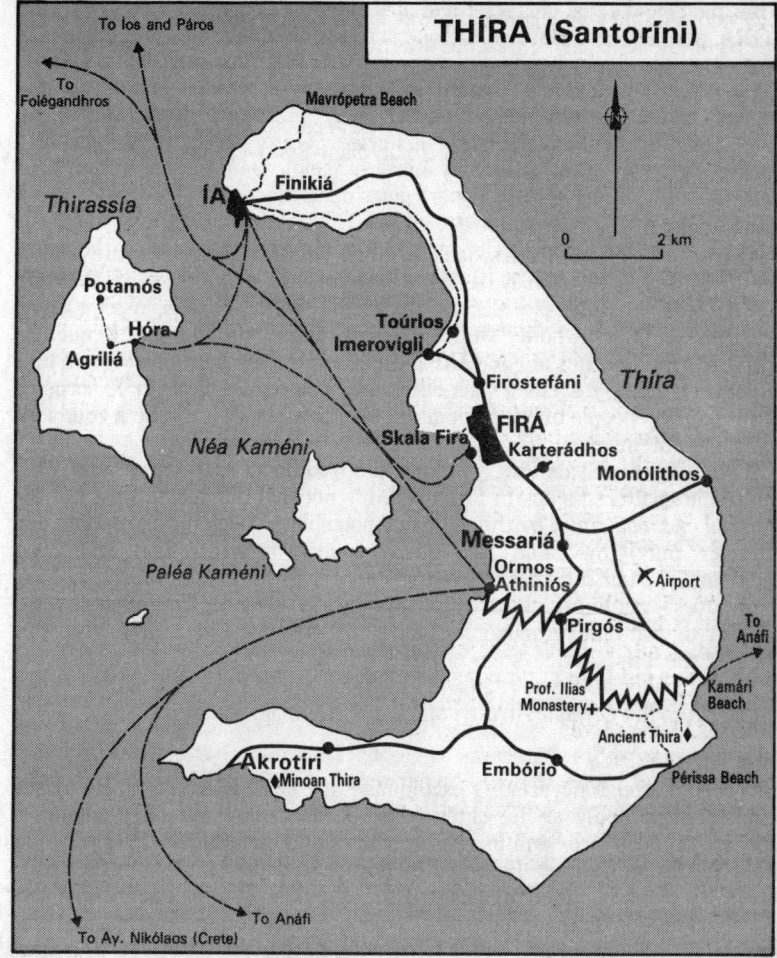

THÍRA (Santoríni)

To Íos and Páros
To Folégandhros
Mavrópetra Beach
Thirassía
Finikiá
ÍA
Potamós
Hóra
Agriliá
Toúrlos
Imerovígli
Néa Kaméni
Firostefáni
Thíra
Skala Firá
FIRÁ
Karterádhos
Monólithos
Messariá
Paléa Kaméni
Ormos
Athiniós
Airport
Pirgós
To Anáfi
Prof. Ilias
Monastery
Kamári
Beach
Ancient Thira
Akrotíri
Minoan Thira
Embório
Périssa Beach
To Anáfi
To Ay. Nikólaos (Crete)
0   2 km

island erupted, its heart sank below the sea, and earthquakes reverberated across the Aegean. Thira was destroyed and it is thought the great Minoan civilisations on Crete fell with it. At this point the island's history became linked with legends of Atlantis, the 'Happy Isles Submerged by Sea'. Plato insisted that the legend was true, and Solon dated the cataclysm to 9000 years before his time – if you're willing to accept a mistake and knock off the final zero, a highly plausible date.

Evidence of the Minoan colony was found at **Akrotíri**, a village buried under banks of volcanic ash at the southwest tip of the island. Tunnels through the ash uncovered structures, two and three storeys high, first damaged by earthquake then buried by eruption; Professor Marinatos, the excavator and now an island hero, was killed by a collapsing wall and is also buried on the site. Lavish frescoes adorned the walls, and Cretan pottery was found stored in a chamber – the frescoes are currently exhibited in Athens, but there are plans to bring them back when a new museum is built. For now, you'll have to content yourself with the (very good) archaeological museum in Firá (see below); Akrotíri itself (daily 9am–3pm) can be reached by bus from FIRÁ or PÉRISSA.

Coming and going

Arriving in Santoríni, ferries dock at either **SKÁLA FIRÁ** or more often – the larger ones especially – at the somewhat grim port of **ÓRMOS ATHINIÓS**, occasionally also at ÍA in the north. **Buses**, astonishingly crammed, connect Athiniós with the island capital Firá and, less frequently, with the main beaches at KAMÁRI and Périssa – disembark quickly and take whatever's going, it's a long walk otherwise. You're also likely to be accosted at Athiniós by people offering rooms all over the island; it can be a good idea to listen to them, given the scramble for beds in Firá especially.

If you alight at Skála Firá, you have the traditional route above you – 580 mule-shit splattered steps to Firá itself. It's not that difficult to walk but the intrepid can also go up by the mules responsible or (weather permitting and summer only) by cable car, quarter-hourly between 7am and 8pm. Incidentally, when it comes to **leaving** – especially for summer/evening ferry departures – get to Athiniós a couple of hours in advance, since crowds reminiscent of war-time evacuations gather on the dockside. Note, too, that though the bus service stops around midnight a shared taxi isn't outrageously expensive. If you're headed for the **airport** near Monólithos, buses run to/from the *Olympic Airways* office in Firá's main square.

Firá

Half-rebuilt after a devastating earthquake in 1956, **FIRÁ** (Thíra, Hóra) still lurches dementedly at the cliff's edge. A stunningly attractive setting, it appears on post cards and tourist brochures and, naturally, it (and you) pay the price for its position. Besieged by hordes of day-trippers from the cruise boats, it's become incredibly tacky of late, the most grossly commercial spot on what can – in summer, at least – seem a grossly commercial island. Gone are the simple restaurants and bakeries of a decade ago, replaced by a mass of supernumerary jewellery and fur boutiques, fast-food places and tourist agencies.

If you insist on staying here, you'll have to move quickly on arrival, particularly if you want one of the better **rooms** with views over the caldera; beds are at a premium in summer and by noon nearly everything is full. Take any reasonable offer, including places just outside the town. Otherwise there are three **youth hostels** in the northern part of town, very cheap, often full to the gills, but not too bad if you have your own bedding and sleep on the roof. In the same neighbourhood, single women can stay at the Dominican convent. Out of season it's easier (and cheaper) to track down rooms; officially, the police only allow hotels to stay open, but you should eventually find someone prepared to put you up.

Firá's cliff-top position is its main attraction but for all that it's not a place to linger. Make time, however, for the **Archaeological Museum** (Mon.–Sat. 9am–3pm, Sun. 9am–1pm, closed Tues.), near the cable car to the north of town. An excellent collection, it includes a curious set of erotic Dionysiac figures.

Buses to points further afield leave Firá from the large rectangular square straight ahead from the top of the stairs. There are enough of them to get around between the town and beaches, but if you want to see the whole island in a couple of days hiring a moped is useful – try any of the firms on the main road to Ía from the bus station square. Bus timetables are posted in the kiosk at the far end of the *platía*: approximately hourly to Ía, Périssa, Akrotíri, half-hourly to Kamári. One place you can easily walk to – in around twenty minutes – is **KARTERÁDHOS**, just south of Firá. It's a small village and a good alternative source of rooms if the capital is full. To this end, **MESSARIÁ**, another 2km further, is also a possibility although the hotels in this pleasant village are on the expensive side.

The rest of theisland

Once outside Firá, the rest of Santoríni comes as a nice surprise. The volcanic soil is highly fertile, and every available inch seems terraced and cultivated. Wheat, cherry-tomatoes, pistachios and grapes are the main crops, all still harvested and planted by hand. The island's *visándo* and *nikhtéri* wines are a little sweet for most tastes but are among the finest produced in the Cyclades.

ÍA, in the northwest of the island, was once a major fishing port of the Aegean but has declined in the wake of economic depression, wars, earthquakes and depleted fish. Partly destroyed in the 1956 quake, it presents a curious mix of pristine white reconstruction and tumbledown ruins clinging to the cliff face – by any standards one of the most dramatic towns of the Cyclades. Ía is also much the calmest place on the island, and with the recent introduction of a post office, part-time bank and bike-hire office there's no longer any reason to feel stuck in Firá. However, **rooms** aren't too easy to come by. The local EOT authorities have restored some of the old houses as guest-lodges, all on the pricey side, and the only other choices are the troglodytic *Pension Lauda* (☎0286/71-204), the *Hotel Anemones* (☎0286/71-220), and the *Hotel Fregata* (☎0286/71-221) – all fairly reasonable. The best value in eating is at *Café Lotza*, where you can dine on such delicacies as *mavromatiká* (black-eyed peas) or *fáva* at the edge of the abyss.

Below the town, 200-odd steps switchback hundreds of metres down to two small harbours: **AMMOÚDHI**, for the fishermen, and **ARMÉNI**, where the ferries dock. Off the cement platform at Ammoúdi you can swim past floating pumice and snorkel among shoals of giant fish, but beware the currents around the church-islet of Áyios Nikólaos. At Arméni, a single taverna specialises in grilled octopus lunches.

It's 12km from Firá to Ía, easy enough by bus but infinitely more satisfying if you walk the stretch from **IMEROVÍGLI**, 3km out of Firá, using a spectacular footpath along the lip of the caldera. Imerovígli has a taverna and one hotel, and if you make the hike on to Ía you'll pass TOÚRLOS on the way, an old Venetian citadel on Cape Skáros. **FINIKIÁ**, 1km east of Ía, has an excellent unofficial **youth hostel** on the north side of the road, and the recommended *Markozanes* and *Finikia* restaurants.

Beaches on Santorini are bizarre – long black stretches of volcanic sand which get blisteringly hot in the afternoon sun. The problem, as always, is that they're no secret and in the summer the crowds can be a bit overpowering. Closest to Firá, **MONÓLITHOS** has a couple of tavernas but is nothing special (though you should be all right camping here, near the airport). Farther south, **KAMÁRI** has surrendered lock, stock and barrel to the package-tour operators and, though there are some **rooms** available, there's not a piece of sand that isn't fronted by concrete villas. Its only virtue seems to be an occasional *kaíki* service to ANÁFI (see next section) in season.

Things are rather better at **PÉRISSA**, around the cape. It's more attractively situated and has lots of cheap rooms, a few decent tavernas (trey the *Hotel Christi*, 100m or so back from the sea), a youth hostel, and an official campsite. The beach extends almost 7km to the west, sheltered by the occasional tamarisk tree.

Kamári and Périssa are separated by the Mésa Vounó headland, on which stood **ancient Thira** (Mon.–Sat. 9am–3pm, Sun. 10am–2.30pm), the post-eruption settlement dating from the ninth century B.C. Expensive taxis, and cheaper buses go up from Kamári, but the best route is on foot from Périssa (half an hour) following a clear path up past the hillside chapel. Though impressively large, most of the ruins (3rd-1st c. B.C.) are difficult to place, but there are temples and houses with mosaics. The view from the theatre, however, is awesome – beyond the stage there's a sheer drop to the sea. When the city was discovered in the 1890s the uniformed band from Firá trooped all the way up to give a concert. You can continue one hour on the path, soon a cobbled way, down to Kamári, slicing across the switchbacks of the road up; part way down you pass a huge cave which contains a tiny shrine and a freshwater spring: the only one on Thíra and a lifesaver on a hot day.

Inland along the same mountain spine, and accessible, alas, by tour bus is the early eighteenth-century monastery of **Profítis Ilías**, now sharing its refuge with Greek radio and TV pylons and antennae of a NATO station which it will hopefully outlive. Normally Greek monasteries will only show visitors their *katholikón*, or main chapel, but here you're free to wander about the old workshops and cells of the monks, too. They're open from 9am to 3pm and have been converted to house a fascinating folklore museum of old rural crafts from winemaking to leatherwork. The easiest approach is probably by taking the Firá–Périssa bus as far as the village of **PÍRGOS**, half an hour's walk below. From near the entrance to the monastery an old footpath then heads across the ridge in about an hour to ancient Thira.

PÍRGOS itself is one of the oldest settlements on the island, a jumble of old houses and alleys that also bears the scars of the 1956 earthquake. It climbs to another Venetian fortress crowned by several churches and you can clamber around the battlements for sweeping views over the entire island and its Aegean neighbours. By way of contrast **MESSARIÁ**, a thirty-minute stroll north, has a skyline consisting solely of massive church domes lording it over the houses huddled in a low bowl.

Thirassía and Kaméni

From either Firá or Ía boat excursions run to the burnt volcanic islets of **PALÉA KAMÉNI** and **NÉA KAMÉNI**, and to the relatively unspoiled islet of **THIRASSÍA**. Néa Kaméni, with its mud-clouded hot springs and shoe-slicing hike to a volcanically active crater, gets mixed reviews, but everybody seems to enjoy Thirassía – part of Santoríni until shorn off by an eruption in the third century B.C. There are three small villages on the islet, some tavernas and rooms, and you could live very simply here while waiting for the once-weekly proper ferry.

Anáfi

An hour's boat ride to the east of Thíra, Anáfi is the end of the line for most of the ferries which call there – and an excellent retreat from mid-season crowds. Once or twice a week there'll be a boat going on to Crete or some of the Dodecanese so it can prove a useful halting post, too.

It is a small, rather harsh island with a population of just under 300, almost all of whom live on the south coast. Here, the harbour village has two tavernas, two shops and a handful of houses, with **HÓRA** adorning a conical hill immediately above. The cliffs are too steep for a proper road and the mule track up can accommodate nothing more than a motorbike, but in any case there are no cars on the island since there is nowhere else for them to go. Exposed and very windy indeed when the *meltémi* is blowing, Hóra has a few

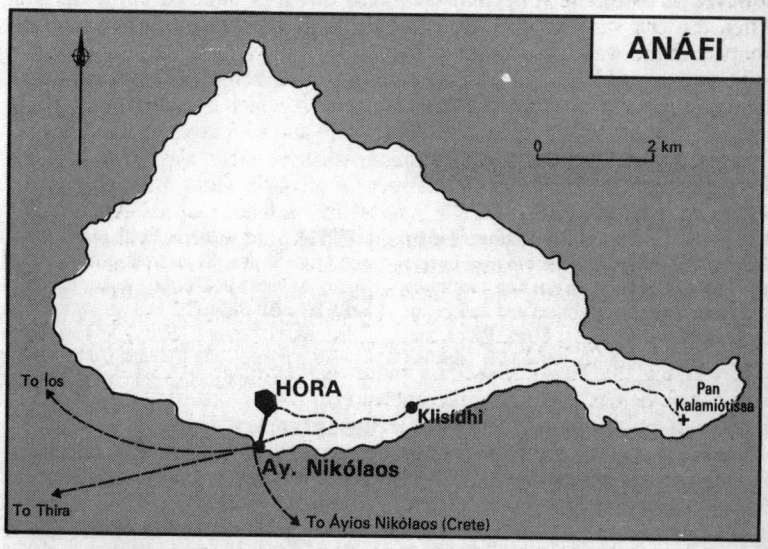

rooms to let but only one taverna and surprisingly few *kafenía*. It is one of those villages where the men sit inside rather than out to drink their coffee and play backgammon, and at first the place seems a somewhat forbidding ghost town. This impression is slowly dispelled, particularly if you know some Greek, as the people of Anáfi are really very hospitable. There may not be a wide choice of food in the tavernas but the few tiny shops have fresh fruit at the right time of year, there's a good bakery, and also a post office.

The port of **ÁYIOS NIKÓLAOS**, with its handful of tavernas serving fresh fish and little crabs, is the best place to be in the evenings, though if you're staying in Hóra there's a stiff climb back – torch essential unless there's a full moon (and you're still sober).

There is a beach with another taverna at **KLISÍDHI**, a short walk along the cliffs to the east of the harbour, and further along (in the southeast corner of the island) is the monastery of **Panayía Kalamiótissa**, built on the site of an ancient temple of Apollo and incorporating part of its masonry. In the mountainous north of the island you come upon a ruined Venetian castle, while numerous tracks lead from Hóra into the interior; most seem to lead nowhere in particular but it's all good walking country. The island is extremely dry, however, and outside the few settlements you'll need to take water with you on any walks.

Even if you come to Anáfi in high season you should expect to be marooned here for several extra days. Although it's nominally the last stop twice a week on various Cyclades ferry routes, the boat will simply skip Anáfi if it's running late – which it generally is. In such a case the only way off the island is by tourist *kaíki* or, in desperation, a real fishing boat, to Kamári on Thíra.

travel details

Most islands in the Cyclades are served by boats from Pireás, but there are also ferries which depart from Lávrio (for Kéa and, much less often, Síros and Kíthnos) and Rafína (for Ándhros, Tínos, Míkonos, Síros, Páros, and Náxos). All three ports are easily reached by bus from Athens.

The frequency of sailings given below is intended to give an idea of services from April to October, when most visitors tour the islands. Expect departures to be at or below the minimum listed level during the winter, with some routes cancelled entirely.

KÉA 1 to 3 daily to Lávrio (2½ hr.); 1 weekly to Kíthnos.

KÍTHNOS 2 to 8 weekly to Pireás (4 hr.); 2 to 8 weekly to Sérifos, Sífnos, and Mílos; 2 to 4 weekly to Kímolos and Lávrio; 1 weekly to Síros.

SÉRIFOS AND SÍFNOS 2 to 8 weekly to Pireás (6 hr.), each other, and Mílos; 1 to 4 weekly to Kímolos, Íos, and Thíra (Santorini); once weekly to Síros; seasonal *kaíki* from Sífnos (Platís Yialós) to Páros.

MÍLOS Daily to Pireás (8 hr.); 2 to 8 weekly to Sífnos (2 hr.), Sérifos, and Kíthnos; daily *kaíki* or ferry to Kímolos; 3 to 5 weekly to Folégandhros, Síkinos, Íos, and Thíra; 1 to 3 weekly to Crete (Áyios Nikólaos and Sitía); 1 weekly to Síros, Anáfi, Kássos, Kárpathos, Hálki, and Rhodes (Ródhos). 1 to 3 daily flights to Athens.

KÍMOLOS Daily *kaíki* to Mílos (Pollónia); 2 to 5 weekly to Sífnos, Sérifos, Kíthnos, and Pireás (6 hr.); 1 or 2 weekly to Folégandhros, Síkinos, Íos, and Thíra; 1 weekly to Síros.

ÁNDHROS At least 2 daily to Rafína (2 hr.), Tínos (2 hr.), and Míkonos; 3 weekly to Síros; 1 weekly to Lávrion.

TÍNOS At least 2 daily to Pireás (5 hr.), Rafína (4 hr.), Ándhros, Síros, and Míkonos.

SÍROS At least 2 daily to Pireás (4 hr.), Rafína (3½ hr.), Tínos (1hr), Míkonos (2 hr.), Náxos, and Páros; 4 to 6 weekly to Amorgós and the islets behind Náxos; 3 a week to Íos, Síkinos, Folégandhros, and Thíra; twice weekly to Ikaría, Sámos, and Astipálea; once weekly to Crete (Áyios Nikólaos and Sitía), Mílos, Kímolos, Sérifos, and Kíthnos.

MÍKONOS At least 2 daily to Pireás (5 hr.), Rafína (3½ hr.), Tínos (1 hr.), Ándhros (3½ hr.) and Síros (2hrs); 2 to 7 weekly *kaíkia* to Délos; occasional *kaíkia* in season to Paros. Many flights daily to Athens and 4 times weekly (in season) to Rhodes, Sámos, Thíra, and Irákli; 2 flights a week to Híos.

PÁROS At least daily to Pireás (7 hr.), Rafína (5 hr.), Náxos, Íos, Thíra, and Síros; 3 a week to Amorgós and the islets behind Náxos; 2 a week to Ikaría, Sámos, Síkinos, Folégandhros, Anáfi, and Astipálea; 1 ferry weekly to assorted Dodecanese islands, and Crete (Irákli). Seasonal *kaíkia* to Andíparos, Míkonos, Sífnos (Platís Yialós), and Náxos (Ayía Ánna). Several daily flights to Athens; 3 weekly planes (in season) to Irákli and Rhodes.

NÁXOS At least daily to Pireás (8 hr.), Rafína (6½ hr.), Páros (1 hr.), Síros, Íos, and Thíra; 2 to 4 weekly to Iráklia, Skhinoússa, Koufoníssi, Dhonoússa, and Amorgós; once a week to select Dodecanese, and Crete (Irákli); seasonal *kaíkia* to Páros (Píso Livádhi).

KOUFONÍSSI, SKHINOÚSSA, IRÁKLIA, AND DHONOÚSSA 2 to 4 weekly to Pireás, Náxos, Páros, Síros, Amorgós, and each other; 1 weekly to Astipálea; plus seasonal *kaíki* to Náxos.

AMORGÓS 4 to 6 ferries weekly to Náxos, Páros, and Síros, some of these continuing to Rafína rather than Pireás; 2 to 4 weekly to Koufoníssi, Skhinoússa, Iráklia, and Dhonoússa; 2 weekly to Astipálea; 1 a week to Kálimnos, Kós,

Níssiros, Tílos, and Rhodes; seasonal *kaíki* to Náxos and the minor islets just listed (see text).

ÍOS At least daily to Pireás (10 hr.), Páros (5 hr.), Náxos (3 hr.), Síros, and Thíra (2 hr.); 1 weekly to Crete (Irákli); 2 to 6 weekly to Síkinos and Folégandhros; 1 to 3 weekly to Mílos, Kímolos, Sérifos, Sífnos, and Kíthnos; 1 or 2 a week to Anáfi. Seasonal *kaíkia* to Síkinos, Folégandhros, and Thíra (Skála Firá).

SÍKINOS and FOLÉGANDHROS 2 to 6 weekly to Pireás (10 hr.) Íos, Thíra, and each other; 1 to 3 weekly to Síros, Páros, Náxos, Kíthnos, Sérifos, Sífnos, Mílos, and Kímolos; 1 to 2 weekly to Anáfi; 1 weekly to Crete (Áyios Nikólaos and/or Sitía), Kássos, Kárpathos, and Rhodes; seasonal *kaíkia* to Íos.

THÍRA At least daily to Pireás (10–12hrs), Páros, Íos, and Náxos; 1 to 6 weekly to Irákli, Crete (5 hr.); 3 to 5 weekly to Síkinos and Folégandhros; 2 to 3 weekly to Anáfi; 1 to 3 weekly to Crete (Áyios Nikólaos and Sitía), Kárpathos, Kássos, Hálki, and Rhodes; 2 weekly to Mílos, Kímolos, Sífnos, Sérifos, and Kíthnos; seasonal *kaíkia* to Anáfi and Íos. Flights at least daily to Athens; 3 or 4 weekly (in season) to Rhodes, Míkonos, and Iráklion.

ANÁFI 2 or 3 weekly to Thíra (2 hr.) and Pireás (18 hr.); 1 to 2 weekly to Crete (Áyios Nikólaos and Sitía), Kássos, Kárpathos, Hálki, and Rhodes; 2 a week to Íos, Náxos, Páros; 1 weekly to Síkinos, Folégandhros, Mílos, and Rafína; seasonal *kaíki* to Thíra (Kamári).

'FLYING DOLPHIN' HYDROFOILS There is a service linking Páros, Náxos, Íos, Thíra, and Crete (Irákli or Réthimno) 1 to 4 times weekly in summer only.

AIRPORTS exist on **Míkonos**, **Thíra**, **Páros**, and **Mílos**, listed in decreasing order of flight frequency per day to/from Athens. In season, or during storms when ferries are idle, you have little chance of getting a seat on less than three days' notice. The Mílos–Athens route is probably the best value for money; the other destinations seem deliberately overpriced, in a (usually unsuccessful) attempt to keep passenger volume manageable.

CHAPTER EIGHT

CRETE

Crete is a great deal more than just another Greek island. Often, especially in the cities or along the developed north coast, it doesn't feel like an island at all, but rather a substantial land in its own right. Which of course it is: a mountainous, wealthy and (at times) surprisingly cosmopolitan one. But when you lose yourself among the mountains, or on the less-known coastal reaches of the south, it has everything you could want of a Greek island and besides: great beaches, remote hinterlands, and enormously hospitable people.

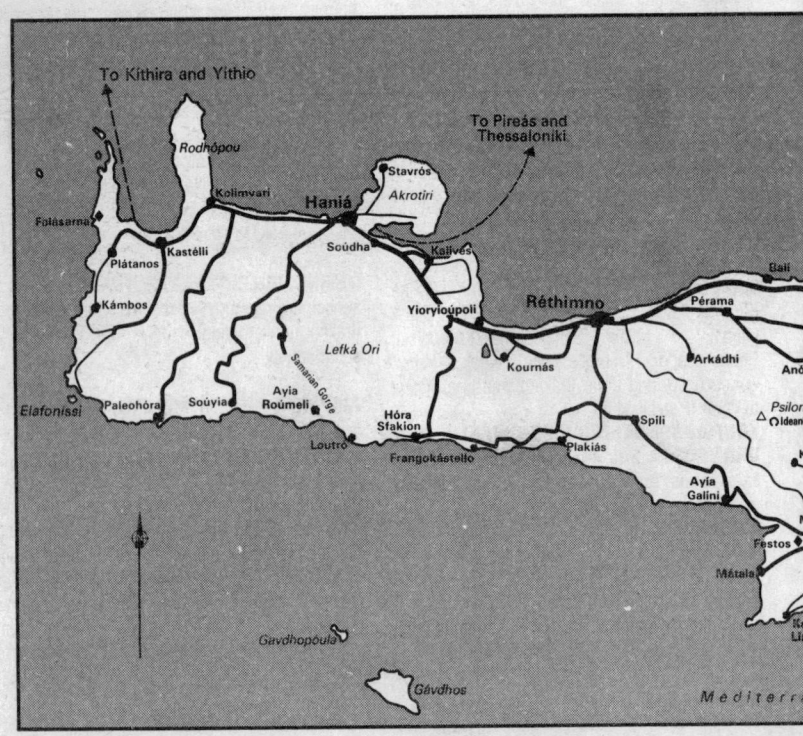

In history Crete is distinguished above all as the home of Europe's earliest civilisation. It was only at the beginning of this century that the legends of King Minos and of a Cretan society which ruled the Greek world in prehistory were confirmed by excavations at Knossos and Festos. Yet the **Minoans** had a remarkably advanced society, the centre of a maritime trading empire as early as 2000 B.C. The artworks produced on Crete at this time are unsurpassed anywhere in the ancient world and it seems clear, wandering through the Minoan palaces and towns, that life on Crete in those days was good. Their peaceful culture survived at least three major natural disasters. Each time the palaces were destroyed, but they were rebuilt on an even grander scale. Only after the last destruction – probably the result of a massive eruption of Thíra (Santoríni) and subsequent tidal waves and earthquakes – do significant numbers of weapons begin to appear in the ruins. This, together with the appearance of the Greek language, has been interpreted to mean that Mycenaean Greeks had taken control of the island. Nevertheless, for nearly 500 years – by far the longest period of peace the island has seen – Crete was home to a culture well ahead of its time.

The Minoans of Crete came originally from Asia Minor; at their height they maintained strong links with Egypt and with the people of Asia Minor,

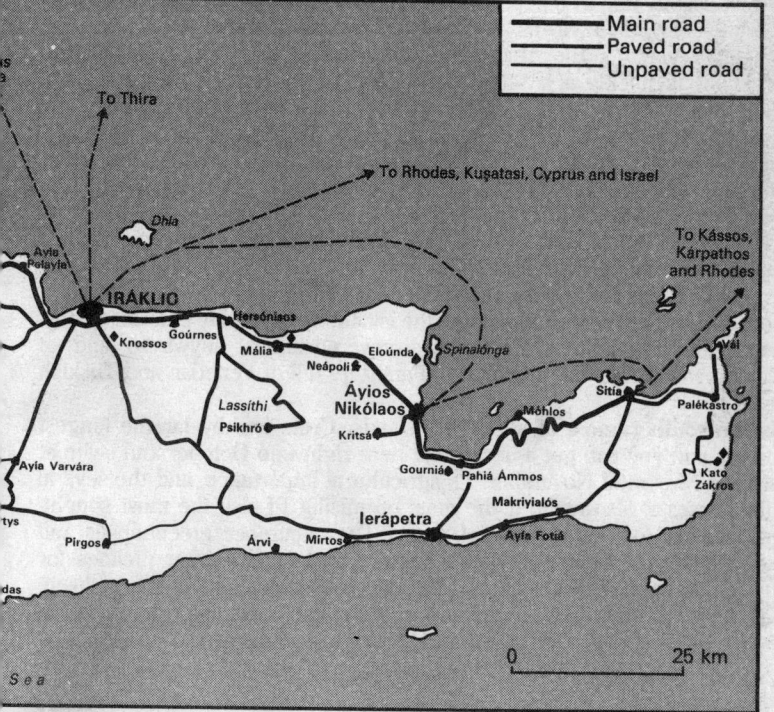

and this position as meeting point – and strategic fulcrum – between east and west has played a major role in Crete's subsequent history. Control of the island passed from Greeks to Romans to Saracens, through the Byzantine Empire to Venice, and finally to Turkey for more than two centuries. During World War II the island was occupied by the Germans and attained the dubious distinction of being the first place to be successfully invaded by paratroops. Each one of these diverse rulers has left some mark on Crete, and more importantly they have forged for the island a personality toughened by endless struggles for independence.

Today, with a flourishing agricultural economy, Crete is one of the few islands which could probably support itself without **tourists**. Nevertheless tourism is heavily promoted. The northeast coast in particular is overdeveloped and, though there are parts of the south and west coasts which have not been spoiled, they are getting harder and harder to find. By contrast, the high mountains of the interior are still barely touched, and one of the best things to do on Crete is to hire a moped and explore the remoter villages, often only a few kilometres off some heavily beaten track.

Every part of Crete has its loyal devotees and it's hard to pick out highlights, but generally if you want to get away from it all you should head west, towards **Haniá** and the smaller, less well-connected places along the south and west coasts. It is in this part of the island also that the White Mountains rise, while below them yawns the famous **Samarian Gorge**.

Whatever you do, the first main priority is to get away from **Iráklio** (Heraklion) as quickly as possible, having paid the obligatory, and rewarding, visit to nearby **Knossos**. The other great Minoan sites cluster around the middle of the island as well: **Festos** and **Ayía Triádha** in the south (with Roman **Gortys** to provide contrast), **Malia** on the north coast. Almost wherever you go, though, you'll find some kind of reminder of the island's history – the town of **Gourniá** near the fleshpots of **Áyios Nikólaos**, the palace of **Zakros** over in the far east, or the lesser sites scattered around the west. For many people, unexpected highlights also turn out to be Crete's Venetian forts, dominant at **Réthimno**, magnificent at **Frangokástello**, and others in various stages of ruin around most of the island; its Byzantine churches, most famously at **Krítsa** but again to be discovered almost anywhere; and, at Réthimno and Haniá, the cluttered old quarters full of Venetian and Turkish relics.

As the southernmost of all Greek islands, Crete has by far the longest summers and you can get a decent tan here right into October and swim at least from May until November. Its agricultural importance, and the several annual harvests, also make it the most promising (if also the most sought-after) location for finding **casual work**. The cucumber greenhouses and pickling factories around Ierápetra have proved to be winter lifelines for many long-term Greek travellers. The one seasonal blight is the *meltémi*, which blows harder here and more continuously than anywhere else in Greece – the best of several reasons for avoiding an **August** visit.

IRÁKLIO, KNOSSÓS AND CENTRAL CRETE

Many visitors to Crete arrive in the island's capital, **Iráklio** (Heraklion), but it's not a beautiful city, nor one where you'll want to stay much longer than it takes to get your bearings and visit the museum and nearby **Knossos**. Iráklio itself, though it has its good points – superb fortifications, a fine market, atmospheric old alleys, and some interesting lesser museums – is for the most part an experience in survival: modern, raucous, traffic-laden, over-crowded and expensive.

The area around the city is less touristy than you might expect, mainly because there are few decent beaches of any size on this central part of the coast. To the west, mountains drop straight into the sea virtually all the way to Réthimno, with just two coastal settlements – **Ayía Pelayía**, a sizeable resort, and **Balí**, which is gradually becoming one. Eastwards the better resorts are at least 40km away, at Hersónissos and beyond, although there is a string of rather half-hearted, unattractive development all the way there. Inland there's agricultural country, the richest on the island, and a series of wealthy but rather dull villages. Directly behind the capital rises Mt. Ioúktas with its characteristic profile of Zeus; to the west the Psilorítis massif spreads around the peak of **Mt. Ída** (Psilorítis), the island's highest. On the south coast there are few roads and little development of any kind, except at **Ayía Galíni** in the southwest, a nominal fishing village long since swamped with tourists, and **Mátala**, which has thrown out the hippies that made it famous and is now crowded with package-trippers. **Léndas** has to some extent occupied Mátala's old niche.

Despite the lack of resorts, there seem constantly to be thousands of people trekking back and forth across the centre of the island. This is largely because of the superb archaeological sites in the south: **Festos**, second of the Minoan palaces, with its attendant villa at **Ayía Triádha**, and **Gortys**, capital of Roman Crete.

Iráklio

The best way to approach **IRÁKLIO** is by sea; that way you see the city as it should be seen, with Ioúktas rising behind and the Psilorítis range to the west. As you get closer it's the city walls which first stand out, still dominating and fully encircling the oldest part of town, and finally you sail in past the great fort defending the harbour entrance. Unfortunately, big ships no longer dock in the old port but at great modern concrete wharves alongside – which neatly sums up Iráklio itself: many of the old parts have been restored from the bottom up, but they're of no relevance to the dust and noise which characterise the city today. These renovations invariably look fake, far too polished and perfect alongside the grime which seems to coat even the most recent new buildings.

From the port the town rises overhead, and you can cut up the stepped alleys for a direct approach to Platía Eleftherías (Liberty Square), the tourist office, and the archaeological museum. The easiest way to the middle of things, though, is to head west along the coast road, past the eastbound bus station, and then up Odhós 25 Avgoústou. Lined with shipping agencies, travel agents and cycle hire places, 25 Avgoústou leads into **Platía Venizélou**. This is crowded with Iráklio's youth, patronising outdoor cafés which are marginally cheaper than those on Eleftherías, and with travellers who've arranged to meet in 'Fountain Square'. The **fountain** itself, built by Venetian governor Francesco Morosini in the seventeenth century and incorporating four lions which were some 300 years old even then, is not particularly spectacular at first glance (especially as it's usually clogged with mud and cigarette ends) but on closer inspection is really a very beautiful work. From the *platía* you can strike up Dedhálou, a pedestrianised street full of tourist shops and restaurants, or continue on 25 Avgoústou to a major traffic junction. To the right, Kalokerinoú leads west out of the city, the **market** lies straight ahead, and Platía Eleftherías is a short walk to the left up Dhikeosínis.

Platía Eleftherías is very much the traditional heart of the city, both in terms of traffic, which swirls around it constantly, and for life in general: lined with expensive cafés and restaurants, and jammed in the evening with strolling hordes. Most of Iráklio's more expensive shops are in the streets leading off the square. The **Archaeological Museum** (open Tues.–Sat. 8am–7pm, Sun. 8am–6pm, closed Mon.) is also just off here, directly opposite the EOT office. Almost every important prehistoric and Minoan find on Crete is included in this fabulous, if bewilderingly large, collection. The museum tends to be crowded – especially when a guided tour stampedes through – but it's worth taking time over. You can't hope to see everything, nor can we attempt to describe it all (several good museum guides are sold here – best is probably the glossy one by J. A. Sakellarakis) but highlights include the town mosaics in Room 2 (galleries are arranged basically in chronological order), the famous inscribed disc from Festos in Room 3 (itself the subject of several books), most of Room 4, especially the magnificent bull's head *rhyton* (drinking vessel), the jewellery in Room 6 (and everywhere), and the engraved black vases in Room 7. Save some of your time and energy for upstairs, too, where the Hall of the Frescoes, with intricately reconstructed fragments of the wall paintings from Knossos and other sites, is especially wonderful.

Of Iráklion's later history, the massive **Venetian walls**, in places up to 45 feet thick, are the most obvious evidence. Though their fabric is incredibly well preserved, access is virtually nonexistent. It is possible – just – to walk on top of them from St. Anthony's bastion over the sea in the west as far as the tomb of Nikos Kazantzakis, Cretan author of *Zorba the Greek*. His epitaph reads 'I believe in nothing, I hope for nothing, I am free'; on weekends Iraklians gather here to pay their respects and get a free view of the soccer matches below.

If the walls seem altogether too much effort, the **port fortifications** are very much easier to see. Stroll out along the jetty (crowded with courting couples after dark) and you can usually get inside the sixteenth-century castle at the harbour entrance, emblazoned with the Venetian Lion of St. Mark. Standing atop this you can begin to understand how Iráklio – or Candia as it was known until the seventeenth century – withstood a 22-year siege before finally falling to the Ottomans. The castle frequently hosts exhibitions which may affect its hours and price, but generally it's open from 9am to 1pm and from 3 to 7pm for a small fee. On the landward side of the port the Venetian *arsenali* can also be seen, their arches rather lost amid the concrete road system all around.

From the harbour, 25 Avgoústou will take you up past most of the rest of what's interesting. The church of **Áyios Títos**, on the left as you approach Platía Venizélou, borders a pleasant little square. It looks magnificent principally because, like most of the churches here, it was adapted by the Turks as a mosque and only reconsecrated in 1925; consequently it has been renovated on numerous occasions. On the top side of this square, abutting 25 Avgoústou, is the Venetian **City Hall** with its famous *loggia*, again almost entirely rebuilt. Just above this, facing Platía Venizélou, is the church of **San Marco**, its steps usually crowded with the overflow of people milling around in the square. Neither of these last two buildings has found a permanent role in its refurbished state, but both are generally open to house some kind of exhibition or craft show.

Finally, slightly away from this circuit but still within the bounds of the walls, there are a couple of lesser museums worth seeing if you have the time. First of these is the collection of **icons** in the church of **Ayía Ekateríni**, an ancient building just below the ugly cathedral, off Kalokerinoú. This is supposedly open from 10.30am to 3.30pm daily except Sunday and additionally on Tuesday, Thursday and Friday afternoons from 4.30 to 6.30pm, but it seems to be one of those places which has always just shut when you get there. If you do get in there's an excellent collection, one which might inspire you to seek out less-known icons in churches around the island. The finest are six large scenes by Mihalis Damaskinos, a near-contemporary of El Greco who fused Byzantine and Renaissance influences. Supposedly both Damaskinos and El Greco studied at Ayía Ekateríni in the sixteenth century when it functioned as a sort of monastic art school.

The **Historical Museum** (open 9am–1pm and 3–5.30pm, daily except Sun.) is some way from here, down near the waterfront next to the westbound bus station. Its display of folk costumes and jumble of local memorabilia includes the reconstructed study of Nikos Kazantakis; there's enough variety to satisfy just about anyone and comic relief in the form of wonderfully nonsensical English labelling.

Iráklio practicalities

Tourist life focuses on the two main squares, Eleftherías and Venizélou, and the alleys between them. This district, crowded with cafés and restaurants, souvenir and jewellery shops, is also where the entire local population turns out in the evenings to parade or to sit and gossip. Lingering here a while over a coffee is irresistible but expensive. For realistic places to stay and to eat you'll need to head to the fringes of this area.

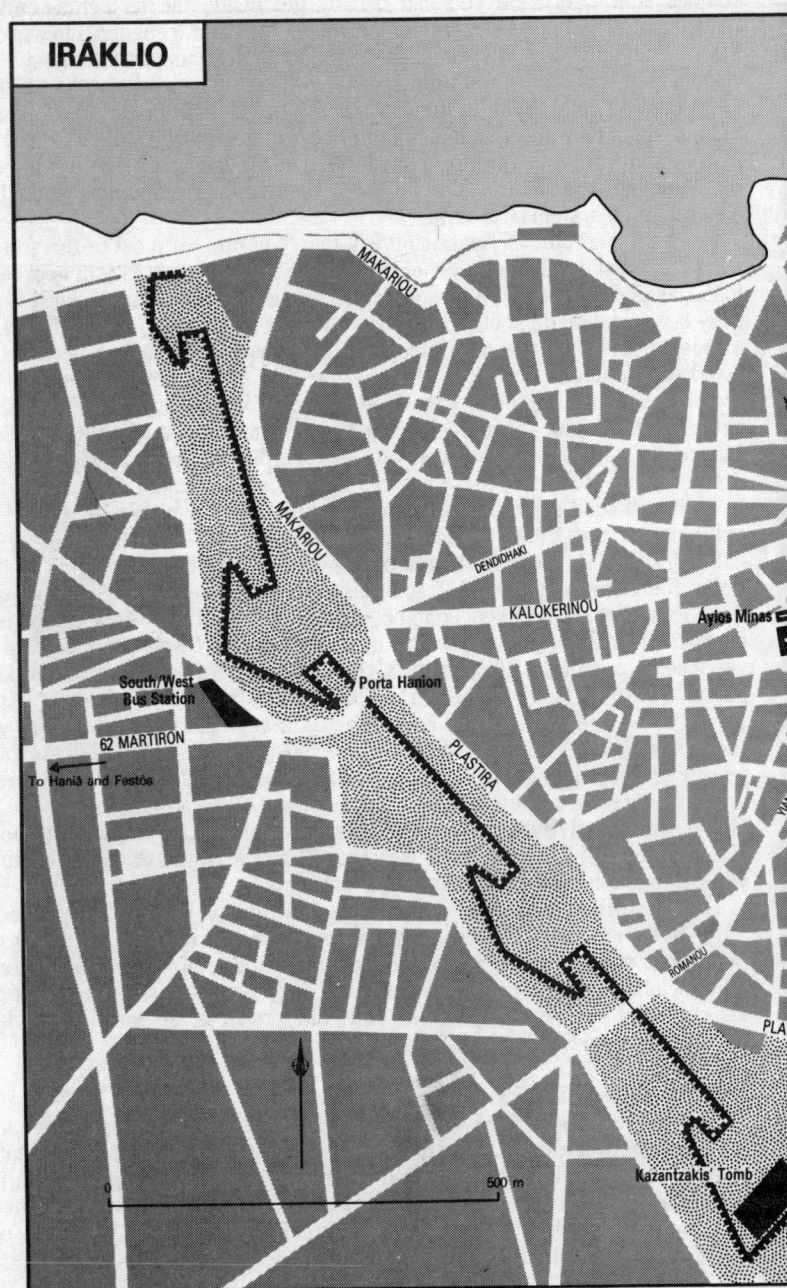

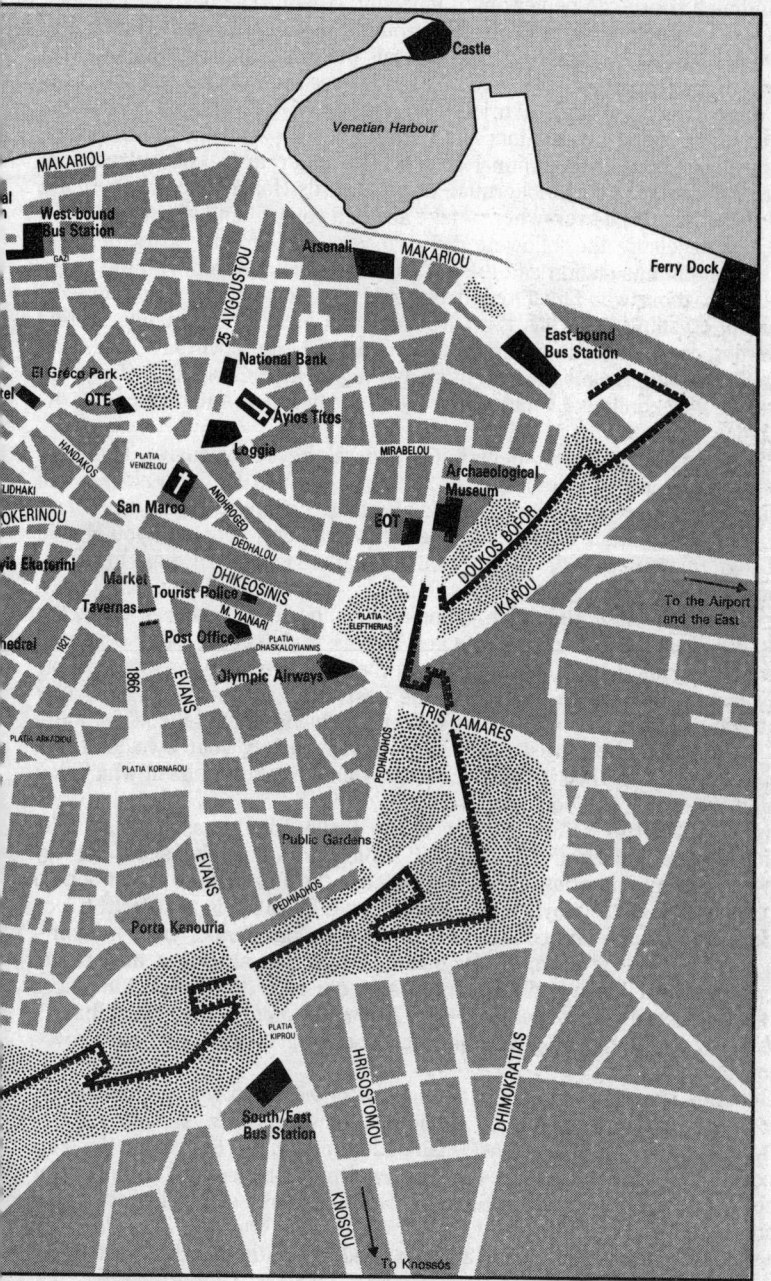

Castle

Venetian Harbour

MAKARIOU

West-bound
Bus Station

Arsenali   MAKARIOU

GAZ

Ferry Dock

25 AVGOUSTOU

East-bound
Bus Station

National Bank

El Greco Park

OTE

Áyios Titos

HANDAKOS

PLATIA
VENIZELOU

Loggia

MIRABELOU

Archaeological
Museum

LIDHAKI

San Marco

ANDROGEO

EOT

DOUKOS BOFOR

OKERINOU

DEDHALOU

ia Ekaterini

DHIKEOSINIS

IKAROU

Market

Tourist Police

Tavernas

M. YIANARI

PLATIA
ELEFTHERIAS

To the Airport
and the East

hedrai

1821

Post Office

PLATIA
DHASKALOYIANNIS

Olympic Airways

1866

EVANS

TRIS KAMARES

PLATIA ARKADIOU

PLATIA KORNAROU

PEDHIADHOS

Public Gardens

EVANS

PEDHIADHOS

Porta Kenouria

HRISOSTOMOU

DHIMOKRATIAS

PLATIA
KIPROU

South/East
Bus Station

KNOSOU

To Knossós

Finding a **room** can be very hard indeed in season. The best place to look is in the area below Platía Venizélou, around the **youth hostel** (Handhákos 24, ☎081/286-281, not the best) and towards the westbound bus station. *Rent Rooms Mary* (Handhákos 48, ☎081/281-135, near the bottom) is good, as is the more expensive and luxurious *Vergina* (☎081/242-739) on Hortátson, closer to the same bus station; *Hotel Hania*, just beyond the youth hostel, offers cheap beds in communal rooms. The other main concentration of affordable rooms is off Kalokerinoú, down towards Haniá Gate but there are odd places scattered everywhere – take any bed you can find when you arrive and look at leisure the following day if necessary. The dusty park between the eastbound bus station and the harbour is always crowded with the sleeping bags of those who failed to find, or couldn't afford, a room; if you're really hard up, crashing here has the advantage that local farmers come around recruiting casual labor in the mornings – but a pleasant environment it's not. Official **camping** means the expensive and regimented *Camping Iráklio*, very large and well-equipped, about 7km west on the beach at Amoudhári (bus #6, see below).

Places to eat are everywhere, but in general they're expensive. There are *souvláki* stalls around the corner of 25 Avgoústou and Platía Venizélou and various other take-out places down Kalokerinoú. For more substantial meals there are few genuine cheapies left downtown, though with care you should find something. Best bet is the alley off the market, leading through to Odhós Evans, which is entirely taken up with tables – the prepared foods are generally not too expensive though anything else can be. The restaurant below the *Hotel Ionia*, on the corner of Evans and Yianári, is also good. Other scattered possibilities include the *Taverna Rizes* at the bottom of Handhákos; a couple of places on the square in front of the post office, and a nameless, partly subterranean taverna on an alley between Dedhálou and Dhikeosínis, more or less opposite the tourist police. If you want to buy your own food, the **Market** on Odhós 1866 is the place to go – an attraction in itself which you should see even if you don't plan to buy.

Iráklio's **Tourist Office** is just below Platía Eleftherías, opposite the archaeological museum. The **Tourist Police** are on Dhikeosínis, halfway between Platía Eleftherías and the market, and the **Post Office** is just behind here, on Platía Dhaskaloyiánnis. The 24-hour **OTE** office is next to El Greco Park, in the square immediately north of Venizélou. **Banks** are common – you can find several down 25 Avgoústou, where the **shipping and travel agents** are. You'll also find **motorbike and car hire** down here, but places off the main road offer better prices; try *Eurocreta/Motospeed* at Hatzidháki 3, just below the archaeological museum. There's a **launderette** close by – follow the signs.

Beaches are some way out, whether east or west of town. In either direction they're easily accessible by public bus, however: #6 west from immediately outside the *Astoria Hotel* (Platía Eleftherías); #1 east from the stop opposite this, under the trees in the centre of the square. Almirós (or Amoudhári) to the west has been subjected to a degree of development – the campsite, several medium-size hotels and one giant one (the *Zeus Beach*, the shadow of the power station at the far end) – and the beach is hard to get to without walking through or past one of these. Amnissós, to the east, seems the better choice, with several tavernas and the added amusement of planes swooping in immediately overhead to land. This is where most locals go on their afternoons off – the farthest of the beaches is the best.

Leaving, **buses** for all points east along the coast road (Malia, Áyios Nikólaos, etc.) leave from the new station by the harbour; west along the main road, to Réthimno and Haniá, from the waterside west of the port, near the *Xenia Hotel*; south and east to Áno Viános, Mírtos and Árvi, from just outside the walls on Platía Kíprou, end of Odhós Evans; southwest to Festos. Mátala, Léndas and Ayía Galíni, or along the old road west, from just outside the Haniá Gate. **For Knossos**, the #2 local bus sets off from the city bus stop (adjacent to the east bus station), runs up 25 Avgoústou (with a stop by Platía Venizélou) and out of town on Odhós 1821 and Evans.

Knossos

The largest of the Minoan palaces, **KNOSSOS** reached its cultural peak over 3000 years ago, though a town of some importance persisted here until well into the Roman era. It lies on a low, largely man-made hill some 5km southeast of Iráklio amid hillsides rich in lesser remains spanning twenty-five centuries, starting at the beginning of the second millenium B.C.

Barely a hundred years ago the palace existed only in mythology. Knossos was the court of the legendary King Minos, whose wife Pasiphae bore the Minotaur: half-bull, half-man. Here the labyrinth was constructed by Daedalus to contain the monster, and youths were brought from Athens as human sacrifice until Theseus arrived to slay the beast, and with Ariadne's help, escape its lair. The discovery of the palace, and the interplay of these legends with fact, is among the most amazing tales of modern archaeology.

Heinrich Schliemann, the excavator of Troy, suspected that a major Minoan palace lay under the various tumuli here but was denied the necessary permission to dig by the local Ottoman authorities at the end of the last century. It remained for Sir Arthur Evans, whose name is indelibly associated with the site, to do so , from 1900 onwards.

The Site
Weekdays 8am–7pm, Sun. 8am–6pm.
As soon as you enter the **palace of Knossos** through the West Court, the ancient ceremonial entrance, it is clear how the legends of the labyrinth grew up around it. Even with a detailed plan, it's almost impossible to find your way around the site with any success. My advice is not to try – wander around for long enough and you'll eventually stumble upon everything. If you're worried about missing the highlights you can always tag along with one of the constant guided tours for a while, catching the patter and then backtracking to absorb the detail when that particular crowd has moved on. You won't get the place to yourself – whenever you come – but exploring on your own does give you the opportunity to appreciate individual parts of the palace in the brief lulls between groups.

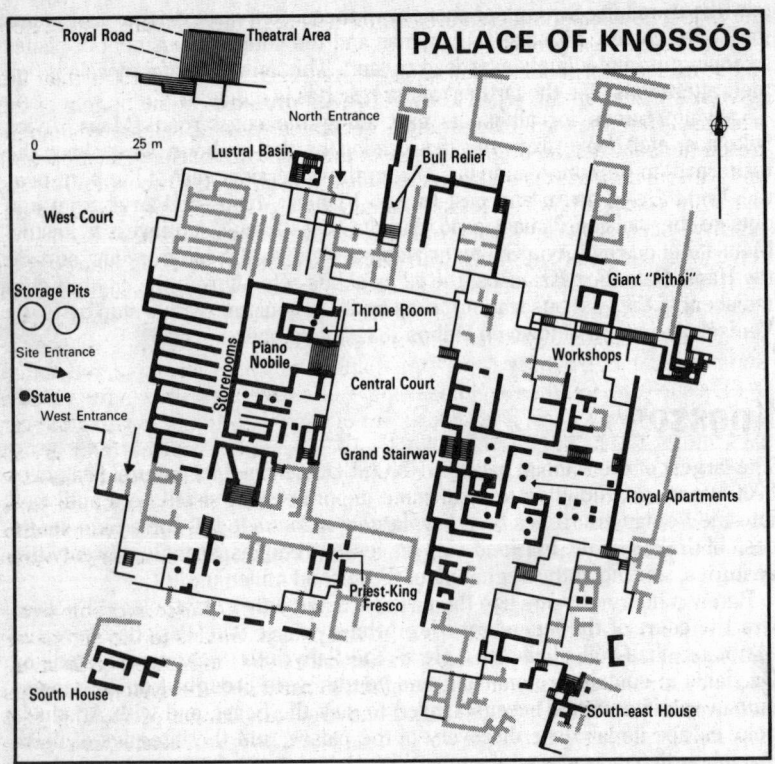

Knossos was liberally 'restored' by Evans, and these restorations have been the source of furious controversy among archaeologists ever since. It has become clear that much of Evans's upper level – the so-called *Piano Nobile* – is pure conjecture. Even so, his guess as to what the palace might have looked like is certainly as good as anyone else's, and it makes the other sites infinitely more meaningful if you have seen Knossos first. Without the restorations, it would be almost impossible to imagine the grandeur of the multi-storey palace or to see the ceremonial stairways, strange, top-heavy pillars and gaily painted walls which distinguish the site. For some idea of the size and complexity of the palace in its original state, take a look at the cutaway drawings (wholly imaginary but probably not too far off) on sale outside.

The superb **royal apartments** around the central staircase are not guess-work, and they are plainly the finest of the rooms at Knossos. The **stairway** itself is a masterpiece of design: not only a fitting approach to these sumptu-ously appointed chambers but also an integral part of the whole plan, its large well bringing light into the lower storeys. Light wells such as these, usually with a courtyard at the bottom, are a constant feature of Knossos and a reminder of just how important creature comforts were to the Minoans, and of how skilled they were at providing them.

For evidence of this luxurious lifestyle you need look no further than the **Queen's Suite**, off the grand **Hall of the Colonnades** at the bottom of the staircase. Here the main living room is decorated with the celebrated dolphin fresco (a duplicate; the original is now in the Iráklio archaeological museum) and with running friezes of flowers and abstract spirals. On two sides it opens out on to courtyards which let in light and air; the smaller one would probably have been planted with flowers. In use, the room would have been scattered with cushions and hung with plush curtains, while doors and further curtains between the pillars would have allowed for privacy, and for cool shade in the heat of the day. This, at least, is what they'd have you believe, and it's a very plausible scenario. Remember, though, that all this is speculation and some of it is pure hype – the dolphin fresco, for example, was found in the courtyard, not the room itself, and would have been viewed from inside as a sort of *trompe l'oeil*, like looking out of a glass-bottomed boat. Whatever the truth, this is an impressive example of Minoan architecture – the more so when you follow the dark passage around to the Queen's **bathroom**, its clay tub protected behind a low wall (and again probably screened by curtains when in use), and to the famous 'flushing' toilet (a hole in the ground with drains to take the waste away – one flushed it by throwing a bucket of water down).

The celebrated **drainage system** was a series of interconnecting terracotta pipes running underneath most of the palace. Guides to the site never fail to point these out as evidence of the advanced state of Minoan civilisation, and they are indeed quite an achievement, in particular the system of baffles and overflows to slow down the runoff and avoid any danger of flooding. Just how much running water there would have been, however, is another matter; the water supply was, and is, at the *bottom* of the hill, and even the combined efforts of rainwater catchment and hauling water up to the palace can hardly have been sufficient to supply the needs of more than a small elite.

Going up the Grand Staircase to the floor above the Queen's domain, you come to a set of rooms generally regarded as the **King's quarters**. These are chambers in a considerably sterner vein; the staircase opens into a grandiose reception chamber known as the **Hall of the Royal Guard**, its walls decorated in repeated shield patterns. Immediately off here is the **Hall of the Double Axes**, believed to be have been the ruler's personal chamber – a double room which would allow for privacy in one portion while audiences were held in the more public section. Its name comes from the double-axe symbol carved into every block of masonry.

Continuing to the top of the grand staircase you emerge on to the broad **Central Court**. Open now, this would once have been enclosed by the walls of the buildings all around. On the far side, in the northwestern corner of the courtyard, is the entrance to another of Knossos's most atmospheric survivals, the **Throne Room**. Here a worn stone throne sits against the wall of a surprisingly small chamber; along the walls around it are ranged stone benches and behind there's a reconstructed fresco of two griffins. In all probability this was the seat of a priestess rather than a ruler – there's nothing like it in any other Minoan palace – but it may just have been an innovation wrought by the Mycenaeans, since it appears that this room dates only from the final period of Knossos's occupation. The weight of visitors has meant that the Throne Room itself is now closed off with a wooden gate, but you can lean over this for a good view, and in the antechamber there's a wooden copy of the throne on which everyone perches to have their picture taken.

The rest you'll see as you wander, contemplating the legends of the place which blur with reality. Try not to miss the giant *pithoi* in the northeast quadrant of the site, an area known as the palace workshops; the storage chambers which you see from behind the Throne Room and the reproduction frescoes in the reconstructed room above it; the Fresco of the Priest-King looking down on the south side of the Central Court; and the relief of a charging bull on its north side. This last would have greeted you if you entered the palace through its north door – here you can see evidence of some kind of gate house and a lustral bath, a sunken area perhaps used for ceremonial bathing and purification. Just outside this gate is the **theatral area** – an open space a little like a stepped amphitheatre which may have been used for ritual performances or dances – and from here the **Royal Road** sets out. Once this probably ran right across the island; nowadays it ends after about a hundred yards in a brick wall beneath the modern road. Circling back around the outside of the palace you get more idea of its scale by looking up at it; on the south side are a couple of small reconstructed Minoan houses worth exploring.

Across a little valley from here, outside the fenced site, is the **Caravanserai** where ancient wayfarers would rest and water their animals. Head out onto the road and you'll find no lack of watering holes for modern travellers either – a string of rather pricey tavernas and tacky souvenir stands. There are several **rooms** places here too, and if you're really into Minoan culture there's a lot to be said for staying out this way to get an early start. Be warned that it's expensive and unashamedly commercial, though.

South: Gortys, Festos and Ayía Triádha

Heading south from Iráklio, the road towards Festos is a pretty good one by the standards of Cretan mountain roads, albeit a dull one too. The country you're heading toward is the richest agricultural land on the island, and right from the start the villages en route are large and businesslike. In the largest of them, AYÍA VARVÁRA, there's a great rock outcrop known as the *Omphalos* (Navel) of Crete, supposed to be the very centre of the island. Past here you descend rapidly to the fertile fields of the Messará plain, where the road joins the main route across the south near the village of ÁYII DHÉKA.

For religious Cretans Áyii Dhéka is something of a place of pilgrimage; its name, 'The Ten Saints', refers to ten early Christians martyred here under the Romans. In a crypt below the modern church you can see the martyrs' tombs, and it's an attractive village to wander around, with several places to eat and even some rooms along the main road. Within easy walking distance, either through the fields or along the main road, sprawls the site of **GORTYS**

(Mon.–Sat. 8am–7pm, Sun. 8am–6pm), ruined capital of the Roman province which included not only Crete but also much of North Africa. Cutting across the fields will give you some idea of the scale of this city at its zenith, approximately the third century A.D.; an enormous variety of other remains, including an impressive theatre, are strewn across your route. Even in Áyii Dhéka itself you'll see Roman pillars and statues lying around in peoples' yards or propping up their walls.

There had been settlement here from the earliest times, but what you find now – and the site has never been systematically excavated – dates almost entirely from the Roman era. At the main entrance to the fenced site, alongside the road, is the ruinous but still impressive basilica of **Áyios Títos**, the saint who converted Crete and was also its first bishop. Beyond this is the *Odeion* which houses the most important discovery on the site, the **Law Code**. These great inscribed blocks of stone were incorporated by the Romans from a much earlier stage of the city's development; they're written in an obscure early Greek/Cretan dialect, and in a style known as *boustrophedon* (ox-plowed), with the lines reading alternately in opposite directions like the furrows of a plowed field. About thirty feet by ten feet in all, this is reputedly the largest Greek inscription ever found. The laws set forth reflect a strictly hierarchical society: five witnesses were needed to convict a free man of a crime, only one for a slave; raping a free man or woman carried a fine of a hundred staters, violating a serf only five.

Some 20km west of Gortys, **MÍRES** is an important market and focal point of transport for the Messará plain – if you're switching buses to get from the beaches on the south coast to the archaeological sites or the west, this is where you'll do it. There are good facilities including a bank, lots of restaurants and plenty of rooms, though there's no particular reason to stay unless you are waiting for a bus or looking for work (it's one of the better places for agricultural jobs). Heading straight for Festos, there's usually no need to stop.

Festos

Open Mon.–Sat. 8am–7pm, Sun. 9am–6pm in season; 10am–4pm and 9am–2pm respectively out of season.

Despite its magnificent setting overlooking the plain of Messará, the palace at **FESTOS** is not as arresting as those at Knossos or Malia. Much of the site is fenced off, and except in the huge central court it is almost impossible to get any sense of the palace as it was; the plan is almost as complex as at Knossos, with none of the reconstruction to bolster the imagination. It's interesting to speculate why the palace was built halfway up a hill rather than on the plain below; certainly not for defence, for this is in no way a good defensive position. Psychological superiority over the peasants or reasons of health are both possible, but it seems quite likely that it was simply the magnificent view – over Psilorítis to the north and the huge plain with the Lassíthi mountains beyond it to the east – which finally swayed the decision. Towards the top of Psilorítis you should be able to make out a small black smudge: the entrance to the Kamáres Cave.

On the ground closer at hand, you can hardly fail to notice the strong similarities between Festos and the other palaces: the same huge rows of storage jars, the great courtyard with its monumental stairway, and the theatral area. Unique to Festos, however, is the third courtyard, in the middle of which are the remains of a furnace used for metalworking. Indeed, this eastern corner of the palace seems to have been home to a number of craftsmen, including potters and carpenters. Oddly enough, Festos was much less ornately decorated than Knossos; there is no evidence, for example, of any of the dramatic Minoan wall paintings.

Ayía Triádha

Open Mon.–Sat. 8.45am–3pm, Sun. 9.30am–2.30pm; closed Fri.

By contrast, some of the finest artworks in the museum at Iráklio came from **AYÍA TRIÁDHA**, less than an hour's walk away. No one is quite sure what this site is, but the most common theory has it as some kind of royal summer villa – smaller than the palaces, but if anything even more lavishly appointed and beautifully situated. In any event it's an attractive place to visit, far less crowded than Festos, with a wealth of interesting little details. Look out in particular for the row of shops in front of what was apparently a marketplace, and for the remains of the paved road which once led down to the Gulf of Messará. The sea itself looks invitingly close, separated from the base of the hill only by Timbáki airfield (mainly used for motor racing these days), but if you try to drive down there it's almost impossible to find your way around the unmarked dust tracks. There's a fourteenth-century church at the site too, worth visiting in its own right for the remains of ancient frescoes.

Practicalities

Take a tour from Iráklio and you'll probably visit all three of these sites in a day and have a lunchtime swim at Mátala thrown in. Doing it by public transport you'll be forced into a rather more leisurely pace, but there's still no reason why you shouldn't get to all three sites and reach Mátala within the day; if necessary it is easy enough to hitch the final stretch. To continue almost anywhere else you'll need to return to Míres first, and possibly spend the night there.

Mátala to Léndas: Iráklio's south coast

MÁTALA is by far the best known of the beaches in Iráklio province, widely promoted and included in tours mainly because of the famous caves cut into the cliffs above its beautiful beach. These ancient tombs used to be almost permanently inhabited by a sizeable hippie community, and you'll still meet people who will assure you that this is *the* travellers' beach on Crete. Not any more it isn't. Nowadays the town is full of package tourists and tries hard to present a respectable image; the cliffs are now cleared and locked up every evening.

A few people still manage to evade the security, or sleep on the beach or in the adjacent campsite, but on the whole the place has changed entirely. The last ten years have seen the arrival of crowds and the development of hotels, discos and restaurants to service them; early afternoon, when the tour buses pull in for their swimming stop, sees the beach packed to overflowing. All of which is not to knock Mátala too much – as long as you're prepared to accept it for what it is, a resort of some size, you'll find the place more than bearable. If the crowds on the town beach get too much, you can climb over the rocks in about twenty minutes (past more caves, many of which *are* inhabited through the summer) to another excellent stretch of sand, known locally as 'Red Beach'. And in the evening, when the trippers have gone, there are some excellent waterside bars and restaurants looking out over invariably spectacular sunsets.

The chief remaining problem concerns prices: rooms are both expensive and oversubscribed, food is good but also not cheap. One way of saving some money and also enjoying a bit more peace is to stay at **PITSÍDHIA** about 5km inland. This is already a well-used option so it's not quite as cheap as you might expect, but there are plenty of rooms, lively places to eat and an affable, young, international crowd. The beach at KALAMÁKI is a good alternative to Mátala if you're staying here: approximately the same distance to walk, though with far less chance of a bus or a lift. Kalamáki itself is beginning to develop somewhat, with a number of rooms and a couple of tavernas, but so far it's a messy and unattractive little place. The beach stretches for miles, surprisingly wild and windswept, lashed by sometimes dangerously rough surf. At the southern end (easier reached by a path off the Pitsídhia–Mátala road) lies KÓMOS, once a Minoan port serving Festos and now the site of a major archaeological excavation. As yet there's not a great deal to be seen, but this is another good beach.

Mátala itself was an important port under the Romans, but the chief harbour for Gortys lay on the other side of Cape Líthinon at **KALÍ LIMÉNES**. Nowadays this is once again a major port – for oil tankers. This has rather spoiled its chances of becoming a major resort, especially when aggravated by the lack of a paved road and proper facilities. Some people like Kalí Liménes: the constant procession of tankers gives you something to look at, there's one very luxurious and not outrageously expensive place offering rooms (about a mile from the village), the coastline is broken up by spectacular cliffs, and as long as there hasn't been a recent oil spill the beaches are reasonably clean and totally empty. But (fortunately) not too many share this enthusiasm.

LÉNDAS, further east along the coast, is far more popular, with a couple of buses daily from Iráklio and a partly justified reputation for being peaceful (sullied by considerable summer crowds). Many people who arrive think they've come to the wrong place: the village at first looks filthy; the beach is small, rocky and dirty, and the rooms are frequently all booked. A number of visitors leave without ever correcting that first impression, for the real attraction of Léndas is not here at all but beyond the point to the west, 2km or so along the coast road. Here there's an enormous, excellent sandy beach, part of it usually taken over by nudists, and a couple of good taverna/bars overlooking it from the roadside. Camping on this beach, or with luck getting one of the few rooms at the tavernas, is a considerably more attractive prospect than staying in the village, though after you've discovered the beach even Léndas itself begins to look more welcoming. At least it has most of the facilities you'll need, including a shop which will change money and numerous places to eat. After you've come to terms with the place you can also explore some less good but quite deserted beaches eastwards, and the scrappy remains of ancient LEVIN by the church. There was an *Asclepion* here around some now-diverted warm springs, but only the odd broken column and fragments of mosaic survive.

If you have your own transport, the roads in these parts are all passable but most are very slow going – there's a line of precipitous hills between the Messará plain and the coast. Along the coast between Léndas and Kalí Liménes there are numerous other little beaches, though nothing spectacular. Public transport is very limited indeed; you'll almost always have to travel via Míres.

East of Iráklio: the package-tour coast

East of Iráklio the startling pace of tourist development in Crete is all too plain to see. The merest hint of a beach is an excuse to build at least one hotel, and these are outnumbered by the concrete shells of resorts-to-be. It's hard to find a room in this monument to the package tour, and expensive if you do. At the city beach of **AMNISSÓS** (#1 bus from Platía Eleftherías) little remains to indicate the once-flourishing port of Knossos aside from a rather dull, fenced-in dig. Nowadays the long stretch of sand is strewn with tourists and litter, but for a day out from Iráklion it's not bad. The taverna is friendly, a campsite offers basic facilities, and no one will object if you sleep on the beach. If you're seriously into antiquities you'll find a more rewarding site in the small villa at Háni Kokkíni, the first of the full-blown resort developments.

As a general rule, the further you go, the better things get: when the road detours all-too-briefly inland, the real Crete – olive groves and stark mountains – asserts itself. You certainly won't see much of it at **GOÚRNES**, where a U.S. Air Force base has been established for years, its aircraft buzzing the beaches for miles around. Not far beyond it is the turning for the direct route up to the Lassíthi plateau, and shortly after that you roll into the first of the really big resorts, **HERSÓNISSOS** (or, more correctly, Límin Hersoníssou; Hersónissos is the attractive village in the hills just behind). If you wanted to stay in a big resort you could do a lot worse than this; there's plenty of nightlife, enough restaurants to keep prices down, and not bad beaches (the Gulf of Malia generally has some of the island's biggest, sandiest ones, all highly developed unfortunately) – but the one thing you won't find is a cheap room. While you're here, take a look at the restored Roman fountain overlooking the sea – sole evidence of the ancient town of Chersonesos.

Without pre-reserved accommodation you'd probably be better off at the still more popular resort of **MÁLIA**, large enough to be a substantial town in its own right. It's very commercial, and the long sandy beach becomes extremely crowded at times, but it's fun if you're prepared to enter into the sybaritic spirit of things. There are dunes at the end of the beach where people sleep out and two campsites. One is just off the beach, the other at the **youth hostel** about fifteen minutes' walk inland. The cheapest rooms are also around the hostel, on the landward side of the main road east of the post office, though the hostel itself is almost impossible to find without detailed directions from someone who is already staying there.

Beyond Mália it's not long before the road leaves the coast, heading across the hills towards Áyios Nikólaos. If you want to escape the frenetic pace of all that has gone before, try continuing to SÍSSI. This little shore village is bypassed by the main road as it cuts inland, and so far has seen only the beginnings of a tourist industry; there are a few villa/apartments, a campsite and a couple of tavernas. It's not much of a beach, but it makes for a refreshing change of pace. On the way you'll have passed Mália's Minoan palace.

The Palace of Malia
Open 8.45am–3pm except Sun.

The archaeological site lies forty minutes' walk east of Malia town on the main road. Any bus will stop, or hire a bike for a couple of hours – it's a pleasant, flat ride. Much less imposing than either Knossos or Festos, Malia in some ways surpasses both. For a start, it's a great deal emptier and you can wander among the remains in relative peace. And while no reconstruction has been attempted, the palace was never reoccupied after its second destruction, so the ground plan is virtually intact. It's a great deal easier to comprehend than Knossos, and if you've seen the reconstructions there, it's easy to envisage this seaside palace in its days of glory. There's a real feeling of an ancient civilisation with a taste for the good life, basking on the rich agricultural plain between the Lassíthi Mountains and the sea.

From this site came the famous gold pendant of two bees (which can be seen in the Iráklio museum or on any postcard stand), allegedly part of a horde which was plundered and whose other treasures can now be found in the British Museum. The beautiful leopard's-head axe, also in the museum at Iráklio, was another of the treasures found here. At the site, look out for the strange indented stone in the central court, which probably held ritual offerings; for the remains of ceremonial stairways; and for the giant *pithoi* which stand like sentinels around the palace. To the south and east, digs are still going on as a large town comes slowly to light.

Leaving the archaeological zone, you can follow the dirt track which runs around it to a lovely stretch of deserted sand. There's a makeshift taverna here, and usually a couple of camper-vans parked, but considering its position it's an amazingly little-visited patch of beach. Moving on, you should again have no difficulty flagging down a bus headed towards Áyios Nikólaos.

West of Iráklio: around Psilorítis

Most people heading west from Iráklio speed straight out on the new coastal highway, non-stop to Réthimno. If you're in a hurry this is not such a bad plan; the road is fast and spectacular, hacked into the sides of mountains which for the most part drop straight to the sea. On the other hand there are no more than a couple of places where you might consider stopping. By contrast the old roads inland are agonizingly slow, but they do pass through a whole string of attractive villages beneath the heights of the Psilorítis range. From here you can set out to explore the mountains and even walk across them to emerge in villages with views of the south coast.

Leaving the city, the **new road** runs at first some distance behind a stretch of highly developed coast, where the hotels compete for shore space with a cement works and power station. As soon as you hit the mountains, though, all this is left behind and there's only the clash of rock and sea to contemplate. Look out as you start to climb for the castle of Paleókastro, beside a bridge which carries the road over a small cove – it is so weathered as to be almost invisible against the brownish face of the cliff. Some 3km below the road, as it rounds the first point, lies the resort of **AYÍA PELAYÍA**. It looks extremely attractive from above – as indeed it is close up – but it is also very commercial and chi-chi: not somewhere to roll up without a reserved room, though out of season you might find a real bargain at an apartment.

Not far beyond there's a turning inland to the village of **FÓDHELE**, allegedly El Greco's birthplace. A plaque from the University of Toledo acknowledges the claim and, true or not, the community has built a small tourist industry on that basis. There are a number of craft shops and some pleasant tavernas where you can sit outside along the river: there's also 'El Greco's house' and a picturesque Byzantine church. None of this amounts to very much but it is a pleasant, relatively unspoiled village if you simply want to sit in peace for a while.

BALÍ, on the coast approximately halfway between Iráklio and Réthimno, also used to be tranquil and undeveloped, and by the standards of this north coast it still is in many ways. The village is built around a couple of small coves some 2km from the main road (a hot walk from the bus), similar to Ayía Pelayía except that the beaches are not quite as good and there are no big hotels. There are, however, plenty of rooms – more every month it seems – and a number of what the brochures no doubt describe as 'modest hotels'. You'll have plenty of company. Nevertheless, this remains one of the best places to stay in the north, with calm swimming in magnificently clear water and reasonable prices for rooms and food. The last and best beach here (follow the signs to 'Paradise') always used to be nudist; whether this will last now that there are rooms to let in a modern building alongside its taverna remains to be seen.

Of the **inland routes** the old main road (via Márathos and Dhamásta) is not the most interesting. This too was something of a bypass in its day and there are few places of any size or appeal, though it's a very scenic drive. If you want to dawdle you're better off on the road which cuts up to Tílissos and then goes via Anóyia. **TÍLISSOS** itself has a significant archaeological site where three Minoan houses were excavated (open Mon.–Sat. 8.45am–3pm,

Sun. 9.30am–2.30pm); unfortunately its reputation is based more on what was found here (many pieces in the Iráklio museum) and on its significance for archaeologists (as a rare glimpse of Minoan life outside the palaces) than on anything which remains to be seen. It deserves at most a quick visit.

ANÓYIA on the other hand is somewhere you might well be tempted to stay, especially if the summer heat is becoming oppressive. Spilling prettily down a hillside close below the highest peaks of the mountains it looks traditional, but closer inspection shows that most of the buildings are actually concrete; the village was destroyed during the war as one of the German reprisals for the abduction of General Kreipe. The reputation which the place has as a handicrafts centre (especially for woven and woollen goods) is at least in part a reflection of the same history – both a conscious attempt to revive the town and the result of grim necessity with so large a proportion of the local men killed. At any rate it worked, for the place is thriving today, thanks at least partly, it seems, to the number of elderly widows keen to subject any visitor to their terrifyingly aggressive sales techniques.

Quite a few people pass through Anóyia during the day but not many of them stay; it shouldn't be hard to find a room in the upper half of town. On the other hand there's almost nowhere to eat: one taverna on the main road where it loops out of the lower village, and a *souvláki* place near the top of the town, neither of which seem to serve anything other than the barbecued lamb which is a local speciality. Vegetarians are advised to buy their own bread and cheese (local cheese is also excellent).

Heading for the mountains, a rough track leads 13km from Anóyia to the Nídha plateau at the base of **Mt. Psilorítis**. Here there's a taverna which used to let rooms but seems now to have been closed to the public altogether, though it is still used by groups of climbers. A short path leads from the taverna to the celebrated Idean Cave (*Idhéon Ándron*), a rival of that on Mt. Dhíkti (p.440) for the title of Zeus's birthplace and certainly associated from the earliest times with the cult of Zeus. Unfortunately for visitors there's now a major new archaeological dig going on inside, which means the whole cave is fenced off, with a miniature railway running into it to carry all the rubble out. In short you can see nothing. The taverna also marks the start of the way to the top of Crete's highest mountain, a climb which is not for the unwary but which for experienced, properly shod hikers is not at all arduous. The route is well-marked with the usual red dots and it should be a six-to-seven-hour round-trip to the chapel at the summit – though in spring thick snow may slow you down.

If you're prepared to camp on the plateau (plenty water but plenty cold too) or can prevail on the taverna to let you in, you could continue on foot next day down to the southern slopes of the range. This is a beautiful hike – at least while the road they're attempting to blast through here is out of sight – and it's also a relatively easy one, four hours or so down a fairly clear path to VORÍZIA, where you can pick up buses again. If you're still interested in caves there's a more rewarding one above the nearby village of **KAMÁRES**, a climb this time of some three hours on a good path. Kamáres has a few rooms and some tavernas, at least one daily bus down to Míres, and an alternate (more difficult) route to the peak of Psilorítis if you want to approach from this direction.

THE EAST

Eastern Crete is dominated by Áyios Nikólaos and its mass tourism; among most Crete aficionados it has a poor reputation. Yet, though you won't want to stay for long in this highly developed resort, but by no means all of the east is like this. Beyond the isthmus and the road south to Ierápetra far fewer people venture, and only Sitía and the famous beach at Vái ever see anything approaching a crowd. Inland too there's interest, especially on the extraordinary Lassíthi plateau – worth a night's stay if only to catch its abidingly rural life.

Neápoli and the Lassíthi plateau

Leaving the palace at Malia, the main road cuts inland towards Neápoli, soon beginning a spectacular climb into the mountains. Set in a high valley, **NEÁPOLI** is a market town little touched by tourism. There is one hotel, a modern church and a tiny museum which rarely opens (but will usually do so on request). Beyond the town it is about twenty minutes before the bus suddenly emerges high above the Gulf of Mirabéllo and Áyios Nikólaos, the island's biggest resort. If you're stopping, Neápoli also marks the second point of access to the **LASSÍTHI PLATEAU**.

Scores of coach tours drive up here daily to view the 'thousands of white-cloth-sailed windmills' which irrigate the high plain, though most groups are disappointed – there are very few working windmills left, and these operate only for limited periods (mainly in June). This is not to say the trip is not justified – it would be for the drive alone – and there are a great many other compensations. The plain itself is a fine example of rural Crete at work, every inch devoted to the cultivation of potatoes, apples, pears, figs, olives and a host of other crops; stay in one of the villages for a night or two and you'll see real life return as the tourists leave. There are plenty of easy rambles around the villages as well, through orchards and past the rusting remains of derelict windmills. You'll find rooms in **TZERMIÁDHON**, the main town, **ÁYIOS KONSTANTÍNOS**, **ÁYIOS YIÓRYIOS** (where there's an entertaining folk museum) and at PSIKHRÓ.

PSIKHRÓ is the base for visiting Lassíthi's other chief attraction, the **Diktean Cave**, birthplace of Zeus. In legend, Zeus's father Kronos was warned that he would be overthrown by a son and accordingly ate all his offspring; on this occasion, however, Rhea, having given birth in the cave, fed Kronos a stone and left the child concealed, protected by the Kouretes who beat their shields outside to disguise his cries. The rest, as they say, is history (or at least myth). There's an obvious path running up to the cave from Psikhró and, whatever you're told, you don't have to have a guide if you don't want one, though you will need some form of illumination. On the other hand it is hard to resist the guides (they're not expensive if you can get a small group together), and much more interesting to go with one. It takes a Cretan imagination to pick out Rhea and the baby Zeus from the lesser stalactites and stalagmites.

Buses run around the plateau to Psikhró direct from Iráklio and from Áyios Nikólaos via Neápoli. Both roads offer spectacular views, coiling through a succession of passes guarded by lines of ruined windmills.

Áyios Nikólaos, Eloúnda and Spinalónga

ÁYIOS NIKÓLAOS ('Ag. Nik'. to the majority of its British visitors) is set around a supposedly bottomless salt lake, now connected to the sea to form an inner harbour. It is supremely picturesque, and exploits this to the full. The lake and port are surrounded by restaurants and bars, all charging well above normal, and the town itself is permanently crammed with tourists, some distinctly surprised to find themselves in a place with no decent beach at all. If you're after clubs, crowds and expensive souvenirs, this is the place for you (likewise if you want to buy foreign newspapers, phone home, practise your English, or catch a bus to almost anywhere in the east).

Finding a cheap **room** however – finding any room for that matter – is virtually impossible in mid-season. Most central, and perhaps your best chance, is the **youth hostel** at Stratigoú Koráka 3, one of the alleys immediately northeast of the lake, between it and the harbour. If you fail here walk up the hill on one of the roads leading out of town and try in all the side streets. There's also a collection of somewhat rundown places on the other side of town near the bus station. The occasional masochist sleeps on the stoney beach right in front of the terminal – but it's not to be advised. Much better, if you're looking to camp, to head southeast for the sandy coves at KALÓ HORIÓ (about 12km) or PAHIÁ ÁMMOS (20km).

The riviera set hangs out the other way, along the coast road to the north, where the hotels come with bungalows, pools, private beaches and five-star cuisine. Between them are scattered cocktail bars – all soft lighting and tinkling pianos – and upmarket discos. **ELOÚNDA**, a resort on a more acceptable scale, is about 8km out along this road. Buses run regularly, but if you feel like hiring a moped it is a spectacular ride, with impeccable views over a gulf dotted with islands and moored supertankers. Just before the village a track (signposted) leads across a causeway to the 'sunken city' of **Olous**. There are restored windmills, Venetian salt pans and a well-preserved dolphin mosaic, but of the sunken city itself no trace beyond a couple of walls in about two feet of water. At any rate swimming is good.

From Eloúnda Kaíkia run to the fortress-rock of **SPINALÓNGA**. As a bastion of the Venetian defence, this tiny islet withstood the Turkish invaders for 45 years after the mainland had fallen; in more recent decades it served as a leper colony. As you watch the boat which brought you disappear to pick up another group, an unnervingly real sense of the desolation of those years descends over the place. **PLÁKA**, back on the mainland, used to be the colony's supply point; now it is a haven from the crowds, with a small pebble beach and a couple of ramshackle tavernas. There are boat trips daily from Áyios Nikólaos to Oloús, Eloúnda and Spinalónga, usually visiting at least one other island along the way.

The other excursion everyone from Áyios Nikólaos takes is inland to **KRITSÁ**, a 'traditional' village about 10km away. Buses run at least every hour from the bus station, and despite the commercialisation it's still a good trip: the local crafts (weaving and embroidery basically, though they sell almost everything here) are fair value and it's also a welcome break from living in the fast lane at 'Ag. Nik'. In fact, if you're looking for somewhere to stay around here, Kritsá has a number of advantages: chiefly availability of rooms, better prices, and something at least approaching a genuinely Greek atmosphere. There are a number of decent places to eat too, though many of them are regular targets of 'Greek Nights Out' from Áyios Nikólaos.

On the approach road some 2km before Kritsá is the lovely Byzantine church of **Panayía Kirá**, inside which are preserved perhaps the most complete set of Byzantine frescoes in Crete (officially open 9am–6pm Mon.–Sat., not Sun.; stiff entrance fee). The fourteenth- and fifteenth-century works have been much retouched, but they're still worth the visit. Excellent (and expensive) reproductions are sold from a shop alongside. Just beyond the church a track leads off towards the archaeological site of **Lato**, a Doric city with a grand hilltop setting. The city itself is extensive but neglected, presumably because visitors and archaeologists on Crete are concerned only with the Minoan era. Ruins aside, you could come here for the views alone: west over Áyios Nikólaos and beyond to the bay and Oloús (which was Lato's port), inland to the Lassíthi mountains.

Gournia and the road east

Just off the main road about 20km southeast of Áyios Nikólaos, **GOURNIA** slumps in the saddle between two low peaks. The most completely preserved Minoan town, its narrow alleys and stairways intersect a throng of one-roomed houses centred on a main square and the house of the local ruler. Although less impressive than the great palaces, the site is strong on revelations about the lives of the ordinary people ruled from Knossos. Its desolation today – you are likely to be alone save for a dozing guard – only serves to heighten the contrast with what must have been a cramped and raucous community 3500 years ago.

It is tempting to cross the road here and take one of the paths through the thyme bushes to the sea for a swim. Don't bother – this seemingly innocent little bay acts as a magnet for every piece of floating detritus dumped off Crete's north coast. There is a slightly better beach, and rooms to let, in the next valley at **Pahiá Ámmos**, about twenty minutes' walk, or in the other direction there's the rather bizarre campsite of *Gournia Moon*, with its own small cove.

This is the narrowest part of the island, and from here a fast new road cuts across the isthmus **to Ierápetra** in the south. In the north, though, the route on **towards Sitía** is one of the most exhilarating in Crete. Carved into cliffs and mountainsides, the road teeters above the coast before plunging inland at Kavoúsi. Of the beaches you see below only **MÓHLOS** is at all accessible, some 5km from the tarmac down a twisting dirt track: here there are a few rooms, a hotel or two and a number of tavernas – all expensive. Nearer Sitía the familiar olive groves are interspersed with vineyards, and in late summer the grapes, spread to dry in the fields and on rooftops, make an extraordinary sight in the varying stages of their slow change from green to gold to brown.

Sitía and the east Coast: Vái beach and Zakros

The port and main town of the relatively unexploited eastern edge of Crete, **SITÍA** is a pleasant if unremarkable place. It offers a plethora of waterside restaurants, a long sandy beach and a lazy lifestyle little affected even by the thousands of visitors in peak season. There's an almost Latin feel to the town – reflected in (or perhaps caused by) the number of French and Italian tourists. For entertainment there's the beach, providing endless fun for snorkellers, or in town a mildly entertaining folklore museum; nightlife centres on a few bars and discos near the ferry dock and out along the beach. The one major excitement is the August **Sultana Festival** – a celebration of the big local export, with traditional dancing and all the locally produced wine you can consume included in the entrance to the fairground.

There are plenty of cheap pensions and **rooms**, a youth hostel on the outskirts, and rarely any problem about sleeping on the beach (though it is worth going a little way out of town to avoid any danger of being rousted by police). You pass the **youth hostel** as you come into Sitía from Áyios Nikólaos on the main road, and there are a few rooms places between here and 'downtown'. More pleasant options, though, can be found in the streets behind the northern stretch of the waterside (the part where all the street cafés are, towards the ferry dock), or – slightly more costly – arrayed behind the eastern beach. For **food**, the waterside places are expensive enough to make you careful about what you eat; there are cheaper options in the streets behind, including a couple of excellent ice-cream parlours.

To Vái beach

Vái beach features alongside Knossos or the Lassíthi plateau on almost every Cretan travel agent's list of excursions. For years it has also been a popular hangout for backpackers camping on the sands. This dual role has created something of a monstrosity – with the vast crowds divided into two hostile camps. At the same time it *is* a superb beach, and the trip there is an enjoyable one.

Leaving Sitía along the beach, the Vái road climbs above a rocky, unexceptional coastline before reaching a fork to the **Monastery of Toploú**. The monastery's forbidding exterior reflects a history of resistance to invaders, but doesn't prepare you for the gorgeous flower-decked cloister within. The blue-robed monks keep out of the way as far as possible, but their cells and refectory are left discreetly on view. In the church is one of the masterpieces of Cretan art, the eighteenth-century icon *Lord Thou Art Great*. Outside you can buy enormously expensive reproductions.

VÁI BEACH itself is famous above all for its palm trees, and the sudden appearance of the grove is indeed an exotic shock. Lying on the fine sand in the early morning, the illusion of a Caribbean island is hard to dismiss. During the day, however, the beach fills as buses arrive in quantities hardly justified by a few palm trees. As everywhere, notices warn that 'Camping is forbidden by law'; for once the authorities seem to mean it and most campers climb over the headlands to the south or north. If you do sleep out, watch your belongings – this seems to be the one place on Crete with crime on any scale. There's an expensive taverna and a café at the beach, plus toilets and showers. By day you can find a bit more solitude by climbing the rocks or swimming to one of the smaller beaches which surround Vái. **ÍTANOS**, 20 minutes' walk north by an obvious trail, has a couple of tiny beaches and some modest ruins of the Classical era.

PALÉKASTRO, some 9km south, is in many ways a better place to stay. Although its beaches can't begin to compare, you'll find several modest places with rooms, a number of reasonable restaurants, and plenty of space to camp out without the crowds (the sea is a couple of kilometres down a dirt track). Palékastro is also the crossroads for the road south, to Zakros.

Zakros

ZÁKROS town is a little under 20km from Palékastro, at the end of the paved road. There are several tavernas and a hotel in the village (where the bus drops you), but the Minoan palace is actually at Káto Zakros, 8km further down a newly paved road to the sea. Part way along you can, if on foot, take a shortcut through an impressive gorge (the 'Valley of the Dead', named for ancient tombs in its sides) but it's usually not difficult to hitch the distance.

The **palace of Zakros** was an important find for archaeologists; it had been occupied only once, and abandoned hurriedly and completely. Later it was forgotten almost entirely and as a result was never plundered or even discovered by archaeologists until very recently – the first major excavation began only in 1960. All sorts of everyday objects – tools, raw materials, food, pottery – were thus discovered intact among the ruins, and a great deal was learned from being able to apply modern techniques (and knowledge of the Minoans) to a major dig from the very beginning. None of this is especially evident when you're at the palace, except perhaps in a particularly simple ground plan, so it's as well that it is also a rewarding visit in terms of the setting. Although the site is some way from the sea, parts of it are often marshy and waterlogged: partly the result of eastern Crete's slow subsidence, partly the fault of a spring which once supplied fresh water to a cistern beside the royal apartments and whose outflow is now silted up. Among the remains of narrow streets and small houses higher up you can keep your feet dry and get an excellent view down over the central court and royal apartments.

The village of **Káto Zakros** is little more than a collection of tavernas, some of which rent out rooms, around a peaceful beach and minuscule fishing anchorage. It's a wonderfully restful place.

Ierápetra and the southeast coast

From Sitía the route south is a cross-country roller-coaster ride until it hits the south coast at **MAKRIYIALÓS**. This little fishing village has one of the best beaches at this end of Crete, with fine sand which shelves so gently you feel you could walk the 200 miles to Africa. Unfortunately in the last few years it has been heavily developed, so while still a very pleasant place to stop for a swim or a bite, it's not somewhere you're likely to find a cheap room.

From here to Ierápetra there's little reason to stop; the few beaches are rocky and the coastal plain submerged under ranks of polyethylene-covered greenhouses. One major exception however is **AYÍA FOTIÁ**, where, hidden from the main road in a wooded valley leading down to a bay, there's quite a travellers' scene going on. Whether you like this depends on just how many other people determined to get away from it all you want to share your solitude with – but at least there are cheap rooms or opportunities to camp out, some café/tavernas with good music, and a fine beach which you reach by walking down the stream bed from the village. Beyond here, beside the road leading in to Ierápetra, are long but exposed stretches of sand, including the appropriately-named 'Long Beach', along which you'll find a couple of large campsites.

IERÁPETRA itself is a cheerless modern supply centre for the region's farmers. It also attracts an amazing number of package tourists and not a few backpackers looking for work, especially out of season. The tavernas along the tree-lined front are scenic enough and the beach, its remotest extremities rarely visited, stretches for a couple of miles to the east. But as a town most people find it pretty uninspiring. Although there has been a port here since Roman times, only the Venetian fort guarding the harbour and a crumbling minaret remain as reminders of better days. What little else has been salvaged is in the one-room museum near the post office. Ierápetra's **youth hostel** is about ten walking minutes away from the town, towards Makriyialós; it can be a useful first source of information about work, so don't be put off by the warden. Other cheap rooms can be found if you search, but in some of the filthiest holes anywhere on the island. The best swimming, unfortunately, is right in front of town from the most crowded sector of the beach.

If you're not heading straight back to the north coast by the fast road, there are a number of small resorts along the beach westwards, though little in the way of public transport. **MÍRTOS** is the first which might actually tempt you to stop, and it's certainly the most accessible, just off the main road with numerous buses to Ierápetra daily and a couple direct to Iráklio. Although developed to a degree, it nonetheless remains tranquil and inexpensive. After Mírtos the main road turns inland towards Áno Viános, then continues across the island towards Iráklio; several places on the coast are reached by a series of rough side tracks. That hasn't prevented one of them, **ÁRVI**, from becoming a larger resort than Mírtos. The beach hardly justifies it but it's an interesting little excursion (with at least one bus a day) if only to see the bananas and pineapples grown down here and to experience the microclimate (noticeably warmer than neighbouring zones, especially in spring or autumn) which encourages them. Two more villages – **KERATÓKAMBOS** and **TSOÚTSOUROS** – look tempting on the map. The first has a rather stony beach and only the most basic of rooms available, but it's popular with Cretan day-trippers and great if you want to escape from the tourist grind for a spell. The second is developed and not really worth the tortuous thirteen-kilometre dirt road in.

If you hope to continue across the south of the island, be warned that there are no buses, and that the road toward Míres, which many maps show as complete, is not. Between Skiniás and Pírgos there are some really appalling stretches and very little traffic. Work seems to have been going on for decades, and progress is painfully slow.

RÉTHIMNO AND ITS HINTERLAND

The relatively low, narrow section of Crete which separates the Psilorítis range from the White Mountains in the west seems at first a nondescript, even dull part of the island. Certainly in scenic terms it has few of the excitements which the west can offer, there are no major archaeological sites as in the east, and many of the villages seem modern and unattractive. On the other hand **Réthimno** itself is an extremely attractive and lively city, with some excellent beaches nearby. And on the south coast, in particular around **Plakiás**, are beaches as fine as any Crete can offer – as you drive towards them the scenery and villages improve by the minute.

Réthimno and the north coast

In the past five years or so, **RÉTHIMNO** has seen a greater influx of tourists than perhaps anywhere else on Crete, with the development of a whole series of large hotels extending almost 10km along the beach to the east. For once, though, the middle of town has been spared, so that at its heart Réthimno remains one of the most beautiful of Crete's major cities (with only Haniá as a serious rival). A wide sandy beach and palm-lined promenade border a labyrinthine tangle of Venetian and Turkish houses lining streets where many of the old men still dress proudly in high boots, *tsalvária* (baggy trousers) and *saríkia* (black head scarves). Ancient minarets lend an exotic air to the skyline, while dominating everything from the west is the superbly preserved outline of the fortress built by the Venetians after a series of pirate raids had devastated the town.

When you get off the bus (there are two terminals, one for long-distance, the other for local services, diagonally opposite each other at the corner of Dhimokratías and Moátsou) walk north toward the sea; the waterside **tourist information office** will be in front of you when you get to the beach. Most of the cheaper **rooms** are to the left as you walk down, around the streets paral-

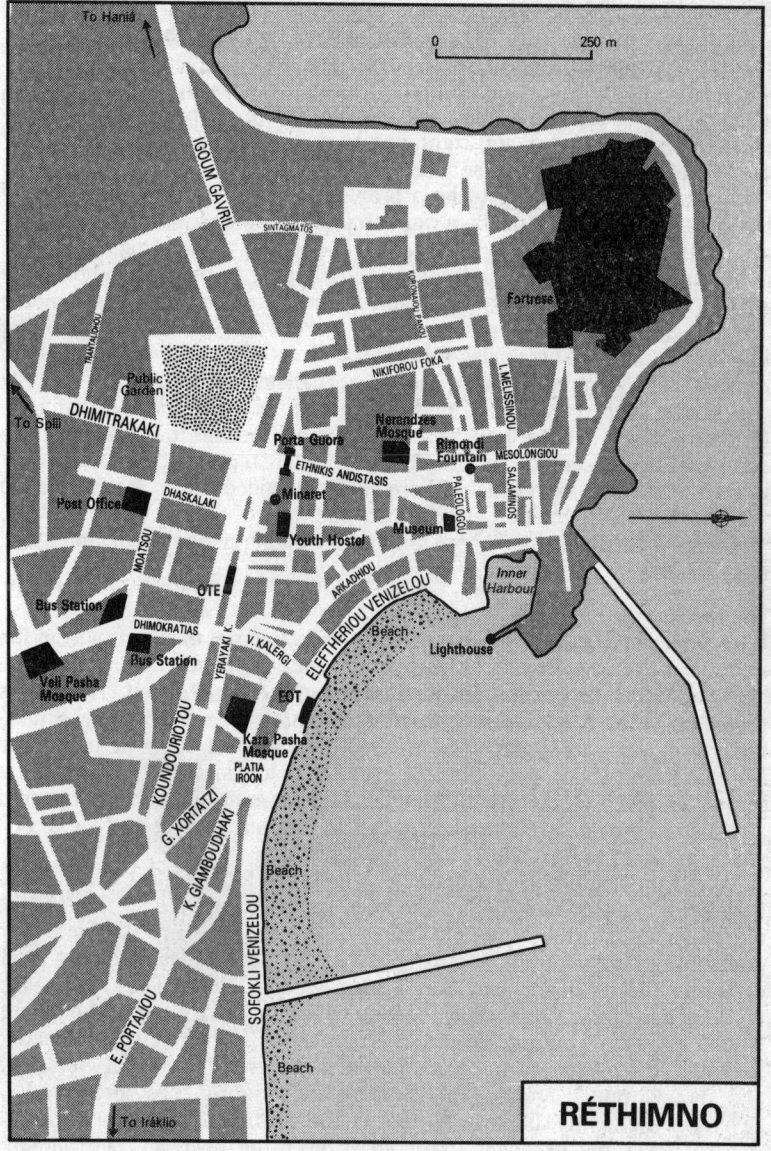

0   250 m

RÉTHIMNO

lel to the esplanade or, continuing in this same direction, behind the old harbour. The best bet is probably to follow Arkadhíou, the street which curves around immediately inland from the beach, looking for 'Rooms' signs up the alleys. A couple of good possibilities here are *Rooms Marcadonis* (V.

Kornárou 1; ☎0831/22-854), or the slightly more luxurious *Pension Vrisinas* (Heréti 10; ☎0831/26-092). For cheaper options the older streets behind the harbour, leading up towards the fortress, are worth exploring. If you can't find a room (quite likely in midsummer) Réthimno's **youth hostel** (Tombázi 41, parallel to Kounouriótou) is a passable alternative, or there are two **campsites** (*Elizabeth* and *Arkadia*) right next to each other about 4km east along the beach, with frequent bus service.

Finding **food** is unlikely to be a problem – there's an unbroken line of tavernas, cafés, and cocktail bars right around the waterside and into the area around the old port – but the prices could be tough if you're struggling with a tight budget. To eat more cheaply you simply have to resist the undeniable attractions of the sea view; you'll find a number of *souvláki* stands along Arkadhíou, or there's an assortment of better-value tavernas around the Rimóndi Fountain. This is also the general area to buy your own food, with **market** stalls set up daily along the top of Andistáseos, towards the old city gate known as the Porta Guora, and a **bakery** (*I Gaspari*) which sells wonderful brown, black and rye bread on the street just behind the fountain. **Bars** and **nightlife** concentrate in the same general area, particularly towards the western end of the town beach, where you'll find video and rock bars like the *Why Not?* or the 'genuine Greek music' offerings of the likes of *Bar Retro*. There are a couple of discos here too, but the bigger ones are out among the large hotels.

The town

With a beach right in the heart of town it's tempting not to stir at all from the sands, but Réthimno repays at least some gentle exploration. For a start you could try checking out the further reaches of the **beach** itself. The waters protected by the breakwaters in front of town have their disadvantages: notably crowds, dubious hygiene (there's said to be a sewer outlet here) and the fact that in so public a place the police tend to crack down on topless bathers by day as much as they do on unofficial campers at night. Less sheltered sands stretch miles to the east, crowded at first but progressively less so if you're prepared to walk a bit.

Away from the beach you don't have far to go for the most atmospheric part of town, immediately behind the inner harbour. Here are the finest of the old buildings and the most interesting of the shops, many still with local craftsmen sitting out front, gossiping as they ply their trades. There's a small **museum** (open 8.45am–3pm, Sun. 9.30am–2.30pm, closed Tues.) housed in the Venetian *loggia*, not a wildly exciting collection but a classy old building. Not far away the **Rimóndi Fountain** is another of the more elegant Venetian survivals. Paleológou, which leads between the two, has several motorbike and moped rental agents. The **Nerandzes mosque**, best preserved of several in Réthimno, is close by too; in the afternoons you can climb the minaret for some excellent (free) views over the town and surrounding countryside.

Follow Andistáseos up and out the Porta Guora and you'll emerge on the main road almost opposite the **Public Gardens**. These are in themselves a green and soothing place to stroll, but most visitors only bother in the latter half of July, when the **Réthimno Wine Festival** is staged here. Though touristy it's a thoroughly enjoyable event, with spectacular local dancing as the evening progresses and the barrels empty. As at the more famous festivals on the mainland the entrance fee includes all the wine you can drink, though you'll need to bring your own cup or else buy one of the souvenir glasses and carafes on sale outside the gardens.

For the most part the rest of the old town is a place simply to wander, with no particular focus but plenty of unexpected old buildings, wall fountains, overhanging wooden balconies, heavy, carved doors and rickety shops to keep you interested. One thing definitely worth seeking out is the **Fortress** (open Tues.–Fri. 8am–8pm; Sat.–Mon. 9.30am–6pm). Close up it's far more dilapidated than it seems from a distance, but it's a wonderfully spooky place, and a supreme vantage point for the sunset.

Around Réthimno

Of all the short trips which could be taken out of Réthimno, the best known is still the most worthwhile. This is to the **monastery of Arkádhi**, some 25km southeast of the city. Immaculately situated in the foothills of the Psilorítis range, Arkádhi is also something of a national Cretan shrine. During the 1866 rebellion against the Turks the monastery became a rebel strongpoint in which, as the Turks gained the upper hand, hundreds of Cretan guerrillas and their families took refuge. Surrounded and, after two days of fighting, on the point of defeat, the defenders ignited a powder magazine just as the Turks entered. Hundreds (some sources claim thousands) were killed, Cretan and Turk alike, and the tragedy did much to promote international sympathy for the cause of Cretan independence. Nowadays you can peer into the roofless vault where the explosion occurred and wander about the rest of the well-restored grounds. The sixteenth-century rococo church survived, and is one of the finest Venetian structures left on Crete; other buildings house a small museum devoted to the exploits of the defenders of the (Orthodox) faith.

Leaving Réthimno **to the west**, the main road climbs for a while above a rocky coastline before descending (after some 5km) to the sea where it runs alongside sandy **beach** for perhaps another 7km. An occasional hotel and a campsite (*George*) offer accommodation, but on the whole there's nothing but a line of straggly bushes between the road and the windswept beach. If you have your own vehicle there are plenty of places to stop here for a swim, and rarely anyone else around. If you want to stay for any time, however, virtually the only base is **YIORYOÚPOLI** at the far end, where the beach is cleaner, wider, and further from the road. It's not exactly unknown – there are a number of houses offering rooms, and several hotels, all full in mid-season – but neither is it heavily developed. Within walking distance inland is **Kournás**, Crete's only lake, set deep in a bowl of hills and almost constantly changing colour. There's a taverna on the shore with a few rooms to let, or you could try for a bed in the nearby village of MOÚRI.

Beyond Yioryoúpoli the main road heads inland, away from a cluster of coastal villages beyond Vámos. It thus misses some spectacular views over the sapphire Bay of Soudha, several quiet beaches, and the setting for the film of *Zorba the Greek*. **KÓKKINO HORIÓ**, the movie location, and nearby **PLÁKA** are indeed postcard-picturesque (more so from a distance), but

KEFALÁS, inland, outdoes both of them. On the exposed north coast there are beaches at **ALMIRÍDHA** and **KALÍVES**, and off the road between them. With luck you can find a room in Almirídha. The much bigger town of Kalíves goes about its agricultural business without the least concession to tourism.

The south coast: to Plakiás and Ayía Galíni via Spíli

There are a couple of alternative routes south from Réthimno, but the main one heads straight out from the centre of town, an initially featureless road due south across the middle of the island. About 23km out, a turning cuts off to the right for Plakiás and Mírthios, following the course of the spectacular Kourtaliótiko ravine.

PLAKIÁS has undergone a major boom and is no longer the pristine village all too many people arrive here expecting. That said, it's still quite low-key, there's a satisfactory beach and a string of good tavernas around the dock; visitors on the whole are young and travelling light. At the height of summer you'll need to arrive early if you hope to find a room; the last to fill are those on the road leading inland, away from the waterside. If needed, there's a **youth hostel** on the edge of town, while the beach is long and nobody is likely to mind if you sleep out on the middle section – but Damnóni (below) is far better if that's your plan. For a stay of more than a day or two, **MÍRTHIOS**, in the hills behind Plakiás and considerably cheaper, also deserves consideration. Here you'll find locals still outnumbering the tourists and something of a travellers' scene based around another popular **youth hostel** (run jointly with the one in Plakiás). The Plakiás bus will usually loop back through Mírthios, but check; otherwise it's less than a five-minute walk from the junction. It takes twenty minutes to walk down to the beach at Plakiás, a little longer to Damnóni, and if you're prepared to walk for an hour or more there are some entirely isolated coves to the west – ask directions in the hostel.

Some of the most tempting beaches in central Crete hide just to the east of Plakiás, albeit ones which are already a very poorly kept secret. Westernmost is **DAMNÓNI**, a term which is generally used to describe the group of three beaches within walking distance east of Plakiás this way. At the first, Damnóni proper, there's a taverna with showers and a wonderfully long strip of sand. At the far end you'll generally find a few people who've dispensed with their clothes – the little cove which shelters the middle of the three beaches, barely accessible except on foot, is entirely nudist. Beyond this, Ammoúdhi Beach has another taverna (with rooms for rent) and a slightly more family atmosphere. To any of these – all considerably more attractive than Plakiás' own beach – you'd have less far to walk, and probably spend less, staying in the village of **LEFKÓYIA**, 2km away. The disadvantages are that Lefkóyia is not itself on the coast, and that besides a couple of tavernas and two or three places letting rooms, it has no facilities at all.

Next in line comes **PRÉVELI**, some 6km southeast of Lefkóyia. It takes its name from a monastery high above the sea which, like every other in Crete, has a proud history of resistance – in this case accentuated by its role in the last war as a shelter for marooned Allied soldiers awaiting evacuation off the south coast. There are fine views and a monument commemorating the rescue operations, but little else to see. Turn left about halfway down the road here, however, and you'll find a path leading down to 'Palm Beach', with a small date-palm grove and solitary drink stand. The beach usually attracts a summer camping community and has a nudist reputation. Sadly, the campers have left the place filthy. Despite them it's a lovely setting, and following the river just upstream you'll find a lagoon of clear water which is sheer paradise.

There are more quite empty beaches east of here – ÁYIOS PÁVLOS, below Saktoúria, for example – but no real road, so getting to them requires either extraordinary hiking dedication or a boat trip from Ayía Galíni. This, Crete's number-one 'picturesque fishing village', is the next stop around the coast, although getting there involves returning to the junction of the main road just north of Koxarés to change buses, or taking the one daily direct service linking Plakiás with Ayía Galíni.

Either way you'll pass through **SPÍLI** shortly after rejoining the main road. A popular coffee break for tours passing this way, Spíli warrants time if you can spare it. Sheltered under a beetling cliff are narrow alleys of ancient houses, all leading up from a square with a famous 24-spouted fountain. With your own transport it's a worthwhile place to stay, peacefully rural at night but with several good rooms places (plus the *Green Hotel* ☎*0832/22-056*) and a variety of onward options in every direction.

If heading for **AYÍA GALÍNI** was your plan, though, maybe you should think again – the 'fishing village' is so picturesque that you can't see it for the tour buses, hotel billboards and English package tourists. Its beach is small and rocky, and apart from some excellent restaurants there seems little reason to come here unless you actively like crowds. The exception is from November to April when most people have left and the mild climate makes it an ideal spot to spend the winter. A lot of long-term travellers do just that, so it's a good place to find work packing tomatoes or polishing cucumbers. One of the better places to stay, if they have space, are the rooms next to the *Hotel Moderno*.

The coastal plain east of here, hidden under acres of polyethylene green-houses and burgeoning concrete sprawl, must be among the ugliest regions in Crete, and TIMBÁKI the dreariest town. Since this is the way to Festos and back to Iráklio, however, you may have no choice but to grin and bear it. More enticingly, it is also the end of what could be an alternative route from Réthimno to the south, via the **Amári Valley**, a road which sees at best one bus a day (to/from Míres). There's little specifically to see or do (though hidden away are a number of frescoed Byzantine churches), but it's an impressive drive under the flanks of the mountains and a reminder of how, in places, rural Crete continues to exist regardless of visitors. It may seem odd that the villages along the way are mostly modern; they were systematically destroyed by the Germans in reprisal for the 1944 kidnapping of General Kreipe.

HANIÁ AND THE WEST

The substantial attractions of Crete's westernmost quarter are all the more enhanced by its lack of visitors; and despite the now-rapid spread of tourist development, the west is likely to remain one of the emptier parts of the island. This is partly because there are no big sand beaches to accommodate resort hotels, and partly because it's so far from the great archaeological sites. But for mountains and empty (if often pebbly) beaches, it's unrivalled.

Haniá itself is one of the best reasons to come here, perhaps the only Cretan city which could be described as enjoyable in itself. The immediately adjacent coast is relatively developed and not overly exciting; for beaches it's the **south coast** you really need. **Paleohóra** is the only place which could really be described as a resort, and even this is on a thoroughly human scale; others are emptier still. **Ayía Rouméli** and **Loutró** can be reached only on foot or by boat; **Hóra Sfakíon** sees hordes passing through but few who stay; **Frangokástello**, with something of everything, may be the best of all of them. Behind these lie the White Mountains – the *Lefká Óri* – and above all the famed walk through the **Gorge of Samariá**.

Haniá

HANIÁ, as any of its residents will tell you, is the spiritual capital of Crete, even if the nominal title has passed (in 1971) to Iráklio. For many it is also by far the island's most attractive city – especially if you can catch it in spring, when the Lefká Óri's snow-capped peaks seem to hover above the roofs. Although it is for the most part a modern city, you might never know it as a tourist. Surrounding the small outer harbour is a wonderful jumble of half-derelict Venetian streets which survived the wartime bombardments, and it is here that life for the visitor is concentrated. Restoration and gentrification – consequences of the tourist boom – have made inroads of late, but it remains an atmospheric place.

Arrival and survival

Large as it is, Haniá is easy to handle once you've reached the centre; you may get lost wandering among the narrow alleys of the old city but that's a relatively small area, and you're never far from the sea or from some other obvious landmark. The **bus station** is on Odhós Kidhonías, within easy walking distance from the action – turn right, then left down the side of Platía 1866 and you'll emerge at a major road junction opposite the top of Hálidhon, the main street of the old quarter leading straight down to the Venetian harbour. **Arriving by boat** you'll anchor about 10km from Haniá at the port of SOÚDHA: there are frequent buses which will drop you by the market on the fringes of the old town, or you can take a taxi. From the **airport** (about 15km) taxis will almost certainly be your only option, though it's worth a quick check to see if any sort of bus (e.g. *Olympic Airways*) you could gate-crash is meeting your flight.

Once into town, it's likely to be a **room** you're hunting down first. There seem to be thousands in Haniá and though in mid-season you may face a long search, everyone seems to find something eventually. Out of season the rooms right over the harbour are worth a try first – surprisingly reasonable at, for example, the *Hotel Piraeus* (corner of Hálidhon and Zambelíou). In season these are not only full but very noisy too. Others will be found mainly to the east of Hálidhon, in the streets around the cathedral (*Pension Fidias* for example) or beyond this into the slightly more confusing, run-down streets of the Spiántza area – all areas for mounting determined searches. Should you fail in the old part of town there are more possibilities in the new districts: some noisy offerings directly opposite the bus station for example, others in the streets running behind the town beach, west of the centre. In desperation you can be almost sure of space at the **youth hostel**, but this, at Dhrakonianoú 33, is a long way from anywhere you might otherwise want to visit (bus #4, #11, #12, and #13 from corner Yianári and Apokorónou, opposite the market).

There are also two **campsites** along the coast to the west: *Camping Hania*, which is just about within walking distance but much easier reached on the local bus to the beaches, and *Camping Ayia Marina* (bigger and better facilities), about 10km out in the village of the same name.

Eating places concentrate around the water, where both the inner and outer harbours are circled by cafés, tavernas and bars. A couple of the cheaper cafés, popular meeting places as well, are on Platía Sindriváni (usually known as Harbor Square) at the bottom of Hálidhon: *Costas* and *Vasilis*. *Costas* is also the place to go (around 6am) if you're looking for work. Otherwise there's little to choose between all of these, and hard as the view and the strolling crowds are to resist you can eat a good deal more cheaply by avoiding the port altogether. Try up Hálidhon or on the narrow streets to the west of it, off Zambelíou: *Jimmy's*, in a sidestreet opposite the cathedral, is particularly popular with English speakers (especially U.S. servicemen from the NATO bases on Akrotíri and Soúdha Bay); the basic *Dhíporto* diner on Skridlóf (east of Hálidhon) is famous for its multilingual menu featuring such exotic delights as 'Pigs' Balls', or *Testicules de Porc* for more refined tastes. There are plenty of still more basic *souvláki* and other fast-food places around, including several just off Platía Sindriváni. *Kentacky Fried Chicken* (*sic*) on Aktí Koundouriótou is appropriately named, but worth noting as the one place still open when you're finally thrown out of the nearby disco-bars.

At least once you'd do better to buy some of your own food, and in any event Haniá's **market**, the finest in Crete, is not to be missed. In addition to the fruit, bread, cheese, fish, meat and vegetables – of which there's a cornucopian abundance – there's the building itself, a splendid, cross-shaped hall reminiscent of a Victorian railway station (and supposedly a replica of the market in Marseilles). Other **shopping** is relatively close by: Odhós Skridlóf has cheap leather goods still not entirely taken over by the tourist trade, and the streets of the new town in front of the market meet more everyday needs: pharmacies, general stores and foreign newspapers on Yianári, designer clothing on Tzanakáki and Konstantínou.

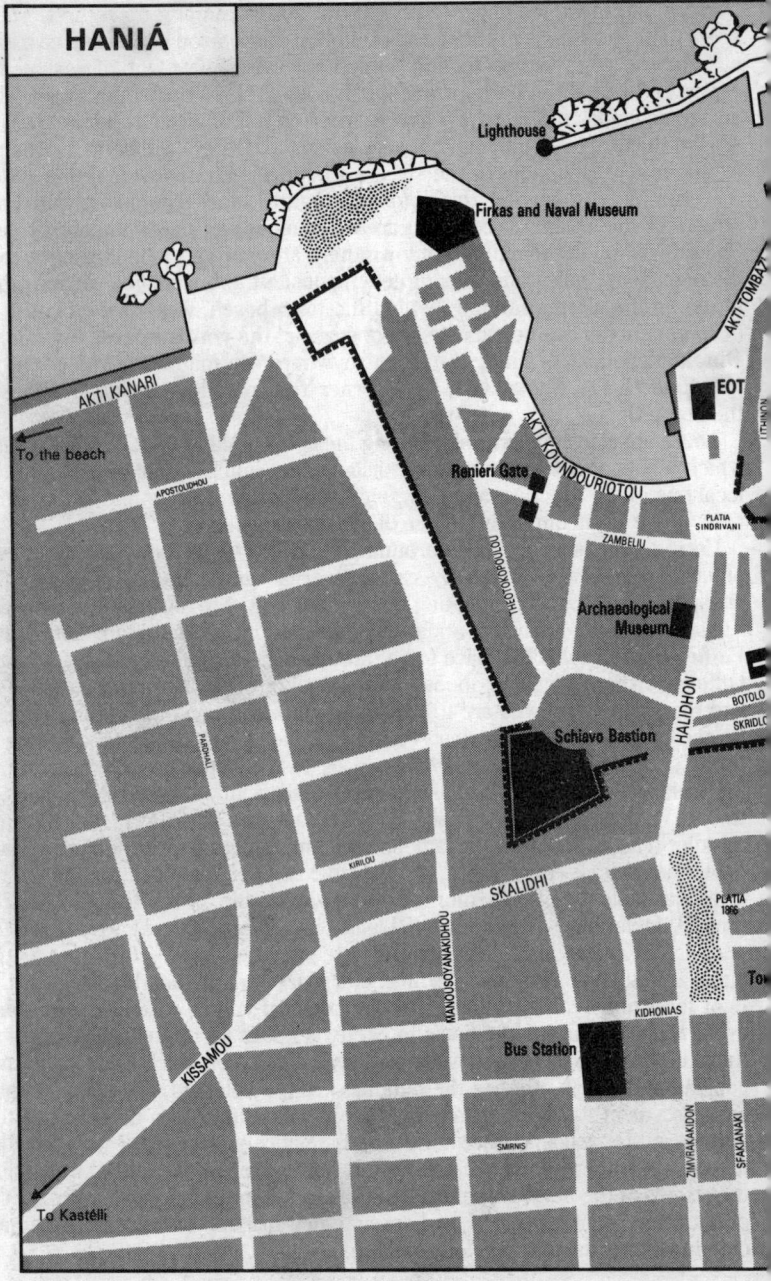

HANIÁ

Lighthouse

Firkas and Naval Museum

AKTITOMBAZ

EOT

ITHINON

AKTI KANARI

To the beach

AKTI KOUNDOURIOTOU

APOSTOLIDHOU

Reniéri Gate

PLATIA
SINDRIVANI

THEOTOKOPOULOU

ZAMBELIU

Archaeological
Museum

HALIDHON

BOTOLO

SKRIDLO

Schiavo Bastion

PARDHNALI

KIRILOU

SKALIDHI

PLATIA
1896

MANOUSOYANAKIOHOU

To

KIDHONIAS

KISSAMOU

Bus Station

SMIRNIS

ZIMVRAKAKIDON

SFAKIANAKI

To Kastélli

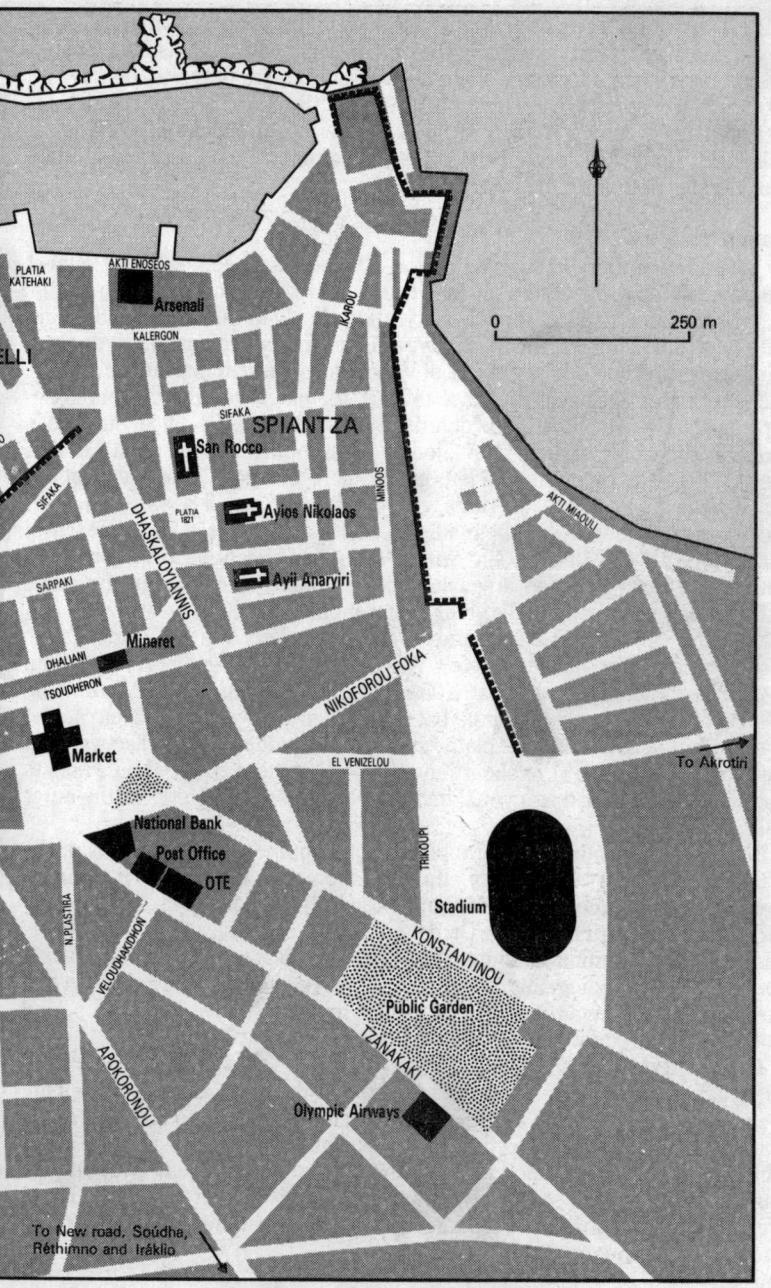

PLATIA
KATEHAKI

AKTI ENOSEOS

Arsenali

KALERGON

ELLI

SIFAKA

SIFAKA

SPIANTZA

San Rocco

SARPAKI

PLATIA
1821

Ayios Nikolaos

DHASKALOYIANNIS

Ayii Anaryiri

DHALIANI

Minaret

TSOUDHERON

Market

KAROU

MINOOS

AKTI MIAOULI

NIKOFOROU FOKA

EL VENIZELOU

To Akrotiri

National Bank

Post Office

OTE

TRIKOUPI

Stadium

N.PLASTIRA

VELOUDHAKIDON

KONSTANTINOU

Public Garden

APOKORONOU

TZANAKAKI

Olympic Airways

To New road, Soúdha,
Réthimno and Iráklio

0   250 m

The **Tourist Office** is on the outer harbour in the strange, domed Mosque of the Janissaries, an extremely helpful branch with full listings posted outside even when it's closed. Main **bank** branches are opposite the market, but for exchange there's one just off Platía Sindriváni and another (which re-opens in the evenings from 6 to 8pm) at the top of Hálidhon. **OTE** is on Tzanakáki, right next to the **post office**; in summer a temporary post office also operates in front of the cathedral.

Around the town

Surprisingly for a city of such antiquity – the site has been occupied almost continuously since Neolithic times – Haniá offers little specifically to see or do. It is, however, a place which is fascinating simply to wander around, stumbling upon surviving fragments of city wall, holes in which ancient Kydonia is being excavated and odd segments of Venetian or Turkish masonry.

The port area is as ever the place to start, the oldest and the most interesting part of town. The little hill which rises behind the tourist office/mosque is **Kastélli**, site of the earliest habitation and core of the Venetian and Turkish towns. There's not a great deal left, but it's here that you'll find traces of the oldest walls (there were two rings, one defending Kastélli alone, a later set encompassing the whole of the medieval city) and the sites of various excavations. Beneath the hill, on the **inner (eastern) harbour**, the arches of sixteenth-century Venetian arsenals survive alongside remains of the outer walls; both are currently undergoing restoration.

Following the esplanade around in the other direction leads to a hefty bastion which now houses Crete's **Naval Museum** (Wed., Fri., and Sun. 10am–2pm, Tue., Thur. and Sat. 10am–2pm and 5–7pm; closed Mon.). The collection's not exactly riveting, but wander in anyway for a look at the seaward fortifications and the platform where the modern Greek flag was first flown on Crete (in 1913). Walk around the back of these restored bulwarks to a street heading inland and you'll find the best preserved stretch of the outer walls.

Behind the harbour lie the less picturesque but more lively sections of the old city. First, a short way up Hálidhon on the right is Haniá's **Archaeological Museum** (8am–7pm, closed Mon.), housed in the Venetian-built church of San Francesco. Damaged as it is, especially from the outside, this remains a beautiful building and a fine little display, even though there's nothing of outstanding interest (the best pieces are all at Iráklio). In the garden a huge fountain and the base of a minaret survive from the period when the Turks converted the church into a mosque.

The **Cathedral**, ordinary and relatively modern, is just a few steps further up Hálidhon on the left. Around it are some of the more animated shopping areas, particularly **Odhós Skrídlof**, with streets leading up to the back of the market beyond. In the direction of the Spiántza quarter are ancient alleys which have yet to feel much effect of the city's modern popularity, still with tumbledown Venetian stonework and overhanging wooden balconies. There are a couple more **minarets** too, one on Dhaliáni, the other in Platía 1821 – a fine traditional square to stop for a coffee.

Once out of the narrow confines of the maritime district, the broad, traffic-choked streets of the **modern city** have a great deal less to offer. Up Tzanakáki, not far from the market, you'll find the **Public Gardens**, a park with strolling couples, a few caged animals (including a few *kri-kri* or Cretan ibex), and a café under the trees; there's also an open-air auditorium which occasionally hosts live music or local festivities. Beyond here you could continue to the **Historical Museum** (weekdays 9.30am–1.30pm and 3–5.30pm) but the effort would be wasted unless you're a Greek-speaking expert on the subject; the place is essentially a very dusty archive with a few photographs on the wall. Perhaps more interesting is the fact that the museum lies on the fringes of Haniá's desirable residential districts – continue to the end of Sfakianáki and then down Iróön Politehníou towards the sea for an insight into how Crete's other half lives. There are several (expensive) garden restaurants down here and a number of fashionable café bars where you can sit outside.

Beaches and bars

Haniá's beaches all lie to the west of the city. For the packed **city beach** this means no more than a ten-minute walk following the shoreline from the naval museum, but for good sand you're better off taking the local bus out along the coast road. This leaves from the east side of Platía 1866 and runs along the coast road as far as **Kalamáki** beach. Kalamáki and the previous stop, **Oasis Beach**, are again pretty crowded but they're a considerable improvement over the beach in Haniá itself. In between you'll find emptier stretches if you're prepared to walk about an hour in all (on sandy beach virtually all the way) from Haniá to Kalamáki, perhaps ten minutes from the road to the beach if you get off the bus at the signs to *Aptera Beach* or *Camping Hania*. Farther afield there are even finer beaches at Ayía Marína to the west, or Stavrós (see overpage) out on the Akrotíri peninsula (reachable by KTEL buses from the main station).

For **nightlife**, it's back to the port. If you really want to do things properly there's only one way to start, an early evening *vólta* among the crowds strolling around the quay. Follow this with an *ouzo* at one of the pavement tables, something to eat, and you're ready to go. Most of the later action takes place in a series of deafening **bars**, generally with small dance floors, just behind the outer harbour. If it all seems a bit raunchier than you'd expect, remember that these places cater to servicemen from the nearby NATO bases at least as much as to visitors – hence the common ploy of employing young female tourists to sit at the bar as decoys (easy money, but soul- and liver-destroying work, and in the long run rarely as uncomplicated as it appears at the outset). Most of the clubs are in the alleys running south off Zambelíou (*Beau Mec* or *Just a Pub* for example) or behind the Plaza Hotel (*Scorpio's*). There are also a couple of straightforward **discos**, mainly for the tourists, complete with cover charges and outrageous prices: *Ariadne* on the edge of the inner harbour, and *Estelle* by the market. *Fangoto*, on Angélou round by the naval museum, is an excellent **jazz** bar which very occasionally features live bands.

On a rather different level, Haniá can also be a good place to catch **local music**. In particular there's a bouzouki bar overlooking the inner harbour from Aktí Tombázi, a grimy and entertaining little dive despite being packed with tourists. For the sort of place Haniotes themselves patronize you'll have to get out of town, probably by taxi (in which case the taxi drivers are the best source of information on what's happening where, especially on nearby village festivals). On a regular basis there are several plate-smashing, dinner-dance style restaurants high on the road out to Akrotíri, all with superb views back over the city.

Around Haniá: the Akrotíri and Rodhopoú peninsulas

Just north of Haniá the AKROTÍRI peninsula loops round to protect the Bay of Soúdha – and a NATO military base and missile-testing area which the Greek socialists have pledged (but so far failed) to remove. In an ironic twist, the peninsula's northwestern coastline is fast developing into a luxury suburb – the beach of HORAFÁKIA, long popular with jaded Haniotes, is surrounded by villas and apartments. **STAVRÓS**, further out, has not yet suffered this fate, and its beach is absolutely superb if you like the calm, shallow water of an almost completely enclosed lagoon. You can rent rooms here, and there are two tavernas. Inland are the monasteries of **Ayía Triádha** and **Gouvernétou**. The former is much more accessible and has a beautiful seventeenth-century church inside its pink-and-ochre cloister; it's also one of the few Cretan monasteries in which genuine monastic life continues. Beyond the latter you can clamber down a craggy path to the abandoned ruins of the monastery of Katholikó and the remains of its narrow (swimmable) harbour.

To the **west of Haniá** extends a coast which was the scene of most of the fighting during the German invasion in 1941. As you leave town an aggressive diving eagle commemorates the German parachutists, and at **MÁLEME** there is a big German cemetry; the Allied cemetry is on the coast just outside Soúdha. There are also beaches, and considerable tourist development, along much of this shore. At **AYÍA MARÍNA** there's a fine sandy beach, and an island offshore said to be a sea monster petrified by Zeus before it could swallow Crete. Seen from the west, its 'mouth' still gapes open. Between **PLATANIÁS** and **KOLIMBÁRI** an almost unbroken strand unfurls, by no means all sandy, but deserted for long stretches between villages. The road here runs through mixed groves of bamboo and oranges; the bamboo windbreaks protect the ripening oranges from the *meltémi*. At Kolimbári the road to Kastélli cuts across the base of another mountainous peninsula, **RODHOPOÚ**. Just off the main road here is the monastery, **Goniás**, with a view most luxury hotels would envy. Every monk in Crete can tell tales of his proud ancestry of resistance to invaders, but here the Turkish cannon balls are still lodged in the walls to prove it, a relic the good fathers are far more proud of than any of the icons.

The Samarian Gorge

From Haniá the Gorge of Samariá can be visited as a day trip or as part of a longer excursion to the south. At over 16km it's Europe's longest gorge and is startlingly beautiful, at its best in spring. Buses leave Haniá for the top at 6.15, 7.30, and 8.30am, plus 4.30pm, and you'll normally be sold a return ticket (valid from Hóra Sfakíon at any time). It's well worth catching the early bus to avoid the full heat of the day while walking through the gorge, though be warned that you will not be alone – there are often as many as four extra coachloads setting off before dawn for the nail-biting climb into the White Mountains.

One way to avoid the early start would be to stay at **OMALÓS** (☎0821/93-269 for info on rooms here) in the middle of the mountain plain from which the gorge descends. But since the village is some way from the start of the track, and the buses arrive as the sun rises, it is almost impossible to get a head start on the crowds. The tourist pavilion at the top is small and expensive (reservations ☎0821/93-237) and a night under the stars a very cold experience. The one significant advantage to staying up here would be if you wanted to undertake some other climbs in the White Mountains, in which case there's a mountain hut about ninety minutes' walk from Omalós or from the top of the gorge (☎0821/24-647 or 0821/30-821 in Haniá for details).

The **GORGE** itself begins at the *Ksilóskalo*, or 'wooden staircase', a stepped path plunging steeply down from the southern lip of the Omalós Plain. Here at the head of the track, opposite the sheer rock face of Mt. Gíngilos, the crowds pouring out of the buses disperse rapidly as keen walkers march purposefully down while others dally over breakfast, contemplating the sunrise for hours. You descend at first through almost alpine scenery: pine forest, wild flowers and very un-Cretan greenery – a verdant shock in the spring, when the stream is also at its liveliest. Small churches and viewpoints dot the route, and about halfway down you pass the abandoned village of **Samariá**, now home to a wardens' station, with picnic facilities and filthy toilets. Farther down, the path levels out and the gorge walls close in until at the narrowest point (the *Sidherespórtes* or 'Iron Gates') one can practically touch both tortured rock faces at once, and, looking up, see them rising sheer for almost a thousand feet.

At an average pace, with regular stops, the walk down takes almost six hours – the upward trek considerably longer. It's hard work (you'll know all about it next day), the path is rough, and solid shoes vital. On the way down there is plenty of water from springs and streams (except some years in September–October), but nothing to eat. The park which surrounds the gorge is the only mainland refuge of the Cretan wild ibex, the *kri-kri* – but don't expect to see one, there are usually far too many people around.

When you finally get down, the village of **AYÍA ROUMELI** is all but abandoned until you reach the beach, a mirage of iced drinks and a cluster of tavernas with rooms to let. If you want to get back to Haniá buy your boat tickets now, especially if you want an afternoon on the beach – the last boat (connecting with the final 6.30pm bus from Hóra Sfakíon) tends to sell out first.

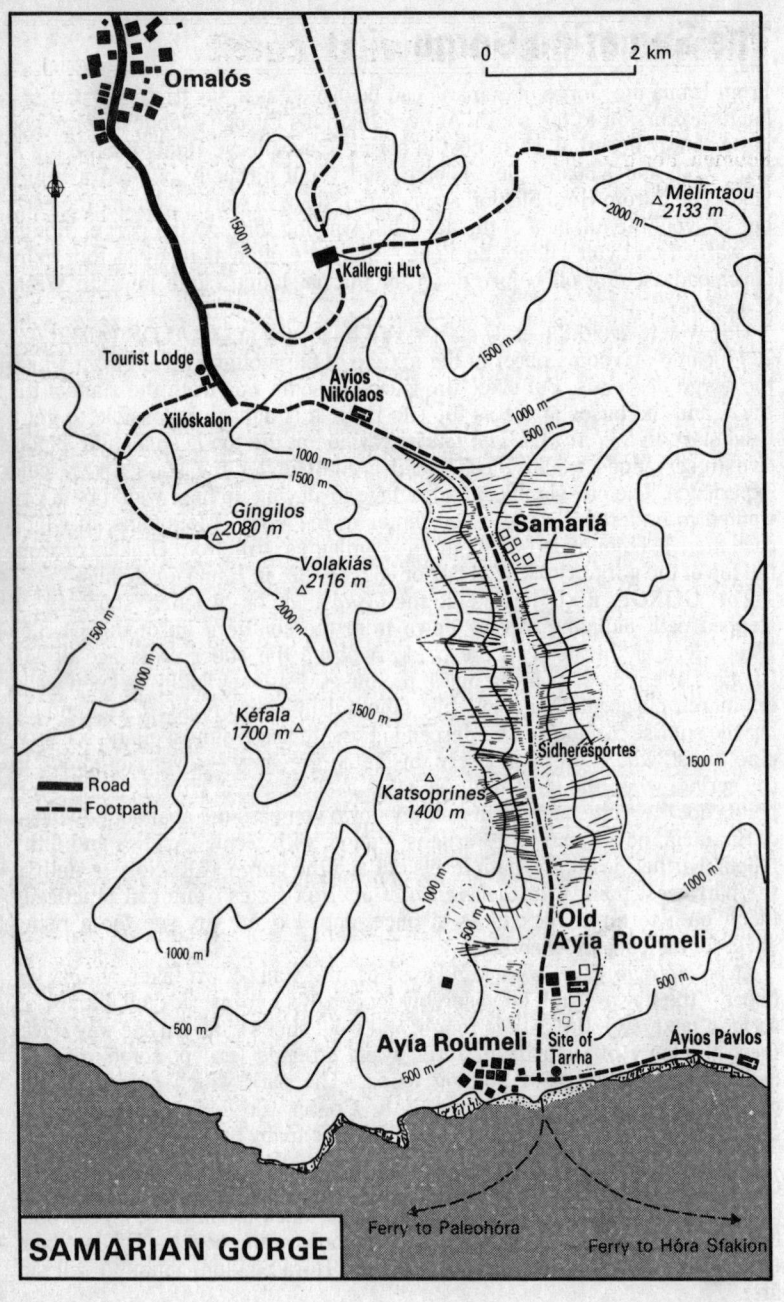

Omalós

0   2 km

Melíntaou
2133 m

1500 m

2000 m

Kallergi Hut

1500 m

Tourist Lodge

Áyios
Nikólaos

1000 m

500 m

Xilóskalon

1000 m

1500 m

Gíngilos
2080 m

Samariá

Volakiás
2116 m

2000 m

1500 m

1000 m

Kéfala
1700 m

1500 m

Sidherespórtes

1500 m

▬▬▬ Road
━ ━ ━ Footpath

Katsoprínes
1400 m

1000 m

500 m

Old
Ayia Roúmeli

1000 m

1000 m

500 m

500 m

Ayía Roúmeli

Site of
Tarrha

Áyios Pávlos

500 m

Ferry to Paleohóra

Ferry to Hóra Sfakíon

SAMARIAN GORGE

Villages of the southwest coast

If you plan to stay on the south coast you should get going as soon as possible for the best chance of finding a room somewhere nicer than Ayía Rouméli. For tranquillity it's hard to beat **LOUTRÓ**, two-thirds of the way to Hóra Sfakíon, and accessible only by boat or on foot. The chief disadvantage of Loutró is its lack of a real beach; most people swim from the rocks around its small bay. If you're prepared to walk, however, there are deserted beaches along the coast to the east. Indeed if you're really into walking there's a coastal trail through Loutró which covers the entire distance between Ayía Rouméli and Hóra Sfakíon, or you could take the daunting zigzag path up the cliff behind to the mountain village of ANÓPOLI. Loutró itself has a number of tavernas and rooms (though not always enough of the latter) and space to camp out on the cape by a ruined fort.

HÓRA SFAKÍON is the more usual terminus for walkers traversing the gorge, with regular boat service along the coast to and from Ayía Rouméli. Consequently it's quite an expensive and not an especially welcoming place; there are plenty of rooms and some excellent tavernas, but for a real beach you should jump straight on the evening bus going toward Plakiás. Plenty of opportunities present themselves en route, one of the most memorable at **FRANGOKÁSTELLO**, a crumbling Venetian attempt to bring law and order to a district which went on to defy both Turks and Germans. Its square, crenellated fort, isolated a few kilometres below a chiselled wall of mountains, looks like it's been spirited out of the High Atlas or Tibet. And speaking of spirits, the place is said to be haunted by ghosts of Greek rebels massacred here in 1829. Every May these *dhrossolítes* (dewy ones) march at dawn across the coastal plain and disappear into the sea near the fort. The rest of the time Frangokástello is peaceful enough, with a superb beach and numbers of tavernas and rooms, but is almost certainly next on the list for mass-market standardisation; electric current and a sporadic disco have already arrived. Slightly further east – and less influenced by tourism or modern life – are the attractive villages of SKALOTÍ and RODHÁKINO, each with basic lodging and food.

In quite the other direction from Ayía Rouméli, less regular boats also head to **SOÚYIA** and on to Paleohóra. Soúyia, until World War II merely the anchorage for Koustoyérako inland, is low key with a long, grey pebble beach and mostly modern building (except for a church with a sixth-century Byzantine mosaic as the foundation). Since a new road has been completed to Haniá the village has started to expand, but except in the very middle of summer it conitnues to make a good fallback for finding a room, eating cheaply and enjoying the beach when the rest of the island is seething with tourists.

Kastélli and the western tip

Apart from being Crete's most westerly town, and the end of the main road, **KASTÉLLI** (KÍSSAMOS, or Kastélli Kissámou as it's variously known) has little going for it. Its beach is rocky and dirty (although showers make it popular with newly arrived campers) and the town is largely bland and modern. It does, however, have a twice-weekly boat to the island of Kíthira, continuing to Yíthio and Monemvassía on the Peloponnese before eventually reaching Pireás. Currently this leaves every Tuesday and Friday (at least through the summer) but since there's every reason not to hang around Kastélli you'd be wise to check first. The agent's office in Kastélli is right on the main square (*Ksirouksákis*; ☎0822/22-655), the dock itself a wearying two-kilometre walk from town.

To the west of Kastélli, in serene contrast, lies some of Crete's loneliest – and for many visitors, finest – coastline. The first place of note on the map is ancient **FALASARNA**, city ruins which mean little to the non-specialist except insofar as they overlook some of the best beaches on Crete, wide and sandy with clean water. There are a handful of tavernas, some of which let a few rooms; otherwise you have to sleep out. Nearest shops are in PLÁTANOS, 5km up the recently paved road, along which there are several daily buses.

So far this whole western coastline remains barely discovered, the road is surfaced only as far as Kámbos, and there is little in the way of official accommodation. SFINÁRI has several houses which let rooms, and a quiet pebble beach a little way below the village. KÁMBOS is similar, but even less visited, its beach a considerable walk down a hill. Beyond them both is the monastery of **Hrissoskalítissa**, hard to get to (though increasingly visited by tours from Haniá or Paleohóra) but well worth the effort for its isolation and nearby beaches; the bus gets as far as VÁTHI, from where the monastery is another two hours' walk away.

Four kilometres beyond Hrisosskalítissa the road leads down to the coast opposite the tiny uninhabited islet of **ELAFONÍSSI**. You can easily wade out to the island with its sandy beaches and rock pools, and the shallow lagoon is warm and crystal-clear. In short it's perfect, but there are only two seasonal tavernas so you may want to bring your own food and water if you plan to stay.

If you can find some way of doing it, a return trip to Kastélli through Élos and Topólia is also recommended; in conjunction with an outward leg along the west coast this would make a stunningly scenic circuit. Near the ocean, villages cling desperately to the high mountainsides, apparently halted by some miracle in the midst of calamitous seaward slides. Around them olives ripen on the terraced slopes, the sea glittering far below. Inland, especially at **Élos**, the main crop is the chestnut, whose huge old trees shade the village streets. In **Topólia** the church of Ayía Sofía is sheltered inside a cave which has been known since Neolithic times. Cutting south from Élos a partly paved road continues through the high mountains towards Paleohóra; on a motorbike, with a sense of adventure and plenty of petrol, it's great: the bus doesn't come this way, villagers still stare at the sight of a tourist, and a host of small, seasonal streams cascade beside or under the track.

Getting down to Paleohóra by the main road, which is paved the whole way, is a lot easier; several daily buses from Haniá make the trip. But although this route also has to wind through the western outriders of the White Mountains, it lacks the excitement of the routes to either side. **KÁNDHANOS**, at the 58-kilometre mark, has been entirely rebuilt since it was destroyed by the Germans for its fierce resistance to their occupation. The original sign erected when the deed was done is preserved on the war memorial: 'Here stood Kandhanos, destroyed in retribution for the murder of 25 German soldiers'.

When the beach at **PALEOHÓRA** finally appears below it is a welcome sight. The little town is built across the base of a peninsula, its harbour on one side, the sand on the other. Above, on the outcrop, Venetian ramparts stand sentinel. These days Paleohóra has become heavily developed and camping on the beach, for example, is a far more risky business than it once was. If innocence and character have been sacrificed in recent years, however, the town is still enjoyable, with a main street filling in the evening with tables as diners spill out of the restaurants, and with a pleasantly chaotic social life. There are scores of places to stay (though not always many vacancies) and there's also a fair-sized campsite; in extremis the beach is still one of the best to sleep out on, with showers, trees and acres of sand. Nearby discos and a rock'n'roll bar, or the soundtrack from the open-air cinema, combine to lull you to sleep. When you tire of Paleohóra and the excellent windsurfing in the bay, there are excursions up the hill – to Prodhrómi, for example – or along a five-hour coastal path to Soúyia.

Alternatively you could take the twice-weekly boat from Paleohóra out to the island of **GÁVDHOS**, the most southerly landmass in Europe. Gávdhos is small (about 10km by 7km at the most) and relatively plain, but it has one major attraction: the enduring isolation which sixty nautical miles of rough sea have helped preserve. Not many people go, and facilities remain pretty basic (if you want to be sure of a room, book one through *Brown's Travel* in Paleohóra). If all you want is a beach to yourself and a taverna to grill your fish, this is the place for you.

travel details

Air/Sea Connections

IRÁKLIO 2 ferries daily to Pireás (12 hr.); 1 to 6 ordinary ferries to/from Thíra; up to 4 weekly hydrofoils linking Iráklio with Thíra, Íos, Náxos, and Páros in season. Ferries to Alexandria (Egypt) and Venice (Italy) every 8 to 10 days and at least weekly to Limassol (Cyprus) and Haifa (Israel). Many daily flights to Athens; seasonally daily to Rhodes, 3 or 4 weekly to Mikonos, Páros, and Thíra; 2 a week to Thessaloníki.

ÁYIOS NIKÓLAOS AND SITÍA 1 to 3 ferries a week to Kássos, Kárpathos, Hálki, and Rhodes; and (in the opposite direction) Anáfi, Thíra, Folégandhros, Síkinos, Mílos, and Pireás (15 hr.)

HANIÁ Daily boat to Piraeus (11 hr.) and one weekly to Thessaloníki; several flights a day to Athens.

KASTÉLLI (KÍSSAMOS) Twice-weekly boat to Yíthio (Peloponnese, 8 hr.), Kíthira, Neápoli, Monemvassía, and Pireás. Currently leaves on Tuesday and Friday mornings.

Main Bus Routes on the Island

Kastélli–Haniá (13 daily from 6am to 8pm; 1 1/2 hr.); Haniá–Réthimno–Iráklio (25 daily from 5.30am to 7.30pm; 4 hr. total); Iráklio–Áyios Nikólaos (20 a day from 6.30am to 8.30pm; 1 1/2 hr.); Áyios Nikólaos–Sitía (8 daily from 6.30am to 9pm; 2 hr.); Iráklio–Ierápetra (10 daily from 7.30am to 6.30pm; 2 1/2 hr.); Iráklio–Festos–Ayía Galíni (9 daily from 6.30am to 5.30 pm; 2/2 1/2 hr.);

Réthimno–Spíli–Ayía Galíni (6 daily from 6.30am to 5pm; 45 min./1 1/2hr.); Haniá–Hóra Sfakíon (4 daily from 8.30am to 3.30pm; 2 hr.); and Haniá–Paleohóra (5 daily from 9am to 5pm; 2 hr.).

Hitching on Crete is poor, rides coming mainly from tourist traffic, so if you can afford it this is one island where hir**ing bicycles, mopeds or motorbikes** makes a lot of difference. There are rental agencies in all the main towns, and most of them will give quite reasonable discounts if you're going for two or more days. Dealers in Réthimno have in the past offered the best rates.

CHAPTER NINE

DODECANESE

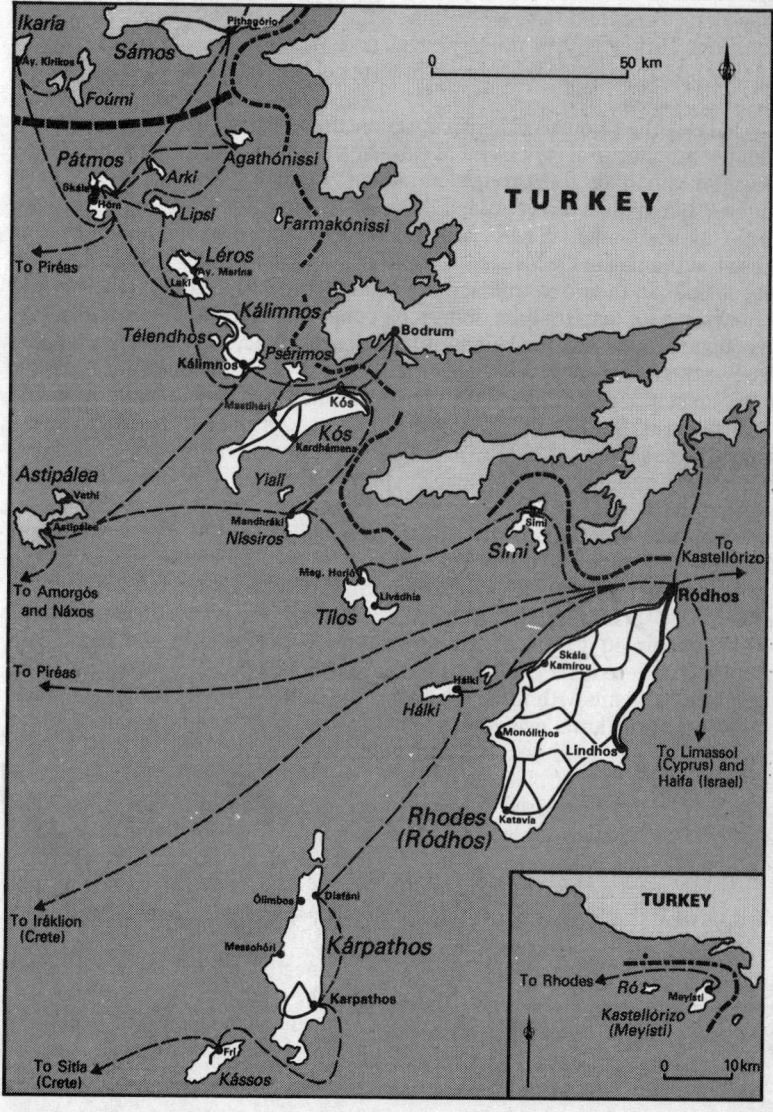

The most distant of the Greek islands, the **Dodecanese** (*Dhodhekánissos*) lie close to the Turkish coast – some, like Kós and Kastellórizo, almost within hailing distance of the shore. Because of this position, and their remoteness from Athens, the islands have always had a turbulent history; they were the scene of ferocious battles between German and British forces in 1943–44 and were only finally included in the modern Greek state in 1948 after centuries of occupation by Crusaders, Turks and Italians. Even now the threat (real or imagined) of invasion from Turkey is very much in evidence. When you ask about the heavy military presence locals talk always in terms of '*when* the Turks come', never '*if . . .*'

Whatever the rigours of the occupations, their legacy includes a wonderful blend of architectural styles and of eastern and western cultures which is the basis for much of the group's attraction. Medieval Rhodes is the most famous, but almost every island has its classical remains, its Crusaders' castle, its traditional villages, and abundant grandiose public buildings. For these last the Italians, who occupied the islands from 1913 to 1943, are mainly responsible. In their determination to beautify the islands and turn them into a showplace for fascism they undertook public works, excavations and reconstruction on a massive scale; and if historical accuracy was sometimes sacrificed in the interests of style, only the expert is likely to complain. A darker more sinister aspect of the Italian administration was the attempted forcible Latinisation of the populace; spoken Greek and Orthodox observance were banned in public from 1920 to 1943. The most tangible reminder of this policy is the great number of older people who speak Italian – or bastardised variants thereof.

Aside from this frequently encountered bilingualism, the Dodecanese themselves display a marked topographic and economic schizophrenia. The dry limestone outcrops of **Kastellórizo**, **Sími**, **Hálki**, **Kássos** and **Kálimnos** have always been forced to rely on the sea for their livelihoods, and the wealth generated by the maritime culture – especially in the nineteenth century – fostered the growth of attractive port towns. The sprawling, relatively fertile giants, **Rhodes** (Ródhos) and **Kós**, have recently seen their traditional agricultural economies almost totally displaced by a tourist industry, attracted by good beaches and nightlife, as well as the Aegean's most exciting ensembles of historical monuments. **Kárpathos** lies somewhere in between, with a (formerly) forested north grafted on to a rocky limestone south; **Tílos**, despite its lack of trees, has ample water, though the green volcano-island of **Níssiros** does not. **Léros** shelters softer contours and more amenable terrain than its map outline would suggest, while **Pátmos** and **Astipálea** at the fringes of the archipelago boast architecture and landscapes more appropriate to the Cyclades.

The largest islands in the group are connected almost daily with each other, and none is hard to reach. Rhodes is the transport hub, with services to Turkey, Israel, Egypt and Cyprus, as well as connections with Crete, the northeastern islands, the Cyclades and the mainland.

Kássos

Barren and depopulated, Kássos attracts few visitors despite being a regular port of call for the ferries. What is left of the population is grouped together in five villages in the north, under the shadow of Kárpathos, leaving most of the island unvisited and inaccessible. There is little sign here of the wealth brought into other islands by emigrant workers, nor, since the island has little to offer them, by tourists; the crumbling houses which line the village streets and the disused terraces covering the land poignantly recall better days.

It's just ten minutes' walk from **FRÍ**, the capital, to the port at EMBORIÓ; indeed the remotest village, **PÓLI**, is only 3km away. There are two hotels in Frí, neither very cheap, and in summer a few rooms. The island's beach, such as it is, is at **Ámmousa,** the other side of the underused airstrip. There's a large cave (**Selai**) nearby, with impressive stalactites.

Striking inland, especially if you're seeking isolation, is more rewarding. Between **AYÍA MARÍNA** and **ARVANITOHÓRI**, the route across the island leaves the road heading south. Civilisation is soon left behind in a silence broken only by the goat bells and an occasional wheeling hawk. Smallholdings and olive groves are still sporadically tended, but no one stays long. After about an hour the Mediterranean appears on the south of the island, a desolate mass of water broken only by the odd ship plying to Cyprus and the Middle East.

The higher fork in the way leads to the mountain chapel and monastery of **Áyios Yióryios**, while the other drops gradually down to the coast. It emerges finally at **Helathrós**, a beautiful cove at the end of a cultivated but uninhabited valley. The beach is small and sandy, the swimming great after the walk, and seabirds of every kind circle the cliffs. With plenty of supplies – hard to come by on Kássos which has little fresh produce – it could be a great place to camp.

Kárpathos

Alone of the the major Dodecanese, Kárpathos was held by the Venetians after the Byzantine collapse and so has no castle of the crusading Knights of St. John. The island has always been something of a backwater, and despite a magnificent coastline of cliffs and rocky promontories constantly interrupted by little beaches, has succumbed surprisingly little to tourism. Only the two ports, Pigádhia and Dhiafáni, are really prepared for a large influx. Most visitors come here for a glimpse of traditional village life, which had until recently carried on quite unaltered for centuries in the isolated north of the island.

Pigádhia (Kárpathos town)

PIGÁDHIA, the capital, is now more often known simply as Kárpathos. It curves around one side of Vróndis Bay, a long sickle of sandy beach stretching beyond. **Hotels** (the *Anessis* and *Avra* are recommended) and **rooms** (a

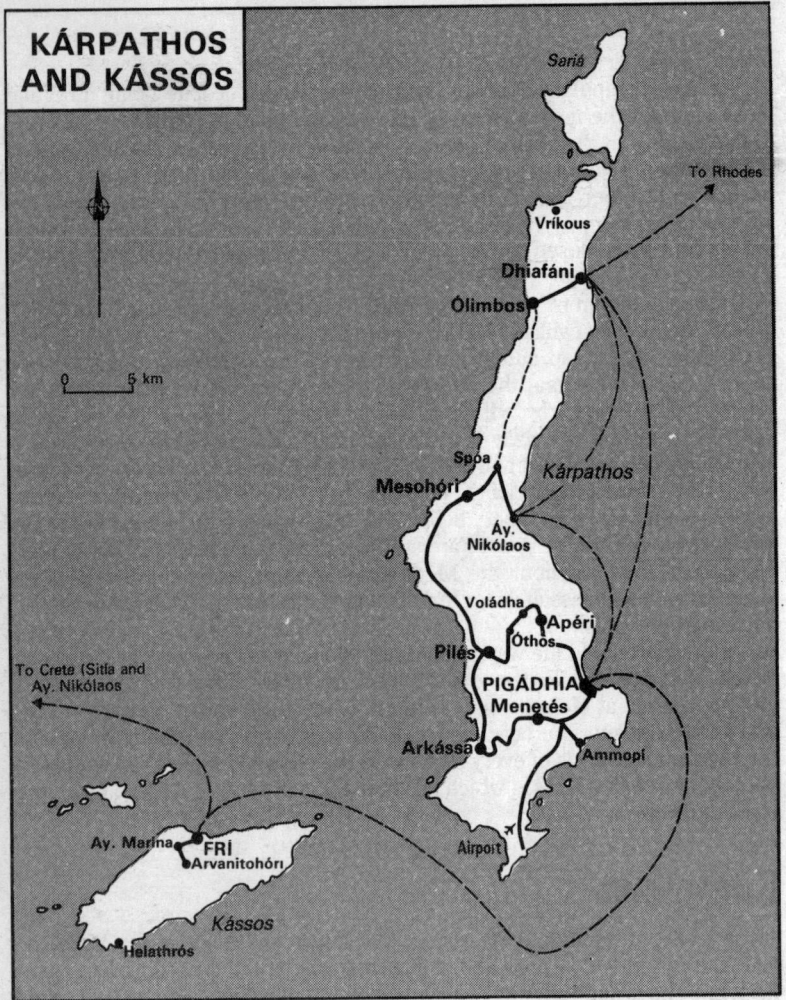

KÁRPATHOS AND KÁSSOS

handful) in town often get full in mid-summer, but the beach to the north is fine to sleep on, particularly under the trees by the ruined fifth-century basilica of **Ayía Fotiní** – you can't miss it. When there is space you'll be offered rooms at the boat docks.

From Pigádhia there are rare buses or expensive taxis to get around the south of the island or, at scandalous expense, you could hire a car or moped; hitching is an attractive, if slow, alternative.

Southern and central Kárpathos

The extreme south of the island appears rocky and forbidding but it provides a worthwhile day's diversion. **AMMOPÍ**, 7km from Pigádhia, is the closest thing on Kárpathos to a developed beach resort: two tiny sandy coves serviced by more seasonal tavernas and rooms than its natural endowments warrant. **MENITÉS**, tucked into the base of a mountain, makes a good visit for its tiny folklore museum and handsome church. **ARKÁSSA**, the end of the bus line, consists of two rows of pastel-hued houses along a stream bed, with rooms and a rudimentary taverna. Unfortunately in recent years a 'holiday village' has sprung up just to seaward.

Five minutes south of this development the relics of **ancient Arkessia** can be found on the promontory, with the mosaic floors of several Byzantine churches. The best of these have been taken to Rhodes while a large section is propped incongruously against a wall of the local school, but what is left in situ, half buried under the sand, is reason enough to visit. Just beyond is the beach, with dunes to camp on. In the other direction the fishing port of **FÍNIKES** boasts another beach and a taverna.

The lush centre of Kárpathos supports a quartet of villages – **APÉRI**, **VOLÁDHA**, **ÓTHOS** and **PILÉS** – blessed with superb hillside settings and ample running water. In these settlements nearly everyone has 'done time' in North America, then returned home with their nest eggs. New Jersey, New York, and Canadian car plates tell you exactly where repatriated islanders struck it rich. Staying in Apéri, you can walk to the isolated beaches of **Aháta** and **Kirá Panayía**.

Heading north, there is a very elusive bus as far as the villages of **SPÓA** and **MESOHÓRI** (for which you must book the night before and on which local residents get priority). It sometimes continues beyond attractive Mesohóri down to the really excellent, and nudist, beach (taverna, rooms) at **Léfkos**, which can alternatively be reached in a few hours's walk from Pilés. Spóa has its own beach annexe, **Áyios Nikólaos**, to which *kaíkia* sail from Pigádhia.

Northern Karpathos

Northern Kárpathos, though connected since 1979 by road with Spóa, continues to exist almost independently of the richer south. There is, for example, no bakery and the women bake in communal, wood-fired ovens.

Most, but not all ferries calling at Pigádhia stop also at Dhiafáni, the northern port; otherwise take a *kaíki* from Pigádhia, the cheapest way between the two except walking. Although its popularity is growing, rooms in **DHIAFÁNI** are still cheap, and life slow. Paths lead north to **Vanánda Beach**, stony but a good place to sleep among the trees, or south to more isolated, nameless strands. Other beaches are accessible only by the small fishing boats, which offer trips in Summer to the uninhabited islet of Sariá or through the narrow strait to Trístomo anchorage and the ruins of **Vrikoús**, once the island's chief port.

Whatever else you do on Kárpathos, a visit to **ÓLIMBOS** is a must. High in the mountains, the village straddles two small peaks, the ridges above studded by windmills. Although the road and electricity, together with a growing number of tourists, are swiftly dragging the place into the twentieth century, it hasn't arrived yet. The women here are immediately striking in their magnificent traditional dress and after a while you notice that they also dominate the village: working in the gardens, carrying goods on their shoulders, or tending the mountain sheep. As on several other of the Dodecanese, property inheritance is matrilineal with houses passing down from mother to eldest daughter upon marriage. Ólimbos men nearly all emigrate or work outside the village, sending money home and returning only at holidays. The long-isolated villagers also speak a unique dialect, said to maintain traces of its Doric and Phrygian origins. Traditional music is still heard regularly and draws considerable crowds of visitors at festival times. From the village, the west coast and tiny port and beach at **Frísses** are a dizzy drop below.

You can get to Ólimbos expensively by taxi from the south, or make the spectacular six-to-seven hour trek from Spóa or Messohóri. Unfortunately a massive fire devastated most of the pine forests around Ólimbos in 1983, making the walk that much less enticing. Alternatively you can stay the night in Dhiafáni and take a less strenuous and possibly more scenic walk up from there. A path – shorter and greatly preferable to the road – leads up a ravine through whatever is left of the forest. A small stream runs beside most of the way, and there is a spring; at your approach snakes slither into hiding and partridges break cover.

As you near the top take the left, lower fork. (The other leads on to Mount Avlóna and down to Vrikoús.) From Avlóna's summit, conditions permitting, you can see Crete to the east and all the islands north as far as Kós. It takes nearly two hours to reach Ólimbos, longer with a pack, but you are well rewarded when you make it. There are several cheap places to stay (*Pension Anixi*, run by a retired member of the local folk dance troupe, is recommended) and a couple of tavernas if your hosts do not cook for you. Be advised, though, that it is impossible to get a room around the dates of any festival.

Rhodes (Ródhos)

It's no accident that Rhodes is among the most visited of Greek islands. Not only is its east coast lined with sandy beaches, but much of the capital is a beautiful and remarkably preserved medieval city. Sadly, it is crammed with tourists – as many as 50,000 a day – throughout the year. For some reason Scandinavians predominate, revelling in the cheap drink; the post office has one box for Sweden, one for the rest of Europe, and smorgasbord is as much a local delicacy as *moussaká*. British package tourists, too, are very much part of the local scene.

Ródhos town

RÓDHOS TOWN divides neatly into two: the old walled city, and the new town which has oozed out around it. Throughout, the tourist is king. In the new town especially, the few buildings which aren't hotels are casinos, bars or discos. Around them stretches the beach (standing room only for latecomers), complete with deckchairs, parasols and showers. At the northernmost point there's a dubious alternative: an uninteresting aquarium and a museum with an extraordinary collection of grotesque freaks of nature (a Cyclopean goat, an eight-legged calf) and apparently rotting stuffed fish.

The **old town** is infinitely more rewarding. First thing to meet the eye, and dominating the northeast sector of the city's fortifications, is the **Palace of the Grand Masters**. Destroyed by an ammunition depot explosion in 1856, it was reconstructed by the Italians as a summer home for Mussolini and Victor Emmanuel III ('King of Italy and Albania, Emperor of Ethiopia'), neither of whom used it much. The exterior is as authentic as possible, but inside things are on an altogether grander scale; a marble staircase leads up to rooms paved with mosaics from Kós, and the furnishings rival many a grand northern European palace. Hidden from view are elevators, central heating, and the other essentials of life as a modern dictator (open Mon.–Sat. 8am–7pm, Sun. 9am–6pm; closed Tues). On Monday and Saturday afternoons there is a supplementary tour of the **city walls** – the only access permitted, if you're interested.

The heavily restored **Street of the Knights** (Odhós Ippotón) leads due east from the Palace Square; the 'Inns' lining it housed the Knights of St. John, according to linguistic/ethnic affiliation, for two centuries. Halfway down peek through a locked gate into a shady garden where a beautiful Turkish fountain runs continuously, surrounded by cannon–balls. At the bottom of the grade the Knights' Hospital has been restored as the **Archaeological Museum** (open Mon.–Sat. 8am–7pm, Sun. 9.30am–2pm; closed Tues.). The star exhibits are two statues of Aphrodite, one dubbed the 'Marine Venus' by Lawrence Durrell.

If you leave the Palace heading straight south, it's hard to miss the most conspicuous Turkish monument in Rhodes, the candy-striped **Suleiman mosque**. The old town is in fact well-sown with mosques and *medressas* (Islamic theological academies), many of them are converted from Byzantine shrines. A couple are still used.

Many of the sizeable Turkish-speaking minority here are descended from Cretan Muslims, deported from that island in 1913 and initially resettled in the run-down village of **Kritika** on the way to the airport road. Native Rhodian Muslims make up the majority of those living in the old town, unconcernedly mixing Greek with Turkish in everday speech. Their most enduring civic contribution is the fantastic **bath house** on Platía Ariónos up in the southwest corner of the old city. One of only a couple of working public baths in Greece, it's a great place to go on a cool, off-season day; open Mon.–Fri. 5am–7pm, slightly shorter hours but cheaper rates on Wed. and Sat.; closed Sun. (For hot days there's a free **public pool** hidden in a triangle of greenery 50m from the tourist office in the new town.)

Heading downhill and east from the Suleiman mosque, **Odhós Sokrátous**, once the heart of the old bazaar, is now the 'Via Turista', packed with souvenir shops and milling foreigners. Beyond the fountain in Platía Ippokrátous, Aristotélous leads into the Platía ton Evreón Martirón (the Square of the

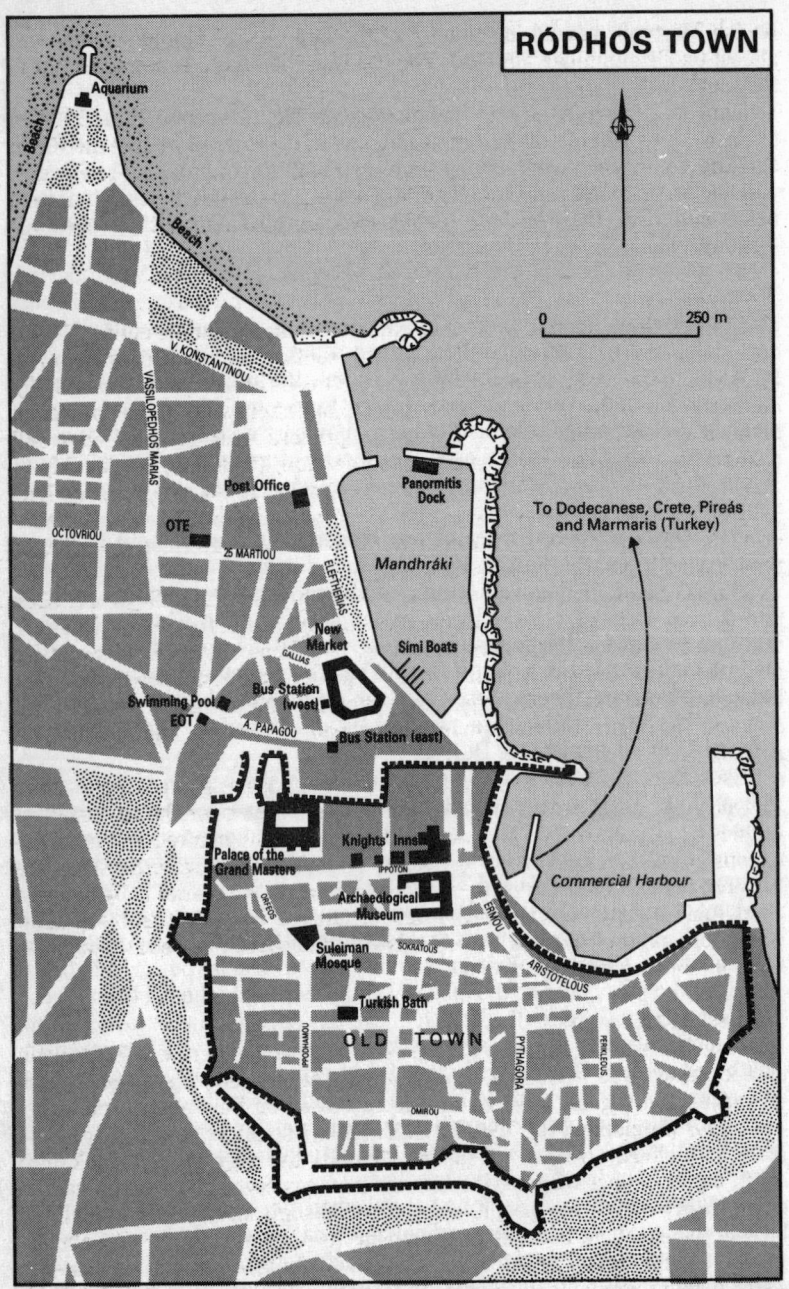

RÓDHOS TOWN

Aquarium

Beach

Beach

V. KONSTANTINOU

VASSILOPEOHOS MARIAS

OCTOVRÍOU

Post Office

OTE

25 MARTIOU

ELEFTHERIAS

Panormítis
Dock

Mandhráki

To Dodecanese, Crete, Pireás
and Marmaris (Turkey)

New
Market

GALLIAS

Bus Station
(west)

Swimming Pool

EOT

A. PAPAGOU

Simi Boats

Bus Station (east)

Knights' Inns
IPPOTON

Palace of the
Grand Masters

OREOU

Archaeological
Museum

SOKRATOUS

ENNOU

Commercial Harbour

Suleiman
Mosque

ARISTOTELOUS

Turkish Bath

OLD TOWN

PYTHAGORA

PERIKLEOUS

IPPODAMOU

OMIROU

0   250 m

Jewish Martyrs), named in memory of the large local community that was almost totally annihilated in 1943. You can visit the ornate **synagogue** just to the south.

Simply to catalogue the principal monuments like this cannot do full justice to the old city. There's an enormous amount of pleasure to be had merely in strolling the streets, under flying archways built for earthquake resistance, past the warm-toned sandstone and lava walls splashed with ochre and blue paint, and over the *hokhláki* (pebble-mosaic) pavement. It all deserves scrutiny.

Practicalities

Cheap pensions abound in Ródhos and are contained almost entirely in the quad bounded by Odhós Omírou on the south, Sokrátous on the north, Perikléos to the east and Ippodhámou in the west. Outside peak season lodging is the one thing still reasonably priced, but at crowded times, or late at night, it's wise to accept the offers of proprietors meeting the ferries and change base next day if necessary. Most **ferries**, (including 2–6 weekly to Marmaris, Turkey) dock in the main, central port. Important exceptions include the *Panormitis* and the seasonal hydrofoils which call near the easternmost antelope column in Mandhráki harbour, and the tourist ferries to Sími leaving from Mandhráki's inner quay.

Eating cheaply can be more of a problem; try the little alleys and back streets away from the Sokrátous area and the square of the Jewish Martyrs, or up near Omírou. Examples include a dirt-cheap restaurant downstairs from the *Hotel Sydney*; a *patsás* (tripe) kitchen on Aristotélous; *Kostas* at Pithágora 62 for moderately expensive seafood; *To Kalo Pedhi*, a primitive but delicious grill just off Sokrátous; and cheap ice cream and pudding at *Anatoliko* nearby at Sokrátous 9.

OTE, the **post office**, **banks**, **EOT** and the police are all in the new town, arrayed around the New Market (a tourist trap). **Buses** for the east coast of Rhodes leave from Odhós Papágou, within sight of the market, and for destinations on the west coast from Odhós Avérof, just outside. Services are frequent but relatively expensive; moped or **motorbike rental** is by contrast good value (partly because of deficient insurance coverage) and will allow you to escape the worst of the crowds on the coast or penetrate inland to some interesting rural spots.

The east coast

Heading down the coast from Ródhos you have to go some way before you escape the crowds from local beach hotels, their numbers swelled by visitors using the regular buses from the capital or on boat and coach tours. The giant promontory of **TSAMBÍKAS**, 26km south of town, is the first place to seriously consider stopping. Actually the very eroded flank of a much larger extinct volcano, the hill has a monastery at the summit said to enjoy superb views; few people enjoy them, though, because they're all too busy at the excellent beaches of Tsambíkas itself (to the south) or Kolímbia (north). At Tsambíkas beach there are a couple of tavernas and the water is warm early in spring (and teeming with people all summer). **KOLÍMBIA**'s tiny harbour – a submerged caldera ringed with volcanic rock – offers similar amenities.

Walking inland from the Kolímbia bus stop you'll reach **Eptá Piyés**, a superb oasis with a tiny reservoir for swimming and an unusual streamside taverna (about 3km). Best overnight base on this stretch of coast is probably **HARÁKI**, a small beach town with rooms and tavernas overlooked by the impressive **feraklós castle**.

LÍNDHOS, Rhodes' number-two tourist draw, irrupts 12km south of here. Like Ródhos town itself, its charm is undermined by the commercialism and the crowds, and there are only a few places to stay not booked semi-permanently by tour companies. It can be a dispiriting sight to see dozens of buses parked nose-to-tail on the access road, and even more on the drive down to the beach, strung like beads on an abacus calculating overdevelopment.

Nevertheless, if you can arrive before or after the tours, when the pebble streets between its immaculately whitewashed houses are empty, Líndhos can still be a beautiful and atmospheric place. The **Byzantine church** is covered with eighteenth-century frescoes, and several of the older houses are open to the public; entrance is free but they tend to expect you to buy something. On the hill above the town, the ancient acropolis with its eminently photogenic Doric **Temple of Athena** (6th c. B.C.) is found inside the **castle** (open Mon.–Sat. 8am–6pm, Sun 8:30am-5pm) – a surprisingly easy blending of two cultures.

Despite the crowds the beach at Líndhos is also one of the finest on the island, and there are other superb stretches to either side. On the south flank of the acropolis hides the small, sheltered **St. Paul's Harbour**, where the apostle is said to have landed, though the apostle would doubtless turn in his grave at the topless Scandinavian sun-worshippers. **LÁRDHOS BAY**, 10km further south, has great dunes behind its beach, and there are intermittent sandy patches all the way down along the sparsely inhabited southeast sector of the island.

The west coast

On the west coast as in the east, the first few kilometres have been surrendered entirely to package tourism. The most important archaeological site on this shore is **KAMIROS**, which with Lindhos and Ialyssos was one of the three powers that united to found the ancient Classical city-state of Ródhos. Soon eclipsed by the new capital, Kamiros was abandoned and only rediscovered in the last century. As a result it is a particularly well-preserved Doric city, doubly worth visiting for its beautiful hillside site (open Mon.–Sat. 8:30am-4pm, Sun. 9am–3:30pm). On the beach below Kamiros there are several tavernas, and more line the route to the modern fishing port of **Skála Kamírou**, 15km to the south. From here a *kaíki* runs daily to the island of **Hálki** (see account following).

Farther down the coastal road, between Kritiniá and Amártos, a side road detours up to **EMBÓNAS**, a somewhat nondescript village at the foot of barren Mt. Atáviros. There's a marked track up to the 1215-metre summit, where there used to be a temple of Zeus. The village itself is more geared to

To Marmaris

To Simi, Tilos, and Kos

To Pireás

To Kastellórizo

RÓDHOS

Triánda
Kremastí
Paradhíssi

Ialyssos   Koskinóu

Soroní   Airport

Faliráki

Kámiros
Petaloúdhes

Sálakos

Afándou

Alimiá   Skála Kamírou

Mt. Profítis Ilías

Eleoússa   Kolímbia

Eptá Piyés   Tsambíkas

Hálki   Kritiniá

Horió   Embóna   Arhángelos

Emborió   Mt. Atáviros

Haráki

Siána   Láerma

Monólithos   LÍNDHOS

Profília   Lárdhos

Apolakiá

Yenádhi

Rhodes (Rhódos)   Skiádhi

To Kárpathos, Kássos and Crete

Katavía

Plimíri

0   10 km

Prassoníssi

RHODES AND HÁLKI

handling tourists than you might expect, as the target of summer 'folk dance tours' from Ródhos town. If the few rooms are full you can beg a bed in the town hall, a practice still honoured in many rural Greek communities.

Back on the southward route, the most attractive village hereabouts is **SIÁNA**, just before Monólithos, the end of the bus line. MONÓLITHOS itself, with its drab, flat-roofed farmhouses, hardly justifies the trip out here, but the dramatic **old castle** atop the steep cliffs to the southwest is draw enough in itself.

The interior

Inland Rhodes is mountainous, wooded, and requires your own vehicle to visit effectively. While a few locales seen together may leave an agreeable impression, no one site justifies the tremendous expense of a taxi or trying to make the best of the inconvenient schedules of the occasional buses.

In retrospect it will probably be the scenery which stands out, along with the last vestiges of the old agrarian life in the slowly depopulating villages. Such young Rhodians as do remain here stay largely to help with the grape harvest in late summer (when there's a fair chance of work for foreigners too). If you have time to spare, and a bit of Greek at your command, traditional hospitality, in the form of a glass of *soúma* (local firewater) or perhaps more, is still very much alive.

Just shy of the airport, turn inland at Triánda for the five-kilometre uphill ride to ancient **Ialyssos** on Filérimos hill. Important as this city was, its visible remains are few; most conspicuous are a subterranean chapel covered with faded frescoes and a Doric fountain. The pine-covered slopes here also shelter the grounds of Filérimos monastery (which you can visit) and a Byzantine castle, but the whole ensemble won't take more than an hour of your time.

Starting from the east coast, if you were to continue inland from Eptá Piyés you'd reach Eleoússa village after some twelve kilometres. Just past this lies the late Byzantine church of **Áyios Nikólaos Foundoúkli** (St. Nicholas of the Hazelnuts), the island's finest, with frescoes from the thirteenth to the fifteenth centuries. Once beyond Eleoússa you must choose between a left fork up to wooded Profítis Ilías, with fine walking country around the former summer residence of the Italian governor, or bearing north toward Soroní on a good road through fine scenery. Part way there's the turning to **Petaloúdhes** or the 'Valley of the Butterflies' which, as on Páros, is actually a Jersey tiger moth valley and which might nowadays more accurately be christened the 'Valley of the Tour Buses'.

The far south

South of a line connecting Monólithos and Lárdhos, you could easily begin to think you had strayed on to another island – at least until you saw the prices. Gone are the spanking new roads and the luxury hotels, and with them most of the crowds. Gone too, however, are the tourist facilities and most of the public transport. Only one daily bus runs to Katavía, along the **east coast**. It's here in the east that you'll find the less developed beaches: often windy, but with dunes which offer shelter and plenty of scope for secluded camping. Tavernas grace the better stretches of sand but there are few places to stay. The main exceptions are at **YENÁDHI**, where you can find rooms in the village and fresh springwater on the beach, and **PLIMÍRI**, way in the south, where the restaurant has some very basic beds.

Beyond Plimíri the road curves inland to **KATAVÍA**, with one or two rooms available if you ask around. In fact there are many empty houses here, but most are locked, awaiting the return of their owners off working in Australia or North America. Only 350 of the registered population of 2000 live he. permanently; this includes a small hamlet of 'Turks' on the edge of the village. A few kilometres north is the fourteenth-century hilltop **monastery of Skiádhi**, which houses a miraculous icon of the Virgin and Child; in the fifteenth century a heretic stabbed the painting, and blood was said to have flowed from the wound in the Mother of God's cheek. The fissure, and suspicious brown stains around it, are still visible.

From Katavía a rough track leads on to Prassoníssi (Leek Island), past the twin roadside shrines marking the spot where two lovers from Katavía took their own lives, stymied by the Greek ecclesiastical law which forbids a man to marry his sister-in-law (or a woman her brother-in-law). **Prassoníssi** is Rhodes' southernmost extremity and the site of a lighthouse run by an elderly couple. In summer you can stroll across the slender sandspit to visit, but winter storms swamp this tenuous link and render the outpost a true island. One virtue of the wide Prassoníssi beach is that the sand is distributed to either side, so you can choose according to which quarter the wind is blowing from.

From Katavía to Monólithos, the **west coast** consists of windswept, totally deserted, sandy beaches. If freelance camping and nudism are your thing, this is the place to indulge, though you'll need your own conveyance or lots of supplies and a stout pair of boots. The nearest town is modern and unexciting **APOLAKIÁ**, a few kilometres inland but equipped with a general store and a few pensions. The logistics of staying in southern Rhodes may seem a bit daunting, but with a little advance planning the beaches are yours to enjoy in surprising isolation.

Hálki

Hálki is a member of the Dodecanese in its own right, though all but 400 of the population have decamped (mostly to Rhodes or to Tarpon Springs, Florida) in the wake of a devasting sponge blight early in this century. Compared to Rhodes the island is marvellously tranquil – the big event of the day is when someone catches a fish – but this may soon change. In 1983 UNESCO designated Hálki as the 'isle of peace and friendship', and made it the seat of an annual summer international youth conference. (Tílos was approached first but declined the honour). As part of the deal, 150 crumbling houses in the harbour town of **EMBORIÓ** were to be restored as guest lodges for the delegates and other interested parties, with UNESCO footing the bill. The single, half-built hotel was in fact finally finished, since the critical lack of fresh water, which had hampered all previous attempts at tourist development, was supposedly remedied by the discovery of ample undersea deposits by a French geological team.

As of 1987 none of these grandiose plans had seriously been acted on. The only tangible sign of 'peace and friendship' was an unending stream of UNESCO and Athenian bureaucrats and their dependents occupying every available bed at unpredictable intervals and staging drunken, musical binges under the guise of 'ecological conferences'. The islanders, fed up with what had obviously turned out to be a scam, sent the freeloaders packing at the end of the year and now intend to run the hotel as a going concern and finish the water projects, thus attracting package tourists (already arriving) and independent travellers. So for a very brief interval there's still time to enjoy the sleepy atmosphere on this tiny (40 square km) limestone speck. In the summer you'll have fierce competition for the handful of rooms in Emborió, and plenty of company at the four tavernas. But if you're staying any length of time, especially in the off-season, you can rent an entire house ridiculously cheaply. There's a **post office** (open as little as possible), three stores, a bakery, and two beaches nearby: one sandy and minute, the other larger and pebbly.

Three kilometres inland lies the old pirate-safe village of **HORIÓ**, abandoned in the 1950s but still crowned by the Knights' castle. Across the way the little church of **Stavrós** is venue for one of the two big island festivals on September 14. There's little else to see or do here, though you can **walk** across the island in an enjoyable couple of hours. The cobble path picks up where the cement 'Tarpon Springs Boulevard' mercifully ends; the latter was donated by the expatriate community in Florida to insure easy Cadillac access to the Stavrós *paniyíri* grounds, though what Hálki really needed (and still needs) is a proper sewage system and salt-free water supply. Walk's end is the monastery of **Áyios Ioánnis Pródhromos**. The caretaking family there can put you up in a cell (except around August 29, the other big festival date); you'll need to bring supplies. The terrain en route is monotonous, but compensated by views over half the Dodecanese and Turkey.

Kastellórizo (Meyísti)

Little more than three nautical miles off the Turkish coast and over seventy from its nearest Greek neighbour (Rhodes), Kastellórizo's official name, Meyísti (Biggest), seems more an act of defiance than a statement of fact. It is the smallest of the Dodecanese, and arriving at night you find its lights quite outnumbered by those of the Turkish town of Kas across the bay.

Less than a century ago there were 15,000 people here, supported by a fleet of schooners which made fortunes transporting goods from the Greek towns of Kalamaki (now Kalkan) and Andifelos (Kas) on the Anatolian mainland. But the advent of steam power and the Italian seizure of the Dodecanese in 1913 sent the island into a decline from which it never recovered. Shipowners failed to modernise their fleets, preferring to sell their ships to the British for the Dardanelles campaign, and the new frontier between the island and republican Turkey, combined with the expulsion of all Anatolian Greeks in 1923, deprived any remaining vessels of their former trade. During the 1930s Kastellórizo enjoyed a brief renaissance when it became a major stopover point for the seaplanes of *Alitalia* and *Air France*, but events at the close of World War II put an end to any hopes of the island's continued viability.

When Italy capitulated to the Allies in the autumn of 1943, a few hundred British commandos occupied Meyísti until displaced by a stronger German force in the spring or early summer of 1944. At some stage during the hasty departure of Commonwealth forces, the fuel dump caught fire and an adjacent arsenal exploded, taking with it more than half of the 2000 houses on Meyísti. Inquiries have concluded that the retreating Allies did some looting, though it was probably Greek pirates engaging in some pillaging of their own who accidentally or deliberately caused the conflagration. In any event the British are not especially popular on Kastellórizo; islanders are further angered by the fact that an Anglo-Greek reparations committee has for almost thirty years delayed payment of reparations to the 850 surviving householders.

Even before these events most of the population had left for Rhodes, Athens, Australia and North America, and today there are barely 200 people living permanently on Kastellórizo. These are largely maintained by remittances from the thousands of emigrants and by subsidies from the Greek government, which fears that the island will revert to Turkey should the number diminish any further. The remaining population concentrates in the northern harbour – the finest, so it is said, between Beirut and Pireás – and its little 'suburb' of **Mandhráki**, just over the fire-blasted hill with its ruined castle of the Knights. Locals may not admit it, but the Anatolian influence on the surviving quayside houses, with their tiled roofs, wooden balconies and long, narrow windows, is evident. One street behind the waterside, though, all is desolation; abandonment having seen to most of the villas which the 1944 fire missed.

Despite its apparently terminal plight, Kastellórizo may have a future of sorts. The government recently dredged the harbour to accommodate cruise ships, completed an airport inland for flights to and from Rhodes, and made the island an official port of entry, a measure calculated to appeal to the yachties who call here. The interesting local **history museum** has been moved one building up from the old **mosque**, and the mosque itself will supposedly re-open as a duty-free shop. Each summer, too, the population is swelled by returnees of 'Kassie' ancestry, some of whom celebrate traditional weddings in the **Áyios Konstantínos** cathedral with its ancient columns pilfered from Patara in Asia Minor.

There is one modern hotel, the *Meyísti*, and a few other **rooms** for let, but despite the recent flurry of activity the island is not prepared for – nor does it get – more than a handful of casual visitors. Water has to be collected in cisterns during the winter, and almost all the food at the three or four quayside tavernas is shipped in from Rhodes, fish being the one inexpensive exception. If you **swim** you'll discover an incredible abundance of multicoloured marine life around these shores, and though there is no beach, the sea is usually clear and flat as glass, perfect for snorkelling off the rocks and steps. Over on the east coast, accessible only by boat, is the grotto of **Parásta**, famed for its stalactites and the strange blue-light effects inside; it's also inhabited by seals, which can be quite aggressive if you get too close. Heat (infernal in summer) permitting, you can walk south and west of the port on good paths past country chapels to **Paleokástro**, site of the Doric city. From the heights you've tremendous views over the elephant's-foot-shaped harbour and surrounding Greek islets across to Turkey. None of these smaller islands are inhabited today but until recently 'The Lady of Rho', one of the islets, resolutely hoisted the Greek flag each day in defiance of the Turks on the mainland; she died a couple of years back, at the age of 104.

Kastellórizo has traditionally depended heavily on produce smuggled across from Kas and for years (during the port captain's siesta, of course) it was fairly easy to arrange a ride over **to Turkey** for the day. Recent reports indicate that this has changed, with the authorities zealously enforcing the rules. This seems ridiculous since both Kastellórizo and Kaş are official ports of entry for the countries involved. The ferry **back to Rhodes** takes six hours, more in bad weather (if it runs at all) and a 'direct' trip to Pireás can last up to 34 hours. Planes to Rhodes are small, expensive STOL craft; in sum Meyísti is not a place to be at the end of a holiday if you're committed to a particular return flight.

Sími

Sími's great problem, lack of water, is in many ways also its greatest asset. However much it might want to, the island can't hope to support more than two or three luxury hotels. Instead hundreds of people are shipped in daily from Rhodes, relieved of their money and sent back. This arrangement suits both the islanders and the few visitors who stay. If you are among the latter, the former become quite friendly once it's clear that you're not a day-tripper. Many foreigners are regular customers and come back several times a year, or even own houses here.

The island's capital consists of **Yialós**, the port, and **Horió**, on the hillside above, collectively known as **SÍMI**. Incredibly, less than a hundred years ago the town was richer and more populous (30,000) than Rhodes. Wealth came, despite the barren land, from a fame in shipbuilding and sponge-diving which go back to pre-Classical times. Vestiges of both activities remain, but the magnificent nineteenth-century mansions are now for the most part roofless and deserted, their windows gaping blankly across the harbour. As on Kastellórizo, a war-time ammunition dump blast – this time set off by the retreating Germans – levelled hundreds of houses up in Horió. Shortly after, the official surrender of the Dodecanese was signed here on May 8, 1945; a plaque commemorates the spot at the present-day *Restaurant Les Katerinettes* and each year on that date there's a fine festival with live music and dancing.

Around the port
The 3000 remaining Simiotes are distributed fairly evenly through the mixture of neoclassical and more typical island dwellings, with most tourist amenities also divided between Horió and the harbour. Down in Yialós, *Sími Tours*, on the waterfront, can sometimes arrange houses for longer periods. Independent travellers planning to stay just a few days have their needs catered for by a trio of inexpensive **pensions** (the *Egli* (☎0241/71-392), *Haska,* (☎0241/71-340), and *Glafkos* (☎0241/71-358)), all grouped around the main *platía*. Before settling on a room make sure that there is water, especially in late summer! Next notch up is represented by the hotels *Zephyros* and *Panormitis*, though if you have the budget for it, you can splurge at the relatively luxurious *Nireus* or *Dorian*.

Best meals in Yialós are found at *Zephyros*, on the waterside near the square, or at the bar/*psistariá O Navtergatis*, 100m back from the quay near the icon painter's shop, though the most popular establishments seem to be *The Trawler* and *Kyriakos's International Restaurant*. Quality and fair price are only relative concepts here, owing to prevailing mercenary attitudes, and you're better advised to forsake the seamier side of Sími (couldn't resist that) for the delights of Horió.

The two stair-paths up, effective against many of the day-trippers and most dramatically climbed towards sunset, deposit you close to assorted shops, the recommended *Yiorgos's Taverna*, and the *Rainbow Hotel*; there are also cheap

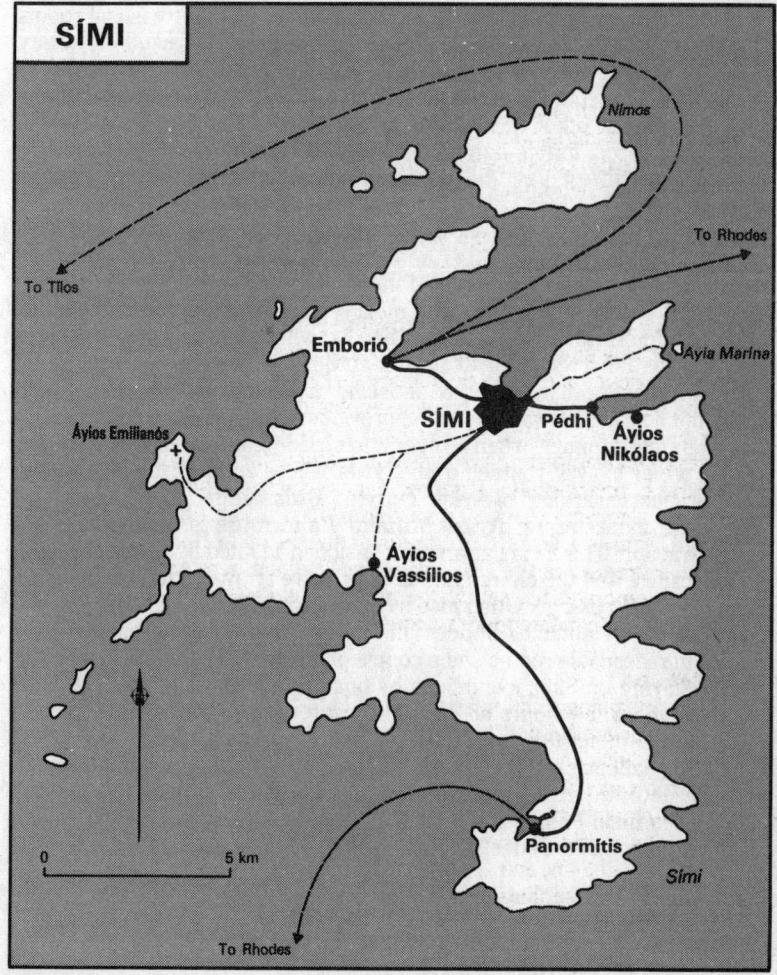

rooms available and all told you'll probably have a better time in this surprisingly large village than down at Yialós. Higher up, the island **museum** contains the usual assortment of local archaeological finds, traditional costumes, antiques and junk salvaged from better days, while at the very pinnacle of things a **castle** occupies the site of Sími's ancient acropolis, surrounded by a dozen chapels.

The island

Sími has no big sandy beaches, but there are plenty of pebbly stretches at the heads of the deep narrow bays which indent the coastline. **PÉDHI**, 45 minutes' walk or a ten-minute regular bus ride from Yialós, is a hamlet in one of Sími's only farming valleys with an average beach, some seasonal rooms and an exorbitantly-priced new hotel. Many will opt for another twenty minutes of walking via goat track on the south shore of Pédhi Bay to **ÁYIOS NIKÓLAOS**, stony but sheltered for camping and with fine swimming and a drinks stall. On the other (north) side of Yialós, you'll find **Nos** beach by the boat-building yards, usable only in the morning. From here a two-kilometre track leads northwest past the water desalinisation plant to very average **Emborió** beach

For energetic walkers with *sturdy* footwear, or those prepared to pay for a boat trip, there are plenty of other better and more secluded coves. You can cross the island – which has retained much of its ancient coniferous cover – in two hours to **Áyios Vassílios**, the most scenic and sheltered of the gulfs, or in a little more time to **Áyios Emilianós**, where you can stay the night (bring supplies) in a wave-lashed cloister at the island's extreme west end. At **Ayía Marína**, you can swim out to an island monastery, but the hour's walk there is not nearly as rewarding as the previous two. The map sold on Sími is accurate in mid-summer, when temperatures rise well, though into the 90°s, you may prefer to avail yourself of the boats. These are, too, the only way to reach the spectacular fjord of **Áyios Yióryios Dhissálona**.

The huge monastery of **Áyios Mihális Panormítis** is Sími's other big tourist attraction. This local patron saint has been adopted by Greek sailors in the Dodecanese and the church has an impressive array of offerings in appreciation for a safe passage. Otherwise it caters mainly for the day-trippers who stop on their way home to Rhodes; the monks' traditional hospitality takes the form of reasonable rooms and a couple of tavernas. There is also a beach. If you're staying on Sími, excursions by boat, or a jeep/walk/boat combination, allow you a few hours at Panormítis, but even so you should make a beeline for the monastery on arrival; too many tourists have had their effect on monastic patience and the church will be closed within a few minutes, not to reopen until the next group (if any) appears. All in all, don't expect too much of; the main impression is of the massive amount of concrete which must have gone into the construction.

Tílos

The small island of Tílos is one of the least visited of the Dodecanese, although it's now on the list of day trips from Rhodes and Kós. Why anyone should want to visit for just a few hours is a mystery, for while it's not a bad place to rest up on the beach or go walking, there is nothing very striking at first glance.

A road (*the* road) runs the seven kilometres from Livádhia, the port, to Megálo Horió, the capital and only other significant habitation. When the boat arrives there is usually some sort of vehicle to take passengers and goods between the two, but at other times you either walk or hitch. Since there are only about fifteen vehicles on the island, the latter can be a slow business.

Of the two villages, **LIVÁDHIA** is the more ready to deal with tourists but the better beaches are around Megálo Horió. Near the harbour there are several **restaurants** (best are *Blue Sky* and *Irini*), two **hotels** and several **rooms** establishments (most reasonable being *Kastello*). Livádhia also has two grocery stores and the usual small-island combination **OTE/post office**.

Staying in **MEGÁLO HORIÓ**, your choices are restricted to two **rooms** outfits and an equal number of **tavernas** which may open only in the evenings. On the other hand you are close to the passable, exposed beach of **Áyios**

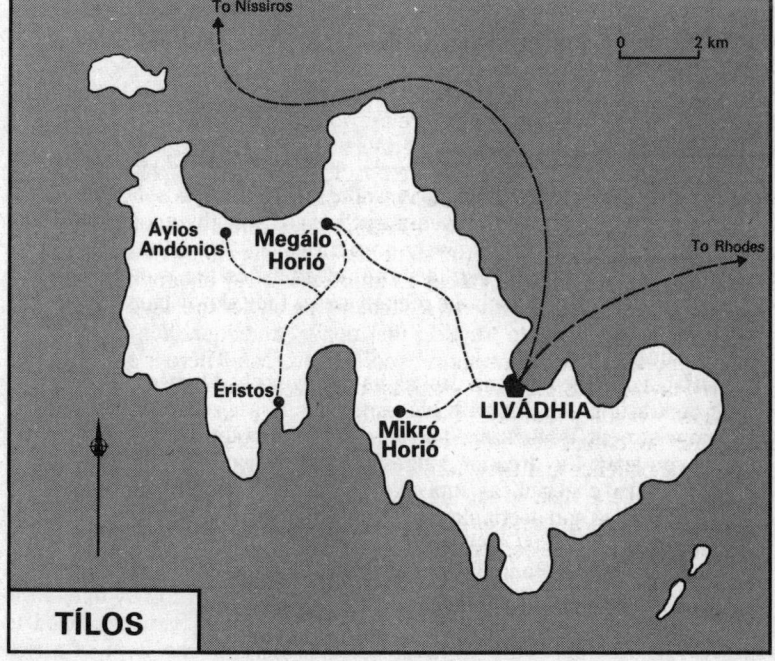

Andónios (one hotel and taverna) on the north shore and the excellent sands at **ÉRISTOS**, 45 minutes due south of Megálo Horió or 1½ hour's walk from Livádhia, and helpfully signposted on the road between the two villages. There are two tavernas near this beach, one of which, the *Nausica*, is particularly good and has rooms to let. It is actually part of a small farm and often has home-grown produce to supplement the freshly caught fish.

Anything fresh is a bonus on Tílos; although the island has ample water it is curiously barren, and even bread has to be imported from Sími or Rhodes. In summer the restaurants do enough business to have vegetables shipped in, but out of season it can be hard to come by any food at all. If worst comes to worst, fishing off the beaches is surprisingly productive.

Things to 'see' on Tílos include the one-roomed **museum** in Megálo Horió, with the usual small-island mixture of archaeological finds, local history and nineteenth-century kitsch. Above the town is a Venetian castle, and on the way to it remains of Pelasgian walls, 12,000-year-old relics of the earliest known Greeks.

Above Livádhia looms another **castle** accessible only to rock climbers, but follow the path which looks as if it leads there and you can clamber down to a small beach on the southwest coast, or go further to totally deserted corners of the island. From the higher points there are views across to Turkey.

Between Livádhia and Érestos is the hamlet of **MIKRÓ HORIÓ**, inhabited until recently but now abandoned to the sheep and goats. In the same direction there's a cave where the petrified bones of several mammoths were discovered during the 1970s – you'll need a guide to get there and a torch when you arrive.

Níssiros

Volcanic Níssiros is noticeably cooler and greener than its southern neighbours, and unlike them has proved attractive and wealthy enough to retain most of its population, staying lively even in winter. The island's income is largely derived from quarrying; offshore towards Kós the islet of Yialí is a vast lump of gypsum on which the miners live as they slowly chip it away.

The north coast
MANDHRÁKI is the port and capital, its tightly packed houses decorated in bright, contrasting colours, with blue swatches of sea visible at the ends of the narrow streets. Whitewashed snakes-and-ladders thread across the pavement as you leave the drearier fringes near the ferry dock, and the bulk of the place looks cheerful, as indeed it is, arrayed around the communal orchard or *kámbos* and overlooked by two ancient fortresses.

Into a corner of the first of these, the predictable Knights' castle, is wedged the little monastery of **Panayía Spilianí**, built on this spot in accordance with the instructions of the Virgin herself, apprehended in a vision by one of the first Christian islanders. Its prestige grew after raiding Saracens failed to discover the vast quantities of silver secreted here, in the form of a rich collection of Byzantine icons.

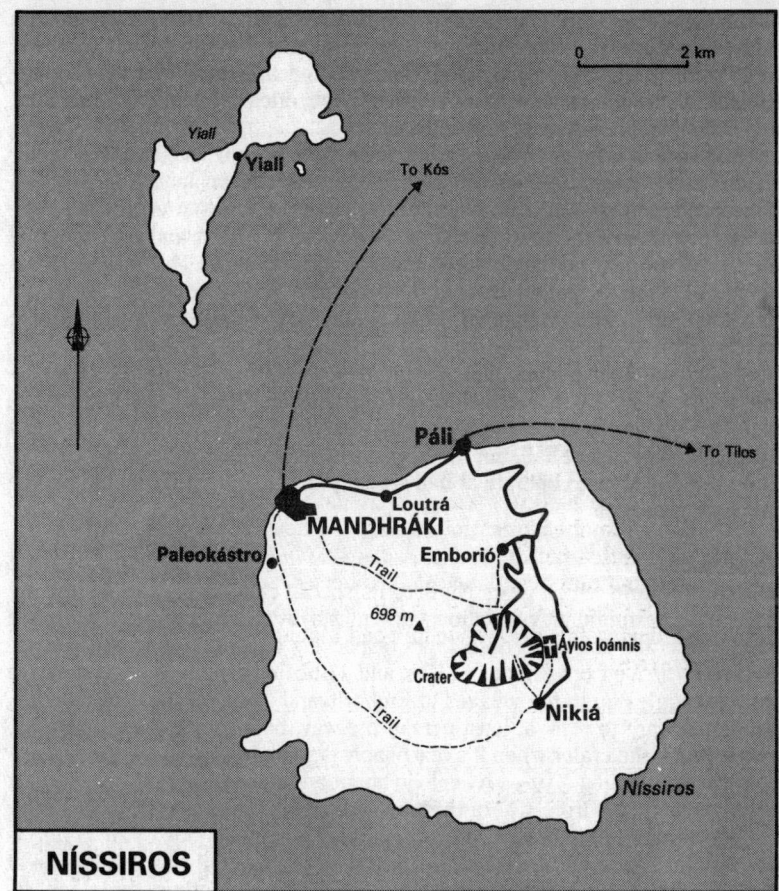

NÍSSIROS

As a defensive bastion, though, 2600-year old **Paleókastro**, twenty minutes' walk out of the Langadháki district, is infinitely more impressive, and one of the most underrated ancient sites in Greece. Back in town there's a small historical **museum** (open Mon.–Sat. 10am-6pm, Sun. 10am–1pm) and next door a *kafenío* serving *soumádha*, the local almond-extract drink.

As far as **practicalities** go, you'll see a handful of hotels and tavernas to the left of the harbour as you disembark from the ferry; best of these, helpful and friendly, are the *Hotel/Restaurant Three Brothers* and the *Romantzo* (with **moped** hire), but in all honesty these are better passed up in favour of the more colourful ones in Mandhráki town proper. Just beyond the public toilets you'll come upon a cluster of pensions (*Maria Intze*, *Porfiris*, plus others) and a decent taverna right on the water. Farther on there's the lively *Taverna Sakkali*, two tavernas named *Nissiros* and several other lodgings, cheapest (if you can get a room) being the *Dhrosia*. In fact it's difficult to go wrong with food or lodging in Mandhráki, and the only no-no would seem to be the *Restaurant Spesial* (sic) *Franzis*, a greasy spoon geared totally to day-trippers. Rounding out the list of facilities, you've a **post office**, a few metered phones, and a bank agent in one of the pharmacies.

The **town beach**, such as it is, lies near the port, but you'll find far better sands east along the coast. Heading out on the main road, the old, now-abandoned spa of **Loutrá** is the first place you encounter; to save time at this point leave the road to clamber over lava boulders and past a ruined ore conveyor-belt to the island's finest **sandy beach**. The swimming is delightful though unfortunately, between the sand fleas and the ugly half-built hotel, you're unlikely to want to stay long or be able to camp on the beach here.

Another kilometre along, and 45 minutes' walk from Mandhráki, the fishing village of **PÁLI** is a more attractive proposition for an overnight base, with three tavernas and as many rooms establishments. Another semi-sandy beach extends east of Páli, but the new spa is nearing completion just behind, and even if it were to operate at half-capacity the human traffic would negate much of its appeal.

The interior

It is the **volcano** which gives Níssiros its special character – and fosters the growth of the abundant vegetation – and no stay would be complete without a visit. There are taxi and coach tours, especially on those days when excursion boats arrive from Rhodes or Kós, and a **public bus** which several days a week struggles up to the villages of Emborió and Nikiá on the crater's edge. But you'll want to walk at least part of the way, both to see the countryside and to reach the crater when it's reasonably deserted.

From Páli a steep stair-path leads in about an hour to EMBORIÓ, a largely abandoned village from where the track continues into the volcanic zone for almost another hour. **NIKIÁ**, the larger village on the far side of the crater, is livelier and spectacularly situated; if you take the bus out this way, pause at the *kafenío* on the unusual round *platía* before descending the steep 45-minute trail to the caldera floor. A few minutes down the hill you can detour on to the signposted path leading north to the eyrie-like **monastery of Áyios Ioánnis Theológos**, with picnic benches, a shady tree and yet another perspective on the volcano.

Approaching from any direction a sulphurous stench drifts out to meet you as the fields and scrub gradually give way to lifeless stone. The sunken crater itself is extraordinary, a Hollywood moonscape of grey, brown and sickly yellow. Its perimeter is pocked with tiny blow holes from which jets of steam pour constantly and around which crystals of pure sulphur form in little tubes and trumpets. The whole floor of the crater seems to hiss, and standing in the middle you can hear the huge cauldron bubbling away below. In legend this is the groaning of Polyvotis, a giant crushed here by the Titans under a huge rock torn from Kós. When there are tourists around a tiny café functions in the centre of the wasteland.

To walk back to Mandhráki, head south from the crater *kafenío* until you pick up a rough track which passes the tiny monastery of Stavrós and then intersects a wide donkey path. This, one of the island's main arteries before the road was built, is still well-maintained and allows superb views over the sea and rural Níssiros. After skirting the last of the volcanic zone and slipping through a pass, it descends gradually and scenically within two hours to Paleókastro and Mandhráki.

Kós

After Rhodes, Kós is easily the most popular island in the Dodecanese, and there are remarkable similarities between the two. On Kós as on Rhodes the harbour is guarded by an imposing castle of the Knights of St. John, the waterside is lined with grandiose Italian public buildings, and minarets and palm trees punctuate extensive Greek and Roman remains. Once again Scandinavian package tourists predominate, filling the hotels behind the beaches. Though sandy and fertile, the hinterland of Kós lacks the wild beauty of Rhodes' interior, and the Rhodes-scale development imposed on an essentially sleepy, small-scale island economy has resulted most obviously in a severe housing crisis (even for locals) and paradoxically higher prices than on Rhodes. In mid-season you'd be lucky to find any sort of room at all.

Kós town

The town of **KÓS** spreads in all directions from the harbour. Around the waterside marches a line of restaurants and bars, not all of them outrageously expensive (try *Taverna Romantika*, the first place encountered when stepping off the ferry) and some cheapish but noisy hotels – *Kalimnos, Elena*, and *Dhodhekanisos* for example. Here too are the **EOT** and tourist police, worth consulting to pick up free maps and check the bus schedules or for help in searching out a **room**. Simple rooms are mostly located towards the back of town near the bus stop or a bit further west, both quiet areas; out here try *Pension Alexis*, Irodhótou 9, or *Pension Vouliakis*, Aryirokástrou 2. Alternatively, there are pensions and cheapish eateries on Avérof (e.g. the *Australia* at no. 39) at the start of Lámbi beach, across the port to the north. The official **campsite** is half an hour's walk along the scrappy beach to the southeast of town, though more intrepid souls lay out their sleeping bags to camp 'freelance' long before that.

Apart from the **castle** (Mon.–Sat. 9am–3pm except Tues., Sun. 9.30am–2.30pm), the town's main attraction lies in its wealth of Hellenistic and Roman remains, many of which were only revealed by an earthquake in 1933 and most of which were restored by the Italians. The largest single section is the ancient **agora**, reached from the castle or from the main square next to the **Archaeological Museum** (same hours as the castle). The **Casa Romana**, a palatial Roman house, and the sections of the ancient town bordered by the **odeion** and the **stadium** are more impressive. Both have well-preserved fragments of mosaic floors, although the best have been carted off to Rhodes.

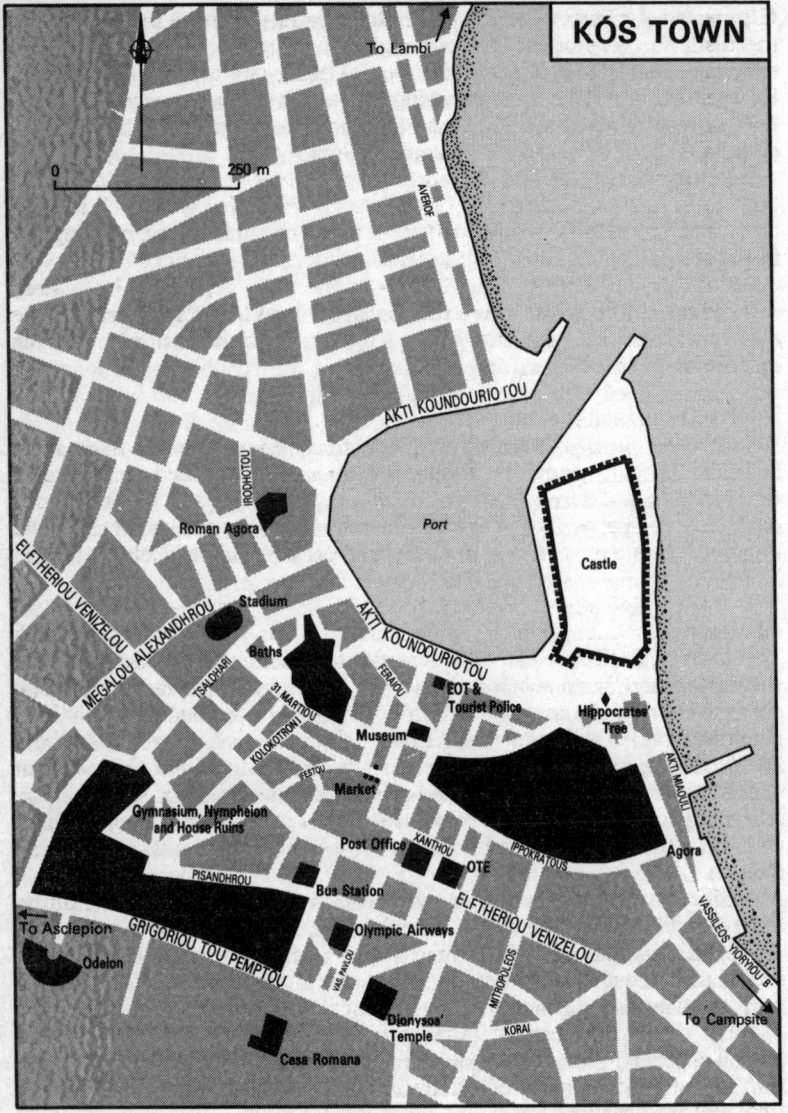

There are so many broken pillars, smashed statues and fragments of bas-relief lying around among the ruins here that no one knows quite what to do with them. The best pieces have been taken for safekeeping into the castle, where most of them are piled up, unmarked and unnoticed. A couple of pillars have even been pressed into service to prop up the branches of

Hippocrates' plane tree. This venerable tree has guarded the entrance to the castle for generations, and although not really elderly enough to have seen the great healer, it has a fair claim to being one of the oldest trees in Europe. Just next door is the imposing eighteenth-century **mosque of Hatzi Hassan**, more intact than the **Defterdar mosque** on Platía Eleftherías, now desecrated by rows of shops on its ground floor.

Kós also boasts an **'old bazaar'**: a lone street, crammed with tourist boutiques, running from behind Platía Ayía Paraskeví (where there's a cheap breakfast bar) and the public market as far as the minaret overlooking the inland archaeological zone. This street is at first called Iféstou but adopts various other aliases along its course. There is one very cheap, nameless **eatery** just seaward of the point where the asphalt of Vassiléos Pávlou crosses the cobbles. Here also you can find a capped **Turkish fountain** with an inscription.

The Asclepion and Platáni

Hippocrates is justly celebrated on Kós; not only does he have a tree named after him, but the star exhibit in the museum is his statue, and the Asclepion (a 45-minute walk from town) is a major tourist attraction. Treatments described by Hippocrates and his followers were still used as recently as a hundred years ago, and his ideas on medical methods and ethics remain influential.

The **Asclepion** whose ruins can be seen today (open Mon.–Sat. 9am-3pm off-season; much longer hours, plus Sunday, in summer) was actually built after the death of Hippocrates, but it is safe to assume that the methods used and taught here were still his. Both a temple to Asclepius and a renowned centre of healing, its magnificent setting on terraces levelled from a hillside overlooking the Turkish mainland reflects the importance given to the environment by these early doctors; springs still provide the site with a constant supply of clean fresh water. There used to be a rival medical school in the ancient town of Cnidus, on the Anatolian coast to the south of Kós, at a time when there was far more contact between the two societies than you'll find today.

A mild social segregation still prevails close at hand in the bi-ethnic village of **PLATÁNI**, on the road to the Asclepion; the Greek Orthodox stay in their single *kafenío* while the Muslim majority hold forth at the three establishments dominating the crossroads. All of the latter serve excellent, cheap, Turkish-style food, far better than you generally get in Kós town. There's a working Ottoman fountain nearby, and the older domestic architecture of Platáni is strongly reminiscent of rural styles in provincial Crete – which, as with part of the community on Rhodes, is where the Muslim population came from early this century.

Just outside Platáni on the road back to the harbour, the **Jewish cemetery** stands in a dark pine grove, 300m from the Muslim graveyard. Dates on the headstones stop ominously after 1940, after which none was allowed the luxury of a natural death. The old **synagogue**, locked and crumbling since the deportations to the concentration camps, is back in Kós town between the ancient *agora* and the waterside.

Around Kós town

If you're looking for anything resembling a deserted **beach** near the capital, you'll need to put in some legwork, or else hire transport. Simplest is to walk out along **LÁMBI BEACH**, which stretches for three kilometres north of town towards Cape Skandhári, the crowds thinning progressively until you hit the off-limits military base. On the same coast, 12km west of Kós town, **Tigáki** is easily accessible by bus, thumb or rented pedal-bicycle, and thus crowded until evening when everyone, except for a few campers or those lucky enough to rent a room, has disappeared. The more unusual but remote **BRÓS THERMÁ** lies thirteen moped-passable kilometres southeast, beyond Paradhísi and around the headland facing Turkey. Here **hot springs** trickle over black sand into the sea, warming it up for early or late-season swims. There's a small seasonal café but no other facilities.

Inland, the main interest of eastern Kós lies in the villages of **Mt. Dhíkeos**, half a dozen settlements reached up the side road from Zipári and nestling among the slopes of the island's only forest. Some, like Evangelístria and Ziá,

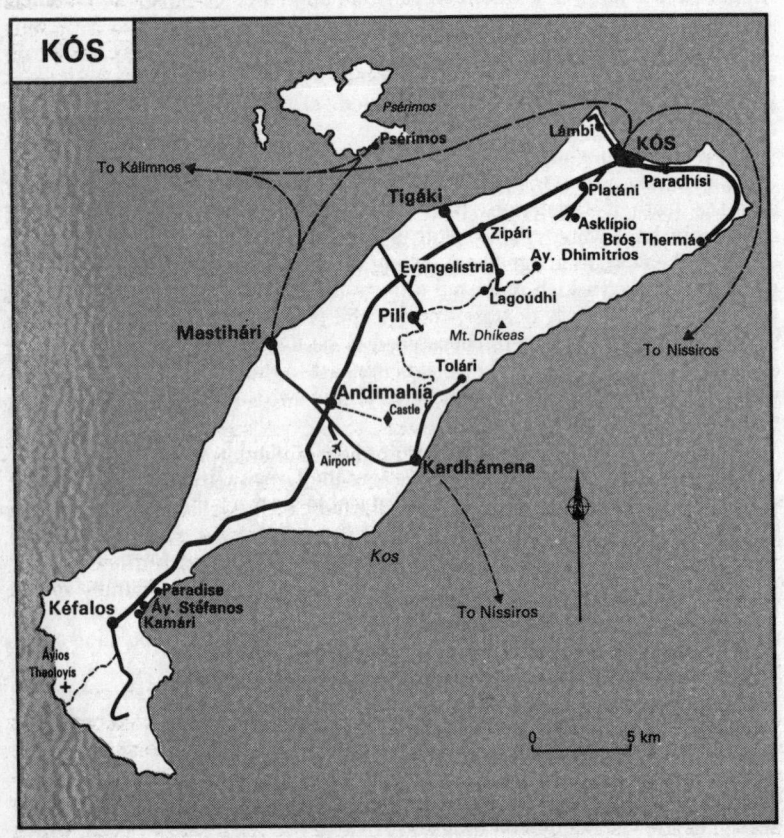

are disappointingly modern or have been sacrificed in the interests of 'Folklore Nights (and Days)'. But others, such as **LAGOÚDHI**, **ÁYIOS YIÓRYIOS**, and **ÁYIOS DHIMÍTRIOS** are still unspoiled. Plus there's always the mountain itself, when bouncing along the rough roads palls. Eventually you'll wind up at **PILÍ**, where above the modern village the ruins of the old cower in the shadow of a clifftop Byzantine castle and several frescoed churches.

Western Kós

In the centre of the island, a giant roundabout near the Andimáhia airport directs traffic towards the northeast (for Kós town), southwest, northwest and southeast.

KARDHÁMENA, on the south coast, is the island's second largest tourist playpen and the runaway local development has banished whatever qualities it may once have had. The beach stretches out east and west from the town, lined to the east with ill-concealed military bunkers and a road as far as **Tolári**, where there is a massive new hotel complex. Kardhámena itself has several reasonable hotels, but since these are perennially reserved by tour companies you've more chance of finding a room in a private house. In season a *kaíki* plies daily to Níssiros. Halfway back up to Andimáhia an enormous **castle** of the Knights of St. John sprawls atop a ridge.

The beach at **MASTIHÁRI**, northwest of the big junction, is smaller than those at Tigáki or Kardhámena, and the town is becoming increasingly built-up, but on the other hand it is the port for *kaíkia* to Kálimnos (package clients shuttled over from the airport have priority) and the tiny Greek islet of Psérimos (see below). The end of the line for buses is KÉFALOS, which squats on a mesa-like hill looking back down the length of Kós. However, most visitors will have descended long before, either at **KAMÁRI** (plentiful accomodation) or **ÁYIOS STÉFANOS** (ditto), where the exquisite remains of a fifth-century basilica overlook tiny Kastrí islet. The beach begins at Kamári and runs five kilometres east, virtually without interruption, to cliff-framed and aptly-named **Paradise beach**. Unfortunately the entire area between Kamári and Áyios Stéfanos has been overshadowed by a huge Club Med complex of bungalows surrounding the main luxury hotel.

Kéfalos itself is the staging point for hikes into the mountainous southwest peninsula. To the west, around the monastery of Áyios Theoloyís, you can still find deserted stretches of coastline, but the nearest is about 6km distant over very rough roads. Along the way you'll be rewarded with views over Kálimnos and Léros to the north, Níssiros and the coast of Turkey to the south.

Psérimos

Psérimos could be an idyllic little island if it wasn't for its proximity to Kós and Kálimnos, which results in day-trippers by the boatload every day of the season. Even in April and October you can be guaranteed at least 100 outsiders a day (which doubles the population), so imagine the scene in high season as the visitors spread themselves along the main sandy beach, which

stretches around the bay in front of the twenty or thirty houses that constitute Psérimos village. There are at least a couple of other less attractive
pebbly beaches to hide away on during the day, no more than thirty walking
minutes away – in fact nowhere on Psérimos is much more than half an
hour's walk away.

When the day-trippers have gone you can, out of season, have the place to
yourself and even in season there won't be too many other overnighters,
since there's a limited number of **rooms** available. There are three small
'hotels', best of which (for cheapness, cleanliness, and friendliness) is the one
run by Katerina Fyloura above her taverna on the eastern side of the harbour.
She has a total of thirteen beds apportioned over five rooms – 1500 to 2000dr
per room – and the food's good too. Katerina also acts as postmistress if you
want to write home, since the island can't support a post office. There's just
one small **store**, not very well-stocked, and most of the island's supplies are
brought in daily from Kálimnos. Eating out, however, won't break the bank
and there's plenty of fresh fish in the handful of tavernas.

The island is most easily reached from Kálimnos, using the wonderful
Pserimos Express which leaves Pothiá harbour each day at 9.30am and returns
at 3pm. The journey takes an hour, and anything less like an express than
this tub is hard to imagine. Then again it is cheap, and even free for a few
weeks at the end of the season, courtesy of the local tourist board.

Astipálea

Both geographically and architecturally, Astipálea would be more at home
among the Cyclades – the island can be seen quite clearly from Thíra and
Amorgós, and it looks and feels more like them than its neighbours to the
east. In antiquity the island's most famous citizen was Kleomedes, a boxer
disqualified from an early Olympic Games for killing his opponent. He came
home so enraged that he demolished the local school, killing all its pupils.
Things have calmed down a bit in the intervening 2500 years and today the
capital, ASTIPÁLEA, is a quiet fishing port.

The harbour of **YIALÓS** dates from the Italian era (Astipálea was the first
island they occupied in the Dodecanese) and most of the settlement between
the quay and the line of nine windmills is even more recent. As you climb up
beyond the port, though, the neighbourhoods get progressively older and
their steep streets are enlivened by the *poúndia* or colourful wooden
balconies of the whitewashed houses. The whole culminates in the
fourteenth-century *kástro*, one of the finest in the Aegean. Until well into this
century over 3000 souls dwelt within, but depopulation and wartime damage
have combined to leave only a desolate shell today; the fine stellar vaulting
over the entrance and a couple of maintained churches remain an attraction.

There are three inexpensive hotels (the *Astynea*, the *Paradisos* and the
Egeon) down in the port, but if you can get them, rooms in the upper town
near the windmills are better. Of the places to eat, only the *Astynea*, on the
wharf, and *I Monaxia*, behind the generator, can be recommended; the

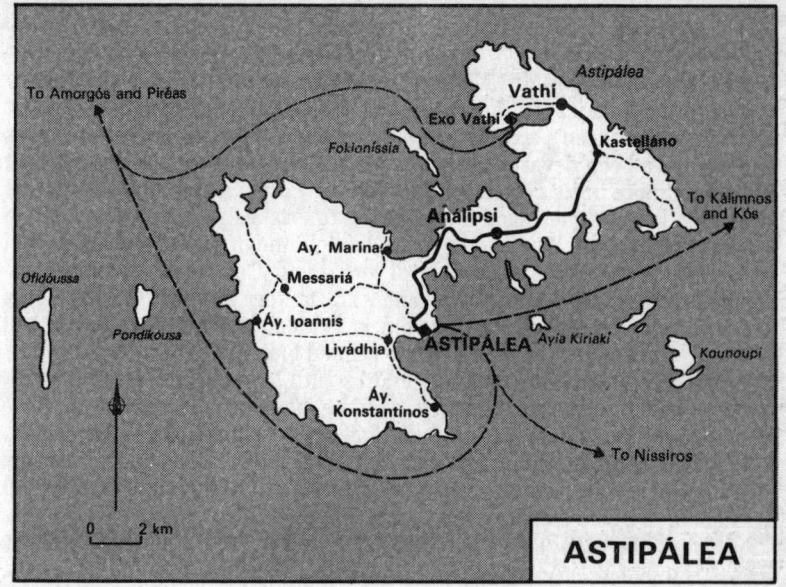

others are execrable. Also, be advised that the islanders have a well-grounded reputation for being indifferent at best, grasping at worst, towards foreigners – surprising considering the paltry numbers of travellers who make it here.

Half an hour's walk from the capital is **LIVÁDHIA**, a fertile green valley with a good beach and shaded restaurants by the waterside. You can camp here or rent a room or bungalow on the beach. **ANÁLIPSI** is about a twelve-kilometre taxi-ride or walk in the other direction; with little except a clean, quiet beach and a small taverna, this makes a nice place to sleep under the stars. The road ends at **VATHÍ**, another quiet fishing village with a superb harbour, which is where the ferry will dock in winter when Astipálea town is too exposed to the prevailing southerlies. At such times, but rarely otherwise, there is a bus between Vathí and Astipálea.

The best outing on the island has to be the two-hour walk from Astipálea to the oasis of **Áyios Ioánnis**. Walk one hour along the dirt track beginning from the fifth or sixth windmill, then bear left at the fork. Another half hour along, puddles on the track are a harbinger of things to come; shortly thereafter you turn left, at the top of a pass, on to a footpath heading for some bony-white rock outcrops. Soon the walled orchards of the farm-monastery of Áyios Ioánnis (not to be confused with a seaside cloister of the same name to the north) comes into view. Just below it a ten-metre waterfall plunges into deep pools fine for bathing. A rather arduous trek down the valley ends at a fine pebbly bay, and proper paths lead directly back to Livádhia if you don't fancy a reprise of the jeep tracks you arrived on.

Kálimnos

Most of the population of Kálimnos lives in or around the port of Pothiá, a wealthy but not very beautiful town famed for its sponge divers. Sadly almost all the Mediterranean's sponges, with the exception of a few deep–water beds off Italy, have been devastated by disease, and only three or four of the fleet of thirty or more boats can currently be usefully occupied. In response to this economic disaster, the island is attempting to establish a tourist industry: so far little developed. The warehouses behind the harbour, however, still process and sell sponges to tourists all year round. During the Italian occupation houses here were painted blue and white to keep alive the Greek colours and irritate the invaders. The custom is beginning to die out, but is still evident; even some of the churches are painted blue.

POTHIÁ has the industrial grit of Síros with little of the latter's charm – the overwhelming impression being of the phenomenal amount of noise engendered by kamikaze motorcyclists and cranked-up juke boxes. **Accommodation** here is rarely a problem, since pension keepers usually meet the ferries, and the *Hotel Alma*, next to the National Bank on Patriarhoú Maximíou, is a safe standby. But **eating**, except at *Stelios Svinos* (across the street from the *Alma*) and the adjacent hot-dog stall, can be expensive. **Buses** run as far as Arninónda in the northwest and Vathí in the northeast, while for more freedom there are plenty of places to hire a **moped**. Chances are you'll want to escape fairly soon to one of the smaller coastal settlements.

Heading northwest across the island, the first place you come to is the old capital, **Horió**, sandwiched between an eroded **castle** of the Knights of St. John and the miniature Byzantine precinct of **Perá Kástro**. The crumbling ruins of the latter are peppered with conspicuously white churches, but it is the castle that especially merits a visit, with its stupendous views over the entire west coast of the island.

From the ridge at Horió the road dips into a cultivated ravine, heading for the consecutive beach resorts of Kandoúni, Mirtiés and Massoúri. All of them are far more developed than is warranted by the scanty shelves of grey sand or pebbles in the vicinity, but at **MIRTIÉS** and **MASSOÚRI** there is at least the possibility of finding a room amid the package-holiday villas, along with views across the strait to the striking, volcanic-plug island of **TÉLENDHOS**. The trip across is arguably the best reason to come to Mirtiés; little boats shuttle to and fro constantly throughout the day. On the islet there is a ruined monastery, a castle, a couple of tiny beaches, several tavernas and two pensions, all in or near the single village. It's also possible to go from Mirtiés directly to Léros aboard the daily *kaíika*.

Beyond Mirtiés bus connections are sparse and you'll do best by moped or group taxi (an institution on Kálimnos). **ARNINÓNDAS** and **EMBORIÓ** both have empty, decent beaches, the latter alongside a couple of good tavernas, rooms and a selection of tamarisks to sleep under.

East from Pothiá, an initially unpromising, forty-minute ride ends dramatically at **VATHÍ**, whose colour provides a startling contrast to the lifeless greys elsewhere on Kálimnos. A long, fertile valley, verdant with orange and tangerine groves, it seems a continuation of the cobalt-blue fjord which penetrates finger-like into the landscape. In the simple port, known as Rína, there are a handful of *kafenía* and tavernas to choose from, as well as a new hotel and a few rooms. For **walkers** the lush valley behind, crisscrossed with rough tractor-tracks and paths, may prove an irresistible lure, but be warned that it will take you the better part of five hours, most of it shadeless once you're out of the orchards, to reach Mirtiés on the opposite coast. The only facilities en route will be in the village of Dhássos at the head of the valley.

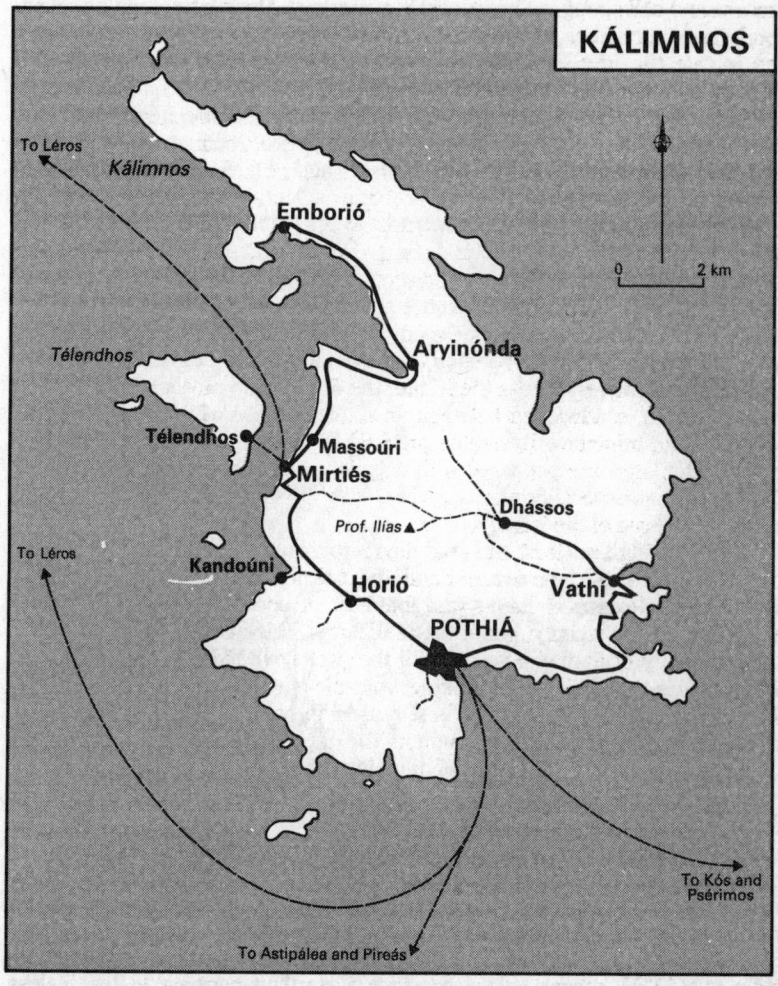

Léros

The Greek fjord reaches its apotheosis on Léros, which is so indented with deep, sheltered anchorages that during the last world war it harboured (in turn) the entire Italian, German, and British fleets. Alas, the bays seem to absorb rather than reflect light, and the island's relative fertility comes across as scruffiness when compared to the crisp lines of its more barren neighbours. These characteristics, coupled with the island's absence until recently from the lists of most major tour operators, mean that barely 10,000 foreigners a year (many of them Italians who grew up on the island), and not many more Greeks, come to stay.

Not that the islanders need, or particularly encourage, tourism; various prisons and sanitariums have long dominated the Lerian economy. During the junta the island was the site of an infamous detention centre. Today, the Lerian mental hospitals are still the repository for 2000 of Greece's more intractable psychiatric cases; and another asylum is home to hundreds of

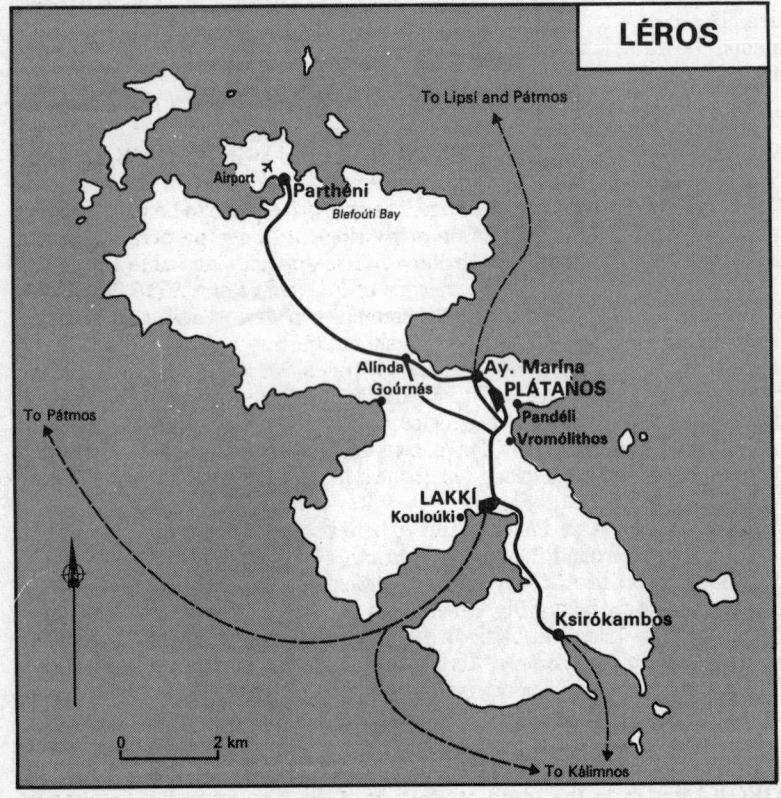

mentally handicapped children. The island's domestic image problem is compounded by its name, the butt of jokes by mainlanders who pounce on its similarity to the word *léra*, connoting dirt and rascality. Islanders are in fact extremely friendly to those who do visit, but their island's role and image seem unlikely to change; indeed in recent years there have been moves to emphasise Léros' role as a purveyor of social services. A network of smaller, halfway-house type facilities will be established on the island, allowing individuals who have been incarcerated for decades to be given more freedom within the community. It is a courageous and humane programme, but certainly not one designed to appeal to the mainstream tourist.

On arrival (invariably at night) the port of **LAKKÍ** is an extraordinary, neon-lit sight, its waterside lined with art deco edifices put up by the Italians. Indeed the whole town, distinctly faded at closer quarters, retains a marvellously seedy elegance in its broad streets laid out around little parks and statues. If you really want to savour it, try the faded grandeur of the C-class *Hotel Léros*. It's on the front about ten minutes' walk from the jetty, and the large rooms almost all have balconies overlooking the bay. There is nowhere much cheaper in Lakkí, though some places offer more in the way of modern facilities. The beach at **Kouloúki**, where there's a taverna and you can sleep among the trees, is in the opposite (west) direction when you get off the boat, away from town.

Better beaches can be found in the five other huge bays which distinguish Léros' coastline. The one **bus** visits every village a few times a day, and shuttles fairly regularly between Lakkí and the capital at **PLÁTANOS**, about an hour's walk away. **Bicycles** and **scooters** can be hired in Lakkí, but in Plátanos as well, which is a nicer and less expensive place to be based for any length of time. Originally built on a low ridge with sea on both sides, and protected by the Byzantine castle above, it has gradually spread in both directions to join up with the fishing villages of **PANDÉLI** and **AYÍA MARÍNA**. Between them the three support a cinema, two discos and a surprisingly lively nightlife in the cafés and bars. It should be easy enough to find a room somewhere here, though not surprisingly amenities are a little better in the two waterside communities. The **castle**, kept in good repair by a series of defenders and once again being restored, is an easy climb above the town. It has superb panoramic views, for reasons of state security you're not allowed to take photographs; the place (open dawn to dusk) is still used as a military observation point.

There's a beach at Pandéli, and a better one at **Vromólithos**, with a taverna, further around the bay to the south. North of Ayía Marína the more developed resort of **ALÍNDA** fronts another long beach lined with villas, a popular spot with holidaying Greeks. On the way you pass a cemetery for British soldiers killed in battle in 1943; immaculately maintained, it stands out here as a grim anomaly. Across the narrowest part of the island from Alínda and reached by a poorly marked side road, **Gournás** is another popular, sandy beach, but strangely with almost no facilities.

Nowhere in this central part of the island is really too far to walk or bicycle if you're reasonably energetic, but **PARTHÉNI** in the north and **XIRÓKAMBOS** to the south are further afield. The former, a tiny hamlet overshadowed by an army base (formerly the junta's political detention centre) and dusty airstrip, has little to recommend it.

five minutes' walk beyond, however, is **Blefoúti Bay**, the island's most isolated (if pebbly) beach, with a lone taverna. On the way to **XIRÓKAMBOS** there's more military development, but the place itself is unaffected; you can find rooms with little difficulty and there are several places to eat and drink, as well as an official **campsite** and a good beach.

Pátmos

Arguably the most beautiful, certainly the best known of the smaller islands in the Dodecanese, Pátmos is unique. It was in a cave here that St. John the Divine (in Greek, *O Theologos*), had his revelation (the Bible's Book of Revelation) and unwittingly shaped the island's destiny. The monastery which commemorates him, founded here in 1088, dominates the island both physically – its fortified bulk towering high above anything else – and, to a considerable extent, politically. While the monks no longer run the island as they did for more than 700 years, their influence has nevertheless stopped the island going the way of Rhodes or Kós. Although there are vast numbers of visitors, and Pátmos is now firmly on the cruise and yacht circuits, they have not been allowed to take the island over. There is little in the way of nightlife – hardly more than a token attempt at a disco – and once outside Skála, the port and main town, development of any kind is appealingly subdued.

The port: Skála and Méloï

Skála initially seems to contradict this image of Patmos. The waterside, with its ritzy-looking cafés and clientele, is a little too sophisticated for its own small-town good. In season it's crowded by day with excursionists from Kós and Rhodes; by night with well-dressed cliques of French, Germans, Brits and Americans. In winter the shops and restaurants close and most of their owners and staff leave for Rhodes; the town itself taking on a somewhat depressed air, with not so much as a cinema for the kids to roar their bikes towards.

If you feel like moving straight out, the most obvious possibility is (walkable) Méloï Beach (see below); Hóra, a bus or taxi-ride up the mountain, is a more authentic base but has few and low-key rooms. If you stay, **accommodation** in **SKÁLA** itself is in demand but there's a reasonable amount of it. *Hotel Patmion* (☎0247/31-313) is a good, modest-priced choice, as is the *Rex* (☎0247/31-242). More likely, however, you'll end up in rooms, hawked vociferously as ever on the quay; they are mostly better than usual quality, though higher than usual prices, too. Unfortunately, the cruise-ship traffic has adversely affected the **eating** picture. Restaurants are generally poor quality, though honourable exceptions are *Grigori's*, on the way to Hóra, and the *Skorpios Creperie*, on your left as you disembark from the ferry. The trendiest bar is certainly the barn-like *Café Arion*, also on the waterside and easily missed with its deceptively small entrance. If you're bewildered, the boat

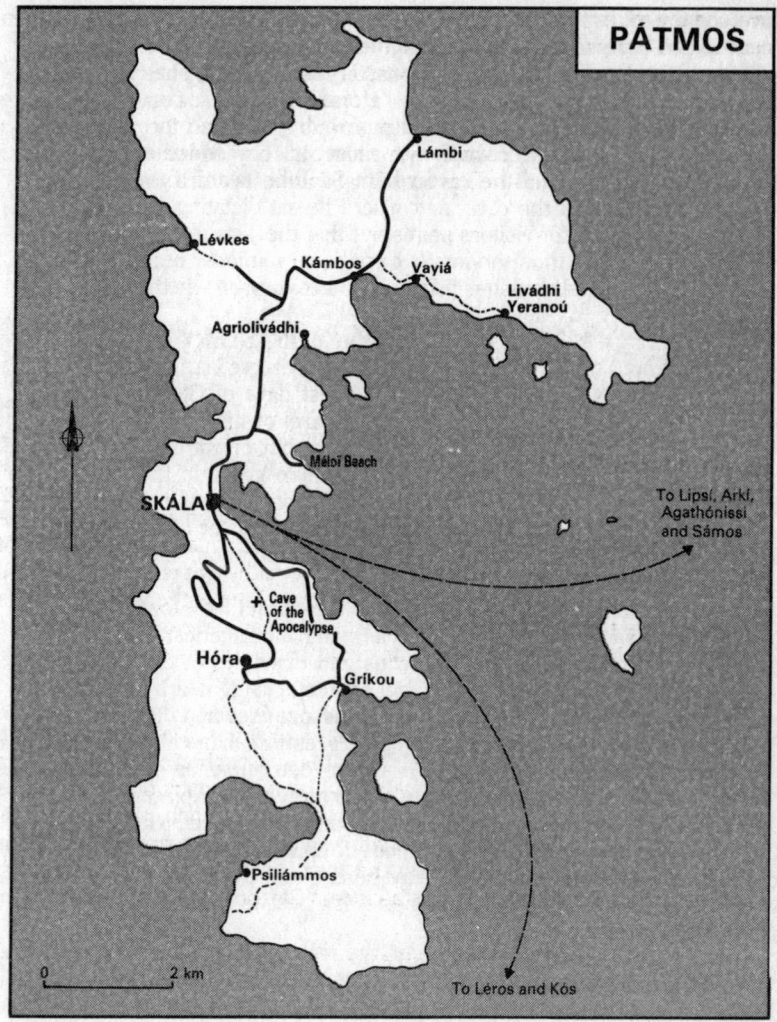

PÁTMOS

Lámbi

Lévkes   Kámbos   Vayiá

Livádhi
Yeranoú

Agriolivádhi

Méloï Beach

SKÁLA   To Lipsí, Arkí,
Agathónissi
and Sámos

Cave
of the
Apocalypse

Hóra   Gríkou

Psiliámmos

0   2 km

To Léros and Kós

docks right opposite the police station; **bus and boat timetables** are posted outside; the (not particularly helpful) tourist police are behind it. Continuing south toward the start of the road to Gríkou is a **moped and motorbike** hire outfit; another more reliable, is by the *Hotel Patmion*.

North, 1½km around the bay, lies **Méloï Beach**, one of the best and most convenient on the island, and of course very popular. There's a good **campsite** here (so 'freelancing' is not appreciated), some rather rustic **rooms** and a couple of reasonable tavernas.

Hóra and the monasteries

For cruise-ship passengers and overnighters alike the first order of business is likely to be heading up to the Monastery of St. John, sheltered behind massive defences in the hilltop capital of Hóra. There is a bus up, but the half-hour walk by a beautiful old cobbled path puts you in a more appropriate frame of mind. Just over halfway, pause at the **Monastery of the Apocalypse**, built around the cave where St. John heard the voice of God issuing from a cleft in the rock, and where he sat dictating His words to a disciple. A leaflet left for visitors points out that the 'fissure . . . (divides) the rock into three parts, thus serving as a continual reminder of the Trinitarian nature of God', and admonishes pilgrims to 'ask yourself whether you are on the side of Christ or of Antichrist'.

This is merely a foretaste, however, of the **MONASTERY OF ST. JOHN**. Behind its imposing fortifications have been preserved a fantastic array of religious treasures dating back to the earliest days of Christianity: relics, icons, books, ceremonial ornaments and apparel of the most extraordinary richness. In short, a fabulous store of delights, but be warned that opening hours are incredibly erratic. Succinct advice is to go on in the morning on Monday, Tuesday, Thursday or Saturday; in the late afternoon on Wednesday or Friday; or any time on Sunday. (In theory the cloister of the Apocalypse adheres to the same schedule.) To be sure of admission, 'modest' dress is essential: definitely no shorts.

Outside St. John's stout walls, **HÓRA** is a beautiful little town whose anti-quated alleys shelter over forty churches and monasteries. The churches, many of them containing beautiful icons and examples of the local skill in wood carving, are almost all locked, but someone living nearby will have the key. Among the best are the church of **Dhiassozoússa** and the monastery of **Zoodhóhos Piyí**. You'll find some good places to eat (notably *Vangelis'* on the square) but in keeping with the islanders' determination not to let casual tourism run roughshod over Pátmos, there are very few places to stay; the foreigners here are mostly long-term occupants, and indeed almost a third of the crumbling mansions have been bought up and restored in the past two decades. If you're determined to stay here – and there are only a total of twenty beds in unsignposted buildings – it's best to make enquiries in the *platía* early in the day.

Around the island

Pátmos, as one local guide proclaims, 'is immense for those who know how to wander in space and time'. The more conventionally propelled may find it easier to get around on foot, or by bus. This is one of the finest islands for **walking**, with a network of paths leading almost everywhere. The over-worked **bus** which connects Skála with Hóra, Kámbos and Gríkou is rather less reliable.

After the extraordinary atmosphere and magnificent scenery, it it **beaches** that are Patmos' principal attraction. From Hóra a good trail heads southeast to the sandiest part of generally overdeveloped **Gríkou Bay** within forty minutes, and a rougher track leads in two hours to the much better beach, with one seasonal taverna, at **Psiliámmos** (there's also a summer *kaíki* service from Skála). More good beaches are found in the north of the island, most of them accessible on foot by following the old paths which (with the exception of some paved or cross-country stretches) parallel the startling, indented eastern shore.

The first beach beyond Méloï, **Agriolivádhi**, is rocky, algae-ridden and without facilities, the next, **Kámbos**, is not much better. But if you strike out east from the latter, **Vayiá** and **Livádhi Yeranoú** are considerably more tempting. From Kámbos you can also head north to the bay of **LÁMBI**, not so practical for swimming when the wind and surf are up, but renowned for an abundance of multicoloured stones. A hamlet of sorts here has a couple of tavernas and rooms, and this is also the most northerly port of call for the daily excursion *kaíkia* which shuttle constantly around the coast in season.

As so often, you'll find the island at its best out of season. It can get cold in winter, but there is a hard core of foreigners who live here year-round, so things never entirely close down. Many of the long-term residents rent houses in **Lévkes**, a fertile valley just west of Kámbos with a lonely and some-times wild beach at its end. It was here that a New Age 'commune' was based before its eviction by the authorities, but very likely there has been no short-age of slightly more mainstream tenants to fill the houses they left behind.

Minor Isles: Lipsí, Arkí and Agathónissi

Of the various islets to the north and east of Pátmos, **LIPSÍ** is the largest and most populated and the one that is beginning to get some summer tourist trade. Most of the inhabitants live around the fine harbour, which is also where most of the food and lodging is located. There is a small **hotel** (*Kalypso*) and **rooms** are also available at the pensions *Flisvos* and *Kolonaki*. Each of these have quite acceptable tavernas either on the premises or next door. Although the islanders are friendly and hospitable, Lipsós is very quiet; little happens.

The island's best **beaches** are in the southeast at KOHLAKOÚRAS and KATSADHIÁ (tavernas open sporadically but don't rely on them) and at PLATÍS YIALÓS, a large, shallow, sandy bay (no food) on the north coast, about an hour's walk along the road leading west from town. A number of paths provide opportunities for a variety of **walks** through the undulating countryside, dotted with blue-domed churches, but you can walk from one end of Lipsí to the other in less than two hours. Other than that there's abso-lutely nothing to do, except maybe listen to the *santoúri* (Levantine hammer dulcimer) player who's rumoured to perform some evenings. But you won't find many better places to do nothing. Lipsí is visited once a week by the *Panormitis*, and there are *kaíkia* from Pátmos and Léros in season.

ARKÍ is considerably more primitive (no electricity, no village as such) and about half the size. The best beach is just offshore on Maráthi Islet, with a taverna catering to the day-trippers who come a couple of times a week from Pátmos.

AGATHÓNISSI is sufficiently remote – much closer to Turkey than Pátmos, in fact – to be out of reach even of these excursions, and its covering of vegetation lives up to its name, which means 'Thorn Island'. However there's a bona fide inland village (**MEGÁLO HORIÓ**) with 150-odd people and two stores; there are two pensions and a few rooms in the port, and you won't starve at the three tavernas. But if you do show up, you'll probably be the only foreigner(s) around; best to come with someone you like a lot, as there'll be no escape for a week!

travel details

To simplify the lists below, the *Panormitis* has been left out. For years this tiny ship has been the only regular lifeline of the smaller islands – it visits them all at least once a week throughout the year. For some time now its schedule has been as follows: Monday, mid-morning, sails from Rhodes to Sími–Tílos–Nísiros–Kós–Kálimnos–Léros–Lipsí–Pátmos–Arkí–Agathónissi and Sámos (Pithagório). Tuesday, early morning, retraces its ports of call as above, arriving in Rhodes 24 hours later. Departs Rhodes mid-morning on Wednesday for Meyísti, returns in the evening. Thursday, early morning, leaves Rhodes for Sími–Tílos–Níssiros–Kós–Kálimnos, backtracks through these islands to Rhodes by late evening. Friday noon, sails from Rhodes for Hálki, Kárpathos (both ports), and Kássos, returning Saturday. Sunday afternoon it again makes the long trek out to Meyísti, returning Monday morning to begin the whole process over again.
In addition there are now expensive hydrofoils based in Rhodes; these depart daily in season, weather permitting, for Sími and Kós, sometimes via Tílos and Níssiros in the latter case, and occasionally make it up as far as Pátmos.

KÁRPATHOS (Pigádhia and Dhiafáni) AND KÁSSOS Twice-weekly **ferries** with each other, Rhodes (7 hr.), Hálki, Crete (Sitía and Áyios Nikólaos, 6 hr.), Thíra, and Pireás; once to Sími, Tílos, Níssiros, Kós, Kálimnos, Astipálea, Amorgós, Páros, Anáfi, Folégandhros, Síkinos, and Mílos. **Note** that in bad weather boats will *not* call at Dhiafáni.

At least 2 daily **flights** between Rhodes and Kárpathos, 2 a week in season between Kássos and Rhodes, via Kárpathos, and 2 summer flights weekly to Crete (Sitía).

HÁLKI Ferries twice a week to Rhodes (1 1/2 hr.), Kárpathos (6 hrs), Kássos, Crete, and Pireás; once to Sími, Tílos, Níssiros, Kós, Kálimnos, Astipálea, Amorgós, Páros, Anáfi, Thíra, Síkinos, Folégandhros, and Mílos. Daily excursion **kaíki** to Rhodes (Skála Kamírou). **Note** that in bad weather only the largest ferries will call.

RHODES 10 a week with Pireás (18–20 hr.); 8 or 9 to Kós (4 hr.) and Kálimnos (5 hr.); 6 weekly to Léros (7 hr.) and Pátmos (8 hr.); twice weekly to Sími (1 hr.), Tílos, Níssiros, Astipálea, Amorgós, Páros, Hálki, Kárpathos (7 hr.), Kássos, Crete (13 hr.); once weekly to Folégandhros, Mílos, Náxos, Síros, Sámos, Híos, Lésvos, Límnos, and Kavála. **Excursion boats** twice daily to Sími, daily to Hálki.
International boat departures include 2 to 6 weekly to Turkey (Marmaris), 2 weekly to Cyprus and Israel, once a week to Egypt.
Several daily **flights** to Athens, 2 a week to Thessaloníki; 2 daily in season to Kárpathos, 2 a week continuing to Kássos; 1 daily to Crete (Iráklio) and Kós, 4 a week in season to Thíra, Míkonos, and Crete (Sitía), 3 weekly to Páros, and 2 weekly to Lésvos. Possibility of **international charter** flight tickets to northern Europe.

KASTELLÓRIZO (MEYÍSTI) Very tenuous means (i.e. hitching a yacht) of getting to Kaş on the Turkish mainland opposite; 3 **flights** weekly to Rhodes.

SÍMI 1 **ferry** weekly to Rhodes, Hálki, Kárpathos, Kássos, Crete, Síros, Náxos, Páros; 2 weekly to Tílos, Níssiros, Kós, Kálimnos, Astipálea, Amorgós, and Pireás. **Excursion boats** twice daily to Rhodes – some, the so-called *epivatikó* are much cheaper.

NÍSSIROS AND TÍLOS Same **ferry** service as Sími, obviously substituting 'Sími' for 'Tílos, Níssiros', but **tourist boats** between Níssiros and Kós (Kós harbour is actually cheaper than Kardhámena).

KOS 8 or 9 weekly to Rhodes (4 hr.), Kálimnos (1 hr.), and Pireás (at least 12 hr.); 6 weekly to Léros (3 hr.) and Pátmos (5 hr.); 2 weekly to Astipálea, Amorgós, Sími, Níssiros, Tílos, Hálki, Kárpathos, Kássos, and Crete; 1 a week to Náxos, Páros, Síros, Sámos, Híos, Lésvos, Límnos, and Kavála. **Excursion boats** at least daily in season from Mastihári and Kós town to Psérimos and Kálimnos, and from Kós town and Kardhámena to Níssiros; less often to Pátmos. **Flights** several times daily to Athens, once daily to Rhodes in summer, 3 weekly in season to Léros, and 1 a week to Sámos and Thessaloníki.

International service includes 1 to 6 boats weekly to Turkey (Bodrum, 1 hr.) and the faint possibility of finding good charter flights to northern Europe.

ASTIPÁLEA Same **ferry** service as Sími, Tílos, and Níssiros, plus seasonal **kaíki** to Kálimnos.

KÁLIMNOS Same **ferry** service as Kós, except no direct connection to Sámos, Híos, Lésvos, etc., plus seasonal **kaíki** to Kós (Mastihári and main port), Psérimos, and Léros (from Mirtiés to Ksirókambos).

LÉROS 6 **ferries** a week to Pireás (12 hr.), Pátmos (1 hr.), Kálimnos (1 hr.), Kós (3 hr.), and Rhodes (7 hr.) Seasonal daily **excursion boats** from Ayía Marína to Lipsí and Pátmos, and from Ksirókambos to Kálimnos. At least daily **flights** to Athens, 3 a week in season to Kós.

PÁTMOS Same **ferry** service as Léros, plus seasonal **tourist boats** to Sámos, Lipsí, and Maráthi on a daily basis.

CHAPTER TEN

EAST AND NORTH AEGEAN ISLANDS

T he seven substantial islands and four minor islets scattered off the coast of Asia Minor and northeast Greece form a rather arbitrary archipelago. Although there is some similarity in architecture and landscape, virtually the only common denominator is the strong individual character of each island. Despite their proximity to modern Turkey, members of the group bear few signs of an Ottoman heritage, especially when compared to Rhodes and Kos. There's the odd minaret or two, and some of the domestic architecture betrays obvious influences from Constantinople, Thrace and further north in the Balkans, but by and large the enduring Greekness of these islands is testimony to the 4000-year Hellenic presence in Asia Minor, which only ended in 1923.

This heritage is duly referred to by the Greek government in its propaganda war with the Turks over the sovereignty of these far-flung outposts. International tensions are, if anything, worse than in the Dodecanese, aggravated by potential undersea oil deposits in the straits between the islands and Turkey. The World Court has found in favour of the Greek position that these islands generate their own continental shelf, as opposed to the Turkish one that the straits fall within the conventional 12-nautical-mile limit of their territorial waters. In a related dispute Turkey has persistently demanded that Greece demilitarise Límnos, astride the sea lanes to and from the Dardenelles, but Greece shows no signs of co-operating.

The resulting heavy military presence can be disconcerting, especially for lone woman travellers, and large tracts of land are off-limits as military reserves. But, as in the Dodecanese, local tour operators do a thriving business shuttling passengers for absurdly high tariffs (caused partly by the need for payoffs at both ends) between the easternmost islands and the Turkish coast with its amazing archaeological sites and watering holes.

The main ports and towns of virtually all these islands are not the quaint picturesque places you become used to in other parts of Greece, with a number of 'real' cities – often with their own industrial base. In most cases you should suppress your initial impulse to take the next boat out, and press on into the worthwhile interiors.

Sámos is the most visited of the 'group', but, if you can leave the crowds behind, perhaps also the most verdant and beautiful. **Ikaría** to the west is relatively unspoiled, and nearby **Foúrni** is a haven for determined solitaries. **Híos** is culturally the most interesting of all, but its natural beauty has been

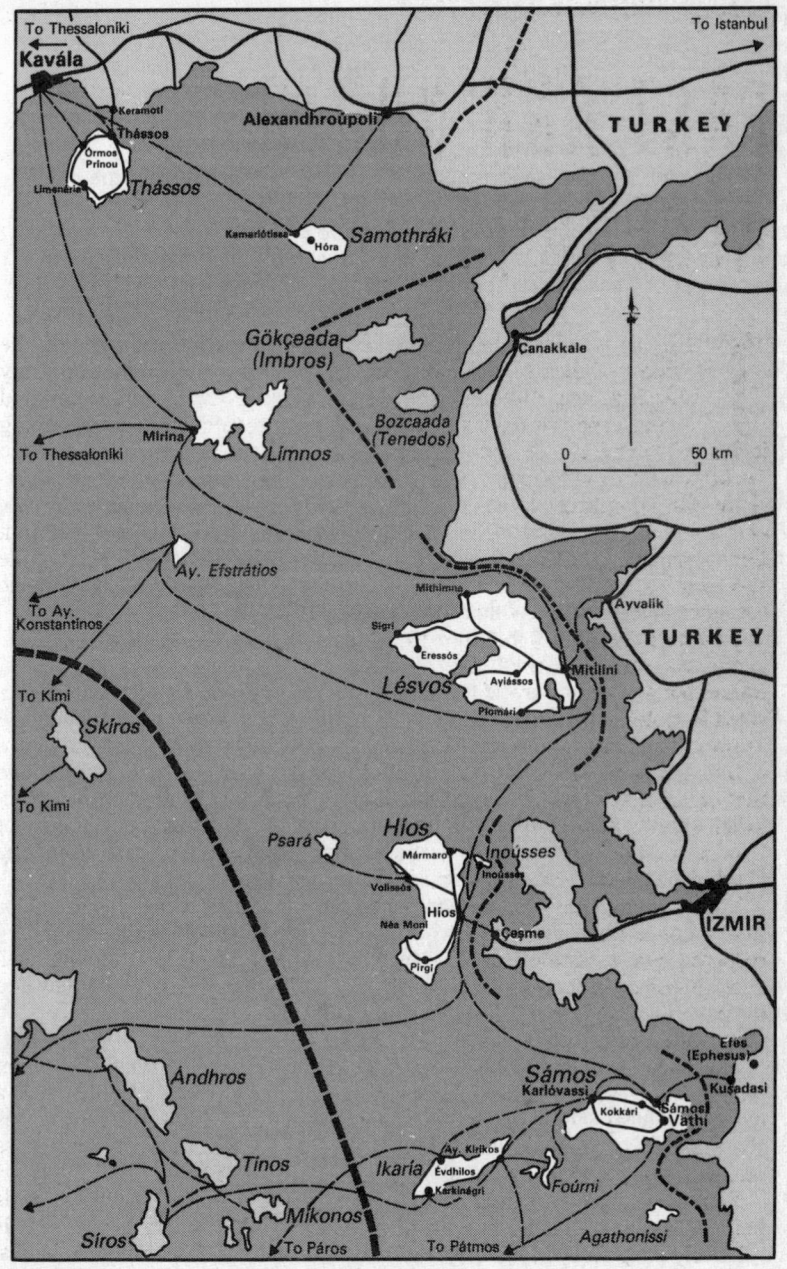

ravaged and the development of tourism has – so far – been deliberately retarded. **Lésvos** is more of an acquired taste, though once you get a feel for the island you may find it hard to leave – the number of repeat visitors grows yearly. By contrast virtually no foreigners and few Greeks visit **Áyios Evstrátios**, and with good reason. **Límnos** is marginally better, but with its appeal confined mostly to the area around the pretty port town.

Samothráki and Thássos to the north are totally isolated from the others except by means of the mainland port Kavála – it's easiest to visit them en route to or from Istanbul. **Samothráki** has one of the most dramatic seaward approaches of any Greek island, and one of the more important ancient sites. The appeal of **Thássos**, on the other hand, is rather broader, with a varied offering of sandy beaches, forested mountains and minor archaeological sites. Cheaply accessible from the mainland, however, it can be overrun in high season.

Sámos

Lush, seductive and well-watered, Sámos was once the wealthiest island in the Aegean and the base of a thriving intellectual community – Epicurus, Pythagoras and Aesop were among the residents – before falling on evil times after the collapse of the Byzantine empire. Ornate two-storey houses in town and village attest to a minor renaissance during the eighteenth and nine-teenth centuries, when the island was semi–autonomous, but the ravages of World War II and mass emigration put a stop to that.

Today the Samian economy is again on the upswing as tourism – too much of it in places – outstrips the traditional livelihoods of winemaking, logging and olive gathering. Comparisons with Crete are tempting: as on that island, the east and most of the northern sectors have been sacrificed, with varying degrees of taste, to the onslaught of chartered-in holiday-makers, while the west and much of the south retain their undeveloped grandeur.

Vathí (Sámos town)

Vathí is the main port and island capital, situated in the northeast. It's modern and uninteresting for the most part, with a waterside dominated by expensive tourist traps and agencies. Only the suburb of Áno Vathí, with its fine old *arhondiká*, is worth pausing for, and perhaps also the **archaeological museum** if it ever re-opens from its lengthy repairs.

The best place to stay, if you can get a room, is the *Pension Ionia*, M. Kalomíri 5, just behind the dock. There are cheap eats around the former bus station, at the corner of Ayíou Nikoláou. (The new bus stop is right over to the other (south) side of town, near the outstanding *Psistaria Katrakazos*). If you're interested in going to **Turkey** (Sámos is directly opposite Kuşadasi and Ephesus), most of the agencies – and departures – are here, though there is some service from Pithagório. Don't forget to check out current Greek regulations about visits to Turkey; *Samos Travel*, by the ferryboat quay, is good for accommodation, information and travel arrangements.

Although Vathí Bay is large it offers poor swimming. Most people inexplicably flock to **Gangoú Beach**, a neglible strip of rocks 1km northeast of the dock. Far better are **Psilí Ámmos** and **Possidhonion** beaches on the southeast tip of Sámos.

The island's **bus service** is reasonable as long as you stick to the tourist corridors of Vathí–Kokkári–Karlóvassi or Vathí–Pithagório, but wretched otherwise. The locals know this so **hitching** is quite good. Otherwise consider hiring a **moped or motorbike** for a day to check out where you might want to base yourself, though rates for these are inevitably higher in Vathí than elsewhere.

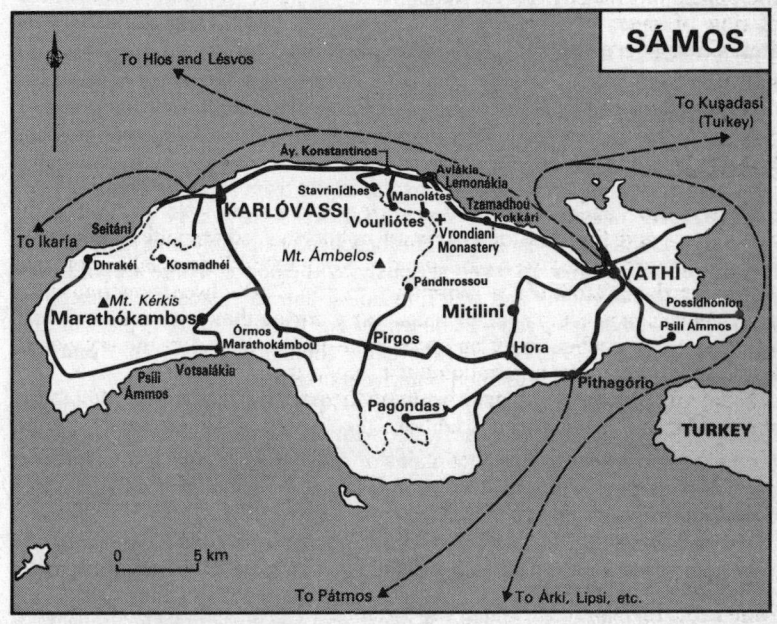

Pithagório

PITHAGÓRIO, renamed in 1955 to honour its native mathematician, Pythagoras, was the ancient capital of the island when, under the tyrant Polycrates (ca. 540–522 B.C.), Samos was a major imperial power. Today it's a dusty town in the shadow of the international airport and, somewhat inexplicably, an established tourist resort. In summer you've little chance of a room and, if you decide to stay, choice is probably limited to a rudimentary campsite in a field behind the town. If you're merely planning to stay the night here in order to catch a boat the following morning, it's better simply to taxi over in time for the departure.

Traces of **ancient Pythagoreion** are much touted in Sámos brochures but assume humbler dimensions as you approach them. The most important site ought to be the **Sanctuary of Hera** (8km north of town, off the airport road), whose principal temple was, after that of Olympian Zeus in Athens, the largest ever built in the Greek world and one of the Seven Ancient Wonders. A single reconstructed column amid a scattered complex of sanctuary buildings does it little justice. Much more interesting if it hasn't been permanently sealed up is the **EUPALINOS TUNNEL**, an aqueduct bored through the mountain just north of the town. Its midsection has collapsed but you should be able to explore a considerable portion of its 900-metre length, though you will need a torch. To get there take the main Vathí road out of town; after a little way a track bears off to the left, past the meagre remains of a theatre, then splits in two – you keep to the left.

The north coast and Mt. Ámbelos villages

Between Vathí and Karlóvassi an idyllic landscape of pine, cypress and orchards gives the lie to any claims of Pithagório's superiority as a resort. Here also are numerous houses sporting tile roofs, beaked chimneys and brightly painted shutters, arranged in settlements crowned by tan churches with blue-and-white-striped turrets instead of the usual simple domes.

KOKKÁRI, one-third of the way to Karlóvassi, is a large fishing village crowning one of twin headlands. The beaches are pebbly and exposed and the 'no camping' signs are taken seriously by the police. There are, however, an abundance of rooms and watering holes, and the place itself (except in high season, when it's a zoo – 25 buses *per day* from Vathí) is so pleasant that you easily forgive the lack of shoreline shelter or sand. *To Kyma* and *Panorama* are the cheapest good waterfront tavernas.

The closest decent beach to Kokkári is **Tzamadhoú** (as in Coleridge's Xanadu), forty minutes' westward walk, with plate-shaped pebbles, a freshwater spring and a taverna, but mountains of rubbish are a poor testament to its popularity. **Tzábo** beach, just west of Avlákia, is cleaner but without water; ditto **Lemonákia**, east of Tzamadhoú.

If Kokkári is overcrowded you might try **ÁYIOS KONSTANTÍNOS**, a very quiet coastal town with plenty of food and lodging. There are no beaches in the immediate vicinity but it does serve as a gateway (Kokkári is anther) to the wonderful villages just inland. A dense and usually signposted network of paths connects the two coastal communities with **Stavrinídhes, Valeondátes, Manolátes, Vourliótes** and the **monastery of Vrondianí**, the island's oldest. In most of these villages you can rustle up a simple meal and perhaps a bed at short notice, and from Manolátes a single path leads further up to the summit of Mt. Ámbelos, and from there onward to **Pándhroson**, the highest south-facing village on Sámos.

Western Sámos

The administrative capital of this region is **KARLÓVASSI**, a sprawling, nondescript town divided into three districts, of which Paleó Kárlovassi (westernmost) is the nicest. Some, though not all, of the Ikaría/Pireás ferries dock here, and buses leave for various points in the southwestern part of the island.

The first stop where you'll be tempted to get off is **Marathókambos**, a pretty, amphitheatrical village overlooking the gulf of the same name, but most passengers will stay on the bus until **Órmos Marathokámbou**, which makes a more functional base for the area's excellent beaches. In Órmos there's a pebbly shore and a dwindling *kaíki*-building industry, but just to the west are some of the only sandy beaches on the island. **Votsalákia** is long, with a few tavernas and rooms. **Psili Ámmos**, 3km beyond (not to be confused with the one further east), is almost as extensive and certainly more scenic, with only a single taverna. The road, passable on a *sturdy* motorbike (don't try it on a moped), continues around Mt. Kérkis to Dhrakéi, with striking views all the way of the mountain and Foúrni island.

There's no bus service if you want to head due west out of Karlóvassi, so you'll have to walk, taxi or hitch. **Potamiá** is a rather dirty, exposed beach an hour distant, redeemed only by an undeveloped hot spring lodged in a grotto and a fine path from Paleó Kárlovassi. Just west of the beach the dirt road peters out and paths continue through the finest scenery on the island. The most popular targets are the beaches of **Mikró Seitáni** (pebbles) and **Megálo Seitáni** (sand), the latter also accessible on foot from Dhrakéi (where the bus calls twice a day). You can also veer inland to the village of **Kosmadhéi**, the start of the easiest route up to the summit of Mt. Kérkis.

Ikaría

Ikaría is physically similar to Sámos though much less visited, and invariably underestimated or slammed by travel writers (like Lawrence Durrell) who probably haven't bothered to see for themselves. Its name is supposed to derive from the unexpected visitation of Icarus, who fell to the sea just off-coast after the wax bindings of his wings melted, and (as any local will patiently explain) the island is itself clearly wing-shaped.

For years the place's main attraction has been a number of hot radioactive springs, principally at **Thérma**, some reputed to cure rheumatism and arthritis and some to make women fertile, though others are so potent that they've long been considered a danger. The unnerving sign which once read 'Welcome to the Island of Radiation' has now been removed.

Ikaría is also one of the Greek Communist Party's strongholds (like Lesvos but unlike Samos, in whose administrative region it is situated), which may explain why the KKE headquarters in Évdhilos is housed in the most impressive building on the waterside. This tendency was accentuated during the long years of right-wing domination in Greece, when (as in prior ages) Ikaria was used as a place of exile for dissidents. Many Ikarians emigrated to North America, and ironically their regular remittances help to support the island's precarious economy.

The island's port and capital is **ÁYIOS KÍRIKOS** on the south coast, where you'll find **banks**, the **post office**, a **tourist office** and **ferry operators**. There are **hotels** and **rooms** too, but while the inhabitants are friendly enough you'll probably want to take the one daily bus to Ikaría's north shore. There are plenty of taxis and hitching is possible. The mountain road from

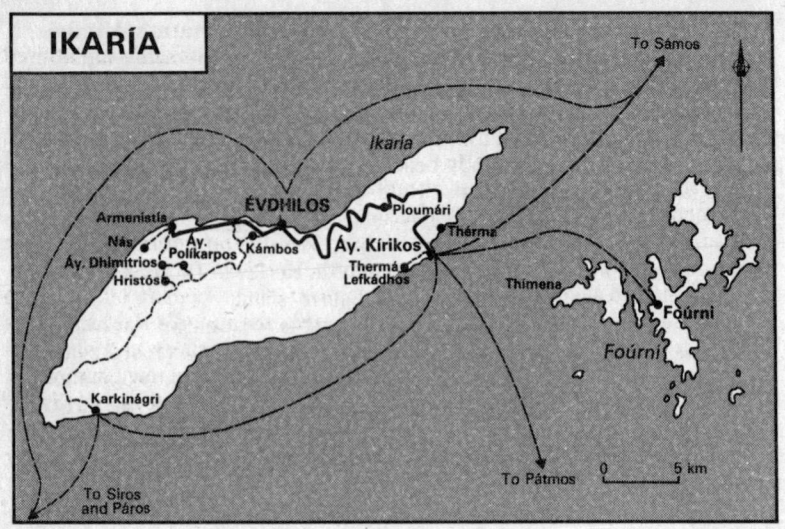

Áyios Kírikos to Évdhilos is one of the most exhilarating on any Greek island, and the long ridge which extends the length of the island is often shrouded in cloud, even in summer when the rest of the Aegean sky is clear.

Northern **ÉVDHILOS**, where ferries also call twice a week (weather permitting), is more agreeable, with an E-class hotel, a fair number of rooms, and pine forests sloping down to the sea on either side. **Kámbos** just to the west has a small museum and the ruins of a Byzantine palace, and nearby are some swimming coves attainable on foot.

The big beaches, however, are at **ARMENISTÍS**, at the end of the bus route in the northwest corner of the island. This village is beginning to get popular with Greek and Northern European youth, who avail themselves of numerous inexpensive rooms and several tavernas. While there are usually quite a number of campers behind the two 300-metre sandy beaches, five or ten minutes' walk east, a word of warning on the life and morals of Ikaría is in order. This is an island more used to Greek rheumatics than surf-seeking backpackers. Nude bathing, above all, is very severely frowned upon, and the locals have rejected an airport because they're not thrilled at the notion of Ikaría going the way of Sámos. An offshoot of such attitudes is that the tourist season here is fairly short, from June to September only, so don't expect too much by way of public transport or tavernas outside those months.

Along the coast west of Armenistís are the hamlets of **Áyios Liskáris**, a church built by a returned Canadian villager on a tiny islet just off its coast, and **Nás** (an hour's walk) with a solitary taverna on a small strip of beach. Striking inland you can walk up to the *Rahés* (Ridges) villages of **Áyios Dhimítrios**, **Áyios Políkarpos** and **Hristós**, and over to the spectacularly-sited and isolated **Karkinágri**, built on so steep a slope that its main communication with the rest of the island is via the occasional *kaíkia* or ferry that heaves to offshore to exchange passengers and supplies.

Foúrni and Thímena

As seen from Mt. Kérkis or Rahés summit, the straits with Sámos are littered with a number of spidery-looking islets. The only ones permanently inhabited are Thímena and Foúrni, which can be reached (weather permitting) by daily *kaíki* (around 1 pm) from Áyios Kírikos, and much less often by services from Karlóvassi or even main-line ferries. All of these exist for the benefit of the locals, and are not a tourist excursion, so you should plan to spend the night since the boat goes straight back.

Apart from the remote hamlet of Hrissomiliá in the north, most of the population of **FOÚRNI** is gathered around the port and the hamlets immediately south of it. The harbour community, its buildings toppling off the steep west-facing shore, is large and lively considering the island's size, and trees lining the main street and quay provide welcome greenery and shade in summer. There are several rooms establishments – inquire, for example, at the *kafenío* owned by Kostas Ahladhis immediately to your left as you disembark – as well as several tavernas near the water and hidden in the backstreets. The friendliness of the inhabitants makes up for the lack of many other amenities.

There is a rather average beach just north of the town, beyond the fish-processing plant, but better ones are found in the opposite direction; follow the track south to the crumbling windmills, then go over the ridge and down a path to the hamlet of **Kámbi**. More paths lead beyond the shady beach here over the cliffs to other secluded swimming-spots.

The islets to the south, visible from any elevation, were once the lair of Algerian pirates, and the word *koursáros* (corsair) crops up frequently in conversation. Today Foúrni is principally a haven for yachters and for *astakós* (Aegean lobster), a sort of oversized saltwater crayfish.

Thímena has two tiny settlements at which the boat calls on its way from Ikaría to Foúrni, and no tourist facilities whatsoever.

Híos

'Craggy Híos', as Homer described his (probable) birthplace, is an island with an eventful history and a strong sense of place. It has always been relatively prosperous, in medieval times through the export of mastic (of which more below) and later by virtue of several shipping dynasties. The shipping magnates and the military authorities have in the past not encouraged tourism, but with the worldwide shipping crisis, resistance is dwindling. Increasing numbers of foreigners are discovering a Híos beyond its large port city – fascinating villages, an important Byzantine monument and a healthy complement of beaches. Sadly, the natural beauty of the island has been much diminished by a series of forest fires in the past decade – only in the far north of the island (around Ayiásmata and Amádhes) and the far south (where there's little to burn) have the woods remained unscathed.

In 1988 the first weekly charters (from Norway) were instituted, and the number of direct flights from northern Europe is expected to increase substantially in succeeding years. Unfortunately there are only about 900 guest beds on the entire island, a sobering figure when you realise that there will be double that number of tourists on any given day in season. Hotels and rooms are proliferating at a dizzying rate, but barely fast enough – properties are often already fully booked by tour companies while still at the foundation stage! Best, therefore, to visit out of season or stay outside the main town; don't expect to be too picky about the standard of accommodation, you will be a lot happier on Híos.

The harbour

Híos town is a bustling commercial centre – a shock coming from most of the other modest little island towns. Yet though it's not an obvious holiday resort, it's worth some time. The city is always full of life, with a shambling old bazaar district, some excellent and authentic tavernas, and a regular evening *volta* (promenade) along the waterfront. All in all, enough to hold your interest.

The **bazaar** extends south and east of the old mosque (now a **Historical Museum** open 10am–1pm Mon.–Sat.) on the main *platía* (Plastíras Square). The official EOT information office, as opposed to the conspicuous but private 'Tourist Information Office' on the quay, is located on Platía Polykhronopoúlou, between the waterside and the *Ionian and Popular Bank*. All of the shipping agencies, whether for hops over to Turkey or a domestic ferry, are within shouting distance of the EOT.

If you've time to kill, wander out to the old Turkish quarter within the decaying walls of a **Genoese fort**, unusually some way inland. As on Sámos, Lésvos and Límnos, the Turks only relinquished control of the island in 1912; in 1822 they committed one of the worst massacres of the War of Independence here, killing 30,000 Hiotes and enslaving some 45,000 others.

Relatively cheap **accommodation** is beginning to proliferate around the cathedral and the bazaar. In addition to such old standbys as the hotels *Filoxenia*, *Palladion* and *Acropolis* (all within sight of each other just behind the quay) and the *Hotel Rodhon* (virtually the only place in the old quarter), you can now also choose from clean and reasonably cheap places like *Hios Rooms*, *Pension Yannis*, *Stella's Rooms* (all near the water) and *Anesis* (in the bazaar but quiet at night).

Eating here can also be a distinct pleasure, more rewarding than the initially obvious rash of fast-food joints run by returned Greek-Americans would seem to promise. Best of the bunch by a long way – don't be put off by its promotion in travel-agency windows – is *O Hotzas*, at the far end of the bazaar on Stefánou Tsourí 74: an outstanding *mezé*, casserole, and barrelled-wine taverna. More centrally, you can get good, cheap, oven-cooked lunches at *Estiatorio Dhimitrakopoulos* on the corner of Sgoutá and Valtarías, a few steps from the long-distance bus terminal. At the far (west) end of the water-side, where the big ferries dock, you'll find the *Ouzeri Theodhosiou* and *Psistaria Freskadha*, along with the inexpensive but good-quality *To Mourayio*. For tremendous yoghurts (imported daily from Mytilíni) there is a milk shop behind the conspicuous *Acropolis*.

The road system radiates out from the capital. Both the blue *astikó* (local) and green long-distance *iperastikó* (long-distance) **buses** can be found near the minaret on Platía Plastíra (also known as Vournáki Square), on opposite sides of the large park. The green vehicles run to most of the villages of the very distinct southern and northern halves of the island, though services to the north are sparse and if you can hire a moped or car, or share a taxi (a very common practice), it's well worth the money. The closest good beach to town is **Karfás** (7km – very frequent blue bus), a long sweep of fine sand with a burgeoning number of rooms and tavernas, crowded only at weekends. *Karatzas* is perhaps the best and cheapest place to eat here, in itself perhaps justifying the trip out.

Central Híos

The monastery of **NÉA MONÍ** founded by the Byzantine emperor Constantine Monamachos IX in 1049 is the most beautiful and important medieval building on any of the Greek islands. Its mosaics rank with those of Dháfni and Óssios Loukás as being among the finest artistic expressions of their age, and its setting, high in the mountains west of the port, is no less memorable. There's a direct bus only on Sunday mornings for mass; at other times you have to take a local bus as far as Karyés (7km) and walk or hitch an equal distance further. Once a powerful and independent community of 600 monks, Néa Moní was pillaged during the atrocities of 1822 and most of its inmates put to the sword. Today the monastery, with its giant refectory and vaulted water cisterns, is maintained by just three nuns; all are in their 80s and they close the buildings from 1 until 4 pm. One of their duties is to keep open for visitors the chapel containing the bones of the 1822 massacre victims from all over the island.

For a really good day's walking you can go on beyond Néa Moní to a pair of extraordinary medieval villages. First met is **AVGÓNIMA**, a jumble of whitewashed houses on a hilltop. The empty, tan buildings of **ANÁVATOS** (11km from Néa Moní; 22 km from Hóra), beyond, are almost indistinguishable from the 300-metre bluff on which they're built. During the 1822 insurrection the 400 inhabitants threw themselves over this cliff rather than surrender to the besieging Turks. As with many of Híos' interior villages, it is still virtually deserted save for a handful of people who remain to grow pistachio nuts and a small amount of other produce. Given the complete absence of facilities you'll either have to sleep out or hitch back at least to Karyés if you want to make it back to town the same day.

Southern Híos

The dry valleys of this part of the island are home to the mastic bush, *Pistacia lentisca* to be precise, which here, alone in Greece, produces an aromatic gum of marketable quantity and quality. The plant itself resembles an ugly miniature baobab, but the resin scraped from it was for centuries the base of paints, cosmetics and chewable jelly beans which became a somewhat addictive staple in Ottoman harems. The wealth engendered by the mastic trade supported a half-dozen *mastikhohoriá* (mastic villages), but the end of imperial Turkey, and the industrial revolution with its petroleum products, knocked the bottom out of the mastic market. Now it's just a curiosity (to be chewed – try the *Elma* brand gum – or drunk as a liqueur) and the *mastikho-*

horiá survive mainly from their tangerines, apricots and olives. The towns themselves are also quite unique – the only settlements on Híos spared by the Turks in 1822 – and at the first opportunity it's worth jumping on a bus headed for Pirgí or Mestá.

PIRGÍ, 24km from the port, is one of the liveliest and most colourful of the villages, its houses elaborately embossed with *ksistá*, geometric patterns cut

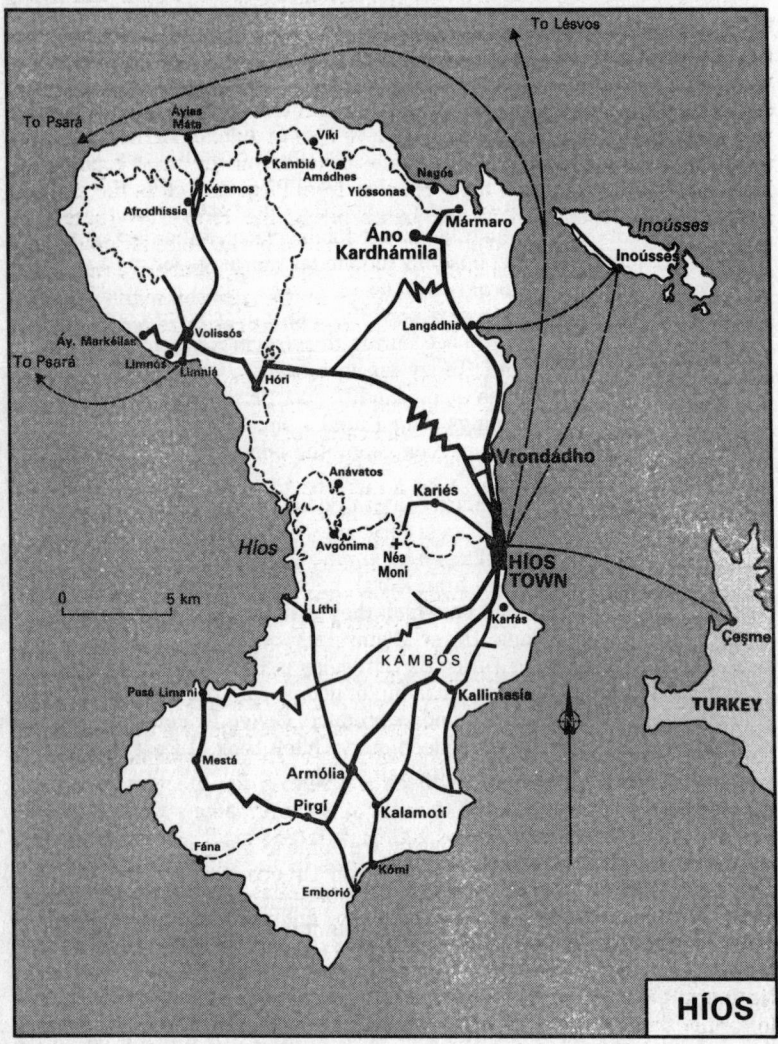

HÍOS

into the plaster and then outlined with paint. On the northeast corner of the central *platía* the fresco-embellished twelfth-century Byzantine church of **Áyii Apóstoli** is tucked under an arcade (open Mon.–Sat. 9am–3:30pm, Sun. 10am–2pm). Pirgí has one hotel, a handful of rooms (some bookable through the **Women's Agricultural and Tourist Co-operative**), a couple of tavernas, and some good beaches nearby.

Closest of these is **EMBORIÓ**, a small fishing community with a few excellent tavernas just 5km from Pirgí (many buses in summer along the side road). The fine dark sand beach of Mávra Voliá lies five minutes' walk southwest from the front – follow the track along a rock shoulder and past a smaller beach. There's another beach 7km distant at ÁYIES PÁNDES, near which, at Káto Fána, are the ruins of a temple of Apollo. **KÓMI**, 4km due south of Kalamotí (which is itself some distance off the main road to the harbour), is the remotest of these beaches from Pirgí, as well as the sandiest and most developed. Not all the buses plying the Pirgí–Híos route pass through Kalamotí, though in summer, as with Emborió, there is some direct service. Should you be stranded the night, a growing number of rooms are available at either Emborió or Kómi. While in the area you might also visit the medieval town of Armólia, which is famous for its ceramics industry.

MESTÁ, 10km west of Pirgí, has a more sombre feel, with its warren of defensively-arranged stone houses doubling as the town's perimeter fortification. From the central *platía*, dominated by a church, a bewildering maze of cool, shaded lanes, provided with anti-earthquake buttresses and tunnels between the usually unpainted houses, wanders off in all directions. Most of the streets end in blind alleys, with a mere half-dozen communicating with the outside world. There are rooms to let here, including a reasonably-priced B-class pension network in restored traditional dwellings, and a good taverna on the main *platía*. Some beaches nearby are accessible by goat trail – ask the way, for example, to **Apothíki**, but avoid the vicinity of Pasá Limáni harbour, which no longer has any ferry service to Rafína.

On your way back to Híos town, or setting out from there by bicycle, you could make a visit the **Kámbos**, a vast plain fertile with citrus groves and ornate old villas built out of a tawny, peanut-brittle masonry. The district was originally settled by the Genoese in the fourteenth century and the sumptuous, three-storey dwellings (many with later Turkish modifications) are unique on the island. Some of them are venues for the yearly summer courses offered by the **Ionic Center** (for information, write to: Strat. Sindhésmou 12, Kolonaki, Athens 106 73; ☎01/364-4448). A limited number of others are being renovated as guesthouses by the authorities, though the scheme will hardly relieve the island's lodging crisis. For a staggering £200–300 *per day*, one to twelve persons may enjoy full board and have their every whim catered to by trained chefs, valets, etc.

Northern Híos

In former times vast pine forests covered this part of the island but generations of shipbuilders, and the disastrous fires of the 1980s, have denuded most of the countryside.

The villages of northern Híos never really recovered from the Turkish massacre. Many are deserted much of the year which means that bus services accordingly sparse. About one-third of the former population now lives in Híos town, venturing out only on the dates of major festivals or to tend their grapes and olives, time which barely adds up to four months of the year. The balance of the northerners, based in Athens or the U.S., visit their ancestral homes for just a few weeks in the summer – making for a very brief, if intense 'season'.

The blue buses run only as far as **VRONDÁDHO**, an amorphous coastal suburb which is the favoured residence of the island's many seafarers. Homer is reputed to have lived and taught here, and just above the little port and pebble beach you can visit his purported lectern, strangely incorporated into a Classical shrine. Accordingly many of the bus shelters are labelled *Dhaskalópetra* (Teacher's Rock).

LANGÁDHIA is probably the first spot where you would be tempted to leave the bus; set, as the name implies, at the mouth of a severe gorge, this attractive fishing settlement has a few rooms and eating-places but no beach worthy of the name. If you are in a terrible hurry to get to Inoússes (see overpage) and have missed the regular ferry, Hristos Moudalos (☎0272/51-568) will shuttle you over from Langádhia – the return price is 10,000dr per boatload.

ÁNO and **KÁTO KARDHÁMILA**, a couple of kilometres apart and almost 40km out of the main town, come as a welcome, green relief from Homer's 'crags', positioned as they are at the edge of a fertile *kámbos*. Káto, better known as **MÁRMARO**, is larger, its waterside streets flanked by the hillside districts of Ráhi and Perivoláki, and indeed it's the second largest community on the island, with a **bank**, **post office** and **OTE** branch. However, neither town is particularly well prepared for visitors, nor is there really much to attract visitors other than some pastel, neoclassical architecture. It's a far better spot for renting a long-term dwelling, which certain numbers of people do each year, than for a short-term **stay**. For tourists there is only the luxury *Hotel Kardamyla* (fronting a pathetic beach regularly supplemented with spread sand), one unmarked pension in Ráhi, whose rooms are obtained by pleading your case at the *Marakaki* sweetshop, and another (last-resort) place up by the shabby disco on the way to the army base. The fishing harbour, fully exposed to the *meltémi*, is strictly businesslike. For **food**, try either the nameless taverna near the sailor's commemorative statue, the nearby *Barba Yannis* snack bar, or one of the seasonal restaurants up by the windmill in Perivoláki. Áno Kardhámila has a single *psistariá*/pizzeria and, while it has no accommodation, makes a good destination for rambles on dirt tracks up through the local orchards.

For a good swim head west for an hour along the coastal cement road, passing the aforementioned mill, to **NAGÓS**, a tiny harbour at the foot of a gorge choked with greenery. The springs have been pipelined out of sight but the 300-metre pebble beach is for all to enjoy, summer winds permitting. You can eat at one taverna and occupy adjacent, unmarked rooms. The town's name is a corruption of *naós*, after a Poseidon temple at the base of the cliff behind; it was a large precinct, covering almost the entire area of the the present-day orchards. Medieval settlers piled soil on top of the remaining flagstones, which made for excellent drainage, and after the island's liberation in 1912 assorted relics, including statues, were excavated – and disappeared. YIÓSSONAS, a fifteen-minute walk west, is a rockier and less sheltered beach but your only chance of relative solitude in high season (July-Sept.) when Nagós throbs with merrymakers twenty hours a day.

Few outsiders venture beyond Yióssonas, although an early-afternoon bus covers the twenty kilometres between Mármaro and Kambiá. AMÁDHES and VÍKI are attractive villages at the base of 1297-metre Pilinéo, the island's summit, which can be climbed from Víki. KAMBIÁ, overlooking a ravine strewn with chapels, has very much of an end-of-the-line feel to it; go to one of the *kafenía* by the church if you want directions for the one-hour path down into and across the gorge to Agriolopó, an abandoned hamlet. From the latter's church a system of tracks (to short cut, always bear right and downhill toward the sea) leads within another ninety minutes to the tumbledown pier and seaweed beach at Ayiásmata..

AYIÁSMATA is one of the strangest spots on the island, consisting of perhaps twenty buildings (four of them churches), including the miraculous grey-and-white baths (6–11am, summer only) after which the place is named. You can stay either at a stone-built hotel or in rooms at the west end of the bay, a truly Fellini-esque setup where working-class Greeks, mostly Hiotes, establish a virtual colony for weeks on end. Rooms are sparse, but the seaview compensates. It is assumed that you will bring most of your own supplies though you can supplement these at a little store in the 'colony'.

The road south out of Ayiásmata passes through strikingly beautiful countryside. Walking is generally obligatory as far as KÉRAMOS and AFRODHÍSSIA, with a short-cut between these villages. Beyond Afrodhíssia, the more attractive of the two, a tarmaç road continues through HÁLANDHRA and NÉA POTAMIÁ – conceivably the ugliest village on Híos – for a total twenty-kilometre (closer to 17km with shortcuts) traverse to Volissós.

VOLISSÓS was once the most important of the island's northern villages, and its old stone houses still curl beneath the hilltop Genoese fort. But today it carries a faintly desolate air, with the bulk of its remaining, mostly elderly inhabitants living in newer buidings around the *platía*. Here there's a post office (but no bank), two stores and an evenings-only taverna. Since the bus only comes this way four times a week, you'll have to plan on staying. This should cause no concern as the area has simply the best beaches on Híos, unspoiled because the adjacent property owners have thus far refused to sell land to developers.

There is no accommodation in Volissós itself but you could ask here about bungalows in Limniá, 1½km below. **LIMNIÁ** also has two tavernas (one seasonal, one permanent) and above the latter are a few rooms. It's a lively and authentic little fishing anchorage, with skippers coming and going from Psará, Híos harbour and even Plomári on Lésvos. You're not far from the fabled beaches either: 1km southeast, at HORÍ, begins an almost boundless sand-and-pebble beach where nudism is permitted, and the more intimate **LÍMNOS** (not to be confused with Limniá) is just a ten-minute jeep-track walk over the headland north of the harbour (or approachable by a longer asphalt road from Volissós). At Límnos there's a single rooms establishment where the dirt track joins the asphalt, and a *psistariá* on the larger of the two excellent sandy coves.

AYÍA MARKÉLLA, 5km further north, stars in many of the local post-cards: a long, stunning beach fronting the monastery of the same name (not particularly interesting but summer taverna and lodging in the grounds). You can happily skip the 'hot' springs out on the headland beyond, however, which turn out to be a tiny cavity of tepid, iron-stained water; most of the summer, anyway, there's enough fresh water in the creek bed behind Ayía Markélla to wash the salt off. Indeed most of the beaches hereabouts seem tailor-made for camping – tolerated due to the shortage of rooms – and except in mid-summer you'll have little company.

Psará and Inoússes

There are also beaches and tavernas on both of Híos's satellite isles. Inoússes, the closer one, has daily ferries from the main harbour in season; Psará is served three or four times weekly. As noted above there are supplementary sailings according to demand from Langádhia and Limniá.

Psará

Psará, like Híos, suffered the massacre in 1822– and it never really recovered. Today there are under 500 inhabitants – quite a contrast with the former population of some 30,000. However, the island, which has had French connections since the early nineteenth century, is currently the subject of a revitalisation project by a Franco-Hellenic team. In 1985 the renovation of the port was completed, and in the following two years the island's first secondary school was opened and cultural and academic links between Psará and Paris were established; there's even a bilingual Greek-French magazine, *Ta Psará*. An airport for interior flights is planned, but it's emphasised that development is to be cultural and for the benefit of the islanders rather than a touristic expansion.

Psará has one hotel (formerly a prison), several pensions, and bed-and-breakfast **accommodation** available in the refectory of a former monastery. There are also a handful of shops and eating places, none of these, alas, yet showing too much of the Parisian influence.

Inoússes

Inoússes has a similar-sized population to Psará – though a very different reputation. For centuries it has provided Greece with many of her wealthiest shipping families: in fact the richest Greek shipowner in the world, Kostas Lemos, comes from Inoússes. This helps explain the large villas and visiting summer yachts in an otherwise ordinary and peaceful Greek island. A macabre local sight is the convent of Evangelismós, endowed by the Pateras family of shipping magnates and containing the mummified body of the reputedly saintly daughter, Irini, and the bones of her father, Panagos; the abbess, presiding over a dozen novices, is Irini's mother. If you want to stay on Inoússes – and there is every reason, despite the stranger elements – there are two D-class hotels.

Lésvos (Mitilíni)

Lésvos, the third largest Greek island after Crete and Évvia, is not only the birthplace of Sappho but also of Aesop, Arion and more recently the primitive artist Theophilos, the poet Odysseus Elytis and the novelist Stratis Myrivilis. Despite these artistic associations, it may not at first strike the visitor as particularly beautiful or interesting, but the rocky volcanic landscape of pine and olive groves (some of the latter 500 years old) grows on you with increased acquaintance, especially so if you have the time and patience to hitchhike or the funds to hire a car or motorbike.

Lovers of medieval and Turkish architecture certainly won't be disappointed. Genoese castles survive at Mitilíni, Mólivos and Ándissa. These date from the late fourteenth century, when Lésvos was given as dowry to a Genoese prince of the Gatelouzi clan following his marriage to the niece of one of the last Byzantine emperors.

Until very recently the enormous olive plantations and the fishing industry supported the inhabitants, but mass-market tourism is now starting to make inroads. As yet Lésvos is still by and large a working island. There are few large hotels outside the capital, Mitilíni, and rooms far outnumber the villa-type of accommodation; there are no official campsites. Buses, too, tend to radiate out from Mitilíni for the benefit of the locals, not the tourists who may want to do an out-and-back day-trip. Furthermore, it must be emphasised that Lésvos is a big place: about 70km by 45km at its widest points, and almost split by the two deep gulfs of Kalloní and Yéra, which means that getting from A to B will usually involve going via C, which could be either Mitilíni or Kalloní, roughly in the middle of the island.

Among the Lésvos's characteristics can be counted a tendency to vote Communist in proportions far greater than elsewhere in Greece, hence the nickname of 'Red Lésvos', and of the mayor of Mólivos, Kostas Doukas – 'The Red Lion of Mólivos'. The village of Pétra also boasts a women's collective, running the main restaurant and letting village rooms, while the tourist office in Mitilíni rejoices in the proud title of *The Co-operative Tourism and Travel Agency of the Union of Agricultural Co-operatives of Lésvos*.

Mitilíni
MITILÍNI is the port and capital, and in Greek fashion sometimes doubles as the name of the island, always something to watch out for when travelling by ferry or plane. The town sprawls around two broad bays divided by a promontory where the Genoese fortress sits – open much of the day but not to be photographed as it's a military security area. Most things of interest to visi-

tors are grouped around the harbour where the ferries dock and the main bazaar street leading northwards behind the banks. The further port is strictly industrial. There are a few old houses in the back streets, a couple of antique stalls in the **market**, an **Archaeological Museum** (under restoration) and a **Popular Art Museum** (open Mon.–Fri. 10am–noon and 4–6pm) near the south harbour. Little else is likely to detain you. The local beaches are disappointing, with the main town beach levying a hefty admission charge.

If you really want to stay, or have to, then the tourist police or private agencies can fix you up with reasonably priced **accommodation**, and there are several large, expensive and noisy hotels on the quay of the southern port. Bear in mind the shortage of accommodation here, however, as well as that of onward transport if you are arriving late in the day. Coming from the airport, buses dovetail poorly with Mitilíni-based buses, and a shared taxi into the town or even further afield may save you a lot of grief.

There are two **bus stations** in Mitilíni. The *astikó* service for nearby villages departs from the middle of the quay, while *iperastikó* coaches leave from a small bus station near Platía Konstantinopóleos at the southern end of the harbour. The **tourist office** is just around the corner from the latter. There are one to four departures daily for the endpoints of Ayiássos, Mandamádhos, Plomári, Polikhnítos, Mólivos, Sígri and Eressós, but the difficulty of organising day-trips are compounded by the deceptive distances over often indifferent roads, and the frequent need to change buses at Kalloní. In short, it's best to decide on a base and stay there for at least a few days, exploring its immediate surroundings on foot or by motorbike, rather than constantly be trying to move on.

Near Mitilíni

Just south of the town, on the road to the airport, you can visit various *pírgi* (tower-mansions) at **Hrissomalloússa** and **Aklidhíou**, built by the wealthy bourgeoisie of the nineteenth century. **Vária**, birthplace of the artist Theophilos, has a museum of his paintings and also the **Teriade Museum** with a comprehensive collection of lithographs by Picasso, Chagall, Matisse, and others. Beyond the airport, and reached easiest by first taking a local bus as far as Loutrá, lies the sandy, isolated beach of **Áyios Ermoyénis**.

Heading north from Mitilíni the beaches are negligible but the startling views across the straits to Turkey make the trip up the coast road to Mandamádhos worthwhile. On the way you can detour to see a Roman aqueduct at Mória, and more tower-mansions (all difficult to find) at Pirgí, Thermís and Pámfilla.

Mandamádhos is famous for its pottery, including the Ali Baba-style *koumári* urns produced by local potters, but more so for the 'black' icon of the Archangel Michael, whose monastery is the powerful focus of a thriving cult. The image (allegedly made from a mixture of mud and blood) is really more idol than icon, both in its lumpy three-dimensionality and in the manner of veneration which seems a holdover from pagan times. First there is the custom of the coin-wish, whereby you press a coin to the Archangel's forehead – if it sticks then your wish will be granted. It's further believed that in carrying out his various errands to bring about the desires of the faithful, the Archangel wears through enough footwear to stock a small shoeshop. Therefore the icon was until recently surrounded not by the usual *támmata* (votive medallions), but by piles of miniature gold and silver shoes left by those he has helped. (The ecclesiastical authorities, perhaps embarrassed by these 'primitive' practices, apparently removed all of the little shoes in 1986.) Just why his devotees should want to encourage this perpetual motion is uncertain, since in Greek folklore the Archangel Michael is also the one who comes for the souls of the dying – and Christianity notwithstanding, the modern Greeks have a no more sanguine attitude toward death than did their ancestors.

Southern Lésvos

Southern Lésvos is oddly shaped. The coast is indented by two great inlets, the gulfs of Kallóní and Yéra, one curving in a northeasterly, the other in a northwestly direction, thus creating a fan-shaped peninsula at the heart of which is the 968-metre Mt. Ólimbos. The gulfs in turn are almost landlocked by virtue of their very narrow outlets to the sea.

PLOMÁRI is the only sizeable coastal town, the second largest on Lésvos, and presents an odd mix of beauty and the distilling industry. Famous for its *oúzo*, it is besieged in summer by hordes of Scandinavian package tourists, but you can usually find a room or two free near the centre of the old, charmingly dilapidated town. The lack of sandy beaches doesn't seem to deter the trippers, and there is excellent swimming about forty minutes' walk to the east at **ÁYIOS ISIDHÓROS** (rooms, tavernas), which is where most of the charter patrons actually stay. Committed misanthropes should walk west past isolated coves in the direction of Melínda, ninety minutes away. The bus line to Plomári goes via the pretty hill settlements of Paleokípos and Pappádhos (as well as Áyios Isidhóros), but if you're hitching or have your own vehicle you could take a shortcut by making use of the ferry at Pérama, across the neck of the Yéra Gulf.

AYIÁSSOS, nestling in a wooded valley under the crest of Mt. Ólimbos, is the most beautiful hill town on Lésvos. The streets are narrow and cobbled and the many traditional houses are all protected. You can walk the fifteen kilometres of dirt tracks from Plomári, but most people arrive by bus from Mitilíni. Ayiássos also boasts the liveliest festival on the island, held on August 15, and there are rooms available for the increasing numbers of visitors, though most restaurants are very plain. Seven months out of the year you can also listen to the town's resident master *santoúri* player, Ioannis Kakourgos, who plays and sells cassettes from his little studio on the market street.

A different bus from Mitilíni goes to nearby **POLIHNÍTOS**. This is not particularly interesting in itself, but close at hand there are some decaying old **hot springs** and, 8km below, an excellent beach at **VATERÁ** (rooms and tavernas). KTEL buses continue once daily as far as Vríssa, 3km above the shore. From here, because of Lesvos' peculiar geography, it's usually a case of retracing your way in to Mitilíni and then out again, unless you're prepared for a spell of zig-zag hitching.

Northern Lésvos

MÓLIVOS (Míthimna) is easily the most attractive spot on Lésvos, a fact which is becoming better known every year. But even in high summer the town's vine-canopied streets seem to absorb quite readily all the package tourists and individual travellers that make their way there. Tiers of sturdy, red-tiled houses, some standing defensively with their rear walls to the sea, mount the slopes between the picturesque harbour and the Genoese **castle**. Closer examination reveals a half dozen weathered **Turkish fountains** along shady, flower-fragrant, stone-paved alleyways, and you can try to gain admission to the **Krallis** and **Yiannakos mansions**. Until proper excavations begin, ancient Míthimna to the north and west is likely to be relatively uninteresting.

Modern dwellings and hotels have unusually been banned from the municipality, and although this inevitably engenders some tweeness it's good to come across a Greek town that knows what it's got and intends to keep it that way. There are plenty of **rooms to let**, and a **tourist office** by the bus stop to help you find them if necessary – though if there are any vacancies when you arrive, the various landladies will be quick to find *you*. The main lower road, straight past the tourist office, heads towards the harbour, where several small **hotels** overlook the water at the end of the road; they are understandably quite pricey. You might instead want to take the road heading upwards

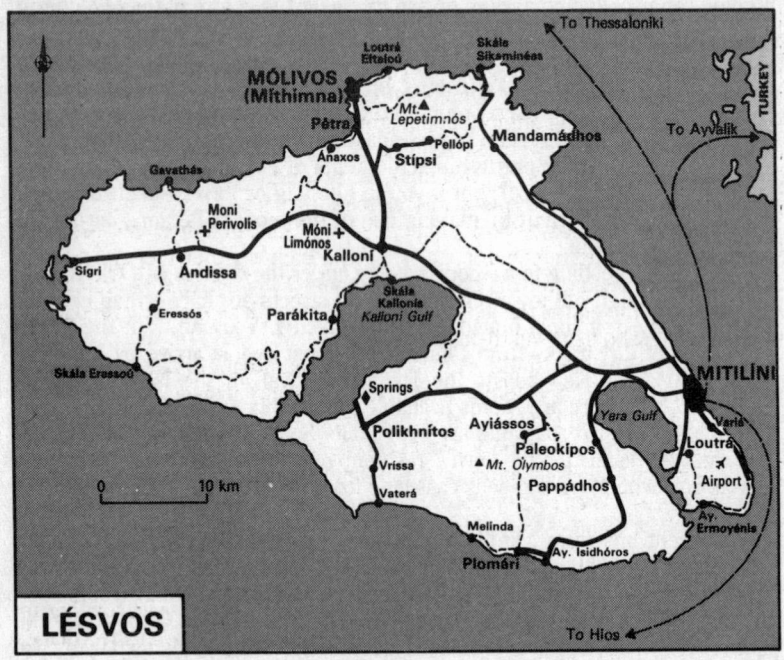

from just beyond the tourist office, past houses with shaded courtyards and, if you're lucky, rooms to go with them. Around the tourist office, too, are several **moped and car hire** places – useful if you're planning to spend several days here, and it's hard to imagine anyone not wanting to. What with a **bank, post office** and **OTE** station, there's no need to move far to transact 'essential' business.

Midsummer sees a **theatre festival** up in the castle as the high point of a generally thriving nightlife, to which the region's political affiliations attract such Communist luminaries as the composer (and KKE MP) Mikis Theodorakis. At least one pub, *To Sokaki*, hosts nightly Greek or Western live music sessions, a good antidote to the pair of extremely loud discos down by the shore. The several **restaurants** on the fishing port are not cheap (except for the easternmost one by the channel entrance) but offer a lovely setting, as do the string of places whose balconies cling to the rock face up in the town.

If or when the pleasures of the town pale, you may care to visit the *Karuna Meditation Retreat Centre* (811 08 Míthimna, Greece) about 2km out of town. This is run by Yiorgos Kassipidhes and his Nepali wife, Yosoda, but write in advance for details of their changing April-to-October programmes of the healing arts, acupuncture and yoga, or simply to reserve a place to stay on your own.

Mólivos itself has few beaches worth mentioning, but **EFTALOÚ**, 5km along a dirt track to the northeast, features some of the finest rustic **thermal baths** in Greece. These are housed in an attractive old domed building, open long hours but with a 100dr admission fee in summer; nearby there are two tavernas, and a growing number of unsightly villas.

Beyond Eftalóu a new coast road runs east to **SKÁLA SIKAMINÉAS** (more commonly known as Sikámia), a delightful fishing village with a pension and tavernas. This is also accessible by inland tracks skirting the base of Mt. Lepetimnós (968m) and connecting Mandamádhos with Mólivos. Stratis Myrivilis, the regional novelist, used a composite of Pétra and Skála Sikamía as the setting for his best-known book, *The Mermaid Madonna*; the tiny church at the end of the jetty in Skála Sikámia will be instantly recognisable to anyone who has read the novel.

PÉTRA is 5km due south of Mólivos and marginally quieter, though it appears that the package companies are now moving in since there are both practical and physical limits to the expansion of Mólivos. The village, not yet very built-up, spreads behind a good sand beach and a seafront *platía*, with plenty of rooms, tavernas and (for the moment) small hotels. As at Pirgí on Híos there is a *Women's Agricultural Tourism Collective*, formed by the town's women in 1984 to offer something other than the usual tourism for the visitors. In addition to opening a **restaurant** in the *platía* (which also serves as a **tourist office** and general information centre), they have made it possible to stay in accommodation affiliated with the collective and, by participating in the proprietors' daily routine, to learn a little more about life in the village. Advance reservations are usually needed (☎0253/41-238).

The town of old stone houses, many with Levantine-style balconies over-hanging the street, takes its name from the giant rock monolith located some distance inland and enhanced by the eighteenth-century **church of the Panyayía Glikofiloússa**. Other local attractions include the sixteenth-century church of Áyios Nikólaos and the intricately decorated **Vareltzidaina mansion**, which can be visited daily except between 1 and 4pm.

There are also a few tavernas well outside Pétra, away from the usual tour-ist beat, so it's worth walking along the unpromising-looking road to the south, past the military sentry post, and picking your way along stretches of beach till you find them. **ANAXÓS**, 3km down this road, with its three restau-rants and kilometre of sand, is the only partly developed spot. From anywhere along this shore you can enjoy beautiful sunsets between and beyond three offshore islets.

STÍPSI, a small town up in the hills a few kilometres east of Pétra, is accessible by one daily bus, offers rooms to let and is a good base for rambles on Lepetimnós, the summit of this hilly and wooded northeast corner of the island. The normal peace of the place can be shattered on occasion, however, when coachloads of tourists descend on the large taverna at the edge of Stípsi for so-called 'Greek Nights'. **PELÓPI**, the next village encountered, proclaims itself the ancestral village of unsuccessful US presidential candidate Mike Dukakis. Perhaps more curious – since the Ottoman Turks rarely left the security of the larger towns – is the former mosque on the main square, now used as a warehouse.

Western Lésvos

KALLONÍ is an unembellished agricultural town more or less in the centre of Lésvos, but it's hard to avoid spending some time here since it's the junc-tion of most KTEL routes. Not all of the buses depart from the busy main street, so if you're waiting to make a connection check where your bus is leaving from. If you have a lot of time to spare, you might make the thirty-minute walk to **SKÁLA KALLONÍ** with its large beach and several restau-rants. The area is noted for its sardines, and a grilled plateful makes a deli-cious lunch.

West of Kallóní the road winds through the hills past the **monastery of Limónos**, which with its promenading peacocks and other farmyard animals, has the rural sleepiness of another age. A former bishop of northern Lésvos acted as curator for the rather informal **folk art museum** consisting of what-ever ancient objects were brought to him by the villagers. After viewing their donations, it seems only polite to leave a monetary one of your own. At **ÁNDISSA**, where there's a Genoese castle, you can detour to the little beach at Gavathás and the frescoed monastery at Perivolís, both some kilometres north.

Most visitors, though, press on to either Sígri or Eressós. The beach at **SKÁLA ERESSOÚ** is generally considered to be the island's best, and as such it's also one of the most crowded, and Skála, after Mólivos and Plomári one of the fastest-growing resorts on the island. There are rooms to let, b sometimes not enough of them, so camping is tolerated; **tavernas** line the water's edge The visitors usually include appreciable numbers of gay women paying homage to the poet **Sappho**, who supposedly lived in ancient Eressós. This was not, as you might suppose, on the site of the village of Eressós 4km inland, but was originally on top of a bluff at one end of the enormous beach.

SÍGRI, on the westernmost tip of Lésvos, is subject to periodic winds. Its main claim to fame is the **petrified forest**, found in the valley between here and Eressós, where stark trunks up to six metres long (not high, as they are mostly fallen) have been created by the combined action of volcanic ash and hot springs. Locals seem amazed that anyone would want to trudge through the stony countryside to look at them, and when you get there you might agree since the trees, while interesting, aren't one of the wonders of the world. Lazy souls might settle for the sample on display in Sígri itself, and the joys of a charming village. The little harbour is guarded by a **Turkish castle**, and the beach on the edge of the village is long and sandy. Other excellent secluded beaches and potential campsites are to be found if you walk further along the coast. There's good cheap eating in Sigri, a few shops, rooms to let, and a small hotel.

Límnos (Lemnos) and Áyios Evstrátios

Límnos is an agricultural garrison island which, despite an airport and creeping lines of asphalt roads, makes few concessions to tourism. The landscape is flat and parched (in summer the water often has to be switched off in the evenings) and, though there are some sandy beaches scattered around the coastline, these are difficult of access. Buses tend to leave **Mírina** (the main town and port) early and often don't return the same day, although there are mopeds and cars for hire.

The few tourists, swelled by a strong military presence, stay mainly in **MÍRINA** (known locally as **KÁSTRO**) on the west coast. It's a pretty town with a fair sprinkling of old Turkish and Thracian houses backing on to the **Genoese-Turkish Castle** (free admission and worth the effort of the climb). There are a couple of small, relatively expensive **hotels**, but you're likely to be met off the boat with the offer of a **room**. For the best and cheapest taverna, simply follow the armed forces.

A good sandy beaches stretches to the north of the harbour, as does a luxury bungalow complex, so it's probably unwise to camp there. Isolated beaches and **campsites** are easy enough to find, however, along the hilly and barren coastline south of Mírina; one of the best, complete with rolling breakers, is just before the village of **THÁNOS**. Moúdhros Bay, which cuts deep into the heart of the island, is best avoided as the shoreline settlements there are shabby and muddy; far better to direct your energies toward the relatively attractive inland villages of KATÁLAKO, SKANDÁLI, and PLATÍ, the last-named a possible base (rooms) just above Thános beach.

Indications of the most advanced Neolithic civilisation in the Aegean have been found at **Poliókhni**, on the east coast of Límnos. Its town walls (ca.

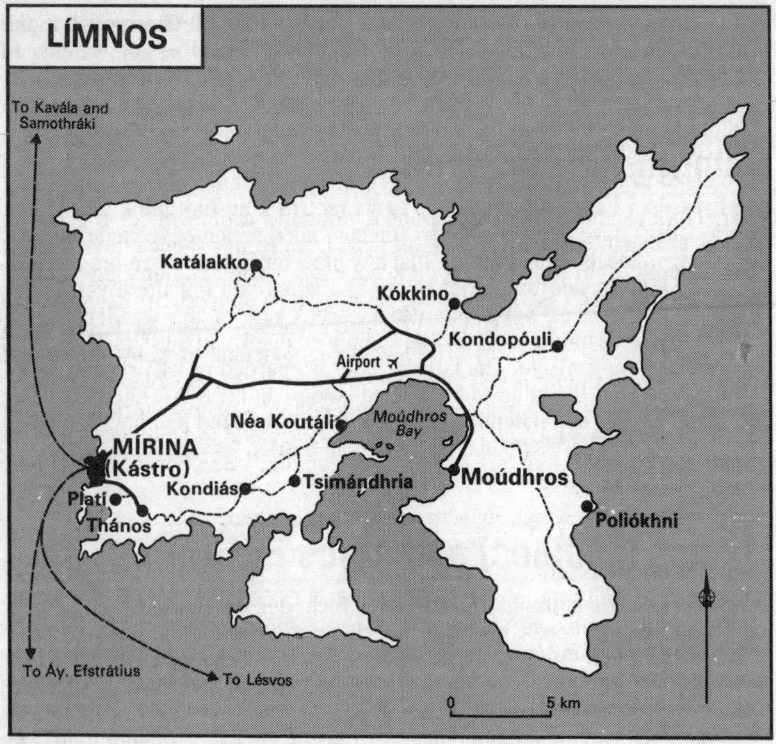

LÍMNOS

To Kavála and Samothráki

Katálakko

Kókkino

Kondopóuli

Airport ✈

Néa Koutáli   Moúdhros Bay

MÍRINA
(Kástro)

Platí   Kondiás   Tsimándhria   Moúdhros

Thános

Poliókhni

To Áy. Efstrátius   To Lésvos

0   5 km

2000 B.C.), interrupted by towers and gates, still stand to five metres in parts. The Italian excavations of the 1930s uncovered four layers of settlement, ranging from a fourth-millennium B.C. city (pre-Troy) to early/late Minoan and Mycenean cultures, but these are hard to make out and even harder to reach.

Áyios Evstrátios

Most easily reached from Límnos, this tiny one-village island is one of the dullest (if not *the* dullest) in the Aegean. The earthquakes that devastated the Sporádes in the mid-1960s also did the same for the community here, which was replaced by ranks of concrete prefab dwellings. If you do decide to get off the boat, you'll find a single pension, exceedingly basic tavernas and shops, and a beach or two. Historically the only outsiders to stay on Áyios Evstrátios have been those who were compelled to do so – it was a place of exile for political prisoners both during the Metaxas regime of the 1930s and the more recent junta.

Still, for the determined, some of the beaches away from the port are in fact quite good, if you don't mind the lengthy walk to get to them, while some of the caves around the island are home to the rare Mediterranean monk seal. But seal-lovers aside, it's hard to imagine too many people wanting to get away from it all to quite the extent that Áyios Evstrátios represents.

Samothráki (Samothrace)

After Thíra, Samothráki has the most dramatic profile of all the Greek islands. Originally colonised by immigrants from Samos (hence the name), it rises abruptly from the sea in a dark mass of granite, culminating in 1600-metre Mt. Fengári. Seafarers have always been guided by its imposing outline, and in legend its summit provided a vantage point for Poseidon to watch over the siege of Troy. The forbidding coastline provides no natural anchorage, and landing is still very much subject to the vagaries of the wind. Yet despite these difficulties, for over a millenium pilgrims journeyed to the island to visit the **Sanctuary of the Great Gods** and to be initiated into its mysteries. The Sanctuary is still the outstanding attraction of the island, which, home to under 3000 people and too remote for most tourists, combines an earthy simplicity with its natural grandeur.

Kamariótissa and Hóra

Boats dock at the little port of **KAMARAIÓTISSA**, where there are a few tavernas, some **rooms to let** and a small pebbly beach where you could unofficially and uncomfortably camp. One of the island's **banks** is here, and **mopeds and scooters** can be hired as well. **Buses** run hourly in season (but only twice weekly in winter) along the north coast to Thermá via Palaeópoli (the site of the Sanctuary) and inland to Hóra, the only village of any size.

Built high in the hills below the ruins of a Byzantine fort, **HÓRA**, too, has **rooms**, along with another bank, the **post office**, the **OTE** branch and three restaurants. All eating places, except one in the port, are likely to be closed in winter. A track leads north to Paleópoli hamlet, and in a stony ravine between it and the plunging, northeasternmost ridgeline of Mt. Fengári lie the remains of the Sanctuary of the Great Gods.

The Sanctuary of the Great Gods

From the late Bronze Age to the last years of the Roman occupation, the mysteries and sacrifices of the cult of the Great Gods were performed on Samothráki. The island was the spiritual focus of the northern Aegean, and its importance in the ancient world was comparable (although certainly secondary) to that of the Mysteries of Eleusis.

The religion of the Great Gods revolved around a hierarchy of ancient Thracian fertility figures: the Great Mother, a subordinate male deity known as Kadmilos, and the potent and ominous twin demons, the *Kabiroi*. When the Samian colonists arrived (traditionally ca. 700 B.C.) they simply syncretised the resident deities with their own – the Great Mother became Demeter, her consort Hermes, and the *Kabiroi* were fused interchangeably with the

Dioskouroi. Around the nucleus of a sacred precinct the newcomers made the beginnings of what is now the Sanctuary.

The mysteries of the cult were never explicitly recorded, since ancient writers feared incurring the wrath of the *Kabiroi*, but it has been established that two levels of initiation were involved. Incredibly, both ceremonies, in direct opposition to the elitism of Eleusis, were open to allcomers, including women and slaves. The lower level of initiation may, as is speculated at Eleusis, have involved a ritual simulation of the life, death and rebirth cycle; in any case, we know that it ended with joyous feasting and can conjecture, since so many clay torches have been found, that it took place at night by their light. The higher level of initiation carried the unusual requirement of a moral standard (the connection of theology with morality – so strong in the later Judeo-Christian tradition – was rarely made at all by the early Greeks). This second level involved a full confession followed by absolution and baptism in bull's blood.

The site (open weekdays 9am–3:30pm, Sun. 10am–4:30pm) is clearly labelled, simple to grasp, and strongly evocative of its proud past. It's a good idea to visit the **museum** (approximately same hours as the site) first, where typical sections of the buildings have been reconstructed and arranged with friezes and statues to give you a fuller idea of their original scale. An

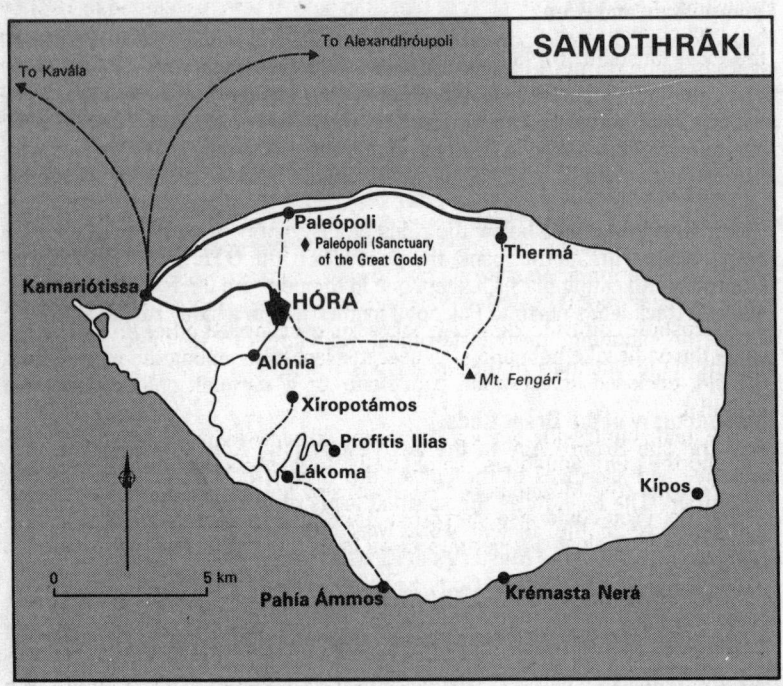

excellent guide by Karl Lehmann – the American excavator of the site – is on sale.

The first structure you come to is the **Anaktoron**, the hall of initiation for the first level of the mysteries, dating in its present form from Roman times. Its inner sanctum was marked by a warning *stele* (now in the museum) and at the southeast corner you can make out the libation pit. Next to it is the **Arsinoeion**, the largest circular ancient building known in Greece. Within its rotunda are the walls of a double precinct (4thC. B.C.) where a rock altar, the earliest preserved ruin on the site, has been uncovered. A little further on, on the same side of the path, you come to the **Temenos**, a rectangular area open to the sky where the feasting probably took place and, edging its rear corner, the conspicuous **Hieron**. Five columns and an architrave of the facade of this large Doric edifice which hosted the higher level of initiation have been erected; dating in part from the fourth century B.C., it was heavily restored in Roman times. Its stone steps have been replaced by modern blocks but the Roman benches for spectators remain in situ, along with the sacred stones where confession was heard.

West of the path you can just discern the outline of the **Theater**, and above it on a ridge is the **Nike Fountain**, famous for the exquisitely sculpted marble centrepiece – the *Winged Victory of Samothrace* – which once stood breasting the wind at the prow of a marble ship. It was discovered in 1863 by the French and carried off to the Louvre, with a copy belatedly forwarded to the local museum. Higher up along the ridge, opposite the rotunda, is an elaborate medieval fortification made entirely of antique material. Finally, on the hill across the river stands a monumental gateway dedicated to the Great Gods by Ptolemy II; many of its blocks lie scattered across the ravine.

The rest of the island

Nine kilometres further east of Paleópoli on the north coast is **THERMÁ**, which with its running streams and plane trees is one of the better places to stay on Samothráki. Despite its one main street and sole expensive hotel (also cheaper rooms to let) it's packed in July and August, when a rather grim seashore campsite 2km away takes the overflow. At other times you can enjoy the namesake hot springs in peace: select from among the modern spa, the old, enclosed stucco-wood bathhouse, or a warmish outdoor pool just behind it.

The lush countryside beyond the rather dispersed village is fine for walking, and the more ambitious can climb the highest mountain in the Aegean, **Mt. Fengári** (the Mountain of the Moon, also known as *Saos*) in a six-hour round trip. (You could also start from Horá but that route is more difficult.) From the top, a clear day permits views from the Trojan plain in the east to Mt. Athos in the west.

Beaches on Samothráki's north shore are uniformly pebbly and exposed; for better ones head for the warmer south flank of the island. A couple of daily buses roll as far as Profítis Ilías, an attractive hill village with good tavernas but no place to stay, via Lákoma, where you alight for the beautiful two-hour walk to **Pahía Ámmos**, an 800-metre sandy beach with a hidden freshwater spring at its eastern end. Nearest supplies are at Lákoma, but this doesn't deter big summer crowds who also arrive by excursion *kaíki*. These also continue past the Krémasta Nerá coastal waterfalls to **Kípos**, another good sand beach with fresh water nearby, at the extreme southeast tip of the island.

Thássos

Just twelve kilometres from the mainland, Thássos has long been a popular resort for northern Greeks, and in recent years has been attracting considerable numbers of foreign (mainly German) tourists. Without being spectacular it is a very beautiful island, its almost circular area covered in gentle slopes of pine, olive and chestnut which rise to a mountainous backbone and plunge to a line of good sand beaches. While it's by no means unspoiled, tourists are spread over six or seven fair-sized villages as well as the two main towns, so enclaves of bars and discos haven't swamped the ordinary Greek life – nut, olive or fruit harvesting, marble quarrying and beekeeping. Beehives often line the roadsides, and many types of local honey can be bought all over the island, as can walnut jam, a thick, treacle-like speciality. Among the less pleasant wildlife is the ubiquitous mosquito, so come prepared. Also, a large area in the southern part of the island was ravaged by fire in 1985, so do heed the many forest-fire prevention warnings and be extra careful if camping. Despite the many 'No Camping' signs, the island is ideal for this, and it's still possible to pitch a tent discreetly in most places.

Thássos town

THÁSSOS TOWN, or **LIMÉNAS/LIMÍN** as it's also known, is the island capital and nexus of life, though not the main port. (Kaválo-based ferries usually stop down the coast at Órmos Prínou, but a few each day continue on to Liménas – worth it for the pine-clad mountain views.) The town, though largely modern, is partly redeemed by its pretty fishing harbour, popular sand beach just east of this, and the substantial remains of the ancient city which pop up between and above the streets. If you want to stay there are several cheap **hotels**, the *Astir*, *Diamandis*, *Viky* and *Angelika*, plus reasonably plentiful rooms, though in summer you should take the first thing offered on arrival. **Eating** out, menus tend to be expensive and bland.

Exploring, the best plan is to hire a moped to circle the island, then use the bus system once you've pinpointed favourite spots. **Car hire** is available but as expensive as anywhere else in Greece; **mopeds or motorbikes** are at standard rates. **Bicycles** are also available, though mainly for the strong of thigh, as there's little flat terrain. **Hitching** is generally good, since distances are usually small. The **bus station** is on the front, near the ferry mooring. The service is good, with about five buses per day doing the full island circuit in season, and several more to and from different villages, with a bias towards the west coast. The 'grand tour' costs well under half the price of a hired scooter.

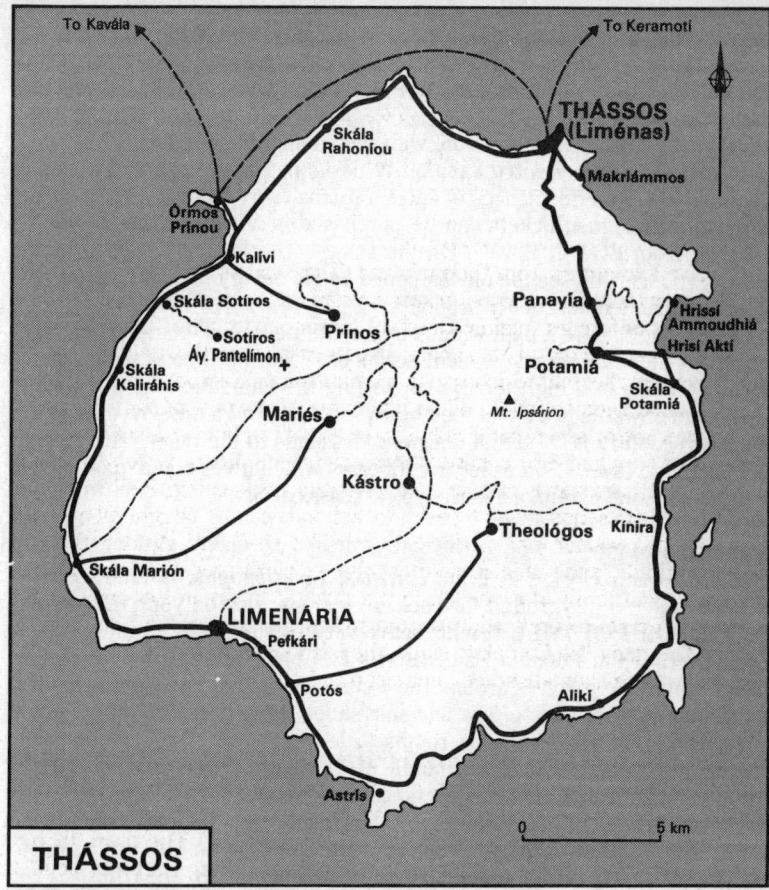

THÁSSOS

There's a privately-run **tourist information agency** on the main street (one back from the waterside but parallel to it), next to the *Just in Time* disco, with the usual maps, timetables and trips, and also a **tourist police** office (open during high season only) near the bus station.

Ancient Thassos abounded in mineral wealth, controlled goldmines on the Thracian mainland and had two safe anchorages, assets which ensured prosperity through Classical, Macedonian and Roman rule. The ruins surrounding the modern town – Limín, incidentally, means 'the harbour' – show traces from each phase of this development. The main excavated area is the **agora**, entered from beside the town **museum** (open Mon.–Sat. 9am–3pm, not Tues.; Sun. 9:30am–2:30pm), a little way back from the modern harbour. It's fenced but rarely locked and, taking advantage of this, best seen towards dusk when a calm, slightly misty air often descends. Prominent are two Roman stoas but you can also make out shops, monuments, passageways and sanctuaries from the remodelled Classical city. And at the far end of the site (away from the sea) a fifth-century B.C. passageway leads through to an elaborate sanctuary of Artemis, a good stretch of Roman road and a few seats of the *odeion*.

Above the town, roughly in line with the smaller fishing port, steps spiral up to a **Hellenistic theatre**, fabulously positioned above a broad sweep of sea and used for performances of ancient drama every Saturday between late July and mid-August; tickets can be purchased in advance from the tourist police or from EOT in Kavála. On the same corner of the headland as the theatre, you can still see the old-fashioned *kaíkia* being built, and gaze across to the uninhabited islet of Thassopoúla.

Beyond the theatre a path winds on to a **Genoese fort**, constructed out of numerous stones from the ancient acropolis. From here you can follow the circuit of **walls** to a high terrace supporting the foundations of a temple of Apollo and onwards to a small rock-hewn sanctuary of Pan. Below it a precarious, sixth-century B.C. 'secret stairway' descends to the outer rank of walls and back into town. It's a satisfying itinerary which gives you a good idea of the structure and extent of a fairly typical Classical city.

Around the coast

The first beach clockwise from Liménas, Makriámmos, is an expensive, restricted-access playground for package tourists; stay on your vehicle until **PANAYÍA** or **POTAMIÁ**, two attractive villages situated on a mountainous ledge overlooking Potamiá Bay. Panayía is a bustling and pretty mountain village where life revolves around the central square with its large plane tree and fountain. There are a few souvenir shops, even here, and small hotels (cheapest is the *Helvetia*) plus rooms to let, but you'll also see sheep and goats being herded through the middle of the village. This is an ideal place for a drink and a meal in the lively evenings, and food tends to be less expensive than elsewhere – try the *Kostas* or *Ethitrio* restaurants. Potamiá proper has a small folk museum (open Mon.–Sat. 9am–noon and 6–9pm), as well as one of the best, marked paths up to the 1204-metre summit of **Mt. Ipsárion**.

There are more tavernas (and a campsite) at the excellent, sandy **HRISSÍ AMMOUDHIÁ** beach, 4km downhill from Panayía at the north end of the bay. No buses go here but it's easy enough to hitch from Panayía or cheap enough to get a taxi. The walk looks short but it's quite heavy going with luggage. Once you get there you can choose between indoor accommodation or 'freelance' camping – the latter popular and untroubled except for early-morning sheep-bell reveilles. **SKÁLA POTAMIÁ** (aka HRISSÍ AKTÍ), at the opposite end, is considerably less attractive with its rocky beach; every building seems to be a souvenir shop, hotel, cafeteria or 'rooms to let'. Skála's main virtue is the local fishing fleet and the corresponding quality of the seafood restaurants.

KÍNIRA is a tiny hamlet further south with a moderate beach, a couple of grocery stores and C-class hotels, a few rooms and a lot of beehives. 'Paradise Beach', nicely situated, sandy, and mainly nudist, lies 1km south, and there are more beautiful and deserted coves beyond in the same direction if you're willing to explore.

The south-facing coast of Thássos has most of the island's best beaches. **ALIKÍ** faces a double bay which almost pinches off a headland. The mixed sand-and-pebble spit gets too popular for its own good in high season, but the water is crystal-clear and the beachside taverna offers good food. The hamlet here (one rooms establishment) is at least worth a stopover. Nearby were ancient marble quarries which supplied the Greek city-states and later the Romans, and on the western cove the pillars of a Doric sanctuary are still visible. It is possible to walk away from the crowds and find some excellent spots for snorkelling, sunbathing and picnics, using the slabs of marble that are scattered around the headland, both above and below the waterline; these have occasionally been eroded into convenient bathtub shapes.

At the extreme south tip of Thássos, **ASTRÍS** has two excellent beaches set in a stunning cliffscape, but the best-appointed local resort – and virtually the only one to function at all outside of summer – is **POTÓS**, where there's a **campsite** plus a fine one-kilometre sand beach facing the sunset. **PEFKÁRI**, 1km west, is essentially an annexe of Potós but the manicured sand has been overwhelmed by the touristic development behind.

As an alternative to Liménas you can base yourself in the marginally quieter and quainter **LIMENÁRIA**, the island's second town, built to house German mining executives brought in by the Turks at the turn of the century. Their remaining mansions lend some distinctive character, but this apart it's a rather ordinary tourist resort, handy mainly for its **banks**, **post office** and **OTE** station.

Continuing clockwise from Limenária to Thássos, the bus service is more frequent, but there's progressively less to stop off for. The various *skáles* (coastal annexes of villages built inland during piratic ages) such as Skála Marión, Skála Kaliráhis and Skála Sotíros, are bleak, straggly and windy, uninviting even on the rare occasions when the shore is sandy.

ÓRMOS PRÍNOU has little to recommend it, other than the ferry connections to Kavála. Buses are usually timed to coincide with the ferries, but if you want to stay, numerous rooms, hotels and quayside tavernas beckon, so someone must like it. There's one more official **campsite** near SKÁLA RAHONÍOU – which is good though the beach is mediocre – as well as rooms, hotels, and some good fish restaurants.

The interior

Few people get around to exploring inland Thássos, but there are several worthwhile rambles around the hill villages besides the aforementioned walk up Mt. Ipsárion from Potamiá. From Potós you can hitch or bus up to **THEOLÓGOS**, a linear community of old houses founded by refugees from Constantinople, which was the island's capital under the Turks (the last of whom only departed, as was the case in most islands in this chapter, after 1923). It has a small square with a couple of cafés under a tree, and a few rooms are available.

From Theológos you can walk down to Kínira on the east coast on a gravel jeep track, or take your chances with narrower trails leading north through the forest. The most interesting return to Potós involves a westward trek, on a variety of surfaces, to **KÁSTRO**, the most naturally fortified of the anti-pirate redoubts. Thirty houses and a church surround a rocky pinnacle which drops off sheer on three sides; summer occupation is becoming the rule after total abandonment in the last century. You could perhaps be put up for the night – there's one taverna, one phone, no power – but without transport you will have to walk or hitch 15km down a dirt road to Limenária.

From Kalívi on the west coast a rough road leads 4km up to **MIKRÓ ÁNO PRÍNOS**, start of the signposted, one-hour walk up to Áyios Pantelímon nunnery. From there you can press on to **SÓTIROS**, an untouched old village to the west, or take the much more confusing way (on lumber roads) to **MARIÉS** in the direction of Kastro. You can often hitch down from the inland villages with people who've been tending their beehives, but take food along for the day – there are often no facilities at all.

travel details

To simplify the lists that follow we've excluded one important boat, the *Alcaeos*. Once a week this links Kavála, Límnos, Lésvos, Híos, Sámos, Kós and Rhodes in each direction, partly compensating for the recent demise of the *Kyklades*.

SÁMOS & IKARÍA 6 to 10 **boats** weekly to Pireás (12 hr.), 1 to 3 a week to Páros, once to Síros, twice (well-spaced) weekly to Híos, weekly (Tues. morning) from Pithagório (Sámos) to nearly all the Dodecanese (the *Panormitis*), plus frequent excursion boats in season from the same port to Pátmos. Daily in season from Sámos to Kuşadasi/Efes (Ephesus); otherwise according to demand. At least 2 daily **flights** from Sámos to Athens and charters to/from many other European cities, with seasonal flights (2 weekly) to Lésvos, Híos, Míkonos, and Kós.

FOÚRNI 1 main-line ferry weekly to Sámos and Pireás; daily *kaíki* to Ikaría; twice weekly to Karlóvassi (Sámos).

HÍOS 5 to 7 **boats** weekly to Pireás (10 hr.) and to Lésvos (4 hr.). Twice weekly to Sámos (4 hrs) and Psará (3 hrs). Weekly ferry to/from Thessaloníki. *Kaíkia* to Inoússes and Psará, 2 to 7 weekly depending on season. 2 to 12 boats weekly, depending on season, to Çeşme in Turkey. At least 2 daily **flights** to Athens, but book well in advance. Seasonal flights (2 weekly) to Sámos, Lésvos, and Míkonos. Weekly charters from Scandanavia.

LÉSVOS 5 to 7 weekly **boats** to Pireás (14 hr.) and Híos (4 hr.). 2 a week to/from Límnos and Kavála. Weekly to Thessaloníki. 1 to 10 weekly to Ayvalik (ancient Kydoni), Turkey. 4 daily **flights** to Athens and Thessaloníki; book well in advance. Seasonal flights to Sámos, Híos, Rhodes (all twice weekly), and Límnos (several weekly), and frequent seasonal charters to/from London and Scandinavia.

LÍMNOS/ÁYIOS EVSTRÁTIOS In addition to the service provided by the *Alcaeos*, the *Skopelos* departs from Áyios Konstantínos Monday night or Tuesday morning to Kavála via Límnos and Áyios Evstrátios, then spends Wednesday and Thursday shuttling between Kavála, Límnos, Áyios Evstrátios and Lésvos, and returns Thursday night or Friday morning from the northernmost ports to Áyios Konstantínos via either Skópelos or Skíathos. The more modest itinerary of the *Aegeus* involves a simple, once-weekly itinerary (usually on the weekend) of Áyios Konstantínos/ Kími–Áyios Evstrátios–Límnos–Kavála and back through the same ports. Crowded daily **flights** from Límnos to Athens (twice) and Thessaloníki (twice); book well in advance. Several weekly flights to Lésvos.

SAMOTHRÁKI 2 or 3 daily **ferries** to/from Alexandhroúpoli (2 hr.) in season, dropping to 5 weekly out of season. Very impractical (costly) connection with other islands via the Kavála once or twice a week.

THÁSSOS 6 to 15 ferries daily (depending on season) between Kavála and Órmos Prínou, with a few of these services extending to Liménas. Between Liménas and Keramotí seasonal frequencies are almost identical. No direct connections with any other island – you must travel via Kavála.

CHAPTER ELEVEN

SPORADES AND EVVIA

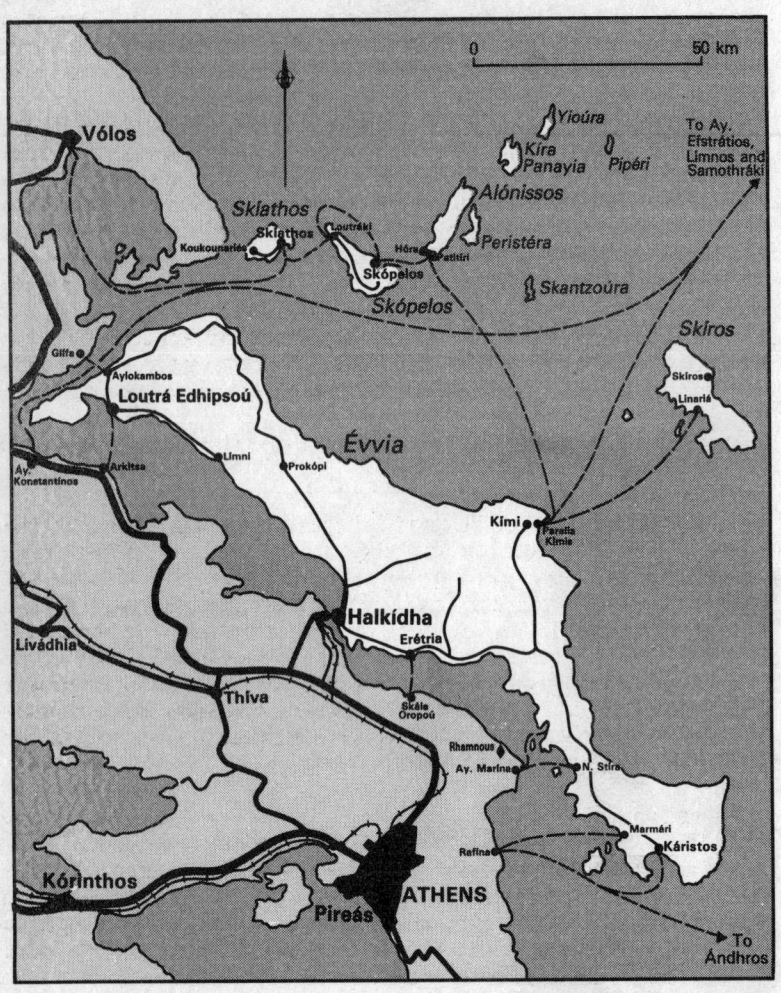

The three northern Sporades – **Skíathos, Skópelos** and **Alónissos** – are archetypal holiday islands. They have good beaches, transparent waters, thick pine forests and (Skíathos notably excepted) remain far from overrun by tourists. None has any prominent historic sites, nor indeed much history until the Middle Ages, and there's absolutely no pressure to do 'educational' things. Any cultural interest is lent by the main towns of each island, all of them graceful late medieval products, except for earthquake-damaged Alónissos. Scattered (as their name, *Sporádhes*, suggests: sporadic) just off the mainland and head-to-tail with each other, they're a very easy group to island-hop and well connected by bus and ferry with Athens via Áyios Konstantínos or Kími, and with Vólos.

Skíros, the fourth island of the archipelago, is slightly isolated from the others, less scenic, but with perhaps the most character, retaining its traditional culture and brilliant white architecture. It is only beginning to get developed, and for an uncommercialised island within six or seven hours of Athens it is hard to beat. The one slight drawback is its onward connections, almost all of which must be made via the Évvian port of Kími.

The huge island of **Évvia** (or Euboea) runs alongside the mainland for over 150km, linked by a bridge at its capital, Halkídha, and by a series of ferry shuttles. Perhaps because it lacks any real island feel or identity it is explored by few foreign tourists. Athenians, in contrast, visit in force, unbothered by such scruples and attracted to half a dozen or so major resorts.

Skíathos

The commercialisation of Skíathos is legendary among foreigners and Greeks – it's a close fourth to that of Corfu, Míkonos and Rhodes. But if you've some time to spare, or a gregarious nature, you might still break your journey here for a day or two. The main disadvantage of the place – that all the population lives in just one town, making everywhere else simply and explicitly a tourist resort – can even be turned to your benefit. Not all of the island is blanketed by concrete villas, so a little walking pays off. **Camping** is actively discouraged however, even in out-of-the-way spots, since summer turns the dry pine needles to tinder. This is a problem you have to be aware of on each of the Sporades islands.

Skíathos Town

SKIÁTHOS TOWN, where the ferries dock, looks great from a distance but as you approach the tourist development becomes all too apparent. Even the little offshore Boúrtzi fortress houses a taverna, and the old quarters (on the slopes away from Odhós Alexándhrou Papadhiamándi) are in danger of being overwhelmed by ranks of hotels, restaurants and 'English' pubs. Skíathos has earned its recent reputation as 'the straight Míkonos'.

In season the few reasonably-priced **hotels** or pensions will be full, though you can usually find a **room**, albeit slightly more expensive than on most islands. There is no official accommodation bureau but instead several tourist agencies. For an honest and helpful approach, try Dimitris Mathinos, a former sea captain with an office at the bottom of A. Papadhiamándi. Avoid lodgings in the flatlands just to the right (north) of A. Papadhiamándi as these tend to be noisy. The best location for accommodation is beyond the *Stamatis* taverna overlooking the fishing harbour – walk high above the water but parallel to it. There's also another concentration of good rooms near the *Filippas* taverna on Kapodhistríou 14. Both of these **eateries** are acceptable – *Stamatis* costs a bit more but is worth it – and *Stavros*, on Evangelístria, plus *I Kova*, also get good marks. The latter is popular with locals and Greek tourists, as is *Zorba's* night club across the way. Other trendy disco-pubs of late seem to be *Banana Bar* and *Stones Pub*, on the same street.

Also near the fishing port, on Platía Tríon Ierarhón, is *Galerie Varsakis*, one of the best *de facto* **folklore** museums in Greece. Many of the older items on display would do the Benaki Museum proud and Mr. Varsakis neither expects, nor wants, to sell the more expensive of these.

The island's only official **campsite** is at **Kólios** beach, approached on the (privately-owned) Koukanariés **bus**, which rolls down the single road every half hour in season (every 2 hr. out).

Rather than the usual bus trip around the island to get your bearings, which is difficult in a place with only one main road, a preferable alternative might well be to take a recce on a boat trip (from the yacht anchorage rather than the ferry harbour) via Lalária, Kástro and Aselinós.

Monasteries around Skíathos town

Better yet, walk: an hour or so on foot out of Skíathos town is the eighteenth-century **Monastery of Evangelístria** (daily 8am–noon and 5–7pm; strict hours), the most interesting of several monasteries on the island and the only one still inhabited; the monks are hospitable and informative about its past. It's claimed that in 1807 the Greek flag was hoisted for the first time ever here, and, among other heroes of the War of Independence, Kolokotronis pledged his oath to fight for freedom. It is exceptionally beautiful, even beyond the grandeur of isolation you find in all Greek monasteries. To reach it walk out of the centre of town on the road toward the airport until, at the point where the asphalt veers hard right, a prominently signposted and waymarked dirt track bears left.

Beyond Evangelístria a track continues to the disused monastery of Harálambos and in a couple more hours you can cross the island completely to the old ruined capital of **Kástro**, built on a windswept headland and connected to the mainland only by rock steps. Among the ruined foundations are three intact chapels, one with fine frescoes, and there's a sheltered sandy bay close by with a spring that's handy for campers. Some tourist agencies schedule boat excursions out here but as often as not you should have the place to yourself.

Beaches

The real business of Skíathos, however, is **beaches**. There are reputed to be over sixty of them on the island, as there need to be to soak up the numbers of summer visitors – at the height of the season the resident population of 4500 can be eclipsed by up to 50,000 outsiders. The beaches on the northeast coast aren't easily accessible, unless you pay for an excursion *kaíki* or are ready for much more arduous treks than those described above. The bus, though, runs along the entire south coast, and from strategic points along the way you can easily reach a good number of beaches. Those before Kalamáki peninsula are unexciting but on the promontory itself, flanked by the campsite and Kanapítsa hamlet, **Rígas, Ayía Paraskeví** and **Vromólimnos** are highly rated, the last offering windsurfing and waterskiing. Most of the popular beaches have at least a drinks/snacks stall; those at Vromólimnos, Aselinós and Troúlos have proper tavernas. The prevailing summer *meltemi* wind blows from the north, so the beaches on the south coast are usually better protected.

From Troúlos a track runs 4km due north to **Mégas Aselinós**, a very good beach with a campsite and a seasonal taverna, never too crowded because it's off the kaíki routes. An alternate fork leads, via the convent of Kounístria (complete with snack bar!) to **Mikrós Aselinós**, just east and even more isolated.

Koukounariés, the very last bus stop, is a majestic sandy bay of clear, gradually deepening water, backed by acres of pines, and despite its popularity it merits at least one visit if only to assess the claim that it's the best beach in Greece. If the scene there is too much, other pleasant beaches are within easy walking distance. **Banana Beach** (aka Krássa), the third cove on the far side of Poúnda headland, is the trendiest of the island's nudist beaches and touted as such in the *Spartacus Gay Guide*. For the less adventurous, the turning for **Ayía Eléni** is the penultimate bus stop, from where you walk one kilometre to the pleasant beach (with drink stall). Or ask the driver to set you down at the start of the thirty-minute path to **Mandhráki** beach, with facilities similar to Ayía Eléni.

Skópelos

More rugged and better cultivated than Skíathos, Skópelos is also very much more attractive. Not that its beaches are any better, its pine forests any thicker, nor its accommodation any less crowded in high season, but it does manage to maintain a character, at least in part, independent of tourism. It is a well-watered place, harvesting olives, plums, pears and almonds. Glóssa and Skópelos, its two main towns, are in addition among the prettiest in the Sporades, clambering uphill along paved steps, their houses distinguished by Venetian-style balconies and grey slate roofs.

The Venetians are only one of the nationalities to have occupied this island at various stages of its history. Others include the French, Romans, Persians and, of course, the Turks. In fact under the Turkish admiral (or pirate) known as *Barbarossa* (Redbeard), the entire population of the island was slaughtered in the sixteenth century.

Loutráki, Glóssa and the west

Most boats call at both ends of Skópelos, stopping first at the small port of **Loutráki** with its thin pebble beach, couple of hotels and few rooms to let. It's been spoilt a little by developments at either end. The café/shop in the square by the harbour is shrouded by beautiful chestnut trees and sells a highly recommended homemade retsina.

High above Loutráki hovers the more preferable **GLÓSSA**, a sizeable and quite beautiful town, totally Greek, several *kafenía*, a taverna and a very few rooms to let. You'll have to ask for the rooms proprietors by name: Stamatis Koukourinis may have a sign out on his old inn-building, and Nikos Larigakis, his brother, and daughter have several premises between them in Loutráki and Glóssa.

Ninety minutes' walk from Glóssa, across to the north coast, will bring you to a beach the locals call **Perivovlioú**. It's indicated only by small blue signposts in Greek and so is little known. The walk itself is worthwhile; it passes a monastery next to a hollow stone cairn containing masses of human bones and skulls. There's also a huge hollow oak tree here, in the heart of which is a small tank of drinking water. The beach, when you get there, is nothing out of the ordinary but there's spring water and a cave for shade.

East of Glóssa, the amazing monastery of **Áyios Ioánnis** is accessible by a new road or a combination of jeep tracks and paths. This is another beautiful, peaceful walk (again about 90 min.), with hawks and nightingales for company. The monastery has a truly dramatic setting perched on the top of a rock high above the sea, though the buildings themselves are modern and rather ugly. There's a water cistern on the rock, and below it a small sandy cove, not particularly good for swimming.

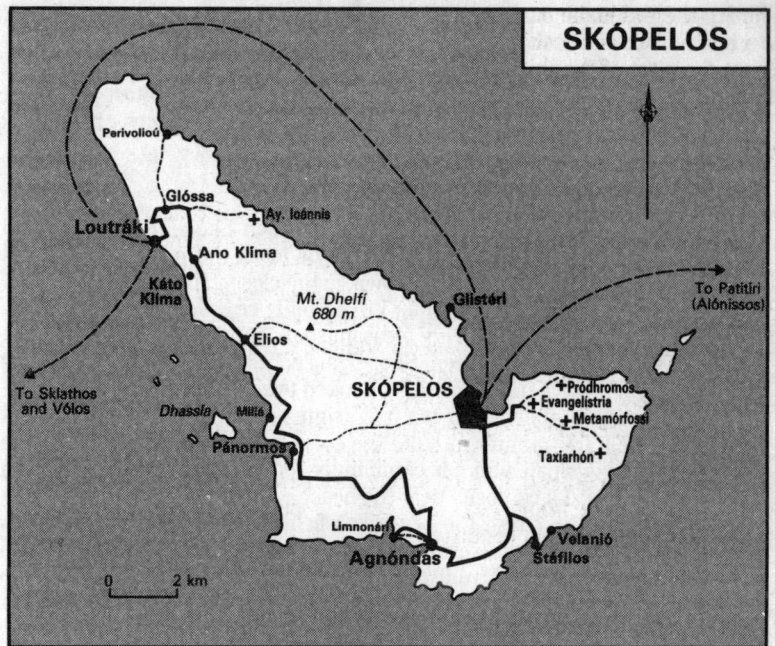

Skopelos town

If you stay on the ferry beyond Loutráki – and this is probably the best plan – you reach **SKÓPELOS TOWN**, sloping down one corner of a huge, almost circular bay. The best way to arrive is by sea, with the town revealed slowly as the boat rounds the final headland. **Hotels** here are few, and mainly tucked away on the far side of the bay, but in the main body of the town there are dozens of **rooms** to let; take up one of the offers when you land, since most are otherwise unadvertised. Nightlife is more subdued than on Skíathos, though there is an ever-increasing number of discos and a dozen or so bars – including a rather pricey jazz bar, *O Platanos*. The three tavernas next to this bar (opposite where the ferries dock) are good for eating. Inland, the bookshop/gallery/café *Armoli* is one of the best of its kind in Greece, with numerous Greek titles in foreign-language translations.

Within the town, spread below the oddly whitewashed ruins of a Venetian **kástro**, are an enormous number of churches – 123 reputedly, though some are small enough to be mistaken for houses – and perched on the slopes opposite the quay are three cloisters, Evangelístria (in view of the town), Metamórfossi and Pródhromos. Visiting hours are usually from 8am to 1pm and from 4 to 7pm (5 to 8pm at Pródhromos). The monastery of **Metamórfossi** was abandoned in 1980 but is now being restored by the monks and is open to visitors again. You should of course dress respectfully, though the hospitable nuns at the two convents will lend you leg-coverings if necessary. Access is simplest by following an old road behind the line of hotels in town to **Evangelístria** (an hour's walk). From there it's an extra half hour's scramble over mule tracks to **Pródhromos**, the remotest and most beautiful of the three. Ignore the new road which goes part way – it's longer and takes away most of the beauty of the walk.

Around the Island

Buses cover the island's one asphalt road between Skópelos and Loutráki about seven times daily, stopping at the paths to all the main beaches and villages. **Stáfilos Beach**, 4km out of town, is the closest, but small and rocky (one taverna lets rooms). It is getting increasingly crowded, but the taverna, shaded by a vast pine tree, is a very pleasant spot. Also worth a mention is the *Terpsis* taverna halfway between Skópelos and Stáfilos, which serves an incredible stuffed chicken that must be booked twelve hours in advance.

There's a very prominent 'No camping' sign at Stáfilos, but to pitch a tent you can just walk five minutes around the coast to **Velanió**, whose pines and surf always draw a small summer community (often nudist). There is spring water in the area and a campsite near the beach.

Farther around the coast, the beachless fishing anchorage of **Agnóndas** (with a combination rooms/restaurant) is the start of a fifteen-minute path (or two-kilometre road) to **Limnonári Beach**, 100 metres of fine sand set in a rather grim and shadeless rock-girt bay. There's a single, seasonal rooms establishment and a taverna, but camping would be a bit cramped.

A much more promising base, if you're after isolation and happy to walk to a nearby beach, is **Pánormos**, a pleasant little hamlet with rooms, tavernas, and a campsite (where people of all income levels may find themselves at times when Skópelos is chock-full). The beach here is gravelly and steeply shelving, but there are small secluded bays close by and, slightly further on at **Miliá**, a tremendous, two-kilometer sweep of tiny pebbles beneath a bank of pines, facing the islet of Dhasía. There's one taverna and just a couple of houses in this languid setting. **Kato** and **Ano Klíma**, on towards Glóssa, both have rooms and tavernas but neither has a particularly appealing beach.

West of Skópelos town various jeep tracks and old paths wind through olive and plum groves toward **Mt. Dhélfi** and the Vathiá forest, or skirt the base of the mountain northeast to Revíthi hill with its fountains and churches, and Karyá, with its '**Sendoúkia**' or ancient tombs. Tracks on the north flank of Dhélfi, beyond Karyá, just conceivably might lead all the way to the Klíma villages, but the main, old trans-island donkey track ends disappointingly in the vicinity of ugly Élios, 9km short of Glóssa.

To the northwest of Skópelos Town, **Glistéri** is a small pebble beach with no shade but a taverna much frequented by locals on Sundays. A fork off the Glistéri and Mt. Dhélfi tracks can be followed across the island to Pánormos within ninety minutes; it's a pleasant walk though the route isn't always obvious. As usual local maps of the island are mostly very inaccurate, even by Greek standards a situation aggravated by the many new tracks bulldozed across the island since the maps were printed. All this makes explorations interesting but sometimes frustrating.

Alónissos

The most remote of the Sporades, Alónissos is – on initial appearance – the least attractive. It has an unfortunate recent history. The vineyards were wiped out by disease in 1950 and the *Hóra* was damaged by an earthquake in 1965. Although its houses were mostly repairable, corruption and the social control policies of the new junta were instrumental in the village's forcible abandonment and the transfer of virtually the entire population down to the previously unimportant anchorage of Patitíri. The result looks a bit soulless, though on closer acquaintance the island turns out to be one of the most traditional – and one of the most friendly – in Greece. Take time and explore.

The monotonous appearance of **PATITÍRI** and the adjoining village of Votsí is characterised by concrete, flat-roofed houses, broken up only by the seafront *kafenía* and the balcony flower boxes with which the locals have tried to cheer the place up. **Rooms** are plentiful and distinctly cheaper than on Skíathos or Skópelos, and the older women who approach you with offers

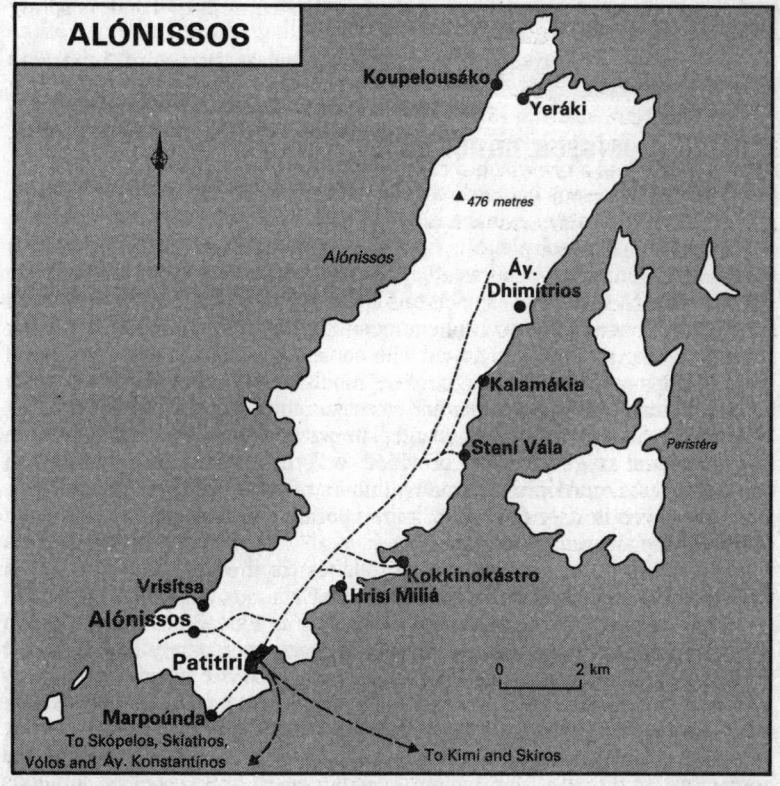

– except in the very busiest season – are often wearing their traditional blue and white costumes. There's also an official **campsite**, *Ikaros Camping*, out on Stení Vála beach.

The **HÓRA** is a fine but steep thirty-minute uphill walk on a donkey track lined by bramble bushes. The town has been substantially restored by Athenians and Germans, who bought the properties at knock-down rates. It has two good tavernas, great sunset views, and a limited number of short-term places to stay. Twenty minutes downhill to the north is the small cove of Vrisítsa (Yialó).

The **beaches** nearest Patitíri and Marpoúnda are nothing special and you're advised to head to the north of the island, either by foot, by moped (expensive and jarring) or excursion *kaíki* (reasonable). Most of the beaches are in the lee of Alónissos' east shore. The best targets include **Hrissí Miliá**, closest to the harbour; **Kokkinokástro**, where you can see the submerged ruins of ancient Ikos; **Stení Vála**, with its campsite, and adjacent **Kalamákia**. All of the above have rudimentary facilities (taverna/drink stall), and Stení Vála is almost a proper village with olive groves, a shop and a small hotel. For real solitaries **Áyios Dhimítrios**, **Koupelousáko** and **Yeráki** much further north can be recommended, but before committing yourself take one of the round-the-island trips available and return to your choice the next day with sufficient groceries.

Beyond Alónissos: minor islets

Northeast of Alónissos half a dozen tiny islets speckle the Aegean. Virtually none of these has any permanent population, nor any ferry service, so the only way you can reach them is by excursion boat. These run only in high season and even then only as weather permits.

PERISTÉRA is the closest islet to Alónissos and was once actually part of it, but subsidence (a common phenomenon in the area) created the narrow straits beween the two. It is graced with some nice sandy beaches and there is rarely anyone around, though some Alonissans do come over for short periods to tend the olive groves, and in season there are the regular evening 'barbecue boats' from the main island. The water supply is uncertain but the islanders must originally have provided wells or cisterns near their small farmhouses. As on Alónissos, small numbers of unofficial campers are tolerated, but there is only one spot, known locally as 'Barbecue Bay', where campfires are allowed.

KIRÁ PANAYÍA, (also known as Pelagós) is the next islet out and is equally fertile and wooded. It's owned by the Orthodox church and there are two monasteries here, one inhabited as recently as 1984. Boats call at a beach and anchorage on the south shore, one of many such sandy stretches and ports around the island, which is popular with yachters. There's no permanent population other than the wild goats. The island boasts a stalactite cave reputed to be that of Homer's Polyphemus (the Cyclops).

Nearby **YIOÚRA** has a similar, even bigger, cave with perhaps better credentials as the one from which Odysseus and his companions escaped.

The main feature, though, is a herd of rare wild goats, distinctive enough to have earned the island the status of a reserve. Two middle-aged couples live here as wardens; part of their job is to unlock the cave for visiting parties and provide a hurricane lamp. You'll need more than just a single source of illumination to see much, however, and getting down into the cavern is fairly strenuous. Apart from the tourist boats, the wardens' only contact with the outside world is a twice-monthly mail-and-provisions boat which, like all other craft, cannot land at the primitive jetty in rough seas.

The above islands are usually visited by the excursion *kaíkia*, but considerably more powers of persuasion will be required to get the fishermen to take you to the remotest three islets.

PIPÉRI, near Yioúra, is a sea-bird and monk seal refuge – permission from EOT (in Athens) is required for access by non-specialists. Tiny, northernmost **PSATHOÚRA** is dominated by its powerful modern lighthouse, though here, as around many of these islands, there's a submerged ancient town, brought low by the endemic subsidence. Roughly halfway between Alónissos and Skíros, green **SKANTZOÚRA**, with a single monastery (still inhabited by one monk) and a few seasonal shepherds, seems a lesser version of Kirá Panayía.

It is altogether possible to be left for a night or more on any of the islands listed, but when acting out your desert-island fantasies be sure to bring more supplies than you need; if the weather worsens suddenly you'll be marooned until such time as small craft can make it out to you! Note also that it will be difficult or impossible to convince anyone to take you out except in midsummer, since the excursion boats serve primarily as fishing boats from September to May. But then the lack of obsequiousness in the face of the tourist trade may be the very reason you've come to Alónissos in the first place.

Skíros (Skyros)

Despite its closeness to Athens, Skíros had until recently remained a very traditional and idiosyncratic island. Any impetus for change had been neutralised by the lack of economic opportunity (and even secondary schooling), forcing the younger Skyrians to live in Athens, and leaving behind a conservative gerontocracy. A *yimnásio* (high school) has at last been provided, and the island has definitely been 'discovered' in the past decade. It's very much of a scene now, the haunt of continental Europeans, chic Athenians, and British, many of whom check into a 'New Age' centre catering to those who feel Skíros by itself isn't enough to 'rethink the form and direction to their lives'. (For details on *The Skíros Centre*, write to 1 Fawley Road, London NW6). The new handful of pubs and discos are probably harbingers of more such to come.

The islanders, meanwhile, remain amazingly friendly and Skíros still ranks as one of the most interesting places in the Aegean. It has a long tradition of ornate woodcarving – a *salonáki Skiriani* (handmade set of chairs) is still

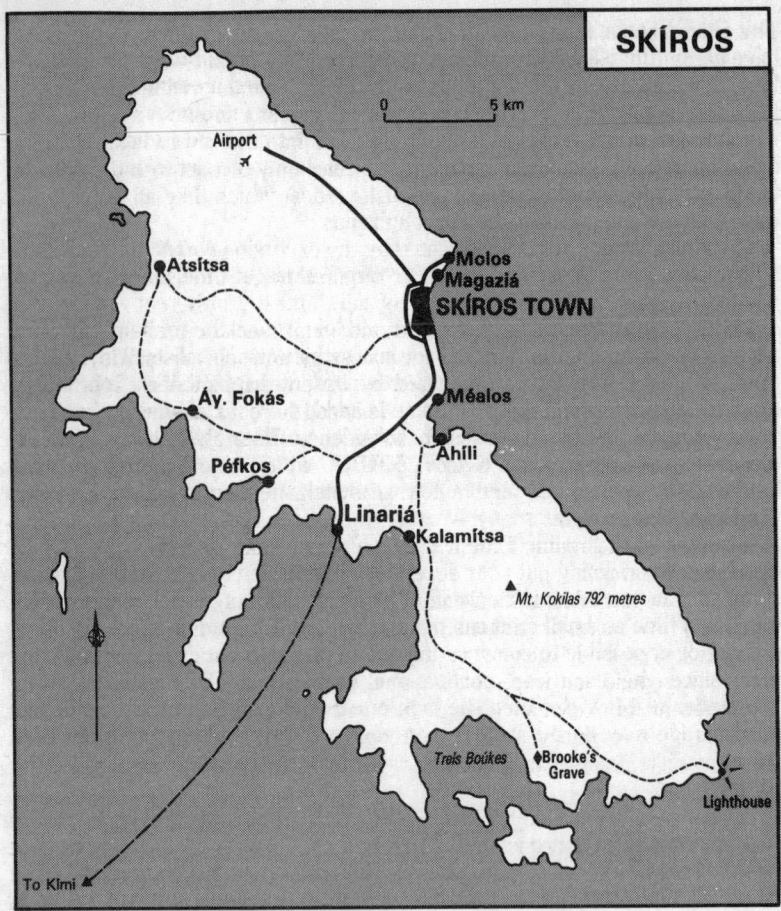

considered an appropriate partial dowry for any young Greek woman – and the men here, especially the older ones, still wear the vaguely Cretan, traditional costume of cap, vest, baggy trousers, leggings and *trohádhia* (Skyrian clogs). The women favour yellow scarves and long embroidered skirts.

If you can possibly coincide with them, Skíros also has some particularly lively, even outrageous, **festivals**. The *Apokriatiká* (pre-Lenten) carnival here is structured around the famous 'Goat Dance' performed by masked revellers in the village streets. Foremost character is the *Yéros*, a menacing figure concealed by a goatskin mask and weighed down by garlands of sheep bells. Accompanying him are *Korélles* and *Kyríes* (transvestites – only the men participate) and *Frangi* (maskers in 'Western' garb). For further details read

Joy Coulentianou's *The Goat Dance of Skyros*, available in Athens and occasionally on the island. The other big annual event takes place near Magaziá beach on August 15, when children race domesticated members of a herd of wild ponies native to Skíros but distantly related to the Shetland pony. They are thought perhaps to be the diminutive horses depicted in the Parthenon frieze, and at any time of the year you might find some of the tame individuals tethered to graze near Hóra.

Linariá and Hóra

Originally Skíros is said to have been two islands but the former units are now connected by a low-lying neck of land and the only real road on the island – running from Linariá, the port, to Skíros *hóra*, the capital. The towns are about 10km apart and there is a bus service which exists principally to meet the ferries and is thus somewhat infrequent. **LINARIÁ** is a little village of part-time fishermen built around a sheltered harbour. There are rooms to let if you want them but there seems to be no problem about sleeping on the beaches. Just over half way to Hóra the bus can let you off at Méalos beach and the turning for the more remote **Ahíli** beach, popular with nudists and freelance campers. Alternatively, walking southeast from Linariá on a dirt road takes you to roomy **Kalamítsa** bay, with a sandy beach and a reasonable solitary taverna.

HÓRA, with its decidedly Cycladic architecture, sits on the landward side of a high rock rising precipitously from the coast. According to legend, King Lycomedes pushed Theseus to his death from its summit; certainly the ancient acropolis and traces of Classical walls can still be made out among the ruins of the Venetian **kástro**. Just within the circuit of the walls, and dominating everything, is the crumbling, tenth-century monastery of Áyios Yióryios, its stones partly incorporated into the later *kástro*, closed for 'restoration'.

Perhaps equally striking, and splendidly incongruous, is the **Memorial to Rupert Brooke** – a bronze nude of 'Immortal Poetry' – at the north end of town (whose nakedness caused a scandal among the townspeople when it was first set up). Brooke, who visited the south of the island very briefly in April 1915, died shortly after of blood poisoning on a French hospital ship anchored offshore and was buried in an olive grove above Treís Boúkes Bay. The site at Treís Boúkes can be reached on foot from Kalamítsá, by *kaíki*, or less romantically, by taxi. Brooke has become something of a local hero, despite his limited acquaintance with Skíros, and ironically was adopted by Kitchener and later Churchill as the paragon of patriotic youth despite his forthrightly expressed socialist and internationalist views.

Back in town, where the brilliant array of white cubist houses cascades from the hillside, there are several **hotels** and plenty of **rooms to let** in private houses. The latter are preferable as they're often exceptionally furnished, with carved partitions and lofts in addition to the above-mentioned furniture, copperware and enamelled plates, which the island's womenfolk seem adept at collecting. **Dining out** involves discrimination between the new boutique-style eateries and the more genuine (though not necessarily inexpensive) *ouzerí*, *inopolía* (wine cellars) and tiny *psistariés*.

Close to the Brooke statue there's an **Archaeological Museum** (Mon.–Sat. 9am–3pm, not Tues., Sun. 9.30am–2.30pm) and the adjacent **Faltaitz Ethnological Museum**, open roughly 10am to 1pm and 4 to 7pm. The latter exhibits a broad selection of domestic items, embroideries, furniture, rare books and models of local houses, as well as hosting a large stock of modern handicrafts for sale.

The official **campsite** is still further down the same hill, near the *Xenia Hotel*; beyond both, the 800-metre-long sandy beach of **Magaziá** extends all the way up to the fishing village of Mólos, which has rooms and tavernas. Camping on the beach doesn't appear a problem – you'll have more trouble from the voracious mosquitoes than from the police or locals.

Around the island

The only practical way of **getting around** Skíros is by foot or by hiring a moped (there are at least a couple of rental places in the main town), though in summer the whimsical bus service also visits the more popular beaches, if that's all you want to do.

Northwest of the town and beach areas a vast agricultural plain blends into large army installations and the airport. It's best to direct your footsteps (or moped) due west, following Kifissós Creek into the pine-filled heart of this half of Skíros, which contrasts sharply with the barren rockiness of the rest. Footpaths to Atsítsa beach, nominally a three-hour walk, can be frustrating; it's more rewarding to follow the dirt track through the fertile Fére Kámbo valley, and stop, 45 minutes out, to have a look at the Byzantine convent of **Áyios Dhimítrios**. You can see its dome among the pines northwest of the track; advance planning can procure the key from *Skyros Travel* but in any case the door may be ajar for a peek at the recently restored, sixteenth-century frescoes.

Atsítsa is shaded by pines (tapped by the Skyrian retsina industry) and sometimes has a lone taverna (with rooms) in operation. There's also an outpost of *The Skyros Centre* here. Elsewhere in the coniferous north, Áyios Fokás and Pévkos Bays are easiest reached by a turning from the paved road near Linariá, though there is (more difficult) access from Atsítsa. **Áyios Fokás** is even more primitive than Atsítsa but **Péfkos** boasts a more-or-less permanent taverna and rooms, as well as the best beach on Skíros.

Évvia (Euboea)

The second largest island (after Crete), Évvia seems more like an extension of the mainland. At Halkídha the connecting bridge has only a seventy-metre channel to span, the island having reputedly been split from the mainland by a blow from Poseidon's trident. There are ferry crossings at no less than six points along its length, and the south of the island is closer to Athens than it is to northern Évvia.

Nevertheless, Évvia *is* an island and in places a very beautiful one. The north, a rolling fertile countryside, is most popular among Greeks, who value its greenery, its beaches and the mineral waters at Loutrá Edhipsoú. The east coast is barren, rocky and largely inaccessible, but the west, right down to Káristos, is much gentler and more cultivated, though increasingly disfigured by industrial operations. All public transport is biased towards this side of the island.

Halkídha

The island capital of **HALKÍDHA** (more formally known as **Halkís**), is by far the largest town on Évvia; heavily industrial, with a shipyard, railway sidings, and cement works. For visitors, it seems a dire place apart from the old Turkish quarter of **Kástro** and its waterside. The entrance to the *kástro* is marked by the mosque now housing the **Byzantine Museum**, and beyond are the remains of the old fortress, an arcaded aqueduct and the unique basilican church of Ayía Paraskeví, an odd structure converted by the Crusaders in the fourteenth century into a Gothic cathedral. There's also a market here for ten days every year at the end of July.

The **waterside** overlooks the Evripós, the narrow channel whose strange currents have baffled scientists for centuries. You can stand on the bridge which spans the narrowest point and watch the water swirling by like a river. Every few hours the current changes and the tide reverses. Aristotle is said to have thrown himself into the waters in despair at his inability to understand what was happening, so if you're puzzled you're in good company. A few *ouzerí* south of the bridge serve grilled octopus, the only other reason for stopping. There's a good **bus service** from Halkídha, serving most parts of the island from a station in the middle of town – head straight inland from the bridge.

South from Halkídha

The coast road heading southeast out of Halkídha is a bad introduction to Évvia. There are some intriguing Venetian towers at **Fílla**, worth a detour if you've your own car, but just what the package tour companies see in the disappointing scenery around Erétria and Amárinthos is not entirely clear – easy connection to Athens, probably.

ERÉTRIA is more notable, with its ancient site, much of which lies under the modern town. Visible remains are dotted around the centre of town (most conspicuously an **agora** and a **Temple of Apollo**) but more interesting are the excavations in the northwest corner, behind the small museum. Here the **theatre** has been uncovered and from its orchestra steps descend to an underground vault used for sudden appearances and disappearances. Beyond the theatre are the ruins of a **gymnasium** and **sanctuary**.

Beyond Alivéri and its cement factories the route mercifully heads inland for **Lépoura** junction, crossing point for travellers going between Káristos and Kími. Just to the south the ancient city of **DHÍSTOS** lies by the shore of a marshy lake (Évvia's largest) 5km south of the modern city town of Kriezá. There are remains of fifth-century B.C. houses and walls, while on the

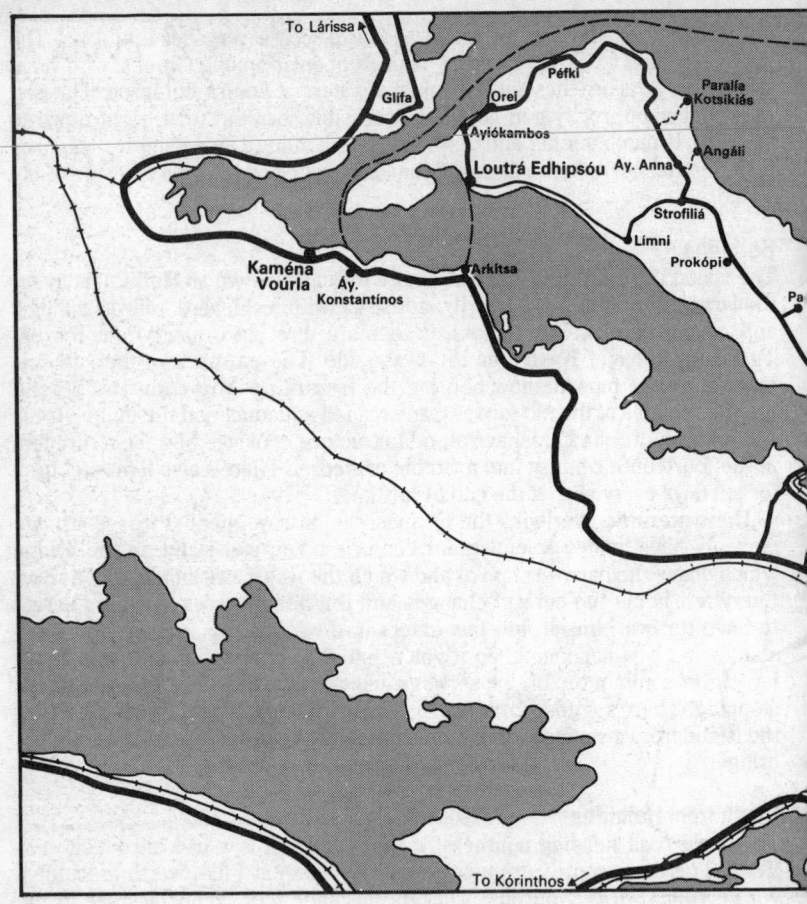

Acropolis perches a Venetian fortress. Continuing south on the main road brings you to the turning for **NÉA STÍRA**, a nondescript seaside resort with a handy ferry connection to Ayía Marína on the Attic peninsula, which gives access to nearby ancient Rhamnous. Much the same can be said for **MARMÁRI**, a few kilometres south, except in this case the ferry link is with Rafína.

Rafína ferries also serve **KÁRISTOS**, at the southern end of the asphalt road system but a vast improvement over these preceding towns. It's a small, pretty port with some good, reasonably-priced restaurants. Unfortunately there's a shortage of affordable accommodation; a nearby sandy beach (to the right as you face the sea) has possibilities of 'freelance' **camping**.

Káristos is also a good base for hikes inland. The most popular destinations are the villages of Páleo Hóra and Míli, graced with orchards and fountains, and beyond these the barren **Mt. Óhi**. This is Évvia's second highest

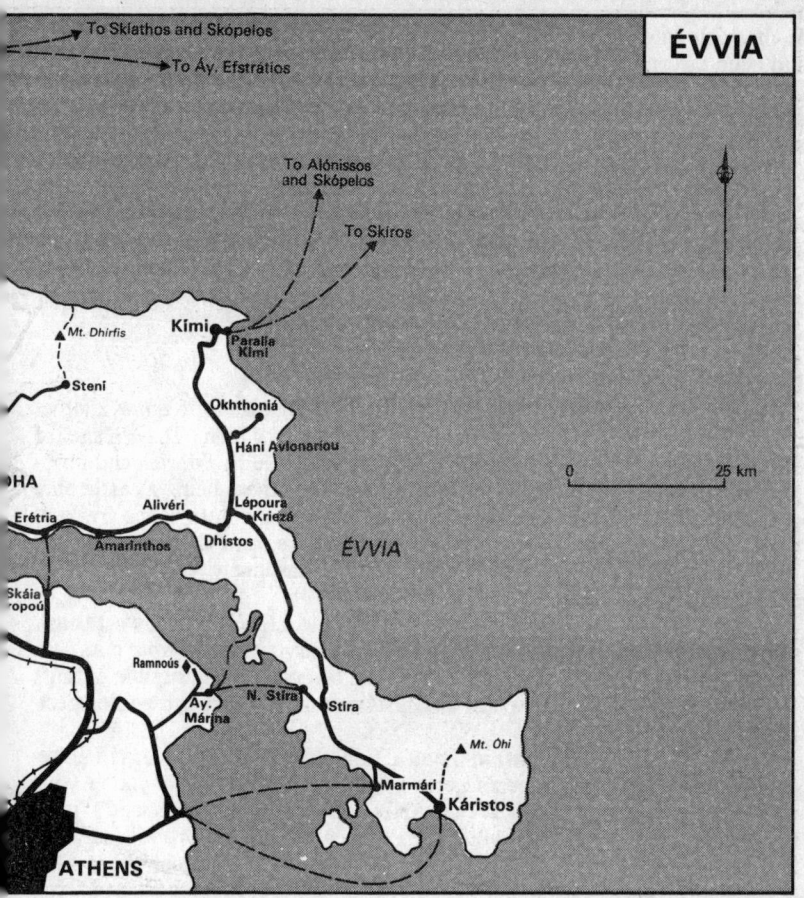

ÉVVIA

To Skíathos and Skópelos

To Áy. Efstrátios

To Alónissos and Skópelos

To Skíros

Mt. Dhírfis

Kími

Paralía Kími

Steni

Okhthoniá

Háni Avlonaríou

0   25 km

HA

Alivéri

Lépoura Kriezá

ÉVVIA

Erétria

Amárinthos

Dhístos

Skáia ropoú

Ramnoús

Ay. Márina

N. Stíra

Stíra

Mt. Óhi

Marmári

Káristos

ATHENS

(1398m) peak, capped by the ancient schist blocks of a Pelasgian building of uncertain function; known as the 'Dragon's House', it is popularly supposed to be haunted.

The northerly fork of the road junction at Lépoura meanders across some of the most peaceful and beautiful countryside in Greece. Just off the road at **HÁNI AVLONARÍOU** stands the Romanesque twelfth-century basilica of **Áyios Dhimítrios**, Évvia's finest. A huge Venetian tower crowns the tiered old houses of Avlonári proper, 2km east. In the same vicinity is the turning for **OKHTHONIÁ**, a hill village above some of the finest deserted sand beaches on the island.

Most travellers, though, stay on the bus until the end of the line at **KÍMI**, built on a green ridge overlooking the sea and its port of Paralía Kími, 4km below. Part way down to the harbour you can visit the **Folklore Museum** (open Mon.–Fri., morning and evening). In the upper town there are a couple of cheapish hotels, the *Kimi* and the *Krinon*, plus some unadvertised rooms, and good tavernas where you can sample the products of the local vineyards. Despite its name, **PARALIA KÍMI** has no real beach, although if you're overnighting before a **ferry across to Skíros** there are plenty of rooms at reasonable prices, and one hotel.

To get up into the rugged country west of Kími you must walk forest paths or return to Halkídha for bus service up to **STENÍ**, a large and beautiful village at the foot of Mt. Dhírfis with a few cheap *psistariés* but just two expensive hotels. Both recommended walking guides (see 'Books' in *Contexts*) describe several worthwhile excursions in the area, most notably to the peaks of Dhírfis and Ksirovoúni and the isolated beach hamlets of Hiliadhoú and Ayía Iríni.

North from Halkídha

The main road north from Halkídha crosses flat farmland for a few kilometres, after which it climbs steeply among forested hills. The village of **PROKÓPI** lies beyond the summit in a valley enclosed by the rich and beautiful woods which are one of its claims to fame, the others being a castle on a precipitous rock and the church of St. John of Russia, whose relics are kept there. These were brought here by Orthodox Turks from Cappadocia in the 1923 population exchange, and Prokópi is still occasionally referred to by its old name of Ahmet Aga.

At **STROFILIÁ** it's possible to take a left fork to **LÍMNI** on the west coast, a small resort with **rooms** and shingle beaches curving gently around its bay. There are also a couple of cheap **hotels** and tavernas, plus possible outings to the monastery down the coast at Galatáki or inland through some spectacular gorges.

The coast road north toward Loutrá Edhipsoú is dangerous and infrequently used. Most traffic bears north (right) at Strofiliá, and if you've your own car the beaches below **AYÍA ÁNNA** are some of the island's best. Otherwise the bus can take you to **PÉFKI**, a seaside resort with **rooms**, tavernas, and a long beach. It's mobbed with Greeks in summer but at such times you can always strike out west along the coast between here and Oreí, a fishing village with two inexpensive hotels and a small beach.

LOUTRÁ EDHIPSOÚ, besides being an important ferry and bus terminus, attracts older, unhealthy Greeks (104 hotels full of them) who come to bathe at the spas renowned since antiquity for curing everything from gallstones to depression. Maybe you should just stay long enough to buy a few bottles of this wonder-water, then cross over to the mainland, either to Ayiókambos, near Oreí, where there are tavernas and rooms to let, or to Glífa, which is more of a proper town, with bus links to Vólos,

travel details

Alkyon Tours, in co-operation with *Loucas Nomicos* ferry lines, hold a virtual monopoly on conventional ferry services to the northern Sporades, and they exploit it. Prices for ferries to and between Skíathos, Skópelos and Alónissos are almost double per nautical mile when compared to Cyclades or Dodecanese lines. On the Kími-Skíros line the *Alkyon/Nomicos* monopoly has been replaced by another, instituted by the Skyrians themselves, who were dissatisfied with the service previously offered.

● SKÍATHOS, SKÓPELOS AND ALÓNISSOS
Regular Ferries
From Áyios Konstantínos 9 weekly to Skíathos (3 hr.) and 7 to Skópelos (Glóssa – 5 hr.), continuing directly to Alónissos (6 hrs) 3 times a week at a maximum. (Heavily reduced service out of season.)
From Kími 4 times a week to Alónissos (3 hr.) and Skópelos (3½ hr.), continuing directly to Glóssa and Skíathos (5½ hr.) twice a week. (Drops to once or twice weekly in spring or autumn, nonexistent in winter).
From Vólos 3 or 4 boats a day to Skíathos (3 hr.) and Skópelos (4 hr.); at least one boat every day to Alónissos (5 hr.) (This is the most consistent service out of season, and always the cheapest).

Flying Dolphins
Much of the year there are 'Flying Dolphin' hydro-foils from Áyios Konstantínos, Vólos and Thessaloníki to all of the Sporades – as always, half the journey time but getting on for double the price of ordinary steamers.
From Áyios Konstantínos At least 1 departure daily to and from Skíathos, Glóssa, Skópelos and Alónissos (3 hr.)
From Vólos 2 to 4 departures daily to Skíathos, Glóssa, Skópelos and Alónissos (2½ hr.), and vice versa. (Service between Skópelos and Alónissos drops to several times a week out of season.) **From Thessaloníki** 3 times weekly in season to Skíathos, Glóssa, Skópelos and Alónissos, and back, via Moudhanía on the Halkidhikí peninsula.

Flights
Skíathos–Athens 3 flights daily.
Skíathos–Thessaloníki 3 flights weekly.

● SKÍROS
Regular Ferries
Skíros is served by conventional ferry only from Kími (2½ hrs) and only by the *Anemoessa*, 'The boat of the Skyrian People'. Services are at least twice a day in season, once daily (around 4pm) otherwise. There is a directly connecting bus service from the Liossíon 260 terminal in Athens.

Flying Dolphins
Twice a week in season the Volos-based **hydrofoil** links Skíros with the other Sporades; be persistent in your efforts to locate it since some locals resent the service and may deny its existence. Tickets can be purchased in Skíros *hóra* and Linariá.

Flights
Skíros–Athens 6 weekly.

● ÉVVIA
Buses
Buses leave Athens for Halkídha every half hour (takes 1½ hr.) from the Liossíon 260 terminal.
Good bus service from Halkídha to most of Évvia.

Trains
19 daily to Halkídha from Athens (Laríssis station); takes 1½ hr.

Ferries
Rafína–Káristos (1 or 2 daily, 2 hr.).
Rafína– Marmári (1 or 2 daily, 1 hr.).
Áyia Márina–Néa Stíra (7 daily, 50 min.). **Skála Oropoú–Erétria** (every hour from 5am–10pm, 25 min.).
Arkítsa–Loutrá Edhipsoú (12 daily from 6.45am–11pm, 50 min.).
Glífa–Ayiókambos (every 2 hrs from 6am–7pm, 30 min.).
Connecting buses from Athens to Rafína (every half hour, 1½ hr.) and to Skála Oropoú from Mavromatéon terminal; to Arkítsa and Glífa from the Liossíon terminal.

CHAPTER TWELVE

THE IONIAN

T he six **Ionian islands**, shepherding their satellites down the west coast of the mainland are both geographically and culturally a mixture of Greece and Italy. Floating on the haze of the Adriatic, their green, even lush, silhouettes come as a shock to those more used to the stark outlines of the Aegean. The fertility is a direct result of the heavy rains which sweep over the archipelago (especially Corfu) from October to March, though in summer the heat can be somnolent rather than bracing.

The islands were the Homeric realm of Odysseus (centred on Ithaca – modern Itháki – or Lefkádha, according to rival theories) and here alone of all modern Greek territory the Ottomans never held sway (except on Lefkádha). After the fall of Byzantium, possession passed to the Venetians and the islands became a keystone in that city state's maritime empire from 1386 until its collapse in 1797. Most of the population must have remained immune to the establishment of Italian as the official language and the arrival of Roman Catholicism, but Venetian influence remains evident and beautiful despite a series of earthquakes in the characteristic island capitals. On Corfu it is mixed with that of the British, who imposed a military 'protectorate' over the Ionian at the close of the Napoleonic Wars before eventually ceding the archipelago to Greece in 1864. There is, however, no question of the islanders' essential Greekness: the poet Solomos, author of the National Anthem, hailed from the Ionians, as did Nikos Mantzelos who provided the music, and the first Greek president, Capodistria.

Tourism has hit **Corfu** in a big way – so much so that it's the only island known to locals and foreigners by different names. None of the other five islands has endured anything like Corfu's scale of development, although it does seem to be beginning on parts of **Zákinthos**. Each of the islands, though, has diverse enough traditions and landscapes to keep island-hopping interesting if you decide to see them all in one journey. And this is easily enough done, with Kefalloniá and (highly recommended) Itháki a neat duo, while the odd ferry continues on south to more isolated Zákinthos.

Kíthira, isolated at the foot of the Peloponnese, traditionally belongs to the Ionian group but since it's easiest reached from Yíthio or Neápoli is covered with the Peloponnese in *Chapter Two*.

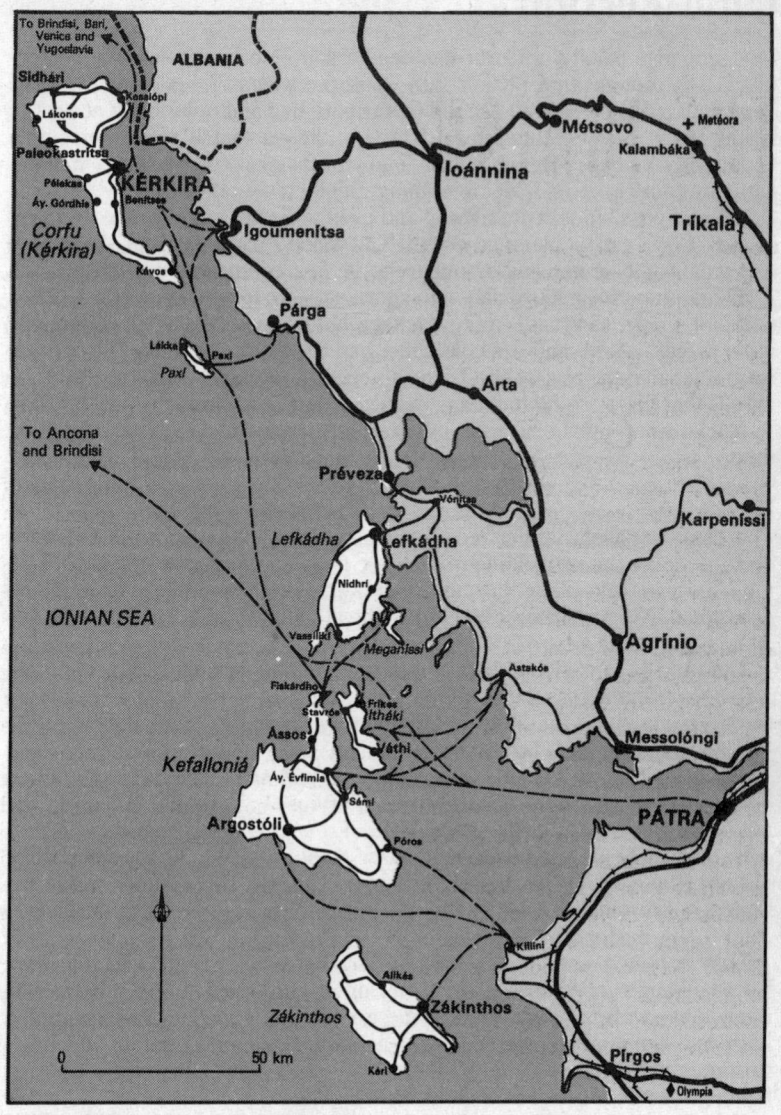

Corfu (Kérkira)

The seductive beauty of Corfu has been a source of inspiration for generations. It is thought that Shakespeare took the island as his setting for *The
Tempest*; Lawrence Durrell echoed this tribute by naming *his* book about the
island *Prospero's Cell*, and Edward Lear enthused that it made him 'grow
younger every hour'. Henry Miller, totally in his element, became euphoric,
lying for hours in the sun 'doing nothing, thinking of nothing'.

It is still possible to feel this way and even at Easter, a busy time on many
islands, Corfu can be pleasantly quiet. The island's natural appeal, the shapes
and scents of its lemon and orange trees, its figs, cypresses and, above all, its
3 million olive trees, all remain an experience – if sometimes a beleaguered
one. For Corfu, sadly, has more package hotels and holiday villas than any
other Greek island, and a whole coast has been virtually ruined. Yet these
contradictions are part of the island's appeal for some travellers. Everyone
agrees that there are far too many people, though the locals themselves have
remained amazingly hospitable, and everyone seems to end up having a good
time.

Kérkira town

The commercialism is apparent the moment you step ashore at the ferry
dock, or cover the two-kilometre distance from the **airport** to the city. From
the latter you can walk, get a cheap taxi (agree on the fare first), or catch the
occasional *Olympic Airways* bus, or the local #5 or #6 blue bus which leaves
500m north of the airport door.

The town is sandwiched between the two hilltop forts of **Paleó** (Old) and
Néo (New) **Froúrio**, relative terms since the older structure was begun by
the Byzantines in the mid-twelfth century, a mere century before the
Venetians began work on the newer citadel. They have both been modified
and damaged by various occupiers and besiegers since, the last contribution
being the neoclassical shrine of Áyios Yióryios, built by the British in the
middle of Paleó during the 1840s. Paleó Froúrio is open from 8am to 7pm
daily, and there's a sound-and-light show most evenings. To the west of the
old fort, the alley-like streets are crammed through the summer with vaca-
tioners converging to 'buy something Greek' from shops which exist solely to
cater to this demand.

This accepted and anticipated, Kérkira is an extremely elegant town.
Evelyn Waugh found it reminded him of Brighton and the parallel is definitely apt – with the addition of some exceptional Venetian churches and a
huge and beautiful concourse, the Spianádha, at the north end of which the
Corfiotes play cricket. (This is one of two main British legacies, the other
being ginger beer or *tsíntsi bírra* as it's called here.)

If you're travelling independently the chances are that you'll arrive fairly
early – or in the middle of the night on a charter flight – which gives you
plenty of time to arrange **accommodation**. Certain individuals waving leaflets in the airport and harbour customs halls might offer to do this for you,
and while many offers are legitimate you should obviously confirm prices,
location and exactly what's being pushed very carefully. The touts begin to

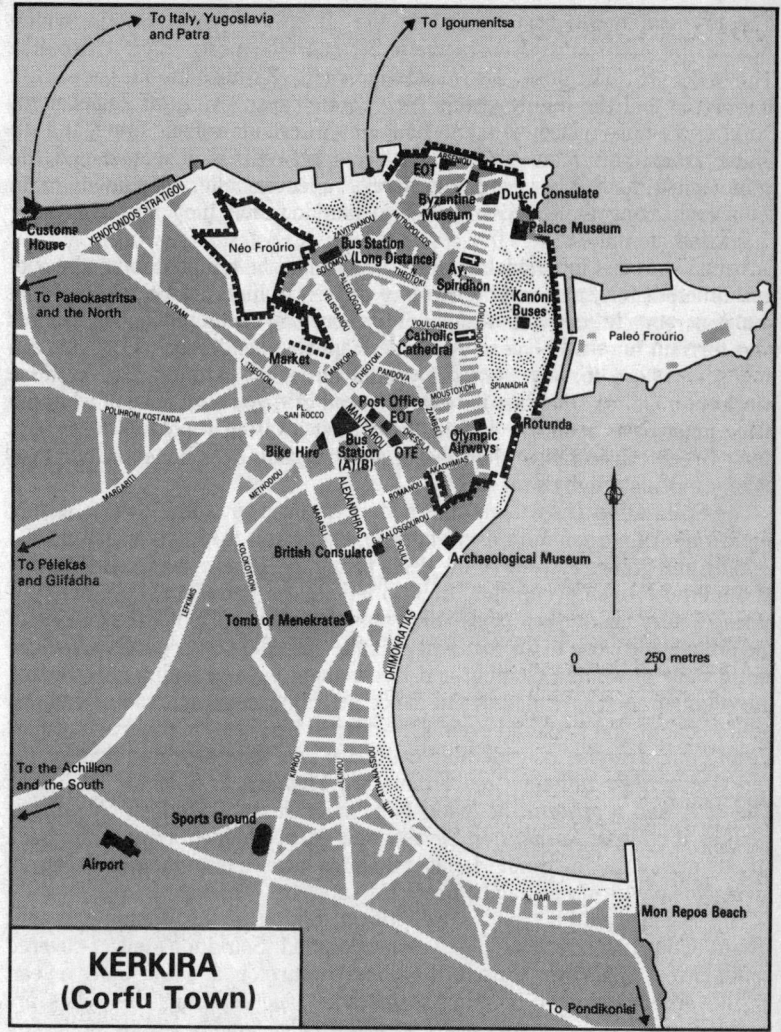

To Italy, Yugoslavia and Patra

To Igoumenítsa

XENOFONDOS STRATIGOU

Customs House

To Paleokastrítsa and the North

EOT

Byzantine Museum

Dutch Consulate

Palace Museum

Néo Froúrio

Bus Station (Long Distance)

Ay. Spiridhon

Kanóni Buses

Paleó Froúrio

Market

Catholic Cathedral

VOULGAREOS

Post Office

EOT

Bike Hire

Bus Station (A) (B)

OTE

Olympic Airways

Rotunda

SPIANADHA

To Pélekas and Glifádha

British Consulate

Archaeological Museum

Tomb of Menekrates

DHIMOKRATIAS

0   250 metres

To the Achillion and the South

Sports Ground

Airport

DAM

Mon Repos Beach

KÉRKIRA (Corfu Town)

To Pondikoníei

appear at about 7am, but our advice is to get into town, use the left-luggage office opposite the main harbour, and get your bearings.

There's a very helpful and professional **tourist office** just east of the Igoumenítsa ferry dock, next door to the Tourist Police. Here you can pick up free maps of the town and island, details of campsites, bus timetables, a list of hotels down to E-class and information on rooms to let in private houses – the likeliest form of summer accommodation, though the tourist office can't make reservations for you. If you do arrive fairly early in the day – and/or the season – you might first check out the cheaper old-town **hotels**, which include the *Metropolis* (Konstantínou 24, near the port), *Elpis* (Parodhos (alleyway) N. Theotóki 4), *Kostantinoupoli* (Zavitsánou 11, near the *Metropolis*) and the highly visible *New York* (Ipapandís 21, off Zavitsánou). Kérkira is a noisy place, so try to find somewhere off a main street. If it's a simple **room** you want, try in the streets between N. Theotóki and the Igoumenítsa dock. There are also several agencies offering student room reductions along Odhós Vassiléos Konstantínou, and they may also have cheap deals to Italy.

Armed with bus timetable and maps, you might be tempted to head out of town immediately, particularly if you've arrived in high season and feel that you've personally seen and bumped into every one of the millions of tourists who turn up here every year. An understandable sentiment, but if you can find somewhere to stay then the capital has a lot to offer. The produce **market** on Odhós Dhessilá, for example, can give you a glimpse of what the place must have been like before the tourist invasion – no less noisy, but tinny Greek music rather than disco, and haggling over honey rather than chanting British rugby songs.

The **Spianádha** (Esplanade) has a more civilised air, and it's worth paying slightly above normal for a drink here to enable you to sit and watch people coming and going. Try one of the cafés facing the **Listón**, an arcaded legacy of the brief French occupation, built to imitate the Parisian Rue de Rivoli. If paying luxury tax on your *tsíntsi bírra* puts you off, stroll along the far side of the promenade close to the fort, where in the splendid flower gardens you can join groups of women chatting and lace-making in the evening sun. During the summer open-air concerts and dance performances occur sporadically on both weekday and weekend evenings – current details from the tourist office.

Eating out, exercise considerable caution if you want anything both cheap and Greek. Two authentic restaurants are *Yisdhakis* at Solomoú 20, off N. Theotóki, and a *psistariá* at Ayíon Pándon 44, just off Voulgaréos. Others, such as the *Hrissi Kardhia* on Sevastianoú 44, are hidden away in the back streets near Kapodhistríou. Menus are almost always prominently displayed, giving you plenty of warning before you sit down.

The island's patron saint is **Spirídhon**, Spiros in the diminutive, after whom about half the male population is named. Spiridhon's silver-covered coffin is kept in his own church on Odhós Vouthrótou, and four times a year, to the accompaniment of much celebration and feasting, the relics are paraded through the streets of Kérkira (on Palm Sunday and the following Saturday, on August 11, and again on the first Sunday in November). Each of these days commemorates a miraculous deliverance of the island credited to the saint – twice from plague during the seventeenth century, from a famine of the sixteenth century and (a more blessed release than either of those for any Greek) from the Turks in the eighteenth century.

The **Archaeological Museum** at Vraíla 3 (behind Garítsa Bay) has a small but interesting collection covering the island's past, ranging from mundane cutlery to fancy jewellery, the prize exhibit being a 2500-year-old gorgon's-head pediment; half-price admission with a student card. **The Palace of St. Michael and St. George** on the Spianádha was built by the British between 1818 and 1823 and now includes a large collection of Asiatic art (Indian, Chinese, Japanese) which shows one more layer of the multi-ethnic history of the island. Close by is the **Solomos Museum** at Arseníou 41, where the Greek national poet lived; it now houses his archives and memorabilia. **The Byzantine Museum** and the **Cathedral** are also worth visiting, but if you get tired of culture and history there's sufficient diversion just wandering around the residential back streets and alleyways.

Five kilometres south of town (bus from the Spianádha), and probably one of Greece's five most popular excursion targets, is the postcard-picturesque **Vlahérna** island, capped by a small monastery and joined to the plush mainland suburb of **Kanóni** by a short causeway. Beyond, the islet of **Pondikoníssi** (Mouse Island), tufted with greenery and a small chapel, is supposed in legend to be a former ship from Odysseus's fleet, petrified by Poseidon in revenge for the blinding of his son Polyphemus.

If you've had a day or two in Kérkira town, though, you may feel like getting away. There are two **bus terminals** out: one for numbered routes through the middle of the island on Platía San Rócco, the other for more remote destinations on Platía Néou Frouríou, just below the fort. **Mopeds** are also available for hire nearby, and at most other main resorts, and are a useful means of acquainting yourself with the various beaches you might want to stay at. Such vehicles obviously get savaged by drivers during the season, so look for agencies with newer ones. Bigger bikes are more reliable and less likely to have been pushed beyond their capacity, but only take them if you're an experienced rider. An incredible number of people have accidents on the gravelly, potholed tracks. In season there are also a few excursion **kaíkia** to certain beaches on the remote southern end of the island.

Northeastern Corfu

The coast north of the port has been remorselessly developed as far as Kassiópi and much of it is probably best written off; there are official campsites at (north to south) Pirgí, Ípsos, Dhassía and Kondokáli (location also of the island's unsavoury youth hostel), but they're large, organised sites with little sense of being in Greece. The beaches vary between pebbly and rocky and are often sullied with rubbish washed up from the mainland. The sea looks murky and polluted too.

Beyond ÍPSOS (about halfway to Kassiópi and best summed up as 'pubs and paragliding') the mood does change slightly for the better. The road runs through olive groves as it rounds **Mt. Pantokrátor** (walkable from the inland villages of Strinílas or Períthia), and from then until it reaches Kassiópi, the beaches (usually rocky coves) are approached along side roads or tracks leading down from the main road. The sea gets cleaner and the company changes; most people in this area are staying in fairly low-key villas scattered round the landscape.

BARBÁTI beach gets crowded by day but is developed only to the extent of a couple of tavernas, and still manages to look like the fishing hamlet it once was. **NISSÁKI** has a number of coves, the first and last accessible by road, the rest by dirt track, and a single vast hotel, the only blot on this particular landscape. **YIMÁRI**, up the road, retains a village-like atmosphere, and even a few independent rooms to let – like gold dust along this stretch of coast.

KALÁMI is where Lawrence Durrell once lived in his 'White House', or so it's claimed; others say it was in nearby Kouloúra. In either case, Kalámi is a pleasant enough settlement, now really a villa/apartment community, with a few rooms to let but poor swimming, while **KOULOÚRA** is a very small port with no rooms to let but a good taverna.

Albania is clearly visible all along this coast, a paltry sea-mile away from the pretty harbour hamlet of **ÁYIOS STÉFANOS**. There is talk of the Albanians allowing organised day-excursions in 1990, if *perestroika* holds out.

KASSIÓPI is the last village on the eastern side of Mt. Pantokrátor. In the early morning, with the tourists still a-bed, its port makes it look deceptively peaceful, though lately it's been taken over entirely and developed by the various tour operators.

The north coast

Initially the stretch of coast west of Kassiópi is barren, and it must be one of the quietest stretches of Corfú shoreline, with no restaurants or shops at all for half a dozen kilometres. The first place to stay is **AYIOS SPIRÍDHON**, where there are restaurants and at least a few campers happily ignoring the obvious 'No camping' signs on the first of the sandy beaches. This is a small beach, however, and if you continue on a little way you'll see a sign to Almirós beach, the start of the continuous strand that sweeps around to Ródha. At this end it's very quiet, with a taverna to keep you fed and the occasional camper van to keep you company.

AHARÁVI, about halfway to Sidhári, is a staid, mostly purpose-built community of villas and apartments, where the supermarket gives you a chance to stock up on your Heinz baked beans. **RÓDHA** was once a small village but has been taken over by the British travel companies. Always a bit windswept, now it seems downright drab, with a soundtrack of *Club 18-30* customers complaining about their hangovers. **KAROUSÁDHES**, just down the coast, has the first 'Rooms for let' signs for miles, and a more laid-back feel despite the two hotels. **SIDHÁRI** has rooms too, and some famous beaches just to the west, but these hardly merit a stop as it's crowded and tatty, though not quite as bad as the Ípsos-to-Kondokáli stretch.

PEROULÁDHES, around the corner, is quite a surprise. For a start it's a genuine, somewhat run-down village. Then there's the beach, reached by a steep path to the brick-red sand below spectacular, wind-eroded cliffs. There's also a restaurant nearby and views across to some of the islets off Corfu's northwest coast.

At windswept, dry **ÁYIOS STÉFANOS** (not to be confused with the previously noted one), it's back to tourist-traps and hastily constructed apartment buildings, quite a contrast to the luscious countryside around. Nearby **ARÍLLAS**, longer established, is marginally more attractive.

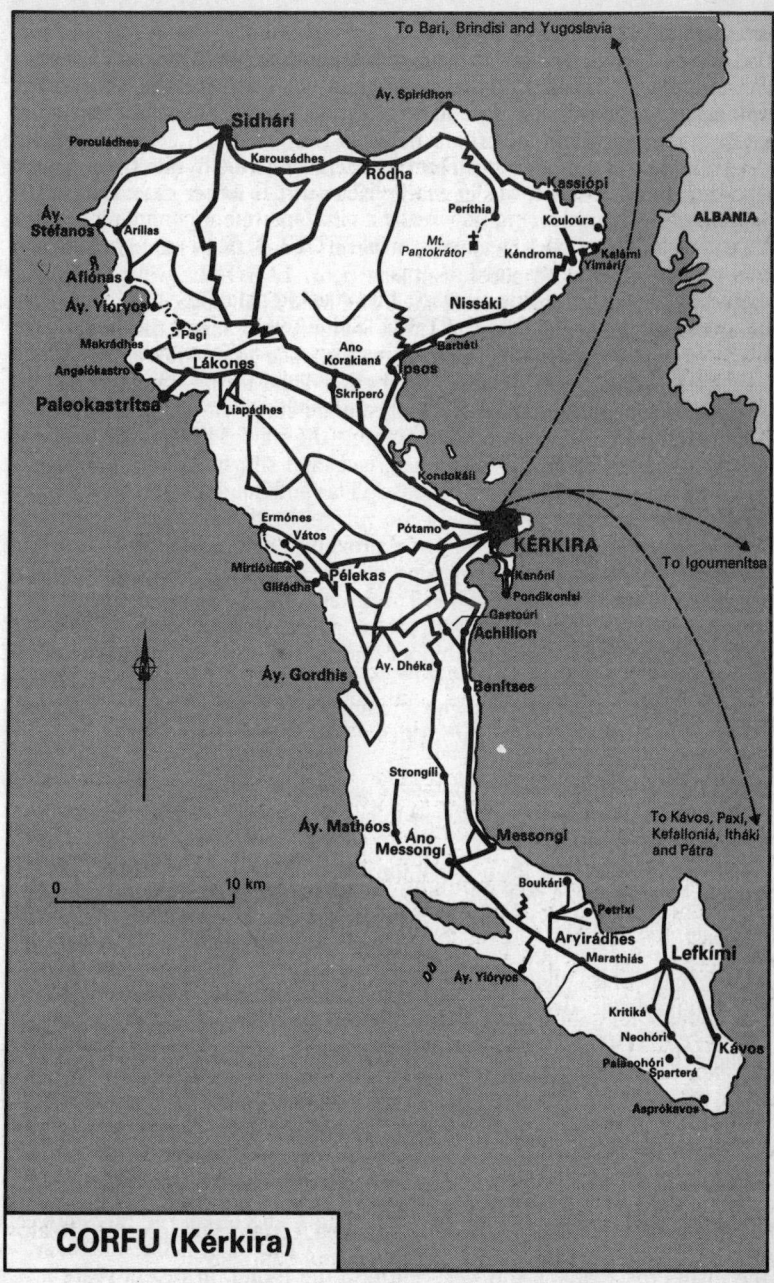

To Bari, Brindisi and Yugoslavia

Áy. Spiridhon

Perouládhes

Sidhári

Karousádhes

Ródha

Kassiópi

Perithia

Kouloúra

Áy. Stéfanos

Arillas

Mt. Pantokrátor

Kéndroma

Kalámi
Ylimárí

ALBANIA

Aflónas

Áy. Yióryos

Nissáki

Makrádhes

Pagí

Ano Korakianá

Barbáti

Angelókastro

Lákones

Ipsos

Paleokastrítsa

Skriperó

Liapádhes

Kondokáli

Ermónes

Vátos

Pótamo

KÉRKIRA

Mirtiótissa

Pélekas

Kanóni

Glifádha

Pondikonísi

To Igoumenitsa

Gastoúri

Achillíon

Áy. Gordhis

Áy. Dhéka

Benítses

Strongili

Áy. Mathéos

Áno Messongí

Messongí

To Kávos, Paxí,
Kefalloniá, Itháki
and Pátra

Boukári

Petríxi

Aryirádhes

Marathiás

Lefkími

Áy. Yióryos

Kritiká

Neohóri

Kávos

Palaiohóri

Sparterá

Asprókavos

0   10 km

CORFU (Kérkira)

The west coast

The overdevelopment that's increasingly evident on the next stretch of coast from Afiónas to Paleokastrítsa is understandable, if lamentable; it's the most striking part of the island, Paleokastrítsa's site especially, with a fine sandy beach in a perfect natural harbour between two headlands. This topography has led it to be identified with Homer's Scheria, where Odysseus was washed ashore and escorted by Nausica to the palace of her father Alcinous, King of the Phaeacians.

The coast north of Paleokastrítsa, however, seems tailor-made for independent travellers, as road access remains poor. **LAKÓNES** village, perched above Paleokastrítsa on a natural shelf, and **MAKRÁDHES**, lost in its olives, are worth stopping for, and the latter stands 300m above the huge sandy beach of **Áyios Yióryios** (rooms, tavernas). Also from Makrádhes a mule path leads within fifteen minutes up the headland to the thirteenth-century Byzantine castle of **Angelókastro**, and commanding vistas in all directions.

PALEOKASTRÍTSA itself has long gone the way of all package locations; it's not so much a resort as an area spread (and still spreading) over five or six coves on a beautiful stretch of coast. Villas and hotels are present in abundance, plus a campsite high up in the village, by the anchorage. The more ordinary end of town is, despite the proximity of the sea, and you'll find rooms to let and some less imposing places to eat. The big outfits seem to prefer locations further up the hill. This is also the one place on Corfu where menus are not so obviously on display, so if it isn't easy to find one to check out prices, eat elsewhere. Even higher than the eateries is the **Monastery of Theotókos** (daily 7am–1pm and 3–8pm), remarkable as much for the numbers of heedless tourists who attempt to visit inappropriately clad (and are barred entry) as for the curiosities within. Go early or late to avoid the bus groups.

LIAPÁDHES, just to the southeast of the bay, seems more of a normal village, with rooms to let and access to beaches that are visible but inaccessible from Paleokastrítsa.

ERMÓNES has one feature that must be unique in Greece: a lift down to the beach. Apart from that and a large hotel, it's not too bad in comparison to some and has a decent beach and eating places. **VÁTOS**, just inland, by a quirk of fate seems to be the one place within easy reach of Kérkira town that isn't developed, isn't flooded with traffic and has an easy relaxed feel to it. It's still a tiny village (with rooms); both tavernas (as so often on Corfu) are called *Spiro's*. Campers pitch tents down towards **MIRTIÓTISSA BEACH**, though they sometimes get rousted and encouraged to use the official site, *Vátos Camping*, near the village. The dirt track down to the sand is steep and has thus far prevented development; the beach itself hosts a nudist section at one end and a small monastery at the other, with relations between the two only occasionally frayed.

In comparison **GLIFÁDHA** is dominated by a huge hotel and its customers; a very popular spot, with more building going on all the time, projects hardly justified by the medium-sized beach. **PÉLEKAS** is likewise busy, as the main crossroads in the west-centre of the island. In recent years it has also acquired a reputation as a watering-hole for the island's hippie/youth crowd. There are a number of unpretentious tavernas and rooms, freelance camping on the closest beach as well as the organised camping at nearby Vátos, and an unofficial hostel to cater to this clientele. A veneer of bourgeois sensibility is applied in the evenings when busloads of tourists arrive from town to admire Pélekas' spectacular sunsets. If you're not the tour-bus sort then there's the #11 bus from Platía San Rócco in Kérkira town.

ÁYIOS GÓRDHIS beach is more remote but that hasn't spared it from the crowds who come to admire the cliff-girt setting, or patronise the rather bizarre *Pink Palace* (certainly pink but hardly a palace), a foreign-run combination holiday village/disco right on the sand.

Journeying further south on the island such cultural excrescences drop off, as does the topography; salt pans, undistinguished villages and flat agricultural plains form the backdrop for such as-yet undefiled beaches as **Áyios Yióryios, Perivóli, Asprókavos** (the southern extreme of Corfu) and the resort of KÁVOS (facing the mainland). Bus services to all these points are sparse though most of the sandy stretches will have at least one seasonal taverna.

At **ÁYIOS YIÓRYIOS** a short walk north will take you to a beautiful undeveloped stretch of surf-pounded sand where you can camp in the dunes at night when such crowds as there are have gone. The town itself is an expanding collection of hotels, apartments and restaurants straggling along the coast and you may prefer the peace of the dunes.

Farther south down the central main road is **MARATHIÁS** and its beach, which is a long trek down a dirt road. The strand is a continuation of the one at Áyios Yióryios, but you'll probably feel slightly more adventurous here, even if you're not alone. There are plenty of restaurants on the beach and on the way down to it, and rooms in the town, along the access road and right on the beach as well. You can also camp in the trees near the bottom or on the beach itself.

If you think you're going to find a quiet village at **KÁVOS**, forget it. Young British package tourists have invaded the place, which is now a perfect spot for pubs, discos and paragliding. The beach is fair but not as good as the last few mentioned and hardly worth making the journey south for.

The southeast coast

As you (sensibly) turn back and work your way up the east coast, LEFKÍMI has a beach to the east but it's not very awe-inspiring and you'd be better off taking the inland, secondary road through such appealing villages as SPARTERÁ, NEOHÓRI and KRITIKÁ. At **ARYIRÁDHES**, another side road bears northeast through a pretty valley en route to a mainly rocky, but crowd-free, coastline. **PETRITÍ**, a working fishing port, is an easy place to find rooms; you share the small unspoiled beach with only a few villa tenants. At **BOUKÁRI** there's a small hotel and a taverna, and more fishermen who still fish, and you can also walk some way around the coast towards the north – as you should do to swim, as there are various crude sewage outlets near the village.

Heading back toward Kérkira town, **ÁYIOS MATHÉOS**, reached on a side road west, seems to be accessible only with your own vehicle; the quiet countryside is hilly and beautiful. A road leads down to the one-taverna beach of **Prasoúnda**, half-sand, half-rock, though both road and beach are good enough to attract a number of drivers in season. Later the road turns into a track which continues south to a more isolated beach, possibly the quietest on Corfu because it takes such determination to get there (though a restaurant has been built).

Once back on the main road north, the east coast from MESSONGÍ onward is a shabby counterpart to the miniature 'Costa del Sol' in the north between Kassiópi and the port. **BENÍTSES** is *the* package resort. Only slightly the more bearable for having engulfed a genuine village, it has a beach littered with beer cans in the evening, and an olive grove with a fish-and-chip shop and a go-kart track. Bad taste reaches its apotheosis, however, near GASTOÚRI village (8km from town), with the incredible **Achillion Palace**, built in a (fortunately) unique blend of Teutonic and neoclassical styles in 1890 by Elizabeth, Empress of Austria. Henry Miller considered it 'the worst piece of gimcrackery' that he'd ever laid eyes on and thought it 'would make an excellent museum for surrealistic art'. Prince Philip (of England) was born there; it is today a casino, though you can just visit the grounds should you wish.

An alternative approach to Kérkira town from the southeast of the island would be to take the quieter inland road north from Áno Messongí, at the crossroads between Messongí and Áyios Mathéos. This leads through the charming villages of STRONGÍLI and ÁYII DHÉKA, both enjoying impressive views.

Paxí (Paxós)

This tiny (12km by 4km) island is devoted almost completely to olive cultivation, and a dire water shortage has prevented the construction of all but one luxury hotel. It is, however, not exactly remote, or unvisited. There are ferries almost every day in season from Corfu and from Párga on the mainland, and seats on the latter must be reserved a day ahead in summer. It used to be that you also had to book rooms on the island in advance, a scheme calculated to stamp out unofficial **camping** and the attendant danger of fire in the precious olive groves, but in recent years the islanders have surrendered to the inevitable and the groves fairly rustle with tents. The island itself has a population of just over two thousand, often matched in season by visitors. It remains quiet and rural, despite the odds.

Most people stay in, or around, the main harbour and village of **GAÍOS**, its three- and four-storey pastel-tinted houses fronting a channel of water which gives it the impression of being built on a river. Opposite is the islet of **Kástro**, which can be reached by boat and offers the best view of the town – one sketched by Edward Lear more than a hundred years ago. There's also the inevitable ruined Venetian fortress on the islet.

This peaceful scene tends to be disrupted for a few hours each day when the excursion boats arrive and fill the tavernas and waterside patisseries with their cargo – in this case both from the mainland and the *Club 18-30* Corfu. But there are plenty of places to escape to, and by evening most of the calm has returned.

Independent travellers are in the minority, with some Scandinavians and just a few Germans and Brits in evidence. The majority of 'resident' visitors come with flight/villa companies, resulting in a safe family atmosphere. The consequences for the solo traveller are mixed. Firstly, many of the properties are reserved by the package companies (though often empty), leaving fewer available rooms, but since most of the villas are out toward Pórto Longós and Lákka, you should, unless you're exceptionally unlucky, eventually find something in or around Gaíos.

When looking for **accommodation**, if you're not met on arrival with the familiar Greek cries of 'Rooms, rooms, yes, yes!', go through the square away from the waterside and take the road that leads out of the town. When you get to the edge of the built-up area turn left at the crossroads/bus stop up a steep concrete road and keep an eye out for the signs. Look out for overcharging, too, and don't be afraid to haggle. A check with the **police station** (behind the waterfront **post office**) confirmed that they sometimes catch people ignoring the officially-fixed prices, which should be displayed. Or maybe you could just take one of the rooms behind the police station itself.

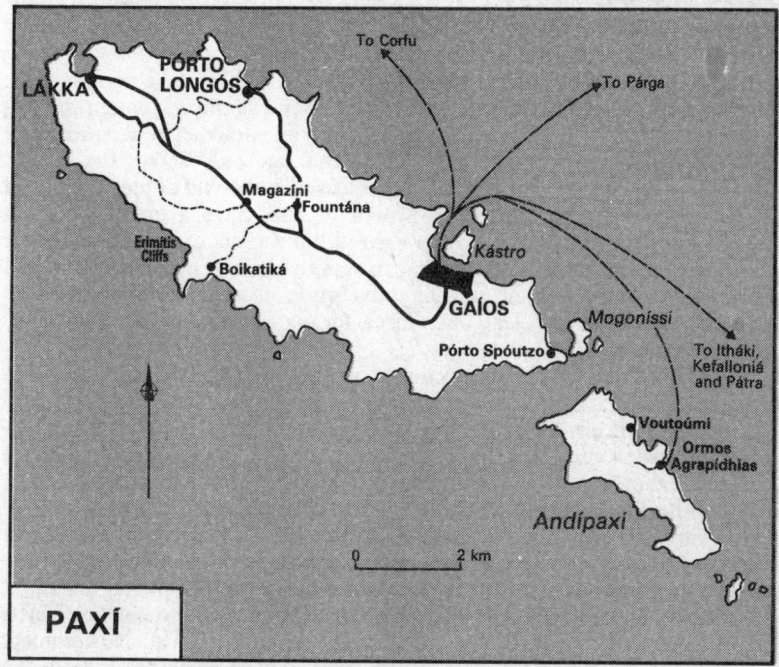

Nobody seems to hassle the campers who settle in around the back of many of the coves.

Food is slightly overpriced, but no more than you would expect on a small island with a short tourist season. The cheapest place with really good food is *Spiro's*, also called *Beautiful Paxi*, which is found by turning right, away from the top of the square, and then immediately left – easily missed as it's small. *Dodo's* also has good food and a wall full of newspaper clippings to prove it. Restaurants tend to push bottled water, and given the water shortage that's understandable, but the tap water is perfectly safe to drink. Probably safer than the *Metaxa* brandy, but if you crave a generous measure of that, try *Costa's Kafenion* just off the main square where you'll pay about one-fifth of the price charged at the trendier bars used by the foreign yachting crowds.

Paxí's single main road splits halfway up the island, with one branch leading to Lákka and the other to Pórto Longós. Both are a walkable distance away, but for the lazy there's the 'Paxos Express', a **bus** that travels between the three main communities about six times a day. **Walking** on the island is good, because distances are small and the masses of olive trees always offer shade. The houses are scattered about, forming many tiny communities in addition to the main three, and there are also said to be over seventy churches on Paxí. The *Greek Islands Club* (one of the main operators to this island) puts out a useful wildflower and walking guide, available in Gaíos and Lákka, which details hard-to-find paths throughout the island. One of these departs from near Magazíni (friendly taverna/rooms) to the enormous chalk-coloured cliffs of Erimítis, which can also be viewed from the cemetery behind the church of Áyii Apóstoli in Boikatiká.

LÁKKA, about 7km northwest of Gáios, has 200 villagers, a peaceful feel, some rooms, fair tavernas, and a pebbly cove for swimming, though the bay in general is rather stagnant. The **aquarium** here shouldn't be missed: not a statement that can be made very often. This one only shows the locally-caught marine life, and the exhibits are released at the end of the season and replaced the following year. The proprietor also takes a great delight in explaining the habits and idiosyncracies of the various creatures, including those that are tame. A recent star turn was the pair of octopi which could unscrew jars to get at their meal of crabs inside; occasionally one would get jealous of the other and leap out. Check for opening times first; floor show not guaranteed.

PÓRTO LONGÓS, facing northeast, is prettier, with better eateries, but accommodation is limited to block-booked holiday villas. This housing shortage doesn't concern the multitudes at the island's premier unofficial **campsite**, one cove south. That, and two more coves southwest of Pórto Longós, constitute the highest concentration of (pebbly) swimming spots on Paxí, along with a like concentration of Italian and Greek holidaymakers.

Get an early start on your ramblings, as all of Paxí's (and Andípaxi's) beaches are exposed to prevailing summer afternoon winds. Contrary to tourist literature propaganda, there is but one sandy beach on the island, at **Mogoníssi**, in the south, where there's also an open-air taverna which boasts 'Theo and Pan, probably the best Greek dancers in the world'. No comment on that, and you'll pay for them in the price of your meal, but at least the menu is varied and the food good. A free bus/boat service leaves Gaíos every evening at 7.30, and there's unofficial camping behind the beach.

Andípaxi

For the best beaches, go to **ANDÍPAXI**, connected several times daily by speedboat (15 min.) or ordinary *kaíki* service from Gaíos. The trip seems expensive for what it is, but the route takes in the spectacular caves on the rocky southern tip of Paxí on the way, and you might also see a few flying fish into the bargain. The boat stops at a couple of beaches before going on to the main anchorage, though there's nothing much there when you arrive so you may as well get off at a beach. There are two tavernas at the first beach, while the second has a bar with food, a panoramic view and prices to match.

Despite its tiny size, Andípaxi is famous for the wine from its vineyards. The two beaches are connected by a dirt road, and for the more intrepid there are paths all over the island. There's no accommodation but camping is tolerated, though the tavernas are not likely to stay open just for you. You will certainly find solitude after sunset on Andípaxi; just don't expect to find too much food and drink.

Lefkádha (Lefkas)

Lefkádha is an oddity; connected to the mainland by a long causeway through salt marshes, you hardly feel it's an island at all. In fact historically it isn't – a canal was cut by Corinthian colonists in 540 B.C. and has been re-dredged (after silting up) at various times since. Strategically it was always important and, approaching the causeway, you pass a series of fortresses, climaxing in the thirteenth-century Frankish **Castle of Santa Maura** which gave its name to the whole island during the Venetian occupation and is still used, on occasion, even today.

Island or no, it was too close to the mainland to avoid a 220-year Turkish tenure beginning in 1467. The Turks were followed by the Venetians, who were overthrown by Napoleon in 1797, until the British took over as Ionian protectors in 1809. It wasn't until 1864 that, like the other Ionian Islands, Lefkádha was reunited with the rest of Greece. It is today the least commercialised of the Ionian group, though the permanent positioning of a 'boat bridge' in 1986, replacing the 30-metre chain ferry to the mainland, may herald the start of tourist expansion.

For the moment, though, it has an unselfconscious charm, lively summer festivals and a strong local *retsina*. Perhaps a good dose of that might help you cope with the island's mosquitoes, which are, it must be said, sometimes a problem – as is the rather overpowering smell from the fishponds in July and August. On the other hand, Lefkádha is a very verdant island and supports the unusual Judas tree and many varieties of orchid, and the mountain villages remain absolutely untouched. The older island women continue to wear the traditional local dress, consisting of two skirts (one forming a bustle), a brown headscarf and a rigid bodice. All bright colours are forsworn out of respect for the state of matrimony and deceased male relatives.

Lefkádha has also been a cradle of sorts for various literati, including two prominent Greek poets, Angelos Sikelianos and Aristotelis Valaoritis, and the short-story writer, Lefcadio Hearn, son of American missionaries. Support of **the arts** continues in the form of an international festival of theatre and folk dancing each August, which attracts visitors from all over the world; on a smaller scale the frequent *bouzoúki* and *klaríno* festivals ensure that the local wine flows well into the early hours. Vlihós, for example, is a small coastal village which has great local *bouzoúki* festivals throughout the summer.

Lefkádha town

The main town, also called **LEFKÁDHA**, looks out from the shore of the shallow lagoon, opposite the mainland fortress. Badly hit by the earthquakes of 1948 and 1953, its **houses** have been rebuilt in an extraordinary fashion, with the upper storeys typically constructed of hardboard and corrugated iron to lay as little stress as possible upon the foundations. Building restrictions forbid the construction of anything over two storeys in height. Add tilted shutters and porches on stilts, plus the numerous **fish traps** out in the lagoon, and Lefkádha is more evocative of the Caribbean than any European port. It's a popular anchorage for the organised yacht flotillas.

The business district, musically energetic at night with strings of light-bulbs overhead, is long and narrow, centred around one main thoroughfare with tiny alleys disappearing to either side. **Hotels** are generally expensive, but three cheapish ones are the *Vyzantion, Averof* and *Patras*. **Restaurants** are among the best in the Ionians; for a good *psistariá* try *Ta Helidhonia*, near the main square at Melá 50, or the conventional *Taverna To Stéki* at Skiadharési 13 nearby. There's a good choice of tavernas on the quayside, but the best restaurant on the island, out near the hospital, is the *Adriatica*. It is pricey, but features unusual vegetarian entrees, an excellent fish pie and other seafood dishes.

Once you've decided to leave town, there's a good **bus** service to the popular coastal resorts of Nidhrí, Vlihós and Vassilikí, as well as to Kariá in the heart of the island. The **bus station** is on the waterfront by the southern yacht harbour. To get anywhere else you'll probably want to hire a **moped**.

Northern Lefkádha

You don't have to go too far to enjoy some of the island's best beaches. **Yíropetra**, sandy but with pebbles that the surf can hurl with bruising force, is the spit bordering the fish-lagoon on the northwest and is a 45-minute walk from town. The main road west of the harbour climbs up to **Faneroméni** monastery, which has beautiful views although it's no longer in use. One point of interest is the *símandro* (oxen's yoke and hammer) which was used to call the congregation to prayer when the German occupying forces forbade the use of a bell.

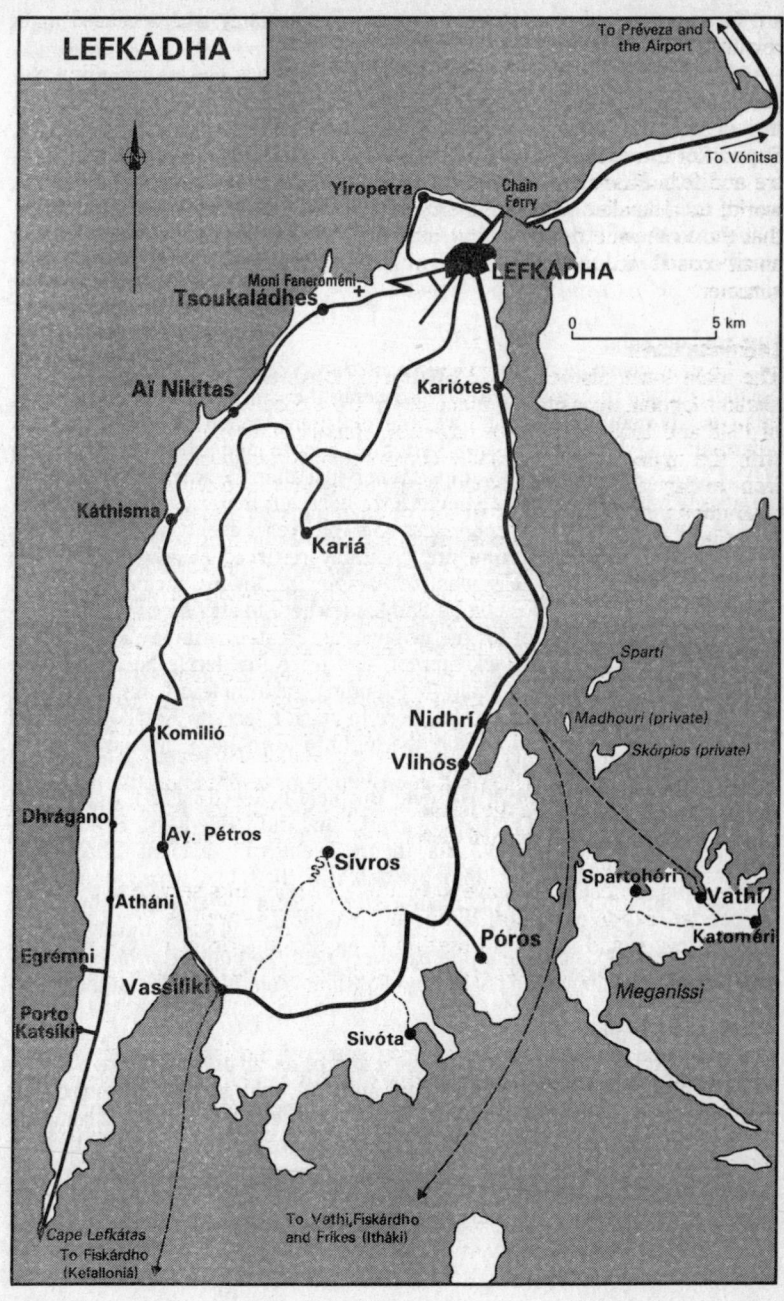

LEFKÁDHA

To Préveza and
the Airport

To Vónitsa

Yíropetra

Chain
Ferry

LEFKÁDHA

Moní Faneroméni

Tsoukaládhes

0   5 km

Kariótes

Aï Nikítas

Káthisma

Kariá

Sparti

Madhouri (private)

Nidhrí

Skórpios (private)

Vlihós

Komilió

Spartohóri

Dhrágano

Ay. Pétros

Sívros

Vathí

Atháni

Póros

Katoméri

Egrémni

Meganíssi

Vassilikí

Porto
Katsíki

Sivóta

Cape Lefkátas
To Fiskárdho
(Kefalloniá)

To Vathi, Fiskárdho
and Frikes (Itháki)

The road then drops down to the resort of **AI-NIKÍTAS**, served by bus a few times daily. Seasonal rooms and tavernas (though no shops yet) are gathered at one end of the kilometre of coarse sand, with camping both on the beach and at a campsite on the road out to Kalamítsi. Continue on by moped or foot to the turning for superb **KÁTHISMA** beach, with much camping, litter and three seasonal tavernas in evidence. A few coves just to the north are nudist but have no facilities; the closest village, up a considerable hill but one of the island's most interesting, is KALAMÍTSI. If the west wind is up, though, all these beaches will be useless, and your efforts are best directed elsewhere. Inland, KARIÁ is a good base for wanderings in the surrounding villages, whether by moped or on foot.

Eastern Lefkádha

On the east coast there are a couple of good **campsites** not too far from Lefkádha town, the one at KARIÓTES being the nearest. The scenery down this coast is quite nondescript, with development limited mostly to vacation villas patronised by Greeks, and there's not a lot to stop for before you reach **NIDHRÍ**. This is a former swamp, drained just after the war, and some have been known to mutter that it should have been left that way. The swimming off the tiny beach is very average, less so if the ever-present yachts have been draining their sumps. **Rooms** are generally reserved in advance by tour companies, but if you really want to sample the town's cocktail bars and discos it should still be possible to find somewhere to stay by trying the tourist agencies or looking out for the usual signs. **Restaurants** are all unbelievably similar in quality (or lack thereof) and price (moderate because of the competition), and the only really outstanding gastronomic features are the two bakeries. If you're just coming here to catch a ferry to Kefalloniá, Itháki or Meganíssi, it's more fun to stay the night in town and shuttle over in the morning with the first bus of the day.

The German archaeologist Wilhelm Dorpfeld believed Nidhrí, rather than Itháki, to be the site of Odysseus's capital and did indeed find Bronze Age tombs on the plain nearby. His theory identifying ancient Itháki with Lefkádha fell into disfavour after his death in 1940, but, wrong or not, his obsessive attempts to give Lefkádha some status over nearby Itháki are honoured by a statue beside the harbour. His tomb is tucked away at Ayía Kiriakí on the opposite side of the bay, very near the house in which he once lived, visible just above the chapel and lighthouse on the far side of the water.

Southern Lefkádha

VLIHÓS, 4km south of Nidhrí at the head of an all-but landlocked bay, is more or less an extension of the resort, and if it's calm swimming you're after then continue to **PÓROS**, where there's a good pebble beach and a campsite below the village itself (rooms/tavernas), though the beach gets both busy and dirty in July and August. The next inlet to the west, **SIVÓTA**, is more protected and remains a delight, its natural harbour making it a favourite with yachts. The campsite is still unofficial and lacks facilities, there are no shops and no more than about twenty houses, but a trip to the nearby fish tavernas should make up for all this.

Of the very few inland settlements only SÍVROS merits a look if you have your own vehicle. The main coastal road eventually ends up in **VASSILIKÍ** (40km from Lefkádha town), where there are plenty of rooms and tavernas under the waterside tamarisks, plus a campsite and ferries south. The somewhat unappetising bay doesn't deter the big windsurfing school here. Boards are for hire, but beginners are forced to confine their efforts to the morning hours since afternoon gusts sweep all except experts from the water. Wind permitting, there are also *kaíki* trips down to the white cliffs of **Cape Lefkátas** (Doukato), which drop 75 abrupt metres into the sea.

Byron's Childe Harold sailed past this point, and 'saw the evening star above, Leucadia's far projecting rock of woe: And hail'd the last resort of fruitless love'. The fruitless love refers to Sappho, who in accord with the ancient legend that you could cure yourself of unrequited love by leaping into these waters, leapt – and died. In her honour the locals know the place as *Kávos tis Kirás*, 'the Lady's Cave', and her act was apparently imitated by the lovelorn youths of Lefkádha for centuries afterwards. And not just the lovelorn, for the act (known as *katapontismós*) was performed annually by scapegoats – always a criminal or a lunatic – selected by priests from the Apollo temple whose ruins lie close by. Feathers, and even live birds, were attached to the sacrificial victim to slow his descent, and waiting boats below took the chosen one, dead or alive, away to some place where the evil that was banished with him could do no further harm to the islanders. The rite continued into the Roman era, when it was little more than a fashionable stunt of decadent youth. These days, every July, Greek hang gliders hold a tournament from these cliffs.

Visitors often find the southwest quadrant of the island dusty and unappealing, though its isolated villages and beaches have some character of their own – and fine views over the Ionian. Heading north from Vassilikí to Áyios Pétros on the mountain route, or south from Lefkádha town on the same road, take the turning at KOMILIÓ (famous for its thyme honey) and continue through Dhrágano and Atháni to the tracks down to the beaches of Egrémni or Pórto Katsíki, and Cape Lefkátas, all signposted by some enterprising local. **PÓRTO KATSÍKI** is a must – a rough track or 100 concrete steps lead down to a long, clean, sandy beach with a turquoise sea and a beautiful white cliff backdrop. There is unofficial camping, and no development of any kind.

Meganíssi and Other Satellites

Lefkádha has a string of satellite islets (Spartí, Madourí, Skórpios and Meganíssi), with the most spectacular view (and only regular access) of these from Nidhrí. **Spartí** is an uninhabited island covered in scrub. **Skórpios** offers its visitors little more as it was the retreat of the (now almost extinct) Onassis family and their staff of forty. Landing is still strictly forbidden, as it is also on the other private island of **Madourí**, the property of the poet Nanos Valaoritis (descendant of Aristotelis) and his family, who are all still very much alive and actively engaged in restoring the ornate mansion which dates from the 1850s.

Meganíssi

MEGANÍSSI, the only conventionally inhabited of these satellite islands, is a twenty-minute ferry or excursion-boat crossing from Nidhrí. It has been for some time a closely-guarded secret among island aficionados, without a post-card or souvenir shop in sight. *Ilios Island Holidays*, however, has discovered it and now takes groups over; their comparatively small operation should do little damage to the island's charms. Meganíssi has a severe water shortage so it is unlikely that any more operators will follow suit. Unfortunately the local fishermen now have to sail as far away as Itháki and Kefalloniá to guarantee a good catch, since the local waters are so overfished. For some, then, a few more tourists would be a welcome incursion. There are no official campsites on the island, but **rooms** are readily available and cheap.

Some excursion boats call at PÓRTO SPÍLIO, from where you follow a winding, uphill concrete road to the village of **SPARTOHÓRI**. From here there is an incredible view across to Lefkádha and Skórpios. The village itself is immaculate, with whitewashed buildings and an abundance of bougainvillea. The locals live from farming and fishing and are genuinely friendly. There are a few tavernas, with only one making any kind of concession to the visiting groups from Nidhrí. **Food** is somewhat limited, but excellently cooked and very cheap. The island's one main road continues from Spartohóri to the village of **KATOMÉRI**, where visitors are likely to be greeted with a free *oúzo* at the taverna and an invitation to join in a game of cards.

Several routes lead over the hills of the island and down through the olive-grove terracing to secluded bays. The most popular of these is AMBELÁKIA, which attracts visiting yacht flotillas. One tour company over-optimistically set up a Club-Med-type operation here; it has now closed down, though the grass huts are still there. You might also get a boat to take you to the caves on the southwest coast which reputedly sheltered submarines during World War II.

The road from Katoméri finishes at **VATHÍ**, the main fishing port on the island and the stop for the regular ferries. Chapels on either side of the harbour entrance bless all boats to grant safe passage, though otherwise it's a rather scruffy place moving at its own pace.

Kefalloniá (Cephallonia, Kefallinía)

Kefalloniá is the largest of the Ionian islands but, initially anyway, the least inviting. Virtually all of its towns and villages were levelled in the 1953 earthquake, and these masterpieces of Venetian architecture had been the one touch of elegance in a severe, mountainous landscape. So it is a very contemporary collection of coastal settlements, at the base of towering escarpments, which greets the visitor on incoming ferries. Beyond, Kefalloniá culminates in the 1632-metre bulk of Mt Énos, declared a national park to protect the fir trees (*Abies cephalonica*) which take their name from the island.

The Kefallonians themselves have a reputation for a certain eccentricity in their better moments – and downright stubbornness in their worst. A typical example is the fact that the bus from Kefalloniá to Athens may well have Lixoúri written on the front. As the station manager explained it: 'The drivers who were born in Lixoúri insist on putting Lixoúri on their buses and refuse to do anything else'. For a long time insular pride dictated a certain gruffness in dealings with outsiders, Greek or non-Greek, until the EOT broadly hinted that they should shape up and take advantage of the most easily exploitable 'development industry'.

Attitudes and facilities have probably changed, but if you want to travel around the island rather than just stay in one resort you're likely to find it a frustrating exercise without your own **transport** – distances are considerable and the bus services still abysmal (though taxis are relatively cheap for shorter trips). Bus times to smaller places are frequently only displayed in Greek, though you're on safer ground with the bigger destinations where both Greek and English timetables are shown. Mopeds and motorbikes are only to be used with discretion, as the terrain is very rough in places, and many grades certainly too steep for underpowered machines. Also bear in mind the distances between and the isolation of so many of the spots on Kefalloniá; come prepared for a bit of impromptu camping. Sleeping on the beaches seems to occur on a small scale here and there without problems.

This said, don't be completely put off as there's a little of everything on Kefalloniá, including some good beaches and a fine if pricey local wine (*Rombola*). And so far the number of tourists remains small.

Sámi and around

Most boats dock at the characterless port of **SÁMI**, built and later rebuilt near the south end of the Itháki straits, more or less on the site of ancient Sámi. This was capital of the island in Homeric times, when Kefalloniá was part of Itháki's maritime kingdom; today the administrative hierarchy is reversed, Itháki being considered the backwater. Most passengers' reaction is to take the first of two daily buses to either Argostóli or Fiskárdho (via Ássos), but before doing so it is worth taking time to visit two remarkable **caves** in the area.

The first, about 2km north of Sámi on the coast road (and then a few hundred metres inland), is **Melissáni**, a blue-tinged cavern partly submerged in brackish water. You're taken by boat (all day, small admission charge) into an inner lake-grotto; its waters, amazingly, emerge from an underground fault which leads the whole way under the island to a point near Argostóli, the *katavóthres*, where the sea gushes endlessly into a subterranean channel. Until the 1953 quake disrupted it, this current was used to drive the famous seamills at the *katavóthres*. That the water, now as then, still ends up in the cave has been shown with fluorescent tracer dye. The other cavern, **Dhrogaráti**, is more conventional (same opening hours and fee); the huge stalagmitic chamber is occasionally used for concerts due to its marvellous acoustics. To get there walk some 4km out of Sámi on the main road to Argostóli, then 500m to the right.

If you need to stay the night in the area after spending the better part of the day seeing the caves, **AYÍA EVFIMÍA**, 10km north of Sámi and astride the bus route to Fiskárdho, makes a good base. There's at least one good taverna in this pretty port town, and regular **ferry service** to Itháki and Astakós on the mainland.

Southern Kefalloniá

Heading southeast from the caves by public transport is virtually impossible. Although there's a left fork toward Póros, Skála and Markópoulo, signposted just before Dhrogaráti, the roads are primitive and hitching unpromising. The simplest approach is to take one bus to Argostóli and then another to the southeast corner of the island.

In any case **PÓROS**, a small resort with a good beach, rooms and adequate restaurants, is one of the better places to stay on Kefalloniá. At least twice a day in season there are useful **ferry links** from here to Zákinthos, and/or Killíni on the Peloponnese. Here, too, the dark plunging mass of Mt. Énos makes its closest approach to the sea. The 5000-foot peak is fairly desolate, with little more than the occasional goat for company, but the views are spectacular; on a clear day you may not quite see forever, but should at least get a glimpse of neighbouring Zákinthos.

The slopes of Énos lend a certain grandeur to the region and dictate the vagaries of the rough roads connecting the many villages nearby which are best explored by moped. Among them **SKÁLA** is an up-and-coming beach resort at the southern extreme of the island. **MARKÓPOULO**, on the asphalt road linking Póros and Argostóli, is the site of a strange phenomenon said to occur yearly around August 15 (The Assumption of the Virgin). Small harmless snakes with cross-like markings on their heads converge on the village church to be grasped rapturously to the bosoms of the faithful.

Driving westward toward Argostóli, you pass first the bay of **Loúrdha** with several sandy beaches, and then, 8km before Argostóli, the turning for **KÁSTRO**, which occupies the site of **Áyios Yióryios** (San Giorgio), the medieval Venetian capital of the island. The old town once supported a population of 15,000 but was destroyed by an earthquake in the seventeenth century; substantial ruins of its castle (open Sun.–Fri. 9.30am–3.30pm except Tues., 9am–1.30pm Sat.), churches and houses can be visited on the hill above the modern village. Byron was impressed by the view from the summit in 1823, when he lived for a few months in the village of Metaxáta some kilometres below; sadly, here as at Messolóngi, the dwelling where he stayed no longer exists.

Argostóli and Lixoúri

ARGOSTÓLI, when you finally arrive, proves to be a large and thriving town marvellously situated on a deep bay within another bay. The place was totally rebuilt after the earthquake, and rooms are expensive, factors partly redeemed by the street life and uncompromisingly Greek feel. For **rooms** try *Spiros Rouhatas*: from the waterside (I. Metaxá) take the street opposite the Lixoúri ferry quay; Spiros's rooms are above his café. The *Adherfí (Brothers) Tzivra* have a restaurant and good, clean (but more expensive) rooms down the side street opposite the petrol pumps next to the bus station. Ask the **tourist office** for rooms and you'll be given a list of names (in Greek) plus phone numbers; the EOT is just off the main square, behind the town hall. There are no E-class **hotels**, just a few D- class, and several pricier ones, some of which will have been seasonally reserved by package companies. Argostóli's not a place to show up unannounced in the middle of August – but also, fortunately, not a place that has yet been swamped by souvenir shops in the manner of Corfu.

One can **eat** well, too, starting at the excellent bakery across from the bus station and winding up at *Kalafatis* and the chicken *psitopolío* (rotisserie) next door, both of these across from the produce market a block from the bus stop. Places like these, and *Adherfi Tzivra*, serve barrelled wine, unlike their counterparts in Platía V. Metaxá. These are larger and more expensive, but apparently the *platía* is *the* place to be.

The **Historical and Cultural Museum** (open Mon.–Fri. 8.30am–2pm and 6.30–8.30pm, Sat. 10–noon) is strong on Victorian travellers' knick-knacks and photographic documentation of Argostóli covering the last century, including the 1953 earthquake and its sad aftermath. There's also an **Archaeological Museum** on the same street as the tourist office. More cultural events are provided by a yearly summer festival; consult EOT for a schedule of events.

The best of Argostóli can be enjoyed without actually staying there, as there are **rooms** at nearby **Lassí** beach and official **camping** at **Fanária** beach, plus more distant but crowded sandy bays at MAKRÍS YIALÓS and PLATÍS YIALÓS, 45 minutes' walk south or a short bus ride from Platía V. Metaxá.

To reach more remote destinations, cross the bay by ferry to **LIXOÚRI**, the base for explorations of Kefalloniá's rugged, westernmost peninsula. The town is a bit downbeat, but could be a quiet, inexpensive place to stay out of season, with some of the cheapest **rooms** being available at the *Restaurant Maria* on Kostí Palamá near the main square. **Eat** here, or opposite the quay at *Antony's* or the place next door.

Walk south out of Lixoúri and things improve fast. After about thirty minutes you reach the first of a series of reasonable sand-and-seaweed beaches. Continue along these and along tracks where necessary until eventually you reach the cape of Áyios Yióryios. Around the corner, and about ninety walking minutes from Lixoúri, is a splendid and completely undeveloped stretch of sand, opposite Vardhianí island. Getting down to it requires persistence, and climbing down the cliffs is not advisable; instead go along the dirt road for a while before striking off to the left. Be warned that there's nowhere to eat or drink along the way once you've passed the *Taverna Apolavsi* way back near the town.

From Argostóli, most people will board a bus bound for Fiskárdho in the north, and the dramatic journey is memorable even if you only turn around and come back again. There are several intermediate stops. **Ayía Kiriakí**, reached by a side road from Angónas, and **Mírtos**, signposted just past Dhivaráta, are two excellent and unexploited sand-and-pebble beaches. Mírtos, with its almost-white sand, fully justifies the long, steep trek down to it.

The main road, hacked out of the palisades on this coast, winds 8km further north to **ÁSSOS**, an unspoiled fishing village built on a narrow isthmus linking it with a castle-crowned headland. There is a good beach nearby, plus several tavernas and rooms. The slight isolation from the highway, and rudimentary direct bus service and facilities, have probably kept it from going the way of picture-postcard **FISKÁRDHO**, notable mainly for having

escaped damage in the earthquake. Today the small village of eighteenth-
and nineteenth-century houses is dominated by tourism, the yacht set is
conspicuous, and so are the boutiques. The place may have more to recommend it out of season. The *Dhendhrinos Taverna* offers value for money and
the same family owns a pension just out of town. Nearby there's reasonable-
to-good swimming off a mixture of rock beaches and reefs, and frequent *kaíki*
and **ferryboat** service to Lefkádha and Itháki.

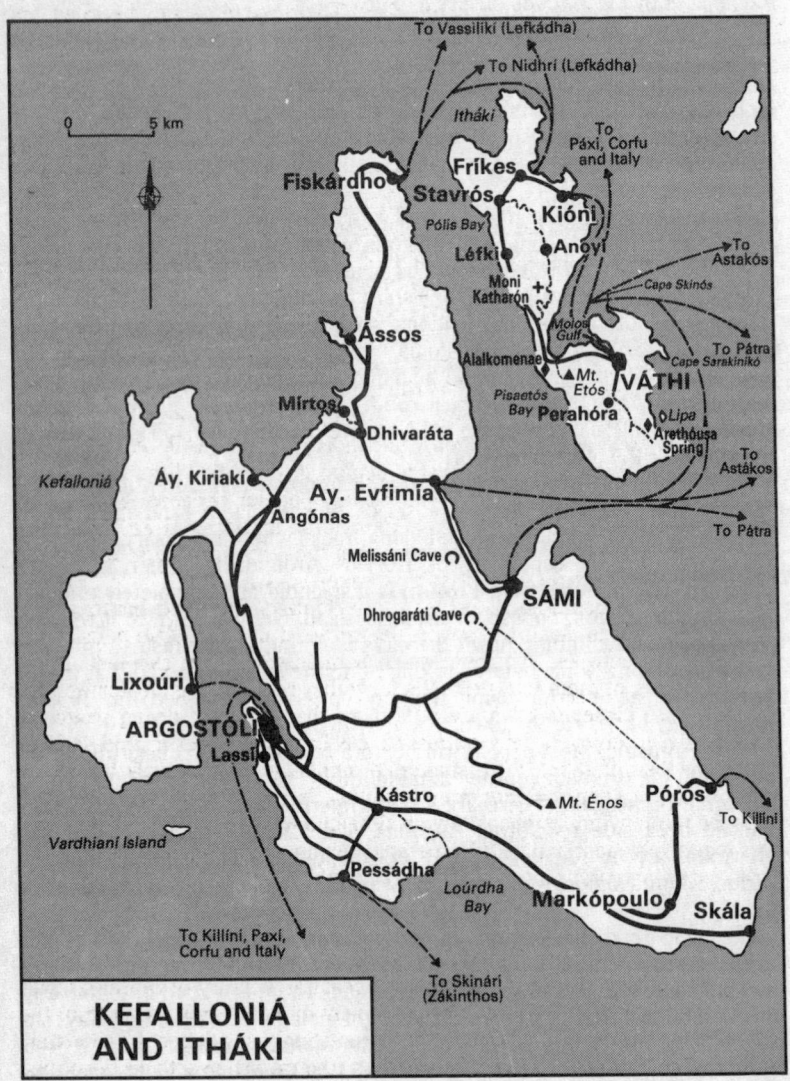

KEFALLONIÁ
AND ITHÁKI

Itháki (Ithaca)

Rugged Itháki, Odysseus's capital, has no substantial archaeological remains but it feels right: '. . . there are no tracks, nor grasslands . . . it is a rocky severe island, unsuited for horses, but not so wretched, despite its small size. It is good for goats . . .' (*The Odyssey*, Book IV, 605; Book XIII, 242). And despite the romance of its name (and its proximity to Corfu) there's still very little tourist development to spoil the place. There are few sandy beaches, but the island is good walking country, with a handful of small fishing villages and various pebbly coves to swim from.

Váthi

Ferries from Pátra, Kefalloniá, Astakós, Corfu or Italy land at the main port and capital of **VÁTHI** (**Itháki**), at the back of a deep bay which seems to close completely around it. In size it is hardly more than a village, its old tiled houses either undamaged or faithfully rebuilt after the terrible 1953 earthquake. There's a conspicuously friendly local feel. Dozens of yachts and cruise ships stop here for a couple of hours but not too many people actually stay – tourist development is for once at a standstill.

Rooms remain fairly easy to come by except during the July music festival and the August/September theatre events; they tend, however, to be inconspicuous, and are best sought by nosing around the back streets south of the ferry dock. There are but two C-class **hotels** at opposite ends of the long quay, the *Odysseus* and the *Mentor*. More choice for **food**, with seven or eight tavernas, though all seem remarkably similar in price and fare. Among the more reliable are: *Psistaria Athinaiki Gonia* (popular because it's the only grill), *To Trehandiri* (cheap casserole food in the bazaar) and *To Thiaki* and *To Kantouni* (adjacent next to the water, near the ferry dock). For dessert the island specialty is *ravani* (syrupy sponge cake).

In season the usual small boats shuttle tourists from the harbour to a series of tiny coves along the peninsula northeast of Váthi. The pebble-and-sand **beaches** between Cape Skinós and Sarakinikó Bay are excellent, many people learning of them too late as the ferry they're departing on steams past. Most of those closer to town are little more than concrete diving platforms (though Byron enjoyed daily swims off the Lazzaretto islet in mid-harbour during his visit of 1823). With some determination you can walk out to the better beaches when the *kaíki* aren't running, but as long as you have good footwear you may prefer to spend your time hiking out to a handful of nearby sites tentatively identified with Homeric locations, or to head further north on Itháki for swimming or more sedentary pastimes.

Odysseus sites

Two paths to 'Odysseus sites' are signposted from Váthi and either of them makes for an easy morning's walk across beautiful country of cypress, olives and vineyards. The **Arethoúsa spring**, ninety minutes' walk south from the port, is down to a trickle in summer but interestingly positioned. Immediately above towers a crag known locally as *Korax* (the raven), exactly as described by Homer in the meeting between Odysseus and his swineherd Eumaeus. To get there take the wide donkey track south out of Váthi, following signs marked '*Krini Arethousas*', and turn down and left on to a narrower path after an hour; a brush fire destroyed the final sign in 1987, so you have to look hard for a red dot on a stone. If you miss the turning, the main thoroughfare continues on to the **Maráthia plateau** (today called Perapigádhi after its capped well), where Eumaeus had his pigsties, but fails to reach remote **Ayíou Andhréou Bay** (accessible only by sea), where Telemachus disembarked to avoid Penelope's suitors who were lying in ambush for him on Asteris Island (the modern Dhaskalío). Below Arethoúsa more tiny paths drop down to a pair of good swimming coves in the lee of Lípa islet.

Perapigádhi shouldn't be confused with **PERAHÓRA**, the old pirate-proof inland village some 2km above the harbour. The upper settlement (one *kafenío*/taverna, one rooms outfit) makes a good return option from Arethoúsa or a trip in itself; obvious paths lead up to it from the olive-swathed plain or there's the direct track, signposted from Odhós Penelópis. The whole bulbous south end of Itháki is in fact crisscrossed with tracks of varying width and surface, and except for the utter lack of water (avoid high summer) makes delightful walking country, whether aimless or purposeful.

Of equally questionable authenticity but gratifying in any case is the **Grotto of the Nymphs** (known locally as *Marmarospíli*), a large cavern about 1km southwest of Váthi, where local knowledge suggests Odysseus, on the advice of Athena, hid the treasure which he had with him on his return to Ithaca. It was certainly known anciently and seems to have once been used as a place of worship. If its attribution is correct then the Bay of Dhexiá (just west of Váthi and below the cave) would be where the Phaecians put in to deposit the sleeping Odysseus and which he failed to recognise as his homeland.

Slightly further on, 380-metre Mt. Aetós looms over the head of the Molos Gulf. On the summit are the ruins of **ancient Alalkomenae**, excavated by Schliemann and mistakenly declared to be the 'Castle of Odysseus'; it's in fact at least 500 years too recent. The site is almost impossible to find, and the search for others is complicated by the studiously inaccurate 'Odysseus sites' maps sold on Itháki. A side road skirts the base of the mountain and crosses the narrowest point on the island to get to pebbly **Pisaetós Bay**, nearly 7km in all from Váthi but with some of the best swimming anywhere near town.

Northern Itháki

The main road out of Váthi continues across the isthmus to the northern half of Itháki, serving the villages of Léfki, Stavrós, Fríkes and Kióni. There are three evenly-spaced daily **buses**, though the north of Itháki is excellent **moped** country. Once a day a *kaíki* also visits the last two of those communities – a cheap and scenic ride used by travellers and locals alike to meet the main-line ferries in Váthi.

STAVRÓS, near the base of the arid island mountain (Korífi, or Nisíti – a re-adoption of its old Homeric name), is a fair-sized village with a couple of relatively expensive tavernas and some rooms. **Pólis Bay**, fifteen minutes' walk below, is rocky but swimmable; people camp here though there are no facilities whatsoever. Supported by a few nearby Mycenean remains, the bay is the archaeologists' current candidate for the main port of ancient Ithaca. One kilometre north of Stavrós, more Mycenaean remains have also been found amid the ruins of a Venetian fort; this, known as **Pelikáta hill**, could perhaps be the site of Odysseus's palace and capital. Speculation is supported by the fact that the place enjoys a marvellous simultaneous view over Pólis Bay and Fríkes Bay. For your own (and even better) personal vantage point over much of Itháki, make your way up the four-kilometre track to the all-but-abandoned village of EXOYÍ in the northwest corner of the island.

FRÍKES is a half-hour walk downhill beyond Stavrós, smaller than the latter but with a handful of tavernas, rooms and a pebbly strip of beach. This is where the seasonal ferries dock, to and from Lefkádha and Fiskárdho on northern Kefalloniá. The port is linked by bus to Váthi. Alternatively, walk forty minutes east to the end of the road at the village of **KIÓNI**, one of the more attractive bases on the island, though its few rooms seem to be booked en masse for the summer by British holiday companies. There's good swimming nearby, free of sea urchins, at the end of the path to Áyios Ilías chapel to the southeast. With Kióni as your starting point you can also walk or moped due south to the still inhabited **convent of Katharón**, via the inland village of **ANOYÍ**, where the proprietress of the one taverna will lend you the keys to the fourteenth-century village church and its excellent frescoes.

Zákinthos (Zante)

Zákinthos, which once exceeded Corfu itself in architectural distinction, was hit hardest by the 1953 Ionian earthquake, and the island's grand old capital was completely destroyed. In the nineteenth century Zante (as the island was known by the Venetians) boasted itself 'the Flower of the Levant'. Today, although some of its beautiful Venetian churches have been restored, it's a rather sad town and the attraction for travellers lies more in the thick vineyards, orchards and olive groves of the interior, and some excellent beaches scattered about the coast.

The island, unusually, is completely self-supporting, and you'll even see the occasional tropical plant, such as banana or bamboo, growing. Spring's the time to see the flowers, and autumn if you want to eat the produce. Any time's a good time for the local wine, served straight from the barrel and, though unbelievably cheap, putting many a bottled Greek wine to shame. At under two hours and a few hundred drachmas from Killíni, on the Peloponnesian mainland, Zákinthos cries out for some of your time.

Pessimists mutter darkly of Zákinthos being turned into another Corfu, and with upwards of 300,000 visitors a year that's understandable. Most tourists, though, are conveniently housed in one place; Laganás, on the south coast. As well as the foreign visitors, July and August also sees an influx of Greek holidaymakers, attracted by the island's proximity to the mainland. If you avoid those months, and steer clear of Laganás and the developing villages of Argási and Tsilívi, there is still a peaceful Zákinthos to be found.

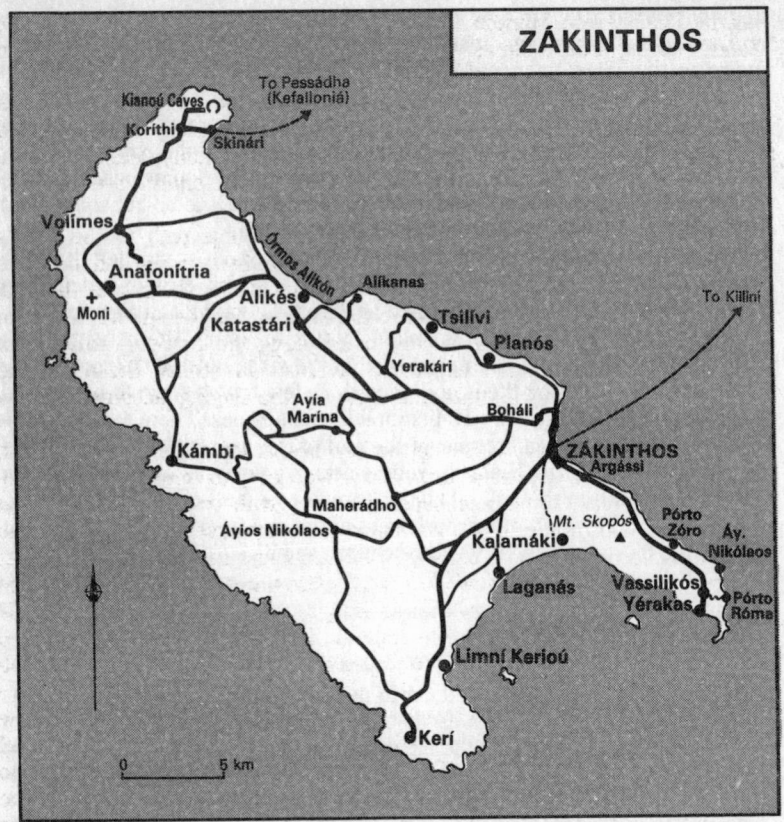

Zákinthos Town

The town, like the island, is known as both **ZÁKINTHOS** and **Zante**. This former 'Venice of the East', rebuilt on the old plan, has bravely tried to recreate some of its style, too, but reinforced concrete can only do so much.

The most tangible hints of former glory are to be found in **Platía Solómou**, the grand and spacious main square. At its north (waterside) corner stands the beautiful fifteenth-century sandstone **church of Áyios Nikólaos**, while paintings and icons salvaged from here and other island churches are displayed in the imposing **Neo-Byzantine Museum** by the town hall. The collection is exceptional, for during the seventeenth and eighteenth centuries Zante became the centre of an Ionian School of painting, given impetus by Cretan refugees unable to practice under Turkish rule. The square itself is named after the island's famous poet **Dionissios Solomos**, who was responsible for introducing demotic Greek (the spoken language of the people) as a literary idiom and who also wrote the words to the Greek national anthem. A small and charming museum is dedicated to him in the nearby Platía Ayíou Márkou (2 blocks up); worthwhile for its glimpses of Zante's strong artistic life as well as to see photographs of the town taken both before and after the earthquake.

The large church of **Áyios Dhioníssios** should be seen, because it has such a dominant influence on Zákinthos' religious life (daily 7am–noon and 4.30-9pm). It was one of the very few buildings left standing after the earthquake, and the murals which cover the interior of the church are undoubtedly impressive.

If you've an evening to fill, walk up an old cobble path to the town's massive **Venetian fortress** which has views south to Pílos and north to Messolóngi; allow for an hour's walk, the 8pm closing time, and the 100-drachma entrance charge. En route to the fortress lies the suburb village of **Boháli**, occupying a natural balcony overlooking the harbour, and with a number of popular though expensive tavernas. In season these are the venues for *kantádhes*, an Italianate style of trio-singing accompanied by guitars and mandolins.

Since most people stay closer to the beaches, at least after the first night, **accommodation** in Zákinthos town is relatively easy to come by and reasonably priced. It tends to be hotel-based, however, with 'rooms to let' signs not much in evidence. Alternatively you could entrust yourself to the people who meet most ferries and who usually have something to offer out of town as well. At the cheaper end in town, try two E-class **hotels**, the *Nea Zakynthos* at Filíkou 7 (the road going up towards Boháli) and the *Oasis* at Koutózi 58 (four streets back from the police station). The D-class hotels are a mixed bag, but include some comfortable places if you're prepared to do the footwork to check them out.

There is a recently-opened **tourist office** on Platía Solómou, next to the imposing National Bank, where you can get advice on private rooms and hotels but cannot make reservations. In short, it shouldn't be too difficult to find accommodation here – unless you foolishly turn up on August 24, the feast of St. Dionysius, when even some of the Greek visitors have to resort to sleeping outside the church for lack of a room. The **tourist police** also have information about accommodation (and bus services), and they're to be found in the police station on the front, sandwiched between Tzouláti and Merkáti Streets, near the church of Áyios Dhioníssios.

Eating out is a bit problematic in Zákinthos town, with restaurants or tavernas thin on the ground. The *Taverna Arekia* comes strongly recommended, but it's a fair walk north along the east road past the EOT beach and next to a tiny church on the left-hand side of the road. You can also work up an appetite by walking a good way in the opposite direction to the *Malavetis Restaurant* at Ayíou Dhionissíou 4 (an approach road to the church). It has a limited menu but it's good and cheap. More central is the *Kalliniko*, next to the OTE office and best value of the places on the Platía Solómou. For a snack bar try *To Posto* at Alex. Róma 59, or stick to the *psistariés* such as *Strouza*, Thesillá 22 (across from the Agrotiki Trapeza) and one halfway up the main arcaded street at Vass. Konstantínos 24.

Zákinthos wines, such as the white *Popolaro*, are among the best in the Ionians, and for dessert or a snack try *mandoláto*, the ubiquitous and delicious honey/egg/almond nougat. It's also worth investing in the very strong and pungent local *grapéria* cheese (taste before you buy). Quality handicrafts are available from the *Zakynthos Women's Cooperative*, just off the waterside.

Beyond the town a broad densely cultivated plain, covered with raisin grapes at various points in their maturation throughout the warm months, extends to the base of the sparsely inhabited mountainous western rim of Zákinthos. To get out there, and to the excellent beaches catalogued below, there is a **bus service** from the station on Odhós Filitá (one block back from the *Fina* pump on the main waterside road), but since the island topography is mostly flat, Zákinthos is an ideal place to hire a **pedal bike**, **moped** or **motorcycle**. *Motorakis* on Leofóros Dhimokratías, opposite the OTE, consistently offers the cheapest prices. If you stick to the buses, though, you'll find a frequent service to Laganás, and reasonably often to places like Tsilívi and Alikés.

Southern Zákinthos

The road heading southeast from the harbour passes under Mt. Skopós on its way to some of the finest scenery and beaches on the island. The first village, ARGÁSSI, should be speedily left behind as it has a poor beach and is quickly being developed into an overblown tourist resort. The first beach where you might be tempted to stop is **Pórto Zóro**, just to the northeast of the road.

VASSILIKÓS straddles a major crossroads and sits within easy striking distance of various good-to-excellent beaches. The village itself is still untouched by the concrete merchants and has rooms to let, with more rooms along the tracks which continue for a couple of kilometres to either ÁYIOS NIKÓLAOS, PÓRTO RÓMA or YÉRAKAS (aka 'Turtle Beach').

Campers congregate under the trees at the smallish but popular **PÓRTO RÓMA** beach; pleasant enough, but nothing more. There are rooms too, though the seasonal tavernas are oversubscribed and overpriced; for eating it's best not to come this far but to stop instead at the small restaurant on the right about 100m down the turning from Vassilikós. This one's simple but good and reasonably-priced, with a fine view south toward Cape Yérakas included.

YÉRAKAS is signposted straight ahead along a dirt road where the asphalt turns abruptly left to Pórto Róma. In the evenings, retrace your steps 200m towards Vassilikós from the Pórto Róma/Yérakas junction and eat at another good taverna that's on the left as you look towards Zákinthos town. There are **rooms** to let around here and much of the way down toward Yérakas. Camping is strictly illegal, and (in the evenings especially) you should take care to steer clear of the well-defined forbidden area where the sea turtles nest. Apropos of wildlife, be warned also that the Zante hunting season extends from late August to mid-March, and the bullets can be flying from early morning! Everywhere in the island you'll see what look like little playhouses on stilts, looking out over olive groves or over the sea; these are the hunters' blinds.

It looks from the map as if Yérakas is the end of the line, but you can in fact walk round the rocky coast quite comfortably towards Laganás. The coast here seems to be home to a number of kingfishers, whose vivid blue feathers flash brilliantly as they fish in the sea. You can continue around the coast for about an hour to an isolated beach below a huge crumbling cliff, but again this is a beach where sleeping out is prohibited.

West of **Kalamáki**, from where a different road will take you back to Zante, the beach becomes progressively muddier and more commercialised until new heights (or depths) are demonstrated at Laganás proper. This is a good juncture for a word about the **loggerhead sea turtles** (*Caretta caretta*), which lay their eggs on the beaches previously noted but also at Laganás Bay. Zákinthos has the greatest known concentration of these creatures in the whole of the Mediterranean, yet local numbers today are down to about 800, roughly half of what they were as recently as the mid-1970s. The majority of these now lay their eggs on two small beaches, whereas until recently they used the whole of the fourteen-kilometre bay. Many of the turtles are injured by motorboats, nests are destroyed by bikes ridden on the beach, and newly-hatched turtles die entangled in deckchairs and umbrellas left out at night on the sand. The Greek government has passed laws designed to protect the loggerheads, but, in addition to the thoughtlessness of visitors, some locals still prefer a beach full of bodies to a sea full of turtles.

KErÍ, in the southwest corner of the island, beyond Laganás, retains some of its pre-earthquake houses and, more curiously, natural tar pools commented on by both Pliny and Herodotus and still used for caulking boats. (There is in fact quite a lot of oil under the Ionian Sea floor and it's only a matter of time before extraction efforts are undertaken). You can also visit the lighthouse nearby and various beaches, particularly at **Limní Kerioú**, a few kilometres before, where as at Kerí you can stay, eat and drink very inexpensively in generally local company.

Northern Zákinthos

Going north or west from Zante town the road threads its way through luxuriantly fertile farmland, punctuated with tumulus-like hills. **TSILÍVI**, 4km out, is the closest beach to town worthy of the name, shallow and sandy with warm water, though the evening breeze whips up the surf. There's an official campsite nearby (*Camping Dafni*).

ORMÓS ALIKÓN, some 13km further along, is a huge gently sloping expanse of sand washed by good breakers; at its eastern end the village of **ALÍKANAS** has a single shop and one exceedingly slow taverna. Villas are block-booked here by a couple of tour companies, and though the place hasn't yet been spoiled there's an alarming amount of building going on. Nearby, however, are two excellent restaurants. *Ta Neraidha*, with a great setting on Alíkanas harbour, always has fresh, well-cooked (if expensive) fish. A friendly family runs *Mantalena*, on the road to Alikés and arguably the best (and cheapest) eatery on the island: a variety of delicious traditional dishes from the kitchen, a genuine house wine from the proprietors' own grapes, and water from a well on the premises.

Towards the northwest end of the bay **ALIKÉS** is an increasingly busy package resort with rooms, restaurants and mopeds available. There are one or two hotels, but as yet nothing like Laganás. In short there's a bit of everything in and around Alikés, including a mosquito problem aggravated by the stagnant water laughingly described as a river. However, plans are afoot to get it flowing again, and hopefully this will be accomplished without carting away too much of the fine sand that is the bay's main asset.

Also from here *kaíkia* sail to the extreme northern tip of the island, where the **Kianóu (Blue) Caves** are some of the more realistically named of the many contenders in Greece. They're terrific for snorkellers, and when you go for a dip here your skin will appear bright blue.

Inland villages

KATASTÁRI, Zákinthos's second largest community, lies just inland from Alikés and beyond it a road takes you the 18km to the cloister of **Anafonítria**. This withstood the earthquake remarkably well, and is today tenanted by a few nuns who will show you the frescoed *katholikón*, a medieval tower, and the purported cell of St. Dionysius, the patron of Zákinthos whose festivals are on August 24 and December 17.

It's in the inland villages like Katastári that you'll witness the ordinary island life, where tourism's no more than the occasional passing coach tour or moped. Stop here and you're likely to be waved over to the *kafeneío* to have an *oúzo* plonked in front of you. **AYÍA MARÍNA**, a few kilometres south, has a church with an impressive Baroque altar screen, and a belfry that's being rebuilt from the remnants left after the 1953 quake. Like most Zákinthos churches, the bells are housed in a separate tower alongside the church itself; each of these ensembles has a different design. Just above Ayía Marína is a taverna rightly boasting one of the best views on the island. From it you can see the whole of the central plain from beyond Alikés in the north to Laganás Bay in the south. There are more fine views from the hilltop village of **ÁNO YERAKÁRI**, one of three Yerakári-settlements within a few hundred yards of each other, and also one of the few interior villages offering **rooms** to let.

Closer to Laganás and Kerí, **MAHERÁDHO** has the spectacularly ornate church of Ayía Mávra, and this is the place to be if you're on the island for her feast day, which usually falls on the first weekend in July.

The road from here to the rural mountain village of **ÁYIOS NIKÓLAOS** is just about passable for a 50cc scooter, but only the sturdiest of dirtbikes – *not* a moped – can traverse some of the mountain roads through the western part of the island. As well as this you also have the local maps to contend with, some of the most inaccurate on sale in the whole of Greece, which is saying a lot. Roads rated as 'major' on these are often little more than goat tracks, or even non-existent; some of the newer and better roads are not shown, while others are placed inaccurately.

The effort of such safaris can be worth it, though, as the sunsets to be viewed from the clifftops on the rocky western coast are spectacular. **KÁMBI** is the favoured place for organised 'Sunset Trips', when the busloads turn up at one particular taverna teetering 300m above the sea on the cliff's edge; there's no denying that the 'performance' here is stunning and you might have the place almost to yourself on an 'off' night. Even higher than the taverna is an enormous cross, erected to commemorate the deaths of Greeks who were thrown off the cliffs during the 1940s. Just whose deaths are commemorated is, sadly, open to dispute. Some say Greeks killed by the Nazis, others say communists killed in the Civil War. Greek memories are long, but subject to partisan selectiveness.

travel details

There are two invaluable boats if you're island-hopping within this group. These are the *Ionis* and *Ionian Glory*, which between them sail daily or nearly so from early June to mid-September from Patras to Brindisi and vice versa, stopping at Kefalloniá (Argostóli – 3 hr.), Itháki (4½ hr.), Paxí (8½ hr.) Corfu (11½ hr.), reaching Brindisi after 18 hr. This route is not included in the island-specific details below.

CORFU (KÉRKIRA) and PAXÍ Roughly hourly (5.30am–10pm) **ferries** from Igoumenítsa to Corfu and vice versa; takes 2 hr. One regular **ferry** plus seasonal *kaíkia*, between Kérkira and Paxí (3 hr.) and a variable number between Paxí and Párga (on the mainland). Additionally, most of the ferryboats plying between Italy and Greece (especially those from Brindisi) call at Corfu (**stopover** is free) on the way; if you want to take advantage of this get it written on your ticket.
Several **flights** daily between Corfu and Athens (45 min.), London, and other British airports. Seasonal flights (twice weekly) to/from Kefalloniá and Zákinthos.

LEFKÁDHA 4 buses daily to and from Athens (7 hr.); also regularly from Préveza, Árta, Ioánnina and Thessaloníki. At least daily **boats**, in season, from Nidhrí to Meganíssi, Kefalloniá (Fiskárdho) and Itháki (Fríkes); from Vassilikí to Kefalloniá (Fiskárdho and Sámi).

ITHÁKI (ITHACA) and KEFALLONIÁ Daily **ferry** connection between Pátra, Itháki (Váthi – 5½ hr.), and Kefalloniá (Sámi). Year-round daily ferries between Astakós on the mainland and Váthi on Itháki, usually continuing to/from Ayía Evfimía on Kefalloniá. Also 3 ferries daily in season (once daily out) between Póros (southeast tip of Kefalloniá) and Killíni (Peloponnese); 2 daily in season (1 out) between Argostóli on Kefalloniá and Killíni; 2 daily in season between Pessádha (Kefalloniá) and Skinári (Zákinthos), which would be a useful link except that buses from Argostóli to Pessádha are rare, and from Skinári to Zákinthos town non-existent; closest services out of Volímes. Seasonal ferries from Kefalloniá (Fiskárdho) to Fríkes and Váthi on Itháki and Nidhrí and Vassilikí on Lefkádha.
Daily **flights** between Argostóli (Kefalloniá) and Athens (45 min.); useful seasonal link to/from Zákinthos and Corfu.

ZÁKINTHOS (ZANTE) Up to 7 ferries a day in summer (3 out of season; 1½ hr.) between Zákinthos and Killíni (Peloponnese). Difficult, twice-daily connection in summer from Skinári to Pessádha (Kefalloniá), as described above. Also expensive **speedboats** (operated by *Alkyonis*) daily in season (sporadic out) between Zákinthos and Pátra.
Daily **flights** between Athens and Zákinthos (45 min.). Twice weekly **flights** to/from Kefalloniá and Corfu; only charter flights between Zákinthos and northern Europe.

Buses from Athens
Combination, inclusive bus-ferry tickets are available from Athens to Kérkira (10 hr.), Kefalloniá (8 hr.), Itháki (7 hr.), and Zákinthos (7 hr.); all leave from the Kifissoú 100 terminal. You can also buy coordinated bus-ferry tickets from Pátra to Zákinthos.

THE HISTORICAL FRAMEWORK

This history is intended to do little more than lend some perspective to your travel, and is heavily weighted toward the era of 'Modern Greece', essentially the twentieth century. For suggestions of in-depth accounts on particular periods, see the 'Books' section.

THE NEOLITHIC, MINOAN AND MYCENEAN AGES

Other than the solitary discovery of a fossilized Neanderthal skull near Thessaloníki, the earliest **evidence of human settlement** in Greece is to be found at Néa Nikomedhía, near Véria. Here, traces of large, rectangular houses dated to around 6000 B.C. have been excavated.

It seems that people originally came to this land in the eastern Mediterranean in fits and starts, predominantly from Anatolia. These **proto-Greeks** settled in essentially peaceful farming communities, made pottery and worshipped Earth/Fertility goddesses – clay statuettes which are still found on the sites of old settlements. This simple way of life eventually disappeared, as people started to tap the land's resources for profit and to compete and exchange in trade.

MINOANS AND MYCENAEANS

Difficult as the time scale is to visualise, the years between 2000 and 1100 B.C. were a time of fluctuating regional dominance based at first upon sea power, with vast royal palaces serving as centres of administration. Particularly important were those at Knossos in Crete, and Mycenae, Tiryns and Argos in the Peloponnese. Crete monopolised the eastern Mediterranean trade routes for a time subsequently called the **Minoan Age**, with the palace at Knossos surviving two earthquakes and a massive volcanic eruption on the island of Thira (Santorini), at some undefinable point between 1500 and 1450 B.C. The most obvious examples of Minoan culture can be seen in frescoes, in jewellery, and in pottery, the distinctive red-and-white design on a dark background marking the peak period of Minoan achievement. When Knossos finally succumbed to disaster, natural or otherwise, around 1400 B.C., it was the flourishing centre of **Mycenae** that assumed the leading role, in turn giving its name to a new 'age'.

This is a period rich in enchanting **fables**: Mycenae boasts Perseus, son of Zeus, as its mythological founder, while the construction of the masonry at the palace of Tiryns is attributed to the immense and one-eyed Cyclops. One ruler of Mycenae, Atreus, is supposed to have hated his brother Thyestes so much that he offered him his own children to eat. Thyestes in turn cursed Atreus and his children, one of whom was Agamemnon, who obligingly fulfilled the terms of the curse by getting murdered by his wife Clytemnestra and her lover. The tombs of the two miscreants can still be seen at Mycenae, in the area between the Lion Gate and the main road.

Just as the fables reflected the prevalence of violence as a means of revenge, **war** had now become a fact of life, instigated and aggravated by trade rivalry and exemplified in the fortifications which were built around the various palaces. The Greece of these years was by no means a united nation; the country was divided into what were in effect a series of splinter groups, owing to the peculiar physical conditions which gave each area access to both mountains and pasture. Settlements flourished according to their proximity to the sea and the fertility of their land; most were self-sufficient, specialising in the production of particular items for trade. Olives, for example, were associated with the region of Attica of which Athens was head, minerals with Melos.

This jigsaw-puzzle of states had also to cope with and assimilate the periodic influx of 'barbarians'. The **Dorians** brought their less refined version of the Greek language from the northern borders and had a devastating influence. They infiltrated the Peloponnese, Rhodes, Kos, Knidos and part of Crete during the eleventh century B.C., flattening the palaces at Pylos, Mycenae, and Tiryns en route. By thereby paralising those vital sea powers they ushered in a so-called Dark Age, a period of enforced introversion of which nothing much is known.

Two trends or events are salient: the almost total supplanting of the mother goddesses by male deities (a process begun under the Mycenaens), and the appearance of an alphabet still recognisable by modern Greeks, which replaced the earlier so-called 'Linear A' and 'Linear B' Minoan/Mycenean scripts.

CITY STATES – AND SPARTA

The ninth century B.C. ushered in the beginnings of the Greek **city-state** (*polis*), and people busied themselves in the intrigues of government and took part in community activities of both industry and leisure. Colonial ventures increased, as did commercial dealings, and the consequent rise in the import trade was gradually to give rise to a new class of manufacturers. The city-state was the life of the people who dwelt within it and each state retained both independence and distinctive style, with the result that the sporadic attempts to unite in a league against an enemy without were always pragmatic and temporary. Features of the two most powerful centres of rivalry are summarised below.

The Dorians had concentrated their power on the Euvrotas river plain, around the town of Sparta; happily for the future of Greece they had avoided settling in Attica. The society of Sparta and its environs was based very much on Dorian military traditions, accentuated by the need to defend the exposed and fertile land on which it stood. Rather than build intricate fortifications, the people of Sparta relied upon an intrinsic military prowess; one imagines a rather stolid society, bent on the pursuit of heroic ideals and adhering staunchly to the state law. Males were subjected to military instruction between the ages of seven and thirty. Weak babies were known periodically to 'disappear'. Girls too had to perform athletic feats of sprinting and wrestling, and even dwellings were more like barracks than houses, which to some extent accounts for the lack of remains in Sparta today.

CLASSICAL ATHENS

Athens, the fulcrum of the state of Attica, was dynamic and exciting in contrast. Home of the administrations of Solon and Pericles, the dramatic talents of Sophlocles and Aristophanes, the oratory of Thucydides and Demosthenes, and the philosophical power of Socrates and Plato, it made up in cultural achievement what it lacked in Spartan virtue. Yet Sparta did not deserve all the military glory. The Athens of the sixth and fifth centuries B.C., the so-called **Classical period** in Greek history, is the Athens which played the major part in repelling the armies of the Persian king Darius at Marathon (490 B.C.) and Salamis (480 B.C.), campaigns depicted later by Aeschylus in *The Persians*.

It was also the Athenian who gave rise to a tradition of democracy, or *demokratia*, meaning literally 'control by the people', although at this stage 'the people' did not include either women or slaves. Each city-state had its *acropolis*, or high town, where religious activity was focused. In Athens there were three organs of government. The *Areopagus*, composed of the city elders, had a steadily decreasing authority and ended up dealing solely with murder cases. Then there was the Council of Five Hundred (men), elected annually by ballot to prepare the business of the Assembly and to attend to matters of urgency. The Assembly gave every free man a political voice; it had sole responsibility for law-making and provided an essential arena for the discussion of important issues. Rule was therefore by amateurs, a genuine council of citizens.

THE PELOPONNESIAN WARS

Bound up in the characteristics of the city-states were inevitable power struggles in which Athens and Sparta above all contended for supremacy – a process which eventually culminated in the Peloponnesian Wars of 431–404 B.C. It was nevertheless a period of intense creativity, particularly in Athens whose actions and pretentions were fast becoming imperial in all but name. Here the Parthenon was constructed, the tragedies of Sophocles performed, and the philosophies of Socrates and Plato expounded. Religion at this stage was polytheistic, ordering all under the aegis of Zeus. In the countryside the proliferation of names and of sanctuary finds suggests a preference for the slightly more mundane Demeter and Dionysus.

After the **Peloponnesian Wars** (nominally won by Sparta) the city-state ceased to function so effectively – partly due to drained resources and political apathy, but to a greater degree a consequence of the increasingly commercial, complex and specialised pressures on everyday life. Trade, originally spurred by the invention of coinage in the sixth century B.C., continued to expand; a revitalised Athens, for example, was exporting wine, oil and manufactured goods, getting corn in return from the Black Sea and from Egypt. The amount of time each man had to devote to the affairs of government decreased and a position in political life became a professional job rather than a natural assumption. Democracy, in a word, had changed. In philosophy there was a shift from the idealists and mystics of the sixth and fifth centuries B.C. to the cynics, stoics, and Epicureans – followers, respectively, of Diogenes, Zeno and Epicurus.

HELLENISTIC AND ROMAN GREECE

The most important factor in the decline of the city-states was meanwhile developing outside their sphere, in the kingdom of Macedonia.

MACEDONIAN EMPIRE

Based at the Macedonian capital of Pella, **Philip II** (359-336) was forging a strong military and unitary force, extending his territories into Thrace and finally establishing control over Athens and southern Greece. **Alexander the Great**, in an extraordinarily brief but glorious thirteen-year reign, extended his father's gains into Persia and Egypt and parts of modern India and Afghanistan.

This unwieldy empire splintered almost immediately upon his death in 323, to be divided into the three Macedonian dynasties of **Hellenistic Greece**: the Antigonids in Macedonia, the Seleucids in Syria and Persia, and the Ptolemies in Egypt. Each were in turn conquered and absorbed by the new Roman Empire, the Ptolemie,s under their queen Cleopatra, last of all.

ROMAN GREECE

Mainland Greece was subdued over some seventy years of campaigns, from 215-146, but **Rome**, having annexed Macedonia, allowed considerable autonomy to the old territories of the city-states. Greek remained the official language of the eastern Mediterranean and its traditions and culture co-existed fairly peacefully with that of the overlords during the next three centuries. In central Greece both Athens and Corinth remained important cities but the emphasis was shifting north – particularly to towns along the new *Via Egnatia*, a military and civil road engineered between Rome and Byzantium via the port of Brundisium (modern Brindisi).

THE BYZANTINE EMPIRE AND MEDIEVAL GREECE

This was a process given even greater impetus, and finality, by the decline of the Roman Empire and its apportioning between eastern and western emperors. In the year A.D. 330 the Emperor Constantine moved his capital to the Greek city of Byzantium and here emerged Constantinople – the 'new Rome' and spiritual and political capital of the **Byzantine Empire**. While the last western Roman emperor was deposed by barbarian Goths in 476, this oriental portion was to be the dominant Mediterranean power for some 800 years and only in 1453 did it collapse completely.

CHRISTIANITY

Christianity had been introduced under Constantine and by the end of the fourth century was the official state religion, its liturgies (still in use in the Greek Orthodox church), creed and New Testament all written in Greek. A distinction has to be drawn here, though, between Greek as a language and culture and as a concept. The Byzantine Empire styled itself Roman, or *Romios*, rather than Hellenic, and moved to eradicate all remaining symbols of pagan Greece. The Delphic Oracle was forcibly closed, and the Olympic Games discontinued, at the end of the fourth century.

The seventh century saw **Constantinople** besieged by Persians, and later Arabs, but the Empire survived, losing only Egypt, the least 'Greek' of its territories. From the ninth to the early eleventh centuries it enjoyed an archetypal 'golden age', both in culture (the church of Óssios Loukás is among the architectual achievements) and in confidence and security. Tied up in the Orthodox Byzantine faith was a sense of spiritual superiority and in Constantinople the emperors saw a 'new Jerusalem' for their 'chosen people'. It was the beginning of a diplomatic and ecclesiastical conflict with the west which was to have disastrous consequences over the next five centuries. In the meantime the eastern and western patriarchs mutually excommunicated each other.

From the seventh through the eleventh centuries **Byzantine Greece**, certainly in the south, became something of a provincial backwater. Administration was absurdly top-heavy and imperial taxation led to semi-autonomous provinces ruled by military generals whose lands were usually acquired from bankrupted peasants. This alienation generated among the poor provided a force for change, with a floating populace ready to turn towards or cooperate with the empire's enemies if terms were an improvement.

Waves of Slavic raiders certainly needed no encouragement to sweep down from the north Balkans throughout this period. At the same time other tribal groups moved down more peaceably from central Europe and were absorbed with little difficulty. According to one theory, the nomadic Vlachs from Romania eventually settled in the Píndhos Mountains and later, from the thirteenth century on, immigrants from Albania most certainly repopulated the islands of Spétses, Ídhra, Ándhros and Évvia as well as parts of Attica.

THE CRUSADES: FRANKISH AND VENETIAN RULE

From the early years of the eleventh century, less welcome and assimilable western forces began to appear. The Normans landed first at Corfu in 1085, and returned again to the mainland, with Papal sanction, a decade later on their way to liberate Jerusalem. Nothing of this, though, was to compare with the **Fourth Crusade** of 1204, when Venetians, Franks and Germans turned their armies directly on Byzantium and sacked and occupied Constantinople. These Latin princes and their followers, intent on new lands and kingdoms, settled in to divide up the best part of the Empire. All of Byzantium that remained were four small peripheral kingdoms or despotates: the most powerful in Nikaea in Asia Minor, less significant ones at Trebizond on the Black Sea, and (in present-day Greece) in Epirus and around Mystra in the Peloponnese.

There followed two extraordinarily involved centuries of manipulation and struggle between Franks, Venetians, Genoese, Catalans and Turks. Byzantine Nikaea recovered the city of Constantinople in 1261 but little of its former territory and power. Instead the focus of Byzantium shifted to the Morea, or Peloponnese, where the autonomous Despotate of **Mystra** eventually succeeded in wresting most of the peninsula from Frankish hands. At the same time it underwent an intense cultural renaissance, strongly evoked in the churches and the shells of the cities remaining today at Mystra, Monemvassía and Yeráki.

TURKISH OCCUPATION

Within a generation of driving out the Franks, the Byzantine Greeks faced a much stronger threat in the expanding empire of the Ottoman **Turks**. Torn apart by internal struggles between their own ruling dynasties, the Palaeologi and Cantacuzenes, and unaided by the Catholic west, they were to prove no match. On Tuesday 29 May 1453, a date still solemnly commemorated by the Orthodox church, Constantinople fell to besieging Muslim Turks. Mystra was to follow within seven years, and Trebizond within nine, by which time virtually all of the old Byzantine Empire lay under Ottoman domination. Only the

Ionian islands and the Cyclades, which remained Venetian, and a few scattered and remote enclaves – like the Máni in the Peloponnese, Sfakiá in Crete and Soúli in Epirus – were able to resist the Turkish advance.

OTTOMAN RULE

Under the 'Dark Ages' of **Ottoman rule** the lands of present-day Greece passed into rural provincialism, taking refuge in the self-protective mode of village life which has only recently been disrupted. Taxes and discipline, sporadically backed up by the genocide of dissenting communities, were inflicted from the Turkish Porte but estates passed into the hands of local chieftains who often had considerable independence. Greek identity meanwhile was preserved through the offices of the Orthodox church which, despite instances of enforced conversion, the Sultans allowed to continue. The monasteries, often secretly, organised schools and became the trustees of Byzantine culture, though this had gone into stagnation after the fall of Constantinople and Mystra, whose scholars and artists emigrated west, adding impetus to the Renaissance.

As Ottoman administration became more and more decentralised and inefficient, individual Greeks rose to local positions of considerable influence and a number of communities achieved a degree of autonomy. Ambelákia village in Thessaly, for example, established an industrial co-operative system to export dyed cloth to Europe, paying only direct taxes to the Sultan. And on the Albanian repopulated islands of the Argo-Saronic, a Greek merchant fleet came into being in the eighteenth century, permitted to trade throughout the Mediterranean. Greeks, too, were becoming organised overseas in the sizeable expatriate colonies of central Europe, which often had affiliations with the semi-autonomous village clusters of Zagória and Pílion.

THE STRUGGLE FOR INDEPENDENCE

Opposition to Turkish rule was becoming widespread, exemplified most obviously by the *Klephts* (brigands) of the mountains. It was not until the nineteenth century, however, that a resistance movement could muster sufficient support and firepower to prove a real challenge to the Turks. In 1770 a Russian-backed uprising had been easily and brutally suppressed but fifty years later the position was different. In Epirus the Turks were over-extended, subduing Ali Pasha's expansionist campaigns; the French revolution had given impetus to the confidence of 'freedom movements'; and the Greek fighters were given financial and ideological underpinnings by the *Filikí Etería*, or 'Friendly Society', a secret political action group recruited principally among the exiled merchants and intellectuals of central Europe. The coalition of *Klephts* and theorists launched their insurrection at the monastery of Ayia Lávra near Peloponnesian Kalávrita, where on 25 March 1821 the Greek banner was first raised openly.

THE WAR OF INDEPENDENCE

To describe in detail the course of the **War of Independence** would be to provoke unnecessary confusion, since much of the rebellion consisted of local and fragmentary guerilla campaigns. What *is* important to understand is that Greeks, though fighting for liberation from the Turks, were not fighting as and for a nation. Motives differed enormously: landowners assumed their role was to lead and sought to retain and reinforce their traditional privileges, while the peasantry saw the struggle as a means towards land redistribution.

Outside Greece, prestige and publicity for the insurrection was promoted by the arrival of around a thousand European **Philhellenes**, almost half of them German, but the most important **Lord Byron**, who died at Messolóngi in April 1824. Though it was the Greek guerilla leaders, above all Theodoros **Kolokotronis**, 'the old man of the Morea', who brought about the most significant military victories of the war, the death of Byron had an immensely important effect on public opinion in the west.

Aid for the Greek struggle had come neither from Orthodox Russia, nor from the western powers of France and Britain, ravaged by the Napoleonic Wars. But by 1827 these three powers had finally agreed to seek autonomy for certain parts of Greece and sent a combined fleet to put pressure on the Sultan's Egyptian army, then ransacking and massacring in the Peloponnese. Events took over and an accidental naval battle in **Navarino Bay** resulted in the destruction of almost the entire Turkish-Egyptian fleet. The following spring Russia itself declared war on the Turks and the Sultan was forced to accept the existence of an autonomous Greece.

In 1830 Greek independence was confirmed by the western powers and **borders** were drawn. These included just 800,000 of the 6 million Greeks living within the Ottoman Empire, and its lands were for the most part the poorest of the Classical and Byzantine territories: Attica, the Peloponnese and the islands of the Argo-Saronic and Cyclades.

THE EMERGING STATE

Modern Greece began as a republic; its first president, Capodistria, concentrated his efforts on building a viable central authority and government in the face of diverse protagonists from the independence struggle. Almost inevitably he was assassinated – in 1831, by two chieftains from the Máni – and perhaps equally inevitably the great western powers stepped in. They created a monarchy, gave limited aid, and set on the throne a Bavarian prince, **Otho**.

The new king proved an autocratic and insensitive ruler, bringing in fellow Germans to fill official posts and ignoring all claims by the landless peasantry for redistribution of the old estates. In 1862 he was eventually forced from the country by a popular revolt, and the Europeans produced a new prince, this time from Denmark, with Britain ceding the Ionian islands to bolster support. **George I**, in fact, proved very much more capable: he built the first railways and roads, introduced land reform in the Peloponnese, and oversaw the first expansion of the Greek borders.

THE MEGÁLI IDHÉA AND THE BALKAN WARS

From the very beginning the single and unquestioned motive force of Greek foreign policy was the **Megáli Idhéa** (Great Idea) of liberating Greek populations outside the country and incorporating the old territory of Byzantium into the kingdom. In 1878 the rich agricultural plains of Thessaly, along with southern Epirus, were ceded to Greece. Less illustriously, the Greeks failed in 1897 to achieve *énosis* (union) with

Crete by attacking Turkish forces on the mainland, and in the process virtually bankrupted the state.

It was from Crete, however, that the most distinguished statesman of modern Greece emerged. **Eleftherios Venizelos**, having led a civilian campaign for his island's liberation, was in 1910 elected as Prime Minister. Two years later he organised an alliance of Balkan powers to fight the two **Balkan Wars** (1912–13), campaigns that saw the Turks virtually driven from Europe. With Greek borders extended to include Crete, the northeast Aegean, nothern Thessaly, central Epirus and parts of Macedonia, the *Megáli Idhéa* was approaching reality. At the same time Venizelos proved himself a shrewd manipulator of domestic Greek public opinion by revising the constitution and introducing a series of liberal social reforms.

Division, however, was to appear with the outbreak of the **First World War**. Venizelos urged Greek entry on the British side, seeing in the conflict possibilities for the 'liberation' of Greeks in Thrace and Asia Minor; the new king, Constantine I, married to a sister of the Kaiser, imposed a policy of neutrality. Eventually Venizelos set up a revolutionary government in Thessaloníki, and in 1917 Greek troops entered the war to join in the Macedonian campaign. On its completion and the capitulation of Bulgaria and Ottoman Turkey, they occupied Thrace, and Venizelos presented at Versailles demands for the predominantly Greek region of Smyrna on the coast of Asia Minor.

It was the beginning of one of the most disastrous episodes in modern Greek history. Venizelos was authorised to move forces into Smyrna in 1919, but by then allied support had evaporated and in Turkey itself a new nationalist movement was taking power under Mustafa Kemal, or Ataturk as he came to be known. In 1920 Venizelos lost the elections and monarchist factions took over, their aspirations unmitigated by the Cretan's skill in foreign diplomacy. Greek forces were ordered to advance upon Ankara in an attempt to bring Ataturk to terms. The '**Anatolian Campaign**' was swiftly brought to a close as Turkish troops forced the Greeks back to the coast and a hurried evacuation from Smyrna. As they left the Turks moved in and systematically massacred the city's Armenian and most of its Greek populations.

THE EXCHANGE OF POPULATIONS

There was now no alternative but for Greece to accept Ataturk's own terms, formalised by the Treaty of Lausanne in 1923, which ordered the **exchange of religious minorities** in each country. Turkey was to accept 390,000 Muslims resident on Greek soil. Greece, mobilised almost continuously for the last decade and with a population of under 5 million, was faced with the resettlement of over 1,300,000 Christian refugees. The *Megáli Idhéa* had ceased to be a viable blueprint.

Changes, inevitably, were intense and far-reaching. The great agricultural estates of Thessaly were finally redistributed, both to Greek tenants and refugee farmers, and huge shanty towns grew into new quarters around Athens, Pireás and other cities, a spur to the country's almost non-existent industry. Politically, too, reaction was swift. A group of army officers moved in after the retreat from Smyrna, 'invited' King Constantine to abdicate and executed five of his ministers. Democracy was nominally restored with the proclamation of a republic, but for much of the next decade changes in government were brought about by factions within the armed forces. Meanwhile, among the urban refugee population, unions were being formed and the Greek Communist Party (KKE) was established. By 1936 it had enough democratic support to hold the balance in parliament, and would have done so had not the army and king decided otherwise.

King George II had been restored by a plebiscite held – and almost certainly manipulated – the previous year, and so presided over an increasingly factionalised parliament. In April 1936 he appointed as prime minister **General John Metaxas**, despite the latter's support from only six elected deputies. Immediately a series of KKE-organised strikes broke out and the king, ignoring attempts to form a broad liberal coalition, dissolved parliament without setting a date for new elections. It was a blatantly unconstitutional move and opened the way for five years of ruthless and at times absurd dictatorship.

Metaxas averted a general strike with military force and proceeded to set up a state based on fascist models of the age. Left-wing and trade union opponents were imprisoned or forced into exile, a state youth movement and secret police set up, and rigid censorship,

extending even to passages of Thucydides, imposed. It was, however, at least a Greek dictatorship, and though Metaxas was sympathetic to Nazi organisation he completely opposed German or Italian domination.

WORLD WAR II AND THE CIVIL WAR

The Italians had unsuccessfully tried to provoke the Greeks by surreptitiously torpedoing the Greek cruiser *Elli* in Tínos harbour on August 15, 1940, but when Mussolini occupied Albania and sent, on October 28, 1940, an ultimatum demanding passage for his troops through Greece, Metaxas responded to the Italian foreign minister with the apocryphal one-word answer *'óhi'* (no). (In fact, his response, in the mutually understood French, was *'C'est la guerre'.*) The date marked the entry of Greece into the **Second World War**, and the gesture is still celebrated as a national holiday.

OCCUPATION AND RESISTANCE

Well prepared, and fighting as a nation in a sudden unity of crisis, the Greeks drove Italian forces from the country and in the operation took control of the long-coveted and predominantly Greek north of Epirus. But the Greek army foolishly frittered away their strength in the snowy mountains of northern Epirus rather than consolidate their gains or defend the Macedonian frontier, and co-ordination with the British never materialised. In April of the following year Nazi mechanised columns swept through Yugoslvia and across the Greek mainland, effectively neutralising the only Axis defeat to date, and by the end of May 1941 airborne and seaborne German invasion forces had completed the occupation of Crete and the other islands.

Metaxas had died before their arrival, but King George and his new self-appointed ministers fled into exile in Cairo; few Greeks, of any political persuasion, were sad to see them go.

The joint **Italian-German-Bulgarian occupation** of Greece was among the bitterest experiences of the European war. Nearly half a million civilians starved to death as all available food was requisitioned to feed occupying armies, and entire villages throughout the mainland and especially Crete were burned and slaughtered at the least suspicion of resistance activity. In the north the Bulgarians desecrated archaeological sites and churches, in their bid to annex 'Slavic' Macedonia.

Primarily in the north, too, the Nazis supervised the deportation to concentration camps of virtually the entire **Greek-Jewish population**. This was at the time a significant community, with Thessaloníki (where ex-UN president and Austrian premier Kurt Waldheim worked for Nazi intelligence) containing the largest Jewish population of any European city.

With a quisling government in Athens – and an unpopular, discredited Royalist group in Cairo – the focus of Greek political and military action over the next four years passed largely to the **EAM**, or National Liberation Front. By 1943 it was in virtual control of most areas of the country, working with the British on tactical operations, with its own army (**ELAS**), navy, and both civil and secret police forces. On the whole it commanded popular support throughout Greece, and offered a framework for the resumption of post-war government.

However, most of its membership was communist, and **Churchill** was determined to reinstate King George II. Even with two years of the war to run it became obvious that there could be no peaceable post-liberation regime other than an EAM-dominated republic. Accordingly in August 1943 representatives from each of the main resistance movements – including two non-communist groups – flew from a makeshift airstrip in Thessaly to ask for guarantees from the 'government' in Cairo that the king would not return unless a plebiscite had first voted in his favour. Neither the Greek nor British authorities would consider the proposal and the one possibility of averting civil war was lost.

EAM returned divided, as perhaps had been the British intention, and a conflict broke out between those who favoured taking peaceful control of any government imposed after liberation, and the hard-line Stalinist ideologues, who believed such a situation should not be allowed to develop. In October 1943, with fears of an imminent British landing force and takeover, ELAS launched a full-scale attack upon its Greek rivals; by the following February, when a ceasefire was arranged, they had wiped out all but the EDES, a right-wing grouping suspected of collaboration with the Germans. At the same time other forces were at work, with both the British and Americans infiltrating units into Greece in order to prevent the establishment of communist government when the Germans began withdrawing their forces.

CIVIL WAR

In fact, as the Germans began to leave in October 1944, most of the EAM leadership agreed to join a British-sponsored 'official' interim government. It quickly proved an error, however, for with 90 percent of the countryside under their control the communists were given only one-third representation, the king showed no sign of renouncing his claims, and in November Allied forces ordered ELAS to disarm. On December 3 all facades were dropped; the police fired on a communist demonstration in Athens and fighting broke out between ELAS and **British troops**, in the so-called **Dhekemvriáná** battle of Athens.

A truce of sorts was negotiated the following spring but the agreement reached at Varkiza was never implemented. The army, police and civil service remained in right-wing hands and while collaborationists were often allowed to retain their positions, left-wing sympathisers, many of whom were not communists, were systematically excluded. The elections of 1946 were won by the right-wing parties, followed by a plebiscite in favour of the king's return. By 1947 guerrilla activity had again reached the scale of a full civil war, and King George had died and been succeeded by his brother Paul (with his consort Frederika). The Americans had now taken over the British role, and putting into action the cold war **Truman doctrine** had taken virtual control of Greece, their first significant post-war experiment in anti-communist intervention. Massive economic and military aid was given to a client Greek government, with a prime minister whose documents had to be countersigned by the American Mission in order to become valid. In the mountains U.S. 'military advisers' supervised campaigns against ELAS and there were mass arrests, court-martials, and imprisonments. Over 3000 executions were recorded, including a number of Jehovah's Witnesses, 'a sect proved to be under communist domination', according to U.S. Ambassador Grady.

By the autumn of 1949, with the Yugoslav-Greek border closed after Tito's rift with Stalin, the last ELAS guerillas finally admitted defeat, retreating into Albania from their last strongholds on Mt. Grámmos. Atrocities had been committed on both sides, including, from the left, widescale destruction of monasteries, and the dubious evacuation of children from 'combat areas' chronicled in Nicholas Gage's (virulently anti-communist) book *Eleni*. Undoubtedly, such errors, as well as the hopelessness of fighting an American-backed army, lost ELAS much support.

RECONSTRUCTION AMERICAN-STYLE: 1950 – 67

It was a demoralised, shattered country which emerged into the Western political orbit of the 1950s. It was also perforce American-dominated, enlisted into the Korean War in 1950 and NATO the following year. The U.S. Embassy foisted upon Greece a winner-take-all electoral system, which was to ensure victory for the right over the next 12 years. All leftist activity was banned; those individuals who were not herded into political 're-education' camps or dispatched by firing squads, legal or vigilante, went into exile throughout Eastern Europe, to return only in the 1980s.

The American-backed party, which won a decisive victory in 1952, was General Papagos's right-wing 'Greek Rally' taken over after his death (and to some extent liberalised) by **Constantine Karamanlis**. Stability of a kind was certainly established in the 1950s and some economic advances registered, particularly after the revival of Greece's traditional German markets, but it was also a decade which saw wholesale depopulation of the villages as migrants sought work in Australia and western Europe, or the larger Greek cities.

The main crisis in foreign policy throughout this period was **Cyprus**, scene of a long terrorist campaign against British rule, and the sporadic threat of a new Greek-Turkish war. A temporary and unworkable solution was forced on the island by Britain in 1960, granting independence without the possibility of self-determination and union with Greece. Much of the traditional Greek-British goodwill was destroyed by the issue, with Britain seen to be acting with regard only for its two military bases, over which it still retains sovereignty.

By 1961, unemployment, the Cyprus issue and the imposition of U.S. nuclear bases on Greek soil were changing the whole political climate, and when Karamanlis was again elected there was strong suspicion of a fraud arranged by the king and army. Strikes became frequent in industry and even agriculture, and King Paul and autocratic, fascist-inclined Queen Frederika were openly attacked in parliament and at protest demonstrations. The far right began to grow uneasy about 'communist resurgence' and, losing confidence in their own electoral influence, arranged the assassination of left-wing deputy Grigoris Lambrakis in Thessaloníki in May 1963. (The assassination, and its subsequent cover-up, is the subject of Vassilis Vassilikos's thriller *Z*, filmed by Costa-Gavras.) It was against this volatile background that Karamanlis resigned, lost the subsequent elections and left the country.

The new government – the first controlled from outside the Greek right since 1935 – was formed by **George Papandreou's** Centre Union Party, and had a decisive majority of nearly fifty seats. It was to last, however, for under two years as conservative forces rallied to thwart its progress. In this the two chief protagonists were the army officers and the new king, 23-year-old **Constantine II**, who was their constitutional Commander-in-Chief.

Since power in Greece has always depended on a co-operative military as well as a network of political appointees, Papandreou's most urgent task in order to govern securely and effectively was to reform the armed forces. His first Minister of Defence proved incapable of the task and, while he was investigating the right-wing plot which was thought to have rigged the 1961 election, 'evidence' was produced of a leftist conspiracy connected with Papandreou's son Andreas (himself a minister in the government). The allegations grew to a crisis and George Papandreou decided to assume the defence portfolio himself, a move which the king refused to give the necessary sanction. Papandreou resigned in order to gain approval at the polls but the king would not order fresh elections, instead persuading members of the Centre Union – chief among them Constantine Mitsotakis, the current conservative party leader – to defect and organise a coalition government. Punctuated by strikes, resignations and mass demonstrations, this lasted for a year and a half until new elections were eventually set for May 28, 1967. They failed to take place.

It was a foregone conclusion that Papandreou's party, having moved toward the left in the course of events, would win massive popular support against the discredited coalition partners. And it was equally certain that there would be some sort of antidemocratic action to try and prevent them f-rom taking power. Constantine was said to have briefed senior generals for a *a coup d'état*, to take place ten days before the elections, but was caught by surprise, as was nearly everyone else, by the **coup of April 21, 1967**, staged by a group of 'unknown' colonels. It was, in the words of Andreas Papandreou, 'the first successful CIA military putsch on the European continent'.

The **colonels' junta**, in control of the means of power, was sworn in by King Constantine and survived a half-hearted counter coup which he attempted to organise. It was an overtly fascist regime, absurdly styling itself as the true Revival of Greek Orthodoxy against western 'corrupting influences', though in reality its ideaology was nothing more than warmed-over dogma from the Metaxas era.

All political activity was banned, trade unions were forbidden to recruit or meet, the press was so heavily censored that many papers stopped printing, and thousands of 'communists' were arrested, imprisoned, and often tortured. Among them were both Papandreous, the composer Mikis Theodorakis (reported as 'unfit to stand trial' after three months' custody) and Amalia Fleming (widow of Alexander). The best known Greek actress, Melina Mercouri, was stripped of her citizenship in absentia and thousands of prominent Greeks joined her in exile. Culturally, the colonels put an end to popular music (closing down most of the authentic Pláka clubs) and inflicted ludicrous censorship on literature and the theatre, including (as under Metaxas) a ban on production of the Classical tragedies.

The colonels lasted for seven years, opposed (especially after the first year) by the majority of the Greek people, excluded from the European community, but propped up and given massive aid by U.S. presidents Lyndon Johnson and Nixon. To the Americans and the CIA the junta's Greece was not an unsuitable client state; human rights considerations were unimportant (then as now), orders were placed for sophisticated military technology, and foreign investment on terms highly unfavourable to Greece was open to multinational corporations. It was a fairly routine scenario for the exploitation of an underdeveloped nation.

Opposition from the beginning was voiced by exiled Greeks in London, the United States and western Europe, but only in 1973 did demonstrations break out openly in Greece. On 17 November the students of Athens **Polytechnic** began an occupation of their buildings. The ruling clique lost its nerve; armoured vehicles stormed the Polytechnic gates and a still-undetermined number of youths were killed. Martial law was tightened and junta chief Colonel Papadopoulos was replaced by the even more noxious and reactionary General Ioannides, head of the secret police.

The end of the ordeal, however, came within a year as the dictatorship embarked on a disastrous political adventure in **Cyprus**. By attempting to topple the Makarios government and impose *énosis* (union) on the island, they provoked a Turkish invasion and occupation of 40 percent of the Cypriot territory. The army finally mutinied and Karamanlis was invited to return from Paris to take office. He negotiated a ceasefire (but no solution) in Cyprus, withdrew temporarily from NATO, and warned that U.S. bases would have to be removed except where they specifically served Greek interest. In November 1974 he was rewarded by a sizeable majority in elections, with a centrist and socialist opposition – the latter PASOK (Panhellenic Socialist Party), a party newly formed and led by Andreas Papandreou.

The government of the majority *Néa Dhimokratía* (New Democracy) party was in every sense a safe conservative option. But to **Karamanlis's** enduring credit it oversaw an effective and firm return to democratic stability, even legitimising the KKE (Communist Party) for the first time in its history. A **refer-**

endum on the monarchy was held – in which 59 percent of Greeks rejected the return of Constantine – and Karamanlis instituted in its place a French-style presidency, which post he himself occupied from 1980 to 1985. Economically there were limited advances although these were more than offset by inflationary defence spending (the result of renewed tension with Turkey), hastily negotiated entrance into the EEC, and the decision to let the drachma float after decades of its being artificially fixed at 30 to the U.S. dollar.

More important, Karamanlis failed to deliver on vital reforms in bureaucracy, social welfare and education; and though the worst figures of the junta were brought to trial the ordinary faces of Greek political life and administration were little changed. By 1981 inflation was hovering around 25 percent, and it was estimated that tax evasion was depriving the state of one-third of its annual budget. In foreign policy the U.S. bases had remained and it was felt that Greece, back in NATO, was still acting as hardly more than an American satellite. The traditional right was demonstrably inadequate to the task at hand.

PASOK: 1981–89

Change – **allayí** – was the watchword of the election campaign which swept Andreas Papandreou's Panhellenic Socialist Movement, better known by the acronym **PASOK**, to power on October 18, 1981. The victory meant a chance for Papandreou to form the first socialist government in Greek history and break a near fifty-year monopoly of authoritarian right-wing rule. With so much at stake the campaign had been passionate even by Greek standards, and PASOK's victory was greeted with euphoria both by the generation whose political voice had been silenced by defeat in the civil war and by a large proportion of the young.

Hopes ran dangerously and naively high. PASOK won 174 of the 300 parliamentary seats and their grudging Communist allies in the KKE captured another 13, one of which was the composer Mikis Theodorakis's. Néa Dhimokratía moved into unaccustomed opposition with 113 deputies. There appeared to be no obstacle to the implementation of a radical **socialist programme**: devolution of power to

local authorities, the socialisation of industry (though it was never clear how this was to be different from nationalisation), improvement of the social services, a purge of bureaucratic inefficiency and malpractice, the end of bribery and corruption as a way of life, an independent and dignified foreign policy following expulsion of U.S. bases, and withdrawal from NATO and the European Community. There was going to be a change of style too, to openness and dialogue. Where Greek political parties had traditionally been the personal followings of charismatic leaders, PASOK was to be a party of ideology and principle, dependent on no single individual member.

The new era started with a bang. The wartime resistance was officially recognised; hitherto, incredibly, they hadn't been allowed to take part in any victory celebrations, wreath-layings or other ceremonies. Peasant women were granted pensions for the first time – 3000 drachmas a month, the same as their outraged husbands – and wages were indexed to the cost of living. Civil marriage was introduced, family law reformed in favour of wives and mothers, and equal rights legislation was put on the statute book. These popular **reformist moves** seemed to mark a total break with the past.

The atmosphere had indeed changed. Greeks no longer lowered their voices to discuss politics in public places or wrapped their opposition newspaper in the respectably conservative *Kathimerini*. At first there were real fears that the climate would be too much for the military and they would once again intervene to choke off a dangerous experiment in democracy, especially when Papandreou assumed the defence portfolio himself in a move strongly reminiscent of his father's attempt to remove King Constantine's appointee in 1965. But Andreas went out of his way to soothe **military susceptibilities**, increasing their salaries, buying new weaponry, and being superfastidious in his attendance at military functions.

THE END OF THE HONEYMOON . . .

Nothing if not a populist, Papandreou promised a bonanza he must have known, as a skilled and experienced economist, he could not deliver. He has as a result pleased nobody on the economic front.

He cannot fairly be blamed – though he is in some reactionary quarters – for the effects of world recession nor for the lack of investment, low productivity, deficiency in managerial and labour skills and other chronic problems besetting the Greek economy. On the other hand, he certainly aggravated the situation in the early days of his first government by allowing his supporters to indulge in violently anti-capitalist rhetoric, which finally closed the purses of any Greek capitalist not already terrified at the mere name of socialism. He also encouraged the prosecution and humiliation of the Tsatsos family, owners of one of Greece's few modern and profitable businesses – cement, in this case – for the illegal export of capital, something of which every Greek with any savings is guilty, including members of this and past governments. And these were **cheap victories**; they were not backed by any programme of nationalisation or public investment. The only nationalisations/socialisations were of hopelessly lame-duck companies, which any sensible capitalist would have been glad to see the back of.

Against this background of a sluggish economy burdened with the additional charges of (marginally) improved social benefits and wage indexing, Papandreou's government had to cope with the effects of world **recession**, which always hit Greece with a delayed effect compared with its more advanced European partners. Shipping, the country's main foreign-currency earner, was devastated, as one glance at the rusting hulks in the bay of Elefsína reveals. Remittances from emigré workers fell off as they joined the lines of the unemployed in their host countries, and tourism receipts diminished under the dual impact of recession and Reagan's warning to Americans to stay away from insecure Athens airport. With huge quantities of imported goods continuing to be sucked into the country in the absence of domestic production, the **foreign debt** topped £10 billion in 1986, with inflation at 25 percent and the balance of payments deficit approaching £1 billion. In addition Greece began to experience the social strains of **unemployment** for the first time. Not that it didn't exist before, as opponents of the government would have one believe; rather it was concealed as under-employment – as well as by the absence of statistics – by the family and by the rural structure of the economy.

The result of all this has been that Papandreou has had to eat his words. The spending spree, joy at the defeat of the right, the popularity of his Greece-for-the-Greeks foreign policy, and some much needed reforms saw him through his first period of office and into a **second term**, with an electoral victory in June 1985 scarcely less triumphant than the first. The complacent and, frankly, dishonest slogan was 'Vote PASOK for Even Better Days'. By October he had imposed a two-year wage freeze and import restrictions, abolished the wage-indexing scheme and devalued the drachma by 15 percent. His fat was pulled out of the fire by none other than that former bogeyman, the **European Community**, which offered a huge two-part loan on condition that this IMF-style **austerity programme** was maintained.

The political fallout of such a classic right-wing deflation, accompanied by shameless soliciting for foreign investment – 'We don't believe in outmoded ideologies', he simpered seductively at a recent conference (i.e. 'Don't worry. We're not socialists') – has been the alienation of the Communists and most of PASOK's own political constituency. Always autocratic, **Papandreou's response to dissent** has been to fire recalcitrant trade union leaders and expel some 300 members of his own party. Assailed by strikes, the government appears to have lost direction completely. In local elections in October 1986 it lost a lot of ground to Néa Dhimokratía, including the mayoralties of the three major cities, Athens, Thessaloníki and Pátra. Papandreou assured the nation that he had taken the message to heart. All that followed was a minor government reshuffle and a panicky attempt to undo the ill-feeling caused by an incredible freeing of rent controls at a time when all wage-earners were feeling the pinch badly. Early in 1987 he went further and sacked all the remaining PASOK veterans in his cabinet, including his son, though it is said, probably correctly, that this was a palliative to public opinion. The new cabinet was so un-Socialist that even the right-wing press called it 'centrist'.

Similar about-faces have taken place in **foreign policy**. The initial anti-U.S., anti-

NATO and anti-E.C. rhetoric was immensely popular, and understandable for a people who have been shamelessly bullied by bigger powers for the past 150 years. There was some high-profile nose-thumbing, like refusing to join EC partners in condeming Jaruzelski's Polish regime, or the Soviet downing of a Korean airliner, or Syrian involvement in terrorist bomb-planting. There were some forgettable embarrassments, too, like suggesting Gaddafi's Libya provided a suitable model for alternative Socialist development and the Mitterand-Gaddafi-Papandreou 'summit' in Crete, which an infuriated Mitterand felt he had been inveigled into on false pretences.

Much was made of a strategic opening to the Arab world. Yasser Arafat, for example, was the first 'head of state' to be received in Athens under the PASOK government. Given Greece's geographical position and historical ties, it was an imaginative and appropriate policy. But if Arab investment was hoped for, it never materialised.

As with all his policies, if you look at what Papandreou does rather than what he says, the picture is much less principled and more 'realistic'. Is he deceiving himself? Or is he cynically manipulating the electorate in order to remain in power? **U.S. bases** are still in Greece, despite sporadic rhetoric. Their future is still shrouded in ambivalent talk about renegotiating the agreements, although the fact that Mr. Schultz dropped in for a chat in 1986 suggests that the Yankee is not the enemy he was. U.S. aid can after all keep the military sweet with expensive new toys. And if NATO were snubbed, who would protect Greece against the perceived threat of Turkish aggression? And where will the sophisticated electronic technology come from that is going to transform the economy? As for the once-reviled European Community, Greece is a net beneficiary and will long continue so – to say nothing of the life-saving loan just negotiated.

... AND THE END OF PASOK?

Up until mid-1988, despite Papandreou's many betrayals, despite the failure to clean up the public services and do away with the system of patronage and corruption, and despite a level of popular displeasure that brought a million striking, demonstrating workers into the streets

(February 1987), no one seriously believed that PASOK could lose the next elections.

Néa Dhimokratía, despite the clamouring for 'the people to vote' of their leader, Konstantinos Mitsotakis, had no coherent programme, and was still discredited by its appalling record in power. Mitsotakis himself is so compromised by a career of wheeling and dealing at great financial advantage to himself that he has long since forfeited both trust and affection. It was his defection which brought down George Papandreou's reforming government in 1965 and started the train of events that culminated in the dictatorship, so the animosity between him and Andreas Papandreou is therefore very deeply felt.

The liberal **centre** no longer existed. The only other real political force were the Communists. The main party, the **KKE**, however, rumble and fulminate from the sidelines in isolated ideological purity, untainted by actually having to wield power and take uncomfortable decisions. Their support looked unlikely to rise much beyond their perennial 10 percent of the vote. They are an old-fashioned party, still hung up on Uncle Joe (Stalin), and led by an old die-hard, Harilaos Florakis. Perhaps the only party with real integrity and ideas on the left is **Ellenikí Aristerá** (The Greek Left), formerly the Euro-wing of KKE. They are led by Leonidas Kirkos, though he is at present their only parliamentary deputy. There are possibilities of Kirkos negotiating a pact with KKE, but whether he will emerge the beneficiary remains to be seen.

However, at the time of writing, it looks like the entire Greek opposition will make gains in the elections due to take place in the first half of 1989. PASOK, and Papandreou in particular, have spent the last six months committing a quite spectacular – and thoroughly humiliating – series of **own goals**.

First were the extraordinary **cavortings of the Prime Minister** himself. Toward the end of 1988, the 70-year-old Papandreou was flown to Britain for open-heart surgery. He took the occasion, with fear of death presumably rocking his judgment, to make public a year-long liaison with a 34-year-old *Olympic Airways* hostess, **Dimitra 'Mimi' Liani**. The affair had been known to most Greeks for some time, and with little ill effect for Papandreou – it had, after all, a certain appeal to the Greek sense of machismo. However, the international news pictures of an old man shuffling about after a taller, young blonde, to the public humiliation of Margaret, his American-born wife, and his family, were unacceptable. In addition to disgust at the spectacle, people began questioning whether Papandreou, the grand old political operator, had lost his touch, his judgment and (some would suggest) his marbles. On New Year's Eve 1989, a night that the Prime Minister traditionally spends with the heads of the army, navy and air force, he was absent — dancing with his mistress and her friends. Even before, on the 1987 anniversary of the Kalamata earthquake, Papandreou, pleading ill health, had failed to attend the ceremonies and was seen instead partying the night away in an Aegean island taverna with Liani. All these instances caused enormous public offence.

Such behaviour might not have damaged PASOK's chance of a third term in power, however, were it not for the emergence and burgeoning of a scandal over the **Bank of Crete**, whose director, Yiorgos Koskotas, a bizarre rags-to-riches con-man, fled to the U.S. after accusations of embezzling at least £120m of deposits. Government ministers seem to have been implicated in the dealings, and they certainly tried to exert pressure to block an audit. Some have quietly resigned; others have left PASOK in disgust at the government's inability, or unwillingness, to clean out the stables. The most dramatic resignation came in March 1989, when Agamemnon Koutsoyorgas, an old friend of Papandreou and number two in the PASOK government, announced that he too was leaving office due to 'slanderous allegations'. In the wake of the Koskotas affair, other suggestions of corruption have surfaced, linking a further series of ministers with pay-offs from illegal **arms dealings**.

The political future for Greece, then, in the spring of 1989, does not look bright. When **elections** take place, a coalition, or narrow Néa Dhimokratía victory, seems likely. And Papandreou, presumably, will go, even if his health holds out. That there is no one of any reasonable stature to take his place looks in the short term to be a disaster. Perhaps, though, it will send a message to the country that years of (mis)rule by charismatic leaders are not necessarily well spent. Real renewal, real *allayí*, probably cannot come until Greece shakes off the stifling legacy of political patronage, bureaucratic obstructiveness, and state despotism, and creates an educational system that teaches its children to think critically rather than to mouth received truths and learn to play the influence game. PASOK may be blamed for not removing these ills, but it cannot be blamed for their existence. They are more than anything the product of many years' rule by repressive, obscurantist and philistine rightist forces.

ARCHAEOLOGY

The great archaeological sites of Greece – Delphi, Olympia, Mycenae, Knossos and the rest – were not always as we see them today. The discovering and then the uncovering of these sites has been the result of much labour: mental and manual. The work is long and painstaking, and has become more so as archaeology has developed: every significant object must be photographed, measured, described and classified in the effort to make sense of the layers of civilization represented on each site. The good archaeologist, though, has always needed to be a polymath – historian, linguist, architect, ceramicist, numismatist, geologist, archaeologist, agriculturist, photographer, artist and diplomat, by turn. Understandably, the profession has tended to attract uncommonly talented and dynamic disciples, drawn by the romance of the past and the challenge of new discovery.

Archaeology until the second half of the nineteenth century was a very hit-and-miss affair. The early students of antiquity went to Greece to draw and make plaster casts of the great masterpieces of classical sculpture. Unfortunately, a number found it more convenient or more profitable to remove the objects wholesale, and may be better described as looters than scholars – see 'Greece's Looted Heritage', following.

The British **Society of Dilettanti** was one of the earliest promoters of Greek culture, financing expeditions to draw and publish antiquities. Founded in the 1730s as a convivial club for young aristocrats who had completed the Grand Tour and fancied themselves arbiters of taste, the Society's main qualification for membership (according to most critics) was drunkenness. Its leading spirit was Sir Frances Dashwood, a notorious rake who founded the infamous Hellfire Club and shocked Europe with the blasphemous orgies held on his estate. Nevertheless, the Society was the first

body organised to sponsor systematic research into Greek antiquities, though it was initially most interested in Italy. Greece, then a backwater of the Ottoman Empire, was not a regular part of the Grand Tour and only the most intrepid adventurers undertook so hazardous a trip.

In the 1740s, two young artists, **James Stuart and Nicholas Revett**, formed a plan to produce a scholarly record of the ancient buildings of Greece before they disappeared altogether. With the support of the society they spent three years in Greece, principally Athens, drawing and measuring the surviving antiquities. The first volume of *The Antiquities of Athens* appeared in 1762, becoming an instant success. The publication of Stuart and Revett's exquisite illustrations gave an enormous fillip to the study of Greek sculpture band architecture, which became the fashionable craze among the educated classes; many European neoclassical town and country houses date from this period.

The Society financed a number of expeditions to Greece, including one to Asia Minor and Attica in 1812. The expedition was to be based in Smyrna, but while waiting in Athens for a ship to Turkey, the party employed themselves in excavations at **Eleusis**, where they uncovered the Temple of Demeter. It was the first archaeological excavation made on behalf of the society, and one of the first in Greece. After extensive explorations in Asia Minor, the participants returned via Attica, where they excavated the **Temple of Nemesis at Rhamnous** and examined the **Temple of Apollo at Sounion**.

The **Greek War of Independence** (1821–28) provided a major impetus to archaeology. Nationhood brought an increased pride in Greece's classical heritage, nowhere more so than in Athens, which succeeded Náfplio as the nation's capital in 1834. As a result of the selection of Prince Otho of Bavaria as the first king of modern Greece in 1832, the **Germans**, whose education system laid great stress on classical learning, were in the forefront of archaeological activity. One of the dominant Teutonic figures during the early years of the new state was **Ludwig Ross**. Arriving in Greece as a student in 1832, he was on hand to show the new king around the antiquities of Athens while Otho considered making the town his capital. Ross was appointed deputy keeper of antiquities to the court, and in 1834 began supervising the **excavation and restoration of the Acropolis**. The work of dismantling the accretion of Byzantine, Frankish and Turkish fortifications began the following year. The graceful Temple of Athena Nike, which had furnished many of the blocks for the fortifications, was rebuilt, And Ross's architect, Leo von Klenze, began the reconstruction of the Parthenon.

The Greeks themselves had begun to focus on their glorious past when the first stirrings of the independence movement were felt. In 1813 the **Philomuse Society** was formed, which aimed to uncover and collect antiquities, publish books and assist students and foreign philhellenes. In 1829 an orphanage on Aegina built by Capodistrias, first President of Greece, became the first Greek **archaeological museum**. Otho's archaeological service was, of course, dominated by Germans, but in 1837 the **Greek Archaeological Society** was founded 'for the discovery, recovery, and restoration of antiquities in Greece'. Its moving spirit was Kyriakos Pittakis, a remarkable figure who during the War of Independence had used his knowledge of ancient literature to discover the Clepsydra spring on the Acropolis – solving the problem of lack of water during the Turkish siege. In the first four years of its existence, the Archeological Society sponsored excavations in Athens at the **Theatre of Dionysius**, the **Tower of the Winds**, the **Propylaia** and the **Erechtheion**. Pittakis also played a major role in the attempt to convince Greeks of the importance of their heritage; antiquities were still being burnt for lime, and looting was a constant threat.

Although King Otho was deposed in 1862 in favour of a Danish princeling, Germans were still in the forefront of Greek archaeology in the 1870s. Two men dominated the scene, Heinrich Schliemann and Ernst Curtius; they could hardly have been more different in character and approach.

Ernst Curtius was a traditionally classical scholar. He had come to Athens in 1837 as tutor to King Otho's family and in 1874 returned to Greece to negotiate the **excavations of Olympia**, one of the richest of Greek sanctuaries and site of the most famous of the ancient panhellenic games. The then German Emperor Wilhelm I intended that the excavation would proclaim to the world the cultural and intellectual pre-eminence of his three-year-old empire. Curtius took steps to set up a **German Archaeological Institute** in Athens and negotiated the **Olympia Convention**, under the terms of which the Germans were to pay for everything and have total control of the dig; all finds were to remain in Greece, though the excavators could make copies and casts; and all finds were to be published simultaneously in Greek and German. Digging began in 1875 on a site buried beneath many feet of river mud, silt and sand. Only one corner of the Temple of Zeus was initially visible, but within months the excavators had turned up statues from the east pediment and the Winged Victory that had stood before the temple. Over forty magnificent sculptures, as well as terracottas, statue bases, and a rich collection of bronzes were uncovered, together with more than 400 inscriptions. The laying bare of this huge complex was a triumph for official German archaeology.

While Curtius was digging at Olympia, a man who represented everything that was anathaema to orthodox classical scholarship was standing archaeology on its head. **Heinrich Schliemann**'s beginnings were not auspicious for one who aspired to dig for ancient cities. The son of a drunken and immoral German pastor, he left school at 14 and spent the next five years as a grocer's assistant. En route to seeking his fortune in Venezuela, he was left for dead on the Dutch coast after a shipwreck. Working as a bookkeeper in Amsterdam, he began to study languages. His phenomenal memory enabled him to master four in his 21st year. Following a six-week study of Russian, Schliemann was sent to St. Petersburg (Leningrad) as a trading agent and had amassed a fortune by the time he was 30. In 1851 he visited California, opened a bank during the Gold Rush and made another fortune. While building for his business interests he still managed to travel widely; in preparation for a trip to the holy city of Mecca he learned Arabic, memorised the Koran in six weeks and had himself circumcised, bathing daily in the sea to heal the wound.

His financial position secure for life, Schliemann was almost ready to tackle his life's ambition – **the search for Troy** and the vindication of his lifelong belief in the truth of Homer's tales of prehistoric cities and heroes. By this time he spoke no less than seventeen languages, and had excavated on the island of Ithaca, writing a book which earned him a doctorate from the University of Rothstock. One element was still lacking, however: a partner to share his ambitions. Having divorced his Russian wife, Schliemann asked his friend the Archbishop of Athens to find him a Greek wife. From among the Archbishop's poor female relations he chose Sophia, thirty years younger than himself, beautiful and intelligent; she would prove a worthy partner.

Although most of the archaeological establishment, led by Curtius, was unremittingly hostile to the millionaire amateur intervening in an area to which they had devoted a lifetime of study, Schliemann sunk his first trench at the hill called Hisarlik, in Northwest Turkey, in 1870; excavation proper began in 1871. Although in his haste to find the city of Priam and Hector and to convince the world of his success, Schliemann dug a huge trench straight through the mound, destroying a mass of important evidence, but he was able nevertheless to identify nine cities, one atop the next. In May of 1873 he discovered the so-called **Treasure of Priam**, a stash of gold and precious jewellery and vessels. It convinced many that the little German had indeed found Troy. Experts however were, and still remain divided over whether the treasure was genuine or whether Schliemann desperate for academic recognition, assembled it from other sources. Tragically it disappeared from Berlin at the end of the World War II and survives now only in photographs.

Three years later Schliemann turned his attentions to **Mycenae**, again inspired by Homer, again following a hunch. Alone among scholars, he sought and found the legendary graves of Mycenean kings *inside* the existing cyclopean wall of the citadel rather than outside, unearthing in the process the magnificent treasures that today form the basis of the prehistoric collection in the National Archaeological Museum in Athens. He dug again at Troy in 1882, assisted by a young architect, Willhelm Dorpfield, who was destined to become one of the great archaeologists of the next century (though his claim for Lefkádha as ancient Ithaca never found popular

acceptance). In 1884 Schliemann returned to Greece to excavate another famous prehistoric citadel, this time at **Tiryns**.

Almost single-handedly, and in the face of unremitting academic hostility, Schliemann, in pursuit of his dream, had revolutionised archaeology and pushed back the knowledge of Greek history and civilization a thousand years. Although some of his results have been shown to have been deliberately falsified in the sacrifice of truth to beauty, his achievement remains enormous.

The last two decades of the nineteenth century saw the discovery of other important classical sites. Excavation began at **Epidaurus** in 1881 under the Greek archaeologist **Panayotis Kavvadias**, who made it his life's work. Meanwhile at **Delphi**, the French, after gaining the permission to transfer the inhabitants of the village to a new town and demolishing the now-vacant village, began digging at the sanctuary of Apollo. Their excavations began in 1892, proved fruitful and continued non-stop for the next eleven years; they have gone on sporadically ever since.

The beginning of the twentieth century saw the domination of Greek archaeology by an Englishman, **Sir Arthur Evans**. An egotistical maverick like Schliemann, he had many characteristics in common with the German: he was independently wealthy; he was middle-aged with a brilliantly successful career behind him when he started his great work; he discovered an unknown civilisation and recovered for Greek history another millenium. Evans excavated the Palace of Minos at Knossos on Crete, discovering one of the oldest and most sophisticated of Mediterranean societies.

Son of a distinguished antiquarian and collector, Evans read history at Oxford, failed to get a fellowship and began to travel. His chief interest was in the Balkans, where he showed a passionate interest in the natiionalist struggles of the people of what is now Yugoslavia against their Turkish overlords. He was in the Bosnia during the insurrection of 1875 and wrote a book on the uprising there; later the *Manchester Guardian* appointed him their special correspondent in the Balkans, and it was his documentation of Turkish atrocities that finally forced a change in British government policy regarding the area. He took enormous risks in the war-torn country, sending back brilliant dispatches and still finding time for exploration and excavation. In 1881 a further insurrection broke out, and Evans was in action again. His dispatches so aggravated the Austrian authorities that they finally deported him.

In 1884, at the age of 33, Evans was appointed curator of the Ashmolean museum in Oxford; the following years saw a series of battles with the university authorities over funding and accommodation. He relieved the tension by travelling whenever he could, and it was in 1893, while in Athens, that his attention was drawn to **Crete**. Evans though very short-sighted, had almost microscopic close vision. In a vendor's stall in Athens he came upon some small drilled stones with tiny engravings in a hitherto unknown language; he was told they came from Crete. He had seen Schliemann's finds from Mycenae, and had been fascinated by this prehistoric culture. Crete, the cross-roads of the Mediterranean, seemed a good place to look for more.

Evans visited Crete in 1894, and headed for the legendary sight of **Knossos**, where a Cretan had already done some impromptu digging, revealing massive walls and a store-room filled with jars. Evans bought a share of the sight, and five years later, after the Turks had been forced off the island, returned to purchase the rest of the land. Excavations began in March 1899 and within a few days evidence of a great complex building was revealed, and artifacts which indicated an astonishingly high level of cultural sophistica-tion. The huge team of excavation workers unearthed elegant courtyards and verandahs, colourful wall paintings, pottery and jewellery and sealstones – the wealth of a civilization which dominated the eastern mediterranean 3500 years ago.

Evans continued to excavate at Knossos for the next thirty years, during which time he established on the basis of changes in the pottery styles the system of dating that remains in use today for classifying Greek prehistory: Early, Middle and Late Minoan (Mycenean on the mainland). He also found time to publish his account of the excavation in a massive six-volume work, *The Palace of Minos*, which appeared intermittently from 1921 to 36. Like Schliemann, Evans also attracted criticism and controversy for his methods – most notably his decision to recon-struct parts of the palace – and many of his interpretations of what he found. Nevertheless, his discoveries and his dedication put him near to the pinnacle of Greek archaeology.

In 1924 Evans gave to the **British School Of Archaeology** the site of Knossos, along with the Villa Ariadne (his residence there) and all other lands within his possession on Crete. At the time the British school was one of several foreign archaeological institutes in Greece; founded in 1886, it had been preceded by the French school, the **German Institute** and the **American School**. Greek archaeology owes much to the work and relative wealth of these foreign schools and others that would follow. They have been responsible for the excavation of many of the most famous sites in Greece: the **Heraion on Sámos** (German), the sacred island of **Delos** (French), sites on **Kós** and in **southern Crete** (Italian), **Corinth** and the **Athenian Agora** (American), to name but a few. Life as a resident foreigner in Greece at the beginning of the century was not for the weak spirited (one unfortunate member of the American school was shot and killed by bandits while on a school trip to visit sites in the Peloponnese), but there were compensations: coveted invitations to afternoon tea with Madame Schliemann, and unlimited access to antiquities in a countryside as yet unscarred.

The years **between the two world wars** saw an expansion of excavation and scholar-ship, most markedly concerning the **prehis-toric civilisations**. Having been shown by Schliemann and Evans what to look for, a new generation of archaeologists was uncovering numerous prehistoric sites on the mainland and Crete, and its members were spending propor-tionately more time studying and interpreting their finds. Digs in the 1920s and 30s had much smaller labour forces (55 workmen under Wace at Mycenae as compared to hundreds who were digging at Knossos in the early days of Evans' excavations) and were supervised by higher numbers of trained archaeologists. Though perhaps not as spectacular as their predecessors, these young scholars would prove just as pioneering as they established the history and clarified the chronology of the newly discovered civilisations.

One of the giants of this generation was **Alan Wace,** who while Director of the British

School of Archaeology from 1913–23 conducted excavations at Mycenae and established a chronological sequence from the nine great tholos tombs on the site. This led Wace to propose a new chronology for prehistoric Greece, and put him in direct conflict with Arthur Evans. Evans believed to the day he died that the mainland citadels had been ruled by Cretan overlords, whereas Wace was convinced of an independent Mycenaean cultural and political development. Evans was by this time a powerful member of the British School Managing Committee, and his published attacks on Wace's claims, combined with the younger archaeologists less than tactful reactions to Evans' dominating personality, resulted in the abrupt halt of the British excavations at Mycenae in 1923 and the no less sudden termination of Wace's job. Wace was pressured to leave Greece, and it was not until 1939 that he eventually returned. In the interval his theories gained growing support from the archaeological community, and are today universally accepted.

Classical archaeology was not forgotten in the flush of excitement over the Mycenaeans and Minoans. The period between the wars saw the continuation of excavation at most established sites, and many new discoveries, among them the sanctuary of Asclepius and its elegant Roman buildings on **Kós**, excavated by the Italians from 1935–43, and the Classical Greek city of **Olynthos**, in northern Greece, which was dug by the American school from 1928–34. After the wholesale removal of houses and apartment blocks that had occupied the site, the American school also began excavations in the **Athenian Agora**, the ancient marketplace, in 1931; work which continues today.

The advent of World War II and the invasion of Greece first by the Italians and then the Germans called a halt to most archaeological work, although not to the activity of the archaeologists themselves, in particular British and American scholars who remained in Greece during the war was **Gorham Stevens**, Director of the American school, an architect whose restoration drawings of the Acropolis remain classics; he converted some of these into postcards which he sold to German and Italian soldiers, the proceeds going to a children's nursery near Athens. **Eugene Vanderpool**, Professor of Archaeology at the American School, also chose to remain behind in Athens, and organised a life-saving soup kitchen for Greek children before being arrested by the Germans and shipped back to Austria. Back in the US and Britain, trained archaeologists were much in demand for the intelligence arm of the war effort, both for their intimate knowledge of the Greek terrain and their acknowledged linguistic abilities, which proved invaluable in decoding enemy messages.

GREECE'S LOOTED HERITAGE

Melina Mercouri's campaign for the return of the Parthenon Marbles to Greece calls into question the whole issue of the looted treasures of the ancient civilisations, and whether they should be restored to their countries of origin. Are the Marbles, housed for a century and a half in the British Museum in London, a special case – a symbol almost of Greece's nationhood? Or should all of Greece's stolen heritage be restored? If the principle of return were pursued to its logical conclusion, many of the great museums of the world would be stripped.

Certainly, the frieze panels and metopes that Lord Elgin's agents sawed and hammered off the Parthenon represent only a tiny proportion of what Greece has lost over the centuries. **Rome** started the process and pursued it vigorously. When the Roman General Mummius laid waste **Corinth** in 146 B.C. as a warning to other Greek city-states to fall into line, that enormously rich city was plundered and vast quantities of statuary taken off to Rome. The Emperor Nero removed 500 statues from **Delphi** among many other depredations including the plunder of **Olympia**. Later, when Rome was under threat from barbarian hordes, the Greek art treasures went to Constantinople, where many were destroyed in the recurrent fires the city suffered. The survivors found their way to Venice and thence to Paris to stock the Emperor's vast 'Musée Napoléon'.

After the Renaissance came the **era of the 'collector'**, the 'scholar', the 'connoisseur'. A Citizen Kane mentality of acquisition for its own sake grew up. From the seventeenth century onwards, collectors were the main threat – English and French gentlemen antiquarians with little to do and with the time, money and resources to grab what they fancied.

If not the worst, **Lord Elgin** was most notorious. As British Ambassador to Constantinople, he used his influence to get the permissions he needed to remove sculptures from the Parthenon. He then proceeded to interpret these permits beyond all reason, subsequently getting the Sultan to rubber-stamp his excesses post facto. His later justification to a Parliamentary Committee that he was saving the marble from being used for mortar by the Turks can be dismissed: we are not talking stray columns and broken statues, but of huge slabs of carved marble sawn off the Parthenon with specially imported marble saws. Perhaps Elgin's abortive plan to borrow a warship to bring the entire Erechteion back to Britain tells us all we need to know about his motives. As he said in a letter: 'Bonaparte has not got such a thing from all his thefts in Italy'.

But Elgin was not alone. Another of Greece's oldest Doric shrines, the **Temple of Aphaia on Aegina** (Éyina), dating from about 490 B.C., was similarly looted. A party of English and German travellers, including **C.R. Cockerell**, later one of the better-known architects of his day and designer of the Ashmolean Museum in Oxford, visited Aegina in 1811. They hired labourers and began to dig, quickly uncovering the main outlines of the temple. On the second day they were startled to find a piece of Parian marble, since the temple was of stone. It was the head of a helmeted warrior, in a perfect state of preservation. Two pediments with seventeen statues depicting scenes from the siege of Troy, as well as many fragments were taken off to Athens while local officials were formally claiming the finds. A bribe of 800 piastres quickly defused the situation.

The four men who jointly 'owned' the marbles had to decide what to do with them. The marbles were shipped to Malta and it was resolved to hold an auction on the island of Zante (Zákinthos), then a British protectorate. The reserve price was 6,000 pounds. Crown Prince Ludwig of Bavaria wanted to create for his future kingdom a collection of antiquities rivalling those of London and Paris – so he too sent an agent to bid. At the time of the auction the British agent was in Malta, believing it was to be held there. Ludwig's agent put in the highest bid, but refused to buy a 'cat in a sack' and would not ratify the purchase until he had been shown plaster casts of the marble in Athens. They are now in the **Museum of Sculptures in Munich**.

The same team held another auction on Zante in May 1814. On sale this time were twenty-three marble slabs from the cella frieze of the **Temple of Apollo Epicurius at Bassae**. High on a lonely hill in Arcadia, the temple was one of the oldest and most complete in Greece. The architect was reputedly Ictinus, builder of the Parthenon, and the temple had been built in the 5th century B.C. to thank Apollo Epicurius – the Helper – for delivering the community from plague. Cockerell copied the capitals at Bassae in his design of the Ashmolean Museum.

Cockerell and his friends arrived at Bassae after abortive digs at Eleusis and Olympia. The local Greeks, fearful of the attitude of the Turkish authorities, had tried to make the visitors leave, but they pretended to have a *firman* (Ottoman authorisation) for what they were doing. Disturbed by the commotion, a fox bolted from under a mass of stone. Cockerell, hanging upside down over the stone, was startled to see a sculptured bas-relief of centaurs and lapiths fighting. Still inverted, he made a hasty sketch, but told no-one what he had found. Since the Greeks refused to dig and the owner of the land turned up with an armed bodyguard, Cockerell and his friends were forced to follow the path of 'legality'. They visited Veli Pasha, ruler of the Morea and son of the notorious Ali Pasha of Ioannina, at Trípoli. Veli issued a *firman* provided he was guaranteed half the spoils. The official dig began in July 1812. Veli, not understanding the value of the finds and in the process of being ousted from his pashalik by the Sultan, sold out his share for 400 pounds, and threw in documents of dubious validity needed for the removal of the marbles from the country. The embarkation at Boúzi was dramatic according to Cockerell: the new Pasha's troops arrived to intervene just as everything had been loaded except one of the earliest known examples of the style of column known as Corinthian. The ship put to sea and fled without it.

At the auction for the Bassae marbles, the British had more success. The Bavarians did not bid, since the goods on sale were artistically inferior to the Aegina marbles. The French bid 8,000 pounds and the British fifteen thousand – presumably a system of sealed bids operated. The marbles are now in the **British Museum**.

The spectacle of governments fighting a war using banknotes instead of bullets in pursuit of national prestige and becoming receivers of stolen goods in the process, cannot have been an edifying one. The auctions had the effect of alerting the British to the value of Elgin's loot, which Ludwig of Bavaria was known to be willing to pay handsomely for. After much horse-trading, Elgin was offered 35,000 pounds and took it. Just as Napoleon's ill-gotten gains were being dispersed from the Louvre following the French defeat at Waterloo, the British Museum was becoming one of the great museums of the world, and the impact of the '**Elgin Marbles**' on European artistic taste was enormous.

These were not, alas, isolated incidents. The French, during the early years of the nineteenth century, had resolved to restock **the Louvre**, now minus its Napoleonic loot, and the Consul-General in Smyrna was instructed that local consuls should purchase any available antiquities. On the site of the Sanctuary of the Great Gods on Samothrace is the Nike Fountain, which once had a magnificently sculptured centrepiece. The French consul found it and made off with it in 1863. Christened the **Winged Victory of Samothrace**, it found its way to Paris, where it remains in the Louvre. In 1820, Viorgos, a farmer on the island of Milos, dug out a tree-stump in the way of his plough and found two halves of a nude female figure, two engraved slabs and a hand holding an apple. There were two French ships moored in the harbour, and Yiorgos told the French consul, no doubt hoping for a quick sale. Uncertain of the statue's value, the consul sought instructions from Smyrna. In the meanwhile, Yiorgos sold the statue to an Armenian priest. There are several conflicting account of what happened next. According to one, when the Armenian tried to send the statue to an official in Constantinople whose favour he was trying to regain, the captain and crew of one of the French ships seized the box it was in by force, tipping off the Armenian priest and his Greek supporters and spilling blood. The Consul was in the thick of the fighting, wielding sword and staff. According to another version, the French bought the statue from the priest for £30. The Venus de Milo, too, made its way to (and remains in) the Louvre.

It was 1874 before the Greek government had the muscle to take a strong stand. The **Olympia Convention** (see preceding piece), signed at a time when the Germans were plundering Asia Minor with their usual single-minded thoroughness, probably saved Greece from depredations on a scale which would have made what had gone before look trivial. It undoubtedly prevented the treasure of Olympia and Mycenae following that of Troy to a German museum.

The **case for the return of Greek art treasures** is a strong one, though there are of course shades of grey. The Venus de Milo is a case in point: this was not a great visible monument being dug up illegally, or at the very least immorally, dismembered, but a statue previously unknown being dug up and sold, on the face of it legally, according to one version. The case for retention is at least arguable.

The British arguments for retaining **the Elgin Marbles**, the Greek *cause célèbre*, are rather more tenuous. Opponents of restoration argue that Elgin acted within the laws of his day; that had he not taken them, they would be now have been destroyed by the Turks, war or acid pollution; and that the British Museum, having bought them in good faith, has looked after them well and exhibits them to the public free of charge; and, most significant, that their return would set a precedent that could denude the museums of the world.

As far as legality goes, the Turkish *firman*, in the surviving Italian translation, allows Elgin to take 'any piece of stone with inscriptions or figures'. That clearly refers to pieces that have already parted company with parent buildings: it can hardly be taken to give permission to saw and chisel great chunks of standing temples. As to the preservation argument, it is hard to support that considering some of the Marbles were shattered during removal, some broken in transit, some lost at sea, some stolen and the survivors left outside for years at the mercy of the English weather. Nor, in fact, have the British Museum looked after them well. As recently as 1939, it became known that for two years the museum cleaners had been rubbing down the sculptures with a solution of ammonia. Prior to this, they had simply been blown with bellows, the dirtier bits being scraped with a blunt copper tool.

The precedent argument can't, of course, be refuted, save by the fact that the marbles are, self-evidently, a very special case – one of the most famous and beautiful structures in existence, and standing for Greece in the eyes of the world. But if the French could be shamed into returning the Venus de Milo, or the Germans the Aegina pediments, so much the better. If Europe is going to have prestige museums of Greek antiquities, then Athens seems as good a location, for tourists and scholars alike, as any.

Michael House and Diane Fortenberry

WILDLIFE

Greek wildlife is arguably the most exciting in the Mediterranean. In spring, the colour, scent and sheer variety of wild flowers, and the resulting wealth of insect life, are breathtaking. Isolated areas, whether they are true islands or remote mountains such as Olympus, have had many thousands of undisturbed years to develop their own individual species. Overall there are some 6000 species of flowering plants (three times that of Britain, for example), many of them unique to Greece.

Around 8000 years ago, Greece was thickly forested. Aleppo and maritime pines grew in coastal regions, giving way to Greek and silver fir and black pine up in the hills and low mountains. But early civilisations changed all that, and most of Greece, like most of Europe, is an artificial mosaic of habitats created by forest clearance followed by agriculture, either row crops or stock-grazing. As long ago as the fourth century B.C., Plato was lamenting the felling of native forests on the hills around Athens. This wasn't all bad for wildlife, though; the scrubby hillsides created by forest clearing and subsequent grazing are one of the richest habitats of all.

Over the last fifty years or so, Greece has on the whole escaped the intensification of agriculture so obvious in Northern Europe. In most of the countryside, crops are still grown in small fields without excessive use of pesticides and herbicides, and flocks of goats graze the hillsides in much the same way as they have done for the last few thousand years. The other side of the coin is that wildlife has been damaged by the rapid development of industry, logging and tourism, all of which have been carried out with little sympathy for the environment. The pollution around Athens and Pireás, in particular, is appalling, and new hotels and resorts have destroyed rich wildlife areas. Happily, there is still enough wildlife to go around, especially if you are prepared to explore a little.

One peculiarly Greek bonus to the naturalist is that wildlife here probably has the longest recorded history of anywhere in the world. Aristotle was a keen naturalist, Theophrastus in the fourth century B.C. was one of the earliest botanists, and Dioscorides, a physician in the first century A.D., wrote a comprehensive book on the herbal uses of plants.

FLOWERS

What you will see depends on where and when you go. Plants will cease flowering (or even living, in the case of annuals) when it is too hot and dry for them — the high summer in Greece does the same to plants as does the winter in northern Europe. So, if you want to see flowers in high summer in Greece, you have to go somewhere cool and moist, which means up a mountain.

The best time to go is **spring**; — which comes to the south coast of Crete in early March, to the northern Píndhos mountains as late as the end of June. In early **summer**, the spring anemones, orchids and rockroses are replaced by plants like the brooms and the chrysanthemums; summer ranges from late April in southern Crete to late July or even August in the high northern mountains.

Once the hot summer is over, things start all over again with some of the **autumn** flowering species such as cyclamens and autumn crocus, flowering from October in the north into December in the south. And the first of the spring bulbs flower in January!

SEASHORE
You might find the spectacular yellow horned poppy growing on shingled banks, and sea stocks and Virginia stocks among the rocks behind the beach. A small pink campion, *Silene colourata*, is often colourfully present. Sand

dunes are rare in Greece, but sometimes there is a flat grazed area behind the beach; these are often good for orchids. Tamarisk trees often grow down to the shore, and there are frequent groves of Europe's largest grass, the giant reed, which can reach 4m high. In the autumn, look for the very large white flowers of the sea daffodil, as well as autumn crocuses on the banks behind the shore. The sea squill also flowers in autumn, with very tall spikes of white flowers rising from huge bulbs.

CULTIVATED LAND

Avoid large fields and plantations, but look for small hay meadows. These are often brilliant with annual 'weeds' in late spring – various chrysanthemum species, wild gladiolus, perhaps wild tulips (especially in the central Peloponnese), and in general a mass of colour such as you rarely see in northern Europe. (Hot summers force plants into flowering at the same time). Small terraces are also good for flowers; you can often find deserted terraces full of cyclamens, anemones and orchids.

LOW HILLSIDES

The pick of the bunch. The trees and shrubs are varied and beautiful, with colourful brooms flowering in early summer, preceded by bushy rockroses – *Cistaceae* – which are a mass of pink or white flowers in spring. Scattered among the shrubs you have the occasional tree, such as the Judas tree, which flowers on bare wood in spring, making a blaze of pink against the green hillsides, and stands out for miles. Lower than the shrubs are the **aromatic herbs** – sage, rosemary, thyme and lavender – with perhaps some spiny species of *Euphorbia*. These occur principally on the *frígana*, limestone slopes scattered with scrubby bushes. (The other hillside type, *maquis*, with its dense prickly scrub, is better for birds).

Below the herbs is the ground layer; peer around the edges and between the shrubs and you will find a wealth of orchids, anemones, grape hyacinths, irises and perhaps fritillaries if you are lucky. The **orchids** are extraordinary; some kinds – the *Ophrys* species – imitate insect colouration in order to attract them for pollination, and have delicate and unusual flowers. They're much smaller and altogether more dignified than the big blowsy tropical orchids that you see in florists' shops. The **irises** are beauties, too; of them, a small, blue species called *Iris sisyrinchium* only flowers in the afternoon, and you can actually sit and watch them open at around midday.

Once the heat of the summer is over, the **autumn bulbs** come into their own, with species of crocus and their relatives, the colchicums and the sternbergias, more squills and finally the autumn cyclamens flowering through into early December.

MOUNTAINS

Good to visit later in the season, with flowers until June in Crete, and well into August on Olympus and in the Píndhos. The rocky mountain gorges are the home of many familiar garden rock plants, such as the aubretias, saxifrages and alyssums, as well as dwarf bellflowers and anemones. The mountains are also the place to see the remaining Greek native coniferous and deciduous forests, and in the woodland glades you will find gentians, cyclamens, violets and perhaps some of the rare and dramatic lilies. Above 1700m or so the forests begin to thin out, with treeline at about 1900m, and in some of these upland meadows you will find the loveliest crocuses, flowering almost before the snow has melted in spring. As in the lowlands, autumn-flowering species of crocus and cyclamen make a visit worthwhile later in the year.

BIRDS

Greece has a good range of the resident **Mediterranean species**, plus one or two very rare ones such as the Ruppells Warbler or the lammergeier vulture, which have most of their European breeding strongholds in Greece. The great thing about birdwatching here is that, if you pick your time right, you can see both resident and **migratory species**. Greece is on the main flyway for species that have wintered in East Africa, but breed in northern Europe; they migrate every spring up the Nile valley, and then move across the eastern Mediterranean, often in huge numbers. This happens from mid-March to mid-May, depending on the species, the weather, and where you are. The return migration in autumn is less spectacular because less concentrated, but still worth watching out for.

On the outskirts of towns and in the fields there are some colourful residents. Small **predatory birds** such as woodchat shrikes, kestrels and red-footed falcons can be seen perched on telegraph wires, and lesser kestrels nest communally and noisily in many small towns and villages. The dramatic pink, black and white hoopoe and the striking yellow and black golden oriole are sparsely represented in woodland and olive groves, and Scops owls (Europe's smallest owl) can often be heard calling around towns at night. They repeat a monotonous single 'poo', sometimes in mournful vocal duets.

Look closely at the **swifts and swallows**, and you will notice a few species not found in northern Europe; some of the swallows will be red-rumped, for example, and you may see the large alpine swift, which has a white belly. The Sardinian warbler dominates the rough scrubby hillsides – the male with a glossy black cap and an obvious red eye.

Wetlands and coastal lagoons are excellent bird territories, especially at spring and autumn migration. Both European species of pelican breed in Greece, and there are a wide variety of herons and egrets, as well as smaller waders such as the avocet and the black-winged stilt, which has ridiculously long, pink legs. The coast is often the best place to see migration, too. Most birds migrate up the coast, navigating by the stars; a thick mist or heavy cloud will force them to land, and you can sometimes see spectacular 'falls' of migrators.

The most exciting birds, however, are to be seen in **the mountains**. Smaller birds like blue rock thrush, alpine chough and rock nuthatch are pretty common, and there is a good chance of seeing large and dramatic birds of prey. The buzzards and smaller eagles are confusingly similar, but there are also golden eagles. The Greek mountains contain all four European species of **vulture**. The small black and white Egyptian vulture, with a one-meter wingspan, is the commonest, but you might also see the black or the griffon vulture, both of which have a three-meter wingspan and look like a flying table! The final vulture is the lammergeier, also with a three-meter wingspan but narrower wings, once almost extinct in Europe but now recovering slowly.

MAMMALS

There's the usual range of small mammals such as rats, mice and voles, and some interesting medium-sized ones – Corfu is the only place I've ever seen a beech marten, for instance.

There is also a fairly typical range of European species such as fox, badger, red squirrel, hare and so on, though the Greek hedgehog is distinctive in having a white breast.

But again it's the **mountains** that host the really exciting species. In the north, the ranges are home to some of the last remnants of big mammals that used to be widespread in the European forests and mountains. Wolves, brown bears, lynx, chamois and wild boar are all present, though the chance of the average traveller seeing one are slim to say the least. The Rhodhópi hills, north of Xánthi on the Bulgarian border, and the Elatía (Kara Dere) valley north of Dhráma, are good places to go to try to see these rare mammals, as are the Píndhos around mounts Gamíla and Smólikas, between Ioánnina and Kónitsa. A rare ibex, known locally as the *kri-kri*, is found around the Samaria gorge in Crete, as well as on some of the islets offshore. But, again, you'll be extremely lucky to see one.

The extremely rare Mediterranean monk seal also breeds on some stretches of remote coast; if spotted, it should be treated with deferent distance – it's endangered and easily scared away from its habitat.

REPTILES AND AMPHIBIANS

A hot, rocky country like Greece suits reptiles well – plenty of sun to bask in and plenty of rocks to hide in – and there are over forty indigenous species, half of the European total. Many of these are the **wall lizards**. Most of the islands have their own special species, but they are all confusingly similar: small lizards with a brownish striped back, often with an orange or yellow belly. Sit and watch a dry, sunny wall almost anywhere in Greece and you're bound to see them. On a few islands, notably the Dodecanese and the northern Cyclades, you may see the agama or Rhodes dragon. Growing up to 30cm, though usually less, they really do look like miniature, spiny-backed dragons with a series of pale diamonds on a brown or grey background. In the bushes of the maquis and *frígana* you may see the Balkan green lizard, a truly splendid, brightly-tinted animal up to half a metre long, most of which is tail; you can often spot it running on its hind legs as if possessed from one bush to another.

At night, **geckos** replace the lizards. Geckos are small (less than 10cm long), have big eyes, and round adhesive pads on their toes which enable them to walk upside down on the ceiling. Sometimes they come into houses, in which case welcome them, since they will keep down the mosquitoes and other biting insects. The **chameleon** is found infrequently in eastern Crete and some of the northern Aegean islands such as Samos. It lives in bushes and low trees, and hunts by day; colour is greenish but variable, for obvious reasons!

The most attractive of Greek reptiles is undoubtedly the **tortoise**. All three European species occur in Greece, but they are pretty similar; all have suffered to different extents from collection for the pet trade. You can still find tortoises easily enough, though, on sunny Greek hillsides. The best time is mid-morning, when they'll be basking between the shrubs and rocks. They come in all sizes depending on age – I've seen them from 5cm to 30cm long. A good way to find them is by ear; they make a constant rustle as they lumber around, and if you find one, look for more, since they often seem to stick together.

A closely related reptile is the **terrapin**, which is basically an aquatic tortoise. Again, both European species occur in Greece, and they're worth looking for in any freshwater lakes or ponds. There are also **sea turtles** in the Ionian; you might be lucky and see one while you're swimming or on a boat, since they sometimes bask on the surface of the water. The one you're most likely to see is the loggerhead turtle (*Caretta caretta*), which can grow up to a metre long. It is endangered, and protected, as discussed in the 'Zákinthos' section of the main guide.

The final group of reptiles are the **snakes**. Greece has plenty of them, but (as in most habitats) they're shy and easily frightened. Although most snakes are nonpoisonous, Greece does have a number of viper species, which are front-fanged venomous snakes, including the nose-horned viper, as poisonous as they come in Europe. Don't get venomous snakes out of perspective – they cause only a handful of deaths a year in Europe – but treat all snakes with respect. If you do get bitten by a snake, sit and wait to see if a swelling develops. If it doesn't, then the snake was harmless or didn't inject venom. If it does, move the area

bitten as little as possible, and get medical attention. Don't try anything fancy like cutting or sucking the wound, but you can bind the limb firmly so as to slow down the blood circulation though not so tightly as to stop the blood flow.

Greek **amphibians** either have tails (newts and salamanders) or they don't (frogs and toads). Newts and salamanders need searching for in ponds at breeding time, and under stones and in moist crevices outside the breeding season. You can't miss the frogs and toads, especially in spring. Greece has the green toad, which has an obvious marbled green and grey back, as well as the common toad. Tree frogs are small, live in trees, and call very noisily at night. They have a stripe down the flank, and vary in colour from bright green to golden brown, depending on where they are sitting – they can change colour like a chameleon.

INSECTS

About a third of all insect species are **beetles**, and these are very obvious in Greece. You might see one of the dung beetles rolling a ball of dung along a path like the mythological Sisyphus, or a rhinoceros-horned beetle digging a hole in a sand dune.

The **grasshopper** and **cricket** family are well represented, and most bits of grass will hold a few. Grasshoppers produce their chirping noise by rubbing a wing against a leg, but crickets do it by rubbing both wings together. **Cicadas**, which most people think of as a type of grasshopper or locust, aren't actually related at all – they're more of a large leafhopper. Their continuous whirring call is one of the characteristic sounds of the Mediterranean noontime, and is produced by the rapid vibration of two cavities called tymbals on either side of the body. If you have time to look closely at bushes and small trees, you might be rewarded with a stick insect or a **praying mantis**, insects that are rarely seen because of their excellent camouflage.

Perhaps the most obvious insects are the **butterflies**, because they're large, brightly coloured, and fly by day. Any time from spring through most of the summer is good for butterflies, and there's usually a second flight of adults of many species in the autumn. Dramatic species include three species of swallowtail, easily told by their large size, yellow and black shading, and long spurs at the back of the hind wings. Cleopatras are large, brilliant yellow butterflies, related to the brimstone of northern Europe, but larger and more colourful. Look out for green hairstreaks – a small green jewel of a butterfly that is particularly attracted to the flowers of the asphodel, a widespread plant of overgrazed pastures and hillsides. One final species typical of southern Greece and the islands are the festoons, unusual butterflies with tropical colour, covered in yellow, red, and black zig-zags.

WHERE TO GO

The locations described in the following pages are a very personal selection. I've visited most of them in spring; but in general, a good site is a good site at any time of the year, except in high summer when everything is burnt to a crisp anyway. It's also usually true that a good flower site will be good for other wildlife.

One possible exception to this is **birds**. They are fickle and mobile animals, and often choose to congregate in fairly unprepossessing places such as windswept estuaries, around rubbish dumps (plenty in Greece!), or smelly sewage plants. Birds adapt well to small-scale agriculture, too, even though the native plants may have been out-competed by olives, artichokes or melons.

If you're looking for wildlife on **the islands**, bear in mind that they're a bit of a special case. In general, the smaller and more remote an island is the smaller its range of species. There is, however, the compensation that remote islands have sometimes developed their own species over the years.

ATHENS AND ATTICA

If your only visit to mainland Greece is a few days stuck in Athens, don't despair of seeing wildlife. The hills of Attica which surround Athens are still rich in wildflowers, and so is the area around the Temple of Sounion, an easy day trip from the capital.

MT. IMITTÓS

Mount Imittós (Hymettus) is a stone's throw from Athens. The monastery of Kessarianí on the lower slopes is surrounded by flowers, with abundant orchids among aromatic bushes of the maquis. This area was treeless by the end of the last war, but is slowly and carefully being replanted. As you go higher on Imittós, and also on the neighbouring mountains of Párnitha and Pendéli, you come through the scrub into some true alpine habitat. Crocuses flower in spring and autumn, cyclamens and anemones grow wherever there is woodland shade (especially true on Párnitha), and near the summits the rock-dwellers flourish, including a lovely species of pink candytuft called *Aethionema saxatile*. All three mountains are an excellent introduction to Greek flowers, and all are readily accessible from Athens. Look out, too, for butterflies and reptiles, including the occasional tortoise.

CAPE SOUNION

Visit Sounion early in the day, before the bus tours arrive, and you'll find a wealth of flowers around the site, especially around the smaller Temple of Athena, since the area around the main temple has been thoughtfully sprayed with herbicides. Among the spring flowers of broom, rockrose and Jerusalem sage you'll find a wide range of orchids and anemones, irises and grape hyacinths. There are flowers later in the year, too, from the mallows and convolvulus of early summer through to the crocuses and cyclamens of the autumn.

THE PELOPONNESE

Some of the ancient sites enjoy hillside settings that are worth exploring for flowers – Epidaurus and Mystra are described below. For mountain flowers, I've chosen the Mt. Killíni massif in the north, and Mt. Taíyettos in the south. Náfplio is worth a trip for its seacliff flowers, and the coastal lagoons near Pírgos for waterbirds.

EPIDAURUS AND NÁFPLIO

The great ancient theatre at Epidarus is in one of the most beautiful settings in Greece, and the surrounding hills are rich in flowers and insects from early spring through early summer, with a variety of colourful anemones, orchids and grape hyacinths. Close by, the seaside fort of Náfplio repays the climb with colourful flowers in the rock crevices, as well as rock nuthatches hunting around the cliffs and walls.

MYSTRA AND MT. TAÍYETTOS

The Byzantine city of Mystra is close to Mt. Taíyettos, and so you can easily combine the natural history of the foothills and the mountains. The hillside immediately behind Mystra has one of the richest spring assemblies of orchids in Greece, followed in early summer by a blaze of colour from the annual flowers.On the lower slopes of Taíyettos, a series of gorges is full of flowers and other wildlife; the Paróri gorge is particularly good. Later in the year, the main Taíyettos ridge offers some of the best hiking in the area, with a combination of pine forests and meadows on the higher slopes.

MT. KILLÍNI

Mt. Killíni and the rest of the range on the southern side of the Gulf of Kórinthos go up to nearly 2500m, and so have plenty of the true mountain flowers in early summer, including crocuses, Star of Bethlehem, saxifrages and gentians. Birds are few but exciting, including many of the big birds of prey.

PÍRGOS

On the west coast, near Olympia, Pírgos has a series of salt lagoons to the south around the Alfiós river delta. Visit these, especially at migration time, for water birds such as herons, egrets, ibis and pelicans.

THESSALY AND CENTRAL GREECE

Four good wildlife spots are described: Mount Olympus in the north of the region, the Pílion peninsula halfway up the east coast, Delphi in the south, and Messolóngi in the southwest. There are others; the Mount Gióna area, just west of Delphi, is good for birds of prey.

MOUNT OLYMPUS

Mount Olympus is especially good for flowers, since the ascent takes you through three distinct habitats, starting with shrubby maquis, moving into beech and native pine forests from 500m to 1700m, and ending up in the true rocky alpine zone above 1800m. July and August are the best months to make the climb. Look out for vultures, eagles and other big birds of prey overhead, and for the beautiful Apollo butterfly – large and white with black and red markings – in the subalpine meadows and clearings.

DELPHI AND MT. PARNASSÓS

The site of **Delphi** is a promising place for sky-watching. The view is magnificent, and there are usually plenty of swifts, swallows, and the odd bird of prey drifting over from the mountains. Delphi has good wild flowers, partly because goats are excluded. Among the ruins themselves are many colourful 'weeds', and higher, above the stadium, you will find goat paths lined with rockroses, anemones, irises, grape hyacinths and orchids. Ancient sites are also excellent for reptiles, since the ruined walls are an ideal habitat. At Delphi, wall lizards abound, and the Balkan green lizards, normally very shy, are particularly tame here.

There are also some excellent coastal headlands around **Galaxídhi**, 17km to the west of Itéa, with tracks winding across *frígana*-covered hillsides full of aromatic herbs; plenty of tortoises here.

North of Aráhova is **Mount Parnassós**. Wait until June for the best of the alpine flowers at the top, but from mid-April through May you'll find many delightful crocus and other bulb species flowering at the edges of the melting snowfields.

THE PÍLION

The Pílion peninsula, east of Vólos, is a glorious mountain habitat, and its villages are superb bases for walking and wildlife exploring. At the top of the mountain range, around the ski resort of Hánia, you'll find the usual spring crocuses and other bulbs. Cyclamens grow in drifts among the pine trees lower down, and still lower you hit the olive groves, finally winding up on rocky hillsides overlooking the sea. In short, it's a microcosm of the major Greek habitats, excellent for all sorts of wildlife.

MESSOLÓNGI

The southwestern corner of the mainland around Messolóngi has a lot of water around, and that makes it a rewarding place for watching birds. The lagoons here are said to be especially good for aquatic birds; look for herons and egrets, and migrating waders in spring and autumn.

EPIRUS

The wild region of Epirus is probably the most spectacular country for walking in in Greece, and the wildlife is correspondingly varied and interesting. The three sites described – the Metéora, Ioánnina, and the Zagóri – are all easily accessible.

THE METÉORA

Even though this is a well-touristed spot because of its extraordinary pinnacle-top monasteries, wildlife is present in abundance. Metéora hangs from the eastern ridge of the Píndhos, with fantastic views down to the plains below. It's too developed for many of the large mammals, but it's one of the best spots in Greece to watch for vultures and eagles, as well as other specialised mountain birds such as alpine choughs.

IOÁNNINA

White storks nest atop the houses in Ioánnina, and the lake on the edge of the town is a worthwhile though polluted site. You can see purple herons in the reeds, feeding on the huge frog population, and egrets and smaller herons. There are large reed beds with breeding warblers, and plenty of wintering duck and other wildfowl. A good spot at any time of the year, and the more so as freshwater is unusual in Greece, so you're likely to see aquatic species that aren't much in evidence elsewhere.

THE ZAGÓRI

This used to be a very remote and wild area, though over the past decade a tourist industry of sorts has developed, centered on the beautiful Víkos Gorge. It is best visited in early summer to get an ideal combination of flowers and weather. Many familiar garden species flower wild in the gorges; the rocks around the monastery at Monodhéndri overlooking the Víkos, for instance, have sheets of purple aubretia and blue bellflowers. The black and white Egyptian vultures are especially evident around here, nesting on cliffs in the many gorges, and I've seen golden and Bonelli's eagles here too. Above villages like the two Pápingos in the foothills of Mt. Gamíla you'll find delicate saxifrages growing on rocky ledges, and there are numerous flowers in the woodland clearings as well. Look for red squirrels in the pine woods, but you'll be lucky (or unlucky) to catch a glimpse of mammals like bear and wildcat.

Further down, you'll find wonderful walks along the gorge of the Voïdhomátis river; there's a specially good one near the village of Arísti. The fringing forest is dark and lush, with cyclamens and ferns. Ramonda, a rare species of gloxinia, grows here on shady crevices with dark green furry leaves and delicate purple flowers. The glades are excellent for butterflies and orchids, and the whole area is rich in woodland birds in early summer.

THE NORTH: MACEDONIA AND THRACE

The extreme north of Greece is known for its birds; the wet marshy deltas of the Néstos, the Áxios and particularly the Évros have huge concentrations of wintering wildfowl and an excellent traffic of wading birds in spring and autumn. Some birds of prey migrate across this region, too; not as many as across the Bosphorus in neighbouring Turkey, but still enough to make it exciting. The forests of the northern borders hold large and shy mammals such as wolves and bears, and the remote Préspa lakes, on the Albanian/Yugoslavian border, waterbirds. Access is difficult to some of the best wildlife areas – not only is transport scarce, making a car very useful, but military permits are essential for some of the eastern areas close to the Turkish border. The spring bird migration is best seen in May, but there are birds through most of the autumn and spring, and winter is the time to see enormous flocks of wild geese and ducks.

AROUND THESSALONÍKI

The northern capital of Thessaloníki is an obvious base, and if you're short of time, there are worthwhile areas within very easy reach. The **Áxios delta** some 10km to the west has wetland birds, and there are salt lagoons next to the sea at **Angelohóri**, which is about the same distance along the coast to the south. Angelohóri is backed by low agricultural land and sand/shingle banks, good for wild flowers and butterflies later in summer. Look hard at any rats you may see around here; if they have a habit of sitting up on their hind legs and looking at you, then they're European susliks, a species of ground squirrel whose range just creeps into northern Greece. Inland, to the northeast of Thessaloníki, is **Lake Korónia** (also called Lake Vassílios). Best viewed from the south, this large lake is fringed with reed-beds and, as it shrinks over the summer, exposes areas of mud which are swarmed eagerly by wading birds out hunting.

Travelling further east from Thessaloníki, ancient **Philippi** has not only ruins but flowers, lizards and tortoises. Zígos, just to the east of

Philippi, is said to have excellent birds and flowers in its small fields and hedgerows. Continuing eastwards, the **Néstos delta**, which forms the Macedonia/Thrace boundary, has been largely drained for agriculture, but still has marshy lagoons full of wetland birds, especially around Keramotí. A better marshy area lies beyond Xánthi at **Pórto Lágo**, where a series of lagoons surrounds the outfall of Lake Vistonídha. The lake itself is best in winter, when it attracts huge numbers of wintering ducks and geese, but Pórto Lágo is best in spring and early summer, and has long been famous for its migratory birds.

THE ÉVROS DELTA

This wetland area, right on the Turkish border, needs a military permit to explore, and photography is forbidden over much of it. But Évros ranks alongside the Camargue in France and the Coto Doñana in Spain as one of the great marshes of Europe, worth a visit at any time of the year except high summer, when biting insects tend to outweigh its other advantages.

THE CYCLADES AND NORTH AEGEAN ISLANDS

Although most of the **Cyclades** tend to be dry and barren, with fewer species than the mainland, there is one obvious exception. This is **Ándhros**, which is green and lush, and has sizeable hills. With its rich vegetation, it's probably the best Cycladic island to visit for wildlife. Good second choices are **Náxos**, with streams for aquatic life, sand dunes, and mountains high enough for large birds, and **Sérifos**, where the high water table fosters creeks with lots of amphibians.

In the **north Aegean**, the islands of **Lésvos** and especially **Sámos** are outstanding. Both are wetter and greener than the islands of the Dodecanese, although they share the Asiatic influence. In the streambeds of Lésvos, for example, there are wild yellow azaleas with their sweet-smelling flowers. Although it's familiar as a garden plant, it's an Asiatic species and occurs nowhere else in Europe. Sámos has two mountain peaks, with a zone of coniferous trees, and here you'll find many of the typical alpine spring flowers such as crocuses and cyclamens; the parent species of our garden hyacinths, *Hyacinthus orientalis*, another Asiatic plant, grows on the lower

slopes. Both Lésvos and Sámos are good for watching bird migration in March and April.

CRETE

Crete is a big enough island to have the full range of Greek habitats, and it's also close to the North African coast, so its plants show a definite influence from there and from Asia. In fact, Crete has about 130 endemic plant species. Being so far south, it has an early spring and would be ideal to visit in March, though flowers continue in the mountains until May or June. The three main mountain ranges rise to over 2000m, with snowfields that persist well into the summer, so Crete offers great choice in its habitats.

PHAESTOS AND AYÍA TRIÁDHA

This complex of ancient Minoan sites in the south of the island is a wonderful place to start looking at Cretan wildlife, best visited in late March, though the month to either side will still find plenty of flowers. A track from the car park leads away from the site into a range of low scrub-covered hills which blossom with spring flowers. Many orchids grow here, including the tall spikes of *Orchis italica*, a striking species with a compact mass of pale pink florets at the top. Look out, too, for the blue flowers of *Nigella arvensis* here, better known as love-in-a-mist.

This classic Greek hillside is completed by lizards and swallowtail butterflies; nightingales and Sardinian warblers sing from the thick scrub, while swifts wheel overhead. There's a river below the site of Ayía Triádha, close by, which is worth exploring for birds.

AYÍA GALÍNI

Though a crowded resort in summer, Ayía Galíni is peaceful in spring. Just to its east is a river outlet below cliffs; lesser kestrels and alpine swifts nest in these, and the reedbeds turn up some interesting birds on migration. A series of tracks leads around to the west, where *frígana* flowers such as orchids and rockroses grow, as well as meadow flowers like gladioli. The ubiquitous pink-and-white anemone-like flowers are a buttercup, *Ranunculus asiaticus*, which just creeps into Europe in Crete and the Dodecanese. Tracks also lead up into low hills to the north; again there are lots of hillside flowers and insects, including the colourful Jerusalem sage, while wild leeks grow amongst the olive groves. Altogether a delightful spot.

ÁYIOS NIKÓLAOS

Although this is now a heavily touristed area, the disused salt pans at Eloúnda are said to be good for birds, and the island of Spinalónga is also worth visiting. Inland, the ancient site at Lato has long been renowned for flowers.

LASSÍTHIS PLATEAU

Since this plateau is higher up, just below Mt. Dhíkti, the peak flowers come a bit later than in the lowlands. The path up to the Dhiktean cave from Psihró is rich with flowers and orchids, and the area also has big birds of prey including vultures and eagles.

SAMARIAN GORGE

The high Omalós plateau shelters mountain birds and flowers, as well as the elusive *kri-kri*, or wild ibex. Down in the gorge itself you'll find cliff-dwelling species of birds such as the brightly-hued rock thrush, and there are colonies of crag martins too – a drab-plumaged bird but a dramatic flier. As for flowers, you'll find orchids, anemones and fritillaries by the paths on the way down, and some rock-loving species on the cliffs. Three to look for are *Linum arboreum*, with brilliant large yellow flowers, the Cretan rock lettuce, nothing like a lettuce but with a long spike of deep blue flowers, and *Ebenus cretica*, another Cretan endemic from the pea family, with pink flowers and downy gray leaves. Don't miss the white peonies which grow around the ruined chapel about 3kms down the track; the flower meadows around the abandoned village of Samariá itself are pretty stunning, too.

THE DODECANESE

The Dodecanese islands, like the islands of the north Aegean, are close to the Turkish coast, and their flowers and even insects have a definite Asia Minor flavour. Rhodes and Kós, the largest islands, are both rewarding; other smaller islands in the group, such as Kálimnos or Sími, tend to have much the same flora and fauna, but less of it. If you find yourself on Kálimnos, take a trip across to the islet of Télendhos; an extraordinary red-and-yellow parasitic plant of the genus *Cytinus* grows in abundance at the foot of its rockroses. It's thinly distributed through southern Greece and the islands, but nowhere else is it so common.

RHODES

Spring comes early on the Dodecanese, so late March or April would be a good time to visit Rhodes, even though the sea is still chilly for swimming then. The north of the island is pretty well developed, but the west coast is wild and spectacular, with high cliffs which you can see near Monolíthos. The higher central parts of Rhodes have birds of prey, and there are good flowers on the pine slopes of Mt. Profítis Ilías, especially cyclamens and the endemic white-flowered Rhodes peony. There are excellent *frígana* and maquis habitats on the east coast, either side of Líndhos; look out for white and pink rockroses and blue sages and conduct a search for lizards, orchids, tortoises and other excitements. The hillside flowers round the ancient site of Kámiros, on the other side of the island from Lindhos, are pretty good too. Birds migrate up the coast between Rhodes and the mainland of Turkey, so it's always worth keeping an eye over the sea for storks and pelicans and the like. The agama or Rhodes dragon is found on Rhodes, though perhaps commoner on Kós.

KÓS

For a small island, Kós is exceptionally endowed with wildlife. There are plenty of hillsides for the classic Greek flowers (and attendant insects and birds), and lots of tortoises too, especially on the hills behind Kardhámena. In the fields behind the beach north of Kardhámena small migratory birds appear in spring. Vultures and small eagles soar over the central spine of mountains, and I would recommend the villages around Píli to anyone. Not only are there good hillsides and mixed woodland for flowers and birds, but the sunset over Kálimnos from the village tavernas is amazing.

On the coast below Píli are some salt pans, which if they are wet can be worth exploring for birds: flamingos, avocets, stilts and spoonbills, plus flowers on the low ground between the salt pans and the sea. In the north, there is a multitude of flowers and butterflies in the fields around the Asclepion. At the other end of the island, the peninsula beyond Kéfalos has wonderful scenery and hillside flowers.

IONIAN ISLANDS

The Ionian islands, from Corfu in the north to Zákinthos in the south, are lusher and greener than most of the other Greek archipelagos, simply because of their high rainfall. The sites described here are all in the north of the group, on Corfu and Paxí.

CORFU

Corfu's strong agricultural development has created a perfect combination of small fields, dense olive groves, and tall cypress trees. You can find rewarding limestone hillsides with a typical *frígana* flora within easy reach of even the more built-up areas. But the northwest of the island offers the best wildlife opportunities.

Just north of **Paleokastrítsa** there is a low range of hills centred on the villages of Pági and Arkadhádes. The slopes near here are territory for orchids and spring flowers, and so are the southern slopes around Vistóna. Fárther up the coast, villages such as Magouládhes, inland from the new resort of **Arílas** have good flowers and woodland birds.

The northern coast is not so interesting, with the exception of **Lake Antonióti**, near Nissós. A small, marshy lake surrounded by woodland, this has a stunning range of orchids – I found over fifteen species in flower one April – and has the added bonus of reedbeds alive with hunting marsh harriers.

Corfu's tallest mountain, Pantokrátor, is also a useful bet. The slopes on the lowlands, especially round Strinílas, are a mixture of open hillside and olive groves, full of orchids, iris and anemones in the spring, with plenty of small birds in the trees. Higher up, towards the radar station at the top, it becomes much more exposed; the rocks around the low shrubs are still excellent for orchids, and you may find fritillaries here as well as one of the loveliest anemones, the blue *Anemone blanda*.

PAXÍ

Paxí, as one of the smallest Ionian islands, has a limited range of species. But it does have a network of small lanes through its olive groves, so it's an easy place to get around on foot. The hillsides north of Gaíos are rewarding for flowers, as is the headland that juts out northwest of Lákka in the north, which has spectacular specimens of the horseshoe orchid *Ophrys ferrum-equinum*. I found the island full of migratory small birds, but that may just have been luck. Look out, however, for Ruppell's warbler, an Ionian and Aegean speciality; I saw a number on the Gaíos town rubbish dump!

Pete Raine

FIELD GUIDES

FLOWERS

Anthony Huxley and William Taylor *Flowers of Greece* (Chatto & Windus). Best book for flower identification. It doesn't describe all the Greek flowers – no book does – but it's an excellent general guide with quality photographic illustrations.

Oleg Polunin *Flowers of Greece and the Balkans* (Oxford University Press). Good on the mountain biomes.

Paul and Jenne Davies *The Wild Orchids of Britain and Europe* (Chatto & Windus). A splendid book for orchid freaks, with details on where to look for them – including sites in Greece.

BIRDS

Petersen, Mountfort and Hollom *Field Guide to the Birds of Britain and Europe* (Collins); **Heinzel, Fitter, and Parslow** *Collins Guide to the Birds of Britain and Europe* (Collins). There are no specific reference books on Greek birds. These two European field guides have the best coverage, with the former, aging but excellent, retaining an edge.

Michael Shepherd *Let's Look at North-East Greece* (Ornitholidays). Useful short guide published by a British birdwatching holiday company.

MAMMALS

Corbet and Ovenden *Collins Guide to the Mammals of Europe* (Collins). As good a guide as they come.

INSECTS

Michael Chinery *Collins Guide to the Insects of Britain and Western Europe* (Collins). This doesn't include Greece, but gives good general information about the main insects you may see.

Higgins and Riley *A Field Guide to the Butterflies of Britain and Europe* (Collins). A field guide that will sort out all the butterflies for you, though it's a bit detailed for the casual naturalist.

REPTILES

Arnold and Burton *Collins Guide to the Reptiles and Amphibians of Britain and Europe* (Collins). A useful guide which infuriatingly for Greek travellers excludes the Dodecanese and eastern Aegean islands.

THE GREEK MINORITIES

The Greek minorities – Vlachs, Sarakat-sáni, Albanians, Turks, Jews and other relict communities – are little known, even within Greece. Indeed to meet Vlachs or Sarakatsáni who remain true to their roots you'll have to get to some fairly remote parts of Epirus. Greco-Turks are another matter, a sizeable community living, as they have done for centuries, in Thrace. The Jews of Greece, as ever, have the saddest history, having been decimated by the Nazi occupiers during the latter stages of World War II.

THE VLACHS

The Vlachs' homeland is in the remote fast-nessess of the Píndhos Mountains in north-western Greece near the Albanian frontier. Traditionally the Vlachs were transhumant shepherds, although some have long led a more settled existence in villages, notably Métsovo. They are an ancient, close-knit community with a strong sense of identity, like their rival shepherd clan, the Sarakatsáni, whom they despise as 'tent-dwellers' and who, in turn, just as passionately despise them for living in houses.

Unlike the Sarakatsans, however, their mother tongue is not Greek, but Vlach, a Romance language, which even today is full of words that anyone with a little Latin can easily recognise: *loop* for wolf, *mulier* for women, *pene* for bread. 'When the Italians invaded Greece', a Vlach told me, 'we could communicate with them easily. Vlach soldiers were often used as interpreters on the Albanian front'.

It used to be thought that the Vlachs were Slavs, descendants of Roman legionaries stationed in the provinces of Illyria and Dacia, who over the centuries had wandered down through the Balkans in search of grazing for their sheep and finally settled in northern Greece, where they had been trapped by the creation of modern frontiers on the disintegration of the Austro-Hungarian and Ottoman empires.

Because of these supposed Slav connections and the old Greek anxieties about the Slavophile, separatist tendencies of the peoples of northern Greece, the Vlachs have been objects of suspicion to the modern state. To their chagrin many villages with Slav-sounding names were renamed during the Metaxas dictatorship of the 1930s, and Vlach schoolchildren forbidden to use their mother tongue.

There is, however, a new theory about their origins, which argues that the Greek Vlachs are of Greek descent and have always inhabited these same regions of the Píndhos Mountains; that during Roman times the Romans found it convenient to train local people as highway guards for the high passes on the old Roman road, the Via Egnatia, which connected Constantinople with the Adriatic. Thus the Vlachs learned their Latin through their association with the Romans and preserved it because of the isolation of their homeland and the exclusive nature of their pastoral way of life.

Sadly, though probably inevitably, the Vlachs' unique traditions are in danger of extinction. A young Vlach lawyer in Athens told me that in his grandfather's day the family had 10,000 sheep, and when they set off on the annual migration from their lowland winter pastures to the mountains it was like a small army on the march, with two or three complete generations together with all their animals and belongings. Nowadays few flocks number more than 250 ewes, and the annual migration takes place in lorries – though a few veterans still do it on foot. Hundreds of Vlachs have sold their flocks and moved to the town or emigrated; many a sheepfold boasts a former Volkswagen-factory hand. There are depressingly few young men among the remaining shepherds. The hardships of their life are too many and the economic returns too small.

Yet to the outsider this ancient pastoral way of life has the magic of the Homeric age about it. I had the good fortune to stay at a Vlach sheepfold near Mt. Grámmos, in northern Epirus. It lies on a grassy plateau at the edge of a vast beech forest at an altitude of nearly 2000 meters, within sight of the guard post on the Albanian frontier where the first shots of the Greeks' Second World War were fired at the invading Italians. It consists of five huts, rebuilt each year from beech branches. Behind the huts an icy stream cascades 50 meters into a rocky gully. Above rises the summit ridge of Grámmos, where violets, gentians and saxifrages bloom among the collapsed dugouts, site of the Greek Communist guerrillas' last stand in the 1946–49 Civil War.

Five families live there; every summer of their lives they have come to this mountain, mostly to these very huts. Among them they have 2000 sheep, divided into two flocks, with the men taking turns to pen them. At the start of summer the ewes still have plenty of milk and need to be milked three times a day by hand. Each morning a train of ponies winds down through the forest carrying the milk to the cheesemaker, who, like the shepherds, comes every season to set up his cheese plant.

The women see to the domestic work, fetching water, cooking and spinning. The huts are kept spotless, the earth floors swept clean as cement. The cooking is done outdoors in big copper cauldrons over open fires.

In the evening it gets cool – by September there is often a frost at night – and each hut has a fire burning on the floor. People gather in one hut or the other for a little socialising. You have to sit down on one of the low beds, made like the rest of the meagre furnishings from beech branches, to avoid being suffocated by the smoke, which collects in the roof of the hut. Apart from the fire, the only light comes from the naked flame of a wick floating in oil.

It is a strange and moving experience to sit in the flickering lamplight listening to the wind and the ceaseless, frantic barking of the sheepdogs scenting wolf in the forest edge, and hear the shepherds tell how one of their number, trapped in Albania by the revolution, had slipped off his sheeps' bells one pitch black night in the 1950s, and driven them over the closely guarded ridge that marks the frontier.

'There was a lot of movement across the frontier after the war', one of them said, 'from both sides. The woods were full of people, you were afraid to go in them. I remember, there was a spring where we watered the sheep, close to the frontier. Many times at night, when I came down for a drink, I would hear voices and creep up behind the rocks to see strangers there. Who knows what they were doing? One time, just after dawn, a man in a suit carrying a small case came up to me and said he wanted to give himself up to me. He was an Albanian doctor. He'd been out on a call, driving through the woods close to the frontier. The woods are very thick there, and he'd just left the car and waited for night to cross into Greece'.

The shepherds are great talkers and have long and detailed memories. The oral tradition is still very much alive among the older ones. 'Our language has no alphabet, so we have no written history. Our grandparents always told us our history'.

Today all Vlachs speak Greek as well as Vlach – in fact, the children, especially of migrants to the cities, often know very little Vlach. Some of the older women, by contrast, speak Greek with a distinctly 'foreign' accent, presumably because they have mixed little outside family circles.

One morning I set out with the sheep and climbed to the top of Mount Grámmos. I found myself sitting on the edge of a crumbling dugout, surrounded by the rusting reminders of war, talking to a shepherd whose sheep were cropping the coarse grass in the scree some way below. 'I was wounded here in 1949, fighting the guerrillas', he said. 'They fought like devils. We couldn't shift them from their positions. They had to send for the planes to get them out'. As I could easily imagine – an infantry assault on these heights must be virtually impossible. I could not help thinking of the guerrillas crouched here in these shallow holes, their last toehold on Greek soil, pinned down, waiting for the planes to come in at eye level and finish them off, like El Sordo in For Whom The Bell Tolls. I wondered what the shepherd felt, leaning there on his crook watching his sheep, their bells the only sound interrupting the silence. 'I had nothing against them', he said. 'They were my brothers. The great powers set us at each other's throats'.

Three hundred meters to the west, and a little lower, we looked down on the Albanian border. Three soldiers were patrolling the Albanian side. As we watched they unslung their rifles and sat down in the sun. Beyond them a flock of Albanian sheep grazed under the eye of their shepherd. 'Those are our people', my shepherd said, 'Vlachs like us. But they haven't even said a *kalí méra* to us in thirty years. They never answer when we call, won't accept a cigarette. They're afraid'. But he told me with some envy that they were government employees on a regular salary and a month's holiday with pay. Their flocks had been nationalised.

Tim Salmon

JEWS AND TURKS OF GREECE

Jews and Turks in Greece are, for historical reasons, best considered together. Since the decline of the Ottoman empire, these two Greek minorities have often suffered similar fates as isolated groups in a non-assimilating culture. Yet it seems that enclaves of each will endure for the forseeable future.

The **Greek Jewish community** is one of the oldest-established in Europe, dating back to the late Classical period. During the Roman and Byzantine eras, the Jews were termed *Romaniote* and colonies flourished throughout the Balkans. In Greece these included Ioánnina, Corfu, Zákinthos, Pátras, Kórinthos, Athens, Halkídha, Véria, Sámos, Crete and, most importantly, Thessaloníki.

OTTOMAN YEARS

The most significant Jewish communities in Greece, however, date back to shortly after the taking of Constantinople by the **Ottomans**. In 1493 Sultan Beyazit II invited Spanish and Portuguese Jews expelled from those countries to settle in the Ottoman empire. The great influx of *Sephardim* (Ladino-speaking Jews) soon swamped the original Romaniote centers, and within two centuries, Ladino, a mix of medieval Spanish and Portuguese with Turkish, Hebrew and Arabic augments, had largely supplanted Greek as the lingua franca of Balkan Jewry. But *Ladinismo* (the medieval Iberian Jewish culture) never penetrated the Romaniote enclaves of Ioánnina, Corfu and Halkídha, which persist to this day.

Turkish officials and their families fanned out across the Balkans to consolidate imperial administration, thus sowing the seeds of the numerous Muslim communities in present-day Bulgaria, Albania, Yugoslavia and Greece. The Ottoman authorities often appointed Jews as civil servants and tax collectors; one, Joseph Nassi, became governor of the Cyclades. As a result Jews became identified with the ruling hierarchy in the eyes of the Orthodox Christian population, and at the outset of the 1821 **War of Independence** the Jewish quarters of Pátra, Kórinthos, Athens and virtually all others within the confines of the nascent Greek state, were put to the sword along with Turkish villagers. Survivors of the various massacres fled north, to the territories that remained under Ottoman control. Within the new Greek kingdom, a small community of Ashkenazi Jews arrived in Athens, along with the Bavarian king Otho, in the 1830s.

UNDER THE GREEK STATE

The **expansion of the Greek nation** thereafter resulted in the decline of both the Greek-Jewish and Greek-Turkish populations. New annexations or conquests (Thessaly in 1878, Epirus, Macedonia, the northeast Aegean and Crete in 1913) provoked a wave of forced or nervous Judaeo-Turkish migration to the other side of the receding Ottoman frontier. While Jews were never forbidden in newly-occupied territory, neither were they explicity welcomed to stay. The Turks – or more correctly, Muslims, since 'Turk' was a generic term for any Mohammedan, even Greeks who had converted to Islam for political or economic advantage – were subject to various expulsion orders.

The **Muslims of Crete**, mostly converted islanders, were forced to choose between apostasy to Christianity or exile. Those who opted to stand by their faith were summarily deposited in the closest Turkish-Muslim settlements over the Ottoman border; Kós town, the nearby village of Platáni, and Rhodes town were three of the more convenient ones.

When the Italians annexed the **Dodecanese** in 1916, the **Muslims** were allowed to remain and they were shortly after made exempt from any of the provisions of the Treaty of Lausanne (which stipulated the wholescale exchange of 'Turk' and 'Greek' populations in the wake of the Asia Minor war). It is not certain exactly how or when the Dodecanese Muslims learned Greek, which they today mix unconcernedly in conversation with Turkish. Obviously secondary education in Greek has been compulsory since 1948, when the Dodecanese were reunited with Greece. But it's more than likely that the Muslim refugees from Crete knew enough Greek both to communicate with neighbouring Christians and to teach the formely purely Turkish villagers the new tongue.

In **Rhodes** there is a long tradition of co-operation between the Muslim and the Jewish communities. In Ottoman days Jews were the only *milet* (subject ethnic group) allowed out after the city gates were closed at dusk, and more recently Muslim and Jewish leaders have consulted on how best to counter government strategies to deprive each of their rights and property. The refugee village of Krítika ('the Cretans') still huddles by the seaside on the way to the airport, and walking through Rhodes' old town it's easy to spot Turkish names on the marquees of various sandalmakers and kebab stands. In **Kós**, Cretan Muslims settled both in the port town and at Platáni, which still has a mixed Greek Orthodox and 'Turkish' population.

During the early 1900s, the same era as the Cretan deportations, the status of mainland Jews and Turks in the path of Greek nationalism was more ambivalent. Even after the respective 1878 and 1913 acquisitions of **Thessaly, Epirus and Macedonia**, Muslim villages continued to exist in these regions. The Tsamídhes, an Albanian Moslem tribe localised in Epirus and Thesprotía, were left alone until 1940–41, when they made the grievous error of siding with the invading Axis armies; they were hunted down and expelled forthwith by first the National Army and later the guerrilla bands.

Thessaloníki in the late nineteenth century was one of the largest Jewish towns in the world. Jews made up 75 percent of the population, and dominated the sailing, shipping and chandlery trades. In addition there were numerous *Dönmeh*, descendants of the false seventeenth century messiah Sabbatai Zvi, who were outwardly Muslims but practiced Judaism in secret. When the city passed to Greek control, the authorities allowed the 'pure' Jews to stay but insisted on the departure of the *Dönmeh*, along with other Turkic Muslims. The *Dönmeh* (Turkish for 'turners', after Zvi's conversion to Islam at swordpoint) insisted that they were 'really' Jews, but to no avail. After 1913 the city began rapidly to lose its Hebraic character; the fire of 1917, emigration to Palestine and the arrival of the Nazis effectively brought an era to a close.

The same period, around the time of World War I, also saw the end of Muslim enclaves on the islands of **Thássos, Samothráki and Sámos**, where the small Jewish community probably accompanied the 'Turks' in their exodus to Smyrna.

Western Thrace, the area from the Néstos River to th203144ros, was the last bastion of Greek Muslims, and it remained so after the

1920–23 Asia Minor War. The **Treaty of Lausanne** (1923) confirmed the right of this minority to remain in situ, in return for a continued Greek Orthodox presence in Istanbul (still known to Greeks as Konstantinópoli), the Prince's Islands, and Tenedos/Imvros Islands.

Over the years the Turks have repeatedly abrogated the terms of the pact and reduced the Turkish 'Greek' Christian population to five percent of pre-1923 levels. The Greeks have more scrupulously honored the bargain and today Muslims make up a third of the population of Greek Thrace, being highly visible in the main towns of Alexandhroúpoli, Komotiní and Xánthi. Muslims control much of the tobacco culture hereabouts and the baggy-trousered women can be glimpsed from the trains which pass through their fields.

The loyalty of these Thr2020ä¥n 'Turks' to the Greek state, however, was amply demonstrated during the last world war. They resisted the invading Bulgarians and Nazis side by side with their Christian compatriots. In return the two occupying forces harassed and deported to death camps many local Muslims. Only the **Pomaks**, a Muslim clan centered around Ehinós, north of Xánthi, collaborated with the Bulgarians, probably on the basis of ethnic affinity. The Pomaks as a group were probably Bogomil-Christian Slavs forcibly converted to Islam in the sixteenth century; they still speak a degenerate dialect of Bulgarian with generous admixtures of Greek and Turkish. During the 1946-49 civil war Thracian Muslims suffered again at the hands of ELAS, who found the deep-seated conservatism of these villagers exasperating and laboured under the misconception that all local Muslims were traitors. Today, though the Orthodox and 'Turkish' Thracian communities live in a fairly easy (if distant) relationship with each other, treatment of these Muslims still functions as a barometer of relations at a more general level between Greece and Turkey. The authorities still keep the Pomaks on a tight rein; they require a travel permit to leave their immediate area of residence, though if you go to visit them you will find them friendly enough, if shy, with the women in gorgeous, distinctive costumes.

But it was the **Jews** rather than the Muslims who suffered the greater catastrophe during **World War II**. Eighty-five percent of a Jewish population of around 80,000 was rounded up by the Nazis in the spring of 1944, never to return. Greek Christians often went to extraordinary lengths to protect their persecuted countrymen, far overshadowing the few instances of sordid betrayal. The city council of Zákinthos and the bishops of Athens and Halkídha put themselves at risk to save many who would otherwise have been killed. Those Jews who remained in the country either went into hiding or joined the guerrillas in the hills. Athens Jewry, indistinguishable from their Orthodox neighbours in appearance and tongue, fared best, but the Ladino-speaking Jews of northern Greece, with their distinctive surnames and customs, were easy targets for their tormentors.

Today barely 5000 Jews remain in Greece. In Thessaloníki there are around 1100 Sephardim, while small Ladino communities continue in Kavála, Sérres, Dhidhimótiho, Tríkala and Véria. Lárissa has a modest number who are still disproportionately important in the clothing trade. However young Jewish women outnumber their male counterparts, with the result that they tend to marry into the Orthodox faith. In Ioánnina, once a major centre of Jewry, less than 100 Romaniote Jews remain. Only 75 or so of the original community of Rhodes survived the war, and many of these are Egyptian Jewish refugees. The *Platía ton Evreón Martirón* (Square of the Jewish Martyrs) is a memorial to the 2000 Jews of Kos and Rhodes slaughtered by the Germans; it occupies the site of the (mostly demolished) old Jewish quarter. Three thousand of today's Greek Jews live in Athens, which is also the home of the National Jewish Museum.

Marc S. Dubin

GREEK PRE-OCCUPATIONS

Greeks are the most openly curious nation in the world. Stop for a few minutes at a kafenío and you will be bombarded with questions, often disarmingly direct ones to the British way of thinking. You'll quickly gather an idea of the Greeks' own preoccupations: money, the family (especially marriage), sex, politics, sports – probably in that order. As these come up so often in conversation, a few words of background on your hosts' expectations of you ...

MONEY You should be able to talk about your job and say how much you earn. Rubbing the thumb and forefinger together is sign language for money and usually means 'Do you get a lot of it?' The price of things, rather than their intrinsic value, often counts for more than it should, and a high price is generally impressive, whatever the object. All foreigners, especially middle-aged ones, and above all, American middle-aged ones, are taken to be wealthy. Although Greeks will harbour jealousy of your riches, this will very rarely turn into any criminal intent. Theft is definitely not a national pastime.

FAMILIES in Greece are close-knit, and marriage is at the centre of Greek life. The possibility of being deliberately, happily single is inconceivable, and hopes for a speedy end to that ignominious status will be sincerely expressed to you. Learn the words for brothers, sisters and other close relatives. They will certainly come up somewhere and sometime. Living together as an unmarried couple is scarcely acceptable, even among more liberal-minded Greeks. Constantly recycled series of comedy films on TV from the 1950s and 1960s revolve almost without exception on the possibility of a couple getting married.

Parents fret about their daughters finding a husband, and it is still a recognised custom for them to provide a dowry (*príka*), often in the form of a house. The government recently passed a law making it illegal for the potential groom to ask for a dowry, but this in itself shows how ingrained the system had become.

This custom is more prevalent in the villages, but most city-dwellers are first- or second-generation internal immigrants from villages, and traditions die hard. Having children is the corollary to getting married, so that's a popular conversational topic, too; concern will be expressed if you're part of a childless couple.

SEX is traditionally restricted to the framework of marriage, but for men the double standard common to all Mediterranean (and most other) cultures has always prevailed. It is assumed that even the nominally celibate inhabitants of monasteries have some fun once in a while. It is further assumed that unattached male travellers, for example, will share and endorse salacious comments about passing women – uncomfortable if you find those values distasteful. Overweening Greek male egos may also find it difficult to understand why unattached foreign women fail to find them irresistible. It is in fact incomprehensible for most men, and not a few women, that anyone should turn down an opportunity to engage in sexual activity; in addition to its procreative role, libido is considered a healthy appetite, a normal, everyday condition to be satisfied like hunger or thirst and over which not too much sleep should be lost – literally or figuratively.

Greeks are refreshingly free of age-ist prejudice on the subject; if the elderly butcher wants to conduct a discreet affair with the widow around the corner, *brávo toús*, more power to them. Similarly, it is no great disgrace to act on (male) homosexual inclinations – but the societal myth holds that all gays are really bisexual and that nobody is a passive partner, a humiliating status. Passive homosexuality, incidentally, is one of the few grounds for exemption from military service.

POLITICS, a decade and a half after freedom from the colonels (see 'Historical Framework'), are still a burning issue. Your political views will be freely sought, and you won't need to travel long in Greece before beginning to recognise the graffiti scrawled on the walls – blue for the conservative *Néa Dhimokratía* party, green for the socialist *PASOK*, and red for the Communist *KKE*. There are, too, party offices in even the smallest villages.

In Greek politics the choice of parties at an election really does mean something, although after the last eight years of *PASOK* (mis)rule, many of the electorate are beginning to wonder. However, if scandals (the Bank of Crete, Andreas Papandreou's liaison with an *Olympic Airways* hostess – again see 'Historical Framework') have taken the place of issues, apathy has not yet entirely set in. Ordinary people take an interest in foreign affairs, whether Greece is directly affected or not. It's good to be able to reciprocate with a little background knowledge on the current Greek situation, even though such knowledge is rarely expected from foreigners.

SPORTS, particularly soccer (*podhósfero*) and basketball (*báskit*), are popular enough for three daily newspapers to be devoted exclusively to the subject. And these papers survive, so they must sell. The Greeks themselves only support successful soccer teams, of whatever nationality, and will invariably follow Liverpool (if under age 30) or Manchester United (if over). The Greek teams take second place, though here, too, people go for success, such as it is, with the regular Greek League winners Panathenaïkós and *Olympiakós*. Greek basketball has a better record of late, with the national team being current European champions.

MATERIALISM is perhaps a lesser foible, but part and parcel of Greek life, nonetheless. *Ksenomanía* (belief in the inherent superiority of overseas products) is a Greek word and a Greek condition. The economy performs a complicated and permanent balancing act on the edge of a precipice, and this is closely connected with the country's inability to produce desirable exports and the thirst for manufactured imports. The government has tried various ways to curb this, including 100 percent taxes on cars, TVs, videos, stereos, etc., and a lengthy advertising campaign with the slogan '*Epiménon Ellínika*' (Insisting on Greek). But all this does little to change Greek perceptions of a world in which foreigners make better quality goods than they do themselves. It is worth noting that in a society as (largely) egalitarian as Greece, gratuitous flaunting of wealth is considered to be in equally bad taste as the shabby garb and affected poverty of certain foreign visitors; there is little to distinguish the owners of the BMWs, the Dobermanns and the designer shades from other Greeks aside from better locks on the door and a higher front fence.

EMPLOYMENT AND EDUCATION That Greece isn't a great producer of manufactured goods is reflected on the employment front. There is constant concern and frustration among the young about the choice of jobs (or lack thereof). Nearly all secondary school students attend until age 18, chasing elusive marks which will entitle them to get into a university. The educational system itself can hardly cope. Schools work on a shift system whereby pupils go in the morning or afternoon, or alternate, because there aren't enough buildings. The universities, too, have similar problems, and graduates find that jobs suited to their qualifications are practically impossible to come by – a problem worsened by the Greek *méson* (literally, 'ways and means') system whereby you need 'connections' to get a good position. Many students go abroad to either western or eastern Europe for a second degree (or even a first) to bolster their qualifications.

POPULAR CULTURE With all this respect for things foreign, coupled with the renowned hospitality towards foreigners (it sometimes seems Greeks are nicer to foreigners than to each other), it's a wonder that Greek culture survives at all. Yet it does, and like so many small nations there is a very strong sense of identity. This comes out in a thousand ways. Children learn Greek dances from an early age, and although they later embrace western music, they don't ignore their own. Thus even a teenage party will normally switch from disco music to Greek towards the end. Greek art and theatre have an enthusiastic following, and artists and actors are taken seriously. Similarly, although foreign-made programmes predominate on TV, most Greeks would prefer that it weren't that way.

Richard Hartle

MUSIC

Music, like most Greek cultural traditions, is a mix of East and West. The older songs, invariably in Eastern-flavoured minor keys or more properly modes (*dhrómi, makamiá*), often have direct precedents in Turkey and Iran, and almost all native Greek instruments are descendants, or near-duplicates, of ones used thoughout the Islamic world. To this Middle Eastern base both Slavs and Italians have added their share, and as a result the repertoire of traditional and more modern Greek pieces is extraordinarily varied. At festival times it's likely you'll happen on some live performances – though Greeks listen and dance increasingly to cassettes these days. Whatever, you certainly shouldn't jump to conclusions after suffering through an evening of endless bouzouki riffs in some plastic tourist taverna.

The following sections detail the main types of music you can expect to hear in various Greek regions.

CRETE, KASSOS AND KARPATHOS

This arc of southern islands is the most promising area in Greece for hearing live music any day of the year. The main instrument here is the *lyra*, a three-stringed fiddle directly related to the Turkish *kemençe*. They are played not on the shoulder but balanced on the thigh, often with tiny bells attached to the bow, which the musician can jiggle for rhythmical accent. The strings are metal, and since the centre one is just a drone the player improvises only on the outer two – a unique, intriguing sound.

Usually the *lyra* is backed up by one or more *laoúta*, similar to the Turkish/Arab *oud* and not unlike the medieval lute. These are rarely used to their full potential but a good player will find the harmonics and overtones of a virtuoso *lyra* piece, at the same time coaxing a pleasing, chime-like tone from his instrument. A *laoúto* solo is an uncommon treat.

In several places in the southern Aegean, notably traditional Kárpathos, a primitive bagpipe, the **askómandra** or **samvoúna**, joins the *lyra* and *laoúto*. During the colonels' dictatorship the playing of the bagpipe in the Cyclades further north was banned lest anyone think the Greeks too primitive – though hopefully, all concerned have recovered from any sense of cultural inferiority. If you remember Kazantzakis's classic novel (or the movie), Zorba himself played a *santoúri*, or hammer dulcimer, for recreation. Today, accomplished players are few and in *Kritikí*, (Cretan music), *Nisiotiká* (island songs) and *rembétika* (see below), it's been relegated to a supporting role. Except in a couple of Athens music halls, you're more likely to see the instruments gathering dust in antique shops.

On a more oddball note, performances by the Irish musician (and long-time Crete resident) Ross Daly are worth looking out for – both in Crete and at various festivals. An ethnomusicologist who plays a dozen traditional instruments, Daly has absorbed influences from all aspects of Cretan musical tradition. Alone or with his group, his vaguely New Age/contemporary interpretations of folk tunes or original compositions are unmistakeable.

AEGEAN ISLANDS

On most of the Aegean islands, and particularly the Cyclades, you'll find the *lyra* replaced by a more familiar-looking **violí**, essentially a western violín. The music is lyrical and usually uptempo. Backing is again often provided by *laoúta* or *santoúria*, though they're sometimes replaced or complemented by various reedwailers such as the *karamúz*, fashioned from two goat horns.

Unlike on Crete, where you can often catch the best music in special clubs or *kéndra*, Aegean island performances tend to be spontaneous and less specialised. Festivals and saints' days in a village square are obviously the most promising times and venues, but my most memorable recital occurred at 10am one Sunday morning when a *kaíki* chugged out of Kímolos harbour with two musicians aboard. They pounded and sawed away on a *laoúto* and a *violí*, singing in the key of ouzo as they circled the ferry *Ionion*. The execution may have been a little imperfect but their spirit was wildly applauded by both passengers and crew; after a repeat performance around the *Kimolos* just behind us, the little boat did one more pass and headed for port.

The folk lyrics of the the Peloponnese, central and western Greece generally hark back to the years of Turkish occupation and to the Independence Movement. The main music is **paleá dhimotiká**, traditional folk ballads with very basic accompaniment on the *klaríno* (clarinet). *Kithára* (guitar), *violí*, and *toumberléki* (lap drum) can also add to the backing.

Most pieces are danceable, and they are divided into such categories as *kalamatianó*, *tsámiko*, *hasaposérviko*, or *syrtó*. Those that are not include the slow, stately *kleftikó*, similar to the *rizítiko* of Crete, both of which relate, baldly or in metaphor, incidents or attitudes from the years of the Ottomans and the rebellions for freedom. Since the songs are strongly associated with national identity it's not surprising that they've been pressed into political service. If you arrive during an election campaign you'll get a free crash course in folk music, each storefront party headquarters blasting out continuous *paleá dhimotiká* interspersed with political harangues. The Communists are apt to include contemporary inspirational music (see below), and the conservatives more likely to bombard you with Greek and western pop.

THRACE AND
THE NORTH

Thrace and Macedonia were in the hands of the Turks only seventy years ago, so music here – louder and less lyrical than in the south – has an unremitting Oriental feel. The Thracian **kavál**, or end-blown flute, is identical to the Turkish articles; so too is the northern bagpipe, or **gaída**. In Macedonia you'll find the **zoúrna**, a screechy, double-reed oboe similar to the Islamic world's *shenai*. It's much in evidence at local festivals, as is the **daoúli**, or deep-toned drum. The *klaríno* and *toumberléki* are not unknown, but even in their presence dances are fast and hard-stamping.

IONIAN ISLANDS

Alone of all modern Greek territory, the Ionian islands never saw Turkish occupation and have a predominantly western musical tradition. The indigenous song-form is Italian both in name, (**kantádhes**) and instrumentation (guitar, mandolin); it's most often heard these days on Lefkádha and Zákinthos.

NÉO KÍMA:
CONTEMPORARY
COMPOSERS

Néo Kíma ('new wave') folk music emerged in small Athenian clubs, or *boîtes*, during the early 1960s. It was in part a rediscovery of the forms of *rembétika* (see below), in part a politicised folk movement, and its young, improvisatory composers strongly identified with the Communists, whose revolutionary songs they revived and adapted. Most of the Athenian boites were closed down during the 1967–74 military junta, and those that survived degenerated into expensive glossy nightclubs. Over the last decade, however, there was something of a revival. See the Athens section for more details.

Though not directly associated with the *Néo Kíma* movement, Mikis Theodorakis and Manos Hadzikakis – the two best-known modern Greek composers – have much in common with its spirit. **Theodorakis** is undoubtedly the most important musical figure modern Greece has produced, and a committed political presence, too, currently a KKE (Communist Party) member of parliament. If you've only ever heard Theodorakis's music for the film of *Zorba the Greek*, check out some of the astonishing settings that he's recorded of poems by Yannis Ritsos. His famous, if somewhat overwrought *March of the Spirit*, premiered in exile (London) in 1969, served as PASOK's theme song for many years.

REMBETIKA

Rembétika is the music of the Greek urban dispossessed – criminals, refugees, drug-users, defiers of social norms. It has existed in some form in Greece since at least the turn of the century. But it is as difficult to define or get to the origins of as jazz or blues, with which it shares marked similarities in spirit and circumstance.

The themes of the songs – illicit love, drug addiction, police oppression, disease and death

– and the tone of the delivery – resignation to the singer's lot, coupled with defiance of authority – will certainly be familiar. But even the word 'rembétika' is of uncertain derivation, the most likely one being rembet, an old Turkish word meaning 'of the gutter', and searches for the birth of rembétika must be conducted in Asia Minor of the last years of the Ottoman empire as well as in Greece proper.

Most outsiders equate Greek music with the bouzoúki, a long-necked, fretted lute derived from the Turkish saz and baglama, though early in this century only a small proportion of Greek musicians used it. Meanwhile, across the Aegean in Smyrna and Constantinople, musical cafés had become popular. Groups usually featured a violinist, a santoúri (hammer dulcimer) player, and a female vocalist, who usually jingled castanets and danced on stage. The style was known as café-amanés or just amanédhes, after both the setting and the frequent repetition of the exclamation aman aman. (An identical exclamation, incidentally, is used in modern Algerian 'rai' music). Despite the sparseness of the instrumentation, this was an elegant, rivetting music, and a style of 'art'-singing requiring considerable skill and harking back to similar vocalisation in Central Asia. Some of its greatest practitioners included 'Dalgas' (Wave), so nicknamed for the undulations and quarter-tones in his voice; Rosa Eskenazi, originally from Thrace; and Dhimitris 'Solonikiye' Semsis, a master fiddler from Macedonia.

The 1923 **exchange of populations** was a key event in the history of rembétika, resulting in the influx of over a million Asia Minor Greeks, many of whom settled in shanty towns around Athens and Pireás. The musicians, like most of the other refugees, were in comparison to the Greeks of the host country extremely sophisticated; many were highly educated, could read and compose music, and had even been unionised in the towns of Asia Minor. It was certainly galling for all of the refugees, who had generally been 'somebody' on the other side of the water, to live on the periphery of the new society in poverty and degradation; most had lost all they had in the hasty evacuation, and many, from inland Anatolia, could speak only Turkish. In their misery they sought relief in another Ottoman institution, the tekés or hashish den.

In the tekédhes of Pireás, Athens and Thessaloníki, a few men would sit on the floor around a charcoal brazier, passing around a nargilés (hookah) filled with Turkish hashish. One of them might begin to improvise a tune on the baglamá or the bouzoúki and begin to sing. The words, either his own or those of the other dervíses ('dervishes' – many rembetic terms were a burlesque of those in the Islamic mystical tradition), would be heavily laced with slang, in the manner of the Harlem jive of the same era – a way of keeping outsiders at bay. As the taksími (long, studied introduction) was completed, one of the smokers might rise and begin to dance a zeibékiko, named after a warrior caste (the zeibeks) of old Anatolia. It would be a slow, intense, introverted performance following an unusual metre (9/8), not for the benefit of others but for himself.

Markos Vamvakaris was one of the greatest performers to emerge from the tekés culture. His proficiency on the bouzoúki was indisputable, though he protested to his friends that his voice, ruined perhaps from too much hash-smoking, was no good for singing. But he bowed to their encouragement and his gravelly, unmistakable sound set the standard for male vocals over the next decade.

But the 'Golden Age' of rembétika – as indeed it was, despite the unhappy lives of many performers – was short-lived. The association of the music with this underworld would proved to be its undoing. The harder-core musicians, with their uncompromising lyrics and lifestyles, were blackballed by the recording industry and 'polite' society; hashish was outlawed in the early 1930s, and police harassment of the tekédhes was stepped up after the Metaxas dictatorship took power in 1936. Even possession of a bouzoúki or a baglamá was a criminal offence. Most of the big names served time in jail; the one bright spot was Thessaloníki, where the police chief, a big rembétika fan, was prepared to turn a blind eye to hash consumption in exchange for being invited to performances.

For a while, the widespread persecution failed to dim the enthusiasm of the mánges (roughly translatable as 'hep cats'). They were notoriously generous and impulsive, if occasionally violent, and enjoyed life to the fullest. Beatings or prison terms were taken in stride;

time behind bars could be used, as it always had been around the Aegean, to make *skaptó* (dug-out) instruments. A *baglamá* could easily be fashioned from a gourd cut in half (the sound box), a piece of wood (the neck), catgut (frets), and wire for strings. Jail songs were composed and became popular in the underworld; the excerpt below (very freely translated from the *mangiká* or argot) is typical:

Down in Lemonadhika there was a ruckus
They caught two pickpockets who acted innocent

They took 'em to the slammer in handcuffs
They'll get a beating if they don't cough up the loot.

Don't beat us, coppers, you know very well
This is our job, and don't ask for bribes.

We lift purses and wallets so we can
Have a regular rest in jail.

Kostas Rouhounas (1934)

Not too surprisingly, the *rembétes* suffered from the disapproval of the puritanical left as well as the puritanical right; the growing Communist Party of the 1930s considered the music and its habitues hopelessly decadent. There was some overlap, however, in the 1940s, as the singers of the *andártika* (resistance songs) learned the lesson of referring in code to issues which were not publicly discussable. Another exception from the later decade was Sotiria Bellou, a *rembétissa* (female rembetic musician) and active Communist.

In general, however, the Metaxas era and World War II spelled the end of the authentic rembetic tradition. Worthwhile material was certainly composed and recorded between 1936 and 1955 – the work of Ioanna Yiorgakopoulou, Vassilis Tsitsanis and Marika Ninou, for example – but most of the later music was perverted beyond recognition by maudlin lyrics and over-orchestration. The addition of an extra string to the *bouzoúki* and its electrification turned a delicate, lightly-strung instrument into an overamplified monstrosity. The presentation, in huge, barnlike clubs, became debased and vulgarised. Virtuoso *bouzoúki* players, assisted by female vocalists, became immensely rich. The clubs themselves were clip-joints where Athenians paid large sums to break plates and to watch dancing whose flashy steps and gyrations were a trav-

esty of the simple dignity and precise, synchronised footwork of the old style.

Ironically, the original *rembétika* was rescued from oblivion by the colonels. Among dozens of other things, the authentic verses were banned. The younger generation coming of age under the dictatorship took a closer look at the forbidden fruit, and derived solace, and deeper meanings, from the nominally apolitical lyrics. When the junta fell in 1974 – and even a little before – there was an outpouring of reissued recordings of the old masters, many of which are still available, and over the next decade live *rembétika* also enjoyed a revival. Today, a number of clubs and groups remain dedicated to the music (see Athens listings), though sadly it seems once again the decline.

Marc S. Dubin
(With thanks to Michael House)

RECORDS

One of the many joys of travelling in Greece is the availability of excellent recordings of Greek music from all eras; after the junta fell, re-releases of the oldest rembétika and other types of music were sponsored by such collecters as Markos Dragoumis and Kostas Hadzidoulis.

In the discography below, the recording artist is cited first, then title, finally label (and stock number if known). Hunting is best, and cheapest, in Greece (see listings in the Athens chapter); in the UK, *Trehantiri* (367 Green Lanes, London N4; ☎01/802-6530) has a fair selection.

Traditional Mainland Music
Greek Traditional Music: A Musical Atlas of Greece (EMI Odeon 3C 064 17966, Unesco Musical Atlas series #8). Don't be put off by the subtitle, this is an excellent collection – as are all the UNESCO projects.
Tragoudhia Keh Hori Tis Stereas ('Songs and Dances of the Mainland'; Minerva 22008). One of the finest collection of *paleá dhimotiká* available.
Yiorgos Mangas (Globe Style, UK). Clarinet virtuoso, with backup band, playing traditional music in a modern, slightly jazzy style.
Kostas Zakinthinos *Pimenika* (Melophone SMEL22). Evocative shepherd's clarinet.

Aristidhis Moskhos *Solo Santouri* (Studio SD22). *Tour de force* by Greece's premier *santoúri* player, who often accompanies Glykeria, Ioannis Markopoulos and others in more commercial settings.

Music of the Mainland (Argo, 1964). British-recorded anthology of unearthly beauty, featuring the famous Halkias clan of musicians from Epirus.

Vassilis Soukas & Takis Karnavas (Pan VOX). Clarinet and vocal, respectively; their first (not later) disc of *paleá dhimotiká*.

Traditional Cretan And Island Music

I Protomastores, 1920-1940 (AEME 11/12). The best Cretan music from between the world wars, in many cases played on instruments which no longer exist.

Ross Daly *Oneirou Topi* ('Places of the Dream'; AEME 311). One of the better discs by the Cretan-resident Irishman and his band, using the whole gamut of Cretan musical heritage – saz, rabab, mandolin, oud, etc. *Ross Daly* (otherwise untitled instrumental, 1986, distributed through Pop 11) is a good example of his more recent 'crossover' style, influenced by Turkish and Indian forms.

Nikos Ksidhakis *Konta sti Doxa mia Stismi* (Lyra 3460). Gypsy songs of small-town (low) life in Macedonia and Thrace. Strongly influenced by *rembétika*, huanting and musically impeccable. Features Ross Daly and Eleftheria Ananitaki.

Mihalis Polyhronakis *Pali tha Vgo na Tradougho* (PAN VOX X33SPV16204). The singing is a bit forced at times but accomplished *laoutó* solos, which you're unlikely to hear live on Crete, redeem it.

Nikos Skevakis *Fotia me Kaei keh Pono* (Panivar 5283). Possibly the best all-round Cretan recording: the *lyra* is not monotonous, the *santoúri* is celestial, the guitarist, laoutist, and lap-drummer play like they mean it.

Tragoudhia kai Hori ton Dhodhekanison ('Songs and Dances of the Dodecanese'; Minerva). *Vióli*, *santoúri* and female voice from Rhodes.

Irini Konitopoulou *Athanata Nisiotika* (Perennial Island Songs) and/or *Nisiotikes Epitihies* (Island Successes). The tape(s), often bootlegged, that are beloved of every island bus driver, and no less good for all that.

Early Rembétika

I Rembetiki Istoria 1922–1955 (EMI 70364-66, 70378-80). This six-volume anthology is a good introduction to rembétika. Vols. 1 and 4 are unalloyed delights, entirely old Smyrnaic and Anatolian pieces; the others are more of a mixed bag.

I Megali tou Rembetikou (Margo 8000-series). By now almost 20 discs, arranged by the artist rather than chronologically. The best are no. 1 (Early performers - Margo 8149), no. 2 (Apostolos Hadzikhristos - Margo 8150), no. 3 (Markos Vamvakaris) and no. 8 (Kostas Roukounas - Margo 8218).

Greek Orientale (Polylyric 9033). Superb selection of Asia Minor *rembétika* from the 1920s and 1930s, with interesting sleeve notes and translations of several lyrics.

Avthentika tragoudhia apo Smirni keh tin poli (Falirea Brothers, 1982). One of the better anthologies of very early material.

Amanedhes (Margo 8222). Good anthology of a very early-rembetic form of 'art singing' with roots in Turkey and Iran.

To Rembetiko Tragoudhi Vol. 1 & 2 (CBS 82302, -03). Recordings made in the U.S. early in this century.

Later Rembétika, including contemporary performers

Marika Ninou & Vasilis Tsitsanis *Marika Ninou at Jimmy the Fat's* (Venus 1053). Poor sound quality (it was a clandestine wire recording) but some of their best material together.

Sotiria Bellou 1946-56 (#5 of the *Megali tou Rebetikou* series; Margo 9103). The Billie Holliday of Greece, without the obnoxious electric backing of later years.

Arhondissa (Margo 8085). Tsitsanis with Bellou and Ninou.

Opisthodhromiki Kompania (Retrogade Company) *Live from Xanthi, Ayiniteio, the 'Kos' Armory* (Lyra 3347). Competent renditions of many Ninou and Hadzikhristos standards.

Rembetiko (CBS 70245). Soundtrack of the film, with music mainly by Stavros Xarhakos, lyrics by the poet Nikos Gatsos. Virtually the only original *rembétika* to be composed in the last 30 years, it carried the film...

Néo Klíma And Miscellaneous

Mikis Theodorakis *With the Horodhia Trikalon* (Olympic SBL 1099-1103, 4 discs). Probably the least bombastic, most accessible of his early (1964-66) material. Rare.

Savinna Yiannatou *Nanourismata* (Lyra 3396). Traditional lullabies with traditional instrumental backing (ney, pan-flutes, clarinet, kanoon, out, laouto, saz, Pontic lyre, guitar, etc.) but with a modern twist.

Heimerini Kolymvites (1981). First recording by a group of architects from Thessaloníki, drawing on *rembétika*, pop and Ionian jazz traditions. The group and record's title, 'Winter Swimmers', is an indication of the surreal lyrics and rich melodies.

Dionysios Savopoulos *Ballos, Pieces of Ten Years, Trapezakia Exo* (Lyra, 1975-83). Jethro Tull meets Bob Dylan – in a Greek context. Not to all tastes, but highly popular and certainly one of the more arresting modern composers to come out of Greece.

Stamatis Kraounakis and **Lina Nikolakopoulou** *Kykloforo, Oploforo* (Polydor 827589, 1985). Hugely successful disc, exploring the boundaries of rock, cabaret and neo klima styles.

FILMS

The Greek film industry suffers from misconceptions and preconceptions similar to those attendant on Greek music – most outsiders' ideas of both seem to have stalled at the level of *Never on Sunday*. Greek movie-making has in fact made great strides in recent years, with some credit due to the accession of PASOK to power. Most productions are technically excellent, though still plagued by lack of adequate funding and tightly written scenarios. Films synopsised below represent a personal selection of the best of the last ten years. You stand a good chance of catching some in Athens (see Art Cinema listings). In London, the National Film Theatre occasionally screens a Greek festival, with subtitles.

Ton Kero ton Ellinon/When the Greeks... (1981, Lakis Papastathis). A rich young bourgeois is held for ransom by nationalist bandits in nineteenth-century Greece and comes in contact with his real heritage for the first time. The bandit chief meanwhile considers joining the state army in this exploration of the tensions which persist in Greece between the rural and the urban.

Angelos (1982, George Katakouzinos). Gut-wrenching portrayal of the career of one of the transvestite homosexual prostitutes who frequent Leofóros Singroú in Athens. Based on an actual case, it drew the second largest audiences in Greece during the year of its release.

Balamos (1982, Stavros Tornes). 'I wanted to buy a horse that would take me to places not easily reached by men'. So saying, the director/narrator Tornes embarks on a fantastic journey to and beyond the gypsy horse-dealing culture of Macedonia.

Rembetiko (1983, Kostas Ferris). Loosely based on the life of singer Marika Ninou, this was both the most expensive Greek production ever (40 million drachmas) and the first cinematic attempt at a social history of *rembétika* music from the Smyrna of the 1920s to Athens of the 1950s. Its grand prize at the Berlin Film Festival of that year reflects more the sumptuous art direction and soundtrack (see discography in 'Music') than any strength of plot, which is strictly melodrama.

Taxidhi sta Kithera/Journey to Kythera (1984, Michael Cacoyannis). The late Manos Katrakis, dean of Greece's old-guard actors, in his last role as an aging communist returning from international exile to an even bleaker form of superfluousness on the island of Kíthira. Tourism arrives, he refuses to sell his share of the land necessary for development and finds himself as isolated as ever.

Stone Years (Pandelis Voulgaris, 1985). Based on a true story of a Communist couple who between them spend 26 years in prison between 1954 and 1974, with only one year of freedom (1966) in which they conceived the child raised in prison. Themis Bazaka won honourable mention at the 1985 Venice Film Festival for her portrayal of the mother Eleni; also adjudged best picture at the 1985 Thessaloníki Festival.

Meteor and Shadow (1985, Takis Spetsiotis). Takis Moskhos' award-winning (Best Actor, Thessaloniki 1985) portrayal of Napoleon Lapathiotis, the drag-queen/junkie poet who scandalised Athens from 1920 until his death in 1944.

The Enchantress (1985, Manoussos Manoussakis). An adaptation of a fairy tale told to the director by his grandmother, wherein the young hero leaves home in search of a beautiful spirit encountered one night near the village spring. A magical mystery tour by an ex-ballpoint pen salesman (!).

Bordello (1985, Nikos Koundouros). Another *Rembetiko*-like period epic by the director of *1922* (1979), which attempted to come to grips with the Asia Minor debacle. *Bordéllo* is set in the Crete of 1897, where a rebellion aginst Ottoman rule has just been crushed and foreign navies lie at anchor to restore order. Madame Hortense and her twelve associates hastily establish a brothel to divert the sailors, secret agents, fortune tellers, rebels in hiding, and (occasionally) the audience.

Marc S. Dubin

BOOKS

MODERN CLASSICS ON GREECE

Patrick Leigh Fermor *Roumeli* (Penguin £3.95), *Mani* (Penguin £3.95). These are not really travelogues; Leigh Fermor is more an aficionado of the vanishing minorities, relict communities and disappearing customs of rural Greece. Authoritative scholarship interspersed with strange and hilarious yarns. Perhaps the best books anyone has written on any aspect of Greece.

Henry Miller *The Colossus of Maroussi* (Penguin, £2.95). Corfu and the soul of Greece in 1939, with Miller, completely in his element, at his most inspired.

Peter Levi *The Hill of Kronos* (Arena, £2.95). Beautifully observed landscape, monuments, and eventually politics as Levi is drawn into resistance to the colonels' junta.

Kevin Andrews *The Flight of Ikaros* (Penguin, £3.95) All is not sweetness and light in this shattering account of an educated, sensitive archaeologist loose in the backcountry during the aftermath of the civil war.

Lawrence Durrell *Prospero's Cell* (Faber, £4.50), *Reflections on a Marine Venus* (Faber, £4.50), *The Greek Islands* (Penguin £6.95). Durrell lived before the last world war with his brother Gerald on Corfu, the subject of *Prospero's Cell* (and the setting of Gerald Durrell's sparkling *My Family and Other Animals*). *Marine Venus* recounts Lawrence's wartime experiences and impressions of Rhodes and other Dodecanese. *Greek Islands* is an impressionistic, dated, but still lyrical guide to the archipelagos.

OLDER ACCOUNTS

Richard Stoneman (ed.) *A Literary Companion to Travel in Greece* (Penguin, £4.95) A wide-ranging anthology of poetry, essays, and fiction from various eras, inspired by the Greek landscape and peoples.

Edward Lear *Journals of a Landscape Painter in Greece & Albania* (Century, £5.95). Highly entertaining journals of two safaris through Greece and Albania in autumn 1848 and spring 1849, by the famous landscape painter and author of *The Book of Nonsense*.

James Theodore Bent *The Cyclades, or Life Among Insular Greeks* (Argonaut Press, Chicago; reprint, 1966). Originally published in 1881, this remains the best account of island customs and folklore; it's also a highly readable, droll account of a year's Aegean travel, including a particularly violent Cycladic winter.

Nikos Kazantzakis *Journey to the Morea* (Cassirer, £4.95). Slightly stilted translation of the Cretan novelist's journey around the Peloponnese and his increasing alienation from the Greece of the 1930s.

Robert Byron *The Station* (Century, £4.95). Not as polished or brilliant as Byron's classic *Road to Oxiana* but a more than interesting account of his travels on Mount Athos and pioneering interest in Byzantine art and architecture.

Sidney Loch *Athos, The Holy Mountain* (Molho Bookstore, Thessaloniki). A tenant of the Phosphori tower in Ouranópoli, on the periphery of Mt. Áthos, from 1924 to 1954, summarises recent Athonite history and the legends surrounding various ikons and monasteries, as gleaned from his years of walking through the monastic republic.

ETHNOGRAPHY

George Megas *Greek Calendar Customs* (The author, through Athens University). Thorough, chronological compendium of festivals throughout the country – though many observances have disappeared since the first, 1952 edition.

Gail Holst *Road to Rembétika: Songs of Love, Sorrow, and Hashish* (Denise Harvey, Athens). The predominant urban musical style of this century, as traced by a Cornell University musicologist. A must if going record-shopping.

Tom Winnifrith *The Vlachs: The History of a Balkan People* (Duckworth, £10.95). Landmark study of the existing Vlach communities in Greece and the rest of the Balkans.

J.K. Campbell *Honour, Family and Patronage* (Oxford University Press, £8.95). A good companion to the above, this is a classic on the Sarakatsáni communities in the mountains of northern Greece, shedding much light on wider aspects of Greek society.

HISTORY

ANCIENT SOURCES

Homer *The Odyssey, The Iliad* (Penguin, £2.95 each). *The Odyssey*, beyond reasonable doubt, is the greatest possible companion when you're battling with or resigning yourself to the vagaries of interisland ferries . . . among other virtues.

M. I. Finley (ed.) *Portable Greek Historians* (Penguin, £3.95). Also well worth travelling with – the best chunks of Herodotus, Thucydides, Xenophon, and Polybius.

Pausanias *The Guide to Greece* (Penguin, £4.95). Written and compiled in the second century A.D., this is an interesting (if slightly academic) companion to a tour of the ancient sites. Functionally edited by Peter Levi, with notes on all modern identifications.

ANCIENT HISTORY

A. R. Burn *Pelican History of Greece* (Penguin, £3.95). Probably the best general introduction to ancient Greece, though for fuller and more interesting analysis you'll do better with one or other of the following.

M. I. Finley *The World of Odyssesus* (Penguin, £3.95). Good on the interrelation of Mycenaean myth and fact.

Oswyn Murray *Early Greece* (Fontana, £3.95). From the Mycenaeans and Minoans through the beginning of the Classical period.

J. K. Davies *Democracy and Classical Greece* (Fontana, £4.95). Established and accessible account of the period and its political developments.

F. W. Walbank *The Hellenistic World* (Fontana, £3.95). From the Macedonian hegemony to the end of the Roman Empire.

BYZANTIUM

Steven Runciman *The Fall of Constantinople, 1453* (Cambridge University Press, £9.95), *Byzantine Style and Civilisation* (Penguin, £5.95). Perhaps the main surprise for first-time travellers to Greece is the fascination of Byzantine monuments, above all at Mystra; these are the best books to begin extending your interest. . .

Michael Psellus *Fourteen Byzantine Rulers* (Penguin £4.95). . . and this, once it's extended, is among the most fascinating contemporary sources, detailing the stormy but brilliant period from 976 to 1078.

MEDIEVAL AND OTTOMAN GREECE

N. Cheetham *Medieval Greece* (Yale University Press, US). Good general survey of the period and its infinite convolutions, with Frankish, Catalan, Venetian, Byzantine and Ottoman struggles for power.

Apostolos Vacalopoulos *The Greek Nation, 1453-1669* and *Origins of the Greek Nation* (Rutgers University Press, US, o/p). The definitive survey of these times.

MODERN GREECE

Richard Clogg *A Short History of Modern Greece* (Cambridge University Press, £6.95). By far the best general study – a short and remarkably clear account of Greece since the decline of Byzantium – though with an emphasis on the events of the last decades.

C.M. Woodhouse *Modern Greece, A Short History* (Faber, £4.95). Briefer and rather more dry than Clogg, with a span from the foundation of Constantinople in 324 to the present. Woodhouse was active in the Greek Resistance during World War II; his perspective is rightwing but he is scrupulous with facts.

Douglas Dakin *The Unification of Greece, 1770-1923* (Ernest Benn, o/p). A lucid account of the foundation of the Greek state and the struggle to extend its boundaries.

John S. Koliopoulos *Brigands with a Cause* (Oxford University Press, £35). History of the brigandage in newly independent Greece and its significance in the struggle for the recovery of territory from Turkey in the later nineteenth century.

Michael Llewellyn Smith *Ionian Vision, Greece in Asia Minor, 1919-22* (Allen Lane, o/p). Standard work on the Anatolian campaign and the confrontation between Greece and Turkey leading to the exchange of populations.

C.M. Woodhouse *The Struggle for Greece, 1941-49* (Hart-Davis, o/p). Masterly (and by no means uncritical) account of this crucial decade, explaining how Greece emerged without a Communist government.

John O. Iatrides (ed.) *Greece in the 1940s: A Nation in Crisis* (University Press of New England, £26.95). Forty essays from different viewpoints and covering all aspects.

Dominique Eudes *The Kapetanios: Partisans and Civil War in Greece, 1943-1949.* (Monthly Review Press, New York, 1972). Fascinating account, by a French Maoist, of why and how ELAS lost the civil war.

C.M. Woodhouse *The Rise and Fall of the Greek Colonels* (Granada, £12.95). Highly readable account of the period of dictatorship.

Richard Clogg *Parties and Elections In Greece* (C. Hurst, £8.95). Scholarly study, published in 1987, of the political structure after the Colonels and an analysis of the (then) contemporary situation with PASOK in power.

BIOGRAPHY

George Psychoundakis *The Cretan Runner* (John Murray, £4.95). Compelling account of the invasion of Crete and subsequent resistance, by a participant. Psychoundakis was a guide and message-runner for all the British protagonists, including Patrick Leigh Fermor, translator of the book.

Oriana Falacci *A Man* (Pocket Books, £3.95). Account of the junta years, relating the author's involvement with Alekos Panagoulis, the anarchist who attempted to assassinate Colonel Papadopoulos in 1968. Issued as a 'novel' in response to threats by those whose names were named.

Vassilis Vassilikos *Z* (Sphere, £2.95). Another 'novel' based very closely on events – the political assassination of Gregoris Lambrakis in Thessaloniki in 1963. It was filmed by Costas Gavras.

Melina Mercouri *I was Born Greek* (Dell 1973; o/p). The title is the start of Melina's response to a junta bureaucrat upon being stripped of her Greek citizenship. She's now Minister of Culture in the PASOK government.

Nicholas Gage *Eleni* (Fontana, £3.95). Controversial account by a Greek-born *New York Times* correspondent who returns to Epirus to avenge the death of his mother, condemned to death by an ELAS tribunal in 1948. Superb descriptions of village life, but very blinkered political 'history' – and the basis of a truly forgettable movie. The book inspired a rebuttal by a Greek leftist, Vassilis Kavvathas, whose family had also been decimated, titled *I Alli Eleni* (The Other Eleni), not as yet translated into English.

FICTION

Nikos Kazantzakis *Zorba the Greek; Christ Recrucified; Report to Greco; Freedom or Death (Captain Mihalis); The Fratricides* (all published by Faber and Faber, £3.95-6.95). The most accessible (and Greece-related) of the numerous novels by the Cretan master. Even with inadequate translation their strength, especially that of *Report to Greco*, shines through.

Stratis Haviaras *When the Tree Sings* (Picador, £3.95), *The Heroic Age* (Penguin, £4.95) Two-part, faintly disguised autobiography about coming of age in Greece in the 1940s. Written in English 'because the experiences depicted in these pages are still too painful to set down in Greek'.

Stratis Myrivilis *The Mermaid Madonna, The Schoolmistress with the Golden Eyes* (Efstathiadis, Athens). Two tempestuous novels set early in the century on the north coast of Lesvos, Myrivilis' homeland.

Alexandros Papadiamantis *The Murderess* (Writers & Readers, £5.95). Turn-of-the-century novel set on Skíathos.

Petros Harris *Chronicle of a Dead City* (Nostos Books, Athens). Short stories set in Athens during the 1940-44 German occupation.

Demetrios Vikelas *Loukas Laras* (Doric Publications, London £3.50). Classic nineteenth-century novel set mainly on Híos.

Stratis Tsirkas *Drifting Cities* (Knopf, long out of print). Epic novel about political intrigue within the exiled Greek armed forces, set in Cairo, Alexandria and Jerusalem of the 1940s.

POETRY

With two Nobel Laureates in recent years – George Seferis and Odysseus Elytis – modern Greece has an extraordinarily intense and dynamic poetic tradition. Translations of all the following are excellent.

George Seferis *Collected Poems, 1924-1955* (Anvil Press, £5.95). Virtually the complete works of the Nobel laureate, with Greek and English verses on facing pages.

Odysseus Elytis *The Axion Esti* (Anvil Press, £4.95); *Selected Poems* (Anvil Press, £8.95)). English-only texts.

C. P. Cavafy, *Collected Poems* (Chatto and Windus, £5.95). The complete works of perhaps the most accessible modern Greek poet, resident for most of his life in Alexandria.

George Pavlopoulos *The Cellar* (Anvil Press, £3.95). Less well-known poet from Pírgos in the Peloponnese. English translation by Peter Levi.

Yannis Ritsos *Ritsos in Parentheses* (Princetown Univ. Press, US). Bilingual anthology of work by the foremost leftist poet.

Angelos Sikelianos *Selected Poems* (Allen and Unwin, £3.95). Small collection by a poet whose work suffers more in translation than the preceding ones.

Modern Greek Poetry (Efsthiadis, Athens). Good collection of translations, predominantly of Seferis and Elytis.

SPECIFIC GUIDES

ARCHAEOLOGY

Evi Melas (ed.) *Temples and Sanctuaries of Ancient Greece: A Companion Guide* (Thames & Hudson, 1973; o/p). Seventeeen very lucid essays on principal sites, written by archaeologists who have worked on them.

A.R. and Mary Burn *The Living Past of Greece: A Time Traveller's Tour of Historic and Prehistoric Places* (Penguin, o/p). Unusual in extent, this covers *all* the main sites, Minoan through to Byzantine and Frankish, with good clear plans and lively text.

REGIONAL GUIDES

Peter Greenhalgh and Edward Eliopoulos *Deep Into Mani* (Faber and Faber, £4.95). A former member of the wartime resistance revisits the Máni forty years after first hiding there, and 25 years after Patrick Leigh Fermor's work, in the company of a British scholar. The result is both the best guide to the region and excellent armchair reading.

John Fisher *The Rough Guide to Crete* (Harrap Columbus, UK, £4.95). Excellent, practical guide to the island by contributor to this *Rough Guide*.

Adam Hopkins *Crete* (Faber and Faber, £4.50). Interesting background history on Crete – not a guide as such.

Stephanie Ginger and Christopher Klint *Athens: A Survival Handbook* (Efstathiadis, Athens). Invaluable if you plan to spend any appreciable time in Athens.

Neville Lewis *Delphi and the Sacred Way* (Michael Haag, £5.95). An account, with ample description of contemporary conditions, and some walking tips, of the route from Athens to Mt. Parnassós, followed in ancient times by religious devotees.

Lycabettus Press Guides (Athens). This series takes in many of the more popular islands and certain mainland highlights; most pay their way both in interest and usefulness – in particular those on Páros, Pátmos and Náfplio.

HIKING

Marc Dubin *Greece on Foot: Mountain Treks, Island Trails* (Cordee, £7.95). Dozens of walks, ranging from two hours to two weeks, split evenly between the mainland and selected islands; extensive preparatory information.

Tim Salmon *The Mountains of Greece: A Walker's Guide* (Cicerone, £7.95). The emphasis in this guide is much more specifically on mountains, and ignores the islands; very strong on the central mainland and Epirus, including a possible route from Delphi to Albania.

Heinz Lothar Stutte and Dietrich Hasse *Meteora* (Cordee, £9.95). Multilingual climbers' guide to the extraordinary monastic rocks of Thessaly. Routes described in topo-form.

Athens has a number of excellent bookshops, at which many of the recommendations below should be available: see the 'Directory' for addresses. In London, the *Hellenic Bookservice* (122 Charing Cross Rd, W1; ☎01/836-2522) and *Zeno's Greek Bookshop* (6 Denmark St, W1; ☎01/836-2522) are knowledgeable specialist dealers, while *The Travel Bookshop* (13 Blenheim Crescent, W11; ☎01/229-5260) is good for out-of-print classics.

ONWARD FROM GREECE

Historically a crossroads between east and west, Greece is well poised for onward travel. It was for many years a first/last stop on the India overland route and remains a good place to pick up cheap flight tickets (see the addresses listed under 'Travel Agencies' in the Athens directory section). Closer at hand, the country's four land borders, and innumerable internationl ferry connections from the port of Pireás, provide equally interesting possibilities.

TURKEY

TURKEY is the most obvious target, though for many people the recent military junta (still essentially in control of the country) and abuses of human rights make travel here feel a distinctly questionable excercise. On the positive side Turks do express a real desire for western contact and their hospitality rivals even that of the Greeks. It's a sad fact that more Britons have seen the film *Midnight Express* than have visited Turkey; but this, and lurid tales of hassles in Istanbul, shouldn't be allowed to colour judgment too much.

Visas are not necessary for British and E.C. passport holders – you're given a stamp for a ninety-day stay on entry. **Inoculations** for typhoid and hepatitis are a good idea, although cholera or malaria precautions are not generally necessary. You can obtain most of these in Athens (see 'Inoculations for travellers' under 'Listings' in the Athens chapter).

The cheapest approach to Turkey is by non-stop bus from Athens or Thessaloníki to Istanbul; it's also not difficult to hitch the route beyond Thessaloníki, as it's a major conduit for long-distance lorry drivers. If you're a student or under 30, however, it's far more pleasant – and not much more expensive – to fly from Athens to Istanbul. Barring student/youth status, take a train (in stages) or an internal flight (reasonable) to Alexandhroúpoli and get a bus or train on from there.

Alternatively, you can cross over to the western coast of Turkey from the islands of Lésvos, Híos, Sámos, Kós and Rhodes. See their respective 'Travel details' for ferry frequencies -- and bear in mind that these services are all heavily reduced (or stop completely) out of season. Best bet for winter travellers is probably the ferry from Rhodes to Marmaris. At all times of the year phone the *limenarhío* (port police) of the island you're planning to depart from for accurate information -- the EOT tends to deny the existence of such boats or any knowledge of their schedules. For the distances involved all the Greek island–Turkish coast ferries are outrageously expensive; all the crossings now cost about £12-20 one-way £20-40 both ways), more than a ticket from any of these islands back to Pireás! Also, anyone on a charter to Rhodes, Kós, Sámos or Lésvos will invalidate their return coupons by staying overnight in Turkey.

All these petty hassles and blatantly political obstructions ennumerated, don't be discouraged from going if you can -- once you're there, costs are more than reasonable and what's to be experienced more than compensates.

Greece has better temples, but in Turkey there are magnificent **ancient cities** scattered all along the coast of what was ancient Aeolia, Ionia, Phrygia and Lycia. Besides the much-touted Efes (Ephesus), there's Bergama (Pergamon), Sart (Sardis), Priene, Milet (Miletus), Aphrodisias, Perge, Aspendos and Side: acres and acres of intact floor plans, colonnades, and huge amphitheatres. Plus there are remains of later Hellenic culture, the Greek-built towns of Ayvalik, Bergama, Antalya, Mugla, Milas, Kalkan and Kas, though you'll get scant recognition of this from Turkish tourist offices.

Coastal resorts like Çeşme, Kuşadasi, Bodrum, and Maramis satisfy sybaritic impulses and are really the only places that tourism has made major inroads in Turkey; Though there are now charters to Dalaman airport, near Marmaris, Antalya and to Izmir (near Efes), the package industry is still in its infancy and the feel of most of these places is very much like the Greece of twenty yearsgo.

For the truly intrepid the **Wild East** beckons: a land so similar to Central Asia that various Afghan refugees have been resettled there, and where you'll also find scattered Armenian, Assyrian, Kurdish and Georgian relics and populations which give the lie to official propaganda asserting the country's homogeneity. For the monumental taste, the interior also offers amazing Hittite sites, Seljuk civil and religious architecture, early Christian and Greek settlements in Cappadocia, and excellent hiking in the Taurus, Cilo and Kaçkar mountains. You can take a **Black Sea** cruise from Trabzon, near the Soviet border, through a half-dozen historic ports (a few hours for stops -- very inexpensive) to Istanbul, which beggars description and must be seen to be believed. The food, too, is some of the best in the world, and if you've any money left over leather goods and *kilims* (flatweave rugs) are of similar calibre.

A good **guidebook** is important. Diana Darke's *Aegean Turkey* and *Eastern Turkey* (Michael Haag) are useful, as, for hikers, is Marc Dubin and Enver Lucas' *Trekking in Turkey* (Lonely Planet). A *Rough Guide* is planned.

EGYPT

There are at least weekly boats throughout the year from Pireás to the port of Alexandrria in **EGYPT**. They cost upwards of £40 for a deck class ticket and take two days -- most sailing via Crete (Iráklio), but a few via Rhodes. Alexandria, an atmospheric but crowded resort, is just under four hours from Cairo by train, at a cost of about £4. Most of the year there are also **flights** virtually daily from Athens to Cairo, not much more expensive than the boats, especialy if you've got a student card.

In addition to the injections suggested for Turkey, cholera shots and malaria tablets should definitely be obtained for travel in Egypt. All nationalities require **visas**, though these can be obtained on arrival at Cairo airport. In Athens, there is an Egyptian consulate at Zalakósta 1. All arriving travellers are required to purchase the equivalent of £80 in Egyptian pounds, at the government 'tourist' rate -- a strategy calculated to stamp out the dwindling black market. Not to worry, even at the official rate such a sum will last one person travelling alone at least two weeks.

Most travellers stick to the major monuments of the **Nile Valley**, but this is a one-dimensional Egypt in more ways than one.

Spend some time as well in some of the Christian towns like Asyut or El Minya, visit off-the-beaten-track temples like Dandara near Qena, and take lorries/buses/trains out to the four **oases** of the western desert. The Coptic monasteries of Wadi Natrun, and two on the Red Sea coast, are fascinating, and the Sinai peninsula contains some of the most beautiful scenery in the world and, despite increasing ease of access, is still years away from despoliation.

A *Rough Guide to Egypt* is due to emerge early in 1990. Best **guidebook** meanwhile is the *Travelaid Guide to Egypt* (Michael Haag).

ISRAEL

From Athens there are also daily flights to **ISRAEL** (Tel Aviv), currently around £35 to £60 one-way. **Boats** from Pireás to Haifa work out about 30 percent cheaper and have the added advantage of sailing via Cyprus, allowing stopover possibilities if you work things out carefully. Many also call at Crete or Rhodes.

Israeli authorities maintain that no **inoculations** are necessary (though typhoid and cholera is certainly still a good idea) and Brotosh and EC citizens do not require **visas**. Keep Israeli stamps out of your passport, though, if you're planning to do any more travelling -- the customs officials are very obliging about detachable visas if you ask *in advance*!

Descriptive adjectives of the country depend largely on the speaker's prejudices, but most agree that there's rarely a dull moment in Israel. The Jewish state, (debatably) the Middle East's only western-style democracy, has apparently completed its imperial phase and must now come to terms with the 1.3 million Arabs inhabiting the occupied territories, who, in conjunction with the 800,000 Arab citizens of Israel, will constitute a bare majority within forty years if present demographic trends continue. Precedents in Lebanon and South Africa are not reassuring but perhaps a solution will be found.

In the meantime there is **Jerusalem**, one of the most fascinating cities on earth, and a plethora of religious and/or archaeological sites within a modest distance. Haifa and Tel Aviv are brassy, modern cities on a generally overdeveloped coast, but the wilderness near the **Dead Sea**, and the **Sea of Galilee** area, more than compensate. And despite rumours to the contrary it is possible to live on a reasonable amount as a traveller, however, positions on *kibbutzim* or *moshavim* are no longer as easy to get.

A *Rough Guide to Israel and the Occupied Territories* is due to emerge in 1989.

CYPRUS

CYPRUS, since the 1974 Turkish invasion and occupation of the north of the island, has been relatively (and unjustly) ignored by many travellers. It's easily and not too expensively reached by ferry from Pireás, Rhodes and Crete, or by flights from Athens and Rhodes. Information and maps are dispensed in Athens by the *Cyprus Tourist Office* at Fillelínon 10 and at all the Greek Cypriot entry points.

To stay overnight in the Turkish sector you need to enter by the Mersin–Famagusta ferry, and make sure that your entry stamp is on a detachable slip of paper. Othewise you may as well get a new passport immediately, as **Turkish Cypriot** stamps cause innumerable problems. Most of the noteworthy resorts, like Girne and Famagusta, are in the northern territory, and **Nicosia**, like Berlin, is a divided city; the main highlights in the south are the Troodhos mountains with their monasteries, and the ruins and beaches at Paphos.

This said, be advised that Cyprus is far more expensive than either Turkey or Greece -- almost as costly as Israel, in fact. And while it makes a pleasant stopover en route to or from any of the above places it doesn't really merit a special trip in itself.

YUGOSLAVIA

Some 90 percent of visitors to Greece who come overland through **YUGOSLAVIA** pass through without getting off the train or bus – and get totally the wrong impression. That particular journey *is* notably grim but a more libellous representation of the country would be hard to find.

Opinions will improve markedly upon breaking the train journey at either **Zagreb**, the gracious capital of the Slovenian republic, or further down the line (justifiably skipping Belgrade) at **Skopje**, interesting in itself but more importantly the gateway for the magnificent **Lake Ohrid** basin. On the limestone-sculpted **Dalmatian coast**, the swimming gets better (and the tourists fewer) as you move southeast to mountainous, earthquake-prone Montenegro.

Buses and planes, are excellent and go everywhere; avoid trains, which are not and do not, except for the showcase lines from Belgrade to Bar (conveniently poised between Kosovo and Montenegro) and the Zagreb–Sarajevo–Mostar–Kardeljevo itinerary, which offers access to the Turkish-flavoured republic of Bosnia and ends just shy of some of the stellar attractions of Dalmatia – Dubrovnik, Korçula and Hvar. As in Greece, the cheapest **places to stay** are rented rooms in people's houses; unlike Greece, relatively few people speak English, so a command of phrasebook Serbo-Croatian is essential.

For a **guidebook**, look no further than our own *Rough Guide*.

LANGUAGE

So many Greeks have been compelled by poverty and other circumstances to work abroad, especially in the English-speaking world, that you'll find someone who speaks some English in almost any village. Add to that the thousands attending language schools or working in the tourist industry – English is the lingua franca of most resorts, with German second – and it is easy to see how so many visitors come back having learnt only half a dozen restaurant words between them. You can certainly get by this way, but it isn't very satisfying.

Greek is not an easy language for English speakers, but it is a beautiful one and even a brief acquaintance will give you some idea of the debt western European languages owe to it. More important than that, the willingness and ability to say even a few words will trans-

form your status from that of dumb tourístas to the honourable one of ksénos, a word which can mean stranger, traveller and guest all rolled into one.

BASIC GREEK

On top of the usual difficulties of learning a new language, Greek presents the additional problem of an entirely separate **alphabet**. Despite initial appearances, this is in practice fairly easily mastered – a skill that will help enormously if you are going to get around independently (see the *Alphabet and transliteration* section below). In addition, certain combinations of letters have unexpected results. This book's transliteration system should help you make intelligible noises but you have to remember that the correct **stress** (marked in the book with à) is absolutely crucial. With the right sounds but the wrong stress people will either fail to understand you, or else understand something quite different from what you intended.

Greek **grammar** is more complicated still: nouns are divided into three genders, all with different case endings in the singular and in the plural, and all adjectives and articles have to agree with these in gender, number and case. (All adjectives are arbitrarily cited in the neuter form in the following lists.) Verbs are even worse. To begin with at least, the best thing is simply to say what you know the way you know it, and never mind the niceties. 'Eat meat hungry' should get a result, however grammatically incorrect. If you worry about your mistakes, you'll never say anything.

LANGUAGE BOOKS

TEACH YOURSELF GREEK COURSES
Breakthrough Greece (Pan; book and two cassettes). Excellent, basic teach-yourself course – completely outclasses the competition.
Greek Language and People (BBC Publications; book and cassette available). More limited in scope but good for acquiring the essentials, and the confidence to try them.
PHRASEBOOKS
Greek Travelmate (Drew; £1.50). Most functional of the pocket phrasebooks. Contemporary phrases and laid out in dictionary form.
Greek At Your Fingertips (Routledge; £3.95).

Expanded edition of the 'Travelmate', with brief sections on grammar.
Tom Stone *Greek Handbook* (Lycabettus Press, Athens). A cross between a cultural guide, phrasebook and dictionary; an excellent emergency manual.
DICTIONARIES
The Oxford Dictionary of Modern Greek (Oxford University Press; £9.95). Considered the best Greek-English, English-Greek dictionary.
Collins Pocket Greek Dictionary (Collins, £4.95). Very nearly as complete as the Oxford and probably better value for the money.

ESSENTIALS

Yes	Néh
No	Óhi
Please	Parakaló
Okay, agreed	Endáksi
Thank you (very much)	Efharistó (polí)
I (don't) understand	(dhen) Katalavéno
Excuse me, do you speak English?	Parakaló, mípos miláte angliká
Sorry/excuse me	Signómi
Today	Símera
Tomorrow	Ávrio
Yesterday	Khthés
Now	Tóra
Later	Argótera
Open	Aniktó
Closed	Klistó
Day	Méra
Night	Níkhta
In the morning	To proí
In the afternoon	To apóyevma
In the evening	To vrádhi
Here	Edhó
There	Ekí
This one	Aftó
That one	Ekíno
Good	Kaló
Bad	Kakó
Big	Megálo
Small	Mikró
More	Perisótero
Less	Ligótero
A little	Lígo
A lot	Polí
Cheap	Ftinó
Expensive	Akrivó
Hot	Zestó
Cold	Krío
With	Mazí
Without	Horís
Quickly	Grígora
Slowly	Sigá
Mr.	Kírios
Mrs.	Kiría
Miss	Dhespinís

QUESTIONS AND REQUESTS

The simplest way of asking a question is to start with *parakaló*, then name the thing you want in an interrogative tone.

Where is the bakery?	Parakaló, o foúrnos?
Can you show me the road to . . . ?	Parakaló, o dhrómos ya . . ?
We'd like a room for two	Parakaló, éna dhomátio ya dhío átoma?
May I have a kilo of oranges?	Parakaló, éna kiló portokália?
Where?	Pou?
How?	Pos?
How many/How much?	Pósi/Póso?

When?	Póte?
Why?	Yatí?
(At what time . . . ?	Ti óra . . . ?
What is/Which is . . . ?	Ti íneh/pió íneh
How much (does it cost)?	Póso káni?
What time does it open?	Ti óra aníyi?
What time does it close?	Ti óra klíni?

TALKING TO PEOPLE

Greek makes the distinction between the informal (*tu/esí*) and formal (*vous/esís*) second person as French does, though only the urban middle class tend to speak this way. Young people, older people and country people nearly always use *esí* even with total strangers. In any event, no one will be too bothered if you get it wrong. By far the most common greeting, on meeting and parting, is *yá sou/yá sas* – literally 'health to you'.

Hello	Hérete
Good morning	Kalí méra
Good evening	Kalí spéra
Good night	Kalí níkhta
Goodbye	Adío
How are you?	Ti kánis/Ti kánete?
I'm fine	Kalá ímeh
And you?	Keh esís?
What's your name?	Pos se léne?
My name is. . .	Meh léne. . .
Speak slower, please	Parakaló, miláte pió sigá
How do you say it in Greek?	Pos léyete sta Eliniká?
I don't know	Dhen kséro
See you tomorrow	Tha se dho ávrio
See you soon	Tha se dho se lígo
Let's go	Páme
Please help me	Parakaló, na me voithíste

ACCOMMODATION

Hotel	Ksenodhohío
A room. . .	Éna dhomátio
for one/two/three people	ya éna/dhío/tría átoma
for one/two/three nights	ya mía/dhío/trís vradhies
with a double bed	meh megálo kreváti
with a shower	meh doús
hot water	zestó neró
cold water	krío neró
Can I see it?	Boró na to dho?
Can we camp here?	Boróume na váloumeh ti skiní edhó?
Campsite	Kamping/Kataskínosi
Tent	Skiní
Youth hostel	Ksenodhohío neótitos

ON THE MOVE

Aeroplane	Aeropláno
Bus	Leoforío
Car	Aftokínito
Motorbike, moped	Mihanáki
Taxi	Taksí

Ship	*Plío/Vapóri/Karávi*	21	*íkosi éna*
Bicycle	*Podhílato*	30	*triánda*
Hitching	*Otostóp*	40	*saránda*
On foot	*Meh ta pódhia*	50	*penínda*
Bus station	*Praktorío-leoforíon*	60	*eksínda*
Bus stop	*Stási*	70	*evdhomínda*
Harbor	*Limáni*	80	*ogdhónda*
What time does it leave?	*Ti óra févyi?*	90	*enenínda*
What time does it arrive?	*Ti óra ftháni?*	100	*ekató*
How many kilometres?	*Pósa hiliómetra?*	150	*ekatón penínda*
How many hours?	*Póses óres?*	200	*dhiakósies/ia*
Where are you going?	*Pou pas?*	500	*pendakósies/ia*
I'm going to. . .	*Páo sto. . .*	1000	*hílies/ia*
I want to get off at. . .	*Thélo na katévo sto. . .*	2000	*dhío hiliádhes*
The road to. . .	*O dhrómos ya. . .*	1,000,000	*éna ekatomírio*
Near	*Kondá*		
Far	*Makriá*	first	*próto*
Left	*Aristerá*	second	*dhéftero*
Right	*Dheksiá*	third	*tríto*
Straight ahead. . .	*Katefthía*		
A ticket to. . .	*Éna isistírio ya. . .*		
A return ticket	*Éna isistírio me epistrofí*	### THE TIME AND DAYS OF THE WEEK	
Beach	*Paralía*	Sunday	*Kiriakí*
Cave	*Spiliá*	Monday	*Dheftéra*
Centre (of town)	*Kéndro*	Tuesday	*Tríti*
Church	*Eklisía*	Wednesday	*Tetárti*
Sea	*Thálasa*	Thursday	*Pémpti*
Village	*Horió*	Friday	*Paraskeví*
Crossroads	*Dhiastávrosi*	Saturday	*Sávato*
		What time is it?	*Ti óra íneh?*
### OTHER NEEDS		One, two, three o'clock	*Mía, dhío, trís*
I eat	*Trógo*	Twenty minutes to four	*Tésseres pará íkosi*
I drink	*Píno*	Five minutes past seven	*Eftá keh pénde*
Bakery	*Foúrnos, psomádhiko*	Half past eleven	*Éndheka keh misí*
Pharmacy	*Farmakío*	Half hour	*misí óra*
Post office	*Tahidhromío*	Quarter hour	*éna tétarto*
Stamps	*Gramatósima*		
Petrol station	*Venzinádhiko*		
Bank	*Trápeza*	### GREEKS' GREEK	
Money	*Leftá/Hrímata*	There are numerous words and phrases which you	
Toilet	*Toualéta*	will hear constantly, even if you rarely have the	
Police	*Astinomía*	chance to use them. These are a few of the most	
Doctor	*Iatrós*	common.	
Hospital	*Nosokomío*		
		Éla	Come (literally) but also Speak to me! You don't say! etc.
### NUMBERS		*Oríste*	What can I do for you? At your service
1	*éna/mía*		
2	*dhío*	*Ti néa?*	What's new?
3	*trís/tría*	*Ti yíneteh?*	What's going on (here)?
4	*téseres/tésera*	*Étsi k'étsi*	So-so
5	*pénde*	*Opá!*	Whoops! Watch it!
6	*éksi*	*Po-po-po!*	Dismay! Concern! Surprise! (like French 'O la la')
7	*eftá*		
8	*okhtó*	*Pedhí mou*	My boy/girl, sonny, friend, etc.
9	*enyá*	*Maláka(s)*	Literally 'wanker', but often used as an informal way of addressing someone.
10	*dhéka*		
11	*éndheka*		
12	*dhódheka*	*Sigá sigá*	Take your time, slow down
13	*dhekatrís*	*Kaló taxídhi*	Bon voyage
14	*dhekatéseres*		
20	*íkosi*		

DHIMOTIKÍ, KATHARÉVOUSSA, AND DIALECTS

Greek may seem complicated in itself, but its impossibilities are multiplied when you consider that for the last century there has been an ongoing dispute between two versions of the language: **katharévoussa** and **dhimotikí**.

When Greece first achieved independence in the nineteenth century, its people were almost universally illiterate, and the language they spoke – **dhimotikí**, 'demotic' or 'popular' Greek – had undergone enormous change since the days of the Byzantine Empire and Classical times. The vocabulary had assimilated countless borrowings from the languages of the various conquerors, in particular the Turks.

It was these peasants who had spilled blood in the revolution, yet the finance and inspiration for the new Greek state, and its early leaders, came from the diaspora – Greek families who had been living in the sophisticated cities of central and eastern Europe, or in Russia. With their European notions about the grandeur of Greece's past, and lofty conception of Hellenism, they set about obliterating the memory of subjection to the Turks in every possible field. And what better way to start than by 'cleansing' the language of its bastard foreign accretions and reviving its Classical purity.

They accordingly set about creating what was in effect a new form of the language, **katharévoussa** (literally, 'cleansed' Greek). The complexities of Classical grammar and syntax were reinstated, and Classical words, long out of use, were reintroduced. To the country's great detriment, *katharévoussa* became the language of the schools and the prestigious professions, government, business, the law, newspapers and academia. Everyone aspiring to membership in the elite strove to master it, and to speak it – even though there was no absolute and defined idea of how many of the words should be pronounced!

The *katharévoussa/dhimotikí* debate has been a highly contentious issue through most of this century. Writers – from Sikelianos and Seferis to Kazantzakis, Myrivilis, and Ritsos – have all championed the demotic in their literature. On the other side, rightwing governments

opportunity. The Metaxas dictatorship of the 1930s changed scores of village names from Slavic to Classical forms (a source of confusion ever since). More recently, the colonels' junta of 1967-74 reversed a decision of the previous government to teach in *dhimotikí* in the schools, bringing back *katharévoussa*, even to cookie wrappers, as part of their fascist ragbag of notions about racial purity and heroic ages. It was a retrograde enough measure in itself, but absolutely devastating for those already in the school system.

Dhimotikí returned once more after the fall of the colonels, and now seems here to stay. It is used in schools, in newspapers (with the exception of the extreme right *Estia*), on radio and TV, and in most official business. The only institution which refuses to bring itself up to date is the church.

This is not to suggest that there is any less **confusion**. K*atharévoussa* **place names** still hold sway on many roadsigns and maps – even though the local people may use the *dhimotikí* form. Thus you will see Leonidhion or Spetsai written, while everyone actually says Leonídhi or Spétses.

DIALECTS

If the lack of any standard Greek were not enough, Greece still offers a rich field of linguistic diversity, both in its dialects and minority languages. Ancient **dialects** are alive and well in many a remote area, and some of them are quite incomprehensible to outsiders. The dialect of Sfákia in Crete is one such. *Tsakónika* (spoken in the east-central Peloponnese) is another, while the dialect of the Sarakatsáni shepherds is said to be the oldest, a direct descendant of the language of the Dorian invaders.

The language of the Sarakatsáni's traditional rivals, the **Vlachs**, on the other hand, is not Greek at all, but a derivative of early Latin, with strong affinities to Romanian. In the Yugoslav and Bulgarian frontier regions you can still hear Slavic **Macedonian** spoken, and right in the heart of Athens you might just hear *arvanítika*, a dialect inherited from eighteenth-century **Albanian** settlers in Attica. In Thrace there is a substantial **Turkish**-speaking population, as well as some speakers of Pomak (a relative of Bulgarian with a large Greco-Turk vocabulary).

THE GREEK ALPHABET: TRANSLITERATION

Set out below is the Greek alphabet, the system of transliteration used in this book, and a brief aid to pronunciation:

Greek	Transliteration	Pronounced
A, α	a	a as in cat
B, β	v	v as in vet
Γ, γ	y/g	y as in yes, except before consonants and a, o or long i, when it's a breathy, throaty version of the g in gap.
Δ, δ	dh	th as in then
E, ε	e	e as in get
Z, ζ	z	z sound
H, η	i	ee sound as in feet
Θ, θ	th	th as in theme
I, ι	i	i as in bit
K, κ	k	k sound
Λ, λ	l	l sound
M, μ	m	m sound
N, ν	n	n sound
Ξ, ξ	ks	ks sound
O, o	o	o as in hot
Π, π	p	p sound
P, ϱ	r	rolled r sound
Σ, σ, ς	s	s sound
T, τ	t	t sound
Y, υ	i	long i, indistinguishable from η
Φ, φ	f	f sound
X, χ	h	harsh h sound, like the ch in loch
Ψ, ψ	ps	ps as in lips
Ω, ω	o	o as in hot, indistinguishable from o

Combinations and dipthongs

AI, αι	e	e as in get
AY, αυ	av/af	av or af depending on following consonant
EI, οι	i	long i, exactly like η
OI, οι	i	long i, identical again
EY, ευ	ev/ef	ev or ef depending on following consonant
OY, ου	ou	ou as in tourist
ΓΓ, γγ	ng	ng as in angle
ΓY, γυ	g/ng	g as in goat at the beginning of a word; ng in the middle
ΜΠ, μπ	b	b as in bar
NT, ντ	d/nd	d at the beginning of a word; nd in the middle
TΣ, τσ	ts	ts as in hits

GREEK TERMS AND ACRONYMS: A GLOSSARY

ACROPOLIS Ancient, fortified hilltop.

ÁYIOS/AYÍA/ÁYII Saint or holy (m/f/pl). Common place name prefix (abbrev. Ag. or Ay.), as: Áyios Nikólaos, St. Nicholas; Ayía Marína, St. Marina; Ayía Saránda, the Forty Holy Martyrs, etc.

AGORA Market and meeting place of an ancient city.

AMPHORA Tall, narrow-necked jar for oil or wine.

APSE Curved recess at the altar end of a church.

ARCHAIC PERIOD Late Iron Age from around 750 B.C. to the start of the Classical period in the fifth century B.C.

ASTIKÓ (intra) city, municipal, local – as in phone calls and bus services.

BASILICA Colonnaded, 'hall-' or 'barn-' type church, most common in northern Greece.

BYZANTINE EMPIRE Created by the division of the Roman Empire in A.D. 395, this, the eastern half, was ruled from Constantinople (the modern Istanbul). In Greece, Byzantine culture peaked twice: in the eleventh century, at Dhafní, Óssios Loukás, Mt. Áthos, Néa Moní, Thessaloníki, etc.), and again at Mystra in the early fifteenth century. Important island centres included Crete, liberally spangled with fifth- to twelfth-century churches, Náxos and Páros. After the fall of Constantinople in 1453, many artisans fled to Venetian-held territory (such as Crete and the Cyclades) and created more magnificent, post-Byzantine works of art.

CLASSICAL PERIOD Essentially from the end of the Persian Wars in the fifth century B.C. until the unification of Greece under Phillip II of Macedon (338 B.C.).

DHIMARHÍO Townhall.

DORIAN Civilisation which overran the Mycenaeans from the north and became their successors through most of Greece, including Crete.

EPARHÍA Greek Orthodox diocese, also the smallest subdivision of a modern province.

FRIEZE Band of sculptures around a temple. Doric friezes consist of tableaus of figures (METOPES) interspersed with grooved panels (TRIGLYPHS); Ionic ones have continuous bands of figures.

FROÚRIO Medieval castle.

GEOMETRIC PERIOD Post-Mycenaean Iron Age era named for the style of its pottery; begins in the early eleventh century B.C. with the arrival of Dorian peoples. By the eighth century B.C., with the development of representational styles, it becomes known as the ARCHAIC period.

HELLENISTIC PERIOD The last and most unified 'Greek empire', created by Philip II and Alexander the Great, finally collapsing with the fall of Corinth to the Romans in 146 B.C.

HÓRA Main town of an island – often with the same name as the island – or a region; literally it means 'the place'.

IKONOSTÁSI Screen between the nave of a church and the altar and apse, often covered in icons; also a wayside shrine.

IONIC Elaborate, decorative development of the older Doric order; Ionic temple columns are slimmer with deeper 'fluted' edges, spiral-shaped capitals, and ornamental bases. CORINTHIAN capitals are a still more decorative development.

IPERASTIKÓ Intercity, long-distance – as in phone calls and bus services.

JANISSARY Member of the Turkish Imperial Guard, often forcibly recruited in childhood from the local population.

KAFENÍO Coffeehouse or café; in a small village the centre of communal life and probably serving as the bus stop too.

KAÍKI (pl. kaíkia) A caique, or medium sized, traditionally wooden boat, used for transporting cargo and passengers; now refers mainly to island excursion boats.

KALDERÍMI Exquisitely engineered, cobbled paths in mountains and islands of Greece; most are a few hundred years old.

KÁMBOS Fertile agricultural plateau, usually near a river mouth.

KÁSTRO Any fortified hill (or a castle), but most usually the oldest, highest, walled-in part of an island *hóra*.

KATHOLIKÓN Central church or chapel of a monastery.

KOÚROS Ancient statue of an idealized young man, usually portrayed with one foot slightly forward of the other; KORAI are the corresponding female figures.

MELTÉMI North wind that blows across the Aegean in summer, starting softly from near the mainland and hitting the Cyclades, the Dodecanese and Crete full on. Its force is gauged by what it knocks over – 'table-weather', 'bell-weather', etc.

MINOAN Crete's great Bronze Age Civilisation which dominated the Aegean from about 2500 to 1400 B.C.

MONÍ Formal term for monastery or convent.

MOREA Medieval term for the Peloponnese.

MYCENAEAN Mainland civilisation centered on Mycenae and the Argolid from about 1700 to 1100B.C.; in some sources held responsible for the final destruction of Minoan culture, and in turn overwhelmed by the Dorians.

NARTHEX Vestibule or entrance hall of a church.

NÉOS, NÉA, NÉO 'New' – often part of town name.

NEOLITHIC Earliest era of settlement in Greece, characterized by the use of stone tools and weapons together with basic agriculture. Divided arbitrarily into Early (ca. 6000 B.C.), Middle (ca. 5000 B.C.), and Late (ca. 3000 B.C.).

NOMÓS Modern Greek province – there are more than fifty of them.

ODEION Small amphitheatre, used for musical performances, minor dramatic productions, or councils.

PALEÓS, PALEÁ, PALEÓ 'Old' – common in town names.

PANAYÍA Virgin Mary.

PANIYÍRI Festival or feast – the local celebration of a holy day.

PANTOCRATOR Literally 'The Almighty', but generally refers to the stern portrayal of Christ in Majesty frescoed or in mosaic on the dome of many Byzantine churches.

PEDIMENT Triangular, sculpted space below the roof of a temple.

PERÍPTERO Street kiosk.

PITHOS (pl. PITHOI) Large ceramic jar for storing oil, grain etc. very common in the Minoan palaces and used in almost identical form in modern Cretan homes.

PLATÍA Square. KENTRIKÍ PLATÍA, central square.

PROPYLAIA Portico or entrance to an ancient building.

SKALA The port of an inland island settlement, nowadays often larger and more important than its namesake but always younger since built after the disappearance of piracy.

STELE Upright stone slab or column, usually inscribed; an ancient tombstone.

STOA Colonnaded walkway in Classical-era marketplace.

TEMENOS Sacred precinct, often used to refer to the sanctuary itself.

THEATRAL AREA Open area found in most of the Minoan palaces with seat-like steps around. May have been a type of theatre or ritual area, but not conclusively proved.

THOLOS Conical or beehive-shaped building, especially a Mycenaean tomb.

ACRONYMS

EA Greek Left (*Ellenikí Aristerá*), formerly the Greek Euro-communist Party (*KKE-Esoterikoú*).

ELAS Popular Liberation Army, the most active resistance group during the 1941-44 occupation.

EPEN Fascist Party, consisting mostly of adherents to the imprisoned Papdopoulos.

EOS Greek Mountaineering Club.

EOT *Ellinikós Organismós Tourismoú*, the NTOG, or tourist organisation.

KKE Communist Party.

KTEL National syndicate of bus companies. Often used conversationally to refer to bus stations.

ND Conservative *Néa Dhimokratía* party.

OSE State railway corporation.

OTE Telephone company.

PASOK Pan-Hellenic Socialist Movement, currently led by Andreas Papandreou and in power since 1981.

INDEX

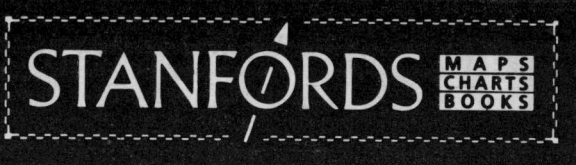